PRENTICE HALL

LITERATURE

GRADE 12
Part 1

COMMON CORE EDITION ©

Upper Saddle River, New Jersey

Boston, Massachusetts

Chandler, Arizona

Glenview, Illinois

ALWAYS LEARNING

PEARSON

Cover Art: (Bkgd) ©Ted Mead/Getty Images, (L) ©James Forte/Getty Images, (B) (c) Tom Merton/OJO Images/ Getty Images, (TL, BC) (c)Blaine Harrington III/CORBIS, (CR) (c)Uli Wiesmeier/zefa/CORBIS.

Taken from:

Prentice Hall Literature, The British Tradition, Common Core Edition
Copyright © 2012 by Pearson Education, Inc.
Published by Prentice Hall
Upper Saddle River, New Jersey 07458

This special edition published in cooperation with Pearson Learning Solutions.

Pearson Learning Solutions, 501 Boylston Street, Suite 900,
Boston, MA 02116
A Pearson Education Company
www.pearsoned.com

Printed in the United States of America

1 2 3 4 5 6 7 8 9 10 V051 16 15 14 13 12 11

000200010271275791

EG

Acknowledgments appear on page R82, which constitutes an extension of this copyright page.

SAT is a registered trademark of the College Entrance Examination Board. ACT is a trademark owned by ACT, Inc.

Wikipedia® is a registered trademark of the Wikimedia Foundation, Inc., ‹http://www.wikimediafoundation.org›

iPod® and Mac® are registered trademarks of Apple Inc.

Use of the trademarks implies no relationship, sponsorship, endorsement, sale, or promotion on the part of Pearson Education, Inc., or its affiliates.

Common Core State Standards © Copyright 2010. National Governors Association Center for Best Practices and Council of Chief State School Officers. All rights reserved.

"Understanding by Design" is registered as a trademark with the United States Patent and Trademark Office by the Association for Supervision of Curriculum Development (ASCD). ASCD claims exclusive trademark rights in the terms "Understanding by Design" and the abbreviation "UbD".

Pearson Education has incorporated the concepts of the Understanding by Design methodology into this text in consultation with Grant Wiggins, one of the creators of the Understanding by Design methodology. The Association for Supervision of Curriculum Development (ASCD), publisher of the "Understanding by Design Handbook" co-authored by Grant Wiggins, has not authorized, approved or sponsored this work and is in no way affiliated with Pearson or its products.

ISBN 10: 1-256-33184-8
ISBN 13: 978-1-256-33184-1

Contributing Authors

The contributing authors guided the direction and philosophy of Pearson Prentice Hall Literature. Working with the development team, they helped to build the pedagogical integrity of the program and to ensure its relevance for today's teachers and students.

Grant Wiggins, Ed.D., is the President of Authentic Education in Hopewell, New Jersey. He earned his Ed.D. from Harvard University and his B.A. from St. John's College in Annapolis. Grant consults with schools, districts, and state education departments on a variety of reform matters; organizes conferences and workshops; and develops print materials and Web resources on curricular change. He is the coauthor, with Jay McTighe, of Understanding by Design and The Understanding by Design Handbook, the award-winning and highly successful materials on curriculum published by ASCD. His work has been supported by the Pew Charitable Trusts, the Geraldine R. Dodge Foundation, and the National Science Foundation. *The Association for Supervision of Curriculum Development (ASCD), publisher of the "Understanding by Design Handbook" co-authored by Grant Wiggins and registered owner of the trademark "Understanding by Design", has not authorized, approved, or sponsored this work and is in no way affiliated with Pearson or its products.*

Jeff Anderson has worked with  struggling writers and readers for almost 20 years. Anderson's specialty is the integration of grammar and editing instruction into the processes of reading and writing. He has published two books, *Mechanically Inclined: Building Grammar, Usage, and Style into Writer's Workshop* and *Everyday Editing: Inviting Students to Develop Skill and Craft in Writer's Workshop,* as well as a DVD, *The Craft of Grammar.* Anderson's work has appeared in *English Journal.* Anderson won the NCTE Paul and Kate Farmer Award for his *English Journal* article on teaching grammar in context.

Arnetha F. Ball, Ph.D., is a  Professor at Stanford University. Her areas of expertise include language and literacy studies of diverse student populations, research on writing instruction, and teacher preparation for working with diverse populations. She is the author of *African American Literacies Unleashed* with Dr. Ted Lardner, and *Multicultural Strategies for Education and Social Change.*

Sheridan Blau is Professor of  Education and English at the University of California, Santa Barbara, where he directs the South Coast Writing Project and the Literature Institute for Teachers. He has served in senior advisory roles for such groups as the National Board for Professional Teaching Standards, the College Board, and the American Board for Teacher Education. Blau served for twenty years on the National Writing Project Advisory Board and Task Force, and is a former president of NCTE. Blau is the author of *The Literature Workshop: Teaching Texts and Their Readers,* which was named by the Conference on English Education as the 2004 Richard Meade Award winner for outstanding research in English education.

William G. Brozo, Ph.D., is a Professor of Literacy at George Mason University in Fairfax, Virginia. He has taught reading and language arts in junior and senior high school and is the author of numerous texts on literacy development. Dr. Brozo'z work focuses on building capacity among teacher leaders, enriching the literate culture of schools, enhancing the literate lives of boys, and making teaching more responsive to the needs of all students. His recent publications include *Bright Beginnings for Boys: Engaging Young Boys in Active Literacy* and the *Adolescent Literacy Inventory.*

Doug Buehl is a teacher, author, and  national literacy consultant. He is the author of *Classroom Strategies for Interactive Learning* and coauthor of *Reading and the High School Student: Strategies to Enhance Literacy;* and *Strategies to Enhance Literacy and Learning in Middle School Content Area Classrooms.*

Jim Cummins, Ph.D, is a professor in the Modern Language Centre  at the University of Toronto. He is the author of numerous publications, including *Negotiating Identities: Education for Empowerment in a Diverse Society.* Cummins coined the acronyms BICS and CAPT to help differentiate the type of language ability students need for success.

Harvey Daniels, Ph.D., has been  a classroom teacher, writing project director, author, and university professor. "Smokey" serves as an international consultant to schools, districts, and educational agencies. He is known for his work on student-led book clubs, as recounted in *Literature Circles: Voice and Choice in Book Clubs & Reading Groups* and *Mini Lessons for Literature Circles.* Recent works include *Subjects Matter: Every Teacher's Guide to Content-Area Reading* and *Content Area Writing: Every Teacher's Guide.*

Jane Feber taught language arts in Jacksonville, Florida, for 36 years. Her innovative approach to instruction has earned her several awards, including the NMSA Distinguished Educator Award, the NCTE Edwin A. Hoey Award, the Gladys Prior Award for Teaching Excellence, and the Florida Council of Teachers of English Teacher of the Year Award. She is a National Board Certified Teacher, past president of the Florida Council of Teachers of English, and the author of *Creative Book Reports* and *Active Word Play*.

Danling Fu, Ph.D., is Professor  of Language and Culture in the College of Education at the University of Florida. She researches and provides inservice to public schools nationally, focusing on literacy instruction for new immigrant students. Fu's books include *My Trouble is My English* and *An Island of English* addressing English language learners in the secondary schools. She has authored chapters in the *Handbook of Adolescent Literacy Research* and in *Adolescent Literacy: Turning Promise to Practice*.

Kelly Gallagher is a full-time English teacher at Magnolia High School in Anaheim, California. He is the former co-director of the South Basin Writing Project at California State University, Long Beach. Gallagher wrote *Reading Reasons: Motivational Mini-Lessons for the Middle and High School, Deeper Reading: Comprehending Challenging Texts 4-12,* and *Teaching Adolescent Writers.* Gallagher won the Secondary Award of Classroom Excellence from the California Association of Teachers of English—the state's top English teacher honor.

Sharroky Hollie, Ph.D., is an  assistant professor at California State University, Dominguez Hills, and an urban literacy visiting professor at Webster University, St. Louis. Hollie's work focuses on professional development, African American education, and second language methodology. He is a contributing author in two texts on culturally and linguistically responsive teaching. He is the Executive Director of the Center for Culturally Responsive Teaching and Learning and the co-founding director of the Culture and Language Academy of Success, an independent charter school in Los Angeles.

Dr. Donald J. Leu, Ph.D., teaches at the University of Connecticut and holds a joint appointment in Curriculum and Instruction and in Educational Psychology. He directs the New Literacies Research Lab and is a member of the Board of Directors of the International Reading Association. Leu studies the skills required to read, write, and learn with Internet technologies. His research has been funded by groups including the U.S. Department of Education, the National Science Foundation, and the Bill & Melinda Gates Foundation.

Jon Scieszka founded GUYS READ,  a nonprofit literacy initiative for boys, to call attention to the problem of getting boys connected with reading. In 2008, he was named the first U.S. National Ambassador for Young People's Literature by the Library of Congress. Scieszka taught from first grade to eighth grade for ten years in New York City, drawing inspiration from his students to write *The True Story of the 3 Little Pigs!*, *The Stinky Cheese Man*, the *Time Warp Trio* series of chapter books, and the *Trucktown* series of books for beginning readers.

Sharon Vaughn, Ph.D., teaches  at the University of Texas at Austin. She is the previous Editor-in-Chief of the *Journal of Learning Disabilities* and the co-editor of *Learning Disabilities Research and Practice*. She is the recipient of the American Education Research Association SIG Award for Outstanding Researcher. Vaughn's work focuses on effective practices for enhancing reading outcomes for students with reading difficulties. She is the author of more than 100 articles, and numerous books designed to improve research-based practices in the classroom.

Karen K. Wixson is Dean of the  School of Education at the University of North Carolina, Greensboro. She has published widely in the areas of literacy curriculum, instruction, and assessment. Wixson has been an advisor to the National Research Council and helped develop the National Assessment of Educational Progress (NAEP) reading tests. She is a past member of the IRA Board of Directors and co-chair of the IRA Commission on RTI. Recently, Wixson served on the English Language Arts Work Team that was part of the Common Core State Standards Initiative.

The selections in this book are presented through the lens of three Essential Questions:

What is the relationship between literature and place?

How does literature shape or reflect society?

What is the relationship of the writer to tradition?

Resources

From Legend to History
The Old English and Medieval Periods (A.D. 449 to 1485)

Celebrating Humanity
The English Renaissance Period (1485 to 1625)

PART TWO: **THE INFLUENCE OF THE MONARCHY**

© **Research Project:** Primary Sources

Contemporary Connection: Connecting Elizabeth I, Past and Present

Comparing Literary Works: Metaphors, Analogies, and Narratives

PART THREE: **DRAMA**

© **Extended Study:** Shakespearean Drama

Comparing Tragedy Past and Present

A Turbulent Time
The Seventeenth and Eighteenth Centuries (1625 to 1798)

PART THREE: **THE TIES THAT BIND**

PART FOUR: **THE ESSAY**

PHLit Online!
www.PHLitOnline.com

Interactive resources provide personalized instruction and activities online.

Literature

▶ Poetry

Informational Text—Literary Nonfiction

▶ Historical and Literary Background

▶ The British Tradition—Reading in the Humanities

Informational Text—Literary Nonfiction

▶ Literature in Context—Reading in the Content Areas

▶ World Literature Connections

Comparing Across World Literature

World Literature Connection

▶ Literary History

▶ Writing Workshops

▶ Communications Workshops

▶ Vocabulary Workshops

SAT PREP ACT Test-Taking Practice

Common Core State Standards Overview

The **Common Core State Standards** will prepare you to succeed in college and your future career. They are separated into four sections—Reading (Literature and Informational Text), Writing, Speaking and Listening, and Language. Beginning each section, the College and Career Readiness Anchor Standards define what you need to achieve by the end of high school. The grade-specific standards that follow define what you need to know by the end of your current grade level.

ⓒ Common Core Reading Standards

College and Career Readiness Anchor Standards

Key Ideas and Details

1. Read closely to determine what the text says explicitly and to make logical inferences from it; cite specific textual evidence when writing or speaking to support conclusions drawn from the text.

2. Determine central ideas or themes of a text and analyze their development; summarize the key supporting details and ideas.

3. Analyze how and why individuals, events, and ideas develop and interact over the course of a text.

Craft and Structure

4. Interpret words and phrases as they are used in a text, including determining technical, connotative, and figurative meanings, and analyze how specific word choices shape meaning or tone.

5. Analyze the structure of texts, including how specific sentences, paragraphs, and larger portions of the text (e.g., a section, chapter, scene, or stanza) relate to each other and the whole.

6. Assess how point of view or purpose shapes the content and style of a text.

Integration of Knowledge and Ideas

7. Integrate and evaluate content presented in diverse formats and media, including visually and quantitatively, as well as in words.

8. Delineate and evaluate the argument and specific claims in a text, including the validity of the reasoning as well as the relevance and sufficiency of the evidence.

9. Analyze how two or more texts address similar themes or topics in order to build knowledge or to compare the approaches the authors take.

Range of Reading and Level of Text Complexity

10. Read and comprehend complex literary and informational texts independently and proficiently.

Grade 12 Reading Standards for Literature

Key Ideas and Details

1. Cite strong and thorough textual evidence to support analysis of what the text says explicitly as well as inferences drawn from the text, including determining where the text leaves matters uncertain.

2. Determine two or more themes or central ideas of a text and analyze their development over the course of the text, including how they interact and build on one another to produce a complex account; provide an objective summary of the text.

3. Analyze the impact of the author's choices regarding how to develop and relate elements of a story or drama (e.g., where a story is set, how the action is ordered, how the characters are introduced and developed).

Craft and Structure

4. Determine the meaning of words and phrases as they are used in the text, including figurative and connotative meanings; analyze the impact of specific word choices on meaning and tone, including words with multiple meanings or language that is particularly fresh, engaging, or beautiful. (Include Shakespeare as well as other authors.)

5. Analyze how an author's choices concerning how to structure specific parts of a text (e.g., the choice of where to begin or end a story, the choice to provide a comedic or tragic resolution) contribute to its overall structure and meaning as well as its aesthetic impact.

6. Analyze a case in which grasping point of view requires distinguishing what is directly stated in a text from what is really meant (e.g., satire, sarcasm, irony, or understatement).

Integration of Knowledge and Ideas

7. Analyze multiple interpretations of a story, drama, or poem (e.g., recorded or live production of a play or recorded novel or poetry), evaluating how each version interprets the source text. (Include at least one play by Shakespeare and one play by an American dramatist.)

8. (Not applicable to literature)

9. Demonstrate knowledge of eighteenth-, nineteenth-, and early-twentieth-century foundational works of American literature, including how two or more texts from the same period treat similar themes or topics.

Range of Reading and Level of Text Complexity

10. By the end of grade 12, read and comprehend literature, including stories, dramas, and poems, at the high end of the grades 11–CCR text complexity band independently and proficiently.

Grade 12 Reading Standards for Informational Text

Key Ideas and Details

1. Cite strong and thorough textual evidence to support analysis of what the text says explicitly as well as inferences drawn from the text, including determining where the text leaves matters uncertain.

2. Determine two or more central ideas of a text and analyze their development over the course of the text, including how they interact and build on one another to provide a complex analysis; provide an objective summary of the text.

3. Analyze a complex set of ideas or sequence of events and explain how specific individuals, ideas, or events interact and develop over the course of the text.

Craft and Structure

4. Determine the meaning of words and phrases as they are used in a text, including figurative, connotative, and technical meanings; analyze how an author uses and refines the meaning of a key term or terms over the course of a text (e.g., how Madison defines *faction* in *Federalist* No. 10).

5. Analyze and evaluate the effectiveness of the structure an author uses in his or her exposition or argument, including whether the structure makes points clear, convincing, and engaging.

6. Determine an author's point of view or purpose in a text in which the rhetoric is particularly effective, analyzing how style and content contribute to the power, persuasiveness, or beauty of the text.

Integration of Knowledge and Ideas

7. Integrate and evaluate multiple sources of information presented in different media or formats (e.g., visually, quantitatively) as well as in words in order to address a question or solve a problem.

8. Delineate and evaluate the reasoning in seminal U.S. texts, including the application of constitutional principles and use of legal reasoning (e.g., in U.S. Supreme Court majority opinions and dissents) and the premises, purposes, and arguments in works of public advocacy (e.g., *The Federalist,* presidential addresses).

9. Analyze seventeenth-, eighteenth-, and nineteenth-century foundational U.S. documents of historical and literary significance (including The Declaration of Independence, the Preamble to the Constitution, the Bill of Rights, and Lincoln's Second Inaugural Address) for their themes, purposes, and rhetorical features.

Range of Reading and Level of Text Complexity

10. By the end of grade 12, read and comprehend literary nonfiction at the high end of the grades 11–CCR text complexity band independently and proficiently.

© Common Core Writing Standards

College and Career Readiness Anchor Standards

Text Types and Purposes

1. Write arguments to support claims in an analysis of substantive topics or texts, using valid reasoning and relevant and sufficient evidence.

2. Write informative/explanatory texts to examine and convey complex ideas and information clearly and accurately through the effective selection, organization, and analysis of content.

3. Write narratives to develop real or imagined experiences or events using effective technique, well-chosen details, and well-structured event sequences.

Production and Distribution of Writing

4. Produce clear and coherent writing in which the development, organization, and style are appropriate to task, purpose, and audience.

5. Develop and strengthen writing as needed by planning, revising, editing, rewriting, or trying a new approach.

6. Use technology, including the Internet, to produce and publish writing and to interact and collaborate with others.

Research to Build and Present Knowledge

7. Conduct short as well as more sustained research projects based on focused questions, demonstrating understanding of the subject under investigation.

8. Gather relevant information from multiple print and digital sources, assess the credibility and accuracy of each source, and integrate the information while avoiding plagiarism.

9. Draw evidence from literary or informational texts to support analysis, reflection, and research.

Range of Writing

10. Write routinely over extended time frames (time for research, reflection, and revision) and shorter time frames (a single sitting or a day or two) for a range of tasks, purposes, and audiences.

Grade 12 Writing Standards

Text Types and Purposes

1. Write arguments to support claims in an analysis of substantive topics or texts, using valid reasoning and relevant and sufficient evidence.

   a. Introduce precise, knowledgeable claim(s), establish the significance of the claim(s), distinguish the claim(s) from alternate or opposing claims, and create an organization that logically sequences claim(s), counterclaims, reasons, and evidence.

   b. Develop claim(s) and counterclaims fairly and thoroughly, supplying the most relevant evidence for each while pointing out the strengths and limitations of both in a manner that anticipates the audience's knowledge level, concerns, values, and possible biases.

   c. Use words, phrases, and clauses as well as varied syntax to link the major sections of the text, create cohesion, and clarify the relationships between claim(s) and reasons, between reasons and evidence, and between claim(s) and counterclaims.

   d. Establish and maintain a formal style and objective tone while attending to the norms and conventions of the discipline in which they are writing.

   e. Provide a concluding statement or section that follows from and supports the argument presented.

2. Write informative/explanatory texts to examine and convey complex ideas, concepts, and information clearly and accurately through the effective selection, organization, and analysis of content.

   a. Introduce a topic; organize complex ideas, concepts, and information so that each new element builds on that which precedes it to create a unified whole; include formatting (e.g., headings), graphics (e.g., figures, tables), and multimedia when useful to aiding comprehension.

   b. Develop the topic thoroughly by selecting the most significant and relevant facts, extended definitions, concrete details, quotations, or other information and examples appropriate to the audience's knowledge of the topic.

   c. Use appropriate and varied transitions and syntax to link the major sections of the text, create cohesion, and clarify the relationships among complex ideas and concepts.

   d. Use precise language, domain-specific vocabulary, and techniques such as metaphor, simile, and analogy to manage the complexity of the topic.

   e. Establish and maintain a formal style and objective tone while attending to the norms and conventions of the discipline in which they are writing.

   f. Provide a concluding statement or section that follows from and supports the information or explanation presented (e.g., articulating implications or the significance of the topic).

3. Write narratives to develop real or imagined experiences or events using effective technique, well-chosen details, and well-structured event sequences.

   a. Engage and orient the reader by setting out a problem, situation, or observation and its significance, establishing one or multiple point(s) of view, and introducing a narrator and/or characters; create a smooth progression of experiences or events.

    b. Use narrative techniques, such as dialogue, pacing, description, reflection, and multiple plot lines, to develop experiences, events, and/or characters.

    c. Use a variety of techniques to sequence events so that they build on one another to create a coherent whole and build toward a particular tone and outcome (e.g., a sense of mystery, suspense, growth, or resolution).

    d. Use precise words and phrases, telling details, and sensory language to convey a vivid picture of the experiences, events, setting, and/or characters.

    e. Provide a conclusion that follows from and reflects on what is experienced, observed, or resolved over the course of the narrative.

Production and Distribution of Writing

4. Produce clear and coherent writing in which the development, organization, and style are appropriate to task, purpose, and audience.

5. Develop and strengthen writing as needed by planning, revising, editing, rewriting, or trying a new approach, focusing on addressing what is most significant for a specific purpose and audience.

6. Use technology, including the Internet, to produce, publish, and update individual or shared writing products in response to ongoing feedback, including new arguments or information.

Research to Build and Present Knowledge

7. Conduct short as well as more sustained research projects to answer a question (including a self-generated question) or solve a problem; narrow or broaden the inquiry when appropriate; synthesize multiple sources on the subject, demonstrating understanding of the subject under investigation.

8. Gather relevant information from multiple authoritative print and digital sources, using advanced searches effectively; assess the strengths and limitations of each source in terms of the task, purpose, and audience; integrate information into the text selectively to maintain the flow of ideas, avoiding plagiarism and overreliance on any one source and following a standard format for citation.

9. Draw evidence from literary or informational texts to support analysis, reflection, and research.

    a. Apply *grades 11–12 Reading standards* to literature (e.g., "Demonstrate knowledge of eighteenth-, nineteenth-, and early-twentieth-century foundational works of American literature, including how two or more texts from the same period treat similar themes or topics").

    b. Apply *grades 11–12 Reading standards* to literary nonfiction (e.g., "Delineate and evaluate the reasoning in seminal U.S. texts, including the application of constitutional principles and use of legal reasoning [e.g., in U.S. Supreme Court Case majority opinions and dissents] and the premises, purposes, and arguments in works of public advocacy [e.g., *The Federalist,* presidential addresses]").

Range of Writing

10. Write routinely over extended time frames (time for research, reflection, and revision) and shorter time frames (a single sitting or a day or two) for a range of tasks, purposes, and audiences.

© Common Core Speaking and Listening Standards

College and Career Readiness Anchor Standards

Comprehension and Collaboration

1. Prepare for and participate effectively in a range of conversations and collaborations with diverse partners, building on others' ideas and expressing their own clearly and persuasively.

2. Integrate and evaluate information presented in diverse media and formats, including visually, quantitatively, and orally.

3. Evaluate a speaker's point of view, reasoning, and use of evidence and rhetoric.

Presentation of Knowledge and Ideas

4. Present information, findings, and supporting evidence such that listeners can follow the line of reasoning and the organization, development, and style are appropriate to task, purpose, and audience.

5. Make strategic use of digital media and visual displays of data to express information and enhance understanding of presentations.

6. Adapt speech to a variety of contexts and communicative tasks, demonstrating command of formal English when indicated or appropriate.

Grade 12 Speaking and Listening Standards

Comprehension and Collaboration

1. Initiate and participate effectively in a range of collaborative discussions (one-on-one, in groups, and teacher-led) with diverse partners on *grades 11–12 topics, texts, and issues,* building on others' ideas and expressing their own clearly and persuasively.

   a. Come to discussions prepared, having read and researched material under study; explicitly draw on that preparation by referring to evidence from texts and other research on the topic or issue to stimulate a thoughtful, wellreasoned exchange of ideas.

   b. Work with peers to promote civil, democratic discussions and decision-making, set clear goals and deadlines, and establish individual roles as needed.

   c. Propel conversations by posing and responding to questions that probe reasoning and evidence; ensure a hearing for a full range of positions on a topic or issue; clarify, verify, or challenge ideas and conclusions; and promote divergent and creative perspectives.

   d. Respond thoughtfully to diverse perspectives; synthesize comments, claims, and evidence made on all sides of an issue; resolve contradictions when possible; and determine what additional information or research is required to deepen the investigation or complete the task.

2. Integrate multiple sources of information presented in diverse formats and media (e.g., visually, quantitatively, orally) in order to make informed decisions and solve problems, evaluating the credibility and accuracy of each source and noting any discrepancies among the data.

3. Evaluate a speaker's point of view, reasoning, and use of evidence and rhetoric, assessing the stance, premises, links among ideas, word choice, points of emphasis, and tone used.

Presentation of Knowledge and Ideas

4. Present information, findings, and supporting evidence, conveying a clear and distinct perspective, such that listeners can follow the line of reasoning, alternative or opposing perspectives are addressed, and the organization, development, substance, and style are appropriate to purpose, audience, and a range of formal and informal tasks.

5. Make strategic use of digital media (e.g., textual, graphical, audio, visual, and interactive elements) in presentations to enhance understanding of findings, reasoning, and evidence and to add interest.

6. Adapt speech to a variety of contexts and tasks, demonstrating a command of formal English when indicated or appropriate. (See grades 11–12 Language standards 1 and 3 for specific expectations.)

© Common Core Language Standards

College and Career Readiness Anchor Standards

Conventions of Standard English

1. Demonstrate command of the conventions of standard English grammar and usage when writing or speaking.

2. Demonstrate command of the conventions of standard English capitalization, punctuation, and spelling when writing.

Knowledge of Language

3. Apply knowledge of language to understand how language functions in different contexts, to make effective choices for meaning or style, and to comprehend more fully when reading or listening.

Vocabulary Acquisition and Use

4. Determine or clarify the meaning of unknown and multiple-meaning words and phrases by using context clues, analyzing meaningful word parts, and consulting general and specialized reference materials, as appropriate.

5. Demonstrate understanding of figurative language, word relationships, and nuances in word meanings.

6. Acquire and use accurately a range of general academic and domain-specific words and phrases sufficient for reading, writing, speaking, and listening at the college and career readiness level; demonstrate independence in gathering vocabulary knowledge when considering a word or phrase important to comprehension or expression.

Grade 12 Language Standards

Conventions of Standard English

1. Demonstrate command of the conventions of standard English grammar and usage when writing or speaking.

   a. Apply the understanding that usage is a matter of convention, can change over time, and is sometimes contested.

   b. Resolve issues of complex or contested usage, consulting references (e.g., *Merriam-Webster's Dictionary of English Usage, Garner's Modern American Usage*) as needed.

2. Demonstrate command of the conventions of standard English capitalization, punctuation, and spelling when writing.

   a. Observe hyphenation conventions.

   b. Spell correctly.

Knowledge of Language

3. Apply knowledge of language to understand how language functions in different contexts, to make effective choices for meaning or style, and to comprehend more fully when reading or listening.

   a. Vary syntax for effect, consulting references (e.g., Tufte's *Artful Sentences*) for guidance as needed; apply an understanding of syntax to the study of complex texts when reading.

Vocabulary Acquisition and Use

4. Determine or clarify the meaning of unknown and multiple-meaning words and phrases based on *grades 11–12 reading and content,* choosing flexibly from a range of strategies.

   a. Use context (e.g., the overall meaning of a sentence, paragraph, or text; a word's position or function in a sentence) as a clue to the meaning of a word or phrase.

   b. Identify and correctly use patterns of word changes that indicate different meanings or parts of speech (e.g., *conceive, conception, conceivable*).

   c. Consult general and specialized reference materials (e.g., dictionaries, glossaries, thesauruses), both print and digital, to find the pronunciation of a word or determine or clarify its precise meaning, its part of speech, its etymology, or its standard usage.

   d. Verify the preliminary determination of the meaning of a word or phrase (e.g., by checking the inferred meaning in context or in a dictionary).

5. Demonstrate understanding of figurative language, word relationships, and nuances in word meanings.

   a. Interpret figures of speech (e.g., hyperbole, paradox) in context and analyze their role in the text.

   b. Analyze nuances in the meaning of words with similar denotations.

6. Acquire and use accurately general academic and domain-specific words and phrases, sufficient for reading, writing, speaking, and listening at the college and career readiness level; demonstrate independence in gathering vocabulary knowledge when considering a word or phrase important to comprehension or expression.

Introductory Unit

COMMON CORE
Workshops

Building Academic Vocabulary

Writing an Objective Summary

Comprehending Complex Texts

Analyzing Arguments

Common Core
State Standards

Reading Literature 2, 4
Reading Informational Text 2, 4, 6, 8, 9
Writing 1.a, 1.b, 1.e, 9, 9.b
Language 6

Building Academic Vocabulary

Academic vocabulary is the language used in school, on standardized tests, and—often—in the business world. Academic terms are more formal and specific than the informal vocabulary most people use among friends and family members. Success in school and later in work requires a clear understanding of different types of academic language. The Common Core State Standards require that you acquire and use grade-appropriate academic words and phrases.

Technical Domain-Specific Academic Vocabulary The literary concepts you will learn throughout this book are one type of academic language. These words are specific to the content area—the subject or discipline—of literature. Other disciplines, such as social studies, the sciences, mathematics, and the arts, have their own academic vocabularies. Some content-area words cross disciplines, or have different meanings when applied to different areas of study.

Technical words are an even more specialized type of domain-specific academic vocabulary. These are words and phrases, such as the following, that identify a precise element in the content area and usually do not appear in other disciplines:

Science: pipette; genome
Music: clef; libretto

Critical Reading and Thinking Terms Many academic terms define modes of thinking, discussing, or writing about ideas. In this book, these words appear in the Critical Reading questions at the ends of the selections. Such academic terms also appear in instructions and writing prompts.

A Note on Etymology
Etymology is the branch of linguistics that deals with word origins and the development of languages. Etymologists trace the history of a word in its own language, and then to even earlier sources in other, more ancient languages. Knowledge of a word's etymology will contribute to your understanding of its meaning and help you determine the meaning of other words that share its history. Etymological information for content-area words appears in the charts on the following pages.

Common Core State Standards

Language 6. Acquire and use accurately general academic and domain-specific words and phrases, sufficient for reading, writing, speaking, and listening at the college and career readiness level; demonstrate independence in gathering vocabulary knowledge when considering a word or phrase important to comprehension or expression.

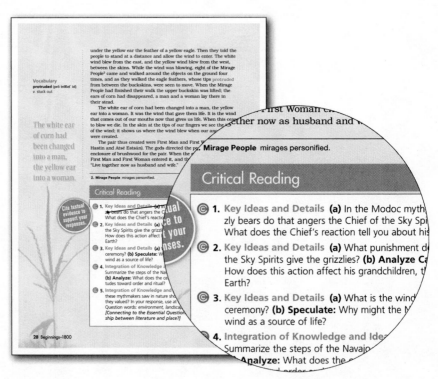

Technical Domain-Specific Academic Vocabulary

Knowledge of technical content-area academic words, and the roots and affixes that compose them, will help you in all your school courses. As you review the charts below, recognize words that apply to content areas other than those specified here.

Technical Domain-Specific Academic Vocabulary: Science

Term	Meaning	Root/Affix
Accelerate	*v.* increase speed	Latin root -*celer-* = swift Words with the same root: accelerator *n.*; celerity *n.*
Catalyst	*n.* something that acts to bring about a result	Latin root -*cata-* = down; away Words with the same root: cataclysm *n.*; catapult *n.*
Chlorophyll	*n.* green pigment found in plant cells	Greek root -*chloro-* = green Words with the same root: chlorine *n.*; chlorosis *n.*
Chromosome	*n.* strand of proteins that carries the genes of a living creature	Greek prefix *chromo-* = color; pigment Words with the same prefix: chromatic *adj.*; chromate *n.*
Cytoplasm	*n.* colorless substance of a cell; outside the nucleus	Greek suffix -*plasm* = molded; formed Words with the same suffix: bioplasm *n.*; protoplasm *n.*
Entropy	*n.* lack of order which increases over time in a system	Greek root -*tropos-* = turning; deviation Words with the same root: tropical *adj.*; trophy *n.*; heliotrope *n.*
Enzyme	*n.* chemical substance produced by living cells that causes changes in other chemicals	Greek suffix -*zyme* = leavening (an agent that causes fermentation) Words with the same suffix: vitazyme *n.*; microzyme *n.*
Mitosis	*n.* method of cell division	Greek suffix -*osis* = action; process Words with the same suffix: prognosis *n.*; psychosis *n.*
Thermometer	*n.* instrument for measuring temperature	Greek root -*therme-* = hot Words with the same root: thermonuclear *adj.*; thermostat *n.*
Viscous	*adj.* having a thick and sticky fluid consistency	Latin prefix *visco-* = sticky Words with the same prefix: viscometer *n.*; viscosity *n.*

Ordinary Language: Ice cubes placed in water will begin to break down.

Academic Language: Ice cubes placed in water will begin the process of entropy.

Exploring Academic Vocabulary: Science

The word *thermometer* combines the Greek roots -*therme-*, which means "heat," and -*metr-*, which means "measure." Using this knowledge, determine the meaning of the following words derived from the same roots:

dynameter   **odometer**   **hypothermia**   **thermography**

Then, use a dictionary to confirm the definitions you proposed. If a general dictionary is not sufficient, consult a specialized science dictionary to find the information you need. Explain how the meaning of each word relates to those of its Greek origins.

Technical Domain-Specific Academic Vocabulary: Mathematics

Term	Meaning	Root/Affix
Correlate	*v.* show mutual relationship between items	Latin prefix *cor-* = together; with Words with the same prefix: correspond *v.*; corrosion *n.*
Exponent	*n.* symbol placed above and to the right of a number or letter to show how many times that quantity is to be multiplied by itself	Latin suffix *-ponent* = to put; place; set Words with the same suffix: component *n.*; proponent *n.*
Inflection	*n.* change of a curve or arc from convex to concave or the reverse	Latin root *-flectere-* = to bend Words with the same root: reflection *n.*; deflect *v.*
Logarithm	*n.* power to which a base must be raised to produce a given number	Greek prefix *logos-* = word; speech; reason Words with the same prefix: logic *n.*; logotype *n.*
Statistics	*n.* numerical facts or data	Latin root *-stat-* = condition; position; state Words with the same root: statistical *adj.*; static *adj.*
Permutation	*n.* one of the ways in which a set of things can be arranged or ordered	Latin root *-mutare-* = change Words with the same root: mutable *adj.;* mutation *n.*
Estimate	*v.* calculate approximately	Middle French root *-estimer-* = value; appraise Words with the same root: estimation *n.*; esteem *v.*
Graphic	*adj.* relating to the use of diagrams, graphs, curves	Greek root *-graph-* = writing; drawing Words with the same root: telegraph *n.*; biography *n.*; autograph *n.*
Configure	*v.* construct; arrange	Latin root *-figura-* = shape; form; figure Words with the same root: disfigure *v.*; effigy *n.*

Ordinary Language: We arranged the **numerical information** in different charts.

Academic Language: We incorporated **statistical data** into charts.

Exploring Academic Vocabulary: Mathematics

The word *correlate* is built on the Latin prefix *cor-* (also *com-* or *con-*), which means "with" or "together." Using this knowledge, determine the meaning of the following words derived from the same prefix:

correspond   **concert**   **compress**   **congruent**

Then, use an online or print dictionary to confirm the definitions you proposed. Explain how the meaning of each word relates to that of its Latin ancestor.

Technical Domain-Specific Academic Vocabulary: Social Studies

Term	Meaning	Root/Affix
Corporation	*n.* organization of many people authorized to act as a single person	Latin root *-corpus-* = body Words with the same root: corporeal *adj.*; incorporate *v.*
Demography	*n.* study of human populations	Greek prefix *demos-* = people Words with the same prefix: demographic *n.*; democracy *n.*
Economy	*n.* system by which a country's money and goods are used and produced	Greek suffix *-nomy* = law; received knowledge Words with the same suffix: economy *n.*; taxonomy *n.*
Invest	*v.* give money to a company in order to receive a profit	Latin root *-vestire-* = dress; clothe Words with the same root: vestment *n.*; investigation *n.*
Admiral	*n.* high-ranking naval officer	Arabic root *-amir-* = leader Words with the same root: emirate *n.*; admiralship *n.*
Curfew	*n.* law requiring a population to stay indoors at a stated hour	Old French root *-covrir-* = to cover Words with the same root: covert *adj.*; coverlet *n.*
Lieutenant	*n.* someone who substitutes for another person of greater authority	Old French root *-lieu-* = place Word with the same root: milieu *n.*
Absolutism	*n.* system of government in which a ruler has unlimited power	Latin prefix *ab-* = away; from Words with the same prefix: absolve *v.*
Civic	*adj.* of a city, citizens, or citizenship	Latin root *-civ-* = citizen Words with the same root: civilian *n.*; civilization *n.*

Ordinary Language:
The government urges citizens to **put money into** local businesses.

Academic Language:
The government urges citizens to **invest in** local businesses.

Exploring Academic Vocabulary: Social Studies

The word *economy* is built on the Greek suffix *–nomy*, which means "law; body of received knowledge." Using this knowledge, determine the meaning of the following words derived from the same suffix:

taxonomy   **autonomy**   **astronomy**   **gastronomy**

Then, use an online or print dictionary to confirm the definitions you proposed. Explain how the meaning of each word relates to that of its Greek ancestor.

Technical Domain-Specific Academic Vocabulary: Technology

Term	Meaning	Root/Affix
Gigabyte	*n.* unit of storage capacity in a computer system equal to 1,073,741,824 bytes	Greek prefix *giga-* = giant Words with the same prefix: gigahertz *n.*; gigantic *adj.*
Macro	*n.* single computer instruction that represents a sequence of operations	Greek prefix *macro-* = long, tall, deep, large Words with the same prefix: macrobiotic *adj.*; macrocosm *n.*
Pixel	*n.* smallest unit of an image on a television or computer screen	Old French suffix *–el* = small one Words with the same suffix: satchel *n.*; model *n.*
Processor	*n.* central part of a computer that does the calculations needed to deal with the information it is given	from Latin root *-cedere-* = to go Words with the same root: proceed *v.*; recede *v.*
Simulation	*n.* situation that produces conditions that are not real but appear real	Latin root *-sim-* = like derived through Indo-European base *sem-/som-* = same; as one Words with the same root: ensemble *v.*; simultaneous *adj.*
Streaming	*n.* method of transmitting data so that it can be delivered and received in a steady stream	German root *-strom-* = current; river Words with the same root: mainstream *n.*; streamline *v.*
Transmitter	*n.* equipment that sends out radio or television signals	Latin prefix *trans-* = across Words with the same prefix: transportation *n.*; transcontinental *adj.*
Debug	*v.* find and correct defects	Latin prefix *de-* = down; from Words with the same prefix: defuse *v.*; defrost *v.*
Export	*v.* in computers, to save data in a format usable by another program	Latin root *-portare-* = to carry Words with the same root: import *v.*; airport *n.*
Binary	*adj.* made up of two parts or things; twofold	Latin root *-bin-* = together; double Words with the same root: binocular *n.*; binomial *n.*

Ordinary Language: I asked the technician to clean up my computer.

Academic Language: I asked the technician to debug my operating system.

Exploring Academic Vocabulary: Technology

The word *simulation* comes from the Latin root *-sim-,* which means "like." This Latin root derives from the Indo-European base *sem-/som-,* which means "same; as one." Using your knowledge of these origins, determine the meaning of the following words derived from the same roots:

resemble   facsimile   verisimilitude   semblance

Then, use a dictionary to confirm the definitions you proposed. Explain how the meaning of each word relates to that of its Indo-European base.

Technical Domain-Specific Academic Vocabulary: The Arts

Term	Meaning	Root/Affix
Allegro	*adv.* faster than allegretto but not so fast as presto	Latin root -*alacer-/-alacris-* = lively; brisk Words with the same root: allegretto *adj.*; *adv.*; alacrity *n.*
Alignment	*n.* arrangement in a straight line	Old French root -*lignier-* = to line Words with the same root: align *v.*; realign *v.*
Craftmanship	*n.* skill used in making handmade objects	Middle English suffix -*schipe*; derived through Anglian suffix -*scip* = state; condition; quality Words with the same suffix: friendship *n.*; dictatorship *n.*
Decrescendo	*n.* gradual decrease in volume	Old French *creissant*; derived through Latin root -*crescere-* = come forth; spring up; grow; thrive Words with the same root: crescent *n.*; increase *v.*
Baritone	*n.* male singing voice lower than a tenor and higher than a bass	Latin root -*tonus-* = sound; tone Words with the same root: monotone *n.*; intonation *n.*
Medium	*n.* material or technique used in art	Latin root -*medius-* = middle Words with the same root: media *n.*; mediate *v.*; median *adj.*
Musicality	*n.* sensitivity to, knowledge of, or talent for music	Latin suffix -*ity* = quality; state; or degree Words with the same suffix: normality *n.*; publicity *n.*
Technique	*n.* method or procedure in rendering an artistic work	Indo-European prefix *tek-* = shape; make Words with the same prefix: technical *adj.*; technician *n.*
Tempo	*n.* speed at which a composition is performed	Latin root -*tempus-* = time Words with the same root: temporal *adj.*; temporary *adj.*

Ordinary Language:
The dancers moved in a perfectly **straight line.**

Academic Language:
The dancers moved in perfect **alignment** on stage.

Exploring Academic Vocabulary: The Arts

The word *craftsmanship* is built on the Anglian suffix *–scip*, which means "state, condition, quality." Using this knowledge, determine the meaning of the following words derived from the same suffix:

musicianship   **readership**   **friendship**   **partnership**

Then, use an online or print dictionary to confirm the definitions you proposed. Explain how the meaning of each word relates to that of its Anglian ancestor.

Vocabulary Across Content Areas

You might recognize words that apply to content areas other than those specified in the charts on the previous pages. For example, notice how the word *accelerator* relates to two different content areas:

> **Science: accelerator** *n.* nerve or muscle that speeds up a body function

> **Automotive Technology: accelerator** *n.* device, such as the foot throttle of an automobile, for increasing the speed of a machine

While the objects referred to in each definition are different, both of their functions relate to the Latin root *–celer–,* meaning "swift." As you read texts for school, recognize similarities in roots or affixes among words in different content areas. This will help you better understand specific terms and make meaningful connections among topics.

Academic Vocabulary: Critical Thinking Terms

Throughout this book, you will encounter academic vocabulary related to the process of critical thinking. Unlike content-area vocabulary, these words apply equally in all school studies. Being familiar with these academic vocabulary words will be useful as you approach high-stakes standardized tests such as the SAT and ACT. Academic vocabulary will also aid you as you encounter business materials in the workplace.

Term (verb form)	Meaning	Root/Affix
Advocate	Speak or write in support of	Latin root *-voc-* = speak; call Related words: advocate *n.*; advocacy *n.*
Anticipate	Prepare for or signal something	Latin prefix *ante-* = before Related words: anticipatory *adj.*; anticipation *n.*
Arrange	Put into order or sequence	Old French root *-rang-* = rank Related words: arrangement *n.*
Assess	Determine importance; size; or value	Latin root *-sed-/-sess-* = sit Related words: assessment *n.*
Categorize	Place in related groups	Greek prefix *kata-/cata-* = down; against Related words: category *n.*; categorical *adj.*
Compare	Examine in order to discover similarities	Latin root *-par-* = equal Related words: comparison *n.*; comparable *adj.*
Conclude	Determination reached through logical reasoning	Latin root *-clud-* = shut Related words: conclusion *n.*; conclusive *adj.*
Contrast	Examine in order to discover differences	Latin prefix *con-/com-* = with; together Related words: contrastable *adj.*
Debate	Discuss opposing reasons; argue	French root *-batre-* = to beat Related words: debatable *adj.*

Term (verb form)	Meaning	Root/Affix
Deduce	Infer from a general principle	Latin root -duc- = to lead Related words: deduction *n.*; deductive *adj.*
Defend	Maintain or support in the face of argument	Latin root -fend- = to strike; push Related words: defense *n.*; defendant *n.*
Describe	Represent in words	Latin root -scrib- = to write Related words: description *n.*; descriptive *adj.*
Design	Create; fashion or construct according to plan	Latin root -sign- = to mark Related words: design *n.*; designer *n.*
Devise	Form in the mind by new combinations of ideas; invent	Latin root -vid- = to separate Related words: devisable *adj.*
Differentiate	Recognize a difference	Latin suffix -ate = act Related words: different *adj.*; differentiation *n.*
Evaluate	Determine significance, worth, or condition through careful study	Old French root -val- = worth; value Related words: evaluation *n.*; evaluative *adj.*
Format	Arrange according to a design or plan	Latin root -form- = form, shape Related words: format *n.*; formation *n.*
Generalize	Draw a larger principle from details	Latin root -genus- = stock; kind Related words: generalization *n.*
Hypothesize	Develop a theory about	Greek prefix *hypo-* = under, beneath Related words: hypothesis *n.*; hypothetically *adv.*
Illustrate	Give examples that support an idea	Latin root -lus- = brighten; illuminate Related words: illustration *n.*; illustrative *adj.*
Interpret	Explain the meaning of	Latin root -inter- = between Related words: interpretation *n.*; interpreter *n.*
Investigate	Make a systematic examination	French root -vestige- = mark; trace; sign Related words: investigation *n.*; investigative *adj.*
Paraphrase	Express in one's own words what another person has said or written	Greek prefix *para-* = beside Related words: paraphraser *n.*
Predict	Foretell on the basis of observation, experience, or reason	Latin root -dic- = speak, tell, say Related words: prediction *n.*; predictable *adj.*
Refute	Prove an argument or statement false or wrong	Latin root -fut- = beat Related words: refutable *adj.*; refutably *adv.*
Sort	Put in place according to kind, class, or nature	Old French root -sortir- = allot; assort Related words: sorter *n.*
Speculate	Use evidence to guess what might happen	Latin root -spec- = look at; view Related words: speculation *n.*; speculative *adj.*
Structure	Create a general plot or outline	Latin root -struct- = to build; assemble Related words: structure *n.*; structural *adj.*
Validate	Prove to be factual or effective	Latin root -val- = be strong Related words: valid *adj.*; validity *n.*

Ordinary Language:
She explained the meaning of the story's symbols.

Academic Language:
She interpreted the meaning of the story's symbols.

Writing an Objective Summary

The ability to write objective summaries is important in college course work and in many careers, such as journalism, business, law, various medical fields, social work, and research. Writing an effective objective summary involves recording the key ideas of a text as well as demonstrating your understanding of the text.

Common Core State Standards

Reading Informational Text
2. Determine two or more central ideas of a text and analyze their development over the course of the text, including how they interact and build on one another to provide a complex analysis; provide an objective summary of the text.

Reading Literature
2. Determine two or more themes or central ideas of a text and analyze their development over the course of the text, including how they interact and build on one another to produce a complex account; provide an objective summary of the text.

Characteristics of an Objective Summary

An effective objective summary is a concise, overview of a text. Following are important elements of an objective summary:

- It is **focused,** relaying the main theme or central idea of a text. It includes specific, relevant details that support that theme or central idea and leaves out unnecessary supporting details.

- It is **brief,** although the writer must be careful to balance brevity and thoroughness and not misrepresent the text by eliminating important parts.

- It is **accurate.** It captures the essence of the longer text it is describing.

- It is **objective.** The writer should refrain from inserting his or her own opinions, judgments, reactions, or personal reflections into the summary.

  Remember that an objective summary is *not* a collection of sentences or paragraphs copied from the original source. It is *not* a long retelling of every event, detail, or point in the original text. Finally, a good summary does *not* include evaluative comments, such as the reader's overall opinion of or reaction to the text.

Checklist for Writing an Objective Summary

Before writing an objective summary, be sure you are well acquainted with the text.

- **Understand the entire passage.** You must clearly understand the text's meaning, including any advanced or technical terminology. In your summary, refer to details from the beginning, middle, and end of the text.

- **Prioritize ideas and details.** Determine the main or central ideas of a text and identify the key supporting details. Make sure you recognize which details are less important so that you do not include them in your objective summary.

- **Identify the author's audience and purpose.** Knowing what the author intended to accomplish in the text as well as what audience it was designed to reach will help you summarize accurately.

INFORMATIONAL TEXT

Model Objective Summary

Note the key elements of an effective objective summary, called out in the sidenotes. Then, write an objective summary of a text you have recently read. Review your summary, and delete any unnecessary details, opinions, or evaluations.

Summary of "The Story of an Hour"

"The Story of an Hour" by ~~the under-appreciated~~ Kate Chopin is a short story about a woman who is told her husband is dead. Set in the late nineteenth century, the story takes place in the home of Mrs. Louise Mallard.

Because of Mrs. Mallard's heart condition, her sister Josephine tells her the news gently. Richards, a family friend, had been in the newspaper office when a telegram was received that told of a railroad disaster, and Brently Mallard was listed as dead. Mrs. Mallard immediately takes in the news and begins to weep, heading to her room alone.

She sits in an armchair and looks out the window. She notices signs of life everywhere, which contrast with her loss. ~~It is so very sad~~.

Then a thought begins to come to her as she looks at the blue patches in the sky. She breathes heavily as she struggles with the full comprehension of the thought that is trying to possess her, but she gives in. She whispers the word: "Free." She repeats the word over and over. Her eyes brighten, her heart beats quickly, and her body relaxes.

She decides that she will cry at the dead body of the man who loved her, but she welcomes the years beyond that. She looks forward to living independently. The thought of freedom is exhilarating.

Josephine begs her to open the door, but Louise refuses.

She imagines the days ahead and prays that her life will be long, remembering that the day before she had dreaded the thought of a long life. She finally lets her sister in ~~and holds her tight around her waist~~. Together they go downstairs to meet Richards.

Brently Mallard, alive and unharmed, then walks through the front door. He was unaware of the accident at the railroad and surprised at the cry of his wife.

The doctors said her weak heart could not stand such joy; they called it the "joy that kills."

A one-sentence synopsis highlighting the theme or central idea of the story can be an effective start to a summary. Relating the setting of the text gives the summary context.

Opinions should not be included in an objective summary.

These sentences are too detailed and too interpretative to be included in an objective summary. More appropriate would be a simpler statement, such as, "Suddenly a thought came to her."

Eliminate unnecessary details.

The writer includes the last phrase in the story because the irony is a key element of the story.

Comprehending Complex Texts

As you prepare for higher education and the workplace, you will be required to read increasingly complex texts. A complex text features one or more of the following qualities:

- challenging vocabulary
- long, complex sentences
- figurative language
- multiple levels of meaning
- unfamiliar settings and situations

The selections in this textbook provide you with a range of readings in many genres. Some of these texts will be quite accessible, while others will be, and should be, more challenging. In order to comprehend and interpret complex texts, practice the reading strategies described here.

Strategy 1: Multi-draft Reading

Good readers develop the habit of rereading texts in order to comprehend them completely. Similar to listening to a song over and over in order to better understand the lyrics and relive the emotional experience, returning to a text enables readers to more fully enjoy and comprehend it. To fully understand a text, try this multi-draft reading strategy:

1st Reading
The first time you read a text, read to gain its basic meaning. If you are reading a narrative text, look for the basics of the plot, character, and setting. If the text is nonfiction, look for central ideas. If you are reading poetry, read first to get a sense of speaker, topic, and mood.

2nd Reading
During your second reading of a text, look for deeper meaning by applying your literary analysis skills. Focus on the artistry or effectiveness of the writing. Look for text structures. Think about why the author chose those organizational patterns. Examine the author's use of language and its effect. For example, consider the effect of rhyme, figurative language, or words with distinct connotations.

3rd Reading
In this reading, search for multiple levels of meaning, considering historical and cultural context. Now is the time to compare and contrast the text with others of its kind you have read. Consider it in the context of its genre, and make connections between texts. You may also make connections between the text and your own experiences. After your third reading, you should be able to evaluate the text's overall effectiveness and its central idea or theme.

Common Core
State Standards

Reading Literature
4. Determine the meaning of words and phrases as they are used in the text, including figurative and connotative meanings; analyze the impact of specific word choices on meaning and tone, including words with multiple meanings or language that is particularly fresh, engaging, or beautiful.

Reading Informational Text
4. Determine the meaning of words and phrases as they are used in a text, including figurative, connotative, and technical meanings; analyze how an author uses and refines the meaning of a key term or terms over the course of a text (e.g., how Madison defines *faction* in *Federalist* No. 10).

9. Analyze seventeenth-, eighteenth- and nineteenth-century foundational U.S. documents of historical and literary significance (including the Declaration of Independence, the Preamble to the Constitution, the Bill of Rights, and Lincoln's Second Inaugural Address) for their themes, purposes, and rhetorical features.

Independent Practice

As you read this poem by John Keats, practice the multi-draft reading strategy by completing a chart like the one below.

On the Grasshopper and Cricket
by John Keats

The poetry of earth is never dead:

When all the birds are faint with the hot sun,

And hide in cooling trees, a voice will run

From hedge to hedge about the new-mown mead;

That is the Grasshopper's—he takes the lead

In summer luxury—he has never done

With his delights; for when tired out with fun

He rests at ease beneath some pleasant weed.

The poetry of earth is ceasing never:

On a lone winter evening, when the frost

Has wrought a silence, from the stove there shrills

The Cricket's song, in warmth increasing ever,

And seems to one in drowsiness half lost,

The Grasshopper's among some grassy hills.

Multi-Draft Reading Chart

	My Understanding
1st Reading Look for key ideas and details that reveal basic meaning.	
2nd Reading Read for deeper meanings. Look for ways in which the author used text structures and language to create effects.	
3rd Reading Integrate knowledge and ideas. Consider cultural and historical context and genre. Connect the text to your own experience.	

Strategy 2: Close Read the Text

Complex texts require close reading and a careful analysis of the writer's choice of words, phrases, and sentences. An awareness of literary and rhetorical techniques and elements, such as parallelism, symbolism, analogy, and text structure, contributes to a deep understanding of a complex text. However, a starting point for close reading is comprehension, which is the foundation for interpretation and analysis. Use the following tips to comprehend the text:

Tips for Close Reading

1. **Break down long sentences into parts.** Look for the subject of the sentence and its verb. Then identify which parts of the sentence modify, or give more information about, its subject.

2. **Reread passages.** When reading complex texts, be sure to reread passages to confirm that you understand their meaning. Look for rhetorical devices and persuasive techniques.

3. **Look for context clues,** such as
   a. Restatement of an idea. For example, in this sentence, *small* restates the adjective *diminutive*.

      She received only a **diminutive** sum, but she was able to make the <u>small</u> amount last the rest of the month.

   b. Definition of sophisticated words. In this sentence, the word *depravity* defines the verb *turpitude*.

      The **turpitude**, or <u>depravity</u>, of the young character in the film stunned the audience to silence.

   c. Examples of concepts and topics. In the following sentence, the underlined text provides examples of words that suggest the meaning of the adjective *melancholy*.

      The **melancholy** territory of gothic literature includes <u>gloomy</u> settings, <u>eerie</u> occurrences, and <u>emotionally troubled</u> characters.

   d. Contrasts of ideas and topics.

      Their **banter** evolved into a <u>serious conversation.</u>

4. **Identify pronoun antecedents.** If long sentences contain pronouns, reread the text to make sure you know to what the pronouns refer. The pronoun *it* in the following sentence refers to the infinitive phrase *to protest injustices,* not to the government.

   The government should assume that **it** is not harmful <u>to protest injustices.</u>
   (The government should assume that to protest injustices is not harmful.)

5. **Look for conjunctions,** such as *and, or, however, accordingly,* and *yet,* to help you understand relationships between ideas.

6. **Paraphrase,** or restate in your own words, passages of difficult text in order to check your understanding. Remember that a paraphrase is essentially a word-for-word restatement of an original text; it is not a summary.

INFORMATIONAL TEXT

Close-Read Model

As you read this document, take note of the sidenotes that model ways to unlock meaning in the text.

from "Defending Nonviolent Resistance"
by Mohandas K. Gandhi

Affection cannot be manufactured or regulated by law. If one has an affection for a person or system, one should be free to give the fullest expression to his disaffection, so long as he does not contemplate, promote, or incite to violence. But the section under which Mr. Banker [a colleague in nonviolence] and I are charged is one under which mere promotion of disaffection is as crime. I have studied some of the cases tried under it, and I know that some of the most loved of India's patriots have been convicted under it. I consider it a privilege, therefore, to be charged under that section. I have endeavored to give in their briefest outline the reasons for my disaffection. I have no personal ill will against any single administrator, much less can I have any disaffection toward the king's person. But I hold it to be a virtue to be disaffected toward a government which in its totality has done more harm to India than any previous system. India is less manly under the British rule than she ever was before. Holding such a belief, I consider it to be a sin to have affection for the system. And it has been a precious privilege for me to be able to write what I have in the various articles, tendered in evidence against me.

In fact, I believe that I have rendered a service to India and England by showing in non-cooperation the way out of the unnatural state in which both are living. In my humble opinion, non-cooperation with evil is as much a duty as is cooperation with good. But in the past, non-cooperation has been deliberately expressed in violence to the evildoer. I am endeavoring to show to my countrymen that violent non-cooperation only multiplies evil and that as evil can only be sustained by violence, withdrawal of support of evil requires complete abstention from violence. Nonviolence implies voluntary submission to the penalty for non-cooperation with evil. I am here, therefore, to invite and submit cheerfully to the highest penalty that be inflicted upon me for what in law is a deliberate crime and what appears to me to be the highest duty of a citizen. The only course open to you, the judge, is either to resign your post, and thus dissociate yourself from evil if you feel that the law you are called upon to administer is an evil and that in reality I am innocent, or to inflict on me the severest penalty if you believe that the system and the law you are assisting to administer are good for the people of this country and that my activity is therefore injurious to the public weal.

Note rhetorical devices, such as Gandhi's use of antithesis—connecting contrasting ideas—here.

The conjunction *But* indicates a contrasting idea: Gandhi has no ill will toward a single person, but he does have disaffection toward the totality of the government.

Look for antecedents. The antecedent of the first *it* comes after the pronoun: *to be disaffected toward a government…* The antecedent of the second *it* is *government*.

Search for context clues. The words in blue are context clues that help you figure out the meaning of the word that appears in yellow.

Break down this long sentence into parts. The text highlighted in yellow conveys the basic meaning of the sentence. The text highlighted in blue provides additional information.

Strategy 3: Ask Questions

Be an attentive reader by asking questions as you read. Throughout this program, we have provided questions for you following each selection. Those questions are sorted into three basic categories that build in sophistication and lead you to a deeper understanding of the texts. Here is an example from this textbook:

Some questions are about **Key Ideas and Details** in the text. You will need to locate and cite explicit information in the text or draw inferences from what you have read.

Some questions are about **Craft and Structure** in the text. To answer these questions, you will need to analyze how the author developed and structured the text. You will also look for ways in which the author artfully used language and how those word choices impacted the meaning and tone of the work.

Critical Reading

1. **Key Ideas and Details (a)** What does the doctor see in the sleepwalking scene, and what does he speculate about the causes for what he sees? **(b) Analyze:** How have Macbeth and Lady Macbeth reversed roles by the end of the play?

2. **Key Ideas and Details (a)** What does Macbeth say when he hears of Lady Macbeth's death? **(b) Draw Conclusions:** What does his reaction to her death reveal about their relationship and his state of mind?

3. **Key Ideas and Details (a)** What does Macbeth say about the witches when he learns that Birnam Wood is apparently moving and that Macduff "was from his mother's womb / Untimely ripped"? **(b) Infer:** What growing realization do these statements about the witches seem to reflect? **(c) Draw Conclusions:** What is Macbeth's state of mind in his final battle with Macduff? Explain.

4. **Craft and Structure (a)** What occurs in Act V, Scene viii, lines 35–75? **(b) Evaluate:** Would the play be complete if it ended with Macbeth's death but omitted these lines? Why or why not?

5. **Integration of Knowledge and Ideas** Do you think a tragedy could be written about an ordinary person living today? Why or why not?

6. **Integration of Knowledge and Ideas** How do Shakespeare's use of comic relief and his revealing of Macbeth's inner turmoil add new dimensions to tragedy? In responding, use at least two of these Essential Question words: *noble, downfall, tradition, classics.* *[Connecting to the Essential Question: What is the relationship of the writer to tradition?]*

Cite textual evidence to support your responses.

Some questions are about the **Integration of Knowledge and Ideas** in the text. These questions ask you to evaluate a text in many different ways, such as comparing texts, analyzing arguments in the text, and using many other methods of thinking critically about a text's ideas.

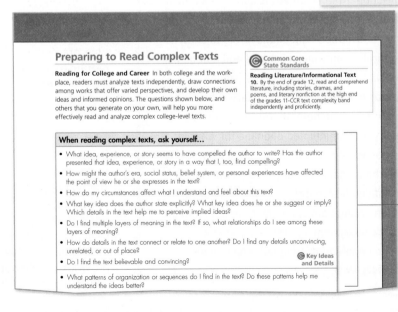

Preparing to Read Complex Texts

Reading for College and Career In both college and the workplace, readers must analyze texts independently, draw connections among works that offer varied perspectives, and develop their own ideas and informed opinions. The questions shown below, and others that you generate on your own, will help you more effectively read and analyze complex college-level texts.

Common Core State Standards

Reading Literature/Informational Text
10. By the end of grade 12, read and comprehend literature, including stories, dramas, and poems, and literary nonfiction at the high end of the grades 11-CCR text complexity band independently and proficiently.

When reading complex texts, ask yourself...

- What idea, experience, or story seems to have compelled the author to write? Has the author presented that idea, experience, or story in a way that I, too, find compelling?
- How might the author's era, social status, belief system, or personal experiences have affected the point of view he or she expresses in the text?
- How do my circumstances affect what I understand and feel about this text?
- What key idea does the author state explicitly? What key idea does he or she suggest or imply? Which details in the text help me to perceive implied ideas?
- Do I find multiple layers of meaning in the text? If so, what relationships do I see among these layers of meaning?
- How do details in the text connect or relate to one another? Do I find any details unconvincing, unrelated, or out of place?
- Do I find the text believable and convincing?
- What patterns of organization or sequences do I find in the text? Do these patterns help me understand the ideas better?

Key Ideas and Details

As you read independently, ask similar types of questions to ensure that you fully enjoy and comprehend any text you choose to read. We have provided sets of questions for you on the Independent Reading pages at the end of each unit.

Ⓒ INFORMATIONAL TEXT

Model

In this example of a complex text, the call-out boxes show questions that an attentive reader might ask while reading.

Sample questions:

The Preamble of the United States Constitution

We the people of the United States, in order to form a more perfect union, establish justice, insure domestic tranquility, provide for the common defense, promote the general welfare, and secure the blessings of liberty to ourselves and our posterity, do ordain and establish this Constitution for the United States of America.

Key Ideas and Details What is the purpose of the Preamble? What is the purpose of the Constitution?

INFORMATIONAL TEXT

Independent Practice

The Bill of Rights

Amendment I Congress shall make no law respecting an establishment of religion, or prohibiting the free exercise thereof; or abridging the freedom of speech, or of the press, or the right of the people peaceably to assemble, and to petition the Government.

Amendment II A well regulated Militia, being necessary to the security of a free State, the right of the people to keep and bear Arms, shall not be infringed.

Amendment III No Soldier shall, in time of peace be quartered in any house, without the consent of the Owner, nor in time of war, but in a manner to be prescribed by law.

Amendment IV The right of the people to be secure in their persons, houses, papers, and effects, against unreasonable searches and seizures, shall not be violated, and no Warrants shall issue, but upon probable cause, supported by Oath or affirmation, and particularly describing the place to be searched, and the persons or things to be seized.

Amendment V No person shall be held to answer for a capital, or otherwise infamous crime, unless on a presentment or indictment of a Grand Jury . . . nor shall any person be subject for the same offence to be twice put in jeopardy of life or limb, nor shall be compelled in any criminal case to be a witness against himself . . . nor shall private property be taken for public use, without just compensation.

Amendment VI In all criminal prosecutions, the accused shall enjoy the right to a speedy and public trial, by an impartial jury of the State and district wherein the crime shall have been committed . . . to be confronted with the witnesses against him . . . and to have the assistance of counsel for his defense.

Amendment VII In Suits at common law, where the value in controversy shall exceed twenty dollars, the right of trial by jury shall be preserved . . .

Amendment VIII Excessive bail shall not be required, nor excessive fines imposed, nor cruel and unusual punishments inflicted. . . .

Craft and Structure What is the effect of parallel structure here? How does this pattern help me follow the ideas and argument? What attitude does the author project?

Integration of Knowledge and Ideas What other U.S. documents have themes similar to those found in the Preamble and the Bill of Rights?

Analyzing Arguments

The ability to evaluate an argument, as well as to make one, is critical for success in college and in the workplace.

What Is an Argument?

Chances are you have used the word *argument* to refer to a disagreement between people. A second definition of *argument* is to present one side of a controversial or debatable issue. Through this type of argument, the writer logically supports a particular belief, conclusion, or point of view. A good argument is supported with reasoning and evidence.

Purposes of Argument

There are three main purposes for writing a formal argument:

- to change the reader's mind about an issue
- to convince the reader to accept what is written
- to motivate the reader to take action, based on what is written

Elements of Argument
Claim (assertion)—what the writer is trying to prove *Example: The penny should be abolished.*
Grounds (evidence)—the support used to convince the reader *Example: There is no profit derived from manufacturing pennies; they actually cost consumers money.*
Justification (reasons)—the link between the grounds and the claim; why the grounds are credible *Example: As a unit of currency, pennies are widely viewed as being obsolete.*

Evaluating Claims

When reading or listening to an argument, critically assess the claims that are made. Analyze the argument to identify claims that are based on fact or that can be proved true. Also evaluate evidence that supports the claims. If there is little or no reasoning or evidence provided to support the claims, the argument may not be sound or valid.

Common Core State Standards

Language
6. Acquire and use accurately grade-appropriate general academic and domain-specific words and phrases, sufficiently for reading, writing, speaking, and listening at the college and career readiness level; demonstrate independence in gathering vocabulary knowledge when considering a word or phrase important to comprehension or expression.

Reading Informational Text
6. Determine an author's point of view or purpose in a text in which the rhetoric is particularly effective, analyzing how style and content contribute to the power, persuasiveness, or beauty of the text.

INFORMATIONAL TEXT
Model Argument

from Philadelphia, and Its Solitary Prison
by Charles Dickens

In the outskirts, stands a great prison, called the Eastern Penitentiary: conducted on a plan peculiar to the state of Pennsylvania. The system here is rigid, strict, and hopeless solitary confinement. I believe it, in its effects, to be cruel and wrong.

In its intention, I am well convinced that it is kind, humane, and meant for reformation; but I am persuaded that those who devised this system of Prison Discipline, and those benevolent gentlemen who carry it into execution, do not know what it is that they are doing. I believe that very few men are capable of estimating the immense amount of torture and agony which this dreadful punishment, prolonged for years, inflicts upon the sufferers; and in guessing at it myself, and in reasoning from what I have seen written upon their faces, and what to my certain knowledge they feel within, I am only the more convinced that there is a depth of terrible endurance in it which none but the sufferers themselves can fathom, and which no man has a right to inflict upon his fellow-creature.

I hold this slow and daily tampering with the mysteries of the brain, to be immeasurably worse than any torture of the body: and because its ghastly signs and tokens are not so palpable to the eye and sense of touch as scars upon the flesh; because its wounds are not upon the surface. . . I hesitated once, debating with myself, whether, if I had the power of saying 'Yes' or 'No,' I would allow it to be tried in certain cases, where the terms of imprisonment were short; but now, I solemnly declare, that with no rewards or honours could I walk a happy man beneath the open sky by day, or lie me down upon my bed at night, with the consciousness that one human creature, for any length of time, no matter what, lay suffering this unknown punishment in his silent cell, and I the cause, or I consenting to it in the least degree.

It seems to me that the objection that nothing wholesome or good has ever had its growth in such unnatural solitude, and that even a dog or any of the more intelligent among beasts, would pine, and mope, and rust away, beneath its influence, would be in itself a sufficient argument against this system. But when we recollect, in addition, how very cruel and severe it is, and that a solitary life is always liable to peculiar and distinct objections of a most deplorable nature, which have arisen here, and call to mind, moreover, that the choice is not between this system, and a bad or ill-considered one, but between it and another which has worked well, and is, in its whole design and practice, excellent; there is surely more than sufficient reason for abandoning a mode of punishment attended by so little hope or promise, and fraught, beyond dispute, with such a host of evils.

The introduction sets the stage for the argument that follows, narrowing the focus from the prison to the system of solitary confinement.

Claim: Solitary confinement is cruel and wrong.

Dickens addresses the counterclaim, stating that the intentions of the system were good, and he assumes that the gentlemen do not know how cruel they are being.

Evidence provided includes that people underestimate the unfathomable suffering from the punishment; the punishment is torture. Dickens draws this conclusion based on what he has seen.

Justification: Basic human rights prohibit cruel, inhumane, or unusual punishment.

Dickens reasons that this punishment is worse than physical torture because no one can see the wounds; he also offers the testimony that he would not assent to this punishment in any case.

The last paragraph summarizes the arguments, and the final sentence restates the claim and asks for action: abandon this mode of punishment.

The Art of Argument: Rhetorical Devices and Persuasive Techniques

Rhetorical Devices

Rhetoric is the art of using language in order to make a point or to persuade listeners. Rhetorical devices such as the ones listed below are accepted elements of argument. Their use does not invalidate or weaken an argument. Rather, the use of rhetorical devices is regarded as a key part of an effective argument.

Rhetorical Devices	Examples
Repetition The repeated use of words, phrases, or sentences	Stop the violence! We want to avoid violence! Stop the violence!
Parallelism The repeated use of similar grammatical structures	The strength of the army, the reach of the navy, and the speed of the air force are considered the source of national pride in the military.
Rhetorical Question Calls attention to the issue by implying an obvious answer	Shouldn't civilized nations avoid cruel punishments, even for the most heinous crimes?
Sound Devices The use of alliteration, assonance, rhyme, or rhythm	The sound of the crowd protesting outside the gate drifted to the inmate's ear and lifted his spirits.
Simile and Metaphor Compares two seemingly unlike things or asserts that one thing *is* another	The words in the book became a salve for her wounded soul.

Persuasive Techniques

Persuasive techniques are often found in advertisements and in other forms of informal persuasion. Although techniques like the ones below are sometimes found in formal arguments, they should be avoided in formal arguments.

Persuasive Techniques	Examples
Bandwagon Approach/Anti-Bandwagon Approach Appeals to a person's desire to belong; encourages or celebrates individuality	Don't be the only one without one! Be the first to own our brand.
Emotional Appeal Evokes people's fear, anger, or desire	Our choices today will ensure the health and prosperity of our children! Of our children's children!
Endorsement/Testimony Employs a well-known person to promote a product or idea	These famous authors, actors, politicians, and CEOs are alumnae of our university!
Loaded Language The use of words that are charged with emotion	It is a crisis of unfathomable proportions.
"Plain Folks" Appeal Shows a connection to everyday, ordinary people	I enjoy a good ol' burger and fries, just like everyone else.
Hyperbole Exaggerates to make a point	I'd give my right arm to end the abuse and neglect of animals.

 EXEMPLAR TEXT

Model Speech

The excerpted speech below includes examples of rhetorical devices and persuasive techniques.

Speech on Conciliation with America, by Edmund Burke

. . . The proposition is peace. Not peace through the medium of war; not peace to be hunted through the labyrinth of intricate and endless negotiations; not peace to arise out of universal discord, fomented from principle, in all parts of the empire; not peace to depend on the juridical determination of perplexing questions, or the precise marking the shadowy boundaries of a complex government. It is simple peace, sought in its natural course and in its ordinary haunts.

Let the colonies always keep the idea of their civil rights associated with your government—they will cling and grapple to you, and no force under heaven will be of power to tear them from their allegiance. But let it be once understood that your government may be one thing and their privileges another, that these two things may exist without any mutual relation - the cement is gone, the cohesion is loosened, and everything hastens to decay and dissolution. As long as you have the wisdom to keep the sovereign authority of this country as the sanctuary of liberty, the sacred temple consecrated to our common faith, wherever the chosen race and sons of England worship freedom, they will turn their faces towards you . . . Slavery they can have anywhere. It is a weed that grows in every soil . . . But until you become lost to all feeling of your true interest and your natural dignity, freedom they can have from none but you. This is the commodity of price, of which you have the monopoly . . . Deny them this participation of freedom, and you break that sole bond which originally made, and must still preserve, the unity of the empire . . . It is the spirit of the English constitution which, infused through the mighty mass, pervades, feeds, unites, invigorates, vivifies, every part of the empire, even down to the minutest member.

Is it not the same virtue which does every thing for us here in England? Do you imagine, then, that it is the Land-Tax Act which raises your revenue? that it is the annual vote in the Committee of Supply, which gives you your army? or that it is the Mutiny Bill which inspires it with bravery and discipline? No! surely, no! It is the love of the people; it is their attachment to their government, from the sense of the deep stake they have in such a glorious institution, which gives you your army and your navy, and infuses into both that liberal obedience without which your army would be a base rabble and your navy nothing but rotten timber . . .

We ought to elevate our minds to the greatness of that trust to which the order of Providence has called us. By adverting to the dignity of this high calling, our ancestors have turned a savage wilderness into a glorious empire, and have made the most extensive and the only honorable conquests, not by destroying, but by promoting the wealth, the number, the happiness of the human race. Let us get an American revenue as we have got an American empire. English privileges have made it all that it is; English privileges alone will make it all it can be.

The repetition of the word *peace* emphasizes its importance, while the paragraph provides a growing, defining context for the term.

This metaphor compares slavery to a weed. Burke uses the metaphor to explain why slavery does not create allegiance to a government.

The alliteration, besides adding to the rhythm of the speech, reinforces the relationship between parts and the whole.

This rhetorical question applies the previous conclusions about the empire to England.

The parallelism in these rhetorical questions builds momentum and leads to the emphatic answer: No!

The strongly rhythmic parallelism in the final sentence provides a memorable conclusion.

Analyzing Legal Meanings and Reasoning

Reading historical and legal texts requires careful analysis of both the vocabulary and the logical flow of ideas that support a conclusion.

Understanding Legal Meanings

The language of historical and legal documents is formal, precise, and technical. Many words in these texts have specific meanings that you need to understand in order to follow the flow of ideas. For example, the second amendment to the U.S. Constitution states that "A well regulated militia being necessary to the security of a free State, the right of the People to keep and bear arms shall not be infringed." To understand this amendment, it is important to know that in this context *militia* means "armed forces," *bear* means "carry," and *infringed* means "denied." To understand legal meanings:

- Use your knowledge of word roots to help you understand unfamiliar words. Many legal terms use familiar Greek or Latin roots, prefixes, or suffixes.

- Do not assume that you know a word's legal meaning: use a dictionary to check the meanings of key words to be certain that you are applying the correct meaning.

- Paraphrase the text to aid comprehension. Replace difficult words with synonyms to make sure you follow the logic of the argument.

Delineating Legal Reasoning

Works of public advocacy, such as court decisions, political proclamations, proposed laws or constitutional amendments, use careful reasoning to support conclusions. These strategies can help you understand the legal reasoning in an argument:

- State the **purpose** of the document in your own words to help you focus on the writer's primary goal.

- Look for the line of reasoning that supports the **arguments** presented. To be valid and persuasive, key arguments should be backed up by clearly stated logical analysis. Be aware of persuasive techniques, such as citing facts and statistics, referring to expert testimonials, and using emotional language with strong connotations.

- Identify the **premises,** or evidence, upon which a decision rests. In legal texts, premises often include **precedents,** which are earlier examples that must be followed or specifically overturned. Legal reasoning is usually based on the decisions of earlier trials. Be sure you understand precedents in order to identify how the court arrived at the current decision.

**Common Core
State Standards**

Reading Informational Text
4. Determine the meaning of words and phrases as they are used in a text, including figurative, connotative, and technical meanings; analyze how an author uses and refines the meaning of a key term or terms over the course of a text.
8. Delineate and evaluate the reasoning in seminal U.S. texts, including the application of constitutional principles and use of legal reasoning and the premises, purposes, and arguments in works of public advocacy.
Writing
9. Draw evidence from literary or informational texts to support analysis, reflection, and research.
9.b. Apply *grades 11–12 Reading Standards* to literary nonfiction.

INFORMATIONAL TEXT

Model Court Decision

Note the strategies used to evaluate legal meanings and reasoning in this Supreme Court decision from 1954 regarding the legality of segregated, "separate, but equal" schools for black and white students.

from *Brown v. Board of Education of Topeka*, Opinion of the Supreme Court by Chief Justice Earl Warren

We come then to the question presented: Does segregation of children in public schools solely on the basis of race, even though the physical facilities and other "tangible" factors may be equal, deprive the children of the minority group of equal educational opportunities? We believe that it does.

In *Sweatt v. Painter*, in finding that a segregated law school for Negroes could not provide them equal educational opportunities, this Court relied in large part on "those qualities which are incapable of objective measurement but which make for greatness in a law school." In *McLaurin v. Oklahoma State Regents*, the Court, in requiring that a Negro admitted to a white graduate school be treated like all other students, again resorted to intangible considerations: ". . . his ability to study, to engage in discussions and exchange views with other students, and, in general, to learn his profession." Such considerations apply with added force to children in grade and high schools. To separate them from others of similar age and qualifications solely because of their race generates a feeling of inferiority as to their status in the community that may affect their hearts and minds in a way unlikely ever to be undone. The effect of this separation on their educational opportunities was well stated by a finding in the Kansas case by a court which nevertheless felt compelled to rule against the Negro plaintiffs: Segregation of white and colored children in public schools has a detrimental effect upon the colored children. The impact is greater when it has the sanction of the law, for the policy of separating the races is usually interpreted as denoting the inferiority of the negro group. A sense of inferiority affects the motivation of a child to learn. Segregation with the sanction of law, therefore, has a tendency to [retard] the educational and mental development of negro children and to deprive them of some of the benefits they would receive in a racially integrated school system. Whatever may have been the extent of psychological knowledge at the time of *Plessy v. Ferguson*, this finding is amply supported by modern authority. Any language in *Plessy v. Ferguson* contrary to this finding is rejected.

We conclude that, in the field of public education, the doctrine of "separate but equal" has no place. Separate educational facilities are inherently unequal.

The word *tangible* comes from the Latin root meaning "to touch." In this decision, the court contrasts tangible, measurable features with intangible features that are difficult to measure.

The court cites two precedents: earlier cases relating to unequal education opportunities for black students.

Here's one way you might break down the ideas in this sentence when you paraphrase: Segregating black students just because of their race makes them feel as if they are less valued by our society. This separation can have a permanent negative influence on their character.

The conclusion makes the **purpose** of the decision clear: to overturn the precedent established by *Plessy v. Ferguson*. The **argument** describes the reasons why the Court no longer considers the reasoning in that earlier case to be valid.

Writing About Legal Meanings

Write a detailed analysis of the phrase "segregation with the sanction of law" in the *Brown v. Board of Education of Topeka* decision. Explain the definitions of the terms as they are used in this context and explain how this phrase relates to the courts decision to outlaw "separate but equal" education.

Composing an Argument

Common Core State Standards

Writing

1.a. Introduce precise, knowledgeable claim(s), establish the significance of the claim(s), distinguish the claim(s) from alternate or opposing claims, and create an organization that logically sequences claim(s), counterclaims, reasons, and evidence.

1.b. Develop claim(s) and counterclaims fairly and thoroughly, supplying the most relevant evidence for each while pointing out the strengths and limitations of both in a manner that anticipates the audience's knowledge level, concerns, values, and possible biases.

1.e. Provide a concluding statement or section that follows from and supports the argument presented.

Choosing a Topic

You should choose a topic that matters to people—and to you. The topic should be debatable or controversial to some degree.

Confirm that you can make an arguable claim. Ask yourself:

1. What am I trying to prove? What ideas do I need to get across?

2. Are there people who would disagree with my claim? What counterclaims would they make?

3. Do I have evidence to support my claim? Is my evidence sufficient and relevant?

If you are able to state what you want to prove and answered "yes" to questions 2 and 3, you have an arguable claim.

Introducing the Claim and Establishing Its Significance

Before you begin writing, determine how much your audience already knows about your chosen topic. Then, provide only as much background information as necessary to introduce your claim. If there are issues surrounding your topic, you will need to clarify them for your audience and narrow the focus to your specific claim. Remember that you are not writing a summary of the topic—you are crafting an argument. Once you have provided context for your argument, you should clearly state your claim, or thesis.

Developing Your Claim With Reasoning and Evidence

Now that you have made your claim, you must support it with evidence, or grounds, and reasons for your claim. A good argument should have at least three solid pieces of evidence to support the claim. Evidence can range from personal experience to researched data or expert opinion. Knowing your audience's knowledge level, concerns, values, and possible biases can help you decide what kind of evidence will have the strongest impact. Make sure your evidence is up to date and comes from a credible source. Always credit your sources.

You should also address opposing counterclaims within the body of your argument. Consider points you have made or evidence you have provided that a person might challenge. Decide how best to refute these counterclaims. One technique for defusing an opponent's claims is to agree with selected parts of them.

Writing a Concluding Statement or Section

Restate your claim in the conclusion of your argument, and summarize your main points. The goal of a concluding section is to provide a sense of closure and completeness to an argument. Make your concluding statement strong enough to be memorable and to leave the reader thinking.

Practice

Exploring both sides of an issue can be a good way to start planning an argument. Complete a chart like the one below to help you plan your own argument.

Topic:	
Issue: _____ _____	
Claim:	Counterclaim:
Grounds (Evidence): 1. _____ 2. _____ 3. _____	Grounds (Evidence): 1. _____ 2. _____ 3. _____
Justification: 1. _____ 2. _____ 3. _____	Justification: 1. _____ 2. _____ 3. _____

When you have completed the chart and developed your own, precise claim, consider the following questions:

1. Who is your audience? What type of evidence can you use to best convince those who do not agree with your claim?

2. Is your evidence strong and difficult to dispute? If not, how can you strengthen it or find better evidence?

3. How will you refute the counterclaim? Are there any parts of the counterclaim you agree with?

Media Literacy Handbook

INTRODUCTION: Today, messages are transmitted across a variety of media modes, such as film, television, radio, and the Internet. As you interact with these messages each day—in images, advertisements, movies, and an array of different contexts—it is important to consider the potential influences of the medium.

- What is the intention of the message?
- How is it communicated?
- How do specific elements of the medium—such as color, image, or font—help convey the message?
- Why might the creator of the message have selected this medium?

These are the key issues of media literacy, the study of messages in the media and their impact.

Camera Shots and Angles

Filmmakers create camera shots and sequences to help them tell stories. Some shots capture an entire scene; others zoom in on specific characters.

Special Effects

Filmmakers use special effects to create on-screen illusions that bring
the imagination to life.

STAR
WARS

Questions About Film Techniques

- What effect is created by the choice of camera angle shown in the image
  at left? Choose another camera angle and explain how that shot might
  convey a different message than the one shown here.

- Study the images above. In what way does the use of special effects
  make the film better for viewers?

Focus and Framing

A sharp focus captures all details in a photographic image. A softer focus lessens the amount of detail that can be seen. The framing of elements within a photograph directs the eye toward a portion of the image.

Lighting and Shadow

Lighting techniques are used in photography to enhance mood and direct the viewer's focus.

Special Techniques

Most images you see today have been manipulated or changed in some way. Even a small change—such as an added graphic element or a difference in shading—can alter the mood of an image.

FROM LUCY: ENGLAN' LADY

James Berry

Questions About Graphics and Photos

- What would be the effect if the image at left used a sharp focus instead of a combination of a sharp and soft focus?

- In what way does the use of color and light create mood in the photo at left?

- What special techniques were applied to the original photograph shown above right? What effect does the use of special techniques create?

Persuasive Techniques
Advertisements use carefully selected visual elements and specific language to appeal to the viewer's emotions.

Text and Graphics

Newspaper and magazine layouts are constructed to capture the eye and quickly convey the important ideas of a story. The use of type fonts, images, and page space direct the eye to portions of the printed page.

Questions About Print Media

- What image or graphic dominates the advertisement at left? In what way does the use of language in the ad enhance its message?

- Which of the above grabs your attention: the image or the graphic on the magazine cover? Explain.

- What do you notice first on the newspaper's front page? What overall effect does the use of type size and fonts create?

How is this book organized?

- **There are six chronological units, starting with Native American beginnings and extending to the present.**
- **Each unit has an introduction that offers multiple perspectives on the history, culture, and literature of the time period.**

A **"Snapshot"** shows you key people, places, and innovations. ▶

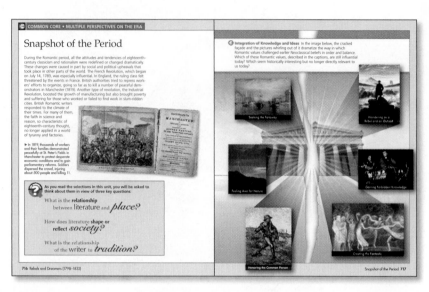

Essential Questions in British and World Literature

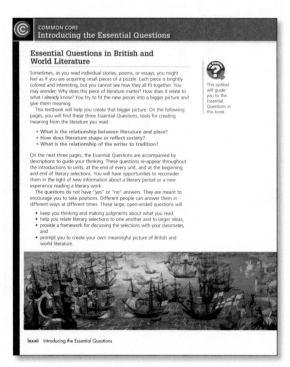

▲ **Essential Questions** help you think about universal themes.

Historical Background
summarizes key events of the era. ▼

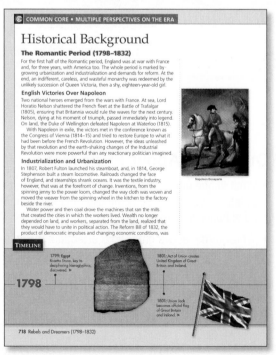

How are the literary selections organized?

- **Each unit contains literary selections from the time period.**
- **Each selection has features to help you better understand the literature.**

Before You Read teaches you important skills and vocabulary. ▶

Vocabulary

averred (ə vurd´) v. stated to be true (p. 824)

sojourn (sō´ jurn) v. stay for a while (p. 831)

expiated (eks´ pē āt´ id) v. atoned for, especially by suffering (p. 838)

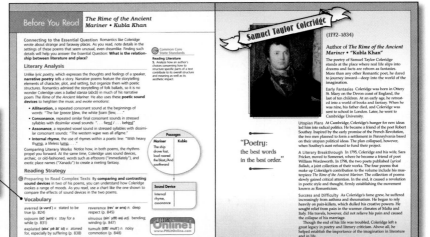

▲ **Author Biography** tells you about the author's life.

Part I

It is an ancient Mariner,
And he stoppeth one of three.
"By thy long gray beard and glittering eye,
Now wherefore stopp'st thou me?"

An ancient Mariner meeteth three Gallants bidden to a wedding feast and detaineth one.

5   "The Bridegroom's doors are opened wide,
And I am next of kin;
The guests are met, the feast is set:
May'st hear the merry din."

Literary Analysis
Poetic Sound Devices
What examples of internal rhymes and assonance can you find in lines 5–8?

◀ **While You Read questions** help you apply the skills as you read.

After You Read helps you practice the skills you have learned. ▶

Skills Practice

After You Read   *The Rime of the Ancient Mariner • Kubla Khan*

Literary Analysis

1. **Craft and Structure** What **sound device** does Coleridge use in the line "It cracked and growled, and roared and howled . . ." (*The Rime of the Ancient Mariner*, line 61)?

2. **Craft and Structure** Find an example of **alliteration** in lines 9–12 of *The Rime of the Ancient Mariner*.

3. **Craft and Structure** Which words in the following line create an **internal rhyme**: "Whiles all the night through fog smoke white…"? (*The Rime of the Ancient Mariner*, line 77)

4. **Craft and Structure** (a) Identify an example of **consonance** in lines 51–54 of *The Rime of the Ancient Mariner*. (b) Identify an example of **assonance** in the same lines.

5. **Craft and Structure** What device dominates the first stanza of "Kubla Khan"? Give three examples.

6. **Craft and Structure** (a) What mood do lines 472–483 of *The Rime of the Ancient Mariner* create? (b) What poetic devices contribute to this mood? Explain.

7. **Comparing Literary Works** Using a chart like the one shown, explain how the characteristics of Coleridge's poetry, including its subjects, settings, events, and uses of language, suit the fantastic subjects he addresses. In discussing his uses of language, specifically consider sound devices.

Poem: _____

Subject	Setting	Events	Language	Why Suitable?

Reading Strategy

8. **Compare and contrast sound devices** in these poems by answering these questions. (a) Identify the mood, or feeling, that Coleridge evokes in lines 1–12 of *The Rime of the Ancient Mariner* and lines 1–11 of "Kubla Khan." (b) How do the sound devices and archaic words used in each poem allow Coleridge to create these moods?

9. (a) Identify four words in "Kubla Khan" that contribute to the poem's exotic, or strange and faraway, atmosphere. (b) Do archaic words in *The Rime of the Ancient Mariner* also make the setting of this poem seem exotic? Why or why not?

10. Which of these two poems uses sound devices to create a greater variety of moods? Quote specific passages to support your points.

PERFORMANCE TASKS
Integrated Language Skills

Vocabulary Acquisition and Use

Word Analysis: Latin Root -journ-
The verb *sojourn*, meaning "to visit for a while," contains the root -*journ*-, derived from French and Latin words meaning "day." In French, the root appears in such words and phrases as *bonjour* ("good day") and *soup du jour* ("soup of the day"). Explain how this root contributes to the meaning of each of these words. If you are unsure of the meaning of any of these words, you may consult a dictionary. Then use each word in an original sentence.

1. adjourn
2. journal
3. journalism
4. journey
5. journeyman

Vocabulary: Antonyms
An antonym is a word that has the opposite meaning of another word. *Freezing* and *boiling* are antonyms, as are *happy* and *sad*. For each word from the vocabulary list on page 818, choose the correct antonym. Then, write an original sentence using both the word and its antonym.

1. averred: (a) claimed, (b) denied, (c) wished
2. sojourn: (a) depart, (b) rest, (c) visit
3. expiated: (a) atoned, (b) sinned, (c) sold
4. reverence: (a) contempt, (b) hope, (c) respect
5. sinuous: (a) dark, (b) narrow, (c) straight
6. tumult: (a) peace, (b) pleasure, (c) wealth

Writing

Explanatory Text Coleridge was not the only nineteenth-century poet to fascinate readers with a mysterious symbolic bird. Find a copy of "The Raven" by the American author Edgar Allan Poe, and read it carefully. Then, write an **essay** comparing the Albatross in *The Rime of the Ancient Mariner* with Poe's Raven as poetic symbols.

Prewriting Gather details about the Albatross and the Raven, grouping them under headings such as "Appearance," "Actions," and "Influence." Remember that symbols are concrete images that stand for a cluster of ideas. For each specific quality or relationship you list in your chart, give the general ideas it suggests.

Drafting As you draft, discuss each category in your chart, linking the details you have listed to your conclusions about the symbolic meaning of each bird. Then, compare the two symbols. Support your ideas with quotations from the works.

Model: Revising for Vivid, Precise Language
The sailors praise the Albatross for bringing good weather,
~~a deadly calm,~~
then blame it for bringing bad weather. The Polar Spirit also
~~wreaks vengeance through extended drought and fast winds.~~
~~uses weather for its vengeance.~~

Vivid words and details make the analysis more interesting and precise.

Revising Review your draft to identify flat, unexciting language. Replace such language with vivid, specific descriptions or claims. Make sure that all quotations are accurate and properly cited.

Special Features Bring British and World Literature to Life and Show Why They Matter Today

Extended Study brings you closer to an author's world or allows you to explore a literary movement or genre in great depth. ▶

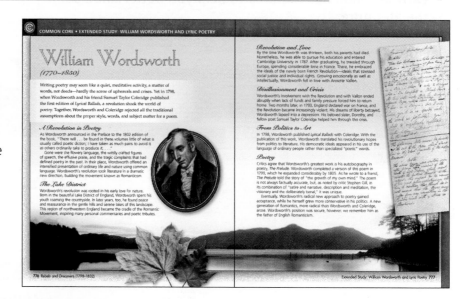

▲ **Illustrations**
help you visualize literary history.

Themes Across Centuries, Genres, or Cultures features essays by today's writers on the topic of the classics. ▼

Contemporary Connections
links the classics to today. ▶

Jane Austen, Movie Star

At first glance, Jane Austen, a nineteenth-century novelist, seems an improbable box-office draw.

She never married, lived with her mother and sister, and died at age 41. Her novels lack sensation of the kind that modern audiences might be thought to crave. They mostly depict the lives of well-brought-up young ladies as they embark on the marriage-go-round.

Yet, since the 1990s, there have been literally dozens of successful film adaptations of Austen's books. Some have been faithful to the original setting of her works, such as the 2005 *Pride and Prejudice* starring Keira Knightley. Other movies, such as *Clueless*, have transplanted plot and characters to more contemporary settings.

In 2007, the film *Becoming Jane* was made about Austen's own life, a fact that would certainly have brought a wry smile to her face.

As Hollywood has discovered, Austen's portrayal of human nature hits the mark every time. Her heroes and heroines may wear top hats and layers of petticoats. They may ride sedately in horse-drawn carriages. However, in their king's English, they speak directly to today's audiences, who see in these characters' dilemmas and decisions reflections of their own.

Lord John Russell

Sir Robert Peel

Thomas Babington Macaulay

THE STORY BEHIND THE DOCUMENTS

Lord John Russell (1792–1878) was the British statesman who introduced the Reform Bill of 1832 in Parliament. A champion of reform, Lord Russell was a leading member of the Whig party when it came to power in 1830 with Lord Grey as prime minister. Some years later, after the Whigs had evolved into the Liberal party, Russell himself served twice as Britain's prime minister. Among his later achievements was passage of a law limiting factory labor to ten hours a day.

Sir Robert Peel (1788–1850) helped lead the Tory party opposition to the Reform Bill of 1832. Peel later served as prime minister twice, first from 1834 to 1835 and later, after reorganizing the Tories as the modern Conservative party, for a much longer period in the 1840s. In 1829, while serving as home secretary in a Tory administration, he established London's police force, whose members are nicknamed "bobbies" in his honor.

Thomas Babington Macaulay (1800–1859) was a well-known nineteenth-century historian and literary critic. Trained as a lawyer, he was also a Whig member of Parliament who, like Lord Russell, spoke in favor of the Reform Bill of 1832. Macaulay first won literary fame with an essay on John Milton. His influential five-volume *History of England* (1849–1861) offered a Whig interpretation of British history, stressing the value of gradual democratic reform.

The Industrial Revolution brought great change to Britain. Large chunks of the population shifted from rural areas to newly emerging urban centers, where the middle class grew and prospered. Britain's political landscape, however, had not changed with the times. Sparsely populated rural areas had disproportionately large representation, while booming new industrial cities like Manchester had none. Some seats in Parliament were completely controlled by a single nobleman or by small self-interested groups. Additionally, landholding and financial restrictions kept much of the population from voting. The result was a Parliament that strongly favored the interests of landowners at the expense of everyone else. The Reform Bill of 1832—often called the First Reform Bill—was an attempt to correct that situation.

▶ **Primary Source: Photography** How does the arrangement of seats in the House of Commons suggest the idea of opposed parties? **[Analyze]**

898 Rebels and Dreamers (1798–1832)

SPEECH IN FAVOR OF REFORM

Lord John Russell

BACKGROUND When the Whigs came to power in 1830, the number one issue on the party's agenda was reform of Britain's election system. To that end, Lord Russell first proposed the Reform Bill on March 1, 1831. The Tory party opposed the bill, with Sir Robert Peel speaking effectively against it. Extracts from both those speeches are presented here.

On the second reading, the bill passed Parliament's House of Commons by just one vote. Recognizing the need for a greater majority, Lord Grey, the Whig prime minister, dissolved Parliament and called for a new election. The Whigs now won many more seats, and the Reform Bill readily passed in the House of Commons—but it was still rejected in Parliament's other chamber, the House of Lords. Finally, the prime minister forced King William IV to name several new members to the House of Lords—members sympathetic to the reforms—and in July of 1832 the bill passed both Houses of Parliament and became law.

Interior of the Commons Chamber, House of Parliament, Westminster, United Kingdom

Lord John Russell's Speech in Favor of Reform

◀ **Primary Sources**
features real documents that made history, and supports in-depth research projects.

COMMON CORE • EXTENDED STUDY: WILLIAM WORDSWORTH AND LYRIC POETRY

Comparing Literary Works
*Poetry of William Wordsworth •
Lyric Poetry from Around the World*

Comparing Lyric Poetry from Around the World

Lyric Poetry Lyric poetry began in song. In fact, the word *lyric* comes from *lyre*, the harplike instrument that ancient Greek poets like Sappho played to accompany their lyric poems. Even before the Greeks, however, people were singing poems expressing faith, love, sorrow, joy, and other strong emotions. Love lyrics survive from ancient Egypt's New Kingdom (c. 1570–1070 B.C.). The philosopher Confucius is said to have compiled the *Book of Songs*, collecting Chinese poetry written as early as 1100 B.C.

Lyric poetry typically has these characteristics:
- It is brief and concise.
- It is communicated by a single speaker expressing personal emotions and observations.
- It uses vivid images to convey ideas and evoke emotions.
- It is musical, often employing rhyme, alliteration, and repetition and following a pattern of rhythm (called meter) or a pattern of syllables.

For lyric poems that you read, fill in a chart like this one. Then, use your charts to answer comparison-and-contrast questions about the poems.

Common Core State Standards

Reading Literature
5. Analyze how an author's choices concerning how to structure specific parts of a text contribute to its overall structure and meaning as well as its aesthetic impact.

Language
4.c. Consult general and specialized reference materials, both print and digital, to find the pronunciation of a word or determine or clarify its precise meaning, its part of speech, its etymology, or its standard usage.

	"The World Is Too Much With Us"	**"I Have Visited Again"**
Form and/or lines	Petrarchan sonnet; 14 lines	
Speaker	Lover of nature	
Observations	Society is too materialistic; nature's beauty is unappreciated.	
Emotions	Unhappiness with society; joy and wonder in nature	
Images	Vivid sights and sounds of wild and pagan sea	
Sound devices	Rhyme, meter, some alliteration, assonance	

Gather Vocabulary Knowledge

These lyric poets use words such as *fathomless*, *treacherous*, and *splendor*. Use a **dictionary** to find each word's part of speech and definition. Then, employ the following reference (printed or electronic) to explore these words:
- **History of Language:** Use a history of English to research each word's etymology, or origins.
- **Book of Quotations:** Use a collection of quotations to find a statement containing some of the words. In a paragraph, explain the nuances in meaning that are evident from the context of the quotation.

Comparing References Compare and contrast what you learn about the words from these specialized references.

Lyric Poetry From Around the World 797

Feature Article

Smithsonian
MAGAZINE

DESIGNING A GLOBE THEATRE FOR THE 21ST CENTURY

By Eric Jaffe

The title defines the article as being about Shakespeare's original theater.

Feature articles frequently use vivid descriptions and colorful language.

The tractor-trailer parked firmly in the Wal-Mart parking lot did no work at all at all places, but the action who performed *Merchant of Venice* right beside it sure did. When the vehicle arrived it deployed into a full-size stage. Behind the set, pneumatic pods inflated to become ticket windows and dressing rooms. Sunlight powered the spotlights and speakers. And when the playhouse folded up and drove off, a screen mounted on the side of the trailer replayed the show for all to see.

This is the Globe Theatre—not the one that housed Shakespeare's best dramas, but one conceived by Jennifer Siegal for a modern audience. Siegal's Globe is part homage to the Elizabethan era's itinerant theatre troupe, part shout-out to today's compact, on-the-go gizmos. The Los Angeles-based architect was one of five designers asked to create a 21st-century Shakespearean theatre for "Reinventing the Globe," a new exhibit at the National Building Museum in Washington, D.C., that opens January 13 and runs through August 2007.

Given only brief guidance and a few months to finish, these architects created modern Globes that challenge conventional thoughts about dramatic performances and the spaces that accommodate them, says Martin Moeller, the exhibition's curator. "When the words stay the same but all else changes, you realize how much power the words have," he says.

Theatre designer John Coyne delivered a truly virtual Globe. To reflect today's cross-cultural world, Coyne's performances would occur simultaneously in several locations. Gigantic screens with live streaming would hang above the stages, and characters would interact in real time. So, speaking in Russian from Moscow, Polonius offers advice to Laertes in New York; standing oceans away, Hamlet pierces Claudius with a venom-tipped sword.

Michelle (pronounced *Mikaleh*) Soran, who did not have theatre design experience, modeled a Globe that would capture an actor's fluidity in the structure itself. He proposed tracing the movements of an actor throughout a performance.

Illustration of Jennifer Siegal's "Globetrotter"—a portable Shakespeare theater.

Informational Text: Feature Article 437

◀ **Reading for Information**
feature nonfiction texts you will encounter in daily life.

Comparing Literature Past and Present
shows the continuity of ideas, themes, and styles. ▶

Essential Questions in British and World Literature

Sometimes, as you read individual stories, poems, or essays, you might feel as if you are acquiring small pieces of a puzzle. Each piece is brightly colored and interesting, but you cannot see how they all fit together. You may wonder, Why does this piece of literature matter? How does it relate to what I already know? You try to fit the new pieces into a bigger picture and give them meaning.

This textbook will help you create that bigger picture. On the following pages, you will find these three Essential Questions, tools for creating meaning from the literature you read:

- **What is the relationship between literature and place?**
- **How does literature shape or reflect society?**
- **What is the relationship of the writer to tradition?**

On the next three pages, the Essential Questions are accompanied by descriptions to guide your thinking. These questions re-appear throughout the introductions to units, at the end of every unit, and at the beginning and end of literary selections. You will have opportunities to reconsider them in the light of new information about a literary period or a new experience reading a literary work.

The questions do not have "yes" or "no" answers. They are meant to encourage you to take positions. Different people can answer them in different ways at different times. These large, open-ended questions will

- keep you thinking and making judgments about what you read,
- help you relate literary selections to one another and to larger ideas,
- provide a framework for discussing the selections with your classmates, and
- prompt you to create your own meaningful picture of British and world literature.

This symbol will guide you to the Essential Questions in this book.

What is the **relationship** between literature and *place?*

From the beginning, England's geography captured the imagination of its writers. Over a thousand years ago, a monk named Bede began a section of his history, "Britain, formerly known as Albion, is an island in the ocean . . ." As you read the selections in this book, think about how England's island existence and dependence on the sea influenced its literature.

The imagination can shape the perception of a place, and writers play a major part in that imagining. How have different generations of England's writers re-imagined their country? How have they shaped remembered or even unreal places, such as a perfect pastoral community that exists only on the pages of a book?

As you read, watch how writers invest places with reality and invent places with imagination. Stay attuned to the variety of responses to the Essential Question: What is the relationship between literature and place?

Thematic Vocabulary

To help as you explore this Essential Question, use words like these:

boundary	colonize	conquest
destruction	empire	geography
immigrant	isolation	mobility
nature		

"This blessed plot, this earth, this realm, this England."

—William Shakespeare, *Richard II*

How does **literature** shape **or** reflect *society?*

We know why we need farmers, carpenters, and doctors, but why do we need writers? Also, how do writers interact with the culture to produce literature that entertains, informs, persuades, challenges, and moves readers?

The writers who create British literature are a vital part of British society. They help to produce its culture, and they are the products of that culture. They are the entertainers who amuse, the critics who confront, and the teachers who share wisdom. Every day, writers celebrate Britain, define it, defy it, and tell its story. As you read this textbook and keep asking this Essential Question, you will become aware of the many relationships between Britain and its writers.

Thematic Vocabulary
To help as you explore this Essential Question, use words like these:

capitalism	dissatisfaction	ideal	independence
industry	loyalty	modernization	
order	revolution	values	

"No man is an island, entire of itself; every man is a piece of the continent, a part of the main." —John Donne, *Meditation 17*

What is the **relationship** of the writer to *tradition?*

The past is not past. It is a living part of the present, and tradition is its embodiment. Literary tradition is the record of how men and women imaginatively responded to their times, what they believed was important and beautiful. It is the record of how they chose to express that beauty, the forms and styles and words and images they used. Tradition is the biography of literature.

Every British writer is, in some way, a product of the British literary tradition and a participant in it. As you keep asking this Essential Question throughout this book, you will be getting to the core of what gives British literature its unique character.

Thematic Vocabulary
To help as you explore this Essential Question, use words like these:

authentic	**conventional**	**interpretation**
monarchy	**philosophy**	**piety**
propriety	**reform**	**struggle**
transformation		

"*Let me imagine . . . what would have happened had Shakespeare had a wonderfully gifted sister, called Judith, let us say.*"

—Virginia Woolf, *A Room of One's Own*

LITERARY MAP OF THE BRITISH ISLES

0 Miles 50 100 150 200
0 Km 50 100 150 200 250 300

N
W E
S

Orkney Islands

Outer Hebrides

NORTH SEA

ENGLAND

Bath Jane Austen writes

Cambridge Alfred, Lord Tennyson studies

Canterbury Destination of Chaucer's pilgrims

Chalfont St Giles John Milton completes *Paradise Lost*

Dorchester Inspiration for Thomas Hardy's Wessex

Dover Matthew Arnold's *Dover Beach*

Haworth The Brontë sisters write

Oxford Samuel Johnson studies

Portsmouth Charles Dickens born

Southwold George Orwell takes his pen name from the river Orwell

Stratford-upon-Avon William Shakespeare born

Tilbury Elizabeth I appears before her troops

Tintagel Legendary birthplace of King Arthur

York W.H. Auden born

SCOTLAND

Ayrshire Robert Burns writes
Dunsinane Macbeth slain

English-Scottish Border
Setting of many early ballads

Atlantic Ocean

Scottish Highlands

Dunsinane

SCOTLAND

Glasgow

EDINBURGH

Ayrshire

English-Scottish Border

Newcastle upon Tyne

Londonderry

NORTHERN IRELAND (U.K.) BELFAST

IRELAND

Galway

DUBLIN

Isle of Man

IRISH SEA

ENGLAND (U.K.)

Haworth York

Liverpool
Manchester Sheffield

Nottingham

Clonmel

CELTIC SEA

WALES (U.K.)

Burmingham

Cambridge Southwold

Stratford-upon-Avon

Tintern Abbey

Oxford Chalfont St Giles Tilbury

Swansea

Cardiff

Bristol Channel

Bristol

Bath

Thames River

Canterbury

Dover

LONDON

Portsmouth

Tintagel
Plymouth

Dorchester

Isle of Wight

Strait of Dover

English Channel

FRANCE

IRELAND
Dublin James Joyce, Jonathan Swift and William Butler Yeats born
Clonmel Laurence Sterne writes
NORTHERN IRELAND
Londonderry Seamus Heaney born
WALES
Swansea Dylan Thomas born

LITERARY MAP OF LONDON

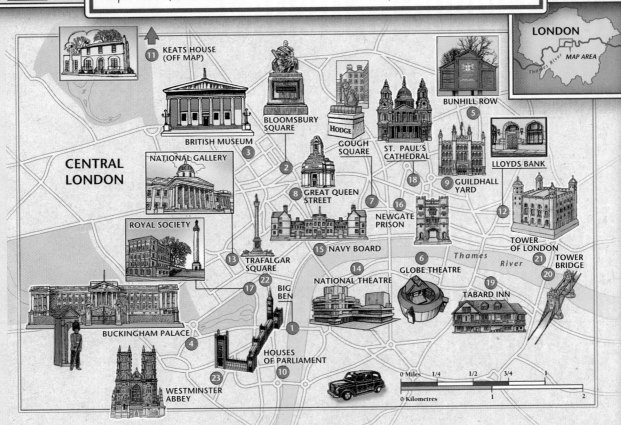

LONDON

MAP AREA

Thames River

KEATS HOUSE (OFF MAP) 11

BRITISH MUSEUM

CENTRAL LONDON

NATIONAL GALLERY 13

ROYAL SOCIETY

BLOOMSBURY SQUARE 2

HODGE

GOUGH SQUARE

ST. PAUL'S CATHEDRAL 18

BUNHILL ROW 5

LLOYDS BANK 12

GUILDHALL YARD 9

GREAT QUEEN STREET 8

NEWGATE PRISON 16

7

TOWER OF LONDON 21

NAVY BOARD 15

TRAFALGAR SQUARE

22

BIG BEN

14 NATIONAL THEATRE

GLOBE THEATRE 6

Thames River

TOWER BRIDGE 20

17

1

BUCKINGHAM PALACE

4

HOUSES OF PARLIAMENT

19 TABARD INN

10

23

WESTMINSTER ABBEY

0 Miles   1/4   1/2   3/4   1

0 Kilometres   1   2

LOCATIONS KEY

1 BIG BEN
Tower clock famous for its accuracy and 13-ton bell

2 BLOOMSBURY SQUARE
Virginia Woolf meets with Bloomsbury Group

3 BRITISH MUSEUM
The oldest public museum in the world features 2.5 miles of galleries

4 BUCKINGHAM PALACE
Office and home of the British monarchy

5 BUNHILL ROW
John Milton writes

6 GLOBE THEATRE
Shakespeare's plays performed

7 GOUGH SQUARE
Samuel Johnson compiles *A Dictionary of the English Language*

8 GREAT QUEEN STREET
William Blake works as an engraver

9 GUILDHALL YARD
Site of Roman amphitheatre

10 HOUSES OF PARLIAMENT
Charles Dickens works as Parliamentary reporter

11 KEATS HOUSE, Hampstead
John Keats born

12 LLOYDS BANK (Corn Hill)
T.S. Eliot works as banker

13 NATIONAL GALLERY
Houses over 2,200 paintings

14 NATIONAL THEATRE
Pinter's plays performed

15 NAVY BOARD
Pepys works, writes *Diary*

16 NEWGATE PRISON/OLD BAILEY
Daniel Defoe, Ben Jonson, Sir Thomas Malory imprisoned

17 ROYAL SOCIETY
Isaac Newton describes gravity and laws of motion

18 ST. PAUL'S CATHEDRAL
John Donne preaches

19 TABARD INN
Chaucer sets the beginning of *The Canterbury Tales* here

20 TOWER BRIDGE
Victorian-era drawbridge

21 TOWER Of LONDON
Sir Walter Raleigh imprisoned

22 TRAFALGAR SQUARE
London's main venue for rallies and outdoor public meetings

23 WESTMINSTER ABBEY, Poet's Corner
Chaucer, Spenser, Dickens, Tennyson, Hardy, Kipling buried

From Legend to History

The Old English and Medieval Periods

"... borne/In the lap
of their shining ship, lined/
With gleaming armor,
going safely/In that oak-hard boat
to where their hearts took them."

—from *Beowulf*

Snapshot of the Period

During the era addressed in this unit, successive waves of invaders came to the British Isles. Each group brought its distinctive culture, including its language. As the different groups fought and eventually united to form a single nation, their languages, too, conflicted and—eventually—combined. The English tongue evolved from Old English to Middle English, the form of the language used by England's greatest medieval poet, Geoffrey Chaucer. Literature, too, evolved—from works transmitted orally, often to the accompaniment of a lyre or harp, to those that were written down.

▲ Design and page from the Book of Kells, an illuminated gospel book created by Irish monks between the late 8th and early 9th century (left). A replica of a lyre found at the Sutton Hoo burial site (right).

 As you read the selections in this unit, you will be asked to think about them in view of three key questions:

What is the **relationship** between literature and *place?*

How does literature **shape or reflect** *society?*

What is the relationship of the **writer** to *tradition?*

Languages Brought Into England

© Integration of Knowledge and Ideas The annotations below identify some of the words invading cultures contributed to English as the language developed into its modern form. What can you infer about each group from the types of words it brought? Explain.

Celts invaded 500 B.C.
- "bard" from *bard* (poet)
- Avon, Thames (names of rivers)

Romans invaded 55 B.C., A.D. 43; left A.D. 407
- "wine" from *vinum*
- "wall" from *vallum*

Anglo-Saxons invasion began A.D. 449
- "bread" from *bread* (crumb)
- "doom" from *doms* (judgment)

Normans invaded 1066
- "attorney" from *atourne* (one appointed)
- "plaintiff" from *plaindre* (make complaint)

Scandinavians invaded in late 700s, 800s, end of 900s
- "anger" from *angr*
- "ransack" from *rann-saka*

The Changing English Language: Psalm 23, verse 1

Modern English (King James Bible) c. 1500 to now ········ The Lord is my shepherd; I shall not want...

Early Middle English c. 1100 to 1500 ···················· Lauerd me steres, noght wante sal me...

Old English before 1100 ·· Drihten me ræt; ne byð me nanes godes wan...

Historical Background

The Old English and Medieval Periods, 449–1485

They came to conquer and stayed to build. First, it was the Romans in A.D. 43 who drove the original Celtic inhabitants of Britain into the north (Scotland) and west (Wales) of the island. Then, in A.D. 449, after the last Roman troops had been summoned home to defend Rome against the barbarian invaders, a group of Germanic tribes, the Angles, the Saxons, and the Jutes, crossed the North Sea and occupied the island the Romans had called Albion. In a short time, "Angle land" became England.

Invasion, Settlement, Assimilation

The next incursion, in A.D. 597, was more peaceful, led by the Roman cleric St. Augustine. He and his followers converted to Christianity the pagans who were there. The Bible of these Christians was written in Latin and they brought Latin learning with them.

In the eighth century, the Danes arrived. At first they raided and looted the towns and monasteries of the northeast, but eventually they settled that area. In 871, when they tried to overrun the rest of the island, they were stopped by Alfred the Great, who is now considered the first King of England. The Danes, too, converted, assimilated, and gave us words like *sky, skill,* and *skate*.

The last successful invasion of England occurred in 1066 when the duke of Normandy in France claimed and won the throne. Known as William the Conqueror, he brought his court and its language to the country he seized. For some time, England was a bilingual country of conquerors and conquered. In his novel *Ivanhoe*, which is set in the Middle Ages, the nineteenth-century writer Sir Walter Scott captures this duality: animals are *swine*, *oxen,* and *calves* on the hoof, but *pork*, *beef,* and *veal* in the kitchen of the noble lord. Even today, we make a last *will* and *testament*, repeating the same meaning in Anglo-Saxon and Norman French, respectively.

TIMELINE

449: Anglo-Saxon Invasion.

449

476: Western Europe Fall of Western Roman Empire.

496: France Clovis, king of Franks, converts to Christianity.

The Feudal Era, 1100–1485

The Normans brought more than their language to the island. They also brought a form of government, social order, and land tenure we call feudalism. This is a vision of the natural and human world as a triangle or pyramid. At the peak is the king and below, in carefully graded steps, are nobles and freemen, down to the serfs who till the land.

Yet all social systems are more fluid than they appear from the outside, and the feudal era in England was a tempestuous time. In 1215, a group of nobles forced King John to sign the Magna Carta. This Great Charter, which limited the powers of the king, marks the beginning of parliamentary government in England. Other kings faced more violent opposition from the nobles and two of them, Edward II in 1327 and Richard II in 1399, were deposed and assassinated. The Black Death, a grim name for the plague, ravaged England in the 14th century and may have killed one-third of the population. Drained by an intermittent series of wars with France, which dragged out for more than one hundred years, England was then torn by a brutal civil war from 1455 to 1485.

At the end of England's bloody civil war, Henry VII came to the throne and all of the forces that had shaped the island kingdom for a thousand years came together in a newly unified state. England was poised to participate in an incredible period of discovery and expansion.

They had come, the conquerors, warriors and priests, the knights and serfs, the outlaws and the righteous, the men, the women, the children, and had settled an island that a glacier had sliced off the European continent. On that relatively small stretch of land, they created a country, a language, and a literature that was to become one of the wonders of the world.

Key Historical Theme: From Many Tribes to One Nation

- For a millennium, England experienced successive waves of invasion.
- The last invaders, the Normans, brought with them the French language and feudalism.
- After a turbulent period, England eventually became a unified state with one language.

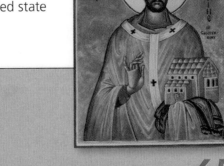

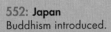

552: Japan
Buddhism introduced.

656

▲ **542: Byzantine Empire** Plague kills half the population of the capital, Constantinople.

591: China
Beginning of book printing.

▲ **597:** St. Augustine founds Christian monastery at Canterbury, Kent.

Essential Questions Across Time

The Old English and Medieval Periods (A.D. 449–1485)

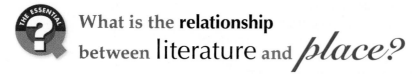

What is the **relationship** between literature and *place?*

In 1399, just before he was deposed and killed, King Richard II returned to England from Ireland. In Shakespeare's version of the scene, the King kneels, touches the sacred soil of England, and says: "Dear earth, I do salute thee with my hand . . . So weeping, smiling, greet I thee, my earth, . . ." This is almost a thousand years after the invading Angles, Saxons, and Jutes set foot on the island's soil, but they neither knelt nor wept. Shakespeare's tragic king, whose feeling for the soil of England is so powerful, shows how the people had shaped a country that had, in turn, shaped them.

How did English writers respond to their island geography?

The Placeless Sea The creation of a sense of place is an important theme in the literature of those who came from elsewhere to dwell on the island. In a way, however, this work of creation begins with an awareness of what is the opposite of place. For islanders, that means the sea, both a protective barrier and an untamable threat. As a watery wilderness, the sea is a kind of placeless place, a vast nowhere that can separate one from home.

"The Seafarer" and "The Wanderer" Two Anglo-Saxon poems chilled by images of the sea, "The Seafarer" and "The Wanderer," are spoken by men on sea voyages. They tell of exile and separation from a remembered home. The bleakness of these poems of lonely struggle is, however, tempered by a different frame of values. Resigned and even bitter as they must have been in their original forms, these poems have come down

TIMELINE

656

712: Spain Seville conquered by Moors.

732: France Charles Martel defeats Moors. ▼

▲ **c. 750:** Surviving version of *Beowulf* composed.

to us in copies made by monks. These monks were aware that Christianity itself begins with a story of exile: Adam and Eve banished from the Garden of Eden. In the Christian tradition, all exile is a model of the exile of humankind from its rightful place in Heaven. In editing "The Seafarer," monks therefore framed the sea-tossed speaker's lament for his life with the overarching Christian theme of exile from Eden, from Heaven, and from God.

The "Sea-Road" The sea also figures in the first epic poem of British literature, *Beowulf*, which contains a distant echo of the journey of the Angles, Saxons, and Jutes to England. In this poem, the hero Beowulf and his men travel by ship to the land of the Danes to face the monster Grendel. The "sea-road," as it is called in the poem, is not merely a threatening watery waste. It is a "road" to fame and honor—and a natural place for these seafaring warriors.

The Mead Hall The destination for Beowulf and his men is not a nation in our modern sense. It is a kingdom, whose capital and command center is Herot, a mead hall. This gathering place—a large building with a single room—probably smelled like a locker room, but it provided warmth, light, food, drink, song, and fellowship for a lord and his warriors. When the monster Grendel comes from the bleak and mysterious darkness to menace Herot, he is striking at the very center of human society, the hearth around which people gather. That is why Beowulf must meet him there and drive him back into the swamp, the dark place from which he comes.

The BRITISH TRADITION

THE CHANGING ENGLISH LANGUAGE
by Richard Lederer

The Beginnings of English

The rise of English as a planetary language is an unparalleled success story that began, long ago, in the middle of the fifth century A.D. Several large tribes of sea rovers—the Angles, Saxons, and Jutes—invaded the islands then known as Britannia. They brought with them a Low Germanic tongue that, in its new setting, became Anglo-Saxon, or Old English. The language came to be called *Englisc*, after *Englaland*, "land of the Angles."

Old English differs so much from modern English that it is harder for us to learn than German is. Still, we can recognize a number of Anglo-Saxon words: *bedd*, *candel*, *eorth*, and *waeter*. Anglo-Saxon words such as these concern the unchanging basics of life. They survived later social upheavals nearly unchanged.

A dramatic evolution in the language came after yet another conquest of England, this one by the Norman French. These Normans (shortened from *Northmen*) had originally been Vikings, but they now spoke French and had taken to French customs. In 1066, under William, Duke of Normandy, the Normans invaded England. One result was that Old Englisc was flooded by the French spoken by the Normans. Examples of French influence include the words *sir*, *madam*, *courtesy*, *honor*, and *royal*. From this infusion of French words emerged a tongue that today we call Middle English.

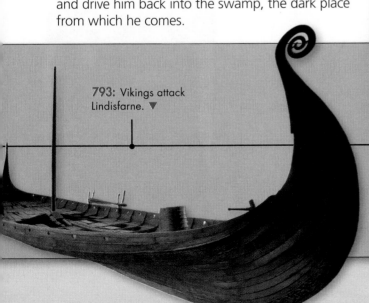

793: Vikings attack Lindisfarne. ▼

▲ 800: Peru Incas build city of Machu Picchu.

861: North Atlantic Vikings discover Iceland.

863

How did literature make a nation of an island?

A Place of Shared Stories In the 8th century, Bede, a learned monk, wrote *A History of the English Church and People*, marking an important stage in England's developing sense of itself as an island-nation. With his knowledge of Latin and history, Bede was not interested in merely telling the story of a single clan's mead hall. Instead, he wrote the history of an entire nation—"Britain, formerly known as Albion."

Through Bede's informative prose, the reader can sense how "the island in the ocean" he describes, with its abundant resources, is on its way to becoming the earth to which Shakespeare's Richard II will kneel. Most importantly, Bede is aware that his island is becoming a nation, a place that is as much a product of its history as of its geography; a country is a geographical area with shared stories.

A Nation Created by Imagination Chaucer's *Canterbury Tales*, England's greatest medieval poem, is all about "shared stories" and a sense of England as a nation of different social types. These various characters are on a pilgrimage to the town of Canterbury. There, in 1170, Thomas à Becket, the Archbishop of Canterbury, was murdered in the cathedral on the orders of his former friend King Henry II, to whom he would not yield in matters of church policy. Becket was canonized, or declared a saint, and the cathedral became a shrine. That is why the pilgrims are traveling there, and they will seal their fellowship by telling one another stories along the way.

For Chaucer and his pilgrims, Canterbury is a somewhat distant goal, a symbol of the ultimate sacred place to which people journey on their life's pilgrimage—Heaven. Such was the ideal. Chaucer's pilgrims, however, have a wide range of motives, desires, and needs, many of which are far from noble. A later great poet and critic, John Dryden, was moved to say of Chaucer: "He has taken into the compass of his *Canterbury Tales* the various manners and humors…of the whole English nation…Not a single character has escap'd him."

In the process of inventing English poetry as we know it, Chaucer presents his pilgrims on the road. England is a place in motion, a nation created by the imagination, by the stories people tell one another. It is these shared stories, with all their humble realities, that transform the British Isles to—in the words of Shakespeare's Richard II—"Dear earth."

ESSENTIAL QUESTION VOCABULARY

These Essential Question words will help you think and write about literature and place:

exile (ek′ sīl′) *n.* long time living away from one's country or community, usually involuntary; banishment

geography (jē äg′ rə fē) *n.* physical features of a region, area, or place

pilgrimage (pil′ grə mij) *n.* long journey to a holy or important place

TIMELINE

863

871: Alfred the Great becomes King of Wessex. ▶

c. 900: **Western Europe** Feudalism develops.

▲ c. 975: Saxon monks copy Old English poems into The Exeter Book.

How does literature **shape or** reflect *society?*

In the ten centuries between the Germanic invasions and the dawn of the modern world, England changed from a place of warrior bands and invading tribes to a country ruled by a king, nobles, and bishops. Indeed, England was increasingly run and organized by merchants and landowners and their representatives in an evolving Parliament. The literature written during this period reflects these changes.

How did writers capture a vanishing world of tribes and clans?

The Hero's Code The world of the Anglo-Saxon epic poem *Beowulf* is that of the tribe and its leader. To become a leader a young warrior must prove himself in battle. So Beowulf crosses the sea to aid his kinsman Hrothgar, who cannot protect his people from the monster Grendel. After his victories over Grendel and Grendel's mother, Beowulf becomes the leader of his own tribe.

Vanishing World, Enduring Values The *Beowulf* poet tells a rousing story, but he also allows his listener to see and feel the world of the hero in both its glory and decline. At the end of the poem, Beowulf, with only the faithful young warrior Wiglaf at his side, battles a dragon and dies for his people. The audience knows that the poet is lamenting not only the death of a hero, but the passing of a hero's way of life.

The BRITISH TRADITION

CLOSE-UP ON HISTORY

Guilds and the Status of Women

By 1000, merchants, traders, and artisans or crafts workers formed a new middle class, ranked between nobles and peasants. This class gained power in medieval towns, with merchants and artisans forming associations called guilds.

The craft guilds of artisans represented workers in one occupation, such as weavers, bakers, or goldsmiths. Guild members made rules to protect the quality of their goods, regulate hours, and set prices. No one except guild members could work in any trade, and becoming a guild member took many years of labor.

Guilds offered opportunities to women, who worked in dozens of crafts and dominated some trades. Young girls became apprentices in trades such as ribbon-making and papermaking. Also, a woman often engaged in the same trade as her father or husband and might inherit his workshop if he died. Chaucer's Wife of Bath, a weaver, represents this type of new middle-class woman.

982: Greenland Eric the Red establishes first Viking Colony. ▼

991: English defeated by Danes at Battle of Maldon.

c. 1020: America Viking Leif Ericson explores Canadian coast.

1040: Macbeth kills Duncan I.

▲**1066:** Normans defeat Saxons at Hastings; William the Conqueror becomes king of England.

1070

How did Chaucer reflect social trends without preaching?

A Poet and His World At the other end of the period, Chaucer provides the most complete example of the poet's interaction with his world.

Chaucer's lifetime, the late fourteenth century, was a turbulent period in English history. The country suffered the devastations of the Black Death and Chaucer vividly describes that plague in "The Pardoner's Tale." In the preaching of dissident theologian John Wycliffe, the country also experienced a foreshadowing of the Protestant Reformation, the Protestant separation from the Catholic Church that would occur in the early sixteenth century. Wycliffe's criticisms of the church reflected a growing discontent with the showy wealth of some religious institutions. In the Prologue to *The Canterbury Tales*, we meet a number of characters who represent various religious orders. Their sometimes questionable behavior suggests the controversy that would lead to the Reformation.

Showing, Not Sermonizing Chaucer, however, does not rant, rave, or preach about corruption among religious orders or other social ills. Instead, he shows us characters like the Monk, who spends more time hunting and feasting than praying and fasting.

Political Turbulence In 1381, England was shaken by The Peasant's Revolt, in which farmers and laborers demanded a greater share in the wealth and governance of the country. King Richard II put the rebellion down, only to lose power himself eighteen years later. London, originally a Roman settlement on the banks of the Thames River, had by this time grown into a great city and a center for international trade.

Rising Middle Class Part of this tumult and change involved the replacement of feudal roles, such as knight and serf, with a newly empowered urban middle class. Chaucer himself was a member of this newly-rising group, as is one of his most memorable characters, the Wife of Bath.

The Writer and Society Writers often address social issues, but not as sociologists. Writers are interested in the human stories, the individual tale rather than the mass phenomenon. Readers are often left to figure out who or what is to blame or praise. The turbulent history of the later Middle Ages is contained in Chaucer's pilgrimage—between the lines.

ESSENTIAL QUESTION VOCABULARY

These Essential Question words will help you think and write about literature and society:

sociologist (sō´ sē äl´ ə jist) *n.* scientist who studies societies and the behavior of people in groups

turbulent (tur´ byə lənt) *adj.* full of commotion or wild disorder

feudal (fyo͞od´ ´l) *adj.* relating to a system in which overlords granted land to lesser lords, or vassals, in return for military service and in which poor farmers worked the land for vassals

TIMELINE

c. 1100: **France** *Song of Roland* written.

1070

1073: Canterbury becomes England's religious center.

▲ 1096: **Europe and Middle East** First Crusade begins.

▲ c. 1130: Oxford becomes a center for learning.

What is the relationship of the writer to *tradition?*

You may first have encountered King Arthur and the Knights of the Round Table in a book, a movie, a comic strip, or even a multi-player game. Their stories have been told, reverently and irreverently, for over a thousand years. These tales, in other words, are traditional; they have been handed down. The word *tradition* comes from the Latin *traditio*, meaning "to hand over, to transmit." Tradition in literature, however, does not simply refer to what a writer receives from the past. It also refers to what a writer does with the inheritance.

How do writers change what they have inherited?

Bequest from the Past The King Arthur stories are a kind of bequest from the past. Different authors accepted this literary inheritance but decided to use it in different ways. For example, the poet who wrote *Sir Gawain and the Green Knight* has his knight-hero submit to a series of tests that teach him something about himself. The tests come from earlier folk tales and romances, or adventure stories about knights, and the poet weaves them into a seamless whole.

Sir Thomas Malory, writing in the fifteenth century at the end of the age of chivalry, uses Arthurian legend in a different way. In his book *Morte d'Arthur* ("Death of Arthur"), Malory gathers many legends of Arthur and his companions to write an elegy, or farewell, to the era of knights.

Changing in the Telling The much earlier Anglo-Saxon epic *Beowulf* also ends on a note of farewell, with the dying hero deserted by all but one faithful follower. It is easy to imagine how this story grew in the retelling. Perhaps in the earliest recitals, the hero sails across the sea to rescue his kinsmen and kill the monster. Then, as new audiences clamor for more, the storyteller adds more exploits. Now, Beowulf must also pursue and kill the monster's mother. Still later, in an episode added by another teller, Beowulf is mortally injured by a dragon. Finally, the monk or monks who copy the tale alter it further, adding Christian elements from their own tradition.

1170: Thomas à Becket, Archbishop of Canterbury, murdered.▼

1214: Mongol leader Genghis Khan captures Peking.

▲ **1215:** King John forced to sign Magna Carta.

1258: First commoners allowed in Parliament.

1270

How did Chaucer respond to and create literary traditions?

Using the Old Geoffrey Chaucer is the supreme literary artist of the English Middle Ages because he is both indebted to traditions and committed to creating them. Consider the idea of his major poem, *The Canterbury Tales*: a varied group of people are thrown together and agree to tell stories to pass the time. In 1353, the Italian author Boccaccio had used the same format in his collection of stories, the *Decameron*, in which a group of aristocrats flee to a castle to avoid the plague and agree to tell one another a hundred tales. Chaucer knew Italian literature and the work of Boccaccio. The idea of a group of stories held together by a frame story is his inheritance.

Making It New Chaucer, however, altered what he inherited. His pilgrims reflect almost all levels of society, from the Knight to the Miller. They are not fleeing from the plague; they are on a religious pilgrimage. Chaucer's approach allows him to explore interesting differences between noble and base motives. For example, the Wife of Bath may be on a pilgrimage not so much to worship at a saint's tomb as to meet her next husband. Chaucer uses each tale to reveal something about the teller.

Inventing The Rhythm of English Poetry Chaucer not only reinvented the frame story; he also reinvented a French verse form to create the iambic pentameter line that would dominate English poetry for hundreds of years. Chaucer knew the ten-syllable lines and rhyming couplets used in French poetry. With the instinct that comes only with real genius, he adapted that form to English. In his rhyming couplets, Chaucer used a line of ten syllables with five alternating accents, the form known as iambic pentameter. This new form, when rediscovered by poets in the sixteenth century, became one of the most enduring traditions in English literature.

Traditions Stretching Backward and Forward The beginnings of literature are lost in the mists of prehistory, when some forms of telling stories came into being. Successive generations used those forms to relate the history of the tribe for each new generation. When these stories came to be written down, traditional forms were established. The wonder of literature in this period is that we can see traditions stretching backward into archeological time and stretching forward to tomorrow.

ESSENTIAL QUESTION VOCABULARY

These Essential Question words will help you think and write about the writer and tradition:

traditional (trə dish'ə nəl) *adj.* relating to or based on old customs, beliefs, and ways of doing things

inheritance (in her'i təns) *n.* goods, ideas, literary creations, or skills received from the past

legend (lej'ənd) *n.* story handed down for generations and believed to be based on actual events

TIMELINE

1270

1275: **China** Marco Polo visits court of Kubla Khan. ▶

1277: England conquers Wales.

1291: **Europe and Middle East** End of Crusades.

1325: **Mexico** Aztecs establish Mexico city and create a dating system with a solar year of 365 days. ▼

CONTEMPORARY CONNECTION

King Arthur: Legendary Hero, Broadway Star!

In medieval Europe, tales circulated of a legendary king named Arthur. He and his knights represented the ideals of chivalry—rules governing the behavior of knights. Since then, Arthur's story has surfaced in many literary and dramatic works. Most recently, it has been brought to life in *Spamalot*, a musical comedy that pokes fun at the legend, as follows:

- King Arthur's kingdom is a Las Vegas resort, not the town of Camelot.

- The knights of the Round Table are a motley crew who have to be talked into performing heroic deeds.

- Arthur's knights underwent trials and ordeals to prove their courage and virtue. *Spamalot*'s crew, however, must prove themselves by producing a Broadway musical.

Despite its silliness, *Spamalot*'s success proves the ongoing fascination with the legend. Tales of romance and courage never go out of style.

▲ **1337:** Beginning of the Hundred Years' War with France.

1348: Black Death begins sweeping through England.

1381: Bible first translated into English.

1429: France Joan of Arc leads French in breaking siege of Orléans.

1453: Germany First Gutenberg Bible printed.▼

1455–1485: The Wars of the Roses.

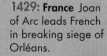

1485

Recent Scholarship

England's Green, Fertile Land

Burton Raffel

We tell jokes about the rainy English climate. A warm ocean current brings that moisture, and makes England the green, fertile land it still is. When the last ice age ended, some three thousand years ago, all across Europe easy hunting ended with it, and people without rich pasturage and easy farming went hungry. The English Channel was not as broad as it is today, and wave after wave of immigrants came pouring across.

Daily Life

Life for England's earliest settlers was in many ways much like that still lived in England, as recently as the early nineteenth century. Cities were, for the most part, a thing of the future, though London was even then beginning to become a rich, bustling port. People lived on and by the land, which was worked by both men and women. Sheep were kept for their wool, pigs for their meat, chickens for their eggs. Most people raised a large percentage of the food they ate. There were no shops where one could buy such necessities as clothing (woven and sewn by hand), though artisans like blacksmiths made tools and other metallic items. Most of the land was owned by nobles, both hereditary and newly created aristocrats, having been made counts and earls as kingly rewards. There were many kingdoms on the island now called England and a good deal of quarreling between and among them.

Kings, Lords, Knights, and Peasants

Society was hierarchical—that is, very little moved upward from the peasant level, and virtually everything proceeded downward from the nobility. No one imagined questioning the necessity for these largely fixed relationships. Without leadership, no community would function, and no stability would have been possible. These were matters as much taken for granted as, today, automobiles and television sets. Most of what we would call "work" was performed by those at the lower levels of society. We have no direct testimony from them, but from drawings and paintings, and surviving documents written by clergy or the minority of

About the Author

Burton Raffel (b. 1928) is a noted scholar and poet. You might also call him a time traveler. His work as a translator of world literature has taken him back in time to Anglo-Saxon England, with his versions of *Beowulf* and "The Seafarer," and to Renaissance France, with his version of Rabelais's *Gargantua and Pantagruel*—to name just two of his many translations. When he is not breaking the time barrier, Raffel serves as a professor of English at the University of Louisiana.

aristocrats who could read and write, there is a sense of relatively prosperous busyness. England was a rich habitat, as its inhabitants well knew. What overseas trading there was usually involved costly goods that only a few could afford. There was a good deal of local trading, most of which was conducted on the barter principle. Aristocrats dressed elaborately and expensively; most others dressed very plainly, both men and women wearing loose-fitting garments very like what we today call "smocks."

People not only worked, but they played. There was a good deal of group dancing: the songs we call "carols" in fact began as dance music. There were harvest and other agricultural festivals, and there were more solemn religious festivals. For both the secular and the holy festivities, there were other entertainments, from storytelling to dramatic presentations.

From Many Kingdoms to One Nation

By the ninth century, some unification of the country's many kingdoms had occurred. Alfred the Great was the most notable English ruler, though still not entirely in control. Immigrants and Anglo-Saxon "natives" pulled and tugged at one another, and continued to fight over the prosperous green land. It was William of Brittany (in France) who finally created as much unity as England was to know for almost another five hundred years. In 1066, at the Battle of Hastings, William the Conqueror defeated an Anglo-Saxon opponent and became the increasingly powerful king of England. The kind of feudal structure he enforced was based on a close accounting of wealth, as reported, at William's direction, by the famous Domesday Book. William's England, now a Norman French "colony," was officially a French-speaking land: indeed, English law courts employed French until the sixteenth century.

But toward the end of the Anglo-Saxon period, we do not know exactly when, someone, somewhere, produced a poetic narrative, probably meant as a guide to proper kingship. This famous book is known as *Beowulf*.

©Collaboration: Speaking and Listening

Burton Raffel refers to the conflict between "Anglo-Saxon 'natives'" and Viking or Danish "immigrants." Suppose you were a council of Viking leaders planning to invade England. Hold a **small group discussion** about the map of Anglo-Saxon Kingdoms below, answering these questions as you make your military plans:

- Which region or regions might aid you in your fight? Why?
- Which regions might oppose your invasion most strongly? Why?
- Would it be easier to sail your war ships down the Ouse River or the Thames? Explain.

The Anglo-Saxon Kingdoms

Integrate and Evaluate Information

1. Use a chart like the one shown to determine the key ideas expressed in the Essential Question essays on pages 6–12. Fill in two ideas related to each Essential Question and note the authors most closely associated with each concept. One example has been done for you.

Essential Question	Key Concept	Key Author
Literature and Place	Exile to a foreign land	"Seafarer" (author unknown)
Literature and Society		
Writer and Tradition		

2. How do the visual sources in this section—artifacts, paintings, photographs, and illustrations—add to your understanding of the ideas expressed in words? Cite specific examples.

3. On page 8, medieval England is described as "a nation of different social types." Using information from the multiple sources presented in this section, explain how this is so. What social structures produced these "types"? How did these social structures change over time, and how did these changes affect the population? Which social structures—and social types—survived, and which were replaced by others? Cite evidence from the multiple sources presented on pages 4–15 in your answer.

©️ 4. **Address a Question** Burton Raffel describes medieval England as a prosperous and bustling island pulsing with commerce, recreation, and, often, war. What stories, images, or events come to mind when you hear the phrase "medieval England"? Integrate details and information from this textbook and other sources—including movies, novels, and games—to support your ideas.

Speaking and Listening: Panel Discussion

The English language is like a large machine that draws its power from two engines. One of these engines is built from the Anglo-Saxon and Scandinavian languages. The other, equally powerful, is fueled by Latin, Greek, and French words. Working in groups, pick one of the following categories:

- Domestic Life
- Law and Politics
- Science and Medicine
- Recreation and Athletics

Choose ten words that belong to your category and determine their current meanings and *etymologies*. Present your findings in a **panel discussion.**

©️**Solve a Research Problem:** In your discussion, explain how usage of certain terms has changed over time. Research and describe any moments in history when the usage of certain words caused conflicts or was contested. Consult reference sources such as dictionaries and encyclopedias, secondary sources that describe the history of the English language, and primary texts—such as literary works—in which the words appear.

©️ **Common Core State Standards**

Reading Informational Text

7. Integrate and evaluate multiple sources of information presented in different media or formats as well as in words in order to address a question or solve a problem.

Language
1.a. Apply the understanding that usage is a matter of convention, can change over time, and is sometimes contested.

Speaking and Listening
1. Initiate and participate effectively in a range of collaborative discussions with diverse partners on *grades 11–12 topics, texts, and issues,* building on others' ideas and expressing their own clearly and persuasively.

ESSENTIAL QUESTION VOCABULARY

Use these words in your responses:

Literature and Place
exile
geography
pilgrimage

Literature and Society
sociologist
turbulent
feudal

Writer and Tradition
traditional
inheritance
legend

Earthly Exile,
Heavenly Home

Connecting to the Essential Question These poems are about people in exile—those forced from and longing for home. As you read, note what the speakers say about their lost homes. This will help you answer the Essential Question: **What is the relationship between literature and place?**

Literary Analysis

A lyric poem expresses the thoughts and feelings of a single speaker. **Anglo-Saxon lyrics,** composed for easy memorization and recitation, contain the following structural elements:

- Lines with **regular rhythms,** usually with four strong beats
- **Caesuras,** pauses for breath in the middle of lines
- **Kennings,** two-word poetic renamings, like "whales' home" for the sea
- **Assonance,** repeated vowel sounds in unrhymed, stressed syllables
- **Alliteration,** repeated initial consonant sounds in stressed syllables

Comparing Literary Works Shaped by these devices, each lyric in this grouping is an **elegy**—a poem mourning the loss of someone or something. Compare and contrast the types of loss experienced by the speakers in these poems. Also, analyze and compare the ways in which the writers used poetic devices to *convey a mood* of sadness.

Reading Strategy

Preparing to Read Complex Texts It is helpful to **understand the historical context** of a literary work, the time in which it was created. Anglo-Saxon England, for example, was a collection of warring kingdoms, not a single nation. In this uncertain situation, people gave loyalty to a lord in return for his protection. Also, men dominated society, and women relied on men for protection. As you read, use a diagram like the one shown to find connections between the characters and settings in these poems and the historical issues of the era.

Vocabulary

admonish (ad män´ ish) *v.* advise; caution (p. 23)

sentinel (sen´ ti nəl) *n.* person or animal that guards (p. 23)

fervent (fʉr´ vənt) *adj.* having great warmth of feeling (p. 23)

rancor (raŋ´ kər) *n.* ill will; continuing and bitter hate (p. 23)

compassionate (kəm pash´ ən it) *adj.* sympathizing; pitying (p. 27)

rapture (rap´ chər) *n.* joy; great pleasure (p. 28)

Common Core
State Standards

Reading Literature
5. Analyze how an author's choices concerning how to structure specific parts of a text contribute to its overall structure and meaning as well as its aesthetic impact.

Event/Idea

The speaker is exiled when his lord dies.

Historical Background

Anglo-Saxon warriors depended on the protection of a powerful lord.

PHLit Online!
www.PHLitOnline.com

from The Exeter Book

"The Seafarer" • "The Wanderer" • "The Wife's Lament"

Imagine what life would be like if there were no television sets and if movies played in theaters only on important occasions. People would gather beforehand, chatting excitedly. The next day, everyone would discuss the film, quoting dialogue and reenacting scenes.

Telling the Story This scenario captures the nature of entertainment during Britain's Anglo-Saxon period, from the fifth to the eleventh century. Few people of the time were able to read, and movies lay centuries in the future. Instead, people turned to traveling storytellers, known as *scops*, who created an oral tradition by memorizing, adapting, and passing along stories and songs. Through the years, many of these works were lost. Others, however, were eventually written down.

An Early Anthology *The Exeter Book* is a collection of manuscripts that includes pieces of this tradition. The book was probably compiled by monks during the reign of Alfred the Great, A.D. 871–899. Without *The Exeter Book,* many stories that came out of the oral tradition would have been lost to us forever. "The Seafarer," "The Wanderer," and "The Wife's Lament" were all discovered in this collection.

Guests Who Came to Stay Those who recited and listened to the tales recorded in *The Exeter Book*—the Anglo-Saxons—were not native to Britain. In the 400s, Roman soldiers stationed in Britain had abandoned the island to defend Rome. The native inhabitants were soon threatened by Picts from Scotland and Scots from Ireland. One British king invited warlike Germanic tribes from Europe to help him defend Britain. These "guests" proved to be the most dangerous invaders of them all. By the 500s, Angles, Saxons, and other Germanic peoples had settled Britain themselves, driving out most of the Britons. By the end of the 600s, these new inhabitants of the island thought of themselves as part of an English nation, and in A.D. 827, King Egbert named Britannia *Englaland,* "land of the Angles."

A Growing Culture The Angles and Saxons brought with them a warrior culture, a seafaring tradition, and pagan beliefs, including a grim, fatalistic view of the world. They were followed by missionaries sent by Rome. Eventually, these missionaries converted Britain to Christianity. Anglo-Saxon culture at the time of *The Exeter Book* was a blend, mixing pagan ideas of fate with Christian faith in heaven, the boasts of proud warriors with lessons about humility. Preserved by scops and monks, this culture gave Britain its first literature.

▲ Anglo-Saxon artifact from the 7th century A.D.: the great gold buckle from the Sutton Hoo ship burial

The Seafarer

Translated by Burton Raffel

BACKGROUND To the Anglo-Saxon people of Britain, home meant something different from what it means for people today. An Anglo-Saxon warrior viewed himself as the follower of a particular lord or king, not as a citizen of a nation. Gathering in the mead-hall, a building dedicated to their feasts, a lord and his warriors would share food, drink, entertainment, and fellowship. Smoky, noisy, smelly, and crowded, the mead-hall was home.

This tale is true, and mine. It tells
How the sea took me, swept me back
And forth in sorrow and fear and pain,
Showed me suffering in a hundred ships,
5 In a thousand ports, and in me. It tells
Of smashing surf when I sweated in the cold
Of an anxious watch, perched in the bow
As it dashed under cliffs. My feet were cast
In icy bands, bound with frost,

The Literature of Exile

"The Seafarer" is about exile, a long stay away from home that is often enforced but sometimes self-imposed. The theme of exile has run through world literature since ancient times. Over the centuries, many writers suffered exile, an experience that colored their work. Some fled for safety. Others were banished for political reasons.

In A.D. 8, for example, the Roman ruler Augustus Caesar sent the poet Ovid into the provinces for writing *The Art of Love*, which was deemed immoral. Ovid remained there until his death, writing *Sorrows*, among other works.

Italian poet Dante Alighieri was sentenced to exile by his political enemies in 1302. Banished from his beloved native city of Florence, he wrote the *Divine Comedy*, an epic that describes a journey through Hell, Purgatory, and Heaven. In the following passage from that work, he evokes the suffering of the outcast: "You shall leave everything you love most:/this is the arrow that the bow of exile/shoots first."

Just as Ovid and Dante went into exile, so did many twentieth-century writers. For example, after the Russian Revolution, poet Marina Tsvetaeva left Moscow, following her husband to Europe, where she wrote poetry filled with longing for her lost home.

Connect to the Literature

Do you think that the exile of the speaker in "The Seafarer" can touch readers in the twenty-first century? Why or why not?

10 With frozen chains, and hardship groaned
Around my heart. Hunger tore
At my sea-weary soul. No man sheltered
On the quiet fairness of earth can feel
How wretched I was, drifting through winter
15 On an ice-cold sea, whirled in sorrow,
Alone in a world blown clear of love,
Hung with icicles. The hailstorms flew.
The only sound was the roaring sea,
The freezing waves. The song of the swan
20 Might serve for pleasure, the cry of the sea-fowl,
The death-noise of birds instead of laughter,
The mewing of gulls instead of mead.[1]
Storms beat on the rocky cliffs and were echoed
By icy-feathered terns and the eagle's screams;
25 No kinsman could offer comfort there,
To a soul left drowning in desolation.
      And who could believe, knowing but
The passion of cities, swelled proud with wine
And no taste of misfortune, how often, how wearily,
30 I put myself back on the paths of the sea.
Night would blacken; it would snow from the north;
Frost bound the earth and hail would fall,
The coldest seeds. And how my heart
Would begin to beat, knowing once more
35 The salt waves tossing and the towering sea!
The time for journeys would come and my soul
Called me eagerly out, sent me over
The horizon, seeking foreigners' homes.
      But there isn't a man on earth so proud,
40 So born to greatness, so bold with his youth,
Grown so brave, or so graced by God,
That he feels no fear as the sails unfurl,
Wondering what Fate has willed and will do.
No harps ring in his heart, no rewards,
45 No passion for women, no worldly pleasures,
Nothing, only the ocean's heave;
But longing wraps itself around him.
Orchards blossom, the towns bloom,
Fields grow lovely as the world springs fresh,

---

1. mead liquor made from fermented honey and water.

50 And all these admonish that willing mind
Leaping to journeys, always set
In thoughts traveling on a quickening tide.
So summer's sentinel, the cuckoo, sings
In his murmuring voice, and our hearts mourn
55 As he urges. Who could understand,
In ignorant ease, what we others suffer
As the paths of exile stretch endlessly on?
    And yet my heart wanders away,
My soul roams with the sea, the whales'
60 Home, wandering to the widest corners
Of the world, returning ravenous with desire,
Flying solitary, screaming, exciting me
To the open ocean, breaking oaths
On the curve of a wave.
                  Thus the joys of God
65 Are fervent with life, where life itself
Fades quickly into the earth. The wealth
Of the world neither reaches to Heaven nor remains.
No man has ever faced the dawn
Certain which of Fate's three threats
70 Would fall: illness, or age, or an enemy's
Sword, snatching the life from his soul.
The praise the living pour on the dead
Flowers from reputation: plant
An earthly life of profit reaped
75 Even from hatred and rancor, of bravery
Flung in the devil's face, and death
Can only bring you earthly praise
And a song to celebrate a place
With the angels, life eternally blessed
80 In the hosts of Heaven.
                  The days are gone
When the kingdoms of earth flourished in glory;
Now there are no rulers, no emperors,
No givers of gold, as once there were,
When wonderful things were worked among them
85 And they lived in lordly magnificence.
Those powers have vanished, those pleasures are dead.
The weakest survives and the world continues,
Kept spinning by toil. All glory is tarnished.

Vocabulary

admonish (ad män´ ish) *v.*
advise; caution

sentinel (sen´ ti nel), *n.*
person or animal that guards

fervent (fur´ vənt) *adj.*
having great warmth of
feeling

rancor (raŋ´ kər) *n.* ill will;
continuing and bitter hate

Literary Analysis
Anglo-Saxon Lyrics
How does the alliteration of
words beginning with *w*, *r*,
and *s* affect the sound and
meaning of lines 59–62?

Literary Analysis
**Anglo-Saxon Lyrics
and the Elegy**
What does the speaker
mourn in lines 81–90?

Reading
Check

What are the "three threats"
mentioned by the speaker?

▲ **Critical Viewing**
In what ways does the mood of this painting match the mood of the speaker's reflections on "The world's honor"?
[Connect]

The world's honor ages and shrinks,
90   Bent like the men who mold it. Their faces
Blanch as time advances, their beards
Wither and they mourn the memory of friends.
The sons of princes, sown in the dust.
The soul stripped of its flesh knows nothing
95   Of sweetness or sour, feels no pain,
Bends neither its hand nor its brain. A brother
Opens his palms and pours down gold
On his kinsman's grave, strewing his coffin
With treasures intended for Heaven, but nothing
100 Golden shakes the wrath of God
For a soul overflowing with sin, and nothing
Hidden on earth rises to Heaven.
          We all fear God. He turns the earth,
He set it swinging firmly in space,
105 Gave life to the world and light to the sky.
Death leaps at the fools who forget their God.
He who lives humbly has angels from Heaven

To carry him courage and strength and belief.
A man must conquer pride, not kill it,
110 Be firm with his fellows, chaste for himself,
Treat all the world as the world deserves,
With love or with hate but never with harm,
Though an enemy seek to scorch him in hell,
Or set the flames of a funeral pyre
115 Under his lord. Fate is stronger
And God mightier than any man's mind.
Our thoughts should turn to where our home is,
Consider the ways of coming there,
Then strive for sure permission for us
120 To rise to that eternal joy,
That life born in the love of God
And the hope of Heaven. Praise the Holy
Grace of Him who honored us,
Eternal, unchanging creator of earth. Amen.

A man must conquer pride, not kill it.

Critical Reading

1. **Key Ideas and Details (a)** Identify three images related to weather in the first stanza. **(b) Interpret:** What does each convey about the speaker's experiences at sea?

2. **Key Ideas and Details (a)** What causes the speaker's heart to "begin to beat"? **(b) Generalize:** How can someone dislike something as much as the seafarer dislikes life at sea and yet be drawn to it?

3. **Key Ideas and Details (a)** What is the seafarer's response to "harps," "rewards," "passion," and the other pleasures of life on the land (lines 44–47)? **(b) Interpret:** Judging from his response to these things, explain whether he is more attached to life on land than he is to life at sea.

4. **Key Ideas and Details (a) Interpret:** What does the speaker mean when he says in lines 58–61, "And yet my heart wanders away, / My soul roams with the sea, . . . / . . . / . . . returning ravenous with desire, . . ."? **(b) Draw Conclusions:** Is the speaker fully at home on land, on the sea, or in neither place? Explain.

5. **Integration of Knowledge and Ideas (a) Interpret:** According to the last section of the poem, where is our home? **(b) Synthesize:** Explain the connection between the poem's concluding message and its depiction of the seafarer's wandering existence.

6. **Integration of Knowledge and Ideas** Can people find a way of life in which they are fully happy, or, like the seafarer, will they always have longings for another place? Explain.

The Wanderer

Translated by
Charles W. Kennedy

Though woefully toiling   on wintry seas
With churning oar   in the icy wave,
Homeless and helpless   he fled from fate.

Oft to the wanderer,   weary of exile,
Cometh God's pity,   compassionate love,
Though woefully toiling   on wintry seas
With churning oar   in the icy wave,
5   Homeless and helpless   he fled from fate.
Thus saith the wanderer   mindful of misery,
Grievous disasters,   and death of kin:
      "Oft when the day broke, oft at the dawning,
Lonely and wretched   I wailed my woe.
10 No man is living,   no comrade left,
To whom I dare fully   unlock my heart.
I have learned truly   the mark of a man
Is keeping his counsel   and locking his lips,
Let him think what he will!   For, woe of heart
15 Withstandeth not fate: a failing spirit
Earneth no help.   Men eager for honor
Bury their sorrow   deep in the breast.
      "So have I also,   often in wretchedness
Fettered[1] my feelings,   far from my kin,
20 Homeless and hapless,[2]   since days of old,
When the dark earth covered   my dear lord's face,
And I sailed away   with sorrowful heart,
Over wintry seas,   seeking a gold-lord,
If far or near   lived one to befriend me
25 With gift in the mead-hall   and comfort for grief.
      "Who bears it, knows   what a bitter companion,
Shoulder to shoulder,   sorrow can be,
When friends are no more.   His fortune is exile,
Not gifts of fine gold;   a heart that is frozen,
30 Earth's winsomeness dead.   And he dreams of the hall-men,
The dealing of treasure,   the days of his youth,
When his lord bade welcome   to wassail[3] and feast.
But gone is that gladness,   and never again
Shall come the loved counsel   of comrade and king.
35   "Even in slumber   his sorrow assaileth,
And, dreaming he claspeth   his dear lord again,
Head on knee, hand on knee,   loyally laying,
Pledging his liege[4]   as in days long past.
Then from his slumber   he starts lonely-hearted,
40 Beholding gray stretches   of tossing sea.
Sea-birds bathing,   with wings outspread,

---

1. Fettered (fet´ ərd) chained; restrained.
2. hapless (hap´ lis) unlucky.
3. wassail (wäs´ əl) a toast in drinking a person's health, or a celebration at which such toasts are made.
4. liege (lēj) lord; sovereign.

The Wanderer **27**

Vocabulary
compassionate (kəm pash´ ən it) *adj.* sympathizing; pitying

Reading Check
What is the wanderer's situation?

Vocabulary
rapture (rap chər) *n.* joy; great pleasure

While hailstorms darken,   and driving snow.
Bitterer then   is the bane of his wretchedness,
The longing for loved one: his grief is renewed.
45 The forms of his kinsmen   take shape in the silence:
In rapture he greets them;   in gladness he scans
Old comrades remembered.   But they melt into air
With no word of greeting   to gladden his heart.
Then again surges   his sorrow upon him;
50 And grimly he spurs   his weary soul
Once more to the toil   of the tossing sea.
      "No wonder therefore,   in all the world,
If a shadow darkens   upon my spirit
When I reflect   on the fates of men—

Reading Strategy
Understand Historical Context How does your knowledge of Anglo-Saxon life help you appreciate the mood of these lines?

55 How one by one   proud warriors vanish
From the halls that knew them,   and day by day
All this earth ages   and droops unto death.
No man may know wisdom   till many a winter
Has been his portion.   A wise man is patient,
60 Not swift to anger,   nor hasty of speech,
Neither too weak,   nor too reckless, in war,
Neither fearful nor fain,[5]   nor too wishful of wealth,
Nor too eager in vow—   ere he know the event.
A brave man must bide[6]   when he speaketh his boast
65 Until he know surely   the goal of his spirit.
      "A wise man will ponder   how dread is that doom
When all this world's wealth   shall be scattered and waste
As now, over all,   through the regions of earth,
Walls stand rime-covered[7]   and swept by the winds.
70 The battlements crumble,   the wine-halls decay;
Joyless and silent   the heroes are sleeping
Where the proud host fell   by the wall they defended.
Some battle launched   on their long, last journey;
One a bird bore   o'er the billowing sea:
75 One the gray wolf slew;   one a grieving earl
Sadly gave   to the grave's embrace.
The Warden of men   hath wasted this world
Till the sound of music   and revel is stilled,
And these giant-built structures   stand empty of life.
80   "He who shall muse   on these moldering ruins,
And deeply ponder   this darkling life,
Must brood on old legends   of battle and bloodshed,
And heavy the mood   that troubles his heart:
'Where now is the warrior?   Where is the war horse?

Literary Analysis
Anglo-Saxon Lyrics
How are caesuras indicated on the page?

---

5. fain (fān) archaic word meaning "eager." In this context it means "too eager."
6. bide (bīd) wait.
7. rime (rīm)**-covered** covered with frost.

85　Bestowal of treasure,　and sharing of feast?
　　Alas! the bright ale-cup,　the byrny-clad[8] warrior,
　　The prince in his splendor—　those days are long sped
　　In the night of the past,　as if they never had been!'
　　And now remains only,　for warriors' memorial,
90　A wall wondrous high　with serpent shapes carved.
　　Storms of ash-spears　have smitten the earls,
　　Carnage of weapon,　and conquering fate.
　　　　"Storms now batter　these ramparts of stone;
　　Blowing snow　and the blast of winter
95　Enfold the earth;　night-shadows fall
　　Darkly lowering,　from the north driving
　　Raging hail　in wrath upon men.
　　Wretchedness fills　the realm of earth,
　　And fate's decrees　transform the world.
100　Here wealth is fleeting,　friends are fleeting,
　　Man is fleeting,　maid is fleeting;
　　All the foundation of earth　shall fail!"
　　　　Thus spake the sage　in solitude pondering.
　　Good man is he　who guardeth his faith.
105　He must never too quickly　unburden his breast
　　Of its sorrow, but eagerly　strive for redress;
　　And happy the man who seeketh for mercy
　　From his heavenly Father,　our fortress and strength.

---

8. **byrny** (bər′ nē)-**clad** dressed in a coat of chain-mail armor.

Critical Reading

1. **Key Ideas and Details (a)** Who are the speakers in the poem?
(b) Analyze: What is the relationship between the two? **(c) Analyze:** What effect does the use of two speakers have on the reader's picture of the wanderer?

2. **Key Ideas and Details (a)** Why does the wanderer go into exile?
(b) Analyze: What images does the poet use to convey his isolation and despair?

3. **Key Ideas and Details (a)** What are "the fates of men" on which the wanderer reflects? **(b) Connect:** Why might the wanderer's own experiences have led him to such brooding thoughts?

4. **Integration of Knowledge and Ideas** According to the poem, how might reflection on "the fates of men" lead to wisdom?

5. **Integration of Knowledge and Ideas** Do you think dwelling on the sorrowful, painful side of life can give a person wisdom and a valuable perspective on life, or do you think it can be harmful? Explain.

Cite textual evidence to support your responses.

The Wife's Lament

Translated by Ann Stanford

I make this song   about me full sadly
my own wayfaring.   I a woman tell
what griefs I had   since I grew up
new or old   never more than now.
5   Ever I know   the dark of my exile.

First my lord went out   away from his people
over the wave-tumult.   I grieved each dawn
wondered where my lord   my first on earth might be.
Then I went forth   a friendless exile
10   to seek service   in my sorrow's need.
My man's kinsmen   began to plot
by darkened thought   to divide us two
so we most widely   in the world's kingdom
lived wretchedly   and I suffered longing.

15   My lord commanded me   to move my dwelling here.
I had few loved ones   in this land
or faithful friends.   For this my heart grieves:
that I should find the man   well matched to me
hard of fortune   mournful of mind
20   hiding his mood   thinking of murder.

Blithe¹ was our bearing   often we vowed
that but death alone   would part us two
naught else.   But this is turned round
now . . .   as if it never were
25   our friendship.   I must far and near
bear the anger   of my beloved.
The man sent me out   to live in the woods
under an oak tree   in this den in the earth.
Ancient this earth hall.   I am all longing.

---

1. **blithe** (blīth) *adj.* cheerful.

30 The valleys are dark   the hills high
the yard overgrown   bitter with briars
a joyless dwelling.   Full oft the lack of my lord
seizes me cruelly here.   Friends there are on earth
living beloved   lying in bed
35 while I at dawn   am walking alone
under the oak tree   through these earth halls.
There I may sit   the summerlong day
there I can weep   over my exile
my many hardships.   Hence I may not rest
40 from this care of heart   which belongs to me ever
nor all this longing   that has caught me in this life.

May that young man   be sad-minded always
hard his heart's thought   while he must wear
a blithe bearing   with care in the breast
45 a crowd of sorrows.   May on himself depend
all his world's joy.   Be he outlawed far
in a strange folk-land—   that my beloved sits
under a rocky cliff   rimed with frost
a lord dreary in spirit   drenched with water
50 in a ruined hall.   My lord endures
much care of mind.   He remembers too often
a happier dwelling.   Woe be to them
that for a loved one   must wait in longing.

Literary Analysis
Anglo-Saxon Lyrics and the Elegy
What does the wife mourn in this elegy?

Critical Reading

Cite textual evidence to support your responses.

1. Key Ideas and Details (a) Why did the wife have to leave her home? **(b) Interpret:** What do lines 25–26 suggest about her reaction to this event?

2. Craft and Structure (a) Generalize: How might a listener feel about his or her griefs after hearing the wife's lament? **(b) Draw Conclusions:** Explain why the poem presents the wife as an image of pure longing, rather than as a person who will one day move on.

3. Integration of Knowledge and Ideas Is the wife justified in her anger and sorrow? Explain.

4. Integration of Knowledge and Ideas How does the Anglo-Saxon sense of home compare with ours? In responding, use at least two of these Essential Question words: *exile, community, refuge, sanctuary*. *[Connecting to the Essential Question: What is the relationship between literature and place?]*

Literary Analysis

© **1. Craft and Structure** Use a graphic organizer like the one shown to find and analyze examples of the following poetic and structural devices in these poems: **regular rhythms, caesuras, kennings, assonance,** and **alliteration.**

Poem	Literary Devices

© **2. Integration of Knowledge and Ideas** **(a)** What makes each of these poems an **elegy**? **(b)** Which poem do you find most moving? In supporting your response, show how poetic devices help call forth your emotions.

Reading Strategy

3. Why is **understanding the historical context,** relating to a warrior's relationship to his lord, important to appreciating the *setting* and the speaker's *character* in "The Wanderer"?

4. How does understanding the role of women in Anglo-Saxon society help you understand the speaker's plight in "The Wife's Lament"?

PERFORMANCE TASKS
Integrated Language Skills

© ## Vocabulary Acquisition and Use

Categorize Vocabulary Using your knowledge of the vocabulary words, decide whether each item contains synonyms only (words similar in meaning) or synonyms and antonyms (words differing in meaning). Explain your choice.

1. admonish, calm, warn

2. fervent, ardent, impassioned

3. compassionate, malicious, kind

4. rancor, bitterness, spite

5. sentinel, guard, watchman

6. rapture, rest, ecstasy

Writing

© **Argument** Write an **editorial** that is an elegy for someone or something that has gone from your neighborhood or school. In your editorial, persuade members of the community that the loss should be regretted. Use persuasive techniques like the following: a *testimonial* to the value of what was lost, from someone your audience will respect; an *emotional appeal* that associates what was lost with things or people that your audience values; *word choice* or language that your readers will find moving.

© **Common Core State Standards**

Writing
1. Write arguments to support claims in an analysis of substantive topics or texts, using valid reasoning and relevant and sufficient evidence.

Language
5. Demonstrate understanding of word relationships and nuances in word meanings.

Focus on Literary Forms
The Epic

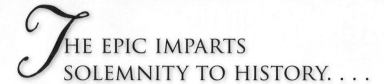

PART 2

THE EPIC IMPARTS SOLEMNITY TO HISTORY. . . .

— VICTOR HUGO

Defining Epics

One of the earliest forms of literature, an **epic** is a long narrative poem written in an elevated style. An epic relates the adventures of a hero in pursuit of goals of national importance. The hero's adventures, which often include a quest, reflect the values of his culture and are usually prominent in the traditions of his people.

Types of Epics In ancient times, stories about heroes were passed down orally. These stories were eventually arranged into larger works called **folk epics** and written down long after they were first composed. Examples include *Beowulf* (Anglo-Saxon), the *Mahabharata* (Indian), and *The Epic of Gilgamesh* (Sumerian). **Literary epics** were composed by individual authors who drew on the conventions of folk epics. Examples include the *Aeneid* by Virgil and *Paradise Lost* by John Milton.

Epic Conventions Most epics share certain literary or formal characteristics called **epic conventions.**

- **Invoking a Muse** At the beginning of an epic, the poet states the subject or purpose of the poem, and then invokes, or calls upon, a muse (a spirit thought to inspire an artist) or supernatural force for help in telling the story. For example, Homer begins the *Iliad*, "Rage—Goddess, sing the rage of Peleus' son Achilles . . ."

- *In Medias Res* The plot begins *in medias res* (Latin for "in the middle of things")—the action is already underway. Homer's *Iliad*, for example, begins during the tenth year of the Trojan War.

- **Elevated Style** See the chart below for a definition and example of the epic convention of elevated style.

Close Read: Characteristics of the Epic

These elements and conventions of an epic appear in the Model text at right.

Epic Hero on a Quest: The epic hero is the central character in an epic. Often of noble or semi-divine birth, he sets out on a quest, a dangerous journey that tests his spirit. Example: *In* Beowulf, *a noble young warrior goes on a quest to rescue a kingdom from a monster.*	**Supernatural Forces:** Supernatural forces include deities, some of whom may watch over the hero, and monsters. Example: *In the ancient Greek epic the* Iliad, *the goddess Athena helps the hero Achilles.*
Valorous Deeds: Valorous deeds are acts that reveal the epic hero's extraordinary qualities and reflect the values cherished by his culture. Example: *Beowulf shows superhuman strength in fighting the monster Grendel with his bare hands.*	**Elevated Style:** An epic contains lofty diction, or word choice, that heightens the importance of the events retold. It may contain catalogs, or lists, of battles, weapons, and royal gifts. Example: *"'Hail, Hrothgar! / Higlac is my cousin and my king; the days / Of my youth have been filled with glory. . . ."* Beowulf, *(lines 236–238)*

Model

About the Text Gilgamesh, the hero of *The Epic of Gilgamesh,* is a Sumerian king who seeks eternal life. He and Urshanabi, a ferryman, have journeyed to meet Utnapishtim, whom the gods saved from a great flood and to whom they have granted immortality. As the excerpt begins, Gilgamesh and Urshanabi prepare to return home.

from *The Epic of Gilgamesh* (translated by N. K. Sandars)

Then Gilgamesh and Urshanabi launched the boat onto the water and boarded it, and they made ready to sail away; but the wife of Utnapishtim the Faraway said to him, "Gilgamesh came here wearied out, he is worn out; what will you give him to carry him back to his own country?" So Utnapishtim spoke, and Gilgamesh took a pole and brought the boat in to the bank. "Gilgamesh, you came here a man wearied out, you have worn yourself out; what shall I give you to carry you back to your own country? Gilgamesh, I shall reveal a secret thing, it is a mystery of the gods that I am telling you. There is a plant that grows under the water, it has a prickle like a thorn, like a rose; it will wound your hands, but if you succeed in taking it, then your hands will hold that which restores his lost youth to a man."

When Gilgamesh heard this he opened the sluices so that a sweet-water current might carry him out to the deepest channel; he tied heavy stones to his feet and they dragged him down to the water-bed. There he saw the plant growing; although it pricked him he took it in his hands; then he cut the heavy stones from his feet, and the sea carried him and threw him onto the shore. Gilgamesh said to Urshanabi the ferryman, "Come here, and see this marvelous plant. By its virtue a man may win back all his former strength. I will take it to Uruk of the strong walls; there I will give it to the old men to eat. Its name shall be 'The Old Men Are Young Again'; and at last I shall eat it myself and have back all my lost youth." So Gilgamesh returned by the gate through which he had come, Gilgamesh and Urshanabi went together. They traveled their twenty leagues and then they broke their fast; after thirty leagues they stopped for the night.

Gilgamesh saw a well of cool water and he went down and bathed; but deep in the pool there was lying a serpent, and the serpent sensed the sweetness of the flower. It rose out of the water and snatched it away, and immediately it sloughed its skin and returned to the well. Then Gilgamesh sat down and wept, the tears ran down his face, and he took the hand of Urshanabi: "O Urshanabi, was it for this that I toiled with my hands, is it for this I have wrung out my heart's blood? For myself I have gained nothing; not I, but the beast of the earth has joy of it now. Already the stream has carried it twenty leagues back to the channels where I found it. I found a sign and now I have lost it. Let us leave the boat on the bank and go."

After twenty leagues they broke their fast, after thirty leagues they stopped for the night; in three days they had walked as much as a journey of a month and fifteen days. When the journey was accomplished they arrived at Uruk, the strong-walled city. Gilgamesh spoke to him, to Urshanabi the ferryman, "Urshanabi, climb up onto the wall of Uruk, inspect its foundation terrace, and examine well the brickwork; see if it is not of burnt bricks; and did not the seven wise men lay these foundations? One third of the whole is city, one third is garden, and one third is field, with the precinct of the goddess Ishtar. These parts and the precinct are all Uruk."

This too was the work of Gilgamesh, the king, who knew the countries of the world. He was wise, he saw mysteries and knew secret things, he brought us a tale of the days before the flood. He went a long journey, was weary, worn out with labor, and returning engraved on a stone the whole story.

Supernatural Forces Utnapishtim is a favorite of the gods, who have granted him immortality. He reveals "a mystery of the gods" that has the supernatural power to restore youth.

Valorous Deeds Gilgamesh dives deep underwater to find the magic plant. He wounds his hands to pluck and secure it. These deeds are valorous, demonstrating courage and perseverance. They are also of great consequence—should Gilgamesh succeed, he will help his people conquer death.

Epic Hero Through his actions, Gilgamesh, like other epic heroes, seeks to better his people. His actions also help to define his culture's concerns and values—the tellers of this epic saw humanity as striving to overcome time and aging.

Elevated Style Note the formal tone and elevated diction of Gilgamesh's lament. The parallel phrases "toiled with my hands" and "wrung out my heart's blood" heighten the intensity.

Themes Across Centuries: Translator's Insights

Burton Raffel Introduces *Beowulf*

A Legendary Tale, Larger Than Life *Beowulf* is a sweeping, action-packed narrative. Written in highly dramatic language, its characters are almost all kings, princes, and their heroic followers. The plot is energized by a pair of powerful man-eating monsters and, at the end, a greedy, fire-spouting dragon. All three are killed by the poem's principal character, Beowulf, who possesses magical qualities of his own. He can swim for days on end; he can breathe for extended periods underwater; his very name tells us in three ways that he is no mere human. He is Beo, or "bear." He is also Wulf, or "wolf." And most important of all, his name does not begin exactly as his father's name, Edgetho: for everyone in Anglo-Saxon England, this break in tradition would have been a dead giveaway of Beowulf's extraordinary character.

A Grand Beginning The story crackles with wonderfully calculated suspense. The hero himself is not introduced at the start. Man-eating Grendel takes the stage, emerging out of the kind of darkness and terror in which Anglo-Saxon life was steeped. Beowulf comes to help the besieged King Hrothgar. (His exciting travel over the deep waves was the first part of the poem I read, over fifty years ago.) The poem carefully explains his heroic, profoundly social motives. Offering himself as a potential sacrifice to Grendel, he fights with and tears an arm off the monster, who flees back into darkness.

Everyone is overjoyed, there is much celebrating—until Grendel's mother enters the scene, hungry (literally) for revenge. Beowulf promptly accepts the challenge, diving far down into the water, finding the lady demon, and in the end killing her in a very close fight. Loaded with praise and gifts, he returns to his own king, to whose throne he succeeds.

The Passage of Time Fifty years later, the old Beowulf's land is terrorized by a fire-breathing dragon. Unlike a good king, and like some of the bad kings in the poem, the dragon fiercely guards and never shares its treasures. Beowulf does not hesitate. But he is old and not as strong as he was. Significantly, he must have help, and is so badly burned that, after the dragon is dead, Beowulf too dies. His people give him a royal burial and a monument, and sing the praises due to a fearless ruler who so totally embodied the virtues of a warrior king.

About the Author

Burton Raffel, the translator of the version of *Beowulf* that follows, has won the Frances Steloff Prize and the Translation Prize for the French-American Foundation. He is the author of numerous poems, screenplays, and novels.

◀ **Critical Viewing**
Which of the dragon's characteristics might a storyteller share with an audience? **[Connect]**

The Spirit of *Beowulf* *Beowulf* is not a pagan poem. There are no pagan gods, no idols, no wanton human sacrifices. Anglo-Saxon England had long since been Christianized when *Beowulf* was composed, but the epic is primarily concerned with social, not religious, issues. Still, if not overtly Christian, *Beowulf*'s close identification with ancient Hebraic ways of life marks it as very much an Old Testament poem. "Almighty God," clearly and repeatedly evoked, operates ethically and holds humans to high moral standards. The creation story of Genesis is beautifully paraphrased. Hell is cited as the home of evil; the Abel and Cain tale is mentioned explicitly. And just as evil is punished, good prevails. The message is that men must learn to behave responsibly, and to love and be faithful to one another, exactly as *Beowulf* has shown that they can.

Critical Reading

1. **Key Ideas and Details (a)** What was the first part of *Beowulf* that Burton Raffel read? **(b) Speculate:** Based on Raffel's introduction, what aspects of the poem do you think led to his lifelong interest in *Beowulf?*

2. **Key Ideas and Details (a)** What specific details of the poem allow Raffel to say so definitely that *Beowulf* is not a pagan poem? **(b) Analyze:** What might the religious dimension of *Beowulf* tell us about the culture that produced it?

   As You Read *Beowulf* . . .

3. **Integration of Knowledge and Ideas** Be ready to compare and contrast your reaction to the poem with Raffel's.

4. **Integration of Knowledge and Ideas** Think about how Raffel's passion for the poem is revealed in his translation.

Before You Read | from *Beowulf*

Connecting to the Essential Question In *Beowulf*, a brave hero battles swamp-dwelling monsters that threaten a kingdom. As you read, notice descriptions of the monsters in *Beowulf*, and consider what the details suggest about Anglo-Saxon ideas about evil. Doing so will help as you explore the Essential Question: **How does literature shape or reflect society?**

Literary Analysis

An **epic** is a long narrative poem, sometimes developed orally, that celebrates heroic deeds and legendary events. Epics, like Homer's *Iliad* from ancient Greece, are among the earliest forms of literature. As such, they reveal the values of the peoples who created them. For example, in *Beowulf*, the action in the mead hall reveals the social and economic relationship between an Anglo-Saxon lord and his followers. This is where the lord provides food, shelter, and fellowship in return for loyalty. It is the center of civilization and all that threatens it is evil. Common features of epics include the following:

- a story told in a serious manner, with elevated language
- a hero battling forces that threaten the world's order

Most epics celebrate the exploits of a **legendary, or epic, hero,** a larger-than-life character. Beowulf's boastful self-confidence, his feats of strength, and his victories in battle make him a classic epic hero. Because he upholds the values of his culture—loyalty, bravery, honor—he can teach modern readers a great deal about the Anglo-Saxon view of the world.

Reading Strategy

Ⓒ Preparing to Read Complex Texts To **determine the main idea or essential message** of a passage, you can *paraphrase* it—identify the key details and restate them in your own words. This strategy will help you understand the long, involved sentences in this translation of *Beowulf*. Use a graphic organizer like the one shown to help you paraphrase such sentences.

Vocabulary

reparation (rep′ ə rā′ shən) *n.* compensation for a wrong (p. 43)

solace (säl′ is) *n.* comfort; relief (p. 44)

purge (pʉrj) *v.* purify; cleanse (p. 48)

writhing (rīth′ iŋ) *adj.* making twisting or turning motions (p. 50)

massive (mas′ iv) *adj.* big and solid; bulky (p. 54)

loathsome (lōth′ səm) *adj.* disgusting (p. 55)

Ⓒ **Common Core State Standards**

Reading Literature
3. Analyze the impact of the author's choices regarding how to develop and relate elements of a story or drama.

Original

High on a wall a Danish watcher / Patrolling along the cliffs saw / The travelers crossing to the shore, their shields / Raised and shining....

Key Details:
guard; saw people; come ashore

Paraphrase

A Danish guard saw strangers come ashore, holding up their shields.

PHLit Online!
www.PHLitOnline.com

ABOUT *BEOWULF*

During Britain's Anglo-Saxon period, from the fifth to the eleventh century, few people were able to read and movies lay centuries in the future. Although the action takes place in sixth-century Scandinavia, *Beowulf* was originally told in Old English, the language spoken by the Anglo-Saxons of England during the years 500 to 1100.

Beowulf, a Geat from a region that is today southern Sweden, sets sail to aid the Danish King Hrothgar in his fight against the monster Grendel. A terrifying swampland creature whose eyes burn "with gruesome light," Grendel has been terrorizing Hrothgar's great banquet hall, Herot, for twelve years. The battle between Beowulf, a young warrior of great strength and courage, and Grendel, his bloodthirsty foe, is the first of three mortal battles that are fought in this long poem.

Forging an Epic The tales in *Beowulf* originate from a time when stories and poems were passed along by word of mouth. In Anglo-Saxon England, traveling minstrels, called *scops*, captivated audiences with long narrative poems. These poems changed and grew as they were passed from one scop to another. *Beowulf* was told and retold in this fashion throughout England for hundreds of years. In the eleventh century, the epic was finally written down.

Beowulf grew out of other, earlier traditions. The monsters and dragons of the tale, the brave warriors steadfastly loyal to their heroic chief, the descent into the eerie regions below the earth—these were familiar elements of Scandinavian or Celtic folk tales. Even a detail as specific as Beowulf's seizure of Grendel's arm can be traced to earlier tales.

A Guide to Life By forging these various traditions into one unified tale and by adding the later influence of Christianity, the Anglo-Saxon scops created a central reference point for their culture. Listening to *Beowulf*, an Anglo-Saxon could learn of bravery and loyalty to one's fellows, of the monsters that spite and hatred could breed, and of the heroism needed to conquer such monsters.

Beowulf and Popular Culture

- Nobel Prize–winner Seamus Heaney's translation of *Beowulf* won the Whitbread Book of the Year Award for Poetry in 1999. (See pages 68–69 for Heaney's comments on his translation.)

- Roger Avary and Neil Gaiman adapted *Beowulf* as a computer animated movie (2007), with voice-overs performed by such stars as Angelina Jolie, Anthony Hopkins, and John Malkovich.

- A *Beowulf* comic-book series was issued in connection with the *Beowulf* movie.

An ancient helmet worn by Anglo-Saxons. ▼

FROM BEOWULF

TRANSLATED BY BURTON RAFFEL

BACKGROUND When *Beowulf* was composed, England was changing from a pagan to a Christian culture. Pagan Anglo-Saxons told grim tales of life ruled by fate, tales in which people struggled against monsters for their place in the world. The missionaries who converted them to Christianity taught them that human beings and their choices of good or evil were at the center of creation. Beowulf reflects both pagan and Christian traditions.The selection opens during an evening of celebration at Herot, the banquet hall of the Danish king Hrothgar (hroth´ gär). Outside in the darkness, however, lurks the murderous monster Grendel.

THE WRATH OF GRENDEL

A powerful monster, living down
In the darkness, growled in pain, impatient
As day after day the music rang
Loud in that hall,[1] the harp's rejoicing
5 Call and the poet's clear songs, sung
Of the ancient beginnings of us all, recalling
The Almighty making the earth, shaping
These beautiful plains marked off by oceans,
Then proudly setting the sun and moon
10 To glow across the land and light it;
The corners of the earth were made lovely with trees
And leaves, made quick with life, with each
Of the nations who now move on its face. And then
As now warriors sang of their pleasure:
15 So Hrothgar's men lived happy in his hall
Till the monster stirred, that demon, that fiend,
Grendel, who haunted the moors, the wild

---

1. hall Herot.

Marshes, and made his home in a hell
Not hell but earth. He was spawned in that slime,
20 Conceived by a pair of those monsters born
Of Cain,[2] murderous creatures banished
By God, punished forever for the crime
Of Abel's death. The Almighty drove
Those demons out, and their exile was bitter,
25 Shut away from men; they split
Into a thousand forms of evil—spirits
And fiends, goblins, monsters, giants,
A brood forever opposing the Lord's
Will, and again and again defeated.
30   Then, when darkness had dropped, Grendel
Went up to Herot, wondering what the warriors
Would do in that hall when their drinking was done.
He found them sprawled in sleep, suspecting
Nothing, their dreams undisturbed. The monster's
35 Thoughts were as quick as his greed or his claws:
He slipped through the door and there in the silence
Snatched up thirty men, smashed them
Unknowing in their beds and ran out with their bodies,
The blood dripping behind him, back
40 To his lair, delighted with his night's slaughter.
        At daybreak, with the sun's first light, they saw
How well he had worked, and in that gray morning
Broke their long feast with tears and laments
For the dead. Hrothgar, their lord, sat joyless

---

2. Cain oldest son of Adam and Eve, who murdered his brother, Abel.

Reading Strategy
Determine the Main Idea by Paraphrasing What are the main ideas in the sentences in lines 34–40?

45 In Herot, a mighty prince mourning
   The fate of his lost friends and companions,
   Knowing by its tracks that some demon had torn
   His followers apart. He wept, fearing
   The beginning might not be the end. And that night
50 Grendel came again, so set
   On murder that no crime could ever be enough,
   No savage assault quench his lust
   For evil. Then each warrior tried
   To escape him, searched for rest in different
55 Beds, as far from Herot as they could find,
   Seeing how Grendel hunted when they slept.
   Distance was safety; the only survivors
   Were those who fled him. Hate had triumphed.
           So Grendel ruled, fought with the righteous,
60 One against many, and won; so Herot
   Stood empty, and stayed deserted for years,
   Twelve winters of grief for Hrothgar, king
   Of the Danes, sorrow heaped at his door
   By hell-forged hands. His misery leaped
65 The seas, was told and sung in all
   Men's ears: how Grendel's hatred began,
   How the monster relished his savage war
   On the Danes, keeping the bloody feud
   Alive, seeking no peace, offering
70 No truce, accepting no settlement, no price
   In gold or land, and paying the living
   For one crime only with another. No one
   Waited for reparation from his plundering claws:
   That shadow of death hunted in the darkness,
75 Stalked Hrothgar's warriors, old
   And young, lying in waiting, hidden
   In mist, invisibly following them from the edge
   Of the marsh, always there, unseen.
           So mankind's enemy continued his crimes,
80 Killing as often as he could, coming
   Alone, bloodthirsty and horrible. Though he lived
   In Herot, when the night hid him, he never
   Dared to touch King Hrothgar's glorious
   Throne, protected by God—God,
85 Whose love Grendel could not know. But Hrothgar's
   Heart was bent. The best and most noble
   Of his council debated remedies, sat
   In secret sessions, talking of terror
   And wondering what the bravest of warriors could do.
90 And sometimes they sacrificed to the old stone gods,
   Made heathen vows, hoping for Hell's

Burton Raffel
Translator's Insight
A normal feud involves two sides: it takes two to tangle. Literary lore suggests that monsters are interested in fights they know they will win.

Vocabulary
reparation (rep´ ə rā´ shən) *n.* compensation for a wrong

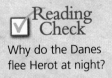

Reading Check

Why do the Danes flee Herot at night?

Support, the Devil's guidance in driving
Their affliction off. That was their way,
And the heathen's only hope, Hell

95   Always in their hearts, knowing neither God
Nor His passing as He walks through our world, the Lord
Of Heaven and earth; their ears could not hear
His praise nor know His glory. Let them
Beware, those who are thrust into danger,

100 Clutched at by trouble, yet can carry no solace
In their hearts, cannot hope to be better! Hail
To those who will rise to God, drop off
Their dead bodies and seek our Father's peace!

THE COMING OF BEOWULF

So the living sorrow of Healfdane's son[3]
105 Simmered, bitter and fresh, and no wisdom
Or strength could break it: that agony hung
On king and people alike, harsh
And unending, violent and cruel, and evil.
    In his far-off home Beowulf, Higlac's[4]
110 Follower and the strongest of the Geats—greater
And stronger than anyone anywhere in this world—
Heard how Grendel filled nights with horror
And quickly commanded a boat fitted out,
Proclaiming that he'd go to that famous king,
115 Would sail across the sea to Hrothgar,
Now when help was needed. None
Of the wise ones regretted his going, much
As he was loved by the Geats: the omens were good,
And they urged the adventure on. So Beowulf
120 Chose the mightiest men he could find,
The bravest and best of the Geats, fourteen
In all, and led them down to their boat;
He knew the sea, would point the prow
Straight to that distant Danish shore.
125   Then they sailed, set their ship

---

3. **Healfdane's** (hā´ alf den´ nəz) **son** Hrothgar.
4. **Higlac's** (hig´ laks) Higlac was the king of the Geats (gā´ ats) and Beowulf's feudal lord and uncle.

Out on the waves, under the cliffs.
Ready for what came they wound through the currents,
The seas beating at the sand, and were borne
In the lap of their shining ship, lined
130 With gleaming armor, going safely
In that oak-hard boat to where their hearts took them.
The wind hurried them over the waves,
The ship foamed through the sea like a bird
Until, in the time they had known it would take,
135 Standing in the round-curled prow they could see
Sparkling hills, high and green
Jutting up over the shore, and rejoicing
In those rock-steep cliffs they quietly ended
Their voyage. Jumping to the ground, the Geats
140 Pushed their boat to the sand and tied it
In place, mail[5] shirts and armor rattling
As they swiftly moored their ship. And then
They gave thanks to God for their easy crossing.
      High on a wall a Danish watcher
145 Patrolling along the cliffs saw
The travelers crossing to the shore, their shields
Raised and shining; he came riding down,
Hrothgar's lieutenant, spurring his horse,
Needing to know why they'd landed, these men
150 In armor. Shaking his heavy spear
In their faces he spoke:
                  "Whose soldiers are you,
You who've been carried in your deep-keeled ship
Across the sea-road to this country of mine?
Listen! I've stood on these cliffs longer
155 Than you know, keeping our coast free
Of pirates, raiders sneaking ashore
From their ships, seeking our lives and our gold.
None have ever come more openly—
And yet you've offered no password, no sign
160 From my prince, no permission from my people
      for your landing

---

5. **mail** flexible body armor made of metal.

Reading Strategy
**Determine the Main
Idea by Paraphrasing**
Paraphrase lines 125–131.
Remember that your
paraphrase need not
follow the word order of
the original.

Reading
Check

Why does Beowulf sail
to Denmark?

Here. Nor have I ever seen,
Out of all the men on earth, one greater
Than has come with you; no commoner carries
Such weapons, unless his appearance, and his beauty,
165 Are both lies. You! Tell me your name,
And your father's; no spies go further onto Danish
Soil than you've come already. Strangers,
From wherever it was you sailed, tell it,
And tell it quickly, the quicker the better,
170 I say, for us all. Speak, say
Exactly who you are, and from where, and why."
　　　　　Their leader answered him, Beowulf unlocking
Words from deep in his breast:
　　　　　　　　　　"We are Geats,
Men who follow Higlac. My father
175 Was a famous soldier, known far and wide
As a leader of men. His name was Edgetho.
His life lasted many winters;
Wise men all over the earth surely
Remember him still. And we have come seeking
180 Your prince, Healfdane's son, protector
Of this people, only in friendship: instruct us,
Watchman, help us with your words! Our errand
Is a great one, our business with the glorious king
Of the Danes no secret; there's nothing dark
185 Or hidden in our coming. You know (if we've heard
The truth, and been told honestly) that your country
Is cursed with some strange, vicious creature
That hunts only at night and that no one
Has seen. It's said, watchman, that he has slaughtered
190 Your people, brought terror to the darkness. Perhaps
Hrothgar can hunt, here in my heart,
For some way to drive this devil out—
If anything will ever end the evils
Afflicting your wise and famous lord.
195 Here he can cool his burning sorrow.
Or else he may see his suffering go on
Forever, for as long as Herot towers
High on your hills."
　　　　　　　　　　The mounted officer
Answered him bluntly, the brave watchman:
200 　　　"A soldier should know the difference between words
And deeds, and keep that knowledge clear
In his brain. I believe your words, I trust in
Your friendship. Go forward, weapons and armor
And all, on into Denmark. I'll guide you
205 Myself—and my men will guard your ship,

Literary Analysis
The Epic and the Legendary Hero
What does Beowulf's way of identifying himself suggest about the values of a warrior culture?

Keep it safe here on our shores,
Your fresh-tarred boat, watch it well,
Until that curving prow carries
Across the sea to Geatland a chosen
210 Warrior who bravely does battle with the creature
Haunting our people, who survives that horror
Unhurt, and goes home bearing our love."
      Then they moved on. Their boat lay moored,
Tied tight to its anchor. Glittering at the top
215 Of their golden helmets wild boar heads gleamed,
Shining decorations, swinging as they marched,
Erect like guards, like sentinels, as though ready
To fight. They marched, Beowulf and his men
And their guide, until they could see the gables
220 Of Herot, covered with hammered gold
And glowing in the sun—that most famous of
    all dwellings,
Towering majestic, its glittering roofs
Visible far across the land.
Their guide reined in his horse, pointing
225 To that hall, built by Hrothgar for the best
And bravest of his men; the path was plain,
They could see their way. . . .

*Beowulf and his men arrive at Herot and are called to see
the King.*

          Beowulf arose, with his men
230 Around him, ordering a few to remain
With their weapons, leading the others quickly
Along under Herot's steep roof into Hrothgar's
Presence. Standing on that prince's own hearth,
Helmeted, the silvery metal of his mail shirt
235 Gleaming with a smith's high art, he greeted
The Danes' great lord:
             "Hail, Hrothgar!
Higlac is my cousin[6] and my king; the days
Of my youth have been filled with glory. Now Grendel's
Name has echoed in our land: sailors
240 Have brought us stories of Herot, the best
Of all mead-halls,[7] deserted and useless when the moon
Hangs in skies the sun had lit,
Light and life fleeing together.
My people have said, the wisest, most knowing
245 And best of them, that my duty was to go to the Danes'
Great king. They have seen my strength for themselves,

---

6. **cousin** here, used as a general term for relative.
7. **mead-halls** To reward his thanes, the king in heroic literature would build a hall
  where mead (a drink made from fermented honey) was served.

▼ **Critical Viewing**
What can you infer about
ancient Scandinavian society
based on the artifacts
displayed on pages 46–47?
[Infer]

Reading
Check

Where does the watchman
bring Beowulf?

Have watched me rise from the darkness of war,
Dripping with my enemies' blood. I drove
Five great giants into chains, chased
250　All of that race from the earth. I swam
In the blackness of night, hunting monsters
Out of the ocean, and killing them one
By one; death was my errand and the fate
They had earned. Now Grendel and I are called
255　Together, and I've come. Grant me, then,
Lord and protector of this noble place,
A single request! I have come so far,
O shelterer of warriors and your people's loved friend,
That this one favor you should not refuse me—
260　That I, alone and with the help of my men,
May purge all evil from this hall. I have heard,
Too, that the monster's scorn of men
Is so great that he needs no weapons and fears none.
Nor will I. My lord Higlac
265　Might think less of me if I let my sword
Go where my feet were afraid to, if I hid
Behind some broad linden[8] shield: my hands
Alone shall fight for me, struggle for life
Against the monster. God must decide
270　Who will be given to death's cold grip.
Grendel's plan, I think, will be
What it has been before, to invade this hall
And gorge his belly with our bodies. If he can,
If he can. And I think, if my time will have come,
275　There'll be nothing to mourn over, no corpse to prepare
For its grave: Grendel will carry our bloody
Flesh to the moors, crunch on our bones
And smear torn scraps of our skin on the walls
Of his den. No, I expect no Danes
280　Will fret about sewing our shrouds, if he wins.
And if death does take me, send the hammered
Mail of my armor to Higlac, return
The inheritance I had from Hrethel, and he
From Wayland.[9] Fate will unwind as it must!"

*That night Beowulf and his men stay inside Herot. While his men
sleep, Beowulf lies awake, eager to meet with Grendel.*

Literary Analysis
The Epic and the Legendary Hero
How do Beowulf's boasts of great deeds and his announcement of his plan establish him as a hero?

Vocabulary
purge (purj) *v.* purify; cleanse

Reading Strategy
Determine the Main Idea by Paraphrasing
Paraphrase Beowulf's plans in lines 264–279.

---

8. **linden** very sturdy type of wood.
9. **Wayland** from Germanic folklore, an invisible blacksmith.

THE BATTLE WITH GRENDEL

285   Out from the marsh, from the foot of misty
Hills and bogs, bearing God's hatred,
Grendel came, hoping to kill
Anyone he could trap on this trip to high Herot.
He moved quickly through the cloudy night,
290 Up from his swampland, sliding silently
Toward that gold-shining hall. He had visited Hrothgar's
Home before, knew the way—
But never, before nor after that night,
Found Herot defended so firmly, his reception
295 So harsh. He journeyed, forever joyless,
Straight to the door, then snapped it open,
Tore its iron fasteners with a touch
And rushed angrily over the threshold.
He strode quickly across the inlaid
300 Floor, snarling and fierce: his eyes
Gleamed in the darkness, burned with a gruesome
Light. Then he stopped, seeing the hall
Crowded with sleeping warriors, stuffed
With rows of young soldiers resting together.
305 And his heart laughed, he relished the sight,
Intended to tear the life from those bodies
By morning; the monster's mind was hot
With the thought of food and the feasting his belly
Would soon know. But fate, that night, intended
310 Grendel to gnaw the broken bones
Of his last human supper. Human
Eyes were watching his evil steps,
Waiting to see his swift hard claws.
Grendel snatched at the first Geat
315 He came to, ripped him apart, cut
His body to bits with powerful jaws,
Drank the blood from his veins and bolted
Him down, hands and feet; death
And Grendel's great teeth came together,
320 Snapping life shut. Then he stepped to another
Still body, clutched at Beowulf with his claws,
Grasped at a strong-hearted wakeful sleeper
—And was instantly seized himself, claws
Bent back as Beowulf leaned up on one arm.
325   That shepherd of evil, guardian of crime,
Knew at once that nowhere on earth
Had he met a man whose hands were harder;
His mind was flooded with fear—but nothing
Could take his talons and himself from that tight

▼ **Critical Viewing**
Why do you think early
Scandinavians adorned their
ships with figures like the
one below? **[Speculate]**

Reading
Check

What happens when
Grendel grabs Beowulf?

Burton Raffel

Burton Raffel
Translator's Insight
Like bullies, monsters immediately think of running, as soon as they find themselves in what might be a fair fight.

Vocabulary
writhing (rīth´ iŋ) *adj.* making twisting or turning motions

Literary Analysis
The Epic
Which details from this description of the battle between Beowulf and Grendel add realism? Which details add epic grandness?

330 Hard grip. Grendel's one thought was to run
From Beowulf, flee back to his marsh and hide there:
This was a different Herot than the hall he had emptied.
But Higlac's follower remembered his final
Boast and, standing erect, stopped
335 The monster's flight, fastened those claws
In his fists till they cracked, clutched Grendel
Closer. The infamous killer fought
For his freedom, wanting no flesh but retreat,
Desiring nothing but escape; his claws
340 Had been caught, he was trapped. That trip to Herot
Was a miserable journey for the writhing monster!
　　　The high hall rang, its roof boards swayed,
And Danes shook with terror. Down
The aisles the battle swept, angry
345 And wild. Herot trembled, wonderfully
Built to withstand the blows, the struggling
Great bodies beating at its beautiful walls;
Shaped and fastened with iron, inside
And out, artfully worked, the building
350 Stood firm. Its benches rattled, fell
To the floor, gold-covered boards grating
As Grendel and Beowulf battled across them.
Hrothgar's wise men had fashioned Herot
To stand forever; only fire,
355 They had planned, could shatter what such skill had put
Together, swallow in hot flames such splendor
Of ivory and iron and wood. Suddenly
The sounds changed, the Danes started
In new terror, cowering in their beds as the terrible
360 Screams of the Almighty's enemy sang
In the darkness, the horrible shrieks of pain
And defeat, the tears torn out of Grendel's
Taut throat, hell's captive caught in the arms
Of him who of all the men on earth
365 Was the strongest.
　　　　　　That mighty protector of men
Meant to hold the monster till its life
Leaped out, knowing the fiend was no use
To anyone in Denmark. All of Beowulf's
Band had jumped from their beds, ancestral
370 Swords raised and ready, determined
To protect their prince if they could. Their courage
Was great but all wasted: they could hack at Grendel
From every side, trying to open
A path for his evil soul, but their points
375 Could not hurt him, the sharpest and hardest iron

Could not scratch at his skin, for that sin-stained demon
Had bewitched all men's weapons, laid spells
That blunted every mortal man's blade.
And yet his time had come, his days
380 Were over, his death near; down
To hell he would go, swept groaning and helpless
To the waiting hands of still worse fiends.
Now he discovered—once the afflictor
Of men, tormentor of their days—what it meant
385 To feud with Almighty God: Grendel
Saw that his strength was deserting him, his claws
Bound fast, Higlac's brave follower tearing at
His hands. The monster's hatred rose higher,
But his power had gone. He twisted in pain,
390 And the bleeding sinews deep in his shoulder
Snapped, muscle and bone split
And broke. The battle was over, Beowulf
Had been granted new glory: Grendel escaped,
But wounded as he was could flee to his den,
395 His miserable hole at the bottom of the marsh,
Only to die, to wait for the end
Of all his days. And after that bloody
Combat the Danes laughed with delight.
He who had come to them from across the sea,
400 Bold and strong-minded, had driven affliction
Off, purged Herot clean. He was happy,
Now, with that night's fierce work; the Danes
Had been served as he'd boasted he'd serve them; Beowulf,
A prince of the Geats, had killed Grendel,
405 Ended the grief, the sorrow, the suffering
Forced on Hrothgar's helpless people
By a bloodthirsty fiend. No Dane doubted
The victory, for the proof, hanging high
From the rafters where Beowulf had hung it, was the monster's
410 Arm, claw and shoulder and all.

*The Danes celebrate Beowulf's victory. That night, though, Grendel's
mother kills Hrothgar's closest friend and carries off her child's
claw. The next day the horrified king tells Beowulf about the two
monsters and their underwater lair.*

THE MONSTERS' LAIR

"I've heard that my people, peasants working
In the fields, have seen a pair of such fiends
Wandering in the moors and marshes, giant
Monsters living in those desert lands.
415 And they've said to my wise men that, as well as they could see,

Reading Strategy
**Determine the Main Idea
by Paraphrasing**
Paraphrase the sentence
in lines 392–397.

Reading
Check

How does Beowulf's battle
with Grendel end?

Reading Strategy
Determine the Main Idea by Paraphrasing
Paraphrase lines 420–431. What do these lines tell you about Grendel's background?

World LITERATURE CONNECTION

Battling Demons in the *Ramayana*

Beowulf's fight with Grendel touches on a universal theme. Tales of heroes who battle monsters or demons are common in world literature. One of the most famous battles occurs in the *Ramayana*, the Hindu epic poem that is as well known in India and other areas of Asia as Bible stories are here. The *Ramayana* is part of a living oral tradition; even today, traveling storytellers recite the tales to large audiences. The hero of this epic is the virtuous prince Rama, husband to beautiful Sita. Rama's enemy is the demon king Ravana, who has ten heads and twenty arms, and lives with his warriors in the land of Lanka. After Ravana kidnaps Sita, Rama must wage battle against the demon king to rescue his wife. While Beowulf's battle with Grendel can be told in a few minutes, Rama's attack on Ravana requires many hours over a series of nights to recite. Both poems feature heroes who ultimately triumph over creatures of supernatural strength and size.

Connect to the Literature

What do you think makes the battle with Grendel feel so compelling, despite the brevity of the description?

One of the devils was a female creature.
The other, they say, walked through the wilderness
Like a man—but mightier than any man.
They were frightened, and they fled, hoping to find help
420 In Herot. They named the huge one Grendel:
If he had a father no one knew him,
Or whether there'd been others before these two,
Hidden evil before hidden evil.
They live in secret places, windy
425 Cliffs, wolf-dens where water pours
From the rocks, then runs underground, where mist
Steams like black clouds, and the groves of trees
Growing out over their lake are all covered
With frozen spray, and wind down snakelike
430 Roots that reach as far as the water
And help keep it dark. At night that lake
Burns like a torch. No one knows its bottom,
No wisdom reaches such depths. A deer,
Hunted through the woods by packs of hounds,
435 A stag with great horns, though driven through the forest
From faraway places, prefers to die
On those shores, refuses to save its life
In that water. It isn't far, nor is it
A pleasant spot! When the wind stirs
440 And storms, waves splash toward the sky,
As dark as the air, as black as the rain
That the heavens weep. Our only help,
Again, lies with you. Grendel's mother
Is hidden in her terrible home, in a place
445 You've not seen. Seek it, if you dare! Save us,
Once more, and again twisted gold,
Heaped-up ancient treasure, will reward you
For the battle you win!"

Beowulf resolves to kill Grendel's monstrous mother. He travels to the lake in which she lives.

THE BATTLE WITH GRENDEL'S MOTHER

Then Edgetho's brave son[10] spoke:

"Remember,
450 Hrothgar, O knowing king, now
When my danger is near, the warm words we uttered,
And if your enemy should end my life

---

10. **Edgetho's brave son** Beowulf. Elsewhere he is identified by such phrases as "the Geats' proud prince" and "the Geats' brave prince."

Then be, O generous prince, forever
The father and protector of all whom I leave
455   Behind me, here in your hands, my beloved
Comrades left with no leader, their leader
Dead. And the precious gifts you gave me,
My friend, send them to Higlac. May he see
In their golden brightness, the Geats' great lord
460   Gazing at your treasure, that here in Denmark
I found a noble protector, a giver
Of rings whose rewards I won and briefly
Relished. And you, Unferth,[11] let
My famous old sword stay in your hands:
465   I shall shape glory with Hrunting, or death
Will hurry me from this earth!"

                                 As his words ended
He leaped into the lake, would not wait for anyone's
Answer; the heaving water covered him
Over. For hours he sank through the waves;
470   At last he saw the mud of the bottom.
And all at once the greedy she-wolf
Who'd ruled those waters for half a hundred
Years discovered him, saw that a creature
From above had come to explore the bottom
475   Of her wet world. She welcomed him in her claws,
Clutched at him savagely but could not harm him,
Tried to work her fingers through the tight
Ring-woven mail on his breast, but tore
And scratched in vain. Then she carried him, armor
480   And sword and all, to her home; he struggled
To free his weapon, and failed. The fight
Brought other monsters swimming to see
Her catch, a host of sea beasts who beat at
His mail shirt, stabbing with tusks and teeth
485   As they followed along. Then he realized, suddenly,
That she'd brought him into someone's battle-hall,
And there the water's heat could not hurt him.
Nor anything in the lake attack him through
The building's high-arching roof. A brilliant
490   Light burned all around him, the lake
Itself like a fiery flame.
                              Then he saw
The mighty water witch and swung his sword,
His ring-marked blade, straight at her head;
The iron sang its fierce song,
495   Sang Beowulf's strength. But her guest

---

11. Unferth Danish warrior who had questioned Beowulf's bravery before the battle with Grendel.

Reading Strategy
Determine the Main Idea by Paraphrasing
Paraphrase lines 467–481.

Burton Raffel
Translator's Insight
True warriors are totally dedicated and fight for fame (honor), not for tangible rewards.

Reading Check
What requests does Beowulf make before he dives into the lake?

Science Connection

Anglo-Saxon Metalwork

The sword that Beowulf discovers is said to have been magically forged by giants—a story reflecting the scarcity and value of swords in Anglo-Saxon times. To form a sword, highly skilled smiths had to heat ore to the melting point of iron (2,800° F), cool it, and then add carbon. The result was a hard, durable metal. A smith's work did not stop at a strong, sharp edge but included the ornamentation of the sword hilt. Handsomely adorned, a sword was at once a deadly weapon and a work of art. Both usable iron and the skills needed to work it were scarce, and a sword's noble owner treasured it, treating it as an individual. Some swords—like Beowulf's Hrunting—were given names.

Connect to the Literature

Besides its ornate hilt, what else makes Hrunting a valuable property?

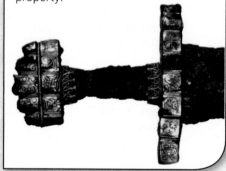

Vocabulary
massive (mas´ iv) *adj.*
big and solid; bulky

Discovered that no sword could slice her evil
Skin, that Hrunting could not hurt her, was useless
Now when he needed it. They wrestled, she ripped
And tore and clawed at him, bit holes in his helmet,
500 And that too failed him; for the first time in years
Of being worn to war it would earn no glory;
It was the last time anyone would wear it. But Beowulf
Longed only for fame, leaped back
Into battle. He tossed his sword aside,
505 Angry; the steel-edged blade lay where
He'd dropped it. If weapons were useless he'd use
His hands, the strength in his fingers. So fame
Comes to the men who mean to win it
And care about nothing else! He raised
510 His arms and seized her by the shoulder; anger
Doubled his strength, he threw her to the floor.
She fell, Grendel's fierce mother, and the Geats'
Proud prince was ready to leap on her. But she rose
At once and repaid him with her clutching claws,
515 Wildly tearing at him. He was weary, that best
And strongest of soldiers; his feet stumbled
And in an instant she had him down, held helpless.
Squatting with her weight on his stomach, she drew
A dagger, brown with dried blood, and prepared
520 To avenge her only son. But he was stretched
On his back, and her stabbing blade was blunted
By the woven mail shirt he wore on his chest.
The hammered links held; the point
Could not touch him. He'd have traveled to the bottom of the earth,
525 Edgetho's son, and died there, if that shining
Woven metal had not helped—and Holy
God, who sent him victory, gave judgment
For truth and right, Ruler of the Heavens,
Once Beowulf was back on his feet and fighting.
530   Then he saw, hanging on the wall, a heavy
Sword, hammered by giants, strong
And blessed with their magic, the best of all weapons
But so massive that no ordinary man could lift
Its carved and decorated length. He drew it
535 From its scabbard, broke the chain on its hilt,
And then, savage, now, angry
And desperate, lifted it high over his head
And struck with all the strength he had left,
Caught her in the neck and cut it through,
540 Broke bones and all. Her body fell
To the floor, lifeless, the sword was wet

With her blood, and Beowulf rejoiced at the sight.
    The brilliant light shone, suddenly,
As though burning in that hall, and as bright as Heaven's
545 Own candle, lit in the sky. He looked
At her home, then following along the wall
Went walking, his hands tight on the sword,
His heart still angry. He was hunting another
Dead monster, and took his weapon with him
550 For final revenge against Grendel's vicious
Attacks, his nighttime raids, over
And over, coming to Herot when Hrothgar's
Men slept, killing them in their beds,
Eating some on the spot, fifteen
555 Or more, and running to his loathsome moor
With another such sickening meal waiting
In his pouch. But Beowulf repaid him for those visits,
Found him lying dead in his corner,
Armless, exactly as that fierce fighter
560 Had sent him out from Herot, then struck off
His head with a single swift blow. The body
jerked for the last time, then lay still.
    The wise old warriors who surrounded Hrothgar,
Like him staring into the monsters' lake,
565 Saw the waves surging and blood
Spurting through. They spoke about Beowulf,
All the graybeards, whispered together
And said that hope was gone, that the hero
Had lost fame and his life at once, and would never
570 Return to the living, come back as triumphant
As he had left; almost all agreed that Grendel's
Mighty mother, the she-wolf, had killed him.
The sun slid over past noon, went further
Down. The Danes gave up, left
575 The lake and went home, Hrothgar with them.
The Geats stayed, sat sadly, watching,
Imagining they saw their lord but not believing
They would ever see him again.
              —Then the sword
Melted, blood-soaked, dripping down
580 Like water, disappearing like ice when the world's
Eternal Lord loosens invisible
Fetters and unwinds icicles and frost
As only He can, He who rules
Time and seasons, He who is truly
585 God. The monsters' hall was full of
Rich treasures, but all that Beowulf took
Was Grendel's head and the hilt of the giants'

▲ **Critical Viewing**
How would this helmet affect the appearance of the person wearing it? **[Infer]**

Vocabulary
loathsome (lōth´ səm)
adj. disgusting

Reading Check
Why do the Danes think Beowulf has been slain?

Jeweled sword; the rest of that ring-marked
Blade had dissolved in Grendel's steaming
590 Blood, boiling even after his death.
And then the battle's only survivor
Swam up and away from those silent corpses;
The water was calm and clean, the whole
Huge lake peaceful once the demons who'd lived in it
595 Were dead.
        Then that noble protector of all seamen
Swam to land, rejoicing in the heavy
Burdens he was bringing with him. He
And all his glorious band of Geats
Thanked God that their leader had come back unharmed;
600 They left the lake together. The Geats
Carried Beowulf's helmet, and his mail shirt.
Behind them the water slowly thickened
As the monsters' blood came seeping up.
They walked quickly, happily, across
605 Roads all of them remembered, left
The lake and the cliffs alongside it, brave men
Staggering under the weight of Grendel's skull,
Too heavy for fewer than four of them to handle—
Two on each side of the spear jammed through it—
610 Yet proud of their ugly load and determined
That the Danes, seated in Herot, should see it.
Soon, fourteen Geats arrived
At the hall, bold and warlike, and with Beowulf,
Their lord and leader, they walked on the mead-hall
615 Green. Then the Geats' brave prince entered
Herot, covered with glory for the daring
Battles he had fought; he sought Hrothgar
To salute him and show Grendel's head.
He carried that terrible trophy by the hair,
620 Brought it straight to where the Danes sat,
Drinking, the queen among them. It was a weird
And wonderful sight, and the warriors stared.

Reading Strategy
Determine Main Idea by Paraphrasing In your own words, paraphrase the events described in lines 596–611.

After being honored by Hrothgar, Beowulf and his fellow Geats return home, where he eventually becomes King. Beowulf rules Geatland for fifty years. When a dragon menaces his kingdom, Beowulf, now an old man, determines to slay the beast. Before going into battle, he tells his men about the royal house and his exploits in its service.

THE LAST BATTLE

And Beowulf uttered his final boast:
"I've never known fear, as a youth I fought
625 In endless battles. I am old, now,
But I will fight again, seek fame still,

If the dragon hiding in his tower dares
To face me."
        Then he said farewell to his followers,
Each in his turn, for the last time:
630   "I'd use no sword, no weapon, if this beast
Could be killed without it, crushed to death
Like Grendel, gripped in my hands and torn
Limb from limb. But his breath will be burning
Hot, poison will pour from his tongue.
635 I feel no shame, with shield and sword
And armor, against this monster: when he comes to me
I mean to stand, not run from his shooting
Flames, stand till fate decides
Which of us wins. My heart is firm,
640 My hands calm: I need no hot
Words. Wait for me close by, my friends.
We shall see, soon, who will survive
This bloody battle, stand when the fighting
Is done. No one else could do
645 What I mean to, here, no man but me
Could hope to defeat this monster. No one
Could try. And this dragon's treasure, his gold
And everything hidden in that tower, will be mine
Or war will sweep me to a bitter death!"
650   Then Beowulf rose, still brave, still strong,
And with his shield at his side, and a mail shirt on his breast,
Strode calmly, confidently, toward the tower, under
The rocky cliffs: no coward could have walked there!
And then he who'd endured dozens of desperate
655 Battles, who'd stand boldly while swords and shields
Clashed, the best of kings, saw
Huge stone arches and felt the heat
Of the dragon's breath, flooding down
Through the hidden entrance, too hot for anyone
660 To stand, a streaming current of fire
And smoke that blocked all passage. And the Geats'
Lord and leader, angry, lowered
His sword and roared out a battle cry,
A call so loud and clear that it reached through
665 The hoary rock, hung in the dragon's
Ear. The beast rose, angry,
Knowing a man had come—and then nothing
But war could have followed. Its breath came first,
A steaming cloud pouring from the stone,
670 Then the earth itself shook. Beowulf
Swung his shield into place, held it
In front of him, facing the entrance. The dragon

Literary Analysis
The Epic
What does Beowulf's speech in lines 630–649 suggest to you about Anglo-Saxon values?

Reading Check
How does Beowulf plan to fight the dragon?

► **Critical Viewing**
What educated guess can you make about Beowulf's bravery from this illustration? **[Infer]**

Coiled and uncoiled, its heart urging it
Into battle. Beowulf's ancient sword
675 Was waiting, unsheathed, his sharp and gleaming
Blade. The beast came closer; both of them
Were ready, each set on slaughter. The Geats'
Great prince stood firm, unmoving, prepared
Behind his high shield, waiting in his shining
680 Armor. The monster came quickly toward him,
Pouring out fire and smoke, hurrying
To its fate. Flames beat at the iron
Shield, and for a time it held, protected
Beowulf as he'd planned; then it began to melt,
685 And for the first time in his life that famous prince
Fought with fate against him, with glory
Denied him. He knew it, but he raised his sword
And struck at the dragon's scaly hide.
The ancient blade broke, bit into
690 The monster's skin, drew blood, but cracked
And failed him before it went deep enough, helped him
Less than he needed. The dragon leaped
With pain, thrashed and beat at him, spouting
Murderous flames, spreading them everywhere.
695 And the Geats' ring-giver did not boast of glorious
Victories in other wars: his weapon
Had failed him, deserted him, now when he needed it
Most, that excellent sword. Edgetho's
Famous son stared at death,
700 Unwilling to leave this world, to exchange it
For a dwelling in some distant place—a journey
Into darkness that all men must make, as death
Ends their few brief hours on earth.
       Quickly, the dragon came at him, encouraged
705 As Beowulf fell back; its breath flared,
And he suffered, wrapped around in swirling
Flames—a king, before, but now
A beaten warrior. None of his comrades
Came to him, helped him, his brave and noble
710 Followers; they ran for their lives, fled
Deep in a wood. And only one of them
Remained, stood there, miserable, remembering,
As a good man must, what kinship should mean.

       His name was Wiglaf, he was Wexstan's son
715 And a good soldier; his family had been Swedish,
Once. Watching Beowulf, he could see
How his king was suffering, burning. Remembering
Everything his lord and cousin had given him,

Reading Strategy
Determine Main Idea by Paraphrasing
In your own words, paraphrase the events of Beowulf's battle with the dragon.

Literary Analysis
The Epic
What do these lines reveal about the values of warrior culture?

Armor and gold and the great estates
720 Wexstan's family enjoyed, Wiglaf's
Mind was made up; he raised his yellow
Shield and drew his sword—an ancient
Weapon that had once belonged to Onela's
Nephew, and that Wexstan had won, killing
725 The prince when he fled from Sweden, sought safety
With Herdred, and found death.[12] And Wiglaf's father
Had carried the dead man's armor, and his sword,
To Onela, and the king had said nothing, only
Given him armor and sword and all,
730 Everything his rebel nephew had owned
And lost when he left this life. And Wexstan
Had kept those shining gifts, held them
For years, waiting for his son to use them,
Wear them as honorably and well as once
735 His father had done; then Wexstan died
And Wiglaf was his heir, inherited treasures
And weapons and land. He'd never worn
That armor, fought with that sword, until Beowulf
Called him to his side, led him into war.
740 But his soul did not melt, his sword was strong;
The dragon discovered his courage, and his weapon,
When the rush of battle brought them together.
          And Wiglaf, his heart heavy, uttered
The kind of words his comrades deserved:
745   "I remember how we sat in the mead-hall, drinking
And boasting of how brave we'd be when Beowulf
Needed us, he who gave us these swords
And armor: all of us swore to repay him,
When the time came, kindness for kindness
750 —With our lives, if he needed them. He allowed us to
          join him,
Chose us from all his great army, thinking
Our boasting words had some weight, believing
Our promises, trusting our swords. He took us
For soldiers, for men. He meant to kill
755 This monster himself, our mighty king,
Fight this battle alone and unaided,
As in the days when his strength and daring dazzled
Men's eyes. But those days are over and gone
And now our lord must lean on younger
760 Arms. And we must go to him, while angry
Flames burn at his flesh, help
Our glorious king! By almighty God,

12. **Onela's / Nephew . . . found death** When Onela seized the throne of Sweden, his two nephews sought shelter with the king of Geatland, Herdred. Wiglaf's father, Wexstan, killed the older nephew for Onela.

Literary Analysis
The Epic and the Legendary Hero
According to Wiglaf, what is Beowulf's relationship with his followers?

I'd rather burn myself than see
Flames swirling around my lord.
765 And who are we to carry home
Our shields before we've slain his enemy
And ours, to run back to our homes with Beowulf
So hard-pressed here? I swear that nothing
He ever did deserved an end
770 Like this, dying miserably and alone,
Butchered by this savage beast: we swore
That these swords and armor were each for us all!"
        Then he ran to his king, crying encouragement
As he dove through the dragon's deadly fumes.

*Wiglaf and Beowulf kill the dragon, but the old king is mortally
wounded. As he dies, Beowulf asks Wiglaf to bring him the treasure
that the dragon was guarding.*

THE SPOILS

775   Then Wexstan's son went in, as quickly
As he could, did as the dying Beowulf
Asked, entered the inner darkness
Of the tower, went with his mail shirt and his sword.
Flushed with victory he groped his way,
780 A brave young warrior, and suddenly saw
Piles of gleaming gold, precious
Gems, scattered on the floor, cups
And bracelets, rusty old helmets, beautifully
Made but rotting with no hands to rub
785 And polish them. They lay where the dragon left them;
It had flown in the darkness, once, before fighting
Its final battle. (So gold can easily
Triumph, defeat the strongest of men,
No matter how deep it is hidden!) And he saw,
790 Hanging high above, a golden
Banner, woven by the best of weavers
And beautiful. And over everything he saw
A strange light, shining everywhere,
On walls and floor and treasure. Nothing
795 Moved, no other monsters appeared;
He took what he wanted, all the treasures
That pleased his eye, heavy plates
And golden cups and the glorious banner,
Loaded his arms with all they could hold.
800 Beowulf's dagger, his iron blade,
Had finished the fire-spitting terror
That once protected tower and treasures
Alike; the gray-bearded lord of the Geats

Reading Strategy
**Determine the Main Idea
by Paraphrasing** What
is the main idea in the
sentence in lines 779–785?

Reading
Check

Why does Wiglaf decide to
come to Beowulf's aid?

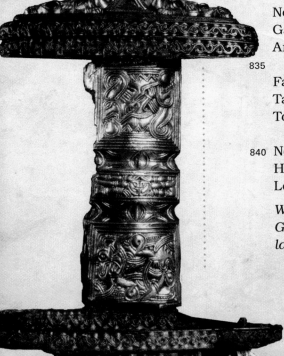

Had ended those flying, burning raids
805 Forever.

Then Wiglaf went back, anxious
To return while Beowulf was alive, to bring him
Treasure they'd won together. He ran,
Hoping his wounded king, weak
And dying, had not left the world too soon.
810 Then he brought their treasure to Beowulf, and found
His famous king bloody, gasping
For breath. But Wiglaf sprinkled water
Over his lord, until the words
Deep in his breast broke through and were heard.
815 Beholding the treasure he spoke, haltingly:
"For this, this gold, these jewels, I thank
Our Father in Heaven, Ruler of the Earth—
For all of this, that His grace has given me,
Allowed me to bring to my people while breath
820 Still came to my lips. I sold my life
For this treasure, and I sold it well. Take
What I leave, Wiglaf, lead my people,
Help them; my time is gone. Have
The brave Geats build me a tomb,
825 When the funeral flames have burned me, and build it
Here, at the water's edge, high
On this spit of land, so sailors can see
This tower, and remember my name, and call it
Beowulf's tower, and boats in the darkness
830 And mist, crossing the sea, will know it."
Then that brave king gave the golden
Necklace from around his throat to Wiglaf,
Gave him his gold-covered helmet, and his rings,
And his mail shirt, and ordered him to use them well:
835 "You're the last of all our far-flung family.
Fate has swept our race away,
Taken warriors in their strength and led them
To the death that was waiting. And now I follow them."
The old man's mouth was silent, spoke
840 No more, had said as much as it could;
He would sleep in the fire, soon. His soul
Left his flesh, flew to glory.

*Wiglaf denounces the warriors who deserted Beowulf. The
Geats burn their king's body on a funeral pyre and bitterly
lament his death.*

THE FAREWELL

       Then the Geats built the tower, as Beowulf
      Had asked, strong and tall, so sailors
845 Could find it from far and wide; working
      For ten long days they made his monument,
      Sealed his ashes in walls as straight
      And high as wise and willing hands
      Could raise them. And the riches he and Wiglaf
850 Had won from the dragon, rings, necklaces,
      Ancient, hammered armor—all
      The treasures they'd taken were left there, too,
      Silver and jewels buried in the sandy

▲ **Critical Viewing**
How would you describe
the mood of this painting?
Does it accurately reflect
the conclusion of *Beowulf*?
Explain. **[Connect]**

Reading
Check

What is Beowulf's last
request?

Ground, back in the earth, again
855 And forever hidden and useless to men.
And then twelve of the bravest Geats
Rode their horses around the tower,
Telling their sorrow, telling stories
Of their dead king and his greatness, his glory,
860 Praising him for heroic deeds, for a life
As noble as his name. So should all men
Raise up words for their lords, warm
With love, when their shield and protector leaves
His body behind, sends his soul
865 On high. And so Beowulf's followers
Rode, mourning their beloved leader,
Crying that no better king had ever
Lived, no prince so mild, no man
So open to his people, so deserving of praise.

Burton Raffel
Translator's Insight
"Mild," in line 868, is not a description of Beowulf as we have seen him. But it is a description often used in the New Testament, more evidence that *Beowulf* is not a pagan poem.

Critical Reading

Cite textual evidence to support your responses.

1. Key Ideas and Details (a) What annoys Grendel and leads to his attacks? **(b) Interpret:** What universal conflict lies behind his war with the Danes?

2. Key Ideas and Details (a) Why does Beowulf travel to Herot? **(b) Infer:** What do his motives for the trip tell you about his character? **(c) Analyze:** How does the contrast between Grendel and Beowulf turn their conflict into a fight between good and evil?

3. Integration of Knowledge and Ideas Beowulf's defeat of Grendel might be described as the defeat of the "dark side" of the warrior's life. Explain.

4. Integration of Knowledge and Ideas Explain how the poem, by keeping Beowulf's memory alive, keeps a culture's values alive.

5. Integration of Knowledge and Ideas Do you think Beowulf's deeds make him a good role model? Explain.

6. Integration of Knowledge and Ideas What does *Beowulf* reveal about the way in which Anglo-Saxons defined evil and good? In responding, use at least two of these Essential Question words: *liminal, boundary, malignant.* *[Connecting to the Essential Question: How does literature shape or reflect society?]*

After You Read | from *Beowulf*

Literary Analysis

**Common Core
State Standards**

© **1. Key Ideas and Details** **Epics** often center on a battle between good and evil. Find evidence in lines 173–198 to indicate that Beowulf is battling for the good.

© **2. Integration of Knowledge and Ideas** An epic reflects the values of the culture that produced it. Use a chart like the one shown to identify three features of *Beowulf* that probably pleased its original audience. For each, draw a conclusion about Anglo-Saxon tastes and values.

Feature	Why Pleasing	Values Reflected
boastful speeches	makes hero seem superhuman	

© **3. Key Ideas and Details** **(a)** What details show the importance of Christian beliefs in the epic? **(b)** What details reveal the importance of pagan warrior values, such as a belief in fate, a taste for boasting, a pride in loyalty, and a desire for fame?

© **4. Integration of Knowledge and Ideas** Frustrated pride may lead to spite, just as loyalty may lead to vengeance, and eagerness for glory may turn into greed. Explain how each creature Beowulf battles represents an extreme and dangerous form of warrior values and behavior.

© **5. Key Ideas and Details** **(a)** List two characteristics that make Beowulf a **legendary, or epic, hero. (b)** Find a passage that shows his more human side. Explain your choice. **(c)** Identify each main character and the traits that make him a hero.

© **6. Integration of Knowledge and Ideas** **(a)** Is Beowulf a believable character, or is he "too heroic"? Explain your answer. **(b)** How does his believability affect your sympathy for him?

© **7. Integration of Knowledge and Ideas** Compare the way the epic commemorates Beowulf with the way our culture celebrates its heroes.

Reading Strategy

8. Determine the main idea of lines 843–861 from *Beowulf* by *paraphrasing* them.

9. (a) Explain which details you did not understand before paraphrasing. **(b)** Compare your paraphrase to the original, citing poetic effects that were lost in your paraphrase.

10. If someone asked you to state the essential message of this epic, which passage would you choose to paraphrase for that person? Why?

Writing
1. Write arguments to support claims in an analysis of substantive topics or texts, using valid reasoning and relevant and sufficient evidence. *(p. 66)*
1.d. Establish and maintain a formal style and objective tone while attending to the norms and conventions of the discipline in which they are writing. *(p. 66)*

Language
3.a. Vary syntax for effect. *(p. 67)*
5. Demonstrate understanding of word relationships. *(p. 66)*

PERFORMANCE TASKS
Integrated Language Skills

ⓒ Vocabulary Acquisition and Use

Word Analysis: Latin Word Root -sol-

The root -sol- comes from the Latin word *solari,* meaning "to relieve, to comfort." The root appears in the word *solace,* which means "an easing of grief, loneliness, or discomfort." With -sol- in mind, answer the following questions. Then, provide a definition of each italicized word.

1. Which character is *inconsolable*?
2. Why might Hrothgar's warriors have felt *disconsolate* after hearing Beowulf's boasts?
3. In what way did Beowulf provide *solace* for Hrothgar's people?
4. How might you *console* the mourning warriors after King Beowulf's death?

Vocabulary: Analogies

An analogy compares two relationships to show their basic similarity. For each item below, analyze the relationship between the first and second words. Then, complete the analogy using a word from the vocabulary list on page 38. Use each word only once, and explain your choice.

1. honest : untruthful :: delightful : _____
2. agreement : discord :: distress : _____
3. elevated : soaring :: huge : _____
4. flee : escape :: rid : _____
5. gift : donation :: reimbursement : _____
6. soothing : disturbing :: unmoving : _____

Writing

ⓒ **Argument** Assuming the role of Beowulf, write a **job application** to Hrothgar, explaining why you are best suited to take on Grendel. Strike the same tone you would use in a real-life job letter. Keep in mind both your *purpose* and your *audience*, and choose words and ideas that are appropriate to both.

Prewriting First, review the text and create a list of Beowulf's best and most noble qualities, as well as his prior experience. Then, review your list, eliminating anything unrelated to the task of battling Grendel.

> **Model: Brainstorming Relevant Ideas**
> _Beowulf's Qualities and Experiences_
> ~~expert sailor~~
> ~~listens to his advisors~~
> survived many wars
> bound giants in chains
> killed monsters of the ocean

Beowulf's sailing and listening skills would not be needed in a battle with Grendel.

Drafting In the first paragraph of your letter, state your purpose and give an overview of your main qualifications for the job. In the body of your letter, describe your qualifications and prior experiences in detail. Remember to maintain a formal yet personable tone.

Revising As you read over your draft, revise any words or phrases that sound too casual, inappropriate, or irrelevant.

Conventions and Style: Coordinating Conjunctions

For a smoother writing style, you can combine short, choppy sentences. One way to combine sentences is by using coordinating conjunctions to join sentence elements. A **coordinating conjunction** connects words or groups of words that have equal importance in the sentence.

Combining Sentences With Coordinating Conjunctions

Choppy	Better
Peace could not be bought with money. Peace could not be bought with land.	Peace could not be bought with money *or* land.
The monster hid in the mist. He terrorized the king's warriors.	The monster hid in the mist *and* terrorized the king's warriors.
The men stayed away from the banquet hall. They feared Grendel.	The men stayed away from the banquet hall, *for* they feared Grendel.

Keep in mind that different coordinating conjunctions show different relationships: *And* shows addition or similarity. *But* and *yet* indicate contrast. *Or* and *nor* indicate a choice. *For* and *so* show a result.

Punctuation Tip: When a coordinating conjunction joins two words, phrases, or subordinate clauses, no comma is needed. When a coordinating conjunction joins three or more elements, insert a comma before each element. When a coordinating conjunction joins two independent clauses, use a comma before the conjunction.

Practice In items 1–4, identify the coordinating conjunction and the words it joins. In items 5–8, use a coordinating conjunction to combine the two sentences.

1. Were pagan or Christian ideas more popular when *Beowulf* was written?
2. The king's council held meetings but could not devise a way to stop the attacks.
3. The people were terrified, but there was one man who could help them.
4. They landed the ship and were greeted by a soldier patrolling the cliffs.
5. He did not take his shield with him to fight Grendel. He did not take his sword either.
6. The monster struggled. He could not escape Beowulf's grip.
7. Her son had been killed. The mother sought revenge.
8. Epics reflect the dominant cultural values of the time. They reflect the dominant religious values too.

© **Writing and Speaking Conventions**_____

A. **Writing** For each pair listed, construct a sentence in which you link the two words or word groups using a coordinating conjunction. Tell what relationship is indicated by the conjunction.

   1. good—evil
   2. outfitted a boat—sailed to a distant land
   3. he killed the monster—the people were grateful

   Example: good—evil
   Sentence: Is the king good or evil?
   Relationship: choice

B. **Speaking** Tell your friends the story of Beowulf's battle with Grendel. Use at least three different coordinating conjunctions.

PH WRITING COACH

Further instruction and practice are available in *Prentice Hall Writing Coach*.

Themes Across Centuries: Translator's Insights

Seamus Heaney Discusses Beowulf

Giving Shape to Poetry A poet in Old English was called a *scop*, pronounced "shop" and meaning "a shaper." But did he do his shaping with a pen on parchment or with sound-patterns in the ear? Was he a scribe or was he a singer? Was *Beowulf* the result of mouth and ear work, or pen and paperwork?

The answer has to be that it was both. We have evidence that the *scop* chanted his poems to the accompaniment of a harp, so the notes he struck with his voice and his instrument were designed to fasten his words into the ear and the memory. But the intricacy of the patterning suggests that over time his live performance developed into a written score, so the heard melody has come down to us as a manuscript, a word which basically means handwritten marks.

The Original *Beowulf* In the original, for example, three lines of one passage of *Beowulf* look like this:

> **Him ðā gegiredan Gēata lēode**
> **ād on eorðan unwāclīcne,**
> **helmum behongen, hilde-bordum.**

Look again and you can see words and traces of words that we still use. "Him," obviously, in line 1; "helmets" and "hung" and "boards" in line 3; and once you realize that the strange letter **ð** is the symbol that Anglo-Saxon scribes used for the "th," you can see "earth" in line 2. But the words were meant to be heard rather than seen, and if you keep looking you can find alliteration that the first audience listened for in every line.

About the Author

Seamus Heaney's poetry focuses on the cities and farms of his homeland in Northern Ireland and the political and religious strife that he has witnessed. Among his translations are *Beowulf* (2000) and Sophocles' drama *Antigone* (2004).

◀ **Critical Viewing**
Why do historians preserve documents like this page from *Beowulf*? **[Speculate]**

The Music of Storytelling Translating an old poem means keeping time, in both the musical and historical sense; it means staying faithful to the original, but not to the point of sounding out of tune. I wanted my version to be a score for performance and tried, therefore, to tune my voice not only to the movement of the Anglo-Saxon lines but to the other voices that had been familiar to me in Northern Ireland. I wrote for my first local accent, imagining the poetry being spoken by old neighbors who always gave their storytelling a natural pace and stress. When I tried out a line, the test would be: do these words sound sure and true if I pretend to be one of those big-voiced elders?

Take, for example, the third line: it tolls like a bell that has been rung four times, and when I translated it I wanted to keep the heavy downbeat of the original alliterating words, so it came out as "hung with helmets, heavy war-shields." I was after a similar effect in later lines such as "funeral fires; fumes of woodsmoke" and "and wailed aloud for their lord's decease."

Still, there is epic pride in the lines as well as elegy, so I wanted them to sound not only mournful but elevated. Ideally, the translator of *Beowulf* will construct something in words that is the equivalent of the burial mound constructed by the Geats, something to make us feel both their hero's greatness and their grief at his loss.

▲ **Critical Viewing**
In what ways does the burial mound pictured here convey both greatness and serenity? **[Interpret]**

Critical Reading

1. **Craft and Structure (a)** According to Heaney's essay, was the original Old English scop a writer or a musician? **(b) Speculate:** In what ways do you think details in this translation of *Beowulf* were influenced by the manner in which the tale was originally told?

2. **Craft and Structure (a)** On what voices does Heaney model his translation? **(b) Infer:** Why might it have helped Heaney to have specific voices in mind as he translated?

   As You Think About *Beowulf* . . .

3. **Integration of Knowledge and Ideas** Many translators have produced versions of *Beowulf*. In what ways might translators' decisions affect your experience with the epic?

Analyzing Functional and Expository Texts

Online Encyclopedia Article • Wikipedia Article

Common Core State Standards

Reading Informational Text
7. Integrate and evaluate multiple sources of information presented in different media or formats as well as in words in order to address a question or solve a problem.

About the Texts

An **online encyclopedia article** is a research source, presented as a Web page on the Internet, that provides information on a given topic. Usually, pages addressing specific topics can be accessed through a search engine within the larger encyclopedia site. Most online encyclopedia articles are written by an expert and feature credible information on the topic of the article, clear identification of the author or sponsor of the Web site, and a list of resources or bibliography consulted by the author. Some sites also provide links to other reliable online resources.

A **Wikipedia article** is an online reference that, unlike a traditional encyclopedia article, can be edited and updated by readers. Wikipedia does not charge an access fee and therefore relies on contributions from amateur writers. This practice has caused some experts to question its accuracy.

Reading Strategy

As you read a digital reference, **evaluate its validity and reliability** as a research tool.

- *Consider the source.* Identify the site's sponsor. Determine whether it promotes a particular agenda, such as to sell products, that could result in biased information.

- *Verify and clarify facts.* Confirm information by consulting other reputable sources in various media or formats. For example, compare the presentation of a topic online, in a book, and in a documentary film. Evaluate the accuracy of one source by measuring it against the others.

As you read, use a chart like this one to evaluate a source's validity:

Digital Resource _____			
Author _____			
Facts to Be Verified	**Sources**	**Discrepancies**	**Result**
1._____	_____	_____	_____
2._____	_____	_____	_____
3._____	_____	_____	_____

Content-Area Vocabulary

These words appear in the selections that follow. They may also appear in other content-area texts:

manuscripts (man′ yo͞o skripts′) *n.* books or documents written by hand before printing was invented

didactic (dī dak′ tik) adj. descriptive of a work that is intended to teach people a moral lesson

fragmentary (frag′ mən ter′ ē) *adj.* consisting of broken pieces; disconnected

forefront (fôr′ frunt′) *n.* the position of most activity or importance

siege (sēj) *n.* the surrounding of a place by an opposing force

Jump to: navigation, search

Q Old English poetry

ENCYCLOPEDIA
BRITANNICA online

Home | Blog | Board | Newsletters | International | Store

English Literature — The Major Manuscripts

The Old English period > Poetry > The major manuscripts

Most Old English poetry is preserved in four **manuscripts** of the late 10th and early 11th centuries. The Beowulf manuscript (British Library) contains *Beowulf*, *Judith*, and three prose tracts; the <u>Exeter Book</u> (Exeter Cathedral) is a miscellaneous gathering of lyrics, riddles, didactic poems, and religious narratives; the <u>Junius Manuscript</u> (Bodleian Library, Oxford)—also called the <u>Caedmon Manuscript</u>, even though its contents are no longer attributed to Caedmon—contains biblical paraphrases; and the <u>Vercelli Book</u> (found in the cathedral library in Vercelli, Italy) contains saints' lives, several short religious poems, and prose homilies. In addition to the poems in these books are historical poems in the <u>Anglo-Saxon Chronicle</u>; poetic renderings of Psalms 51–150; the 31 Metres included in <u>King</u> <u>Alfred the Great</u>'s translation of <u>Boethius</u>'s *De consolatione philosophiae (Consolation of Philosophy)*; magical, **didactic**, elegiac, and heroic poems; and others, miscellaneously interspersed with prose, jotted in margins, and even worked in stone or metal.

> Underlined words in blue are hyperlinks or connections to other sources.

Related Topics

<u>Poetry</u>

from the English literature *article*

The Norman Conquest worked no immediate transformation on either the language or the literature of the English. Older poetry continued to be copied during the last half of the 11th century; two poems . . .

<u>Development as a poet</u>

from the Pound, Ezra *article*

Unsettled by the slaughter of World War I and the spirit of hopelessness he felt was pervading England after its conclusion, Pound decided to move to Paris, publishing before he left two of his most . . .

<u>lament</u>

a nonnarrative poem expressing deep grief or sorrow over a personal loss. The form developed as part of the oral tradition along with heroic poetry and exists in most languages. Examples include . . .

<u>Chadwick, H. Munro</u>

English philologist and historian, professor of Anglo-Saxon at the University of Cambridge (1912–41), who helped develop an integral approach to Old English studies.

ENCYCLOPEDIA
BRITANNICA **online**

Home | Blog | Board | Newsletters | International | Store

The major manuscripts
from the English literature *article*

Most Old English poetry is preserved in four manuscripts of the late 10th and early 11th centuries. The Beowulf manuscript (British Library) contains *Beowulf, Judith,* and three prose tracts; the . . .

The Eddaic verse forms
from the Scandinavian literature *article*

Three metres are commonly distinguished in Eddaic poetry: the epic measure, the speech measure, and the song measure. Most narrative poems were in the first measure, which consisted of short lines of . . .

Alliterative verse
from the English literature *article*

Virtually all Old English poetry is written in a single metre, a four-stress line with a syntactical break, or caesura, between the second and third stresses, and with alliteration linking the two . . .

Lattimore, Richmond

American poet and translator renowned for his disciplined yet poetic translations of Greek classics.

Caedmon

first Old English Christian poet, whose **fragmentary** hymn to the creation remains a symbol of the adaptation of the aristocratic-heroic Anglo-Saxon verse tradition to the expression of Christian . . .

The golden age of Bede
from the United Kingdom *article*

Within a century of Augustine's landing, England was in the **forefront** of scholarship. This high standard arose from a combination of influences: that from Ireland, which had escaped the decay caused . . .

Exeter Book

the largest extant collection of Old English poetry. Copied c. 975, the manuscript was given to Exeter Cathedral by Bishop Leofric (died 1072). It begins with some long religious poems: the Christ, . . .

Jump to: navigation, search

🔍 Davy Crockett

Davy Crockett

From Wikipedia, *the free encyclopedia*

Colonel David Crockett (August 17, 1786 - March 6, 1836) was a celebrated 19th-century American folk hero, frontiersman, soldier and politician; usually referred to as Davy Crockett and by the popular title "King of the Wild Frontier." He represented Tennessee in the U.S. House of Representatives, served in the Texas Revolution, and died at the age of 49 at the Battle of the Alamo.

■ Born	David Crockett August 17, 1786 Greene County, Tennessee
■ Died	March 6, 1836 (aged 49) Alamo Mission, San Antonio, Republic of Texas Killed in action
■ Occupation	Pioneer, Soldier, Trapper, Explorer, State Assemblyman, Congressman
■ Title	Colonel
■ Spouse	Polly Finley (1806–1815) her death Elizabeth Patton (1816–1836) his death

Contents

- 1 Early years
- 2 Political career
- 3 Texas Revolution
- 5 Death
- 8 Crockett in media
- 11 References
- 12 Further reading
- 13 External links

> Any user can edit Wikipedia articles, so it is important to verify facts found here against other sources.

[edit] Birth and Childhood

Davy Crockett was born near the Nolichucky River in Greene County, Tennessee, on August 17th,1786. David was the fifth of nine children of John and Rebecca Hawkins Crockett. His father was one of the Overmountain Men who fought in the American Revolutionary War battle of Kings Mountain. The Crocketts moved to Morristown, Tennessee sometime during the 1790s and built a cabin. A museum now stands on this site and is a reconstruction of that cabin.[1]

Shortly after being sent to school, Crockett ran away from home and spent several years roaming from town to town. During this period, Crockett claims to have visited most of the towns and villages throughout Tennessee and learned the majority of his skills as a backwoodsman, hunter and trapper.

[edit] Political Career

On September 17, 1821, Crockett was elected to the Committee of Propositions and Grievances. In 1826 and 1828 he was elected to the United States House of Representatives. As a Congressman, Crockett supported the rights of squatters, who were barred from buying land in the West without already owning property. He also opposed President Andrew Jackson's Indian Removal Act, and his opposition to Jackson caused his defeat when he ran for re-election in 1831; however, he won when he ran again in 1833. In 1835, he was narrowly defeated for re-election.[2]

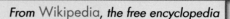

From Wikipedia, *the free encyclopedia*

[edit] Texas Revolution

On October 31, 1835, Crockett left Tennessee for Texas, writing "I want to explore Texas well before I return." He traveled along the Kawesch Glenn, a southwest trail. He arrived in Nacogdoches, Texas, in early January 1836. On January 14, 1836, Crockett and 65 other men signed an oath before Judge John Forbes to the Provisional Government of Texas for six months. "I have taken the oath of government and have enrolled my name as a volunteer and will set out for the Rio Grande in a few days with the volunteers from the United States." Each man was promised about 4,600 acres (19 km²) of land as payment. On February 6, Crockett and about five other men rode into San Antonio de Bexar and camped just outside of the town. They were later greeted by James Bowie and Antonio Menchacha and taken to the home of Don Erasmo Seguin.

William Barret Travis was the commander in charge at the siege at the Alamo. He appealed for help against the Mexican forces, to which Davy Crockett responded. The Texas forces of 180–250 were overwhelmed by the attacking 1,300-1,600 Mexican soldiers. The Mexican commanders understood their superiority of numbers and position and offered free passage to all concerned. Travis, supported by his entire force except one, refused to surrender.[3]

[edit] Death

All that is known for certain about the fate of Davy Crockett is that he died at the Battle of the Alamo.

> This warning alerts you that the information in one section of the article has not been adequately cited and may not be reliable.

This section does not cite any references or sources.
Please improve this section by adding citations to reliable sources. Unverifiable material may be challenged and removed.

[edit] References

1. Crockett Tavern Museum
2. A Century of Lawmaking for a New Nation: U.S. Congressional Documents and Debates, 1774-1875. The Library of Congress, URL accessed 2007-08-01.
3. Roots Web. "David Crockett, Tennesse.

> This section indicates the article's sources and allows the user to verify its information.

[edit] Further reading

- Crockett, David, *A Narrative of the Life of David Crockett of the State of Tennessee;* University of Nebraska Press.
- Levy, Buddy, *The Real Life Adventures of David Crockett;* Putnam Press.

Critical Reading

1. Key Ideas and Details (a) Identify three distinct features of the Britannica page. Consider both content and components provided for navigation. **(b)** Which feature would be most helpful to you in evaluating the site's reliability and credibility? Explain your choice.

2. Key Ideas and Details What other sources might you use to evaluate the validity and reliability of the Britannica article? Explain your choices.

3. Key Ideas and Details (a) What is the main difference between Wikipedia and other encyclopedias? **(b)** Which feature or features of the Wikipedia page could you use to evaluate the site's validity and reliability? Explain your choices.

4. Content-Area Vocabulary (a) Explain how the Latin words *manus,* ("hand") and *scribere* ("to write") contribute to the meaning of the word *manuscript.* **(b)** Determine the meaning of these other words derived from the Latin word *manus: manacle, manicure, manipulate, manual,* and *manage.* Use a dictionary to verify the meanings you determined.

Common Core State Standards

Writing

2. Write informative/explanatory texts to examine and convey complex ideas, concepts, and information clearly and accurately through the effective selection, organization, and analysis of content.

2.c. Use appropriate and varied transitions to clarify the relationships among complex ideas and concepts.

Language

4.d. Verify the preliminary determination of the meaning of a word or phrase.

⏱ Timed Writing

Explanatory Text [40 minutes}

Format

In an **analytical essay,** you break a topic into its elements and examine each one. Write at least one paragraph about each element, and include smooth transitions between ideas.

Write an **analytical essay** in which you **evaluate** the validity and reliability of various digital reference tools. Consider the pages shown here, as well as other sources you may have consulted in the past. Discuss the credibility of the various sites, as well as the information and features each offers. Also, explain how you can use other sources in various media to further verify the credibility of an online reference. End with a discussion of why it is important to verify the reliability of information presented online and elsewhere.

Academic Vocabulary

When you **evaluate** a text, you state your own judgment about it. Be sure to support your judgment with specific details from the texts.

5-Minute Planner

Complete these steps before you begin to write:

1. Read the prompt carefully. List key words.

2. Write a thesis that clearly responds to the prompt.

3. Scan the texts shown here and jot down other details that relate to the prompt.

4. Briefly sketch an outline for your essay. **TIP** In a Timed Writing situation an outline can be a simple numbered list.

5. Reread the prompt, and begin drafting.

Beowulf: From Ancient Epic to Graphic Novel

It was the superhero in *Beowulf,* the sword-wielding slayer of monsters, that drew comics creator Gareth Hinds to the eighth-century epic. It was the warrior's heroism and realistic fighting style, however, that led the artist in Hinds to render the story as a graphic novel. Above all, as Hinds told one interviewer, *Beowulf* is "an incredibly cool story."

It is so cool and powerful that this tale of a warrior-chieftain has found its way into movies (the latest one directed by Robert Zemeckis, with writer Neil Gaiman sharing a screenwriting credit), TV, and opera. In Hinds's chosen medium, the dragon looks remarkably similar to the one in the movie *Alien* and Beowulf has the fit body of a comic-book superhero.

For his graphic novel, Hinds employed three different art styles: pen and ink, with computer coloring using Adobe Photoshop; paint on wooden panels; and black wash over black ink. All pre-press work was done on his own computer. Thus, while Beowulf's narrative may be timeless, Hinds's techniques are as up-to-the-minute as Hollywood's transformations of paper comic books into movie blockbusters.

Gareth Hinds
artist of *Beowulf*

Gareth Hinds was always drawing when he was child. "I was basically born into it," he says. "But I had a lot of really good training and encouragement along the way. And I'm a very strong believer in the power of good art instruction." So it was only natural that he would study art in school, earning two Bachelors of Fine Art, from Rochester Institute of Technology and Parsons School of Design. He used a grant to self-publish his first graphic novel, *Bearskin*, a Grimm's fairy tale, in 1997. The next year he self-published *Beowulf.* His version of Shakespeare's *King Lear* came out in 2007.

Hinds advises aspiring artists to "become well-rounded." Also, the key to artistic success, he insists, is to "tell a story that is meaningful to ordinary people."

from BEOWULF

GARETH HINDS

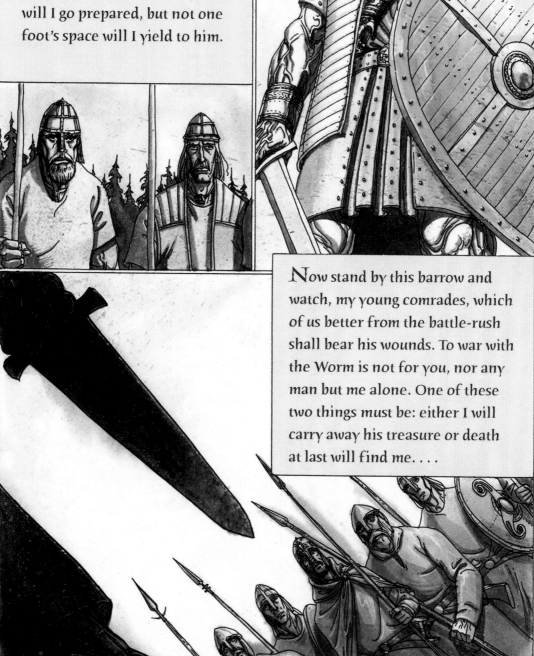

As in the old time with Grendel, I would not use sword or other weapon against this Worm. But I know not how, without these, I could fell such an enemy. Thus will I go prepared, but not one foot's space will I yield to him.

Now stand by this barrow and watch, my young comrades, which of us better from the battle-rush shall bear his wounds. To war with the Worm is not for you, nor any man but me alone. One of these two things must be: either I will carry away his treasure or death at last will find me. . . .

Critical Reading

1. **Respond:** In this section from his graphic novel, Hinds depicts the lead-up to the battle with the dragon. Does the way in which Hinds portrays characters and scenes agree with how you pictured them? Why or why not?

2. **(a) Analyze:** In what visual ways does Hinds build suspense for the battle with the dragon? **(b) Analyze:** How do the words in the text boxes work with the images to create suspense?

3. **(a) Classify:** Where does Hinds use close-ups, middle-distance views, and long-distance perspectives in telling the story? **(b) Evaluate:** Do you think he effectively combines these different perspectives? Explain.

Use these questions to hold a class discussion of *Beowulf*:

4. **(a)** How does storytelling with pictures and words differ from storytelling with words alone? **(b)** What are the advantages and disadvantages of each method? Explain.

5. Do you find it surprising that a very new form, the graphic novel, draws its subject matter from a very old form, an ancient epic? Why or why not?

A National Spirit

Connecting to the Essential Question In this selection, a monk living many years ago describes the distant British Isles for European readers. As you read, notice details that suggest Bede is describing a place that is far away from the known world. Finding such details will help you think about the Essential Question: **What is the relationship between literature and place?**

Common Core State Standards

Reading Informational Text

5. Analyze and evaluate the effectiveness of the structure an author uses in his or her exposition, including whether the structure makes points clear, convincing, and engaging.

Literary Analysis

Historical writing tells the story of past events using reliable evidence, such as eyewitness reports and documents. Bede, however, lived at a time when even educated people were more superstitious and less informed. Also, as occurs in any era, his biases and beliefs affected his accounts. In Bede's historical writing, therefore, you will find the following:

- Statements of fact: "Britain, formerly known as Albion, is an island"
- Superstitions: belief that snakes die from breathing Ireland's air
- Personal beliefs: "All are united in their study of God's truth"

Look for examples of each of these elements as you read.

Reading Strategy

Preparing to Read Complex Texts Bede's purpose is to introduce readers to a new place, Britain. Naturally, he tries to do this as clearly as possible. **Analyze the clarity of meaning** he achieves by focusing on these elements of his writing:

- *Patterns of organization*, such as the order in which he discusses Britain and Ireland, and his way of combining facts, examples, description, and narration, or the telling of a story
- *Hierarchical structures,* such as the relative importance he gives to different aspects of Britain
- *Repetition of main ideas*, such as Britain's positive qualities
- *Word choice*; for example, the use of factual language
- *Clear syntax*, or easy-to-understand sentence structure

As you read, use a chart like the one shown to analyze the clarity of Bede's discussion.

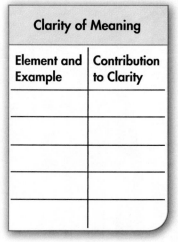

Clarity of Meaning	
Element and Example	**Contribution to Clarity**

Vocabulary

promontories (präm´ ən tôr´ ēz) *n.* peaks of high land sticking out into a body of water (p. 85)

cultivated (kul´ tə vāt´ əd) *v.* grown (p. 85)

innumerable (i nōō´ mer ə bəl) *adj.* too many to count (p. 85)

migrated (mī´ grāt´ əd) *v.* moved from one region or country to another (p. 86)

www.PHLitOnline.com

BEDE (673–735)

Author of *A History of the English Church and People*

▲ Detail of a manuscript by the 8th century English Benedictine monk and scholar, the Venerable Bede.

It was as if the lights had gone out. In the fifth century, the Roman Empire abandoned Britain. Rome was the center of the most advanced civilization in the West. As part of the Roman Empire, Britain had been connected with a larger world of trade and culture. Roman missionaries taught reading and writing as they preached Christianity. Roman soldiers patrolled Britain's borders. Once Rome withdrew, however, Britain was isolated, threatened by invasion from without and by strife from within.

Keeping Learning Alive Monasteries, particularly in Ireland, kept knowledge alive during these dark times. Monks studied Latin, the language of the Roman Empire. They laboriously copied books. The more scholarly monks wrote new works.

Much of what we know about England before A.D. 700 is based on the work of one such monk, Bede. A contemporary of the unknown author of *Beowulf*, Bede was the most learned scholar of his day. Although he wrote forty books on various subjects, his reputation would be secure on the basis of one—*A History of the English Church and People*, for which Bede is called the father of English history.

A Daily Reminder Bede was born in Wearmouth (now Sunderland) in northeastern England. At age seven, he entered the nearby monastic school of Jarrow. A diligent student, he stayed on as a priest and scholar. Although Bede lived his whole life at Jarrow, he wrote in Latin, so his work was accessible to scholars throughout the West. His pupils carried his writings to Europe. His work, famous in his own lifetime for its scholarship, has become a part of daily life—Bede helped originate the dating of events from the birth of Christ, a cornerstone of the Western calendar.

A Scholarly Work In the *History,* Bede describes the conquest of Britain by the Anglo-Saxon tribes after the departure of the Romans. His main concern, however, was the expansion of Christianity in England. Bede gathered information from many kinds of documents, interviewed knowledgeable monks, and, in general, proceeded very much like a modern historian.

In the century after his death, Bede's history was translated from Latin into English for King Alfred. In the same century, Bede was honored with the title "the Venerable [respected] Bede."

from

A HISTORY OF THE ENGLISH CHURCH AND PEOPLE

Translated by Leo Sherley-Price

BACKGROUND Although the majority of British people in Bede's day were illiterate and written records were scarce, monasteries such as the one to which Bede belonged were dedicated to continuing a tradition of learning. Through the monastery, Bede had access to books and other documents, as well as contact with other learned monks. Using these sources, he was able to generate his history of Britain. His fellow Britons may have been illiterate, but Bede had in mind a larger world of readers for his work—the Church to which he belonged and the Roman civilization in which it participated. Bede wrote his account of Britain for such readers, starting at the beginning with the basics.

THE SITUATION OF BRITAIN AND IRELAND: THEIR EARLIEST INHABITANTS

Britain, formerly known as Albion, is an island in the ocean, facing between north and west, and lying at a considerable distance from the coasts of Germany, Gaul, and Spain, which together form the greater part of Europe.

It extends 800 miles northwards, and is 200 in breadth, except where a number of promontories stretch farther, the coastline round which extends to 3,675 miles. To the south lies Belgic Gaul,[1] from the nearest shore of which travelers can see the city known as Rutubi Portus, which the English have corrupted to Reptacestir.[2] The distance from there across the sea to Gessoriacum,[3] the nearest coast of the Morini, is 50 miles or, as some write it, 450 furlongs.[4] On the opposite side of Britain, which lies open to the boundless ocean, lie the isles of the Orcades.[5] Britain is rich in grain and timber; it has good pasturage for cattle and draft animals,[6] and vines are cultivated in various localities. There are many land and sea birds of various species, and it is well known for its plentiful springs and rivers abounding in fish. There are salmon and eel fisheries, while seals, dolphins, and sometimes whales are caught. There are also many varieties of shellfish, such as mussels, in which are often found excellent pearls of several colors: red, purple, violet, and green, but mainly white. Cockles[7] are abundant, and a beautiful scarlet dye is extracted from them which remains unfaded by sunshine or rain; indeed, the older the cloth, the more beautiful its color. The country has both salt and hot springs, and the waters flowing from them provide hot baths, in which the people bathe separately according to age and sex. As Saint Basil says: "Water receives its heat when it flows across certain metals, and becomes hot, and even scalding." The land has rich veins of many metals, including copper, iron, lead, and silver. There is also much black jet[8] of fine quality, which sparkles in firelight. When burned, it drives away snakes, and, like amber, when it is warmed by friction, it clings to whatever is applied to it. In old times, the country had twenty-eight noble cities, and innumerable castles, all of which were guarded by walls, towers, and barred gates.

Since Britain lies far north toward the pole, the nights are short in summer, and at midnight it is hard to tell whether the evening twilight still lingers or whether dawn is approaching; for in these northern latitudes the sun does not remain long below the horizon at night. Consequently both summer days and winter nights are long, and when the sun withdraws

---

1. **Belgic Gaul** France.
2. **Reptacestir** Richborough, part of the city of Sandwich.
3. **Gessoriacum** Boulogne, France.
4. **furlongs** units for measuring distance; a furlong is equal to one eighth of a mile.
5. **Orcades** Orkney Isles.
6. **draft animals** animals used for pulling loads.
7. **Cockles** edible shellfish with two heart-shaped shells.
8. **jet** *n.* type of coal.

Vocabulary

promontories
(präm´ ən tôr´ ēz) *n.* peaks of high land sticking out into the water

cultivated
(kul´ tə vāt´ əd) *v.* grown

innumerable
(i n$\overline{oo}$´ mər ə bəl) *adj.* too many to count

Reading Strategy

Analyze Clarity of Meaning If Britain is unknown to many of his readers, why does it make sense for Bede to begin with a geographical description?

Literary Analysis

Historical Writing
Find two facts in this paragraph. Then, identify one claim for which you might need more evidence.

Reading Check

According to Saint Basil, how does water from the hot springs receive its heat?

southwards, the winter nights last eighteen hours. In Armenia,[9] Macedonia,[10] and Italy, and other countries of that latitude, the longest day lasts only fifteen hours and the shortest nine.

At the present time there are in Britain, in harmony with the five books of the divine law, five languages and four nations—English, British, Scots, and Picts. Each of these have their own language, but all are united in their study of God's truth by the fifth, Latin, which has become a common medium through the study of the scriptures. The original inhabitants of the island were the Britons, from whom it takes its name, and who, according to tradition, crossed into Britain from Armorica,[11] and occupied the southern parts. When they had spread northwards and possessed the greater part of the islands, it is said that some Picts from Scythia[12] put to sea in a few long ships and were driven by storms around the coasts of Britain, arriving at length on the north coast of Ireland. Here they found the nation of the Scots, from whom they asked permission to settle, but their request was refused. Ireland is the largest island after Britain, and lies to the west. It is shorter than Britain to the north, but extends far beyond it to the south towards the northern coasts of Spain, although a wide sea separates them. These Pictish seafarers, as I have said, asked for a grant of land to make a settlement. The Scots replied that there was not room for them both, but said: "We can give you good advice. There is another island not far to the east, which we often see in the distance on clear days. Go and settle there if you wish; should you meet resistance, we will come to your help." So the Picts crossed into Britain, and began to settle in the north of the island, since the Britons were in possession of the south. Having no women with them, these Picts asked wives of the Scots, who consented on condition that, when any dispute arose, they should choose a king from the female royal line rather than the male. This custom continues among the Picts to this day. As time went on, Britain received a third nation, that of the Scots, who migrated from Ireland under their chieftain Reuda, and by a combination of force and treaty, obtained from the Picts the settlements that they still hold. From the name of this chieftain, they are still known as Dalreudians, for in their tongue *dal* means a division.

Ireland is broader than Britain, and its mild and healthy climate is superior. Snow rarely lies longer than three days, so that

---

9. **Armenia** region between the Black and the Caspian seas, now divided between the nations of Armenia and Turkey.
10. **Macedonia** region in the eastern Mediterranean, divided among Greece, Yugoslavia, and Bulgaria.
11. **Armorica** Brittany, France.
12. **Scythia** ancient region in southeastern Europe.

ATLAS PAGE
THE BRITISH ISLES

An atlas is a book of maps and other information on a country's physical landscape, political makeup, and economic resources. Modern atlases benefit from satellite technology and computer-generated maps. You can use this atlas page to verify and clarify — check the accuracy and clarity of — facts that Bede provides about Britain's geography and resources.

CONNECT TO THE LITERATURE

Use this modern atlas entry for Ireland and the United Kingdom to check the accuracy and clarity of three of Bede's statements of fact about the British Isles.

> At its widest the United Kingdom is 300 miles (500 km) across. From the northern tip of Scotland to the southern coast of England, it is about 600 miles (1,000 km). No part is more than 75 miles (120 km) from the sea.
>
> The greatest distance from north to south in Ireland is 302 miles (486 km), and from east to west it is 171 miles (275 km).

Republic of Ireland / **United Kingdom**

Natural Resources

United Kingdom	Republic of Ireland
coal, petroleum, natural gas, iron ore, lead, zinc, gold, tin, limestone, salt, clay, chalk, gypsum, potash, silica sand, slate, arable land	natural gas, peat, copper, lead, zinc, silver, barite, gypsum, limestone, dolomite

Animal Life

United Kingdom	Republic of Ireland
Red Deer, badgers, otters, foxes, stoats, weasels, rodents hedgehogs, moles, shrews, rabbits, newts, frogs, toads, lizards, snakes	Red Deer, badgers, otters, foxes, stoats, rodents, hedgehogs, shrews, rabbits, newts, frogs

Climate: Republic of Ireland

Month	Average Max Temp F°	Average Min Temp F°	Daily Hours of Sunshine	Days of Rainfall
March	50	37.4	3	11
June	64.4	48.2	6	12
September	62.6	48.2	4	15
December	46.4	35.6	2	18

Land Area

United Kingdom	Republic of Ireland
total: 94,526 sq mi	total: 27,135 sq mi
land: 93,278 sq mi	land: 26,599 sq mi
water: 1,247 sq mi	water: 537 sq mi
coastline: 7,723 mi	coastline: 900 mi

Climate: United Kingdom

Month	Max Temp F°	Min Temp F°	Hours of Sunshine	Days of Rainfall
March	47.3	35.42	4	13
June	62.4	47.1	7	11
September	61	47.3	5	13
December	44.4	34.7	1	15

United Kingdom	Republic of Ireland
mostly rugged hills and low mountains; level to rolling plains in east and southeast	mostly level to rolling interior plain surrounded by rugged hills and low mountains; sea cliffs on west coast

Sunlight: In Britain, daily sunshine hours range from between one and two in midwinter to between five and seven in midsummer.

from A History of the English Church and People **87**

Literary Analysis
Historical Writing
Find one example of a superstition in this paragraph.

there is no need to store hay in summer for winter use or to build stables for beasts. There are no reptiles, and no snake can exist there, for although often brought over from Britain, as soon as the ship nears land, they breathe its scented air and die. In fact, almost everything in this isle enjoys immunity to poison, and I have heard that folk suffering from snakebite have drunk water in which scrapings from the leaves of books from Ireland had been steeped, and that this remedy checked the spreading poison and reduced the swelling. The island abounds in milk and honey, and there is no lack of vines, fish, and birds, while deer and goats are widely hunted. It is the original home of the Scots, who, as already mentioned, later migrated and joined the Britons and Picts in Britain. There is a very extensive arm of the sea, which originally formed the boundary between the Britons and the Picts. This runs inland from the west for a great distance as far as the strongly fortified British city of Alcuith.[13] It was to the northern shores of this firth[14] that the Scots came and established their new homeland.

---

13. Alcuith Dumbarton, Scotland.
14. firth narrow arm of the sea.

Critical Reading

 1. Key Ideas and Details **(a)** What background does Bede give about British scarlet dye? **(b) Infer:** What does this information suggest about the lifestyle or economy of the country?

 2. Key Ideas and Details **(a) Interpret:** In what way does Latin unite England? **(b) Interpret:** According to Bede, what factor is most important in uniting people and giving them a common identity?

 3. Integration of Knowledge and Ideas **Evaluate:** Does Bede do a good job answering readers' questions about England? Explain, giving three examples of possible questions.

 4. Integration of Knowledge and Ideas In what ways does Britain's remote location influence Bede's description of it? In responding, use at least two of these Essential Question words: *geography, proximity, isolation.* **[Connecting to the Essential Question: What is the relationship between literature and place?]**

Cite textual evidence to support your responses.

Literary Analysis

Common Core State Standards

1. Integration of Knowledge and Ideas Evaluate Bede's **historical writing** in terms of the evidence he supplies. On a chart like this one, *clarify* several claims Bede makes about Britain or Ireland. For each claim, list his supporting evidence, *verify* it against evidence from a modern atlas page (p. 87), and indicate whether you feel he gives enough support for the claim.

Claim/Clarify	Evidence	Evaluation/Verify

2. Integration of Knowledge and Ideas How do Bede's attitudes and beliefs color the information he provides? Support your answer with examples from the selection.

3. Integration of Knowledge and Ideas **(a)** In Bede's account, contrast factors that are dividing England with those that are uniting it. **(b)** Which factors seem stronger? Why?

Writing
1. Write arguments to support claims in an analysis of substantive topics or texts, using valid reasoning and relevant and sufficient evidence.

Language
5. Demonstrate understanding of word relationships.

Reading Strategy

4. Analyze the clarity of meaning in Bede's writing, taking into account the contributions of elements such as *patterns of organization*, *hierarchic structures*, *repetition of main ideas*, *word choice*, and *syntax*.

5. It is the year 3000, and a writer wants Earthlings to appreciate the value of a new colony on Mars. How could Bede's use of word choice, repetition, and patterns of organization serve as a model for this writer?

PERFORMANCE TASKS
Integrated Language Skills

Vocabulary Acquisition and Use

Categorize Vocabulary Using the list of vocabulary words on page 82, analyze the relationship between the words in each item. Are they synonyms (words with similar meanings) or a combination of synonyms and antonyms (words with opposite meanings)? Use a dictionary if necessary.

1. promontories, capes, headlands

2. grew, destroyed, cultivated

3. innumerable, few, scarce

4. migrated, traveled, journeyed

Writing

Argument Review Bede's *History* as if you were an eighth-century European reader looking for business opportunities. Then, write a **business memo** convincing people to invest in an enterprise in Britain or Ireland. Explain your plan clearly and persuasively, citing passages from the selection to support your points. Use a heading that specifies To, From, Subject, and Date.

Literary History: Chaucer's World

The Canterbury Tales . . .
is actually a story about stories.

Chaucer's Guided Tour of Medieval Life and Literature

Rich people, poor people, stock brokers, artists, farmers, street vendors . . . with all of the different lifestyles in our culture, you may wonder what single event could gather together people from all parts of society. Geoffrey Chaucer found in his own society an orderly, even joyous event that gathered people from diverse backgrounds and occupations—a pilgrimage, or journey to a sacred spot. It is such a pilgrimage that gathers together the diverse characters in his masterpiece, *The Canterbury Tales.*

The Journey Begins Like modern travelers, medieval pilgrims must have been eager to while away their time traveling. Chaucer uses this fact to set his story in motion. *The Canterbury Tales* begins with a Prologue, in which the Narrator, presumably Chaucer himself, meets twenty-nine other pilgrims at the Tabard Inn, located in a suburb of London. As the pilgrims prepare for their journey, the host of the Inn, Harry Bailey, sets a challenge. To make the journey more entertaining, he suggests that each pilgrim tell two stories on the way to Canterbury and two stories on the return trip. The person who tells the best tale will be treated to a feast hosted by the other pilgrims. The pilgrims accept the challenge, and Bailey himself decides to join them and judge the competition.

Each of the following sections of the work consists of one of the pilgrim's tales. Brief transitions, as one storyteller finishes and another begins, link the stories. In this way, the work is actually a story about stories, twenty-four different tales set within the overarching tale of the pilgrimage.

Snapshots of an Era In the Prologue, Chaucer sketches a brief but vivid portrait of each pilgrim, creating a lively sense of medieval life. In itself, the Prologue is a great literary achievement. As critic Vincent Hopper notes,

> The description of the various pilgrims turn in rapid sequence from an article of clothing to a point of character and back again with no apparent organization or desire for it. Yet so effective is this artful artlessness that each pilgrim stands out sharply as a type of medieval personality and also as a highly individualized character. . . .

Chaucer begins his survey of medieval society with the courtly world, which centered on the nobility. Medieval nobles such as Chaucer's Knight held land granted them by a lord or king, for whom they fought in times of war. In the middle ranks of medieval society were learned professionals, such as Chaucer's Doctor, and wealthy businessmen. The lower orders included craftsmen, storekeepers, and minor administrators, such as the Reeve and the Manciple. The various ranks of the Church, a cornerstone of medieval society, are represented by characters from the Prioress to the Summoner.

However, as Chaucer writes about character ranks and types, he presents them as real people, individuals who defy categorizing. For example, though all outward appearances suggest that the Merchant is wealthy, he is, in fact, deeply in debt—a secret he keeps from some of his fellow travelers. Such breaks in stereotype provide readers with an even greater insight into the daily lives of medieval people.

A Literary Tour The popular genres in Chaucer's day included romances (tales of chivalry), *fabliaux* (short, bawdy, humorous stories), the stories of saints' lives, sermons, and allegories (narratives in which characters represent abstractions such as Pride or Honor). Each pilgrim chooses to tell a type of tale consistent with his or her character, and each of the major forms of medieval literature is represented. Chaucer wrote much of the *Tales* using his own form, the heroic couplet, a pair of rhyming lines with five stressed syllables each. For this important innovation, along with his other achievements, he is known as the father of English poetry.

The Endless Road Traveling with Chaucer's pilgrims, a reader may feel that the world is a big place but that, somehow, all of its pieces fit together. *The Canterbury Tales* reminds us that every journey from here to there is filled with stories, waiting to be told.

Speaking and Listening: Discussion

© Comprehension and Collaboration Imagine you are taking a long bus or plane trip with a group of modern-day travelers. With a group, discuss the types of people traveling with you. Come up with your own cast of characters for a modern-day version of *The Canterbury Tales*. Use these questions to guide your **discussion:**

- What different kinds of people make up our society today? Identify six types and build a character that matches each.

- In what ways might many of these individuals break the stereotype they outwardly appear to fit?

- What kind of tale might each character tell?

Choose a point person to share your ideas with the class.

Geoffrey Chaucer (1343?–1400)

Son of a merchant, page in a royal house, soldier, diplomat, and royal clerk, Geoffey Chaucer saw quite a bit of the medieval world. His varied experiences helped prepare him to write *The Canterbury Tales*. This masterpiece provides the best contemporary picture we have of fourteenth-century England. Gathering characters from different walks of life, Chaucer takes the reader on a journey through medieval society.

The Poet's Beginning The exact date of Geoffrey Chaucer's birth is unknown, but official records furnish many details of his active life. Born into a middle-class family, Chaucer was sent in his early teens to work as page to the wife of Lionel of Antwerp, a son of the reigning monarch, Edward III. Through this position, middle-class Chaucer was introduced to the aristocratic society of England. In 1359, while serving in the English Army in France, Chaucer was captured and held prisoner. King Edward paid a £16 (sixteen-pound) ransom for his release—a sum that was eight times what a simple laborer might make in a year. In 1366, Chaucer married Philippa Pan, a lady-in-waiting to the queen. Their eldest child, Thomas, continued his father's rise in the world, marrying a noblewoman and acquiring great wealth.

The Poet Matures Chaucer began writing in his twenties, practicing his skills as a poet as he rose through the ranks of medieval society. His early poems were based on the works of European poets. These were followed by various translations of French poetry. His first major work, *The Book of the Duchess*, was probably completed in early 1369, almost one year after the death of Blanche of Lancaster, for whose grieving husband, John of Gaunt, he wrote the poem. As Chaucer grew older, he developed a mature style of his own and displayed a deep insight into human character.

The Canterbury Tales

Chaucer wrote *The Canterbury Tales* in his later years. No one knows for certain what prompted him to begin this work. Chaucer's inspiration may have come from his own participation in the pilgrimage to Canterbury. A pilgrimage is a long journey to a shrine or holy site, undertaken by people who wish to express their devotion. The Canterbury Cathedral was the focus of devotion because St. Thomas à Becket was murdered there in 1170. Chaucer certainly had the opportunity to observe many pilgrims starting their journeys—a window of his London home overlooked the pilgrim road that led to Canterbury.

In this masterwork, each character tells a tale on the way to Canterbury. Just as the tellers of *The Canterbury Tales* come from the length and breadth of medieval society, the tales encompass medieval literature—from romance to comedy, from rhyme to prose, from crude humor to religious mysteries. Only 24 of the projected 120 tales were finished, but they stand together as a complete work.

The Father of English Poetry

In his own lifetime, Geoffrey Chaucer was considered the greatest English poet. Recognized as a shrewd storyteller, he was also praised by a contemporary as the first to "rain the gold dewdrops of speech and eloquence" into English literature. Throughout history, new generations of poets writing in English have studied his work for both inspiration and insight.

Chaucer lies buried in Westminster Abbey. In recognition of his unique position in England's literary tradition, Westminster's honorary burial area for distinguished writers, the Poets' Corner, was established around his tomb. The words in Middle English at the right are from Chaucer's poem *Troilus and Criseyde*. They are not on his tomb, but they serve to measure both his distance from us and his closeness to us.

Ye knowe eek, that in forme of speche is chaunge

Withinne a thousand yeer, and wordes tho

That hadden prys, now wonder nyce and straunge

Us thinketh hem; and yet they spake hem so,

And spedde as wel in love as men now do . . .

CHAUCER'S SHARP EYE FOR DRESS

Do you dress to impress? Or for success?
Medieval Dress Codes In the 14th century, rules dictating style depended on whether you were rich, middle-class, or poor. No one below the rank of knight could wear fur, for example; merchants could wear the same clothes as knights only if they were five times wealthier, and women were forbidden from wearing silk head coverings.

In the Prologue to *The Canterbury Tales*, Chaucer relies on the details of the pilgrims' clothing and a general knowledge of the do's and don'ts of fashion laws to reveal their personalities, positions on the social ladder, and attempts at modesty or deception.

Modest Dress The Knight's coarse tunic "stained and dark" could have fooled fashion watchers into believing he was without rank. Yet knights were members of the nobility and were allowed to adorn themselves with fur and gold.

Pleasure Loving A Franklin, a member in good standing of the top tier of 14th century hierarchy, was a pleasure-loving fellow. This landowner carried "a little purse of silk…" that Chaucer aptly describes as "white as morning milk."

The Wife of Bath's "flowing mantle" hid her "large hips," her handkerchiefs were finely woven, her stockings "were of the finest scarlet red" and her shoes "soft and new." Her clothing revealed her as a member of the middle class.

Clothing That Suits the Profession A Doctor in the group was adorned alarmingly in "blood-red garments…lined with taffeta," almost as if he were advertising his profession. Yet Chaucer wrote that the Doctor watched every cent and was "rather close as to expenses."

Bottom line: No matter what you wear or when you live, your clothes say a lot about who you are, where you fit, and what you aspire to be.

Knight   Franklin   Wife of Bath   Doctor

Before You Read

from *The Canterbury Tales: The Prologue*

Connecting to the Essential Question In the Prologue to *The Canterbury Tales*, Chaucer describes different medieval social types. Briefly describe some social types at your school. In describing social types, you probably described their clothes. As you read, note what Chaucer's descriptions of clothes reveal about his characters. Doing so will help you explore the Essential Question: **How does literature shape or reflect society?**

Literary Analysis

As you read the Prologue, look for these forms of **characterization**—techniques of revealing character:

- **Direct characterization** presents direct statements about a character, like Chaucer's statement that the Knight "followed chivalry. . . ."
- **Indirect characterization** uses actions, thoughts, dialogue, and description to reveal a character's personality. By saying the Knight Is "not gaily dressed," Chaucer suggests that he is not vain.

Each character in the selection represents a different segment of society in Chaucer's time. By using characterization to reveal the virtues and faults of each, Chaucer provides **social commentary,** writing that offers insight into society, its values, and its customs. As you read, determine what Chaucer's characters suggest about his views of English society and of life.

Reading Strategy

 **Preparing to Read Complex Texts** When you do not understand a long, involved sentence you are reading, repair your comprehension by **questioning.** For example, you may have trouble understanding the eighteen-line sentence at the start of Chaucer's Prologue. To analyze the sentence, ask the questions *When?, Who?, Where?, What?, Why?,* and *How?* to identify essential information. Use a chart like the one shown to finish analyzing Chaucer's first sentence.

Vocabulary

solicitous (sə lis′ ə təs) *adj.*
showing care or concern (p. 101)

garnished (gär′ nisht) *adj.*
decorated; trimmed (p. 102)

absolution (ab′ sə lo͞o′ shən) *n.*
act of freeing someone of a sin or criminal charge (p. 103)

commission (kə mish′ ən) *n.*
authorization; act of giving authority to an individual (p. 105)

sanguine (saŋ′ gwin) *adj.*
confident; cheerful (p. 106)

prevarication (pri var′ i kā′ shən)
n. evasion of truth (p. 115)

Common Core State Standards

Reading Literature
1. Cite strong and thorough textual evidence to support analysis of what the text says explicitly as well as inferences drawn from the text, including determining where the text leaves matters uncertain.
3. Analyze the impact of the author's choices regarding how to develop and relate elements of a story or drama.

Analyze Difficult Sentences	
When?	in April
Who?	people; palmers
Where?	
What?	
Why?	
How?	

www.PHLitOnline.com

from the Canterbury Tales
The Prologue

Geoffrey Chaucer
translated by Nevill Coghill

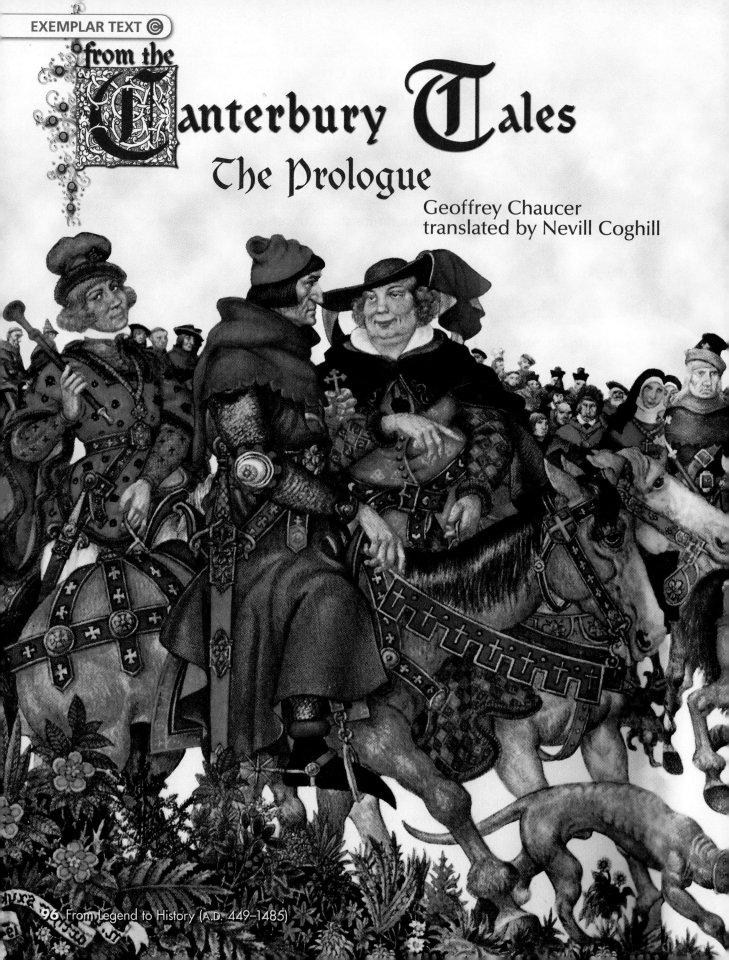

Lines 1–18 of the Prologue in Chaucer's original Middle English are followed by the entire Prologue in a modern translation.

Whan that Aprill with his shoures soote
The droghte of March hath perced to the roote,
And bathed every veyne in swich licour
Of which vertu engendred is the flour;
5 Whan Zephirus eek with his sweete breeth
Inspired hath in every holt and heeth
The tendre croppes, and the yonge sonne
Hath in the Ram his halve cours yronne,
And smale foweles maken melodye,
10 That slepen al the nyght with open ye
(So priketh hem nature in hir corages);
Thanne longen folk to goon on pilgrimages,
And palmeres for to seken straunge strondes,
To ferne halwes, kowthe in sondry londes;
15 And specially from every shires ende
Of Engelond to Caunterbury they wende,
The hooly blisful martir for to seke,
That hem hath holpen whan that they were seeke.

When in April the sweet showers fall
And pierce the drought of March to the root, and all
The veins are bathed in liquor of such power
As brings about the engendering of the flower,
5 When also Zephyrus[1] with his sweet breath
Exhales an air in every grove and heath
Upon tender shoots, and the young sun
His half-course in the sign of the Ram[2] has run,
And the small fowl are making melody
10 That sleep away the night with open eye
(So nature pricks them and their heart engages)
Then people long to go on pilgrimages
And palmers[3] long to seek the stranger strands[4]
Of far-off saints, hallowed in sundry lands,
15 And specially, from every shire's end
In England, down to Canterbury they wend
To seek the holy blissful martyr,[5] quick
To give his help to them when they were sick.

1. **Zephyrus** (zef′ ə rəs) the west wind.
2. **Ram** Aries, the first sign of the zodiac. The pilgrimage began on April 11, 1387.
3. **palmers** pilgrims who wore two crossed palm leaves to show that they had visited the Holy Land.
4. **strands** shores.
5. **martyr** St. Thomas à Becket, the Archbishop of Canterbury, who was murdered in Canterbury Cathedral in 1170.

It happened in that season that one day

20 In Southwark,[6] at The Tabard,[7] as I lay
    Ready to go on pilgrimage and start
    For Canterbury, most devout at heart,
    At night there came into that hostelry
    Some nine and twenty in a company

25 Of sundry folk happening then to fall
    In fellowship, and they were pilgrims all
    That towards Canterbury meant to ride.
    The rooms and stables of the inn were wide;
    They made us easy, all was of the best.

30 And shortly, when the sun had gone to rest,
    By speaking to them all upon the trip
    I soon was one of them in fellowship
    And promised to rise early and take the way
    To Canterbury, as you heard me say.

35   But nonetheless, while I have time and space,
    Before my story takes a further pace,
    It seems a reasonable thing to say
    What their condition was, the full array
    Of each of them, as it appeared to me

40 According to profession and degree,
    And what apparel they were riding in;
    And at a Knight I therefore will begin.
    There was a *Knight*, a most distinguished man,
    Who from the day on which he first began

45 To ride abroad had followed chivalry,
    Truth, honor, generousness and courtesy.
    He had done nobly in his sovereign's war
    And ridden into battle, no man more,
    As well in Christian as heathen places,

50 And ever honored for his noble graces.
        When we took Alexandria,[8] he was there.
    He often sat at table in the chair
    Of honor, above all nations, when in Prussia.
    In Lithuania he had ridden, and Russia,

55 No Christian man so often, of his rank.
    When, in Granada, Algeciras sank
    Under assault, he had been there, and in
    North Africa, raiding Benamarin;
    In Anatolia he had been as well

60 And fought when Ayas and Attalia fell,

Reading Strategy
Questioning
According to lines 43–46, what values does the Knight follow?

Literary Analysis
Characterization
What do lines 54–65 indirectly suggest about the Knight's character?

---

6. **Southwark** (suth´ ərk) suburb of London at the time.
7. **The Tabard** (ta´ bərd) an inn.
8. **Alexandria** site of one of the campaigns fought by Christians against groups who posed a threat to Europe during the fourteenth century. The place names that follow refer to other battle sites in these campaigns, or crusades.

For all along the Mediterranean coast
He had embarked with many a noble host.
In fifteen mortal battles he had been
And jousted for our faith at Tramissene
65 Thrice in the lists, and always killed his man.
This same distinguished knight had led the van[9]
Once with the Bey of Balat,[10] doing work
For him against another heathen Turk;
He was of sovereign value in all eyes.
70 And though so much distinguished, he was wise
And in his bearing modest as a maid.
He never yet a boorish thing had said
In all his life to any, come what might;
He was a true, a perfect gentle-knight.
75 Speaking of his equipment, he possessed
Fine horses, but he was not gaily dressed.
He wore a fustian[11] tunic stained and dark
With smudges where his armor had left mark;
Just home from service, he had joined our ranks
80 To do his pilgrimage and render thanks.
　　　He had his son with him, a fine young *Squire*,
A lover and cadet, a lad of fire
With locks as curly as if they had been pressed.
He was some twenty years of age, I guessed.
85 In stature he was of a moderate length,
With wonderful agility and strength.
He'd seen some service with the cavalry
In Flanders and Artois and Picardy[12]
And had done valiantly in little space
90 Of time, in hope to win his lady's grace.
He was embroidered like a meadow bright
And full of freshest flowers, red and white.
Singing he was, or fluting all the day;
He was as fresh as is the month of May.
95 Short was his gown, the sleeves were long and wide;
He knew the way to sit a horse and ride.
He could make songs and poems and recite,
Knew how to joust and dance, to draw and write.
He loved so hotly that till dawn grew pale
100 He slept as little as a nightingale.
Courteous he was, lowly and serviceable,
And carved to serve his father at the table.

Reading Strategy
Questioning What motivates the Squire in lines 85–90?

Reading
Check

What are some of the military accomplishments of the Knight?

---

9. van the part of the army that goes before the rest (short for *vanguard*).
10. Bey of Balat pagan leader.
11. fustian (fus´ chǝn) *n.* coarse cloth of cotton and linen.
12. Flanders . . . Picardy regions in Belgium and France.

There was a *Yeoman*[13] with him at his side,
No other servant; so he chose to ride.
105 This Yeoman wore a coat and hood of green,
And peacock-feathered arrows, bright and keen
And neatly sheathed, hung at his belt the while
—For he could dress his gear in yeoman style,
His arrows never drooped their feathers low—
110 And in his hand he bore a mighty bow.
His head was like a nut, his face was brown.
He knew the whole of woodcraft up and down.
A saucy brace[14] was on his arm to ward
It from the bow-string, and a shield and sword
115 Hung at one side, and at the other slipped
A jaunty dirk,[15] spear-sharp and well-equipped.
A medal of St. Christopher[16] he wore
Of shining silver on his breast, and bore
A hunting-horn, well slung and burnished clean,
120 That dangled from a baldric[17] of bright green.
He was a proper forester I guess.
       There also was a *Nun*, a Prioress.[18]
Her way of smiling very simple and coy.
Her greatest oath was only "By St. Loy!"[19]
125 And she was known as Madam Eglantyne.
And well she sang a service,[20] with a fine
Intoning through her nose, as was most seemly,
And she spoke daintily in French, extremely,
After the school of Stratford-atte-Bowe;[21]
130 French in the Paris style she did not know.
At meat her manners were well taught withal;
No morsel from her lips did she let fall,
Nor dipped her fingers in the sauce too deep;
But she could carry a morsel up and keep
135 The smallest drop from falling on her breast.
For courtliness she had a special zest,
And she would wipe her upper lip so clean
That not a trace of grease was to be seen
Upon the cup when she had drunk; to eat,

▲ **Critical Viewing**
Compare this portrait with Chaucer's description of the Yeoman. What details did the artist choose to change or omit? **[Compare and Contrast]**

---

13. *Yeoman* (yō′ mən) *n.* attendant.
14. brace bracelet.
15. dirk *n.* dagger.
16. St. Christopher patron saint of travelers.
17. baldric *n.* belt worn over one shoulder and across the chest to support a sword.
18. Prioress *n.* in an abbey, the nun ranking just below the abbess.
19. St. Loy St. Eligius, patron saint of goldsmiths and courtiers.
20. service daily prayer.
21. Stratford-atte-Bowe nunnery near London.

140 She reached a hand sedately for the meat.
    She certainly was very entertaining,
    Pleasant and friendly in her ways, and straining
    To counterfeit a courtly kind of grace,
    A stately bearing fitting to her place,
145 And to seem dignified in all her dealings.
    As for her sympathies and tender feelings,
    She was so charitably solicitous
    She used to weep if she but saw a mouse
    Caught in a trap, if it were dead or bleeding.
150 And she had little dogs she would be feeding
    With roasted flesh, or milk, or fine white bread.
    And bitterly she wept if one were dead
    Or someone took a stick and made it smart;
    She was all sentiment and tender heart.
155 Her veil was gathered in a seemly way,
    Her nose was elegant, her eyes glass-gray;
    Her mouth was very small, but soft and red,
    Her forehead, certainly, was fair of spread,
    Almost a span[22] across the brows, I own;
160 She was indeed by no means undergrown.
    Her cloak, I noticed, had a graceful charm.
    She wore a coral trinket on her arm,
    A set of beads, the gaudies[23] tricked in green,
    Whence hung a golden brooch of brightest sheen
165 On which there first was graven a crowned *A*,
    And lower, *Amor vincit omnia.*[24]
        Another *Nun*, the chaplain at her cell,
    Was riding with her, and *three Priests* as well.
        A *Monk* there was, one of the finest sort
170 Who rode the country; hunting was his sport.
    A manly man, to be an Abbot able;
    Many a dainty horse he had in stable.
    His bridle, when he rode, a man might hear
    Jingling in a whistling wind as clear,
175 Aye, and as loud as does the chapel bell
    Where my lord Monk was Prior of the cell.
    The Rule of good St. Benet or St. Maur[25]
    As old and strict he tended to ignore;
    He let go by the things of yesterday

---

22. **span** nine inches.
23. **gaudies** large green beads that marked certain prayers on a set of prayer beads.
24. *Amor vincit omnia* (ä´ môr´ vin´ chit ôm´ nē ä´) "love conquers all" (Latin).
25. **St. Benet or St. Maur** St. Benedict, author of monastic rules, and St. Maurice, one of his followers. Benet and Maur are French versions of Benedict and Maurice.

Vocabulary
solicitous (sə lis´ ə təs) *adj.* showing care or concern

Literary Analysis
Characterization
What can you infer about the Prioress based on this detailed description of her jewelry?

Reading Check

How does the Nun show her "sympathies and tender feelings"?

180 And took the modern world's more spacious way.
He did not rate that text at a plucked hen
Which says that hunters are not holy men
And that a monk uncloistered is a mere
Fish out of water, flapping on the pier,

185 That is to say a monk out of his cloister.
That was a text he held not worth an oyster;
And I agreed and said his views were sound;
Was he to study till his head went round
Poring over books in cloisters? Must he toil

190 As Austin[26] bade and till the very soil?
Was he to leave the world upon the shelf?
Let Austin have his labor to himself.
    This Monk was therefore a good man to horse;
Greyhounds he had, as swift as birds, to course.

195 Hunting a hare or riding at a fence
Was all his fun, he spared for no expense.
I saw his sleeves were garnished at the hand
With fine gray fur, the finest in the land,
And on his hood, to fasten it at his chin

200 He had a wrought-gold cunningly fashioned pin;
Into a lover's knot it seemed to pass.
His head was bald and shone like looking-glass;
So did his face, as if it had been greased.
He was a fat and personable priest;

205 His prominent eyeballs never seemed to settle.
They glittered like the flames beneath a kettle;
Supple his boots, his horse in fine condition.
He was a prelate fit for exhibition,
He was not pale like a tormented soul.

210 He liked a fat swan best, and roasted whole.
His palfrey[27] was as brown as is a berry.
    There was a *Friar,* a wanton[28] one and merry
A Limiter,[29] a very festive fellow.
In all Four Orders[30] there was none so mellow,

215 So glib with gallant phrase and well-turned speech.
He'd fixed up many a marriage, giving each
Of his young women what he could afford her.
He was a noble pillar to his Order.
Highly beloved and intimate was he

▲ **Critical Viewing**
What can you infer from this picture about the Monk's style of living? List three details supporting your conclusion. **[Infer]**

Vocabulary
garnished (gär′ nisht) *adj.*
decorated; trimmed

---

26. **Austin** English version of St. Augustine, who criticized lazy monks.
27. **palfrey** *n.* saddle horse.
28. **wanton** *adj.* jolly.
29. **Limiter** friar who is given begging rights for a certain limited area.
30. **Four Orders** There were four orders of friars who supported themselves by begging: Dominicans, Franciscans, Carmelites, and Augustinians.

220 With County folk[31] within his boundary,
    And city dames of honor and possessions;
    For he was qualified to hear confessions,
    Or so he said, with more than priestly scope;
    He had a special license from the Pope.
225 Sweetly he heard his penitents at shrift[32]
    With pleasant absolution, for a gift.
    He was an easy man in penance-giving
    Where he could hope to make a decent living;
    It's a sure sign whenever gifts are given
230 To a poor Order that a man's well shriven,[33]
    And should he give enough he knew in verity
    The penitent repented in sincerity.
    For many a fellow is so hard of heart
    He cannot weep, for all his inward smart.
235 Therefore instead of weeping and of prayer
    One should give silver for a poor Friar's care.
    He kept his tippet[34] stuffed with pins for curls,
    And pocket-knives, to give to pretty girls.
    And certainly his voice was gay and sturdy,
240 For he sang well and played the hurdy-gurdy.[35]
    At sing-songs he was champion of the hour.
    His neck was whiter than a lily-flower
    But strong enough to butt a bruiser down.
    He knew the taverns well in every town
245 And every innkeeper and barmaid too
    Better than lepers, beggars and that crew,
    For in so eminent a man as he
    It was not fitting with the dignity
    Of his position, dealing with a scum
250 Of wretched lepers; nothing good can come
    Of dealings with the slum-and-gutter dwellers,
    But only with the rich and victual-sellers.
    But anywhere a profit might accrue
    Courteous he was and lowly of service too.
255 Natural gifts like his were hard to match.
    He was the finest beggar of his batch,
    And, for his begging-district, payed a rent;
    His brethren did no poaching where he went.
    For though a widow mightn't have a shoe,
260 So pleasant was his holy how-d'ye-do
    He got his farthing from her just the same

---

31. **County folk** The phrase refers to rich landowners.
32. **shrift** *n.* confession.
33. **well shriven** *adj.* absolved of his sins.
34. **tippet** *n.* hood.
35. **hurdy-gurdy** stringed instrument played by cranking a wheel.

Literary Analysis
Characterization
In lines 244–254, is Chaucer
using direct characterization
or indirect characterization?
Explain.

Reading Check

How does the Friar
earn his living?

▼ **Critical Viewing**
What can you infer from this picture about the Oxford Cleric's style of living?
[Infer]

Before he left, and so his income came
To more than he laid out. And how he romped,
Just like a puppy! He was ever prompt
265 To arbitrate disputes on settling days
(For a small fee) in many helpful ways,
Not then appearing as your cloistered scholar
With threadbare habit hardly worth a dollar,
But much more like a Doctor or a Pope.
270 Of double-worsted was the semi-cope[36]
Upon his shoulders, and the swelling fold
About him, like a bell about its mold
When it is casting, rounded out his dress.
He lisped a little out of wantonness
275 To make his English sweet upon his tongue.
When he had played his harp, or having sung,
His eyes would twinkle in his head as bright
As any star upon a frosty night.
This worthy's name was Hubert, it appeared.
280   There was a *Merchant* with a forking beard
And motley dress, high on his horse he sat,
Upon his head a Flemish[37] beaver hat
And on his feet daintily buckled boots.
He told of his opinions and pursuits
285 In solemn tones, and how he never lost.
The sea should be kept free at any cost
(He thought) upon the Harwich-Holland range,[38]
He was expert at currency exchange.
This estimable Merchant so had set
290 His wits to work, none knew he was in debt,
He was so stately in negotiation,
Loan, bargain and commercial obligation.
He was an excellent fellow all the same;
To tell the truth I do not know his name.
295   An *Oxford Cleric,* still a student though,
One who had taken logic long ago,
Was there; his horse was thinner than a rake,
And he was not too fat, I undertake,
But had a hollow look, a sober stare;

---

36. semi-cope cape.
37. Flemish from Flanders.
38. Harwich-Holland range the North Sea between England and Holland.

300 The thread upon his overcoat was bare.
He had found no preferment in the church
And he was too unworldly to make search
For secular employment. By his bed
He preferred having twenty books in red
305 And black, of Aristotle's[39] philosophy,
To having fine clothes, fiddle or psaltery.[40]
Though a philosopher, as I have told,
He had not found the stone for making gold.[41]
Whatever money from his friends he took
310 He spent on learning or another book
And prayed for them most earnestly, returning
Thanks to them thus for paying for his learning.
His only care was study, and indeed
He never spoke a word more than was need,
315 Formal at that, respectful in the extreme,
Short, to the point, and lofty in his theme.
The thought of moral virtue filled his speech
And he would gladly learn, and gladly teach.
  A *Sergeant at the Law* who paid his calls,
320 Wary and wise, for clients at St. Paul's[42]
There also was, of noted excellence.
Discreet he was, a man to reverence,
Or so he seemed, his sayings were so wise.
He often had been Justice of Assize
325 By letters patent, and in full commission.
His fame and learning and his high position
Had won him many a robe and many a fee.
There was no such conveyancer[43] as he;
All was fee-simple[44] to his strong digestion,
330 Not one conveyance could be called in question.
Nowhere there was so busy a man as he;
But was less busy than he seemed to be.
He knew of every judgment, case and crime
Recorded, ever since King William's time.
335 He could dictate defenses or draft deeds;
No one could pinch a comma from his screeds,[45]

Spiral Review
Understanding Historical Context
What inferences can you make about the economic ideas of the time based on the suggestion that the Clerk's attitude toward money is unusual?

Vocabulary
commission (kə mish′ ən) *n.* authorization; act of giving authority to an individual

Reading Check
What are the Cleric's interests?

---

39. Aristotle's (ar′ is tät′ əlz) referring to the Greek philosopher (384–322 B.C.).
40. psaltery (sôl′ tər ē) ancient stringed instrument.
41. stone . . . gold At the time, alchemists believed that a "philosopher's stone" existed that could turn base metals into gold.
42. St. Paul's London cathedral near the center of legal activities in the city. Lawyers often met near there to discuss cases.
43. conveyancer one who draws up documents for transferring ownership of property.
44. fee-simple unrestricted ownership.
45. screeds long, boring speeches or pieces of writing.

And he knew every statute off by rote.
He wore a homely parti-colored coat
Girt with a silken belt of pin-stripe stuff;
340 Of his appearance I have said enough.
　　　There was a *Franklin*[46] with him, it appeared;
White as a daisy-petal was his beard.
A sanguine man, high-colored and benign,
He loved a morning sop[47] of cake in wine.
345 He lived for pleasure and had always done,
For he was Epicurus'[48] very son,
In whose opinion sensual delight
Was the one true felicity in sight.
As noted as St. Julian[49] was for bounty
350 He made his household free to all the County.
His bread, his ale were the finest of the fine
And no one had a better stock of wine.
His house was never short of bake-meat pies,
Of fish and flesh, and these in such supplies
355 It positively snowed with meat and drink
And all the dainties that a man could think.
According to the seasons of the year
Changes of dish were ordered to appear.
He kept fat partridges in coops, beyond,
360 Many a bream and pike were in his pond.
Woe to the cook whose sauces had no sting
Or who was unprepared in anything!
And in his hall a table stood arrayed
And ready all day long, with places laid.
365 As Justice at the Sessions[50] none stood higher;
He often had been Member for the Shire.[51]
A dagger and a little purse of silk
Hung at his girdle, white as morning milk.
As Sheriff he checked audit, every entry.
370 He was a model among landed gentry.
　　　A *Haberdasher*, a *Dyer*, a *Carpenter*,
A *Weaver* and a *Carpet-maker* were
Among our ranks, all in the livery
Of one impressive guild-fraternity.[52]

Vocabulary
sanguine (san´ gwin) *adj.*
confident; cheerful

Reading Strategy
Questioning What
question do lines 346–348
answer about the main idea
in line 345?

Literary Analysis
Characterization
What are the Franklin's
interests?

---

46. *Franklin* wealthy landowner.
47. **sop** piece.
48. **Epicurus'** (ep´ i kyoor´ əs) referring to a Greek philosopher (341–270 B.C.) who
    believed that happiness is the most important goal in life.
49. **St. Julian** patron saint of hospitality.
50. **Sessions** court sessions.
51. **Member . . . Shire** Parliamentary representative for the county.
52. **guild-fraternity** In the Middle Ages, associations of men practicing the same craft
    or trade, called guilds, set standards for workmanship and protected their members
    by controlling competition.

375 They were so trim and fresh their gear would pass
     For new. Their knives were not tricked out with brass
     But wrought with purest silver, which avouches
     A like display on girdles and on pouches.
     Each seemed a worthy burgess,[53] fit to grace
380 A guild-hall with a seat upon the dais.
     Their wisdom would have justified a plan
     To make each one of them an alderman;
     They had the capital and revenue,
     Besides their wives declared it was their due.
385 And if they did not think so, then they ought;
     To be called "*Madam*" is a glorious thought,
     And so is going to church and being seen
     Having your mantle carried like a queen.
          They had a *Cook* with them who stood alone
390 For boiling chicken with a marrow-bone,
     Sharp flavoring-powder and a spice for savor.
     He could distinguish London ale by flavor,
     And he could roast and seethe and broil and fry,
     Make good thick soup and bake a tasty pie.
395 But what a pity—so it seemed to me,
     That he should have an ulcer on his knee.
     As for blancmange,[54] he made it with the best.
          There was a *Skipper* hailing from far west;
     He came from Dartmouth, so I understood.
400 He rode a farmer's horse as best he could,
     In a woolen gown that reached his knee.
     A dagger on a lanyard[55] falling free
     Hung from his neck under his arm and down.
     The summer heat had tanned his color brown,
405 And certainly he was an excellent fellow.
     Many a draught of vintage, red and yellow,
     He'd drawn at Bordeaux, while the trader snored.
     The nicer rules of conscience he ignored.
     If, when he fought, the enemy vessel sank,
410 He sent his prisoners home; they walked the plank.
     As for his skill in reckoning his tides,
     Currents and many another risk besides,
     Moons, harbors, pilots, he had such dispatch
     That none from Hull to Carthage was his match.
415 Hardy he was, prudent in undertaking;
     His beard in many a tempest had its shaking,
     And he knew all the havens as they were
     From Gottland to the Cape of Finisterre,

Literary Analysis
Characterization and Social Commentary
What point is Chaucer making about the relationship between these men and their wives?

Literary Analysis
Characterization
What picture of the Skipper is created by the mixture of details about his heartlessness with details about his competence?

Reading Check
What are two characteristics of the Skipper?

---

53. burgess member of a legislative body.
54. blancmange (blə mänzh′) at the time, the name of a creamy chicken dish.
55. lanyard loose rope around the neck.

Reading Strategy
Questioning In the
sentence in lines 421–428,
what is said about *how* the
Doctor practices medicine?

And every creek in Brittany and Spain;
420   The barge he owned was called *The Maudelayne*.
        A *Doctor* too emerged as we proceeded;
No one alive could talk as well as he did
On points of medicine and of surgery,
For, being grounded in astronomy,
425   He watched his patient's favorable star
And, by his Natural Magic, knew what are
The lucky hours and planetary degrees
For making charms and magic effigies.
The cause of every malady you'd got
430   He knew, and whether dry, cold, moist or hot;[56]
He knew their seat, their humor and condition.
He was a perfect practicing physician.
These causes being known for what they were,
He gave the man his medicine then and there.
435   All his apothecaries[57] in a tribe
Were ready with the drugs he would prescribe,
And each made money from the other's guile;
They had been friendly for a goodish while.
He was well-versed in Aesculapius[58] too
440   And what Hippocrates and Rufus knew
And Dioscorides, now dead and gone,
Galen and Rhazes, Hali, Serapion,
Averroes, Avicenna, Constantine,
Scotch Bernard, John of Gaddesden, Gilbertine.[59]
445   In his own diet he observed some measure;
There were no superfluities for pleasure,
Only digestives, nutritives and such.
He did not read the Bible very much.
In blood-red garments, slashed with bluish-gray
450   And lined with taffeta,[60] he rode his way;
Yet he was rather close as to expenses
And kept the gold he won in pestilences.
Gold stimulates the heart, or so we're told.
He therefore had a special love of gold.
455   A worthy *woman* from beside Bath[61] city
Was with us, somewhat deaf, which was a pity.
In making cloth she showed so great a bent

---

56. **The cause . . . hot** It was believed that the body was composed of four "humors" (cold
    and dry, hot and moist, hot and dry, cold and moist) and that diseases resulted from a
    disturbance of one of these "humors."
57. **apothecaries** (ə päth′ə ker′ ēz) persons who prepared medicines.
58. **Aesculapius** (es′ kyoo lā′ pē əs) in Roman mythology, the god of medicine and healing.
59. **Hippocrates . . . Gilbertine** famous physicians and medical authorities.
60. **taffeta** (taf′ i tə) fine silk fabric.
61. **Bath** English resort city.

She bettered those of Ypres and of Ghent.[62]
In all the parish not a dame dared stir
460 Towards the altar steps in front of her,
And if indeed they did, so wrath was she
As to be quite put out of charity.
Her kerchiefs were of finely woven ground;[63]
I dared have sworn they weighed a good ten pound,
465 The ones she wore on Sunday, on her head.
Her hose were of the finest scarlet red
And gartered tight; her shoes were soft and new.
Bold was her face, handsome, and red in hue.
A worthy woman all her life, what's more
470 She'd had five husbands, all at the church door,
Apart from other company in youth;
No need just now to speak of that, forsooth.
And she had thrice been to Jerusalem,
Seen many strange rivers and passed over them;
475 She'd been to Rome and also to Boulogne,
St. James of Compostella and Cologne,[64]
And she was skilled in wandering by the way.
She had gap-teeth, set widely, truth to say.
Easily on an ambling horse she sat
480 Well wimpled[65] up, and on her head a hat
As broad as is a buckler[66] or a shield;
She had a flowing mantle that concealed
Large hips, her heels spurred sharply under that.
In company she liked to laugh and chat
485 And knew the remedies for love's mischances,
An art in which she knew the oldest dances.

A holy-minded man of good renown
There was, and poor, the *Parson* to a town,
Yet he was rich in holy thought and work.
490 He also was a learned man, a clerk,
Who truly knew Christ's gospel and would preach it
Devoutly to parishioners, and teach it.
Benign and wonderfully diligent,
And patient when adversity was sent
495 (For so he proved in great adversity)
He much disliked extorting tithe[67] or fee,
Nay rather he preferred beyond a doubt
Giving to poor parishioners round about

▼ **Critical Viewing**
What does the Wife
of Bath's pose convey
about her character?
[Analyze]

The Wife of Bath, Arthur Szyk for *The Canterbury Tales*

Reading Check
What is the Parson's main
characteristic?

---

62. Ypres (ē′ prə) **and of Ghent** (gent) Flemish cities known for wool making.
63. ground composite fabric.
64. Jerusalem . . . Rome . . . Boulogne . . . St. James of Compostella . . . Cologne famous pilgrimage sites at the time.
65. wimpled wearing a scarf covering the head, neck, and chin.
66. buckler small round shield.
67. tithe (tīth) one tenth of a person's income, paid as a tax to support the church.

Literary Analysis
Characterization and
Social Commentary
How does Chaucer use his characterization of the Parson to comment on the way priests ought to behave?

From his own goods and Easter offerings
500 He found sufficiency in little things.
Wide was his parish, with houses far asunder,
Yet he neglected not in rain or thunder,
In sickness or in grief, to pay a call
On the remotest, whether great or small,
505 Upon his feet, and in his hand a stave.
This noble example to his sheep he gave,
First following the word before he taught it,
And it was from the gospel he had caught it.
This little proverb he would add thereto
510 That if gold rust, what then will iron do?
For if a priest be foul in whom we trust
No wonder that a common man should rust;
And shame it is to see—let priests take stock—
A soiled shepherd and a snowy flock.
515 The true example that a priest should give
Is one of cleanness, how the sheep should live.
He did not set his benefice to hire[68]
And leave his sheep encumbered in the mire
Or run to London to earn easy bread
520 By singing masses for the wealthy dead,
Or find some Brotherhood and get enrolled.
He stayed at home and watched over his fold
So that no wolf should make the sheep miscarry.
He was a shepherd and no mercenary.
525 Holy and virtuous he was, but then
Never contemptuous of sinful men,
Never disdainful, never too proud or fine,
But was discreet in teaching and benign.
His business was to show a fair behavior
530 And draw men thus to Heaven and their Savior,
Unless indeed a man were obstinate;
And such, whether of high or low estate,
He put to sharp rebuke to say the least.
I think there never was a better priest.
535 He sought no pomp or glory in his dealings,
No scrupulosity had spiced his feelings.
Christ and His Twelve Apostles and their lore
He taught, but followed it himself before.
      There was a *Plowman* with him there, his brother.
540 Many a load of dung one time or other
He must have carted through the morning dew.
He was an honest worker, good and true,

---

68. set . . . hire pay someone else to perform his parish duties.

Living in peace and perfect charity,
And, as the gospel bade him, so did he,
545 Loving God best with all his heart and mind
And then his neighbor as himself, repined
At no misfortune, slacked for no content,
For steadily about his work he went
To thrash his corn, to dig or to manure
550 Or make a ditch; and he would help the poor
For love of Christ and never take a penny
If he could help it, and, as prompt as any,
He paid his tithes in full when they were due
On what he owned, and on his earnings too.
555 He wore a tabard⁶⁹ smock and rode a mare.
There was a *Reeve*,⁷⁰ also a *Miller*, there,
A College *Manciple*⁷¹ from the Inns of Court,
A papal *Pardoner*⁷² and, in close consort,
A Church-Court *Summoner*,⁷³ riding at a trot,
560 And finally myself—that was the lot.

        The *Miller* was a chap of sixteen stone,⁷⁴
A great stout fellow big in brawn and bone.
He did well out of them, for he could go
And win the ram at any wrestling show.
565 Broad, knotty and short-shouldered, he would boast
He could heave any door off hinge and post,
Or take a run and break it with his head.
His beard, like any sow or fox, was red
And broad as well, as though it were a spade;
570 And, at its very tip, his nose displayed
A wart on which there stood a tuft of hair,
Red as the bristles in an old sow's ear.
His nostrils were as black as they were wide.
He had a sword and buckler at his side,
575 His mighty mouth was like a furnace door.
A wrangler and buffoon, he had a store
Of tavern stories, filthy in the main.
His was a master-hand at stealing grain.
He felt it with his thumb and thus he knew
580 Its quality and took three times his due—
A thumb of gold, by God, to gauge an oat!
He wore a hood of blue and a white coat.
He liked to play his bagpipes up and down
And that was how he brought us out of town.

---

69. **tabard** loose jacket.
70. ***Reeve*** estate manager.
71. ***Manciple*** buyer of provisions.
72. ***Pardoner*** one who dispenses papal pardons.
73. ***Summoner*** one who serves summonses to church courts.
74. **sixteen stone** 224 pounds. A stone equals 14 pounds.

▲ **Critical Viewing**
Compare this portrait of the Miller with lines 561–584. What details did the illustrator choose to change or omit? **[Compare and Constrast]**

Reading Check

What is the Plowman like?

Reading Strategy
Questioning What are the two subjects of the comparison in lines 594–604?

585 The *Manciple* came from the Inner Temple;
All caterers might follow his example
In buying victuals; he was never rash
Whether he bought on credit or paid cash.
He used to watch the market most precisely
590 And go in first, and so he did quite nicely.
Now isn't it a marvel of God's grace
That an illiterate fellow can outpace
The wisdom of a heap of learned men?
His masters—he had more than thirty then—
595 All versed in the abstrusest legal knowledge,
Could have produced a dozen from their College
Fit to be stewards in land and rents and game
To any Peer in England you could name,
And show him how to live on what he had
600 Debt-free (unless of course the Peer were mad)
Or be as frugal as he might desire,
And they were fit to help about the Shire
In any legal case there was to try;
And yet this Manciple could wipe their eye.

605 The *Reeve* was old and choleric and thin;
His beard was shaven closely to the skin,
His shorn hair came abruptly to a stop
Above his ears, and he was docked on top
Just like a priest in front; his legs were lean,
610 Like sticks they were, no calf was to be seen.
He kept his bins and garners[75] very trim;
No auditor could gain a point on him.
And he could judge by watching drought and rain
The yield he might expect from seed and grain.
615 His master's sheep, his animals and hens,
Pigs, horses, dairies, stores and cattle-pens
Were wholly trusted to his government.
And he was under contract to present
The accounts, right from his master's earliest years.
620 No one had ever caught him in arrears.
No bailiff, serf or herdsman dared to kick,
He knew their dodges, knew their every trick;
Feared like the plague he was, by those beneath.
He had a lovely dwelling on a heath,
625 Shadowed in green by trees above the sward.[76]
A better hand at bargains than his lord,
He had grown rich and had a store of treasure
Well tucked away, yet out it came to pleasure

---

75. garners *n.* buildings for storing grain.
76. sward *n.* turf.

His lord with subtle loans or gifts of goods,
630 To earn his thanks and even coats and hoods.
When young he'd learnt a useful trade and still
He was a carpenter of first-rate skill.
The stallion-cob he rode at a slow trot
Was dapple-gray and bore the name of Scot.
635 He wore an overcoat of bluish shade
And rather long; he had a rusty blade
Slung at his side. He came, as I heard tell,
From Norfolk, near a place called Baldeswell.
His coat was tucked under his belt and splayed.
640 He rode the hindmost of our cavalcade.
There was a *Summoner* with us in the place
Who had a fire-red cherubinnish face,[77]
For he had carbuncles.[78] His eyes were narrow,
He was as hot and lecherous as a sparrow.
645 Black, scabby brows he had, and a thin beard.
Children were afraid when he appeared.
No quicksilver, lead ointments, tartar creams,
Boracic, no, nor brimstone,[79] so it seems,
Could make a salve that had the power to bite,
650 Clean up or cure his whelks[80] of knobby white.
Or purge the pimples sitting on his cheeks.
Garlic he loved, and onions too, and leeks,
And drinking strong wine till all was hazy.
Then he would shout and jabber as if crazy,
655 And wouldn't speak a word except in Latin
When he was drunk, such tags as he was pat in;
He only had a few, say two or three,
That he had mugged up out of some decree;
No wonder, for he heard them every day.
660 And, as you know, a man can teach a jay
To call out "Walter" better than the Pope.
But had you tried to test his wits and grope
For more, you'd have found nothing in the bag.
Then "*Questio quid juris*"[81] was his tag.
665 He was a gentle varlet and a kind one,
No better fellow if you went to find one.
He would allow—just for a quart of wine—

▲ **Critical Viewing**
What can you infer from this picture about the Summoner's personality? List three details supporting your conclusion. **[Infer]**

Reading
Check
How do serfs and herdsmen view the Reeve?

---

77. fire-red . . . face In the art of the Middle Ages, the faces of cherubs, or angels, were often painted red.
78. carbuncles (kär´ buŋ´ kəlz) *n.* pus-filled boils resulting from a bacterial infection under the skin.
79. quicksilver . . . brimstone various chemicals and chemical compounds, used as remedies. *Quicksilver* is a name for mercury. *Brimstone* is a name for sulfur.
80. whelks *n.* pustules; pimples.
81. "Questio quid juris" "The question is, What is the point of law?" (Latin).

Any good lad to keep a concubine
A twelvemonth and dispense it altogether!
670 Yet he could pluck a finch to leave no feather:
And if he found some rascal with a maid
He would instruct him not to be afraid
In such a case of the Archdeacon's curse
(Unless the rascal's soul were in his purse)
675 For in his purse the punishment should be.
"Purse is the good Archdeacon's Hell," said he.
But well I know he lied in what he said;
A curse should put a guilty man in dread,
For curses kill, as shriving brings, salvation.
680 We should beware of excommunication.
Thus, as he pleased, the man could bring duress
On any young fellow in the diocese.
He knew their secrets, they did what he said.
He wore a garland set upon his head
685 Large as the holly-bush upon a stake
Outside an ale-house, and he had a cake,
A round one, which it was his joke to wield
As if it were intended for a shield.
  He and a gentle *Pardoner* rode together,
690 A bird from Charing Cross of the same feather,
Just back from visiting the Court of Rome.
He loudly sang "*Come hither, love, come home!*"
The Summoner sang deep seconds to this song,
No trumpet ever sounded half so strong.
695 This Pardoner had hair as yellow as wax,
Hanging down smoothly like a hank of flax.
In driblets fell his locks behind his head
Down to his shoulder which they overspread;
Thinly they fell, like rat-tails, one by one.
700 He wore no hood upon his head, for fun;
The hood inside his wallet had been stowed,
He aimed at riding in the latest mode;
But for a little cap his head was bare
And he had bulging eyeballs, like a hare.
705 He'd sewed a holy relic on his cap;
His wallet lay before him on his lap,
Brimful of pardons come from Rome all hot.
He had the same small voice a goat has got.
His chin no beard had harbored, nor would harbor,
710 Smoother than ever chin was left by barber.
I judge he was a gelding, or a mare.

▲ **Critical Viewing**
How well does this picture
of the Pardoner match
Chaucer's description of him
in lines 695–710? **[Assess]**

As to his trade, from Berwick down to Ware
There was no pardoner of equal grace,
For in his trunk he had a pillowcase
715 Which he asserted was Our Lady's veil.
He said he had a gobbet[82] of the sail
Saint Peter had the time when he made bold
To walk the waves, till Jesu Christ took hold.
He had a cross of metal set with stones
720 And, in a glass, a rubble of pigs' bones.
And with these relics, any time he found
Some poor up-country parson to astound,
On one short day, in money down, he drew
More than the parson in a month or two,
725 And by his flatteries and prevarication
Made monkeys of the priest and congregation.
But still to do him justice first and last
In church he was a noble ecclesiast.
How well he read a lesson or told a story!
730 But best of all he sang an Offertory,[83]
For well he knew that when that song was sung
He'd have to preach and tune his honey-tongue
And (well he could) win silver from the crowd.
That's why he sang so merrily and loud.
735   Now I have told you shortly, in a clause,
The rank, the array, the number and the cause
Of our assembly in this company
In Southwark, at that high-class hostelry
Known as *The Tabard*, close beside *The Bell*.
740 And now the time has come for me to tell
How we behaved that evening; I'll begin
After we had alighted at the inn,
Then I'll report our journey, stage by stage,
All the remainder of our pilgrimage.
745 But first I beg of you, in courtesy,
Not to condemn me as unmannerly
If I speak plainly and with no concealings
And give account of all their words and dealings,
Using their very phrases as they fell.
750 For certainly, as you all know so well,
He who repeats a tale after a man

Literary Analysis
Characterization
What facts in lines 719–726 indirectly characterize the Pardoner?

Vocabulary
prevarication (pri var´ i kā´ shən) *n.* evasion of truth

Reading Strategy
Questioning Why does Chaucer apologize in the sentence starting with line 745?

Reading
Check

What two things does Chaucer promise to tell the reader?

---

82. gobbet piece.
83. Offertory song that accompanies the collection of the offering at a church service.

The Literature of Social Observation

Chaucer was just one author in a long tradition of British writers who detailed ironic observations of social types. Four centuries later, for instance, eighteenth-century writers such as Joseph Addison held up a mirror to middle-class society, describing the typical characters of the day and their follies.

The tradition of social commentary bloomed with the invention of the novel, a form built around keen observations of character and society. Yet the novel emphasized the individual in a way that earlier literature often did not. The characters of nineteenth-century novelist Charles Dickens, for instance, take on their social roles with extravagant, individual style. In a sense, though, Dickens was only following Chaucer. In pilgrims such as the Wife of Bath, the Skipper, and the Host, you can already detect a spark of vital individuality, deeper than any social role.

Connect to the Literature

Identify three ways in which the Wife of Bath both fits and defies the stereotype of a woman of her time.

Is bound to say, as nearly as he can,
Each single word, if he remembers it,
However rudely spoken or unfit,
755 Or else the tale he tells will be untrue,
The things invented and the phrases new.
He may not flinch although it were his brother,
If he says one word he must say the other.
And Christ Himself spoke broad[84] in Holy Writ,
760 And as you know there's nothing there unfit,
And Plato[85] says, for those with power to read,
"The word should be as cousin to the deed."
Further I beg you to forgive it me
If I neglect the order and degree
765 And what is due to rank in what I've planned.
I'm short of wit as you will understand.
　　　Our *Host* gave us great welcome; everyone
Was given a place and supper was begun.
He served the finest victuals you could think,
770 The wine was strong and we were glad to drink.
A very striking man our Host withal,
And fit to be a marshal in a hall.
His eyes were bright, his girth a little wide;
There is no finer burgess in Cheapside.[86]
775 Bold in his speech, yet wise and full of tact,
There was no manly attribute he lacked,
What's more he was a merry-hearted man.
After our meal he jokingly began
To talk of sport, and, among other things
780 After we'd settled up our reckonings,
He said as follows: "Truly, gentlemen,
You're very welcome and I can't think when
—Upon my word I'm telling you no lie—
I've seen a gathering here that looked so spry,
785 No, not this year, as in this tavern now.
I'd think you up some fun if I knew how.
And, as it happens, a thought has just occurred
And it will cost you nothing, on my word.
You're off to Canterbury—well, God speed!
790 Blessed St. Thomas answer to your need!
And I don't doubt, before the journey's done

---

84. broad bluntly.
85. Plato Greek philosopher (427?–347? B.C.).
86. Cheapside district in London.

You mean to while the time in tales and fun.
Indeed, there's little pleasure for your bones
Riding along and all as dumb as stones.
795 So let me then propose for your enjoyment,
Just as I said, a suitable employment.
And if my notion suits and you agree
And promise to submit yourselves to me
Playing your parts exactly as I say
800 Tomorrow as you ride along the way,
Then by my father's soul (and he is dead)
If you don't like it you can have my head!
Hold up your hands, and not another word."
      Well, our consent of course was not deferred,
805 It seemed not worth a serious debate;
We all agreed to it at any rate
And bade him issue what commands he would.
"My lords," he said, "now listen for your good,
And please don't treat my notion with disdain.
810 This is the point. I'll make it short and plain.
Each one of you shall help to make things slip
By telling two stories on the outward trip
To Canterbury, that's what I intend,
And, on the homeward way to journey's end
815 Another two, tales from the days of old;
And then the man whose story is best told,
That is to say who gives the fullest measure
Of good morality and general pleasure,
He shall be given a supper, paid by all,
820 Here in this tavern, in this very hall,
When we come back again from Canterbury.
And in the hope to keep you bright and merry
I'll go along with you myself and ride
All at my own expense and serve as guide.
825 I'll be the judge, and those who won't obey
Shall pay for what we spend upon the way.
Now if you all agree to what you've heard
Tell me at once without another word,
And I will make arrangements early for it."
830   Of course we all agreed, in fact we swore it
Delightedly, and made entreaty too
That he should act as he proposed to do,

Literary Analysis
Characterization What
does the Host's decision
to accompany the pilgrims
suggest about him?

Become our Governor in short, and be
Judge of our tales and general referee,
835 And set the supper at a certain price.
We promised to be ruled by his advice
Come high, come low; unanimously thus
We set him up in judgment over us.
More wine was fetched, the business being done;
840 We drank it off and up went everyone
To bed without a moment of delay.
     Early next morning at the spring of day
Up rose our Host and roused us like a cock,
Gathering us together in a flock,
845 And off we rode at slightly faster pace
Than walking to St. Thomas' watering-place;[87]
And there our Host drew up, began to ease
His horse, and said, "Now, listen if you please,

---

87. St. Thomas' watering-place a brook two miles from the inn.

▶ **Critical Viewing**
What can you infer about
the personalities of these
monks from this illustration?
[Infer]

My lords! Remember what you promised me.
850 If evensong and matins will agree[88]
Let's see who shall be first to tell a tale.
And as I hope to drink good wine and ale
I'll be your judge. The rebel who disobeys,
However much the journey costs, he pays.
855 Now draw for cut[89] and then we can depart;
The man who draws the shortest cut shall start."

---

88. If evensong . . . agree "if what you said last night holds true this morning."
89. draw for cut draw lots, as when pulling straws from a bunch; the person who pulls the short straw is "it."

Critical Reading

1. **Key Ideas and Details** **(a)** List three characteristics of the Nun. **(b) Deduce:** What details does Chaucer include in his description of the Nun to make gentle fun of her? Explain.

2. **Key Ideas and Details** **(a)** Identify two of the main characteristics of the Friar and the Parson. **(b) Compare and Contrast:** What are some of the ways in which the Friar and the Parson differ?

3. **Key Ideas and Details** Judging from the descriptions of the Friar and the Parson, what does Chaucer think can cause a religious person to fail in his or her duty?

4. **Key Ideas and Details** How does Chaucer's attitude toward the Monk differ, if at all, from his attitude toward the Friar? Explain.

5. **Integration of Knowledge and Ideas** **(a) Apply:** What modern character types match the characters in the Prologue? **(b) Apply:** What types would Chaucer not have anticipated? Explain.

6. **Integration of Knowledge and Ideas** **(a) Analyze:** From what segments of medieval society do the pilgrims come? **(b) Draw Conclusions:** What does their participation in a common pilgrimage suggest about the times?

7. **Integration of Knowledge and Ideas** Judging from his pilgrims, do you think Chaucer believes people are basically good, basically evil, or often a mix of the two? Give examples to support your answer.

8. **Integration of Knowledge and Ideas** Do you think Chaucer's view of people is justified? Explain.

9. **Integration of Knowledge and Ideas** Explain what a description of clothing reveals about a character and about medieval society. Use two of these Essential Question words: *echelon, distinct, approbation, condemn.* **[Connecting to the Essential Question: How does literature shape or reflect society?]**

Cite textual evidence to support your responses.

After You Read | from *The Canterbury Tales: The Prologue*

Literary Analysis

1. Key Ideas and Details Give three details that Chaucer uses to **characterize** the Doctor. For each, note whether the characterization is **direct** or **indirect**.

2. Key Ideas and Details **(a)** Find one example of each of the following kinds of details in Chaucer's characterizations: direct statement, physical description, character's action. **(b)** Explain how your examples of physical description and action indirectly characterize that pilgrim.

3. Craft and Structure **(a)** Identify an example in which Chaucer uses mild sarcasm in describing a character. **(b)** Explain how his *tone*, or attitude, changes the meaning of the description.

4. Craft and Structure Choose the character sketch you find most effective. Explain the method Chaucer uses to make the sketch so vivid.

5. Integration of Knowledge and Ideas Use a chart like the one shown to reflect on the **social commentary** in the Prologue. **(a)** What social comment does Chaucer make in his sketch of the Pardoner? **(b)** What does the sketch of the Knight suggest were some of the virtues promoted by medieval society?

Character	Detail	Implication About Society

6. Integration of Knowledge and Ideas Most of Chaucer's characters are named after a profession. What does this emphasis on the characters' social roles suggest about medieval society?

7. Integration of Knowledge and Ideas **(a)** If Chaucer were writing today, what three kinds of pilgrims might he consider adding to the group? Explain your choices. **(b)** Describe how each of your twenty-first-century pilgrims would dress and speak.

Reading Strategy

8. Suppose you were having trouble understanding the sentence in lines 47–50. Practice **repairing your comprehension** of the sentence by **questioning**. What essential information do you discover by asking *When?, Who?, Where?, What?, Why?,* and *How?*

9. Use the same questioning technique to analyze the sentence in lines 529–533.

10. Find and analyze another sentence from the Prologue, especially one that continues through many lines. Remember that asking basic questions will help you unlock its meaning.

Common Core State Standards

Writing
5. Develop and strengthen writing as needed by planning, revising, editing, rewriting, or trying a new approach, focusing on addressing what is most significant for a specific purpose and audience. *(p. 121)*

Language
4.a. Use context as a clue to the meaning of a word or phrase. *(p. 121)*

© Vocabulary Acquisition and Use

Word Analysis: Latin Suffix -tion

The suffix -tion means "the act or process of" or "the result of the act or process of." For example, prevaricate means "to distort the truth"; prevarication means "the act of distorting the truth." Likewise, absolve means "to free someone of a sin"; absolution refers to the act of freeing some one from a sin, and also to the state of freedom that results from being absolved. With a small group, write a short paragraph about some of Chaucer's pilgrims. Include at least four of the following words in your paragraph:

1. flirtation	**4.** devotion
2. decoration	**5.** negotiation
3. narration	**6.** digestion

Then, choose two of the words used in your paragraph. For each, write a sentence explaining how the suffix -tion helps contribute to the meaning of the word.

Vocabulary: Context Clues

The context of a word is the other words, phrases, and sentences that come before and after the word and that may provide clues to its meaning. For each underlined word that appears below, explain how clues in the paragraph help you infer the word's contextual meaning.

A motley group of pilgrims gathered for a journey. The first was a stout, <u>sanguine</u> cook who greeted each newcomer with a jolly "Hallo!" The second was a noblewoman whose gowns were <u>garnished</u> with emeralds and pearls. The third, a young clerk, was traveling on <u>commission</u> from his employer; he made his errand sound so lofty and important that the other pilgrims suspected him of <u>prevarication</u>. The fourth, a widow, believed the clerk was telling the truth and behaved in a kind, <u>solicitous</u> manner toward him. The fifth said he was naught but a sinner, and that he sought naught but <u>absolution</u> for his crimes.

Writing

© **Narrative Text** A blog is a Web site where entries on a particular subject are written and posted in reverse chronological order on a single homepage. Show your understanding of the Prologue by starting a **pilgrimage blog.** Write an introduction as the Host. Then, add postings from several pilgrims in which they express their thoughts, hopes, and fears about the journey.

Prewriting First, decide on a pilgrimage-related topic—the more controversial, the better. Review Chaucer's description of each character and jot down several opinions each might hold about this topic.

Drafting As you draft your postings, use language that strongly expresses each pilgrim's personality.

Revising As you revise, check to make sure you have written each posting in character and that you have stayed on topic. Revise language that slips out of character, and delete details that are irrelevant.

Model: Revising for a Consistent Voice

The Franklin says:

I find the idea of rationing our provisions to be ~~interesting, but a bit extreme~~ not only impractical, but downright insulting! It is my custom to carry an abundant supply of cake and beverage, and to indulge at will—and also to share what I have with fellow-travelers.

The Franklin is a cheerful character, so the angry language doesn't fit. The revision strikes a polite and cordial tone.

Critical Commentary

Geoffrey Chaucer: Father of English Literature

Long had our dull Fore-Fathers slept Supine,
Nor felt the Raptures of the Tuneful Nine;
Till Chaucer first, a merry Bard, arose;
And many a Story told in Rhyme and Prose.

This stanza, penned by English author Joseph Addison in 1694, expresses the general view of Chaucer expressed by most English writers who followed him. The "Tuneful Nine," or Muses—that is, the nine goddesses said to inspire the arts—were asleep in England until Chaucer came along. Addison's contemporary John Dryden, the great pioneer of English literary criticism, called Chaucer "the father of English poetry":

> *From Chaucer the purity of the English tongue began. . . . As he is the father of English poetry, so I hold him in the same degree of veneration as the Grecians held Homer or the Romans Virgil.*

▲ This imaginary British pound note depicts Chaucer as the Father of English Literature.

Romantic Age author William Hazlitt hailed Chaucer as "the first to tune his native tongue" and named him as a person from the past whom he would most like to meet:

> *He was himself a noble, manly character, standing before his age and striving to advance it; a pleasant humorist withal, who . . . would make as hearty a companion as mine host of the Tabard.*

The attitude toward Chaucer is summed up by twentieth-century author G. K. Chesterton:

> *. . . Shakespeare and Milton were the greatest sons of their country; but Chaucer was the Father of his Country, rather in the style of George Washington. And apart from that, he made something that has altered all Europe more than the Newspaper: the Novel. He was a novelist when there were no novels.*

Ⓒ **Key Ideas and Details** In what ways does the Prologue show Chaucer being (in Chesterton's words) "a novelist when there were no novels"? Explain.

Before You Read | from *The Pardoner's Tale*

Connecting to the Essential Question In this tale told by Chaucer's Pardoner, greed is an important motivation. Consider what you have observed about the power of greed. As you read, look for examples of greed in this tale, and notice its effects on the characters and action. Considering the influence of this motive will help you explore the Essential Question: **How does literature shape or reflect society?**

Literary Analysis

Allegories are narratives that have both literal and deeper, symbolic meanings. "The Pardoner's Tale" is a kind of allegory called an *exemplum,* Latin for "example." The tale is an exemplum against the sin of greed, and the Pardoner uses the tale to illustrate the point of one of his sermons, "Love of money is the root of all evil."

To teach its lesson effectively, an allegory must be easily understood and remembered by the listeners. For this reason, an allegory may use certain basic storytelling patterns, or **archetypal narrative elements,** found in folk literature around the world. These elements include the following:

- Characters, events, and other things that come in threes
- A test of the characters' morality
- A mysterious guide who helps point the way
- A just ending that rewards good or punishes evil

Because it is structured to contain such elements, the basic story in this tale survived retellings as it traveled from ancient India to Europe. As you read, note the archetypal elements that make the allegory and its moral clear and memorable.

Reading Strategy

© Preparing to Read Complex Texts If you cannot fully understand a passage at first, **reread** it and the surrounding passages. Rereading can help you clarify characters' identities, the sequence or causes of events, and puzzling language. As you read "The Pardoner's Tale," use a diagram like the one shown to clarify difficult passages.

Vocabulary

pallor (pal′ ər) *n.* unnatural lack of color; paleness (p. 129)

hoary (hôr′ ē) *adj.* white or gray with age (p. 129)

tarry (tar′ ē) *v.* to delay or linger (p. 132)

apothecary (ə päth′ ə ker′ ē) *n.* pharmacist; druggist (p. 132)

deftly (deft′ lē) *adv.* skillfully; with ease and quickness (p. 132)

sauntered (sôn′ tərd) *v.* walked at an unhurried pace (p. 132)

© Common Core State Standards

Reading Literature
5. Analyze how an author's choices concerning how to structure specific parts of a text contribute to its overall structure and meaning.

Passage

"He gathered lots and hid them in his hand...."

Reread Earlier Passage

"'We draw for lots and see the way it goes; / The one who draws the longest, lucky man,...'"

Clarification

"Drawing lots" must be like drawing straws: The one who draws the longest is "it."

PHLit
Online!
www.PHLitOnline.com

from The Pardoner's Tale **123**

from
The Pardoner's Tale

Geoffrey Chaucer
translated by Nevill Coghill

The Pardoner's Prologue

"My lords," he said, "in churches where I preach
I cultivate a haughty kind of speech
And ring it out as roundly as a bell;
I've got it all by heart, the tale I tell.
5   I have a text, it always is the same
And always has been, since I learnt the game,
Old as the hills and fresher than the grass,
Radix malorum est cupiditas."[1]

⟫⟫⬥⟪

*The Pardoner explains how he introduces
himself to a congregation, showing official documents
and offering relics as cures for various problems.
Next, he explains how he preaches.*

⟫⟫⬥⟪

"Then, priestlike in my pulpit, with a frown,
10   I stand, and when the yokels[2] have sat down,
I preach, as you have heard me say before,
And tell a hundred lying mockeries[3] more.
I take great pains, and stretching out my neck
To east and west I crane about and peck
15   Just like a pigeon sitting on a barn.
My hands and tongue together spin the yarn
And all my antics[4] are a joy to see.
The curse of avarice and cupidity[5]
Is all my sermon, for it frees the pelf.[6]
20   Out come the pence, and specially for myself,
For my exclusive purpose is to win

---

1. *Radix malorum est cupiditas* Latin for "Greed is the root of all evil."
2. **yokels** (yō´ kəlz) *n.* unsophisticated people living in a rural area.
3. **mockeries** (mäk´ ər ēz) n. stories that are untrue.
4. **antics** (an´ tikz) *n.* playful, silly, or ludicrous acts.
5. **avarice** (av´ ə ris) **and cupidity** (kyōō pid´ ə tē) *n.* desire to gain
    wealth; greed (synonyms).
6. **pelf** (pelf) n. ill-gotten gains of money or wealth.

And not at all to castigate[7] their sin.
Once dead what matter how their souls may fare?
They can go blackberrying, for all I care!
25   "Believe me, many a sermon or devotive
Exordium[8] issues from an evil motive.
Some to give pleasure by their flattery
And gain promotion through hypocrisy,
Some out of vanity, some out of hate;
30 Or when I dare not otherwise debate
I'll put my discourse into such a shape,
My tongue will be a dagger; no escape
For him from slandering falsehood shall there be,
If he has hurt my brethren[9] or me.
35 For though I never mention him by name
The congregation guesses all the same
From certain hints that everybody knows,
And so I take revenge upon our foes
And spit my venom forth, while I profess
40 Holy and true—or seeming holiness.
        "But let me briefly make my purpose plain;
I preach for nothing but for greed of gain
And use the same old text, as bold as brass,
Radix malorum est cupiditas.
45 And thus I preach against the very vice
I make my living out of—avarice.
And yet however guilty of that sin
Myself with others I have power to win
Them from it, I can bring them to repent;
50 But that is not my principal intent.
Covetousness[10] is both the root and stuff
Of all I preach. That ought to be enough.
        "Well, then I give examples thick and fast
From bygone times, old stories from the past.
55 A yokel mind loves stories from of old,
Being the kind it can repeat and hold.
What! Do you think, as long as I can preach
And get their silver for the things I teach,
That I will live in poverty, from choice?
60 That's not the counsel of my inner voice!
No! Let me preach and beg from kirk[11] to kirk

Reading Strategy
Rereading Reread
lines 41–44 to determine
the "principal intent" of the
Pardoner's sermons.

---

7. **castigate** (kas´ ti gāt´) *v.* to punish severely.
8. **Exordium** (eg zôr´ dē əm) *n.* the opening part of an oration.
9. **brethren** (bre*th*´ rən) *n.* brothers.
10. **Covetousness** (kuv´ ət əs nis) *n.* greed, especially for what belongs to others.
11. **kirk** *n.* church.

And never do an honest job of work,
No, nor make baskets, like St. Paul, to gain
A livelihood. I do not preach in vain.
65 There's no apostle I would counterfeit;
I mean to have money, wool and cheese and wheat
Though it were given me by the poorest lad
Or poorest village widow, though she had
A string of starving children, all agape.
70 No, let me drink the liquor of the grape
And keep a jolly wench in every town!
     "But listen, gentlemen; to bring things down
To a conclusion, would you like a tale?
Now as I've drunk a draught of corn-ripe ale,
75 By God it stands to reason I can strike
On some good story that you all will like.
For though I am a wholly vicious man
Don't think I can't tell moral tales. I can!
Here's one I often preach when out for winning;
80 Now please be quiet. Here is the beginning."

The Pardoner's Tale

     It's of three rioters I have to tell
Who, long before the morning service bell,[12]
Were sitting in a tavern for a drink.
And as they sat, they heard the hand-bell clink
85 Before a coffin going to the grave;
One of them called the little tavern-knave[13]
And said "Go and find out at once—look spry!—
Whose corpse is in that coffin passing by;
And see you get the name correctly too."
90 "Sir," said the boy, "no need, I promise you;
Two hours before you came here I was told.
He was a friend of yours in days of old,
And suddenly, last night, the man was slain,
Upon his bench, face up, dead drunk again.

---

12. long before . . . bell long before 9:00 A.M.
13. tavern-knave serving boy.

Reading Strategy
Rereading Reread lines 66–71 to find out what the Pardoner means by saying, "I do not preach in vain."

Literary Analysis
Allegory Which details in the opening sentence enable the audience to form a quick opinion of the main characters?

Reading
Check

What vice does the Pardoner admit to having, even though he preaches against it?

95　There came a privy[14] thief, they call him Death,
　　Who kills us all round here, and in a breath
　　He speared him through the heart, he never stirred.
　　And then Death went his way without a word.
　　He's killed a thousand in the present plague,[15]
100　And, sir, it doesn't do to be too vague
　　If you should meet him; you had best be wary.
　　Be on your guard with such an adversary,
　　Be primed to meet him everywhere you go,
　　That's what my mother said. It's all I know."
105　　　The publican[16] joined in with, "By St. Mary,
　　What the child says is right; you'd best be wary,
　　This very year he killed, in a large village
　　A mile away, man, woman, serf at tillage,[17]
　　Page in the household, children—all there were.
110　Yes, I imagine that he lives round there.
　　It's well to be prepared in these alarms,
　　He might do you dishonor." "Huh, God's arms!"
　　The rioter said, "Is he so fierce to meet?
　　I'll search for him, by Jesus, street by street.
115　God's blessed bones! I'll register a vow!
　　Here, chaps! The three of us together now,
　　Hold up your hands, like me, and we'll be brothers
　　In this affair, and each defend the others,
　　And we will kill this traitor Death, I say!
120　Away with him as he has made away
　　With all our friends. God's dignity! Tonight!"
　　　　They made their bargain, swore with appetite,
　　These three, to live and die for one another
　　As brother-born might swear to his born brother.
125　And up they started in their drunken rage
　　And made towards this village which the page
　　And publican had spoken of before.
　　Many and grisly were the oaths they swore,
　　Tearing Christ's blessed body to a shred;[18]
130　"If we can only catch him, Death is dead!"
　　　　When they had gone not fully half a mile,
　　Just as they were about to cross a stile,
　　They came upon a very poor old man
　　Who humbly greeted them and thus began,
135　"God look to you, my lords, and give you quiet!"

---

14. **privy** secretive.
15. **plague** the Black Death, which killed over a third of the population of Europe from 1347–1351. The plague reached England in 1348.
16. **publican** innkeeper.
17. **tillage** plowing.
18. **Tearing . . . shred** their oaths included such expressions as "God's arms" and "God's blessed bones."

Literary Analysis
Allegory and Archetypal Elements What details of the publican's comments add to the sense of danger?

Reading Strategy
Rereading What lines explain the "bargain" the rioters are said to have made in line 122?

To which the proudest of these men of riot
Gave back the answer, "What, old fool? Give place!
Why are you all wrapped up except your face?
Why live so long? Isn't it time to die?"

140 The old, old fellow looked him in the eye
And said, "Because I never yet have found,
Though I have walked to India, searching round
Village and city on my pilgrimage,
One who would change his youth to have my age.

145 And so my age is mine and must be still
Upon me, for such time as God may will.

"Not even Death, alas, will take my life;
So, like a wretched prisoner at strife
Within himself, I walk alone and wait

150 About the earth, which is my mother's gate,
Knock-knocking with my staff from night to noon
And crying, 'Mother, open to me soon!
Look at me, mother, won't you let me in?
See how I wither, flesh and blood and skin!

155 Alas! When will these bones be laid to rest?
Mother, I would exchange—for that were best—
The wardrobe in my chamber, standing there
So long, for yours! Aye, for a shirt of hair[19]
To wrap me in!' She has refused her grace,

160 Whence comes the pallor of my withered face.

"But it dishonored you when you began
To speak so roughly, sir, to an old man,
Unless he had injured you in word or deed.
It says in holy writ, as you may read,

165 'Thou shalt rise up before the hoary head
And honor it.' And therefore be it said
'Do no more harm to an old man than you,
Being now young, would have another do
When you are old'—if you should live till then.

170 And so may God be with you, gentlemen,
For I must go whither I have to go.'

"By God," the gambler said, "you shan't do so,
You don't get off so easy, by St. John!
I heard you mention, just a moment gone,

175 A certain traitor Death who singles out
And kills the fine young fellows hereabout.
And you're his spy, by God! You wait a bit.
Say where he is or you shall pay for it,
By God and by the Holy Sacrament!

180 I say you've joined together by consent

---

19. shirt of hair here, a shroud.

▲ **Critical Viewing**
What moral might a medieval illustration like this one have served to teach? **[Hypothesize]**

Vocabulary
pallor (pal´ ər) *n.* unnatural lack of color; paleness

hoary (hôr´ ē) *adj.* white or gray with age

Reading
Check

What do the three rioters swear to do?

from The Pardoner's Tale **129**

Literary Analysis
Allegory and
Archetypal Elements
What archetypal role does
the old man play?

To kill us younger folk, you thieving swine!"
     "Well, sirs," he said, "if it be your design
To find out Death, turn up this crooked way
Towards that grove, I left him there today
185 Under a tree, and there you'll find him waiting.
He isn't one to hide for all your prating.[20]
You see that oak? He won't be far to find.
And God protect you that redeemed mankind,
Aye, and amend you!" Thus that ancient man.
190   At once the three young rioters began
To run, and reached the tree, and there they found
A pile of golden florins[21] on the ground,
New-coined, eight bushels of them as they thought.
No longer was it Death those fellows sought,
195 For they were all so thrilled to see the sight,
The florins were so beautiful and bright,
That down they sat beside the precious pile.
The wickedest spoke first after a while.
"Brothers," he said, "you listen to what I say.
200 I'm pretty sharp although I joke away.
It's clear that Fortune has bestowed this treasure
To let us live in jollity and pleasure.
Light come, light go! We'll spend it as we ought.
God's precious dignity! Who would have thought
205 This morning was to be our lucky day?
     "If one could only get the gold away,
Back to my house, or else to yours, perhaps
For as you know, the gold is ours, chaps—
We'd all be at the top of fortune, hey?

Reading Strategy
Rereading Reread
lines 206–211 to clarify the
remark in line 212.

210 But certainly it can't be done by day.
People would call us robbers—a strong gang,
So our own property would make us hang.
No, we must bring this treasure back by night
Some prudent way, and keep it out of sight.
215 And so as a solution I propose
We draw for lots and see the way it goes;
The one who draws the longest, lucky man,
Shall run to town as quickly as he can
To fetch us bread and wine—but keep things dark—
220 While two remain in hiding here to mark
Our heap of treasure. If there's no delay,
When night comes down we'll carry it away,
All three of us, wherever we have planned."
     He gathered lots and hid them in his hand
225 Bidding them draw for where the luck should fall.

---

20. prating chatter.
21. florins coins.

It fell upon the youngest of them all,
And off he ran at once towards the town.
     As soon as he had gone, the first sat down
And thus began a parley²² with the other:
230 "You know that you can trust me as a brother;
Now let me tell you where your profit lies;
You know our friend has gone to get supplies
And here's a lot of gold that is to be
Divided equally amongst us three.
235 Nevertheless, if I could shape things thus
So that we shared it out—the two of us—
Wouldn't you take it as a friendly act?"
     "But how?" the other said. "He knows the fact
that all the gold was left with me and you;
240 What can we tell him? What are we to do?"
     "Is it a bargain," said the first, "or no?
For I can tell you in a word or so
What's to be done to bring the thing about."
"Trust me," the other said, "you needn't doubt
245 My word. I won't betray you, I'll be true."
     "Well," said his friend, "you see that we are two,
And two are twice as powerful as one.
Now look; when he comes back, get up in fun
To have a wrestle; then, as you attack,
250 I'll up and put my dagger through his back
While you and he are struggling, as in game;
Then draw your dagger too and do the same.
Then all this money will be ours to spend,
Divided equally of course, dear friend.
255 Then we can gratify our lusts and fill
The day with dicing at our own sweet will."
Thus these two miscreants²³ agreed to slay
The third and youngest, as you heard me say.
     The youngest, as he ran towards the town,
260 Kept turning over, rolling up and down
Within his heart the beauty of those bright
New florins, saying, "Lord, to think I might
Have all that treasure to myself alone!
Could there be anyone beneath the throne
265 Of God so happy as I then should be?"
     And so the Fiend,²⁴ our common enemy,
Was given power to put it in his thought
That there was always poison to be bought,

---

22. **parley** discussion.
23. **miscreants** villains.
24. **Fiend** Satan.

▲ **Critical Viewing**
Compare this illustration to the one on page 129. What point might the artist make by depicting contrasting individuals being taken by death? **[Compare and Contrast]**

Reading
Check

What does the old man say the rioters will find under the tree? What do they find there?

from The Pardoner's Tale **131**

And that with poison he could kill his friends.
270 To men in such a state the Devil sends
Thoughts of this kind, and has a full permission
To lure them on to sorrow and perdition;[25]
For this young man was utterly content
To kill them both and never to repent.
275 　　And on he ran, he had no thought to *tarry*,
Came to the town, found an *apothecary*
And said, "Sell me some poison if you will,
I have a lot of rats I want to kill
And there's a polecat too about my yard
280 That takes my chickens and it hits me hard;
But I'll get even, as is only right,
With vermin that destroy a man by night."
　　The chemist answered, "I've a preparation
Which you shall have, and by my soul's salvation
285 If any living creature eat or drink
A mouthful, ere he has the time to think,
Though he took less than makes a grain of wheat,
You'll see him fall down dying at your feet;
Yes, die he must and in so short a while
290 You'd hardly have the time to walk a mile,
The poison is so strong, you understand."
　　This cursed fellow grabbed into his hand
The box of poison and away he ran
Into a neighboring street, and found a man
295 Who lent him three large bottles, He withdrew
And *deftly* poured the poison into two.
He kept the third one clean, as well he might,
For his own drink, meaning to work all night
Stacking the gold and carrying it away.
300 And when this rioter, this devil's clay,
Had filled his bottles up with wine, all three,
Back to rejoin his comrades *sauntered* he.
　　Why make a sermon of it? Why waste breath?
Exactly in the way they'd planned his death
305 They fell on him and slew him, two to one.
Then said the first of them when this was done,
"Now for a drink. Sit down and let's be merry,
For later on there'll be the corpse to bury."
And, as it happened, reaching for a sup,
310 He took a bottle full of poison up
And drank and his companion, nothing loth,
Drank from it also, and they perished both.

---

25. **perdition** damnation.

◄ **Critical Viewing**
What does this illustration say about the relationship between material wealth and death? **[Interpret]**

There is, in Avicenna's long relation²⁶
Concerning poison and its operation,
315 Trust me, no ghastlier section to transcend
What these two wretches suffered at their end.
Thus these two murderers received their due,
So did the treacherous young poisoner too.

O cursed sin! O blackguardly excess!
320 O treacherous homicide! O wickedness!
O gluttony that lusted on and diced!
O blasphemy that took the name of Christ
With habit-hardened oaths that pride began!
Alas, how comes it that a mortal man,
325 That thou, to thy Creator, Him that wrought thee,

Literary Analysis
Allegory In addition to avarice, or greed, against what sins does the exemplum preach in lines 319–323?

Reading
Check

What explanation does the rioter give to the Apothecary for buying the poison?

---

26. Avicenna's long relation book on medicines written by Avicenna (980–1037), an Arab physician, which contains a chapter on poisons.

That paid His precious blood for thee and bought thee,
Art so unnatural and false within?
    Dearly beloved, God forgive your sin
And keep you from the vice of avarice!
330 My holy pardon frees you all of this,
Provided that you make the right approaches,
That is with sterling rings, or silver brooches.
Bow down your heads under this holy bull![27]
Come on, you women, offer up your wool!
335 I'll write your name into my ledger; so!
Into the bliss of Heaven you shall go.
For I'll absolve you by my holy power,
You that make offering, clean as at the hour
When you were born. . . . That, sirs, is how I preach.
340 And Jesu Christ, soul's healer, aye, the leech
Of every soul, grant pardon and relieve you
Of sin, for that is best I won't deceive you.

---

27. **holy bull** an official proclamation by the Catholic Church.

Critical Reading

Cite textual evidence to support your responses.

1. **Key Ideas and Details (a)** When the story opens, what are the rioters doing, and what captures their attention? **(b) Generalize:** What sort of people are they? Explain how you know.

2. **Integration of Knowledge and Ideas** The Pardoner is quite open about the manipulative use to which he puts the tale. Do the Pardoner's reasons for telling the story detract from its moral truth? Explain.

3. **Integration of Knowledge and Ideas** The tale refers to the time of the plague. **(a)** What does the tale suggest about the effects of such a disaster on society? Support your answer. **(b) Apply:** Can stories such as this one encourage people to behave well even in times of crisis? Explain.

4. **Integration of Knowledge and Ideas** Do you think the desire for gain is ultimately destructive, as the Pardoner's tale suggests, or can it lead to positive consequences? Explain.

5. **Integration of Knowledge and Ideas** What can you learn about life in the Middle Ages from "The Pardoner's Tale"? Use at least two of these Essential Question words in your response: *role, principles, reproach, excess.* [*Connecting to the Essential Question: How does literature shape or reflect society?*]

After You Read | from *The Pardoner's Tale*

Literary Analysis

© 1. Key Ideas and Details (a) Explain why "The Pardoner's Tale" is an **allegory,** and cite a passage to support your point. **(b)** Then, explain how the allegory of "The Pardoner's Tale" proves that greed is the root of all evil.

© 2. Integration of Knowledge and Ideas Identify two ways in which "The Pardoner's Tale" differs from modern short stories.

© 3. Craft and Structure (a) Why is it ironic, or surprising, that the Pardoner tells this story? **(b)** What point might Chaucer be making about moral tales by assigning this one to a rogue?

© 4. Craft and Structure (a) What role does the old man perform in the story? **(b)** What might he symbolize? **(c)** Explain the way in which the old man's presence in the tale benefits the Pardoner and motivates his listeners to adopt a more wholesome existence.

© 5. Integration of Knowledge and Ideas (a) On a chart like the one shown, explain how the tale illustrates the **archetypal elements** listed.

Patterns of Three	Test of Characters	Mysterious Guide	Just Ending

(b) Then, work with a partner to add to your response. Share your combined answers with the class.

© 6. Key Ideas and Details What other familiar elements does the story include?

© 7. Integration of Knowledge and Ideas Why do you think many tales feature things that come in threes?

© 8. Integration of Knowledge and Ideas Do you think that archetypal elements are more likely to be found in tales told orally or in written stories? Explain.

Reading Strategy

9. Find a passage that you had trouble understanding when you first read it. Improve your comprehension by **rereading** the lines leading up to the passage. Then, explain what the passage means. If you have already clarified the passage in this way, explain how you did so.

10. In line 112, the publican tells the rioters, "He might do you dishonor." Reread the previous lines. Then, use the information they provide to explain the publican's meaning.

11. In line 319, the Pardoner speaks of "blackguardly excess" as well as homicide. Reread earlier lines to clarify what he means.

Common Core State Standards

Writing

1.a. Introduce precise, knowledgeable claim(s), establish the significance of the claim(s), distinguish the claim(s) from alternate or opposing claims, and create an organization that logically sequences claim(s), counterclaims, reasons, and evidence. *(p. 136)*

Language

6. Acquire and use accurately general academic and domain-specific words and phrases, sufficient for reading, writing, speaking, and listening at the college and career readiness level; demonstrate independence in gathering vocabulary knowledge when considering a word or phrase important to comprehension or expression. *(p. 136)*

PERFORMANCE TASKS

Integrated Language Skills

© Vocabulary Acquisition and Use

Word Analysis: Greek Prefix *apo-*

The word apothecary, meaning "druggist," combines the Greek prefix *apo-,* meaning "away; off; separate," with a form of a Greek word for "put." An apothecary is one who "puts away," or stores, prescriptions. This prefix can often be found in *scientific terms* and in other words, too.

Write an alternate definition for each numbered word that contains the word *away, off,* or *separate.* An example appears first.

apoapsis *n.* farthest point from gravitational center in the orbit of any satellite

alternate definition: <u>away</u> or separated from gravitational center in a satellite's orbit

1. **apology** *n.* words of regret for an offense

2. **apogee** *n.* the highest or farthest point

3. **apostle** *n.* a person sent on a special mission

Vocabulary: Relate New to Familiar Words

Associating a new word with an already familiar word can help you remember the meaning of the new word. For each of the following items, replace the italicized familiar word with one of the words from the vocabulary list.

1. Death *strolled* down the moonlit lane.

2. His long, craggy face shone with an eerie *paleness*.

3. His long *whitened* beard fluttered in the silent breeze.

4. When a black cat crossed his path, Death stepped *easily* over its scrawny back.

5. Suddenly, Death picked up his pace. "This is no time to *dally*," he thought.

6. "I feel like death, and the *pharmacist* is closing shop in five minutes!"

Writing

© **Argumentative Text** In the final lines of his tale, the Pardoner preaches passionately on the subject of greed (among other sins). Write a **sermon**—a persuasive talk about some aspect of morality—on greed. Your sermon should be directed toward a contemporary audience.

Prewriting First, brainstorm for a list of modern-day examples of greed. Then jot down a few answers to this question: What ill effects do these forms of greed cause for an individual or for society at large?

Drafting Begin your sermon with a strong *claim* or a vivid image. Then, spend the remainder of your sermon developing this claim or image. Support your central idea with examples, arguments, emotional appeals, and word choice *suited to a con-*temporary audience.

Revising As you read your draft, imagine that you disagree with each key point you encounter. Then revise to acknowledge and refute that opposing argument.

Model: Revising to Refute Opponents

may be convenient for a large family, but it is nevertheless
Owning a large, gas-guzzling vehicle ʌis- irresponsible. It consumes twice the fuel of smaller cars and puts twice as much pollution into the atmosphere. It therefore gives *you,* the owner, a double ownership in the problem of global warming...

The writer revises to anticipate what the opposition might say.

Before You Read | *The Wife of Bath's Tale*

Connecting to the Essential Question In her tale, the feisty Wife of Bath asserts the idea that husbands and wives should be equal in marriage. As you read, identify passages in which the Wife of Bath supports the idea of "selfsame sovereignty," or equality in marriage. This will help you address the Essential Question: **How does literature shape or reflect society?**

Common Core
State Standards

Reading Literature
3. Analyze the impact of the author's choices regarding how to develop and relate elements of a story or drama.

Literary Analysis

A **frame story** contains—or frames—another story or group of stories. In *The Canterbury Tales,* the frame story is the characters' pilgrimage to Canterbury Cathedral described in the Prologue. Within the frame story are the tales told by the characters on their journey. Here are some ways in which the frame story develops a work of literature:

- Individual tales reflect the description of the storytellers' personalities and lives that you find in the frame story.
- A tale may itself contain a frame story and an inner tale. "The Wife of Bath's Tale" has such a structure.
- The **setting** of the frame story, the time and place of its action, may not match the settings of individual tales. For example, the events in the Prologue occur around Chaucer's time, but the Wife of Bath sets her frame story much earlier, during the reign of King Arthur.

Analyze these interactions and consider their effects as you read "The Wife of Bath's Tale."

Reading Strategy

Preparing to Read Complex Texts You may encounter unfamiliar words while reading. If so, repair your comprehension by **checking context clues**—words and phrases in the surrounding passage that shed light on the meaning of a word. Common context clues are synonyms, antonyms, and examples that clarify a word's meaning. Use a chart like the one shown to find context clues as you read.

Passage
"Hundreds of years ago, in days of yore"

↓

Context Clue
Unfamiliar Word: *yore* Context Clue: Hundreds of years ago Relation to Word: Similar in meaning

↓

Conclusion
If days of *yore* took place hundreds of years ago, *yore* must mean time long past.

Vocabulary

implored (im plôrd´) *v.* begged earnestly (p. 140)

relates (ri lāts´) *v.* tells (p. 141)

contemptuous (kən temp´ choo əs) *adj.* scornful (p. 145)

bequeath (bē kwēth´) *v.* hand down as an inheritance (p. 146)

prowess (prou´ is) *n.* heroism; distinction (p. 147)

esteemed (ə stēmd´) *adj.* highly respected; held in high regard (p. 147)

rebuke (ri byook´) *v.* criticize strongly (p. 149)

www.PHLitOnline.com

THE WIFE of BATH'S TALE

Geoffrey Chaucer
translated by Nevill Coghill

W hen good King Arthur ruled in ancient days,
   (A king that every Briton loves to praise.)
This was a land brim-full of fairy folk.
The Elf-Queen and her courtiers joined and broke
Their elfin dance on many a green mead,   5
Or so was the opinion once, I read,
Hundreds of years ago, in days of yore.
But no one now sees fairies any more.
For now the saintly charity and prayer
Of holy friars seem to have purged the air;   10
They search the countryside through field and stream
As thick as motes[1] that speckle a sun-beam,
Blessing the halls, the chambers, kitchens, bowers,
Cities and boroughs, castles, courts and towers,
Thorpes,[2] barns and stables, outhouses and dairies, 15
And that's the reason why there are no fairies.
Wherever there was wont to walk an elf
To-day there walks the holy friar himself
As evening falls or when the daylight springs,
Saying his matins[3] and his holy things,   20
Walking his limit round from town to town.
Women can now go safely up and down.
By every bush or under every tree;
There is no other incubus but he,
So there is really no one else to hurt you   25
And he will do no more than take your virtue.
          Now it so happened, I began to say,
Long, long ago in good King Arthur's day,
There was a knight who was a lusty liver.
One day as he came riding from the river   30
He saw a maiden walking all forlorn
Ahead of him, alone as she was born.
And of that maiden, spite of all she said,
By very force he took her maidenhead.
          This act of violence made such a stir,   35
So much petitioning of the king for her,
That he condemned the knight to lose his head
By course of law. He was as good as dead
(It seems that then the statutes took that view)

---

1. **motes** dust particles.
2. **Thorpes** villages.
3. **matins** morning prayers.

◀ **Critical Viewing** Which details in this picture of the Wife of
Bath suggest she is a self-confident middle-class woman? **[Analyze]**

40 But that the queen, and other ladies too,
    implored the king to exercise his grace
    So ceaselessly, he gave the queen the case
    And granted her his life, and she could choose
    Whether to show him mercy or refuse.

45   The queen returned him thanks with all her might,
    And then she sent a summons to the knight
    At her convenience, and expressed her will:
    "You stand, for such is the position still,
    In no way certain of your life," said she,

Reading Strategy
Checking Context Clues
Use the surrounding lines to
determine the meaning of
the word *concede* in line 54.

50 "Yet you shall live if you can answer me:
    What is the thing that women most desire?
    Beware the axe and say as I require.
        "If you can't answer on the moment, though,
    I will concede you this: you are to go

55 A twelvemonth and a day to seek and learn
    Sufficient answer, then you shall return.
    I shall take gages[4] from you to extort
    Surrender of your body to the court."
        Sad was the knight and sorrowfully sighed,

60 But there! All other choices were denied,
    And in the end he chose to go away
    And to return after a year and day
    Armed with such answer as there might be sent
    To him by God. He took his leave and went.

65   He knocked at every house, searched every place,
    Yes, anywhere that offered hope of grace.
    What could it be that women wanted most?
    But all the same he never touched a coast,
    Country or town in which there seemed to be

70 Any two people willing to agree.
        Some said that women wanted wealth and treasure,
    "Honor," said some, some "Jollity and pleasure,"
    Some "Gorgeous clothes" and others "Fun in bed,"
    " To be oft widowed and remarried," said

75 Others again, and some that what most mattered
    Was that we should be cossetted[5] and flattered.
    That's very near the truth, it seems to me;

---

4. gages guarantees.
5. cossetted pampered.

A man can win us best with flattery.
To dance attendance on us, make a fuss,
80 Ensnares us all, the best and worst of us.
      Some say the things we most desire are these:
Freedom to do exactly as we please,
With no one to reprove our faults and lies,
Rather to have one call us good and wise.
85 Truly there's not a woman in ten score
Who has a fault, and someone rubs the sore,
But she will kick if what he says is true;
You try it out and you will find so too.
However vicious we may be within
90 We like to be thought wise and void of sin.
Others assert we women find it sweet
When we are thought dependable, discreet
And secret, firm of purpose and controlled,
Never betraying things that we are told.
95 But that's not worth the handle of a rake;
Women conceal a thing? For Heaven's sake!
Remember Midas?[6] Will you hear the tale?
      Among some other little things, now stale,
Ovid relates that under his long hair
100 The unhappy Midas grew a splendid pair
Of ass's ears; as subtly as he might,
He kept his foul deformity from sight;
Save for his wife, there was not one that knew.
He loved her best, and trusted in her too.
105 He begged her not to tell a living creature
That he possessed so horrible a feature.
And she—she swore, were all the world to win,
She would not do such villainy and sin
As saddle her husband with so foul a name;
110 Besides to speak would be to share the shame.
Nevertheless she thought she would have died
Keeping this secret bottled up inside;
It seemed to swell her heart and she, no doubt,
Thought it was on the point of bursting out.
115   Fearing to speak of it to woman or man,
Down to a reedy marsh she quickly ran
And reached the sedge. Her heart was all on fire
And, as a bittern[7] bumbles in the mire,

6. **Midas** In mythology, King Midas had the magic touch that turned everything to gold. Here, Chaucer makes reference to Ovid's *Metamorphoses*.
7. **bittern** small wading bird.

Reading Strategy
Checking Context Clues
Which context clues might help you figure out the meaning of *ensnares* in line 80?

Vocabulary
relates (ri lāts′) *v.* tells

Literary Analysis
Frame Story
What clues in lines 97–99 signal the beginning of a tale-within-a-tale?

Reading Check

What punishment does the queen demand of the knight?

▲ **Critical Viewing**
In what ways does this illustration depict the knight's role on the field of battle and in the royal court? **[Analyze]**

She whispered to the water, near the ground,
120   "Betray me not, O water, with thy sound!
      To thee alone I tell it: it appears
      My husband has a pair of ass's ears!
      Ah! My heart's well again, the secret's out!
      I could no longer keep it, not a doubt."
125   And so you see, although we may hold fast
      A little while, it must come out at last,
      We can't keep secrets; as for Midas, well,
      Read Ovid for his story; he will tell.

              This knight that I am telling you about
130   Perceived at last he never would find out
      What it could be that women loved the best.
      Faint was the soul within his sorrowful breast
      As home he went, he dared no longer stay;
      His year was up and now it was the day.

135   As he rode home in a dejected mood
      Suddenly, at the margin of a wood,
      He saw a dance upon the leafy floor
      Of four and twenty ladies, nay, and more.
      Eagerly he approached, in hope to learn
140   Some words of wisdom ere he should return;
      But lo! Before he came to where they were,
      Dancers and dance all vanished into air!
      There wasn't a living creature to be seen
      Save one old woman crouched upon the green.
145   A fouler-looking creature I suppose
      Could scarcely be imagined. She arose
      And said, "Sir knight, there's no way on from here.
      Tell me what you are looking for, my dear,
      For peradventure that were best for you;
150   We old, old women know a thing or two."

              "Dear Mother," said the knight, "alack the day!
      I am as good as dead if I can't say
      What thing it is that women most desire;
      If you could tell me I would pay your hire."
155   "Give me your hand," she said, "and swear to do
      Whatever I shall next require of you
      —If so to do should lie within your might—
      And you shall know the answer before night."
      "Upon my honor," he answered, "I agree."

160 "Then," said the crone, "I dare to guarantee
Your life is safe; I shall make good my claim.
Upon my life the queen will say the same.
Show me the very proudest of them all
In costly coverchief or jewelled caul[8]
165 That dare say no to what I have to teach.
Let us go forward without further speech."
And then she crooned her gospel in his ear
And told him to be glad and not to fear.
　　　They came to court. This knight, in full array,
170 Stood forth and said, "O Queen, I've kept my day
And kept my word and have my answer ready."
　　　There sat the noble matrons and the heady
Young girls, and widows too, that have the grace
Of wisdom, all assembled in that place,
175 And there the queen herself was throned to hear
And judge his answer. Then the knight drew near
And silence was commanded through the hall.
　　　The queen then bade the knight to tell them all
What thing it was that women wanted most.
180 He stood not silent like a beast or post,
But gave his answer with the ringing word
Of a man's voice and the assembly heard:
　　　"My liege and lady, in general," said he,
"A woman wants the self-same sovereignty
185 Over her husband as over her lover,
And master him; he must not be above her.
That is your greatest wish, whether you kill
Or spare me; please yourself. I wait your will."
　　　In all the court not one that shook her head
190 Or contradicted what the knight had said;
Maid, wife and widow cried, "He's saved his life!"
　　　And on the word up started the old wife,
The one the knight saw sitting on the green,
And cried, "Your mercy, sovereign lady queen!
195 Before the court disperses, do me right!
'Twas I who taught this answer to the knight,
For which he swore, and pledged his honor to it,
That the first thing I asked of him he'd do it,
So far as it should lie within his might.
200 Before this court I ask you then, sir knight,

---

8. **coverchief. . .caul** kerchief, and a decorative cap, both worn as headgear by medieval women.

To keep your word and take me for your wife:
For well you know that I have saved your life.
If this be false, deny it on your sword!"
        "Alas!" he said, "Old lady, by the Lord
205 I know indeed that such was my behest,
But for God's love think of a new request,
Take all my goods, but leave my body free."
"A curse on us," she said, "if I agree!
I may be foul, I may be poor and old,
210 Yet will not choose to be, for all the gold
That's bedded in the earth or lies above,
Less than your wife, nay, than your very love!"
        "My love?" said he. "By Heaven, my damnation!
Alas that any of my race and station
215 Should ever make so foul a misalliance!"
Yet in the end his pleading and defiance
All went for nothing, he was forced to wed.
He takes his ancient wife and goes to bed.

Now peradventure some may well suspect
220 A lack of care in me since I neglect
To tell of the rejoicings and display
Made at the feast upon their wedding-day.
I have but a short answer to let fall;
I say there was no joy or feast at all,
225 Nothing but heaviness of heart and sorrow.
He married her in private on the morrow
And all day long stayed hidden like an owl,
It was such torture that his wife looked foul.
        Great was the anguish churning in his head
230 When he and she were piloted to bed;
He wallowed back and forth in desperate style.
His ancient wife lay smiling all the while;
At last she said, "Bless us! Is this, my dear,
How knights and wives get on together here?
235 Are these the laws of good King Arthur's house?
Are knights of his all so contemptuous?
I am your own beloved and your wife,
And I am she, indeed, that saved your life;
And certainly I never did you wrong.

◄ **Critical Viewing**
In what ways does this picture help you visualize the kind of medieval nobles who listened to the knight's answer? **[Connect]**

Reading Strategy
Checking Context Clues
What is the meaning of *anguish* in line 229? Identify the context clues that helped you to determine the meaning.

Vocabulary
contemptuous
(kən temp´ chōō əs) *adj.*
scornful

Reading
Check

In addition to becoming the knight's wife, what more does the old woman demand?

Then why, this first of nights, so sad a song?
You're carrying on as if you were half-witted
Say, for God's love, what sin have I committed?
I'll put things right if you will tell me how."
  "Put right?" he cried. "That never can be now!

245
Nothing can ever be put right again!
You're old, and so abominably plain,
So poor to start with, so low-bred to follow;
It's little wonder if I twist and wallow!
God, that my heart would burst within my breast!"

250
  "Is that," said she, "the cause of your unrest?"
  "Yes, certainly," he said, "and can you wonder?"
  "I could set right what you suppose a blunder,
That's if I cared to, in a day or two,
If I were shown more courtesy by you.

255
Just now," she said, "you spoke of gentle birth,
Such as descends from ancient wealth and worth.
If that's the claim you make for gentlemen
Such arrogance is hardly worth a hen.
Whoever loves to work for virtuous ends,

260
Public and private, and who most intends
To do what deeds of gentleness he can,
Take him to be the greatest gentleman.
Christ wills we take our gentleness from Him,
Not from a wealth of ancestry long dim,

265
Though they **bequeath** their whole establishment
By which we claim to be of high descent.
Our fathers cannot make us a bequest

Literary Analysis
Frame Story
By the standards set forth in lines 255–262, is the Knight from the Prologue a gentleman? Why or why not?

Vocabulary
bequeath (bē kwēth′)
v. hand down as an inheritance

LITERATURE IN CONTEXT

Selfsame Sovereignty

The Wife of Bath uses the story of the knight and the old woman to express her own belief in selfsame sovereignty, or equality in marriage between a husband and wife. Whether such an idea meant that women shared ownership of property and family wealth, or whether it meant they had an equal share in decision-making, such a belief was definitely well ahead of the times.

In medieval England, women could inherit property only if there were no male heirs in the family. Usually, property was entailed, or assigned to the male survivors, the women being left under the men's care until marriage or death. Moreover, at marriage a woman was often required to renounce any further claims to her father's property. Often, any property she did bring to the marriage was immediately forfeited to her husband, leaving her with virtually no further claim to it. Only in 1857 did Great Britain's Married Women's Property Acts first allow a woman the right to property in her own name.

Connect to the Literature

The Wife of Bath refuses to play a subordinate role in her society. In what ways does Chaucer's description of the Wife of Bath, as well as her tale, suggest that she was an unusual woman for her time?

Of all those virtues that became them best
And earned for them the name of gentleman,
270 But bade us follow them as best we can.
        "Thus the wise poet of the Florentines,
Dante[9] by name, has written in these lines,
For such is the opinion Dante launches:
'Seldom arises by these slender branches
275 prowess of men, for it is God, no less,
Wills us to claim of Him our gentleness.'
For of our parents nothing can we claim
Save temporal things, and these may hurt and maim.
        "But everyone knows this as well as I;
280 For if gentility were implanted by
The natural course of lineage down the line,
Public or private, could it cease to shine
In doing the fair work of gentle deed?
No vice or villainy could then bear seed.
285   "Take fire and carry it to the darkest house
Between this kingdom and the Caucasus,[10]
And shut the doors on it and leave it there,
It will burn on, and it will burn as fair
As if ten thousand men were there to see,
290 For fire will keep its nature and degree,
I can assure you, sir, until it dies.
        "But gentleness, as you will recognize,
Is not annexed in nature to possessions,
Men fail in living up to their professions;
295 But fire never ceases to be fire.
God knows you'll often find, if you enquire,
Some lording full of villainy and shame.
If you would be esteemed for the mere name
Of having been by birth a gentleman
300 And stemming from some virtuous, noble clan,
And do not live yourself by gentle deed
Or take your fathers' noble code and creed,
You are no gentleman, though duke or earl.
Vice and bad manners are what make a churl.
305   "Gentility is only the renown
For bounty that your fathers handed down,
Quite foreign to your person, not your own;
Gentility must come from God alone.
That we are gentle comes to us by grace

---

9. Dante Dante Alighieri (dän′ tā al əg yer′ ē) (1265–1321) Italian poet who wrote the *Divine Comedy.*
10. Caucasus (kō′ kə səs) mountain range between southeastern Europe and western Asia.

Vocabulary

prowess (prou′ is) *n.*
heroism; distinction

esteemed (ə stēmd′) *adj.*
highly respected

Reading
Check

According to the old woman,
what makes a man a
gentleman?

310　And by no means is it bequeathed with place.
　　　　"Reflect how noble (says Valerius)[11]
　　Was Tullius surnamed Hostilius,
　　Who rose from poverty to nobleness.
　　And read Boethius, Seneca no less,
315　Thus they express themselves and are agreed:
　　'Gentle is he that does a gentle deed.'
　　And therefore, my dear husband, I conclude
　　That even if my ancestors were rude,
　　Yet God on high—and so I hope He will—
320　Can grant me grace to live in virtue still,
　　A gentlewoman only when beginning
　　To live in virtue and to shrink from sinning.
　　　　"As for my poverty which you reprove,
　　Almighty God Himself in whom we move,
325　Believe and have our being, chose a life
　　Of poverty, and every man or wife
　　Nay, every child can see our Heavenly King
　　Would never stoop to choose a shameful thing.
　　No shame in poverty if the heart is gay,
330　As Seneca and all the learned say.
　　He who accepts his poverty unhurt
　　I'd say is rich although he lacked a shirt.
　　But truly poor are they who whine and fret
　　And covet what they cannot hope to get.
335　And he that, having nothing, covets not,
　　Is rich, though you may think he is a sot.[12]
　　　　"True poverty can find a song to sing.
　　Juvenal says a pleasant little thing:
　　'The poor can dance and sing in the relief
340　Of having nothing that will tempt a thief.'
　　Though it be hateful, poverty is good,
　　A great incentive to a livelihood,
　　And a great help to our capacity
　　For wisdom, if accepted patiently.
345　Poverty is, though wanting in estate,
　　A kind of wealth that none calumniate.[13]
　　Poverty often, when the heart is lowly,

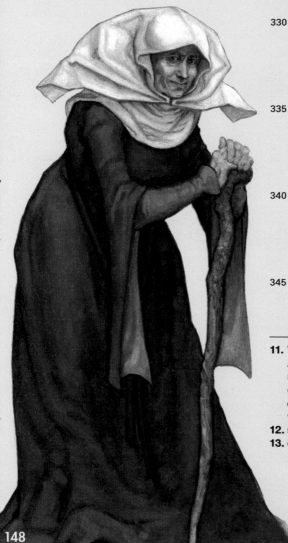

▼ Critical Viewing
Compare the illustrations of
the crone and maiden. Why
is the crone better able to
teach the knight a lesson?
[Speculate]

---

11. **Valerius . . . Seneca** Valerius (və lir′ ē əs) Maximus was a first-century
A.D. Roman author who collected historical anecdotes. Tullius Hostilius
rose from humble beginnings to become a legendary king of Rome. Boethius (bō ē′ thē əs) was a Roman philosopher whose *The Consolation
of Philosophy* is a recognized source for Chaucer's writings. Seneca
was a Roman philosopher and dramatist.
12. **sot** fool.
13. **calumniate** (kə lum′ ne āt′) slander.

Brings one to God and teaches what is holy,
Gives knowledge of oneself and even lends
350 A glass by which to see one's truest friends.
And since it's no offence, let me be plain;
Do not rebuke my poverty again.

  "Lastly you taxed me, sir, with being old.
Yet even if you never had been told
355 By ancient books, you gentlemen engage
Yourselves in honor to respect old age.
To call an old man 'father' shows good breeding,
And this could be supported from my reading.

  "You say I'm old and fouler than a fen.
360 You need not fear to be a cuckold, then.
Filth and old age, I'm sure you will agree,
Are powerful wardens upon chastity.
Nevertheless, well knowing your delights,
I shall fulfil your worldly appetites.

365   "You have two choices; which one will you try?
To have me old and ugly till I die,
But still a loyal, true and humble wife
That never will displease you all her life,
Or would you rather I were young and pretty
370 And chance your arm what happens in a city
Where friends will visit you because of me,
Yes, and in other places too, maybe.
Which would you have? The choice is all your own."

  The knight thought long, and with a piteous groan
375 At last he said, with all the care in life,
"My lady and my love, my dearest wife,
I leave the matter to your wise decision.
You make the choice yourself, for the provision
Of what may be agreeable and rich
380 In honor to us both, I don't care which;
Whatever pleases you suffices me."

  "And have I won the mastery?" said she,
"Since I'm to choose and rule as I think fit?"
"Certainly, wife," he answered her, "that's it."
385 "Kiss me," she cried. "No quarrels! On my oath
And word of honor, you shall find me both,
That is, both fair and faithful as a wife;
May I go howling mad and take my life
Unless I prove to be as good and true
390 As ever wife was since the world was new!
And if to-morrow when the sun's above
I seem less fair than any lady-love,

Vocabulary
rebuke (ri byŏŏk´) v.
criticize strongly

Reading
Check

Identify two benefits that the
old woman says can come
with poverty.

Than any queen or empress east or west,
Do with my life and death as you think best.
395 Cast up the curtain, husband. Look at me!"
          And when indeed the knight had looked to see,
Lo, she was young and lovely, rich in charms.
In ecstasy he caught her in her arms,
His heart went bathing in a bath of blisses
400 And melted in a hundred thousand kisses,
And she responded in the fullest measure
With all that could delight or give him pleasure.
          So they lived ever after to the end
In perfect bliss; and may Christ Jesus send
405 Us husbands meek and young and fresh in bed,
And grace to overbid them when we wed.
And—Jesu hear my prayer!—cut short the lives
Of those who won't be governed by their wives;
And all old, angry niggards of their pence,[14]
410 God send them soon a very pestilence!

14. **niggards** (nig′ ərdz) **of their pence** misers stingy with their money.

Literary Analysis
Frame Story
Which words serve as a clue that the interior story is finished and that the Wife has turned her attention toward her riding companions?

Critical Reading

Cite textual evidence to support your responses.

1. Key Ideas and Details (a) What punishment does the king initially order for the knight? **(b) Speculate:** Why might the king willingly allow his wife to effect a different punishment instead? **(c) Apply:** What philosophy about relationships do the king and queen share with the Wife of Bath?

2. Key Ideas and Details (a) What character flaw is the tale-within-a-tale of Midas's wife meant to illustrate? **(b) Evaluate:** In your opinion, does this inner story undercut the main point of the Wife's tale? Explain.

3. Key Ideas and Details (a) What bargain does the knight make with the old woman? **(b) Analyze:** Why do you think the queen forces the knight to keep his part of the bargain?

4. Key Ideas and Details (a) What final choice does the old woman offer the knight? **(b) Infer:** In what way does his response show that he has finally learned his lesson about the nature of women? **(c) Make a Judgment:** Has the knight experienced sufficient punishment and redemption for his crime? Explain.

5. Integration of Knowledge and Ideas By discussing selfsame sovereignty, was Chaucer reflecting or trying to influence social trends? In responding, use at least two of these words: *parity, independence, reciprocate. [Connecting to the Essential Question: How does literature shape or reflect society?]*

After You Read *The Wife of Bath's Tale*

Literary Analysis

Common Core State Standards

Language
3. Apply knowledge of language to understand how language functions in different contexts, to make effective choices for meaning or style, and to comprehend more fully when reading or listening. *(p. 152)*

4. Determine or clarify the meaning of unknown and multiple-meaning words and phrases based on *grades 11–12 reading and content,* choosing flexibly from a range of strategies. *(p. 152)*

1. Integration of Knowledge and Ideas Reread the description of the Wife of Bath in the General Prologue, or the **frame story** for the Wife's tale. **(a)** Compare the characteristics of the Wife to those of the old woman in the Wife's tale. **(b)** Do you think the Wife identifies with the old woman? Why or why not?

2. Integration of Knowledge and Ideas In the frame story, the Host declares he will judge the pilgrims' tales on their "good morality and general pleasure" (Prologue line 818), their ability to teach a moral or lesson, and the entertainment value for the listeners. As the Host, how would you respond to the Wife's tale? **(a)** Use the first two boxes in the chart below to note details from the tale. **(b)** Then, use the details to determine a final judgment.

Good Morality/ Lesson	General Pleasure/ Entertainment Value	Final Judgment

3. Craft and Structure In what ways does the **setting** of "The Wife of Bath's Tale" compare or contrast with the setting of the frame story, the pilgrimage to Canterbury?

4. Key Ideas and Details (a) In what ways do the details of the setting in lines 135–144 echo the description of "ancient days" in lines 3–7? **(b)** Describe the way these details hint at, or foreshadow, the happy ending of the tale.

5. Integration of Knowledge and Ideas In what ways is a story like "The Wife of Bath's Tale" an important commentary on the lives of medieval women?

6. Integration of Knowledge and Ideas (a) In today's society, where might you find individuals who would agree with the Wife and the philosophy she illustrates with her story? **(b)** Who might argue against such opinions?

7. Analyzing Visual Information: Does the caricature of Chaucer on this page suggest that he knew and appreciated many people like the characters he invented? Why or why not?

Reading Strategy

8. (a) If you were unfamiliar with the word "dejected," in line 135, how might you repair your comprehension by **checking context clues**? **(b)** Identify three words you might use instead of "dejected" that would retain the meaning of the lines around the word.

9. Define the word "suffices" as it is used in line 381, explaining which context clues enabled you to determine its meaning.

10. Which type of context clue—synonyms, antonyms, examples, or another type of clue—has been most useful to you in figuring out the meaning of new words? Explain.

PERFORMANCE TASKS
Integrated Language Skills

⊚ Vocabulary Acquisition and Use

Multiple-Meaning Words in Context

Many English words have more than one meaning. For example, *relates* as a verb with an object can mean "tells a story or recounts," or, as a verb without an object, "to have or establish a relation (to)." Often, the meaning of the word changes according to its part of speech, which can be determined by the context. Note these examples:

The Wife relates her tale.
He relates to what she is saying.

In the first sentence, that *relates* takes an object provides a clue to its correct meaning, as does the fact that the object, "tale," is a narrative. In the second sentence, *relates* does not take an object, suggesting that it means "to have or establish a relation (to)."

For each of the following, explain how context helps you know which definition corresponds to the italicized word.

1. The Wife *relates* best to submissive men.

    a. tells   **b.** has a relation to

2. Is her desire for power merely an *act*?

    a. to take action **b.** performance

3. If so, her *bluff* is as compelling as her tale!

    a. lie   **b.** high, steep bank

Vocabulary: Logical or Illogical?

Review the vocabulary words on page 137. Then, for each item below, revise the sentence so that the underlined vocabulary word is used logically. Be sure not to change the vocabulary word.

Example: When the dark clouds moved in, the water in the puddles <u>glistened</u>.

After the dark clouds moved away, the water in the puddles <u>glistened</u>.

1. Let us give less consideration to the rights of women, the Wife of Bath <u>implored</u>.

2. The story the Wife of Bath <u>relates</u> is a warning against the destructiveness of greed.

3. When asked what women wanted most, the knight replied in a <u>contemptuous</u> way.

4. The old woman in the tale says that our fathers <u>bequeath</u> us their wealth and virtue.

5. According to the old wife in the story, the <u>prowess</u> of men is their fierceness.

6. The Wife's tale suggests that gentlemen should be <u>esteemed</u> only for their rank.

7. The old woman in the Wife's tale changes into a young woman because the knight continues to <u>rebuke</u> her.

Using Resources to Build Vocabulary

Lively Descriptive Adjectives and Their Connotations
In the Prologue, Chaucer uses lively adjectives to help you visualize his characters. For example, in line 299, he refers to the Oxford Cleric's "hollow look" and "sober stare." Following are other examples of lively adjectives:

    motley (line 281)   wary (line 320)   trim (line 375)
    fresh (line 375)   stout (line 562)   broad (line 565)

Review these words in context. Then, use a *print or digital thesaurus* to find synonyms for each. Rewrite the passage by replacing the word with a synonym. Next, read your new lines, and briefly explain how they differ from Chaucer's originals. Tell how the *connotative meanings,* or associations, of the adjectives make them better or worse for describing the characters, although their *denotative meanings,* or definitions, are similar.

Writing

Argumentative Text Chaucer's outlandish, rule-breaking pilgrims have long been the subject of critical speculation. Through such characters, did Chaucer hope to reform the flawed institutions they represent—the church, the nobility, the government, and marriage, among others? Or did he intend to censure the pilgrims themselves and others like them?

Perhaps he meant to do neither. In his book *Chaucer and the Energy of Creation,* critic Edward I. Condren writes:

> *To view Chaucer as a reformer . . . is to overlook his evident love affair with the world he creates—a world he neither condemns, endorses, burdens with ideology, nor seeks to improve, but a world he shows as a dynamic, human, endlessly fascinating entity unto itself.*

Do you agree or disagree with Condren's take on Chaucer? Do you, too, believe that the poet's main intent was to capture life in all its teeming glory, or do you suspect that he had an agenda of reform or censure? Write an **essay** in which you evaluate Condren's view and state your own judgment about Chaucer's purpose, supporting your claims with evidence from the texts.

Prewriting Before formulating an opinion, review the texts with an open mind. Gather details, including *imagery* and *figures of speech*, that describe pilgrims acting unconventionally and evoke your emotions. Is the *tone* of each detail comically affirming or darkly disapproving?

Drafting Use these steps as you compose your essay:

- In your introduction, include a *thesis* statement supporting or refuting Condren's remark. Try to express your thesis in a way that engages the interest of the reader.

- In your essay, *support your thesis* with information and examples from your prewriting notes. Return to the texts for additional support, if necessary.

- Close the essay by restating your thesis and by echoing your strongest evidence.

Revising Your essay may discuss social and religious institutions that some readers may value. Review your draft, placing a star next to passages that might lead to *misunderstandings*. For each star, rephrase the idea so that your meaning is clear and your tone is inoffensive.

Common Core State Standards

Writing

1.a. Create an organization that logically sequences claims, counterclaims, reasons, and evidence.

1.e. Provide a concluding statement or section that follows from and supports the argument presented.

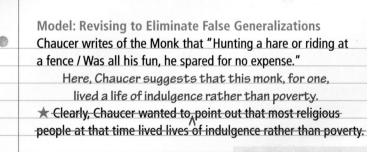

Model: Revising to Eliminate False Generalizations

Chaucer writes of the Monk that "Hunting a hare or riding at a fence / Was all his fun, he spared for no expense."

Here, Chaucer suggests that this monk, for one, lived a life of indulgence rather than poverty.

★ Clearly, Chaucer wanted to point out that most religious people at that time lived lives of indulgence rather than poverty.

The generalization "most religious people" makes a false generalization from Chaucer's passage. The writer replaces it with a specific reference to the monk.

PERFORMANCE TASKS

Integrated Language Skills

Conventions and Style: Correlative Conjunctions

Too many short sentences can make your writing sound dull or stilted. When two short sentences have related ideas, you might be able to combine them using a **correlative conjunction,** a word pair connecting similar words or groups of words.

Combining: Correlative Conjunctions

The correlative conjunction you should use depends on the relationship between the ideas.

Two Short Sentences
The Carpenter is not described in detail. The Weaver isn't either.
The young man was the knight's Squire. He was also the knight's son.
The Cleric will buy books. The Cleric might take a course instead.

Combined
Neither the Weaver *nor* the Carpenter is described in detail.
The young man was *not only* the knight's Squire *but also* his son.
The Cleric will *either* buy books *or* take a course.

Practice In items 1–5, supply a correlative conjunction to complete the sentence. In items 6–10, use a correlative conjunction to combine the two sentences.

1. Each pilgrim must _____ tell four stories _____ pay for the journey.
2. The parson shows _____ generosity _____ patience in his behavior toward others.
3. The old woman urges the knight to respect _____ poverty _____ old age.
4. The travelers briefly considered _____ to accept _____ reject the Host's proposal.
5. Knights were supposed to be _____ honest _____ generous.
6. The narrator is a storyteller. The characters are storytellers too.
7. The host of the tavern serves as a travel guide. He serves as a judge of the tales.
8. The pardoner is greedy. He is hypocritical.
9. The knight must answer the queen's question correctly. Otherwise, he must surrender himself to the court.
10. The old man had not hurt the rioters by his words. He had not hurt them by his actions.

Punctuation Tip: Do not use a comma to separate items joined by a correlative conjunction, except when they are independent clauses.

© **Writing and Speaking Conventions**_____

A. Writing For each pair, write a sentence using a correlative conjunction to link the words or phrases.

1. entertainment—competition
2. honorable—courteous
3. read the poem aloud—listen to a recording

   Example: entertainment—competition

   Sentence: The stories serve as both an entertainment and a competition.

PH **WRITING COACH**

Further instruction and practice are available in *Prentice Hall Writing Coach.*

B. Speaking Describe a pilgrimage you have taken or would like to take. Include at least two sentences with correlative conjunctions.

GALLERY OF FRAME STORIES

To delay her execution, Scheherazade...

... tells stories that she leaves incomplete until the next night.

The Thousand and One Nights
MEDIEVAL ARABIA

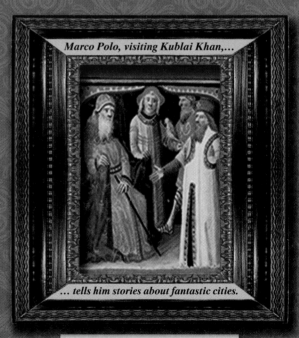

Escaping the plague, residents of Florence, Italy,...

... tell stories to entertain one another.

The Decameron
BY GIOVANNI BOCCACCIO (ITALIAN; 1313–1375)

Pilgrims traveling to Canterbury, England,...

... enter into a storytelling competition.

The Canterbury Tales
BY GEOFFREY CHAUCER (ENGLISH; 1343?–1400)

Marco Polo, visiting Kublai Khan,...

... tells him stories about fantastic cities.

Invisible Cities (1972)
BY ITALO CALVINO (ITALIAN; 1923–1985)

Comparing Literary Works

from *The Canterbury Tales* •
from the *Decameron:*
Federigo's Falcon

Comparing Frame Stories Across Cultures

Frame Stories A frame story is a type of narrative in which the author creates one long story that contains within it another story or group of stories. It has been used as a literary device by writers from diverse time periods and regions. Early frame stories, like those of *The Thousand and One Nights*, wove together tales from a variety of sources. Chaucer did so when he wrote *The Canterbury Tales*, but he also developed stories and characters of his own. Here are some advantages of a frame story:

- ties together stories of all different kinds
- presents fantastic stories in the realistic context of the frame
- captures the natural quality of oral storytelling

As you read the selection from the *Decameron*, use a chart like the one shown to compare it with the selections from *The Canterbury Tales*.

	The Canterbury Tales	*Decameron*
Frame-story setting	England in the 1300s	
Storytellers' backgrounds	people of all ages from different walks of life	
Storytellers' purpose for gathering	to make a pilgrimage to Becket's shrine in Canterbury	
Storytellers' purpose for storytelling	to pass the time and compete for best story	
Types of stories within the frame	stories of many kinds set in many times and places	

Gather Vocabulary Knowledge

In the third paragraph of the excerpt from the *Decameron,* Boccaccio uses the words *pre-eminence, eloquence,* and *sumptuous.* Read the paragraph, and then use the following exercises to further explore the words.

- **Context** Reread the words and try to define them using context—the words immediately surrounding the word you are trying to define. Then, use a print or online **dictionary** to verify your definitions and to find the parts of speech.
- **Etymologies** Use a print or online dictionary or a book of etymologies to determine the etymologies, or origins, of the three words.

After you have familiarized yourself with the words, form a small group with classmates and use the words in a brief paragraph about attending a formal event at a banquet hall or a palace. Then, elect a speaker and share your writing with the rest of the class.

Common Core State Standards

Reading Literature
10. By the end of grade 12, read and comprehend literature, including stories, at the high end of the grades 11–CCR text complexity band independently and proficiently.

Language
4.a. Use context as a clue to the meaning of a word or phrase.
4.c. Consult general and specialized reference materials, both print and digital, to find the pronunciation of a word or determine or clarify its precise meaning, its part of speech, or its etymology.
6. Demonstrate independence in gathering vocabulary knowledge when considering a word or phrase important to comprehension or expression.

www.PHLitOnline.com

Giovanni Boccaccio *(1313–1375)*

Author of the *Decameron: Federigo's Falcon*

When Giovanni Boccaccio (jō vän´ ē bō kä´ chō) was ten years old, his father, an associate of a well-known banking firm, sent the boy away from his native Florence to work at the firm's bank in Naples. Here he remained for many years, attending the court of Robert of Anjou, who ruled Naples at the time.

Enjoying the splendor and sophistication of Robert's court, Boccaccio showed little interest in becoming a businessman or a lawyer, as his father wanted him to do. Instead, he began writing— something he did prolifically for the rest of his life.

A Wider Worldview In 1340, financial problems caused Boccaccio's family to recall him to Florence, where at first he found the middle-class life not to his tastes. However, the change broadened his understanding of all different kinds and classes of people, an experience that would prove useful in his writing. In time, he became more sympathetic to Florence and its citizens, even engaging in local politics and serving as a Florentine ambassador.

Scholarship and Authorship In 1350, Boccaccio met the Italian poet and scholar Francesco Petrarch, with whom he began a lifelong friendship. Petrarch encouraged Boccaccio's writing, including many scholarly works in Latin.

However, while Boccaccio himself was proudest of these works, it is for an Italian work that he is best remembered. That masterpiece is the *Decameron*, a collection of stories that reveal his impressive literary versatility while exploring deeply human universal themes of love, loss, deception, fate, and honor.

"Human it is to have compassion on the unhappy."

from the Decameron

Giovanni Boccaccio
translated by G.H. McWilliam

BACKGROUND In 1348, bubonic plague swept Europe, killing more than half the population of Florence, including Boccaccio's parents. The *Decameron* begins with a group of ten young aristocrats—seven women and three men— taking up residence on a country estate where they hope to wait out the plague in Florence. To entertain themselves, each of them tells one story a day for ten days—the name Decameron means "ten days." Each day they elect a "king" or "queen" to preside over the day's storytelling and suggest the theme of the stories. "Federigo's Falcon" is told on the fifth day.

Federigo's Falcon

Comparing Frame Stories Why do you think the "queen" introduces another storyteller, Coppo di Borghese Domenichi, in the third paragraph of the story?

Vocabulary
courtly (kôrt′ ly)
adj. elegantly dignified; polite

Once Filomena had finished, the queen, finding that there was no one left to speak apart from herself (Dioneo being excluded from the reckoning because of his privilege[1]), smiled cheerfully and said:

It is now my own turn to address you, and I shall gladly do so, dearest ladies, with a story similar in some respects to the one we have just heard. This I have chosen, not only to acquaint you with the power of your beauty over men of noble spirit, but so that you may learn to choose for yourselves, whenever necessary, the persons on whom to bestow your largesse,[2] instead of always leaving these matters to be decided for you by Fortune, who, as it happens, nearly always scatters her gifts with more abundance than discretion.

You are to know, then, that Coppo di Borghese Domenichi, who once used to live in our city and possibly lives there still, one of the most highly respected men of our century, a person worthy of eternal fame, who achieved his position of pre-eminence by dint of his character and abilities rather than by his noble lineage, frequently took pleasure during his declining years in discussing incidents from the past with his neighbors and other folk. In this pastime he excelled all others, for he was more coherent, possessed a superior memory, and spoke with greater eloquence. He had a fine repertoire, including a tale he frequently told concerning a young Florentine called Federigo, the son of Messer Filippo Alberighi, who for his deeds of chivalry and courtly manners was more highly spoken of than any other squire in Tuscany.[3] In the manner of most young men of gentle breeding, Federigo lost his heart to a noble lady, whose name was Monna[4] Giovanna, and who in her time was considered one of the loveliest and most adorable women to be found in Florence. And with the object of winning her love, he rode at the ring, tilted,[5] gave sumptuous banquets, and distributed a large number of gifts, spending money

---

1. **Dioneo . . privilege** Because he is considered very witty, Dioneo is granted the privilege of telling a story on any theme that is always the last story of the day.
2. **largesse** (lär jes′) *n.* generous gifts.
3. **squire in Tuscany** well-born landowner in the Italian region where Florence is located.
4. **Monna** a title of respect similar to *Lady* in English.
5. **tilted** jousted; engaged in a medieval contest in which horsemen in armor attempted to unseat one another by thrusting lances.

without any restraint whatsoever. But since she was no less chaste than she was fair, the lady took no notice, either of the things that were done in her honor, or of the person who did them.

In this way, spending far more than he could afford and deriving no profit in return, Federigo lost his entire fortune (as can easily happen) and reduced himself to poverty, being left with nothing other than a tiny little farm, which produced an income just sufficient for him to live very frugally, and one falcon of the finest breed in the whole world. Since he was as deeply in love as ever, and felt unable to go on living the sort of life in Florence to which he aspired, he moved out to Campi, where his little farm happened to be situated. Having settled in the country, he went hunting as often as possible with his falcon, and, without seeking assistance from anyone, he patiently resigned himself to a life of poverty.

Now one day, while Federigo was living in these straitened circumstances, the husband of Monna Giovanna happened to fall ill, and, realizing that he was about to die, he drew up his will. He was a very rich man, and in his will he left everything to his son, who was just growing up, further stipulating that, if his son should die without legitimate issue, his estate should go to Monna Giovanna, to whom he had always been deeply devoted.

Shortly afterward he died, leaving Monna Giovanna a widow, and every summer, in accordance with Florentine custom, she went away with her son to a country estate of theirs, which was very near Federigo's farm. Consequently this young lad of hers happened to become friendly with Federigo, acquiring a passion for birds and dogs; and, having often seen Federigo's falcon in flight, he became fascinated by it and longed to own it, but since he could see that Federigo was deeply attached to the bird, he never ventured to ask him for it.

And there the matter rested, when, to the consternation of his mother, the boy happened to be taken ill. Being her only child, he was the apple of his mother's eye, and she sat beside his bed the whole day long, never ceasing to comfort him. Every so often she asked him whether there was anything he wanted, imploring him to tell her what it was, because if it was possible to acquire it, she would move heaven and earth to obtain it for him.

After hearing this offer repeated for the umpteenth time, the boy said:

"Mother, if you could arrange for me to have Federigo's falcon, I believe I should soon get better."

On hearing this request, the lady was somewhat taken aback, and began to consider what she could do about it. Knowing that Federigo had been in love with her for a long time, and that she had never deigned to cast so much as a single glance in his direction, she said to herself: "How can I possibly go to him, or even send anyone, to ask him for this falcon, which to judge from all I have heard is the

Vocabulary
frugally (froo͞ʹ gə lē)
adv. in a way that is careful with money

◀ Critical Viewing
In what ways might this portrait be an accurate representation of Federigo?
[Analyze]

Reading Check
What remains of Federigo's fortune after pursuing Monna Giovanna?

finest that ever flew, as well as being the only thing that keeps him alive? And how can I be so heartless as to deprive so noble a man of his one remaining pleasure?"

Her mind filled with reflections of this sort, she remained silent, not knowing what answer to make to her son's request, even though she was quite certain that the falcon was hers for the asking.

At length, however, her maternal instincts gained the upper hand, and she resolved, come what may, to satisfy the child by going in person to Federigo to collect the bird, and bring it back to him. And so she replied:

"Bear up, my son, and see whether you can start feeling any better. I give you my word that I shall go and fetch it for you first thing tomorrow morning."

Next morning, taking another lady with her for company,[6] his mother left the house as though intending to go for a walk, made her way to Federigo's little cottage, and asked to see him. For several days, the weather had been unsuitable for hawking, so Federigo was attending to one or two little jobs in his garden, and when he heard, to his utter astonishment, that Monna Giovanna was at the front door and wished to speak to him, he happily rushed there to greet her.

When she saw him coming, she advanced with womanly grace to meet him. Federigo received her with a deep bow, whereupon she said:

"Greetings, Federigo!" Then she continued: "I have come to make amends for the harm you have suffered on my account, by loving me more than you ought to have done. As a token of my esteem, I should like to take breakfast with you this morning, together with my companion here, but you must not put yourself to any trouble."

"My lady," replied Federigo in all humility, "I cannot recall ever having suffered any harm on your account. On the contrary I have gained so much that if ever I attained any kind of excellence, it was entirely because of your own great worth and the love I bore you. Moreover I can assure you that this visit which you have been generous enough to pay me is worth more to me than all the money I ever possessed, though I fear that my hospitality will not amount to very much."

So saying, he led her unassumingly into the house, and thence into his garden, where, since there was no one else he could call upon to chaperon her, he said:

"My lady, as there is nobody else available, this good woman, who is the wife of the farmer here, will keep you company whilst I go and see about setting the table."

Though his poverty was acute, the extent to which he had squandered his wealth had not yet been fully borne home to Federigo; but on this particular morning, finding that he had nothing to set before

---

6. taking . . . company It was not considered proper for a young woman of the upper classes to go out by herself.

the lady for whose love he had entertained so lavishly in the past, his eyes were well and truly opened to the fact. Distressed beyond all measure, he silently cursed his bad luck and rushed all over the house like one possessed, but could find no trace of either money or valuables. By now the morning was well advanced, he was still determined to entertain the gentlewoman to some sort of meal, and, not wishing to beg assistance from his own farmer (or from anyone else, for that matter), his gaze alighted on his precious falcon, which was sitting on its perch in the little room where it was kept. And having discovered, on picking it up, that it was nice and plump, he decided that since he had nowhere else to turn, it would make a worthy dish for such a lady as this. So without thinking twice about it he wrung the bird's neck and promptly handed it over to his housekeeper to be plucked, dressed, and roasted carefully on a spit. Then he covered the table with spotless linen, of which he still had a certain amount in his possession, and returned in high spirits to the garden, where he announced to his lady that the meal, such as he had been able to prepare, was now ready.

The lady and her companion rose from where they were sitting and made their way to the table. And together with Federigo, who waited on them with the utmost deference, they made a meal of the prize falcon without knowing what they were eating.

On leaving the table they engaged their host in pleasant conversation for a while, and when the lady thought it time to broach the subject she had gone there to discuss, she turned to Federigo and addressed him affably as follows:

"I do not doubt for a moment, Federigo, that you will be astonished at my impertinence when you discover my principal reason for coming here, especially when you recall your former mode of living and my virtue, which you possibly mistook for harshness and cruelty. But if you had ever had any children to make you appreciate the power of parental love, I should think it certain that you would to some extent forgive me.

"However, the fact that you have no children of your own does not exempt me, a mother, from the laws common to all other mothers. And being bound to obey those laws, I am forced, contrary to my own wishes and to all the rules of decorum and propriety, to ask you for something to which I know you are very deeply attached—which is only natural, seeing that it is the only consolation, the only pleasure, the only recreation remaining to you in your present extremity of fortune. The gift I am seeking is your falcon, to which my son has taken so powerful a liking, that if I fail to take it to him I fear he will succumb to the illness from which he is suffering, and consequently I shall lose him. In imploring you to give me this falcon, I appeal, not

Vocabulary
deference (def´ ər əns) *n.* courteous regard or respect

affably (af´ ə blē) *adv.* in a friendly manner

impertinence (im purt´ ə nəns) *n.* rudeness; impudence

Reading Check

Why has Monna Giovanna visited Federigo?

to your love, for you are under no obligation to me on that account, but rather to your noble heart, whereby you have proved yourself superior to all others in the practice of courtesy. Do me this favor, then, so that I may claim that through your generosity I have saved my son's life, thus placing him forever in your debt."

When he heard what it was that she wanted, and realized that he could not oblige her because he had given her the falcon to eat, Federigo burst into tears in her presence before being able to utter a single word in reply. At first the lady thought his tears stemmed more from his grief at having to part with his fine falcon than from any other motive, and was on the point of telling him that she would prefer not to have it. But on second thoughts she said nothing, and waited for Federigo to stop crying and give her his answer, which eventually he did.

"My lady," he said, "ever since God decreed that you should become the object of my love, I have repeatedly had cause to complain of Fortune's hostility towards me. But all her previous blows were slight by comparison with the one she has dealt me now. Nor shall I ever be able to forgive her, when I reflect that you have come to my poor dwelling, which you never deigned to visit when it was rich, and that you desire from me a trifling favor which she has made it impossible for me to concede. The reason is simple, and I shall explain it in few words.

"When you did me the kindness of telling me that you wished to breakfast with me, I considered it right and proper, having regard to your excellence and merit, to do everything within my power to prepare a more sumptuous dish than those I would offer to my ordinary guests. My thoughts therefore turned to the falcon you have asked me for and, knowing its quality, I reputed it a worthy dish to set before you. So I had it roasted and served to you on the trencher this morning, and I could not have wished for a better way of disposing of it. But now that I discover that you wanted it in a different form, I am so distressed by my inability to grant your request that I shall never forgive myself for as long as I live."

In confirmation of his words, Federigo caused the feathers, talons and beak to be cast on the table before her. On seeing and hearing all this, the lady reproached him at first for killing so fine a falcon, and serving it up for a woman to eat; but then she became lost in admiration for his magnanimity[7] of spirit, which no amount of poverty had managed to diminish, nor ever would. But now that her hopes of obtaining the falcon had vanished she began to feel seriously concerned for the health of her son, and after thanking Federigo for his hospitality and good intentions, she took her leave of him, looking all despondent, and returned to the child. And to his mother's indescribable sorrow, within the space of a few days, whether through his dis-

Vocabulary
despondent (di spän′ dənt) *adj.* hopeless; dejected

---

7. magnanimity (mag′ nə nim′ ə tē) *n.* noble generosity.

appointment in not being able to have the falcon, or because he was in any case suffering from a mortal illness, the child passed from this life.

After a period of bitter mourning and continued weeping, the lady was repeatedly urged by her brothers to remarry, since not only had she been left a vast fortune but she was still a young woman. And though she would have preferred to remain a widow, they gave her so little peace that in the end, recalling Federigo's high merits and his latest act of generosity, namely to have killed such a fine falcon in her honor, she said to her brothers:

"If only it were pleasing to you, I should willingly remain as I am; but since you are so eager for me to take a husband, you may be certain that I shall never marry any other man except Federigo degli Alberighi."

Her brothers made fun of her, saying:

"Silly girl, don't talk such nonsense! How can you marry a man who hasn't a penny with which to bless himself?"

"My brothers," she replied, "I am well aware of that. But I would sooner have a gentleman without riches, than riches without a gentleman."

Seeing that her mind was made up, and knowing Federigo to be a gentleman of great merit even though he was poor, her brothers fell in with her wishes and handed her over to him, along with her immense fortune. Thenceforth, finding himself married to this great lady with whom he was so deeply in love, and very rich into the bargain, Federigo managed his affairs more prudently, and lived with her in happiness to the end of his days.

Comparing Frame Stories Which words let you know that the interior story has finished?

Critical Reading

Cite textual evidence to support your responses.

1. **Key Ideas and Details (a)** What early efforts does Federigo make to win Monna Giovanna's love? **(b) Summarize:** How does she respond to those efforts? **(c) Analyze:** What does her behavior reveal about her character?

2. **Key Ideas and Details (a) Connect:** In what ways do Federigo's gestures of hospitality when Monna Giovanna visits reflect his former life as a wealthy gentleman? **(b) Infer:** Why is killing the bird such a sacrifice for him? **(c) Analyze:** What does his sacrifice show about his character?

3. **Key Ideas and Details (a) Infer:** Why is it difficult for Monna Giovanna to ask Federigo for the falcon? **(b) Analyze:** What does her making the request show about her character?

4. **Integration of Knowledge and Ideas (a) Evaluate:** Do you think Monna Giovanna makes the right decision in marrying Federigo in the end? **(b) Support:** Cite reasons and story details to support your evaluation.

After You Read

from *The Canterbury Tales* ▪
from the *Decameron:*
Federigo's Falcon

Comparing Frame Stories

 **Common Core
State Standards**

Writing
1. Write arguments to support claims in an analysis of substantive topics or texts, using valid reasoning and relevant and sufficient evidence.
10. Write routinely over extended time frames and shorter time frames for a range of tasks, purposes, and audiences.

1. **Integration of Knowledge and Ideas (a)** In the **frame story** of Boccaccio's *Decameron*, what is the premise or reason for the storytelling? **(b)** How is that premise like and unlike the premise for the storytelling in Chaucer's work? **(c)** Which premise makes for a more effective frame story? Why?

2. **Integration of Knowledge and Ideas** One advantage of a frame story is that it can capture, in written form, the qualities of oral storytelling. Which author, Boccaccio or Chaucer, better conveys those qualities? Explain.

3. **Integration of Knowledge and Ideas** Consider this statement: Frame stories are not effective for revealing character because the only action people perform is telling stories. Explain why you agree or disagree with this assertion, citing evidence from "Federigo's Falcon" and *The Canterbury Tales* as support.

Timed Writing

Argumentative Text: Essay

Although Chaucer and Boccaccio both use the device of the frame story, they do not always deal with similar themes in exactly the same way.

Assignment: Write an **interpretation of a literary text** in which you compare and contrast the theme of "Federigo's Falcon" with the theme of "The Wife of Bath's Tale" or "The Pardoner's Tale." **[40 minutes]**
Your essay should explore these types of questions:

- How does the sequence of events and outcome of each tale offer a clue to its theme?
- How does the theme of each tale reflect or suggest the personality, background, or motives of the character in the frame story who narrates the tale?
- What do the themes of the two tales have in common, and how are they different?

As you write, support your ideas with accurate and detailed references to the texts.

USE ACADEMIC VOCABULARY

As you write, use academic language, including the following words or their related forms:

compare
contrast
insight
interpret

For more about academic language, see the vocabulary charts in the introduction to this book.

5-Minute Planner

Complete these steps before you begin to write:

1. Read the assignment carefully. Identify key words and phrases.
2. Scan the selections, looking for details related to your assignment.
   TIP As you scan, jot down quotations that you might use in your essay.
3. Write a rough outline for your essay.
4. Reread the prompt and begin drafting.

Perils and Adventures

Connecting to the Essential Question Many characters in these selections are knights who observe a code of honorable behavior called chivalry. As you read, look for passages in these selections that reveal the kind of behavior that chivalry requires. Finding these passages will help as you answer the Essential Question: **What is the relationship of the writer to tradition?**

Common Core State Standards

**Reading Literature
2.** Provide an objective summary of the text.

Literary Analysis

Romances are narratives that tell of strange, sometimes supernatural events in exotic settings. **Medieval romances** are adventure stories with kings, knights, and damsels in distress. The medieval romances in this grouping are based on **legends,** anonymous traditional stories about the past that may have been inspired by real events and people. Legends, like these relating to King Arthur and his knights, often feature the following:

- heroic figures and memorable deeds
- quests, or searches for something important; contests; and tests
- patterns, such as events repeated three times

Medieval writers created romances by adding to legends such elements as vivid descriptions, plot twists, and accounts of the reactions and motives of characters. As you read, look for these elements and compare and contrast their use in these selections.

Reading Strategy

© **Preparing to Read Complex Texts** You can **determine the main idea, or essential message,** of a work or a passage in several different ways. One method is to **summarize** a whole work or a portion of it by identifying and briefly restating its main ideas and relevant details. An effective summary will only include factual information, and not your personal opinions about what you have read. As you read, use a chart like the one shown to summarize key ideas and details.

Passage

"Ah, traitor unto me and untrue," said King Arthur, "now hast thou betrayed me twice. Who would have weened that thou that has been to me so loved and dear…, and would betray me for the riches of this sword."

⬇

Summary

King Arthur charges his knight with betraying him twice out of greed.

Vocabulary

adjure (a jʊʊr′) *v.* request solemnly; appeal to earnestly (p. 175)

adroitly (ə drɔit′ lē) *adv.* with physical or mental skill (p. 181)

largesse (lär jes′) *n.* nobility of spirit (p. 183)

entreated (en trēt′ id) *v.* made an earnest appeal; pleaded (p. 186)

peril (per′ əl) *n.* exposure to harm or injury (p. 187)

interred (in turd′) *v.* buried in the earth (p. 194)

PHLit Online!
www.PHLitOnline.com

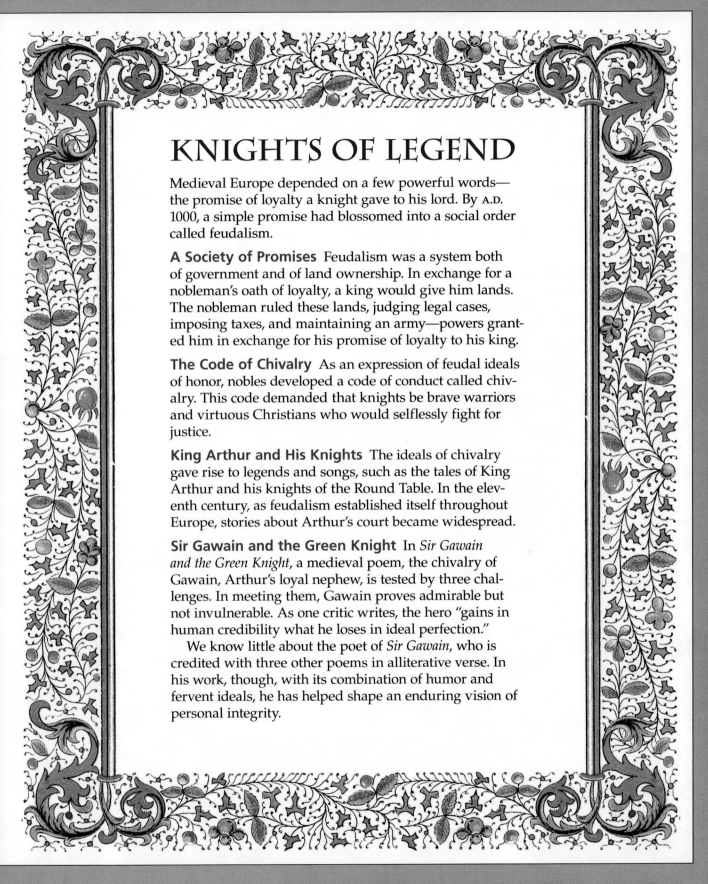

KNIGHTS OF LEGEND

Medieval Europe depended on a few powerful words—the promise of loyalty a knight gave to his lord. By A.D. 1000, a simple promise had blossomed into a social order called feudalism.

A Society of Promises Feudalism was a system both of government and of land ownership. In exchange for a nobleman's oath of loyalty, a king would give him lands. The nobleman ruled these lands, judging legal cases, imposing taxes, and maintaining an army—powers granted him in exchange for his promise of loyalty to his king.

The Code of Chivalry As an expression of feudal ideals of honor, nobles developed a code of conduct called chivalry. This code demanded that knights be brave warriors and virtuous Christians who would selflessly fight for justice.

King Arthur and His Knights The ideals of chivalry gave rise to legends and songs, such as the tales of King Arthur and his knights of the Round Table. In the eleventh century, as feudalism established itself throughout Europe, stories about Arthur's court became widespread.

Sir Gawain and the Green Knight In *Sir Gawain and the Green Knight*, a medieval poem, the chivalry of Gawain, Arthur's loyal nephew, is tested by three challenges. In meeting them, Gawain proves admirable but not invulnerable. As one critic writes, the hero "gains in human credibility what he loses in ideal perfection."

We know little about the poet of *Sir Gawain*, who is credited with three other poems in alliterative verse. In his work, though, with its combination of humor and fervent ideals, he has helped shape an enduring vision of personal integrity.

Arthur answer gave
And said, "Sir courteous knight,
If contest here you crave,
55 You shall not fail to fight."

"Nay, to fight, in good faith, is far from my thought;
There are about on these benches but beardless children,
Were I here in full arms on a haughty[4] steed,
For measured against mine, their might is puny.
60 And so I call in this court for a Christmas game,
For 'tis Yule, and New Year, and many young bloods about;
If any in this house such hardihood claims,
Be so bold in his blood, his brain so wild,
As stoutly to strike one stroke for another,
65 I shall give him as my gift this gisarme[5] noble,
This ax, that is heavy enough, to handle as he likes,
And I shall bide the first blow, as bare as I sit.
If there be one so wilful my words to assay,
Let him leap hither lightly, lay hold of this weapon;
70 I quitclaim it forever, keep it as his own,
And I shall stand him a stroke, steady on this floor,
So you grant me the guerdon to give him another, sans blame.[6]
    In a twelvemonth[7] and a day
    He shall have of me the same;
75   Now be it seen straightway
    Who dares take up the game."

If he astonished them at first, stiller were then
All that household in hall, the high and the low;
The stranger on his green steed stirred in the saddle,
80 And roisterously his red eyes he rolled all about,
Bent his bristling brows, that were bright green,
Wagged his beard as he watched who would arise.
When the court kept its counsel he coughed aloud,
And cleared his throat coolly, the clearer to speak:
85 "What, is this Arthur's house," said that horseman then,
"Whose fame is so fair in far realms and wide?
Where is now your arrogance and your awesome deeds,
Your valor and your victories and your vaunting words?
Now are the revel and renown of the Round Table
90 Overwhelmed with a word of one man's speech,
For all cower and quake, and no cut felt!"

Literary Analysis
Medieval Romance
What aspect of medieval romances does the Green Knight's appearance illustrate?

Reading
Check

How does the Green Knight challenge Arthur's court?

---

4. **haughty** (hôt′ ē) *adj.* lofty.
5. **gisarme** (gi zärm′) *n.* battle-ax.
6. **I shall . . . blame** "I will stand firm while he strikes me with the ax provided that you reward me with the opportunity to do the same to him without being blamed for it."
7. **twelvemonth** a year.

With this he laughs so loud that the lord grieved;
The blood for sheer shame shot to his face, and pride.
    With rage his face flushed red,
95   And so did all beside.
    Then the king as bold man bred
    Toward the stranger took a stride.

And said, "Sir, now we see you will say but folly,
Which whoso has sought, it suits that he find.
100 No guest here is aghast of your great words.
Give to me your gisarme, in God's own name,
And the boon you have begged shall straight be granted."
He leaps to him lightly, lays hold of his weapon;
The green fellow on foot fiercely alights.
105 Now has Arthur his ax, and the haft[8] grips,
And sternly stirs it about, on striking bent.
The stranger before him stood there erect,
Higher than any in the house by a head and more;
With stern look as he stood, he stroked his beard,
110 And with undaunted countenance drew down his coat,
No more moved nor dismayed for his mighty dints
Than any bold man on bench had brought him a drink of wine.
    Gawain by Guenevere
    Toward the king doth now incline:
115   "I beseech, before all here,
    That this melee may be mine."

"Would you grant me the grace," said Gawain to the king,
"To be gone from this bench and stand by you there,
If I without discourtesy might quit this board,
120 And if my liege lady[9] misliked it not,
I would come to your counsel before your court noble.
For I find it not fit, as in faith it is known,
When such a boon is begged before all these knights,
Though you be tempted thereto, to take it on yourself
125 While so bold men about upon benches sit,
That no host under heaven is hardier of will,
Nor better brothers-in-arms where battle is joined;
I am the weakest, well I know, and of wit feeblest;
And the loss of my life would be least of any;
130 That I have you for uncle is my only praise;
My body, but for your blood, is barren of worth;
And for that this folly befits not a king,
And 'tis I that have asked it, it ought to be mine,
And if my claim be not comely let all this court judge in sight."

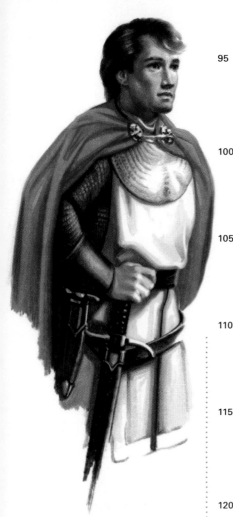

▲ **Critical Viewing**
Read Gawain's description
of himself in lines 128–130.
In what ways does this
illustration of Gawain
contrast with those lines?
[Compare and Contrast]

---

8. haft *n.* handle of a weapon or tool.

9. liege (lēj) **lady** Guenevere, the wife of the lord, Arthur, to whom Gawain is bound to give service and allegiance.

135   The court assays the claim,
            And in counsel all unite
            To give Gawain the game
            And release the king outright.

      Then the king called the knight to come to his side,
140 And he rose up readily, and reached him with speed,
      Bows low to his lord, lays hold of the weapon,
      And he releases it lightly, and lifts up his hand,
      And gives him God's blessing, and graciously prays
      That his heart and his hand may be hardy both.
145 "Keep, cousin," said the king, "what you cut with this day,
      And if you rule it aright, then readily, I know,
      You shall stand the stroke it will strike after."
      Gawain goes to the guest with gisarme in hand,
      And boldly he bides there, abashed not a whit.
150 Then hails he Sir Gawain, the horseman in green:
      "Recount we our contract, ere you come further.
      First I ask and adjure you, how you are called
      That you tell me true, so that trust it I may."
      "In good faith," said the good knight, "Gawain am I
155 Whose buffet befalls you,[10] whate'er betide after,
      And at this time twelvemonth take from you another
      With what weapon you will, and with no man else alive."
            The other nods assent:
            "Sir Gawain, as I may thrive,
160   I am wondrous well content
            That you this dint[11] shall drive."

      "Sir Gawain," said the Green Knight, "By God, I rejoice
      That your fist shall fetch this favor I seek,
      And you have readily rehearsed, and in right terms,
165 Each clause of my covenant with the king your lord,
      Save that you shall assure me, sir, upon oath,
      That you shall seek me yourself, wheresoever you deem
      My lodgings may lie, and look for such wages[12]
      As you have offered me here before all this host."
170 "What is the way there?" said Gawain, "Where do you dwell?
      I heard never of your house, by Him that made me,
      Nor I know you not, knight, your name nor your court.
      But tell me truly thereof, and teach me your name,
      And I shall fare forth to find you, so far as I may,
175 And this I say in good certain, and swear upon oath."
      "That is enough in New Year, you need say no more,"

---

10. Whose . . . you "whose blow you will receive."
11. dint *n.* blow.
12. wages *n.* payment; that is, a strike with the ax.

Literary Analysis
Medieval Romance
How are Gawain's words in lines 128–134 and the court's decision consistent with the ideals of chivalry?

Vocabulary
adjure (ə joor´) *v.* request solemnly; appeal to earnestly

Reading Check

What does Gawain do to the Green Knight?

Said the knight in the green to Gawain the noble,
"If I tell you true, when I have taken your knock,
And if you handily have hit, you shall hear straightway
180 Of my house and my home and my own name;
Then follow in my footsteps by faithful accord.
And if I spend no speech, you shall speed the better:
You can feast with your friends, nor further trace my tracks.[13]
    Now hold your grim tool steady
185   And show us how it hacks."
    "Gladly, sir; all ready,"
    Says Gawain; he strokes the ax.

The Green Knight upon ground girds him with care:
Bows a bit with his head, and bares his flesh:
190 His long lovely locks he laid over his crown,
Let the naked nape for the need be shown
Gawain grips to his ax and gathers it aloft—
The left foot on the floor before him he set—
Brought it down deftly upon the bare neck,
195 That the shock of the sharp blow shivered the bones
And cut the flesh cleanly and clove it in twain,[14]
That the blade of bright steel bit into the ground.
The head was hewn off and fell to the floor;
Many found it at their feet, as forth it rolled;
200 The blood gushed from the body, bright on the green,
Yet fell not the fellow, nor faltered a whit,
But stoutly he starts forth upon stiff shanks,
And as all stood staring he stretched forth his hand,
Laid hold of his head and heaved it aloft,
205 Then goes to the green steed, grasps the bridle,
Steps into the stirrup, bestrides his mount,
And his head by the hair in his hand holds,
And as steady he sits in the stately saddle
As he had met with no mishap, nor missing were his head.
210   His bulk about he haled,
    That fearsome body that bled;
    There were many in the court that quailed
    Before all his say was said.

For the head in his hand he holds right up;
215 Toward the first on the dais directs he the face,
And it lifted up its lids, and looked with wide eyes,
And said as much with its mouth as now you may hear:
"Sir Gawain, forget not to go as agreed,

Reading Strategy
Summarizing How would you summarize the event described in lines 188–213?

Literary Analysis
Medieval Romance
What two characteristics of a medieval romance are reflected in lines 214–231?

---

13. If I tell you . . . tracks The Green Knight tells Gawain that he will let him know where he lives after he has taken the blow. If he is unable to speak following the blow, there will be no need for Gawain to know.
14. clove it in twain split it in two.

And cease not to seek till me, sir, you find,
220 As you promised in the presence of these proud knights.
To the Green Chapel come, I charge you, to take
Such a dint as you have dealt—you have well deserved
That your neck should have a knock on New Year's morn.
The Knight of the Green Chapel I am well-known to many,
225 Wherefore you cannot fail to find me at last;
Therefore come, or be counted a recreant[15] knight."
With a roisterous rush he flings round the reins,
Hurtles out at the hall door, his head in his hand,
That the flint fire flew from the flashing hooves.
230 Which way he went, not one of them knew
Nor whence he was come in the wide world so fair.
  The king and Gawain gay
  Make a game of the Green Knight there,
  Yet all who saw it say
235   'Twas a wonder past compare.

Though high-born Arthur at heart had wonder,
He let no sign be seen, but said aloud
To the comely queen, with courteous speech,
"Dear dame, on this day dismay you no whit;
240 Such crafts are becoming at Christmastide,
Laughing at interludes, light songs and mirth,
Amid dancing of damsels with doughty knights.
Nevertheless of my meat now let me partake,
For I have met with a marvel, I may not deny."
245 He glanced at Sir Gawain, and gaily he said,
"Now, sir, hang up your ax, that has hewn enough,"
And over the high dais it was hung on the wall
That men in amazement might on it look,
And tell in true terms the tale of the wonder.
250 Then they turned toward the table, those two together,
The good king and Gawain, and made great feast,
With all dainties double, dishes rare,
With all manner of meat and minstrelsy both,
Such happiness wholly had they that day in hold.
255   Now take care, Sir Gawain,
  That your courage wax not cold
  When you must turn again
  To your enterprise foretold.

—————————
15. recreant *adj.* cowardly.

▲ **Critical Viewing**
Identify two elements in this illustration of Arthur that portray him as a powerful ruler. **[Analyze]**

Reading
Check

What happens after Gawain chops off the Green Knight's head?

from Sir Gawain and the Green Knight **177**

The following November, Sir Gawain sets out to fulfill his promise to the Green Knight. For weeks, he travels alone through the cold, threatening woods of North Wales. Then, after he prays for shelter, he comes upon a wondrous castle on Christmas Eve, where he is greeted warmly by the lord of the castle and his lady. The lord assures Sir Gawain that the Green Chapel is nearby and promises to provide him with a guide to lead him there on New Year's Day. Before the lord and Sir Gawain retire for the night, they agree to exchange whatever they receive during the next three days. Sir Gawain keeps his pledge for the first two days, but he fails to give the lord the magic green girdle that the lady gives him on the third day, because she gives it with the promise that it will protect him from harm. The next day, Gawain sets out for the Green Chapel. His guide urges him not to proceed, but Gawain feels that it would be dishonorable not to fulfill his pledge. He is determined to accept his fate; however, he wears the magic green girdle that the lady has given him.

▼ **Critical Viewing**
Examine this illustration of Gawain's journey through the wilderness. Why might Gawain be tempted to stay in the castle and give up his quest? **[Speculate]**

He puts his heels to his horse, and picks up the path;
260 Goes in beside a grove where the ground is steep,
Rides down the rough slope right to the valley;
And then he looked a little about him—the landscape was wild,
And not a soul to be seen, nor sign of a dwelling,
But high banks on either hand hemmed it about,
265 With many a ragged rock and rough-hewn crag;
The skies seemed scored by the scowling peaks.
Then he halted his horse, and hoved there a space,
And sought on every side for a sight of the Chapel,
But no such place appeared, which puzzled him sore,
270 Yet he saw some way off what seemed like a mound,
A hillock high and broad, hard by the water,
Where the stream fell in foam down the face of the steep
And bubbled as if it boiled on its bed below.
The knight urges his horse, and heads for the knoll;
275 Leaps lightly to earth; loops well the rein
Of his steed to a stout branch, and stations him there.
He strides straight to the mound, and strolls all about,
Much wondering what it was, but no whit the wiser;
It had a hole at one end, and on either side,
280 And was covered with coarse grass in clumps all without,
And hollow all within, like some old cave,
Or a crevice of an old crag—he could not discern aright.
    "Can this be the Chapel Green?
    Alack!" said the man, "Here might
285   The devil himself be seen
    Saying matins[16] at black midnight!"

16. **matins** *n.* morning prayers.

"Now by heaven," said he, "it is bleak hereabouts;
This prayer house is hideous, half covered with grass!
Well may the grim man mantled in green
290 Hold here his orisons,[17] in hell's own style!
Now I feel it is the Fiend, in my five wits,
That has tempted me to this tryst,[18] to take my life;
This is a Chapel of mischance, may the mischief take it!
As accursed a country church as I came upon ever!"
295 With his helm on his head, his lance in his hand,
He stalks toward the steep wall of that strange house.
Then he heard, on the hill, behind a hard rock,
Beyond the brook, from the bank, a most barbarous din:
Lord! it clattered in the cliff fit to cleave it in two,
300 As one upon a grindstone ground a great scythe!
Lord! it whirred like a mill-wheel whirling about!
Lord! it echoed loud and long, lamentable to hear!
Then "By heaven," said the bold knight, "That business up there
Is arranged for my arrival, or else I am much misled.

305   Let God work! Ah me!
     All hope of help has fled!
     Forfeit my life may be
     But noise I do not dread."

Then he listened no longer, but loudly he called,
310 "Who has power in this place, high parley to hold?
For none greets Sir Gawain, or gives him good day;
If any would a word with him, let him walk forth
And speak now or never, to speed his affairs."
"Abide," said one on the bank above over his head,
315 "And what I promised you once shall straightway be given."
Yet he stayed not his grindstone, nor stinted its noise,
But worked awhile at his whetting before he would rest,
And then he comes around a crag, from a cave in the rocks,
Hurtling out of hiding with a hateful weapon,
320 A Danish ax[19] devised for that day's deed,
With a broad blade and bright, bent in a curve,
Filed to a fine edge—four feet it measured
By the length of the lace that was looped round the haft.
And in form as at first, the fellow all green,
325 His lordly face and his legs, his locks and his beard,
Save that firm upon two feet forward he strides,
Sets a hand on the ax-head, the haft to the earth;
When he came to the cold stream, and cared not to wade,

17. orisons *n.* prayers.
18. tryst (trist) *n.* meeting.
19. Danish ax long-bladed ax.

Literary Analysis
Medieval Romance and Legend In what way does Gawain's speech in lines 287–294 add a dimension to the story that might not have been present in the original legend?

Reading Check

What is the Green Knight doing when Gawain arrives at the Green Chapel?

from Sir Gawain and the Green Knight **179**

He vaults over on his ax, and advances amain
330 On a broad bank of snow, overbearing and brisk of mood.
     Little did the knight incline
     When face to face they stood;
     Said the other man, "Friend mine,
     It seems your word holds good!"

335 "God love you, Sir Gawain!" said the Green Knight then,
"And well met this morning, man, at my place!
And you have followed me faithfully and found me betimes,
And on the business between us we both are agreed:
Twelve months ago today you took what was yours,
340 And you at this New Year must yield me the same.
And we have met in these mountains, remote from all eyes:
There is none here to halt us or hinder our sport;
Unhasp your high helm, and have here your wages;
Make no more demur[20] than I did myself
345 When you hacked off my head with one hard blow."
"No, by God," said Sir Gawain, "that granted me life,
I shall grudge not the guerdon[21] grim though it prove;
And you may lay on as you like till the last of my part be paid."
     He proffered, with good grace,
350   His bare neck to the blade,
     And feigned a cheerful face:
     He scorned to seem afraid.

Then the grim man in green gathers his strength,
Heaves high the heavy ax to hit him the blow.
355 With all the force in his frame he fetches it aloft,
With a grimace as grim as he would grind him to bits;
Had the blow he bestowed been as big as he threatened,
A good knight and gallant had gone to his grave.
But Gawain at the great ax glanced up aside
360 As down it descended with death-dealing force,
And his shoulders shrank a little from the sharp iron.
Abruptly the brawny man breaks off the stroke,
And then reproved with proud words that prince among knights.
"You are not Gawain the glorious," the green man said,
365 "That never fell back on field in the face of the foe,
And now you flee for fear, and have felt no harm:
Such news of that knight I never heard yet!
I moved not a muscle when you made to strike,
Nor caviled[22] at the cut in King Arthur's house;
370 My head fell to my feet, yet steadfast I stood,
And you, all unharmed, are wholly dismayed—

▲ **Critical Viewing**
In what ways does this illustration of the Green Knight compare or contrast with your mental image of him? **[Compare and Contrast]**

Literary Analysis
Medieval Romance
How do Gawain's actions in lines 359–387 reflect or depart from the ideals of knighthood?

---

20. demur (dē mʉr) protest; delay.
21. guerdon *n.* reward.
22. caviled raised trivial objections

Wherefore the better man I, by all odds, must be."
        Said Gawain, "Strike once more;
        I shall neither flinch nor flee;
375   But if my head falls to the floor
        There is no mending me!"

    "But go on, man, in God's name, and get to the point!
    Deliver me my destiny, and do it out of hand,
    For I shall stand to the stroke and stir not an inch
380 Till your ax has hit home—on my honor I swear it!"
    "Have at thee then!" said the other, and heaves it aloft,
    And glares down as grimly as he had gone mad.
    He made a mighty feint, but marred not his hide;
    Withdrew the ax adroitly before it did damage.
385 Gawain gave no ground, nor glanced up aside,
    But stood still as a stone, or else a stout stump
    That is held in hard earth by a hundred roots.
    Then merrily does he mock him, the man all in green:
    "So now you have your nerve again, I needs must strike;
390 Uphold the high knighthood that Arthur bestowed,
    And keep your neck-bone clear, if this cut allows!"
    Then was Gawain gripped with rage, and grimly he said,
    "Why, thrash away, tyrant, I tire of your threats;
    You make such a scene, you must frighten yourself."
395 Said the green fellow, "In faith, so fiercely you speak
    That I shall finish this affair, nor further grace allow."
        He stands prepared to strike
        And scowls with both lip and brow;
        No marvel if the man mislike
400   Who can hope no rescue now.

    He gathered up the grim ax and guided it well:
    Let the barb at the blade's end brush the bare throat;
    He hammered down hard, yet harmed him no whit
    Save a scratch on one side, that severed the skin;
405 The end of the hooked edge entered the flesh,
    And a little blood lightly leapt to the earth.
    And when the man beheld his own blood bright on the snow,
    He sprang a spear's length with feet spread wide,
    Seized his high helm, and set it on his head,
410 Shoved before his shoulders the shield at his back,
    Bares his trusty blade, and boldly he speaks—
    Not since he was a babe born of his mother
    Was he once in this world one half so blithe—
    "Have done with your hacking—harry me no more!
415 I have borne, as behooved, one blow in this place;
    If you make another move I shall meet it midway
    And promptly, I promise you, pay back each blow with brand.

Vocabulary
adroitly (ə droit´ lē) *adv.*
with physical or mental skill

Reading Strategy
Summarizing
Summarize what happens
after the Green Knight's third
stroke with the ax.

Reading Check

How does Gawain react
when the Green Knight first
lifts his axe?

▲ Critical Viewing
In view of what has happened, how might Gawain feel when he remembers this image of the Green Knight's wife?
[Speculate]

One stroke acquits me here;
So did our covenant stand
420   In Arthur's court last year—
Wherefore, sir, hold your hand!"

He lowers the long ax and leans on it there,
Sets his arms on the head, the haft on the earth,
And beholds the bold knight that bides there afoot,
425 How he faces him fearless, fierce in full arms,
And plies him with proud words—it pleases him well.
Then once again gaily to Gawain he calls,
And in a loud voice and lusty, delivers these words:
"Bold fellow, on this field your anger forbear!
430 No man has made demands here in manner uncouth,
Nor done, save as duly determined at court.
I owed you a hit and you have it; be happy therewith!
The rest of my rights here I freely resign.
Had I been a bit busier, a buffet, perhaps,
435 I could have dealt more directly; and done you some harm.
First I flourished with a feint, in frolicsome mood,
And left your hide unhurt—and here I did well
By the fair terms we fixed on the first night;
And fully and faithfully you followed accord:
440 Gave over all your gains as a good man should.
A second feint, sir, I assigned for the morning
You kissed my comely wife—each kiss you restored.
For both of these there behooved but two feigned blows by right.
    True men pay what they owe;
445   No danger then in sight.
    You failed at the third throw,
    So take my tap, sir knight.

"For that is my belt about you, that same braided girdle,
My wife it was that wore it; I know well the tale,
450 And the count of your kisses and your conduct too,
And the wooing of my wife—it was all my scheme!
She made trial of a man most faultless by far
Of all that ever walked over the wide earth;
As pearls to white peas, more precious and prized,
455 So is Gawain, in good faith, to other gay knights.
Yet you lacked, sir, a little in loyalty there,
But the cause was not cunning, nor courtship either,
But that you loved your own life; the less, then, to blame."
The other stout knight in a study stood a long while,
460 So gripped with grim rage that his great heart shook.
All the blood of his body burned in his face
As he shrank back in shame from the man's sharp speech.
The first words that fell from the fair knight's lips:

"Accursed be a cowardly and covetous heart!
465 In you is villainy and vice, and virtue laid low!"
Then he grasps the green girdle and lets go the knot,
Hands it over in haste, and hotly he says:
"Behold there my falsehood, ill hap betide it!
Your cut taught me cowardice, care for my life,
470 And coveting came after, contrary both
To largesse and loyalty belonging to knights.
Now am I faulty and false, that fearful was ever
Of disloyalty and lies, bad luck to them both! and greed.
   I confess, knight, in this place,
475   Most dire is my misdeed;
   Let me gain back your good grace,
   And thereafter I shall take heed."

Then the other laughed aloud, and lightly he said,
"Such harm as I have had, I hold it quite healed.
480 You are so fully confessed, your failings made known,
And bear the plain penance of the point of my blade,
I hold you polished as a pearl, as pure and as bright
As you had lived free of fault since first you were born.
And I give you sir, this girdle that is gold-hemmed
485 And green as my garments, that, Gawain, you may
Be mindful of this meeting when you mingle in throng
With nobles of renown—and known by this token
How it chanced at the Green Chapel, to chivalrous knights.
And you shall in this New Year come yet again
490 And we shall finish out our feast in my fair hall with cheer."

Vocabulary
largesse (lär jes´) *n.* nobility of spirit

Reading Strategy
Summarizing How would you summarize Sir Gawain's response to the Green Knight in lines 459–477?

Critical Reading

1. **Key Ideas and Details** **(a)** How do Arthur's knights first respond to the Green Knight's challenge? **(b) Analyze:** Why does the Green Knight laugh at their response?

2. **Key Ideas and Details** **(a)** What does Gawain offer to do? **(b) Analyze:** How does he make his offer seem humble, not boastful?

3. **Key Ideas and Details** **(a) Interpret:** In lines 464–477, how does Sir Gawain react when he considers his own actions? **(b) Draw Conclusions:** What has Sir Gawain learned from his second encounter with the Green Knight?

4. **Integration of Knowledge and Ideas** Using the example of Sir Gawain, explain whether it is more important to achieve goals or to learn from mistakes.

Cite textual evidence to support your responses.

Author of *Morte d'Arthur*

SIR THOMAS MALORY
(1405?–1471)

When people today hear the name Sir Thomas Malory, they may think of knights in shining armor, daring quests, and heroic rescues. They may not think of a convicted felon who spent much of his life in jail! The Malory they recall is the author of the most complete surviving collection of Arthurian legends, *Morte d'Arthur*. Yet, some historians have claimed that he is the same Thomas Malory who was jailed for such crimes as cattle-stealing, extortion, and assault—and who once escaped custody by swimming a moat!

Malory the Prisoner Few facts about Malory's life are known with certainty. It is said that he loved hunting and tournaments as well as Arthurian lore. Scholars generally hold that the author of *Morte d'Arthur* spent much of his life in prison. Some maintain, though, that he was jailed as a prisoner of war, not as a rustler.

A Book From Behind Bars Whatever the reason for his imprisonment, Malory probably wrote *Morte d'Arthur* from behind bars. Even as a prisoner, a knight such as Malory would have been granted access to books, such as the Arthurian texts that Malory translated and adapted.

A Legend Reborn *Morte d'Arthur* is not merely a retelling of existing legends. Fired by his own belief in the ideals of knighthood—and perhaps embittered by the decline of these ideals in a time of civil war—Malory forged the Arthurian legends into a visionary cycle of bold adventure, spiritual quests, and heart-rending betrayal. This great work was given its name by William Caxton, the man who established the first printing press in England. Caxton published *Morte d'Arthur* after its author's death, ensuring its enduring fame.

FROM
MORTE D'ARTHUR

SIR THOMAS MALORY

This selection begins after King Arthur has traveled to France at the insistence of his nephew, Gawain, to besiege his former friend and knight, Lancelot, for his involvement with Queen Guenevere. However, the king's attempts to punish Lancelot are halfhearted, and he is soon forced to abandon them altogether when he learns that his illegitimate son, Mordred, has seized control of England. Arthur leads his forces back to England, and Mordred attacks them upon their landing. Gawain is killed in the fighting, but before he dies, he manages to send word to Lancelot that Arthur is in need of his assistance.

So upon Trinity Sunday at night King Arthur dreamed a wonderful dream, and in his dream him seemed[1] that he saw upon a chafflet[2] a chair, and the chair was fast to a wheel, and thereupon sat King Arthur in the richest cloth of gold that might be made. And the King thought there was under him, far from him, an hideous deep black water, and therein was all manner of serpents, and worms, and wild beasts, foul and horrible. And suddenly the King thought that the wheel turned upside down, and he fell among the serpents, and every beast took him by a limb. And then the King cried as he lay in his bed, "Help, help!"

And then knights, squires, and yeomen awaked the King, and then he was

◀ **Critical Viewing**
Compare and contrast the details in this picture with those in Malory's account of Arthur's dream. **[Compare and Contrast}**

---

1. **him seemed** It seemed to him.
2. **chafflet** platform.

so amazed that he wist[3] not where he was. And then so he awaked until it was nigh day, and then he fell on slumbering again, not sleeping nor thoroughly waking. So the King seemed[4] verily that there came Sir Gawain unto him with a number of fair ladies with him. So when King Arthur saw him, he said, "Welcome, my sister's son. I weened ye had been dead. And now I see thee on-live, much am I beholden unto Almighty Jesu. Ah, fair nephew and my sister's son, what been these ladies that hither be come with you?"

"Sir," said Sir Gawain, "all these be ladies for whom I have foughten for when I was man living. And all these are those that I did battle for in righteous quarrels, and God hath given them that grace, at their great prayer, because I did battle for them for their right, that they should bring me hither unto you. Thus much hath given me leave God, for to warn you of your death. For and ye fight as tomorn[5] with Sir Mordred, as ye both have assigned, doubt ye not ye must be slain, and the most party of your people on both parties. And for the great grace and goodness that Almighty Jesu hath unto you, and for pity of you and many more other good men there shall be slain, God hath sent me to you of his special grace to give you warning that in no wise ye do battle as tomorn, but that ye take a treaty for a month from today. And proffer you largely[6] you so that tomorn ye put in a delay. For within a month shall come Sir Lancelot with all his noble knights and rescue you worshipfully and slay Sir Mordred and all that ever will hold with him."

Then Sir Gawain and all the ladies vanished. And anon the King called upon his knights, squires, and yeomen, and charged them wightly[7] to fetch his noble lords and wise bishops unto him. And when they were come the King told them of his avision,[8] that Sir Gawain had told him and warned him that, and he fought on the morn, he should be slain. Then the King commanded Sir Lucan the Butler and his brother Sir Bedivere the Bold, with two bishops with them, and charged them in any wise to take a treaty for a month from today with Sir Mordred. "And spare not: proffer him lands and goods as much as ye think reasonable."

So then they departed and came to Sir Mordred where he had a grim host of an hundred thousand, and there they entreated Sir Mordred long time. And at the last Sir Mordred was agreed for to have Cornwall and Kent by King Arthur's days, and after that, all England, after the days of King Arthur.

Then were they condescended[9] that King Arthur and Sir Mordred should meet betwixt both their hosts, and each of them should bring

---

3. **wist** knew.
4. **the King seemed** It seemed to the King.
5. **and . . . tomorn** "if you fight tomorrow."
6. **proffer you largely** make generous offers.
7. **wightly** quickly.
8. **avision** dream.
9. **condescended** agreed.

fourteen persons. And so they came with this word unto Arthur. Then said he, "I am glad that this is done," and so he went into the field.

And when King Arthur should depart, he warned all his host that, and they see any sword drawn, "Look ye come on fiercely and slay that traitor Sir Mordred, for I in no wise trust him." In like wise Sir Mordred warned his host that "And ye see any manner of sword drawn, look that ye come on fiercely, and so slay all that ever before you standeth, for in no wise I will not trust for this treaty." And in the same wise said Sir Mordred unto his host, "For I know well my father will be avenged upon me."

And so they met as their pointment[10] was and were agreed and accorded thoroughly. And wine was fetched and they drank together. Right so came an adder out of a little heathbush, and it stung a knight in the foot. And so when the knight felt him so stung, he looked down and saw the adder. And anon he drew his sword to slay the adder, and thought none other harm. And when the host on both parties saw that sword drawn, then they blew beams,[11] trumpets, horns, and shouted grimly. And so both hosts dressed them together. And King Arthur took his horse and said, "Alas, this unhappy day!" and so rode to his party, and Sir Mordred in like wise.

And never since was there never seen a more dolefuller battle in no Christian land, for there was but rushing and riding, lunging and striking; and many a grim word was there spoken of either to other, and many a deadly stroke. But ever King Arthur rode throughout the battle[12] of Sir Mordred many times and did full nobly, as a noble king should do, and at all times he fainted never. And Sir Mordred did his devoir[13] that day and put himself in great peril.

And thus they fought all the long day, and never stinted[14] till the noble knights were laid to the cold earth. And ever they fought still till it was near night, and by then was there an hundred thousand laid dead upon the down. Then was King Arthur wood-wroth[15] out of measure when he saw his people so slain from him. And so he looked about him and could see no more of all his host, and good knights left no more on-live, but two knights: the t'one was Sir Lucan the Butler and the other his brother Sir Bedivere. And yet they were full sore wounded.

"Jesu, mercy," said the King, "where are all my noble knights become? Alas that ever I should see this doleful day! For now," said King Arthur, "I am come to mine end. But would to God," said he,

> And when they were come the King told them of his avision, that Sir Gawain had told him and warned him that, and he fought on the morn, he should be slain.

Vocabulary
peril (per´ əl) *n.* exposure to harm or injury

Reading Check
What causes the two armies to start fighting?

---

10. **pointment** arrangement.
11. **beams** type of trumpet.
12. **battle** battalion.
13. **devoir** (də vwär´) *n.* duty (from the French; obsolete).
14. **stinted** stopped.
15. **wood-wroth** wild with rage.

"that I wist now where were that traitor Sir Mordred that has caused all this mischief."

Then King Arthur looked about and was ware where stood Sir Mordred leaning upon his sword among a great heap of dead men.

"Now give me my spear," said King Arthur unto Sir Lucan, "for yonder I have espied the traitor that all this woe hath wrought."

"Sir, let him be," said Sir Lucan, "for he is unhappy. And if ye pass this unhappy day ye shall be right well revenged upon him. And, good lord, remember ye of your night's dream, and what the spirit of Sir Gawain told you tonight, and yet God of his great goodness hath preserved you hitherto. And for God's sake, my lord, leave off by this, for, blessed be God, ye have won the field: for yet we been here three on-live, and with Sir Mordred is not one on-live. And therefore if ye leave off now, this wicked day of destiny is past."

"Now, tide[16] me death, tide me life," said the King, "now I see him yonder alone, he shall never escape mine hands. For at a better avail shall I never have him."

"God speed you well!" said Sir Bedivere.

Then the King got his spear in both his hands and ran toward Sir Mordred, crying and saying, "Traitor, now is thy deathday come!"

And when Sir Mordred saw King Arthur he ran until him with his sword drawn in his hand, and there King Arthur smote Sir Mordred under the shield, with a thrust of his spear, throughout the body more than a fathom. And when Sir Mordred felt that he had his death's wound, he thrust himself with the might that he had up to the burr[17] of King Arthur's spear, and right so he smote his father King Arthur with his sword holden in both his hands, upon the side of the head, that the sword pierced the helmet and the casing of the brain. And therewith Sir Mordred dashed down stark dead to the earth.

And noble King Arthur fell in a swough[18] to the earth, and there he swooned oftentimes, and Sir Lucan and Sir Bedivere ofttimes heaved him up. And so, weakly betwixt them, they led him to a little chapel not far from the seaside, and when the King was there, him thought him reasonably eased. Then heard they people cry in the field. "Now go thou, Sir Lucan," said the King, "and do me to

16. **tide** befall.
17. **burr** hand guard.
18. **swough** forcible movement

◀ **Critical Viewing**
In this picture of the battle between King Arthur and Sir Mordred, which details contribute to the grim mood? Explain. **[Analyze]**

Reading Strategy
Summarizing Summarize the events leading to the death of Mordred and the mortal wounding of King Arthur.

Reading Check

What does Sir Lucan urge King Arthur to do?

wit[19] what betokens that noise in the field."

So Sir Lucan departed, for he was grievously wounded in many places. And so as he walked he saw and harkened by the moonlight how that pillagers and robbers were come into the field to pill and to rob many a full noble knight of brooches and bracelets and of many a good ring and many a rich jewel. And who that were not dead all out there they slew them for their harness and their riches. When

▼ Critical Viewing In this picture of Sir Bedivere and the dying Arthur, do you think the boat that Bedivere sees is real or supernatural? Why? **[Interpret]**

19. **me to wit** "let me know."

Sir Lucan understood this work, he came to the King as soon as he might and told him all what he had heard and seen. "Therefore by my read,"[20] said Sir Lucan, "it is best that we bring you to some town."

"I would it were so," said the King, "but I may not stand, my head works so. Ah, Sir Lancelot," said King Arthur, "this day have I sore missed thee. And alas that ever I was against thee, for now have I my death, whereof Sir Gawain me warned in my dream."

Then Sir Lucan took up the King the t'one party[21] and Sir Bedivere the other party; and in the lifting up the King swooned and in the lifting Sir Lucan fell in a swoon that part of his guts fell out of his body, and therewith the noble knight's heart burst. And when the King awoke he beheld Sir Lucan how he lay foaming at the mouth and part of his guts lay at his feet.

"Alas," said the King, "this is to me a full heavy sight to see this noble duke so die for my sake, for he would have helped me that had more need of help than I. Alas that he would not complain him for his heart was so set to help me. Now Jesu have mercy upon his soul."

Then Sir Bedivere wept for the death of his brother.

"Now leave this mourning and weeping gentle knight," said the King, "for all this will not avail me. For wit thou well, and might I live myself, the death of Sir Lucan would grieve me evermore. But my time passeth on fast," said the King. "Therefore," said King Arthur unto Sir Bedivere, "take thou here Excalibur my good sword and go with it to yonder water's side; and when thou comest there I charge thee throw my sword in that water and come again and tell me what thou sawest there."

"My lord," said Sir Bedivere, "your commandment shall be done, and I shall lightly[22] bring you word again."

So Sir Bedivere departed. And by the way he beheld that noble sword, that the pommel and the haft[23] was all precious stones. And then he said to himself, "If I throw this rich sword in the water, thereof shall never come good, but harm and loss." And then Sir Bedivere hid Excalibur

20. **read** advice.
21. **party** side.
22. **lightly** quickly.
23. **pommel** . . . **haft** hilt and hand guard.

Literary Analysis
Medieval Romance
What note of realism does this one-sentence paragraph strike?

Reading Check

What does Arthur ask Sir Bedivere to do with Excalibur?

▶ **Critical Viewing**
What do you think the three women around the dead or dying Arthur are doing? Explain. **[Infer]**

under a tree. And so, as soon as he might, he came again unto the King and said he had been at the water and had thrown the sword into the water.

"What saw thou there?" said the King.

"Sir," he said, "I saw nothing but waves and winds."

"That is untruly said of thee," said the King. "And therefore go thou lightly again and do my commandment; as thou art to me loved and dear, spare not, but throw it in."

Then Sir Bedivere returned again and took the sword in his hand. And yet him thought sin and shame to throw away that noble sword. And so eft[24] he hid the sword and returned again and told the King that he had been at the water and done his commandment.

"What sawest thou there?" said the King.

"Sir," he said, "I saw nothing but waters wap and waves wan."[25]

"Ah, traitor unto me and untrue," said King Arthur, "now hast thou betrayed me twice. Who would have weened that thou that has been to me so loved and dear, and thou art named a noble knight, and would betray me for the riches of this sword. But now go again lightly, for thy long tarrying putteth me in great jeopardy of my life, for I have taken cold. And but if thou do now as I bid thee, if ever I may see thee I shall slay thee mine own hands, for thou wouldest for my rich sword see me dead."

Literary Analysis
Medieval Romance
What element does the appearance of the hand add to the tale?

Then Sir Bedivere departed and went to the sword and lightly took it up, and so he went to the water's side; and there he bound the girdle about the hilts, and threw the sword as far into the water as he might. And there came an arm and an hand above the water and took it and clutched it, and shook it thrice and brandished; and then vanished away the hand with the sword into the water. So Sir Bedivere came again to the King and told him what he saw.

"Alas," said the King, "help me hence, for I dread me I have tarried overlong."

Then Sir Bedivere took the King upon his back and so went with him to that water's side. And when they were at the water's side, even fast[26] by the bank floated a little barge with many fair ladies in it; and among them all was a queen; and all they had black hoods, and all they wept and shrieked when they saw King Arthur.

"Now put me into that barge," said the King; and so he did softly. And there received him three ladies with great mourning, and so they set them down. And in one of their laps King Arthur laid his head, and then the queen said, "Ah, my dear brother, why have ye tarried so long from me? Alas, this wound on your head hath caught overmuch cold." And anon they rowed fromward the land, and Sir Bedivere beheld all those ladies go froward him.

---

24. **eft** again.
25. **waters . . . wan** waters lap and waves grow dark.
26. **fast** close.

from Morte d'Arthur 193

Literary Analysis
Medieval Romance and Legend Does the description of Sir Bedivere's reaction sound more like a description you might find in a folk tale or in a modern short story? Explain.

Vocabulary
interred (in turd´) *v.* buried in the earth

Reading Strategy
Summarizing What happens to Sir Bedivere after Arthur departs on the barge?

Then Sir Bedivere cried and said, "Ah, my lord Arthur, what shall become of me, now ye go from me and leave me here alone among mine enemies?"

"Comfort thyself," said the King, "and do as well as thou mayest, for in me is no trust for to trust in. For I must into the vale of Avilion[27] to heal me of my grievous wound. And if thou hear nevermore of me, pray for my soul."

But ever the queen and ladies wept and shrieked, that it was pity to hear. And as soon as Sir Bedivere had lost sight of the barge he wept and wailed, and so took the forest and went all that night.

And in the morning he was ware, betwixt two bare woods, of a chapel and an hermitage. Then was Sir Bedivere glad, and thither he went, and when he came into the chapel he saw where lay an hermit groveling on all fours, close thereby a tomb was new dug. When the hermit saw Sir Bedivere he knew him well, for he was but little tofore Bishop of Canterbury, that Sir Mordred put to flight.

"Sirs," said Sir Bedivere, "what man is there here interred that you pray so fast for?"

"Fair son," said the hermit. "I wot not verily but by guessing. But this same night, at midnight, here came a number of ladies and brought here a dead corpse and prayed me to inter him. And here they offered an hundred tapers, and gave me a thousand gold coins."

"Alas," said Sir Bedivere, "that was my lord King Arthur, which lieth here buried in this chapel."

Then Sir Bedivere swooned, and when he awoke he prayed the hermit that he might abide with him still, there to live with fasting and prayers:

"For from hence will I never go," said Sir Bedivere, "by my will, but all the days of my life here to pray for my lord Arthur."

"Sir, ye are welcome to me," said the hermit, "for I know you better than ye think that I do: for ye are Sir Bedivere the Bold, and the full noble duke Sir Lucan the Butler was your brother."

Then Sir Bedivere told the hermit all as you have heard tofore, and so he stayed with the hermit that was beforehand Bishop of Canterbury. And there Sir Bedivere put upon him poor clothes, and served the hermit full lowly in fasting and in prayers.

Thus of Arthur I find no more written in books that been authorized, neither more of the very certainty of his death heard I nor read, but thus was he led away in a ship wherein were three queens; that one was King Arthur's sister, Queen Morgan le Fay, the other was the Queen of North Galis, and the third was the Queen of the Waste Lands.

Now more of the death of King Arthur could I never find, but that these ladies brought him to his grave, and such one was interred there which the hermit bare witness that was once Bishop of

---

27. **Avilion** legendary island where Arthur is said to dwell until his return.

Canterbury. But yet the hermit knew not in certain that he was verily the body of King Arthur; for this tale Sir Bedivere, a knight of the Table Round, made it to be written.

Yet some men say in many parts of England that King Arthur is not dead, but carried by the will of our Lord Jesu into another place; and men say that he shall come again, and he shall win the Holy Cross. Yet I will not say that it shall be so, but rather I would say: here in this world he changed his life. And many men say that there is written upon the tomb this:

HIC IACET ARTHURUS, REX QUONDAM, REXQUE FUTURUS[28]

---

28. HIC . . . FUTURUS Here lies Arthur, who was once king and king will be again.

Critical Reading

1. **Key Ideas and Details (a)** What warning does King Arthur receive in his dream? **(b)** How do circumstances frustrate his attempt to heed this warning? **(c) Interpret:** How does this series of events make the ending of the tale seem fated?

2. **Key Ideas and Details (a)** What is the relationship between Mordred and Arthur? **(b) Interpret:** How does the conflict between them emphasize the theme of betrayal in the tale?

3. **Integration of Knowledge and Ideas (a) Compare and Contrast:** How does the description of Sir Lucan's death contrast with the speech in which Arthur bemoans his passing? **(b) Draw Conclusions:** What conclusions can you draw from this contrast about the range of medieval taste in literature?

4. **Integration of Knowledge and Ideas** At the tale's end, rightful authority has been betrayed and may yet return, but it is not here now. What idea of leadership and loyalty in the present does this ending suggest?

5. **Integration of Knowledge and Ideas** Do you think leaders are "Arthurs"—those who should receive perfect obedience— or should people sometimes question their leader's decisions? Explain.

6. **Integration of Knowledge and Ideas** Do the authors of these selections accept or question the code of chivalry? In your response, use at least two of these Essential Question words: *traditional, ideal, conform.* **[Connecting to the Essential Question: What is the relationship of the writer to tradition?]**

Cite textual evidence to support your responses.

Literary Analysis

1. Craft and Structure (a) Identify three characteristics of Sir Gawain that make him an ideal hero for a **medieval romance.** Explain each answer. **(b)** Identify a shortcoming of his, and explain what it suggests about the theme of human weakness in medieval romance.

2. Key Ideas and Details In the excerpt from *Morte d'Arthur,* how do the supernatural events surrounding King Arthur's death link the story to the future?

3. Craft and Structure (a) Compare the characterization of Gawain (*Sir Gawain,* lines 459–477) with Malory's description of Bedivere as he reacts to the dying Arthur. Use a graphic organizer like the one shown. **(b)** Explain which author has done more to add literary elements, such as plot twists, descriptions, and characterization.

	Gawain's Reactions	Bedivere's Reactions
What He Says		
What He Does		
What He Feels		

4. Comparing Literary Works (a) Which of these elements of romance is least emphasized in *Sir Gawain:* chivalry, a far-off setting, the supernatural, adventure, or love? Explain. **(b)** Which is least emphasized in *Morte d'Arthur?* **(c)** What characteristics of a **legend** do the two selections share?

5. Analyzing Visual Information Using your knowledge of Arthurian legend, explain the humor in the cartoon shown here.

Reading Strategy

6. You are retelling *Sir Gawain and the Green Knight* to an audience of fifth graders. To prepare, **summarize the main idea or essential message** you would stress and the relevant details you would include.

7. As Sir Bedivere, summarize for a curious traveler who is visiting your hermitage the events leading up to King Arthur's death.

8. Based on your reading of these selections, summarize the main idea behind the code of chivalry and note the key ways in which it governed a knight's behavior.

Common Core State Standards

Writing

3. Write narratives to develop real or imagined experiences or events using effective technique, well-chosen details, and well-structured event sequences. *(p. 197)*

3.d. Use precise words and phrases, telling details, and sensory language to convey a vivid picture of the experiences, events, setting, and/or characters. *(p. 197)*

Language

4.a. Use context as a clue to the meaning of a word or phrase. *(p. 197)*

Integrated Language Skills

◎ Vocabulary Acquisition and Use

Word Analysis: The Word Root -droit-

The word *adroitly*, meaning "with physical or mental skill," is based on the French root *-droit-*, meaning "right." This root meaning reveals a historical bias toward right-handedness. The bias can be seen even more clearly in the Latin root *sinister*, meaning "left," "left-hand," or "unlucky." Answer these questions relating to *-droit-*.

1. Given that the prefix *mal-* means "bad," what might *maladroit* mean?

2. *Gauche* means "socially maladroit" in English. Which of these two words might it mean in French: "left" or "right"?

3. Which would you consider more *adroit*: a smooth left-handed layup in basketball or a clumsy right-handed air ball?

4. Using your knowledge of the root, briefly describe a duel between two knights—Sir Art the Adroit and Sir Mort the Maladroit.

Vocabulary: True or False?

Using your knowledge of the underlined vocabulary words, indicate whether each of the following statements is more likely to be true or false. Then, explain your answer.

1. A giant is lunging toward you, brandishing an ax. You would most likely <u>adjure</u> him to stop.

2. If his first swing was low and close, you might leap <u>adroitly</u> onto a nearby tabletop.

3. In the same moment, you might recognize the extent of your <u>peril.</u>

4. You might then beg the giant to abandon his <u>largesse</u> and take pity on small, helpless you.

5. If you have <u>entreated</u> the giant in just the right way, he might suddenly cease his attack and beg for forgiveness.

6. At that point, you might feel extraordinarily <u>interred</u>.

Writing

◎ **Narrative Text** As Sir Gawain approaches the Green Chapel, he reacts by expressing himself in an interior monologue—a device in which a character speaks only to himself or herself, revealing thoughts, feelings, and personality traits. Write an **interior monologue** in which Gawain reacts to another event in the story. In your monologue, create a distinctive voice for Gawain. Have him react to unfolding events in a *specific place*.

Prewriting List characteristics of Gawain, and jot down notes on the dramatic situation he is confronting. What would he think about the situation? How would he feel?

Drafting Writing in the first person, have Gawain "discuss" the situation with himself and so reveal both the events and the *significance of the events* to which he reacts. Make sure that key details explaining the situation emerge early. Refer to prewriting notes to ensure that you convey Gawain's character.

Revising Star sections of your draft in which Gawain's feelings are especially strong. Review these passages, replacing dull phrases with vivid expressions of his personality or reactions.

> **Model: Using Reactions to Develop a Narrative**
> By St. Peter's sail, will no one answer this strange knight's challenge? I would, forsooth, were it not presumptuous-seeming and—what! Arthur himself is answering!

> When Gawain interrupts himself to remark on a new disturbance, the reader sees the situation through the character's reactions.

Primary Sources

Letters
Letters of
Margaret Paston

Ballads
Four Folk
Ballads

 **Common Core State Standards**

Reading Informational Text
7. Integrate and evaluate multiple sources of information presented in different media or formats as well as in words in order to address a question or solve a problem.

About the Text Forms

A **letter** is a written communication to a person or group. In the centuries before telephones and e-mail, letters were a basic means of sharing information over a distance. Carried on foot, by horse, or by ship, letters were written for business and diplomatic reasons as well as personal ones. Today, letters from earlier eras are primary sources of information that shed light on the events, personalities, and daily life of times past.

During the Middle Ages, most people could neither read nor write. One of the ways in which they transmitted information was in story poems set to music, called **ballads.** Telling of sensational events and everyday calamities, **folk ballads** were anonymously composed and passed orally from singer to singer among the common folk. They often use four-line *stanzas,* in which only the second and fourth lines rhyme, and contain *dialogue* and repeated lines or phrases called **refrains.** Today, folk ballads of old are still being sung. As primary sources, they provide valuable glimpses into the lives and attitudes of ordinary people.

As you prepare to read these texts, consider questions you have about English life in the late Middle Ages. Look for answers among the details these primary sources provide.

Reading Strategy

The scholars who prepare primary sources for publication often include text aids to help you understand these sources from a different era. You can improve your comprehension of primary sources by **analyzing, evaluating, and applying information from text features.** Such features may include *introductory and side notes* that give background or *footnotes* that clarify unfamiliar terms or words in *dialect,* the variety of a language spoken by people in a particular region or group.

Letters and ballads can both reflect and influence their times. As you read, consider how passages in Margaret Paston's letters show her responding to and trying to influence events. Also consider how ballads hint at certain *assumptions* about love and death and speculate how people in medieval times may have reacted to those assumptions.

Note-Taking Guide

Primary-source documents are a rich source of information for researchers. As you read these documents, use a note-taking guide like the one shown to organize relevant and accurate information.

1 Type of Document (check one)
   ☐ Newspaper   ☐ Letter   ☐ Diary   ☐ Map   ☐ Government Document
   ☐ Advertisement   ☐ Speech   ☐ Other (specify): _____

2 Date(s) or Period Composed _____

3 Author (if known) _____
   Author's Position (if known) _____

4 Intended Audience _____

5 Purpose and Message
   a Why was this document composed? (check the main purpose)
      ☐ to entertain   ☐ to inform   ☐ to persuade   ☐ to describe   ☐ to reflect
   b Which word or words best describe the tone?   ☐ personal
      ☐ formal   ☐ humorous   ☐ dramatic   ☐ emotional   ☐ unsentimental
   c Summarize the message or main events in a sentence or two.
      _____
      _____

   d What does this document show about life in the time and place in which it was composed?
      _____
      _____

> **Reading Strategy**
> **Using Text Features**
> Features such as introductory notes, side notes, and footnotes may clarify details about time and place. As you read, analyze and apply information from text features to better understand the documents.

This guide was adapted from the **U.S. National Archives** document analysis worksheet.

Vocabulary

aldermen (ôl´ dər mən) *n.* chief officers in a shire, or county (p. 202)

succor (suk´ ər) *v.* help; aid; relieve (p. 202)

certify (sʉrt´ ə fī´) *v.* declare a thing true or accurate; verify; attest (p. 202)

remnant (rem´ nənt) *n.* what is left over; remainder (p. 202)

ransacked (ran´ sakt´) *v.* searched through to find goods to rob; looted (p. 203)

asunder (ə sun´ dər) *adv.* into parts or pieces (p. 203)

assault (ə sôlt´) *v.* violently attack (p. 203)

bar (bär) *n.* one of the vertical lines dividing written music into equal sections called measures (p. 205)

measure (mezh´ ər) *n.* a section of written music between two vertical lines called bars (p. 205)

melody (mel´ ə dē) *n.* a sequence of single tones that together create a tune or song (p. 205)

THE STORY BEHIND THE DOCUMENTS

Dating from 1477, this letter from the Paston collection may be the first Valentine message in English. Margery Brews writes to her fiancé, John Paston, "Be my olde Valentine."

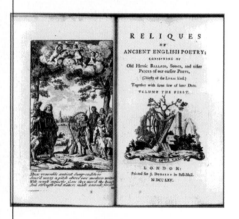

Percy's *Reliques of Ancient English Poetry*, shown above, popularized medieval ballads and inspired Romantic poets William Wordsworth and Samuel Taylor Coleridge to write their own ballads.

Margaret Paston (1423–1484) was born Margaret Mautby in the eastern English county of Norfolk. In about 1442 she married John Paston, a Norfolk lawyer and landowner. The Pastons had only recently acquired their wealth, however, and had to fight hard to keep it. During John's frequent visits to London to work on legal matters, it fell to his wife to run the estates, settle land disputes, and defend Paston manors against hostile raids.

Because they were often separated, Margaret and John exchanged many letters discussing family matters, local politics, and the everyday business of running an estate. Their letters are part of the more than one thousand Paston family documents originally preserved as evidence for lawsuits. Today these documents are a treasure trove of information about life in fifteenth-century England.

In the fifteenth century, when the weak rule of Henry VI plunged England into chaos, many families like the Pastons were able to rise from poverty, taking properties for which their legal claim was not firm. In one instance, the powerful Duke of Suffolk challenged the Pastons' claim to the manor of Hellesdon and bribed the mayor of the city of Norwich (nôr´ ij) to help force the Pastons out. Although Margaret Paston, with a garrison of sixty warriors, repelled the first attacks, the duke eventually seized and looted Hellesdon. In the first two letters presented here, Margaret writes to her husband with news of the duke's success. In the third letter, composed after her husband's death, she writes to her son Sir John Paston about defending another Paston property called Caister.

Unlike Margaret and John Paston, most people in the fifteenth century could not write or read. One way the common folk passed along sensational news and entertaining stories was in brief storytelling poems set to music called folk ballads.

The first English folk ballads probably go back to the twelfth century, but many more date to the Pastons' era of the fifteenth. Anonymously composed and transmitted orally from singer to singer, folk ballads exist in many different versions. The four presented here are versions from the border area between England and Scotland and use words and pronunciations in Scots dialect.

In 1765, Bishop Thomas Percy collected and published folk ballads in a book called *Reliques of Ancient English Poetry*. As other collections followed, people began to appreciate the literary value of folk ballads and the fascinating glimpses they offered of daily life and attitudes among people in times past.

▶ **Critical Viewing** The Paston manor homes were often attacked. Judging from this photograph of a manor house, how easy would it have been to defend such a building? Explain. **[Speculate]**

Letters of
MARGARET PASTON

Margaret Paston

Primary Sources
Letters What does this letter show about the loyalties of others to a newly wealthy family like the Pastons?

Vocabulary
aldermen (ôl´ dər mən) *n.* chief officers in a shire, or county

succor (suk´ ər) *v.* help; aid; relieve

certify (su̇rt´ ə fī´) *v.* declare a thing true or accurate; verify; attest

remnant (rem´ nənt) *n.* what is left over; remainder

Margaret Paston to John Paston
17 October 1465
Norwich

. . . The Duke came to Norwich on Tuesday at 10 o'clock with some 500 men. And he sent for the mayor and aldermen with the Sheriffs, desiring them in the King's name that they should make enquiry of the constables of every ward in the City as to what men had gone to help or succor your men at any time during these gatherings and, if they could find any, that they should take and arrest and correct them, and certify to him the names by 8 o'clock on Wednesday. Which the Mayor did and will do anything that he may for him and his men. . . .

I am told that the old Lady [the Dowager Duchess] and the Duke are fiercely set against us on the information of Harleston, the bailiff of Costessey . . . and such other false shrews which would have this matter carried through for their own pleasure. . . . And as for Sir John Heveningham, Sir John Wingfield and other worshipful men, they are but made their doggebolds [lackeys], which I suppose will cause their disworship hereafter. I spoke with Sir John Heveningham and informed him of the truth of the matter and of all our demeaning at Drayton, and he said he would that all things were well, and that he would inform my Lord what I told him, but that Harleston had all the influence with the Duke here, and at this time he was advised by him and Dr. Aleyn.

The lodge and the remnant of your place was beaten down on Tuesday and Wednesday and the Duke rode on Wednesday to Drayton and so forth to Costessey while the lodge at Hellesdon was being beaten down. And this night at midnight Thomas Slyforth . . . and others had a cart and fetched away featherbeds and all our stuff that was left at the parson's and Thomas Waters' house to be kept. . . . I pray you send me word how I shall act—whether you wish that I abide at Caister or come to you at London. . . .

Margaret Paston to John Paston
27 October 1465
Norwich

. . . Please you to know that I was at Hellesdon on Thursday last and saw the place there, and, in good faith, nobody would believe how foul and horrible it appears unless they saw it. There come many people daily to wonder at it, both from Norwich and many other places, and they speak of it with shame. The Duke would have been a £1000 better off if it had not happened, and you have the more good will of the people because it was so foully done. They made your tenants of Hellesdon and Drayton, with others, break down the walls of both the place and the lodge—God knows full much against their wills, but they dare not refuse for fear. I have spoken with your tenants of Hellesdon and Drayton and comforted them as well as I can. The Duke's men ransacked the church and bore away all the goods that were left there, both of ours and of the tenants, and even stood upon the high altar and ransacked the images and took away those that they could find, and put the parson out of the church till they had done, and ransacked every man's house in the town five or six times. . . . As for lead, brass, pewter, iron, doors, gates and other stuff of the house, men from Costessey and Cawston have it, and what they might not carry away they have hewn asunder in the most spiteful manner. . . .

At the reverence of God, if any worshipful and profitable settlement may be made in your matters, do not forsake it, to avoid our trouble and great costs and charges that we may have and that may grow hereafter. . . .

<hr />

The following letter was sent to Sir John Paston, Margaret's knighted son. Caister, a castle with many manors and estates, had been willed to the Paston family by Sir John Fastolf, for whom John Paston worked as financial advisor. There followed years of legal wrangles during which the Pastons faced numerous challenges to the will. Because her husband had died the year before, Margaret turned to her son Sir John for help defending Caister. Sir John sent his younger brother, also named John, to protect the castle. John failed, however, surrendering the castle after his protector, King Edward IV, was captured during the Wars of the Roses.

Margaret Paston to Sir John Paston
11 July 1467
Norwich

. . . Also this day was brought me word from Caister that Rising of Fritton had heard in divers places in Suffolk that Fastolf of Cowhawe gathers all the strength he may and intends to assault Caister and to enter there if he may, insomuch that it

Reading Strategy
Text Features What does this note clarify about the social position of the Pastons and the dangers they faced?

Reading Check
What has the Duke done against the Pastons?

is said that he has five score men ready and daily sends spies to know what men guard the place. By whose power or favor or support he will do this I know not, but you know well that I have been afraid there before this time, when I had other comfort than I had now: I cannot guide nor rule soldiers well and they set not by [do not respect] a woman as they should by a man. Therefore I would that you should send home your brothers or else Daubeney to take control and to bring in such men as are necessary for the safeguard of the place. . . . And I have been about my livelode to set a rule therein, as I have written to you, which is not yet all performed after my desire, and I would not go to Caister till I had done. I do not want to spend more days near thereabouts, if I can avoid it; so make sure that you send someone home to keep the place and when I have finished what I have begun I shall arrange to go there if it will do any good— otherwise I had rather not be there. . . .

. . . I marvel greatly that you send me no word how you do, for your enemies begin to grow right bold and that puts your friends in fear and doubt. Therefore arrange that they may have some comfort, so that they be not discouraged, for if we lose our friends, it will be hard in this troublous world to get them again . . .

Critical Reading

Cite textual evidence to support your responses.

© **1. Key Ideas and Details (a)** What does the duke force the Pastons' tenants to do? **(b) Interpret:** How does Margaret Paston feel about the duke's actions, and how does she expect the tenants to feel?

© **2. Craft and Structure (a) Analyze:** Cite examples of emotional appeals and logical reasons that Margaret Paston uses in requesting help from her husband and son. **(b) Draw Conclusions:** What sort of relationship does she have with her husband and son?

© **3. Integration of Knowledge and Ideas (a) Generalize:** What do the letters suggest to you about life in the Middle Ages? **(b) Evaluate:** What do you think is the most important difference, positive or negative, between life then and today? Why?

TWA CORBIES

BACKGROUND *During the Middle Ages, death before the age of thirty-five was the norm. The stark facts of life and death promoted the unsentimental outlook of medieval folk ballads.*

As I was walking all alane,
I heard twa corbies[1] making a mane.[2]
The tane unto the tither did say,
"Whar sall we gang and dine the day?"

5 "In behint yon auld fail dyke,[3]
I wot[4] there lies a new-slain knight;
And naebody kens[5] that he lies there
But his hawk, his hound, and his lady fair.

"His hound is to the hunting gane,
10 His hawk to fetch the wild-fowl hame,
His lady's ta'en anither mate,
So we may mak our dinner sweet.

"Ye'll sit on his white hause-bane,[6]
And I'll pike out his bonny blue e'en;[7]
15 Wi' ae lock o' his gowden hair
We'll theek[8] our nest when it grows bare.

"Mony a one for him maks mane,
But nane sall ken whar he is gane.
O'er his white banes, when they are bare,
20 The wind sall blaw for evermair."

---

1. **twa corbies** two ravens.
2. **mane** moan.
3. **fail dyke** bank of earth.
4. **wot** know.
5. **kens** knows.
6. **hause-bane** neck-bone.
7. **e'en** eyes.
8. **theek** thatch.

LORD RANDALL

Reading Strategy
Text Features What words and pronunciations in Scots dialect are explained in the first two footnotes? Why do you think there are no footnotes for the dialect in lines 1–3?

O where hae ye been, Lord Randall, my son?
O where hae ye been, my handsome young man?"
"I hae been to the wild wood; mother, make my bed soon,
For I'm weary wi' hunting, and fain[1] wald[2] lie down."

5   "Where gat ye your dinner, Lord Randall, my son?
Where gat ye your dinner, my handsome young man?"
"I dined wi' my true-love; mother, make my bed soon,
For I'm weary wi' hunting, and fain wald lie down."

"What gat ye to your dinner, Lord Randall, my son?
10 What gat ye to your dinner, my handsome young man?"
"I gat eels boil'd in broo;[3] mother, make my bed soon,
For I'm weary wi' hunting, and fain wald lie down."

Primary Sources
Folk Ballads What do the details in the fourth stanza of "Lord Randall" reveal about medieval life among the nobility?

"What became of your bloodhounds, Lord Randall, my son?
What became of your bloodhounds, my handsome young man?"
15 "O they swell'd and they died; mother, make my bed soon,
For I'm weary wi' hunting, and fain wald lie down."

"O I fear ye are poison'd, Lord Randall, my son!
O I fear ye are poison'd, my handsome young man!"
"O yes! I am poison'd; mother, make my bed soon,
20 For I'm sick at the heart, and I fain wald lie down."

1. **fain** gladly.
2. **wald** would.
3. **broo** broth.

Critical Reading

Cite textual evidence to support your responses.

1. **Key Ideas and Details (a)** Besides the two corbies, or ravens, who are the only ones that know where the new-slain knight lies? **(b) Infer:** Who or what do you think has caused the knight's death? Why?

2. **Craft and Structure (a) Infer:** How would you describe the corbies' tone in discussing the knight's death? **(b) Interpret:** What does the tone suggest about the medieval attitude toward death?

3. **Integration of Knowledge and Ideas (a) Analyze Cause and Effect:** Do you think Lord Randall was poisoned, or do you think he is simply sick at heart? Cite details to support your analysis. **(b) Draw Conclusions:** What view of love does "Lord Randall" express?

GET UP AND BAR THE DOOR

It fell about the Martinmas time,[1]
    And a gay time it was then,
When our goodwife got puddings to make,
    She's boild them in the pan.

5   The wind sae cauld blew south and north.
    And blew into the floor;
Quoth our goodman to our goodwife,
    "Gae out and bar the door."

"My hand is in my hussyfskap,[2]
10   Goodman, as ye may see;
An it should nae be barrd this hundred year,
    It's no be barrd for me."[3]

They made a paction[4] tween them twa.
    They made it firm and sure.
15 That the first word whaeer shoud speak,
    Shoud rise and bar the door.

Then by there came two gentlemen,
    At twelve o'clock at night,
And they could neither see house nor hall,
20   Nor coal nor candlelight.

"Now whether is this a rich man's house,
    Or whether it is a poor?"
But neer a word wad ane o' them[5] speak,
    For barring of the door.

25 And first they[6] ate the white puddings,
    And then they ate the black:

1. **Martinmas time** November 11.
2. **hussyfskap** household duties.
3. **An it should . . . me** "If it has to be barred by me, then it will not be barred in a hundred years."
4. **paction** agreement.
5. **them** the man and his wife.
6. **they** the strangers.

▲ **Primary Source: Art**
What does this painting tell you about domestic life in medieval times? **[Infer]**

Reading Check

What is it that neither the husband nor the wife wants to do?

Tho muckle[7] thought the goodwife to hersel,
    Yet neer a word she spake.

Then said the one unto the other,
30   "Here, man, take ye my knife;
Do ye tak aff the auld man's beard,
    And I'll kiss the goodwife."

"But there's nae water in the house,
    And what shall we do than?"
35 "What ails ye at the pudding broo,[8]
    That boils into[9] the pan?"

O up then started our goodman,
    An angry man was he:
"Will ye kiss my wife before my een,
40   And scad[10] me wi pudding bree?"[11]

Then up and started our goodwife,
    Gied three skips on the floor:
"Goodman, you've spoken the foremost word;
    Get up and bar the door."

Reading Strategy
Text Features How do the footnotes for this ballad help explain or clarify what occurs?

---

7. **muckle** much.
8. **What . . . broo** "What's the matter with pudding water?"
9. **into** in.
10. **scad** scald.
11. **bree** broth.

Critical Reading

Cite textual evidence to support your responses.

1. **Key Ideas and Details (a)** What agreement do the goodman and his wife make? **(b) Analyze:** What situation and/or character traits prompt them to make this agreement?

2. **Key Ideas and Details (a) Interpret:** To what class of society do the goodman and his wife belong? Cite details to support your answer. **(b) Draw Conclusions:** What does the strangers' treatment of them suggest about the dangers people of this class faced in medieval times?

3. **Key Ideas and Details (a) Summarize:** What dilemma does the couple face when the strangers arrive? **(b) Analyze:** In what way does the wife "win"? In what way do neither she nor her husband win? **(c) Interpret:** What point about stubbornness does the ballad make?

BARBARA ALLAN

It was in and about the Martinmas time,[1]
 When the green leaves were a-fallin';
That Sir John Graeme in the West Country
 Fell in love with Barbara Allan.

5 He sent his man down through the town
 To the place where she was dwellin':
"O haste and come to my master dear,
 Gin[2] ye be Barbara Allan."

O slowly, slowly rase[3] she up,
10 To the place where he was lyin',
And when she drew the curtain by:
 "Young man, I think you're dyin'."

"O it's I'm sick, and very, very sick,
 And 'tis a' for Barbara Allan."
15 "O the better for me ye sal[4] never be,
 Though your heart's blood were a-spillin'.

"O dinna ye mind,[5] young man," said she,
 "When ye the cups were fillin',
That ye made the healths gae round and round,
20 And slighted Barbara Allan?"

He turned his face unto the wall,
 And death with him was dealin':
"Adieu, adieu, my dear friends all,
 And be kind to Barbara Allan.

---

1. **Martinmas time** November 11.
2. **Gin** if.
3. **rase** rose.
4. **sal** shall.
5. **dinna ye mind** don't you remember.

Primary Sources
Folk Ballads What does the phrase "his man" tell you about the society of the time?

Reading Check

Why does Sir John Graeme send his man to Barbara Allan?

25 And slowly, slowly rase she up,
    And slowly, slowly left him;
And sighing said she could not stay,
    Since death of life had reft[6] him.

    She had not gane a mile but twa,[7]
30   When she heard the dead-bell knellin',
And every jow[8] that the dead-bell ga'ed[9]
    It cried, "Woe to Barbara Allan!"

"O mother, mother, make my bed,
    O make it soft and narrow:
35 Since my love died for me today,
    I'll die for him tomorrow."

Primary Sources
Folk Ballad Who speaks the dialogue in the last stanza? What general purpose does all the dialogue in the ballad serve?

---

6. **reft** deprived.
7. **not . . . twa** gone but two miles.
8. **jow** stroke.
9. **ga'ed** made.

Critical Reading

Cite textual evidence to support your responses.

© 1. **Key Ideas and Details (a)** What reason does Sir John give for his ailment? **(b)** What reason does Barbara Allan give for acting unconcerned about his plight? **(c) Interpret:** What is another reason she might put on a show of indifference?

© 2. **Key Ideas and Details Interpret:** Do you think Barbara Allan loved Sir John before her visit, or do you think the knowledge that he is dying inspires her love? Explain.

© 3. **Integration of Knowledge and Ideas (a) Summarize:** Sum up Barbara Allan's realization and feelings in the final stanza. **(b) Interpret:** What does the ballad suggest is the ultimate expression of love? **(c) Evaluate:** Do you agree with this view? Why or why not?

© 4. **Integration of Knowledge and Ideas (a) Analyze:** What chain of causes and effects leads to the outcome of the story in this ballad? **(b) Infer:** What do these events suggest about attitudes toward love among the common folk who listened to ballads? Explain.

The Sound of Medieval Music

Nobody knows for sure when the old English and Scottish folk ballads were first composed, who their authors were, or how they were performed. Based on versions in circulation today, we can guess that the narratives were sung and that the singers probably accompanied themselves on string instruments such as harps or lutes. Musicians playing woodwinds similar to recorders and flutes, as well as percussion instruments like the tabor, may have joined in. A bagpiper might even have contributed an interlude between verses.

Medieval musicians tuned their instruments differently from the way most Western musicians do today, and were probably influenced by Middle Eastern scales. The Islamic rule of the Iberian Peninsula (711–1492) and the Crusades (1095–1291) had introduced Europeans to Arabic vocal and instrumental traditions. During the Middle Ages, North African and Middle Eastern tonalities probably colored much of the music in Europe and the British Isles.

CONNECT TO THE LITERATURE

How would music enhance or detract from the stories in these ballads? Explain.

▲ Medieval musicians often combined string instruments with drums, horns, and bagpipes.

BAGPIPES
In the Middle Ages, bagpipes were played throughout Britain and Scotland as well as India and North Africa. With its loud, plaintive sound, it was the perfect instrument for the outdoors.

PIPE and TABOR
The pipe and tabor could be played by one person, who beat the tabor with one hand, while playing the pipe with the other. The tabor, a simple drum, is still used in the British Isles.

HARP
The word *harp* comes from Anglo-Saxon and Old German and originally meant, "to pluck." Triangular harps were used in Scotland as far back as the 9th century. Strings were made of twisted animal gut, horsehair, or even silk.

LUTE and PLECTRUM
The European lute was the predecessor to the modern guitar. It was an offspring of the oud, a stringed instrument introduced into Spain by the Arabs, during Islamic rule (711–1492). Like the oud, the early medieval lute was plucked with a pencil-thin tool called a plectrum.

Letters ▪ Ballads

Comparing Primary Sources

Refer to your Note-Taking Guide to complete these questions.

1. How are the perspectives on death and violence expressed in Paston's letters and in the ballads similar and different? Cite specific details to support your analysis.

2. Using a Venn diagram like this one, compare and contrast the letters and ballads with regard to their forms, audiences, and purposes.

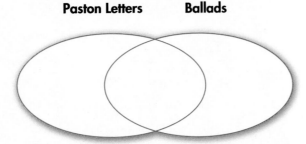

Paston Letters   **Ballads**

3. **(a)** Cite two questions about life in England during the Middle Ages that these texts can help you answer. Explain. **(b)** Which texts do you find more informative, and in what ways?

Vocabulary Acquisition and Use

New Vocabulary Answer each question. Then, explain how your understanding of the italicized vocabulary word helped you answer.

1. Who will *succor* the poor and needy, a kind person or a cruel one?

2. Who will *assault* a village, an invading army or a tired traveler?

3. Would a *remnant* of a meat loaf be the first piece or the last?

4. Which can more easily be torn *asunder*, a stone or a piece of paper?

Content-Area Vocabulary Use your knowledge of the italicized vocabulary words to decide whether each statement is true or false. Explain your answers.

1. A *measure* generally contains just one note.

2. To teach someone a song, you might hum the *melody*.

3. The *bar* tells you how quickly or slowly to play a piece of music.

4. *Aldermen* generally had influence in their communities.

5. When you *certify* something, you challenge it in court.

Etymology Study The word *ransacked*, from the Old Norse *rann*, meaning "house," and *saka*, meaning "seek," comes from the common medieval practice of attacking a place in search of valuables. A synonym of *ransacked* often used today is *looted*. Use a print or an online thesaurus to find two more synonyms for this word.

 **Common Core State Standards**

Writing

7. Conduct short as well as more sustained research projects to answer a question or solve a problem; narrow or broaden the inquiry when appropriate; synthesize multiple sources on the subject, demonstrating understanding of the subject under investigation.

8. Gather relevant information from multiple authoritative print and digital sources, using advanced searches effectively; assess the strengths and limitations of each source in terms of the task, purpose, and audience; integrate information into the text selectively to maintain the flow of ideas, avoiding plagiarism and overreliance on any one source and following a standard format for citation.

Language

6. Acquire and use accurately general academic and domain-specific words and phrases, sufficient for reading, writing, speaking, and listening at the college and career readiness level; demonstrate independence in gathering vocabulary knowledge when considering a word or phrase important to comprehension or expression.

Research Task

Topic: The Manor in Medieval England

Margaret Paston and her husband owned several significant properties, including two manor houses—the Hellesdon Manor and the Manor at Gresham. A manor was more than just a house. Under Feudalism, it was the center—both physical and symbolic—of the related economic system called Manorialism.

Assignment: With a group, write a **research report** on the English manor and the social order it represented. Discuss how key architectural elements reflect economic and legal relationships between the occupants of the manor and the people who lived in the surrounding area. Consider the following items:

- The relationship of the manor house to the surrounding land
- Activities, such as legal proceedings, that took place in a manor home
- The typical layout of the manor home, including the great hall, and the uses of these features
- Changes in manor homes as Feudalism waned in England

Formulate your research plan. In a group, brainstorm to formulate research questions about English manors and Manorialism. Then, discuss and decide on a plan to answer those questions.

Gather sources. Use library and computer searches to locate and explore a full range of relevant sources that answer the research questions. Organize the information into categories that address specific aspects of your topic. For all sources you consult, keep records that include the information you will need to construct thorough citations.

Synthesize information. When you synthesize information, you can decide which ideas and evidence to use and which to discard, arriving at the best response to your research question. A graphic organizer can clarify information and help you to compare and contrast it. For example, by listing specific features of a typical manor, you can better understand the picture of medieval life they convey.

RESEARCH TIP

There are many online sites dealing with specific English manor homes. You may want to include graphics from these sites and cite them in your report.

Model: Using a Chart to Synthesize Information

Item	Description	Picture of Culture It Conveys

Organize and present your ideas. Write your report on the English manor and Manorialism. Account for both the physical features of these structures as well as the social, legal, and economic system they represent. Include specific examples, and include graphic elements that will help your readers understand your ideas and evidence. Be sure to cite all sources, both print and electronic, accurately.

Use a checklist like the one shown to evaluate your work.

Research Checklist

- ☐ Have I answered the research questions?
- ☐ Have I organized information to support my central ideas?
- ☐ Have I accurately and thoroughly cited my sources?
- ☐ Have I presented my reasons clearly?

Write a Narrative

Common Core
State Standards

Writing

3. Write narratives to develop real or imagined experiences or events using effective technique, well-chosen details, and well-structured event sequences.

3.d. Use telling details to convey a vivid picture of the experiences, events, setting, and/or characters.

5. Develop and strengthen writing as needed by planning, focusing on addressing what is most significant for a specific purpose and audience.

Autobiographical Narrative The best stories are often true—they tell about real events in a writer's life. From memories of childhood to funny anecdotes to dramatic encounters, true stories touch and inspire us. Such stories are called **autobiographical narratives.** Follow the steps outlined in this workshop to write your own autobiographical narrative.

Assignment Write an autobiographical narrative about an event in your life that marked a significant change or led to an important insight.

What to Include Your autobiographical narrative should include the following elements:

- Characters, with a focus on one main character—you, the writer
- A setting with specifically located scenes and incidents and with *concrete sensory details* such as sights, sounds, and smells
- A *sequence of events* that forms a plot and whose *significance* is clear
- Conflict between characters or between a character and another force
- Insights that you gained from the experience

To preview the criteria on which your autobiographical narrative may be assessed, see the rubric on page 221.

www.PHLitOnline.com

To get a feel for autobiographical narratives, read this mentor text in which Elizabeth McCracken describes the thrill of scary stories. Notice how she uses the idea of a "room" in both a literal and a figurative way.

from: Introduction to *Frankenstein*

Like most seven-year-olds, I was never really alone except in dreams. Someone was always in a nearby room. I liked the terrifying movies I saw on TV, so many different versions of Frankenstein—Frankenstein, Bride of Frankenstein, Abbott and Costello Meet Frankenstein. I liked fairy tales with dark woodcuts of dense forests that might hide any number of monsters. Fear was the only room I had to myself.

WRITE GUY
Jeff Anderson, M.Ed.

What Do You Notice?

Read the highlighted sentence several times. Then, with a partner, discuss the qualities that make it special. You might consider the following elements:

- Word choice
- Sentence Length
- Rhythm
- Structure

Share your group's observations with the class.

Prewriting and Planning

Choosing Your Topic

To choose an event for your essay, use one of these strategies:

- **Listing** Create a chart with three columns, labeled *People*, *Places*, and *Events*. List memorable parts of your life under each column. Then, look for connections among the items you listed. When you find a connection, circle the items and draw an arrow to link them. Review your connections for narrative ideas.

- **Using Sentence Starters** Complete these sentences to generate ideas:

  - The funniest thing happened when _____.
  - My favorite holiday was _____.
  - My strongest memory from childhood is _____.

Narrowing Your Topic

Find your insight. Make your topic more specific by focusing on one idea you want to convey. Narrow a general topic to focus on one key event that highlights a meaningful insight.

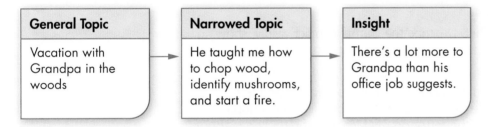

General Topic	Narrowed Topic	Insight
Vacation with Grandpa in the woods	He taught me how to chop wood, identify mushrooms, and start a fire.	There's a lot more to Grandpa than his office job suggests.

Gathering Details

Look for concrete details. List specific details you will include. Consider sensory details that convey the sights, sounds, and smells of the scenes. Look for details about characters' actions, movements, thoughts, words, and gestures. As you collect details, think about where each one will fit best in your narrative. Estimate about how much space and emphasis you will give to specific elements. The plan shown works for many narratives.

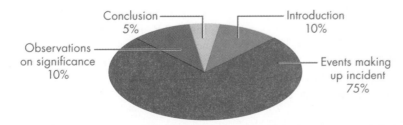

Drafting

Common Core State Standards

Writing

3.b. Use narrative techniques, such as dialogue, pacing, description, reflection, and multiple plot lines, to develop experiences, events, and/or characters.

3.e. Provide a conclusion that follows from and reflects on what is experienced, observed, or resolved over the course of the narrative.

Shaping Your Writing

Start out strong. Catch your readers' interest with a strong opening. Consider the options in this chart.

Opening Strategy	Example
Introduce a Character: A description of a character is effective if your narrative centers on a relationship.	Bob doesn't say much, no matter what may be going on, but when you see that gleam in his eye, you know you're in trouble.
Focus on Setting: This approach works well if time and place are critical elements.	The wind whistled through the cracks in the attic window.
Begin with Dialogue: An intriguing line of dialogue can quickly pull readers in.	"I said, did anybody leave this package on the counter?"

Pace your writing. Make sure you do not get bogged down in insignificant details. Establish background information quickly and then set your main incident in motion.

Providing Elaboration

Highlight a striking conflict. Describe the central conflict vividly, showing your readers the reason for the conflict instead of just telling them.

Flat: Grandpa wanted me to chop wood, but I didn't know how.

Vivid: "Henry, do me a favor and chop up a few logs, OK?" I nodded and hurried out to the woodpile so Grandpa wouldn't see the terror on my face. What did I know about chopping wood? The ax taunted me. Just thinking about swinging it made my toes hurt because I knew the ax was way more likely to land on my foot than the log.

End well. Devise an interesting closing. You might put the finishing touch on your story or leave readers hoping for more. Consider ending with an epilogue about what happened after the incident, a summary of your insights, or an unanswered question related to the conflict.

Model: Devising a Good Closing

I was sweating and my muscles ached, but there was my pile of chopped-up logs. I felt proud, as if this two-foot-high stack of wood was a house I had built with my own hands. The discarded splinters seemed like my own fears, cast away in the act of chopping.

> The writer ends on a note of accomplishment, providing an insight into the experience.

Writers on Writing

Burton Raffel On Shaping a Narrative

Burton Raffel is the author of the introduction to *Beowulf* (p. 36).

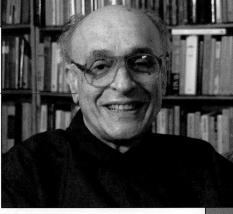

This is an excerpt from an autobiographical piece I wrote about thirty years ago. It tries to re-create, in adult language, some of those well-rubbed but rarely verbalized feelings that all small children surely have. Children are not simply the "small adults" that our civilization used to think they were. Nor is childhood merely another, though different, route to the same landing place.

"I realized that I was inventing a reality that wasn't real."

—*Burton Raffel*

from *Out in the Backyard of My Mind*

When I think of myself, as a small child, I remember, first, the sensation of offensive clothing—floppy clothing. Clothing buttoned and snapped and fastened in places I could not reach and affixed for reasons I knew I would not approve of if I could have understood what they were. I remember my shirts strapped to my back, somehow; and I remember ghastly knickers of worn corduroy, hanging baggy at the knees; and floppy coats that had belonged to cousins and uncles unseen, handed down, a little shabbier and floppier each time, until they came to me. I remember the faintly dank smell of cheap wool (mixed with what?), and especially its coarse, hairy feel— and the good, powdery smell and full softness of a big brown automobile lap robe, always and still called "the horse blanket." Skin was no better: if I was ever without clothing, in those days, I do not remember it, nor remember any pleasure from it. And I can remember hiding from my nakedness. Not just the way all little children do, sometimes, but compulsively, fiercely. One summer—I was eight, I think—my mother had a serious operation and I spent two months with a relative. Two summer months, and hot work of it, playing outdoors, but I did not know how to take a bath by myself and I would not let anyone give me a bath; no one unauthorized was to be allowed to see me unclothed.

These first two sentences are not "laundry lists": their detail is simply what they, and the piece as a whole, are about.

The details of the third sentence introduce a quiet shift in focus, from myself to the exterior world: walking, first, and then cars.

The last sentences move the focus of the piece even further into society.

Revising

Revising Your Overall Structure

Clarify the time and place. Be sure that you have clearly indicated *shifts in time and place* and have *paced actions* to accommodate these *changes*.

1. Star any place where the time or location changes.

2. Underline in red the words you have used to indicate the change. Have a partner check to make sure that each shift is clear and complete and that the actions do not seem abrupt.

3. Revise by adding transitional phrases or descriptive words. Insert a paragraph break to highlight the impact of a time or place shift.

Common Core State Standards

Writing
3.c. Use a variety of techniques to sequence events so that they build on one another to create a coherent whole and build toward a particular tone and outcome.

5. Develop and strengthen writing as needed by revising, focusing on addressing what is most significant for a specific purpose and audience.

Model: Revising to Clarify Time and Place

That day was more than nine years ago. I have lived in America now for nearly ten years.

It was a good experience, to be surprised by the taste of a drink. Today, I struggle to hold on to everything about myself that makes me un-American.

> Added information shows a gap in time.

Peer Review: Share your draft with a classmate. Explain why you made your revision choices, and ask your reader to give you feedback about the time and place shifts you included.

Revising Your Content

Add significance. Consider conveying the significance of events to your audience by adding an **interior monologue,** in which a character reacts to events and reveals his or her feelings and thoughts about them.

Revising Your Sentences

Eliminate unnecessary tense changes. Even though you may be moving back and forth in time in your narrative, do not change tenses unnecessarily. Do not shift tenses without a good reason.

Original Sentence:

It was midnight when the vote tally is finally complete.

Corrected Sentence:

It was midnight when the vote tally was finally completed.

Developing Your Style

Vivid Word Choice

Word Choice Choose strong verbs and adjectives that bring the characters, events, setting, and conflict of your autobiographical narrative to life. Avoid words that are weak, dull, or vague.

Weak: I drank the soda and it was delicious.

Strong: I took a sip of the soda and savored its tangy surprises: a tart kick of lime and extra-fizzy bubbles that tickled the inside of my mouth and made me feel as if I were smelling a lime air freshener.

Instead of settling for general, overused verbs and adjectives, take time to find precise, vivid examples.

Find It in Your Reading

Read the selection "Letters of Margaret Paston" on pages 201–204.

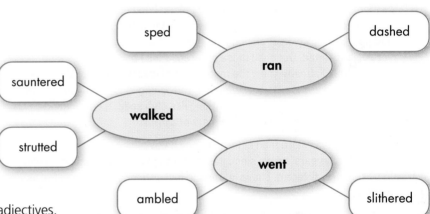

1. Find two sentences from Paston's letters in which the author uses strong verbs and two sentences in which the author uses strong adjectives.

2. Choose two words from the selection that you find particularly vivid.

Apply It to Your Writing

Review the draft of your autobiographical narrative, focusing on your choice of words. Follow these steps as you read:

- Circle any words that seem dull, weak, or vague. Also circle any uses of jargon or clichés.

- Challenge yourself to replace each circled word with a more vivid alternative, especially one that brings a setting to life with concrete sensory details of sights, sounds, and smells.

- Use a thesaurus or dictionary, and check to be sure that your new words accurately reflect what you want to say about your characters, setting, or conflict.

PH WRITING COACH

Further instruction and practice are available in *Prentice Hall Writing Coach*.

A Toast to the Future

I came to this country on a plane. Just a kid, not even eight years old yet, I sat on the center aisle of a huge 747 in Chicago waiting to fly to Los Angeles. These names—Chicago, Los Angeles—were abstract to me. All I knew was that I was in America, the place where everybody drives a nice car and lives in a great house or apartment and the bad guys always lose. At least, that was what the television back in Romania had shown me.

I was very thirsty, sitting in that center aisle. I kept asking my mom when they were going to bring us drinks. I don't know how much time went by before the cart came around, but it finally arrived.

That moment was my first real encounter with America. There were so many cans to choose from, so many colors. I had no idea which one to take. I chose the blue one since blue was my favorite color. I opened it up and poured it in my clear plastic cup. The soda was also clear, and I was very disappointed. Out of all those different cans I had to choose club soda, a drink I already knew the taste of. But I was wrong. I took a sip, and to my joyous surprise, it was sweet and refreshing, and the bubbles tickled the inside of my mouth. It tasted nothing like club soda. It was a good experience, to be surprised by the taste of a drink.

That day was more than nine years ago. I have lived in America now for nearly ten years. I have since passed through feelings of isolation and fears of being different. I have learned to make friends and to lead life as I want to.

Today, I struggle to hold on to everything about myself that makes me un-American. I try not to forget the Romanian language, I try to remember that I was not born in America. I think about Romania every day. I will not forget it, ever. A Romanian flag hangs in my bedroom alongside pictures of American rock stars. The thought of my homeland always makes me feel a certain way. I feel a kind of bittersweet feeling, calm, a feeling of happiness. I picture a warm sunny day on which I am walking alone on the little winding street that surrounded our building complex.

When I think of the future, though, I have a simple hope. I hope the future will be like the moment one tastes the first sip of sweet, crisp, bubbly soda, when a second before it looked like just plain old club soda.

Mircea clearly establishes the setting of his story.

The narrative centers on the conflict of cultures.

Mircea devotes several sentences to the choice of sodas, using pacing to focus his reader's attention and build interest.

Vivid sensory details draw a reader into Mircea's experience. See Developing Your Style, p. 219.

Mircea clearly states the insight he has gained and poetically links it to the narrative.

Editing and Proofreading

Focus on punctuation. To punctuate direct quotations, place commas or periods inside the final quotation mark and place semicolons or colons outside it. Place a question mark inside the closing quotation mark only if it is part of the quotation.

> **Inside:**   My grandfather asked, "Where do you think you're going?"
>
> **Outside:** Will I be able to say "I'm sorry"?

Focus on spelling. When the prefix *ex-* means "out," do not use a hyphen after it: *extract, export, exhaust*. When it means "former," use a hyphen: *ex-president, ex-wife*.

Spiral Review: Conventions Earlier in this unit, you learned about correlative conjunctions (page 154). Check your narrative to be sure you have used those conventions correctly.

Publishing, Presenting, and Reflecting

Consider one of the following ways to share your writing with your classmates.

Maintain a portfolio. Follow your growth as a writer by keeping your autobiographical narrative with other works in a writing portfolio.

Publish a literary magazine. Collect your classmates' narratives for publication in a student magazine, which you might post on the Internet. Have writers provide illustrations and introductions for their works.

Reflect on your writing. Jot down your thoughts on the experience of writing an autobiographical narrative. Begin by answering this question: What did you learn about yourself as a writer by completing this narrative?

Rubric for Self-Assessment

Evaluate your reflective essay using the following criteria and rating scale.

Common Core State Standards

Writing
5. Develop and strengthen writing as needed by editing, focusing on addressing what is most significant for a specific purpose and audience.
6. Use technology, including the Internet, to produce, publish, and update individual or shared writing products in response to ongoing feedback, including new arguments or information.

Language
2.a. Observe hyphenation conventions.
2.b. Spell correctly.

PH WRITING COACH

Further instruction and practice are available in *Prentice Hall Writing Coach*.

Criteria	Rating Scale
	not very very
Focus: How well do you describe yourself, the main character, and the other characters in your narrative?	1 2 3 4 5
Organization: How effectively do you organize the sequence of events?	1 2 3 4 5
Support/Elaboration: How well do you use details to describe scenes and events?	1 2 3 4 5
Style: How vivid is your word choice, especially your use of strong verbs and adjectives to bring characters, events, settings, and conflicts to life?	1 2 3 4 5
Conventions: How correct is your grammar, especially your use of punctuation?	1 2 3 4 5

Evaluate Persuasive Speech

Common Core State Standards

Speaking and Listening
3. Evaluate a speaker's point of view, reasoning, and use of evidence and rhetoric, assessing the stance, premises, links among ideas, word choice, points of emphasis, and tone used.

Persuasive speech, also called argument, includes a range of uses, from a presidential address to a lawyer's closing remarks. Persuasion happens whenever one person speaks to convince another to think or act in a certain way.

Types of Propositions

Persuasive speech includes four types of propositions.

Propositions	Example
Fact—asserts that something is	Average annual temperatures have been rising.
Value—claims that something is good or bad or is better or worse than something else	Kenneth Branagh's adaptation of *Hamlet* is the best.
Problem—demonstrates that a problem exists	Our team's name, The Ants, is a problem because…
Policy—argues that something should be done	Our school should start a debate club.

Identify Persuasive Techniques

Persuasive Appeals Different types of persuasive speech rely on varied types of appeals, evidence, and patterns of logic:

- **Ethos, an ethical appeal,** cites the speaker's authority, as in a famous surgeon endorsing a heart medicine.
- **Pathos, an emotional appeal,** tugs at the audience's emotions, as in an ad that uses a smiling infant to sell baby food.
- **Logos, a logical appeal,** applies reasoning and facts to build convincing arguments.

Syllogisms are arguments made up of two premises and a conclusion. Example: "All men are mortal. Socrates is a man. Socrates is mortal."

Inductive reasoning draws a conclusion from examples. Example: "I touched three icicles and they were cold. I think all icicles are cold."

Deductive reasoning applies a general principle to specific cases. Example: "I know ice is frozen, so I know this icicle will be cold."

Analogies are comparisons. A letter of recommendation comparing your writing to a professional's will probably create a good impression.

Identify Persuasive Techniques (continued)

Uses of Language Effective speakers use various techniques to achieve clarity, force, and aesthetic effect:

- **rhetorical questions:** questions not meant to be answered but used to establish solidarity with an audience
- **parallelism:** repetition of similar ideas in similar grammatical forms
- **figurative language:** nonliteral language, such as similes and metaphors, that add interest and encourage active listening

Negative Techniques Speakers may also resort to *negative persuasive techniques,* including the misuse of logic, in order to sway listeners. Many **logical fallacies,** such as those listed below, may seem plausible at first:

- *ad hominem* **attack:** an attack on a person's character
- **false causality:** the idea that A happened before B, so A caused B
- **red herring:** an irrelevant distraction from more important points
- **overgeneralization:** a conclusion based on too little evidence
- **bandwagon effect:** the idea that you should do something because everyone does it

Activities: Evaluate Persuasive Speech

Ⓒ Comprehension and Collaboration With a classmate, complete the following activities, using the evaluation form shown below to guide your work.

A. Find a persuasive speech in a play or on the Internet. Describe the proposition and evaluate the use of specific persuasive techniques.

B. Identify logical fallacies in three different speeches. Then, discuss why the speakers might have resorted to using fallacies.

Evaluation Form for Persuasive Speech

Name of Speech _____

Media Type _____

Intended Audience _____

Purpose _____

Type of Proposition _____

Appeal to Ethos _____

Appeal to Pathos _____

Appeal to Logos (Include syllogisms or analogies, if possible) _____

Uses of Language _____

Negative Persuasive Techniques _____

In your opinion, does this speaker argue persuasively and ethically? Why or
   why not? _____

Vocabulary Workshop

Using Dictionaries and Other Resources

A **dictionary** is a reference tool that contains information about words. Each entry lists the word's correct spelling and pronunciation, grammatical function, meanings, and etymology, or origin. **Print dictionaries** are organized alphabetically. **Electronic dictionaries** offer a search list or require you to enter your word. **Specialized dictionaries** define words and phrases in a particular field, such as medicine, law, art, or literature.

Sample Dictionary Entry

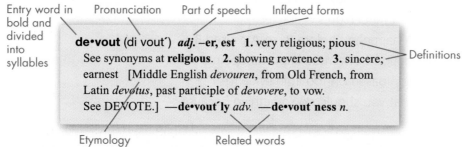

Entry word in bold and divided into syllables

Pronunciation   Part of speech   Inflected forms

de•vout (di vout´) *adj.* –**er, est** **1.** very religious; pious
See synonyms at **religious**. **2.** showing reverence **3.** sincere; earnest [Middle English *devouren*, from Old French, from Latin *devōtus*, past participle of *devovere*, to vow.
See DEVOTE.] —**de•vout´ly** *adv.* —**de•vout´ness** *n.*

Definitions

Etymology   Related words

A **thesaurus** is a reference tool providing, for each entry, lists of synonyms and some antonyms. The synonyms share the *denotative*, or literal, meaning of the entry word. However, they do not always share the *connotative* meaning, or associations a word suggests. For example, *precise* and *prim* have similar meanings, but *precise* has a positive connotation while *prim* suggests a self-conscious fussiness. After choosing a synonym, it is a good idea to check its meaning in a dictionary to see how it will fit in your sentence.

Sample Thesaurus Entry

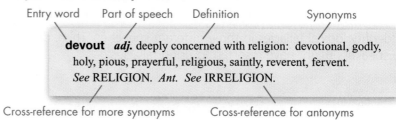

Entry word   Part of speech   Definition   Synonyms

devout *adj.* deeply concerned with religion: devotional, godly, holy, pious, prayerful, religious, saintly, reverent, fervent.
See RELIGION. *Ant. See* IRRELIGION.

Cross-reference for more synonyms   Cross-reference for antonyms

Practice

Directions: Answer each question as directed.

1. Use a dictionary to discover the etymology of *barbarous*. Analyze the word's origin and explain how it relates to the etymology of *brave*.

2. Analyze a thesaurus entry for *brave*. **(a)** Choose two words with positive connotations. Use each in a sentence about Beowulf or another epic hero. **(b)** Then, choose two synonyms with negative connotations. Use each in a sentence that illustrates its meaning.

3. Use a dictionary to trace the etymologies of these words: *shield, destiny, fame, hero, dragon, sword.* Which derive from Old English?

4. Trace the etymologies of these words: *kingdom, nation.*

Common Core State Standards

Language
4.a. Use context as a clue to the meaning of a word or phrase.
4.c. Consult general and specialized reference materials, both print and digital, to find the pronunciation of a word or determine or clarify its precise meaning, its part of speech, its etymology, or its standard usage.
4.d. Verify the preliminary determination of the meaning of a word or phrase.

Vocabulary Acquisition and Use: Context Clues

Context clues are words or phrases that help readers clarify the meanings of unfamiliar words in a text. By using context clues, you can determine the word or words that complete a sentence. Sentence Completion questions appear in most standardized tests. In these types of questions, you are given sentences with one or more missing words. Your task is to use the context to choose the correct word or words to complete each sentence logically. Try this strategy: (1) Read the sentence. (2) Read *all* of the answer choices, and mark those that might work. (3) Of the ones you marked, choose the answer that works best.

Practice

Test-Taking Tip
Immediately rule out any answer choices you know are wrong.

This exercise is modeled after the Sentence Completion exercises that appear in the Critical Reading section of the SAT.

Directions: Each of the following sentences is missing one or two words. Choose the word or set of words that best completes each sentence.

1. Violent, ___?___ creatures such as Grendel appear frequently in heroic literature.
   A. fervent
   B. solicitous
   C. genteel
   D. loathsome
   E. compassionate

2. The beast often makes it a habit to ___?___ and consume the people of a nearby community.
   A. assault
   B. purge
   C. cultivate
   D. befriend
   E. purge

3. Before the entire village has been torn ___?___, a noble traveler—often a distant kinsman—will arrive on the scene.
   A. adroitly
   B. aloft
   C. asunder
   D. obliquely
   E. apologetically

4. Next, at his own ___?___, the hero will confront the mighty beast.
   A. predicament
   B. peril
   C. prevarication
   D. pallor
   E. prowess

5. Though he is sometimes wounded, the hero takes ___?___ in his sacrifice.
   A. rancor
   B. prevarication
   C. absolution
   D. solace
   E. reparation

6. The hero proves his ___?___ from death.
   A. solace
   B. immunity
   C. largesse
   D. authority
   E. vulnerability

Test-Taking Practice

Reading Test: Natural Science Passages

Natural science passages are one type of reading selection found on standardized tests. These passages may relate to biology, chemistry, geology, or other sciences. They may have a social or historical perspective as well. Natural science passages are informational, but they also express the author's point of view either directly or indirectly. Questions following these passages may focus on main idea, text structure, and author's purpose. They will also test your comprehension of key facts and details.

 Common Core State Standards

RI.11-12.1, RI.11-12.2, RI.11-12.3, RI.11-12.4, RI.11-12.5; L.11-12.3, L.11-12.4, L.11-12.6
[For the full wording of the standards, see the standards chart in the front of your textbook.]

Practice

The following exercise is modeled after the ACT Reading Test, Natural Science section. The full reading test has 40 questions.

Directions: Read the following passage, taken from Bede's *A History of the English Church and People*. Then, choose the best answer to each question.

Ireland is broader than Britain, and its mild and healthy climate is superior. Snow rarely lies longer than three days, so that there is no need to store hay in summer for winter use or to build stables for beasts. There are no reptiles, and no snake can exist there, for
5 although often brought over from Britain, as soon as the ship nears land, they breathe its scented air and die. In fact, almost everything in this isle enjoys immunity to poison, and I have heard that folk suffering from snakebite have drunk water in which scrapings from the leaves of books from Ireland had been steeped, and that this
10 remedy checked the spreading poison and reduced the swelling. The island abounds in milk and honey, and there is no lack of vines, fish, and birds, while deer and goats are widely hunted. It is the original home of the Scots, who, as already mentioned, later migrated and joined the Britons and Picts in Britain. There is a very extensive
15 arm of the sea, which originally formed the boundary between the Britons and the Picts. This runs inland from the west for a great distance as far as the strongly fortified British city of Alcuith. It was to the northern shores of this firth that the Scots came and established their new homeland.

Strategy

Scan, then read.

- **First, scan the passage.** Take 20 seconds to skim the text. Look for a main topic and a few key terms.

- **Second, read the passage in full.** Ask yourself: *What information is most important? How does the author present this information?*

1. It can reasonably be inferred that at the time of the writing
   A. the environment in northern Europe was drastically different than it is today.
   B. the geography of northern Europe had recently and dramatically shifted.
   C. many people in Europe were suffering from poor health.
   D. most people in Europe knew little about Ireland.

2. Which of the following statements best paraphrases lines 2–3?
   F. Winter weather is harsh, but summer is easy on both animals and farmers.
   G. Because the snow is quick-melting, it does not interfere with the storage of hay or the building of shelters.
   H. Mild, dry winters eliminate the need for hay storage and animal shelters.
   J. The animals are hearty enough to go without food or shelter during the mild winter months.

3. The author includes the detail about the snakebite remedy (lines 7–10) in order to
   A. entertain his readers with a local legend.
   B. support the idea that Ireland's environment is healthful.
   C. encourage his readers to try the remedy for themselves.
   D. illustrate how uncivilized Ireland is.

4. The author writes that the island "abounds in milk and honey" (line 11).
   This phrase
   F. symbolizes the island's people.
   G. denotes the contents of the island.
   H. identifies an important limitation.
   J. connotes wholesome abundance.

5. In the context of the passage, the main function of lines 12–19 is to
   A. situate the island of Ireland in relation to Britain.
   B. provide background information about the Scots.
   C. indicate that Britain is home to many different peoples.
   D. suggest that Ireland is largely free of inhabitants.

6. Which conclusion can best be drawn about the author of the passage?
   F. He is native to Ireland.
   G. He is objective and credible.
   H. His motives are questionable.
   J. He has a background in medicine.

7. In the context of lines 14–18, it can reasonably be inferred that a *firth* is
   A. the shore of an island.
   B. a unit of measurement.
   C. an arm of the sea.
   D. the outer boundary of a city.

Grammar and Writing: Editing in Context

Some tests feature a passage with numbered sentences or parts of sentences, some of which contain errors in grammar, style, and usage. Your task is to choose the best version of the sentence from the choices offered. Some questions may also refer to the passage as a whole or to the numbered paragraphs contained in the passage.

Practice

This exercise is modeled after the ACT English Test.

Directions: For each underlined sentence or portion of a sentence, choose the best alternative. If an item asks a question about the underlined portion, choose the best answer to the question.

[1]

Edith May Pretty had lived on the Sutton Hoo estate near Suffolk, England, for twelve years. <u>The word *hoo* means "spur of a hill."</u> Mrs. Pretty, her
₁
husband, <u>nor</u> her son had never quite been sure what to make of the
₂
nineteen large mounds visible throughout the grounds. Now infested with rabbits, the mounds were rumored to hold ancient mysteries.

[2]

<u>After</u> her husband died, Pretty's curiosity got the best of her. In 1938, she
₃
hired an archaeologist named Basil Brown to open some of the smaller mounds, which held a few interesting treasures, <u>so</u> nothing as wondrous or
₄
mysterious as legend had predicted. Unsatisfied, Pretty instructed Brown to open Mound One, the largest of them all.

[3]

In the spring of 1939, Brown and two helpers began to dig a trench from the east end of the mound. Soon, the men encountered some large iron rivets, <u>or</u> fasteners, laid out in a <u>long, repetitive pattern,</u> like a subterranean
₅ ₆
ribcage. As more of the pattern emerged, the men realized that they were standing in the remains of the bottom hull of a colossal boat. More than 80 feet long, the ship had served as the burial vessel of an Anglo-Saxon king. Fully equipped for the afterlife, the ship's hold contained forty-one items of solid gold, silverware inscribed in Greek, a silver dish bearing the stamp of the

---

Strategy

Try out each answer.
Mentally test each answer before you choose one of them. The one that sounds the best is probably correct.

Byzantine emperor, and a bronze bowl from the Middle East. In addition to satisfying Edith May Pretty's curiosity, this astounding archaeological discovery greatly expanded contemporary understanding of Anglo-Saxon culture.

1. Upon reviewing paragraph 1, the writer considers deleting the indicated sentence. If the writer were to delete the sentence, the paragraph would primarily lose
   A. an explanation of one of the essay's central concepts.
   B. a colorful detail that draws the reader into the essay.
   C. an impressive fact that establishes the writer's credibility.
   D. nothing; it should be deleted.

2. F. NO CHANGE
   G. and
   H. but also
   J. though

3. What is the function of this word?
   A. It is used as a correlative conjunction.
   B. It is used as a coordinating conjunction.
   C. It is used as a subordinating conjunction.
   D. It has no function and should be deleted.

4. F. NO CHANGE
   G. than
   H. or
   J. but

5. A. NO CHANGE
   B. as though
   C. nor
   D. and

6. F. NO CHANGE
   G. repetitive pattern
   H. long pattern
   J. pattern

7. What is the most accurate summary of paragraph 3?
   A. It contains specific information and historical details.
   B. It describes the great Anglo-Saxon archaeological discovery that was made.
   C. It is the conclusion of the story.
   D. It persuades people to study archaeology.

8. *This question refers to the passage as a whole.* What is the main idea of this passage?
   F. Archaeology is a more established science today than it once was.
   G. People should be more curious.
   H. Old rumors may be true.
   J. Old tales, curiosity, and hard work lead to an important discovery.

 ## Timed Writing: Position Statement [30 minutes]

Burton Raffel, translator of *Beowulf,* has remarked that one of the most satisfying aspects of that poem is "the poet's insight into people." One might also argue that Bede, author of *A History of the English Church and People*, had equally deep insight into people and places.

In your view, which kind of text—a work of fiction like *Beowulf* or a work of nonfiction like Bede's *History*—sheds greater light on an ancient culture and its people? Write an essay developing your view on this issue. Support your position with reasoning and examples based on your reading, studies, or observations.

Academic Vocabulary

An **issue** is a debatable idea. There is no one right or wrong position on an issue. Choose the position for which you can offer the strongest support.

Performance Tasks

Directions: *Follow the instructions to complete the tasks below as required by your teacher. As you work on each task, incorporate both general academic vocabulary and literary terms you learned in this unit.*

**Common Core
State Standards**

RL.11-12.1; RL.11-12.3, RL.11-12.5; RI.11-12.5; W.11-12.1.d, W.11-12.1.e, W.11-12.2; SL.11-12.1, SL.11-12.4, SL.11-12.6
[For the full wording of the standards, see the standards chart in the front of your textbook.]

Writing

Task 1: Literature [RL.11-12.1; W.11-12.2]
Analyze Character

Write an **essay** *in which you analyze a character from a literary work in this unit.*

- Select a character who is central to the work in which he or she appears.

- Describe the character as fully as possible, based on the information provided in the work. Details in the text may provide either direct information or indirect clues about the character.

- Once you have described the character, analyze the character's significance in the work. For example, the character may stand for a type of person or may be archetypal. He or she may have a particular role or motivation.

- Remember to support your inferences with evidence from the text.

- Provide a conclusion that follows from the information you presented and also creates a sense of closure.

Task 2: Informational Text [RI.11-12.5; W.11-12.1.e]
Analyze Text Structure

Write an **essay** *in which you analyze how a text's structure contributes to its meaning in a nonfiction work from this unit.*

- Choose a work of nonfiction from this unit in which the author's choices concerning text structure help to clarify and develop central ideas.

- Determine which text structure is being used. Evaluate the way in which the structure helps to introduce and clarify points.

- Include a judgment as to how effective the author's use of text structure is.

- Provide examples from the text to support your ideas.

- Use a variety of sentence lengths in your writing. Combine short, choppy sentences by using coordinating or correlative conjunctions.

- End your essay with a conclusion that follows from your discussion and sums up your main points.

Task 3: Literature [RL.11-12.5; W.11-12.1.d]
Analyze Poetic Structure

Write an **essay** *in which you analyze how an author's choices concerning structure add to the overall meaning of a poem.*

- Choose a poem from this unit and briefly describe its overall structure and important structural elements. For example, the length of a poem or a distinct rhythm might be considered structural choices.

- Write a thesis sentence that describes the impact that the structure of the poem has upon its meaning.

- Discuss the relationship between structure and meaning in detail, providing evidence from the text to support your reasoning.

- Establish and maintain a formal style and objective tone in your writing.

- Finish your essay with a strong conclusion that sums up your main points and makes a statement about the relationship between poetic form and meaning.

Speaking and Listening

Make Inferences

*Conduct a **small group discussion** exploring inferences that can be made about culture based upon one of the literary works in this unit.*

- Choose a work that contains clues about the culture in which it originated.
- Identify details that point to values, beliefs, the historical framework, and the social structure of the culture.
- Explain how these details help you to make connections and draw inferences about the culture.
- Prepare for the discussion. Create a list of questions based on your analysis designed to stimulate discussion.
- As group members contribute, build on their ideas. Pose further questions and point to evidence from the work.
- Respond thoughtfully to diverse perspectives and points of view.

Analyze Story Elements

*Prepare and deliver an **oral presentation** in which you analyze and evaluate the presentation and development of story elements in a literary work from this unit.*

- Explain which work you chose and briefly summarize the setting, situation, characters, conflict, and plot.
- Discuss how the author orders events and how he or she introduces and develops characters or new situations.
- Explain how the author's choices about the development of the story elements contribute to the narrative's larger meaning or themes.
- Apply the conventions of Standard English grammar and usage in your speaking.
- As you present, speak clearly and loudly enough to be understood by your audience.

Analyze Text Structure

*Prepare and deliver an **oral presentation** in which you analyze the effect of text structure on the meaning as well as the artistry and beauty of a literary work from this unit.*

- Identify a work in which the structure of the text is deeply connected to its meaning and is also aesthetically significant. Caesuras, rhyming quatrains, or frame story structure are all examples of text structures.
- Define the text structure and its impact on the text's meaning.
- Discuss what you perceive to be artful or aesthetically pleasing about this text structure and in what way it engaged you as a reader. Draw a conclusion as to why the author made specific choices regarding structure.
- Present your interpretation and supporting evidence in an organized and clear way, so that your audience can follow your reasoning.

How does literature shape or reflect society?

What is Home? Over the thousand years covered in this unit, England evolved from a collection of clans to a more unified nation. You can trace this evolution in the different ideas of home expressed by various writers.

Assignment Choose three works from this unit that express different perspectives on the significant idea of home. Write a **comparison-and-contrast essay** about these perspectives, showing how the idea of home changed over time.

Featured Titles

In this unit, you have read a variety of British literature of the Old English and Medieval periods. Continue to read works related to this era on your own. Select books that you enjoy, but challenge yourself to explore new topics, new authors, and works offering varied perspectives or approaches. The titles suggested below will help you get started.

LITERATURE

Beowulf: A Verse Translation
Translated by Burton Raffel

Epic This Old English poem tells how Beowulf heroically defeats three fearsome monsters: Grendel, Grendel's mother, and a dragon. Thrill to the ultimate in gore from a time when audiences heard their heroic tales told aloud instead of going to the multiplex to see them.

[An excerpt from Beowulf *appears on page 40 of this book. Build knowledge by reading the full text.]*

The Canterbury Tales
Geoffrey Chaucer
Translated by Nevil Coghill   EXEMPLAR TEXT

Poetry As part of a storytelling contest, each character in this medieval classic tells a tale while on a pilgrimage from London to Canterbury Cathedral. The stories range from bawdy and hilarious to innocent and virtuous, depending on the personality of the storyteller.

[An excerpt from The Canterbury Tales *appears on page 96 of this book. Build knowledge by reading the full text.]*

Sir Gawain and the Green Knight
Translated by Brian Stone

Poetry In this acclaimed medieval romance, Sir Gawain is the young nephew of King Arthur. The Green Knight tests Gawain's chivalric ideals by posing three challenges.

[An excerpt from Sir Gawain and the Green Knight *appears on page 170 of this book. Build knowledge by reading the full text.]*

The Once and Future King
T. H. White
Ace, 1987

Novel In this modern classic, White retells a variety of exciting tales about the legendary King Arthur and his Knights of the Round Table. White's humorous, imaginative, and suspenseful retellings will delight today's readers.

INFORMATIONAL TEXTS

Historical Texts

The Ecclesiastical History of the English People
Bede
Translated by Leo Sherley-Price

History Written in A.D. 731 by a Christian monk named Bede, this book describes England from the first-century invasion by the Romans to Anglo-Saxon life in Bede's own day. It is a fascinating account of the ebb and flow of peoples and belief systems in the early centuries of Britain.

[An excerpt from the same work—using the slightly different title A History of the English Church and People*—appears on page 84 of this book. Build knowledge by reading the full text.]*

The Book of Margery Kempe
Margery Kempe
Translated by B. A. Windeatt

Autobiography Considered the first autobiography in English, this book was dictated to a priest. It narrates the spiritual and everyday struggles of one woman in the fifteenth century as she deals with bankruptcy, the pressures of maintaining a household with fourteen children, and divine revelations that send her on pilgrimages far from home.

Contemporary Scholarship

A Distant Mirror: The Calamitous 14ᵗʰ Century
Barbara W. Tuchman
Ballantine Books, 1978

History Told from the perspective of nobleman Enguerrand de Coucy (1340–1397), this book explores important events in the fourteenth century, including the Black Death, The Hundred Years' War, and the Crusades.

The Story of English
Robert McCrum, Robert MacNeil, and William Cran

Linguistics This book presents a stimulating and comprehensive record of spoken and written English—from its Anglo-Saxon origins to the present day, when English is the dominant language of commerce and culture, with more than one billion English speakers throughout the world.

Preparing to Read Complex Texts

Reading for College and Career In both college and the workplace, readers must analyze texts independently, draw connections among works that offer varied perspectives, and develop their own ideas and informed opinions. The questions shown below, and others that you generate on your own, will help you more effectively read and analyze complex college-level texts.

Common Core State Standards

Reading Literature/Informational Text
10. By the end of grade 12, read and comprehend literature, including stories, dramas, and poems, and literary nonfiction at the high end of the grades 11-CCR text complexity band independently and proficiently.

When reading complex texts, ask yourself...

- What idea, experience, or story seems to have compelled the author to write? Has the author presented that idea, experience, or story in a way that I, too, find compelling?

- How might the author's era, social status, belief system, or personal experiences have affected the point of view he or she expresses in the text?

- How do my circumstances affect what I understand and feel about this text?

- What key idea does the author state explicitly? What key idea does he or she suggest or imply? Which details in the text help me to perceive implied ideas?

- Do I find multiple layers of meaning in the text? If so, what relationships do I see among these layers of meaning?

- How do details in the text connect or relate to one another? Do I find any details unconvincing, unrelated, or out of place?

- Do I find the text believable and convincing?

© **Key Ideas and Details**

- What patterns of organization or sequences do I find in the text? Do these patterns help me understand the ideas better?

- What do I notice about the author's style, including his or her diction, uses of imagery and figurative language, and syntax?

- Do I like the author's style? Is the author's style memorable?

- What emotional attitude does the author express toward the topic, the story, or the characters? Does this attitude seem appropriate?

- What emotional attitude does the author express toward me, the reader? Does this attitude seem appropriate?

- What do I notice about the author's voice—his or her personality on the page? Do I like this voice? Does it make me want to read on?

© **Craft and Structure**

- Is the work fresh and original?

- Do I agree with the author's ideas entirely, or are there elements I find unconvincing?

- Do I disagree with the author's ideas entirely, or are there elements I can accept as true?

- Based on my knowledge of British literature, history, and culture, does this work reflect the British tradition? Why or why not?

© **Integration of Ideas**

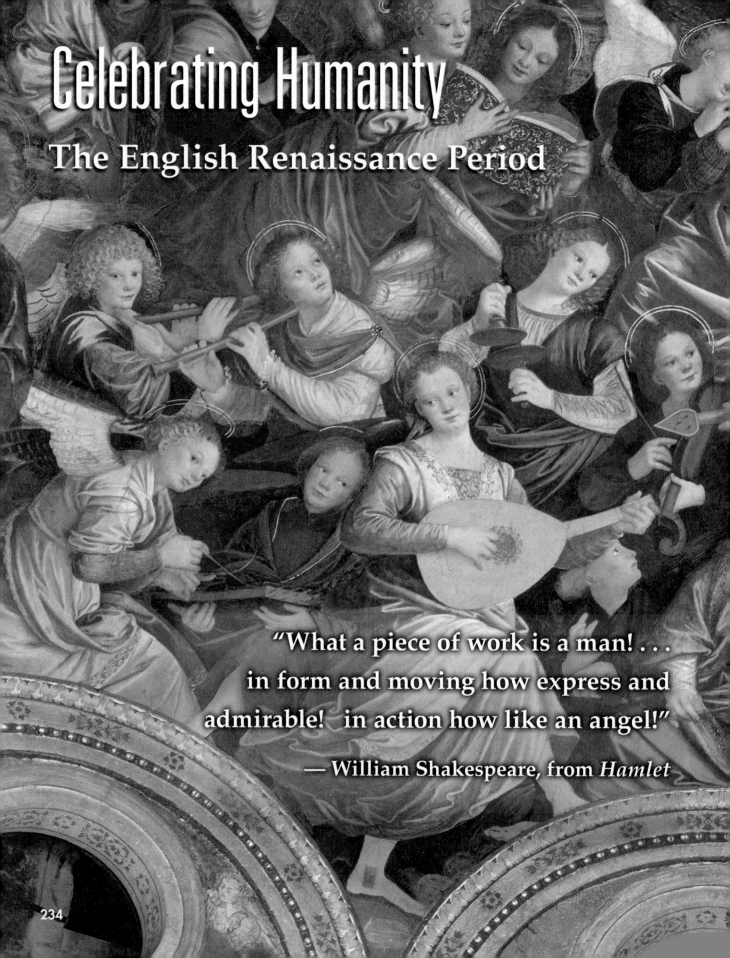

Celebrating Humanity
The English Renaissance Period

"What a piece of work is a man! . . .
in form and moving how express and
admirable! in action how like an angel!"

— William Shakespeare, from *Hamlet*

PHLit
Online!
www.PHLitOnline.com

Hear It!
- Selection summary audio
- Selection audio

See It!
- Author videos
- Essential Question video
- Get Connected videos
- Background videos
- More about the authors
- Illustrated vocabulary words
- Vocabulary flashcards

Do It!
- Interactive journals
- Interactive graphic organizers
- Grammar tutorials
- Interactive vocabulary games
- Test practice

Snapshot of the Period

Renaissance and Reformation

Two major movements influenced the thought and literature of this period: the Renaissance and the Reformation. The Renaissance, meaning "rebirth," was characterized by innovations in art, science, and exploration, and a rediscovery of long-neglected classical works. Beginning in Italy, it gradually spread northward. Renaissance scholars of northern Europe, like Erasmus, attempted to reform the Catholic Church. The German theologian Martin Luther, however, initiated the movement known as the Reformation (reform-ation), which led to the founding of Protestantism. Luther stressed the Bible, rather than the Pope, as the source of authority and the importance of faith, rather than good works, for salvation.

Of the two major English works of this period, Shakespeare's plays and the King James Bible, the first is a product of the Renaissance and the second a product of the Reformation.

▲ This 16th-century engraving shows the new technology of book printing. The printing press, developed by Gutenberg in the mid-15th century, helped spread the ideas of the Renaissance and the Reformation.

As you read the selections in this unit, you will be asked to think about them in view of three key questions:

What is the **relationship** between literature and *place?*

How does literature **shape or** reflect *society?*

What is the relationship of the **writer** to *tradition?*

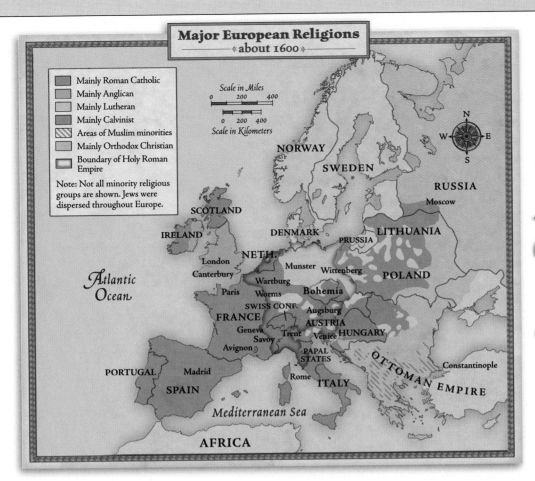

Major European Religions
about 1600

Legend:
- Mainly Roman Catholic
- Mainly Anglican
- Mainly Lutheran
- Mainly Calvinist
- Areas of Muslim minorities
- Mainly Orthodox Christian
- Boundary of Holy Roman Empire

Note: Not all minority religious groups are shown. Jews were dispersed throughout Europe.

Scale in Miles
0   200   400

Scale in Kilometers
0   200   400

NORWAY
SWEDEN
RUSSIA
Moscow
SCOTLAND
IRELAND
DENMARK
LITHUANIA
PRUSSIA
NETH.
London
Munster
Wittenberg
Canterbury
Wartburg
POLAND
Paris
Worms
Bohemia
Atlantic Ocean
SWISS CONF.
Augsburg
FRANCE
AUSTRIA
Geneva
Trent
Venice
HUNGARY
Savoy
Avignon
PAPAL STATES
OTTOMAN EMPIRE
Constantinople
PORTUGAL
Madrid
Rome
ITALY
SPAIN
Mediterranean Sea
AFRICA

A Time of Change in Religion & Science

Ⓒ Integration of Knowledge and Ideas The Reformation led to sharp religious divisions in Europe, shown on the map above. Which territories were controlled by Roman Catholics and which by Protestant denominations—Anglican, Calvinist, or Lutheran? How does this map help explain the war between England and Spain, which broke out in 1588? Review the timeline below. Which Renaissance inventions shown would you consider the most important? Why?

Renaissance Inventions

1496
paper mill; wall paper

1581
pendulum

1590
microscope

1608
telescope

Historical Background

The English Renaissance Period (1485–1625)

The two major European movements of this period, the Renaissance and the Reformation, both involved a return to old sources that led to cultural innovations.

Renaissance and Reformation: Going Back to Move Forward

The Renaissance, which means "rebirth," sought to revive the learning of ancient Greece and Rome. It was a secular movement that encouraged voyages of discovery and emphasized human aspiration. During this period, the very dimensions of the world shifted and enlarged, as Europeans discovered new parts of the globe, and Polish scientist Nicolaus Copernicus first proposed that the sun, not the Earth, was the center of the solar system. Renaissance ideas blossomed first in the Italian city states (1350–1550) and slowly spread northward, giving rise to the English Renaissance (1485–1625).

The Reformation, inspired by the ideas of the German theologian Martin Luther (1483–1546), began in part as a reaction against what many perceived as corruption in the Catholic Church. Reformation thinkers wanted to return to what they took to be a more pure idea of Christianity. Once again, an attempt to return to early ideas led to something new, as reformers created a denomination of Christianity known as Protestantism.

The Drama of English History

England became swept up in both of these two wider European movements, sometimes in a dramatic, even bloody, fashion. In the late 1400s, England was beginning to heal after thirty years of civil war. By the early 1500s, the country had plunged into the religious controversies of the Reformation. At the same time, the spirit of the Renaissance breathed new life into the arts.

The story begins in 1485, when Henry Tudor became King Henry VII, ending a civil war and reconciling the two factions in the war, the House of York and the the House of Lancaster. With him began the reign of the Tudors. His son, Henry VIII, inherited a strong, stable country. Henry VIII married his older brother's widow, Catherine of Aragon, and she bore him

TIMELINE

1485: Henry VII becomes the first Tudor king. ▼

1497: Africa Vasco da Gama rounds Cape of Good Hope.

1503: Italy Leonardo da Vinci paints *Mona Lisa.* ▶

1485

1492: Columbus lands in Western Hemisphere.

1500: *Everyman* first performed.

238 Celebrating Humanity (1485–1625)

a daughter, Mary. However, Henry then fell in love with Anne Boleyn, a beautiful lady of the court. He also wanted a male heir, which Catherine had not provided him. He therefore petitioned the Pope for a divorce on the grounds that his marriage to his brother's widow was invalid.

Henry had written a treatise attacking Luther, and the Pope had designated Henry "Defender of the Faith," a title English monarchs retain to this day. However, when the Pope denied his petition to remarry, Henry refused to comply, marrying Anne Boleyn in 1533 and eventually severing all ties with Rome. In 1534, he established the Protestant Church of England with himself at its head. Religious affiliation and allegiance to the king were suddenly united.

The woman who was to become perhaps the greatest of England's monarchs, Elizabeth I, was born to Henry and Anne Boleyn in 1533. Before Elizabeth took the throne in 1558, Catholics and Protestants struggled for control of the country, and Elizabeth's ascent to the throne was marked by turmoil and death. When Elizabeth took power, however, she firmly established England as a Protestant nation and ushered in a golden age of prosperity and peace. The greatest threat to her rule came in 1588, when Catholic Spain assembled an armada, or fleet of warships, to conquer England. Elizabeth rallied her people, and the English fleet, aided by bad weather, shattered the armada. This glorious moment produced a surge of spirit and sense of power that swept the entire nation.

Elizabeth I never married and had no heir. The final days of her reign were clouded with questions of who would succeed her. In 1603, James I became her successor and the first of the ill-starred Stuart line. By the end of his reign, his struggles with Parliament foreshadowed the civil war that would come during the reign of his son, Charles I.

Key Historical Theme: Going Back to Create Something New

- Renaissance scholars turned to classical authors for inspiration, and Reformation thinkers broke with the Catholic Church in their attempt to return Christianity to its original principles.

- Renaissance ideas stimulated literary, artistic, and scientific achievement in England.

- Influenced by the Reformation, England became a Protestant country.

1509: **Italy** Michelangelo paints ceiling of Sistine Chapel. ▼

1513: Ponce de León explores Florida. ▶

1512: First masque performed.

1514

Essential Questions Across Time

The English Renaissance Period (1485–1625)

 What is the **relationship** between literature and *place?*

What did England come to mean?

"This England" It was in a theater that one of the most enduring descriptions of England was delivered. In Shakespeare's *Richard II*, first performed in 1595, the Duke of Lancaster, John of Gaunt, articulates his vision of what England should be: "This blessed plot, this earth, this realm, this England." His words reflect the exhilaration that followed the defeat of the Spanish Armada in 1588. At the time, Spain was one the world's superpowers, feared for her military might. Spain was also a champion of the Catholic Church, which Henry VIII had rejected. By defeating the Armada, England had established its place as a player in the drama of world history.

The Age of Exploration England also sought a place on the world stage through exploration. Fueled by the Renaissance thirst for knowledge, European navigators ventured far and wide, aided by the invention of the compass and by advances in astronomy. Their explorations culminated in Columbus's arrival in the Americas in 1492. England's participation in the Age of Exploration began in 1497, when the Italian-born explorer John Cabot, sailing for an English company, reached present-day Canada. Cabot laid the basis for future English claims in North America.

Forging a Literature of England Even as England was redefining itself politically as a world power, its poets and dramatists were taking a new hold on the English language, transforming it into an instrument of new literary power. The English poets Edmund Spenser, Sir Philip Sidney, and William Shakespeare pioneered new forms of the sonnet and wrote extended sonnet sequences (see p. 246). Embarking on his own voyage of discovery,

> **ESSENTIAL QUESTION VOCABULARY**
>
> These Essential Question words will help you think and write about literature and place:
>
> **exhilaration** (eg zil´ə rā´shən) *n.* liveliness; high spirits
>
> **pastoral** (pas´tər əl) *n.* genre of literature portraying rural life as peaceful and simple
>
> **climate** (klī´mət) *n.* prevailing or average weather conditions of a place

TIMELINE

1514

◀ **1518: Africa** Algiers and Tunisia founded.

1521: Italy Pope Leo X excommunicates Martin Luther.

1532: France Rabelais publishes *Gargantua and Pantagruel*, Book 1.

1532: Peru Pizzaro conquers Incas.

Shakespeare explored the heights and depths of the English language in his plays, rediscovering the words of philosophers and kings as well as of rogues and laborers, and adding along the way his own coinages. Through redefinitions of forms and new uses of English, the poets of England created a literature that was truly of England, strong enough to, in turn, influence writers across the world.

What was London's role in this literary explosion?

Theater in London During this period, London, a bustling port city on the river Thames, thrived, becoming a center of world commerce. As the wealth and population of the city grew, theater came to flourish there. Actors were regarded as disreputable by Puritanical city officials. As a result, plays were staged in theaters outside the city limits, on the south bank of the Thames. That is where the famous Globe theater, home for Shakespeare's troupe, opened in 1599. Drama was edging London southward. As the city grew, more writers came, attracted by the presence of the theaters, of patrons, and of publishers.

Londoners' Rural Dreams As poets and writers flocked to smoky London—soft coal was the principal source of heat—they dreamed about the country. Following the models of the classical literature they had studied, they turned to the pastoral as a literary form. (*Pastor* is the Latin word for shepherd.) Greek and Roman literature had depicted shepherds and shepherdesses tending flocks in some innocent garden world. Walking the wet and stinking streets of London, poets imagined a green and carefree world, the world of English poet Christopher Marlowe's "The Passionate Shepherd to His Love."

The BRITISH TRADITION

THE CHANGING ENGLISH LANGUAGE, by Richard Lederer

"A Man of Fire-New Words"

Time has proved the truth of what Shakespeare's contemporary, Ben Jonson, said of him: "He was not of an age but for all time." William Shakespeare's words, as well as his works, were not just of an age, but for all time. He was, quite simply, the greatest word maker who ever lived. Of the 20,138 different words that Shakespeare employs in his plays, sonnets, and other poems, his is the first known use of more than 1,700 of them.

Consider the following list of thirty representative words that, as far as we can tell, Shakespeare was the first to use in writing: aerial, amazement, assassination, auspicious, baseless, bedroom, bump, castigate, countless, courtship, critic, dishearten, dislocate, dwindle, exposure, frugal, generous, gloomy, hurry, impartial, invulnerable, lapse, laughable, lonely, majestic, monumental, perusal, pious, sneak, useless.

The striking compound that Shakespeare fashioned to describe a character in *Love's Labour's Lost* is an important label for the playwright himself: "a man of fire-new words."

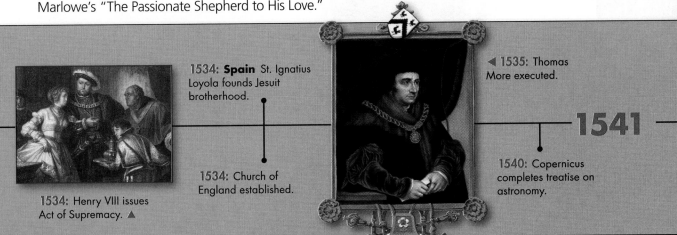

1534: **Spain** St. Ignatius Loyola founds Jesuit brotherhood.

1534: Church of England established.

1534: Henry VIII issues Act of Supremacy. ▲

◄ 1535: Thomas More executed.

1541

1540: Copernicus completes treatise on astronomy.

How does literature **shape or** reflect *society?*

What to believe? That was the question, and it was a question that affected everything, from religion, to politics, to the very nature of the Earth and the universe.

Why was belief an issue?

Changing Beliefs The official religion of England changed four times in less than thirty years. This series of upheavals began in 1534, when King Henry VIII took England out of the Catholic camp and made it a Protestant country.

Political Allegiance and Religious Belief The new link between politics and religion often had tragic consequences. Consider Sir Thomas More, a trusted advisor of King Henry VIII. A man of principle, More would not support Henry's petition for divorce. After he refused to acknowledge Henry as the head of the Church of England, Henry had him executed. More's tragic end announced a new, sometimes fatal struggle between warring religious convictions.

   Mary I, daughter of Henry VIII and Catherine, became queen in 1553. She denied the validity of the church her father founded and used the power of the state to return the country to Catholicism. Those she thought the worst heretics she had burned at the stake, but this only fortified the resolve of those who had embraced Protestantism. Her successor, Elizabeth I, re-established the monarch's supremacy in the Church of England, restoring Protestantism as the country's official religion. Elizabeth strove for moderation in religious matters. Even so, she contended with Catholic plots against her throne and eventually had Mary, Queen of Scots—her Catholic cousin and rival—executed.

Other Shifts in Belief Even as Protestantism had shaken the Pope's claim to be at the center of the religious world, developments in science

TIMELINE

1547: Henry VIII dies.

1541

◀ **1549:**
The Book of Common Prayer issued.

1563: More than 20,000 Londoners die in plague.

1558: Elizabeth I becomes queen.

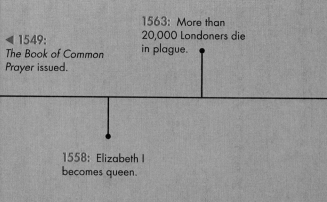

High Fashion in the Elizabethan Age

A more trivial version of the question, What to believe?, is the question, What to wear? For the Elizabethan nobility, however, that second question was almost as urgent as the first. Women and men alike took dress very seriously. Noblewomen looked like dolls on display, tightly laced into dresses that resembled giant bells. Noblemen were arrayed like showy peacocks in close-fitting jackets and wide collars that seemed to serve up their heads on plates of lace. As demonstrated in the accompanying portraits—one of Queen Elizabeth I and one of Nicholas Hilliard—clothing was elaborate and theatrical in an age that loved the drama and also loved to dramatize itself.

Two devices that helped create these theatrical effects were the ruff and the farthingale, both of which came from the Spanish court. Even after the English navy defeated the Spanish Armada in 1588, Spanish fashions held sway among the English nobility. The ruff was a pleated, starched collar worn by both sexes. It varied in size, but as you can see from the portrait of Hilliard, it could expand to the size of a large platter. The farthingale was a linen underskirt stretched over a thick iron wire that supported a skirt or dress and gave it the bell shape that Elizabeth's dress has in the portrait.

and exploration were overturning old pictures of the universe. Explorers confirmed that the Earth is round, not flat. They discovered the Americas, previously unknown to Europeans, and estimates of the size of the Earth doubled. Add to these discoveries the new Copernican theory that the sun, not the Earth, is at the center of the solar system, and the result was the upending of centuries of belief.

◀ **1564:** William Shakespeare born.

1567: South America 2 million Indians die of typhoid.

1567: Brazil Rio de Janeiro founded by Portuguese. ▶

1569

How did writers respond to problems of belief?

One True Bible Protestantism emphasized the authority of scripture, and to answer concerns about existing translations, King James I convened a group of fifty-four scholars to produce a new translation of the Bible. There would be one, authentic, accurate version for the entire realm. The scholars he commissioned to translate the work produced a Bible that remains a standard text and a masterpiece of English writing. (See page 246 for more details.) However, it did not resolve all conflicts. Even as men and women now read the same words, they argued about what those words meant.

The Place of the Individual Just as the Renaissance emphasized the glory of humanity and the value of the individual, Reformation thinkers such as Luther stressed the role of the individual's faith in achieving salvation. At the same time, religious controversy could demand an individual decision about what to believe. The new prominence of the individual is mirrored in the literature of the period. From Astrophel's complaints in Sidney's sonnet sequence *Astrophel and Stella* to the powerful soliloquies in Shakespeare's plays, in which characters lay bare the conflicts that tear at their souls, Elizabethan literature turned a new eye on the inner life.

Deciding What to Believe Columbus, Luther, and Copernicus never came to England, but they shaped the new worlds in which everyone had to learn to live all over again. It was a time of incredible turmoil: intellectual, religious, political, artistic. In the midst of that turmoil, ordinary people struggled to decide what to believe, how to worship, and whom to obey. The glorious literature of the period gave them new terms in which to think, opening the way to modern ideas of the individual.

ESSENTIAL QUESTION VOCABULARY

These Essential Question words will help you think and write about literature and society:

petition (pə tish´ən) *n.* solemn request to a person or group in authority

heretics (her´ə tiks) *n.* those holding opinions at odds with accepted religious beliefs

turmoil (tur´moil´) *n.* commotion; uproar; confusion

TIMELINE

▲ **1579:** Sir Francis Drake lands near site of San Francisco on his voyage around the globe.

1569

1582: Italy Pope Gregory XIII introduces new calendar. ▼

c. 1582: Sir Philip Sidney writes *Astrophel and Stella.*

What is the relationship of the writer to *tradition?*

Renaissance and Reformation are the words that define the period. *Renaissance* means rebirth and refers to the revival of classical learning at this time. Reformation was the re-forming of the church, bringing it back to its earlier, basic forms. Both went back to older traditions to make something new.

What did writers rediscover in the classics?

Humanism The ancient language of Latin had never gone away—its study was still an important part of an education. What was rediscovered in this period was not a language, but the "purer" forms in which the classical writers of ancient Greece and Rome wrote. The classics also offered a view of life different from the Christian vision that had dominated Europe. Ancient Greek and Roman authors offered ethics without reference to heaven and hell and philosophy that was about the natural world, not about the supernatural. They emphasized what it was to be human, so the new way of thinking based on the classics was called Humanism.

How did rediscovery encourage originality?

Translation and Invention The champions of Humanism wanted the classics to reach a wide audience. They therefore undertook a series of translations that made the ancient works more widely available while at the same time enriching the English language. English poet and dramatist George Chapman translated the *Iliad,* the ancient Greek poet Homer's epic poem about the fall of ancient Troy. Sir Thomas North translated the ancient writer Plutarch's brief biographies of famous Greeks and Romans and provided Shakespeare with material for five plays. Perhaps most important, when the English poet Henry Howard, Earl of Surrey, translated the *Aeneid*, the Roman poet Virgil's epic on the founding of Rome, he used unrhymed lines of iambic pentameter. This supple form, "blank verse," was quickly adapted for the stage, and Elizabethan playwright Christopher

1588: English navy defeats Spanish Armada.

1590: Edmund Spenser publishes *The Faerie Queen,* Part I.

◄ **1594:** Shakespeare writes *Romeo and Juliet.*

1595: South America Sir Walter Raleigh explores Orinoco River.

1597

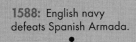

Marlowe's version of blank verse, his "mighty line," inspired Shakespeare to imitate it and then make it his special instrument. The invention of blank verse shows that, as often happened in this period, the return to older sources led to innovations.

A New Form of Drama The drama itself was a mixture of two traditions, one native and one classical. The native tradition began in the medieval church and involved the reenactment of scenes from the Bible. These "plays" moved into the marketplace, adding depictions of the struggles of vice and virtue. Shakespeare probably saw such performances as a boy. Onto this native stock of theatrical representation, the new writers grafted classical models of comedy and tragedy. The result was a new form of English drama.

Borrowing and Reinventing One of the most enduring forms of English poetry, the sonnet, entered the English tradition through translation. In this period, writers from all over Europe borrowed ideas and literary models from Italy, where the Renaissance began. English poets imported a fourteen-line Italian poem called the *sonetto*. Sidney, Spenser, and Shakespeare worked individual variations on the challenging form (see page 241), as would poets of later centuries.

In religion, how did writers move forward by going back?

Remaking the Bible, in English Translation was crucial to the Reformation as well. When James I came to the throne, it was obvious that the Church of England, in existence for sixty-nine years, should have one recognized English Bible. There were English translations, but none was standard. King James appointed a committee of scholars to make a new translation. Not only did they consult the Latin version of St. Jerome, which had been used in Europe for more than a thousand years, but working with Latin, Greek, and Hebrew texts, in a blend of the new learning and the new religious fervor, they produced the required Bible, a masterpiece of English prose.

Once again, writers had gone back to traditional sources and used them to make something new and enduring. Other translations may now be used in church services, but as long as English is spoken, "The Lord is my shepherd" will be remembered.

ESSENTIAL QUESTION VOCABULARY

These Essential Question words will help you think and write about the writer and tradition:

ethics (eth´iks) *n.* study of standards of conduct and moral judgment

theology (thē äl´ə jē) *n.* study of religious doctrines and matters of divinity

innovations (in´ ə vā´shənz) *n.* new methods or devices

TIMELINE

1599: Globe theater opens. ▼

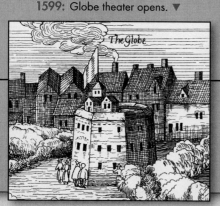

1597

1603: Elizabeth I dies.

1600: East India Company founded.

▲ 1606: Guy Fawkes executed for Gunpowder Plot.

William Shakespeare: To Be or Not to Be . . . A Rocker!

Shakespeare's sonnets may seem an unlikely inspiration for contemporary musicians, composers, and singers. In 2007, however, the Royal Shakespeare Company commissioned pop artists to set their favorite sonnet to music. Here are some of the surprising results:

- Irish singer Gavin Friday found his inspiration in Sonnet 40: "Take my loves, love, yea take them all. . . ." One reviewer wrote that Friday's performance was "extraordinary," describing his intonation of the sonnet as "a kind of strangulated speech-song."

- Former 10,000 Maniacs lead singer Natalie Merchant picked melancholy Sonnet 73, with its reflections on advancing age: "To love that well which thou must leave ere long."

- Romanian violinist Alexander Balanescu's choice was Sonnet 43, with its speaker's expression of longing to see his love: "All days are nights to see till I see thee."

- Electronic artist Mira Calix decided on Sonnet 130, a parody of love poetry, which begins, "My mistress's eyes are nothing like the sun." Calix liked "the idea that it appears to be a diss."

For artists and audience alike, the experience proved the timelessness of the sonnets. As Merchant commented in wonder, "How could an Englishman writing at the beginning of the seventeenth century and I have so much in common?"

1607: North America British colony established at Jamestown.

1618: Germany Kepler proposes laws of planetary motion.

1623: First patent laws passed.

1609: Italy Galileo builds first telescope.

▲ **1620: North America** Pilgrims land at Plymouth Rock.

1625

1625: James I dies.

Recent Scholarship

Life in Elizabethan and Jacobean England

Sir Frank Kermode

L ondon expanded greatly during the reign of Queen Elizabeth I, becoming one of the largest and wealthiest European capitals. Essentially a medieval city, its southern boundary was the River Thames, which was also its principal thoroughfare. To the north was the old Roman wall, but the city was spreading beyond it. Upstream was Westminster, the historic seat of the court and the national government. And across the river was Southwark, outside the jurisdiction of the City of London and therefore the favored site for enterprises, including theaters, deplored by the virtually autonomous and puritanical city government.

The population was swollen by country people, escaping the restrictions of rural life and famine, and by immigrants from Europe. The narrow, traffic-crowded streets were lined by shops and workshops, by civic mansions and rich halls of the trade guilds, and by the Inns of Court, haunts of lawyers and young gentlemen continuing their studies after leaving Oxford or Cambridge. The class system was strict—clothes were appropriate to rank, whether gentleman, citizen, craftsman, or laborer.

About the Author

Sir Frank Kermode is a literary critic who has written in-depth analyses of works ranging from the Bible to those of Shakespeare and beyond. He is a former professor of modern English at University College, London, and was knighted by Queen Elizabeth in 1991.

Shakespeare, new to London, probably took time to settle down. His London was the area around the old St. Paul's cathedral. The theaters were across the river in wicked Southwark. Westminster, site of Whitehall Palace, was a couple of miles to the west. There, in ancient halls, the great affairs of state were decided. There the queen contended with the Pope and her other foreign and domestic enemies. Later, James catered to his favorites and dreamed of establishing absolute monarchy and universal peace. However, their majesties both liked plays, so there was hope for an aspiring playwright. There was the prospect of pleasure and success, though there was also risk. Perhaps that's why Shakespeare left his family in Stratford: to take his place in the London theater—and eventually, literary immortality.

The Challenges of Urban Life

London was not clean or healthy. Sanitation was crude—the Thames was a beautiful sewer. Deadly diseases—plague, malaria, smallpox—ensured a high mortality rate. Cheats, tricksters, and thieves abounded. Men carried weapons—swords or pistols—in the street. Meanwhile, as the fields and woods were built over, access to country air grew more difficult.

Inflation was unchecked but money flowed freely. Among the expensive luxuries of the day were ostentatious clothes and tobacco, a recent import from the New World. London was perpetual bustle, noise, and display. Imagine how a young man from the provinces, like Shakespeare, might react to it. Shakespeare's Stratford, though a sturdy community with its own guilds and its good grammar school, hardly offered adequate preparation for London, a great port and the gateway to the larger world. The splendor of the river and the mansions lining its bank won the keen admiration of foreign visitors, who compared its magnificence to that of Paris and other great European cities.

From Stratford to London

In Shakespeare's day, the journey from Stratford to London took four days on foot, two on a horse.

© Speaking and Listening: Collaboration

Sir Frank Kermode refers to London's "perpetual bustle, noise and display." With a few classmates, study the picture showing the display at a feast held across the river from the Tower of London (c. 1570). Then, participate in a **small group discussion** pointing out the features of the scene that might have interested Shakespeare. Look for such items as these:

- a nobleman riding with a hawk on his arm
- children dressed like little adults
- fashionably dressed people strolling
- a servant holding a shield on his back

Integrate and Evaluate Information

 Common Core
State Standards

Reading Informational Text

7. Integrate and evaluate multiple sources of information presented in different media or formats as well as in words in order to address a question or solve a problem.

Speaking and Listening

4. Present information, findings, and supporting evidence, conveying a clear and distinct perspective, such that listeners can follow the line of reasoning, alternative or opposing perspectives are addressed, and the organization, development, substance, and style are appropriate to purpose, audience, and a range of formal and informal tasks.

5. Make strategic use of digital media in presentations to enhance understanding of findings, reasoning, and evidence and to add interest.

1. Use a chart like the one shown to determine the key ideas expressed in the Essential Question essays on pages 240–246. Fill in two ideas related to each Essential Question and note the authors most closely associated with each concept. One item has been completed for you.

Essential Question	Key Concept	Key Author
Literature and Place		
Literature and Society		
Writer and Tradition	New uses of the sonnet	William Shakespeare

2. Review the visual images in this section. Choose one that, in your view, is representative of the movement known as the Renaissance, and one that is representative of the movement known as the Reformation. Explain your choices.

3. Both the Renaissance and the Reformation sought to recover earlier perspectives: the former by reviving the literature of ancient Greece and Rome, and the latter by returning to Christian scripture (rather than the pope) for religious guidance. (a) Describe one effect of Renaissance ideas on the literature of the time. (b) Explain how the Renaissance and Reformation shaped new ideas of the individual.

© 4. **Address a Question:** In his essay on pages 248–249, Sir Frank Kermode writes that Renaissance London "was not clean or healthy" but that the splendor and vitality of the city was widely admired. Would you like to have visited London during this period in history? Why or why not? Integrate information from this textbook and other sources, such as an online history of the city, to support your ideas.

Speaking and Listening: "Welcome" Talk

Shakespearean drama had its home in London's Globe theater. Destroyed by Puritans in the mid-1600s, the Globe was rebuilt in 1997. Today, the new Globe serves as a theater, information center and exhibition space.

Play the role of a docent, or tour guide, at the new Globe, and prepare a multimedia **"welcome" talk** for visitors. Your talk should include a brief history of the original Globe theater, as well as a description of the resources at the modern Globe. Make sure to address alternative views of the theater's history and construction. To accompany your talk, prepare a brief slide presentation that includes photographs or diagrams of the theater. Select images that will lend interest or that will help your audience understand your points.

© **Solve a Research Problem:** This assignment requires you to research both the history and present-day existence of the Globe. Begin by formulating a research plan. Review both print and media sources, and consult the ones that you determine will provide reliable information about the Globe. You may also want to contact an actual Globe docent for information about the talks given to visitors.

ESSENTIAL QUESTION VOCABULARY

Use these words in your responses:

Literature and Place
exhilaration
pastoral
climate

Literature and Society
petition
heretics
turmoil

Writer and Tradition
ethics
theology
innovations

PART 1

Lovers and Their Lines

Before You Read

from *Spenser's Sonnets* •
from *Sidney's Sonnets*

Connecting to the Essential Question Like modern song-writers, Elizabethan poets used strongly emotional language to express their love. As you read, notice the different poetic forms these poets used to express love. This will help you answer the Essential Question: **What is the relationship of the writer to tradition?**

Literary Analysis

A **sonnet** is a fourteen-line lyric poem with a single theme. Each line in a sonnet is usually in iambic pentameter—five groups of two syllables, each with the accent on the second syllable. Sonnet forms include these:

- The **Petrarchan sonnet** is divided into an eight-line octave, rhyming *abbaabba*, followed by a six-line sestet, rhyming *cdecde*. Often, the octave poses a problem that is answered in the sestet. Contrasts between the octave and the sestet allow poets to develop meaning and achieve beautiful effects.
- The **Spenserian sonnet** rhymes *abab bcbc cdcd ee*.

In a **sonnet sequence,** sonnets are linked by theme or person addressed.

Comparing Literary Works Notable writers of the Elizabethan Age, such as Spenser and Sidney, made their mark by writing sonnet sequences. To connect one hundred or more poems without growing dull, they used a basic fictional situation: The speaker in the sequence is deeply in love, but his love is often unfulfilled.

As you read, compare Spenser's and Sidney's uses of this basic situation.

Reading Strategy

© **Preparing to Read Complex Texts** To better understand what you read, **determine the main idea or essential message** of literary works or passages. For instance, you can determine the main idea of a passage of poetry by *paraphrasing* it, or restating it in your own words. First read the passage to find a complete thought. Then, separate the essential from the nonessential information, and express the essential information in your own language. Use a chart like the one shown to help you write a paraphrase.

Vocabulary

deign (dān) *v.* condescend; lower oneself (p. 254)

assay (a sā´) *v.* try (p. 256)

devise (di vīz´) *v.* work out or create; plan (p. 256)

wan (wän) *adj.* sickly; pale (p. 259)

languished (laŋ´ gwisht) *adj.* weakened; dulled (p. 259)

balm (bäm) *n.* ointment or other thing that heals or soothes (p. 260)

Common Core State Standards

Reading Literature
5. Analyze how an author's choices concerning how to structure specific parts of a text contribute to its overall structure and meaning as well as its aesthetic impact.

Poet's Lines

"One day I wrote her name upon the strand,/ But came the waves and washèd it away:"

Paraphrase

One day the speaker wrote his beloved's name in the sand at the beach, but the waves came and erased his writing.

www.PHLitOnline.com

EDMUND SPENSER

(1552–1599)

Author of *Spenser's Sonnets*

Born into a working-class family, Edmund Spenser attended the Merchant Taylors' School on a scholarship and managed to work his way through Cambridge University. During his university years, Spenser published his first poems.

Pay for Poetry Unlike many other poets of the day, Spenser depended on the payments he received for his work. When the queen's treasurer balked at paying him, he sent this verse to the queen: "I was promised on a time / To have reason for my rhime. / From that time unto this season / I have received nor rhime, nor reason." Spenser was paid immediately.

The Faerie Queene In 1580, Spenser took a position as secretary to the Lord Deputy of Ireland. On a visit to Ireland in 1589, Sir Walter Raleigh (see p. 265) read and was impressed with one of Spenser's unfinished poems. He persuaded Spenser to take the first three books of this long poem to London for publication. That poem became Spenser's greatest work, *The Faerie Queene*.

Written in an intentionally archaic style, *The Faerie Queene* recounts the adventures of several knights, each representing a virtue. This allegory of good and evil, dedicated to Queen Elizabeth I (who appears as the Faerie Queene in the poem), brought Spenser a small pension.

A Poet's Poet Spenser was an innovative poet. In *The Faerie Queene*, he created a new type of nine-line stanza, which was later named for him. He also created a sonnet form, known as the Spenserian sonnet, containing a unique structure and rhyme scheme. His sonnet sequence *Amoretti* is unique among such works—it is addressed to the poet's own wife, not some inaccessible, idealized beauty.

The noblest mind the best contentment has.

—*Edmund Spenser*

SONNET 1
EDMUND SPENSER

Happy ye leaves when as those lily hands,
Which hold my life in their dead doing[1] might,
Shall handle you and hold in love's soft bands,
Like captives trembling at the victor's sight,
5 And happy lines, on which with starry light,
Those lamping[2] eyes will deign sometimes to look
And read the sorrows of my dying spright,[3]
Written with tears in heart's close[4] bleeding book.
And happy rhymes bathed in the sacred brook
10 Of Helicon[5] whence she derived is,
When ye behold that angel's blessed look,
My soul's long lacked food, my heaven's bliss.
Leaves, lines, and rhymes, seek her to please alone,
Whom if ye please, I care for other none.

1. **doing** killing.
2. **lamping** flashing.
3. **spright** spirit.
4. **close** secret.
5. **Helicon** In Greek mythology, the mountain home of the Muses, goddesses of the arts.

Vocabulary
deign (dān) v. condescend; lower oneself

World
LITERATURE
IN CONTEXT

Francesco Petrarch, Father of the Sonnet (1304–1374)
The 16th century English sonnet was inspired by an Italian tradition. Two hundred years earlier, Francesco Petrarch, a scholar and poet born near Florence, Italy, had written the *Canzoniere* ("Song-book"), a sonnet sequence, or linked group of sonnets, dedicated to a woman named Laura.

Petrarch did not invent the sonnet form, but he perfected it, giving his name to the Petrarchan sonnet based on an octave and a sestet rhyming *abbaabba* and *cdecde* (or *cdcdcd*). He also created the sonnet sequence and wrote his lyrics in everyday Italian rather than Latin, the literary language of the time.

Connect to the Literature

How did Spenser and Sidney modify the form of the Petrarchan sonnet?

▶ **Critical Viewing**
This picture shows the Muses at the site of Hippocrene, the fountain from which the waters of poetic inspiration were said to flow. Which details in the picture suggest poetic inspiration?
[Interpret]

SONNET 35
EDMUND SPENSER

My hungry eyes through greedy covetize,[1]
Still[2] to behold the object of their pain,
With no contentment can themselves suffice:
But having pine[3] and having not complain.
5 For lacking it they cannot life sustain,
And having it they gaze on it the more:
In their amazement like Narcissus[4] vain
Whose eyes him starved: so plenty makes me poor.
Yet are mine eyes so fillèd with the store
10 Of that fair sight, that nothing else they brook,
But loathe the things which they did like before,
And can no more endure on them to look.
All this world's glory seemeth vain to me,
And all their shows but shadows, saving she.

1. **covetize** v. desire excessively.
2. **Still** adv. always.
3. **pine** v. yearn.
4. **Narcissus** in Greek mythology, a youth who fell in love with his own reflection in a pool, wasted away with yearning, and was changed after his death into the narcissus flower.

SONNET 75
EDMUND SPENSER

One day I wrote her name upon the strand,[1]
But came the waves and washèd it away:
Again I wrote it with a second hand,
But came the tide, and made my pains his prey.
5   "Vain man," said she, "that dost in vain assay,
A mortal thing so to immortalize,
For I myself shall like to this decay,
And eek[2] my name be wipèd out likewise."
"Not so," quod[3] I, "let baser things devise
10 To die in dust, but you shall live by fame:
My verse your virtues rare shall eternize,
And in the heavens write your glorious name.
Where whenas death shall all the world subdue,
Our love shall live, and later life renew."

---

1. **strand** beach.
2. **eek** also.
3. **quod** said.

Vocabulary
assay (a sā´) *v.* try

devise (di vīz´) *v.* work out or create; plan

Critical Reading

Cite textual evidence to support your responses.

1. **Key Ideas and Details** **(a)** In Sonnet 1, what are the three things the speaker addresses? **(b) Interpret:** What does the speaker hope their combined effect will be on the lady?

2. **Key Ideas and Details** **(a)** In Sonnet 35, what do the speaker's eyes desire? **(b) Interpret:** Describe the state that desire produces in him.

3. **Key Ideas and Details** **(a)** In Sonnet 75, why does the lady say the speaker's efforts are futile? **(b) Summarize:** Summarize the speaker's response. **(c) Draw Conclusions:** What connection does the poem make between immortality and poetry?

4. **Integration of Knowledge and Ideas** Are these speakers over-reacting to their situations?

Sir Philip Sidney

(1554–1586)

Author of *Sidney's Sonnets*

Sir Philip Sidney was a courtier, scholar, poet, and soldier—a true "Renaissance man." He attended both Oxford and Cambridge, and furthered his knowledge by traveling extensively through Europe. He became a favorite in the court of Queen Elizabeth I.

Groomed for Success Nephew of the earl of Leicester and son of the statesman Sir Henry Sidney, Philip Sidney was certainly well connected. Throughout his life, though, he carried himself with remarkable modesty. His schoolmate and, later, biographer Fulke Greville remarked on his "staidness of mind, [and] lovely and familiar gravity."

A Brave Soldier Around 1580, Sidney fell out of favor with the queen when he wrote a letter urging her not to marry the duke of Anjou. Eventually, he regained status with her and was knighted in 1583. In 1586, during a military engagement against the Spanish Catholics in Holland, Sidney was severely wounded. As he lay on the battle-field, he bravely insisted that the water offered to him be given to another wounded soldier. Twenty-six days later he died, to the great grief of his country.

Pioneering Sonneteer Sidney wrote the first great sonnet sequence in English, *Astrophel and Stella*. Before Sidney, Sir Thomas Wyatt and others had writ-ten excellent sonnets, but Sidney's were the first linked by subject matter and theme. Each sonnet addresses an aspect of Astrophel's love for Stella. This sonnet sequence was inspired by Penelope Devereux (Stella), to whom Sir Philip (Astrophel) had been engaged. The engagement was later broken, and Penelope married Lord Rich. Yet, for most readers, Stella's name will forever be linked with Astrophel's.

Either I will find a way,

or I will make one.

—Sir Philip Sidney

SONNET 31

SIR PHILIP SIDNEY

With how sad steps, O Moon, thou climb'st the skies!
How silently, and with how wan a face!
What, may it be that even in heavenly place
That busy archer[1] his sharp arrows tries?
5   Sure, if that long-with-love-acquainted eyes
Can judge of love, thou feel'st a lover's case.
I read it in thy looks, thy languished grace,
To me, that feel the like, thy state descries.[2]
Then even of fellowship, O Moon, tell me
10 Is constant love deemed there but want of wit?[3]
Are beauties there as proud as here they be?
Do they above love to be loved, and yet
Those lovers scorn whom that love doth possess?
Do they call virtue there ungratefulness?

Vocabulary
wan (wän) *adj.* sickly; pale
languished (laŋ´ gwisht) *adj.* weakened; dulled

◀ **Critical Viewing**
Which details suggest that the subject of this portrait might be the speaker in Sonnet 31? **[Connect]**

---

1. **busy archer** Cupid, the Roman god of love.
2. **descries** reveals.
3. **wit** intelligence.

SONNET 39

SIR PHILIP SIDNEY

Vocabulary
balm (bäm) *n.* ointment
or other thing that heals
and soothes

Literary Analysis
The Sonnet How does the
rhyme scheme of lines 1–8
make this sonnet different
from a typical Spenserian or
Petrarchan sonnet?

Come sleep! O sleep, the certain knot of peace,
The baiting place[1] of wit, the balm of woe,
The poor man's wealth, the prisoner's release,
The indifferent[2] judge between the high and low;
5   With shield of proof[3] shield me from out the prease[4]
Of those fierce darts Despair at me doth throw:
O make in me those civil wars to cease;
I will good tribute pay, if thou do so.
Take thou of me smooth pillows, sweetest bed,
10   A chamber deaf to noise, and blind to light,
A rose garland, and a weary head:
And if these things, as being thine by right,
Move not thy heavy grace, thou shalt in me,
Livelier than elsewhere, Stella's image see.

---

1. **baiting place** place for refreshment.
2. **indifferent** impartial.
3. **proof** proven strength.
4. **prease** crowd.

Critical Reading

Cite textual evidence to support your responses.

1. **Key Ideas and Details (a)** In Sonnet 31, how does the moon appear to the speaker? **(b) Infer:** To what does the speaker attribute the moon's mood? **(c) Analyze:** How does the speaker reveal his own situation by addressing the moon?

2. **Key Ideas and Details (a)** What benefits does the speaker attribute to sleep in lines 1–4 of Sonnet 39? **(b)** What "reward" does he promise sleep in lines 13–14? **(c) Interpret:** Judging from this "reward," why does he crave sleep?

3. **Craft and Structure** What, if anything, do the regular rhymes and briefness of the sonnet form add to these poets' expressions of love? Explain. In your response, use at least two of these Essential Question words: *form, imitation, influence, Renaissance. [Connecting to the Essential Question: What is the relationship of the writer to tradition?]*

After You Read

 from *Spenser's Sonnets* • from *Sidney's Sonnets*

Literary Analysis

1. Craft and Structure Reread Sidney's Sonnets 31 and 39, and analyze their rhyme schemes. Do these **sonnets** more closely follow the **Spenserian** or the **Petrarchan** form? Explain.

2. Craft and Structure Review Spenser's three sonnets. Then, explain what poets can achieve in a **sonnet sequence** that they cannot in individual poems. Consider such factors as shifting moods and developing characters.

3. Comparing Literary Works Using a chart like the one here, compare and contrast one of Sidney's sonnets with one of Spenser's.

Petrarchan/ Spenserian?	Speaker's Situation	Addressed to...	Types of Images	Speaker's Conclusion

4. Craft and Structure **(a)** Compare the person or thing addressed in each of the sonnets you entered in the chart. **(b)** Explain how the basic **sonnet sequence** situation justifies or motivates each choice of addressee.

5. Craft and Structure **(a)** Compare the dominant purpose of each sonnet in the chart—to express hope, to persuade, to complain, and so on. **(b)** Explain how the sonnet sequence situation justifies or motivates each purpose.

6. Integration of Knowledge and Ideas Explain how, in each sonnet, the writer goes beyond the basic sonnet situation to give a general insight into the nature of love or life.

7. Integration of Knowledge and Ideas **(a)** Renaissance poets compared those they loved to "perfect" things in nature or to timeless figures from mythology. To what "perfect" things do songwriters compare their loves today? **(b)** In what other ways are modern songwriters similar to or different from Renaissance sonneteers?

Reading Strategy

8. Reread the octave of Sidney's Sonnet 39. **(a) Determine the essential message** of lines 1–4 by writing a *paraphrase* of them. **(b)** Then, paraphrase lines 5–8. **(c)** What problem do lines 1-8 set up?

9. (a) Reread and then paraphrase the sestet of Sonnet 39. You may break the sestet into smaller sections for paraphrasing. **(b)** What does the sestet suggest about the reason for the problem in the octave? Explain.

Common Core State Standards

Writing
2. Write informative/ explanatory texts to examine and convey complex ideas, concepts, and information clearly and accurately through the effective selection, organization, and analysis of content. *(p. 262)*
4. Produce clear and coherent writing in which the development, organization, and style are appropriate to task, purpose, and audience. *(p. 262)*

Language
4.a. Use context as a clue to the meaning of a word or phrase. *(p. 262)*
4.b. Identify and correctly use patterns of word changes that indicate different meanings or parts of speech. *(p. 262)*

Integrated Language Skills

© Vocabulary Acquisition and Use

Word Analysis: Patterns of Word Changes

Words often change form and *meaning* when they serve different *functions*. For example, the verb *languish,* which means "to become weak," has the past participle form *languished.* This form can be used as an adjective ("languished grace") or as a verb ("He languished under the weight of illness"). Other forms of the word are *languid,* an adjective that means "drooping" or "weak," and the noun *languor,* meaning "weakness."

For each sentence below, decide what function or meaning the missing word should have. Then identify the form of *languish* that belongs in the blank, explaining each choice.

1. His _____ was caused by overexertion.
2. The worker's movements were _____ at the end of the day.
3. Everyone _____ in the heat.

Vocabulary: Context Clues

Context clues are words and phrases in a text that help you reason out the meaning of an unfamiliar word. For each underlined word below, explain how clues in the sentence help you identify the word's *contextual meaning.*

1. The young woman <u>languished</u>, weakened by neglect.
2. Her <u>wan</u> complexion matched the washed-out hue of her hankie.
3. Even a glimpse of her beloved would be a soothing <u>balm</u> to her broken heart.
4. Desperate, she began to <u>devise</u> an array of complicated plans.
5. Then, she grew haughty; she would never <u>deign</u> to answer his call.
6. Just let him <u>assay</u> an approach, she muttered.

Writing

© **Explanatory Text** As a technical writer, you have been contracted to compose a *manual* explaining *procedures* for putting together a Petrarchan sonnet. The manual will be used by the company's newest sonneteers, so it should be clear, accurate, and easy to follow. It should also employ and briefly define the *technical* terms for each element of the sonnet, including *octave, sestet, iambic pentameter,* and *rhyme scheme.*

Prewriting Consider using some or all of the following: a preface, a table of contents, an overview of the product, in-depth descriptions of each part, step-by-step instructions, an FAQ section (Frequently Asked Questions), and a Where to Find Help page.

Model: Anticipating Reader Confusion

II. The Sestet
The second half of the sonnet is made up of a *sestet.*
A **sestet** is a group of six lines with the rhyme scheme *cdecde.*

The writer has anticipated and answered the following questions: *What is a sestet? What is its rhyme scheme?*

Drafting As you draft your manual, keep your readers in mind. Define all technical terms and put all concepts into clear, concise language.

Revising Revise with an eye to format. Have you included too much information on a single page? Can your reader glance at a page and understand what the page contains? Add headings, bullets, boldfacing, and other text features as needed.

Conventions and Style: Subordinating Conjunctions

For a smoother flow and more variety in your writing, try using subordinating conjunctions to combine sentences. A **subordinating conjunction** joins two complete ideas by making one idea subordinate to, or dependent on, the other.

Common Subordinating Conjunctions

after	as though	if	unless
although	because	now that	until
as if	before	since	when
as soon as	even though	so that	while

When you use **subordination** to combine sentences, you show which idea is more important.

Use Subordination to Combine Sentences

Simple Sentences: Philip Sidney regained the queen's favor. Then he was knighted.
Combined: Philip Sidney was knighted *after* he regained the queen's favor.

Simple Sentences: The speaker describes leaves. He is really talking about a book.
Combined: *Although* the speaker describes leaves, he is really talking about a book

Practice In items 1–5, supply an appropriate subordinating conjunction to complete each sentence. In items 6–10, combine the two sentences using a subordinating conjunction.

1. According to the poet's guess, the moon is sad _____ it has lost in love.
2. Poets often compare lovers to the moon or stars, _____ their beloved is perfect.
3. The poems will keep her memory alive _____ she dies.
4. The moon appears _____ it feels weak or sick.
5. He asks for smooth pillows, a comfortable bed, and a dark and quiet room _____ he can sleep soundly.
6. He has looked at her. He does not want to look at anything else.
7. The writing is finished. The sea washes it away.
8. He will still love her. She does not return his feelings.
9. He wants to please her. He loves her.
10. The poet addresses the moon. He acts as if the moon understands him.

© Writing and Speaking Conventions

A. Writing For each pair of ideas, construct a sentence that uses a subordinating conjunction to join the ideas.

1. the poet is happy—he is gazing at his beloved

2. her name was washed away—the tide came in

> **Example:** the moon climbs the skies—it does so with sad steps
> **Sentence:** Although the moon climbs the skies, it does so with sad steps.

Punctuation Tip: Use a comma after a subordinate clause that comes at the beginning of a sentence but not, in most cases, before a subordinate clause that comes at the end of a sentence.

B. Speaking Choose one of the sonnets and summarize it to a classmate. In your summary, correctly use two subordinating conjunctions.

PH WRITING COACH

Further instruction and practice are available in *Prentice Hall Writing Coach*.

Connecting to the Essential Question As you read, notice which poem's setting is shaped more by the imagination and which by observation of the world. Making this distinction will help you answer this Essential Question: **What is the relationship between literature and place?**

Literary Analysis

Works in the **pastoral** tradition, in poetry or prose, celebrate the pleasures of country life. This tradition, dating back to ancient Greece, was developed by authors writing for an urban audience. These conventions of the pastoral allowed city dwellers to imagine a country life:

- shepherds addressing or describing a beloved shepherdess
- a natural setting that seems perfect in every respect
- simple pleasures and games, including singing contests

Comparing Literary Works While addressing pastoral conventions differently, Marlowe and Raleigh touch on a number of **universal themes:** the link between love and the delights of youth and nature, and the relationship of love to time—love conquering time or being conquered by it.

Note the variations in these themes as you read. Also, consider this *nuance:* Although Raleigh seems to be writing against the pastoral tradition, is he in some way part of it?

Reading Strategy

 **Preparing to Read Complex Texts** As you read a poem, determine if it contains multiple themes. Then, decide how multiple themes add to the meaning of the poem. For example, do the themes build on or contradict each other?

When reading a pair of related poems, **analyze similar themes** in the two by comparing and contrasting their *patterns of organization* and *repetition*. For example, Marlowe and Raleigh use similar patterns of organization to create contrasting versions of pastoral themes. Use a chart like the one on this page to help you summarize each poem and then compare and contrast themes.

Vocabulary

melodious (mə lō′ dē əs) *adj.* sweet-sounding; tuneful; pleasing to hear (p. 266)

madrigals (ma′ dri gəlz) *n.* short love poems set to music (p. 266)

reckoning (rek′ ən iŋ) *n.* accounting (p. 268)

gall (gôl) *n.* bitter feeling; deep spite (p. 268)

wither (with′ ər) *v.* dry up (p. 268)

© **Common Core State Standards**

Reading Literature

2. Determine two or more themes or central ideas of a text and analyze their development over the course of the text, including how they interact and build on one another to produce a complex account.

Marlowe
Stanza #1   **argument** Come be my love and enjoy the countryside with me.   **key words** live, love, pleasures   **themes** pastoral, love and youth

Raleigh
Stanza #1   **response** I would be your love if you were telling the truth.   **repeated words** live, love, pleasures   **themes** anti-pastoral, untruthful lover

www.PHLitOnline.com

(1564–1593)

CHRISTOPHER MARLOWE

Author of **"The Passionate Shepherd to His Love"**

Killed before the age of thirty, Christopher Marlowe nonetheless managed to achieve renown as a brilliant playwright and poet. He spent his college days writing plays and serving as a government agent.

A Pioneer in Drama *Tamburlaine,* Marlowe's first drama, dazzled the public with its dynamic characterization of the tyrant-hero. All of Marlowe's subsequent plays may be seen as variations on a single theme: the larger-than-life hero who "overreaches," seeking to dominate everything around him.

The most famous example is the protagonist in *Doctor Faustus,* who thirsts for supreme knowledge and sells his soul to the devil. Marlowe matched the grandeur of his heroes with the grandeur of language, forging blank verse into a powerfully expressive medium for the first time in English drama.

A Life of Intrigue Marlowe has been described as a scoundrel, a ladies' man, and a hothead. By all accounts, his personal magnetism attracted both friends and enemies. When the court of Queen Elizabeth I wrote a letter implying that Marlowe had performed important government services, rumors flew about that he was a spy.

A Violent Death Marlowe was knifed to death in a tavern brawl in 1593. To this day, scholars question whether his death was really caused by his drunken refusal to pay his bill or whether he was murdered because of his undercover activities on behalf of the government.

(1554?–1618)

SIR WALTER RALEIGH

Author of **"The Nymph's Reply to the Shepherd"**

Sir Walter Raleigh is famed for having been a courtier, a navigator, a poet, and a historian.

A Charmed Life The half-brother of a famous sailor and an explorer, Raleigh began to satisfy his taste for adventure early in life, when he volunteered as a teenager for army service in France. A favorite of Queen Elizabeth I, he was given estates and prestigious appointments. In 1584, he set up a colony in Virginia.

Disaster When it was discovered that Raleigh had been secretly married to one of the queen's maids of honor, he and his wife were imprisoned in the Tower of London for a time but then released. Following the queen's death in 1603, Raleigh was accused of conspiring against King James I and was imprisoned again in the Tower, where he remained for thirteen years. He was eventually released to seek out gold along the Orinoco River in Venezuela. Despite a royal command not to engage in battle with Spain, Raleigh's fleet entered Spanish territory. In the ensuing fight, Raleigh lost his son and was forced to return to England. There, Raleigh was executed for disobeying the king's orders.

Literary Achievements Raleigh was a friend of some of the leading poets of his age, including Sir Philip Sydney and Edmund Spenser. Like them, he wrote elegant verse, rich in vivid imagery and classical allusions. Among Raleigh's numerous prose works is an ambitious book entitled *The History of the World* (1614), composed while he was in prison.

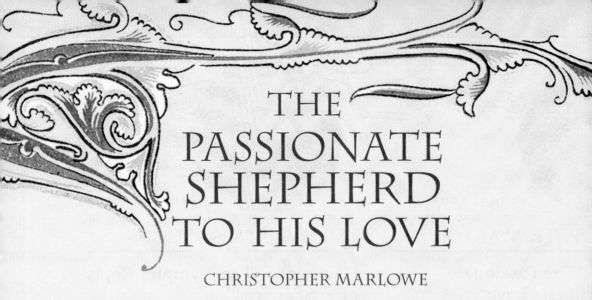

THE PASSIONATE SHEPHERD TO HIS LOVE

CHRISTOPHER MARLOWE

Come live with me, and be my love,
And we will all the pleasures prove[1]
That valleys, groves, hills, and fields,
Woods, or steepy mountain yields.

5 And we will sit upon the rocks,
Seeing the shepherds feed their flocks,
By shallow rivers to whose falls
Melodious birds sing madrigals.

And I will make thee beds of roses,
10 And a thousand fragrant posies,
A cap of flowers, and a kirtle[2]
Embroidered all with leaves of myrtle;

A gown made of the finest wool,
Which from our pretty lambs we pull;
15 Fair lined slippers for the cold,
With buckles of the purest gold;

A belt of straw and ivy buds,
With coral clasps and amber studs;
And if these pleasures may thee move,
20 Come live with me, and be my love.

The shepherds' swains shall dance and sing
For thy delight each May morning;
If these delights thy mind may move,
Then live with me and be my love.

---

1. **prove** experience.
2. **kirtle** skirt.

Literary Analysis
Pastoral
Which details in this stanza idealize the landscape?

Vocabulary
melodious (mə lō′ dē əs) *adj.* sweet-sounding; tuneful; pleasing to hear

madrigals (ma′ dri gəlz) *n.* short love poems set to music

▶ **Critical Viewing**
The poem's speaker views the countryside as a luxurious source of pleasure and the perfect escape from urban life. Which details in this painting reflect such an ideal? **[Connect]**

THE NYMPH'S REPLY TO THE SHEPHERD

SIR WALTER RALEIGH

BACKGROUND "The Passionate Shepherd to His Love" and "The Nymph's Reply to the Shepherd" are examples of reply poems. Many poets travel in similar social circles, and their association with each other sometimes motivates them to construct poems in response to one another's work. In addition to Sir Walter Raleigh, for example, John Donne also wrote a reply poem, "The Bait," to Marlowe's "The Passionate Shepherd to His Love." Such linkages can be found in many literary epochs and cultures: for example, twentieth-century Chinese poet Shu Ting composed a poem, titled "Also All," in response to Bei Dao's poem "All."

Reading Strategy
Analyzing Similar Themes
How do the first four lines of this poem compare with the opening lines of "The Passionate Shepherd to His Love"?

Vocabulary
reckoning (rek´ ən iŋ) *n.* accounting

gall (gôl) *n.* bitter feeling; deep spite

wither (with´ ər) *v.* dry up

If all the world and love were young
And truth in every shepherd's tongue
These pretty pleasures might me move
To live with thee, and be thy love.

5 Time drives the flocks from field to fold,
When rivers rage and rocks grow cold,
And Philomel[1] becometh dumb,
The rest complains of cares to come.

The flowers do fade, and wanton fields
10 To wayward winter reckoning yields:
A honey tongue, a heart of gall,
Is fancy's spring, but sorrow's fall.

Thy gowns, thy shoes, thy beds of roses,
Thy cap, thy kirtle,[2] and thy posies
15 Soon break, soon wither, soon forgotten,
In folly ripe, in reason rotten.

---

1. **Philomel** the nightingale.
2. **kirtle** skirt.

Thy belt of straw and ivy buds,
Thy coral clasps and amber studs,
All these in me no means can move
20 To come to thee and be thy love.

But could youth last and love still breed,
Has joy no date[3] nor age no need,
Then these delights my mind might move,
To live with thee and be thy love.

---

3. **date** ending.

Critical Reading

Cite textual evidence to support your responses.

1. **Key Ideas and Details (a)** In "The Passionate Shepherd to His Love," what does the speaker ask his love to do in the first stanza? **(b) Interpret:** What kind of future life together does the speaker envision?

2. **Key Ideas and Details (a)** What happens to the nightingale in line 7 of "The Nymph's Reply"? **(b) Compare and Contrast:** According to lines 5 through 8, in what ways is the nymph's world different from that of the shepherd? **(c) Analyze:** Which words in this stanza evoke a feeling of ruin or despair? Explain.

3. **Key Ideas and Details (a)** According to lines 21–22 of "The Nymph's Reply," what might persuade the nymph to live with the shepherd? **(b) Speculate:** Do you think these lines would console the shepherd? **(c) Analyze:** How does the nymph present a realistic portrayal of time and change?

4. **Integration of Knowledge and Ideas** If you were the shepherd, what counterargument might you make in response to the "The Nymph's Reply"?

5. **Integration of Knowledge and Ideas** What is the good, if any, of using literature to imagine an ideal setting? In your answer, use at least two of these Essential Question words: *perfection, escape, pastoral, realistic.* *[Connecting to the Essential Question: What is the relationship between literature and place?]*

Literary Analysis

1. Key Ideas and Details Although both Marlowe and Raleigh's poems reflect the **pastoral** tradition, the speakers present opposing views of rural life. **(a)** Use a chart like the one shown to identify details that signal the shepherd's idealized view and the nymph's more realistic view of country life.

Shepherd's Idealism	Nymph's Realism

(b) Based on their attitudes toward nature, what conclusions can you draw about the personalities of the shepherd and the nymph?

2. Craft and Structure In line 16 of "The Nymph's Reply to the Shepherd," in what way does the speaker's word choice reveal a striking balance of opposites to illustrate the theme of the harmful effects of time?

3. Integration of Knowledge and Ideas (a) In what ways can Raleigh's poem be considered anti-pastoral? **(b)** Is it a *nuance* or *ambiguity* of Raleigh's poem that it is also part of the pastoral tradition? For instance, could you argue that this shepherd and nymph are engaged in a pastoral singing contest? Explain.

4. Integration of Knowledge and Ideas The worth of love is one of the **universal themes** explored in these poems, but the speakers present contrasting views. **(a)** Compare and contrast the views of each speaker on the worth and reliability of love. **(b)** Although these speakers, a shepherd and a nymph, are supposedly part of the same landscape, how are they "worlds apart"? **(c)** Compare their syntax, or sentence structure.

5. Comparing Literary Works Renaissance lyric poems often linked the inevitable passage of time with the Latin motto *carpe diem*, meaning "seize the day," or enjoy yourself in the present. **(a)** How does this motto apply to each of these poems? **(b)** How is this theme universal, rather than specific to a particular culture?

6. Analyzing Visual Information Does this caricature of Sir Walter Raleigh suggest he might have shared the Nymph's cynical view of love proposals? Explain.

Reading Strategy

7. (a) If you **analyze similar themes** in both poems, what similarities and *repetitions* do you find in them? **(b)** How does Raleigh's *pattern of organization* make it easier for him to contrast his views on pastoral, love, and time with those of Marlowe?

8. (a) What experiences might have shaped the nymph's attitudes in "The Nymph's Reply"? **(b)** If you were the nymph, what kind of future might you project for the shepherd?

Common Core State Standards

Writing

2.c. Use appropriate and varied transitions and syntax to link the major sections of the text, create cohesion, and clarify the relationships among complex ideas and concepts. *(p. 271)*

Language

4.a. Use context as a clue to the meaning of a word or phrase. *(p. 271)*

ⓒ Vocabulary Acquisition and Use

Word Analysis: *gall*

The *medical etymology* of the word *gall* goes back to the Greek word *chole*, or "bile." Bile is the bitter yellowish fluid secreted by the liver to aid in digestion. In ancient Greek medicine, bile referred to one of two bodily humors, or fluids: black bile, thought to cause melancholy, or yellow bile, thought to cause anger. The other two humors were blood, which made a person cheerful and confident; and phlegm, which made a person calm and detached. In a healthy person, these four fluids were thought to be held in balance. This theory remained the most common view of the human body in Europe until the 1800s.

In each sentence below, replace *gall* with a word of similar meaning.

1. The gall of defeat was difficult to swallow.
2. He could no longer contain his gall and began to yell.

Vocabulary: Context Clues

Review the vocabulary words on page 264. Then, for each item below, explain how the meaning of the vocabulary word and the *context* in which it is used help you identify each statement as correct or incorrect.

1. The poet adapted her works as *madrigals* and participated in a performance of them.
2. Her strong, *melodious* voice was perfectly suited to the poems' deep emotion.
3. At the end of the stunning performance, she even had the *gall* to sing several encores and take additional bows.
4. According to one *reckoning*, the show drew the largest crowd in the whole history of the opera house.
5. These facts suggest the conclusion that the poet's fame will *wither* within days.

Writing

ⓒ **Informative Text** Marlowe's and Raleigh's poems present opposing points of view on the same subject. Write an **essay** in which you develop a *coherent thesis*, or consistent central idea, about the poems' *similarities and differences*. Focus on the viewpoints expressed by the speakers in the poems.

Prewriting Use a chart like the one shown to compare the poems. Then, draw a conclusion about their similarities and differences.

Model: Compare and Contrast Essay	Love	Nature	Time	World
"The Passionate Shepherd"	sees it as life's highest pleasure			
"The Nymph's Reply"	sees it as a mistake			

Using generalizations here will help the writer see major similarities and differences in the speakers' viewpoints.

Drafting Incorporate your conclusion into a clear thesis statement. Then, in the body of your essay, develop this thesis by comparing the viewpoints expressed in the poems. Use transition words and phrases such as *similarly*, *in contrast*, and *by comparison*.

Revising Revise your draft, focusing on redundant ideas. Remove any words or sentences that do not directly relate to or support your thesis.

Connecting to the Essential Question Shakespeare changed the structure of the Petrarchan sonnet. As you read, identify some of the differences between the Shakespearean and the Petrarchan sonnet. Noting these differences will help you answer the Essential Question: **What is the relationship of the writer to tradition?**

Literary Analysis

A **Shakespearean sonnet** has fourteen lines, with five iambic feet to the line (an iambic foot is an unstressed syllable followed by a stressed one).

Unlike Petrarchan and Spenserian sonnets, a Shakespearean sonnet follows the rhyme scheme *abab cdcd efef gg,* giving it this structure:

• three **quatrains,** or four-line stanzas

• a rhyming **couplet** that dramatically restates or redefines a theme

As you read, notice Shakespeare's quatrains and couplets. Also notice how his sentences often continue past lines and sometimes past quatrains.

Though all Shakespearean sonnets have fourteen rhyming lines, there are no rules about the number or types of sentences. Shakespeare uses this freedom of **syntax,** or sentence structure, to create dazzling dramatic effects. By saving his main idea until the end of one long sentence (lines 13–14), he makes Sonnet 106 build like a lawyer's statement to a jury.

Reading Strategy

Preparing to Read Complex Texts A sonnet's rhyme scheme, stanzas, and syntax are text structures. You can better understand a sonnet by **analyzing its text structures,** noticing how they contribute to the sonnet's clarity of meaning and aesthetic impact. For example, each quatrain helps develop the main problem or argument, which the couplet then dramatically restates or redefines. Use a chart like the one shown to analyze each sonnet's *pattern of organization*.

Vocabulary

scope (skōp) *n.* range of perception or understanding (p. 275)

sullen (sul´ ən) *adj.* gloomy; dismal (p. 275)

chronicle (krän´ i kəl) *n.* historical record of events in chronological order (p. 275)

prefiguring (prē fig´ yər iŋ) *v.* foreshadowing (p. 275)

impediments (im ped´ ə mənts) *n.* obstacles (p. 276)

alters (ôl´ tərz) *v.* changes (p. 276)

Common Core State Standards

Reading Literature
5. Analyze how an author's choices concerning how to structure specific parts of a text contribute to its overall structure and meaning as well as its aesthetic impact.

Language
3.a. Apply an understanding of syntax to the study of complex texts when reading.

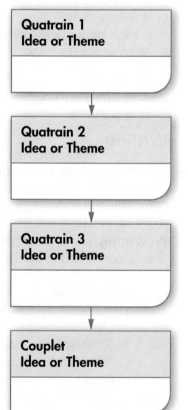

Quatrain 1
Idea or Theme

Quatrain 2
Idea or Theme

Quatrain 3
Idea or Theme

Couplet
Idea or Theme

www.PHLitOnline.com

William Shakespeare (1564–1616)

Author of *Sonnet 29* • *Sonnet 106* • *Sonnet 116* • *Sonnet 130*

Shakespeare may be the most admired author of all time. If he were living today, he would be a celebrity, and the facts of his life would be widely available in magazine articles, books, and Web pages. Instead, we know few facts about him, and these few had to be painstakingly traced from legal and church records or deduced from references in his work.

Bare-Bones Biography Shakespeare was born in the country town of Stratford-on-Avon and probably attended the town's free grammar school. When he was eighteen, he married twenty-six-year-old Anne Hathaway. They had a daughter, Susanna, and twins, Hamnet and Judith.

Shakespeare acquired a public reputation as an actor and a playwright. In addition, he was part owner of a London theater called the Globe, where many of his plays were performed. (For more about Shakespeare and his work as a dramatist, see pages 316–319.)

The Sonnet In the years 1592–1594, London's theaters were closed because of an outbreak of the plague. This general misfortune may have had at least one benefit: It may have provided the time that Shakespeare needed to write some of his 154 sonnets.

In writing a long sequence of sonnets, Shakespeare was being fashionable. Elizabethan poets enjoyed the sonnet form, writing fourteen-line lyric poems to both real and imaginary lovers.

The great Italian poet Petrarch (1304–1374) pioneered the writing of sonnet sequences. His sequence charts each pang and longing of the speaker's unfulfilled love for an idealized lady. This poetic device led to endless inventiveness—the beloved's beauty invites extravagant comparisons, and she provides a focus for the poet's ingenuity.

Shakespeare's Sequence Like the sonnet sequences of other poets, Shakespeare's 154 sonnets are numbered. Most of them are addressed to a handsome, talented young man, urging him to marry and have children who can carry on his talents. Readers treasure Shakespeare's masterful use of the sonnet to bring the fundamental experiences of life—time, death, love, and friendship—into tight focus.

> "*Not marble nor the gilded monuments Of princes shall outlive this pow'rful rhyme . . .*"
>
> —William Shakespeare, from Sonnet 55

Sonnet 29

WILLIAM SHAKESPEARE

When in disgrace with fortune and men's eyes,
I all alone beweep my outcast state,
And trouble deaf heaven with my bootless[1] cries,
And look upon myself and curse my fate,
5 Wishing me like to one more rich in hope,
Featured like him, like him with friends possessed,
Desiring this man's art, and that man's scope,
With what I most enjoy contented least.
Yet in these thoughts myself almost despising,
10 Haply[2] I think on thee, and then my state,
Like to the lark at break of day arising
From sullen earth, sings hymns at heaven's gate;
    For thy sweet love remembered such wealth brings
    That then I scorn to change my state with kings.

1. bootless futile.
2. Haply *adv.* by chance.

Vocabulary

scope (skōp) *n.* range of perception or understanding
sullen (sul´ ən) *adj.* gloomy; dismal

◄ Critical Viewing
In what ways does the style of this illustration reflect the style of Shakespeare's sonnets? **[Connect]**

Sonnet 106

WILLIAM SHAKESPEARE

When in the chronicle of wasted time
I see descriptions of the fairest wights,[1]
And beauty making beautiful old rhyme,
In praise of ladies dead and lovely knights,
5 Then in the blazon[2] of sweet beauty's best
Of hand, of foot, of lip, of eye, of brow,
I see their antique pen would have express'd
Even such a beauty as you master now.
So all their praises are but prophecies
10 Of this our time, all you prefiguring;
And, for they look'd but with divining eyes,
They had not skill enough your worth to sing:
    For we, which now behold these present days,
    Have eyes to wonder, but lack tongues to praise.

1. wights (wīts) *n.* human beings; people.
2. blazon *n.* here, catalog of lover's physical attributes.

Vocabulary

chronicle (krän´ i kəl) *n.* historical record of events in chronological order
prefiguring (prē fig´ yer iŋ) *v.* foreshadowing

Reading Check

What is the speaker's state of mind at the end of Sonnet 29?

Sonnet 116

WILLIAM SHAKESPEARE

Let me not to the marriage of true minds
Admit impediments. Love is not love
Which alters when it alteration finds,
Or bends with the remover to remove.
5 O, no! It is an ever-fixèd mark
That looks on tempests and is never shaken;
It is the star to every wandering bark,[1]
Whose worth's unknown, although his height be
    taken.[2]
Love's not Time's fool, though rosy lips and cheeks
10 Within his bending sickle's compass[3] come;
Love alters not with his brief hours and weeks,
But bears it out even to the edge of doom.[4]
    If this be error, and upon me proved,
    I never writ, nor no man ever loved.

---

1. **star . . . bark** the star that guides every wandering ship: the North Star.
2. **Whose . . . be taken** whose value is unmeasurable, although navigators measure its height in the sky.
3. **compass** range; scope.
4. **doom** Judgment Day.

Critical Reading

1. **Key Ideas and Details (a)** With whom is the speaker in Sonnet 29 in "disgrace"? **(b) Analyze:** What overall effect does this disgrace have on the speaker's state of mind?

2. **Key Ideas and Details (a)** According to line 12 of Sonnet 29, what causes the shift in the speaker's mood? **(b) Analyze:** How would you describe the shifting moods in the sonnet?

3. **Integration of Knowledge and Ideas (a)** Identify two images in Sonnet 116 that show the effects of time. **(b) Compare and Contrast:** Compare the effects of time on love with the ideal of love in the poem.

Cite textual evidence to support your responses.

The Mystery of the
SONNETS

For centuries, readers have puzzled over Shakespeare's sonnet sequence, which tells a story of love and betrayal. The early poems address a beautiful young man, whom the poet urges to get married and have children. The later poems concern a dark-haired woman, who torments the poet with jealousy. Midway through the sequence, a rival poet makes an appearance, further complicating the situation.

Were these characters real people? Or were they simply creations of Shakespeare's dramatic imagination? Literary detectives have proposed various historical figures as the characters in the sonnets. But the only facts we know for sure are that the sonnet sequence was published in 1609 and dedicated to a "Mr. W.H."

CONNECT TO THE LITERATURE

Does knowing the story told by the sonnets make reading individual sonnets more interesting? Why or why not?

Title page from the 1609 edition of *Shake-Speares Sonnets.* ▼

WILLIAM HERBERT

Some think William Herbert, the third Earl of Pembroke and a patron of the arts, was the young man of the sonnets. Shakespeare's "First Folio" was dedicated to him.

GEORGE CHAPMAN

His powerful translation of Homer inspired John Keats. Chapman is thought by many to be the rival poet of Shakespeare's Sonnets.

WILLIAM SHAKESPEARE

Nicholas Hilliard painted this portrait, which some believe to be the young Shakespeare, in 1588.

CHRISTOPHER MARLOWE

Poet and dramatist Christopher Marlowe (1564–1593) may have been the rival poet.

EMILIA BASSANO

Some historians think Emilia Bassano, the daughter of a court musician, was Shakespeare's mysterious "Dark Lady."

HENRY WRIOTHESLY

The third Earl of Southampton, Wriothesly became Shakespeare's patron in 1593. Many believe he was the "fair youth" of the sonnets.

Sonnet 130

WILLIAM SHAKESPEARE

Literary Analysis
The Shakespearean Sonnet Identify the rhyme scheme of the sonnet's first quatrain.

Spiral Review
Check Context Clues Based on the context of the poem as a whole, what is the meaning of the term "false compare" in the last line?

My mistress' eyes are nothing like the sun,
Coral is far more red than her lips' red;
If snow be white, why then her breasts are dun;
If hairs be wires, black wires grow on her head.
5   I have seen roses damasked,[1] red and white,
But no such roses see I in her cheeks;
And in some perfumes is there more delight
Than in the breath that from my mistress reeks.[2]
I love to hear her speak. Yet well I know
10   That music hath a far more pleasing sound.
I grant I never saw a goddess go;[3]
My mistress, when she walks, treads on the ground.
        And yet, by heaven, I think my love as rare
        As any she belied[4] with false compare.

---

1. **damasked** variegated.
2. **reeks** emanates.
3. **go** walk.
4. **belied** (bē līd´) misrepresented.

Critical Reading

Cite textual evidence to support your responses.

1. **Key Ideas and Details** **(a)** How are the mistress's eyes, lips, cheeks, breath, and voice inferior, according to Sonnet 130? **(b) Interpret:** Why does the speaker say she "treads on the ground"?

2. **Integration of Knowledge and Ideas** **(a)** In Sonnet 130, what does the final couplet say about the speaker's feelings? **(b) Interpret:** What general truth does the couplet suggest? **(c) Draw Conclusions:** In his sonnets, Petrarch worshiped his mistress. Why has Sonnet 130 been called anti-Petrarchan?

3. **Integration of Knowledge and Ideas** What advantages or disadvantages does the Shakespearean sonnet have compared with the Petrarchan sonnet? Explain. In your response, use at least two of these Essential Question words: *complex, innovative, dramatic.* *[Connecting to the Essential Question: What is the relationship of the writer to tradition?]*

Literary Analysis

**Common Core
State Standards**

Writing
2.b. Develop the topic
thoroughly by selecting
the most significant and
relevant facts, extended
definitions, concrete
details, quotations, or
other information and
examples appropriate to
the audience's knowledge
of the topic. *(p. 280)*

Language
5. Demonstrate
understanding of word
relationships. *(p. 280)*

© 1. Craft and Structure (a) Identify the three quatrains and the couplet
of the **Shakespearean sonnet** using Sonnet 106 as an example.
(b) Which rhyming words represent the *a*'s, *b*'s, *c*'s, *d*'s, *e*'s, *f*'s,
and *g*'s of the rhyme scheme?

© 2. Craft and Structure Choose a sonnet and use a chart like the one
shown to map out its **syntax.**

Number of Sentences	Number of Lines in Each Sentence	Syntax is Straightforward or Complicated?

© 3. Craft and Structure (a) Which two of the sonnets use complicated
syntax, featuring sentences full of phrases and clauses? **(b)** Compare the
complicated syntax of these sonnets with the simpler syntax of the other
two sonnets. **(c)** In each case, explain how effectively the elaborate or the
simple syntax conveys the meaning.

© 4. Key Ideas and Details Explain how Shakespeare uses references to
other poetry in Sonnets 106 and 130. In each case, how do these references support the argument he is making?

© 5. Integration of Knowledge and Ideas If Shakespeare had adapted one
of these sonnets to the Petrarchan form (an eight-line octet followed by
a six-line sestet), how might the new form have affected the way he presented his message?

© 6. Integration of Knowledge and Ideas (a) Which sonnet do you think
best expresses modern attitudes? Support your choice with examples. **(b)** Do
you think the sonnet is a form suited to today's world? Why or why not?

Reading Strategy

7. (a) Analyze text structures in Shakespeare's sonnets by listing the main
idea of each section of Sonnets 106 and 116. **(b)** Does each idea correspond to a quatrain or couplet? Explain.

8. Analyze the effects of the couplet in each of these sonnets. Does it
restate what has been said, provide a different perspective on it, or
reverse it? Cite evidence from the poems to support your point.

9. In Sonnet 29, line 9 marks a turn in the meaning. By contrast, in
Sonnet 116, lines 1–12 express a single thought in different ways. Which
pattern of organization do you prefer, a sonnet that swerves in meaning
or one that builds to a conclusion? Why?

Integrated Language Skills

© Vocabulary Acquisition and Use

Word Analysis: Greek Root -chron-

The word *chronicle* contains the Greek root -*chron*-, meaning "time." This root is important in words relating to history. For example, a chronicle is a record of events arranged in their order of occurrence. Keeping in mind the meaning of -*chron*-, match the following words with their definitions.

1. chronology

2. chronicler

3. chronological

4. chronometer

a. person who records events by date

b. arranged in order of occurrence

c. a list of important events by date

d. a device that measures time

Vocabulary: Analogies

An *analogy* is a comparison of two pairs of words that have the same relationship. For each item, determine the relationship between the first and second words. Then, using a word from the vocabulary list on page 272, fill in the blank to complete the analogy. Explain your choice.

1. Humming : singing :: _____ : occurring

2. Careful : rash :: _____ : cheerful

3. Principles : beliefs :: _____ : obstacles

4. Wavers : decides :: _____ : preserves

5. Desk : drawer :: _____ : entry

6. Speed : reduced :: _____ : limited

Writing

© **Argumentative Text** In his sonnets, Shakespeare uses imagery—words that appeal to the senses—to suggest the complexities of love. In an **essay,** analyze the imagery in one of his sonnets. Consider how the images are used both to communicate central ideas and to evoke readers' emotions. Support your ideas and reasoning with relevant quotations and details from the poem.

Prewriting Describe the images in a sonnet of your choice. Next to each image, note the idea that it expresses and its relationship to other images in the poem. Use a chart like the one shown.

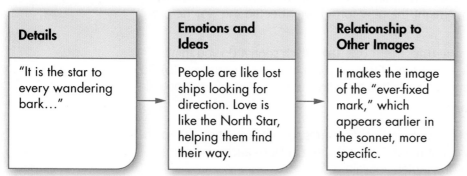

Details	Emotions and Ideas	Relationship to Other Images
"It is the star to every wandering bark…"	People are like lost ships looking for direction. Love is like the North Star, helping them find their way.	It makes the image of the "ever-fixed mark," which appears earlier in the sonnet, more specific.

Drafting Begin with a strong thesis statement. Then, use details to support your ideas. Note relationships of similarity, contrast, or development among images.

Revising Review your analysis. If necessary, refine your thesis to fit the details or add details as support. Then, consider your audience's knowledge of the topic. If you think that any of your points will not be easily understood, add clarifications, such as defining a difficult word or explaining a connection you have made.

The Influence of the Monarchy

PART 2

Primary Sources

Speech
Speech Before
Her Troops

Eyewitness Account
Examination of Don Luis
de Córdoba

 **Common Core**
State Standards

Reading Informational Text
2. Determine two or more central ideas of a text and analyze their development over the course of the text, including how they interact and build on one another to provide a complex analysis; provide an objective summary of the text.

About the Text Forms

A **speech,** or talk given to an audience, is one of the oldest means of communication, serving purposes like these: to persuade, entertain, or inform. Before recording technology was invented, a speech was always immediate. Those not present had to read, or be read, a written record of the speaker's words. Such transcripts are valuable primary sources.

An **eyewitness account** is an oral or written narrative of events by someone who saw what happened. Even if it has some inaccuracy or bias, an eyewitness account of historical events can still be a valuable primary source, especially when considered along with other accounts of the same events.

Reading Strategy

One of the best ways of remembering the details in a primary source and understanding the relationships between them is by **summarizing,** or briefly restating the writer's central ideas and listing the key facts that support these ideas.

Once you have summarized the central ideas and key supporting details in a text, identify ways in which the central ideas interact. Here is an example:

Central Idea 1: Elizabeth I loves and trusts her people.
Supporting Detail: She has come to address them even though her advisers warn of treachery.
Central Idea 2: She will reward her troops.
Supporting Detail: She knows that they deserve reward.
Interaction of Ideas: Her promise reflects her love.

After reading each of these primary sources, summarize it. Then, use your summary to analyze the development of central ideas and their interaction. Prepare for your summary by using *anecdotal scripting*—note-taking—as you read.

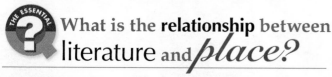 **What is the relationship between literature and *place*?**

England was at war, but the troops were still unpaid. What might inspire them to go on? Elizabeth I had an answer. As you read her speech, consider what her leadership and her words suggest about the answer to the Essential Question shown above.

 **PHLit Online!** www.PHLitOnline.com

Note-Taking Guide

Primary source documents are a rich source of information for researchers. As you read these documents, use a note-taking guide like the one shown to organize relevant and accurate information.

1 Type of Document (check one)
☐ Newspaper ☐ Letter ☐ Diary ☐ Map ☐ Speech ☐ Advertisement
☐ Government Document ☐ Eyewitness Account ☐ Memorandum ☐ Other

2 Date of Document _____

3 Author _____
Author's Position _____

4 Original Audience _____

5 Purpose and Importance

a What was the original purpose? _____
Write down two details that support your answer. _____
_____

b What are the key ideas or observations in this document? _____
_____

c What does this document show about the time and place in which it was composed? _____
_____

Reading Strategy
Summarizing Information
Sometimes you need to organize the basic information found in a primary source document. One way of doing this is **summarizing,** briefly restating main points and key details. As you read, summarize the key ideas in each document.

This guide was adapted from the **U.S. National Archives** document analysis worksheet.

Vocabulary

treachery (trech´ ər ē) *n.* betrayal of trust or loyalty (p. 285)

tyrants (tī´ rənts) *n.* cruel, oppressive rulers (p. 285)

realms (relmz) *n.* regions under the rule of a king or queen (p. 287)

stead (sted) *n.* position being filled by a replacement (p. 287)

obedience (ō bē´ dē əns; ō bēd´ yəns) *n.* the act of following orders or instructions (p. 287)

concord (kän´ kôrd´) *n.* friendly relations; harmony (p. 287)

valor (val´ ər) *n.* courageous behavior (p. 287)

galleons (gal´ ē ənz) *n.* large sailing ships used for war or trade (p. 289)

THE STORY BEHIND THE DOCUMENTS

Elizabeth I (1533–1603), who became England's queen in 1558 when she was barely out of her teens, ruled at a time when few thought a woman could succeed as a leader. The young queen, however, using courage and judgment, brought stability and prosperity to her nation. Today she is often named as England's greatest monarch. A dramatic moment in her reign came when King Philip II of Spain sent an Armada, or war fleet, to invade England. Her speech to her troops at this dangerous time reveals her skill as an inspirational leader.

Don Luis de Córdoba was a Spanish aristocrat, the son of a high official in Philip II's court. Sailing with the Armada, he survived the fighting, but his ship was wrecked off the west coast of Ireland. There the English executed most Armada survivors, but the high-born Don Luis was allowed to live. His eyewitness account of his experiences provides a valuable record of a major historical event.

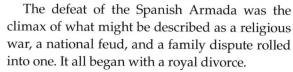

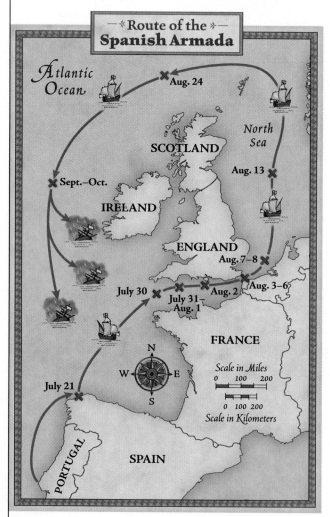

The defeat of the Spanish Armada was the climax of what might be described as a religious war, a national feud, and a family dispute rolled into one. It all began with a royal divorce.

In 1533, King Henry VIII of England, a headstrong man, divorced the Spanish princess Catherine of Aragon to marry Anne Boleyn. This caused him to split with the Roman Catholic Church. As a result, England became a Protestant nation. Spain remained a champion of Roman Catholicism. In addition, England and Spain were rivals for colonial possessions in the New World.

Family disputes added fuel to the fires. Mary, daughter of Henry VIII and Catherine of Aragon, became England's queen and wed the future king of Spain, Philip II. Philip and Bloody Mary, as she was called for persecuting Protestants, tried to make England Catholic again. Mary was highly suspicious of her Protestant half-sister and royal rival, Elizabeth. With Protestants rebelling and maybe plotting to bring Elizabeth to the throne, Mary kept Elizabeth in the Tower of London or under house arrest.

When Mary died and Elizabeth became queen, most of England welcomed the change. Roman Catholics at home and abroad, however, schemed to overthrow Elizabeth. Philip II of Spain was at the heart of such conspiracies. In 1588, he sent a large fleet, the Spanish Armada, to conquer England and bring it back into the Catholic fold.

SPEECH BEFORE HER TROOPS

Queen Elizabeth I

▲ These Dangers Averted medals celebrated the defeat of the Spanish Armada.

BACKGROUND *By the 1580s, Philip II was king of Portugal as well as Spain and ruled over vast New World colonies. He also ruled the Spanish Netherlands (today's Netherlands and some adjoining areas), where his repression of Protestants prompted the Dutch to rebel. Philip's Protestant half-sister-in-law, Elizabeth I, queen of England, aided the Dutch rebels and quietly support-ed attacks on Spanish ships by English sea captains. In 1587, when a plot to replace her with her Catholic cousin Mary, Queen of Scots, ended in failure, Elizabeth had Mary executed. A year later, Philip sent his Armada of warships to collect troops fight-ing in the Netherlands and invade England.*

With Elizabeth's navy fighting the Spanish fleet, her land forces massed in the English port of Tilbury, anticipating an invasion that never came. Nerves frayed and soldiers began to grumble about delays in pay. Then Elizabeth, dramatically dressed in a white gown and silver breast-plate, appeared before the troops and made the following famous speech.

Primary Sources

Speech When Elizabeth delivered this speech, which words in the first two sentences do you think she emphasized? Why?

Vocabulary

treachery (trech′ ər ē) *n.* betrayal of trust or loyalty

tyrants (tī′ rənts) *n.* cruel, oppressive rulers

My loving people, we have been persuaded by some, that are careful of our safety, to take heed how we commit ourselves to armed multitudes,[1] for fear of treachery: but I assure you, I do not desire to live to distrust my faithful and loving people. Let tyrants fear; I have always so behaved myself that, under God, I have placed my chiefest strength and safeguard in the loyal hearts and good will of my subjects. And therefore I am come amongst you at this time, not as for my recreation or sport, but being resolved, in the midst and heat of the battle, to live or die amongst you all; to lay down, for my God, and for my kingdom, and for my people, my honor and my blood, even the dust. I know I have but the body of a weak and

---

1. armed multitudes troops with weapons, like those she is addressing.

feeble woman; but I have the heart of a king, and of a king of England, too; and think foul scorn that Parma[2] or Spain, or any prince of Europe, should dare to invade the borders of my realms: to which, rather than any dishonor should grow by me, I myself will take up arms; I myself will be your general, judge, and rewarder of every one of your virtues in the field. I know already, by your forwardness, that you have deserved rewards and crowns;[3] and we do assure you, on the word of a prince, they shall be duly paid you. In the mean my lieutenant general shall be in my stead, than whom never prince commanded a more noble and worthy subject; not doubting by your obedience to my general, by your concord in the camp, and by your valor in the field, we shall shortly have a famous victory over the enemies of my God, of my kingdom, and of my people.

---

2. **Parma** Alessandro Farnese (1545–1592), duke of the Italian state of Parma and commander of Philip II's troops fighting rebels in the Spanish Netherlands.
3. **crowns** coins depicting the monarch's head, used to pay the troops.

Critical Reading

1. **Key Ideas and Details** **(a)** According to the speech, what have Elizabeth's advisers warned her not to do, and why does she do it anyway? **(b) Interpret:** What effect is the inclusion of this information designed to have on her audience?

2. **Key Ideas and Details** **(a)** What does Elizabeth tell her audience she already knows, and what does she promise to do? **(b) Analyze Cause and Effect:** How do you think her audience reacted to this information? Why?

3. **Craft and Structure** **(a) Analyze:** Where does Elizabeth exaggerate in her speech? **(b) Evaluate:** Do you think the exaggeration makes her speech more or less persuasive? Explain your answer.

Cite textual evidence to support your responses.

◄ **Critical Viewing** What does this rendering of Elizabeth indicate about the importance of pageantry—ceremony and theatrical presence—in her court? Explain your reasoning. **[Interpret]**

Examination of
DON LUIS DE CÓRDOBA

BACKGROUND: THE SPANISH ARMADA VS. THE ENGLISH FLEET

	Spain	England
Statistics	about 130 ships: 40 are 1st rate best warships: large, slow, with fewer and lighter guns; gunners not well trained	about same number best warships: small, fast, with more and heavier guns; gunners well trained
Battle Plan	• sail up English Channel • at Flanders, pick up troops for invasion	• attack early • break up Spanish battle formation
Results	• English outmaneuver Spanish but do no real damage • Spanish fleet anchors off Calais (ka lā´), France • English set boats afire and send them toward Spanish fleet • Spanish formation breaks up; English win decisive battle • Bad weather drives Spanish away; they sail northward • Many Spanish ships, including Don Luis de Córdoba's, are wrecked on the west coast of Ireland	

Primary Sources
Eyewitness Account
How might the circumstances under which Don Luis was questioned affect the accuracy of his information?

Don Lewes from Cordoba in Andalucia:[1] Captain of the men shipwrecked on the shore of the land of Sir Murrough ne Doe (Galway), says that when the Spanish fleet got near to Plymouth, there were 140 different types of boats including 96 great ships for the battle, and the rest were pataches[2] and small boats for transport. Off the coast of Plymouth, they met about 70 of Queen Elizabeth's ships. The Queen's ships gained the weather gage[3] and shot at them. They kept going towards Calais and returned fire for 2 or 3 hours. During this battle, Don Pedro and his ship were captured, as he was left behind the fleet when a cannon ball broke the main mast. The next day was calm and therefore nothing happened between them, except that a Spanish ship of 700 ton was burned accidentally, but most of the men were rescued. On the 3rd day they fought for 5 or 6 hours without losing any ships. On the 4th day they fought for 4 hours without losing any ships. On the

---

1. **Andalucia** the region of southern Spain where the city of Córdoba is located.
2. **pataches** *n.* small, fast, well-armed Portuguese ships that sailed with the Armada.
3. **gained the weather gage** positioned the ships so that the wind blew into their sails, giving them the advantage of more speed.

5th day they reached Calais where they anchored and chained themselves together and at the same time, 25 more ships came to join the Queen's fleet. During the night, the Spanish saw 6 ships on fire sailing down upon them, which forced them to cut their cables and set sail; at this point a great ship was burned amongst them, and a galleas[4] was shipwrecked on the sands. After this, the English ships entered into a fierce fight with the Spanish, in which 2 of the greatest Spanish Galleons were so beaten, that they were forced to come ashore at Flanders and sent the men to their other ships. That day, if the fire had not stopped them, they were going to put 7000 men on the shore at Calais to go to the prince (Duke) of Parma to find out his plans. He was going to be in charge of them and they had some unopened orders addressed to him, which were lost in the burnt ship. When they were stopped by this fire, they were broken and so fought very hard, and after 3 days moved out of the sight of the (English) coast, so that the Queen's ships left them and returned home, celebrating by firing off a lot of cannons. After this, the Duke of Medina moved his remaining ships together and found that he had lost 6 ships. He ordered his forces to return to Spain. But around Norway, the great storm took them and beat them towards our coast; the Duke had already warned them about the dangers of our coastline.

Vocabulary
galleons (gal´ ē ənz) *n.* large sailing ships used for war or trade

Reading Strategy
Summarizing Information
Summarize the information that Don Luis supplies about events near Norway.

---

4. galleas *n.* a large warship powered by both oars and sails.

Critical Reading

1. **Key Ideas and Details (a) Summarize:** What happened off the coast of Plymouth? **(b) Infer:** Why do you think Don Luis mentions that the English got the advantage from the wind?

2. **Key Ideas and Details (a)** What was the purpose of the "ships of fire," or fireships, that the English sent out? **(b) Infer:** How do you think Don Luis felt as he told what happened near Calais? Why?

3. **Key Ideas and Details (a) Analyze Cause and Effect:** What prevented the Duke of Parma from giving and receiving orders? **(b) Draw Conclusions:** What do the details suggest about communications among the Spanish forces?

Cite textual evidence to support your responses.

Speech ▪ Eyewitness Account

Comparing Primary Sources

Refer to your Note-Taking Guide to complete these questions.

1. **(a)** Contrast the authors' purposes and audiences in these documents arising from the same historical event. **(b)** How do these contrasts explain the differences in tone, or attitude?

2. **(a)** Use a chart like the one below to identify one statement from each document and what it reveals about this historic battle. **(b)** From which document do you learn more? Explain.

Author	Statement	What It Reveals
Queen Elizabeth I		
Don Luis de Córdoba		

3. **(a)** Summarize each source, listing the central ideas along with key supporting details. **(b)** For each source, analyze the development and interaction of central ideas, explaining whether they reinforce or contrast with each other.

4. Write a paragraph exploring how each primary source, in its own way, would be useful to historians studying the Armada.

© Vocabulary Acquisition and Use

Using New Vocabulary Choose the Word Bank word that is most clearly related to the situation in each sentence. Explain your choices.

treachery   stead   obedience   valor

1. A child heeded all the instructions her parents gave her.
2. A spy pretending to be a friend betrayed the king's trust.
3. The soldier showed great courage during the battle.
4. When the teacher fell ill, a substitute filled in for her.

Content-Area Vocabulary Identify the letter of the choice that is a synonym for the boldfaced word. Then, use the word in a sentence.

5. **tyrants:** **(a)** monarchs **(b)** trends **(c)** dictators **(d)** quarrels
6. **realms:** **(a)** kingdoms **(b)** treaties **(c)** truths **(d)** valuables
7. **galleons:** **(a)** ropes **(b)** amounts **(c)** kitchens **(d)** warships

Etymology Study *Concord* comes from the Latin word *concordia,* meaning "agreement," which includes the Latin root *cord,* meaning "heart." People or things in *concord* seem to have the same heart. The words *accord* and *cordial* have the same Latin root.

Using an online or print dictionary, explain how the root's meaning is reflected in each of these words.

 Common Core State Standards

Writing
7. Conduct short as well as more sustained research projects to answer a question or solve a problem; narrow or broaden the inquiry when appropriate; synthesize multiple sources on the subject, demonstrating understanding of the subject under investigation. *(p. 291)*

8. Gather relevant information from multiple authoritative print and digital sources, using advanced searches effectively; assess the strengths and limitations of each source in terms of the task, purpose, and audience; integrate information into the text selectively to maintain the flow of ideas, avoiding plagiarism and overreliance on any one source and following a standard format for citation. *(p. 291)*

Language
6. Acquire and use accurately general academic and domain-specific words and phrases, sufficient for reading, writing, speaking, and listening at the college and career readiness level; demonstrate independence in gathering vocabulary knowledge when considering a word or phrase important to comprehension or expression.

Research Task

Topic: The Defeat of the Spanish Armada

News traveled slowly in 1588. When Queen Elizabeth I delivered her "Speech Before Her Troops" to rally them against the expected Spanish invasion, the Armada had already been defeated. Using effective research, you can find out about the battle faster, and perhaps more fully, than Elizabeth could.

Assignment: Write a **research report** about one of these aspects of the battle with the Spanish Armada:

- historical causes of the conflict
- forces and weapons of each side
- military tactics used by each side
- sequence of the battle's events

During the battle with the Armada, the English attacked the Spanish fleet with fireships.

Formulate a research plan. Brainstorm and consult with others to decide upon a topic. Formulate an open-ended research question to address your topic, such as "In the battle with the Spanish Armada, what were the differences between the English and the Spanish tactics?" Then, formulate a plan for in-depth research on your topic.

Gather sources. Follow your plan, determining, locating, and exploring the full range of relevant sources.

- Gather evidence, distinguishing between reliable and unreliable sources. Avoid overreliance on one source.
- Systematically organize information to support your central idea. Outline your ideas using a conceptual map or timeline.

RESEARCH TIP

Be sure to separate factual data and the complex inferences you make based on the data. Also, differentiate among primary, secondary, and other sources.

Model: Using a Timeline to Organize Information

July 20 Armada sets sail for England.	**July 27** Armada anchors off Calais.	**July 29** English use fireships.

Use a checklist like the one shown to evaluate your work.

Research Checklist

- ☐ Have I answered the research question?
- ☐ Have I gathered and synthesized information from reliable sources?
- ☐ Have I organized all the information clearly?
- ☐ Have I cited sources accurately, using a style manual?

Synthesize information. Critique your research process at each step, modifying your process or research question as needed. Differentiate between theories and evidence, and determine whether the evidence for a theory is weak or strong. As you draft, maintain a flow by selecting and synthesizing related, relevant ideas from your sources.

Organize and present ideas. Provide an analysis that does not simply restate facts but supports and develops your personal opinions. Give your report sufficient length and depth to address the complexities of the topic. Avoid plagiarism, citing your sources for ideas not your own, following a standard format.

Connecting Elizabeth I, Past and Present

Famous actresses have portrayed Elizabeth I over the years, including Sarah Bernhardt and Helen Mirren. It was, however, a young unknown who in 1998 portrayed the transformation of Elizabeth on screen from a fragile, endangered girl to one of the most respected and iconic monarchs in history. In doing so, Australian actress Cate Blanchett also transformed herself into a star.

Blanchett, who even as a child loved to perform, studied Elizabeth I's letters to better understand the monarch. "It was there I could see the mechanics of her brain and her thought processes," she explained, "and the way she was able to play people off against each other, as well as her extraordinary intelligence."

The young actress came to think of Elizabeth herself as a kind of actress, and once said of her: "You know, she was in her element in front of a large crowd. She had the instincts of a performer. . . ."

Cate Blanchett has played royalty more than once. After starring as Elizabeth I in Indian director Shekhar Kapur's *Elizabeth*, which earned her an Academy Award Best Actress nomination, she portrayed the Elf Queen Galadriel in the immensely popular *The Lord of the Rings* trilogy (2001–2003). In 2005, Blanchett won the Oscar for Best Supporting Actress for her role as Hollywood cinema queen Katharine Hepburn in *The Aviator*.

*Cate Blanchett's performance in **Elizabeth** made the Australian actress into a celebrity.*

John Lahr
Drama Critic/Interviewer

John Lahr, who interviewed Cate Blanchett for *The New Yorker* magazine, has show business blood in his *veins*. His father, Bert Lahr, played *The Wizard of Oz*'s Cowardly Lion.

As a senior drama critic for *The New Yorker*, Lahr is interested in how actors create their public images as well as how they perform on stage and screen. "When you become a public personality and have a public persona, you have created 'you,'" he once said. "The public 'you' is your greatest invention."

In interviewing Blanchett, however, Lahr encountered an actress who seemed to disappear into the characters she portrayed.

from DISAPPEARING ACT

Interview with Cate Blanchett
conducted *by John Lahr*

Blanchett grew up in Ivanhoe, a leafy suburb of Melbourne, beside the Yarra River. She was the middle child, between an older brother, Bob, who had a mild case of cerebral palsy, and Genevieve. (Bob works as a computer programmer; Genevieve is studying architecture, after a successful career as a stage designer.)

Of the siblings, Blanchett was, by her own admission, the most adventurous. "I felt very free as a child," she said. Together, she and Genevieve invented characters, which Blanchett would play, for days at a time, around the house. "My sister and I would dress me up in something," she said "I'd pull a face or a stance; she'd give them names and an identity."

When Blanchett was around nine, her enthusiasm for performance took the form of knocking on strangers' doors to see if she could talk her way inside their homes with a tall tale about a lost dog. "It was the adrenaline rush, really," she said. "My friends hid in the bushes. I remember the woman at the door saying, 'I haven't seen a dog. Come in. I'll ask my husband.' I looked at the bushes thinking, Oh, my God, what am I doing? I remember the look in this woman's eyes when she started to think, You haven't lost a dog, have you? It suddenly had become a real thing."

Blanchett continued, "My whole childhood was like that. If someone dared me, I'd do it."

"Cate is willing to throw herself into a chaotic state out of which something will arise," the director Shekhar Kapur told me. "The fluidity you get in Cate is also because of the contradictions inside her." Blanchett is both candid and private, gregarious and solitary, self-doubting and daring, witty and melancholy. It was these contradictions that prompted Kapur to cast her as Elizabeth I in *Elizabeth*, one of the films that made Blanchett an international star.

Blanchett's mother, June, was a jazz-loving schoolteacher. Her Texas-born father, Robert, who met June when his Navy ship broke down in Melbourne, had, according to Blanchett, "a very dry sense of humor." He had quit school at fourteen—"I went to the school for bums," he told his daughter. Robert put himself through night school, worked at a television station, returned to Australia to marry June, and got into advertising. Then, when Blanchett was ten, he died. "I was playing the piano," she has recalled. "He walked past the window. I waved goodbye. He was going off to work. He had a heart attack that day. He was only forty."

The fact that she hadn't embraced him before he left haunted Blanchett. "I developed this ritual where I couldn't leave the house until I could actually physically say goodbye to everyone," she said. . . .

After Robert died, Blanchett developed a passion for horror movies. "I loved being terrified," she said. "It used to be a badge of honor if you could sit through *Halloween II*." Some of the thrill of horror movies lies in the thrill of surviving them, of, in a sense, cheating death. It's a thrill that carries over, as Upton [her husband] pointed out, to acting. "You go onstage and you're alive," he said. "You walk offstage, then the character's gone. You survive the experience. . . ."

"The fluidity you get in Cate is also because of the contradictions inside her."

Critical Reading

1. **(a)** How would Blanchett perform as a child? **(b) Infer:** Why did Blanchett enjoy this kind of performance?

2. **(a)** According to the interviewer, what is part of the thrill of horror movies? **(b) Interpret:** What connection does Blanchett's husband see between this thrill and the experience of acting? Explain.

3. **(a) Summarize:** Briefly summarize the childhood experiences Blanchett discusses in this interview. **(b) Draw Conclusions:** How might her childhood experiences, actions, and interests have helped her develop skills she needs to act?

Use these questions to focus a class discussion of "Disappearing Act":

4. In what ways are actresses and monarchs—like Cate Blanchett and Elizabeth I—both performers? Explain the reasons for your answer.

5. **(a)** How might creating a public image, as actresses and monarchs do, be a kind of deception? **(b)** How might it be a true expression of an individual's personality?

Connecting to the Essential Question The King James Bible has been for centuries an important book for many Protestants. As you read, identify qualities of language and rhythm that contribute to the appeal and influence of this great prose work. This will help you answer the Essential Question: **How does literature shape or reflect society?**

Literary Analysis

The Bible conveys themes of faith in a few genres, including these:

- **Psalms**—sacred songs or lyric poems in praise of God.
- **Sermons**—speeches offering religious or moral instruction. The Sermon on the Mount contains the basic teachings of Christianity.
- **Parables**—simple stories from which a moral or religious lesson can be drawn. The most famous are in the New Testament.

Comparing Literary Works Psalms, sermons, and parables all convey deep messages about life. Each communicates a message in a manner suited to its form. Psalms are songs. To engage an audience, psalms may feature vivid figurative language including **metaphors**—comparisons of unlike things. To help listeners understand, sermons may feature **analogies**—explanations comparing abstract relationships to familiar ones. Parables are **narratives**—stories illustrating a message.

As you read, compare the methods by which each selection conveys its message and the appeal and effectiveness of each.

Reading Strategy

 **Preparing to Read Complex Texts** In some portions of the Bible, the *main idea* is implied rather than directly stated. You can **determine the main idea** by *making inferences*—identifying key details in the text and then relating them to other details and to your own experience. When making inferences, consider what the text suggests as well as what it leaves uncertain. Use a chart like the one shown.

Vocabulary

righteousness (rī´ chəs nis) *n.* the characteristic of acting in a just, virtuous manner (p. 299)

stature (stach´ ər) *n.* height; level of achievement (p. 301)

prodigal (präd´ i gəl) *adj.* recklessly wasteful (p. 302)

entreated (en trēt´ id) *v.* begged; pleaded with (p. 304)

transgressed (trans grest) *v.* over-stepped or broke (a law or commandment) (p. 304)

Common Core State Standards

Reading Literature
1. Cite strong and thorough textual evidence to support analysis of what the text says explicitly as well as inferences drawn from the text, including determining where the text leaves matters uncertain.
4. Determine the meaning of words and phrases as they are used in the text, including figurative and connotative meanings.

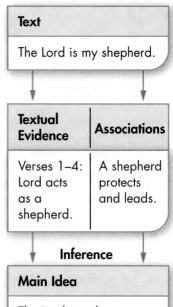

Text	
The Lord is my shepherd.	

Textual Evidence	Associations
Verses 1–4: Lord acts as a shepherd.	A shepherd protects and leads.

Inference

Main Idea
The Lord watches over faithful people, protecting them from danger.

PHLit Online!
www.PHLitOnline.com

FROM THE KING JAMES BIBLE

The King James Bible (completed 1611)

For centuries, the Bible was the cornerstone of European culture—the ultimate reference for rulers and priests, the ultimate authorization for laws and religious practices, a treasury of images and subjects for art. Yet, the book was inaccessible to the majority of Europeans. During the Reformation, in the 1500s, the need for a closer study of the Bible was widely acknowledged, which led to translations of the work into the vernacular, or common languages. For the first time, this grounding work became widely accessible.

The King James Bible, the authoritative English translation, was created at the command of King James I. In 1604, James commissioned fifty-four scholars and clergymen to compare all known texts of the Bible and prepare the definitive English edition.

Early Bibles The Bible, a collection of books developed over more than 1,200 years, consists of two main parts—the Old Testament, written in Hebrew, and the New Testament, written in Greek. In about A.D. 405, St. Jerome finished translating the Bible into Latin. This translation, the Vulgate, remained the standard Bible of the West for centuries. King James's translators, though, were to review the original sources, as well as translations of the work.

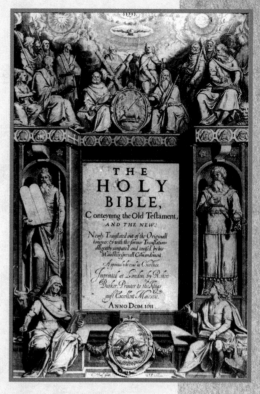

▲ Title page of the 1611 edition of the King James Bible

A Systematic Plan The project was carefully organized from the start. The books of the Bible were divided among six groups of scholars in Westminster, Oxford, and Cambridge.

The groups took four years to produce their initial drafts. Then, two scholars from each region spent nine months in London reviewing and revising the draft. After laboring for seven years, the group produced one of the great works of English literature. The King James Bible has been called "the only classic ever created by a committee."

Tyndale's Legacy The King James Bible was not the first English translation of the book. James's translators were greatly influenced by William Tyndale's translation. Tyndale, a Protestant chaplain and tutor in England, fled clerical oppression at home and published his translation of the New Testament in Germany. Before he had completed work on the Old Testament, however, he was arrested for heresy and executed near Brussels, Belgium, in 1536.

As England became more Protestant, Tyndale came to be viewed, not as a heretic, but as a hero. King James's committee closely followed the magnificent diction and rhythms of Tyndale's groundbreaking translation.

PSALM 23

FROM THE KING JAMES BIBLE

BACKGROUND Up to the middle 1400s, Bibles were painstakingly copied by hand. The resulting manuscripts, though often quite beautiful, were rare and costly. When the German inventor Johann Gutenberg devised a method of printing with movable type, widespread distribution of the Bible began.

Psalm 23 and Psalm 137 come from the Book of Psalms, a section of the old testament composed of 150 sacred songs. Many of the psalms are attributed to David, the young shepherd who killed Goliath and eventually became King of Israel. Psalm 23 is frequently recited at funerals, in times of trouble, and when people are in need of comfort.

1 The Lord is my shepherd; I shall not want.

2 He maketh me to lie down in green pastures: he leadeth me beside the still waters.

3 He restoreth my soul: he leadeth me in the paths of righteousness for his name's sake.

4 Yea, though I walk through the valley of the shadow of death, I will fear no evil: for thou art with me; thy rod and thy staff they comfort me.

5 Thou preparest a table before me in the presence of mine enemies; thou anointest my head with oil; my cup runneth over.

6 Surely goodness and mercy shall follow me all the days of my life: and I will dwell in the house of the Lord forever.

Vocabulary
righteousness
(rī´ chəs nis) *n.* the characteristic of acting in a just, virtuous manner

Literary Analysis
Metaphor
What is the central metaphor of Psalm 23?

◀ **Critical Viewing** Which details in this artist's portrayal of King David show him as a composer of the Book of Psalms? **[Analyze]**

PSALM 137

FROM THE KING JAMES BIBLE

1 By the rivers of Babylon, there we sat down, yea, we wept, when we remembered Zion.

2 We hanged our harps upon the willows in the midst thereof.

3 For there they that carried us away captive required of us a song; and they that wasted us required of us mirth, saying, Sing us one of the songs of Zion.

4 How shall we sing the Lord's song in a strange land?

5 If I forget thee, O Jerusalem, let my right hand forget her cunning.

6 If I do not remember thee, let my tongue cleave to the roof of my mouth; if I prefer not Jerusalem above my chief joy.

7 Remember, O Lord, the children of Edom in the day of Jerusalem; who said, Raze it, raze it, even to the foundation thereof.

8 O daughter of Babylon, who art to be destroyed; happy shall he be, that rewardeth thee as thou hast served us.

9 Happy shall he be, that taketh and dasheth thy little ones against the stones.

Critical Reading

Cite textual evidence to support your responses.

© **1. Craft and Structure (a)** What image is developed in the opening verses of Psalm 23? **(b) Infer:** Why might this image provide comfort to listeners? **(c) Draw Conclusions:** How does the inclusion of the images of the valley of death and of enemies strengthen the psalm?

© **2. Key Ideas and Details (a) Infer:** Which clues in Psalm 137 suggest that the author is living in exile? Explain. **(b) Connect:** In what ways is the psalm itself an answer to the question in verse 4?

© **3. Key Ideas and Details (a) Interpret:** In what ways does Psalm 137 combine sadness and anger? **(b) Evaluate:** Do you think the anger expressed in the psalm makes it less appealing? Why or why not?

© **4. Integration of Knowledge and Ideas** What type of music, if any, would serve as the best accompaniment for Psalm 137? Why?

S FROM THE SERMON ON THE MOUNT

FROM THE KING JAMES BIBLE MATTHEW 6: 24-30

24 No man can serve two masters: for either he will hate the one, and love the other; or else he will hold to the one, and despise the other. Ye cannot serve God and mammon.[1]

25 Therefore I say unto you, Take no thought for your life, what ye shall eat, or what ye shall drink; nor yet for your body, what ye shall put on. Is not the life more than meat, and the body than raiment?[2]

26 Behold the fowls of the air: for they sow not, neither do they reap, nor gather into barns; yet your heavenly Father feedeth them. Are ye not much better than they?

27 Which of you by taking thought can add one cubit unto his stature?

28 And why take ye thought for raiment? Consider the lilies of the field, how they grow; they toil not, neither do they spin:

29 And yet I say unto you, That even Solomon[3] in all his glory was not arrayed like one of these.

30 Wherefore, if God so clothe the grass of the field, which to day is, and to morrow is cast into the oven, *shall he* not much more *clothe* you, O ye of little faith?

---

1. **mammon** (mamʹ ən) *n.* money, personified as a false god.
2. **raiment** (rāʹ mənt) *n.* clothing; wearing apparel.
3. **Solomon** (sälʹ ə mən) *n.* tenth-century B.C. king of Israel.

Literary Analysis
Psalm, Sermon, and Parable
Why is the strategy of asking the audience questions particularly suited to a sermon?

Vocabulary
stature (stachʹ ər) *n.* height; level of achievement

Critical Reading

© 1. **Key Ideas and Details** **(a)** What human activities do the fowls and lilies of the sermon avoid? **(b) Analyze:** How does this "omission" affect their lives? **(c) Interpret:** Describe the attitude towards life that Jesus advocates.

Cite textual evidence to support your responses.

© 2. **Key Ideas and Details** Does Jesus, the speaker of this sermon, mean that his followers should literally "take no thought for life"? Explain.

© 3. **Integration of Knowledge and Ideas** Explain what a life lived like the lilies might be like.

₽from the
₽arable
of the
₽rodigal ₷on

FROM THE KING JAMES BIBLE LUKE 15: 11-32

World
LITERATURE
CONNECTION

Parables Around the World
The oral traditions of Zen Buddhists, Islamic Sufis and Jewish Hassidim all use parables to teach ideas about morality, philosophy and religion.

A Sufi story tells of a man who is chased by a hungry tiger. Finally the man turns around and cries to the tiger, "Why don't you leave me alone?" "Why don't you stop being so appetizing?" responds the tiger. This parable points out that there is always more than one way to see a situation.

Connect to the Literature

In what way does The Parable of the Prodigal Son challenge long-standing attitudes?

11 And he said, A certain man had two sons:

12 And the younger of them said to his father, Father, give me the portion of goods that falleth to me. And he divided unto them his living.

13 And not many days after the younger son gathered all together, and took his journey into a far country, and there wasted his substance with riotous living.

14 And when he had spent all, there arose a mighty famine in that land; and he began to be in want.

15 And he went and joined himself to a citizen of that country; and he sent him into his fields to feed swine.

16 And he would fain[1] have filled his belly with the husks that the swine did eat: and no man gave unto him.

17 And when he came to himself, he said, How many hired servants of my father's have bread enough and to spare, and I perish with hunger!

18 I will arise and go to my father, and will say unto him, Father, I have sinned against heaven, and before thee,

19 And am no more worthy to be called thy son: make me as one of thy hired servants.

20 And he arose, and came to his father. But when he was yet a great way off, his father saw him, and had compassion, and ran, and fell on his neck, and kissed him.

21 And the son said unto him, Father, I have sinned against heaven, and in thy sight, and am no more worthy to be called thy son.

---

1. fain *adv.* gladly.

▶ **Critical Viewing** Which verses from the selection are best illustrated by this painting? Explain. **[Interpret]**

22 But the father said to his servants, Bring forth the best robe, and put *it* on him; and put a ring on his hand, and shoes on *his* feet:

23 And bring hither the fatted calf, and kill *it*; and let us eat, and be merry:

24 For this my son was dead, and is alive again; he was lost, and is found. And they began to be merry.

25 Now his elder son was in the field: and as he came and drew nigh to the house, he heard music and dancing.

26 And he called one of the servants, and asked what these things meant.

27 And he said unto him, Thy brother is come; and thy father hath killed the fatted calf, because he hath received him safe and sound.

28 And he was angry, and would not go in: therefore came his father out, and entreated him.

29 And he answering said to *his* father, Lo, these many years do I serve thee, neither transgressed I at any time thy commandment: and yet thou never gavest me a kid, that I might make merry with my friends:

30 But as soon as this thy son was come, which hath devoured thy living with harlots, thou hast killed for him the fatted calf.

31 And he said unto him, Son, thou art ever with me, and all that I have is thine.

32 It was meet[2] that we should make merry, and be glad: for this thy brother was dead, and is alive again; and was lost, and is found.

---

2. **meet** *adj.* fitting.

Vocabulary

entreated (en trēt´ id) *v.* begged; pleaded with

transgressed (trans grest´) *v.* overstepped or broke (a law or commandment)

Critical Reading

Cite textual evidence to support your responses.

@ 1. **Key Ideas and Details** **(a)** What causes the younger son to return home? **(b) Compare and Contrast:** Contrast the father's and the older son's responses to the younger son's return.

@ 2. **Key Ideas and Details** **(a)** What specific complaint does the older son make? **(b) Assess:** How effectively does the father address his concerns?

@ 3. **Integration of Knowledge and Ideas** **(a) Interpret:** Why does the father say that the younger son is "alive again"? **(b) Apply:** In what circumstances might the lesson of the parable apply today?

@ 4. **Integration of Knowledge and Ideas** What made the King James Bible so influential? In your response, use at least two of the following Essential Question words: *majestic, clarity, solemn, preach.* *[Connecting to the Essential Question: How does literature shape or reflect society?]*

Literary Analysis

**Common Core
State Standards**

Writing
3. Write narratives to develop real or imagined experiences or events using effective technique, well-chosen details, and well-structured event sequences. *(p. 306)*

3.d. Use precise words and phrases, telling details, and sensory language to convey a vivid picture of the experiences, events, setting, and/or characters. *(p. 306)*

Language
1.a. Apply the understanding that usage is a matter of convention, can change over time, and is sometimes contested. *(p. 306)*

1. Key Ideas and Details (a) What is the message of the selection from the Sermon on the Mount? **(b)** Why is the form of a **sermon** suited to this lesson?

2. Key Ideas and Details (a) What is the chief moral lesson of the Parable of the Prodigal Son? **(b)** Why is the form of a **parable** suited to this lesson?

3. Craft and Structure (a) Contrast the styles of the **psalm,** the sermon, and the parable. **(b)** How is the style of each selection appropriate to its purpose?

4. Integration of Knowledge and Ideas The **metaphor** of the shepherd in Psalm 23, the **analogy** of the birds in the Sermon on the Mount, and the **narrative** in the Parable of the Prodigal Son are all designed to appeal to their original audience of uneducated, rural folk. Explain, using a chart like the one below.

Images: Familiar / Unfamiliar?	Simple / Difficult?	Memorable? Why?

5. Comparing Literary Works Of the following, which did you find easiest to understand: the metaphor of the shepherd, the analogy of the lilies, or the lesson of the prodigal son? For each, explain what was clear and what was complex.

Reading Strategy

6. For Psalm 23, **determine the main idea** by *making inferences* about the meaning of this quotation: "I will dwell in the house of the Lord forever." Consider, for example, what "the house of the Lord" might mean and why the word *dwelling* may have a connotation stronger than that of the word *living*.

7. What inference can you make from the fact that this excerpt from the Sermon on the Mount closes with "O ye of little faith"?

8. After reading the Parable of the Prodigal Son, what inference can you make about the value the Bible places on forgiveness?

9. Do you think that mercy and forgiveness are more important than, less important than, or equal in importance to justice? Explain, using examples from the parable.

10. Make inferences about the meaning of this quote from the Sermon on the Mount: "Which of you by taking thought can add one cubit unto his stature?"

Vocabulary Acquisition and Use

Word Analysis: Latin Root -stat-

The word *stature*, meaning "height when standing," comes from the Latin root -stat-, sometimes spelled -stit-, which means "to stand" or "to set up." Over time, the word *stature* has taken on a figurative meaning in addition to its literal one: though it sometimes refers to a person's actual height, it can also refer to a person's prominence or position in society or in some other organization or ranking.

Use the meaning of the root -stat- to match the following words with their definitions.

1. statue　　　　　**a.** to set up a procedure

2. stationary　　　 **b.** standing still

3. institute　　　　 **c.** rank

4. constitution　　 **d.** a figure that stands

5. status　　　　　 **e.** act of setting up

Vocabulary: Synonyms

Write a complete sentence to answer each question. For each item, use a vocabulary word from page 296 in place of the underlined words.

1. In what jobs or professions would a person need a good deal of <u>fairness</u> and <u>honesty</u>?

2. What might you say to a friend who was being <u>recklessly wasteful</u> with money she had borrowed?

3. Why do you think people often identify with a book or movie character who has <u>broken a law</u>?

4. Why might a person who is <u>begged</u> for something respond less favorably than one who is asked politely?

5. In your view, why is social <u>standing</u> so important to so many people?

Writing

Narrative Text Write a **parable** in the King James style about a modern-day issue or situation that supports a moral in which you believe. Study the style of the Parable of the Prodigal Son, and adapt it to your purposes.

Prewriting Choose a moral to teach, and sketch the plot of a story to illustrate it. Then reread the Parable of the Prodigal Son, taking notes on the style in which it is told.

Drafting Follow your notes as you draft, setting out the events of your story in clear sequence. Emphasize those elements—character traits or events—that will lead the reader to understand your parable. Use sensory details to make the scenes vivid and specific in your reader's mind. Conclude the parable with a moral.

Revising Highlight parts of your work that do not fit the general style you have adopted. Rewrite marked passages for consistency.

> **Model: Revising for Consistent Style**
> And, lo, the bully descended like a wolf on the playground. "Out of my way, meathead," he said.
> ~~laid about him mightily.~~
> And he ⋀ ~~started wailing on the nearest person.~~

The revision maintains the style: formal, simple, biblical-sounding narration contrasting with the character's slang dialogue.

Focus on Literary Forms
Drama

"DRAMA IS LIFE WITH THE DULL BITS CUT OUT."

— ALFRED HITCHCOCK

Defining Drama

Drama is a form of literature that tells a story through performances by actors.

Types of Drama The ancient Greeks developed drama into a sophisticated art form. They created two broad categories of drama: tragedy and comedy.

- **Tragedies** end with the downfall or death of the protagonist, or main character. In ancient Greek and Shakespearean tragedy, the main character is the *tragic hero*—an outstanding person of high rank who falls to his or her ruin.
- **Comedies** feature ordinary protagonists in conflicts that are resolved happily.

Elements of Drama The text of a play consists of dialogue and stage directions.

- **Dialogue** The term **dialogue** refers to the lines characters speak in conversation with each other. Playwrights also use these types of speech: **monologues,** or long speeches delivered by one character to others; **asides,** or private remarks to another character or to the audience that are not heard by other characters onstage; and **soliloquies,** or speeches voicing a character's inner thoughts, not heard by others.
- **Stage Directions** Many playwrights include **stage directions,** or instructions, about the setting, costumes, lighting, scenery, and props, or objects used onstage. Stage directions may also indicate how and when characters should move and with what expression they should deliver their lines.

Close Read: Elements of Shakespearean Drama These literary elements appear in the Model text.

Soliloquy: A soliloquy is a long speech expressing private thoughts, not heard by others. Example: *Before murdering King Duncan, Macbeth delivers a soliloquy expressing his fears and doubts, beginning "If it were done when 'tis done . . . "* (Macbeth, I, vii, 1).	**Internal Conflict and Characterization:** An internal conflict is a character's struggle with his or her own conflicting motivations. In his soliloquies, Shakespeare turns a powerful psychological spotlight on characters' internal conflicts. Example: ***"Hamlet.** To be or not to be, that is the question. . . ."* (Hamlet, III, i, 62)
Imagery: The mind's power to make sense of the world is part of Shakespearean drama. Imagery, or word pictures, in the dialogue shows characters' minds and hearts at work. Example: ***"Romeo.** But soft! What light through yonder window breaks? / It is the East, and Juliet is the sun!"* (Romeo and Juliet, II, ii, 2–3)	**Blank Verse:** Shakespeare's noble characters often speak in a type of poetry called blank verse, consisting of unrhymed lines each containing five stressed syllables. Each stressed syllable is preceded by an unstressed syllable in a "da-DUM, da-DUM" rhythm. Example: ***"Antony.** O mighty Caesar! Dost thou lie so low?"* (Julius Caesar, III, i, 148)

Model

About the Text In Shakespeare's *Hamlet,* Hamlet's uncle Claudius has murdered Hamlet's father, the king of Denmark, and then married Hamlet's mother, taking the throne of Denmark. In this soliloquy, Claudius ponders his crime.

from *The Tragedy of Hamlet,* Act III, Scene iii, Lines 39–75
William Shakespeare

KING CLAUDIUS

O, my offence is rank, it smells to heaven;
40 It hath the primal eldest curse[1] upon't,
A brother's murder. Pray can I not,
Though inclination be as sharp as will:
My stronger guilt defeats my strong intent;
And, like a man to double business bound,
45 I stand in pause where I shall first begin,
And both neglect. What if this cursed hand
Were thicker than itself with brother's blood,
Is there not rain enough in the sweet heavens
To wash it white as snow? Whereto serves mercy
50 But to confront the visage of offence?[2]
And what's in prayer but this two-fold force,
To be forestalled ere we come to fall,
Or pardon'd being down? Then I'll look up;
My fault is past. But, O, what form of prayer
55 Can serve my turn? 'Forgive me my foul murder'?
That cannot be; since I am still possess'd
Of those effects for which I did the murder,
My crown, mine own ambition and my queen.
May one be pardon'd and retain the offence?
60 In the corrupted currents of this world
Offence's gilded hand may shove by justice,
And oft 'tis seen the wicked prize itself
Buys out the law: but 'tis not so above;
There is no shuffling, there the action lies
65 In his true nature; and we ourselves compell'd,
Even to the teeth and forehead of our faults,
To give in evidence. What then? What rests?
Try what repentance can. What can it not?
Yet what can it when one can not repent?
70 O wretched state! O bosom black as death!
O limed[3] soul, that, struggling to be free,
Art more engaged! Help, angels! Make assay!
Bow, stubborn knees; and, heart with strings of steel,
Be soft as sinews of the newborn babe!
75 All may be well.

1. **primal eldest curse** the curse of Cain. In the Bible, Cain killed his brother Abel.

2. **Whereto serves mercy . . . visage of offence?** What is mercy's purpose if not to contest condemnation?

3. **limed** trapped, as a bird caught in birdlime, a sticky substance used in traps.

Soliloquy In this speech, Claudius reveals his thoughts alone onstage, confessing that he has murdered his brother, who was Hamlet's father and the king of Denmark.

Blank Verse The rhythm of the blank verse helps carry Claudius's analysis of prayer and forgiveness to its conclusion.

Internal Conflict In these lines Claudius elaborates on his internal conflict—the fact that he is "to double business bound." He cannot truly repent of the murder as long as he is still attached to what it has brought him: a crown and a wife.

Imagery The contrast between the images of "strings of steel" and "sinews of the newborn babe" reflects Claudius's agonized struggle—he is torn between his stubborn attachment to his crime and his desire to repent.

Literary History: Shakespeare's Globe

"Can this cockpit hold
The vasty fields of France? Or may we cram
Within this wooden O the very casques
That did affright the air at Agincourt?"

—*Shakespeare, from* Henry V

The Elizabethan Theater

English drama came of age during the reign of Elizabeth I, developing into a sophisticated and popular art form. Although playwrights like Shakespeare were mainly responsible for the great theatrical achievements of the time, audiences and theater buildings were equally important.

Before the reign of Elizabeth I, traveling theater companies put on plays wherever they could find an audience, often performing in the open courtyards of inns. Spectators watched from the ground or from balconies or galleries above.

England's First Playhouse

When Shakespeare was twelve years old, an actor named James Burbage built London's first theater, called simply The Theater. Actors—even prominent and well-to-do actors like James Burbage—were frowned upon by the city fathers. Nonetheless, they were wildly popular with the common people and were called on frequently to perform at court. A man like Burbage enjoyed a reputation somewhat like a rock star's today.

The Globe In 1597, the city fathers closed down The Theater. In late 1598, Richard Burbage (James Burbage's son) and his men dismantled it and hauled it in pieces across the Thames to Southwark. It took them six months to rebuild it, and when they did, they renamed it the Globe.

Scholars disagree about what the Globe actually looked like because there are no surviving drawings from the time or detailed descriptions. Shakespeare refers to the building in *Henry V* as "this wooden O." The building had to have been small enough for the actors to be heard, and we know that performances drew as many as 2,500 to 3,000 people. These truly packed houses must have been uncomfortable—especially when you consider that people of the era didn't bathe or change their clothes very often! Most spectators stood throughout the performance. Some of the audience sat in a gallery behind the performers. Though they saw only the actors' backs and probably could not hear very well, they were content to be seen by the rest of the audience.

There were no sets or lighting at the Globe. Plays were performed in sunlight, and a playwright's words alone had to create moods like the one in the eerie first scene of *Macbeth.* Holding an audience spellbound was complicated by the fact that most spectators ate and drank throughout the performance.

The first Globe met its demise in 1613, when a cannon fired as part of a performance of *Henry VIII* ignited the theater's thatched roof. Everyone escaped unharmed, but the Globe burned to the ground. Although the theater was rebuilt, the Puritans had it permanently closed in 1642.

The New Globe

Building a replica of Shakespeare's Globe was the American actor Sam Wanamaker's dream. After long years of fundraising and construction, the theater opened to its first full season on June 8, 1997, with a production of *Henry V.* Like the earlier Globe, this one is made of wood, with a thatched roof and lime plaster covering the walls. The stage and the galleries are covered, but the "bear pit," where the modern-day groundlings stand, is open to the skies.

Perhaps the most striking aspect of seeing Shakespeare's plays performed at the Globe is the immediacy of the action. The performers, as Benedict Nightingale noted in the *London Times,* "are talking to you, asking you questions, involving you in their fears." Is that not what theater is all about?

A performance at the modern Globe

Speaking and Listening: Discussion

Ⓒ **Comprehension and Collaboration** Today, most patrons expect a certain level of comfort and technical sophistication when attending a theatrical event—whether a concert, a Broadway show, or a school assembly.

With a group, discuss your experiences while attending live performances. Use these questions to guide your discussion:

- In what ways do modern shows compare with what you have read about Elizabethan theater?
- Do you think live theater is more popular or less popular today than in Shakespeare's day? Explain.

Choose a point person to share your group's ideas with the class.

Literary History: Shakespeare on Film

Adapting Shakespeare

William Shakespeare wrote for the same audience that filmmakers write for today. Recognizing his wide appeal, filmmakers have adapted many of Shakespeare's plays as films. On these two pages, you will see examples of some of the more notable adaptations.

◄ The 1956 science-fiction film *Forbidden Planet* adapted Shakespeare's drama *The Tempest*, transforming the play's mysterious island into a distant planet.

Japanese director Akira Kurosawa's samurai epic *Throne of Blood* (1957) is considered one of the best film adaptations of *Macbeth*. Toshiro Mifune (shown here) plays the character based on Shakespeare's tragic hero. ▶

◀ The musical *West Side Story* (1961) updated *Romeo and Juliet* to the mean streets of New York City. The warring families of Shakespeare's drama become rival gangs.

Common Core State Standards

Reading Literature
7. Analyze multiple interpretations of a story, drama, or poem, evaluating how each version interprets the source text.

In 1996, Claire Danes (shown here) played Juliet to Leonardo DiCaprio's Romeo in Baz Luhrmann's version of *Romeo and Juliet*. Luhrmann used Shakespeare's dialogue, but set the play in a hip modern suburb. ▶

Reading Literature: Group Discussion

Ⓒ Analyzing Multiple Interpretations After reading Shakespeare's *Macbeth*, view two or more productions of the play. Consider the 1948 film version directed by Orson Welles as well as any current theatrical versions. Then, in small groups, compare the interpretations you viewed. Use these prompts to guide discussion:

- Did the characters in each version match the characters you imagined while reading *Macbeth*? Were the portrayals effective?
- Describe and evaluate the use in each production of techniques specific to the medium—for film, for example, you might discuss the use of camera point of view, including distance shots and close-ups.
- Did the production depart from Shakespeare's text by introducing, updating, or omitting elements? Evaluate each change.

Based on your discussion, evaluate the effectiveness of each production.

Themes Across Centuries: Scholar's Insights

Sir Frank Kermode on *Macbeth*

Macbeth's **Dramatic History** *Macbeth,* first performed in 1606, is a play about the murder of a good king of Scotland, its cruel consequences for his country, and the final overthrow of the murderous usurper. Shakespeare takes many liberties with history, for King Duncan was not really a saintly character and Macbeth not a particularly evil one. Banquo is presented in a favorable light because he was held to be the ancestor of King James, the Scottish king who inherited Elizabeth's throne in 1603. Shakespeare's company was called The King's Men; as servants of the king, they had good reason to praise his ancestry and his virtues. Considering the period background, the play is remarkable for the allusions it makes to events in the early years of James's reign.

Portraying the Tumult of Mind and Conscience Yet these allusions are matters of secondary interest to the modern reader. *Macbeth* is a work of the author's full maturity. He had already written the tragedies *Hamlet, Othello,* and *King Lear* and had learned how to represent not merely outward actions but the tumults of the mind and conscience.

In the passage shown from Act I, Macbeth is at the moment of decision, the interim between desire and action, debating within himself whether to go ahead with the plot he devised with his wife to murder the king, their guest. He is weighing the benefits that act would bring him against the powerful reasons for not doing it. He knows that time won't stand still when Duncan is dead. The killing will start a train of events calling for further action.

He is willing to risk judgment after death but knows it will happen in this life. In the here and now. And he gives ordinary social, human reasons for not committing the crime: He is Duncan's kinsman and his host. Moreover, for a subject to kill an innocent monarch is an offense so horrible that his imagination foretells the dreadful disturbances and great sorrows that must ensue. And he admits he has no motive except overweening ambition.

About the Author

Literary critic Sir Frank Kermode wrote the award-winning *Shakespeare's Language* in 2000. Other works by Kermode include *The Uses of Error* (1991) and *An Appetite for Poetry* (1989).

▼ **Critical Viewing**
What general traits might be worthy of note in a tribute to a young king, like James I pictured here? **[Speculate]**

The Actions of a Common Man The reason why Macbeth's soliloquy is so famous is not that it concerns the early history of Scotland, and the foundation of the Stuart dynasty, but that it gives incomparably vivid expression to an acute crisis of conscience. For a moment, Macbeth is every man or woman, who must, in the course of his or her life, be faced by the need to decide which of two choices is the right one.

The language of this soliloquy is sometimes unusual and full of feverish excitement. But, at first, do not bother too much about the details; just allow yourself to be swept along by the movement of passionate thought.

This soliloquy indicates the extraordinary range and flexibility of the play's language, incomparably greater than English could have provided even fifty or sixty years before. This new fluency owes something to sixteenth-century Bible translations.

Religious and Ethical Thought As this soliloquy also reflects, *Macbeth* is notable for complying with native ethical traditions. Shakespeare is not often explicitly religious, but Macbeth speaks as one aware of the Christian religion—he understands the danger to his soul, yet gives his "eternal jewel" to "the common enemy of man" (3.1.68–69). Behind such remarks there is a great weight of religious and ethical thought.

> *"He's here in double trust:*
> *First, as I am his kinsman and his subject,*
> *Strong both against the deed; then, as his host,*
> *Who should against his murderer shut the door,*
> *Not bear the knife myself. Besides, this Duncan*
> *Hath borne his faculties so meek, hath been*
> *So clear in his great office, that his virtues*
> *Will plead like angels, trumpet-tongue'd, against*
> *The deep damnation of his taking-off . . .*
> *I have no spur*
> *To prick the sides of my intent, but only*
> *Vaulting ambition, which o'erleaps itself*
> *And falls on th'other."* — Macbeth, Act I, Scene vii

Critical Reading

1. **Key Ideas and Details** **(a)** What English king did Shakespeare intend to honor by writing *Macbeth?* **(b) Speculate:** What benefits might a company of actors and playwrights reap by presenting their king in a favorable light?

2. **Key Ideas and Details** **(a)** According to Kermode, what reason does Macbeth provide for wanting to kill King Duncan? **(b) Speculate:** If, in the course of the play, Macbeth is punished for killing the king, what message might this send to the audience in Shakespeare's day?

As You Read Macbeth . . .

3. **Integration of Knowledge and Ideas** Note moments in which Banquo and most kings in the play are presented in a positive light as a way to honor James I of England.

4. **Integration of Knowledge and Ideas** Look for evidence that supports Kermode's characterization of Macbeth as "every man or woman . . . faced by the need to decide which of two choices is the right one."

WILLIAM SHAKESPEARE

(1564–1616)

Because of his deep understanding of human nature, his compassion for all types of people, and the power and beauty of his language, William Shakespeare is regarded as the greatest writer in English. Nearly four hundred years after his death, Shakespeare's plays continue to be read widely and produced throughout the world. They have the same powerful impact on today's audiences as they had when they were first staged.

THE PLAYWRIGHT IN HIS OWN TIME

It is a myth that we know absolutely nothing about Shakespeare's life. As critic Irving Ribner attests, "we know more about him than we do about virtually any other of his contemporary dramatists, with the exception of Ben Jonson." Shakespeare was born on April 23, 1564, in Stratford-on-Avon,

"The poet's eye, in a fine frenzy rolling,
Doth glance from heaven to earth, from earth
*   to heaven;*
And, as imagination bodies forth
The forms of things unknown, the poet's pen
Turns them to shapes, and gives to airy nothing
A local habitation and a name."

—William Shakespeare,
from *A Midsummer Night's Dream*

which is northwest of London. (The date is based on a record of his baptism on April 26.) Stratford, with a population of about two thousand in Shakespeare's day, was the market town for a fertile agricultural region.

Shakespeare's father, John, was a successful glove maker and businessman who held a number of positions in the town's government. His mother, whose maiden name was Mary Arden, was the daughter of John's landlord. Their marriage, therefore, boosted the Shakespeare family's holdings. Nevertheless, there is evidence that in the late 1570s, John Shakespeare began to suffer financial reverses.

SHAKESPEARE'S EDUCATION

No written evidence of Shakespeare's boyhood exists—not even a name on a school attendance list. However, given his father's status, it is highly probable that he attended the Stratford Grammar School, where he acquired a knowledge of Latin.

Although Shakespeare did not go on to study at a university, his attendance at the grammar school from ages seven to sixteen would have provided him with a good education. Discipline at such a school was strict, and the school day lasted from 6:00 A.M. in the summer (7:00 in the winter) until 5:00 P.M. From 11:00 to 1:00, students were dismissed to eat lunch with their families. At 3:00, they were allowed to play for a quarter of an hour!

SHAKESPEARE'S MARRIAGE AND FAMILY

Shakespeare's name enters the official records again in November 1582, when he received a license to marry Anne Hathaway. The couple had a

Speaking Shakespeare

You may not realize the extent to which you already "speak" Shakespeare. For example, have you ever used or heard any of these phrases used in *Macbeth*?

He's full of *milk of human kindness* (I, v, 17)
Don't worry about it, *what's done is done!* (II, ii, 12)
That will last until *the crack of doom*. (IV, i, 117)
She finished the jobs in *one fell swoop*. (IV, iii, 219)

Shakespeare invented each of these now common phrases, which were unknown in English before their appearance in *Macbeth*. Look for them as you read and discover if their meanings have changed since Shakespeare's time.

daughter, Susanna, in 1583, and twins, Judith and Hamnet, in 1585. Beyond names and years in which his children were born, we know little about his family life. Some writers have made much of the fact that Shakespeare left his wife and children behind when he went to London not long after his twins were born. However, he visited his family in Stratford regularly during his years as a playwright, and they may have lived with him for a time in London.

ACTOR AND PLAYWRIGHT

It is uncertain how Shakespeare became connected with the theater in the late 1580s and early 1590s. By 1594, however, he had become a part owner and the principal playwright of the Lord Chamberlain's Men, one of the most successful theater companies in London.

In 1599, the company built the famous Globe theater on the south bank of the Thames River, in Southwark. This is where most of

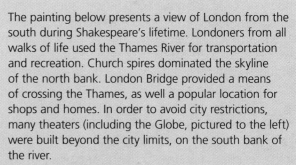

The painting below presents a view of London from the south during Shakespeare's lifetime. Londoners from all walks of life used the Thames River for transportation and recreation. Church spires dominated the skyline of the north bank. London Bridge provided a means of crossing the Thames, as well a popular location for shops and homes. In order to avoid city restrictions, many theaters (including the Globe, pictured to the left) were built beyond the city limits, on the south bank of the river.

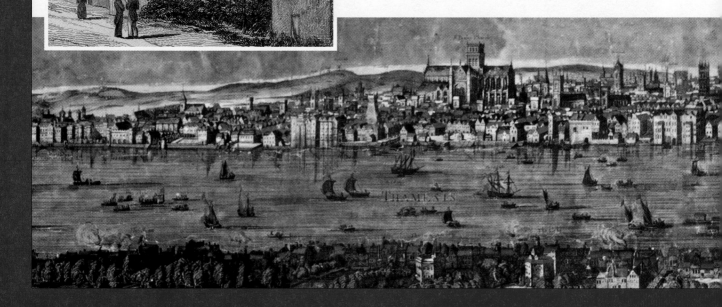

Shakespeare's plays were performed. When James I became king in 1603, after the death of Elizabeth I, James took control of the Lord Chamberlain's Men and renamed the company the King's Men.

RETIREMENT

In about 1610, Shakespeare retired to Stratford, where he continued to write plays. He was a prosperous middle-class man, who profited from his share in a successful theater company. Six years later, on April 23, 1616, he died and was buried in Holy Trinity Church in Stratford. Because it was a common practice to move bodies after burial to make room for others, Shakespeare wrote the following as his epitaph:

> Blest be the man that spares these stones,
> And curst be he that moves my bones.

HIS LITERARY RECORD

Shakespeare did not think of himself as a man of letters. He wrote his plays to be performed and did not bring out editions of them for the reading public. The first published edition of his work, called the First Folio, was issued in 1623 by two members of his theater company, John Heminges and Henry Condell. It contained thirty-six of the thirty-seven plays now attributed to him.

Shakespeare's varied output includes romantic comedies, like *A Midsummer Night's Dream* and *As You Like It*; history plays, like *Henry IV*, Parts 1 and 2; tragedies, like *Romeo and Juliet, Hamlet, Othello, King Lear,* and *Macbeth*; and later romances, like *The Tempest*. In addition to his plays, he wrote 154 sonnets and three longer poems.

MACBETH
SHAKESPEARE'S SOURCES

FACT AND LEGEND

By Shakespeare's time, the story of the eleventh-century Scottish king Macbeth was a mixture of fact and legend. Shakespeare and his contemporaries, however, probably regarded the account of Macbeth in Raphael Holinshed's *Chronicles of England, Scotland, and Ireland* as completely factual. The playwright drew on the *Chronicles* as a source for the play, yet, as you will see, he freely adapted the material for his own purposes.

HOLINSHED'S CHRONICLES

Holinshed's account contains a description of a meeting between Macbeth and the witches. His account also tells how Macbeth and his friends, angry at the naming of King Duncan's son Malcolm as Prince of Cumberland, ambush and slay Duncan. However, the historical Macbeth's claim to the throne has some basis. (See page 408 for an explanation of the ancient Scottish custom of choosing kings.) Finally, Holinshed indicates that Banquo is Macbeth's accomplice in the assassination. Lady Macbeth, prominent in Shakespeare's play, does not play a significant role in Holinshed.

SHAKESPEARE'S MACBETH

Shakespeare took what he needed from the *Chronicles* and shaped it into a tragic plot. Seeing the theatrical possibilities of the meeting with the witches, Shakespeare staged such an encounter in Act I, Scene iii. However, he changed Holinshed's account in order to make King Duncan an innocent victim: Shakespeare's Macbeth does not have a legitimate claim to the throne. Further, Shakespeare used another story in the *Chronicles*—one in which a wife urges her husband to kill a friend and guest—as the basis for the character Lady Macbeth. She becomes Macbeth's co-conspirator, replacing Banquo. Shakespeare, of course, had political motives for holding Banquo innocent. Banquo was considered the ancestor of the new king, James I!

Before You Read | *Macbeth, Act I*

Connecting to the Essential Question In *Macbeth*, a noble person's downfall results from a character flaw. As you read, note that *Macbeth*, unlike classical tragedies, includes comedy in its portrayal of a noble character's downfall. Finding such moments will help you answer the Essential Question: **What is the relationship of the writer to tradition?**

Literary Analysis

During the late 1500s, **Elizabethan drama** blossomed. Using models from ancient Greece and Rome, writers reintroduced **tragedies**—plays in which disaster befalls a character. Dramatists also began writing their plays in carefully crafted unrhymed verse, using rich language and vivid imagery.

Because the Globe, like other Elizabethan theaters, had no lighting, plays were performed in broad daylight. There were also no sets, so the words of the play had to create the illusion of time and place for the audience.

Playwrights made key choices about how to develop and relate character. One device they used was called a **soliloquy,** a long speech usually made by a character who is alone (the Latin *solus* means "alone"). This speech reveals thoughts and feelings to the audience. In Shakespeare's tragedies, the greatest works of Elizabethan drama, tragic characters reveal secret desires or fears through their soliloquies.

As you read the following soliloquies in this act, note the inner struggles each reveals.

- Lady Macbeth's soliloquy, Act I, Scene v, lines 1–30
- Macbeth's soliloquy, Act I, Scene vii, lines 1–28

Reading Strategy

Ⓒ Preparing to Read Complex Texts Like many dramas, Shakespeare's plays were meant to be performed, not read. By **analyzing information from text features** like introductory *background notes*, *stage directions* in brackets, *illustrations*, and *footnotes* on the side of the text, you can picture the action in your mind. You can also better understand the meaning and tone of the characters' words. Use a chart like the one shown to analyze information from text features and clarify the meaning of passages.

Vocabulary

valor (val´ ər) *n.* bravery (p. 324)

treasons (trē´ zənz) *n.* betrayals of one's country (p. 330)

imperial (im pir´ ē əl) *adj.* having supreme authority (p. 330)

surmise (sər mīz´) *n.* imaginings; speculation (p. 331)

sovereign (säv´ rən) *adj.* supreme in power or authority (p. 336)

Ⓒ Common Core State Standards

Reading Literature
3. Analyze the impact of the author's choices regarding how to develop and relate elements of a story or drama.

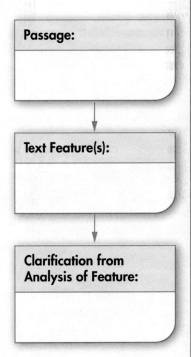

Passage:

Text Feature(s):

Clarification from Analysis of Feature:

www.PHLitOnline.com

THE TRAGEDY OF
MACBETH
WILLIAM SHAKESPEARE

Background

The Elizabethans viewed the universe, in its ideal state, as both orderly and interconnected. They believed that a great chain linked all beings, from God on high to the lowest beasts and plants. They also believed that universal order was based on parallels between different realms. Just as the sun ruled in the heavens, for example, the king ruled in the state and the father in the family. Because everything was linked, a disturbance in one area would cause a disturbance in others. In keeping with this concept of order, a Shakespearean tragedy shows how a tragic hero's bad choices can disturb the whole universe. As *Macbeth* gets under way, notice the parallel disorders in the mind of the hero, the weather, and the kingdom.

CHARACTERS

DUNCAN, King of Scotland

MALCOLM } his sons
DONALBAIN

MACBETH
BANQUO
MACDUFF
LENNOX } noblemen
ROSS   of Scotland
MENTEITH
ANGUS
CAITHNESS

FLEANCE, son to Banquo
SIWARD, Earl of Northumberland, general of
      the English forces
YOUNG SIWARD, his son

SEYTON, an officer attending on Macbeth
SON TO MACDUFF
AN ENGLISH DOCTOR
A SCOTTISH DOCTOR
A PORTER
AN OLD MAN
THREE MURDERERS
LADY MACBETH
LADY MACDUFF
A GENTLEWOMAN attending
      on Lady Macbeth
HECATE
WITCHES
APPARITIONS
LORDS, OFFICERS, SOLDIERS,
      ATTENDANTS, AND MESSENGERS

Setting: Scotland; England

ACT I

Scene i. *An open place.*

[*Thunder and lightning. Enter* THREE WITCHES.]

FIRST WITCH. When shall we three meet again?
In thunder, lightning, or in rain?

SECOND WITCH. When the hurlyburly's done,
When the battle's lost and won.

5 **THIRD WITCH.** That will be ere the set of sun.

FIRST WITCH. Where the place?

SECOND WITCH.   Upon the heath.

THIRD WITCH. There to meet with Macbeth.

FIRST WITCH. I come, Graymalkin.[1]

SECOND WITCH. Paddock[2] calls.

THIRD WITCH.   Anon![3]

10 **ALL.** Fair is foul, and foul is fair.
Hover through the fog and filthy air.   [*Exit.*]

Scene ii. *A camp near Forres, a town in northeast Scotland.*

[*Alarum within.[1] Enter* KING DUNCAN, MALCOLM, DONALBAIN, LENNOX,
with ATTENDANTS, *meeting a bleeding* CAPTAIN.]

Reading Strategy
Analyze Text Features
Who or what are Graymalkin and Paddock in lines 8 and 9? How do you know?

1. **Graymalkin** first witch's helper, a gray cat.

2. **Paddock** second witch's helper, a toad.

3. **Anon** at once.

1. **Alarum within** trumpet call offstage.

Reading
Check

Where, when, and with whom will the witches next meet?

▲ **Critical Viewing** Examine Fuseli's rendering of the witches. Does the mood he creates correspond to the mood in Act I, Scene i? Why or why not? **[Connect]**

2. **sergeant** officer.

3. **broil** battle.

4. **choke their art** prevent each other from swimming.

5. **Western Isles** the Hebrides, off Scotland.

6. **Of kerns and gallowglasses** with lightly armed Irish foot soldiers and heavily armed soldiers.

7. **damned quarrel** accursed cause.

8. **Showed . . . whore** falsely appeared to favor Macdonwald.

9. **minion** favorite.

Vocabulary
valor (val´ ər) *n.* marked courage or bravery

KING. What bloody man is that? He can report,
　As seemeth by his plight, of the revolt
　The newest state.

MALCOLM. 　　　　　　This is the sergeant[2]
　Who like a good and hardy soldier fought
5 'Gainst my captivity. Hail, brave friend!
　Say to the king the knowledge of the broil[3]
　As thou didst leave it.

CAPTAIN. 　　　　　　Doubtful it stood,
　As two spent swimmers, that do cling together
　And choke their art.[4] The merciless Macdonwald—
10 Worthy to be a rebel for to that
　The multiplying villainies of nature
　Do swarm upon him—from the Western Isles[5]
　Of kerns and gallowglasses[6] is supplied;
　And fortune, on his damnéd quarrel[7] smiling,
15 Showed like a rebel's whore:[8] but all's too weak:
　For brave Macbeth—well he deserves that name—
　Disdaining fortune, with his brandished steel,
　Which smoked with bloody execution,
　Like **valor**'s minion[9] carved out his passage

20   Till he faced the slave;
       Which nev'r shook hands, nor bade farewell to him,
       Till he unseamed him from the nave to th' chops,[10]
       And fixed his head upon our battlements.

   KING. O valiant cousin! Worthy gentleman!

25 **CAPTAIN.** As whence the sun 'gins his reflection[11]
       Shipwracking storms and direful thunders break,
       So from that spring whence comfort seemed to come
       Discomfort swells. Mark, King of Scotland, mark:
       No sooner justice had, with valor armed,
30   Compelled these skipping kerns to trust their heels
       But the Norweyan lord,[12] surveying vantage,[13]
       With furbished arms and new supplies of men,
       Began a fresh assault.

   KING.   Dismayed not this
       Our captains, Macbeth and Banquo?

   CAPTAIN.   Yes;
35   As sparrows eagles, or the hare the lion.
       If I say sooth,[14] I must report they were
       As cannons overcharged with double cracks;[15]
       So they doubly redoubled strokes upon the foe.
       Except[16] they meant to bathe in reeking wounds,
40   Or memorize another Golgotha,[17]
       I cannot tell—
       But I am faint; my gashes cry for help.

   KING. So well thy words become thee as thy wounds;
       They smack of honor both. Go get him surgeons.

                        [*Exit* CAPTAIN, *attended.*]

[*Enter* ROSS *and* ANGUS.]

       Who comes here?

45 **MALCOLM.**   The worthy Thane[18] of Ross.

   LENNOX. What a haste looks through his eyes! So should he look
       That seems to[19] speak things strange.

   ROSS.   God save the king!

   KING. Whence cam'st thou, worthy Thane?

   ROSS.   From Fife, great King;
       Where the Norweyan banners flout the sky
50   And fan our people cold.
       Norway[20] himself, with terrible numbers,
       Assisted by that most disloyal traitor
       The Thane of Cawdor, began a dismal[21] conflict;
       Till that Bellona's bridegroom, lapped in proof,[22]

Literary Analysis
Elizabethan Drama
What offstage scene does the captain describe in this speech (lines 7–23)?

10. **unseamed . . . chops** split him open from the navel to the jaws.

11. **'gins his reflection** rises.

12. **Norweyan lord** king of Norway.

13. **surveying vantage** seeing an opportunity.

14. **sooth** truth.

15. **cracks** explosives.

16. **except** unless.

17. **memorize . . . Golgotha** (gôl′ gə thə) make the place as memorable for slaughter as Golgotha, the place where Christ was crucified.

18. **Thane** Scottish title of nobility.

19. **seems to** seems about to.

20. **Norway** king of Norway.

21. **dismal** threatening.

22. **Bellona's . . . proof** Macbeth is called the mate of Bellona, the goddess of war, clad in tested armor.

Literary Analysis
Elizabethan Drama
How do Lennox's words here (lines 46–47) supply a clue for the actor playing Ross?

Reading Check
What role has Macbeth played in the battle?

23. self-comparisons counter movements.

24. lavish insolent.

25. composition terms of peace.

26. St. Colme's Inch island near Edinburgh, Scotland.

27. our bosom interest my heart's trust.

28. present immediate.

Reading Strategy

Analyze Information from Text Features

What information about the setting for Scene iii do you learn from the italicized stage directions?

1. Killing swine It was commonly believed that witches killed domestic animals.

2. Aroint thee Be off.

3. rump-fed ronyon fat-rumped, scabby creature.

4. Aleppo trading center in Syria.

5. sieve It was commonly believed that witches often sailed in sieves.

6. rat . . . tail According to popular belief, witches could assume the form of any animal, but the tail would always be missing.

7. they blow to which the winds blow.

8. card compass.

9. penthouse lid eyelid.

10. forbid cursed.

55 Confronted him with self-comparisons,[23]
Point against point, rebellious arm 'gainst arm,
Curbing his lavish[24] spirit: and, to conclude,
The victory fell on us.

KING.   Great happiness!

ROSS.   That now
Sweno, the Norways' king, craves composition;[25]
60 Nor would we deign him burial of his men
Till he disbursed, at Saint Colme's Inch,[26]
Ten thousand dollars to our general use.

KING. No more that Thane of Cawdor shall deceive
Our bosom interest:[27] go pronounce his present[28] death,
65 And with his former title greet Macbeth.

ROSS. I'll see it done.

KING. What he hath lost, noble Macbeth hath won.

[*Exit.*]

Scene iii. A heath near Forres.

[*Thunder. Enter the* THREE WITCHES.]

FIRST WITCH. Where hast thou been, sister?

SECOND WITCH. Killing swine.[1]

THIRD WITCH. Sister, where thou?

FIRST WITCH. A sailor's wife had chestnuts in her lap,
And mounched, and mounched, and mounched.
5   "Give me," quoth I.
"Aroint thee,[2] witch!" the rump-fed ronyon[3] cries.
Her husband's to Aleppo[4] gone, master o' th' Tiger:
But in a sieve[5] I'll thither sail,
And, like a rat without a tail,[6]
10 I'll do, I'll do, and I'll do.

SECOND WITCH. I'll give thee a wind.

FIRST WITCH. Th' art kind.

THIRD WITCH. And I another.

FIRST WITCH. I myself have all the other;
15 And the very ports they blow,[7]
All the quarters that they know
I' th' shipman's card.[8]
I'll drain him dry as hay:
Sleep shall neither night nor day
20 Hang upon his penthouse lid;[9]
He shall live a man forbid:[10]

Weary sev'nights[11] nine times nine
Shall he dwindle, peak,[12] and pine:
Though his bark cannot be lost,
25   Yet it shall be tempest-tossed.
Look what I have.

SECOND WITCH. Show me, show me.

FIRST WITCH. Here I have a pilot's thumb,
Wracked as homeward he did come.

[Drum within.]

30 **THIRD WITCH.** A drum, a drum!
Macbeth doth come.

ALL. The weird[13] sisters, hand in hand,
Posters[14] of the sea and land,
Thus do go about, about:
35   Thrice to thine, and thrice to mine,
And thrice again, to make up nine.
Peace! The charm's wound up.

[Enter MACBETH *and* BANQUO.*]*

MACBETH. So foul and fair a day I have not seen.

BANQUO. How far is 't called to Forres? What are these
40   So withered, and so wild in their attire,
That look not like th' inhabitants o' th' earth,
And yet are on 't? Live you, or are you aught
That man may question? You seem to understand me,
By each at once her choppy[15] finger laying
45   Upon her skinny lips. You should be women,
And yet your beards forbid me to interpret
That you are so.

MACBETH.   Speak, if you can: what are you?

FIRST WITCH. All hail, Macbeth! Hail to thee, Thane of Glamis!

SECOND WITCH. All hail, Macbeth! Hail to thee, Thane of Cawdor!

50 **THIRD WITCH.** All hail, Macbeth, that shalt be King hereafter!

BANQUO. Good sir, why do you start, and seem to fear
Things that do sound so fair? I' th' name of truth,
Are you fantastical,[16] or that indeed
Which outwardly ye show? My noble partner
55   You greet with present grace[17] and great prediction
Of noble having[18] and of royal hope,
That he seems rapt withal:[19] to me you speak not.
If you can look into the seeds of time,
And say which grain will grow and which will not,

11. **sev'nights** weeks.

12. **peak** waste away.

13. **weird** destiny-serving.

14. **Posters** swift travelers.

Literary Analysis
Elizabethan Drama
What descriptive details does Banquo use in his speech about the witches (lines 39–47)?

15. **choppy** chapped.

16. **fantastical** imaginary.

17. **grace** honor.

18. **having** possession.

19. **rapt withal** entranced by it.

Reading Check

What has Macbeth earned through his exploits?

▲ **Critical Viewing** Which of the two soldiers on the right do you think is Macbeth? Explain your reasoning. **[Deduce]**

Literary Analysis
Elizabethan Drama
How could Elizabethan actors have made this scene with the witches mysterious without help from special lighting effects?

20. **happy** fortunate.

21. **imperfect** incomplete.

22. **Sinel's** (sī′ nəlz) Macbeth's father's.

23. **owe** own.

24. **intelligence** information.

60   Speak then to me, who neither beg nor fear
       Your favors nor your hate.

FIRST WITCH. Hail!

SECOND WITCH. Hail!

THIRD WITCH. Hail!

65 **FIRST WITCH.** Lesser than Macbeth, and greater.

SECOND WITCH. Not so happy,[20] yet much happier.

THIRD WITCH. Thou shalt get kings, though thou be none.
       So all hail, Macbeth and Banquo!

FIRST WITCH. Banquo and Macbeth, all hail!

70 **MACBETH.** Stay, you imperfect[21] speakers, tell me more:
       By Sinel's[22] death I know I am Thane of Glamis;
       But how of Cawdor? The Thane of Cawdor lives,
       A prosperous gentleman; and to be King
       Stands not within the prospect of belief,
75   No more than to be Cawdor. Say from whence
       You owe[23] this strange intelligence?[24] Or why

Upon this blasted heath you stop our way
With such prophetic greeting? Speak, I charge you.

[WITCHES *vanish*.]

BANQUO. The earth hath bubbles as the water has,
80   And these are of them. Whither are they vanished?

MACBETH. Into the air, and what seemed corporal[25] melted
As breath into the wind. Would they had stayed!

BANQUO. Were such things here as we do speak about?
Or have we eaten on the insane root[26]
85   That takes the reason prisoner?

MACBETH. Your children shall be kings.

BANQUO.   You shall be King.

MACBETH. And Thane of Cawdor too. Went it not so?

BANQUO. To th' selfsame tune and words. Who's here?

[*Enter* ROSS *and* ANGUS.]

ROSS. The King hath happily received, Macbeth,
90   The news of thy success; and when he reads[27]
Thy personal venture in the rebels' fight,
His wonders and his praises do contend
Which should be thine or his.[28] Silenced with that,
In viewing o'er the rest o' th' selfsame day,
95   He finds thee in the stout Norweyan ranks,
Nothing afeard of what thyself didst make,
Strange images of death.[29] As thick as tale
Came post with post,[30] and every one did bear
Thy praises in his kingdom's great defense,
And poured them down before him.

100 **ANGUS.**   We are sent
To give thee, from our royal master, thanks;
Only to herald thee into his sight,
Not pay thee.

ROSS. And for an earnest[31] of a greater honor,
105   He bade me, from him, call thee Thane of Cawdor;
In which addition,[32] hail, most worthy Thane!
For it is thine.

BANQUO. [*Aside*] What, can the devil speak true?

MACBETH. The Thane of Cawdor lives: why do you dress me
In borrowed robes?

ANGUS.   Who was the thane lives yet,
110   But under heavy judgment bears that life
Which he deserves to lose. Whether he was combined[33]

25. **corporal** real.

26. **insane root** henbane or hemlock, believed to cause insanity.

Reading Strategy
Analyze Information from Text Features
What does Banquo mean by the "insane root" (line 84)?

27. **reads** considers.

28. **His wonders . . . his** His admiration contends with his desire to praise you.

29. **Nothing . . . death** killing, but not being afraid of being killed.

30. **As thick . . . post** as fast as could be counted came messenger after messenger.

31. **earnest** pledge.

32. **In which addition** with this new title.

33. **combined** allied.

Reading Check
What do the witches promise Macbeth and Banquo?

34. **line** support.

35. **vantage** assistance.

36. **wrack** ruin.

Vocabulary

treasons (trē´ zənz) *n.*
betrayals of one's country or
oath of loyalty

37. **behind** still to come.

Reading Strategy

**Analyze Information from
Text Features**

Using the side notes,
how would you rephrase
lines 120–121?

38. **home** fully.

39. **enkindle you unto**
encourage you to hope for.

40. **Cousins** often used as
a term of courtesy between
fellow noblemen.

41. **swelling . . . theme**
stately idea that I will be
King.

Vocabulary

imperial (im pir´ ē əl) *adj.*
of an empire; having
supreme authority

42. **suggestion** thought of
murdering Duncan.

43. **seated** fixed.

44. **Against . . . nature**
in an unnatural way.

With those of Norway, or did line[34] the rebel
With hidden help and vantage,[35] or that with both
He labored in his country's wrack,[36] I know not;
115 But treasons capital, confessed and proved,
Have overthrown him.

MACBETH.   [*Aside*] Glamis, and Thane of Cawdor:
The greatest is behind.[37] [*To* ROSS *and* ANGUS]
Thanks for your pains.
[*Aside to* BANQUO] Do you not hope your children shall be
kings,
When those that gave the Thane of Cawdor to me
Promised no less to them?

120 **BANQUO.** [*Aside to* MACBETH] That, trusted home,[38]
Might yet enkindle you unto[39] the crown,
Besides the Thane of Cawdor. But 'tis strange:
And oftentimes, to win us to our harm,
The instruments of darkness tell us truths,
125 Win us with honest trifles, to betray 's
In deepest consequence.
Cousins,[40] a word, I pray you.

MACBETH.   [*Aside*] Two truths are told,
As happy prologues to the swelling act
Of the imperial theme.[41]—I thank you, gentlemen.—
130 [*Aside*] This supernatural soliciting
Cannot be ill, cannot be good. If ill,
Why hath it given me earnest of success,
Commencing in a truth? I am Thane of Cawdor:
If good, why do I yield to that suggestion[42]
135 Whose horrid image doth unfix my hair
And make my seated[43] heart knock at my ribs,
Against the use of nature?[44] Present fears
Are less than horrible imaginings.

▶ **Critical Viewing** In
what ways does the design
of this crown reflect the
belief that kings were
divinely appointed? Explain
your reasoning. [**Analyze**]

My thought, whose murder yet is but fantastical
140 Shakes so my single[45] state of man that function
Is smothered in surmise, and nothing is
But what is not.

BANQUO.   Look, how our partner's rapt.

MACBETH. [*Aside*] If chance will have me King, why,
chance may crown me,
Without my stir.

BANQUO.   New honors come upon him,
145 Like our strange[46] garments, cleave not to their mold
But with the aid of use.

MACBETH.   [*Aside*] Come what come may,
Time and the hour runs through the roughest day.

BANQUO. Worthy Macbeth, we stay upon your leisure.[47]

MACBETH. Give me your favor.[48] My dull brain was wrought
150 With things forgotten. Kind gentlemen, your pains
Are registered where every day I turn
The leaf to read them. Let us toward the King.
[*Aside to* BANQUO] Think upon what hath chanced,
and at more time,
The interim having weighed it,[49] let us speak
Our free hearts[50] each to other.

155 **BANQUO.**   Very gladly.

MACBETH. Till then, enough. Come, friends.

[*Exit.*]

Scene iv. Forres. The palace.

[*Flourish.*[1] *Enter* KING DUNCAN, LENNOX, MALCOLM, DONALBAIN,
and ATTENDANTS.]

KING. Is execution done on Cawdor? Are not
Those in commission[2] yet returned?

MALCOLM.   My liege,[3]
They are not yet come back. But I have spoke
With one that saw him die, who did report
5 That very frankly he confessed his treasons,
Implored your Highness' pardon and set forth
A deep repentance: nothing in his life
Became him like the leaving it. He died
As one that had been studied[4] in his death,
10 To throw away the dearest thing he owed[5]
As 'twere a careless[6] trifle.

45. single unaided, weak.

Reading Strategy
Analyze Information from Text Features
What does the stage direction for line 153 indicate to the actor playing Macbeth?

46. strange new.

Vocabulary
surmise (sər mīz´) *n.* imaginings; speculation

47. stay upon your leisure await your convenience.

48. favor pardon.

49. The interim . . . it when we have had time to think about it.

50. Our free hearts our minds freely.

1. Flourish trumpet fanfare.

2. in commission commissioned to oversee the execution.

3. liege (lèj) *n.* lord or king.

4. studied rehearsed.

5. owed owned.

6. careless worthless.

Reading Check

As Macbeth thinks about what the witches have promised, what "horrid image" frightens him?

KING. There's no art
To find the mind's construction[7] in the face:
He was a gentleman on whom I built
An absolute trust.

7. **mind's construction** person's character.

[*Enter* MACBETH, BANQUO, ROSS, *and* ANGUS.]

O worthiest cousin!
15   The sin of my ingratitude even now
Was heavy on me: thou art so far before,
That swiftest wing of recompense is slow
To overtake thee. Would thou hadst less deserved,
That the proportion both of thanks and payment
20   Might have been mine![8] Only I have left to say,
More is thy due than more than all can pay.

8. **Would . . . mine** If you had been less worthy, my thanks and payment could have exceeded the rewards you deserve.

MACBETH. The service and the loyalty I owe,
In doing it, pays itself.[9] Your Highness' part
Is to receive our duties: and our duties
25   Are to your throne and state children and servants;
Which do but what they should, by doing every thing
Safe toward[10] your love and honor.

9. **pays itself** is its own reward.

10. **Safe toward** with sure regard for.

KING. Welcome hither.
I have begun to plant thee, and will labor
To make thee full of growing. Noble Banquo,
30   That hast no less deserved, nor must be known

▼ **Critical Viewing** How does this Scottish castle reflect the mood of the play? **[Connect]**

No less to have done so, let me enfold thee
And hold thee to my heart.

BANQUO.   There if I grow,
The harvest is your own.

KING.   My plenteous joys,
Wanton[11] in fullness, seek to hide themselves
35   In drops of sorrow. Sons, kinsmen, thanes,
And you whose places are the nearest, know,
We will establish our estate upon
Our eldest, Malcolm,[12] whom we name hereafter
The Prince of Cumberland: which honor must
40   Not unaccompanied invest him only,
But signs of nobleness, like stars, shall shine
On all deservers. From hence to Inverness,[13]
And bind us further to you.

MACBETH. The rest is labor, which is not used for you.[14]
45   I'll be myself the harbinger,[15] and make joyful
The hearing of my wife with your approach;
So, humbly take my leave.

KING.   My worthy Cawdor!

MACBETH. [Aside] The Prince of Cumberland! That is a step
On which I must fall down, or else o'erleap,
50   For in my way it lies. Stars, hide your fires;
Let not light see my black and deep desires:
The eye wink at the hand;[16] yet let that be   [Exit.]
Which the eye fears, when it is done, to see.

KING. True, worthy Banquo; he is full so valiant,
55   And in his commendations I am fed;
It is a banquet to me. Let's after him,
Whose care is gone before to bid us welcome.
It is a peerless kinsman.   [Flourish. Exit.]

Scene v. Inverness. Macbeth's castle.

[Enter MACBETH'S WIFE, alone, with a letter.]

LADY MACBETH. [Reads] "They met me in the day of
success; and I have learned by the perfect'st report
they have more in them than mortal knowledge.
When I burned in desire to question them further,
5   they made themselves air, into which they vanished.
Whiles I stood rapt in the wonder of it, came
missives[1] from the King, who all-hailed me 'Thane
of Cawdor'; by which title, before, these weird sisters
saluted me, and referred me to the coming on
10   of time, with 'Hail, King that shalt be!' This have I

Macbeth, Act I, Scene v **333**

thought good to deliver thee,[2] my dearest partner of
greatness, that thou mightst not lose the dues of
rejoicing, by being ignorant of what greatness is
promised thee. Lay it to thy heart, and farewell."

15 Glamis thou art, and Cawdor, and shalt be
What thou art promised. Yet do I fear thy nature;
It is too full o' th' milk of human kindness
To catch the nearest[3] way. Thou wouldst be great,
Art not without ambition, but without
20 The illness[4] should attend it. What thou wouldst highly,
That wouldst thou holily; wouldst not play false,
And yet wouldst wrongly win. Thou'dst have, great Glamis,
That which cries "Thus thou must do" if thou have it;
And that which rather thou dost fear to do
25 Than wishest should be undone.[5] Hie thee hither,
That I may pour my spirits in thine ear,
And chastise with the valor of my tongue
All that impedes thee from the golden round[6]
Which fate and metaphysical aid doth seem
To have thee crowned withal.

[*Enter* MESSENGER.]

30   What is your tidings?

MESSENGER. The King comes here tonight.

LADY MACBETH.   Thou'rt mad to say it!
Is not thy master with him, who, were't so,
Would have informed for preparation?

MESSENGER. So please you, it is true. Our thane is coming.
35 One of my fellows had the speed of him,[7]
Who, almost dead for breath, had scarcely more
Than would make up his message.

LADY MACBETH.   Give him tending;
He brings great news.   [*Exit* MESSENGER.]
                        The raven himself is hoarse
That croaks the fatal entrance of Duncan
40 Under my battlements. Come, you spirits
That tend on mortal[8] thoughts, unsex me here,
And fill me, from the crown to the toe, top-full
Of direst cruelty! Make thick my blood,
Stop up th' access and passage to remorse[9]
45 That no compunctious visitings of nature[10]
Shake my fell[11] purpose, nor keep peace between
Th' effect[12] and it! Come to my woman's breasts,
And take my milk for gall,[13] you murd'ring ministers,[14]
Wherever in your sightless[15] substances
50 You wait on[16] nature's mischief! Come, thick night,

Literary Analysis
**Elizabethan Drama
and Soliloquy**
What does Lady Macbeth's
soliloquy in lines 15–30
reveal about her ambitions
and plans?

3. **nearest** quickest.

4. **illness** wickedness.

5. **that which . . . undone**
What you are afraid of
doing you would not wish
undone once you have
done it.

6. **round** crown.

7. **had . . . him** overtook him.

8. **mortal** deadly.

9. **remorse** compassion.

10. **compunctious . . . nature**
natural feelings of pity.

11. **fell** savage.

12. **effect** fulfillment.

13. **milk for gall** kindness in
exchange for bitterness.

14. **ministers** agents.

15. **sightless** invisible.

16. **wait on** assist.

◀ **Critical Viewing** This is an artist's rendering of nineteenth-century actress Ellen Terry playing Lady Macbeth. Judging by the picture, how do you think Terry would have spoken lines 38-54 in Act I, Scene v? **[Deduce]**

17. **pall** enshroud.
18. **dunnest** darkest.

And pall[17] thee in the dunnest[18] smoke of hell,
That my keen knife see not the wound it makes,
Nor heaven peep through the blanket of the dark,
To cry "Hold, hold!"

[*Enter* MACBETH.]

                        Great Glamis! Worthy Cawdor!
55   Greater than both, by the all-hail hereafter!
Thy letters have transported me beyond
This ignorant[19] present, and I feel now
The future in the instant.[20]

MACBETH.   My dearest love,
Duncan comes here tonight.

LADY MACBETH.   And when goes hence?

MACBETH. Tomorrow, as he purposes.

19. **ignorant** unknowing.
20. **instant** present.

Reading Check

What does Lady Macbeth feel is Macbeth's weakness?

21. beguile the time deceive the people tonight.

22. dispatch management.

23. look up clear appear innocent.

Vocabulary

sovereign (säv´ rən) *adj.* supreme in power, rank, or authority

24. To alter . . . fear to show a disturbed face will arouse suspicion.

1. *Hautboys* oboes announcing the arrival of royalty.

2. seat location.

3. gentle soothed.

4. temple-haunting martlet martin, a bird that usually nests in churches. In Shakespeare's time, *martin* was a slang term for a person who is easily deceived.

5. approve show.

6. mansionry nests.

7. jutty projection.

8. coign of vantage advantageous corner.

9. procreant (prō´ krē ənt) **cradle** nest where the young are hatched.

10. haunt visit.

11. The love . . . trouble Though my visit inconveniences you, you should ask God to reward me for coming, because it was my love for you that prompted my visit.

12. single business feeble service.

13. rest your hermits remain your dependents bound to pray for you. Hermits were often paid to pray for another person's soul.

---

60 **LADY MACBETH.**   O, never
    Shall sun that morrow see!
    Your face, my Thane, is as a book where men
    May read strange matters. To beguile the time,[21]
    Look like the time; bear welcome in your eye,
65   Your hand, your tongue: look like th' innocent flower,
    But be the serpent under 't. He that's coming
    Must be provided for: and you shall put
    This night's great business into my dispatch;[22]
    Which shall to all our nights and days to come
70   Give solely sovereign sway and masterdom.

MACBETH. We will speak further.

LADY MACBETH.   Only look up clear.[23]
    To alter favor ever is to fear.[24]
    Leave all the rest to me.   [*Exit.*]

Scene vi. Before Macbeth's castle.

[*Hautboys.*[1] *Torches. Enter* KING DUNCAN, MALCOLM, DONALBAIN, BANQUO, LENNOX, MACDUFF, ROSS, ANGUS, *and* ATTENDANTS.]

KING. This castle hath a pleasant seat;[2] the air
    Nimbly and sweetly recommends itself
    Unto our gentle[3] senses.

BANQUO.   This guest of summer,
    The temple-haunting martlet,[4] does approve[5]
5   By his loved mansionry[6] that the heaven's breath
    Smells wooingly here. No jutty,[7] frieze,
    Buttress, nor coign of vantage,[8] but this bird
    Hath made his pendent bed and procreant cradle.[9]
    Where they most breed and haunt,[10] I have observed
    The air is delicate.

[*Enter* LADY MACBETH.]

10 **KING.**   See, see, our honored hostess!
    The love that follows us sometime is our trouble,
    Which still we thank as love. Herein I teach you
    How you shall bid God 'ield us for your pains
    And thank us for your trouble.[11]

LADY MACBETH.   All our service
15   In every point twice done, and then done double,
    Were poor and single business[12] to contend
    Against those honors deep and broad wherewith
    Your Majesty loads our house: for those of old,
    And the late dignities heaped up to them,
    We rest your hermits.[13]

20 **KING.**   Where's the Thane of Cawdor?
     We coursed[14] him at the heels, and had a purpose
     To be his purveyor:[15] but he rides well,
     And his great love, sharp as his spur, hath holp[16] him
     To his home before us. Fair and noble hostess,
     We are your guest tonight.

25 **LADY MACBETH.**   Your servants ever
     Have theirs, themselves, and what is theirs, in compt,[17]
     To make their audit at your Highness' pleasure,
     Still[18] to return your own.

     KING.   Give me your hand.
     Conduct me to mine host: we love him highly,
30   And shall continue our graces towards him.
     By your leave, hostess.   [*Exit.*]

Scene vii. Macbeth's castle.

[*Hautboys. Torches. Enter a* SEWER,[1] *and diverse* SERVANTS *with dishes and service over the stage. Then enter* MACBETH.]

     MACBETH. If it were done[2] when 'tis done, then 'twere well
     It were done quickly. If th' assassination
     Could trammel up the consequence, and catch,
     With his surcease, success;[3] that but this blow
5   Might be the be-all and the end-all—here,
     But here, upon this bank and shoal of time,
     We'd jump the life to come.[4] But in these cases
     We still have judgment here; that we but teach
     Bloody instructions, which, being taught, return
10   To plague th' inventor: this even-handed[5] justice
     Commends[6] th' ingredients of our poisoned chalice[7]
     To our own lips. He's here in double trust:
     First, as I am his kinsman and his subject,
     Strong both against the deed; then, as his host,
15   Who should against his murderer shut the door,
     Not bear the knife myself. Besides, this Duncan
     Hath borne his faculties[8] so meek, hath been
     So clear[9] in his great office, that his virtues
     Will plead like angels trumpet-tongued against
20   The deep damnation of his taking-off;
     And pity, like a naked newborn babe,
     Striding the blast, or heaven's cherubin[10] horsed
     Upon the sightless couriers[11] of the air,
     Shall blow the horrid deed in every eye,
25   That tears shall drown the wind. I have no spur
     To prick the sides of my intent, but only
     Vaulting ambition, which o'erleaps itself
     And falls on th' other—

14. **coursed** chased.

15. **purveyor** advance supply officer.

16. **holp** helped.

17. **compt** trust.

18. **Still** always.

Literary Analysis
Elizabethan Drama
What details does Banquo use in Scene vi, lines 3–10 to paint a word picture of Macbeth's castle?

1. **sewer** chief butler.

2. **done** over and done with.

3. **If . . . success** if the assassination could be done successfully and without consequence.

4. **We'd . . . come** I would risk life in the world to come.

5. **even-handed** impartial.

6. **commends** offers.

7. **chalice** cup.

8. **faculties** powers.

9. **clear** blameless.

10. **cherubin** angels.

11. **sightless couriers** unseen messengers (the wind).

Literary Analysis
Elizabethan Drama and Soliloquy
What doubts does Macbeth reveal in his soliloquy (lines 1–28)?

Reading Check
What deed does Lady Macbeth urge her husband to perform?

[*Enter* LADY MACBETH.]

How now! What news?

LADY MACBETH. He has almost supped. Why have you
left the chamber?

MACBETH. Hath he asked for me?

30 **LADY MACBETH.**   Know you not he has?

MACBETH. We will proceed no further in this business:
He hath honored me of late, and I have bought[12]
Golden opinions from all sorts of people,
Which would be worn now in their newest gloss,
Not cast aside so soon.

35 **LADY MACBETH.**   Was the hope drunk
Wherein you dressed yourself? Hath it slept since?
And wakes it now, to look so green and pale
At what it did so freely? From this time
Such I account thy love. Art thou afeard
40 To be the same in thine own act and valor
As thou art in desire? Wouldst thou have that
Which thou esteem'st the ornament of life,[13]
And live a coward in thine own esteem,
Letting "I dare not" wait upon[14] "I would,"
Like the poor cat i' th' adage?[15]

45 **MACBETH.**   Prithee, peace!
I dare do all that may become a man;
Who dares do more is none.

LADY MACBETH.   What beast was 't then
That made you break[16] this enterprise to me?
When you durst do it, then you were a man;
50 And to be more than what you were, you would
Be so much more the man. Nor time nor place
Did then adhere,[17] and yet you would make both.
They have made themselves, and that their[18] fitness now
Does unmake you. I have given suck, and know
55 How tender 'tis to love the babe that milks me:
I would, while it was smiling in my face,
Have plucked my nipple from his boneless gums,
And dashed the brains out, had I so sworn as you
Have done to this.

MACBETH.   If we should fail?

LADY MACBETH.   We fail?
60 But[19] screw your courage to the sticking-place[20]
And we'll not fail. When Duncan is asleep—
Whereto the rather shall his day's hard journey
Soundly invite him—his two chamberlains

---

12. **bought** acquired.

Reading Strategy
Analyze Text Features
In line 42, what does Lady
Macbeth mean by the
"ornament of life"?

13. **ornament of life** the
crown.

14. **wait upon** follow.

15. **poor . . . adage** from an
old proverb about a cat
who wants to eat fish but
is afraid of getting its paws
wet.

16. **break** reveal.

17. **Did then adhere** was then
suitable (for the assassination)

18. **that their** their very.

19. **But** only.

20. **sticking-place** the notch
that holds the bowstring of
a taut crossbow.

Will I with wine and wassail[21] so convince,[22]
65 That memory, the warder of the brain,
Shall be a fume, and the receipt of reason
A limbeck only:[23] when in swinish sleep
Their drenchéd natures lies as in a death,
What cannot you and I perform upon
70 Th' unguarded Duncan, what not put upon
His spongy[24] officers, who shall bear the guilt
Of our great quell?[25]

MACBETH.   Bring forth men-children only;
For thy undaunted mettle[26] should compose
Nothing but males. Will it not be received,
75 When we have marked with blood those sleepy two
Of his own chamber, and used their very daggers,
That they have done 't?

LADY MACBETH.   Who dares receive it other,[27]
As we shall make our griefs and clamor roar
Upon his death?

MACBETH.   I am settled, and bend up
80 Each corporal agent to this terrible feat.
Away, and mock the time[28] with fairest show:
False face must hide what the false heart doth know.   [*Exit.*]

21. **wassail** carousing.
22. **convince** overpower.
23. **That . . . only** that memory, the guardian of the brain, will be confused by the fumes of the drink, and the reason become like a still, distilling confused thoughts.
24. **spongy** sodden.
25. **quell** murder.
26. **mettle** spirit.
27. **other** otherwise.
28. **mock the time** mislead the world.

Critical Reading

@ 1. **Key Ideas and Details (a)** What statements do the witches and Macbeth make about "foul and fair"? **(b) Interpret:** What meaning (or meanings) does each remark have?

@ 2. **Key Ideas and Details (a)** Describe Banquo's and Macbeth's reactions to the witches. **(b) Compare and Contrast:** Compare and contrast their reactions to the witches.

@ 3. **Key Ideas and Details (a)** In his soliloquy at the beginning of Scene vii, what arguments against killing Duncan does Macbeth express? **(b) Analyze Cause and Effect:** Which of these arguments seems to influence him the most? Explain.

@ 4. **Integration of Knowledge and Ideas (a)** What is Lady Macbeth's opinion of her husband's character? **(b) Analyze:** How does she use her knowledge of his character to convince him to kill Duncan?

Cite textual evidence to support your responses.

After You Read *Macbeth, Act I*

Literary Analysis

© **1. Craft and Structure (a)** What vivid image, typical of **Elizabethan drama,** does Shakespeare create when Macbeth says to Ross, "why do you dress me / In borrowed robes?" (Act I, Scene iii, lines 108–109)? **(b)** What uneasiness in Macbeth does this word picture reveal?

© **2. Craft and Structure** How does Macbeth's encounter with the witches show that the play will probably be a **tragedy?**

© **3. Integration of Knowledge and Ideas** Does Macbeth's meeting with the witches suggest that evil is something people choose, a force that seeks people out, or some combination of the two? Explain.

© **4. Integration of Knowledge and Ideas** Identify a person in history who is similar to a character in Macbeth. Then, explain your choice.

© **5. Integration of Knowledge and Ideas** Using a chart like this one, analyze the details of setting in the lines shown. Then, indicate how modern sets and lighting might produce such a setting.

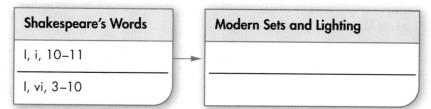

Shakespeare's Words	Modern Sets and Lighting
I, i, 10–11	
I, vi, 3–10	

© **6. Craft and Structure** What do each of the following **soliloquies** reveal about their speaker's thoughts and plans: **(a)** Lady Macbeth, Act I, Scene v, lines 1–30 and **(b)** Macbeth, Act I, Scene vii, lines 1–28?

© **7. Craft and Structure** In Act I, which type of speech directed to the audience is more effective in revealing Macbeth's thoughts: asides or a soliloquy? Explain.

© **8. Integration of Knowledge and Ideas** Do Lady Macbeth's and Macbeth's soliloquies add to the sense that the characters are moving toward disaster? Why or why not?

Reading Strategy

9. (a) Analyze information from text features such as stage directions, side notes, and illustrations to describe the action in Act I, Scene i, and the beginning of Act I, Scene v. **(b)** Which text features were most helpful in describing the action? Provide reasons for your choice or choices.

10. Use the side notes to clarify the meaning of the following terms: **(a)** anon, **(b)** Thane, **(c)** cousins.

**Common Core
State Standards**

Writing
3. Write narratives to develop real or imagined experiences or events using effective technique, well-chosen details, and well-structured event sequences. *(p. 341)*

3.d. Use precise words and phrases, telling details, and sensory language to convey a vivid picture of the experiences, events, setting, and/or characters. *(p. 341)*

Language
4.a. Use context as a clue to the meaning of a word or phrase. *(p. 341)*

5. Demonstrate understanding of nuances in word meanings. *(p. 341)*

Integrated Language Skills

Vocabulary Acquisition and Use

Word Analysis: Denotations and Connotations of Political Words

A word's **denotation** is its dictionary meaning—what it means, free of associations it might call to mind. A word's **connotation** is the set of associations and feelings that it stirs up. The denotation of *liege* is "king" or "subject." In addition to these denotative meanings, the word carries connotations of deep allegiance between ruler and subject. Another word with strong connotations is the adjective *sovereign*, suggesting a formal and absolute power, unlike its weaker synonym *dominant*.

For each of these political words, use a thesaurus to find a word with the same denotation but weaker connotations. Then, explain your choice.

1. reign (n.)   3. monarch   5. dominion
2. imperial   4. realm   6. majesty

Vocabulary: Context Clues

Each sentence below features an underlined word from the vocabulary list on page 321. If the word's meaning makes sense in the context, identify the sentence as logical. If not, identify the sentence as illogical and revise it to make it logical. Do not change the vocabulary word.

1. Macbeth's fearfulness in battle proved that he was a man of <u>valor</u>.
2. The <u>imperial</u> air with which Macbeth commanded caused others to obey him instantly.
3. Macbeth's assassination plan was aided by his habit of engaging in anxious <u>surmise</u>.
4. The witches had appealed to Macbeth's image of himself as <u>sovereign</u>.
5. Duncan believed in Macbeth and knew he was capable of <u>treason</u>.

Writing

Narrative Text As Macbeth, write a **speech** introducing the visiting Duncan to your household. Include details you would use in a real-life introduction of a speaker.

Prewriting List facts about Duncan, such as his title and accomplishments. Then, list the traits that make him a good king.

Drafting Begin with a flattering anecdote. Then use your prewriting lists to craft an engaging narrative account of his life and accomplishments.

Revising Revise to add subtlety by telling a flattering story about Duncan that may not be widely known to the listeners. Also, place stars next to boring, overused words or phrases. Then, replace them with language that is more vivid and specific. Use words and phrases that would seem flattering to Duncan but also ironically suggest your plan to do away with him.

Model: Revising for Subtlety

These last weeks have been difficult for our liege. We can only

hope that his time among us will provide a ~~tired~~ king with   *fading*

long spell of bodily repose   *this realm*

a ~~bit of rest~~, and that he shall leave ~~our home~~ in a state

heavenly rejuvenation.

of ~~renewal and health.~~

The writer replaces weak, everyday words and phrases with language that is both lofty—befitting a king—and subtly suggestive of treason.

Before You Read *Macbeth, Act II*

Literary Analysis

Blank verse—unrhymed iambic pentameter—was invented during the English Renaissance to reflect natural speech. An **iamb** consists of an unstressed syllable followed by a stressed syllable (˘ ´). In iambic pentameter, there are five such feet (units) to the line. *Macbeth* is written mainly in blank verse, as follows:

> Mĕthóught Ĭ héard ă vóice cr̆y, "Sléep nŏ móre!" (II,ii,34)

For interest, Shakespeare varies his meter, as when he begins this line with a **trochaic foot** (´ ˘): "List'ning their fear, I could not say 'Amen'" (II, ii, 28). Another variation is the **anapestic foot** (˘ ˘ ´). As you read, listen for the rhythm as well as the meaning of the dialogue.

Shakespeare sometimes interrupts his blank verse with **prose,** which is writing that is not divided into poetic lines and lacks a definite rhythm. In his tragedies, lower-ranking characters often speak in prose to provide **comic relief,** a humorous break from a tense mood. Notice this effect as you read the Porter's speech at the start of Act II, Scene iii. By using different line structures, such as blank verse or prose, for specific characters, Shakespeare adds to the overall meaning of the play.

Reading Strategy

ⓒ **Preparing to Read Complex Texts** A key *pattern of organization* in Shakespeare's blank verse is the way in which sentences and blank verse lines interact. By **analyzing** that interaction, you can better understand how Shakespeare achieves **clarity of meaning.** In making your analysis, follow sentences past line endings. For instance, you must follow this sentence past the end of the line to learn what the owl does:

> *"It was the owl that shrieked, the fatal bellman,*
> *Which gives the stern'st good-night. . . ." (II, ii, 3–4).*

Use a chart like this one to distinguish between lines and sentences.

Vocabulary

augment (ôg ment´) *v.* make greater; enlarge (p. 344)

palpable (pal´ pə bəl) *adj.* capable of being touched or felt (p. 344)

stealthy (stel´ thē) *adj.* sly (p. 344)

multitudinous (mul´ tə tō͞od´ ´n əs) *adj.* existing in great numbers (p. 348)

equivocate (ē kwiv´ ə kāt´) *v.* to use terms that have two or more meanings to mislead purposely or deceive (p. 348)

predominance (prē däm´ ə nəns) *n.* superiority (p. 354)

Common Core State Standards

Reading Literature
5. Analyze how an author's choices concerning how to structure specific parts of a text contribute to its overall structure and meaning as well as its aesthetic impact.

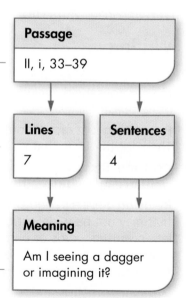

Passage
II, i, 33–39

Lines	Sentences
7	4

Meaning
Am I seeing a dagger or imagining it?

Review and Anticipate

In Act I, we learn that Macbeth has distinguished himself in battle. Returning from the battle-field, he and Banquo meet three witches who predict that Macbeth will not only be rewarded by King Duncan, but that he will become king himself. However, the witches also greet Banquo as a father of kings. Motivated by the witches' prophecies, Macbeth considers killing Duncan. The assassination becomes more likely when the king decides to visit Macbeth's castle. Lady Macbeth, on hearing about the witches' predictions and the king's visit, resolves that she and her husband will kill Duncan. When Macbeth hesitates, she urges him on. As Act II begins, they are about to perform this evil deed.

ACT II

Scene i. Inverness. Court of Macbeth's castle.

[*Enter* BANQUO, *and* FLEANCE, *with a torch before him.*]

BANQUO. How goes the night, boy?

FLEANCE. The moon is down; I have not heard the clock.

BANQUO. And she goes down at twelve.

FLEANCE.   I take't, 'tis later, sir.

BANQUO. Hold, take my sword. There's husbandry[1] in heaven.
5   Their candles are all out. Take thee that[2] too.
     A heavy summons[3] lies like lead upon me,
     And yet I would not sleep. Merciful powers,
     Restrain in me the cursèd thoughts that nature
     Gives way to in repose!

[*Enter* MACBETH, *and a* SERVANT *with a torch.*]

                                         Give me my sword!

10   Who's there?

MACBETH. A friend.

BANQUO. What, sir, not yet at rest? The King's a-bed:
     He hath been in unusual pleasure, and
     Sent forth great largess to your offices:[4]
15   This diamond he greets your wife withal,
     By the name of most kind hostess; and shut up[5]
     In measureless content.

MACBETH.   Being unprepared,
     Our will became the servant to defect,
     Which else should free have wrought.[6]

1. husbandry thrift.

2. that probably his sword belt.

3. summons weariness.

4. largess . . . offices gifts to your servants' quarters.

5. shut up retired.

6. Being . . . wrought Because we did not have enough time to prepare, we were unable to entertain as lavishly as we wanted to.

BANQUO.   All's well.

20 I dreamt last night of the three weird sisters:
To you they have showed some truth.

MACBETH.   I think not of them.
Yet, when we can entreat an hour to serve,
We would spend it in some words upon that business,
If you would grant the time.

BANQUO.   At your kind'st leisure.

25 **MACBETH.** If you shall cleave to my consent, when 'tis,[7]
It shall make honor for you.

BANQUO.   So[8] I lose none
In seeking to augment it, but still keep
My bosom franchised[9] and allegiance clear,
I shall be counseled.

MACBETH.   Good repose the while!

30 **BANQUO.** Thanks, sir. The like to you!

[*Exit* BANQUO *with* FLEANCE.]

MACBETH. Go bid thy mistress, when my drink is ready,
She strike upon the bell. Get thee to bed.

[*Exit* SERVANT.]

Is this a dagger which I see before me,
The handle toward my hand? Come, let me clutch thee.
35 I have thee not, and yet I see thee still.
Art thou not, fatal vision, sensible[10]
To feeling as to sight, or art thou but
A dagger of the mind, a false creation,
Proceeding from the heat-oppressèd brain?
40 I see thee yet, in form as palpable
As this which now I draw.
Thou marshal'st[11] me the way that I was going;
And such an instrument I was to use.
Mine eyes are made the fools o' th' other senses,
45 Or else worth all the rest. I see thee still;
And on thy blade and dudgeon[12] gouts[13] of blood,
Which was not so before. There's no such thing.
It is the bloody business which informs[14]
Thus to mine eyes. Now o'er the one half-world
50 Nature seems dead, and wicked dreams abuse[15]
The curtained sleep; witchcraft celebrates
Pale Hecate's offerings;[16] and withered murder,
Alarumed by his sentinel, the wolf,
Whose howl's his watch, thus with his stealthy pace,
55 With Tarquin's[17] ravishing strides, towards his design
Moves like a ghost. Thou sure and firm-set earth,

---

7. cleave . . . 'tis join my cause when the time comes.

8. So provided that.

Vocabulary
augment (ôg ment´) *v.* make greater; enlarge

9. bosom franchised heart free (from guilt).

10. sensible able to be felt.

Vocabulary
palpable (pal´ pə bəl) *adj.* capable of being touched or felt

11. marshal'st leads.

12. dudgeon wooden hilt.

13. gouts large drops.

14. informs takes shape.

15. abuse deceive.

16. Hecate's (hek´ə tēz) **offerings** offerings to Hecate, the Greek goddess of witchcraft.

Vocabulary
stealthy (stel´ thē) *adj.* sly

17. Tarquin's of Tarquin, a Roman tyrant.

Hear not my steps, which way they walk, for fear
Thy very stones prate of my whereabout,
And take the present horror from the time,
60   Which now suits with it.[18] Whiles I threat, he lives:
Words to the heat of deeds too cold breath gives.

[*A bell rings.*]

I go, and it is done: the bell invites me.
Hear it not, Duncan, for it is a knell
That summons thee to heaven, or to hell.   [*Exit.*]

Scene ii. Macbeth's castle

[*Enter* LADY MACBETH.]

LADY MACBETH. That which hath made them drunk hath made
           me bold;
What hath quenched them hath given me fire. Hark! Peace!
It was the owl that shrieked, the fatal bellman,
Which gives the stern'st good-night.[1] He is about it.
5   The doors are open, and the surfeited grooms[2]
Do mock their charge with snores. I have drugged their possets,[3]
That death and nature do contend about them,
Whether they live or die.

MACBETH.   [*Within*] Who's there? What, ho?

LADY MACBETH. Alack, I am afraid they have awaked
10   And 'tis not done! Th' attempt and not the deed
Confounds[4] us. Hark! I laid their daggers ready;
He could not miss 'em. Had he not resembled
My father as he slept, I had done 't.

[*Enter* MACBETH.]

                    My husband!

MACBETH. I have done the deed. Didst thou not hear a noise?

15 **LADY MACBETH.** I heard the owl scream and the crickets cry.
Did not you speak?

MACBETH.   When?

LADY MACBETH.   Now.

MACBETH.   As I descended?

LADY MACBETH. Ay.

MACBETH. Hark!
Who lies i' th' second chamber?

LADY MACBETH.   Donalbain.

20 **MACBETH.** This is a sorry[5] sight.

LADY MACBETH. A foolish thought, to say a sorry sight.

Spiral Review
Soliloquy In what way
do lines 31–61 introduce
a new sound into poetry,
the "sound" of someone
thinking aloud on stage?

18. **take . . . it** remove the horrible silence that suits this
moment.

1. **bellman . . . good-night** It
was customary for a bell to
be rung at midnight outside
a condemned person's
cell on the night before an
execution.

2. **surfeited grooms** overfed
servants.

3. **possets** warm bedtime
drinks.

4. **Confounds** ruins.

Literary Analysis
Blank Verse Notice that
the iambic pentameter of
line 16 is shared in dialogue
between Macbeth and Lady
Macbeth. Why might the
playwright have chosen this
artistry?

5. **sorry** miserable.

**Reading
Check**

What deed have Macbeth
and Lady Macbeth
performed?

MACBETH. There's one did laugh in 's sleep, and one cried "Murder!"
That they did wake each other. I stood and heard them.
But they did say their prayers, and addressed them
Again to sleep.

25 **LADY MACBETH.** There are two[6] lodged together.

MACBETH. One cried "God bless us!" and "Amen" the other,
As they had seen me with these hangman's hands:
List'ning their fear, I could not say "Amen,"
When they did say "God bless us!"

LADY MACBETH.   Consider it not so deeply.

30 **MACBETH.** But wherefore could not I pronounce "Amen"?
I had most need of blessing, and "Amen"
Stuck in my throat.

LADY MACBETH.   These deeds must not be thought
After these ways; so, it will make us mad.

MACBETH. Methought I heard a voice cry "Sleep no more!
35 Macbeth does murder sleep"—the innocent sleep,
Sleep that knits up the raveled sleave[7] of care,
The death of each day's life, sore labor's bath,
Balm of hurt minds, great nature's second course,[8]
Chief nourisher in life's feast—

LADY MACBETH.   What do you mean?

40 **MACBETH.** Still it cried "Sleep no more!" to all the house:
"Glamis hath murdered sleep, and therefore Cawdor
Shall sleep no more: Macbeth shall sleep no more."

LADY MACBETH. Who was it that thus cried? Why, worthy Thane,
You do unbend[9] your noble strength, to think
45 So brainsickly of things. Go get some water,
And wash this filthy witness[10] from your hand.
Why did you bring these daggers from the place?
They must lie there: go carry them, and smear
The sleepy grooms with blood.

MACBETH.   I'll go no more.
50 I am afraid to think what I have done;
Look on 't again I dare not.

LADY MACBETH.   Infirm of purpose!
Give me the daggers. The sleeping and the dead
Are but as pictures. 'Tis the eye of childhood
That fears a painted devil. If he do bleed,
55 I'll gild[11] the faces of the grooms withal,
For it must seem their guilt.   [*Exit. Knock within.*]

Vocabulary

multitudinous (mul´ tə tōōd´ 'n əs) *adj.* existing in great numbers

12. **incarnadine** (in kär´ nə dīn) redden.

13. **Your constancy . . . unattended** Your firmness of purpose has left you.

14. **watchers** up late.

Literary Analysis

Blank Verse, Prose, and Comic Relief

How do the shift from verse to prose in Scene iii and the porter's remarks affect the mood?

1. **porter** doorkeeper.

2. **should have old** would have plenty of.

3. **Beelzebub** (bē el´ zə bub´) the chief devil.

4. **a farmer . . . plenty** a farmer who hoarded grain, hoping the prices would come up after a bad harvest.

5. **enow** enough.

Vocabulary

equivocate (ē kwiv´ ə kāt´) *v.* to use terms that have two or more meanings to mislead purposely or deceive

6. **an equivocator . . . scale** a liar who could make two contradictory statements and swear both were true.

7. **stealing . . . hose** stealing some cloth from the hose while making them.

8. **goose** pressing iron.

MACBETH.   Whence is that knocking?
How is 't with me, when every noise appalls me?
What hands are here? Ha! They pluck out mine eyes!
Will all great Neptune's ocean wash this blood
60   Clean from my hand? No; this my hand will rather
The multitudinous seas incarnadine,[12]
Making the green one red.

[*Enter* LADY MACBETH.]

LADY MACBETH.   My hands are of your color, but I shame
To wear a heart so white. [*Knock.*] I hear a knocking
65   At the south entry. Retire we to our chamber.
A little water clears us of this deed:
How easy is it then! Your constancy
Hath left you unattended.[13] [*Knock.*] Hark! more knocking.
Get on your nightgown, lest occasion call us
70   And show us to be watchers.[14] Be not lost
So poorly in your thoughts.

MACBETH.   To know my deed, 'twere best not know myself.   [*Knock.*]
Wake Duncan with thy knocking! I would thou couldst!

[*Exit.*]

Scene iii. Macbeth's castle.

[*Enter a* PORTER.[1] *Knocking within.*]

PORTER.   Here's a knocking indeed! If a man were porter
of hell gate, he should have old[2] turning the key.
[*Knock.*] Knock, knock, knock! Who's there, i' th'
name of Beelzebub?[3] Here's a farmer, that
5   hanged himself on th' expectation of plenty.[4] Come
in time! Have napkins enow[5] about you; here you'll
sweat for 't. [*Knock.*] Knock, knock! Who's there, in
th' other devil's name? Faith, here's an equivocator,
that could swear in both the scales against
10   either scale;[6] who committed treason enough for
God's sake, yet could not equivocate to heaven. O,
come in, equivocator. [*Knock.*] Knock, knock, knock!
Who's there? Faith, here's an English tailor come
hither for stealing out of a French hose:[7]
15   come in, tailor. Here you may roast your goose.[8]
[*Knock.*] Knock, knock; never at quiet! What are you?
But this place is too cold for hell. I'll devil-porter it no
further. I had thought to have let in some of all
professions that go the primrose way to th'
20   everlasting bonfire. [*Knock.*] Anon, anon!
[*Opens an entrance.*] I pray you, remember the porter.

[*Enter* MACDUFF *and* LENNOX.]

MACDUFF. Was it so late, friend, ere you went to bed,
    That you do lie so late?

25 **PORTER.** Faith, sir, we were carousing till the second
    cock:[9] and drink, sir, is a great provoker of three
    things.

MACDUFF. What three things does drink especially
    provoke?

PORTER. Marry, sir, nose-painting, sleep, and urine.
30   Lechery, sir, it provokes and unprovokes; it provokes
    the desire, but it takes away the performance: there-
    fore much drink may be said to be an equivocator
    with lechery: it makes him and it mars him; it
    sets him on and it takes him off; it persuades him
35   and disheartens him; makes him stand to and not
    stand to; in conclusion equivocates him in a sleep,
    and giving him the lie, leaves him.

MACDUFF. I believe drink gave thee the lie[10] last night.

PORTER. That it did, sir, i' the very throat on me: but I
40   requited him for his lie, and, I think, being too strong
    for him, though he took up my legs sometime, yet I
    make a shift to cast[11] him.

MACDUFF. Is thy master stirring?

[*Enter* MACBETH.]

    Our knocking has awaked him; here he comes.

LENNOX. Good morrow, noble sir.

45 **MACBETH.**   Good morrow, both.

MACDUFF. Is the king stirring, worthy Thane?

MACBETH.   Not yet.

MACDUFF. He did command me to call timely[12] on him:
    I have almost slipped the hour.

MACBETH.   I'll bring you to him.

MACDUFF. I know this is a joyful trouble to you;
50   But yet 'tis one.

MACBETH. The labor we delight in physics pain.[13]
    This is the door.

MACDUFF.   I'll make so bold to call,
    For 'tis my limited service.[14]   [*Exit* MACDUFF.]

LENNOX. Goes the king hence today?

---

9. second cock 3:00 A.M.

10. gave thee the lie laid
you out.

11. cast vomit.

Literary Analysis
Blank Verse and Prose
Why is it appropriate for
the dialogue in lines 43–44
to change back from prose
to blank verse?

12. timely early.

13. labor . . . pain labor we
enjoy cures discomfort.

14. limited service assigned
duty.

Reading Check

To what gate does the
porter compare the gate
of Macbeth's castle?

MACBETH.   He does: he did appoint so.

55 **LENNOX.** The night has been unruly. Where we lay,
Our chimneys were blown down, and, as they say,
Lamentings heard i' th' air, strange screams of death,
And prophesying with accents terrible
Of dire combustion[15] and confused events
60 New hatched to th' woeful time: the obscure bird[16]
Clamored the livelong night. Some say, the earth
Was feverous and did shake.

MACBETH.   'Twas a rough night.

LENNOX. My young remembrance cannot parallel
A fellow to it.

[*Enter* MACDUFF.]

65 **MACDUFF.** O horror, horror, horror! Tongue nor heart
Cannot conceive nor name thee.

MACBETH AND LENNOX.   What's the matter?

MACDUFF. Confusion[17] now hath made his masterpiece.
Most sacrilegious murder hath broke ope
The Lord's anointed temple,[18] and stole thence
The life o' th' building.

70 **MACBETH.**   What is 't you say? The life?

LENNOX. Mean you his Majesty?

MACDUFF. Approach the chamber, and destroy your sight
With a new Gorgon:[19] do not bid me speak;
See, and then speak yourselves. Awake, awake!

[*Exit* MACBETH *and* LENNOX.]

75 Ring the alarum bell. Murder and Treason!
Banquo and Donalbain! Malcolm! Awake!
Shake off this downy sleep, death's counterfeit,

Reading Strategy
Analyzing Clarity of Meaning
Read lines 55–62 aloud. How many sentences are there in these lines?

15. combustion confusion.

16. obscure bird bird of darkness, the owl.

17. Confusion destruction.

18. The Lord's anointed temple the King's body.

Reading Strategy
Analyzing Clarity of Meaning In the latter part of Macduff's speech, lines 75–81, where should you not pause at the ends of lines?

19. Gorgon Medusa, a mythological monster whose appearance was so ghastly that those who looked at it turned to stone.

LITERATURE IN CONTEXT

Cultural Connection

Elizabethan Concepts of Monarchy
For the Elizabethans, the monarch was God's representative on Earth. For this reason, the expression "the Lord's anointed" is used to describe the head of state. Killing the ruler, therefore, was not just an act of political assassination; it was also a horrifying desecration of religious values.

Connect to the Literature
How does Macduff's line 68 reflect this concept of monarchy?

And look on death itself! Up, up, and see
The great doom's image!²⁰ Malcolm! Banquo!
80   As from your graves rise up, and walk like sprites,²¹
To countenance²² this horror. Ring the bell.

[*Bell rings. Enter* LADY MACBETH.]

   LADY MACBETH. What's the business,
That such a hideous trumpet calls to parley²³
The sleepers of the house? Speak, speak!

   MACDUFF.   O gentle lady,
85   'Tis not for you to hear what I can speak:
The repetition, in a woman's ear,
Would murder as it fell.

[*Enter* BANQUO.]

                                     O Banquo, Banquo!
Our royal master's murdered.

   LADY MACBETH.   Woe, alas!
What, in our house?

   BANQUO.   Too cruel anywhere.
90   Dear Duff, I prithee, contradict thyself,
And say it is not so.

[*Enter* MACBETH, LENNOX, *and* ROSS.]

   MACBETH. Had I but died an hour before this chance,
I had lived a blessed time; for from this instant
There's nothing serious in mortality:²⁴
95   All is but toys.²⁵ Renown and grace is dead,
The wine of life is drawn, and the mere lees²⁶
Is left this vault²⁷ to brag of.

[*Enter* MALCOLM *and* DONALBAIN.]

   DONALBAIN. What is amiss?

   MACBETH.   You are, and do not know 't.
The spring, the head, the fountain of your blood
100   Is stopped; the very source of it is stopped.

   MACDUFF. Your royal father's murdered.

   MALCOLM.   O, by whom?

   LENNOX. Those of his chamber, as it seemed, had done 't:
Their hands and faces were all badged²⁸ with blood;
So were their daggers, which unwiped we found
105   Upon their pillows. They stared, and were distracted.
No man's life was to be trusted with them.

   MACBETH. O, yet I do repent me of my fury,
That I did kill them.

20. great doom's image
likeness of Judgment Day.

21. sprites spirits.

22. countenance be in
keeping with.

23. parley war conference.

Spiral Review
Metaphor In line 96,
what does Macbeth mean
by "The wine of life"?

24. serious in mortality
worthwhile in mortal life.

25. toys trifles.

26. lees dregs.

27. vault world.

Literary Analysis
Blank Verse Where is
there a pause in line 100?
How does it reinforce the
meaning?

28. badged marked.

**Reading
Check**

According to Lennox,
what evidence proves that
the guards killed Duncan?

▲ **Critical Viewing** This painting depicts the moment when Macbeth comes from murdering Duncan (II, ii, 14). However, it also captures the nature of the relationship between Macbeth and Lady Macbeth in the first part of the play. What do their facial expressions and body language suggest about that relationship? **[Interpret]**

MACDUFF.	Wherefore did you so?

MACBETH. Who can be wise, amazed, temp'rate and furious,
110 Loyal and neutral, in a moment? No man.
The expedition[29] of my violent love
Outrun the pauser, reason. Here lay Duncan,
His silver skin laced with his golden blood,
And his gashed stabs looked like a breach in nature
115 For ruin's wasteful entrance: there, the murderers,
Steeped in the colors of their trade, their daggers
Unmannerly breeched with gore.[30] Who could refrain,
That had a heart to love, and in that heart

29. **expedition** haste.

30. **breeched with gore**
covered with blood.

Courage to make 's love known?

LADY MACBETH.   Help me hence, ho!

MACDUFF. Look to the lady.

120 **MALCOLM.** [*Aside to* DONALBAIN] Why do we hold our tongues,
That most may claim this argument for ours?[31]

DONALBAIN. [*Aside to* MALCOLM] What should be spoken here,
Where our fate, hid in an auger-hole,[32]
May rush, and seize us? Let's away:
Our tears are not yet brewed.

125 **MALCOLM.** [*Aside to* DONALBAIN] Nor our strong sorrow
Upon the foot of motion.[33]

BANQUO.   Look to the lady.

[LADY MACBETH *is carried out.*]

And when we have our naked frailties hid,[34]
That suffer in exposure, let us meet
And question[35] this most bloody piece of work,
130 To know it further. Fears and scruples[36] shake us.
In the great hand of God I stand, and thence
Against the undivulged pretense[37] I fight
Of treasonous malice.

MACDUFF.   And so do I.

ALL.   So all.

MACBETH. Let's briefly[38] put on manly readiness,
And meet i' th' hall together.

135 **ALL.**   Well contented.

[*Exit all but* MALCOLM *and* DONALBAIN.]

MALCOLM. What will you do? Let's not consort with them.
To show an unfelt sorrow is an office[39]
Which the false man does easy. I'll to England.

DONALBAIN. To Ireland, I; our separated fortune
140 Shall keep us both the safer. Where we are
There's daggers in men's smiles; the near in blood,
The nearer bloody.[40]

MALCOLM.   This murderous shaft that's shot
Hath not yet lighted,[41] and our safest way
Is to avoid the aim. Therefore to horse;
145 And let us not be dainty of leave-taking,
But shift away. There's warrant[42] in that theft
Which steals itself[43] when there's no mercy left.

[*Exit.*]

31. **That most . . . ours** who are the most concerned with this topic.

32. **auger-hole** tiny hole, an unsuspected place because of its size.

33. **Our tears . . . motion** We have not yet had time for tears nor to turn our sorrow into action.

34. **when . . . hid** when we have put on our clothes.

35. **question** investigate.

36. **scruples** doubts.

37. **undivulged pretense** hidden purpose.

38. **briefly** quickly.

Reading Strategy
Analyzing Clarity of Meaning How do the brief sentences in lines 136–138 reinforce the meaning?

39. **office** function.

40. **the near . . . bloody** The closer we are in blood relationship to Duncan, the greater our chance of being murdered.

41. **lighted** reached its target.

42. **warrant** justification.

43. **that theft . . . itself** stealing away.

Reading Check

What do Malcolm and Donalbain decide to do?

Scene iv. Outside Macbeth's castle.

[*Enter* ROSS *with an* OLD MAN.]

OLD MAN. Threescore and ten I can remember well:
Within the volume of which time I have seen
Hours dreadful and things strange, but this sore[1] night
Hath trifled former knowings.

ROSS.   Ha, good father,
5   Thou seest the heavens, as troubled with man's act,
Threatens his bloody stage. By th' clock 'tis day,
And yet dark night strangles the traveling lamp:[2]
Is 't night's predominance, or the day's shame,
That darkness does the face of earth entomb,
When living light should kiss it?

10 **OLD MAN.**   'Tis unnatural,
Even like the deed that's done. On Tuesday last
A falcon, tow'ring in her pride of place,[3]
Was by a mousing owl hawked at and killed.

ROSS. And Duncan's horses—a thing most strange
         and certain—
15   Beauteous and swift, the minions of their race,
Turned wild in nature, broke their stalls, flung out,
Contending 'gainst obedience, as they would make
War with mankind.

OLD MAN.   'Tis said they eat[4] each other.

ROSS. They did so, to th' amazement of mine eyes,
That looked upon 't.

[*Enter* MACDUFF.]

20   Here comes the good Macduff.
How goes the world, sir, now?

MACDUFF.   Why, see you not?

ROSS. Is 't known who did this more than bloody deed?

MACDUFF. Those that Macbeth hath slain.

ROSS.   Alas, the day!
What good could they pretend?[5]

MACDUFF.   They were suborned:[6]
25   Malcolm and Donalbain, the king's two sons,
Are stol'n away and fled, which puts upon them
Suspicion of the deed.

ROSS.   'Gainst nature still.
Thriftless ambition, that will ravin up[7]
Thine own life's means! Then 'tis most like

---

1. sore grievous.

2. traveling lamp the sun.

Vocabulary
predominance (prē däm´ ə nəns) *n.* superiority

3. tow'ring . . . place soaring at its summit.

4. eat ate.

Literary Analysis
Blank Verse What rhythmic variation in the blank verse do you find at the beginning of line 23?

5. pretend hope for.

6. suborned bribed.

7. ravin up devour greedily.

30   The sovereignty will fall upon Macbeth.

MACDUFF. He is already named, and gone to Scone[8]
To be invested.

ROSS.   Where is Duncan's body?

MACDUFF. Carried to Colmekill,
The sacred storehouse of his predecessors
And guardian of their bones.

35 **ROSS.**   Will you to Scone?

MACDUFF. No, cousin, I'll to Fife.[9]

ROSS.   Well, I will thither.

MACDUFF. Well, may you see things well done there.
    Adieu,
Lest our old robes sit easier than our new!

ROSS. Farewell, father.

40 **OLD MAN.** God's benison[10] go with you, and with those
That would make good of bad, and friends of foes!

                                     [*Exit.*]

8. Scone (skoōn) where Scottish kings were crowned.

9. Fife where Macduff's castle is located.

10. benison blessing.

Critical Reading

1. Key Ideas and Details (a) Describe Macbeth's and Lady Macbeth's reactions to the murder just after it is committed. **(b) Compare and Contrast:** Compare and contrast their reactions to the deed.

2. Key Ideas and Details (a) What kind of gate does the porter imagine he is tending? **(b) Interpret:** In what way is the porter's playful fantasy a comment on Macbeth's situation?

3. Integration of Knowledge and Ideas (a) What two strange occurrences are reported in this act? **(b) Interpret:** Why would Shakespeare include reports of such occurrences at this point in the play? **(c) Connect:** In what way do these strange occurrences relate to the Elizabethan notion of an orderly and interconnected universe?

4. Key Ideas and Details (a) Analyze: What question does Ross ask that indicates he doubts the grooms committed the murder? Explain. **(b) Infer:** Is Ross satisfied by the answer? Explain.

5. Integration of Knowledge and Ideas Do you think a political assassination like the one Macbeth commits is ever justifiable? Why or why not?

Cite textual evidence to support your responses.

Critical Commentary

from **"On the Knocking at the Gate in *Macbeth*"**

Thomas De Quincey

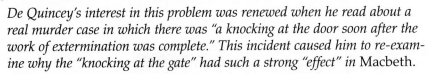

English author Thomas De Quincey published his influential essay on Macbeth *in 1823, more than 200 years after the first performance of the play. In the essay, he does not only express his ideas about the play, but he models the process of criticism: It begins when a reader has a problem with a text that he or she cannot easily solve.*

From my boyish days I had always felt a great perplexity on one point in *Macbeth*. It was this: the knocking at the gate, which succeeds to the murder of Duncan, produced to my feelings an effect for which I never could account. The effect was, that it reflected back upon the murder a peculiar awfulness and a depth of solemnity; yet, however obstinately I endeavored with my understanding to comprehend this, for many years I never could see why it should produce such an effect.

De Quincey's interest in this problem was renewed when he read about a real murder case in which there was "a knocking at the door soon after the work of extermination was complete." This incident caused him to re-examine why the "knocking at the gate" had such a strong "effect" in Macbeth.

. . . at length I solved it to my own satisfaction; and my solution is this. Murder in ordinary cases, where the sympathy is wholly directed to the case of the murdered person, is an incident of coarse and vulgar horror; and for this reason, that it flings the interest exclusively upon the natural but ignoble instinct by which we cleave to life . . .

He goes on to discuss a topic familiar to anyone who enjoys reading thrillers: How can an author help an audience understand the mind of a murderer?

Such an attitude would little suit the purposes of the poet. What then must he do? He must throw the interest on the murderer. Our sympathy must be with him; (of course I mean a sympathy of comprehension, a sympathy by which we enter into his feelings, and are made to understand them,—not a sympathy of pity or approbation.) . . . in the murderer, such a murderer as a poet will condescend to, there must be raging some great storm of passion,—jealousy, ambition, vengeance, hatred,—which will create a hell within him; and into this hell we are to look.

In *Macbeth*, for the sake of gratifying his own enormous and teeming faculty of creation, Shakespeare has introduced two murderers: and, as usual in his hands, they are remarkably discriminated: but, though in Macbeth the strife of mind is greater than in his wife, the tiger spirit not so awake, and his feelings caught chiefly by contagion from her,—yet, as both were finally involved in the guilt of murder, the murderous mind of necessity is finally to be presumed in both. . . .

Here, De Quincey expresses his central idea, that the "knocking at the gate" symbolizes a return to "ordinary life." By contrast, such a return only emphasizes the horror of the murder.

. . . All action in any direction is best expounded, measured, and made apprehensible, by reaction. Now apply this to the case in *Macbeth*. Here, as I have said, the retiring of the human heart and the entrance of the fiendish heart was to be expressed and made sensible. Another world has stepped in; and the murderers are taken out of the region of human things, human purposes, human desires. They are transfigured: Lady Macbeth is "unsexed"; Macbeth has forgot that he was born of woman; both are conformed to the image of devils; and the world of devils is suddenly revealed.

But how shall this be conveyed and made palpable? In order that a new world may step in, this world must for a time disappear. The murderers, and the murder, must be insulated—cut off by an immeasurable gulf from the ordinary tide and succession of human affairs—locked up and sequestered in some deep recess; we must be made sensible that the world of ordinary life is suddenly arrested—laid asleep—tranced—racked into a dread armistice: time must be annihilated; relation to things without abolished; and all must pass self-withdrawn into a deep . . . suspension of earthly passion.

Hence it is, that when the deed is done, when the work of darkness is perfect, then the world of darkness passes away like a pageantry in the clouds: the knocking at the gate is heard; and it makes known audibly that the reaction has commenced: the human has made its reflux upon the fiendish; the pulses of life are beginning to beat again; and the re-establishment of the goings-on of the world in which we live, first makes us profoundly sensible of the awful parenthesis that had suspended them.

Ⓒ **Key Ideas and Details** Why did the "knocking at the gate" puzzle De Quincey? What does De Quincey conclude about the scene that puzzled him?

After You Read *Macbeth, Act II*

Literary Analysis

© 1. Craft and Structure To analyze Shakespeare's use of **blank verse,** complete a chart like this one by identifying the rhythm of each of the lines indicated.

Line	Iambic Feet	Trochaic or Anapestic Feet
"It is the bloody business which informs...."		
"'Macbeth does murder sleep' —the innocent sleep,..."		

© 2. Craft and Structure Mark stressed and unstressed syllables in Act II, Scene ii, lines 59–62.

© 3. Craft and Structure Identify three metrical variations in Act II, Scene ii, lines 59–62.

© 4. Craft and Structure (a) Contrast the Porter's speech (Act II, Scene iii, lines 1–21) with the two speeches at the end of Act II, Scene ii to show that the Porter's speech is written in **prose** form. **(b)** Why might prose be suitable for a "low" character? **(c)** How does the speech offer **comic relief?**

© 5. Integration of Knowledge and Ideas The nineteenth-century English writer Thomas De Quincey argued that the scene with the Porter reinforces the shock of the king's murder by a striking contrast: "The re-establishment of the goings-on of the world in which we live, first makes us profoundly sensible of the awful [episode] that had suspended them." (For a larger excerpt from De Quincey's essay, see pages 356–357.) Do you agree or disagree? Explain.

© 6. Integration of Knowledge and Ideas Macbeth has a strong imagination. In what way does this trait both prompt him to commit a crime and make it hard for him to commit it?

Reading Strategy

7. Analyze how Shakespeare achieves **clarity of meaning** by focusing on the interaction between sentences and blank verse lines. **(a)** How many sentences are there in Act II, Scene i, lines 62–64? **(b)** In reading these lines for meaning, would you pause at any of the line ends? Explain.

8. (a) Experiment by using two different ways of reading the sentences in Act II, Scene i, lines 56–61, beginning, "Thou sure . . ." First read them by pausing after each line of blank verse. Then, read them by following sentences past the ends of lines. Which way was clearer? Why? **(b)** In your own words, express the meaning of this passage.

Common Core State Standards

Writing

1. Write arguments to support claims in an analysis of substantive topics or texts, using valid reasoning and relevant and sufficient evidence. *(p. 359)*

1.a. Introduce precise, knowledgeable claim(s), establish the significance of the claim(s), distinguish the claim(s) from alternate or opposing claims, and create an organization that logically sequences claims, counterclaims, reasons, and evidence. *(p. 359)*

Integrated Language Skills

Vocabulary Acquisition and Use

Word Analysis: Latin Word Root -voc-

The word *equivocate*, meaning "to speak in two equal voices" or "to mislead," is based on the Latin root -*voc*-, meaning "voice" or "calling." Words with the root -*voc*- are useful in interpreting *Macbeth*, whose protagonist is haunted by many voices: the stern voice of his wife; the prophetic voices of witches; the accusing voices of ghosts; and the disturbing voice of his own conscience.

With a small group, write a paragraph that describes Macbeth's central conflict or conflicts. Use at least four of the -*voc*- words listed below in your description. Use a dictionary if necessary.

vocalize	invocation	vocation
advocate	irrevocable	provoke

Then, choose two of the words in your paragraph and write a sentence explaining how the root -*voc*- helps create each word's meaning.

Vocabulary: Antonyms

Antonyms are words with opposite meanings. For each sentence, replace the underlined term with an antonym from the vocabulary list on page 342. The antonym should make the sentence logical. Change the form of the vocabulary word if necessary.

1. Macbeth's success in battle gave him a sense of <u>inferiority</u>.
2. He was willing to use <u>straightforward</u> means to become king.
3. Before murdering Duncan, his doubts and fears were <u>few</u>.
4. As Macbeth approached the king's bedchamber, the sense of fear was <u>intangible</u>.
5. The Witches' prophecy served to <u>diminish</u> Macbeth's sense of ambition.
6. He learned the witches always <u>told the truth</u>.

Writing

Argumentative Text Reread De Quincey's essay (pages 356–357) on the porter scene. Then, write an **essay** agreeing or disagreeing with his interpretation. Support your ideas with detailed references to the text.

Prewriting Reread Scenes ii and iii of Act II, noting your own feelings and reactions. Then, reread De Quincey's comments. Note how your responses to the scene are like or unlike his.

Drafting Begin by stating your agreement or disagreement in a clear thesis. Then, support your thesis with references to the tone, mood, style, or "sound" of the porter's language. Next, anticipate those who may disagree with your view by providing logical counterarguments.

Revising Review your essay to be sure it is clear and logically organized. Make sure to comment on every quotation you include, and check to see that each claim you make is supported.

A comparison of the writer's own ideas and de Quincey's reveals that both felt perplexed in response to the Porter's soliloquy.

Model: Comparing Responses

The first thing I felt when I began reading the Porter's speech was confusion. I was confused not only by his archaic expressions, but also by his exasperated response to something as routine as a knock at the door. Answering the door is, after all, a porter's job.

De Quincey says he felt "an effect for which [he] could never account."

Before You Read — *Macbeth, Act III*

Literary Analysis

Conflict—the struggle between two forces—is what creates drama.

- An **external conflict** is a struggle between two characters or groups.

- An **internal conflict** is a struggle within a character.

The action, or series of events, of a play is developed and ordered by an author so that it reaches a **climax**—the point at which the internal and external conflicts are greatest. The impact of the climax on the play as a whole is twofold: The tension is at its highest and the conflicts are resolved.

In Act III of *Macbeth,* notice how the rising action leads the new king to a state dinner and the sight of a guest—a guest who should not be there!

In connection with that dinner, Macbeth makes this critical remark to Banquo in Act III, Scene i, line 27: "Fail not our feast." This invitation is an example of dramatic irony, a device that Shakespeare uses to heighten conflict. **Dramatic irony** occurs when the words or actions of a character take on a meaning for the audience or readers different from the one the character intends.

Observe how Macbeth's remark takes on dramatic irony as events unfold, and becomes a different kind of invitation, answered by a different kind of guest.

Reading Strategy

© **Preparing to Read Complex Texts** Connecting different passages in a text will also enable you to **identify cause-and-effect relationships**—to show, for example, how an earlier event or remark (cause) leads to a later one (effect). The Witches' prophecy that Banquo will father kings may be a cause that has many effects in Act III. Use a graphic organizer like the one shown to trace those effects.

Vocabulary

indissoluble (in′ di säl′ yo͞o bəl) *adj.* not able to be undone (p. 361)

dauntless (dônt′ lis) *adj.* fearless; cannot be intimidated (p. 362)

predominant (prē däm′ ə nənt) *adj.* foremost; powerful (p. 363)

infirmity (in fʉr′ mə tē) *n.* physical or mental defect; illness (p. 371)

malevolence (mə lev′ ə ləns) *n.* ill will; spitefulness (p. 375)

Common Core State Standards

Reading Literature
3. Analyze the impact of the author's choices regarding how to develop and relate elements of a story or drama.

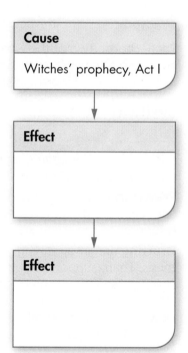

Cause
Witches' prophecy, Act I

↓

Effect

↓

Effect

www.PHLitOnline.com

Review and Anticipate

In Act II, Lady Macbeth drugs Duncan's guards, enabling Macbeth to kill the king. Macbeth then kills the guards, too, so that he can more easily blame them for the king's murder. Duncan's sons, Malcolm and Donalbain, flee, afraid that they will be assassinated by a kinsman eager to claim the throne. Because they run away, some suspect them of killing their father. As the act closes, it seems that Macbeth will be named king. Act III begins with Macbeth on the throne—as the witches had predicted. All seems to be going well for him, but he feels threatened by Banquo.

ACT III

Scene i. Forres. The palace.

[*Enter* BANQUO.]

> **BANQUO.** Thou hast it now: King, Cawdor, Glamis, all,
> As the weird women promised, and I fear
> Thou play'dst most foully for 't. Yet it was said
> It should not stand[1] in thy posterity,
> 5 But that myself should be the root and father
> Of many kings. If there come truth from them—
> As upon thee, Macbeth, their speeches shine—
> Why, by the verities on thee made good,
> May they not be my oracles as well
> 10 And set me up in hope? But hush, no more!

[*Sennet*[2] *sounded. Enter* MACBETH *as King,* LADY MACBETH, LENNOX, ROSS, LORDS, *and* ATTENDANTS.]

> **MACBETH.** Here's our chief guest.
>
> **LADY MACBETH.**   If he had been forgotten,
> It had been as a gap in our great feast,
> And all-thing[3] unbecoming.
>
> **MACBETH.** Tonight we hold a solemn[4] supper, sir,
> And I'll request your presence.
>
> 15 **BANQUO.**   Let your Highness
> Command upon me, to the which my duties
> Are with a most indissoluble tie
> For ever knit.
>
> **MACBETH.** Ride you this afternoon?
>
> **BANQUO.**   Ay, my good lord.
>
> 20 **MACBETH.** We should have else desired your good advice
> (Which still hath been both grave and prosperous[5])

◄ **Critical Viewing**
After wielding a dagger like this against Duncan, can Macbeth expect to rule in peace? Explain. **[Predict]**

1. **stand** continue.

2. *Sennet* trumpet call.

3. **all-thing** altogether.

4. **solemn** ceremonious.

5. **grave and prosperous** weighty and profitable.

Vocabulary
indissoluble (in´ di säl´ yoo bəl) *adj.* not able to be dissolved or undone

Reading Check
What does Banquo suspect about Macbeth?

In this day's council; but we'll take tomorrow.
Is't far you ride?

BANQUO. As far, my lord, as will fill up the time
'Twixt this and supper. Go not my horse the better,[6]
I must become a borrower of the night
For a dark hour or twain.

MACBETH. Fail not our feast.

BANQUO. My lord, I will not.

MACBETH. We hear our bloody cousins are bestowed
In England and in Ireland, not confessing
Their cruel parricide, filling their hearers
With strange invention.[7] But of that tomorrow,
When therewithal we shall have cause of state
Craving us jointly.[8] Hie you to horse. Adieu,
Till you return at night. Goes Fleance with you?

BANQUO. Ay, my good lord: our time does call upon 's.

MACBETH. I wish your horses swift and sure of foot,
And so I do commend you to their backs.
Farewell.   [*Exit* BANQUO.]
Let every man be master of his time
Till seven at night. To make society
The sweeter welcome, we will keep ourself
Till suppertime alone. While[9] then, God be with you!

[*Exit* LORDS *and all but* MACBETH *and a* SERVANT.]

Sirrah,[10] a word with you: attend those men
Our pleasure?

ATTENDANT. They are, my lord, without the palace gate.

MACBETH. Bring them before us.   [*Exit* SERVANT.]
To be thus[11] is nothing, but[12] to be safely thus—
Our fears in Banquo stick deep,
And in his royalty of nature reigns that
Which would be feared. 'Tis much he dares;
And, to[13] that dauntless temper of his mind,
He hath a wisdom that doth guide his valor
To act in safety. There is none but he
Whose being I do fear: and under him
My genius is rebuked,[14] as it is said
Mark Antony's was by Caesar. He chid[15] the sisters,
When first they put the name of King upon me,
And bade them speak to him; then prophetlike
They hailed him father to a line of kings.
Upon my head they placed a fruitless crown
And put a barren scepter in my gripe,[16]

---

6. Go not . . . better unless my horse goes faster than I expect.

7. invention lies.

8. cause . . . jointly matters of state demanding our joint attention.

9. While until.

10. Sirrah common address to an inferior.

11. thus king.

12. but unless.

Vocabulary
dauntless (dônt´ lis) *adj.* fearless; cannot be intimidated

13. to added to.

14. genius is rebuked guardian spirit is cowed.

15. chid scolded.

16. gripe grip.

Thence to be wrenched with an unlineal hand,
No son of mine succeeding. If 't be so,
65   For Banquo's issue have I filed[17] my mind;
For them the gracious Duncan have I murdered;
Put rancors in the vessel of my peace
Only for them, and mine eternal jewel[18]
Given to the common enemy of man,[19]
70   To make them kings, the seeds of Banquo kings!
Rather than so, come, fate, into the list,
And champion me to th' utterance![20] Who's there?

[*Enter* SERVANT *and* TWO MURDERERS.]

Now go to the door, and stay there till we call.

[*Exit* SERVANT.]

Was it not yesterday we spoke together?

  MURDERERS. It was, so please your Highness.

75 **MACBETH.**   Well then, now
Have you considered of my speeches? Know
That it was he in the times past, which held you
So under fortune,[21] which you thought had been
Our innocent self: this I made good to you
80   In our last conference; passed in probation[22] with you,
How you were born in hand,[23] how crossed, the instruments,
Who wrought with them, and all things else that might
To half a soul[24] and to a notion[25] crazed
Say "Thus did Banquo."

  FIRST MURDERER.   You made it known to us.

85 **MACBETH.** I did so; and went further, which is now
Our point of second meeting. Do you find
Your patience so predominant in your nature,
That you can let this go? Are you so gospeled,[26]
To pray for this good man and for his issue,
90   Whose heavy hand hath bowed you to the grave
And beggared yours for ever?

  FIRST MURDERER.   We are men, my liege.

  MACBETH. Ay, in the catalogue ye go for[27] men;
As hounds and greyhounds, mongrels, spaniels, curs,
Shoughs, water-rugs[28] and demi-wolves, are clept[29]
95   All by the name of dogs: the valued file[30]
Distinguishes the swift, the slow, the subtle,
The housekeeper, the hunter, every one
According to the gift which bounteous nature
Hath in him closed,[31] whereby he does receive
100   Particular addition,[32] from the bill

---

17. filed defiled.

18. eternal jewel soul.

19. common . . . man the Devil.

20. champion me to th' utterance Fight against me to the death.

21. held . . . fortune kept you from good fortune.

22. passed in probation reviewed the proofs.

23. born in hand deceived.

24. half a soul halfwit.

25. notion mind.

26. gospeled ready to forgive.

27. go for pass as.

28. Shoughs (shuks), **water-rugs** shaggy dogs, long-haired dogs.

29. clept called.

30. valued file classification by valuable traits.

Vocabulary
predominant (prē däm´ ə nənt) *adj.* foremost; powerful

Reading Strategy
Identifying Cause-and-Effect Relationships
What does the first murderer mean in line 91 when he answers Macbeth, "We are men"?

31. closed enclosed.

32. addition distinction (to set it apart from other dogs).

Reading Check

What has caused Macbeth to hire these murderers?

That writes them all alike: and so of men.
Now if you have a station in the file,[33]
Not i' th' worst rank of manhood, say 't,
And I will put that business in your bosoms
105 Whose execution takes your enemy off,
Grapples you to the heart and love of us,
Who wear our health but sickly in his life,[34]
Which in his death were perfect.

SECOND MURDERER.   I am one, my liege,
Whom the vile blows and buffets of the world
110 Hath so incensed that I am reckless what
I do to spite the world.

FIRST MURDERER.   And I another
So weary with disasters, tugged with fortune,
That I would set[35] my life on any chance,
To mend it or be rid on 't.

MACBETH.   Both of you
Know Banquo was your enemy.

115 **BOTH MURDERERS.**   True, my lord.

MACBETH. So is he mine, and in such bloody distance[36]
That every minute of his being thrusts
Against my near'st of life:[37] and though I could
With barefaced power sweep him from my sight
120 And bid my will avouch[38] it, yet I must not,
For certain friends that are both his and mine,
Whose loves I may not drop, but wail his fall[39]
Who I myself struck down: and thence it is
That I to your assistance do make love,
125 Masking the business from the common eye
For sundry weighty reasons.

SECOND MURDERER.   We shall, my lord,
Perform what you command us.

FIRST MURDERER.   Though our lives—

MACBETH. Your spirits shine through you. Within this hour at most
I will advise you where to plant yourselves,
130 Acquaint you with the perfect spy o' th' time,
The moment on 't;[40] for 't must be done tonight,
And something[41] from the palace; always thought[42]
That I require a clearness:[43] and with him—
To leave no rubs[44] nor botches in the work—
135 Fleance his son, that keeps him company,
Whose absence is no less material to me
Than is his father's, must embrace the fate
Of that dark hour. Resolve yourselves apart:[45]

---

33. file ranks.

34. wear . . . life are sick as long as he lives.

35. set risk.

36. distance disagreement.

37. near'st of life most vital parts.

38. avouch justify.

39. wail his fall (I must) bewail his death.

Literary Analysis
Conflict What conflict does Macbeth express in lines 116–126?

40. the perfect . . . on't exact information of the exact time.

41. something some distance.

42. thought remembered.

43. clearness freedom from suspicion.

44. rubs flaws.

45. Resolve yourselves apart Make your own decision.

I'll come to you anon.

MURDERERS.   We are resolved, my lord.

140 **MACBETH.** I'll call upon you straight.[46] Abide within.
     It is concluded: Banquo, thy soul's flight,
     If it find heaven, must find it out tonight.   [*Exit.*]

46. **straight** immediately.

Scene ii. The palace.

[*Enter* MACBETH'S LADY *and a* SERVANT.]

LADY MACBETH. Is Banquo gone from court?

SERVANT. Ay, madam, but returns again tonight.

LADY MACBETH. Say to the King, I would attend his leisure
     For a few words.

SERVANT.   Madam, I will.   [*Exit.*]

LADY MACBETH.   Nought's had, all's spent,
5   Where our desire is got without content:
     'Tis safer to be that which we destroy
     Than by destruction dwell in doubtful joy.

[*Enter* MACBETH.]

     How now, my lord! Why do you keep alone,
     Of sorriest fancies your companions making,
10   Using those thoughts which should indeed have died
     With them they think on? Things without all remedy
     Should be without regard: what's done is done.

MACBETH. We have scotched[1] the snake, not killed it:
     She'll close[2] and be herself, whilst our poor malice
15   Remains in danger of her former tooth.[3]
     But let the frame of things disjoint,[4] both the worlds[5] suffer,
     Ere we will eat our meal in fear, and sleep
     In the affliction of these terrible dreams
     That shake us nightly: better be with the dead,
20   Whom we, to gain our peace, have sent to peace,
     Than on the torture of the mind to lie
     In restless ecstasy.[6] Duncan is in his grave;
     After life's fitful fever he sleeps well.
     Treason has done his worst: nor steel, nor poison,
25   Malice domestic, foreign levy,[7] nothing,
     Can touch him further.

LADY MACBETH.   Come on.
     Gentle my lord, sleek o'er your rugged looks;
     Be bright and jovial among your guests tonight.

MACBETH. So shall I, love; and so, I pray, be you:

Reading Strategy
Identifying Cause-and-Effect Relationships
What causes Lady Macbeth to say what she does in lines 4–7?

1. **scotched** wounded.

2. **close** heal.

3. **in . . . tooth** in as much danger as before.

4. **frame of things disjoint** universe collapse.

5. **both the worlds** heaven and earth.

6. **ecstasy** frenzy.

7. **Malice . . . levy** civil and foreign war.

Reading Check

What does Macbeth ask the murderers to do?

Literary Analysis
Conflict and Irony What is ironic about Macbeth's idea for disguising the couple's real conflict with Banquo (Scene ii, lines 30–35)?

8. **Present him eminence** Honor him.

9. **Unsafe . . . lave** We are unsafe as long as we have to wash.

10. **vizards** (viz′ ərdz) masks

11. **nature's . . . eterne** Nature's lease is not eternal.

12. **jocund** (jäk′ ənd) cheerful; jovial

13. **shard-borne** borne on scaly wings.

30   Let your remembrance apply to Banquo;
        Present him eminence,⁸ both with eye and tongue:
        Unsafe the while, that we must lave⁹
        Our honors in these flattering streams
        And make our faces vizards¹⁰ to our hearts,
        Disguising what they are.

35 **LADY MACBETH.**   You must leave this.

    MACBETH. O, full of scorpions is my mind, dear wife!
        Thou know'st that Banquo, and his Fleance, lives.

    LADY MACBETH. But in them nature's copy's not eterne.¹¹

    MACBETH. There's comfort yet; they are assailable.
40   Then be thou jocund.¹² Ere the bat hath flown
        His cloistered flight, ere to black Hecate's summons
        The shard-borne¹³ beetle with his drowsy hums
        Hath rung night's yawning peal, there shall be done

A deed of dreadful note.

LADY MACBETH.   What 's to be done?

45 **MACBETH.** Be innocent of the knowledge, dearest chuck,[14]
Till thou applaud the deed. Come, seeling[15] night,
Scarf up[16] the tender eye of pitiful day,
And with thy bloody and invisible hand
Cancel and tear to pieces that great bond[17]
50 Which keeps me pale! Light thickens, and the crow
Makes wing to th' rooky[18] wood.
Good things of day begin to droop and drowse,
Whiles night's black agents to their preys do rouse.
Thou marvel'st at my words: but hold thee still;
55 Things bad begun make strong themselves by ill:
So, prithee, go with me.   [*Exit.*]

Scene iii. Near the palace.

[*Enter* THREE MURDERERS.]

FIRST MURDERER. But who did bid thee join with us?

THIRD MURDERER.   Macbeth.

SECOND MURDERER. He needs not our mistrust; since he delivers
Our offices[1] and what we have to do
To the direction just.[2]

FIRST MURDERER.   Then stand with us.
5   The west yet glimmers with some streaks of day.
Now spurs the lated traveler apace
To gain the timely inn, and near approaches
The subject of our watch.

THIRD MURDERER.   Hark! I hear horses.

BANQUO. [*Within*] Give us a light there, ho!

SECOND MURDERER.   Then 'tis he. The rest
10   That are within the note of expectation[3]
Already are i' th' court.

FIRST MURDERER.   His horses go about.[4]

THIRD MURDERER. Almost a mile: but he does usually—
So all men do—from hence to th' palace gate
Make it their walk.

[*Enter* BANQUO *and* FLEANCE, *with a torch*]

SECOND MURDERER. A light, a light!

THIRD MURDERER.   'Tis he.

15 **FIRST MURDERER.**   Stand to 't

14. **chuck** term of endearment.

15. **seeling** eye-closing. Falconers sometimes sewed a hawk's eyes closed in order to train it.

16. **Scarf up** blindfold.

17. **great bond** between Banquo and fate.

18. **rooky** full of rooks, or crows.

Reading Strategy
Identifying Cause-and-Effect Relationships
To what specific action do you think Macbeth is indirectly referring in lines 45–56?

1. **offices** duties.

2. **direction just** exact detail.

3. **within . . . expectation** on the list of expected guests.

4. **His . . . about** His horses have been taken to the stable.

Reading Check
What does Macbeth tell Lady Macbeth and what does he hold back from her?

BANQUO. It will be rain tonight.

FIRST MURDERER.   Let it come down.

[*They set upon* BANQUO.]

BANQUO. O, treachery! Fly, good Fleance, fly, fly, fly!

[*Exit* FLEANCE.]

Thou mayst revenge. O slave! [*Dies.*]

THIRD MURDERER. Who did strike out the light?

5. way thing to do.

FIRST MURDERER.   Was't not the way?[5]

20 **THIRD MURDERER.** There's but one down; the son is fled.

SECOND MURDERER. We have lost best half of our affair.

FIRST MURDERER. Well, let 's away and say how much is done.

[*Exit.*]

Scene iv. The palace.

[*Banquet prepared. Enter* MACBETH, LADY MACBETH, ROSS, LENNOX, LORDS, *and* ATTENDANTS.]

1. degrees ranks. At state banquets, guests were seated according to rank.

MACBETH. You know your own degrees;[1] sit down:
    At first and last, the hearty welcome.

LORDS. Thanks to your Majesty.

2. society company.

MACBETH. Ourself will mingle with society[2]
5   And play the humble host.
    Our hostess keeps her state,[3] but in best time
    We will require[4] her welcome.

3. keeps her state remains seated on her throne.

4. require request.

LADY MACBETH. Pronounce it for me, sir, to all our friends,
    For my heart speaks they are welcome.

[*Enter* FIRST MURDERER.]

10 **MACBETH.** See, they encounter thee with their hearts' thanks.
    Both sides are even: here I'll sit i' th' midst:
    Be large in mirth; anon we'll drink a measure[5]
    The table round. [*Goes to* MURDERER] There's blood upon thy face.

5. measure toast.

MURDERER. 'Tis Banquo's then.

6. thee . . . within you outside than he inside.

15 **MACBETH.** 'Tis better thee without than he within.[6]
    Is he dispatched?

MURDERER. My lord, his throat is cut; that I did for him.

MACBETH. Thou art the best o' th' cutthroats.
    Yet he's good that did the like for Fleance;

7. nonpareil without equal.

20   If thou didst it, thou art the nonpareil.[7]

MURDERER. Most royal sir, Fleance is 'scaped.

MACBETH. [*Aside*] Then comes my fit again: I had else been perfect,
    Whole as the marble, founded as the rock,
    As broad and general as the casing⁸ air:
25   But now I am cabined, cribbed, confined, bound in
    To saucy⁹ doubts and fears.—But Banquo's safe?

MURDERER. Ay, my good lord: safe in a ditch he bides,
    With twenty trenchèd¹⁰ gashes on his head,
    The least a death to nature.¹¹

MACBETH.   Thanks for that.
30   [*Aside*] There the grown serpent lies; the worm that's fled
    Hath nature that in time will venom breed,
    No teeth for th' present. Get thee gone. Tomorrow
    We'll hear ourselves¹² again.   [*Exit* MURDERER.]

LADY MACBETH.   My royal lord,
    You do not give the cheer.¹³ The feast is sold
35   That is not often vouched, while 'tis a-making,
    'Tis given with welcome.¹⁴ To feed were best at home;
    From thence, the sauce to meat is ceremony;¹⁵
    Meeting were bare without it.

[*Enter the* GHOST *of* BANQUO *and sits in* MACBETH'S *place.*]

MACBETH.   Sweet remembrancer!
    Now good digestion wait on appetite,
    And health on both!

40 **LENNOX.**   May't please your Highness sit.

MACBETH. Here had we now our country's honor roofed,¹⁶
    Were the graced person of our Banquo present—

8. **as . . . casing** as unrestrained as the surrounding.

9. **saucy** insolent.

10. **trenchèd** trenchlike.

11. **nature** natural life.

12. **hear ourselves** talk it over.

13. **give the cheer** make the guests feel welcome.

14. **The feast . . . welcome** The feast at which the host fails to make the guests feel welcome while the food is being prepared is no more than a bought dinner.

15. **From . . . ceremony** Ceremony adds a pleasant flavor to the food.

16. **our . . . roofed** the most honorable men in the country under one roof.

Reading Check

What do the murderers fail to do?

LITERATURE IN CONTEXT

Cultural Connection

Stagecraft at the Globe

It took some sophisticated Elizabethan theatrics to manage entrances and exits such as those of Banquo's ghost. (Macbeth reacts to the ghost in this picture.) In the farthest reaches of the Globe Theater's stage was a small area called the rear stage, which was open to the audience but enclosed by a wall at the back and cloth hangings on the sides. A trapdoor in the floor of the rear stage was the means by which Banquo's ghost made an entrance. The trapdoor operated silently, and it was not completely visible to the audience.

Connect to the Literature

What other characters in *Macbeth* might have used a trapdoor for exits or entrances? Explain.

Who may I rather challenge for unkindness
Than pity for mischance![17]

ROSS.   His absence, sir,
45   Lays blame upon his promise. Please 't your Highness
To grace us with your royal company?

MACBETH. The table's full.

LENNOX. Here is a place reserved, sir.

MACBETH. Where?

LENNOX. Here, my good lord. What is 't that moves your Highness?

MACBETH. Which of you have done this?

50 **LORDS.**   What, my good lord?

MACBETH. Thou canst not say I did it. Never shake
Thy gory locks at me.

ROSS. Gentlemen, rise, his Highness is not well.

LADY MACBETH. Sit, worthy friends. My lord is often thus,
55   And hath been from his youth. Pray you, keep seat.
The fit is momentary; upon a thought[18]
He will again be well. If much you note him,
You shall offend him and extend his passion.[19]
Feed, and regard him not.—Are you a man?

60 **MACBETH.** Ay, and a bold one, that dare look on that
Which might appall the devil.

LADY MACBETH.   O proper stuff!
This is the very painting of your fear.
This is the air-drawn dagger which, you said,
Led you to Duncan. O, these flaws[20] and starts,
65   Impostors to true fear, would well become
A woman's story at a winter's fire,
Authorized[21] by her grandam. Shame itself!
Why do you make such faces? When all's done,
You look but on a stool.

MACBETH.   Prithee, see there!
70   Behold! Look! Lo! How say you?
Why, what care I? If thou canst nod, speak too.
If charnel houses[22] and our graves must send
Those that we bury back, our monuments
Shall be the maws of kites.[23]   [*Exit* GHOST.]

75 **LADY MACBETH.**   What, quite unmanned in folly?

MACBETH. If I stand here, I saw him.

LADY MACBETH.   Fie, for shame!

---

17. Who . . . mischance
whom I hope I may re-
proach for being absent
due to discourtesy rather
than pity because he has
had an accident.

Reading Strategy
**Identifying Cause-and-
Effect Relationships**
How might you connect
Macbeth's agitation with his
knowledge that Fleance has
escaped?

Literary Analysis
Conflict How does the
incident with Banquo's ghost
convey Macbeth's inner
conflict?

18. upon a thought in a
moment.

19. passion suffering.

20. flaws gusts of wind;
outbursts of emotion.

21. Authorized vouched for.

22. charnel houses vaults
containing human bones
dug up in making new
graves.

23. our . . . kites Because the
dead will be devoured by
birds of prey, our tombs
will be the bellies of those
birds.

Scene from Macbeth, Cattermole, The Folger Shakespeare Library, Washington, D.C.

◀ **Critical Viewing**
In what ways does the artist's use of light and shadow suggest the conflict in Act III, Scene iv? **[Interpret]**

MACBETH. Blood hath been shed ere now, i' th' olden time,
Ere humane statute purged the gentle weal;[24]
Ay, and since too, murders have been performed
Too terrible for the ear. The time has been

80 That, when the brains were out, the man would die,
And there an end; but now they rise again,
With twenty mortal murders on their crowns,[25]
And push us from our stools. This is more strange
Than such a murder is.

LADY MACBETH.   My worthy lord,
Your noble friends do lack you.

85 **MACBETH.**   I do forget.
Do not muse at me, my most worthy friends;
I have a strange infirmity, which is nothing
To those that know me. Come, love and health to all!
Then I'll sit down. Give me some wine, fill full.

[*Enter* GHOST.]

90 I drink to th' general joy o' th' whole table,
And to our dear friend Banquo, whom we miss;
Would he were here! To all and him we thirst,[26]
And all to all.

LORDS.   Our duties, and the pledge.

MACBETH. Avaunt![27] and quit my sight! Let the earth hide thee!
95 Thy bones are marrowless, thy blood is cold;

24. Ere . . . weal before humane laws civilized the state and made it gentle.

25. mortal . . . crowns deadly wounds on their heads.

Vocabulary
infirmity (in fur′ mə tē) *n.* physical or mental defect; illness

26. thirst drink.

27. Avaunt Be gone!

Reading Check
Why is Macbeth startled at the feast?

28. **speculation** sight.

29. **Hyrcan** (hər´ kən) from Hyrcania, a province of the ancient Persian and Macedonian empires south of the Caspian Sea.

30. **that** Banquo's shape.

31. **desert** place where neither of us could escape.

32. **inhabit** remain indoors.

33. **admired** amazing.

34. **overcome us** come over us.

35. **disposition. . . owe** my own nature.

Reading Strategy
Identifying Cause-and-Effect Relationships
What effects do you think Macbeth's behavior will have on the guests?

36. **Stand . . . going** Do not wait to depart in order of rank.

37. **Augures and understood relations** omens and the relationship between the omens and what they represent.

38. **maggot-pies and choughs** (chufs) magpies and crows.

39. **man of blood** murderer.

40. **at odds** disputing.

Thou hast no speculation[28] in those eyes
Which thou dost glare with.

LADY MACBETH.   Think of this, good peers,
But as a thing of custom, 'tis no other.
Only it spoils the pleasure of the time.

100 **MACBETH.** What man dare, I dare.
Approach thou like the rugged Russian bear,
The armed rhinoceros, or th' Hyrcan[29] tiger;
Take any shape but that,[30] and my firm nerves
Shall never tremble. Or be alive again,
105 And dare me to the desert[31] with thy sword.
If trembling I inhabit[32] then, protest me
The baby of a girl. Hence, horrible shadow!
Unreal mock'ry, hence!   [*Exit* GHOST.]
                    Why, so: being gone,
I am a man again. Pray you, sit still.

LADY MACBETH. You have displaced the mirth, broke the
110   good meeting,
With most admired[33] disorder.

MACBETH.   Can such things be,
And overcome us[34] like a summer's cloud,
Without our special wonder? You make me strange
Even to the disposition that I owe,[35]
115 When now I think you can behold such sights,
And keep the natural ruby of your cheeks,
When mine is blanched with fear.

ROSS.   What sights, my lord?

LADY MACBETH. I pray you, speak not: He grows worse and worse;
Question enrages him: at once, good night.
120 Stand not upon the order of your going,[36]
But go at once.

LENNOX.   Good night; and better health
Attend his Majesty!

LADY MACBETH.   A kind good night to all!

                    [*Exit* LORDS.]

MACBETH. It will have blood, they say: blood will have blood.
Stones have been known to move and trees to speak;
125 Augures and understood relations[37] have
By maggot-pies and choughs[38] and rooks brought forth
The secret'st man of blood.[39] What is the night?

LADY MACBETH. Almost at odds[40] with morning, which is which.

MACBETH. How say'st thou, that Macduff denies his person

At our great bidding?

130 **LADY MACBETH.**　　　　Did you send to him, sir?

MACBETH. I hear it by the way, but I will send:
There's not a one of them but in his house
I keep a servant fee'd.[41] I will tomorrow,
And betimes[42] I will, to the weird sisters:
135　More shall they speak, for now I am bent[43] to know
By the worst means the worst. For mine own good
All causes shall give way. I am in blood
Stepped in so far that, should I wade no more,
Returning were as tedious as go o'er.
140　Strange things I have in head that will to hand,
Which must be acted ere they may be scanned.[44]

LADY MACBETH. You lack the season of all natures,[45] sleep.

MACBETH. Come, we'll to sleep. My strange and self-abuse[46]
Is the initiate fear that wants hard use.[47]
145　We are yet but young in deed.　　　　　　　　　*[Exit.]*

Scene v. *A witches' haunt.*

[*Thunder. Enter the* THREE WITCHES, *meeting* HECATE.]

FIRST WITCH. Why, how now, Hecate! you look angerly.

HECATE. Have I not reason, beldams[1] as you are,
Saucy and overbold? How did you dare
To trade and traffic with Macbeth
5　In riddles and affairs of death;
And I, the mistress of your charms,
The close contriver[2] of all harms,
Was never called to bear my part,
Or show the glory of our art?
10　And, which is worse, all you have done
Hath been but for a wayward son,
Spiteful and wrathful; who, as others do,
Loves for his own ends, not for you.
But make amends now: get you gone,
15　And at the pit of Acheron[3]
Meet me i' th' morning: thither he
Will come to know his destiny.
Your vessels and your spells provide,
Your charms and everything beside.
20　I am for th' air; this night I'll spend
Unto a dismal and a fatal end:
Great business must be wrought ere noon.
Upon the corner of the moon
There hangs a vap'rous drop profound;

41. fee'd paid to spy.

42. betimes quickly.

43. bent determined.

Literary Analysis
Conflict How do lines 136–139 in Scene iv mark a turning point in Macbeth's inner conflict?

44. scanned examined.

45. season . . . natures preservative of all living creatures.

46. My . . . self-abuse my strange delusion.

47. initiate . . . use beginner's fear that will harden with experience.

1. beldams hags.

2. close contriver secret inventor.

3. Acheron (ak´ ər än´) hell; in Greek mythology the river of Hades.

Reading Check
Why will Macbeth visit "the weird sisters" again?

4. **sleights** devices.

5. **artificial sprites** spirits created by magic.

6. **confusion** ruin.

7. **security** overconfidence.

25   I'll catch it ere it come to ground:
And that distilled by magic sleights[4]
Shall raise such artificial sprites[5]
As by the strength of their illusion
Shall draw him on to his confusion.[6]
30   He shall spurn fate, scorn death, and bear
His hopes 'bove wisdom, grace, and fear:
And you all know security[7]
Is mortals' chiefest enemy.

[*Music and a song.*]

  Hark! I am called; my little spirit, see,
35   Sits in a foggy cloud and stays for me.   [*Exit.*]

[*Sing within,* "Come away, come away," *etc.*]

FIRST WITCH. Come, let's make haste; she'll soon be
back again.   [*Exit.*]

Scene vi. The palace.

[*Enter* LENNOX *and another* LORD.]

1. **hit** coincided with.

2. **Which . . . farther** from which you can draw your own conclusions.

3. **borne** managed.

4. **cannot . . . thought** can fail to think.

5. **fact** deed.

6. **thralls** slaves.

7. **an 't** if it.

8. **broad** unguarded.

9. **due of birth** birthright; claim to the throne.

LENNOX. My former speeches have but hit[1] your thoughts,
Which can interpret farther.[2] Only I say
Things have been strangely borne.[3] The gracious Duncan
Was pitied of Macbeth: marry, he was dead.
5   And the right-valiant Banquo walked too late;
Whom, you may say, if 't please you, Fleance killed,
For Fleance fled. Men must not walk too late.
Who cannot want the thought,[4] how monstrous
It was for Malcolm and for Donalbain
10   To kill their gracious father? Damnèd fact![5]
How it did grieve Macbeth! Did he not straight,
In pious rage, the two delinquents tear,
That were the slaves of drink and thralls[6] of sleep?
Was not that nobly done? Ay, and wisely too;
15   For 'twould have angered any heart alive
To hear the men deny 't. So that I say
He has borne all things well: and I do think
That, had he Duncan's sons under his key—
As, an 't[7] please heaven, he shall not—they should find
20   What 'twere to kill a father. So should Fleance.
But, peace! for from broad[8] words, and 'cause he failed
His presence at the tyrant's feast, I hear,
Macduff lives in disgrace. Sir, can you tell
Where he bestows himself?

LORD.   The son of Duncan,
25   From whom this tyrant holds the due of birth,[9]

Lives in the English court, and is received
Of the most pious Edward[10] with such grace
That the malevolence of fortune nothing
Takes from his high respect.[11] Thither Macduff
30 Is gone to pray the holy King, upon his aid[12]
To wake Northumberland and warlike Siward;[13]
That by the help of these, with Him above
To ratify the work, we may again
Give to our tables meat, sleep to our nights,
35 Free from our feasts and banquets bloody knives,
Do faithful homage and receive free honors:[14]
All which we pine for now. And this report
Hath so exasperate the King that he
Prepares for some attempt of war.

LENNOX.   Sent he to Macduff?

40 **LORD.** He did: and with an absolute "Sir, not I,"
The cloudy[15] messenger turns me his back,
And hums, as who should say "You'll rue the time
That clogs[16] me with this answer."

LENNOX.   And that well might
Advise him to a caution, t' hold what distance
45 His wisdom can provide. Some holy angel
Fly to the court of England and unfold
His message ere he come, that a swift blessing
May soon return to this our suffering country
Under a hand accursed!

LORD.   I'll send my prayers with him.   [*Exit.*]

Critical Reading

1. **Key Ideas and Details (a)** What does Macbeth think as he anticipates the murder of Banquo? **(b) Compare and Contrast:** Compare and contrast Macbeth's thoughts about Banquo's murder with his thoughts before the murder of Duncan.

2. **Key Ideas and Details (a)** In the banquet scene, what complaint does Macbeth make about murdered men? **(b) Analyze:** Is there anything humorous or even ridiculous in this complaint? Why or why not? **(c) Connect:** Does Shakespeare use humor for comic relief in this scene, as he does in the earlier scene with the porter? Explain.

3. **Integration of Knowledge and Ideas** Has the relationship between Macbeth and Lady Macbeth changed? Explain.

4. **Integration of Knowledge and Ideas** What does the murder of Banquo suggest about the effects of evil on evildoers? Explain.

Cite textual evidence to support your responses.

After You Read *Macbeth, Act III*

Literary Analysis

1. **Craft and Structure (a)** Why is Macbeth involved in an **external conflict** with Banquo? **(b)** In what way does Macbeth fail to resolve this conflict?

2. **Craft and Structure** Complete a chart like the one below to show the intensification of **conflict** and the movement toward a climax in Act III.

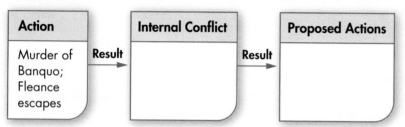

3. **Craft and Structure (a)** How is Macbeth's behavior at the banquet a sign of an **internal conflict? (b)** How does he temporarily resolve this conflict?

4. **Key Ideas and Details** Macbeth is personifying evil. Who do you think will lead the forces of good in a campaign against him? How do you know?

5. **Craft and Structure (a)** Identify three examples of **dramatic irony** in Macbeth's speeches to Banquo in Act III, Scene i, lines 20–38. **(b)** In what way do these examples achieve an aesthetic purpose for Shakespeare by heightening the tension?

6. **Craft and Structure** How does the dramatic irony in Act III, Scene iv, lines 41–44 create an expectation of a tense encounter?

7. **Integration of Knowledge and Ideas** What camera shots would you use to film the banquet scene for a movie version of *Macbeth?* Explain.

Reading Strategy

8. **Identify causes and effects** in the play by explaining how the Witches' prophecy that Banquo will father kings could be viewed as the cause of the following items: **(a)** the question Macbeth asks of Banquo, "'Goes Fleance with you?'" (III, i, 35); **(b)** Macbeth's recruiting of the murderers (III, iii)

9. Some critics suggest that the third murderer is Macbeth himself. Argue for or against this interpretation, supporting your points by showing what would cause Macbeth to join the two murderers in person or what would cause him not to join them.

10. In Act III, Scene vi, a lord tells Lennox that Duncan's son is being sheltered at the English court and that Macduff has gone there to seek his aid. What effects do you think will result from Macduff's visit?

Common Core State Standards

Writing

3. Write narratives to develop real or imagined experiences or events using effective technique, well-chosen details, and well-structured event sequences. *(p. 377)*

3.a. Engage and orient the reader by setting out a problem, situation, or observation and its significance, establishing one or multiple point(s) of view, and introducing a narrator and/or characters; create a smooth progression of experiences or events. *(p. 377)*

3.d. Use precise words and phrases, telling details, and sensory language to convey a vivid picture of the experiences, events, setting, and/or characters. *(p. 377)*

5. Develop and strengthen writing as needed by planning, revising, editing, rewriting, or trying a new approach, focusing on addressing what is most significant for a specific purpose and audience. *(p. 377)*

Language

4.a. Use context as a clue to the meaning of a word or phrase. *(p. 377)*

Vocabulary Acquisition and Use

Word Analysis: Latin Prefix *mal-*

The Latin prefix *mal-* means "bad or badly, poorly, or wrong." *Malevolence*, therefore, means "ill will." The prefix *mal-* can also mean "not," as in *malcontent*. With a group, write a short paragraph describing several qualities that would make a person a poor leader, giving an example of each. Use at least three of the *mal-* words listed below. If any of the words are unfamiliar, refer to a dictionary to clarify their meanings.

maladjusted	malformed
malady	maladministration
malfunction	malicious

Then, for each of the *mal-* words used in your description, tell whether the prefix most nearly means "bad or badly," "poorly," "wrong," or "not."

Vocabulary: Context Clues

The context of a word—the words, phrases and sentences that surround it—may provide clues to its meaning. In the paragraph below, explain how context clues help you identify the meaning of the underlined vocabulary words:

A <u>predominant</u> nobleman in the court of King Malicia heard rumors of foul play in the neighboring kingdom of Maloria. "Though your reign is <u>indissoluble</u>, my liege," he said to the king, "I am afraid the one next door is a little flimsy." "Does the King of Maloria suffer from physical illness or mental <u>infirmity</u>?" the king queried. "Both, my liege," replied the nobleman. "Though he thinks himself <u>dauntless</u>, he is actually a cowering ninny." "Perfect!" cackled the king. "My unchecked <u>malevolence</u> shall soon make me the evil ruler of not one kingdom, but two!"

Writing

Narrative Text Write a **soliloquy** for a lord returning from Macbeth's banquet. At the beginning of the soliloquy, have him clearly establish his point of view (a guest at Macbeth's banquet). Then, have your character relate the events he has seen and explain why they are important.

Prewriting Reread Scene iv. List Macbeth's most striking words and actions, your lord's reactions, and possible sensory details of the scene.

Drafting Using your prewriting list, draft the soliloquy in **blank verse,** unrhymed iambic pentameter. Mimic Shakespeare's style and diction.

Revising Reread your soliloquy to strengthen its figurative language. First, place a star next to descriptive words and phrases that sound too literal. Then, replace each with an imaginative comparison or word picture.

Model: Revising for Figurative Language

     face as dazed as death

And then the king, with ~~pale and frightened face,~~

rose slowly, staring at—nay, toward—the wall

    danced

where nothing ~~was~~ except for shadows dark.

The writer replaces the lackluster adjectives with a vivid and eerie comparison. Next, she replaces the flat *to-be* verb with a lively action verb. These changes help the audience "see" what is being described.

Before You Read | *Macbeth, Act IV*

Literary Analysis

Imagery is the language that writers use to re-create sensory experiences and stir emotions. It is what helps you see, hear, feel, smell, and taste, rather than just read or listen to words. Shakespeare uses imagery to pack sensory experiences and strong emotions into almost every line. Further, he creates these patterns of images that run through the whole play:

- Blood
- Ill-fitting clothes
- Babies and children, sometimes killed by Macbeth and sometimes threatening him

These images reinforce important themes in the play. The last group of images suggests that Macbeth is in some way warring against the future, which babies and children represent. As you read, link patterns of images to the play's central ideas.

Some images are powerful because they are **archetypal**—they relate to ideas and emotions expressed by people in many cultures. In Act IV, for example, **images of banishment from an ideal world**—shrieking, groaning, and bleeding—indicate that Macbeth's Scotland resembles an underworld region where the dead are punished. Look for such archetypal images as you read.

Reading Strategy

@ **Preparing to Read Complex Texts** You will better understand and enjoy a literary work if you **analyze its text structures,** or the way it is put together. In *Macbeth,* Shakespeare uses a type of text structure that involves relationships among images and among patterns of images. For example, as indicated above, you will see patterns of images relating to blood and to babies and children.

Use a graphic organizer like the one shown to figure out how a pattern of images reinforces a theme in the play. Then, analyze how the development and relationship of these images adds to the impact and meaning of the play.

Vocabulary

pernicious (pər nish´ əs) *adj.* fatal; deadly (p. 384)

judicious (joō dish´ əs) *adj.* showing good judgment (p. 385)

sundry (sun´ drē) *adj.* various; miscellaneous (p. 389)

intemperance (in tem´ pər əns) *n.* lack of restraint (p. 390)

avarice (av´ ə ris) *n.* greed (p. 390)

credulous (krej´ oō ləs) *adj.* tending to believe too readily (p. 391)

@ **Common Core State Standards**

Reading Literature
3. Analyze the impact of the author's choices regarding how to develop and relate elements of a story or drama.

Language
1.a. Apply the understanding that usage is a matter of convention, can change over time, and is sometimes contested. *(Literature in Context: Vocabulary Connection, p. 388)*

Image Pattern: Blood

Examples:
• IV, i, 37
•
•
•

↓

Relation to Theme:

www.PHLitOnline.com

Review and Anticipate

Macbeth hires murderers to kill Banquo and Banquo's son, Fleance. The murderers botch the job, killing Banquo but allowing Fleance to escape. Then, at a state banquet, Macbeth is shocked to see the ghost of Banquo sitting in the king's chair. Macbeth decides to visit the witches again, determined to know "the worst." At the end of Act III, we learn that Malcolm is in England preparing to invade Scotland and that Macduff has gone to join him. Act IV will be a turning point in the play. Macbeth seeks help from the witches to secure his power. The forces of good, however, are beginning to gather against him.

ACT IV

Scene i. A witches' haunt.

[*Thunder. Enter the* THREE WITCHES.]

FIRST WITCH. Thrice the brinded[1] cat hath mewed.

SECOND WITCH. Thrice and once the hedge-pig[2] whined.

THIRD WITCH. Harpier[3] cries. 'Tis time, 'tis time.

FIRST WITCH. Round about the caldron go:
5   In the poisoned entrails throw.
     Toad, that under cold stone
     Days and nights has thirty-one
     Swelt'red venom sleeping got,[4]
     Boil thou first i' th' charmèd pot.

10 **ALL.** Double, double, toil and trouble;
     Fire burn and caldron bubble.

SECOND WITCH. Fillet of a fenny snake,
     In the caldron boil and bake;
     Eye of newt and toe of frog,
15   Wool of bat and tongue of dog,
     Adder's fork[5] and blindworm's[6] sting,
     Lizard's leg and howlet's[7] wing,
     For a charm of pow'rful trouble,
     Like a hell-broth boil and bubble.

20 **ALL.** Double, double, toil and trouble;
     Fire burn and caldron bubble.

THIRD WITCH. Scale of dragon, tooth of wolf,
     Witch's mummy, maw and gulf[8]
     Of the ravined[9] salt-sea shark,
25   Root of hemlock digged i' th' dark,

▲ **Critical Viewing**
What is the significance of a burning caldron—like this one—to the play? **[Connect]**

1. **brinded** striped.

2. **hedge-pig** hedgehog.

3. **Harpier** one of the spirits attending the witches.

4. **Swelt'red . . . got** venom sweated out while sleeping.

5. **fork** forked tongue.

6. **blindworm's** small, limbless lizard's.

7. **howlet's** small owl's.

8. **maw and gulf** stomach and gullet.

9. **ravined** ravenous.

Reading Check

What are the witches doing as the act begins?

Edmund Dulac
19 11

Liver of blaspheming Jew,
Gall of goat, and slips of yew
Slivered in the moon's eclipse,
Nose of Turk and Tartar's lips,[10]
30   Finger of birth-strangled babe
Ditch-delivered by a drab,
Make the gruel thick and slab:[11]
Add thereto a tiger's chaudron,[12]
For th' ingredience of our caldron.

35 **ALL.** Double, double, toil and trouble;
    Fire burn and caldron bubble.

   SECOND WITCH. Cool it with a baboon's blood,
    Then the charm is firm and good.

[*Enter* HECATE *and the other* THREE WITCHES.]

   HECATE. O, well done! I commend your pains;
40   And every one shall share i' th' gains:
    And now about the caldron sing,
    Like elves and fairies in a ring,
    Enchanting all that you put in.

[*Music and a song:* "Black Spirits," *etc. Exit* HECATE *and the other* THREE WITCHES.]

   SECOND WITCH. By the pricking of my thumbs,
45   Something wicked this way comes:
    Open, locks,
    Whoever knocks!

[*Enter* MACBETH.]

   MACBETH. How now, you secret, black, and midnight hags!
    What is 't you do?

   ALL.   A deed without a name.

50 **MACBETH.** I conjure you, by that which you profess,
    Howe'er you come to know it, answer me:
    Though you untie the winds and let them fight
    Against the churches; though the yesty[13] waves
    Confound[14] and swallow navigation up;
55   Though bladed corn be lodged[15] and trees blown down;
    Though castles topple on their warders' heads;
    Though palaces and pyramids do slope[16]
    Their heads to their foundations; though the treasure
    Of nature's germens[17] tumble all together,
60   Even till destruction sicken, answer me
    To what I ask you.

   FIRST WITCH.   Speak.

10. **blaspheming Jew . . . Tartar's lips** For many in Shakespeare's audience, the words *Jew, Turk,* and *Tartar* evoked stereotypical enemies of Christianity.

11. **slab** sticky.

12. **chaudron** (shô′ drən) entrails.

◄ **Critical Viewing**
Has this artist captured the spirit of the witches as it is portrayed in IV, i? Explain. **[Evaluate]**

Reading Strategy
Analyzing Text Structures
How does the pattern of images in Scene i reinforce the scene's meaning?

13. **yesty** foamy.

14. **Confound** destroy.

15. **lodged** beaten down.

16. **slope** bend.

17. **nature's germens** seeds of all life.

Reading Check

What does Macbeth demand of the witches?

Literary Analysis

Imagery How do the apparitions that Macbeth sees in Scene i, lines 68, 76, and 86 connect with the patterns of imagery in the play?

18. farrow young pigs.

19. gibbet (jib´ it) gallows.

SECOND WITCH.   Demand.

THIRD WITCH.   We'll answer.

FIRST WITCH. Say, if th' hadst rather hear it from our mouths,
    Or from our masters?

MACBETH.   Call 'em, let me see 'em.

65   **FIRST WITCH.** Pour in sow's blood, that hath eaten
    Her nine farrow;[18] grease that's sweaten
    From the murderer's gibbet[19] throw
    Into the flame.

ALL.   Come, high or low,
    Thyself and office[20] deftly show!

[*Thunder.* FIRST APPARITION: *an Armed Head.*[21]]

20. office function.

21. *an Armed Head* symbol of Macduff.

MACBETH. Tell me, thou unknown power—

FIRST WITCH.   He knows thy thought:
70   Hear his speech, but say thou nought.

FIRST APPARITION. Macbeth! Macbeth! Macbeth! Beware Macduff!
    Beware the Thane of Fife. Dismiss me: enough.

                                 [*He descends.*]

22. harped hit upon.

MACBETH. Whate'er thou art, for thy good caution thanks:
    Thou hast harped[22] my fear aright. But one word more—

75   **FIRST WITCH.** He will not be commanded. Here's another,
    More potent than the first.

[*Thunder.* SECOND APPARITION: *a Bloody Child.*[23]]

23. *a Bloody Child* symbol of Macduff at birth.

SECOND APPARITION. Macbeth! Macbeth! Macbeth!

MACBETH. Had I three ears, I'd hear thee.

SECOND APPARITION. Be bloody, bold, and resolute! Laugh to scorn
80   The pow'r of man, for none of woman born
    Shall harm Macbeth.   [*Descends.*]

24. take . . . fate get a guarantee from fate (by killing Macduff).

MACBETH. Then live, Macduff: what need I fear of thee?
    But yet I'll make assurance double sure,
    And take a bond of fate.[24] Thou shalt not live;
85   That I may tell pale-hearted fear it lies,
    And sleep in spite of thunder.

25. *a Child . . . hand* symbol of Malcolm.

[*Thunder.* THIRD APPARITION: *a Child Crowned, with a tree in his hand.*[25]]

                           What is this,
    That rises like the issue of a king,
    And wears upon his baby-brow the round
    And top of sovereignty?[26]

26. top of sovereignty crown.

ALL.   Listen, but speak not to 't.

THIRD APPARITION. Be lion-mettled, proud, and take no care
90   Who chafes, who frets, or where conspirers are:
       Macbeth shall never vanquished be until
       Great Birnam Wood to high Dunsinane Hill
       Shall come against him.   *[Descends.]*

       MACBETH.   That will never be.
95   Who can impress[27] the forest, bid the tree
       Unfix his earth-bound root? Sweet bodements,[28] good!
       Rebellious dead, rise never, till the Wood
       Of Birnam rise, and our high-placed Macbeth
       Shall live the lease of nature,[29] pay his breath
100   To time and mortal custom.[30] Yet my heart
       Throbs to know one thing. Tell me, if your art
       Can tell so much: shall Banquo's issue ever
       Reign in this kingdom?

       ALL.   Seek to know no more.

       MACBETH. I will be satisfied. Deny me this,
105   And an eternal curse fall on you! Let me know.
       Why sinks that caldron? And what noise is this?

[Hautboys.]

       FIRST WITCH. Show!

       SECOND WITCH. Show!

       THIRD WITCH. Show!

110   **ALL.** Show his eyes, and grieve his heart;
       Come like shadows, so depart!

[A show of eight KINGS *and* BANQUO, *last* KING *with a glass*[31] *in his hand.]*

       MACBETH. Thou art too like the spirit of Banquo. Down!
       Thy crown does sear mine eyelids. And thy hair,
       Thou other gold-bound brow, is like the first.
115   A third is like the former. Filthy hags!
       Why do you show me this? A fourth! Start, eyes!
       What, will the line stretch out to th' crack of doom?
       Another yet! A seventh! I'll see no more.
       And yet the eighth appears, who bears a glass
120   Which shows me many more: and some I see
       That twofold balls and treble scepters[32] carry:
       Horrible sight! Now I see 'tis true;
       For the blood-boltered[33] Banquo smiles upon me,
       And points at them for his.[34] What, is this so?

125   **FIRST WITCH.** Ay, sir, all this is so. But why
       Stands Macbeth thus amazedly?
       Come, sisters, cheer we up his sprites,
       And show the best of our delights:

27. impress force into service.

28. bodements prophecies.

29. lease of nature natural lifespan.

30. mortal custom natural death.

31. glass mirror.

Literary Analysis
Imagery What does Macbeth learn from the images of the eight kings?

32. twofold . . . scepters coronation emblems and insignia of the kingdoms of England, Scotland, and Ireland, united in 1603 when James VI of Scotland became James I of England.

33. blood-boltered with his hair matted with blood.

34. his his descendants.

Reading Check

What do the three apparitions tell Macbeth, and what further vision does he see?

35. antic round grotesque circular dance.

I'll charm the air to give a sound,
130   While you perform your antic round,[35]
That this great king may kindly say
Our duties did his welcome pay.

[*Music.* THE WITCHES *dance, and vanish.*]

Vocabulary
pernicious (pər nish′ əs)
adj. fatal; deadly

MACBETH. Where are they? Gone? Let this pernicious hour
Stand aye accursèd in the calendar!
Come in, without there!

[*Enter* LENNOX.]

135 **LENNOX.**   What's your Grace's will?

MACBETH. Saw you the weird sisters?

LENNOX.   No, my lord.

MACBETH. Came they not by you?

LENNOX.   No indeed, my lord.

MACBETH. Infected be the air whereon they ride,
And damned all those that trust them! I did hear
140   The galloping of horse. Who was 't came by?

LENNOX. 'Tis two or three, my lord, that bring you word
Macduff is fled to England.

MACBETH.   Fled to England?

LENNOX. Ay, my good lord.

36. anticipat'st foretold.

37. The flighty . . . it The fleeting plan is never fulfilled unless it is carried out at once.

38. firstlings . . . heart first thoughts, impulses.

MACBETH. [*Aside*] Time, thou anticipat'st[36] my dread exploits.
145   The flighty purpose never is o'ertook
Unless the deed go with it.[37] From this moment
The very firstlings of my heart[38] shall be
The firstlings of my hand. And even now,
To crown my thoughts with acts be it thought and done:
150   The castle of Macduff I will surprise;
Seize upon Fife; give to th' edge o' th' sword

39. trace succeed.

His wife, his babes, and all unfortunate souls
That trace[39] him in his line. No boasting like a fool;
This deed I'll do before this purpose cool:
155   But no more sights!—Where are these gentlemen?
Come, bring me where they are.

[*Exit.*]

Scene ii. Macduff's castle.

[*Enter* MACDUFF'S WIFE, *her* SON, *and* ROSS.]

LADY MACDUFF. What had he done, to make him fly the land?

ROSS. You must have patience, madam.

LADY MACDUFF.   He had none:
   His flight was madness. When our actions do not,
   Our fears do make us traitors.

   ROSS.   You know not
5   Whether it was his wisdom or his fear.

   LADY MACDUFF. Wisdom! To leave his wife, to leave his babes,
   His mansion and his titles,[1] in a place
   From whence himself does fly? He loves us not;
   He wants the natural touch:[2] for the poor wren,
10   The most diminutive of birds, will fight,
   Her young ones in her nest, against the owl.
   All is the fear and nothing is the love;
   As little is the wisdom, where the flight
   So runs against all reason.

   ROSS.   My dearest coz,[3]
15   I pray you, school[4] yourself. But, for your husband,
   He is noble, wise, _judicious_, and best knows
   The fits o' th' seasons,[5] I dare not speak much further:
   But cruel are the times, when we are traitors
   And do not know ourselves;[6] when we hold rumor
20   From what we fear,[7] yet know not what we fear,
   But float upon a wild and violent sea
   Each way and move. I take my leave of you.
   Shall not be long but I'll be here again.
   Things at the worst will cease, or else climb upward
25   To what they were before. My pretty cousin,
   Blessing upon you!

   LADY MACDUFF. Fathered he is, and yet he's fatherless.

   ROSS. I am so much a fool, should I stay longer,
   It would be my disgrace and your discomfort.[8]
   I take my leave at once.   [_Exit_ ROSS.]

30   **LADY MACDUFF.**   Sirrah, your father's dead;
   And what will you do now? How will you live?

   SON. As birds do, mother.

   LADY MACDUFF.   What, with worms and flies?

   SON. With what I get, I mean; and so do they.

   LADY MACDUFF. Poor bird! thou'dst never fear the net nor lime,[9]
35   The pitfall nor the gin.[10]

   SON. Why should I, mother? Poor birds they are not set for.
   My father is not dead, for all your saying.

   LADY MACDUFF. Yes, he is dead: how wilt thou do for a father?

   SON. Nay, how will you do for a husband?

Literary Analysis
Imagery What image is suggested by Lady Macduff's use of the words "fly" and "flight" in lines 8 and 13?

1. **titles** possessions.

2. **wants . . . touch** lacks natural affection.

3. **coz** cousin.

4. **school** control.

Vocabulary
judicious (jōō dish′ əs) _adj._ showing good judgment

5. **fits o' th' season** disorders of the time.

6. **when . . . ourselves** when we are treated as traitors but do not know of any treason.

7. **when . . . fear** believe rumors based on our fears.

8. **It . . . discomfort:** I would disgrace myself and embarrass you by weeping.

Literary Analysis
Imagery What does the imagery in Scene ii, lines 34–35 suggest about what might happen?

9. **lime** birdlime, a sticky substance smeared on branches to catch birds.

10. **gin** trap.

Reading Check
Where has Macduff gone, and how will Macbeth revenge himself against Macduff?

11. **sell** betray.

12. **for thee** for a child.

13. **swears and lies** takes an oath and breaks it.

14. **enow** enough.

15. **in . . . perfect** I am fully informed of your honorable rank.

16. **doubt** fear.

17. **homely** simple.

18. **fell** fierce.

40 **LADY MACDUFF.** Why, I can buy me twenty at any market.

SON. Then you'll buy 'em to sell[11] again.

LADY MACDUFF. Thou speak'st with all thy wit, and yet i' faith,
With wit enough for thee.[12]

SON. Was my father a traitor, mother?

45 **LADY MACDUFF.** Ay, that he was.

SON. What is a traitor?

LADY MACDUFF. Why, one that swears and lies.[13]

SON. And be all traitors that do so?

LADY MACDUFF. Every one that does so is a traitor, and must
be hanged.

50 **SON.** And must they all be hanged that swear and lie?

LADY MACDUFF. Every one.

SON. Who must hang them?

LADY MACDUFF. Why, the honest men.

SON. Then the liars and swearers are fools; for there are liars and
55 swearers enow[14] to beat the honest men and hang up them.

LADY MACDUFF. Now, God help thee, poor monkey! But how wilt
thou do for a father?

SON. If he were dead, you'd weep for him. If you would not, it were
60 a good sign that I should quickly have a new father.

LADY MACDUFF. Poor prattler, how thou talk'st!

[*Enter a* MESSENGER .]

MESSENGER. Bless you, fair dame! I am not to you known,
Though in your state of honor I am perfect.[15]
65 I doubt[16] some danger does approach you nearly:
If you will take a homely[17] man's advice,
Be not found here; hence, with your little ones.
To fright you thus, methinks I am too savage;
To do worse to you were fell[18] cruelty,
70 Which is too nigh your person. Heaven preserve you!
I dare abide no longer.   [*Exit* MESSENGER.]

LADY MACDUFF.   Whither should I fly?
I have done no harm. But I remember now
I am in this earthly world, where to do harm
Is often laudable, to do good sometime
75 Accounted dangerous folly. Why then, alas,
Do I put up that womanly defense,
To say I have done no harm?—What are these faces?

[*Enter* MURDERERS.]

MURDERER. Where is your husband?

LADY MACDUFF. I hope, in no place so unsanctified
Where such as thou mayst find him.

80 **MURDERER.**   He's a traitor.

SON. Thou li'st, thou shag-eared[19] villain!

MURDERER.   What, you egg!

                          [*Stabbing him.*]

    Young fry[20] of treachery!

SON.   He has killed me, mother:
    Run away, I pray you!   [*Dies.*]

            [*Exit* LADY MACDUFF *crying "Murder!" followed by* MURDERERS.]

19. **shag-eared** hairy-eared.

20. **fry** offspring

Reading Check

Whom do Macbeth's men kill?

▼ **Critical Viewing**
This engraving shows the murderers menacing Macduff's family. In what way does the artist capture the defiance reflected in Act IV, Scene ii, line 81?
[Interpret]

Literary Analysis

Imagery How do the images in Scene iii, lines 1–4 help establish a contrast between Malcolm and Macduff?

1. **Bestride . . . birthdom** Protectively stand over our native land.

2. **Like . . . dolor** similar cry of anguish.

3. **deserve . . . me** earn by betraying me to Macbeth.

4. **wisdom** It is wise.

Scene iii. England. Before the King's palace.

[*Enter* MALCOLM *and* MACDUFF.]

> **MALCOLM.** Let us seek out some desolate shade, and there
> Weep our sad bosoms empty.
>
> **MACDUFF.**   Let us rather
> Hold fast the mortal♦ sword, and like good men
> Bestride our down-fall'n birthdom.[1] Each new morn
> 5 New widows howl, new orphans cry, new sorrows
> Strike heaven on the face, that it resounds
> As if it felt with Scotland and yelled out
> Like syllable of dolor.[2]
>
> **MALCOLM.**   What I believe, I'll wail;
> What know, believe; and what I can redress,
> 10 As I shall find the time to friend,♦ I will.
> What you have spoke, it may be so perchance.
> This tyrant, whose sole♦ name blisters our tongues,
> Was once thought honest:♦ you have loved him well;
> He hath not touched you yet. I am young; but something
> 15 You may deserve of him through me;[3] and wisdom[4]
> To offer up a weak, poor, innocent lamb
> T' appease an angry god.
>
> **MACDUFF.** I am not treacherous.

LITERATURE IN CONTEXT

Vocabulary Connection

♦ Shifting Meanings

Because language is always changing, some words used by Shakespeare have shifted in meaning.

Mortal (IV, iii, 3) means "deadly," which is somewhat unlike its current meaning, "subject to death or decay."

Friend (IV, iii, 10), which today is a noun, is used as a verb meaning "to be friendly."

Sole (IV, iii, 12), which now means "single" or "one and only," is used as an intensifier meaning "very."

Honest (IV, iii, 13) has the broad sense of "good."

As you read, be alert to shifts in meaning like these, and use the context of a word or phrase as well as the side notes to help you determine Shakespeare's meaning.

Connect to the Literature

What possible meanings might the word *recoil* have in line 19?

MALCOLM. But Macbeth is.
A good and virtuous nature may recoil
20 In an imperial charge. But I shall crave your pardon;
That which you are, my thoughts cannot transpose:
Angels are bright still, though the brightest⁵ fell:
Though all things foul would wear⁶ the brows of grace,
Yet grace must still look so.⁷

MACDUFF. I have lost my hopes.

25 **MALCOLM.** Perchance even there where I did find my doubts.
Why in that rawness⁸ left you wife and child,
Those precious motives, those strong knots of love,
Without leave-taking? I pray you,
Let not my jealousies be your dishonors.
30 But mine own safeties.⁹ You may be rightly just
Whatever I shall think.

MACDUFF. Bleed, bleed, poor country:
Great tyranny, lay thou thy basis sure,
For goodness dare not check thee: wear thou thy wrongs:
The title is affeered.¹⁰ Fare thee well, lord:
35 I would not be the villain that thou think'st
For the whole space that's in the tyrant's grasp
And the rich East to boot.

MALCOLM. Be not offended:
I speak not as in absolute fear of you.
I think our country sinks beneath the yoke;
40 It weeps, it bleeds, and each new day a gash
Is added to her wounds. I think withal
There would be hands uplifted in my right;¹¹
And here from gracious England¹² have I offer
Of goodly thousands: but, for all this,
45 When I shall tread upon the tyrant's head,
Or wear it on my sword, yet my poor country
Shall have more vices than it had before,
More suffer, and more sundry ways than ever,
By him that shall succeed.

MACDUFF. What should he be?

50 **MALCOLM.** It is myself I mean, in whom I know
All the particulars of vice so grafted¹³
That, when they shall be opened,¹⁴ black Macbeth
Will seem as pure as snow, and the poor state
Esteem him as a lamb, being compared
With my confineless harms.¹⁵

55 **MACDUFF.** Not in the legions
Of horrid hell can come a devil more damned
In evils to top Macbeth.

---

5. **the brightest** Lucifer.

6. **would wear** desire to wear.

7. **so** like itself.

8. **rawness** unprotected state or condition.

9. **safeties** protections.

10. **affeered** legally confirmed.

Literary Analysis
Imagery Why are the images Malcolm uses to describe Scotland in lines 39–41 more effective than a simple statement that the country is in trouble and getting worse?

11. **in my right** on behalf of my claim.

12. **England** king of England.

Vocabulary
sundry (sun′ drē) *adj.*
various; miscellaneous

13. **grafted** implanted.

14. **opened** in bloom.

15. **confineless harms** unbounded evils.

Reading Check

How does Malcolm describe himself to Macduff?

16. **Luxurious** lecherous.

17. **Sudden** violent.

18. **continent impediments** restraints.

Vocabulary

intemperance (in tem´ pər əns) *n.* lack of restraint

19. **nature** man's nature.

20. **Convey** secretly manage.

21. **affection** character.

Vocabulary

avarice (av´ ə ris) *n.* greed

22. **stanchless** never-ending.

23. **summer-seeming** summerlike.

24. **of** that killed.

25. **foisons** (foi´ zənz) plenty.

26. **mere own** own property.

27. **portable** bearable.

28. **division . . . crime** variations of each kind of crime.

29. **confound** destroy.

MALCOLM.   I grant him bloody,
Luxurious,[16] avaricious, false, deceitful,
Sudden,[17] malicious, smacking of every sin
60 That has a name: but there's no bottom, none,
In my voluptuousness: your wives, your daughters,
Your matrons and your maids, could not fill up
The cistern of my lust, and my desire
All continent impediments[18] would o'erbear,
65 That did oppose my will. Better Macbeth
Than such an one to reign.

MACDUFF.   Boundless intemperance
In nature[19] is a tyranny; it hath been
Th' untimely emptying of the happy throne,
And fall of many kings. But fear not yet
70 To take upon you what is yours: you may
Convey[20] your pleasures in a spacious plenty,
And yet seem cold, the time you may so hoodwink.
We have willing dames enough. There cannot be
That vulture in you, to devour so many
75 As will to greatness dedicate themselves,
Finding it so inclined.

MALCOLM.   With this there grows
In my most ill-composed affection[21] such
A stanchless[22] avarice that, were I King,
I should cut off the nobles for their lands,
80 Desire his jewels and this other's house:
And my more-having would be as a sauce
To make me hunger more, that I should forge
Quarrels unjust against the good and loyal,
Destroying them for wealth.

MACDUFF.   This avarice
85 Sticks deeper, grows with more pernicious root
Than summer-seeming[23] lust, and it hath been
The sword of[24] our slain kings. Yet do not fear.
Scotland hath foisons[25] to fill up your will
Of your mere own.[26] All these are portable,[27]
90 With other graces weighed.

MALCOLM. But I have none: the king-becoming graces,
As justice, verity, temp'rance, stableness,
Bounty, perseverance, mercy, lowliness,
Devotion, patience, courage, fortitude,
95 I have no relish of them, but abound
In the division of each several crime,[28]
Acting it many ways. Nay, had I pow'r, I should
Pour the sweet milk of concord into hell,
Uproar the universal peace, confound[29]

All unity on earth.

100 **MACDUFF.**   O Scotland, Scotland!

MALCOLM. If such a one be fit to govern, speak:
I am as I have spoken.

MACDUFF.   Fit to govern!
No, not to live. O nation miserable!
With an untitled[30] tyrant bloody-sceptered,
105 When shalt thou see thy wholesome days again,
Since that the truest issue of thy throne[31]
By his own interdiction[32] stands accursed,
And does blaspheme his breed?[33] Thy royal father
Was a most sainted king: the queen that bore thee,
110 Oft'ner upon her knees than on her feet,
Died[34] every day she lived. Fare thee well!
These evils thou repeat'st upon thyself
Hath banished me from Scotland. O my breast,
Thy hope ends here!

MALCOLM.   Macduff, this noble passion,
115 Child of integrity, hath from my soul
Wiped the black scruples, reconciled my thoughts
To thy good truth and honor. Devilish Macbeth
By many of these trains[35] hath sought to win me
Into his power; and modest wisdom[36] plucks me
120 From over-credulous haste: but God above
Deal between thee and me! For even now
I put myself to thy direction, and
Unspeak mine own detraction,[37] here abjure
The taints and blames I laid upon myself,
125 For[38] strangers to my nature. I am yet
Unknown to woman, never was forsworn,
Scarcely have coveted what was mine own,
At no time broke my faith, would not betray
The devil to his fellow, and delight
130 No less in truth than life. My first false speaking
Was this upon myself. What I am truly,
Is thine and my poor country's to command:
Whither indeed, before thy here-approach,
Old Siward, with ten thousand warlike men,
135 Already at a point,[39] was setting forth.
Now we'll together, and the chance of goodness
Be like our warranted quarrel![40] Why are you silent?

MACDUFF. Such welcome and unwelcome things at once
'Tis hard to reconcile.

[*Enter a* DOCTOR.]

140 **MALCOLM.** Well, more anon. Comes the King forth, I pray you?

Reading Strategy
Analyzing Text Structures
How does the image in Act IV, Scene iii, line 98 echo those in Act I, Scene v, line 17 and Act I, Scene v, lines 47–48?

30. **untitled** having no right to the throne.

31. **truest . . . throne** child of the true king.

32. **interdiction** exclusion.

33. **blaspheme his breed** slander his ancestry.

34. **Died** prepared for heaven.

35. **trains** enticements.

36. **modest wisdom** prudence.

Vocabulary
credulous (krej´ ōō ləs) *adj.* tending to believe too readily

37. **detraction** slander.

38. **For** as.

39. **at a point** prepared.

40. **the chance . . . quarrel** May our chance of success equal the justice of our cause.

Reading Check
What response by Macduff convinces Malcolm that Macduff is being honest?

43. **presently amend** immediately recover.

DOCTOR. Ay, sir. There are a crew of wretched souls
    That stay[41] his cure: their malady convinces
    The great assay of art;[42] but at his touch,
    Such sanctity hath heaven given his hand,
    They presently amend.[43]

145 **MALCOLM.**   I thank you, doctor.

                                        [*Exit* DOCTOR.]

MACDUFF. What's the disease he means?

MALCOLM.   'Tis called the evil:[44]
    A most miraculous work in this good King,
    Which often since my here-remain in England
    I have seen him do. How he solicits heaven,
150 Himself best knows: but strangely-visited people,
    All swoll'n and ulcerous, pitiful to the eye,
    The mere[45] despair of surgery, he cures,
    Hanging a golden stamp[46] about their necks,
    Put on with holy prayers: and 'tis spoken,
155 To the succeeding royalty he leaves
    The healing benediction. With this strange virtue
    He hath a heavenly gift of prophecy,
    And sundry blessings hang about his throne
    That speak him full of grace.

                        [*Enter* ROSS.]

44. **evil** scrofula (skräf´ yə lə), skin disease called "the king's evil" because it was believed that it could be cured by the king's touch.

45. **mere** utter.
46. **stamp** coin.

MACDUFF.   See, who comes here?

160 **MALCOLM.** My countryman; but yet I know him not.

MACDUFF. My ever gentle[47] cousin, welcome hither.

MALCOLM. I know him now: good God, betimes[48] remove
    The means that makes us strangers!

ROSS.   Sir, amen.

MACDUFF. Stands Scotland where it did?

ROSS.   Alas, poor country!
165 Almost afraid to know itself! It cannot
    Be called our mother but our grave, where nothing[49]
    But who knows nothing is once seen to smile;
    Where sighs and groans, and shrieks that rent the air,
    Are made, not marked, where violent sorrow seems
170 A modern ecstasy.[50] The dead man's knell
    Is there scarce asked for who,[51] and good men's lives
    Expire before the flowers in their caps,
    Dying or ere they sicken.

MACDUFF.   O, relation
    Too nice,[52] and yet too true!

47. **gentle** noble.

48. **betimes** quickly.

Reading Strategy
Analyzing Text Structures
Connect the images in lines 164-173 with similar images revealing Scotland as a hellish place.

49. **nothing** no one.

50. **modern ecstasy** ordinary emotion.

51. **The dead . . . who** People can no longer keep track of Macbeth's victims.

52. **nice** exact.

MALCOLM. What's the newest grief?

175 **ROSS.** That of an hour's age doth hiss the speaker;[53]
Each minute teems[54] a new one.

MACDUFF. How does my wife?

ROSS. Why, well.

MACDUFF. And all my children?

ROSS. Well too.

MACDUFF. The tyrant has not battered at their peace?

ROSS. No; they were well at peace when I did leave 'em.

180 **MACDUFF.** Be not a niggard of your speech: how goes 't?

ROSS. When I came hither to transport the tidings,
Which I have heavily borne, there ran a rumor
Of many worthy fellows that were out;[55]
Which was to my belief witnessed[56] the rather,
185 For that I saw the tyrant's power[57] afoot.
Now is the time of help. Your eye in Scotland
Would create soldiers, make our women fight,
To doff[58] their dire distresses.

MALCOLM. Be 't their comfort
We are coming thither. Gracious England hath
190 Lent us good Siward and ten thousand men;
An older and a better soldier none
That Christendom gives out.

ROSS. Would I could answer
This comfort with the like! But I have words

53. **That . . . speaker** Report of the grief of an hour ago is hissed as stale news.

54. **teems** gives birth to.

Literary Analysis
Imagery Why do you think Ross uses such an exaggerated image in lines 186–188?

55. **out** in rebellion.

56. **witnessed** confirmed.

57. **power** army.

58. **doff** put off.

Reading Check
What report from Scotland does Ross bring?

▼ **Critical Viewing**
How does this castle compare with your image of Inverness? **[Connect]**

That would be howled out in the desert air,
Where hearing should not latch[59] them.

195 **MACDUFF.**   What concern they?
The general cause or is it a fee-grief[60]
Due to some single breast?

ROSS.   No mind that's honest
But in it shares some woe, though the main part
Pertains to you alone.

MACDUFF.   If it be mine,
200   Keep it not from me, quickly let me have it.

ROSS. Let not your ears despise my tongue for ever,
Which shall possess them with the heaviest sound
That ever yet they heard.

MACDUFF.   Humh! I guess at it.

ROSS. Your castle is surprised; your wife and babes
205   Savagely slaughtered. To relate the manner,
Were, on the quarry[61] of these murdered deer,
To add the death of you.

MALCOLM.   Merciful heaven!
What, man! Ne'er pull your hat upon your brows;
Give sorrow words. The grief that does not speak
210   Whispers the o'er-fraught[62] heart and bids it break.

MACDUFF. My children too?

ROSS.   Wife, children, servants, all
That could be found.

MACDUFF.   And I must be from thence!
My wife killed too?

ROSS.   I have said.

MALCOLM.   Be comforted.
Let's make us med'cines of our great revenge,
215   To cure this deadly grief.

MACDUFF. He has no children. All my pretty ones?
Did you say all? O hell-kite![63] All?
What, all my pretty chickens and their dam
At one fell swoop?

MALCOLM. Dispute it[64] like a man.

220 **MACDUFF.**   I shall do so;
But I must also feel it as a man.
I cannot but remember such things were,
That were most precious to me. Did heaven look on,
And would not take their part? Sinful Macduff,

59. **latch** catch.
60. **fee-grief** personal grief.

Literary Analysis
Imagery How does
the image in line 206
emphasize the ghastly fate of
Macduff's family?

61. **quarry** heap of game slain
in a hunt.

62. **o'er-fraught** over-
burdened.

63. **hell-kite** hellish bird
of prey.

64. **Dispute it** Counter your
grief.

◀ **Critical Viewing**
What emotions does this
actor playing Macduff
project? Explain. **[Interpret]**

225 They were all struck for thee! Naught[65] that I am,
Not for their own demerits but for mine
Fell slaughter on their souls. Heaven rest them now!

MALCOLM. Be this the whetstone of your sword. Let grief
Convert to anger; blunt not the heart, enrage it.

66. front to front face to face.

230 **MACDUFF.** O, I could play the woman with mine eyes,
And braggart with my tongue! But, gentle heavens,
Cut short all intermission; front to front[66]
Bring thou this fiend of Scotland and myself;
Within my sword's length set him. If he 'scape,
235 Heaven forgive him too!

MALCOLM. This time goes manly.
Come, go we to the King. Our power is ready;

67. Our . . . leave We need only to take our leave.

Our lack is nothing but our leave.[67] Macbeth

68. Put . . . instruments urge us onward as their agents.

Is ripe for shaking, and the pow'rs above
Put on their instruments.[68] Receive what cheer you may.
240 The night is long that never finds the day. *[Exit.]*

Critical Reading

Cite textual evidence to support your responses.

© **1. Key Ideas and Details (a)** What are the predictions made by the second and third apparitions? **(b) Analyze:** Why does Macbeth readily accept these predictions?

© **2. Key Ideas and Details (a)** What happens to Macduff's family? **(b) Infer:** What does the fate of Macduff's family suggest about Macbeth's state of mind?

© **3. Key Ideas and Details (a)** How does Malcolm test Macduff? **(b) Analyze:** What does this test reveal about both Malcolm and Macduff? Explain.

© **4. Integration of Knowledge and Ideas (a)** How does Macduff respond when asked to take the news about his family "like a man"? **(b) Interpret:** How would you characterize Macduff, based on his reaction to the murder of his wife and son? **(c) Compare and Contrast:** Compare and contrast Macduff's understanding of manhood with definitions of it earlier in the play.

© **5. Integration of Knowledge and Ideas (a) Hypothesize:** If Shakespeare were alive today, would he argue that evildoers are primarily influenced by genetics, upbringing, or their own free choice? Base your answer on evidence from Act IV. **(b) Evaluate:** Would you agree with his position? Explain.

After You Read *Macbeth, Act IV*

Literary Analysis

1. Craft and Structure Identify a passage in Act IV that has vivid **imagery.** Using a chart like the one shown, indicate the emotions that the images express.

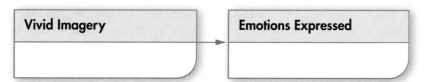

Vivid Imagery	→	Emotions Expressed

2. Craft and Structure **(a)** In Act IV, Scene i and Act IV, Scene ii, find images that show children and babies are in danger from Macbeth and also threaten him. **(b)** Why is Macbeth at war with the future, which babies and children represent?

3. Craft and Structure **(a)** Find two passages in Act IV, Scene iii with images of sickness. **(b)** Explain how these images relate to the conflict between Macbeth and Malcolm.

4. Craft and Structure In Act IV, Scene iii, identify two **archetypal images of banishment from an ideal world,** images that describe Scotland in terms of weeping, bleeding, or both.

5. Integration of Knowledge and Ideas What do the images of banishment from an ideal world and the references to the Christian underworld indicate about Macbeth's rule over Scotland? Explain.

Reading Strategy

6. Analyze the text structure of *Macbeth* by identifying three patterns of imagery that occur throughout Act IV. Remember that a pattern of imagery is a series of related images—for example, images of blood.

7. Explain how each of the patterns of imagery you identified relates to an important theme—an insight into life or comment on life—in the play.

8. Demonstrate how several patterns of imagery work together to convey the play's meaning.

9. (a) Would *Macbeth* be less rich if Shakespeare had not used imagery to reinforce the themes of his play? Why or why not? **(b)** Is it necessary for the reader to experience the images with his or her senses to make them truly effective? Explain.

10. Some critics have argued that a pattern of imagery is a text structure that appeals to a reader's mind, emotions, and senses. Do you agree or disagree? Why?

Common Core State Standards

Writing

2.b. Develop the topic thoroughly by selecting the most significant and relevant facts, extended definitions, concrete details, quotations, or other information and examples appropriate to the audience's knowledge of the topic. *(p. 398)*

2.f. Provide a concluding statement or section that follows from and supports the information or explanation presented. *(p. 398)*

5. Develop and strengthen writing as needed by planning, revising, editing, rewriting, or trying a new approach, focusing on addressing what is most significant for a specific purpose and audience. *(p. 398)*

Language

4.d. Verify the preliminary determination of the meaning of a word or phrase. *(p. 398)*

PERFORMANCE TASKS
Integrated Language Skills

Ⓒ Vocabulary Acquisition and Use

Word Analysis: Latin Word Root -cred-

The Latin root -cred- means "belief." For example, to be *credulous* is "to believe something too readily." The word *creed*, meaning "belief," can also be traced back to this root, as can the word *credentials*, meaning "qualifications," or traits that make a person trustworthy or believable.

Working with a partner, use the word parts shown below to build six -cred- words. Then, write the meanings of these words.

in-	-ulous
dis-	-ulity
mis-	-ible

When you are done, verify your words and definitions by referring to a dictionary.

Vocabulary: Analogies

An analogy compares two relationships to show their similarity. For each item, determine the relationship between the first and second words. Then, complete the analogy using a word from the vocabulary list on page 378. Use each word only once, and explain your choice.

1. *suspicion : trust ::* _____ : *generosity*
2. *expensive : costly ::* _____ : *assorted*
3. *independent : adult ::* _____ : *child*
4. *formality : ease ::* _____ : *self-control*
5. *offensive : rude ::* _____ : *sensible*
6. *invulnerable : susceptible ::* _____ : *harmless*

Writing

Ⓒ **Informative Text** *Archetypal images of banishment from an ideal world*—otherwise known as the archetype of the "fall"— often appear in works dealing with the loss of innocence or with a character's descent into a state of evil. Write an **essay** analyzing Shakespeare's use of such images in *Macbeth*. Identify the "ideal world" from which one or more characters are expelled, as well as the causes of this banishment. Remember to trace the descent into evil by means of Shakespeare's imagery.

Prewriting Create a flow chart like the one shown to trace a central character's "fall." Identify imagery reflecting the ideal state in which the character exists at first. Then list reasons why this ideal state does not last. (The reasons may be internal character traits, external events, or both.) Finally, describe the evil into which the character has fallen.

Drafting Begin with a statement that summarizes the fall from the ideal state shown in your prewriting chart. Develop your essay by indicating the ways Shakespeare uses imagery to picture this fall. Support your points by making *specific and detailed references* to the text, and note how these passages might affect *readers' or viewers' emotions.*

Revising Revise to add breadth and depth to your essay. Consider adding comparisons or references to other works of literature that use archetypal images of banishment. Alternatively, provide a concluding section about *nuances or complexities* that make Shakespeare's use of these archetypal images more convincing than that of other authors.

Model: Charting a Character's Fall

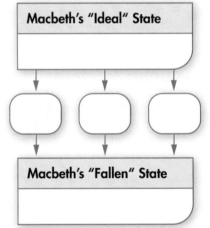

Critical Commentary

"Macbeth as King"

Ian Johnston

Ian Johnston teaches at Malaspina-University College, Nanaimo, BC, Canada. His analysis of Macbeth's character in the later acts of the play comes from his lecture entitled "Introduction to Macbeth."

. . . It is worth asking ourselves what in Macbeth commands our attention throughout the second half of this play. After all, he is in many respects the least admirable tragic hero of all. In characters like Othello, Romeo, Cleopatra, Lear, Antony, Hamlet . . . we can usually find something to admire. We may not like them (they are not very likable people), but there is something in their characters or their situations on which we can hang some sympathy, even if there is not enough for us to rationalize away their actions. But Macbeth is a mass murderer, who does away with friends, colleagues, woman and children, often for no apparent reason other than his own desires. Why do we keep our attention focused on him?

▲ Macbeth demands to know the future from the Witches.

The answer, I think, has to do with the quality of his mind, his horrible determination to see the entire evil business through. Having, with the murder of Duncan, taken charge of the events which shape his life, he is not now going to relinquish the responsibility for securing his desires. The most remarkable quality of the man in this process is the clear-eyed awareness of what is happening to him personally. He is suffering horribly throughout, but he will not crack or seek any other remedy than what he alone can deliver. If that means damning himself even further, then so be it.

This stance certainly does not make Macbeth likable or (from our perspective) in many respects admirable. But it does confer a heroic quality upon his tragic course of action. He simply will not compromise with the world, and he will pay whatever price that decision exacts from him, even though as his murderous career continues he becomes increasingly aware of what it is costing him.

© **Key Ideas and Details** According to Johnston, is Macbeth among Shakespeare's more admirable tragic heroes? Explain.

Before You Read | *Macbeth, Act V*

Literary Analysis

Shakespearean tragedy usually contains these elements:

- A central character of high rank and personal quality, yet with a **tragic flaw** or weakness
- Causally related events that lead this character to disaster, at least partly through his or her flaw
- An experience of pity, fear, and awe for the audience
- Lively action that creates a vivid spectacle and the use of comic scenes to temper and offset the mood of sadness

As you read, consider how Shakespeare introduces Macbeth as a character (as a war hero) and how the author then develops the character, adding complexity and depth and ultimately revealing a tragic flaw. Note, too, how Shakespeare chooses to include plot events that lead to Macbeth's downfall and that make his tragic flaw evident.

Reading a Shakespearean tragedy is often uplifting despite the disasters that befall the hero. This positive experience results from the **tragic impulse,** which shows the tragic hero acting nobly.

Reading Strategy

 **Preparing to Read Complex Texts** As products of a certain time, great plays reflect the beliefs of their period. To better understand a great play, therefore, you should **relate the work to the major themes and issues of its period.** Following are ways to uncover the philosophical, political, and religious influences that shaped *Macbeth*'s characters and settings:

- Be aware of the importance Elizabethans placed on the king's role in maintaining social order and how they linked order in the heavens with order in society.
- Compare the ideas that characters express with modern ideas.

In using the second method, focus on the ideas expressed by the doctor in Act V, Scene i. Use a chart like the one shown to compare his ideas with those a modern psychiatrist might express.

Vocabulary

perturbation (pʉr´ tər bā´ shən) *n.* disturbance (p. 401)

recoil (ri koil´) *v.* to draw back in fear, surprise, or disgust (p. 405)

antidote (an´ tə dōt´) *n.* remedy (p. 406)

pristine (pris´ tēn´) *adj.* original; unspoiled (p. 407)

clamorous (klam´ ər əs) *adj.* noisy (p. 410)

harbingers (här´ bin jərz) *n.* forerunners (p. 410)

vulnerable (vul´ nər ə bəl) *adj.* exposed to attack or harm (p. 412)

**Common Core
State Standards**

**Reading Literature
3.** Analyze the impact of the author's choices regarding how to develop and relate elements of a story or drama.

Comparison of Beliefs

Doctor in *Macbeth*

↓

Modern Psychiatrist

www.PHLitOnline.com

Review and Anticipate

In Act IV, Macbeth learns from the witches that he must "Beware Macduff!" but that he need not fear any man "of woman born." He also learns he will never be vanquished until the forest itself marches against him. However, he sees a vision indicating that Banquo will indeed father a long line of kings.

Armed with his new knowledge, Macbeth orders the murder of Macduff's wife and son. Macduff himself is in England to join forces with Malcolm and is overcome when he hears the news. Nevertheless, he and Malcolm will lead an army against Macbeth.

Act V will determine the outcome as Macbeth, grown reckless in evil, battles against Malcolm and his men.

ACT V

Scene i. Dunsinane. In the castle.

[*Enter a* DOCTOR OF PHYSIC *and a* WAITING-GENTLEWOMAN.]

DOCTOR. I have two nights watched with you, but can perceive no truth in your report. When was it she last walked?

GENTLEWOMAN. Since his Majesty went into the field.[1] I have seen
5   her rise from her bed, throw her nightgown upon her, unlock her closet,[2] take forth paper, fold it, write upon 't, read it, afterwards seal it, and again return to bed; yet all this while in a most fast sleep.

DOCTOR. A great perturbation in nature, to receive at
10   once the benefit of sleep and do the effects of watching![3] In this slumb'ry agitation, besides her walking, and other actual performances, what, at any time, have you heard her say?

15 **GENTLEWOMAN.** That, sir, which I will not report after her.

DOCTOR. You may to me, and 'tis most meet[4] you should.

GENTLEWOMAN. Neither to you nor anyone, having no witness to confirm my speech.

[*Enter* LADY MACBETH, *with a taper.*]

  Lo you, here she comes! This is her very guise,[5] and, upon my
20   life, fast asleep! Observe her; stand close.[6]

DOCTOR. How came she by that light?

GENTLEWOMAN. Why, it stood by her. She has light by her continually. 'Tis her command.

25 **DOCTOR.** You see, her eyes are open.

▲ Critical Viewing
Who will slay Macbeth with a sword like this one? **[Predict]**

1. **field** battlefield.
2. **closet** chest.

Vocabulary
perturbation (pʉr´ tər bā´ shən) *n.* disturbance

3. **effects of watching** deeds of one awake.
4. **meet** suitable.

5. **guise** custom.
6. **close** hidden.

Reading Check

Why has the gentlewoman summoned the doctor?

GENTLEWOMAN. Ay, but their sense[7] are shut.

DOCTOR. What is it she does now? Look, how she rubs her hands.

GENTLEWOMAN. It is an accustomed action with her,
30   to seem thus washing her hands: I have known her
    continue in this a quarter of an hour.

LADY MACBETH. Yet here's a spot.

DOCTOR. Hark! She speaks. I will set down what comes
35   from her, to satisfy[8] my remembrance the more strongly.

LADY MACBETH. Out, damned spot! Out, I say! One: two:
    why, then 'tis time to do 't. Hell is murky. Fie, my
    lord, fie! A soldier, and afeard? What need we fear
    who knows it, when none can call our pow'r to
40   accompt?[9] Yet who would have thought the old man
    to have had so much blood in him?

DOCTOR. Do you mark that?

LADY MACBETH. The Thane of Fife had a wife. Where is
    she now? What, will these hands ne'er be clean? No
45   more o' that, my lord, no more o' that! You mar all
    with this starting.

DOCTOR. Go to, go to! You have known what you should not.

GENTLEWOMAN. She has spoke what she should not, I am
50   sure of that. Heaven knows what she has known.

LADY MACBETH. Here's the smell of the blood still. All the
    perfumes of Arabia will not sweeten this little hand.
    Oh, oh, oh!

55 **DOCTOR.** What a sigh is there! The heart is sorely charged.[10]

GENTLEWOMAN. I would not have such a heart in my
    bosom for the dignity[11] of the whole body.

DOCTOR. Well, well, well—

GENTLEWOMAN. Pray God it be, sir.

60 **DOCTOR.** This disease is beyond my practice. Yet I have
    known those which have walked in their sleep who
    have died holily in their beds.

LADY MACBETH. Wash your hands; put on your nightgown;
    look not so pale! I tell you yet again, Banquo's
65   buried. He cannot come out on 's[12] grave.

DOCTOR. Even so?

LADY MACBETH. To bed, to bed! There's knocking at
    the gate. Come, come, come, come, give me your hand!

7. **sense** powers of sight.

8. **satisfy** support.

9. **to accompt** into account.

Literary Analysis
Shakespearean Tragedy
Does the sleepwalking scene suggest that Lady Macbeth is a tragic heroine? Explain.

10. **charged** burdened.

11. **dignity** worth.

◀ **Critical Viewing**
Identify four details from the sleepwalking scene (V, i) the artist illustrates in this picture. **[Connect]**

12. **on 's** of his.

Reading Check

What does Lady Macbeth do and say as she sleepwalks?

70   What's done cannot be undone. To bed, to bed, to bed!

                                                            [*Exit* LADY MACBETH.]

DOCTOR. Will she go now to bed?

GENTLEWOMAN. Directly.

DOCTOR. Foul whisp'rings are abroad. Unnatural deeds
    Do breed unnatural troubles. Infected minds
    To their deaf pillows will discharge their secrets.
75   More needs she the divine than the physician.
    God, God forgive us all! Look after her;
    Remove from her the means of all annoyance,[13]
    And still keep eyes upon her. So good night.
    My mind she has mated[14] and amazed my sight:
80   I think, but dare not speak.

GENTLEWOMAN.   Good night, good doctor.

                                                               [*Exit.*]

Scene ii. *The country near Dunsinane.*

[*Drum and colors. Enter* MENTEITH, CAITHNESS, ANGUS, LENNOX, SOLDIERS.]

MENTEITH. The English pow'r[1] is near, led on by Malcolm,
    His uncle Siward and the good Macduff.
    Revenges burn in them; for their dear causes
    Would to the bleeding and the grim alarm
    Excite the mortified man.[2]

5 **ANGUS.**   Near Birnam Wood
    Shall we well meet them; that way are they coming.

CAITHNESS. Who knows if Donalbain be with his brother?

LENNOX. For certain, sir, he is not. I have a file[3]
    Of all the gentry: there is Siward's son,
10   And many unrough[4] youths that even now
    Protest[5] their first of manhood.

MENTEITH.   What does the tyrant?

CAITHNESS. Great Dunsinane he strongly fortifies.
    Some say he's mad; others, that lesser hate him,
    Do call it valiant fury: but, for certain,
15   He cannot buckle his distempered cause
    Within the belt of rule.[6]

ANGUS.   Now does he feel
    His secret murders sticking on his hands;
    Now minutely revolts upbraid his faith-breach.[7]
    Those he commands move only in command,
20   Nothing in love. Now does he feel his title

Reading Strategy
Relating a Work to the Issues of Its Period
What can you infer about medicine during this time from the doctor's words in lines 72–80?

13. annoyance injury.

14. mated baffled.

1. pow'r army.

2. Would . . . man would incite a dead man to join the bloody, grim call to arms.

3. file list.

4. unrough beardless.

5. Protest assert.

Literary Analysis
Shakespearean Tragedy
Do you agree with those whom Caithness quotes in Scene ii, line 13? Is Macbeth "mad"? Why or why not?

6. rule self-control.

7. minutely . . . faith-breach every minute revolts rebuke his disloyalty.

Hang loose about him, like a giant's robe
Upon a dwarfish thief.

MENTEITH.   Who then shall blame
His pestered[8] senses to recoil and start,
When all that is within him does condemn
Itself for being there?

25 **CAITHNESS.**   Well, march we on,
To give obedience where 'tis truly owed.
Meet we the med'cine of the sickly weal,[9]
And with him pour we, in our country's purge,
Each drop of us.[10]

LENNOX.   Or so much as it needs
30 To dew the sovereign flower and drown the weeds.[11]
Make we our march towards Birnam.

[*Exit, marching.*]

Scene iii. Dunsinane. In the castle.

[*Enter* MACBETH, DOCTOR, *and* ATTENDANTS.]

MACBETH. Bring me no more reports; let them fly all![1]
Till Birnam Wood remove to Dunsinane
I cannot taint[2] with fear. What's the boy Malcolm?
Was he not born of woman? The spirits that know
5 All mortal consequences[3] have pronounced me thus:
"Fear not, Macbeth; no man that's born of woman
Shall e'er have power upon thee." Then fly, false thanes,
And mingle with the English epicures.[4]
The mind I sway[5] by and the heart I bear
10 Shall never sag with doubt nor shake with fear.

[*Enter* SERVANT.]

The devil damn thee black, thou cream-faced loon.[6]
Where got'st thou that goose look?

SERVANT. There is ten thousand—

MACBETH.   Geese, villain?

SERVANT.   Soldiers, sir.

MACBETH. Go prick thy face and over-red thy fear.
15 Thou lily-livered boy. What soldiers, patch?[7]
Death of thy soul! Those linen[8] cheeks of thine
Are counselors to fear. What soldiers, whey-face?

SERVANT. The English force, so please you.

MACBETH. Take thy face hence.   [*Exit* SERVANT.]

Seyton!—I am sick at heart.

8. **pestered** tormented.

Vocabulary
recoil (ri koil´) *v.* to draw back in fear, surprise, or disgust

9. **med'cine . . . weal**
Malcolm and his supporters are "the medicine" that will heal "the sickly" commonwealth.

10. **Each . . . us** every last drop of our blood.

11. **dew . . . weeds** water the royal flower (Malcolm) and drown the weeds (Macbeth).

1. **let . . . all** let them all desert me!

2. **taint** become infected.

3. **mortal consequences** future human events.

4. **epicures** gluttons.

5. **sway** move.

6. **loon** fool.

7. **patch** fool.

8. **linen** pale as linen.

Reading Check
Why is Macbeth unafraid even though Malcolm's army is marching against him?

9. **push** effort.

10. **disseat** unthrone.

11. **the sear** withered state.

Literary Analysis
Shakespearean Tragedy
Do lines 20–28 evoke
sympathy for Macbeth?
Explain.

12. **moe** more.

13. **skirr** scour.

Reading Strategy
**Relating a Work to the
Issues of Its Period**
Would a modern psychiatrist
answer as the doctor does
in lines 45–46? Why or why
not?

14. **Raze out** erase.

Vocabulary
antidote (an´ tə dōt´)
n. remedy

20   When I behold—Seyton, I say!—This push[9]
Will cheer me ever, or disseat[10] me now.
I have lived long enough. My way of life
Is fall'n into the sear,[11] the yellow leaf,
And that which should accompany old age,
25   As honor, love, obedience, troops of friends,
I must not look to have; but, in their stead,
Curses not loud but deep, mouth-honor, breath,
Which the poor heart would fain deny, and dare not.
Seyton!

[*Enter* SEYTON.]

SEYTON. What's your gracious pleasure?

30   **MACBETH.**   What news more?

SEYTON. All is confirmed, my lord, which was reported.

MACBETH. I'll fight, till from my bones my flesh be hacked.
Give me my armor.

SEYTON.   'Tis not needed yet.

MACBETH. I'll put it on.
35   Send out moe[12] horses, skirr[13] the country round.
Hang those that talk of fear. Give me mine armor.
How does your patient, doctor?

DOCTOR.   Not so sick, my lord,
As she is troubled with thick-coming fancies
That keep her from her rest.

MACBETH.   Cure her of that.
40   Canst thou not minister to a mind diseased,
Pluck from the memory a rooted sorrow,
Raze out[14] the written troubles of the brain,
And with some sweet oblivious antidote
Cleanse the stuffed bosom of that perilous stuff
Which weighs upon the heart?

DOCTOR.   Therein the patient
45   Must minister to himself.

MACBETH. Throw physic[15] to the dogs, I'll none of it.
       Come, put mine armor on. Give me my staff.
       Seyton, send out.—Doctor, the thanes fly from me.—
50   Come, sir, dispatch. If thou couldst, doctor, cast
       The water[16] of my land, find her disease
       And purge it to a sound and *pristine* health,
       I would applaud thee to the very echo,
       That should applaud again.—Pull 't off,[17] I say.—
55   What rhubarb, senna, or what purgative drug,
       Would scour these English hence? Hear'st thou of them?

DOCTOR. Ay, my good lord; your royal preparation
       Makes us hear something.

MACBETH.   Bring it[18] after me.
       I will not be afraid of death and bane[19]
60   Till Birnam Forest come to Dunsinane.

DOCTOR. [*Aside*] Were I from Dunsinane away and clear,
       Profit again should hardly draw me here.   [*Exit.*]

Scene iv. *Country near Birnam Wood.*

[*Drum and colors. Enter* MALCOLM, SIWARD, MACDUFF, SIWARD'S SON,
MENTEITH, CAITHNESS, ANGUS, *and* SOLDIERS, *marching.*]

MALCOLM. Cousins, I hope the days are near at hand
       That chambers will be safe.[1]

MENTEITH.   We doubt it nothing.

SIWARD. What wood is this before us?

MENTEITH.   The Wood of Birnam.

MALCOLM. Let every soldier hew him down a bough
5   And bear 't before him. Thereby shall we shadow[2]
       The numbers of our host, and make discovery[3]
       Err in report of us.

SOLDIERS.   It shall be done.

SIWARD. We learn no other but the confident tyrant
       Keeps still in Dunsinane, and will endure
       Our setting down before 't.[4]

10 **MALCOLM.**   'Tis his main hope,
       For where there is advantage to be given
       Both more and less[5] have given him the revolt,
       And none serve with him but constrained things
       Whose hearts are absent too.

Side notes:

15. **physic** medicine.

16. **cast the water** diagnose the illness.

Vocabulary
pristine (pris´ tēn´) *adj.*
original; unspoiled

17. **Pull 't off** Pull off a piece of armor, which has been put on incorrectly in Macbeth's haste.

18. **it** his armor.

19. **bane** destruction.

Literary Analysis
Shakespearean Tragedy
How does Malcolm's order in Scene iv, lines 4–7 increase the sense of tension surrounding the play's outcome and Macbeth's fate?

1. **That . . . safe** that people will be safe in their own homes.

2. **shadow** conceal.

3. **discovery** those who see us.

4. **setting down before 't** laying seige to it.

5. **more and less** people of high and low rank.

Reading Check
How will Malcolm's men disguise themselves?

MACDUFF.   Let our just censures
15   Attend the true event,[6] and put we on
      Industrious soldiership.

SIWARD.   The time approaches,
      That will with due decision make us know
      What we shall say we have and what we owe.[7]
      Thoughts speculative their unsure hopes relate,

20   But certain issue strokes must arbitrate:[8]
      Towards which advance the war.[9]   [*Exit, marching.*]

Scene v. Dunsinane. Within the castle.

[*Enter* MACBETH, SEYTON, *and* SOLDIERS, *with drum and colors.*]

MACBETH. Hang out our banners on the outward walls.
      The cry is still "They come!" Our castle's strength
      Will laugh a siege to scorn. Here let them lie
      Till famine and the ague[1] eat them up.

5   Were they not forced[2] with those that should be ours,
      We might have met them dareful,[3] beard to beard,
      And beat them backward home.

                    [*A cry within of women.*]

                                    What is that noise?

SEYTON. It is the cry of women, my good lord.   [*Exit.*]

MACBETH. I have almost forgot the taste of fears:
10   The time has been, my senses would have cooled
      To hear a night-shriek, and my fell[4] of hair

      Would at a dismal treatise[5] rouse and stir

LITERATURE IN CONTEXT

History Connection

The Real Macbeth

The real Macbeth, who ruled Scotland from 1040 to 1057, did, in fact, become king by killing King Duncan. However, Macbeth's claim to the throne was legitimate due to the ancient Scottish custom of tanistry.

   According to this system, the ablest, oldest male in an extended royal family could declare war on his competitors for the crown. The real Macbeth declared war on King Duncan and killed him fairly in battle. Eventually, Duncan's son Malcolm led a Northumbrian invasion force into Scotland. In 1057, he killed Macbeth.

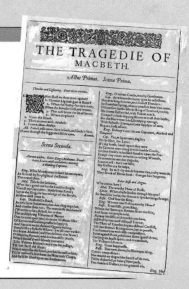

Connect to the Literature

Use this history of the real Macbeth to predict the end of the play.

As life were in 't. I have supped full with horrors.
Direness, familiar to my slaughterous thoughts,
Cannot once start⁶ me.

[*Enter* SEYTON.]

15   Wherefore was that cry?

SEYTON. The queen, my lord, is dead.

MACBETH. She should⁷ have died hereafter;
There would have been a time for such a word.⁸
Tomorrow, and tomorrow, and tomorrow
20   Creeps in this petty pace from day to day,
To the last syllable of recorded time;
And all our yesterdays have lighted fools
The way to dusty death. Out, out, brief candle!
Life's but a walking shadow, a poor player
25   That struts and frets his hour upon the stage
And then is heard no more. It is a tale
Told by an idiot, full of sound and fury
Signifying nothing.

[*Enter a* MESSENGER.]

Thou com'st to use thy tongue; thy story quickly!

30 **MESSENGER.** Gracious my lord,
I should report that which I say I saw,
But know not how to do 't.

MACBETH.   Well, say, sir.

MESSENGER. As I did stand my watch upon the hill,
I looked toward Birnam, and anon, methought,
The wood began to move.

35 **MACBETH.**   Liar and slave!

MESSENGER. Let me endure your wrath, if 't be not so.
Within this three mile may you see it coming;
I say a moving grove.

MACBETH.   If thou speak'st false,
Upon the next tree shalt thou hang alive,
40   Till famine cling⁹ thee. If thy speech be sooth,¹⁰
I care not if thou dost for me as much.
I pull in resolution, and begin
To doubt th' equivocation of the fiend
That lies like truth: "Fear not, till Birnam Wood
45   Do come to Dunsinane!" And now a wood
Comes toward Dunsinane. Arm, arm, and out!
If this which he avouches¹¹ does appear,
There is nor flying hence nor tarrying here.

---

6. start startle.

7. should inevitably would.

8. word message.

Literary Analysis
Shakespearean Tragedy and the Tragic Impulse
This speech in lines 17–28 is a powerful expression of life's futility. Is Macbeth's story really "a tale/Told by an idiot, full of sound and fury/Signifying nothing"? Why or why not?

Literary Analysis
Shakespearean Tragedy
In lines 42–50, how does Macbeth's allusion to the witches' prophecies disclose a growing awareness of his own doom?

9. cling wither.

10. sooth truth.

11. avouches asserts.

Reading Check

To what two things does Macbeth compare life when he hears Lady Macbeth is dead?

▶ **Critical Viewing**
Do you think this picture
portrays the fight between
Macbeth and Young
Siward (V, vii, 10–11) or
that between Macbeth and
Macduff (V, viii, 34–35)?
Explain. **[Make a Judgment]**

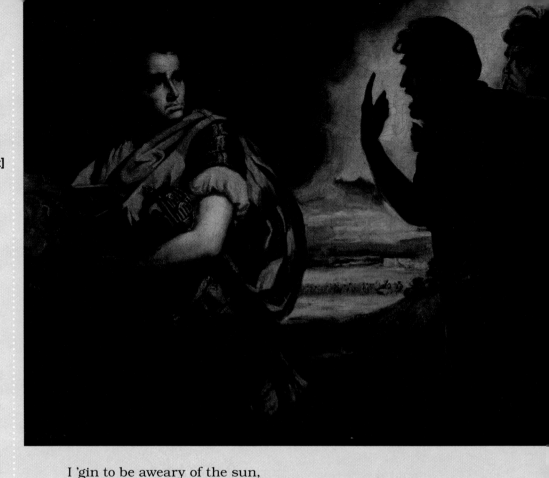

I 'gin to be aweary of the sun,
50   And wish th' estate o' th' world were now undone.
Ring the alarum bell! Blow wind, come wrack!
At least we'll die with harness[12] on our back.   [*Exit.*]

12. harness armor.

Scene vi. Dunsinane. Before the castle.

[*Drum and colors. Enter* MALCOLM, SIWARD, MACDUFF, *and their army,
with boughs.*]

MALCOLM. Now near enough. Your leavy[1] screens throw down,
And show like those you are. You, worthy uncle,
Shall, with my cousin, your right noble son,
Lead our first battle.[2] Worthy Macduff and we
5   Shall take upon 's what else remains to do,
According to our order.[3]

1. leavy leafy.

2. battle battalion.

3. order plan.

SIWARD.   Fare you well.
Do we find the tyrant's power[4] tonight,
Let us be beaten, if we cannot fight.

4. power forces.

MACDUFF. Make all our trumpets speak; give them all breath.
10   Those clamorous harbingers of blood and death.

[*Exit. Alarums continued.*]

Vocabulary
clamorous (klam´ ər əs)
adj. noisy

harbingers (här´ bin jərz)
n. forerunners

Scene vii. *Another part of the field.*

[*Enter* MACBETH.]

MACBETH. They have tied me to a stake; I cannot fly,
But bearlike I must fight the course.¹ What's he
That was not born of woman? Such a one
Am I to fear, or none.

[*Enter* YOUNG SIWARD.]

YOUNG SIWARD. What is thy name?

5 **MACBETH.**   Thou'lt be afraid to hear it.

YOUNG SIWARD. No; though thou call'st thyself a hotter name
Than any is in hell.

MACBETH.   My name's Macbeth.

YOUNG SIWARD. The devil himself could not pronounce a title
More hateful to mine ear.

MACBETH.   No, nor more fearful.

10 **YOUNG SIWARD.** Thou liest, abhorrèd tyrant; with my sword
I'll prove the lie thou speak'st.

[*Fight, and* YOUNG SIWARD *slain.*]

MACBETH.   Thou wast born of woman.
But swords I smile at, weapons laugh to scorn,
Brandished by man that's of a woman born.   [*Exit.*]

[*Alarums. Enter* MACDUFF.]

MACDUFF. That way the noise is. Tyrant, show thy face!
15 If thou be'st slain and with no stroke of mine,
My wife and children's ghosts will haunt me still.
I cannot strike at wretched kerns, whose arms
Are hired to bear their staves.² Either thou, Macbeth,
Or else my sword, with an unbattered edge,
20 I sheathe again undeeded.³ There thou shouldst be;
By this great clatter, one of greatest note
Seems bruited.⁴ Let me find him, Fortune!
And more I beg not.   [*Exit. Alarums.*]

[*Enter* MALCOLM *and* SIWARD.]

SIWARD. This way, my lord. The castle's gently rend'red:⁵
25 The tyrant's people on both sides do fight;
The noble thanes do bravely in the war;
The day almost itself professes yours,
And little is to do.

MALCOLM.   We have met with foes
That strike beside us.⁶

1. **bearlike . . . course** like a bear chained to a stake being attacked by dogs, I must fight until the end.

Literary Analysis
Shakespearean Tragedy
In Scene vii, does Macbeth show signs of bravery or is he just overconfident because of what the witches said? Explain.

2. **staves** spears.

3. **undeeded** unused.

4. **bruited** reported.

5. **gently rend'red** easily surrendered.

6. **strike . . . us** deliberately miss us.

Reading Check

What is the outcome of the hand-to-hand combat between Macbeth and Young Siward?

SIWARD.   Enter, sir, the castle.

[*Exit. Alarum.*]

Scene viii. Another part of the field.

[*Enter* MACBETH.]

MACBETH. Why should I play the Roman fool, and die
  On mine own sword?[1] Whiles I see lives,[2] the gashes
  Do better upon them.

[*Enter* MACDUFF.]

MACDUFF.   Turn, hell-hound, turn!

MACBETH. Of all men else I have avoided thee.
5   But get thee back! My soul is too much charged
  With blood of thine already.

MACDUFF.   I have no words:
  My voice is in my sword, thou bloodier villain
  Than terms can give thee out![3]

                [*Fight. Alarum.*]

MACBETH.   Thou losest labor:
  As easy mayst thou the intrenchant[4] air
10   With thy keen sword impress[5] as make me bleed:
  Let fall thy blade on vulnerable crests;
  I bear a charmèd life, which must not yield
  To one of woman born.

MACDUFF.   Despair thy charm,
  And let the angel[6] whom thou still hast served
15   Tell thee, Macduff was from his mother's womb
  Untimely ripped.[7]

MACBETH. Accursèd be that tongue that tells me so,
  For it hath cowed my better part of man![8]
  And be these juggling fiends no more believed,
20   That palter[9] with us in a double sense;
  That keep the word of promise to our ear,
  And break it to our hope. I'll not fight with thee.

MACDUFF. Then yield thee, coward,
  And live to be the show and gaze o' th' time:[10]
25   We'll have thee, as our rarer monsters[11] are,
  Painted upon a pole,[12] and underwrit,
  "Here may you see the tyrant."

MACBETH.   I will not yield,
  To kiss the ground before young Malcolm's feet,
  And to be baited with the rabble's curse.
30   Though Birnam Wood be come to Dunsinane,

---

1. **play . . . sword** die like Brutus or Cassius, who killed themselves with their own swords in the moment of defeat.

2. **Whiles . . . lives** so long as I see living men.

3. **terms . . . out** words can describe you.

4. **intrenchant** incapable of being cut.

5. **impress** make a dent in.

Vocabulary
vulnerable (vul´ nər ə bəl) *adj.* exposed to attack or harm

6. **angel** fallen angel; fiend.

7. **his . . . ripped** Macduff's mother died before giving birth to him.

8. **better . . . man** courage.

9. **palter** juggle.

10. **gaze o' th' time** spectacle of the age.

11. **monsters** freaks.

12. **Painted . . . pole** pictured on a banner stuck on a pole by a showman's booth.

And thou opposed, being of no woman born,
Yet I will try the last. Before my body
I throw my warlike shield. Lay on, Macduff;
And damned be him that first cries "Hold, enough!"

[*Exit, fighting. Alarums.*]

[*Re-enter fighting, and* MACBETH *slain. Exit* MACDUFF, *with* MACBETH.
Retreat and flourish.[13] *Enter, with drum and colors,*
MALCOLM, SIWARD, ROSS, THANES, *and* SOLDIERS.]

13. *Retreat and flourish*
trumpet call to withdraw
and fanfare.

35 **MALCOLM.** I would the friends we miss were safe arrived.

SIWARD. Some must go off;[14] and yet, by these I see,
So great a day as this is cheaply bought.

14. **go off** die.

MALCOLM. Macduff is missing, and your noble son.

ROSS. Your son, my lord, has paid a soldier's debt:
40   He only lived but till he was a man;
The which no sooner had his prowess confirmed
In the unshrinking station[15] where he fought,
But like a man he died.

15. **unshrinking station**
place where he stood
firmly.

SIWARD.   Then he is dead?

ROSS. Ay, and brought off the field. Your cause of sorrow
45   Must not be measured by his worth, for then
It hath no end.

SIWARD.   Had he his hurts before?

ROSS. Ay, on the front.

SIWARD.   Why then, God's soldier be he!
Had I as many sons as I have hairs,
I would not wish them to a fairer death:
And so his knell is knolled.

Reading Strategy
**Relating a Work to the
Issues of Its Period**
What does Siward's reaction
to the death of his son
reveal about the values of
patriotism and honor at this
time (lines 47–53)?

50 **MALCOLM.**   He's worth more sorrow,
And that I'll spend for him.

SIWARD.   He's worth no more:
They say he parted well and paid his score:
And so God be with him! Here comes newer comfort.

[*Enter* MACDUFF, *with* MACBETH'S *head.*]

MACDUFF. Hail, King! for so thou art: behold, where stands
55   Th' usurper's cursèd head. The time is free.[16]
I see thee compassed with thy kingdom's pearl,[17]
That speak my salutation in their minds,
Whose voices I desire aloud with mine:
Hail, King of Scotland!

16. **The . . . free** Our country
is liberated.

17. **compassed . . . pearl**
surrounded by the noblest
people in the kingdom.

ALL.   Hail, King of Scotland!

[*Flourish.*]

Reading
Check
Who finally slays Macbeth?

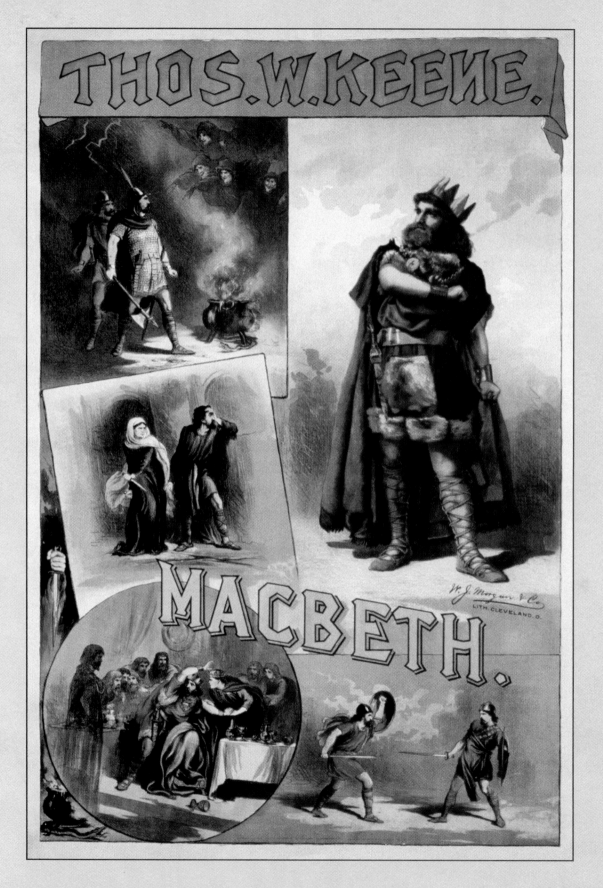

60 **MALCOLM.** We shall not spend a large expense of time
        Before we reckon with your several loves,[18]
        And make us even with you.[19] My thanes and kinsmen,
        Henceforth be earls, the first that ever Scotland
        In such an honor named. What's more to do,
65   Which would be planted newly with the time[20]—
        As calling home our exiled friends abroad
        That fled the snares of watchful tyranny,
        Producing forth the cruel ministers
        Of this dead butcher and his fiendlike queen,
70   Who, as 'tis thought, by self and violent hands
        Took off her life—this, and what needful else
        That calls upon us, by the grace of Grace
        We will perform in measure, time, and place:[21]
        So thanks to all at once and to each one,
75   Whom we invite to see us crowned at Scone.

[*Flourish. Exit all.*]

18. **reckon . . . loves** reward
each of you for your devotion.

19. **make . . . you** pay what
we owe you.

20. **What's . . . time** what
remains to be done at the
beginning of this new age.

21. **in measure . . . place**
fittingly at the appropriate
time and place.

◀ **Critical Viewing**
Based on the scenes shown
in the poster, summarize the
play. **[Summarize]**

Critical Reading

Cite textual
evidence to
support your
responses.

1. **Key Ideas and Details (a)** What does the doctor see in the
sleepwalking scene, and what does he speculate about the causes
for what he sees? **(b) Analyze:** How have Macbeth and Lady
Macbeth reversed roles by the end of the play?

2. **Key Ideas and Details (a)** What does Macbeth say when he
hears of Lady Macbeth's death? **(b) Draw Conclusions:** What
does his reaction to her death reveal about their relationship and
his state of mind?

3. **Key Ideas and Details (a)** What does Macbeth say about the
witches when he learns that Birnam Wood is apparently moving and that Macduff "was from his mother's womb / Untimely
ripped"? **(b) Infer:** What growing realization do these statements
about the witches seem to reflect? **(c) Draw Conclusions:** What is
Macbeth's state of mind in his final battle with Macduff? Explain.

4. **Craft and Structure (a)** What occurs in Act V, Scene viii,
lines 35–75? **(b) Evaluate:** Would the play be complete if it ended
with Macbeth's death but omitted these lines? Why or why not?

5. **Integration of Knowledge and Ideas** Do you think a tragedy
could be written about an ordinary person living today? Why or
why not?

6. **Integration of Knowledge and Ideas** How do Shakespeare's
use of comic relief and his revealing of Macbeth's inner turmoil
add new dimensions to tragedy? In responding, use at least two of
these Essential Question words: *noble, downfall, tradition, classics.*
*[Connecting to the Essential Question: What is the relation-
ship of the writer to tradition?]*

After You Read *Macbeth, Act V*

Literary Analysis

**Common Core
State Standards**

Language
4.c. Consult general and specialized reference materials, both print and digital, to find the pronunciation of a word or determine or clarify its precise meaning, its part of speech, its etymology, or its standard usage. *(p. 417)*

Ⓒ 1. **Craft and Structure** Identify all the elements of **Shakespearean tragedy** in *Macbeth,* citing examples from the play.

Ⓒ 2. **Key Ideas and Details** Use a chart like this one to show how Banquo's response to the witches emphasizes Macbeth's **tragic flaw.**

Ⓒ 3. **Key Ideas and Details** What role does Lady Macbeth play in Macbeth's choice of evil?

Ⓒ 4. **Key Ideas and Details** **(a)** How does Macbeth's tragic flaw lead him to disaster? **(b)** Once Macbeth kills Duncan, can he turn back? Why or why not?

Ⓒ 5. **Key Ideas and Details** Find three passages that show how Macbeth's imagination adds to the tragedy. Support your choices.

Ⓒ 6. **Integration of Knowledge and Ideas** **(a)** What positive qualities does Macbeth display in Act V? Explain. **(b)** How do Macbeth's positive qualities contribute to the **tragic impulse** revealed in the play?

Ⓒ 7. **Integration of Knowledge and Ideas** In what way does the tragic impulse involve going beyond limitations? Support your answer with references to the play.

Reading Strategy

8. **Relate the play to the major themes and issues of its period** by answering these questions: **(a)** How does the belief in witches influence the setting and the characters? **(b)** How do Elizabethan beliefs in the importance of order add to the tragedy?

9. **(a)** What do the doctor's remarks lead you to infer about Elizabethan concepts of and treatments for mental illness? **(b)** Compare and contrast Elizabethan concepts of mental illness with those of today.

Integrated Language Skills

ⓒ Vocabulary Acquisition and Use

Word Analysis: Latin Root -turb-

The root -turb- means "to disturb." To experience *perturbation* is to experience "a great disturbance." Knowing the meaning of the root -turb-, define the italicized words below. Then, verify your definitions with a dictionary.

1. At the beginning of the play, a captain reports on the *turbulence* of the battle that is being fought.
2. As the events in *Macbeth* suggest, the Middle Ages was a *turbulent* period in the history of Scotland.
3. Elizabethans believed that a *perturbation* in the heavens meant disorder in society.
4. Macbeth's reaction shows he is extremely *perturbed* by Fleance's escape.
5. After being stirred, the witches' potion was *turbid*.

Using Resources to Build Vocabulary

Descriptive Adjectives: Words Relating to Tragedy

The genre of tragedy carries its own lexicon, or vocabulary. This lexicon includes words—many of them Greek in origin—that relate to different elements of the form or to aspects of the tragic characters themselves. Here are some of these words:

agon	chorus
apostrophe	hamartia
catastrophe	hubris
catharsis	peripeteia

Use a dictionary or a digital resource to look up the meanings of these words, and record their definitions. Then, write a brief description of *Macbeth* using at least three of the words.

Vocabulary: Sentence Completion

Use a word from the vocabulary list on page 400 to complete the sentence, and explain your choice. Use each word only once.

1. The movement of Birnam Wood began with a _____ rustling of trees.
2. The first trees that approached Dunsinane were _____ of the army that followed.
3. Farmers were shocked to see the untouched, _____ wood suddenly move.
4. The trees' unexpected motion made several of the farmers _____ in amazement.
5. This shocking event also made them feel _____ to other strange happenings.
6. They all confessed to a feeling of _____ in their hearts.
7. It was a feeling for which there was no _____.

"It is a tale told by an idiot, full of sound and fury, signifying nothing, and No. 1 on the best-seller list."

PERFORMANCE TASKS
Integrated Language Skills

Writing

 Argumentative Text Shakespeare critic Stephen Greenblatt has this to say about Macbeth's plot to assassinate King Duncan:

> The lure is strong enough . . . to make him ignore the threat of divine judgment in the afterlife, but still for a fateful moment he holds back:
>
> *We still have judgement here, that we but teach*
> *Bloody instructions which, being taught, return*
> *To plague th'inventor.*
>
> . . . [I]t is not in some imagined other world that your actions will be judged; it is here and now. Judgment in effect means punishment: whatever violent or dishonest things you do will inevitably serve as a lesson for others to do to you.

In an **analytical essay**, evaluate Greenblatt's commentary. Do you agree that Macbeth dreads the earthly consequences of his actions more than he dreads the fate of his soul—or do you think the opposite is true?

Prewriting Use these steps as you prepare to draft your essay:

- Skim the text, looking for imagery, language, or other stylistic devices that shed light on the nature of Macbeth's crisis. Make a list of these elements.

- Review your list as a whole, and decide whether it supports Greenblatt's conclusion, supports the opposite conclusion, or strikes you as utterly ambiguous. If you decide in favor of ambiguity, ask yourself what thematic purpose such ambiguity might serve.

- Express your position in a sentence or two.

Drafting Introduce the drama, Greenblatt's opinion, and your own. Then, choose two or three key passages to analyze. As you draft, refer to your strongest evidence by quoting it.

Revising Review your draft to ensure that you have considered not only the literal meanings of Macbeth's words, but also any underlying currents of tone, mood, or irony. Could subtle elements of your key passages lead someone to draw a different conclusion? If so, revise to anticipate and address these potential interpretations. Finally, be sure you include correct references and citations.

© **Common Core State Standards**

Writing

1.a. Introduce precise, knowledgeable claim(s), establish the significance of the claim(s), distinguish the claim(s) from alternate or opposing claims, and create an organization that logically sequences claim(s), counterclaims, reasons, and evidence.

5. Develop and strengthen writing as needed by planning, focusing on addressing what is most significant for a specific purpose and audience.

Language

1. Demonstrate command of the conventions of standard English grammar and usage when writing or speaking. *(p. 419)*

Model: Including References and Citations

As he contemplates the murder of Duncan, Macbeth expresses a concern for eternal consequences—namely, damnation. He speculates that Duncan has been "So clear in his great office, / that his virtues / Will plead like angels trumpet-tongued against / The deep damnation of his taking-off" (I.vii.18–20). Even as Macbeth worries about damnation, though, he is more worried that "pity... Shall blow the horrid deed in every eye," here on earth.

A direct reference to Macbeth's first soliloquy strengthens the analysis. Parenthetical citations indicate act, scene, and line numbers.

Conventions and Style: Adjective and Adverb Clauses

A subordinate clause that modifies a noun or pronoun is called an **adjective clause.** Adjective clauses tell *what kind* or *which one* about the word they modify. When you see a relative pronoun or a relative adjective at the beginning of a subordinate clause, you may be looking at an adjective clause.

Using Adjective and Adverb Clauses

Example: Macbeth kills Duncan, *who is the king of Scotland.*

The adjective clause, introduced by the relative pronoun *who*, modifies the proper noun *Duncan.*

An **adverb clause** is a subordinate clause that modifies a verb, adjective, adverb, or verbal by telling *where, when, in what way, to what extent, under what condition,* or *why.* Adverb clauses start with subordinating conjunctions such as *although, as if, before, unless, wherever,* and *while.*

Example: *Until he heard the witches' prophecy,* Macbeth harbored no thoughts of murder.

Here, the adverb clause modifies the verb *harbored.* The subordinating conjunction is *until.*

Punctuation Tip: When an adverb clause starts a sentence, it is followed by a comma. If an adverb clause ends a sentence, it is usually not preceded by a comma.

Practice Identify each adjective clause and each adverb clause, and tell what word or words it modifies.

1. They encounter the three witches as they are crossing a moor.
2. He remembers everything that the witches have said.
3. Lady Macbeth's ambition is even greater than her husband's.
4. The bloody dagger seems to lead him to the room where the king sleeps.
5. Macbeth becomes king after he kills Duncan.
6. Lady Macbeth, who is plagued by guilt, starts walking in her sleep.
7. She cannot clean the imaginary bloodstains that she sees on her hands.
8. When Macbeth hears of his wife's death, he falls into a state of despair.
9. He hires murderers because he sees Banquo as a threat.
10. Macduff joins Prince Malcolm, who has raised an army to challenge the tyrannical new king.

Ⓒ **Writing and Speaking Conventions** _____

A. Writing Use each subordinate clause below in a sentence. Then tell which word the clause modifies and what type of clause it is.

1. after he wins a military battle
2. who ruled Scotland
3. because his wife persuaded him

   Example: after he wins a military battle

   Sentence: After he wins a military battle, Macbeth is made Thane of Cawdor.

   Word Modified; Type of Clause: is made; adverb clause

B. Speaking Describe a set design for your favorite scene from *Macbeth.* Include at least one adjective clause and one adverb clause.

PH WRITING COACH

Further instruction and practice are available in *Prentice Hall Writing Coach.*

THE CHANGING TRAGIC HERO

RENAISSANCE ENGLAND
The Tragedy of Macbeth
—William Shakespeare (1564 – 1616)

ANCIENT GREECE
Oedipus the King
—Sophocles (496–406 B.C.)

EARLY 19TH-CENTURY GERMANY
Faust
—Johann Wolfgang von Goethe (1749–1832)

LATE 19TH-CENTURY NORWAY
A Doll's House
—Henrik Ibsen (1828–1906)

20TH-CENTURY AMERICA
Death of a Salesman
—Arthur Miller (1915–2005)

Comparing Literary Works

from *Macbeth* by William Shakespeare
• from *Oedipus the King* by Sophocles •
from *Faust* by Wolfgang Von Goethe

Comparing Tragedy Past and Present

Tragedy Tragedy had its origins in ancient Greece, where Aeschylus, Sophocles, and Euripides created immortal verse dramas. Greek tragedy typically featured a high-born figure (called the **tragic hero**) whose **tragic flaw**—a mistake or unwise decision—leads to ruin. The audience felt sorrow and pity for the hero's plight. A chorus commented on the action, and fate or supernatural elements also played a role.

Rediscovered in the Renaissance, ancient tragedies served as models for a golden age of European drama, including the masterpieces of Shakespeare. In the nineteenth century, Romantic verse tragedies, like Goethe's *Faust*, focused on the protagonist's urge to go beyond all limits. Later in the century, this type of drama gave way to modern realistic tragedies like those of Ibsen and Chekhov. Such tragedies featured ordinary heroes whose downfall stemmed from social ills. More recent playwrights, like Arthur Miller, continued in this realistic vein.

As you read the selections from *Oedipus the King* and *Faust*, use a chart like the one shown to compare them to Shakespeare's *Macbeth*.

	Macbeth	*Oedipus*	*Faust*
tragic hero	Scottish nobleman		
tragic flaw	murders king and others due to excessive ambition		
fate/supernatural elements	witches and apparitions predict the future		
style elements	verse for high-born characters; soliloquies; asides; no chorus		

© Gather Vocabulary Knowledge

The words *account, reckoning, infinite,* and *constitutionally* appear in these excerpts. Use a **dictionary** to find each word's definition. Then, use other references to explore these words:

- **Specialized Dictionaries:** Use specialized dictionaries, such as those that focus on politics, to discover whether the words have technical meanings. When you encounter the word, decide whether the author intended the technical meaning or not.

- **Book of Quotations:** Use an online or print collection of quotations to find a quotation that contains each of the words. In a sentence or two, analyze the word's connotations in the context of the quotation.

Common Core State Standards

Reading Literature
10. By the end of grade 12, read and comprehend literature, including dramas, at the high end of the grades 11–CCR text complexity band independently and proficiently.

Language
6. Demonstrate independence in gathering vocabulary knowledge when considering a word or phrase important to comprehension or expression.

Macbeth • *Oedipus the King* • *Faust* **421**

SOPHOCLES
(496 B.C.–406 B.C.)

Sophocles' (säf´ ə klēz´) life corresponded with the splendid rise and tragic fall of fifth-century Athens. At 16, he was one of the young men chosen by the city to perform a choral ode, dancing and singing in a public celebration of the Athenian naval victory over the Persians at Salamis. In 442 B.C., he was one of the treasurers of the imperial league, which was organized to resist Persia. With Pericles, Sophocles served as one of the generals in the war against the island of Samos, which later tried to secede from the Athenian league. In 413 B.C., he was also appointed to a special government committee when the Athenian expedition to Sicily failed. He died in 406 B.C., two years before Athens surrendered to Sparta in the Peloponnesian War.

Winning Playwright Sophocles' life also coincided with the rise and fall of the Golden Age of Greek tragedy. His career as a dramatist began in 468 B.C. when he entered the Dionysia (dī´ ə nē´ sē ə), the annual theatrical competition dedicated to the god Dionysus (dī´ ə nī´ səs). Competing against the established and brilliant playwright Aeschylus (es´ ki ləs), Sophocles won first prize. Over the next 62 years, he wrote more than 120 plays, 24 of which won first prize; those that did not come in first placed second. Yet only seven of Sophocles' plays have survived intact.

Enriching the Drama Greek plays had their origins in religious festivals honoring the god Dionysus. At first, a chorus narrated stories of the god's life in song. The choral leader would occasionally step forward to recite part of the story alone. Eventually, the recitation grew longer and involved a second speaker. Sophocles increased the number of singers in the chorus and introduced a third speaking part. The addition of a third actor allowed for more dramatically complex dialogue than that of the earlier plays. Sophocles also introduced technical innovations to Greek tragedy, which was presented in an open-air theater with few props. For instance, he was the first to use a crane that lowered actors "miraculously" onto the stage.

Faithfulness to Human Experience In addition to his technical innovations, Sophocles is known for his fidelity to universal human experience. In his plays, the world order consists of human beings, nature, and the inscrutable forces of the gods and fate. Sophocles suggests that while gods can predetermine or influence human action, they do not necessarily define one's character. People are responsible for finding out who they are and where they belong; they must then take moral responsibility for their lives.

"Numberless are the world's wonders, but none / More wonderful than man."
—Sophocles

from *Oedipus* the King

Translated by David Grene

— BACKGROUND According to the myth on which Sophocles' play is based, King Laius and Queen Jocasta of Thebes learn from an oracle that their son will kill his father and marry his mother. Horrified, they pin together their baby son's feet and give him to a servant to leave on Mount Cithaeron to die. The servant instead gives the baby to a shepherd, who gives him to King Polybus and Queen Merope of Corinth. They name him Oedipus, meaning "swollen feet," and raise him as their own. When Oedipus learns from the oracle that he will kill his father and marry his mother, he thinks this fate refers to Polybus and Merope and so flees Corinth. Enraged by a chariot driver who tries to run him off the road, he kills the driver and his passenger. He then comes to Thebes, which is being terrorized by a monster called the Sphinx, which will let no one enter Thebes until the riddle it poses is solved. Oedipus solves the riddle and, as a reward, marries the recently widowed Jocasta, becoming king of Thebes. He has two sons and two daughters and rules successfully for twenty years. Then a plague breaks out, and the oracle says that it will not end until Laius' murderer is exiled from Thebes.

The following selection, which concludes the play, occurs soon after Oedipus learns that Jocasta is his biological mother and that the man he killed on the road was Laius, his biological father. Horrified by their sins, Jocasta has taken her own life, and Oedipus has blinded himself.

OEDIPUS: . . . come—it's unfit to say what is unfit
to do.—I beg of you in God's name hide me
1520   somewhere outside your country, yes, or kill me,
or throw me into the sea, to be forever
out of your sight. Approach and deign to touch me

Reading
Check

What does Oedipus learn
from the oracle?

for all my wretchedness, and do not fear.
No man but I can bear my evil doom.

1525 **CHORUS:** Here Creon comes in fit time to perform
or give advice in what you ask of us.
Creon is left sole ruler in your stead.

OEDIPUS: Creon! Creon! What shall I say to him?
How can I justly hope that he will trust me?
In what is past I have been proved towards him
1530 an utter liar.

[*Enter* CREON.]

CREON: Oedipus, I've come
not so that I might laugh at you nor taunt you
with evil of the past. But if you still
are without shame before the face of men
1535 reverence at least the flame that gives all life,
our Lord the Sun, and do not show unveiled
to him pollution such that neither land
nor holy rain nor light of day can welcome.

[*To a* SERVANT.]

Be quick and take him in. It is most decent
that only kin should see and hear the troubles
1540 of kin.

OEDIPUS: I beg you, since you've torn me from
my dreadful expectations and have come
in a most noble spirit to a man

Comparing Tragedies
What important information does the chorus supply to the audience in these lines?

Vocabulary
reverence (rev´ rəns) *v.* show great respect

LITERATURE IN CONTEXT

The Greek Chorus and Players

In Greek tragedies, the role of the chorus was central to the production and to the meaning of the play. The chorus consisted of 12 or 15 dancers called *choreuts,* who were young men about to enter the military. The chorus danced as it sang, moving from right to left during the strophe (strō´ fē), then left to right during the antistrophe (an tis´ trə fē).

Originally, plays included only one actor in addition to the chorus. Thespis, from whom we derive the English word *thespian,* or actor, is said to have been the first actor. The dramatist Aeschylus (es´ kə ləs) is said to have introduced the second actor, and Sophocles the third.

In most dramas, actors played several different parts each. Their costumes were long, flowing garments and expressive masks, which they changed as they changed characters. The actors' shoes also featured a high wooden sole called a *cothurnus* (kō thər´ nəs) to make the individual look taller and more impressive and to heighten visibility in the vast theater.

Connect to the Literature

What roles does the chorus perform at the beginning and end of this excerpt? Also, in what ways does the picture on page 427 help you visualize how the chorus performs?

that has used you vilely[1]—do a thing for me.
1545   I shall speak for your own good, not for my own.

CREON: What do you need that you would ask of me?

OEDIPUS: Drive me from here with all the speed you can
    to where I may not hear a human voice.

CREON: Be sure, I would have done this had not I
1550   wished first of all to learn from the God the course
    of action I should follow.

OEDIPUS: But his word
    has been quite clear to let the parricide,[2]
    the sinner, die.

CREON: Yes, that indeed was said.
    But in the present need we had best discover
1555   what we should do.

OEDIPUS: And will you ask about
    a man so wretched?

CREON: Now even you will trust
    the God.

OEDIPUS: So. I command you—and will beseech you—
    to her that lies inside that house give burial
1560   as you would have it; she is yours and rightly
    you will perform the rites for her. For me—
    never let this my father's city have me
    living a dweller in it. Leave me live
    in the mountains where Cithaeron is, that's called
1565   my mountain, which my mother and my father
    while they were living would have made my tomb.
    So I may die by their decree who sought
    indeed to kill me. Yet I know this much:
    no sickness and no other thing will kill me.
1570   I would not have been saved from death if not
    for some strange evil fate. Well, let my fate
    go where it will.
                Creon, you need not care
    about my sons; they're men and so wherever
    they are, they will not lack a livelihood.
1575   But my two girls—so sad and pitiful—
    whose table never stood apart from mine,
    and everything I touched they always shared—
    O Creon, have a thought for them! And most
    I wish that you might suffer me to touch them
1580   and sorrow with them.

---

1. vilely (vīl´ ly) *adv.* wickedly
2. parricide (par´ ə sīd) *n.* someone who murders his or her father.

Comparing Tragedies
What does Oedipus' request to Creon show about his attitude toward Thebes? As a **tragic hero**, what noble qualities does he reveal?

Vocabulary
rites (rīts) *n.* ceremonies; rituals

Comparing Tragedies
What role does Oedipus believe fate has played in his life?

Reading Check

What information does Creon want to learn from the God?

[*Enter* ANTIGONE *and* ISMENE, OEDIPUS' *two daughters.*]
O my lord! O true noble Creon! Can I
really be touching them, as when I saw?
What shall I say?
Yes, I can hear them sobbing—my two darlings!
and Creon has had pity and has sent me
1585   what I loved most?
Am I right?

CREON: You're right: it was I gave you this
because I knew from old days how you loved them
as I see now.

1590 **OEDIPUS:**   God bless you for it, Creon,
and may God guard you better on your road
than he did me!
                    O children,
where are you? Come here, come to my hands,
a brother's hands which turned your father's eyes,
1595   those bright eyes you knew once, to what you see,
a father seeing nothing, knowing nothing,
begetting you from his own source of life.
I weep for you—I cannot see your faces—
I weep when I think of the bitterness
1600   there will be in your lives, how you must live
before the world. At what assemblages
of citizens will you make one? to what
gay company will you go and not come home
in tears instead of sharing in the holiday?
1605   And when you're ripe for marriage, who will he be,
the man who'll risk to take such infamy
as shall cling to my children, to bring hurt
on them and those that marry with them? What
curse is not there? "Your father killed his father
1610   and sowed the seed where he had sprung himself
and begot you out of the womb that held him."
These insults you will hear. Then who will marry you?
No one, my children; clearly you are doomed
to waste away in barrenness unmarried.
1615   Son of Menoeceus[3], since you are all the father
left these two girls, and we, their parents, both
are dead to them—do not allow them wander
like beggars, poor and husbandless.
They are of your own blood.
1620   And do not make them equal with myself
in wretchedness; for you can see them now
so young, so utterly alone, save for you only.

Vocabulary

infamy (in´ fə mē) *n.* very
bad reputation; disgrace

---

3. Son of Menoeceus (mə nē´ sē əs) Creon.

Touch my hand, noble Creon, and say yes.
If you were older, children, and were wiser,

1625 there's much advice I'd give you. But as it is,
let this be what you pray: give me a life
wherever there is opportunity
to live, and better life than was my father's.

CREON: Your tears have had enough of scope; now go within the
1630   house.

OEDIPUS: I must obey, though bitter of heart.

CREON: In season, all is good.

OEDIPUS: Do you know on what conditions I obey?

CREON: You tell me them,
1635   and I shall know them when I hear.

OEDIPUS: That you shall send me out
to live away from Thebes.

CREON: That gift you must ask of the God.

▼ **Critical Viewing**
What does this image of
Oedipus and the Chorus
suggest about their
relationship? Explain.
[Interpret]

Reading
Check

Why does Oedipus weep for
his daughters?

OEDIPUS: But I'm now hated by the Gods.

1640 **CREON:**   So quickly you'll obtain your prayer.

OEDIPUS: You consent then?

CREON: What I do not mean, I do not use to say.

OEDIPUS: Now lead me away from here.

CREON: Let go the children, then, and come.

1645 **OEDIPUS:** Do not take them from me.

CREON: Do not seek to be master in everything,
for the things you mastered did not follow you throughout your
life.

[*As* CREON *and* OEDIPUS *go out.*]

CHORUS: You that live in my ancestral Thebes, behold this
Oedipus,—
him who knew the famous riddles and was a man most
masterful;
1650 not a citizen who did not look with envy on his lot—see him
now and see the breakers of misfortune swallow him!
Look upon that last day always. Count no mortal happy till
he has passed the final limit of his life secure from pain.

Comparing Tragedies
What does the final speech of the chorus stress about the events depicted in the play?

Critical Reading

Cite textual evidence to support your responses.

© **1. Key Ideas and Details (a)** In order to end the plague in Thebes, what command did Oedipus apparently make about the person who murdered Laius? **(b) Analyze:** What about this command is ironic, or surpising and unexpected?

© **2. Key Ideas and Details (a)** What does Oedipus ask Creon to do regarding Jocasta's body and his daughters' future? **(b) Analyze:** What do these requests show about Oedipus' character?

© **3. Craft and Structure (a)** In his final remark, what does Creon tell Oedipus not to seek? **(b) Interpret:** Based on this final scene, what do you think is the theme or central message of the play?

© **4. Integration of Knowledge and Ideas (a) Make a Judgment:** At the play's end, do you think Oedipus is ennobled by suffering? **(b) Support:** Provide reasons and cite detailed and accurate references from the play to support your opinion.

Johann Wolfgang von Goethe
(1749–1832)

Because of the tremendous diversity of his talents and interests, Johann (yō hän´) Wolfgang von Goethe (gö´ tə) is best described as a true Renaissance man. He was not only a gifted writer but also a scientist, a painter, a statesman, a philosopher, and an educator.

The son of a wealthy lawyer, Goethe was born in the German town of Frankfurt am Main. After receiving a thorough education from private tutors, he was sent to the University of Leipzig to study law. More interested in the arts than in law, Goethe spent most of his free time writing poetry, studying art, and attending concerts. Nonetheless, he finished his legal studies in 1771.

A Developing Novelist Goethe practiced law for a brief period, during which he wrote *The Sorrows of Young Werther* (1774), an autobiographical novel inspired by an unhappy love affair and the suicide of one of his friends. One of the most important novels of the eighteenth century, *The Sorrows of Young Werther* earned Goethe international fame.

A year after the novel's publication, Goethe accepted an invitation to the court of the reigning duke of Weimar, Charles Augustus. Goethe lived in Weimar for the rest of his life, and for ten years he served as the duke's chief minister. In 1780, he traveled to Italy in an effort to dedicate time and energy to his writing.

Shortly after returning to Weimar, Goethe fell in love with Christiane Vulpius, whom he later married. Through a close friendship with the noted German writer Friedrich von Schiller (1759–1805), Goethe gained valuable guidance and assistance in revising a number of his important works.

A Legendary Figure Probably the most notable of these works was *Faust*. With Schiller's advice and direction, Goethe revised an early draft of the play, adding a prologue. Unfortunately, Schiller died three years before *Faust, Part I* (1808) was published.

The final and greatest achievement of Goethe's literary career was the completion of *Faust, Part II*. The poet's vision of the legendary Faust transformed the traditional character into a newer, more sympathetic one that has fascinated readers and scholars for centuries. Goethe had begun his work on *Part II* while still a young man; because he contributed to the piece throughout his life, *Faust, Part II* ultimately reflects the deep philosophy of life and wry wisdom of the poet's mature years. Goethe never knew of the success of *Faust, Part II,* as it was published in 1832, a few months after his death.

> "As soon as you trust yourself, you will know how to live."
> — Goethe

From
FAUST

Johann Wolfgang von Goethe
translated by Louis MacNeice

BACKGROUND Georg Faust, or Faustus, was a German
scholar and traveling magician who lived from about 1480
to 1540. According to legend, Faust sold his soul to the devil
in exchange for youth, knowledge, and magical powers. In
Goethe's version of the legend, Faust's interests reflect ideas of
Romanticism, the literary and artistic movement.

This scene comes from Faust, Part I. *Mephistopheles, or the
devil, is urging Faust to formalize their contract by signing it
"with one little drop of blood."*

FAUST: Only do not fear that I shall break this contract.
What I promise is nothing more
Than what all my powers are striving for.
250   I have puffed myself up too much, it is only
Your sort that really fits my case.
The great Earth Spirit has despised me
And Nature shuts the door in my face.
The thread of thought is snapped asunder,
255   I have long loathed knowledge in all its fashions.
In the depths of sensuality
Let us now quench our glowing passions!
And at once make ready every wonder
Of unpenetrated sorcery!
260   Let us cast ourselves into the torrent of time,
Into the whirl of eventfulness,
Where disappointment and success,
Pleasure and pain may chop and change
As chop and change they will and can;
265   It is restless action makes the man.

MEPHISTOPHELES: No limit is fixed for you, no bound;
If you'd like to nibble at everything
Or to seize upon something flying round—
Well, may you have a run for your money!
270   But seize your chance and don't be funny!

FAUST: I've told you, it is no question of happiness.

Comparing Tragedies
In what ways are Faust's
motivations (lines 260–265)
similar to and different
from those of Macbeth and
Oedipus?

The most painful joy, enamored hate, enlivening
Disgust—I devote myself to all excess.
My breast, now cured of its appetite for knowledge,
275 From now is open to all and every smart,
And what is allotted to the whole of mankind
That will I sample in my inmost heart,
Grasping the highest and lowest with my spirit,
Piling men's weal and woe upon my neck,
280 To extend myself to embrace all human selves
And to founder in the end, like them, a wreck.

MEPHISTOPHELES: O believe *me*, who have been chewing
These iron rations many a thousand year,
No human being can digest
285 This stuff, from the cradle to the bier[1]
This universe—believe a devil—
Was made for no one but a god!
He exists in eternal light
But us he has brought into the darkness
290 While *your* sole portion is day and night.

FAUST: I will all the same!

MEPHISTOPHELES: That's very nice.
There's only one thing I find wrong;
Time is short, art is long.
You could do with a little artistic advice.
295 Confederate with one of the poets
And let him flog his imagination
To heap all virtues on your head,
A head with such a reputation:
Lion's bravery,
300 Stag's velocity,
Fire of Italy,
Northern tenacity.
Let *him* find out the secret art
Of combining craft with a noble heart
305 And of being in love like a young man,
Hotly, but working to a plan.
Such a person—*I'd* like to meet him;
"Mr. Microcosm"[2] is how I'd greet him.

FAUST: What am I then if fate must bar
310 My efforts to reach that crown of humanity
After which all my senses strive?

---

1. bier (bir) *n.* coffin and its supporting platform.
2. Mr. Microcosm man regarded as the epitome of the world.

Comparing Tragedies
How is Goethe's verse, as translated by Louis MacNeice, different from the verse used by Shakespeare?

Vocabulary
tenacity (tə nas′ ə tē) *n.* persistence; stubbornness

Reading Check

To what does Faust devote himself?

MEPHISTOPHELES:
You are in the end . . . what you are.
You can put on full-bottomed wigs with a million locks,
You can put on stilts instead of your stocks,
315   You remain for ever what you are.

FAUST: I feel my endeavors have not been worth a pin
When I raked together the treasures of the human mind,
If at the end I but sit down to find
No new force welling up within.
320   I have not a hair's breadth more of height,
I am no nearer the Infinite.

MEPHISTOPHELES: My very good sir, you look at things
Just in the way that people do;
We must be cleverer than that
325   Or the joys of life will escape from you.
Hell! You have surely hands and feet,
Also a head and you-know-what;
The pleasures I gather on the wing,
Are they less mine? Of course they're not!
330   Suppose I can afford six stallions,
I can add that horse-power to my score
And dash along and be a proper man
As if my legs were twenty-four.
So good-bye to thinking! On your toes!
335   The world's before us. Quick! Here goes!
I tell you, a chap who's intellectual
Is like a beast on a blasted heath
Driven in circles by a demon
While a fine green meadow lies round beneath.

340 **FAUST:** How do we start?

MEPHISTOPHELES: We just say go—and skip.
But please get ready for this pleasure trip.

[*Exit* FAUST.]

Only look down on knowledge and reason,
The highest gifts that men can prize,
345   Only allow the spirit of lies
To confirm you in magic and illusion,
And then I have you body and soul.
Fate has given this man a spirit
Which is always pressing onward, beyond control,
350   And whose mad striving overleaps

◀ **Critical Viewing**
How does this painting convey the powers of nature that Faust has experienced?

Comparing Tragedies
Do either Macbeth or Oedipus long, like Faust, for "the Infinite"? Explain.

Reading
Check

What does Mephistopheles urge Faust to do?

All joys of the earth between pole and pole.
Him shall I drag through the wilds of life
And through the flats of meaninglessness,
I shall make him flounder and gape and stick

355 And to tease his insatiableness
Hang meat and drink in the air before his watering lips;
In vain he will pray to slake his inner thirst,
And even had he not sold himself to the devil
He would be equally accursed.

Vocabulary
insatiableness (in sā′ shə bəl nəs) *n.* the quality of being impossible to fill

Critical Reading

Cite textual evidence to support your responses.

1. **Key Ideas and Details (a)** To what does Faust say he devotes himself and what does he reject? **(b) Analyze:** How do what he pursues and what he rejects explain what he means by "the Infinite"? **(c) Interpret:** In what ways do Faust's pursuits reflect the Romantics' desire to go beyond ordinary life?

2. **Key Ideas and Details (a) Interpret:** What does Mephistopheles' simile comparing an intellectual to a beast (lines 336–339) suggest about his attitude toward intellectuals? **(b) Infer:** Why does Mephistopheles want Faust and others to "look down on knowledge and reason"?

3. **Key Ideas and Details (a) Analyze:** What quality in Faust does Mephistopheles count on to gain control of him? **(b)** In the final lines, what does Mephistopheles predict will happen to Faust? **(c) Speculate:** Do you agree with this prediction? Why or why not?

4. **Integration of Knowledge and Ideas (a) Connect:** Some critics have called contemporary society, with its devotion to constantly developing technology, Faustian. What do you think they mean? **(b) Make a Judgment:** Do you believe our society is Faustian? Why or why not?

After You Read ▪ *Macbeth • Oedipus the King • Faust*

Comparing Tragedies

**Common Core
State Standards**

1. Integration of Knowledge and Ideas **(a)** What is similar about the social status of Macbeth and Oedipus? **(b)** How might the social status of these **tragic heroes** contribute to the awe—a mixed feeling of respect and dread—that the audience feels in watching the **tragedy? (c)** What other elements in each of the three selections help create awe? Explain.

2. Key Ideas and Details How would you define the **tragic flaw** of each hero?

3. Integration of Knowledge and Ideas *Faust* has a chorus of sorts, though it does not appear in this selection; *Macbeth*, however, has no chorus in the usual sense. **(a)** In your opinion, do the Witches in *Macbeth* perform some of the roles that a chorus does? Why or why not? **(b)** Would adding a chorus like that in a Greek drama strengthen or weaken *Macbeth*? Explain.

Writing
2. Write informative/ explanatory texts to examine and convey complex ideas, concepts, and information clearly and accurately through the effective selection, organization, and analysis of content.
10. Write routinely over extended time frames and shorter time frames for a range of tasks, purposes, and audiences.

 Timed Writing

Explanatory Text: Essay

Macbeth and the excerpts you have read reveal how the structure and elements in the work of dramatists changed over time.

Assignment: Write an **explanatory essay** in which you compare and contrast two plays from different periods. Evaluate how the dramatic structure and elements changed from one play to the other. **[40 minutes]**

Use questions like these to focus your analysis.
- Is the play structured to teach a moral, show the downfall of a noble character, or allow for the happy resolution of a misunderstanding?
- Are the characters personifications, social types, or complex individuals?

As you write, follow the conventions of a strong analytical essay:
- Begin your essay with a clear thesis statement.
- Use a clear organizational schema for conveying ideas.
- Support your thesis with relevant and substantial evidence, including well-chosen details from the texts.

As you draft, write legibly. Use appropriate capitalization and punctuation.

5-Minute Planner

Complete these steps before you begin to write:
1. Read the assignment carefully. Take note of key words and phrases.
2. Jot down some initial thoughts. Then, scan the plays for evidence that supports your ideas. **TIP** Create a chart in which to record quotations or details related to each play.
3. Create an outline for your essay that identifies the central idea of each paragraph.
4. Reread the prompt, and draft your essay.

USE ACADEMIC VOCABULARY

As you write, use academic language, including the following words or their related forms:

comparison
contrast
distinguish
resolution

For more about academic language, see the vocabulary charts in the introduction to this book.

Analyzing Functional and Expository Texts

Feature Article • Theater Review

Common Core State Standards

Reading Informational Text
6. Determine an author's point of view or purpose in a text in which the rhetoric is particularly effective, analyzing how style and content contribute to the power, persuasiveness, or beauty of the text.

About the Texts

A **feature article** is an informative or entertaining piece of nonfiction writing, found in a print or online periodical, that focuses on a topic of general interest such as a trend, local performance, or significant person. Features include an enticing *lead,* or opening, and a body that provides in-depth analysis.

A **theater review** is a feature article in which the writer gives facts and details about a theatrical production, as well as his or her opinion of it. Some of its features include an overview of the work; a "quick review" device, such as a star ranking indicating quality; and details of where and when the production can be viewed.

Reading Strategy

An **author's purpose** is his or her reason for writing—to inform, to persuade, or to entertain. An **author's perspective,** or **point of view,** on a topic consists of his or her beliefs, judgments, and attitudes about that topic. As you read, **evaluate the author's purpose and perspective** as it is reflected in the following elements:

- The title
- The author's *style,* or overall manner of expression, and *tone,* or the attitude he or she conveys through word choice (formal or informal, serious or light, sarcastic or straightforward); typically established by the lead
- The points made with anecdotes and direct quotes, as well as the facts and interesting details the author chooses to include

Use a chart like the one shown to evaluate the author's purpose.

Text Structures	Example	Effect on Meaning
Title		
Lead		
Positive/Negative Adjectives		
Direct Quotes		
Facts and Details		

Content-Area Vocabulary

These words appear in the selections that follow. They may also appear in other content-area texts:

pneumatic (noo mat′ ik) *adj.* run or powered by compressed air

excavation (eks′ kə vā′ shən) *n.* the process of making a hole or a cavity by digging and removing

contemporaneous (kən tem′ pə rā′ nē əs) *adj.* originating, existing, or happening during the same period of time

regime (rə zhēm′) *n.* a system of management or government that is in power

Smithsonian
M A G A Z I N E

The title indicates the topic of the article—efforts to design a modern equivalent of the Globe, Shakespeare's original theater.

DESIGNING A GLOBE THEATRE FOR THE 21ST CENTURY

By Eric Jaffe

Feature articles frequently use vivid descriptions and informal language.

The tractor-trailer planted firmly in the Wal-Mart parking lot did not seem out of place, but the actors who performed *Merchant of Venice* right beside it sure did. When the vehicle arrived it deployed into a full-size stage. Behind the set, **pneumatic** pods inflated to become ticket-windows and dressing rooms. Sunlight powered the spotlights and speakers. And when the play-house folded up and drove off, a screen mounted on the side of the trailer replayed the show for all to see.

This is the Globe Theatre—not the one that housed Shakespeare's best dramas, but one conceived by Jennifer Siegal for a modern audience. Siegal's Globe is part homage to the Elizabethan era's itinerant theatre troupe, part shout-out to today's compact, on-the-go gizmos. The Los Angeles-based architect was one of five designers asked to create a 21st-century Shakespearean theatre for "Reinventing the Globe," a new exhibit at the National Building Museum in Washington, D.C., that opens January 13 and runs through August 2007.

Illustration of Jennifer Siegal's "Globetrotter"—a portable Shakespeare theater

Given only brief guidance and a few months to finish, these architects created modern Globes that challenge conventional thoughts about dramatic performances and the spaces that accommodate them, says Martin Moeller, the exhibition's curator. "When the words stay the same but all else changes, you realize how much power the words have," he says.

Theatre designer John Coyne delivered a truly virtual Globe. To reflect today's cross-cultural world, Coyne's performances would occur simultaneously in several locations. Gigantic screens with live streaming would hang above the stages, and characters would interact in real time. So, speaking in Russian from Moscow, Polonius offers advice to Laertes in New York; standing oceans away, Hamlet pierces Claudius with a venom-tipped sword.

Michele (pronounced *Mi-keleh*) Saee, who did not have theatre design experience, modeled a Globe that would capture an actor's fluidity in the structure itself. He proposed tracing the movements of an actor throughout a performance

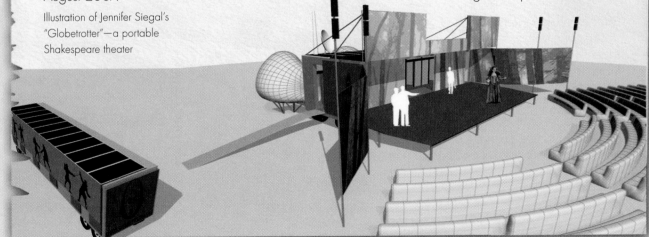

using electronic monitors then, with the help of a computer, turning these motions into a three-dimensional image that would become the building. "It's like those photos at night where you see red and white lights streaking down the road," Moeller says. "It's almost like you have a history built into one image."

David Rockwell's transparent Globe is intended to erase the barrier between outdoor and indoor settings. H3, the architectural firm guided by Hugh Hardy, created a floating Globe that could bounce around to various New York City boroughs, like so many bar-hopping hipsters, as a way to increase public access.

Siegel, who is the founder of the Office of Mobile Design, says her portable Globe, dubbed the "Globetrotter," is ready to go into production with the right client.

"We're a mobile society that deals with communication devices in a compact way, and theatre can be represented in a similar take," she says. "It doesn't have to be going to this old, stodgy building. It could be much more accessible, transient and lighter."

In some ways, conceptualizing a Globe Theatre for the future requires as much imagination as re-creating the one that stood in Shakespeare's day. Despite the playhouse's prominence, historians still argue over many aspects of the theatre, says Franklin J. Hildy of the University of Maryland, an advisor to the London Globe reconstruction that opened in 1997.

Notable uncertainties include the shape of the stage (some say it was rectangular, others square); how many sides the structure had (with ranges from 16 to 24); even the size of the building itself (some call the diameter 100 feet across, others 90).

Globe reconstructions work off evidence from seven maps of London in that day, texts from Shakespeare's plays and a site **excavation** (the original theatre, built in 1599, burned down in 1613 and was restored in the same place). Perhaps the most crucial historical document is a contract to build the Fortune theatre, a **contemporaneous** playhouse, which instructs builders to copy many of the Globe's dimensions.

Of the Globe's certainties, the stage that jutted out into the crowd was one of its most impressive attributes, says Hildy. "Everywhere you looked there was life, audience, energy." Standing patrons, known as groundlings, surrounded the stage, often shouting at the actors, cracking hazelnut shells—even sitting on stage.

Though Shakespeare's work also appeared at the Rose and Curtain theatres, the Globe hosted most of his famous dramas—including *Hamlet*, *King Lear* and *Macbeth*—which explains part of its lasting allure, Hildy says.

"The sense has always been that you could feel a closer connection to Shakespeare if you could understand how he saw theatre, how he saw his plays staged," he says. "Shakespeare was working during one of the most successful periods that theatre has ever had. There seems to be a relationship between buildings and that success."

> The writer gives the reader historical background to put the current project in context.

The restored Globe Theatre in London

The New York Times

April 26, 2007

Theater Review / 'Macbeth'

The Scottish Play, Told With Sound and Fury and Puppets

By LAWRENCE VAN GELDER

> The "lead" in this review makes the reader wonder what this theatrical production is all about.

A puppet **regime** has seized control of the stage of the New Victory Theater. Plotting bloody murder, it slaughters men, women and children in pursuit of power until condign vengeance wreaks its ruin.

"Macbeth" is back in a captivating production that allies the actorly talents of the Chicago Shakespeare Theater with the remarkable talents of the Colla Marionette Company (Compagnia Marionettistica Carlo Colla e Figli) of Italy, which traces its origins to 1835.

In this swift-moving presentation (95 minutes including intermission), playing through Sunday, thirteen puppeteers out of sight above the stage combine with seven actors seated in semidarkness facing the action to render a forceful, visually captivating and clearly articulated version of Shakespeare's tragedy.

Here legions of troops march, caparisoned horses carry caped and tartan-bedecked Scottish noblemen, evil unfolds in the depths of great castles, a flock of birds flutters overhead, and the weird sisters and their fiery cauldron disgorge the prophecies that will lead Macbeth and his lady to deadly doings.

The New York Times

Humans, animals, witches—all 130 of them are puppets, most of them three feet tall. Their deeds and misdeeds are carried out in eye-catching sylvan settings and in the corridors and on the parapets of castles whose perspectives make them seem to have been built of genuine stone. In the blackouts between scenes, music composed by Fabio Vacchi intensifies the atmosphere of tension and foreboding.

At least since 1846-7, when Giuseppe Verdi and his librettist Francesco Maria Piave applied themselves to transforming "Macbeth" to opera, Italy has been no stranger to abridging this tragedy; this production retains the play's highlights, including Lady Macbeth's sleepwalking scene, Banquo's ghost, the witches' recipe and the coming of Birnam Wood to Dunsinane.

With puppetry directed by Eugenio Monti Colla and spoken word directed by Kate Buckley, the two companies engineer a shining collaboration.

This "Macbeth" is recommended for audiences 12 and older. For all and in all respects, it is an uncommon treat.

"Macbeth" runs through Sunday at the New Victory Theater.

> The reviewer offers information on where and when performances take place.

> The reviewer supports his point of view or purpose with specific details.

Critical Reading

1. Key Ideas and Details (a) In the feature article, what does the author say is the reason different versions of the Globe Theater were created? **(b)** Why does the author consider it important to conceptualize a Globe Theater for the future?

2. Key Ideas and Details (a) What is the author's purpose and perspective in the feature article? **(b)** Explain two ways in which he uses direct quotes to support his perspective.

3. Craft and Structure (a) What facts and details in the theater review support the author's opinion of the performance? **(b)** Describe the style and the tone of the review. **(c)** What perspective do this style and tone help to express?

4. Content-Area Vocabulary The Latin prefix *trans-* means "across" or "through." The Latin verb *parēre* means "to be visible." Together, they contribute to the meaning of *transparent*, which means "clear" or "through which things are visible." Using your knowledge of the prefix *trans-,* give the meaning of each of these words: *transmit, transcribe,* and *transpose.* Then, verify your preliminary determination of the meaning of each word by looking it up in a dictionary.

Common Core State Standards

Reading Informational Text

7. Integrate and evaluate multiple sources of information presented in different media or formats as well as in words in order to address a question or solve a problem.

Writing

2.b. Develop the topic thoroughly by selecting the most significant and relevant facts, extended definitions, concrete details, quotations, or other information and examples appropriate to the audience's knowledge of the topic.

Language

4.d. Verify the preliminary determination of the meaning of a word or phrase.

Timed Writing

Informative Text [40 minutes]

Format

In a **compare-and-contrast** essay, you analyze the similarities and differences between two or more things. One way to organize your essay is to discuss similarities first and differences second.

Write a **compare-and-contrast** essay in which you analyze and compare the **aesthetic and cultural considerations** that influence modern producers and theater designers when they stage Shakespeare. Integrate ideas and examples from both the feature article and the theater review, providing context as required by your audience's background knowledge. Evaluate the importance and ultimate consequence for theater of each factor you discuss.

Academic Vocabulary

Aesthetic and cultural considerations are ideas concerning style, beauty, and the power of a work to express the experiences of its audience.

5-Minute Planner

Complete these steps before you begin to write.

1. Read the prompt carefully. Underline key words.

2. Scan the texts for details about the reasons people have for adapting Shakespeare. **TIP** Pay special attention to quotations from participants and to descriptions of the impact of their work, as well as to signal words indicating purpose, such as "as a way to."

3. Decide which points you will discuss.

4. Reread the prompt, and begin drafting.

Write a Persuasive Essay

**Common Core
State Standards**

Writing
1. Write arguments to support claims in an analysis of substantive topics or texts, using valid reasoning and relevant and sufficient evidence.
5. Develop and strengthen writing as needed by planning, revising, editing, rewriting, or trying a new approach, focusing on addressing what is most significant for a specific purpose and audience.

Persuasive, or Argumentative, Essay English Renaissance writers such as Sir Thomas More argued vigorously for their humanistic ideals in **persuasive essays,** also called *argumentative essays.* A persuasive essay is a prose work that presents a case for or against a position using supporting evidence and convincing language. Follow the steps outlined in this workshop to write your own persuasive essay.

Assignment Write a persuasive essay on an issue of importance to you.

What to Include To succeed, your persuasive essay must feature the following elements:

- a thesis statement that clearly states your position and the action you want readers to take
- well-organized evidence that supports your argument, such as facts, examples, statistics, and personal experience
- responses to alternate or opposing claims
- information that will appeal to your audience's logic and emotions, and that will inspire trust in your credibility and character
- compelling persuasive language that maintains a formal tone
- transitions and varied syntax used to link ideas
- an effective conclusion that sums up the argument

To preview the criteria on which your persuasive essay may be judged, see the rubric on page 449.

To get a feel for persuasive writing, read this excerpt. Notice how Queen Elizabeth I appeals to both her audience's logic and emotions.

from: Speech Before Her Troops

My loving people, we have been persuaded by some, that are care-ful of our safety, to take heed how we commit ourselves to armed multitudes, for fear of treachery; but I assure you, I do not desire to live to distrust my faithful and loving people. Let tyrants fear; I have always so behaved myself that, under God, I have placed my chiefest strength and safeguard in the loyal hearts and good will of my sub-jects. And therefore I am come amongst you at this time, not as for my recreation or sport, but being resolved, in the midst and heat of the battle, to live or die amongst you all; to lay down, for my God, and for my kingdom, and for my people, my honor and my blood, even the dust.

WRITE GUY
Jeff Anderson, M.Ed.

What Do You Notice?

Read the highlighted sentence several times. Then, with a partner, discuss the qualities that make it special. You might consider the following elements:

- word choice
- sentence length
- use of punctuation
- vivid details

Share your group's observations with the class.

Prewriting and Planning

Choosing Your Topic

Use one of the following strategies to find a topic that provokes in you a strong reaction:

- **Conduct a news scan.** Read newspapers or listen to news programs to learn about current, controversial issues. Avoid issues on which your only opinion is "I like _____" or "I dislike _____." Pick a topic on which you take a clearly articulated stand.

  Weak: I don't like the proposed changes to update the mall.

  Strong: Rather than piecemeal projects, our community needs a coherent revitalization plan.

- **Monitor online discussions.** Internet message boards often contain heated disagreements. Look for boards sponsored by local schools, government agencies, or media sources. Scan message boards for topics that receive many responses—a high number of posts about a topic may indicate controversy.

Narrowing Your Topic

Once you have identified a general interest, focus on a specific aspect that you can fully and completely support. Consider the needs of your intended audience as you make notes about your topic.

My Interest: Health Care   Narrower Topic: Preventive Care

Gathering Details

Gather facts and arguments to support your position. Use libraries, the Internet, personal interviews, or other resources. Make note also of any facts that contradict your opinion, so you can prepare counterarguments. You might begin by filling out a chart like the one shown.

Purpose	Audience	My Arguments	Counterarguments to Address
To persuade seniors to apply early to college	Seniors at my school	• Choosing early admissions may improve your chances of acceptance. • Applications will just hang over your head if you delay.	• Some schools do not offer early admissions. • Getting in early may limit your financial aid package.

Drafting

Shaping Your Writing

Showcase your thesis statement. Introduce a knowledgeable claim on the issue in your first paragraph. To establish the significance of your thesis, begin with examples, facts, or a brief anecdote that will grab readers' attention. Then state your viewpoint in the final sentence of the first paragraph. The chart shown explains some patterns you can use in your introduction.

Develop ideas. Use the body of your writing to defend your ideas. As you develop your argument, help readers understand what is at stake by clearly distinguishing your thesis from opposing claims and then refuting them. Present claims and counterclaims in logical sequence. Make sure you present the strongest evidence on both sides, addressing your audience's concerns and questions. Then, conclude your essay with a memorable restatement of your thesis idea and a clear call for action—a statement of what you want done.

Providing Elaboration

Use rhetorical devices to present appeals. You can use rhetorical devices to grab your audience's interest and persuade them that you are right.

- **Repetition:** Repeat key words to focus your argument.

  Example: The plan is convenient, but is convenience more important than safety?

- **Parallelism:** Repeated grammatical structures can create a memorable rhythm.

  Example: The safety of every student, every teacher, and every visitor is at stake.

- **Analogies:** Use comparisons to help readers grasp ideas.

  Example: Allowing parking along the field is as dangerous as allowing motorcycles to enter a bicycle race.

You can use rhetorical devices to make the following kinds of appeals:

- **Logical appeals** present ideas based on reasoning.
- **Ethical appeals** establish the credibility of information.
- **Emotional appeals** tap into an audience's feelings.

Use a chart like the one shown to develop a list of appeals.

The Importance of Preventative Health Care	
Logical Appeal	If you take good care of yourself, then you reduce your chances of being inconvenienced by a cold or flu.
Ethical Appeal	Doctors say that, whenever possible, prevent yourself and others from catching a cold.
Emotional Appeal	Just a little care can help you avoid the drippy nose, scratchy throat, and aching muscles of a cold or flu.

Common Core State Standards

Writing
1.a. Introduce precise, knowledgeable claim(s), establish the significance of the claim(s), distinguish the claim(s) from alternate or opposing claims, and create an organization that logically sequences claim(s), counterclaims, reasons, and evidence.
1.b. Develop claim(s) and counterclaims fairly and thoroughly, supplying the most relevant evidence for each while pointing out the strengths and limitations of both in a manner that anticipates the audience's knowledge level, concerns, values, and possible biases.
1.e. Provide a concluding statement or section that follows from and supports the argument presented.

Developing Opening Paragraphs

Pattern 1
- Example
- Example $\rightarrow$ Thesis statement

Pattern 2
- Fact
- Fact $\rightarrow$ Thesis statement

Pattern 3
- Brief anecdote $\rightarrow$ Thesis statement

Writers on Writing

Frank Kermode On Persuasion

> Frank Kermode is the author of *"Life in Elizabethan and Jacobean England"* (p. 248).

This passage is excerpted from my essay in *Daedalus, The Journal of the American Academy of Arts and Sciences.* It briefly considers the notion of the common reader from the eighteenth century up to the present day. To Dr. Samuel Johnson, the common reader of the eighteenth century was identified as a member of the leisured class. Now, it is argued, the term applies to people who have benefited by a college education.

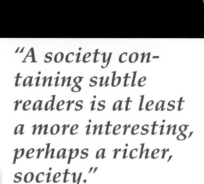

"A society containing subtle readers is at least a more interesting, perhaps a richer, society."

—Sir Frank Kermode

from *The Common Reader*

I have assumed that the modern Common Reader passes through a college or university. The number of people now teaching literature in such institutions is probably greater than the total of critics who formerly existed throughout history, and they must have some effect on the millions of readers who frequent their classes. Does good come of this? The eminent American critic Richard Poirier says he sees "no reason in the world" why common readers should care to read the classics or serious contemporary fiction and poetry; "I don't think it makes them better people, better citizens, better anything." By some criteria he must be right. Indeed, it is immodest to propose that by making people read these things we are improving them, ethically or civically. All we dare claim is that we are making them better readers. We might or might not go on to claim that bad reading has often had disastrous consequences; or that a society containing subtle readers is at least a more interesting, perhaps a richer, society than one that does not; or that good readers are likely to be more resistant to the exploitative forces of "the ruling system." But we should not say we are improving them, except as readers.

← The arts of reading are now entrusted to college and university teachers. Should we assume that this is a wholly good thing?

← Richard Poirier, an eminent critic, denies that enhanced reading skills confer ethical benefits on the student.

← Even if his argument is persuasive, it could be maintained that skillful reading has other socially beneficial effects.

Revising

Revising Your Overall Structure

Arrange arguments in a logical order. Review your writing to make sure that your evidence is arranged logically and effectively. Follow these steps.

1. Clearly show the connections between ideas, such as the connections between your thesis and supporting reasons, using transition words and phrases, such as *because, therefore, due to,* and *consequently.*

2. In addition, use varied syntax to show the connections between ideas. For example, a complex sentence, combining a dependent and an independent clause, can clearly show the relation between claims and reasons: e.g., *Because the numbers are increasing, immediate action is required.* A compound sentence, joining two or more independent clauses, can be used to link two equally important reasons or to contrast claims and counterclaims: e.g., *Opponents say the plan is the only one that will work, but my alternative has proven effective.*

3. Experiment with arranging your arguments in order of importance, either from least important to most important, or vice versa.

Common Core State Standards

Writing

1.c. Use words, phrases, and clauses as well as varied syntax to link the major sections of the text, create cohesion, and clarify the relationships between claim(s) and reasons, between reasons and evidence, and between claim(s) and counterclaims.

4. Produce clear and coherent writing in which the development, organization, and style are appropriate to task, purpose, and audience.

Language

3.a. Vary syntax for effect, consulting references for guidance as needed; apply an understanding of syntax to the study of complex texts when reading.

Model: Using Transition Words

In order to play a sport,

ʌYou are required to pass your classes, which of course motivates athletes to make good grades.

The transition words *in order to* indicate cause and effect.

Revising Your Word Choice

Replace weak language with powerful words or images. To strengthen your arguments, circle passages that are vague or lack force. For each one, brainstorm for charged words, vivid images, and dramatic analogies to help you make your points.

Peer Review: Share your draft with a partner. Discuss your ideas for replacing dull language. Together, choose the most vivid words or phrases.

Vague	Getting into a good college can be tough.	Suddenly, you get nervous about choosing a college.
Vivid	Like a thousand cattle trying to pass through the same gate, vast numbers of students across the nation apply each year for a limited number of places at colleges.	Suddenly, a feeling bubbles up from the pit of your stomach, an achy, acidic feeling of panic.

Developing Your Style

Making Sure Your Ideas Are Well Organized

Your persuasive essay probably contains both facts and opinions. Facts can include statistics, examples, and anecdotes. When your facts are well organized, they support your opinions, as in this example:

Opinion: I think we should carpet the school hallway.

Supporting Facts: The carpeting will reduce noise. Mr. Porter, of the maintenance staff, says it will be easier to clean than the existing floors.

As you review the way your facts and opinions are organized, look for logical fallacies, or false connections between ideas:

A **hasty generalization** is based on only a few facts or samples.

Example: I tasted one apple and it was sweet. Therefore, all of the apples in the basket must be sweet.

A **non sequitur** (Latin for "it does not follow") draws a conclusion that does not follow from the evidence given.

Example: Members of Congress are elected by the people and make the laws. Members of Congress know what is best for the people.

A **false analogy** ignores key differences between compared items.

Example: Children are like little adults. Like adults, children can be trusted to make their own financial decisions.

Find It in Your Reading

Read or review "Speech Before Her Troops" by Elizabeth I, page 285.

1. Find two facts and two opinions that she includes in her speech.

2. Find an argument she makes and explain whether it is logical or not.

Apply It to Your Writing

Review your draft. For each paragraph in your draft, follow these steps:

1. Underline the facts or statistics you have used to support your position. Check to see that your facts come from current, reliable sources and that you have cited them accurately.

2. Circle the opinions you have used to support your arguments. Verify that the opinions can be validated by facts, expert opinions, or logical arguments.

3. Evaluate the appeals you have made and revise any faulty logic.

PH WRITING COACH

Further instruction and practice are available in *Prentice Hall Writing Coach*.

Why It Is Important To Be a Student Athlete

You may believe that being a student athlete is a big waste of time. If so, you probably think about having to spend most of your free time at practice or competitions, or about having to stay up late at night doing homework that most students do right after school. You might fear not being able to go to that big party this weekend because of the example you are supposed to be. While it's true that being a student athlete is a huge commitment that calls for a lot of sacrifices and takes a lot of time, it is more than worth it. Every teenager with the opportunity to play a sport should take advantage of it.

One of the main priorities for teenagers is preparing for the "real world." When teenagers go off on their own, there are many things they need to be able to do to make it in the world. They need to be able to take on responsibilities, make smart decisions, set and work for goals, and manage their time well. All of these things are also required by student athletes in order to be successful. So, athletes actually have practice in these important skills outside of the sport itself that lead them to find success as adults.

Most teenagers today want to go to college, and—let's face it—unless you have good grades, you're probably not going to be able to get in. For student athletes, making good grades is a pressing need all the way through school. In order to play a sport, you are required to pass your classes, which of course motivates athletes to make good grades. Along with making good grades come more scholarship opportunities for student athletes.

Maintaining good health is important to everyone. Research shows that healthy habits begun young dramatically improve good health throughout life. When you are a student athlete, you are physically fit from running, lifting weights, or whatever it is your sport requires of you to be prepared. Healthy eating is another component to good health, and the diets that your coaches put you on take care of that. Student athletes learn how to take care of their bodies, making them healthier than most other people.

Take advantage of the opportunities and great outcomes that being a student athlete can bring. If you decide to participate in school athletics, you will find that your life will improve all around.

Kristen ends her introduction with a clear thesis statement that she defends in the body of the essay.

Kristen lists examples and facts—she identifies the many benefits of school athletics. See Developing Your Style, p. 447.

With this paragraph, Kristen addresses the needs of the audience beyond school.

Editing and Proofreading

Focus on commonly confused words. Look for words that are commonly mistaken for one another: for example, *adapt* and *adopt*, *accept* and *except*, or *affect* and *effect*. If necessary, consult a dictionary or handbook to make sure you are using the correct word.

Focus on spelling. The "er" sound can be spelled with different letter combinations. Review your spelling of each word with this sound.

Spiral Review: Conventions Earlier in this unit, you learned about subordinating conjunctions (p. 263) and adjective and adverb clauses (p. 419). Check your persuasive essay to be sure you have used those conventions correctly.

Publishing, Presenting, and Reflecting

Consider one of the following ways to share your writing.

Deliver a speech. Use your persuasive essay as the basis for a speech. See the Communications Workshop on page 450 for presentation strategies.

Submit a letter to the editor. Condense your persuasive essay and re-format it as a letter to the editor for publication in your school or community newspaper.

Create an advertising campaign. Present the key ideas from your essay in a public service print campaign that includes posters and a brochure. Or create a public service announcement for radio broadcast.

Reflect on your writing. Jot down your thoughts on the experience of writing a persuasive essay. Begin by answering this question: How did rhetorical devices help you make your points?

Rubric for Self-Assessment

Evaluate your persuasive essay using the following criteria and rating scale.

Criteria	Rating Scale				
	not very				very
Focus: How clear is your thesis statement?	1	2	3	4	5
Organization: How effectively do you organize your arguments?	1	2	3	4	5
Support/Elaboration: How well do you use evidence and a variety of appeals to support your position?	1	2	3	4	5
Style: How well do you use rhetorical devices, such as parallelism, repetition, and analogies?	1	2	3	4	5
Conventions: How correct is your grammar, especially your use of commonly confused words?	1	2	3	4	5

Common Core State Standards

Writing

5. Develop and strengthen writing as needed by planning, revising, editing, rewriting, or trying a new approach, focusing on addressing what is most significant for a specific purpose and audience.

Language

1.b. Resolve issues of complex or contested usage, consulting references as needed.

2.b. Spell correctly.

Deliver a Persuasive Speech

Persuasive speech is language that is used to influence people's thoughts or actions. Most people use persuasion spontaneously as they negotiate their daily lives. In formal speaking situations, however, you must plan persuasive arguments and strategies.

Topic and Thesis

The first step to developing a persuasive speech is to choose a topic about which you are passionate. Jot down a list of issues that interest you. Then, create an arguable **thesis**—your position, or perspective, on the topic. A strong thesis statement is direct and clear, and the goal of your speech should be to persuade your audience to accept the position you set forth in your thesis statement.

Argument and Reasoning

Know your audience. Think carefully about your **audience:** who they are and the values or concerns they share. Understanding your audience will help you develop persuasive appeals that will reach them. There are three main types of persuasive appeals:

- **Ethical Appeal:** Establish your authority as a speaker, by acknowledging both sides of the topic and referring to credible sources.

- **Emotional Appeal:** Present information and evidence in a way that evokes listeners' emotions.

- **Logical Appeal:** Support your thesis with sound *facts* and *reasons*.

You can use different forms of argument to structure your line of reasoning. Use *inductive reasoning* to draw a conclusion after examining specific cases. *Deductive reasoning* involves applying an established principle or conclusion to a specific case. A *syllogism* is a series of three statements or ideas: a general statement, a specific statement, and a conclusion, such as "Reading will improve a student's vocabulary. I need to improve my vocabulary. Therefore, I should read more." An *analogy* is a comparison of one thing to something seemingly unrelated.

Address alternative perspectives. Identify alternative or opposing viewpoints to your position, and answer them in your speech by including logical counterarguments.

Select effective language techniques. As you write your speech, vary your *diction*, or word choice. The use of *Standard American English*—the formal English taught in school—ensures your ideas are clear. Limited use of *informal expressions* or slang can build a bridge to your audience. Keep your audience's knowledge level in mind if you use *technical language* to discuss scientific or technical topics. You may need to define technical terms to ensure that your audience follows your argument.

Common Core State Standards

Speaking and Listening

1.d. Respond thoughtfully to diverse perspectives; synthesize comments, claims, and evidence made on all sides of an issue; resolve contradictions when possible; and determine what additional information or research is required to deepen the investigation or complete the task. *(p. 451)*

4. Present information, findings, and supporting evidence, conveying a clear and distinct perspective, such that listeners can follow the line of reasoning, alternative or opposing perspectives are addressed, and the organization, development, substance, and style are appropriate to purpose, audience and a range of formal and informal tasks.

Also focus on your *syntax,* or sentence structure. The language devices shown in the chart below can make your speech precise and powerful.

Rhetorical Questions	Parallel Structure	Concrete Images	Figurative Language
questions asked for effect that do not require an answer	repetition of grammatical patterns	vivid descriptions of events, places, or people	symbolic or nonliteral language, like similes and metaphors

Activities: Deliver and Discuss a Persuasive Speech

© **Comprehension and Collaboration** For both activities, use an evaluation form like the one shown below.

A. *Rehearse* your speech for friends. Then, deliver it to your class. Afterward, discuss your speech with the class. Respond thoughtfully to classmates' comments and questions. Then, have your audience fill out an evaluation form like the one shown below.

B. Review classmates' comments, synthesizing them by noting where they overlap. Conduct any research needed to answer the concerns raised, and then develop and present an **impromptu speech** offering a *rebuttal,* or answer to your audience's critique of your arguments.

Evaluation Form for Delivery of a Speech

Name of Speech ———————————————————

Thesis ———————————————————————

Types of Persuasive Appeals:

    Ethical: ☐   Example: ———————————————

    Emotional: ☐   Example: —————————————

    Logical: ☐   Example: ———————————————

Diction:

    Standard English ☐   Informal Language ☐   Technical Language ☐

    Examples: ———————————————————

Syntax and Language Devices:

    Rhetorical Questions ☐   Parallel Structure ☐

    Concrete Images ☐   Figurative Language ☐

    Examples: ———————————————————

What would the speaker's opponents say in response to this argument?

———————————————————————————

What did the speaker do well? What could be improved? ———————

———————————————————————————

Words from Mythology

During the Renaissance, many words with origins in Greek and Roman mythology entered the English language. The renewed interest in the cultures of ancient Greece and Rome inspired English translations of classical writers. As these bodies of literature became familiar, English writers made allusions to their settings, characters, and events. From there, it was a short step to inventing related words that conveyed similar meanings. The chart explains the mythological origin of some common words:

Words	Origin
furious	In Greek mythology, the three **Furies** were the spirits of punishment.
martial	In Roman mythology, **Mars** was the god of war, second in importance only to Jupiter.
mercurial	In Roman mythology, **Mercury** was the winged messenger, fleet of foot.
narcissistic	In Greek mythology, the beautiful youth **Narcissus** fell in love with his own reflection in a pool. He pined away as a result of his unrequited love for himself.
titanic	In Greek mythology, the **Titans** were the race of giants who came before the gods of Olympus.

These words can be found in the literature we read today. For example, in the tragedy *Othello*, Shakespeare writes, "I know not where is that Promethean heat, / That can thy light relume." The allusion is to Prometheus, a figure from Greek mythology who stole fire from heaven. Today, *Promethean* is defined as "creative" or "courageously original." Knowing the classical or Biblical origins of words can help you understand their meanings when you encounter them in your reading.

Practice

Directions: Complete the analogies below, using the chart above to help you. Then, explain the relationship between each pair of words.

1. mercurial : permanent :: _____ : titanic

   a. quick   **b.** small   **c.** sinking   **d.** huge

2. gentle : mild :: martial : _____

   a. military   **b.** enemy   **c.** warlike   **d.** soft

Directions: Use each of these words in sentences that show your understanding of their meaning as inferred from their origins.

3. a. furious   **b.** narcissistic   **c.** mercurial

Common Core State Standards

Language

4.a. Use context as a clue to the meaning of a word or phrase.

5. Demonstrate understanding of word relationships.

6. Acquire and use accurately general academic and domain-specific words and phrases, sufficient for reading, writing, speaking, and listening at the college and career readiness level.

Vocabulary Acquisition and Use

Context clues are words or phrases that help readers clarify the meanings of unfamiliar words in a text. By using context clues, you can determine the word or words that complete a sentence. Sentence Completion questions appear in most standardized tests. In these types of questions, you are given sentences with one or more missing words. Your task is to use the context to choose the correct word or words to complete each sentence logically. Try this strategy: (1) Read the entire sentence and anticipate a word that would logically complete it. (2) Scan the answer choices for that word. (3) If the word you anticipated is not there, look for a synonym.

Practice

This exercise is modeled after the Sentence Completion exercises that appear in the Critical Reading section of the SAT.

Directions: Each of the following sentences is missing one or two words. Choose the word or set of words that best completes each sentence.

Test-Taking Tip
Immediately rule out any answer choices you *know* are wrong.

1. Elizabeth, daughter of Henry VIII, was only 25 years old when she became England's ___?___ queen.
   A. melodious
   B. prodigal
   C. sovereign
   D. pernicious
   E. sanguine

2. Elizabeth proved ___?___, assuming the throne with rigor and wit.
   A. dauntless
   B. sullen
   C. multitudinous
   D. wan
   E. skeptical

3. She tolerated neither ___?___ nor insults, though she herself could be both ___?___ and inconstant.
   A. valor . . . predominant
   B. treasons . . . predominant
   C. valor . . . sullen
   D. treasons . . . sullen
   E. challenge . . . agreeable

4. Unwilling to compromise her power, the "Virgin Queen" would never ___?___ to take a husband.
   A. move
   B. scope
   C. deign
   D. raze
   E. vote

Test-Taking Practice

Critical Reading Test: Paired Passages

Paired reading passages are one type of critical reading passage. Paired passages may be fiction or nonfiction, prose or poetry, and vary in length. Questions that follow will refer to each passage individually and to both passages as a unit. As you read, note similarities and differences between the passages, especially the authors' attitudes, word choices, and styles.

Common Core State Standards

RL.11-12.1, RL.11-12.2, RL.11-12.4; L.11-12.3, L.11-12.4, L.11-12.6
[For the full wording of the standards, see the standards chart in the front of your textbook.]

Strategy

- **Read Passage 1**, and answer the questions that refer only to the first passage.
- **Read Passage 2**, and answer the questions that refer only to the second passage.
- Finally, answer the **compare-and-contrast** questions.

Practice

The following exercise is modeled after the SAT Paired Passages Critical Reading section. This section usually includes 48 questions.

Directions: Read both passages. Then, answer the questions. Passage 1 is by Christopher Marlowe. Passage 2 is by Sir Walter Raleigh.

PASSAGE 1

The Passionate Shepherd to His Love

Come live with me, and be my love,
And we will all the pleasures prove
That valleys, groves, hills, and fields,
Woods, or steepy mountain yields.

5 And we will sit upon the rocks,
Seeing the shepherds feed their flocks,
By shallow rivers to whose falls
Melodious birds sing madrigals.

And I will make thee beds of roses,
10 And a thousand fragrant posies,
A cap of flowers, and a kirtle
Embroidered all with leaves of myrtle;

A gown made of the finest wool,
Which from our pretty lambs we pull;
15 Fair lined slippers for the cold,
With buckles of the purest gold;

A belt of straw and ivy buds,
With coral clasps and amber studs;
And if these pleasures may thee move,
20 Come live with me, and be my love.

The shepherds' swains shall dance and sing
For thy delight each May morning;
If these delights thy mind may move,
Then live with me and be my love.

PASSAGE 2

The Nymph's Reply to the Shepherd

If all the world and love were young
And truth in every shepherd's tongue
These pretty pleasures might me move
To live with thee, and be thy love.

5 Time drives the flocks from field to fold,
When rivers rage and rocks grow cold,
And Philomel becometh dumb,
The rest complains of cares to come.

The flowers do fade, and wanton fields
10 To wayward winter reckoning yields:
A honey tongue, a heart of gall,
Is fancy's spring, but sorrow's fall.

Thy gowns, thy shoes, thy beds of roses,
Thy cap, thy kirtle, and thy posies
15 Soon break, soon wither, soon forgotten,
In folly ripe, in season rotten.

Thy belt of straw and ivy buds,
Thy coral clasps and amber studs,
All these in me no means can move
20 To come to thee and be thy love.

But could youth last and love still breed,
Has joy no date nor age no need,
Then these delights my mind might move,
To live with thee and be thy love.

1. Which of the following best states the theme of Passage 1?

   A. Love can be felt only in natural surroundings.

   B. Nature provides the raw materials for all human needs.

   C. The pleasures of love are akin to the pleasures of nature.

   D. Love should be both mentally and emotionally stimulating.

   E. The delights of nature far outweigh those of romance.

2. It can most reasonably be inferred from Passage 1 that the speaker

   A. feels a deep connection to nature

   B. has impure motives

   C. is disenchanted with his daily life

   D. has long suffered from unrequited love

   E. is unschooled in the art of love

3. In line 19 of Passage 1, *move* most nearly means

   A. relocate

   B. stir

   C. offend

   D. find

   E. perplex

4. Which of the following best summarizes Passage 2?

   A. Nature may endure, but love is quick to die.

   B. Love does not require gifts or complicated arguments.

   C. Though nature is temporary, our love is permanent.

   D. To love is to ignore the cares and trials of mortality.

   E. Like nature and youth, love is fleeting.

5. It can be inferred that the speaker of Passage 2 finds "truth in every shepherd's tongue" (line 2)

   A. rarely

   B. only when convenient

   C. frequently

   D. only in nature

   E. occasionally

6. It would be most accurate to say that

   A. Passage 1 is a parody of Passage 2

   B. Passage 1 is an excerpt of Passage 2

   C. Passage 2 is a response to Passage 1

   D. Passage 2 is a poor imitation of Passage 1

   E. Passage 2 allegorizes Passage 1

7. The speaker of Passage 2 would most likely describe the speaker of Passage 1 as

   A. deceptive

   B. unintelligent

   C. romantic

   D. naive

   E. remote

Editing in Context: Grammar and Writing

Editing-in-context segments often appear in the writing sections of standardized tests. They are made up of a reading passage with numbered sentences. The passages are usually drafts of student essays that contain errors in grammar, style, and usage. For each question, you must decide which of four possible answers will best correct a given sentence.

Practice

This exercise is modeled after the Identifying Sentence Errors portion of the SAT Writing test. The test usually includes 18 such questions.

Directions: Each of the following sentences contains either a single error or no error at all. The error, if there is one, is underlined and lettered. If a sentence contains an error, select the letter of that underlined part. If the sentence is correct, select choice E.

Strategy

"Listen" for Errors
Read the sentence straight through. If you mentally "trip" over one of the underlined portions, it's probably wrong.

1. During the **sixteenth century**—the first
   A
   century of the **printed book**—writers
   B
   from all **levels of society** sought to have
   C
   his works published. **No error**
   D   E

   A.
   B.
   C.
   D.
   E.

2. However, it was **one** of the **more**
   A
   dangerous eras in history **for** those
   B   C
   whose names appeared in print.
   D
   No error
   E

   A.
   B.
   C.
   D.
   E.

3. All books were **censored** by various
   A
   government and church authorities,
   B
   whom in turn were **accountable to** the
   C   D
   monarch. **No error**
   E

   A.
   B.
   C.
   D.
   E.

4. **Even** the most innocent **complement**
   A   B
   could be construed as slander; even the
   most straightforward observation could
   C
   be **mistaken** for deceit. **No error**
   D   E

   A.
   B.
   C.
   D.
   E.

5. Punishments <u>came</u> in <u>a range of forms</u> and
   _A   _B
degrees; <u>it</u> was sometimes a mere reprimand,
         _C
<u>sometimes</u> a decade in prison. <u>No error</u>
_D   _E

   A.
   B.
   C.
   D.
   E.

6. For this reason, the medieval <u>practice</u>
                               _A
of circulating <u>unpublished</u> manuscripts
               _B
continued <u>to thrive</u> <u>well</u> into the 1700s.
           _C   _D
<u>No error</u>
   _E

   A.
   B.
   C.
   D.
   E.

7. For courtiers and <u>others of</u> high rank, writing
                     _A
and circulating anonymous texts <u>were</u> a
                                 _B
<u>relatively safest</u> way of expressing dissent or
             _C
<u>affection</u>. <u>No error</u>
     _D   _E

   A.
   B.
   C.
   D.
   E.

 ## Timed Writing: Position Statement [25 minutes]

In *Utopia*, Sir Thomas More writes: "When a ruler enjoys wealth and pleasure while all about him are grieving and groaning, he acts as a jailor rather than as a king."

Write an essay in which you agree or disagree with More's statement. Do you consider it an overstatement, or a painful truth? What value, if any, might it hold for leaders of our own time? Use reasons and examples from your own knowledge and experience to support your ideas.

> **Academic Vocabulary**
>
> Read the prompt and the assignment twice carefully. Note key words, such as *agree* or *disagree*, that clarify the assignment.

Performance Tasks

Follow the instructions to complete the tasks below as required by your teacher. As you work on each task, incorporate both general academic vocabulary and literary terms you learned in this unit.

Common Core State Standards

RL.11-12.1, RL.11-12.3, RL.11-12.4, RL.11-12.5; RI.11-12.2, RI.11-12.6; W.11-12.1, W.11-12.2; SL.11-12.4, SL.11-12.5
[For the full wording of the standards, see the standards chart in the front of your textbook.]

Writing

Task 1: Literature [RL.11-12.3; W.11-12.1]
Analyze the Development of a Drama

*Write an **essay** in which you analyze how the author of one of the dramatic works in this unit develops and relates the key elements of the play.*

- Explain which play you chose and briefly summarize the plot.
- Identify key choices the author made in writing the drama. For example, consider where the play is set, how the action is ordered, and how the characters are introduced and developed. Consider also the way in which these elements relate to each other.
- Analyze the impact of the author's choices, discussing how these decisions affect both the play's meaning and the reader's experience.
- Organize ideas so that each idea builds on the one it follows to create a unified whole.
- Provide a concluding section that follows from the explanation presented. In your conclusion, sum up your analysis of the author's key choices and their impact. Include a memorable statement of your opinion of the work.

Task 2: Literature [RL.11-12.4; W.11-12.1]
Analyze Shakespearean Language

*Write an **essay** in which you analyze Shakespeare's word choice in one of the acts of* Macbeth, *which appears in this unit.*

- Identify specific examples of language that you find especially effective in one of the acts of *Macbeth.* Consider the following elements: figures of speech, such as similes or metaphors; specific words that are particularly interesting or beautiful; and connotative meanings that are especially rich or striking. Explain your choices and the reasons for them.
- Identify any words in the act that readers may not understand. Explain the meanings of these words. If any have multiple meanings, explain which ones are most important.
- Consider how the combined word choices in the act you are analyzing develop the author's tone.
- Cite specific examples from the play to support your ideas. Quote precisely and accurately. Introduce each example with a sentence or phrase that shows its connection to the idea you intend it to illustrate.

Task 3: Informational Text [RI.11-12.2; W.11-12.2]
Analyze the Development of Central Ideas

*Write an **essay** in which you analyze the development of two or more central ideas in a work of literary nonfiction from this unit.*

- Choose a work of nonfiction from this unit, and clearly identify and explain at least two central ideas expressed in the work.
- Discuss how the author introduces and develops each idea.
- Support your claim, identifying specific details that shape and refine each central idea.
- Explain how the central ideas interact and build on one another—reinforcing, adding to, or refining each other—to create a complex analysis of the topic of the work.
- To ensure that readers understand your analysis, include an objective summary of the work.

Speaking and Listening

Task 4: Literature [RL.11-12.5; SL.11-12.4]
Analyze Text Structure

*Prepare and deliver an **oral presentation** in which you analyze the structure of a poem in this unit.*

- Identify the poem you will analyze, and explain why you chose it.

- Begin your presentation by discussing the overall structure of your chosen poem. For example, does it follow simple chronological order, or does it move about in time? Who is the speaker, and who is being addressed? Do the divisions between stanzas or other sections reflect and reinforce shifts in ideas?

- Identify a specific section of the poem that you will analyze in your presentation. For example, you may discuss how the poem begins, how events are ordered, or how it ends (happily, tragically, or inconclusively). Discuss how the specific section or aspect of the poem contributes to the overall structure.

- Discuss the aesthetic, or artistic, impact of the author's structural choices.

- Explain how the structure affects the poem's overall meaning. Support your ideas with evidence from the text.

Task 5: Literature [RL.11-12.1; SL.11-12.5]
Draw Inferences

*Prepare and deliver an **oral presentation** in which you cite textual evidence to support inferences drawn from a poem in this unit.*

- Identify the poem you chose. Explain the poem's explicit meaning or key idea. Quote from the text to support your point.

- Identify any ideas or emotions that the speaker suggests but does not explicitly state. Cite details from the poem that help you draw these inferences. Explain how you tied these details together to see connections that suggest implicit meanings.

- Discuss ideas or emotions the poem leaves uncertain or open to interpretation. Consider the reasons for and effects of this ambiguity.

- Incorporate digital media that enhances your presentation. For example, consider images, audio, graphics, or textual elements that help illustrate and clarify your ideas or those expressed in the poem.

Task 6: Informational Text [RI.11-12.6; SL.11-12.4]
Determine Author's Point of View

*Prepare and deliver an **oral presentation** in which you determine the author's point of view and analyze his or her style in a nonfiction work from this unit.*

- Introduce the work you chose. Explain the author's purpose, topic, and central ideas.

- Describe the author's point of view. Explain how the author's stance affects his or her discussion of the topic and helps to shape the central idea.

- Discuss specific aspects of the author's rhetoric and style. Cite details and examples from the text to support your position.

- Define technical language or uncommon words to address your audience's knowledge level of your subject.

 What is the relationship of the writer to tradition?

Something Old, Something New The old rhyme about weddings says that a bride should wear "something old" together with "something new." In that spirit, many writers in this unit combined old and new.

Assignment Choose three authors from this unit who drew from tradition to create something new. Write a **literary analysis** showing how each author used a traditional theme, genre, or stylistic device but refreshed it with a new or inventive approach.

Featured Titles

In this unit, you have read a variety of literature of the English Renaissance. Continue to read works related to this era on your own. Select books that you enjoy, but challenge yourself to explore new topics, new authors, and works offering varied perspectives or approaches. The titles suggested below will help you get started.

LITERATURE

The Tragedy of Hamlet
William Shakespeare   EXEMPLAR TEXT

 Drama In this classic tale of murder and revenge, Hamlet learns that his uncle has murdered his father in order to seize the crown. Urged on by the ghost of his father, Hamlet swears he will kill his uncle. However, Hamlet is paralyzed by indecision, delaying his revenge until events themselves speed the story to a bloody conclusion.

[Shakespeare's play The Tragedy of Macbeth begins on page 322 of this book. Build knowledge by reading another tragedy by this author.]

The Tempest
William Shakespeare

 **Drama** After his evil brother steals his kingdom, the magician Prospero and his daughter are stranded on a remote island. Years later, when a tempest shipwrecks his brother on the same island, Prospero has the opportunity for revenge, reconciliation, or both—if only his magic powers do not fail him.

The Sonnets
William Shakespeare

 **Poetry** This collection contains all 154 of Shakespeare's sonnets, along with commentary and illustrations. This version includes an introduction by the poet W. H. Auden.

[Four of Shakespeare's sonnets appear on pages 275–278 of this book. Build knowledge by reading all of his sonnets.]

Don Quixote
Miguel de Cervantes   EXEMPLAR TEXT

 **Novel** Don Quixote, an aging man from La Mancha, Spain, sets out with his companion Sancho Panza on a quest filled with misadventures. He is determined to save maidens, right wrongs, and revive the code of chivalry. The fact that these adventures take place largely in Quixote's head only adds to the satiric hilarity.

INFORMATIONAL TEXTS

Historical Texts

Utopia
Sir Thomas More
NuVision Publications, 2007

 Philosophy More describes an idealized city-state governed by reason. In a wide-ranging work that anticipates the hot-button issues of the next several centuries, he addresses such topics as women's rights, education, religion, and war.

Contemporary Scholarship

Galileo's Daughter
Dava Sobel

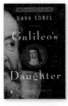 **Science** This scientific biography tells of Galileo's relationship with Virginia, his eldest daughter and confidante. Her letters, translated and masterfully woven into the narrative, illuminate and humanize the life of this towering figure in the fields of astronomy and physics.

The Children of Henry VIII
Alison Weir
Ballantine Books, 1997

 Historical Narrative Six times married, King Henry VIII of England left four prospective heirs to the throne after his death. This narrative describes the tumultuous period when three of Henry's children reigned in succession—Edward VI, Mary I, and, finally, Queen Elizabeth I.

A Year in the Life of William Shakespeare: 1599
James Shapiro

 Biography Thirty-five-year-old William Shakespeare wrote four plays in 1599. In this biography, James Shapiro discusses how the turbulent events of the time influenced *Henry V, Julius Caesar, As You Like It,* and *Hamlet.*

Preparing to Read Complex Texts

Reading for College and Career In both college and the workplace, readers must analyze texts independently, draw connections among works that offer varied perspectives, and develop their own ideas and informed opinions. The questions shown below, and others that you generate on your own, will help you more effectively read and analyze complex college-level texts.

 **Common Core State Standards**

Reading Literature/Informational Text
10. By the end of grade 12, read and comprehend literature, including stories, dramas, and poems, and literary nonfiction at the high end of the grades 11-CCR text complexity band independently and proficiently.

When reading complex texts, ask yourself...

- What idea, experience, or story seems to have compelled the author to write? Has the author presented that idea, experience, or story in a way that I, too, find compelling?

- How might the author's era, social status, belief system, or personal experiences have affected the point of view he or she expresses in the text?

- How do my circumstances affect what I understand and feel about this text?

- What key idea does the author state explicitly? What key idea does he or she suggest or imply? Which details in the text help me to perceive implied ideas?

- Do I find multiple layers of meaning in the text? If so, what relationships do I see among these layers of meaning?

- How do details in the text connect or relate to one another? Do I find any details unconvincing, unrelated, or out of place?

- Do I find the text believable and convincing?

© **Key Ideas and Details**

- What patterns of organization or sequences do I find in the text? Do these patterns help me understand the ideas better?

- What do I notice about the author's style, including his or her diction, uses of imagery and figurative language, and syntax?

- Do I like the author's style? Is the author's style memorable?

- What emotional attitude does the author express toward the topic, the story, or the characters? Does this attitude seem appropriate?

- What emotional attitude does the author express toward me, the reader? Does this attitude seem appropriate?

- What do I notice about the author's voice—his or her personality on the page? Do I like this voice? Does it make me want to read on?

© **Craft and Structure**

- Is the work fresh and original?

- Do I agree with the author's ideas entirely, or are there elements I find unconvincing?

- Do I disagree with the author's ideas entirely, or are there elements I can accept as true?

- Based on my knowledge of British literature, history, and culture, does this work reflect the British tradition? Why or why not?

© **Integration of Ideas**

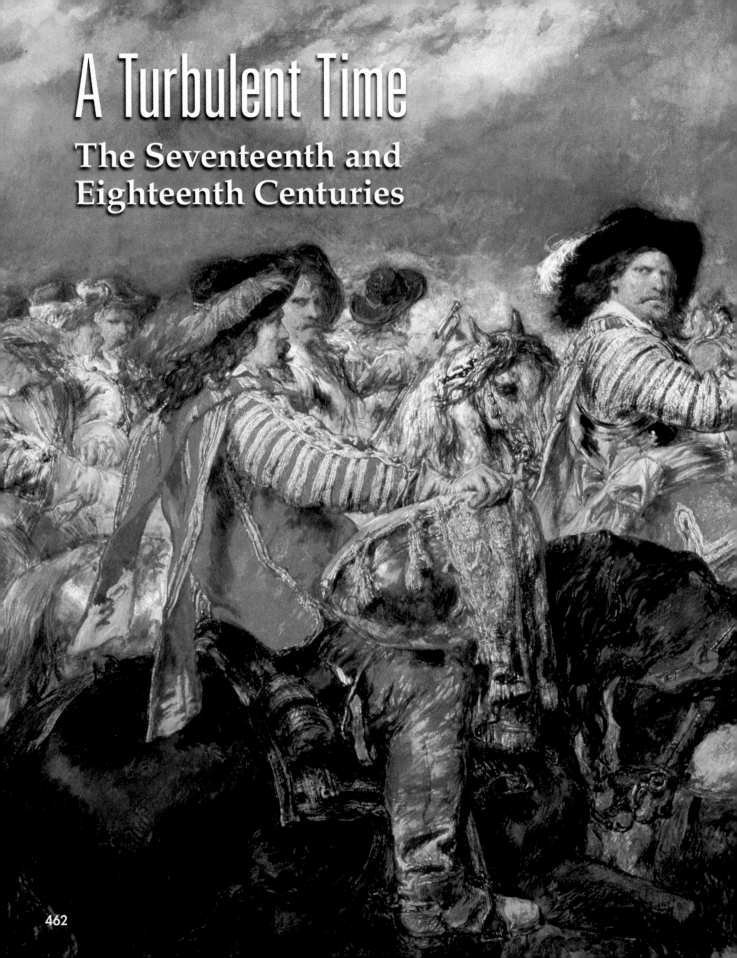

A Turbulent Time

The Seventeenth and Eighteenth Centuries

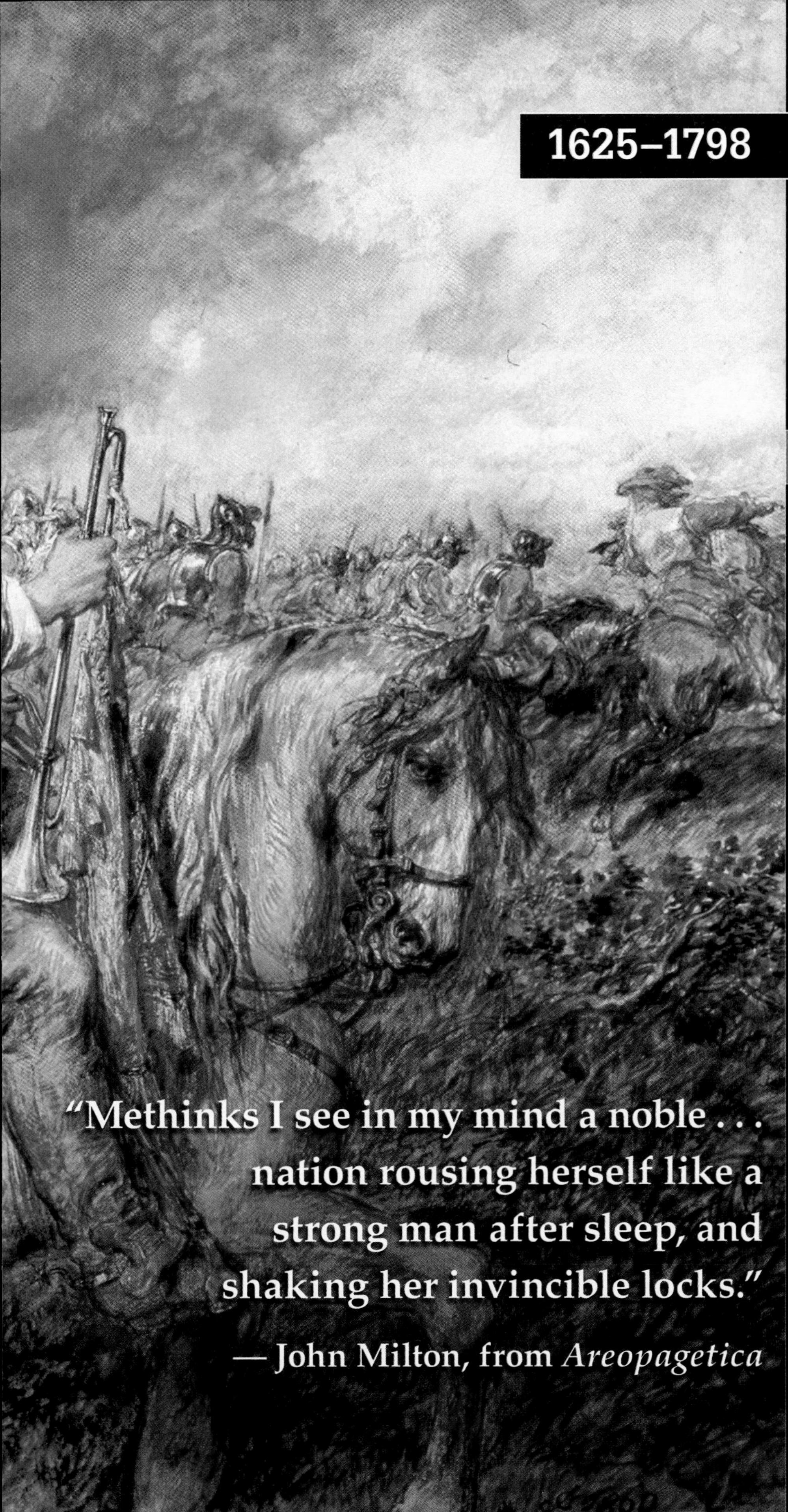

Unit 3

1625–1798

"Methinks I see in my mind a noble . . . nation rousing herself like a strong man after sleep, and shaking her invincible locks."

— John Milton, from *Areopagetica*

PHLit Online!
www.PHLitOnline.com

Hear It!
- Selection summary audio
- Selection audio

See It!
- Au hor videos
- Essential Question video
- Get Connected videos
- Background videos
- More about the authors
- Illustrated vocabulary words
- Vocabulary flashcards

Do It!
- Interactive journals
- Interactive graphic organizers
- Grammar tutorials
- Interactive vocabulary games
- Test practice

Snapshot of the Period

Social turmoil and new growth define this period and its literature. The guns of the English Civil War, which pitted the king against Parliament, echo through the work of poets Andrew Marvell, Richard Lovelace, and John Milton. The Industrial and Agricultural revolutions, sparked by the use of new machines in production and in farming, led to the growth of cities, an increase in urban poverty, and the rise of the middle class. These developments influenced the work of Samuel Pepys, Daniel Defoe, Samuel Johnson, and Joseph Addison, each of whom chronicled the life of the middle class or catered to its leisure needs. At the end of the period, political revolutions in America and in France prepared the way for the revolution in literature known as Romanticism.

The surrender of British General Cornwallis to George Washington at Yorktown, Virginia (1781), led to America's victory in the Revolution.

James Watt's steam engine, shown here, helped bring about the Industrial Revolution.

 As you read the selections in this unit, you will be asked to think about them in view of three key questions:

What is the **relationship** between literature and *place?*

How does literature **shape or reflect** *society?*

What is the relationship of the **writer** to *tradition?*

CAVALIERS vs. ROUNDHEADS

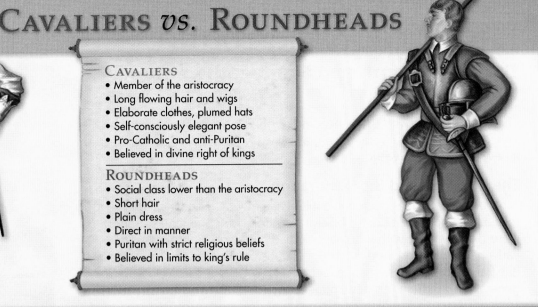

CAVALIERS
- Member of the aristocracy
- Long flowing hair and wigs
- Elaborate clothes, plumed hats
- Self-consciously elegant pose
- Pro-Catholic and anti-Puritan
- Believed in divine right of kings

ROUNDHEADS
- Social class lower than the aristocracy
- Short hair
- Plain dress
- Direct in manner
- Puritan with strict religious beliefs
- Believed in limits to king's rule

THE INTRODUCTION OF COFFEE TO ENGLAND is a story in which exploration, trade, slavery, the growth of cities, and the rise of the middle class all play a role.

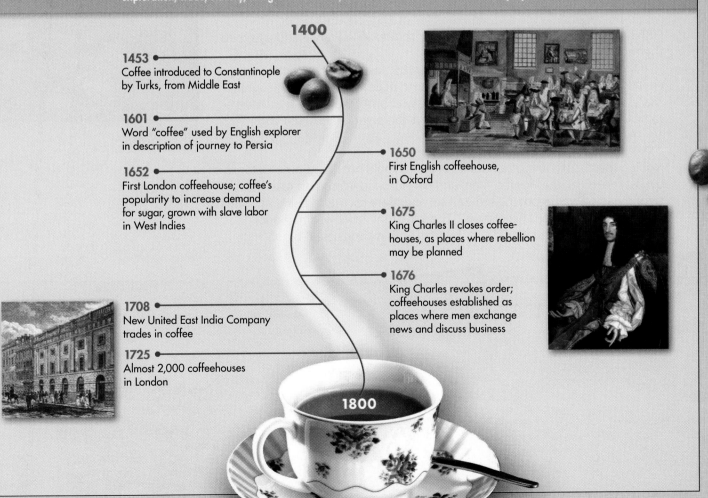

1400

1453
Coffee introduced to Constantinople by Turks, from Middle East

1601
Word "coffee" used by English explorer in description of journey to Persia

1652
First London coffeehouse; coffee's popularity to increase demand for sugar, grown with slave labor in West Indies

1650
First English coffeehouse, in Oxford

1675
King Charles II closes coffee-houses, as places where rebellion may be planned

1676
King Charles revokes order; coffeehouses established as places where men exchange news and discuss business

1708
New United East India Company trades in coffee

1725
Almost 2,000 coffeehouses in London

1800

Historical Background

The Seventeenth and Eighteenth Centuries (1625–1798)

The period begins with the beheading of one king and ends with the beheading of another. In between, a civil war and five revolutions created a new and different world.

The Civil War and the Restoration

A proud king, Charles I, struggled with Parliament over political and religious authority until, in 1642, civil war broke out. The king's supporters were the Cavaliers, with long hair, plumed hats, and high boots. The Parliamentary forces were the "Roundheads," with cropped hair, black hats, and sturdy shoes. Their leaders included Oliver Cromwell, a stern general who thought his new model army could bring divine justice to England. After six brutal years, Charles was defeated, captured, and tried by his "subjects." Condemned to death, he was beheaded in January 1649.

A dead king does not, however, guarantee a democratic or effective government. Impatient with quarreling Parliamentary factions, Cromwell seized power and served as Lord Protector of England until his death (1653–1658). In 1660, Charles II returned from exile in France and assumed the throne in a restored monarchy.

When Charles died without an heir in 1685, his brother, a Catholic convert, became James II. James also had no male heirs, and his daughter, Mary, was a staunch Protestant. The uneasy country was willing to have James as king while it waited for Mary, but the aging king had a son.

"The Glorious Revolution"

Nobles, merchants, and other power brokers would not stand for a Catholic dynasty. In 1688, they invited Mary and her husband William to take the throne. James was deposed, and William and Mary succeeded him, an event hailed as "The Glorious Revolution." The will of the governed had once again determined who would rule, but this time without great bloodshed.

Charles I

TIMELINE

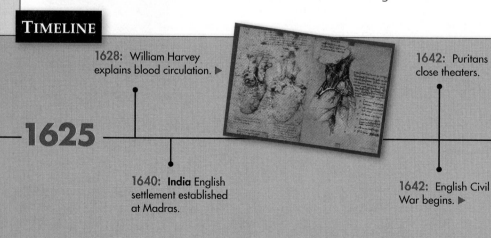

1628: William Harvey explains blood circulation. ▶

1642: Puritans close theaters.

1625

1640: **India** English settlement established at Madras.

1642: English Civil War begins. ▶

Parliament stepped in again in 1701, passing the Act of Settlement to keep the crown in Protestant hands. In 1714, George, the Elector of Hanover in Germany, became king. George I did not speak English and cared little for the country, and Parliament assumed almost complete control.

Other Revolutions

The Industrial Revolution, an explosion of manufacturing involving new technology and new energy sources such as steam, began in the 1700s. Powerful new machinery linked with crop rotation, larger farms, and improved transportation led to an Agricultural Revolution, creating a new abundance with which fewer farmers could feed the swelling population of the cities.

The fourth revolution began in 1775 and ended in 1781. England, a mighty military power, was defeated by American troops fighting on their own soil. America became independent but maintained connections of language, politics, culture, and literature that enriched both countries.

The fifth revolution of the period began on July 14, 1789, when the people of Paris stormed the Bastille, a hated symbol of royal oppression. Shortly after this, King Louis XVI was beheaded and the old order was shattered. Government without kings, already established in America, had now displaced a monarchy in Europe.

At the end of the American Revolution, when Lord Cornwallis led his defeated troops out of Yorktown, the band played a popular tune: "The World Turned Upside Down." It is a good theme song for the whole era.

Key Historical Theme: Civil War and Revolutions

- Struggles between king and Parliament led to a bloody civil war, culminating in the execution of Charles I, and subsequently, to a bloodless revolution deposing Charles II's successor, James II.

- Industrial and Agricultural revolutions boosted manufacturing and farming production.

- Revolutions in America and France showed that people could change their form of government.

1643: France Louis XIV becomes king.

1649: Charles I beheaded.

◄ **1660:** Monarchy restored.

1660

1644: China Ming Dynasty ends.

1653: Oliver Cromwell becomes Lord Protector. ►

1658: Oliver Cromwell dies. Puritan government collapses.

Essential Questions Across Time

The Seventeenth and Eighteenth Centuries (1625–1798)

? **What is the relationship between literature and *place?***

Bustling city versus quiet country: that age-old division is central to the period. For most of the time, it is the city of London that matters, but gradually, it is the rural landscape that comes to dominate.

How was London the capital of literature, too?

Old London The London of the seventeenth-century poets John Donne, Ben Jonson, and the young John Milton was still the old city of narrow, unpaved streets and timber houses. The river Thames was the main thoroughfare. It was easier to sail to a distant destination than walk or ride, and with only one bridge, ferries were needed to connect the two banks of the river.

During the civil war and the Protectorate of Cromwell, all eyes focused on the Houses of Parliament. These were not the imposing buildings in which Parliament sits today, made famous by postcards. (Those buildings were erected in the 1840s!) Although much smaller, they were still the stages on which the political dramas of the day were enacted.

In 1660, a new king returned from exile, and London threw off its Puritan black, reopened the theaters the triumphant Puritans had closed in 1642, welcomed actresses on the stage for the first time, and celebrated.

London Disasters Become London Literature The party did not last long, however. The Puritans said it was divine retribution on a scandalous court; historians say it was flea-bearing rats from the busy wharves on the Thames. In 1664, the plague struck and

TIMELINE

1664: North America
Britain seizes
New Netherlands.

1666: Great Fire of London. ▶

1660

◀ **1682: North America**
La Salle claims Louisiana
for France.

the streets of London were filled with carts carrying dead bodies to lime pits. Then, in 1666, a great fire broke out and large areas of London were incinerated. Samuel Pepys captured these twin disasters in his *Diary*, displaying a reporter's cool eye and a citizen's warm concern.

Pepys was writing only for himself, or so he thought (the *Diary*, written in code, was "translated" and published in the 19th century). At least two generations later, however, Daniel Defoe interviewed survivors of the plague and studied records to re-create that perilous time for a broad public, writing the fictional *A Journal of the Plague Year*.

How did roads lead to novels?

Just as London was rebuilt after the fire, the countryside was also being transformed by a series of turnpikes for stagecoaches and canals for barges. The primary purpose was business, but as people took advantage of the new mobility the coach roads offered, a new literary form took inspiration from the road: the novel.

The novel pictured all kinds of characters in their wanderings. Henry Fielding's humorous and good-humored *Tom Jones* was a prime example of a novel on the road. (One later writer, the French novelist Stendhal, would even define a novel as a mirror traveling down a road, reflecting the life around it.)

How did a new gathering place capture a new readership?

All roads still led to London, especially for the bright and ambitious. In London, they would encounter a new kind of gathering place. Suddenly,

---

The BRITISH TRADITION

THE CHANGING ENGLISH LANGUAGE, BY RICHARD LEDERER

No Harmless Drudge, He

On April 15, 1755, Dr. Samuel Johnson—blind in one eye, impoverished, and incompletely educated—produced the first modern *Dictionary of the English Language*.

Johnson set himself the task of making a different kind of dictionary, one of the first that would include all the words in the English language, not just the difficult ones. In addition, he would show how to divide words into syllables and where words came from. He would establish a consistent system of defining words and draw from his own gigantic learning to provide, for the first time in any dictionary, illustrative quotations from famous writers.

Underfunded and working almost alone in a Fleet Street garret room, Johnson defined some 43,000 words and illuminated their meanings with more than 114,000 supporting quotations.

Johnson defined a lexicographer as "a writer of dictionaries, a harmless drudge . . ." However, he was obviously far more than a harmless drudge, and his two-volume dictionary was by far the most comprehensive and readable that had appeared.

WORKS of JOHN LOCKE, Esq

1684: **China** All ports opened to foreign trade.

1688: Glorious Revolution.

1690: John Locke publishes his *Two Treatises of Government.* ▶

1685: James II becomes king.

◀ 1689: Bill of Rights becomes law.

1695

like mushrooms sprung up overnight, these places were all over the city. There seemed to be one on every corner. Who could account for the unstoppable spread of the coffee house? Will's and White's were among the most fashionable, but they all had many regulars.

They were popular because they offered not only coffee, the beverage that was all the rage at the time, but a place to hang out, to meet friends, to smoke a pipe, and to read the essays in those new-fangled magazines people were talking about. The titles of two famous magazines of the time, *The Tatler* and *The Spectator*, suggest that periodicals were an extension of the observation and gossip that took place around the city and especially in coffee houses. Such gossip, however, was still respectable for a self-conscious and social-climbing middle class—a coffee house was more proper than a tavern.

Samuel Johnson, who had ridden from Litchfield to London to seek literary fame and fortune—sharing a horse with future actor David Garrick, according to legend—embodied the London man of letters at this time. He famously remarked that if a man were tired of London, he was tired of life. In his greatest literary achievement, the *Dictionary of the English Language*, Johnson defined in a single book all the words worth knowing, just as London itself defined all the life worth living.

How did the countryside begin to influence literature?

Even as Johnson was speaking, however, the times were changing. One of the most popular and influential poems of the second half of the eighteenth century is not set in London, but in a country churchyard. Thomas Gray's "Elegy Written in a Country Churchyard" is a sober and thoughtful poem, and its meditative tone is completely different from the biting satire that flourished in an urban world. A mood of nocturnal reverie became the dominant mood of poetry.

Removed from the din and dirt of the city, poets looked to country landscapes for inspiration, moral examples, and consolation. The country replaced the city as the setting and subject for literature.

> **ESSENTIAL QUESTION VOCABULARY**
>
> These Essential Question words will help you think and write about literature and place:
>
> **mobility** (mō bil´ ə tē´) *n.* ability to move freely from place to place
>
> **meditative** (med´ ə tāt´ iv) *adj.* deeply thoughtful
>
> **urban** (ʉr´ bən) *adj.* characteristic of the city, as opposed to the country

TIMELINE

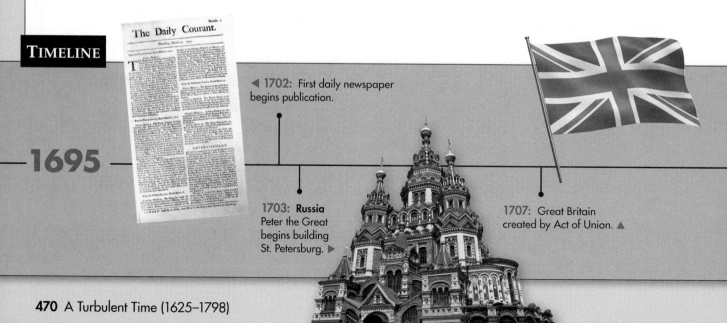

◀ **1702:** First daily newspaper begins publication.

1703: Russia Peter the Great begins building St. Petersburg. ▶

1707: Great Britain created by Act of Union. ▲

— 1695 —

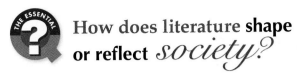

How does literature shape or reflect *society?*

The turmoil of the period raised profound questions about order. Civil war toppled a king and so posed the question, What holds the social order together? Fueled by religious differences, the war dramatized still other fundamental questions: If human beliefs differ irreconcilably, what can one know about the order of the world or about the right way to behave? Even economic growth opened questions. Members of the new middle class, their place in the world secured by prosperity, not birth, were haunted by the question, What is my place in the social order? The literature of the time was dedicated to answering such questions.

How did Milton's Grace become Newton's Gravity?

For John Milton, who lived through the Civil War, serving as Cromwell's secretary, literature, religion, and civic duty were all related. His epic *Paradise Lost* takes disobedience as its theme: the rebellious pride of Satan leading to the willful disobedience of Eve. Writing in the dark days when the Puritan religious government had failed, he intended his epic poem "to justify the ways of God to men."

At almost the same time that Milton published *Paradise Lost*, one of England's towering geniuses provided a different vision of God's ways in the world. In 1687, Isaac Newton published his *Mathematical Principles of Natural Philosophy* and everything changed. Newton demonstrated that the universe was governed by natural physical principles. Newton himself was a deeply religious man, but others read his work as proof that the world operated without the constant attention of a divine being. Gravity replaced grace. Some believed in a divine watchmaker who created and wound up the universe and then let it tick on its own.

Belief in a benevolent but detached God was called Deism. Pope's *Essay on Man* tells us: "Know then thyself, presume not God to scan." More and more, emphasis would be placed on understanding humans in their own world and according to the natural laws of that world.

ESSENTIAL QUESTION VOCABULARY

These Essential Question words will help you think and write about literature and society:

civic (siv´ik) *adj.* relating to citizenship and affairs of government

rational (rash´ ən əl) *adj.* of or based on reason

proportion (prō pôr´ shən) *n.* balance; desirable relationship among parts

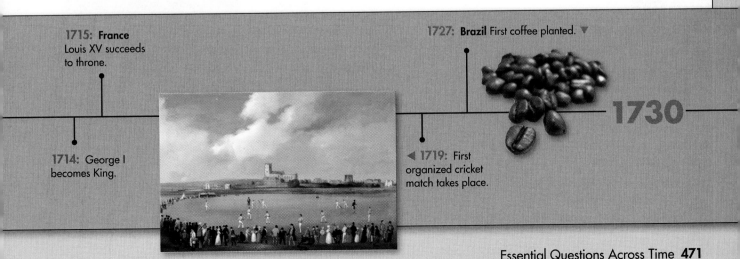

1715: France Louis XV succeeds to throne.

1727: Brazil First coffee planted. ▼

1730

1714: George I becomes King.

◀ **1719:** First organized cricket match takes place.

Essential Questions Across Time **471**

Why did literature focus on conduct?

Satire and Proportion In this new world, writers examined conduct through the lens of reason, not revelation. As a result, satire flourished. Satire ridicules conduct that is not rational, that is out of proportion. Pope's *Rape of the Lock* is a mock epic in which a trivial incident is treated as something earth-shaking. Swift's *Gulliver's Travels* is, with its tiny Lilliputians and giant Brobdingnagians, a study in proportion and the disproportionate things that humans do.

The "How-to" Genres The literary essay began as a "how-to" genre, teaching rational conduct to the new middle classes and helping them find their own identity. As Addison says in his essay "The Aims of *The Spectator*," he hopes the "morning lectures" in his new periodical will provide "instruction agreeable, and ... diversion useful."

The novel also had its start in the "how-to" fashion. Samuel Richardson, a publisher, wrote a book of advice on conduct for apprentices. He then began a series of model letters on problems of conduct in daily life. In 1740, these turned into *Pamela*. Often cited as the first English novel, *Pamela* is epistolary in form; it is a series of letters by a young servant whose virtue is, unsuccessfully, assailed by her master.

Religious belief was also caught up in this question of appropriate conduct. John Wesley founded Methodism, which grew from his early commitment to self-examination and self-discipline, the "method" of belief and worship. His preaching was very influential because it met the need for a renewed sense of personal religious experience.

The BRITISH TRADITION

CLOSE-UP ON DAILY LIFE

Proper Behavior for Children

The eighteenth-century focus on proper conduct applied to children as well. One book on this subject was entitled *Rules for Children's Behavior: At Church, at Home, at Table, in Company, in Discourse, at School, abroad, and among Boys . . .* (1701). Following are some of the "Rules for Behavior in Company":

Sit not down in the presence of Superiors without bidding.

Sing not nor hum in thy mouth while thou art in company.

Play not wantonly like a Mimic with thy Fingers or Feet.

Stand not wriggling with thy body hither and thither, but steady and upright.

In coughing or sneezing make as little noise as possible.

If thou cannot avoid yawning, shut thy Mouth with thine Hand or Handkerchief before it, turning thy Face aside.

Laugh not aloud, but silently Smile upon occasion.

TIMELINE

1740: Prussia Frederick the Great succeeds to the throne. ▼

1749: Henry Fielding publishes *Tom Jones*.

1730

1745: Last Jacobite rebellion in Scotland.

1752: North America Benjamin Franklin invents lightning rod. ▲

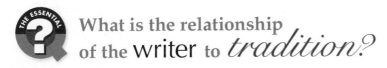

What is the relationship of the writer to *tradition?*

In this period, some literary traditions reach a magnificent conclusion, and some wholly new forms emerge from the chaos of civil war and revolution to meet the needs of a growing, literate, middle-class audience.

What effects did the Renaissance and Reformation have?

From Love to Religion John Donne is a child of the Renaissance—the rebirth of classical learning and themes that began in the fifteenth century—and Reformation—the efforts to reform Christianity that led to the birth of Protestantism. He begins as a witty love poet and ends as the Dean of the old St. Paul's Cathedral, which burned in 1666. His early lyrics continue the Elizabethan tradition, but his Holy Sonnets change the sonnet from a love poem into a religious meditation.

Work Based on the Classics Ben Jonson's poetry is restrained and graceful, like the classical poetry he admired. Poets who succeeded him, "The Tribe of Ben," produced brilliant poems on the *carpe diem* theme. *Carpe diem* is Latin for "seize the day," and the speakers in the poems, male, urge their audience, female, to forget inhibitions and take advantage of the fleeting hours of life. Andrew Marvell's "To His Coy Mistress" adds a serious undertone suggesting the real ravages of time.

Renaissance and Reformation John Milton's work embodies almost all the traditions of both the Renaissance and Reformation. Able to read Greek, Latin, Hebrew, French, and Italian, he wanted to give English an epic poem to match those of Homer and Virgil. He first considered an epic based on the legends of King Arthur because Homer and Virgil had based their epics on mythic histories of their countries.

A devout son of the Reformation, however, he decided that the fit subject for an English epic was the Bible's story of creation and fall. When the hated monarchy had been restored, the poet, blind and disillusioned with politics, dictated his poem about the fall from Eden and the promise of a redeemer who will restore the human race to its rightful heritage.

1756: Britain enters Seven Years War.

1761: First exhibition of agricultural machines opens in London. ▶

1765

1759: Canada British troops capture Quebec. ▶

1764: London introduces practice of numbering houses.

How did Milton create a new role for the poet?

Poet as Prophet In his writing, Milton addressed the English as if he were an Old Testament prophet, thundering at a people that had broken its covenant with God. Milton created the role of poet as prophet, a poet reminding a nation of the path from which it had strayed. This idea of the poet had a strong influence on subsequent literature. In the Romantic period, the poets William Blake and Percy Bysshe Shelley assume the role. Another Romantic, Wordsworth, despairing of the state of England in 1802, writes: "Milton! thou shouldst be living at this hour / England hath need of thee."

What new forms arose for new audiences?

The Heroic Couplet Milton's influence was not felt immediately. With the end of the civil war and Puritan rule, poets sought a new mode of expression for a new social order. That mode was the heroic couplet, iambic pentameter lines linked in rhyming pairs. This form perfectly suited an urban aristocratic society that valued clever talk. With the genius of Alexander Pope, the form reaches its peak. The variations he creates within the rigid form give his poetry its vitality.

The Essay and the Novel Two new forms came into being in this period to meet the demands of a new middle-class audience: the essay and the novel. Both require a literate audience with money to spend on periodicals and books and leisure time to fill—an audience who want to read about people like themselves and people they would like to be.

The essay is a secular sermon, teaching lessons about life. Where sermons are delivered in houses of worship, essays depended on publication in periodicals to reach their audience. At the same time, periodicals relied on essays to attract readers. That marriage produced an enduring form whose offspring includes today's newspaper columns and television news commentary shows.

The novel had its roots in quasi-religious narratives: the life story of a man or woman struggling to survive and be virtuous in a world that is hostile, evil, or simply indifferent. Coming into flower in the middle of the eighteenth century, the novel is the beginning of a style of literature—self-conscious, self-analytical, socially concerned—that will dominate coming centuries.

John Milton

TIMELINE

1776: North America
American Revolution begins. ▼

1765

1773: North America
Boston Tea Party. ▶

CONTEMPORARY CONNECTION

John Milton: Epic Poet or Computer Visionary?

John Milton wrote his great epic *Paradise Lost* in the mid-1600s. So, what could Milton's poetic description of hell possibly have in common with artificial intelligence, the technology of thinking machines? Pandemonium, that's what!

Paradise Lost describes how Satan was ousted from heaven and set up his own domain. Milton actually created the word *Pandemonium* to name Satan's capital city. It is based on the Greek word *pan*, meaning "all," and the Latin word *daemonium*, meaning "demons." Pandemonium is the place where all the demons gather to argue about which diabolical scheme they will pursue next. Satan, of course, makes the final decision.

In 1958, Oliver Selfridge, a computer pioneer, thought Milton's word for the capital of the nether world was perfect to describe a system of processing information. In pandemonium as it refers to computers, there are four levels of demons. Demons are the working parts of a computer program. The lowest demons receive data. Higher-level demons accumulate and "shout" out their data. Like Satan, the top demon makes the decision about which shout is the loudest and should be followed up.

Certainly, Milton could not have anticipated this use for his word. Being an inventive thinker himself, though, he would probably have applauded it!

1784: France
First school for the blind established.

1789: France
Revolution begins with storming of Bastille. ▶

1798: William Wordsworth and Samuel Taylor Coleridge publish *Lyrical Ballads*.

1798

Recent Scholarship

Richard Rodriguez

Talks About the Time Period

From Small Towns to Big Cities

In high school, whenever teachers assigned texts of British literature, I responded most to the idea of London. I lived in Sacramento, at that time, more a town than a city. By senior year, because my body and mind were growing, I began to feel the need of a city—a place of contest and ambition. I left home, as so many seekers of fortune in English novels leave home, for the city.

London, Market for Commodities and Ideas

London at the beginning of the eighteenth century was becoming the center of the world. Most of the world's commodities and many of the world's ideas passed through London. A city of so much invested interest was interested. People required news: of ships, of trade, of exploration. To get the news, people required newspapers. Londoners also wanted to read about themselves, about plays and books, about fashions and personalities.

About the Author

Richard Rodriguez (b. 1944) is a distinguished nonfiction author and journalist who often presents his views on public television. His books include *Hunger of Memory: The Education of Richard Rodriguez* (1982), *Days of Obligation: An Argument with My Mexican Father* (1992), and *Brown: The Last Discovery of America* (2001; 2003).

Birth of *The Spectator*

In 1711, an ex-soldier and ex-scholar named Richard Steele published a journal called *The Spectator*. *The Spectator*'s innovation was to notice and to comment upon the social and moral life of London. Steele enlisted a young writer named Joseph Addison to contribute to the paper. Addison developed the persona of *The Spectator*:

> "I am frequently seen in most public places. . . . [But] I live in the world rather as a spectator of mankind than as one of the species. . . ."

Addison's essays are fictional observations of real places and real habits. They remain among the best records we have of how several classes of men and women behaved and thought and spoke in London in the eighteenth century.

Joining "the conversation of cities"

It was my ambition, when I left my schoolbooks behind, to join the conversation of cities. I became a journalist. My fate, as Addison might have foretold: In order to write, one must seek solitude. To create a public voice, one must choose loneliness.

Addison benefited from his solitude as a spectator; he was thrilled to have found readers in the male clubs and coffee houses of London. And he also wanted women readers.

When I was in high school and teachers instructed me to compose an essay, I never wondered about my reader. My reader was the teacher—her ear a pair of spectacles, her voice a fluent red ink.

What one never learns in high school about writing is just how large the world is and how a writer in the world must find an audience—must seduce, amuse, or infuriate a stranger's attention.

The Beginning and End of Print

The reading audience of eighteenth-century London was avid, middle class, growing as the city was growing—whereas we live near the end of a long age of print. Now, fewer people read for their news; fewer still for their pleasure. Today's blogger, tossing words into the void of the Web, must sense this. I sense it, writing for newspapers. Yet one is confident that one is, somehow, recorded. One lives in the age of mass media, after all.

But writing, although lonely, cannot be completed alone. In order to write, in order to continue writing, the writer needs to find, as Addison found, a reader—"you"—someone willing to complete the meaning of this sentence by the act of reading.

© Speaking and Listening: Collaboration

Rodriguez compares his career to that of British author Joseph Addison (1672–1719), who, says Rodriguez, "was thrilled to have found readers in the male clubs and coffee houses of London." These coffee houses were places where people exchanged news and ideas, as well as conducted business.

With a partner, study the picture of an eighteenth-century coffee house shown here. Then, formulate a **media evaluation** that answers the following questions:

- What techniques did the artist use to convey a favorable or unfavorable impression of such a place?
- What social and personal values was the artist promoting?

LONDON COFFEE-HOUSES, PAST AND PRESENT.

Integrate and Evaluate Information

1. Use a chart like the one shown to determine the key ideas expressed in the Essential Question essays on pages 468–474. Fill in two ideas related to each Essential Question and note the authors most closely associated with each concept. One item has been provided for you.

Essential Question	Key Concept	Key Author
Literature and Place	Threats to London	Samuel Pepys
Literature and Society		
Writer and Tradition		

2. Review the visual sources that appear on the timeline on pages 466–475. Make two generalizations about life during the seventeenth and eighteenth centuries based on the images. Cite specific examples from the essays on these pages to support your generalizations.

3. The seventeenth and eighteenth centuries were marked by civil war and revolution. Choose either the English civil war or the Glorious Revolution and describe the perspectives of those involved in the conflict. What did each side seek? To what was it opposed? What long-term changes in English society did the event help to create? Cite evidence from the multiple sources presented on pages 464–475, as well as from other sources you consult, such as encyclopedias, in your response.

4. **Address a Question:** In his essay on pages 476–477, Richard Rodriguez recalls that "It was my ambition, when I left my schoolbooks behind, to join the conversation of cities." What "conversations" define your town or city? What forums give citizens a "public voice"? How could you use these forums to "join the conversation"? Integrate information from this textbook and other sources, such as blogs, to support your ideas.

Speaking and Listening: Debate

With other students, form two small groups, the Roundheads and the Cavaliers, and **debate** the following resolution: *A king rules by divine right and cannot be deposed.* Argue for and against the resolution before an audience of your classmates.

Solve a Research Problem: To participate effectively in the debate, you and your teammates will need to research the following topics:

- the divine right of kings
- Parliament's rights to limit the king's power
- Anglican and Roman Catholic beliefs versus Puritan beliefs

Before you begin, formulate a research plan that includes a variety of print and online sources. Assign a different task to each team member. Before the debate, share information and rehearse arguments. As you present your evidence in the debate, cite the texts you consulted.

 **Common Core State Standards**

Reading Informational Text
7. Integrate and evaluate multiple sources of information presented in different media or formats as well as in words in order to address a question or solve a problem.

Speaking and Listening
1. Initiate and participate effectively in a range of collaborative discussions with diverse partners on *grades 11–12 topics, texts, and issues,* building on others' ideas and expressing their own clearly and persuasively.

1.a. Come to discussions prepared, having read and researched material under study; explicitly draw on that preparation by referring to evidence from texts and other research on the topic or issue to stimulate a thoughtful, well-reasoned exchange of ideas.

ESSENTIAL QUESTION VOCABULARY

Use these words in your responses:

Literature and Place
mobility
meditative
urban

Literature and Society
civic
rational
proportion

Writer and Tradition
literate
heritage
prophet

The War Against Time

PART 1

Before You Read | *Works of John Donne*

Connecting to the Essential Question John Donne was called *witty* not only because his work was amusing, but also because it used clever comparisons. A poetic device that Donne invented was the odd but clever comparison of things that at first seem very different. Noting such comparisons will help as you answer the Essential Question: **What is the relationship of the writer to tradition?**

Literary Analysis

Donne and his followers wrote **metaphysical poetry**—poetry characterized by intellectual displays and concern with metaphysical, or philosophical, issues. It uses the following poetic devices:

- **Conceits** are extended comparisons that link objects or ideas not commonly associated. For example, Donne compares two lovers to the two legs of a drawing compass.
- **Paradoxes** are images or descriptions that appear self-contradictory but that reveal a deeper truth: "Death, thou shalt die."

Interpret the conceits and paradoxes you find in Donne's work, and analyze how word choices result in poetry that is fresh and engaging.

Reading Strategy

© **Preparing to Read Complex Texts** To understand these poems, **analyze the author's perspective,** or view the author is taking, and **how word choice affects meaning and tone.** Remember that Donne's work is divided into a youthful period, during which he wrote love poems, and a later phase, during which he wrote religious works. Donne's poems are arranged in rough chronological order, so you can see evidence of his change of heart. Also, even though the speaker in each poem is not necessarily Donne himself, the poet is closely identified with the speaker. Use a chart like the one shown to infer the speaker's situation and motivation—these, in turn, will give you clues to the author's perspective.

Vocabulary

profanation (präf´ ə nā´ shən) *n.* action showing disrespect for something sacred (p. 484)

laity (lā´ i tē) *n.* those not initiated into a priesthood (p. 484)

trepidation (trep´ ə dā´ shən) *n.* trembling (p. 484)

contention (kən ten´ shən) *n.* dispute; argument (p. 489)

piety (pī´ ə tē) *n.* devotion to sacred duties (p. 489)

covetousness (kuv´ ət əs nis) *n.* greediness (p. 490)

Common Core State Standards

Reading Literature
4. Analyze the impact of specific word choices on meaning and tone, including words with multiple meanings or language that is particularly fresh, engaging, or beautiful.

Speaker's Words

"Sweetest love, I do not go, For weariness of thee, … "

Situation

He has to leave his beloved.

Motivation

He is reassuring her that he is not leaving because he is tired of her.

PHLit
Online!
www.PHLitOnline.com

John Donne (1572?–1631)

Works of John Donne

Donne's life and poetry seem to fall neatly into two contradictory parts. Wild, young Jack Donne wrote clever love poems read by sophisticated aristocrats. In later life, sober Dr. John Donne, Dean of St. Paul's and the most popular preacher in England, published widely read meditations and sermons. Contradiction and conflict were the stuff of Donne's life; they are also at the heart of his poetic style. As Jack or as John, Donne the writer excelled at dramatizing— and wittily resolving—the contradictions of life.

Religious Conflict A distant relative of Sir Thomas More, Donne was raised a Catholic. In the England of Queen Elizabeth I, Catholics faced prejudice and restrictive laws. Although Donne studied at Oxford and Cambridge, he never obtained his degree, probably because of his refusal to compromise his Catholicism by swearing an oath acknowledging the supremacy of the king over the church. Later, he abandoned Catholicism and joined the official Church of England. To this day, scholars debate whether Donne experienced a genuine conversion.

A Secret Marriage After taking part in two naval expeditions against the Spanish, Donne served as private secretary to one of the queen's highest-ranking officials, Sir Thomas Egerton. Bright, clever, and charming, Donne secretly wed Anne More, his employer's niece, in 1601. Again, scholars throw doubt on Donne's motives. Some hold that he married for love; others maintain that he hoped his marriage to the daughter of an influential family would promote his career. If Donne counted on this possibility, though, he was sadly mistaken. Anne's father disapproved of the union, and so Donne's marriage temporarily ruined his chances for social advancement.

For many years, the devoted couple lived plagued by poverty and illness, in the midst of which Donne still managed to write influential poetry. He eked out a living writing religious tracts and serving as temporary secretary to several aristocrats. Donne finally attained a secure position in 1615 when, at the insistence of King James, he entered the clergy.

Success After serving as a royal chaplain, Donne became dean of St. Paul's Cathedral in London in 1621, a post he held until his death. He became one of the most popular preachers of his day. No longer the writer of sly or witty passionate verses, he published widely read sermons and religious meditations. Jack Donne's days were over, and John Donne's fame was spreading.

Fair Is My Love, Edwin A. Abbey. The
Harris Museum and Art Gallery, Preston

Song
John Donne

▲ **Critical Viewing**
How does the relationship
of the man and woman in
this painting compare with
the relationship described in
the poem? **[Compare and
Contrast]**

Sweetest love, I do not go,
　　For weariness of thee,
Nor in hope the world can show
　　A fitter love for me;
5　　　But since that I
Must die at last, 'tis best
To use¹ myself in jest,
　　Thus by feigned² deaths to die.

Yesternight the sun went hence,
10　　And yet is here today;
He hath no desire nor sense,
　　Nor half so short a way;

1. **use** condition.
2. **feigned** (fānd) *adj.* imagined.

Then fear not me,
But believe that I shall make
15 Speedier journeys, since I take
More wings and spurs than he.

O how feeble is man's power,
That if good fortune fall,
Cannot add another hour,
20 Nor a lost hour recall!
But come bad chance,
And we join to it our strength,
And we teach it art and length,
Itself o'er us to advance.

25 When thou sigh'st, thou sigh'st not wind,
But sigh'st my soul away;
When thou weep'st, unkindly kind,
My life's blood doth decay.
It cannot be
30 That thou lovest me as thou say'st,
If in thine my life thou waste,
That art the best of me.

Let not thy divining heart
Forethink me any ill,
35 Destiny may take thy part,
And may thy fears fulfill;
But think that we
Are but turned aside to sleep.
They who one another keep
40 Alive, ne'r parted be.

Critical Reading

1. Key Ideas and Details (a) What does the speaker say his reason is for leaving? **(b) Infer:** To what remark of his beloved might he be responding in this poem?

2. Key Ideas and Details (a) Analyze: How would you outline the speaker's argument? **(b) Speculate:** What might the argument's effect on the beloved be?

3. Integration of Knowledge and Ideas Imagine that the speaker's beloved is in tears as he is leaving. Why might the speaker have chosen to present his feelings in the form of witty arguments?

4. Integration of Knowledge and Ideas The speaker uses exaggeration to persuade his beloved. Do you think exaggeration is a useful or a valid persuasive tool? Explain.

Cite textual evidence to support your responses.

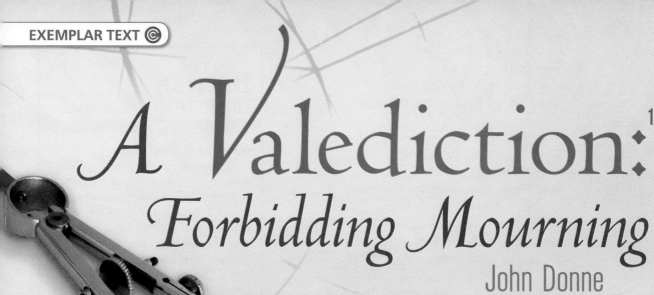

A Valediction:[1]
Forbidding Mourning
John Donne

As virtuous men pass mildly away,
    And whisper to their souls to go,
Whilst some of their sad friends do say
    The breath goes now, and some say, No;

5 So let us melt, and make no noise,
    No tear-floods, nor sigh-tempests move,
'Twere profanation of our joys
    To tell the laity our love.

Moving of th'earth brings harms and fears,
10   Men reckon what it did and meant;
But trepidation of the spheres,[2]
    Though greater far, is innocent.

Dull sublunary[3] lovers' love
    (Whose soul is sense) cannot admit
15 Absence, because it doth remove
    Those things which elemented it.[4]

But we by a love, so much refined,
    That our selves know not what it is,

Vocabulary
profanation (präf′ ə nā′ shən) *n.* action showing disrespect for something sacred

laity (lā′ i tē) *n.* those not initiated into a priesthood

trepidation (trep′ ə dā′ shən) *n.* trembling

Reading Strategy
Analyzing Perspective
Why does the speaker turn parting into a proof of the strength of his love?

---

1. **valediction** farewell speech.
2. **trepidation of the spheres** movements of the stars and planets that are inconsistent with a perfect circular orbit.
3. **sublunary** (sub′ loo nər′ ē) referring to the region below the moon, considered in early astronomy to be the domain of changeable and perishable things.
4. **Those things . . . elemented it** the basic materials or parts of their love.

Inter-assurèd of the mind,[5]
20   Care less, eyes, lips, and hands to miss.

Our two souls therefore, which are one,
      Though I must go, endure not yet
A breach, but an expansion,
      Like gold to airy thinness beat.

25 If they be two, they are two so
      As stiff twin compasses[6] are two;
Thy soul the fixed foot, makes no show
      To move, but doth, if th'other do.

And though it in the center sit,
30   Yet when the other far doth roam,
It leans, and hearkens after it,
      And grows erect, as that comes home.

Such wilt thou be to me, who must
      Like th'other foot, obliquely[7] run;
35 Thy firmness makes my circle just,[8]
      And makes me end where I begun.

If they be two,
they are two so
As stiff twin
compasses are two...

---

5. **Inter-assurèd of the mind** mutually confident of each other's thoughts.
6. **twin compasses** the two legs of a drawing compass.
7. **obliquely** at an angle; not straight.
8. **just** true; perfect.

Critical Reading

1. **Key Ideas and Details (a)** According to the speaker, how should he and his beloved part? **(b) Infer:** What does he think that this manner of parting shows about their love? **(c) Interpret:** Describe two other claims the speaker makes to show how special their love is.

2. **Key Ideas and Details** The poem compares the lovers to the legs of a compass—she is fixed in place while he moves. What does the comparison indicate about their relationship?

3. **Integration of Knowledge and Ideas** The speaker links love with the order and stability of the world. Support this insight with details from the poem.

4. **Integration of Knowledge and Ideas** Do you, like the speaker, see love as a union of two souls, or do you think that lovers should be independent? Explain.

Cite textual evidence to support your responses.

HOLY SONNET 10

John Donne

Sir Thomas Aston *at the Deathbed of His Wife,* John Souch, Manchester City Art Galleries

Death be not proud, though some have called thee
Mighty and dreadful, for thou art not so;
For those whom thou think'st thou dost overthrow,
Die not, poor death, nor yet canst thou kill me.
5 From rest and sleep, which but thy pictures[1] be,
Much pleasure; then from thee much more must flow,
And soonest our best men with thee do go,
Rest of their bones, and soul's delivery.[2]
Thou art slave to fate, chance, kings, and desperate men,
10 And dost with poison, war, and sickness dwell,
And poppy,[3] or charms can make us sleep as well
And better than thy stroke; why swell'st[4] thou then?
One short sleep past, we wake eternally,
And death shall be no more; Death, thou shalt die.

◀ **Critical Viewing** The painting shows Lady Aston both when she is alive and when she is dead. Compare the relationship between death and life implied by the painting with that developed in Holy Sonnet 10. **[Compare and Contrast]**

Literary Analysis
Metaphysical Poetry
What paradox does the speaker use to end his argument with Death?

1. **pictures** images.
2. **And . . . delivery** Our best men go with you to rest their bones and find freedom for their souls.
3. **poppy** opium.
4. **swell'st** swell with pride.

Critical Reading

1. **Key Ideas and Details (a)** What "pictures" of death does the speaker mention? **(b) Infer:** What positive lesson about death does the speaker draw from this resemblance?

2. **Key Ideas and Details (a) Interpret:** In what sense is death a slave (line 9)? **(b) Connect:** How does this point justify the opening line?

3. **Key Ideas and Details (a) Interpret:** What does the statement "Death, thou shalt die" mean? **(b) Draw Conclusions:** Why might the speaker react to death by challenging its "strength" and "pride"?

4. **Integration of Knowledge and Ideas** Does the speaker sound like a man talking himself out of fear or like one who has triumphed over fear? Explain.

Cite textual evidence to support your responses.

Meditation 17

John Donne

Nunc lento sonitu dicunt, Morieris.
(NOW, THIS BELL TOLLING SOFTLY FOR ANOTHER,
SAYS TO ME, THOU MUST DIE.)

▼ **Critical Viewing**
The building in this image stands remote and alone. How does this image contrast with the message Donne delivers in his sermon? **[Compare and Contrast]**

Perchance he for whom this bell tolls may be so ill as that he knows not it tolls for him; and perchance I may think myself so much better than I am as that they who are about me and see my state may have caused it to toll for me, and I know not that. The church is catholic,[1] universal, so are all her actions; all that she does belongs to all. When she baptizes a child, that action concerns me; for that child is thereby connected to that head which is my head too, and ingrafted into that body[2] whereof I am a member. And when she buries a man, that action concerns me: all mankind is of one author and is one volume; when one man dies, one chapter is not torn out of the

---

1. **catholic** applying to humanity generally.
2. **head . . . body** In the Bible, St. Paul calls Jesus the head (spiritual leader) of all men (1 Corinthians 11:3) and a body in which the faithful are unified (1 Corinthians 12:12).

book, but translated into a better language; and every chapter must be so translated. God employs several translators; some pieces are translated by age, some by sickness, some by war, some by justice; but God's hand is in every translation, and his hand shall bind up all our scattered leaves again for that library where every book shall lie open to one another. As therefore the bell that rings to a sermon calls not upon the preacher only, but upon the congregation to come, so this bell calls us all; but how much more me, who am brought so near the door by this sickness. There was a contention as far as a suit[3] (in which both piety and dignity, religion and estimation,[4] were mingled) which of the religious orders should ring to prayers first in the morning; and it was determined that they should ring first that rose earliest. If we understand aright the dignity of this bell that tolls for our evening prayer, we would be glad to make it ours by rising early, in that application, that it might be ours as well as his whose indeed it is. The bell doth toll for him that thinks it doth; and though it intermit again, yet from that minute that that occasion wrought upon him, he is united to God. Who casts not up his eye to the sun when it rises? but who takes off his eye from a comet when that breaks out? Who bends not his ear to any bell which upon any occasion rings? but who can remove it from that bell which is passing a piece of himself out of this world? No man is an island, entire of itself; every man is a piece of the continent, a part of the main.[5] If a clod be washed away by the sea, Europe is the less, as well as if a promontory were, as well as if a manor of thy friend's or of thine own were. Any man's death diminishes me because I am involved in mankind, and therefore never send to know for whom the bell

---

3. **suit** lawsuit.
4. **estimation** self-esteem.
5. **main** mainland.

Vocabulary
contention (kən ten′ shən) *n.* dispute; argument

piety (pī′ ə tē) *n.* devotion to sacred duties

Literary Analysis
Metaphysical Poetry In the sentence beginning, "No man is an island," what extended metaphor does Donne use to show one person's relationship to all humankind?

Reading Check

According to Donne, for whom does the bell toll?

...Therefore never send to know for whom the bell tolls; it tolls for thee.

tolls; it tolls for thee. Neither can we call this a begging of misery or a borrowing of misery, as though we were not miserable enough of ourselves but must fetch in more from the next house, in taking upon us the misery of our neighbors. Truly it were an excusable covetousness if we did; for affliction is a treasure, and scarce any man hath enough of it. No man hath affliction enough that is not matured and ripened by it, and made fit for God by that affliction. If a man carry treasure in bullion, or in a wedge of gold, and have none coined into current money,[6] his treasure will not defray him as he travels. Tribulation is treasure in the nature of it, but it is not current money in the use of it, except we get nearer and nearer our home, heaven, by it. Another man may be sick too, and sick to death, and this affliction may lie in his bowels as gold in a mine and be of no use to him; but this bell that tells me of his affliction digs out and applies that gold to me, if by this consideration of another's danger, I take mine own into contemplation and so secure myself by making my recourse to my God, who is our only security.

Vocabulary
covetousness (kuv′ ət əs nis) *n.* greediness

---

6. **current money** currency; wealth in spendable form.

Critical Reading

Cite textual evidence to support your responses.

1. **Key Ideas and Details** **(a)** What event does the tolling bell announce? **(b) Analyze:** Why does Donne say the tolling bell applies to him as well as to others?

2. **Key Ideas and Details** **(a)** What reason does Donne give for saying, "Any man's death diminishes me"? **(b) Interpret:** What does Donne mean by "No man is an island, entire of itself; every man is a piece of the continent"? **(c) Analyze:** How does the comparison of humanity to a continent support the idea that one death affects all people?

3. **Key Ideas and Details** **(a) Analyze:** In Donne's metaphor, when does the "treasure" of affliction turn into "current [spendable] money"? **(b) Interpret:** Why does Donne find affliction valuable? **(c) Connect:** In what sense does the tolling bell "apply" one person's affliction to another?

4. **Integration of Knowledge and Ideas** Donne says that, once one takes the bell as tolling for oneself, one is "united to God." In urging people to think about their own deaths, what might he be implying about people's attachment to worldly things such as money, success, and popularity?

5. **Integration of Knowledge and Ideas** Does the statement "No man is an island" still apply today? Why or why not? In your response, use at least two of these Essential Question words: *theme, unity, individual.* **[Connecting to the Essential Question: What is the relationship of the writer to tradition?]**

Literary Analysis

1. Craft and Structure Identify and interpret a **conceit** that the speaker in "Song" uses to reassure his beloved. Explain what things are being compared.

2. Craft and Structure (a) What **paradox** does the speaker use in the fourth stanza of "Song"? **(b)** Explain the truth underlying this contradiction.

3. Craft and Structure (a) Identify a conceit in Holy Sonnet 10. **(b)** Explain the speaker's point in making the comparison.

4. Integration of Knowledge and Ideas In Meditation 17, Donne uses a conceit comparing suffering and treasure. **(a)** Use a chart like the one shown to analyze the forms of treasure he discusses. **(b)** Explain how each relates to suffering.

Main Idea: There are two forms of suffering, just as there are two forms of treasure.		
First Form of Treasure: _____	Second Form of Treasure: _____	Relationship Between Forms of Treasure: _____

5. Integration of Knowledge and Ideas (a) What important differences distinguish "Song" and "Valediction" from Holy Sonnet 10? **(b)** Identify an element of metaphysical poetry that all three share, giving examples from each.

6. Craft and Structure In the poems, the speaker uses conceits and paradoxes to move from uncertainty (his own or his listener's) to certainty. In Meditation 17, he uses these devices to inspire uncertainty in his listener. Explain, using examples from each work.

Reading Strategy

7. Analyze how the author's perspective affects meaning by tracing a shift of attitude and perspective in Donne's work. **(a)** How does the perspective in "Song" and "A Valediction: Forbidding Mourning" differ from that in Holy Sonnet 10? **(b)** In what ways does this change affect the meaning, or essential message, Donne communicates in each poem?

8. (a) In each of Donne's works, who is the speaker and what is the speaker's situation? **(b)** What is each speaker's motivation? **(c)** How do the speaker's situation and motivation provide a clue to Donne's perspective in each poem?

9. Choose a line from each work, and describe how knowledge of the speaker's situation and motivation helps you understand the text.

10. During World War II, the British used the phrase "No man is an island" to justify joining the fight against Nazi Germany. Do you think this use of Donne's words accurately reflected his perspective and meaning? Explain.

Common Core State Standards

Writing
3.a. Create a smooth progression of experiences or events. *(p. 492)*
5. Develop and strengthen writing as needed by planning, revising, editing, rewriting, or trying a new approach, focusing on addressing what is most significant for a specific purpose and audience. *(p. 492)*

Language
1. Demonstrate command of the conventions of standard English grammar and usage when writing or speaking. *(p. 493)*
1.b. Resolve issues of complex or contested usage, consulting references as needed. *(p. 493)*
5. Demonstrate understanding of word relationships in word meanings. *(p. 492)*

Integrated Language Skills

© Vocabulary Acquisition and Use

Word Analysis: Latin Prefix *con-*

The word *contention* begins with the Latin prefix *con-*, which means "together" or "with." *Contention* comes from a Latin word meaning "to strive or struggle with."

Use at least four of the *con-* words listed here to write a paragraph about the works by Donne you have read. If any of the words are unfamiliar, use a dictionary to clarify their meanings.

concentrate	conflict
confront	connect
consequence	console
construct	contact

Then, choose two of the words you used and write a sentence identifying how the prefix *con-* helps create their meaning.

Vocabulary: Analogies

Analogies show the relationships between pairs of words. Complete each analogy using a word from the vocabulary list on page 480. In each, your choice should create a word pair that matches the relationship between the first two words given. Then, explain your answers.

1. *Crime* is to *law* as _____ is to *faith*.
2. The _____ is to the *clergy* as *civilians* are to *military personnel*.
3. *Nervousness* is to _____ as *happiness* is to *smiling*.
4. *Jealousy* is to *envy* as _____ is to *quarrel*.
5. _____ is to *religion* as *patriotism* is to *the nation*.
6. *Hunger* is to *food* as _____ is to *money*.

Writing

© **Narrative Text** Imagine that a publisher has asked you to prepare a *biographical narrative* about John Donne. The essay will introduce a collection of Donne's work by highlighting the most important events of his life. Your assignment is to write a **plan** for your narrative.

Prewriting Review the biographical and background information on Donne in the text. Select the key events in his life, both personal and professional. You can also consult literary encyclopedias in print or online to gather more information.

Drafting Following your prewriting notes, write an outline for your narrative with the correct *sequence of events* that helps your reader to smoothly follow the progress of Donne's life.

Revising Read through your outline and revise points to make sure you can use them to communicate clearly the *significance of key events* to your audience.

> **Model: Revising to Clarify Significance**
> **Weak explanation:** 1615—Donne *became* a clergyman
> **Strong explanation:** 1615—Donne *gained security by entering* the clergy

Specific language best communicates the significance of events.

Conventions and Style: Comparative and Superlative Adjectives and Adverbs

Adjectives and adverbs can take three different forms, as shown in the chart below.

Forms of Adjectives and Adverbs		
Positive	**Comparative**	**Superlative**
sweet	sweeter	sweetest
witty	wittier	wittiest
mildly	more mildly	most mildly
willingly	more willingly	most willingly
much	more	most
good	better	best

The comparative degree is for comparing *two* persons, places, or things. The superlative is for comparing *three or more.* Some comparatives and superlatives are formed by adding a suffix to the modifier (*-er* or *-est,* respectively). Others are formed by using (respectively) *more* or *most.* Consult a dictionary of English usage as needed to determine correct usage.

Practice Supply the correct form of the adjective or adverb shown in parentheses.

1. The mature John Donne was _____ than his younger counterpart, Jack. (*religious*)
2. She thought he was the _____ man she had ever met. (*charming*)
3. T. S. Eliot praised Donne's works _____ than many earlier critics had. (*highly*)
4. He says she is the _____ woman for him. (*good*)
5. The speaker says that he will travel _____ than the sun. (*fast*)
6. Death takes the _____ men when they are young. (*fine*)
7. It was determined that whoever rose _____ should be called to prayer first. (*early*)
8. Donne says a person who suffers becomes _____ than one who does not. (*mature*)
9. "Song" is _____ than "Valediction." (*long*)
10. Which of the three poems did you enjoy _____? (*much*)

Using the Comparative	Using the Superlative
The days of his youth were *wilder* than those of his later life.	At one time, Donne was the most *popular* preacher in England.
During his lifetime, Donne's sermons were read *more widely* than his love poems.	Some people thought John Donne was the *best* poet at that time.

Ⓒ Writing and Speaking Conventions

A. **Writing** For each adjective or adverb below, write one sentence using the comparative form and one using the superlative form.

   1. carefully   **2.** proud   **3.** mighty   **4.** great   **5.** deeply

   Then, consult a dictionary of English usage to ensure that you have correctly formed comparatives and superlatives.

B. **Speaking** As Death, write and present a response to Donne's argument in Holy Sonnet 10. Correctly use at least one comparative form and one superlative form. Consult a dictionary of English usage to check your formation of comparatives and superlatives.

> **PH WRITING COACH**
> Further instruction and practice are available in *Prentice Hall Writing Coach.*

Connecting to the Essential Question In his poetry, Ben Jonson favored qualities like balance, clarity, and proportion, virtues he associated with classical literature. As you read, notice passages in Jonson's poems that reflect the classical virtues of balance and clarity. Identifying these passages will help as you answer the Essential Question: **What is the relationship of the writer to tradition?**

Common Core State Standards

Reading Literature
4. Analyze the impact of specific word choices on meaning and tone, including words with multiple meanings or language that is particularly fresh, engaging, or beautiful.

Literary Analysis

A **lyric** is a brief, melodic poem expressing personal thoughts or feelings. In ancient Greece, lyrics were recited or sung to the accompaniment of a lyre (hence the name lyr-ic).

Styles of lyric poetry are often influenced by the *historic period*. Renaissance England, Ben Jonson's era, admired classical Greece. It is natural, therefore, that Jonson used an ancient Greek form called an **epigram** (from the Greek for "inscription"). Epigrams include these features:

- Short lines with bouncy rhythms

- Paradoxical twists, as in "Drink to me only with thine eyes . . ."

- Parallel structures, as in "Still to be neat, still to be dressed, . . ."

As you read, analyze the elements that make Jonson's lines memorable.

Reading Strategy

Preparing to Read Complex Texts By **comparing and contrasting elements** in several poems, you can better understand how Jonson expresses a range of feelings. Remember that these elements are the cumulative result of particular word choices:

- *tone*, or writer's attitude toward the subject

- *mood*, the emotions called up by the poem

- *style*, the author's general approach, varying from highly personal to impersonal and distant

Use the chart shown to compare these elements, including word choices that contribute to them, and to note how Jonson uses them to achieve his *aesthetic purposes*, or goals.

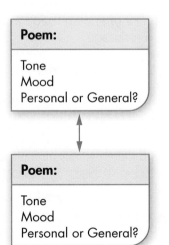

Poem:

Tone
Mood
Personal or General?

Poem:

Tone
Mood
Personal or General?

Vocabulary

fate (fāt) *n.* destiny; fortune (p. 497)

lament (lə ment´) *v.* express grief over; mourn (p. 497)

presumed (pri zoomd´) *v.* taken for granted; assumed (p. 498)

sound (sound) *adj.* healthy; undamaged (p. 498)

divine (di vīn´) *adj.* heavenly; holy (p. 500)

wreath (rēth) *n.* circle of flowers (p. 500)

PHLit Online!
www.PHLitOnline.com

Ben Jonson (1572–1637)

Author of "On My First Son" • "Still to Be Neat" • "Song: To Celia"

Ben Jonson lived a nearly mythic life. Even in his physical stature, he seemed a little larger than life—he was a big man with boundless energy and enormous courage. Brilliant in his poetry and dangerous in a duel, a classical scholar and a veteran soldier, an astute critic and a brassy talker, Jonson had a colorful, sometimes violent career that culminated in his reputation as an esteemed judge of literature. The friend as well as the chief rival of Shakespeare and Donne, he set literary tastes for a generation of poets.

A Poet at War Adopted in infancy, Jonson worked for his stepfather, a bricklayer, while attending the equivalent of high school under a private tutor. Too poor to study at a university, Jonson joined the army and fought in the wars for Dutch independence from Spain. The brawny Jonson at one point met an enemy champion in single combat before the massed armies of Holland and Spain. Jonson won.

Scandal and Success After returning to England, Jonson became an actor. Despite his turbulent life—jailed for his part in a "slanderous" play, almost hanged for killing a fellow actor in a duel, and even suspected of plotting against the king—Jonson became a major dramatist.

The Importance of a Poet Jonson's own opinion of his work and status may be judged by the fact that when he published his collected works in 1616, he entitled the volume *The Works of Benjamin Jonson*—a style of title used largely with celebrated ancient authors. With this gesture, Jonson may have become the first English-language poet to claim true professional dignity for himself.

Varied Styles Jonson's experiences ranged from tavern brawls to elegant entertainments, and his poetic styles are equally varied. He favored satire in his dramas, poking fun at contemporary character types in plays such as *Volpone* and *The Alchemist.*

Jonson wrote many of his poems in an impersonal style, one suited to inscriptions on monuments. Others are filled with nasty wit. As diverse as his styles are, though, one of his consistent strengths is the clear, direct expression of ideas.

A Lasting Influence In his varied experiences and diverse literary output, Jonson might seem to sum up the age in which he lived. Yet his importance does not end with the seventeenth century. Jonson's influence on writers is still felt today, and his plays continue to be produced.

ON MY FIRST SON

Ben Jonson

Farewell, thou child of my right hand,[1] and joy;
    My sin was too much hope of thee, loved boy,
Seven years thou wert lent to me, and I thee pay,
    Exacted by thy fate, on the just[2] day.
5 O, could I lose all father,[3] now. For why
    Will man lament the state he should envy?
To have so soon scaped world's, and flesh's rage,
    And, if no other misery, yet age?
Rest in soft peace, and, asked, say here doth lie
10   Ben Jonson his best piece of poetry.
For whose sake, henceforth, all his vows be such,
    As what he loves may never like[4] too much.

---

1. **child . . . hand** literal translation of the Hebrew name Benjamin, the name of Jonson's son. Jonson's son was born in 1596 and died in 1603.
2. **just** exact.
3. **lose . . . father** shed an identity as a father.
4. **like** possibly meant in the old sense of "please."

Vocabulary

fate (fāt) *n.* destiny

lament (lə ment′) *v.* express grief over; mourn

Literary Analysis

Lyric Do you think this poem was written to create a sense of permanence? Explain.

Critical Reading

1. **Key Ideas and Details (a)** What is the sin the speaker refers to in line 2? **(b) Interpret:** Why does the speaker call this feeling a sin?

2. **Key Ideas and Details (a) Interpret:** Why does the speaker wish to "lose all father, now"? **(b) Interpret:** What does he vow in lines 11–12? **(c) Draw Conclusions:** Why would grief lead to these reactions?

3. **Key Ideas and Details (a) Interpret:** Does the speaker ever present his feelings of grief directly? Explain. **(b) Evaluate:** Why might this manner of presenting grief strengthen the impression made on the reader?

4. **Integration of Knowledge and Ideas (a) Apply:** Contrast the ideas in lines 5–8 with contemporary attitudes. **(b) Evaluate:** Which makes more sense to you?

Cite textual evidence to support your responses.

Still to Be Neat

Ben Jonson

Vocabulary
presumed (pri zōōmd´)
v. taken for granted; assumed

sound (sound) *adj.* healthy;
undamaged

Reading Strategy
**Comparing and
Contrasting** How does the
mood of lines 11–12 of "Still
to Be Neat" contrast with
that of the final lines of "On
My First Son?

▶ **Critical Viewing**
Given his sentiments in the
poem, of what details of this
woman's appearance would
Jonson approve? Explain.
[Connect]

Still[1] to be neat, still to be dressed,
As you were going to a feast;
Still to be powdered, still perfumed;
Lady, it is to be presumed,
5 Though art's hid causes[2] are not found,
All is not sweet, all is not sound.

Give me a look, give me a face,
That makes simplicity a grace;
Robes loosely flowing, hair as free;
10 Such sweet neglect more taketh me
            Than all th'adulteries[3] of art.
They strike mine eyes, but not my heart.

---

1. **Still** always.
2. **causes** reasons.
3. **adulteries** adulterations; corruptions.

Portrait of Mrs. Richard Brinsley Sheridan, Thomas Gainsborough, National Gallery of Art, Washington, D.C.

Critical Reading

Cite textual
evidence to
support your
responses.

1. **Key Ideas and Details** **(a)** To what style of dress and grooming
is the speaker reacting in the first stanza? **(b) Interpret:** What are
the "hid causes" that he suspects lie behind this style? **(c) Infer:**
Why does he prefer the style of "sweet neglect"?

2. **Key Ideas and Details** **(a) Analyze:** How does Jonson use repetition to support his meaning? **(b) Evaluate:** How might Jonson's
ideas about fashion apply to his own poem?

3. **Integration of Knowledge and Ideas** Which trends in modern
advertising can you connect with the ideas in the poem?

SONG: To Celia

Ben Jonson

Literary Analysis

Lyric What features of epigrams does Jonson use in lines 1–4?

Vocabulary

divine (di vīn´) *adj.* heavenly; holy

wreath (rēth) *n.* circle of flowers

Drink to me only with thine eyes,
And I will pledge with mine:
Or leave a kiss but in the cup,
And I'll not look for wine.
5 The thirst that from the soul doth rise,
Doth ask a drink divine:
But might I of Jove's[1] nectar sup,
I would not change for thine.

I sent thee late[2] a rosy wreath,
10 Not so much honoring thee,
As giving it a hope, that there
It could not withered be.
But thou thereon did'st only breathe,
And sent'st it back to me;
15 Since when it grows and smells, I swear,
Not of itself, but thee.

---

1. **Jove's** Jupiter's. In Roman mythology, Jupiter is the ruler of the gods.
2. **late** recently.

Critical Reading

Ⓒ **1. Key Ideas and Details (a)** For what does the soul thirst in lines 5–6 of "Song: To Celia"? **(b) Interpret:** Explain how this idea of the soul's thirst extends the image in lines 1–2.

Ⓒ **2. Key Ideas and Details (a) Assess:** How much do you know about the speaker of "Song: To Celia" or his beloved? **(b) Make a Judgment:** How would more information affect your appreciation of the poem?

Ⓒ **3. Integration of Knowledge and Ideas** Does Jonson's poem seem artificial or false by today's standards, or does it capture true sentiment? Explain.

Ⓒ **4. Integration of Knowledge and Ideas** Does Jonson's emphasis on clarity lessen the emotional impact of his work? In your response, use at least two of these Essential Question words: *classic, precise, artificial.* *[Connecting to the Essential Question: What is the relationship of the writer to tradition?]*

Literary Analysis

 **Common Core State Standards**

Writing

1.a. Introduce precise, knowledgeable claim(s), establish the significance of the claim(s), distinguish the claim(s) from alternate or opposing claims, and create an organization that logically sequences claim(s), counterclaims, reasons, and evidence. *(p. 502)*

Language

1. Demonstrate command of the conventions of standard English grammar and usage when writing or speaking. *(p. 503)*

4. Determine or clarify the meaning of unknown and multiple-meaning words and phrases based on *grades 11–12 reading and content*, choosing flexibly from a range of strategies. *(p. 502)*

1. Craft and Structure Jonson favored a form of **lyric** called an *epigram*, a term that comes from a Greek word meaning "inscription." Would "On My First Son" be suitable as an inscription on the subject's tombstone? Explain.

2. Craft and Structure Identify three pairs of parallel phrases or clauses in "Still to Be Neat."

3. Craft and Structure (a) Explain how the phrase "sweet neglect" in "Still to Be Neat" appears paradoxical, or self-contradictory, but makes memorable sense. **(b)** How does the *irony—a surprising difference from the expected*—of the phrase add to its effect?

4. Craft and Structure Use a chart like the one shown to identify and characterize lines that give "Song: To Celia" the style of an epigram.

"Bouncy" Rhythms	Parallelism	Witty Wordings	Paradoxes
Lines:	Lines:	Lines:	Lines:

Reading Strategy

5. Comparing Literary Works (a) Compare and contrast elements in Jonson's work by contrasting the tone of lines 9–12 of "On My First Son" with that of lines 1–6 of "Still to Be Neat." **(b)** How do these different tones allow Jonson to achieve different *aesthetic purposes* in these lyrics?

6. Comparing Literary Works (a) For each lyric, identify one or two words or images that help create the *mood.* **(b)** Compare and contrast the moods called up by each of these poems.

7. Comparing Literary Works (a) Identify two details of Jonson's *style* in "On My First Son" that make it a sincere personal statement of grief. Explain. **(b)** Identify two details of Jonson's *style* in "Song: To Celia" that give it a formal, impersonal quality. Explain your choices. **(c)** Are both *aesthetic purposes*—sincerity and formality—equally valuable? Why or why not?

8. Comparing Literary Works (a) Which details in "Still to Be Neat" give it a generalized quality? **(b)** Which details make it seem heartfelt? **(c)** Compare the sentiment in this poem with the sentiment of the other two lyrics.

9. In what occupations today might the elements of Jonson's brief, witty writing style be effective? Explain.

© Vocabulary Acquisition and Use

Multiple-Meaning Words

Many English words have more than one meaning, such as *sound*, which Jonson uses in "Still to Be Neat." From the context of the lines, you know that the word means "healthy" rather than "noise." Use context clues to determine the meanings of the italicized words in these sentences.

1. After the choir sang, the *divine* delivered his sermon.

2. The agent struggled to *divine* the secret of the coded message.

3. Winning the *prize* thrilled the contestant.

Next, think of another word with multiple meanings and write two sentences in which you use it in different ways. Exchange your sentences with a partner, and use context clues to determine the meanings of each other's word. If context is not sufficient to determine the meaning, use a print or an online dictionary.

Vocabulary: Synonyms

A **synonym** is a word that has the same meaning as another word. Replace each italicized word below with a synonym from the vocabulary list on page 494. Use each vocabulary word only once.

1. "I always *regret* my mistakes of the past," said the sad man.

2. The sunlight streaming into the cathedral produced a feeling of the *sacred*.

3. The *garland* of leaves, colored red and green, brightened the door.

4. The carpenter thought the wood was *strong* and good for building.

5. He felt that an evil *doom* awaited him.

6. The judge told the jury to *suppose* that the accused was innocent.

Writing

© **Argumentative Text** Some critics complain that Jonson's poetic style is dull. Critic Douglas Bush defends the poet from these criticisms: " … Jonson demanded … the ageless classical virtues of clarity, unity, symmetry, and proportion. … His poems are wholes, not erratic displays of verbal fireworks." Drawing on details from the selections, write a **response** to this idea.

Prewriting Note uses of *imagery*, *language*, or *stylistic devices* that illustrate or contradict each "classical virtue" that Bush cites. Determine whether your examples support or refute Bush's claim and decide whether you agree or disagree with his view.

Drafting Write a draft of your response that begins by summarizing Bush's point and stating your position. As you write, support your generalizations with *accurate and detailed references* to Jonson's writing.

Revising Review your draft, highlighting generalizations and looking for supporting details for each. Make sure that all quotations are accurate and properly referenced.

For instance, the lines "But might I of Jove's nectar sup / I would not change for thine" unify the images of drinking. The reference to Jove, though, is artificial.

Model: Adding Support
Jonson may achieve unity, but in some cases it is at the expense of spontaneous feeling. What is the virtue of formal unity if the poem seems lifeless?

Added details from the poem strengthen support for the generalization.

Conventions and Style: Participles, Gerunds, and Infinitives

One way to make your writing smoother is to combine short sentences using participles, gerunds, and infinitives. A **participle** is a verb form, usually ending in *-ing* or *-ed*, that can be used as an adjective. A **gerund** is a verb form ending in *-ing* that acts as a noun. An **infinitive** is a verb form that appears with the word *to* and acts as a noun, an adjective, or an adverb. You can add modifiers and complements to these verb forms to make **phrases,** or groups of words without a subject or a verb.

Combining with Participial, Gerund, and Infinitive Phrases

Choppy	Better
Ben Jonson was adopted in infancy. Ben Jonson grew up poor.	*Adopted in infancy*, Ben Jonson grew up poor. (participial phrase modifying *Ben Jonson*)
He joined the army. He chose a course.	*Joining the army* was the course he chose. (gerund phrase as the subject)
Jonson could not attend a university. Jonson was not wealthy enough.	Jonson was not wealthy enough *to attend a university*. (infinitive phrase acting as an adverb modifying the adverb *enough*)

Practice In items 1–5, identify the italicized phrase as a participial, gerund, or infinitive phrase. In items 6–10, use the type of phrase indicated in parentheses to combine the two sentences into one, more involved sentence.

1. Her hair, *flowing freely*, was beautiful.
2. *Using a lot of makeup* can hide facial flaws.
3. His goal was *to give clear, brief expression to his ideas*.
4. Jonson, *regarded as a great judge of literature*, guided the trends of his time.
5. The speaker says he hopes *to avoid ever loving anyone so deeply again*.
6. He lost his son. It was a painful experience. (gerund)
7. Jonson returned to England. Jonson became an actor. (participial)
8. The speaker longs for one thing. The speaker would like to forget his identity as a father. (infinitive)
9. Jonson was influenced by the poetry of the ancient Greeks. Jonson liked to write poems with a social function. (participial)
10. Jonson employed satire, a type of humor. Jonson poked fun at contemporary character types. (infinitive)

Writing and Speaking Conventions

A. Writing Use each phrase in a sentence and tell what type of phrase it is.

1. writing with a direct style
2. to dress simply
3. saying goodbye to a child

   Example: writing with a direct style
   Sentence: Writing with a direct style, Jonson became popular.
   Type of Phrase: participial phrase

B. Speaking Respond to the ideas in "Still to Be Neat" as though you are a woman living in Ben Jonson's time. Use at least one participial phrase, one gerund phrase, and one infinitive phrase.

PH **WRITING COACH**

Further instruction and practice are available in *Prentice Hall Writing Coach*.

Connecting to the Essential Question These poets all promote the idea of seizing pleasure in the moment. As you read, notice passages in which a poet gives a personal twist to the theme *Seize pleasure now.* Finding such passages will help as you answer the Essential Question: **What is the relationship of the writer to tradition?**

Literary Analysis

Each poem in this grouping expresses a version of the **carpe diem theme** (kär′ pē dē′ em). *Carpe diem* is Latin for "seize the day." The theme might be summed up as: "Time is fleeting, so act decisively to enjoy yourself."

This theme has a classical origin, with the Roman poet Horace being the first to use the phrase *carpe diem*. It was also popular in love poems of the 16th and 17th century, like the ones in this grouping. In such lyrics, a male speaker usually tries to convince a female to grasp the opportunity for love. The *carpe diem* theme may build upon other themes in a poem, such as the fleeting nature of youth or the relationship between human-kind and nature.

Reading Strategy

© **Preparing to Read Complex Texts** In reading, it is helpful to **analyze and evaluate similar themes** across a variety of selections. Marvell, Herrick, and Suckling all use the *carpe diem* theme, but they do so in different ways:

- Marvell approaches the theme with a mix of whimsical fancy and passionate urgency.
- Herrick delivers a more traditional version of the theme, using familiar imagery to depict the passing seasons.
- Suckling gives the theme a new twist. The speaker in his poem advises a friend to abandon, rather than pursue, a problematic lover.

As you read, use a chart like the one shown to continue analyzing and evaluating how each of these poets expresses this classic theme.

Vocabulary

coyness (koi′ nis) *n.* shyness; aloofness, often as part of a flirtation (p. 507)

amorous (am′ ə res) *adj.* full of love or desire (p. 508)

languish (laŋ′ gwish) *v.* become weak; droop (p. 508)

prime (prīm) *n.* best stage of a thing or process (p. 510)

wan (wän) *adj.* sickly pale; faint or weak (p. 513)

prevail (pri vāl′) *v.* win; achieve a goal (p. 513)

© **Common Core State Standards**

Reading Literature
2. Determine two or more themes or central ideas of a text and analyze their development over the course of the text, including how they interact and build on one another to produce a complex account.

Carpe Diem Theme

Marvell

Herrick

Suckling

PHLit Online!
www.PHLitOnline.com

ANDREW MARVELL

(1621–1678)

Author of "To His Coy Mistress"

Marvell showed an extraordinary adaptability in a turbulent time. Although he was the son of a Puritan minister and frowned on the abuses of the monarchy, he enjoyed close friendships with supporters of Charles I in the king's dispute with Parliament. He also opposed the government of Oliver Cromwell, leader of the Puritan rebellion and then ruler of England.

Beginning in 1651, however, Marvell worked for Lord Fairfax, the commanding general of the Parliamentary army. Still later, he tutored Cromwell's ward. Marvell gained the sponsorship of the Puritan and great English poet John Milton, whose assistant he became.

Marvell wrote masterful poetry in various veins—some works share the metaphysical qualities of Donne's verse, while others have the classical qualities recommended by Jonson. Although he was thought of chiefly as a satirist until the nineteenth century, much of his work has become classic.

"We would sit down, and think which way
To walk, and pass **our long love's day.**"

The Interrupted Sleep, François Boucher. The Metropolitan Museum of Art

TO HIS COY **MISTRESS**

Andrew Marvell

Had we but world enough, and time,
This coyness lady were no crime.
We would sit down, and think which way
To walk, and pass our long love's day.
5   Thou by the Indian Ganges' side
Should'st rubies find; I by the tide
Of Humber[1] would complain. I would
Love you ten years before the Flood,
And you should if you please refuse
10   Till the conversion of the Jews.[2]
My vegetable love should grow
Vaster than empires, and more slow;
An hundred years should go to praise
Thine eyes, and on thy forehead gaze;
15   Two hundred to adore each breast,
But thirty thousand to the rest;
An age at least to every part,
And the last age should show your heart.
For, lady, you deserve this state,[3]
20   Nor would I love at lower rate.
   But at my back I always hear
Time's wingèd chariot hurrying near:
And yonder all before us lie
Deserts of vast eternity.
25   Thy beauty shall no more be found,
Nor, in thy marble vault, shall sound

Vocabulary
coyness (koi′ nis) *n.*
shyness; aloofness, often
as part of a flirtation

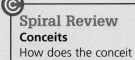

Spiral Review
Conceits
How does the conceit
in lines 1–20 help
set a humorous tone?

Reading Check
What is the lady's crime?

---

1. **Humber** river flowing through Hull, Marvell's home town.
2. **conversion of the Jews** according to Christian tradition, the Jews were to be converted immediately before the Last Judgment.
3. **state** dignity.

◄ **Critical Viewing** In what way do both the painting and the poem illustrate the traditional roles of men and women in courtship? **[Connect]**

My echoing songs; then worms shall try
That long-preserved virginity,
And your quaint honor turn to dust,
30 And into ashes all my lust:
The grave's a fine and private place,
But none I think do there embrace.
    Now therefore, while the youthful hue
Sits on thy skin like morning dew,
35 And while thy willing soul transpires[4]
At every pore with instant fires,
Now let us sport us while we may,
And now, like amorous birds of prey,
Rather at once our time devour
40 Than languish in his slow-chapped[5] power.
Let us roll all our strength, and all
Our sweetness, up into one ball,
And tear our pleasures with rough strife
Thorough[6] the iron gates of life:
45 Thus, though we cannot make our sun
Stand still, yet we will make him run.

4. **transpires** breathes out.
5. **slow-chapped** slow-jawed.
6. **Thorough** through.

Vocabulary
amorous (am´ ə res) *adj.*
full of love or desire

languish (laŋ´ gwish) *v.*
become weak; droop

Literary Analysis
Carpe Diem **Theme**
What new twist does the speaker apply in order to "solve" the problem of fleeting time?

Critical Reading

Cite textual evidence to support your responses.

1. **Key Ideas and Details** **(a)** Name three things the speaker and his mistress would do and the time each would take if time were not an issue. **(b) Connect:** How do these images relate to the charge the speaker makes against his lady in lines 1–2?

2. **Key Ideas and Details** **(a) Infer:** Why would the speaker be willing to spend so much time waiting for his mistress? **(b) Interpret:** How does this willingness take the sting out of his complaint?

3. **Craft and Structure** **(a) Analyze:** What future does the speaker foresee for himself and his love in lines 25–30? **(b) Connect:** How do the images in lines 21–30 answer the images in the first part of the poem?

4. **Craft and Structure** Why does the speaker save the urgent requests in lines 33–46 for the end?

5. **Integration of Knowledge and Ideas** **(a) Compare and Contrast:** Compare the attitudes toward time at the beginning, middle, and end. **(b) Evaluate:** Is Marvell's idea of love realistic or idealistic? Explain.

Robert Herrick

(1591–1674)

Author of "To the Virgins, to Make Much of Time"

Born into a family of London goldsmiths, Herrick went to Cambridge when he was twenty-two and graduated at the age of twenty-nine. After graduation, he served as a military chaplain. As a reward for his services, he was assigned to a parish in rural England. Here, he performed his churchly duties and wrote religious verse and musical love poems.

Although not politically active, Herrick was evicted from his parish by the Puritans and allowed back only with the Restoration of Charles II. While barred from his church, Herrick returned to his native and beloved London, where he published his poetry in *Noble Numbers* and *Hesperides* (the title comes from an ancient Greek name for a mythical garden at the edge of the world).

Published during a turbulent time and largely ignored by his contemporaries, these verses were rediscovered in the nineteenth century. Today, Herrick is included among the English poets of the seventeenth century who are still worth remembering.

Reading poems like "To the Virgins, to Make Much of Time," modern readers might suppose that Herrick was a bit of a rake or playboy. That impression seems to be further confirmed by a poem like "Upon the Loss of His Mistresses": "I have lost, and lately, these / Many dainty mistresses . . .," whom he goes on to name: Julia, Sappho, Anthea, Electra, Corinna, and Perilla.

The perhaps disappointing biographical truth is that this poet, so rakish in his verse, lived for many years rather soberly as a bachelor church official in the west of England. As one critic points out, the name of Herrick's maid was Prudence.

To the Virgins, to Make Much of Time

Robert Herrick

Gather ye rosebuds while ye may,
    Old time is still a-flying;
And this same flower that smiles today
    Tomorrow will be dying.

5   The glorious lamp of heaven, the sun,
    The higher he's a-getting,
The sooner will his race be run,
    And nearer he's to setting.

That age is best which is the first,
10   When youth and blood are warmer;
But being spent, the worse, and worst
    Times still succeed the former.

Then be not coy, but use your time,
    And, while ye may, go marry;
15   For, having lost but once your prime,
    You may forever tarry.[1]

---

1. tarry (tar´ ē) v. delay.

Literary Analysis
Carpe Diem Theme
Which images in lines 5–8 capture the *carpe diem* theme?

Vocabulary
prime (prīm) *n.* best stage of a thing or process

▲ **Critical Viewing**
This painting by John William Waterhouse was directly inspired by Herrick's poem. Which details in it correspond to images in the poem? **[Connect]**

Cite textual evidence to support your responses.

Critical Reading

1. **Key Ideas and Details** **(a)** What advice does the speaker give women in lines 1–4? **(b) Interpret:** What does the advice mean?

2. **Key Ideas and Details** **(a) Interpret:** What does the poem suggest about passing time? **(b) Connect:** How does the last stanza answer these concerns?

Sir John Suckling (1609–1642)

Author of "Song"

In some ways, Sir John Suckling lived a life more romantic than Marvell's or Herrick's. A privileged young courtier, Suckling inherited his vast estates when he was only eighteen. He later served as a gentleman in the privy chamber of Charles I. Praised as the cleverest of conversationalists, Suckling was said to be able to compose a poem at a moment's notice. He incorporated some of his best lyrics, including the poem "Song," into plays that he lavishly produced at his own expense.

Suckling's military exploits proved less successful than his poems, however. The cavalry troop he raised and lavishly uniformed for the king was defeated in Scotland, and Suckling was mocked for caring more about his men's uniforms than about their military abilities. After joining a failed Royalist plot to rescue a royal minister from prison, he fled to France, where he died in despair at the age of thirty-three. His poems, though, preserve the dash and spirit of his younger days.

▼ **Critical Viewing** Consider the
speaker's words in "Song." What
might the young lover pictured here
be writing? Explain. **[Speculate]**

SONG

Sir John Suckling

Why so pale and wan, fond lover?
    Prithee, why so pale?
Will, when looking well can't move her,
    Looking ill prevail?
5   Prithee, why so pale?

Why so dull and mute, young sinner?
    Prithee, why so mute?
Will, when speaking well can't win her,
    Saying nothing do't?
10   Prithee, why so mute?

Quit, quit, for shame; this will not move,
    This cannot take her.
If of herself she will not love,
    Nothing can make her:
15   The devil take her!

Vocabulary
wan (wän) *adj.* sickly pale; faint or weak

prevail (pri vāl') *v.* win; achieve a goal

Reading Strategy
Analyze Similar Themes How does the speaker's attitude toward his listener in lines 11–15 compare to the speaker's attitude in lines 33–46 of "To His Coy Mistress?"

Critical Reading

1. Key Ideas and Details (a) How does the young lover look and act according to the first ten lines of "Song"? **(b) Analyze:** Explain why the speaker treats the friend's behavior as if it were an attempt to achieve a goal.

2. Key Ideas and Details (a) Interpret: In the final stanza, what helpful shift in perspective does the speaker encourage? **(b) Draw Conclusions:** What attitude toward love does the last stanza reflect?

3. Key Ideas and Details (a) Analyze: What features of the poem make it suitable as song lyrics? **(b) Hypothesize:** Which would be a good audience for such a song: uneducated farmers, young aristocrats, or both? Explain, using details from the poem.

4. Integration of Knowledge and Ideas Do these poets merely repeat the *carpe diem* theme, or do they give it new life? Explain. Use two of these Essential Question words in your response: *universal, contemporary, derivative.* *[Connecting to the Essential Question: What is the relationship of the writer to tradition?]*

Cite textual evidence to support your responses.

Literary Analysis

1. Craft and Structure Contrast the treatment of the **carpe diem** theme in the three poems using a chart like the one shown.

Carpe Diem Images	Qualities: Fanciful? Simple?

Statement of Plea	Humorous? Passionate? Reasonable?

2. Integration of Knowledge and Ideas This theme has appeared in literature over a long period of time. What do you think accounts for its popularity?

Reading Strategy

3. Analyze and evaluate similar themes by noting which of these authors presents the *carpe diem* theme most effectively. Consider such factors as word choice, imagery, interaction with other themes, and sense of drama.

PERFORMANCE TASKS
Integrated Language Skills

Vocabulary Acquisition and Use

Compare the meaning of each underlined vocabulary word with its **context,** or surrounding words, to determine whether the statement is true or false. Write T or F, and explain your answer.

1. He had not eaten for days, and his cheeks were <u>wan</u>.

2. *The <u>Prime</u> of Miss Jean Brodie* is probably about a woman near death.

3. If a plant is not regularly watered, it will <u>languish</u>.

4. The soccer team that scores the most goals will <u>prevail</u>.

5. <u>Coyness</u> shows commitment to a relationship.

6. An <u>amorous</u> couple is affectionate.

Writing

Argumentative Text Public-service announcements (PSAs) urge people to act wisely. Use the *carpe diem* theme in a **PSA** that calls on people to do something beneficial, such as exercise to maintain health.

- Decide whether you will write a radio or television ad.
- Write the script and revise it to make sure you use effective evidence, logical evidence, and emotional appeals to persuade your audience.

Common Core State Standards

Writing
1. Write arguments to support claims in an analysis of substantive topics or texts, using valid reasoning and relevant and sufficient evidence.

A Nation Divided

▲ Critical Viewing
What feeling does this portrayal of Adam and Eve convey? **[Interpret]**

Literary History: Milton's World

In the 1650s, the aged John Milton decided to retell the Biblical story of the creation, fall, and redemption of humanity in two epics, Paradise Lost *and* Paradise Regained. *With these works, Milton reaffirmed Britain's core values after a decade of war.*

Making "Darkness Visible": Milton's Epic Ambition

Milton had compelling reasons for telling this story. By 1652, he was completely blind. Unable to write, he dictated the poem to his daughters, who copied down each word. As he worked, the world crumbled around him. The monarchy he had opposed was restored to England, and he went to jail for a time. Blind, disgraced, and disillusioned, Milton nevertheless persevered. Over perhaps ten years, he dictated nearly 11,000 lines of poetry. The result, critics agree, is the greatest epic in the English language, *Paradise Lost.*

An Overview Like many epic poems, *Paradise Lost* begins in the middle. Milton introduces Satan, who, along with his angel allies, has done the unthinkable—rebelled against God. Expelled from Heaven, they have plummeted into Hell, a place devoid of light, life, and even form: "one great furnace flamed, yet from those flames / No light, but rather darkness visible / Served only to discern sights of woe."

Satan's war with Heaven is Milton's invention. The remainder of the story is the familiar one of Christian tradition. God has forbidden Adam and Eve to eat fruit from the Tree of the Knowledge of Good and Evil. Bent on revenge, Satan tempts Eve into eating the apple. She then persuades Adam to partake. This event, the Fall of Adam and Eve, leads to their (and so humanity's) expulsion from the Garden of Eden. They leave Paradise with a sense of hope: "The World was all before them, where to choose / Their place of rest, and Providence their guide. . . ."

A Cosmic Commentary Apart from telling this grand story, large portions of *Paradise Lost* are dedicated to another grand project— "to justify the ways of God to men." In the story, God sends the angel Raphael to Paradise to warn Adam of the necessity of obedience. In their conversation, Milton is able to speak on a few issues that were controversial in his day.

- **Reason and Free Will** Humanity can see the difference between right and wrong. With that ability comes the freedom to choose between the two.

- **Free Will and Predestination** God knows everything that is, was, and will be. Yet God's foreknowledge does not mean that people's choices are determined in advance by God. People have free will.

By affirming free will, Milton broke with some of the sternest Puritans of his day, who held that men and women were predestined to salvation or damnation. Milton's epic story finds individuals responsible for their own actions and fate and so grants them dignity.

Words in the Void In a sense, *Paradise Lost* is Milton's answer to the great historical crisis through which Britain had just passed. Puritans, including Milton, had challenged the official Church of England. They demanded a return to what they saw as the original principles of the Christian religion. At the same time, religious controversy led to the Civil War (1642–1649) in which Parliament eventually put its own king, Charles I, to death.

These upheavals shattered the symbolic centers of English life and culture, Church and King. With *Paradise Lost*, Milton helped the nation find its bearings again by retelling the central story of its culture. In the figure of Satan, he commemorated the destructive forces that had recently torn through the nation. At the same time, the fall of Satan symbolically puts rebellious urges into their proper place—the netherworld of Hell. It was these tasks, perhaps, that drove the blind Milton to rise above adversity and deliver this epic to his country.

Milton's Legacy Over the centuries, Milton's story of the Fall has become as well known as the biblical version. It has influenced writers as diverse as the poets William Blake, the visionary; and John Keats, the introspective dreamer; as well as the novelist George Eliot, a formidable social critic. By the nineteenth century, study of Milton's epic was considered an essential part of a respectable education, and even relatively uneducated people could be expected to have two books in their homes—the King James Bible and *Paradise Lost*. In telling a story to heal his own time, Milton fed the imaginations of generations to come.

Speaking and Listening: Discussion

© Comprehension and Collaboration Since the time of Milton, many writers have attempted to heal the wounds of collective trauma through works of literature.

With a group, discuss your thoughts about the ways in which literature can bring understanding or closure to people after a period of historical crisis. Use these questions to guide your discussion:

- What examples can you cite in which literature, including drama, deals with a real historical crisis?
- Do you think such literature can have meaning for people who have not lived through the crisis in question? If so, how?

Organize your conclusions into a **report** to share your ideas with the class.

John Milton

(1608–1674)

John Milton is regarded as one of the greatest poets of the English language, yet he owes this regard to comparatively few poems. Much of his work is in Latin, not English, and during the fifteen years he spent writing political pamphlets and other prose works, he wrote little poetry. Although other poets have surpassed him in quantity, Milton's masterpiece, the epic *Paradise Lost,* is enough to establish him as the equal of Chaucer and Shakespeare. Milton himself never lacked self-confidence, setting his sights on poetic greatness at the start of his career.

A Privileged Childhood

Milton was born in London to a middle-class family and grew up in a highly cultured environment. His father, a professional scribe who drew up contracts and lent money, was also a composer and musician of considerable ability. Deeply religious, Milton's father was devoted to the Protestant cause. At the age of thirteen, Milton started his formal education, the equivalent of high school. He was also tutored at home. He mastered Greek, Latin, and Hebrew, as well as several modern European languages. After this thorough education, Milton went on to college.

God's Poet

When Milton entered Christ's College at Cambridge University, he had already decided to prepare himself for a career as a great poet ("God's poet" was how he described himself). It appears that for a time he also considered entering the ministry. The religious and political situation at the time, though, was quite uncertain, so Milton devoted himself to a life of study. After earning his degrees from Cambridge, he withdrew to his father's house, first at Hammersmith, then at Horton in Buckinghamshire, for nearly six years, where, it is said, he read everything that was written in the ancient and modern languages at his command. It was during this long period of study that he wrote one of his best-known poems, "Lycidas." That work, together with the poems "L'Allegro" and "Il Penseroso," written during his student days, marked the young Milton as a gifted poet destined for fame.

A Man of Ideals

Following his studies, Milton went to continental Europe for a planned two-year Grand Tour, during which he called on the astronomer Galileo (1564–1642). While he was away, Parliament rebelled against King Charles I, eventually replacing the monarchy with a government led by Oliver Cromwell. Learning of the revolt, Milton cut short his trip and returned to England. He began writing pamphlets for the Puritan cause, criticizing the control of the bishops over the English church.

Public Service, Private Loss

In 1649, when the Puritans decided to execute Charles I, Milton wrote a treatise defending this act. Impressed by Milton's brilliantly presented opinions, Cromwell made him Secretary of State for Foreign Tongues. This position required Milton to translate official documents into Latin and to write in defense of the new government against Royalist attacks. It was while serving in this position that he lost his eyesight.

In 1660, Milton's fortunes took a turn for the worse. The monarchy was restored, and Milton was imprisoned for a time. (His friend, the poet Andrew Marvell, may have been instrumental in gaining his release.) Blind and stripped of most of his property, Milton withdrew once again into words—he wrote *Paradise Lost* (1667), the greatest epic of the English language.

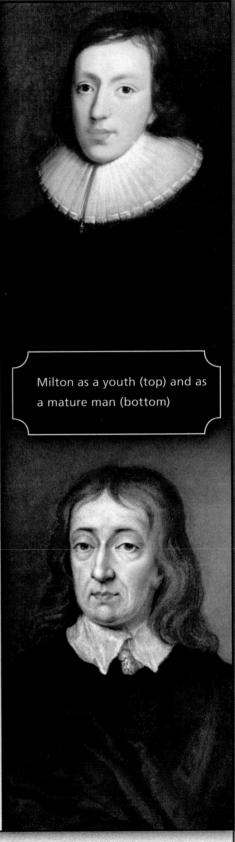

Milton as a youth (top) and as a mature man (bottom)

Milton & POP CULTURE

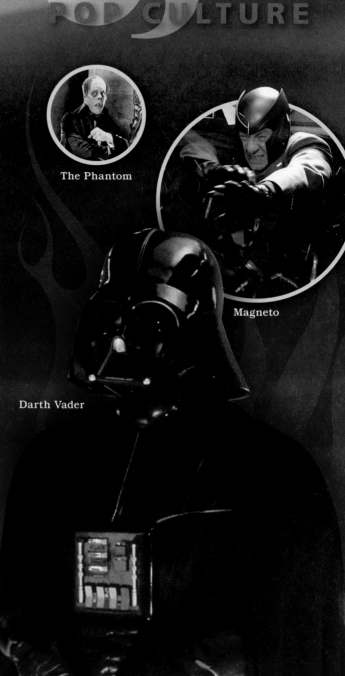

The Phantom

Magneto

Darth Vader

DARK HEROES

In Milton's 17th-century epic poem *Paradise Lost*, God casts Satan out of Heaven and into Hell. The fallen angel is vivid and dark at the same time. In this respect, Satan is like other larger-than-life figures who, though villainous, rivet our attention. While none are more powerful than the Devil, there are many dark-hero figures in popular culture.

- Darth Vader, unforgettable villain of the *Star Wars* movies, is one. Brutal enforcer of Empire rule, Vader was instantly memorable for the helmet that covered his face and by his voice (James Earl Jones's menacing tones).

- Magneto, another enemy of true heroes, was introduced in the first issue (1963) of *X-Men*, the comic written by Stan Lee and illustrated by Jack Kirby. Like Satan, he is the head of an army, not the dark angels of Hell but the Brotherhood of Evil Mutants.

- The physically deformed musical genius, Erik, better known as the Phantom, made his first frightening appearance in Gaston Leroux's novel *The Phantom of the Opera* in 1910. Since then, this despairing and daring villain has appeared in a movie and a musical, both based on the original novel.

Regardless of media—poem, novel, film, comic, or Broadway show—stories of dark heroes continue to fascinate audiences.

Before You Read | *Poetry of John Milton*

Connecting to the Essential Question John Milton brings to life a well-known story of the time, about angels who rebelled against God. As you read, notice vivid passages in Milton's description of the underworld in *Paradise Lost*. Seeing such descriptions in your mind's eye will help you answer the Essential Question: **What is the relationship of the writer to tradition?**

Literary Analysis

An **Italian,** or **Petrarchan, sonnet** is a fourteen-line lyric poem with a distinctive structure. The first eight lines, called the octave, rhyme *abbaabba* and present a problem. A six-line sestet with a variable rhyme scheme responds to the octave. In Milton's Italian sonnets, the structure of the octave and the sestet contributes to the structure, meaning, and aesthetic pleasure of the entire sonnet.

An **epic** is a long narrative poem about a hero. For seventeenth-century English writers, ancient epic poets such as Homer—the blind, half-mythical author of the *Iliad* and the *Odyssey*—set the standard for literary greatness. Milton uses the following features of Homeric epics in *Paradise Lost:*

- A story that begins in the middle of the action (*in medias res*)
- An opening invocation in which the poet calls for divine aid in telling his story
- Extended similes, comparisons using *like* or *as*

Look for these epic elements as you read *Paradise Lost,* and analyze how in the sonnets, the structure of the parts contributes to the structure and meaning of the poem.

Reading Strategy

Preparing to Read Complex Texts If you do not understand a passage, repair your comprehension by **using a graphic organizer** like the one shown. This organizer can help you break down long, confusing sentences into smaller parts: main clauses, which can stand by themselves, and supporting clauses, which cannot.

Vocabulary

semblance (sem′ bləns) *n.* appearance; image (p. 522)

illumine (i lo͞o′ mən) *v.* light up (p. 526)

transgress (trans gres′) *v.* violate a law or command (p. 526)

guile (gīl) *n.* artful trickery (p. 527)

obdurate (äb′ do͝or it) *adj.* stubborn (p. 527)

tempestuous (tem pes′ cho͞o əs) *adj.* turbulent; stormy (p. 528)

transcendent (tran sen′ dənt) *adj.* exceeding beyond all limits (p. 529)

ignominy (ig′ nə min′ ē) *n.* humiliation; dishonor (p. 529)

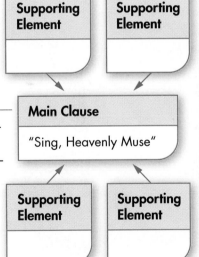

Supporting Element

Supporting Element

Main Clause

"Sing, Heavenly Muse"

Supporting Element

Supporting Element

www.PHLitOnline.com

Sonnet VII

("How soon hath Time") JOHN MILTON

Vocabulary
semblance (sem´ bləns)
n. appearance; image

How soon hath Time, the subtle thief of youth,
    Stolen on his wing my three and twentieth year!
    My hasting days fly on with full career,[1]
    But my late spring no bud or blossom showeth.
5 Perhaps my semblance might deceive[2] the truth,
    That I to manhood am arrived so near,
    And inward ripeness doth much less appear,
    That some more timely-happy spirits[3] endueth.[4]
Yet be it less or more, or soon or slow,
10   It shall be still[5] in strictest measure even
    To that same lot,[6] however mean or high,
Toward which Time leads me, and the will of Heaven;
    All is, if I have grace to use it so,
    As ever in my great Taskmaster's eye.

---

1. **career** speed.
2. **deceive** prove false.
3. **timely-happy spirits** others who seem to be more accomplished poets at the age of twenty-four.
4. **endueth** endows.
5. **still** always.
6. **lot** fate.

Critical Reading

Cite textual evidence to support your responses.

1. **Key Ideas and Details** **(a)** What occasion leads Milton to the thoughts in the poem? **(b) Infer:** Judging from the image in lines 1–2, how does Milton view this occasion?

2. **Key Ideas and Details** **(a)** To what season does Milton compare his time of life? **(b) Infer:** Why does he say that this season "no bud or blossom showeth"? **(c) Interpret:** What is his feeling about this situation?

3. **Key Ideas and Details** **(a) Infer:** To what does Milton trust himself and his life in lines 9–14? **(b) Interpret:** In what way does this act of trust answer his worries in the first part of the poem?

Sonnet XIX

("When I consider how my light is spent")
JOHN MILTON

When I consider how my light is spent
    Ere half my days, in this dark world and wide,
    And that one talent[1] which is death to hide,
    Lodged with me useless, though my soul more bent
5 To serve therewith my Maker, and present
    My true account, lest he returning chide;
    "Doth God exact day labor, light denied?"
    I fondly[2] ask; but Patience to prevent
That murmur, soon replies, "God doth not need
10   Either man's work or his own gifts; who best
    Bear his mild yoke, they serve him best. His state
Is kingly. Thousands[3] at his bidding speed
    And post[4] o'er land and ocean without rest:
    They also serve who only stand and wait."

---

1. **talent** allusion to the parable of the talents (Matthew 25: 14–30). The servant who earns interest for his master on five talents (a large unit of money) is commended. The servant who hides and then returns a talent is condemned to "outer darkness."
2. **fondly** foolishly.
3. **Thousands** thousands of angels.
4. **post** travel.

Critical Reading

1. **Key Ideas and Details (a)** According to the poem, at what point in his life did the speaker's eyesight fail? **(b) Infer:** In line 2, how does his way of identifying this point in his life emphasize the despair he feels?

2. **Key Ideas and Details (a)** What has happened to the speaker's "one talent"? **(b) Infer:** Why does blindness have this effect on his talent?

3. **Key Ideas and Details (a) Connect:** In lines 3–6, what connection does the speaker make between the use of one's talent and service to God? **(b) Interpret:** What dilemma does this connection create for him? **(c) Interpret:** What does his question in line 7 mean?

4. **Key Ideas and Details (a) Infer:** What answers the speaker? **(b) Interpret:** How does this new speaker interpret the idea of service to God?

5. **Integration of Knowledge and Ideas** Do you think that this poem could inspire a contemporary person who is facing a physical challenge? Explain.

> **Cite textual evidence to support your responses.**

From Paradise Lost

John Milton

BACKGROUND

Paradise Lost was written as the dust was settling after years of war and turmoil. From 1642 to 1660, the government of England went from a monarchy to a commonwealth (rule by Parliament) to a protectorate (rule by one man, Oliver Cromwell) to a monarchy. During this two-decade period, no matter which side a person was on, he or she experienced both defeat and triumph.

Perhaps Milton wrote *Paradise Lost* because he sensed that the nation needed an anchor, a literary work that would once again help define and unite a culture. His explanation of God's reason for allowing suffering in the world, and the dark, proud figure of the rebel Satan pitted against God in civil war, must have led readers to reflect on England's own civil war.

▶ **Critical Viewing** How is Milton's time period—an era in which England was torn apart by civil war and religious conflict—reflected in this painting? **[Connect]**

Of man's first disobedience, and the fruit
Of that forbidden tree, whose mortal[1] taste
Brought death into the world, and all our woe,
With loss of Eden, till one greater Man[2]
5 Restore us, and regain the blissful seat,
Sing Heavenly Muse,[3] that on the secret top
Of Oreb, or of Sinai,[4] didst inspire
That shepherd, who first taught the chosen seed,
In the beginning how the Heavens and Earth
10 Rose out of Chaos: or if Sion hill[5]
Delight thee more, and Siloa's brook[6] that flowed
Fast[7] by the oracle of God, I thence
Invoke thy aid to my adventurous song,
That with no middle flight intends to soar
15 Above the Aonian mount,[8] while it pursues
Things unattempted yet in prose or rhyme.
And chiefly thou O Spirit,[9] that dost prefer
Before all temples the upright heart and pure,
Instruct me, for thou know'st; thou from the first
20 Wast present, and with mighty wings outspread
Dovelike sat'st brooding on the vast abyss
And mad'st it pregnant: what in me is dark
Illumine, what is low raise and support;
That to the height of this great argument[10]
25 I may assert Eternal Providence,
And justify the ways of God to men.
  Say first, for Heaven hides nothing from thy view
Nor the deep tract of Hell, say first what cause
Moved our grand[11] parents in that happy state,
30 Favored of Heaven so highly, to fall off
From their Creator, and transgress his will

Vocabulary
illumine (i loo´ mən) v. light up

transgress (trans gres´) v. violate a law or command

1. **mortal** deadly.
2. **one . . . Man** Christ.
3. **Heavenly Muse** Urania, the muse of astronomy and sacred poetry in Greek mythology. Here, Milton associates Urania with the holy spirit that inspired Moses ("That shepherd") to receive and interpret the word of God for the Jews ("the chosen seed"). To convey the message of God to his people, Moses wrote the first five books of the Bible, including Genesis, the book on which *Paradise Lost* is based.
4. **Oreb** (ōr´ eb) **. . . Sinai** (sī´ nī´) alternate names for the mountain where God communicated the laws to Moses.
5. **Sion** (sī´ ən) **hill** hill near Jerusalem on which the temple ("the oracle of God") stood.
6. **Siloa's** (sī lō´ əz) **brook** stream near Sion hill.
7. **Fast** close.
8. **Aonian** (ā ō´ nē ən) **mount** Mount Helicon in Greek mythology, home of the Muses. Milton is drawing a comparison between the epic he is now presenting and the epics written by the classical poets, Homer and Virgil.
9. **Spirit** the Holy Spirit, the voice that provided inspiration for the Hebrew prophets.
10. **argument** theme.
11. **grand** first in importance and in time.

For[12] one restraint,[13] lords of the world besides?[14]
Who first seduced them to that foul revolt?
The infernal Serpent; he it was, whose *guile*

35 Stirred up with envy and revenge, deceived
The mother of mankind, what time his pride
Had cast him out from Heaven, with all his host
Of rebel angels, by whose aid aspiring
To set himself in glory above his peers,

40 He trusted to have equaled the Most High,
If he opposed; and with ambitious aim
Against the throne and monarchy of God
Raised impious war in Heaven and battle proud,
With vain attempt. Him the Almighty Power

45 Hurled headlong flaming from the ethereal sky
With hideous ruin and combustion down
To bottomless perdition, there to dwell
In adamantine[15] chains and penal fire,
Who durst defy the Omnipotent to arms.

50 Nine times the space that measures day and night
To mortal men, he with his horrid crew
Lay vanquished, rolling in the fiery gulf,
Confounded though immortal. But his doom
Reserved him to more wrath; for now the thought

55 Both of lost happiness and lasting pain
Torments him; round he throws his baleful eyes
That witnessed[16] huge affliction and dismay,
Mixed with *obdurate* pride and steadfast hate.
At once as far as angels' ken,[17] he views

60 The dismal situation waste and wild:
A dungeon horrible, on all sides round,
As one great furnace flamed, yet from those flames
No light, but rather darkness visible
Served only to discover sights of woe,

65 Regions of sorrow, doleful shades, where peace
And rest can never dwell, hope never comes
That comes to all; but torture without end
Still urges,[18] and a fiery deluge, fed
With ever-burning sulfur unconsumed:

70 Such place eternal justice had prepared
For these rebellious, here their prison ordained

---

12. For because of.
13. one restraint commandment that Adam and Eve should not eat of the fruit of the tree of knowledge.
14. besides in every other respect.
15. adamantine (ad´ ə man´ tēn´) *adj.* unbreakable.
16. witnessed gave evidence of.
17. ken view; scope of knowledge.
18. urges afflicts.

▶ **Critical Viewing**
What traditional associations with sin explain this artist's rendering of one of Milton's fallen angels? **[Hypothesize]**

In utter darkness, and their portion set
As far removed from God and light of Heaven
As from the center thrice to the utmost pole.[19]

75   O how unlike the place from whence they fell!
There the companions of his fall, o'erwhelmed
With floods and whirlwinds of tempestuous fire,
He soon discerns, and weltering by his side
One next himself in power, and next in crime,

80   Long after known in Palestine, and named
Beelzebub.[20] To whom the archenemy,
And thence in Heaven called Satan, with bold words
Breaking the horrid silence thus began:
   "If thou beest he; but O how fallen! how changed

85   From him, who in the happy realms of light

Vocabulary
tempestuous
(tem pes´ choo əs) *adj.*
turbulent; stormy

---

19. **center . . . . pole** three times the distance from the center of the universe (Earth) to the outermost sphere of the universe.
20. **Beelzebub** (bē el´ zə bub´) traditionally, the chief devil, or Satan. In this poem, Satan's chief lieutenant among the fallen angels.

Clothed with transcendent brightness didst outshine
Myriads though bright: if he whom mutual league,
United thoughts and counsels, equal hope
And hazard in the glorious enterprise,
90 Joined with me once, now misery hath joined
In equal ruin: into what pit thou seest
From what height fallen, so much the stronger proved
He with his thunder:[21] and till then who knew
The force of those dire arms? Yet not for those,
95 Nor what the potent Victor in his rage
Can else inflict, do I repent or change,
Though changed in outward luster, that fixed mind
And high disdain, from sense of injured merit,
That with the Mightiest raised me to contend,
100 And to the fierce contention brought along
Innumerable force of spirits armed
That durst dislike his reign, and me preferring,
His utmost power with adverse power opposed
In dubious battle on the plains of Heaven,
105 And shook his throne. What though the field be lost?
All is not lost; the unconquerable will,
And study[22] of revenge, immortal hate,
And courage never to submit or yield:
And what is else not to be overcome?
110 That glory never shall his wrath or might
Extort from me. To bow and sue for grace
With suppliant knee, and deify his power
Who from the terror of this arm so late
Doubted[23] his empire, that were low indeed,
115 That were an ignominy and shame beneath
This downfall; since by fate the strength of gods
And this empyreal substance[24] cannot fail,
Since through experience of this great event,
In arms not worse, in foresight much advanced,
120 We may with more successful hope resolve
To wage by force or guile eternal war
Irreconcilable, to our grand Foe,
Who now triumphs, and in the excess of joy
Sole reigning holds the tyranny of Heaven."
125 So spake the apostate angel, though in pain,
Vaunting aloud, but racked with deep despair;
And him thus answered soon his bold compeer.[25]

21. **He . . . thunder** God.
22. **study** pursuit.
23. **Doubted** feared for.
24. **empyreal** (em pir´ ē əl) **substance** the indestructible substance of which Heaven, or the empyrean, is composed.
25. **compeer** comrade; equal.

Vocabulary
transcendent
(tran sen´ dənt) *adj.*
exceeding beyond all limits

Literary Analysis
Epic Poetry What details in these lines might suggest to some readers that Satan is the hero of Milton's epic?

Literary Analysis
Epic Poetry In what way does Milton's vision of the opposition between Satan and God fit the expectation that epics tell of famous battles?

Vocabulary
ignominy (ig´ nə min´ ē)
n. humiliation; dishonor

Reading Check

Whom does Satan discover lying next to him?

Reading Strategy
Using Graphic Organizers
Complete a chart to break
the sentence into main and
supporting clauses.

"O prince, O chief of many thronèd Powers,
That led the embattled Seraphim[26] to war

130 Under thy conduct, and in dreadful deeds
Fearless, endangered Heaven's perpetual King,
And put to proof his high supremacy,
Whether upheld by strength, or chance, or fate!
Too well I see and rue the dire event[27]

135 That with sad overthrow and foul defeat
Hath lost us Heaven, and all this mighty host
In horrible destruction laid thus low,
As far as gods and heavenly essences
Can perish: for the mind and spirit remains

140 Invincible, and vigor soon returns,
Though all our glory extinct, and happy state
Here swallowed up in endless misery.
But what if he our conqueror (whom I now
Of force[28] believe almighty, since no less

145 Than such could have o'erpowered such force as ours)
Have left us this our spirit and strength entire
Strongly to suffer and support our pains,
That we may so suffice[29] his vengeful ire,
Or do him mightier service as his thralls

150 By right of war, whate'er his business be
Here in the heart of Hell to work in fire,
Or do his errands in the gloomy deep?
What can it then avail though yet we feel
Strength undiminished, or eternal being

155 To undergo eternal punishment?"
Whereto with speedy words the Archfiend replied:
  "Fallen cherub, to be weak is miserable,
Doing or suffering:[30] but of this be sure,
To do aught[31] good never will be our task,

160 But ever to do ill our sole delight,
As being the contrary to his high will
Whom we resist. If then his providence
Out of our evil seek to bring forth good,
Our labor must be to pervert that end,

165 And out of good still[32] to find means of evil;
Which oft times may succeed, so as perhaps
Shall grieve him, if I fail not,[33] and disturb

Literary Analysis
Epic Poetry What
assumptions about the epic
struggle between good and
evil does Milton make in
lines 159–168?

---

26. Seraphim (ser′ ə fim′) the highest order of angels.
27. event outcome.
28. Of force necessarily.
29. suffice satisfy.
30. doing or suffering whether one is active or passive.
31. aught anything.
32. still always.
33. if . . . not unless I am mistaken.

His inmost counsels from their destined aim.
But see the angry Victor[34] hath recalled
170   His ministers of vengeance and pursuit
Back to the gates of Heaven: the sulfurous hail
Shot after us in storm, o'erblown hath laid
The fiery surge, that from the precipice
Of Heaven received us falling, and the thunder,
175   Winged with red lightning and impetuous rage,
Perhaps hath spent his shafts, and ceases now
To bellow through the vast and boundless deep.
Let us not slip[35] the occasion, whether scorn,
Or satiate[36] fury yield it from our Foe.
180   Seest thou yon dreary plain, forlorn and wild,
The seat of desolation, void of light,
Save what the glimmering of these livid flames
Casts pale and dreadful? Thither let us tend
From off the tossing of these fiery waves,
185   There rest, if any rest can harbor there,
And reassembling our afflicted powers,[37]
Consult how we may henceforth most offend
Our Enemy, our own loss how repair,
How overcome this dire calamity,
190   What reinforcement we may gain from hope,
If not what resolution from despair."
   Thus Satan talking to his nearest mate,
With head uplift above the wave, and eyes
That sparkling blazed; his other parts besides
195   Prone on the flood, extended long and large,
Lay floating many a rood,[38] in bulk as huge
As whom the fables name of monstrous size,
Titanian, or Earthborn, that warred on Jove,
Briareos or Typhon,[39] whom the den
200   By ancient Tarsus[40] held, or that sea beast
Leviathan,[41] which God of all his works
Created hugest that swim the ocean stream:
Him haply slumbering on the Norway foam

---

34. angry Victor God.
35. slip fail to take advantage of.
36. satiate (sā´ shē āt´) satisfied.
37. afflicted powers overthrown armies.
38. rood old unit of measure equal to seven or eight yards.
39. Titanian (tī tā´ nē ən) **. . . Earthborn . . . Briareos** (brī ar´ ē əs) **. . . Typhon** (tī´ fən) In classical mythology, both the Titans, led by Briareos, who had a hundred hands, and the Giants (Earthborn), led by Typhon, a hundred-headed serpent monster, fought with Jove. As punishment for their rebellion, both Briareos and Typhon were thrown into the underworld.
40. Tarsus (tär´ səs) capital of Cilicia (sə lish´ ə). Typhon is said to have lived in Cilicia near Tarsus.
41. Leviathan (lə vī´ ə thən) in the Bible, a great sea monster.

Reading Check

What does Satan tell Beelzebub their sole purpose will be?

Spiral Review
Imagery
How might the violent imagery in lines 209–241 and elsewhere in the poem relate to the English civil wars?

The pilot of some small night-foundered skiff,
205 Deeming some island, oft, as seamen tell,
With fixed anchor in his scaly rind
Moors by his side under the lee, while night
Invests[42] the sea, and wished morn delays:
So stretched out huge in length the Archfiend lay
210 Chained on the burning lake, nor ever thence
Had risen or heaved his head, but that the will
And high permission of all-ruling Heaven
Left him at large to his own dark designs,
That with reiterated crimes he might
215 Heap on himself damnation, while he sought
Evil to others, and enraged might see
How all his malice served but to bring forth
Infinite goodness, grace and mercy shown
On man by him seduced, but on himself
220 Treble confusion, wrath and vengeance poured.
Forthwith upright he rears from off the pool
His mighty stature; on each hand the flames
Driven backward, slope their pointing spires, and rolled
In billows leave in the midst a horrid vale.
225 Then with expanded wings he steers his flight
Aloft, incumbent[43] on the dusky air
That felt unusual weight, till on dry land
He lights, if it were land that ever burned
With solid, as the lake with liquid fire;
230 And such appeared in hue, as when the force
Of subterranean wind transports a hill
Torn from Pelorus, or the shattered side
Of thundering Etna,[44] whose combustible
And fueled entrails thence conceiving fire,
235 Sublimed[45] with mineral fury, aid the winds,
And leave a singèd bottom all involved[46]
With stench and smoke: such resting found the sole
Of unblessed feet. Him followed his next mate,
Both glorying to have scaped the Stygian[47] flood
240 As gods, and by their own recovered strength,
Not by the sufferance[48] of supernal[49] power.
    "Is this the region, this the soil, the clime,"
Said then the lost Archangel, "this the seat

---

42. Invests covers.
43. incumbent lying.
44. Pelorus (pə lôr′ əs) . . . **Etna** volcanic mountains in Sicily.
45. Sublimed vaporized.
46. involved enveloped.
47. Stygian (stij′ ē ən) of the river Styx, which, in Greek mythology, encircled Hades (hā′ dēz′), the home of the dead.
48. sufferance permission.
49. supernal (sə purn′ əl) heavenly.

That we must change[50] for Heaven, this mournful gloom
245 For that celestial light? Be it so, since he
Who now is sovereign can dispose and bid
What shall be right: farthest from him is best,
Whom reason hath equaled, force hath made supreme
Above his equals. Farewell happy fields,
250 Where joy forever dwells. Hail horrors! Hail
Infernal world! and thou, profoundest Hell
Receive thy new possessor, one who brings
A mind not to be changed by place or time.
The mind is its own place, and in itself
255 Can make a Heaven of Hell, a Hell of Heaven.
What matter where, if I be still the same,
And what I should be, all but less than he
Whom thunder hath made greater? Here at least
We shall be free; the Almighty hath not built
260 Here for his envy, will not drive us hence:
Here we may reign secure, and in my choice
To reign is worth ambition though in Hell:

---

50. change exchange.

Literary Analysis
Epic Poetry and Poetic Ambition In what way is the attitude expressed in lines 250–258 fitting both for a hero and a poet?

Reading Check

What does Satan say about the mind?

◄ **Critical Viewing**
Why might the English Civil War have made Milton think of a battle between angels like the one depicted in this picture? **[Connect]**

Better to reign in Hell than serve in Heaven.
But wherefore[51] let we then our faithful friends,
265 The associates and copartners of our loss
Lie thus astonished[52] on the oblivious[53] pool,
And call them not to share with us their part
In this unhappy mansion, or once more
With rallied arms to try what may be yet
Regained in Heaven, or what more lost in Hell?"

51. **wherefore** why.
52. **astonished** stunned.
53. **oblivious** causing forgetfulness.

Critical Reading

@ 1. **Key Ideas and Details (a)** Summarize the story of Adam and Eve as Milton tells it in lines 28–36. **(b) Connect:** How is the fall of Adam and Eve connected to the fall of Satan and his cohorts?

@ 2. **Key Ideas and Details (a)** Lines 59–74 describe Hell. What does Milton indicate are its main features? **(b) Interpret:** Explain Satan's reaction in lines 94–99 to his fall into Hell.

@ 3. **Key Ideas and Details (a) Infer:** In lines 116–124, what kind of war does Satan propose to wage against Heaven? **(b) Interpret:** Judging from lines 105–116, what is his motive for such a war? **(c) Hypothesize:** How will this war lead to the fall of Adam and Eve?

@ 4. **Integration of Knowledge and Ideas (a) Interpret:** Explain how Satan's attitude toward Hell in lines 250–252 proves that he is "one who brings / A mind not to be changed by place or time" (lines 252–253). **(b) Draw Conclusions:** Explain how the mind "Can make a Heaven of Hell, a Hell of Heaven" (line 255).

@ 5. **Integration of Knowledge and Ideas (a) Summarize:** Characterize Satan, supporting your description with quotations from the text. **(b) Evaluate:** To what extent does Satan seem admirable? To what extent despairing? Explain.

@ 6. **Integration of Knowledge and Ideas (a) Interpret:** What does Milton mean when he says he wants to "justify the ways of God to men" (line 26)? **(b) Assess:** How good a start has Milton made toward this goal? Explain.

@ 7. **Integration of Knowledge and Ideas** Focus on an especially strong passage in *Paradise Lost*. What devices—word choice, rhythm, characterization, description—help Milton reinvent the story of the fallen angels? In your response, use at least two of these Essential Question words: *invent, innovation, tradition*. *[Connecting to the Essential Question: What is the relationship of the writer to tradition?]*

Cite textual evidence to support your responses.

Critical Commentary

from "A Defense of Poetry"
Percy Bysshe Shelley

from *Surprised by Sin*
Stanley Fish

Poets and critics have long debated whether Satan in Paradise Lost *is an evil villain or the secret hero of the poem. Romantics like Percy Bysshe Shelley viewed Satan as a heroic Romantic rebel. Writing in 1821, Shelley made the case for that perspective.*

Milton's Devil as a moral being is as far superior to his God, as one who perseveres in some purpose, which he has conceived to be excellent in spite of adversity and torture, is to one who in the cold security of undoubted triumph inflicts the most horrible revenge upon his enemy, not from any mistaken notion of inducing him to repent of a perseverance in enmity, but with the alleged design of exasperating him to deserve new torments. Milton has so far violated the popular creed (if this shall be judged to be a violation) as to have alleged no superiority of moral virtue to his god over his devil. And this bold neglect of a direct moral purpose is the most decisive proof of the supremacy of Milton's genius. . . .

Writing exactly 150 years later, the critic Stanley Fish argued that, far from being an admirable rebel, Milton's Satan has no will or identity of his own.

. . . Satan's independence is an illusion because he is in bondage to the freedom to do as he likes and he becomes the captive of momentary purposes and the plaything of master strategists (God, Milton) who make of him what they will; his will does not exist (he has no "deepest self"), except in a Satanic never-never-Land where evil could be someone's good. This reversal is impossible in a universe where God is God and when Satan admits "myself am Hell" he, in effect, says "myself am not," since hell is the state of disunion from God's sustaining power and hence a state of nonbeing . . . Perhaps the most ironic of his boasts is this one: "What matter where, if I be still the same" (I.256). The sameness of evil is the sameness of chaos, a stability of instability where the identity and form of any atom or cluster of atoms is a matter of chance unless an ordering power is imposed; Satan is condemned to restless wandering until God or some deputy of God finds a use for him and endows him with motives and opinions and powers to fit the role "imposed from without."

Ⓒ **Key Ideas and Details** What admirable qualities does Shelley attribute to Satan? Why does Fish declare that "Satan's independence is an illusion"?

After You Read *Poetry of John Milton*

Literary Analysis

© 1. Craft and Structure **(a)** Which **Italian sonnet** has the more regular pattern of rhymes in the sestet? **(b)** Does this regularity strengthen the "solution" the sestet gives to the problem set out in the octave? Explain.

© 2. Craft and Structure **(a)** In Sonnet XIX, how does sentence structure break with the pattern of octave and sestet? **(b)** What effect is achieved?

© 3. Key Ideas and Details **(a)** What major event has occurred before the beginning of Milton's **epic? (b)** How does picking up the story after this event follow the conventions of epic form?

© 4. Craft and Structure A traditional epic character has a powerful personality. How does Milton make Satan a suitable epic character?

© 5. Integration of Knowledge and Ideas In Sonnets VII and XIX, Milton reflects on setbacks to his poetic ambition. Use a chart like the one shown to compare the two poems.

Speaker's Situation	Effect on Ambition	Solution	How Solution Helps

© 6. Integration of Knowledge and Ideas **(a)** Explain how, by writing *Paradise Lost*, Milton aspires to the literary greatness of Homer and the Bible. Provide lines from the poem in support. **(b)** Does Milton's ambition contradict the moral of Sonnet XIX: "They also serve who only stand and wait"? Why or why not?

© 7. Integration of Knowledge and Ideas **(a)** What ideas about the power of a poet might lines 254–255 of *Paradise Lost* suggest? **(b)** What parallel, if any, can you draw between the situation of Satan and the ambition of a poet? Explain.

© 8. Integration of Knowledge and Ideas Using your knowledge of *Paradise Lost*, explain the humor of the cartoon shown on this page.

Reading Strategy

9. (a) Identify a passage that was hard to understand. **(b)** Explain how to repair comprehension by **using a graphic organizer** to break down sentences into main and supporting clauses.

10. (a) Identify the main clause in lines 1–8 of Sonnet XIX. **(b)** Explain what each supporting clause adds to its meaning.

Common Core State Standards

Language

4.c. Consult general and specialized reference materials, both print and digital, to find the pronunciation of a word or determine or clarify its precise meaning, its part of speech, its etymology, or its standard usage. *(p. 537)*

6. Acquire and use accurately general academic and domain-specific words and phrases, sufficient for reading, writing, speaking, and listening at the college and career readiness level. *(p. 537)*

©**The New Yorker Collection**, 1988, J. B. Handelsman, from *cartoonbank.com*. All Rights Reserved.

"We're Birds of Paradise all right— paradise lost!"

© Vocabulary Acquisition and Use

Word Analysis: Latin Root -lum-

The Latin root -lum-, found in *illumine*, means "light" or "lamp." It is the basis for many words used in *science* to describe light.

Review the list of words and definitions containing -lum-. Then, use the context of the sentences that follow to determine which words fit best in the sentences that follow. Use each word only once and explain your answers.

illuminant *n.* something giving off light

illuminate *v.* shed light on

lumens *n.* units of light

luminous *adj.* emitting light

1. "This clue may _____ the entire mystery," exclaimed the detective.
2. A more efficient light bulb generates more _____ while using less power.
3. The _____ full moon made the path ahead of them clear.
4. A flickering torch served as their only _____.

Vocabulary: Synonyms

A **synonym** is a word that has a similar meaning as another word. Write a complete sentence to answer each question that follows. In your answer, replace the underlined word or words with a synonym taken from the vocabulary list on page 521.

1. Does a good portrait give more than a <u>likeness</u> of its subject?
2. What did they use to <u>shine on</u> the dark pool?
3. What do shoplifters want when they <u>commit a wrong</u>?
4. How does <u>sneakiness</u> benefit a spy?
5. How would an <u>inflexible</u> child act?
6. What effect did the <u>violent</u> events have on the crowd?
7. How did the audience feel about the <u>unmatchable</u> musical performance?
8. Did the corrupt senator's <u>shame</u> affect anyone else?

Using Resources to Build Vocabulary

Epic Style: Words for the Nether World

In *Paradise Lost*, one of Milton's greatest challenges is to create a vivid picture of Hell. He meets this challenge by using words like the ones below to describe the underworld:

desolation	dreary
forlorn	glimmering
gloom	horrid
mournful	wild

Note how the *connotations*, or associations, of these words serve Milton's purpose. Then, use a print or an electronic *dictionary* or *thesaurus* to find **antonyms**—words with the opposite meaning—of these words. Identify which of those antonyms you think Milton might use to describe Heaven and explain why.

PERFORMANCE TASKS
Integrated Language Skills

Writing

Argumentative Text Twentieth-century literary critic Douglas Bush said this of *Paradise Lost*: "Its characterization of Satan is one of the supreme achievements of world literature." Clearly Satan is the villain of the poem. Is he more than that? Do you feel any admiration or sympathy for him as you read?

Write an **essay** in which you present and defend your analysis of the character of Satan in *Paradise Lost*. Consider both positive and negative aspects of his character. In your essay, explain how your view of Satan influences your interpretation of *Paradise Lost* itself.

Prewriting Study the *imagery, language, events, universal themes, speeches,* and *stylistic devices* that Milton uses to characterize Satan. Refer to the Critical Commentary on page 535 to spark your own ideas.

- Use a chart like the one shown to take your notes.
- Consider how Milton balances these positive and negative elements.
- Think about other villains from literature or movies. How does Milton's treatment of Satan compare to the way these villains are presented?
- Write a sentence or two to serve as the thesis of your essay, and develop an outline that shows how you will support the thesis.

Common Core State Standards

Writing
1.a. Introduce precise, knowledgeable claim(s), and create an organization that logically sequences claim(s), reasons, and evidence.
1.b. Develop claim(s) fairly and thoroughly, supplying the most relevant evidence for each.
1.e. Provide a concluding statement or section that follows from and supports the argument presented.

Negative Aspects	Positive Aspects
introduction to Satan: (lines 34–40) he is arrogant and destructive	strong will: "All is not lost" (line 106)
"durst defy the Omnipotent" (line 49)	resourceful: "We may with more successful hope resolve / To wage by force or guile eternal war" (lines 120–121)
"obdurate pride and steadfast hate" (line 58)	

Drafting Write a draft of your essay that follows your outline and incorporates evidence from the text of *Paradise Lost* to support your points. State your thesis in the opening paragraph, support it in the body of the essay, and conclude the essay by summarizing what you have proved.

Revising Revise your essay to make it clear and effective.

- Review your draft, making sure you have included *accurate and detailed references to the text* to support your points.
- If your opening paragraph is not lively, consider quoting from the poem or contrasting Satan with another villain to catch readers' attention.
- Check quotations to be sure they are accurate and properly referenced.
- Read the essay carefully to make sure it is grammatically correct and that all words are spelled correctly.

Conventions and Style: Misplaced and Dangling Modifiers

One way to make your writing clearer is to avoid misplaced and dangling modifiers. A **misplaced modifier** seems to modify the wrong word in a sentence because it is too far away from the word it really modifies. A **dangling modifier** does not sensibly modify any word because the word it should modify does not appear in the sentence. Always check your writing for any words, phrases, or clauses that are misplaced or dangling modifiers.

Fix Misplaced and Dangling Modifiers

Misplaced	Better
Milton hoped to one day achieve poetic greatness *early in his career*. (phrase)	Early in his career, Milton hoped to one day achieve poetic greatness.

Dangling	Better
Seeking revenge against God, Eve is tempted into eating the forbidden fruit. (phrase)	Seeking revenge against God, Satan tempts Eve into eating the forbidden fruit.
While he was working as a translator for the government, his eyesight was lost. (clause)	While he was working as a translator for the government, Milton lost his eyesight.

Practice Fix each misplaced or dangling modifier to make the sentence clear and sensible. You may have to change the wording slightly. In items 1–5, the misplaced or dangling modifier is in italics.

1. Milton dictated the poem to his daughters, *blind and unable to write*.
2. *Gifted*, Milton's destiny was to become a famous poet.
3. *At the age of fourteen*, Milton's formal education was begun.
4. *Learning about the revolt against the king*, Milton's tour of Europe was cut short.
5. His blindness is the burden he bears, *which he calls a "mild yoke."*
6. Losing the battle, Hell becomes the rebellious angels' place of banishment.
7. Satan initiates a battle with God motivated by pride and willfulness.
8. The speaker reflects that time has stolen his youth on his birthday.
9. Concerned about his career progress, comfort is found in the speaker's faith.
10. Satan decides he will make humans commit acts of evil during his conversation with Beelzebub.

© Writing and Speaking Conventions

A. Writing Write a sentence using each phrase or clause as a modifier. Then, tell what word or words the phrase or clause modifies.

   1. getting older   **2.** during middle age   **3.** who serves God

   Example: getting older
   Sentence: The poet, getting older, wrote about time.
   Word Modified: poet

B. Speaking Write and perform a dialogue in which Satan tries to rally his fellow devils. Correctly use one word, one phrase, and one clause as modifiers.

> **PH** | **WRITING COACH**
>
> Further instruction and practice are available in *Prentice Hall Writing Coach*.

EPICS
in World Literature

Match numbers on the left with pictures on the right to see illustrations of some of these world epics.

1 *Iliad and Odyssey* (c. 800–700 B.C.)
ancient Greek epics attributed to Homer

Mahabharata (200 B.C.–A.D. 400)
Indian epic attributed to Vyasa

Song of Roland (c. A.D. 1100)
French epic

2 *Song of My Cid* (c. 1140)
Spanish epic

3 *Divine Comedy* (1308–1321)
Italian epic by Dante Alighieri

4 *Paradise Lost* (1667) and
Paradise Regained (1671)
English epics by John Milton

5 *The Song of Hiawatha* (1855)
American epic by Henry Wadsworth Longfellow

Sundiata (1960)
West African epic, created as a novel by D. T. Niane

6 *Omeros* (1990)
Caribbean epic by Derek Walcott

Comparing Literary Works

from *Paradise Lost* • from the
Divine Comedy: Inferno

Comparing Epics Around the World

The Epic Tradition Epics are long narrative poems describing the adventures of noble characters. Among the earliest epics are *Gilgamesh*, from the Middle East, and the ancient Greek epics attributed to Homer, the *Iliad* and the *Odyssey*. One of the first epics with a known author is the Roman poet Virgil's *Aeneid.* Christian authors Dante Alighieri (the *Divine Comedy*) and John Milton (*Paradise Lost*) imitated classical models and developed their great works using these traditional elements of epics:

- amazing events, such as great battles, and vast settings
- larger-than-life main characters and supernatural creatures who take an interest in human affairs
- themes expressing important cultural values and beliefs
- an elevated style using a serious tone and lofty poetic language

As you read, use a chart like the one shown to help you compare the elements of the excerpt from Dante's epic with those from Milton's *Paradise Lost*. Consider the impact of the choices that each author made.

**Common Core
State Standards**

Reading Literature
3. Analyze the impact of the author's choices regarding how to develop and relate elements of a story or drama.

Language
6. Demonstrate independence in gathering vocabulary knowledge when considering a word or phrase important to comprehension or expression.

	Divine Comedy: Inferno	*Paradise Lost*
subject		the Fall of Humanity
main character(s)		Satan; larger-than-life supernatural character
setting(s)		vivid depictions of Heaven and Hell
theme(s)		original sin; pride and disobedience
style		serious tone; lofty poetic language; blank verse

© Gather Vocabulary Knowledge

Dante used related forms of the words *cowered, awe,* and *writhes.* Use a **dictionary** to find each word's part of speech and definition. Then, employ the following references to further explore these words:

- **History of Language:** Use a history of English to research each word's origins. Write a paragraph about the word's emergence in English.
- **Book of Quotations:** Use an online or print collection of quotations to find a quotation containing one of the words. In a paragraph, explain nuances in meaning that are evident from the context of the quotation.

Comparing References Compare and contrast what you learn about the words from these and other related references, printed or electronic.

Dante
Alighieri
(1265–1321)

Dante Alighieri (dän´ tā al əg yer´ ē), whose visions of Hell have haunted readers for centuries, is widely considered one of the greatest poets of western civilization. T. S. Eliot wrote, "Dante and Shakespeare divide the modern world between them; there is no third."

Political Chaos Dante was born into a poor but noble family in the Italian city of Florence. At the time, Italy was not a unified nation but a collection of independent city-states where internal political struggles and interstate rivalries often led to warfare. Elected to help run Florence's government, Dante and his party were overthrown in civil warfare that led to exile from his beloved city in 1302. His experience of exile would play an important role in his writing.

Pioneering Italian In Dante's time, most European writers wrote in Latin, the language of scholarship and the Church. Dante believed that poets should write in the vernacular, or language of the people—in his case, Italian. In 1304, he published *De Vulgari Eloquentia,* which argued for the use of the vernacular. He wrote many lyric poems in Italian, and his crowning achievement, the *Divine Comedy,* was also an Italian work.

The Love of His Life Appearing in the *Divine Comedy* is a woman named Beatrice, to whom Dante also dedicated his early love poems. Scholars believe she is based on a real-life person, Beatrice Portinari. Yet evidence suggests that Dante saw the real Beatrice only twice in his life—first when he was nine and then nine years later. Nevertheless, for Dante, Beatrice came to represent an ideal love figure, the guiding force that led him from despair.

> "Midway in our life's journey, I went astray/from the straight road and woke to find myself/**alone in a dark wood. . . .**"

FROM THE DIVINE COMEDY:
Inferno
Dante Alighieri
translated by John Ciardi

BACKGROUND In his *Divine Comedy*, Dante uses an organizing principle based on the number three, drawn from the Christian concept of the Holy Trinity. Documenting his imagined visit to Hell, Purgatory, and Heaven, he divides the epic into three parts—*Inferno*, *Purgatorio*, and *Paradiso*.

In Paradise, Dante will be guided by his beloved Beatrice. For his trip through Hell to Purgatory, however, Dante's guide is the poet Virgil, to whom Dante pays homage by calling him "my Master." Virgil takes Dante through the nine circles of Hell, organized by gravity of the sin involved. In this final canto of *Inferno*, the two reach the ninth circle, by the frozen waters of Cocytus[1], where those guilty of the worst sin, treachery, are found. They include Judas Iscariot, who betrayed Jesus, and Brutus and Cassius, two Roman senators who plotted to assassinate the Roman leader Julius Caesar. They also include the angel-turned-devil Satan, here called Lucifer, the ulti-mate traitor who rebelled against God.

▲ **Critical Viewing**
How does the artist's depiction of Lucifer in this engraving compare and contrast with Dante's portrayal of him?
[Compare and Contrast]

---

1. Cocytus (kō sīt´ əs) Greek: "river of wailing."

Canto XXXIV

Ninth Circle: Cocytus
Round Four: Judecca
The Center

Compound Fraud
The Treacherous to Their Masters
Satan

"On march the banners of the King,"[2] Virgil begins as the Poets face the last depth. He is quoting a medieval hymn, and to it he adds the distortion and perversion of all that lies about him. "On march the banners of the King—of Hell." And there before them, in an infernal parody of Godhead, they see Satan in the distance, his great wings beating like a windmill. It is their beating that is the source of the icy wind of Cocytus, the exhalation of all evil.

All about him in the ice are strewn the sinners of the last round, *Judecca*, named for Judas Iscariot.[3] These are the *Treacherous to Their Masters*. They lie completely sealed in the ice, twisted and distorted into every conceivable posture. It is impossible to speak to them, and the Poets move on to observe Satan.

He is fixed into the ice at the center to which flow all the rivers of guilt; and as he beats his great wings as if to escape, their icy wind only freezes him more surely into the polluted ice. In a grotesque parody of the Trinity, he has three faces, each a different color, and in each mouth he clamps a sinner whom he rips eternally with his teeth. *Judas Iscariot* is in the central mouth: *Brutus* and *Cassius*[4] in the mouths on either side.

Having seen all, the Poets now climb through the center, grappling hand over hand down the hairy flank of Satan himself—a last supremely symbolic action—and at last, when they have passed the center of all gravity, they emerge from Hell. A long climb from the earth's center to the Mount of Purgatory awaits them, and they push on without rest, ascending along the sides of the river Lethe, till they emerge once more to see the stars of Heaven, just before dawn on Easter Sunday.

Comparing Epics
What aspect of Dante's style is illustrated in lines 4–5?

> "On march the banners of the King of Hell,"
> my Master said. "Toward us. Look straight ahead:
> can you make him out at the core of the frozen shell?"
> Like a whirling windmill seen afar at twilight,

---

2. **On ... King** This hymn was written in the sixth century by Venantius Fortunatus, Bishop of Poitiers. The original celebrates the Holy Cross and is part of the service for Good Friday, to be sung at the moment of uncovering the cross.
3. **Judas Iscariot** (is ker′ ē ət) disciple who betrayed Jesus; see the Bible, Matthew 26:14, 48.
4. **Brutus and Cassius** They took part in a plot to assassinate Julius Caesar.

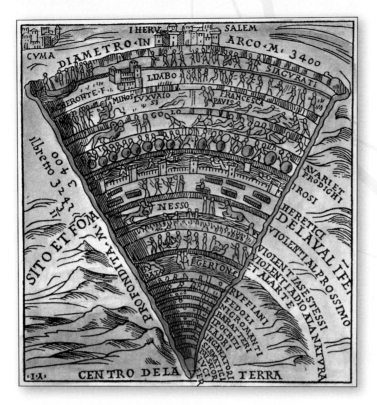

◀ **Critical Viewing** Where on this map of the *Inferno* do Dante and Virgil now find themselves? Use information from the background on the facing page of hints. **[Analyze]**

Vocabulary
cowered (kou´ ərd) *v.* crouched, as from fear or cold

5   or when a mist has risen from the ground—
      just such an engine rose upon my sight
stirring up such a wild and bitter wind
      I cowered for shelter at my Master's back,
      there being no other windbreak I could find.
I stood now where the souls of the last class
10   (with fear my verses tell it) were covered wholly;
      they shone below the ice like straws in glass.
Some lie stretched out; others are fixed in place
      upright, some on their heads, some on their soles;
      another, like a bow, bends foot to face.
15 When we had gone so far across the ice
      that it pleased my Guide to show me the foul creature[5]
      which once had worn the grace of Paradise,
he made me stop, and, stepping aside, he said:
      "Now see the face of Dis![6] This is the place
20   where you must arm your soul against all dread."
Do not ask, Reader, how my blood ran cold
      and my voice choked up with fear. I cannot write it:
      this is a terror that cannot be told.
I did not die, and yet I lost life's breath:
25   imagine for yourself what I became,
      deprived at once of both my life and death.

---

5. the foul creature Lucifer.
6. Dis (dis) in Greek mythology, the god of the lower world or the lower world itself. Here, it stands for Lucifer.

Comparing Epics
What background information about Lucifer, or Satan, do lines 33–35 share with Milton's epic?

Vocabulary
awe (ô) *n.* feelings of reverence, fear, and wonder

The Emperor of the Universe of Pain
    jutted his upper chest above the ice;
    and I am closer in size to the great mountain
30 the Titans[7] make around the central pit,
    than they to his arms. Now, starting from this part,
    imagine the whole that corresponds to it!
If he was once as beautiful as now
    he is hideous, and still turned on his Maker,
35   well may he be the source of every woe!
With what a sense of **awe** I saw his head
    towering above me! for it had three faces:[8]
    one was in front, and it was fiery red;
the other two, as weirdly wonderful,
40   merged with it from the middle of each shoulder
    to the point where all converged at the top of the skull;
the right was something between white and bile;
    the left was about the color one observes
    on those who live along the banks of the Nile.
45 Under each head two wings rose terribly,
    their span proportioned to so gross a bird:

---

7. Titans giant deities who were overthrown by Zeus and the Olympian gods of Greece.
8. three faces There are many interpretations of these three faces. The common theme in all of them is that the faces are a perversion of the qualities of the Trinity.

▼ Critical Viewing
Which elements in this engraving emphasize Virgil's role as guide and protector of Dante? **[Analyze]**

> **If he was once as beautiful as now
> he is hideous, and still turned on his Maker,
> well may he be the source of every woe!**

I never saw such sails upon the sea.
They were not feathers—their texture and their form
    were like a bat's wings—and he beat them so
50   that three winds blew from him in one great storm:
it is these winds that freeze all Cocytus.
    He wept from his six eyes, and down three chins
    the tears ran mixed with bloody froth and pus.[9]
In every mouth he worked a broken sinner
55   between his rake-like teeth. Thus he kept three
    in eternal pain at his eternal dinner.
For the one in front the biting seemed to play
    no part at all compared to the ripping: at times
    the whole skin of his back was flayed away.
60 "That soul that suffers most," explained my Guide,
    "is Judas Iscariot, he who kicks his legs
    on the fiery chin and has his head inside.
Of the other two, who have their heads thrust forward,
    the one who dangles down from the black face
65   is Brutus: note how he writhes without a word.
And there, with the huge and sinewy arms, is the soul,
    of Cassius,—But the night is coming on[10]
    and we must go, for we have seen the whole."
Then, as he bade, I clasped his neck, and he,
70   watching for a moment when the wings
    were opened wide, reached over dexterously[11]
and seized the shaggy coat of the king demon;
    then grappling matted hair and frozen crusts
    from one tuft to another, clambered down.
75 When we had reached the joint where the great thigh
    merges into the swelling of the haunch,
    my Guide and Master, straining terribly,
turned his head to where his feet had been
    and began to grip the hair as if he were climbing;[12]
80   so that I thought we moved toward Hell again.

---

9. bloody froth and pus the gore of the sinners he chews, which is mixed with his saliva.
10. the night is coming on It is now Saturday evening.
11. dexterously *adv.* skillfully.
12. as if he were climbing They have passed the center of gravity and so must turn around and start climbing.

Comparing Epics
What is unusual about the climate in this final circle of Dante's Hell?

Vocabulary
writhes (rīthz) *v.* twists and turns the body, as in agony

Reading Check
What torture do Judas Iscariot, Brutus, and Cassius suffer?

"Hold fast!"

my Guide said, and his breath came shrill/with labor and exhaustion.

"There is no way/but by such stairs to rise above such evil."

Vocabulary
shrill (shril) *adj.* high and sharp in tone; high-pitched

Vocabulary
nimble (nim´ bəl) *adj.* able to move quickly and lightly

"Hold fast!" my Guide said, and his breath came shrill
  with labor and exhaustion. "There is no way
  but by such stairs to rise above such evil."
At last he climbed out through an opening
85 in the central rock, and he seated me on the rim;
  then joined me with a nimble backward spring.
I looked up, thinking to see Lucifer
  as I had left him, and I saw instead
  his legs projecting high into the air.
90 Now let all those whose dull minds are still vexed
  by failure to understand what point it was
  I had passed through, judge if I was perplexed.
"Get up. Up on your feet," my Master said.
  "The sun already mounts to middle tierce,[13]
95 and a long road and hard climbing lie ahead."
It was no hall of state we had found there,

---

13. middle tierce According to the church's division of the day for prayer, tierce is the period from about six to nine A.M. Middle tierce, therefore, is seven-thirty. In going through the center point, Dante and Virgil have gone from night to day. They have moved ahead twelve hours.

but a natural animal pit hollowed from rock
with a broken floor and a close and sunless air.
"Before I tear myself from the Abyss,"

100   I said when I had risen, "O my Master,
explain to me my error in all this:
where is the ice? and Lucifer—how has he
been turned from top to bottom: and how can the sun
have gone from night to day so suddenly?"

105   And he to me: "You imagine you are still
on the other side of the center where I grasped
the shaggy flank of the Great Worm of Evil
which bores through the world—you were while I climbed down,
but when I turned myself about, you passed

110   the point to which all gravities are drawn.
You are under the other hemisphere where you stand;
the sky above us is the half opposed
to that which canopies the great dry land.
Under the midpoint of that other sky

115   the Man[14] who was born sinless and who lived
beyond all blemish, came to suffer and die.
You have your feet upon a little sphere
which forms the other face of the Judecca.
There it is evening when it is morning here.

120   And this gross Fiend and Image of all Evil
who made a stairway for us with his hide
is pinched and prisoned in the ice-pack still.
On this side he plunged down from heaven's height,
and the land that spread here once hid in the sea

125   and fled North to our hemisphere for fright:[15]
And it may be that moved by that same fear,
the one peak[16] that still rises on this side
fled upward leaving this great cavern[17] here."
Down there, beginning at the further bound

---

14. **the Man** Jesus, who suffered and died in Jerusalem, which was thought to be the middle of the Earth.
15. **fled North . . . for fright** Dante believed that the Northern Hemisphere was mostly land and the Southern Hemisphere, mostly water. Here, he explains the reason for this state of affairs.
16. **the one peak** the Mount of Purgatory.
17. **this great cavern** the natural animal pit of line 97. It is also "Beelzebub's dim tomb," line 130.

◄ **Critical Viewing** What evidence is there from this image that Dante and Virgil have made it out of hell? **[Analyze]**

Comparing Epics
Would the description of Lucifer in line 107 apply to the Satan of Milton's epic? Why or why not?

Reading Check
What "stairway" did Virgil take to climb out of Hell?

And this gross Fiend and Image of all Evil
who made a stairway for us with his hide
is pinched and prisoned in the ice-pack still.

where a round opening brought in sight the blest
and beauteous shining of the Heavenly cars.
And we walked out once more **beneath the Stars.**

130   of Beelzebub's[18] dim tomb, there is a space
        not known by sight, but only by the sound
of a little stream[19] descending through the hollow
        it has eroded from the massive stone
        in its endlessly entwining lazy flow."

135 My Guide and I crossed over and began
        to mount that little known and lightless road
        to ascend into the shining world again.
    He first, I second, without thought of rest
        we climbed the dark until we reached the point

140   where a round opening brought in sight the blest
    and beauteous shining of the Heavenly cars.
    And we walked out once more beneath the Stars.[20]

---

18. **Beelzebub's** (bē el′ zə bubz′) Beelzebub, which in Hebrew means "god of flies," was another name for Lucifer or Satan.
19. **a little stream** Lethe (lē′ thē); in classical mythology, the river of forgetfulness, from which souls drank before being born. In Dante's symbolism, it flows down from Purgatory, where it has washed away the memory of sin from the souls who are undergoing purification. That memory it delivers to Hell, which draws all sin to itself.
20. **Stars** As part of his total symbolism, Dante ends each of the three divisions of the *Divine Comedy* with this word. Every conclusion of the upward soul is toward the stars, symbols of hope and virtue. It is just before dawn of Easter Sunday that the Poets emerge— a further symbolism.

Critical Reading

1. Key Ideas and Details (a) In lines 22–23, what does Dante say he cannot describe? **(b) Analyze:** How does he nevertheless communicate his experience?

2. Key Ideas and Details (a) What do the three figures in Lucifer's mouth all have in common, and what do they have in common with Lucifer? **(b) Interpret:** Why do you think Dante situates these sinners in frozen waters? **(c) Infer:** Why do you think he feels no sympathy for these sinners, as he did for many sinners in earlier circles of Hell?

3. Key Ideas and Details (a) Which aspect of Brutus's torture does Virgil emphasize in line 65? **(b) Interpret:** Why might language be denied to the inhabitants of the ninth circle of Hell?

After You Read

from *Paradise Lost* •
from the *Divine Comedy:
Inferno*

Comparing Epics

1. Integration of Knowledge and Ideas Compare and contrast the ways in which Dante and Milton portray Satan (or Lucifer) in their **epics.** **(a)** What is similar about these epic villains? **(b)** How do they differ physically and in terms of personality?

2. Integration of Knowledge and Ideas **(a)** What is similar and different about the sinful behavior being criticized in each epic? **(b)** Based on the two excerpts, do you think these epics are teaching the same values? Why or why not?

3. Craft and Structure How effective is each selection in achieving the elevated style appropriate to an epic? Cite specific passages to support your opinions.

4. Integration of Knowledge and Ideas Is there evidence in the texts themselves that Dante's epic was written in the Middle Ages and Milton's in the seventeenth century? Explain.

⏱ Timed Writing

Informative Text: Essay

Epics traditionally show their heroes braving the underworld or other dangerous, often supernatural settings to perform great deeds.

Assignment: Write an essay in which you compare and contrast the impact of the authors' choices as to how to portray setting. **[40 minutes]**
Address questions such as these to focus your analysis:

- What do the imagery and descriptive language these authors use to portray Hell have in common? How do they differ?

- What is the effect of Dante's firsthand impression of Hell compared to the effect of Milton's all-knowing narrator?

- Which setting do you find more unusual? Why?

- Which universal themes do these settings suggest? Explain.

As you draft your essay, remember to do the following:

- Write an essay of sufficient length to address the questions you decide to consider.

- Include relevant and substantial evidence and well-chosen details.

- Write legibly and use appropriate capitalization and punctuation conventions.

5-Minute Planner

Complete these steps before you begin to write:

1. Read the assignment carefully. Identify key words and phrases.

2. Weigh the similarities and differences between the two selections.
   TIP As you scan the texts, jot down details that you might use.

3. Create a rough outline for your essay.

4. Reread the prompts, and draft your essay.

© Common Core State Standards

Writing
2. Write informative/explanatory texts to examine and convey complex ideas, concepts, and information clearly and accurately through the effective selection, organization, and analysis of content.

10. Write routinely over extended time frames and shorter time frames for a range of tasks, purposes, and audiences.

USE ACADEMIC VOCABULARY

As you write, use academic language, including the following words or their related forms:

categorize
classify
determine
indicate

For more information about academic language, see the vocabulary charts in the introduction to this book.

Connecting to the Essential Question If you talk about your trip down "the road of life," you are using the same symbolism as Bunyan does in his book. As you read, note religious ideas that influence Bunyan's hero, Christian, in this episode of his life's trip. Identifying these ideas will help as you answer the Essential Question: **How does literature shape or reflect society?**

Literary Analysis

Used in different types of narratives, **allegory** is a literary form in which all the parts of a story have a symbolic meaning. Many works of fiction use *symbols*—objects, people, or places that stand for something beyond themselves. In an allegory, however, every element of the story is symbolic. The allegory in *The Pilgrim's Progress* can therefore be read in two ways:

- On the *literal* level, it tells the story of an adventure-packed journey.
- On the *symbolic* level, it tells the complex account of a Christian soul's journey through life to salvation.

The purpose of an allegory is to teach a moral lesson. To make his lesson clear, Bunyan uses names that reveal the symbolic meanings of characters. A character who assists the hero, for example, is named Help. As you read the excerpt from this allegory, analyze the author's choices of names for the characters. Then, consider the lessons that the allegory teaches as well as the multiple themes that it expresses.

Reading Strategy

 **Preparing to Read Complex Texts** By **analyzing the text structure** of an allegory—its literal and symbolic levels—you can better appreciate its *meaning*. Remember, too, that you will be reading just one episode of a longer journey that stands for a Christian soul's search for salvation.

- Review the map on page 556 to see the whole journey.
- Use a chart like the one shown to interpret the meaning of specific characters and places in this part of the journey.

Vocabulary

heedless (hēd´ lis) *adj.* not taking notice; inattentive (p. 554)

wallowed (wäl´ ōd) *v.* rolled around in mud, water, etc. (p. 554)

burden (bʉrd´ ən) *n.* something that weighs one down; a heavy load or responsibility (p. 554)

endeavored (en dev´ ərd) *v.* made a serious attempt; tried (p. 554)

dominions (də min´ yənz) *n.* governed territories (p. 555)

substantial (səb stan´ shəl) *adj.* large in size or strength (p. 555)

Common Core State Standards

Reading Literature
2. Determine two or more themes or central ideas of a text and analyze their development over the course of the text, including how they interact and build on one another to produce a complex account.

Interpreting an Allegory	
Overall symbolism	Christian's journey = a Christian's journey through life to salvation
Specific symbols with names that signal their meaning	Christian = a Christian Celestial City = heaven
Specific symbols not signaled by their names	
Main message or lesson	

JOHN BUNYAN

Author of *The Pilgrim's Progress*

The son of a tinker, or traveling mender of pots and pans, John Bunyan had little formal education. Yet he went on to produce *The Pilgrim's Progress*, one of the most widely read books in the English language.

Finding Faith Born near Bedford in central England, Bunyan learned only the basics of reading and instead worked as his father's apprentice, a path on which he would have continued had warfare not intervened. Drafted into the army, he fought on the Parliamentary side in the English Civil Wars. In about 1648, he married a member of a Puritan sect to which he converted. The two religious tracts his wife brought into their home also helped him improve his reading.

Testaments of Faith By 1655, Bunyan had become a popular preacher at his Bedford church. Five years later, however, when Charles II was restored to the throne, it became illegal to preach outside the Church of England. Arrested and jailed for twelve years, Bunyan spent the time profitably, studying the Bible and using it as a guide in writing several books, including a religious autobiography, *Grace Abounding*. He began *The Pilgrim's Progress* during a second, shorter prison term, publishing the first part in 1678 and a second part six years later.

Combining simple yet vivid language and characters with humor and suspense, *The Pilgrim's Progress* proved enormously popular. It went through ten printings in the author's lifetime, was translated into over a hundred languages, and has outsold every other religious work in English except the King James Bible.

"I BETOOK ME TO MY BIBLE AND BEGAN TO TAKE
GREAT PLEASURE IN READING; BUT ESPECIALLY
WITH THE HISTORICAL PART THEREOF....
I BEGAN TO LOOK INTO IT WITH NEW EYES AND
READ AS I NEVER DID BEFORE."

from
THE PILGRIM'S PROGRESS

JOHN BUNYAN

Now I saw in my dream, that just as they had ended this talk, they drew near to a very miry Slough that was in the midst of the plain, and they, being heedless, did both fall suddenly into the bog. The name of the Slough was Despond.[1] Here therefore they wallowed for a time, being grievously bedaubed with the dirt, and Christian, because of the burden that was on his back, began to sink in the mire.

Pliable. Then said Pliable, Ah, neighbor Christian, where are you now?

Christian. Truly, said Christian, I do not know.

IT IS NOT ENOUGH TO BE PLIABLE

Pliable. At that Pliable began to be offended, and angerly, said to his fellow, Is this the happiness you have told me all this while of? If we have such ill speed at our first setting out, what may we expect, 'twixt this and our journey's end? May I get out again with my life you shall possess the brave country alone for me. And with that he gave a desperate struggle or two, and got out of the mire on that side of the Slough which was next to his own house. So away he went, and Christian saw him no more.

Christian in trouble, seeks still to get further from his own house.

Wherefore Christian was left to tumble in the Slough of Despond alone; but still he endeavoured to struggle to that side of the Slough that was still further from his own house, and next to the Wicket Gate; the which he did, but could not get out, because of the burden that was upon his back; but I beheld in my dream, that a man came to him, whose name was Help, and asked him what he did there.

Christian. Sir, said Christian, I was bid go this way by a man called Evangelist, who directed me also to yonder Gate, that I might escape the wrath to come; and as I was going thither, I fell in here.

THE PROMISES

Help. But why did you not look for the steps?

Christian. Fear followed me so hard, that I fled the next way, and fell in.

HELP LIFTS HIM OUT

Help. Then, said he, Give me thy hand; so he gave him his hand, and he drew him out, and set him upon sound ground, and bid him go on his way.

---

1. Despond (di spänd´) *n.* despair; hopelessness.

Vocabulary

heedless (hēd´ lis) *adj.* not taking notice; inattentive

wallowed (wäl´ ōd) *v.* rolled around in mud, water, etc.

burden (bʉrd´ ən) *n.* something that weighs one down; a heavy load or responsibility.

endeavored (en dev´ ərd) *v.* made a serious attempt; tried

WHAT MAKES THE SLOUGH OF DESPOND

Then I stepped to him that plucked him out, and said, "Sir, where-fore, since over this place is the way from the City of Destruction, to yonder Gate, is it, that this plat[2] is not mended, that poor travellers might go thither with more security?" And he said unto me, "This miry Slough is such a place as cannot be mended; it is the descent whither the scum and filth that attends conviction for sin doth contin-ually run, and therefore is it called the Slough of Despond: for still as the sinner is awakened about his lost condition, there ariseth in his soul many fears, and doubts, and discouraging apprehensions, which all of them get together, and settle in this place; and this is the reason of the badness of this ground.

"It is not the pleasure of the King that this place should remain so bad; his labourers also, have, by the direction of His Majesty's survey-ors, been for above this sixteen hundred years, employed about this patch of ground, if perhaps it might have been mended; yea, and to my knowledge," saith he, "here hath been swallowed up at least twenty thousand cart loads; yea, millions of wholesome instructions, that have at all seasons been brought from all places of the King's dominions (and they that can tell, say they are the best materials to make good ground of the place); if so be it might have been mended, but it is the Slough of Despond still, and so will be when they have done what they can.

THE PROMISES OF FORGIVENESS AND ACCEPTANCE TO LIFE BY FAITH IN CHRIST

"True, there are by the direction of the law-giver, certain good and substantial steps, placed even through the very midst of this Slough; but at such time as this place doth much spew out its filth, as it doth against change of weather, these steps are hardly seen; or if they be, men through the dizziness of their heads step besides; and then they are bemired to purpose, notwithstanding the steps be there; but the ground is good when they are once got in at the Gate."

---

2. **plat** a flat, low-lying piece of ground.

Critical Reading

1. **Key Ideas and Details** **(a) Summarize:** Sum up what happens to Christian at the Slough of Despond. **(b) Interpret:** What human mood or attitude might the Slough of Despond represent?

2. **Integration of Knowledge and Ideas** What does the selection show about the role of faith in Bunyan's society? In your response, use at least two of these Essential Question words: *devout, piety, redeem.* *[Connecting to the Essential Question: How does literature shape or reflect society?]*

Literary Analysis
Allegory
On the symbolic level of this allegory, to what might the steps refer?

Reading Strategy
Analyzing Allegory
What does the King symbolize?

Vocabulary
dominions (də min′ yənz) *n.* governed territories or lands
substantial (səb stan′ shəl) *adj.* having substance; large in size or strength

"IT IS NOT THE PLEASURE OF THE KING THAT THIS PLACE SHOULD REMAIN SO BAD ... BUT THE GROUND IS GOOD WHEN THEY ARE ONCE GOT IN AT THE GATE."

MAPPING ALLEGORY

An allegory is like an extended metaphor in which every detail has a literal and a symbolic meaning:

LITERAL MEANING	ALLEGORICAL MEANING
Main character a man named Christian	**Main character** stands for any Christian person
Other characters people named Pliable, Help, Mr. Worldly Wiseman, and so forth	**Other characters** stand for ways in which others help or hinder a Christian person
Plot a journey from one city to another	**Plot** a spiritual journey toward salvation
Setting a variety of places on the journey, including swamps, hills, towns, fairs	**Setting** each place stands for a different stage on the road toward salvation; for example, the Slough of Despond stands for a feeling of despair.

This map shows some of the places Christian visits on his allegorical journey from sin to salvation.

Slough of Despond

Mount Sinai

Beelzebub's Castle

Valley of the Shadow of the Death

Celestial City

Mouth of Hell

CONNECT TO THE LITERATURE

If John Bunyan were alive today, how might he use advanced technology to create his religious allegory?

After You Read | from *The Pilgrim's Progress*

Literary Analysis

© 1. Craft and Structure Using details from the selection, explain why *The Pilgrim's Progress* is an **allegory.** Use a chart like the one shown to record elements of the allegory's symbolism.

Character/Place	Symbolic Role in a Christian's Life Journey

© 2. Integration of Knowledge and Ideas (a) What moral lesson or lessons do you think Bunyan was trying to teach in this episode? **(b)** Judging by this episode, how would you explain the popular appeal of *The Pilgrim's Progress*?

Reading Strategy

3. Analyzing text structures will help you appreciate the two levels of an allegory. **(a)** Briefly summarize the literal level of meaning in this episode of the allegory—what happens in the story? **(b)** Then, summarize the symbolic meaning of the events instead of just retelling them.

4. How does the title, *The Pilgrim's Progress,* help clarify the basic overall symbolism of the plot?

PERFORMANCE TASKS
Integrated Language Skills

© Vocabulary Acquisition and Use

Use your knowledge of the underlined vocabulary words to determine whether each statement is true or false. Then, explain your answers.

1. A million dollars is a <u>substantial</u> amount of money.
2. A dog that just <u>wallowed</u> in something is likely to be dry.
3. A monarch rules over his or her <u>dominions</u>.
4. By misbehaving, Jill <u>endeavored</u> to please her teacher.
5. A <u>heedless</u> student listens carefully to what the teacher says.
6. A heavy suitcase can be a <u>burden</u> for a traveler.

Writing

© Informative Text Imagine that a film is being made of *The Pilgrim's Progress* and your job is to cast the parts. Write a **casting memo** suggesting actors who might play the roles in this selection. Describe the qualities each performer will need or the reasons you think a particular star will suit a particular role. Cite details from the selection to justify your ideas. Use a standard memo format, including headings indicating From, To, Subject, and Date.

© Common Core State Standards

Writing
2.b. Develop the topic thoroughly by selecting the most significant and relevant facts, extended definitions, concrete details, quotations, or other information and examples appropriate to the audience's knowledge of the topic.

Connecting to the Essential Question The two authors of these selections have different opinions on the role of women in society. Briefly explain whether you consider yourself a traditionalist, a reformer, or neither with regard to this issue. As you read, notice what the speakers in these poems say about or to female characters. Understanding this contrast will help as you answer the Essential Question: **How does literature shape or reflect society?**

Common Core State Standards

Reading Literature
4. Analyze the impact of specific word choices on meaning and tone, including words with multiple meanings or language that is particularly fresh, engaging, or beautiful.

Literary Analysis

Although they seem to be opposite, tradition and reform go together.

- **Tradition** is a society's approved values, beliefs, roles, and practices.
- **Reform** attempts to change traditional practices and ideas.

Amelia Lanier is a clear reformer, fighting against stereotypes of women, whereas Richard Lovelace fights for tradition, going to war and prison for his king and his honor. As you read, note the appearance of themes of tradition and reform in their works.

Comparing Literary Works Even when reformers' proposals are radical, they are often based on traditional beliefs. Lanier, for example, turns to the Bible, a traditional text, to support her new ideas about the equality of men and women. Lovelace, a supporter of the traditional power of his king, finds a new kind of freedom in love and integrity.

Both use a key strategy for interpreters of a tradition: They explore the multiple meanings of value terms such as *strength, honor,* and *freedom.* By redefining such terms, they find new ways to apply traditional ideas. As you read, analyze the impact of the authors' use of these words and the *political, religious, and philosophical assumptions* that their use suggests.

Poem
"Eve's Apology"

↓

Historical Context
Seventeenth-century women's rights were restricted; story of Eve was used to justify these restrictions

Reading Strategy

Preparing to Read Complex Texts As you read a work, **relate it to the major themes and issues of its historical period** by identifying ideas, assumptions, and references that are typical of its era. Consider also which ideas may be responses to events of the period. To understand how Lanier's and Lovelace's poems reflect their era, complete a chart like the one shown for each work.

Vocabulary

breach (brēch) *n.* breaking or being broken; failure to observe the terms of an agreement (p. 561)

discretion (di skresh′ ən) *n.* care in what one does and says (p. 561)

reprove (ri proov′) *v.* rebuke or find fault for an action (p. 561)

inconstancy (in kän′ stən sē) *n.* fickleness; changeableness (p. 563)

www.PHLitOnline.com

Amelia Lanier (1569–1645)

Author of "Eve's Apology in Defense of Women"

Amelia Lanier (also spelled "Lanyer") saw the need for women's rights three hundred years before the women's movement for equality. Daring to question her society's vision of women and the limited roles it allowed them, she anticipated future ideas of justice for women.

From Court Life to Working Woman Lanier had ties to the royal court, where her father, Baptista Bassano, was a musician to Queen Elizabeth I. Lanier's husband, Alphonso, and her son, Henry, were also court musicians. Despite her court connections, however, Lanier and her husband were not wealthy. When her husband died in 1613, Lanier sought to make a living by opening a school outside London.

A Radical Work In 1611, Lanier published a volume of poetry called *Salve Deus Rex Judaeorum (Hail, God, King of the Jews)*. In this groundbreaking work, of which "Eve's Apology in Defense of Women" is a section, Lanier questioned the privileges of the upper class and called for women's social and religious equality with men.

Although a woman sat on the throne of England during much of Lanier's lifetime, few women in her day published poetry. The poems in *Salve Deus Rex Judaeoroum* reflect her sense that women were underrepresented in the culture of the time. Sections of the work praise her female patrons, while others re-evaluate the role of women in stories from the Bible.

"Dark Lady" or Visionary? In later times, Lanier was perhaps more famous as a possibility for Shakespeare's "dark lady" (the mysterious woman to whom he addresses some of his sonnets) than for her poetry. As scholars have explored the political undercurrents of past literature, though, interest in Lanier has revived. Today, Lanier is considered a visionary feminist who spoke out against injustice.

from
Eve's Apology in Defense of Women

Amelia Lanier

BACKGROUND During the late sixteenth and early seventeenth centuries, a war of words raged, known as "the debate about women." The issue: Were women by nature idle, vain, and immoral, or were they by nature good? Most of the debaters turned to the biblical story of Eve to support their points. Eve, their assumption went, was the first woman and the image of all women after her, so all women share her nature. Lanier's poem, making the same assumption, joins the controversy with powerful pro-woman arguments.

Literary Analysis
Tradition and Reform
On what tradition does Lanier draw in these lines?

But surely Adam cannot be excused,
Her fault though great, yet he was most to blame;
What weakness offered, strength might have refused,
Being Lord of all, the greater was his shame:
5   Although the serpent's craft had her abused,
God's holy word ought all his actions frame,
    For he was Lord and King of all the earth,
    Before poor Eve had either life or breath.

Who being framed by God's eternal hand,
10   The perfectest man that ever breathed on earth;
And from God's mouth received that strait command,
The breach whereof he knew was present death:
Yea, having power to rule both sea and land,
Yet with one apple won to lose that breath
15   Which God had breathéd in his beauteous face,
Bringing us all in danger and disgrace.

And then to lay the fault on patience's back,
That we poor women must endure it all;
We know right well he did discretion lack,
20   Being not persuaded thereunto at all;
If Eve did err, it was for knowledge sake,
The fruit being fair persuaded him to fall:
No subtle serpent's falsehood did betray him,
If he would eat it, who had power to stay him?

25   Not Eve, whose fault was only too much love,
Which made her give this present to her dear,
That what she tasted, he likewise might prove,
Whereby his knowledge might become more clear;
He never sought her weakness to reprove,
30   With those sharp words, which he of God did hear:
Yet men will boast of knowledge, which he took
From Eve's fair hand, as from a learned book.

Critical Reading

1. Key Ideas and Details (a) According to Lanier, what motive did Eve have for tasting of the Tree of Knowledge? **(b)** According to Lanier, why did Eve offer Adam a taste of the apple? **(c) Summarize:** Describe Eve's character according to Lanier.

2. Key Ideas and Details (a) According to the last stanza, what should Adam have done? **(b) Infer:** What view of Adam is suggested by Lanier's description of him?

3. Key Ideas and Details According to the poem, in what way do men apply a double standard to the story of the Fall?

4. Integration of Knowledge and Ideas Explain why the interpretation of this story was so important in seventeenth-century arguments about the nature of women.

Cite textual evidence to support your responses.

RICHARD LOVELACE (1618–1657)

Author of "To Lucasta, on Going to the Wars" • "To Althea, from Prison"

Richard Lovelace, son of a wealthy family and firm supporter of his king, had the misfortune to live at a time when the English monarchy was under violent assault. The Civil War that culminated in the execution of the king plunged the privileged Lovelace into prison and poverty.

Looks and Talent Before England's Civil War, Lovelace profited by his association with royalty. It is said that, charmed by this winning young man, the king and queen ordered Oxford to grant him a degree before he had completed his studies! Lovelace did not, however, lack talent. While at Oxford, he wrote a play, painted, and played music.

The Price of Loyalty Lovelace was about twenty-six when Parliament challenged the king's authority and civil war broke out. Perhaps because of his personal charm, Lovelace was chosen to demand that Parliament restore the king's authority. Parliament was not impressed, though, and Lovelace was immediately arrested.

A Daring Life While imprisoned, Lovelace wrote "To Althea, From Prison," a moving affirmation of the value of personal integrity, even if it meant imprisonment. When released, he rejoined Charles's forces and spent his fortune equipping the king's army. Upon Charles's defeat in 1645, Lovelace joined the wars against Spain.

An Untimely End Returning to England years later, Lovelace was again imprisoned by the Puritans. During this time, he prepared for publication the volume that included "To Lucasta, on Going to the Wars." No one knows for certain how Lovelace's life ended, but it is believed that the charming young man who had won the heart of his king and queen died in discouragement and poverty at the age of thirty-nine.

To Lucasta, on Going to the Wars

RICHARD LOVELACE

Background TENSIONS BETWEEN THE CHURCH OF ENGLAND AND THE PURITANS WHO WISHED TO REFORM IT HAD RISEN TO A DANGEROUS LEVEL. FOREIGN WARS HAD LED TO A MONEY SHORTAGE. CHARLES I MADE THE SITUATION WORSE BY MISHANDLING PARLIAMENT, BY PRESSURING NOBLES FOR MONEY, AND BY FORCING COMMONERS TO SERVE IN HIS ARMIES. IN 1642, ENGLAND'S PARLIAMENT WENT TO WAR AGAINST ENGLAND'S KING. LOVELACE, A LOYAL SUPPORTER OF CHARLES, WAS TWICE IMPRISONED BY THE KING'S OPPONENTS.

> Tell me not, Sweet, I am unkind,
>   That from the nunnery
> Of thy chaste breast, and quiet mind,
>   To war and arms I fly.
>
> 5 True, a new mistress now I chase,
>   The first foe in the field;
> And with a stronger faith embrace
>   A sword, a horse, a shield.
>
> Yet this inconstancy is such,
> 10   As you too shall adore;
> I could not love thee, Dear, so much,
>   Loved I not honor more.

Reading Strategy
Relating a Work to Its Historical Period How does understanding the historical period in which Lovelace was writing help you interpret lines 7–8?

Vocabulary
inconstancy (in kän´ stən sē)
n. fickleness; changeableness

To Althea, from Prison

Richard Lovelace

When love with unconfined wings
    Hovers within my gates,
And my divine Althea brings
    To whisper at the grates;
5 When I lie tangled in her hair
    And fettered to her eye,
The gods[1] that wanton[2] in the air
    Know no such liberty.

When flowing cups run swiftly round,
10   With no allaying Thames,[3]
Our careless heads with roses bound,
    Our hearts with loyal flames;
When thirsty grief in wine we steep,
    When healths[4] and drafts[5] go free,
15 Fishes that tipple in the deep,
    Know no such liberty.

---

1. **gods** The word *gods* is replaced by *birds* in some versions of this poem.
2. **wanton** play.
3. **cups . . . Thames** (temz) wine that has not been diluted by water (from the river Thames).
4. **healths** toasts.
5. **drafts** drinks.

When, like committed linnets,[6] I
    With shriller throat shall sing
The sweetness, mercy, majesty,
20   And glories of my King;
When I shall voice aloud how good
    He is, how great should be,
        Enlarged[7] winds that curl the flood,
        Know no such liberty.

25   Stone walls do not a prison make,
    Nor iron bars a cage;
Minds innocent and quiet take
    That for an hermitage;[8]
If I have freedom in my love,
30   And in my soul am free,
Angels alone that soar above,
    Enjoy such liberty.

---

6. committed linnets caged finches.
7. Enlarged released.
8. hermitage (hur´ mi tij) a place of religious seclusion.

Literary Analysis
Tradition and Reform
In lines 25–28, how does Lovelace use the multiple associations of *walls* to shift from the idea of a prison to the idea of a place of religious seclusion?

Critical Reading

© 1. **Key Ideas and Details (a)** What does the speaker "now . . . chase" in line 5 of "To Lucasta"? **(b) Interpret:** In what sense does the speaker admit to having two loves? **(c) Draw Conclusions:** In the final two lines, why does the strength of the speaker's love for Lucasta depend on the strength of his other love?

© 2. **Key Ideas and Details (a)** In "To Althea," what are three things the poet does in prison? **(b) Interpret:** Explain the kind of "liberty" these activities possess.

© 3. **Key Ideas and Details (a)** In the fourth stanza of "To Althea," which two freedoms does the poet say are most important? **(b) Interpret:** What is the meaning of lines 25–26? **(c) Evaluate:** Do you agree with Lovelace's views on freedom? Explain.

© 4. **Integration of Knowledge and Ideas** Which of these authors do you think was reflecting dominant social attitudes about women? Which was trying to influence or change those attitudes? Explain. In your response, use at least two of these Essential Question words: *values, independence, reform.* *[Connecting to the Essential Question: How does literature shape or reflect society?]*

Cite textual evidence to support your responses.

Literary Analysis

1. Key Ideas and Details (a) In "Eve's Apology," what traditional assumptions is Lanier trying to **reform? (b)** What **tradition** does she use to aid her, and why? **(c)** How does she reinterpret this tradition to make her point?

2. Integration of Knowledge and Ideas (a) In "To Althea, from Prison," what tradition does Lovelace defend? **(b)** Compare the spirit of lines 29–32 with the principles of a reformer such as Gandhi or Martin Luther King, Jr.

3. Comparing Literary Works (a) In "Eve's Apology," lines 1–8, what conclusion about the Fall does Lanier draw from Adam's strength? **(b)** How does she shift between *weakness* as "moral weakness" and as "powerlessness" to make her point? **(c)** Use a chart like the one shown to note a similar shift in the meaning of *freedom* in "To Althea."

Meaning 1	Meaning 2	Reasoning Behind Shift	Valid?

Reading Strategy

4. Relate poems to their historical period by showing how issues, events, or political assumptions of the period help you interpret these passages: **(a)** "Eve's Apology," lines 25–32 **(b)** "To Lucasta," lines 11–12 **(c)** "To Althea," lines 17–24.

PERFORMANCE TASKS
Integrated Language Skills

Vocabulary Acquisition and Use

Choose the letter of each word's antonym (opposite). Explain each choice.

1. breach: **(a)** violation **(b)** cooperation **(c)** compliance
2. discretion: **(a)** valor **(b)** loudness **(c)** outspokenness
3. reprove: **(a)** forgive **(b)** support **(c)** balance
4. inconstancy: **(a)** flirtatiousness **(b)** faithfulness **(c)** certainty

Writing

Narrative Text Today, as in Lovelace's time, soldiers bid farewell to spouses, parents, or other loved ones when going off to war. Write a brief **dramatic scene** portraying such an event.

- Decide what relationship the characters will have.
- Use *dialogue* to reveal the characters' *emotions*.
- Revise your script to include stage directions where necessary.

Common Core State Standards

Writing
3.b. Use narrative techniques, such as dialogue, pacing, description, reflection, and multiple plot lines, to develop experiences, events, and/or characters.

The Ties That Bind

PART 3

Primary Sources

Diary
The Diary of Samuel Pepys

Policy Statement
Charles II's Declaration to London, 1666

Common Core State Standards

Reading Informational Text
1. Cite strong and thorough textual evidence to support analysis of what the text says explicitly as well as inferences drawn from the text, including determining where the text leaves matters uncertain.
3. Analyze a complex set of ideas or sequence of events and explain how specific individuals, ideas, or events interact and develop over the course of the text.

About the Text Forms

A **diary** is an account of a person's experiences and reactions kept daily or at frequent intervals. Some people keep diaries just for themselves. Others hope one day to publish their diaries and so may be more careful in what they say or how they say it. As primary sources, diaries can offer a personal perspective on historical figures and events or provide valuable information about everyday life in the writer's times.

A **policy statement** is an official statement in which a government, a business, or another organization states principles or guidelines to follow. It often addresses a particular situation and aims to achieve a particular result. As primary sources, policy statements can show the political, social, or economic concerns at a particular time.

Reading Strategy

To get the most out of a primary source, follow these steps. As you complete your reading of the text or of a section of the text

- *summarize* what the writer has said, restating the most important ideas
- *draw conclusions* about what the writer says implicitly, identifying his or her assumptions, or unstated beliefs, and implied, or suggested, meanings
- *analyze* the relations among ideas, events, and people in the text, considering how they interact and develop
- **verify and clarify facts.** First, identify factual claims—claims that you can confirm or disprove. Check each claim in another source, noting whether the second source confirms or disconfirms it. In addition, identify unclear passages and determine whether other sources help clarify them.

Support your summary and analysis with strong textual evidence—relevant quotations from the text. Note any points at which the text leaves matters uncertain, and determine the possible reasons for the uncertainty.

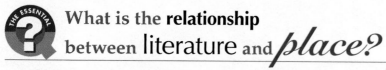

What is the relationship between literature and *place*?

As you read, consider the glimpses of seventeenth-century London that each document provides and the way it reflects the city's concerns.

Note-Taking Guide

Primary-source documents are a rich source of information for researchers. As you read these documents, use a note-taking guide like the one shown to organize relevant and accurate information.

1 Type of Document (check one)

☐ Newspaper ☐ Letter ☐ Diary ☐ Speech ☐ Advertisement

☐ Government Document ☐ Eyewitness Account ☐ Memorandum ☐ Other

2 Date of Document _____

3 Author _____

Author's Position _____

4 Original Audience _____

5 Purpose and Importance

a What was the original purpose?_____

Write down two details that support your answer. _____

_____

_____

b List two important ideas, statements, or observations from this document.

_____

_____

c What does this document show about the time and place in which it

was composed?_____

_____

_____

Reading Strategy
Verifying and Clarifying Facts
Identify facts and statements you may want to verify and clarify using other sources.

This guide was adapted from the **U.S. National Archives** document analysis worksheet.

Vocabulary

apprehensions (ap rē hen´ shənz) *n.* fears; concerns (p. 572)

abated (ə bāt´ id) *v.* lessened (p. 572)

lamentable (lam´ ən tə bəl) *adj.* causing grief; distressing (p. 573)

combustible (kəm bus´ tə bəl) *adj.* capable of being ignited and burned; flammable (p. 574)

malicious (mə lish´ əs) *adj.* deliberately harmful; destructive (p. 576)

accounts (ə kountz´) *n.* records of money received and paid out; financial records (p. 577)

pernicious (pər nish´ is) *adj.* causing great injury, destruction, or ruin; deadly (p. 579)

magistrate (maj´ is trāt) *n.* a local official who administers the law or serves as a judge (p. 579)

eminent (em´ ə nənt) *adj.* noteworthy; of high rank; distinguished (p. 579)

notorious (nō tôr´ ē əs) *adj.* widely but unfavorably known; having a bad reputation (p. 579)

deliberation (di lib´ ər ā´ shən) *n.* careful consideration and discussion before reaching a decision (p. 579)

THE STORY BEHIND THE DOCUMENTS

Samuel Pepys

Samuel Pepys (pēps) (1633–1703), author of perhaps the most famous diary in English, was in a good position to report on his era. The son of a London tailor, Pepys became a clerk in the navy in 1660 and continued on a rapid rise to fame and fortune, eventually serving as a member of Parliament and secretary of the navy. Pepys began his diary in 1660 and continued it for nine years, when failing eyesight forced him to abandon the project. Writing for himself alone, he used a little-known shorthand that was not deciphered until the nineteenth century, when the diary was published. Today the diary offers a detailed and intimate account of events great and small in Restoration London.

Charles II (1630–1685) was restored to the throne in 1660, the same year Pepys began his diary. Charles's coronation —vividly described in the diary—came after years of exile during the period of England's civil war and subsequent Puritan rule. Excessive in his personal life, he tried to govern with moderation, punishing a few people directly responsible for the execution of his father, Charles I, but otherwise allowing different factions to share in governing. He also supported the arts and, to further scientific advancement, sponsored establishment of the Royal Society—an organization that numbered Samuel Pepys among its early presidents.

The return of the monarchy was greeted with much jubilation in a nation tired of Puritan austerity. Then twin disasters struck: a Great Plague broke out in 1664 and swept through London the following year, and the Great Fire of London devastated the city just one year after that. Samuel Pepys gives vivid and detailed accounts of both events in his diary. In his policy statement of 1666, Charles II responds to the Great Fire by ordering London's citizens to institute practices that would help prevent such calamities in the future.

Charles II

from THE DIARY

Samuel Pepys

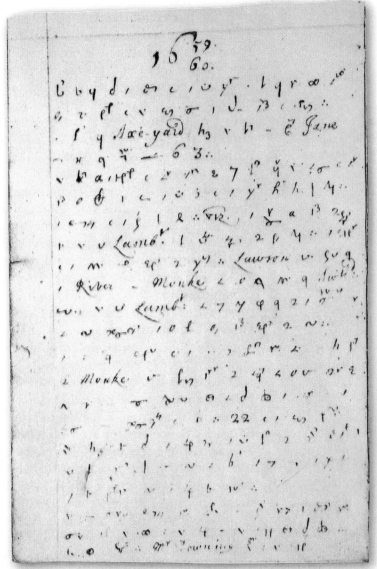

First page of Samuel Pepys's Diary 31 May 1669, Pepys Library, Magdalene College, Cambridge

The Plague

Sept. 3, 1665. (Lord's Day.) Church being done, my Lord Bruncker, Sir J. Minnes, and I up to the vestry[1] at the desire of the Justices of the Peace, Sir Theo. Biddulph and Sir W. Boreman and Alderman Hooker, in order to the doing something for the keeping of the plague from growing; but Lord! to consider the madness of the people of the town, who will (because they are forbid) come in crowds along with the dead corps[2] to see them buried; but we agreed on some orders for

▲ **Critical Viewing**
What evidence on this page of the diary suggests that Pepys never meant to share his writing with the world? **[Infer]**

1. **vestry** (ves′ trē) *n.* church meeting-room.
2. **corps** corpses.

the prevention thereof.[3] Among other stories, one was very passionate, methought of a complaint brought against a man in the town for taking a child from London from an infected house. Alderman Hooker told us it was the child of a very able citizen in Gracious Street, a saddler,[4] who had buried all the rest of his children of the plague, and himself and wife now being shut up and in despair of escaping, did desire only to save the life of this little child; and so prevailed to have it received stark-naked into the arms of a friend, who brought it (having put it into new fresh clothes) to Greenwich; where upon hearing the story, we did agree it should be permitted to be received and kept in the town. Thence with my Lord Bruncker to Captain Cocke's, where we mighty merry and supped, and very late I by water to Woolwich, in great apprehensions of an ague. . . .

Sept. 14, 1665. When I come home I spent some thoughts upon the occurrences of this day, giving matter for as much content on one hand and melancholy on another, as any day in all my life. For the first; the finding of my money and plate,[5] and all safe at London, and speeding in my business of money this day. The hearing of this good news to such excess, after so great a despair of my Lord's doing anything this year; adding to that, the decrease of 500 and more, which is the first decrease we have yet had in the sickness since it begun: and great hopes that the next week it will be greater. Then, on the other side, my finding that though the bill[6] in general is abated, yet the city within the walls is increased, and likely to continue so, and is close to our house there. My meeting dead corpses of the plague, carried to be buried close to me at noonday through the city in Fanchurch Street. To see a person sick of the sores, carried close by me by Grace church in a hackney coach.[7] My finding the Angell Tavern at the lower end of Tower Hill, shut up, and more than that, the alehouse at the Tower Stairs, and more than that, the person was then dying of the plague when I was last there, a little while ago, at night, to write a short letter there, and I overheard the mistress of the house sadly saying to her husband somebody was very ill, but did not think it was of the plague. To hear that poor Payne, my waiter, hath buried a child, and is dying himself. To hear that a laborer I sent but the other day to Dagenhams, to know how they did there, is dead of the plague; and that one of my own watermen, that carried me daily, fell sick as soon as he had landed me on Friday morning last, when I had been all night upon the water (and I believe he did get his infection that day at Brainford), and is now dead of the plague. To hear

Vocabulary
apprehensions (ap´ rē hen´ shənz) *n.* fears; concerns

Vocabulary
abated (ə bāt´ id) *v.* lessened

Primary Sources
Diary
What do the incomplete sentences and names in the entry for September 14, 1665, suggest about the audience for whom Pepys was writing?

---

3. **but we . . . thereof** Funeral processions were forbidden in London during the plague. However, the law was often ignored.
4. **saddler** *n.* person who makes, sells, and repairs saddles.
5. **plate** valuable serving dishes and flatware.
6. **bill** weekly list of burials.
7. **hackney coach** carriage for hire.

that Captain Lambert and Cuttle are killed in the taking these ships; and that Mr. Sidney Montague is sick of a desperate fever at my Lady Carteret's, at Scott's Hall. To hear that Mr. Lewes hath another daughter sick. And, lastly, that both my servants, W. Hewer and Tom Edwards, have lost their fathers, both in St. Sepulcher's parish, of the plague this week, do put me into great apprehensions of melancholy, and with good reason. But I put off the thoughts of sadness as much as I can, and the rather to keep my wife in good heart and family also. After supper (having eat nothing all this day) upon a fine tench[8] of Mr. Shelden's taking, we to bed.

The Fire of London

Sept. 2, 1666. (Lord's day.) Some of our maids sitting up late last night to get things ready against our feast today, Jane called us up about three in the morning, to tell us of a great fire they saw in the city. So I rose and slipped on my nightgown, and went to her window, and thought it to be on the back side of Mark Lane at the farthest; but, being unused to such fires as followed, I thought it far enough off; and so went to bed again and to sleep. About seven rose again to dress myself, and there looked out at the window, and saw the fire not so much as it was and farther off. So to my closet to set things to rights after yesterday's cleaning. By and by Jane comes and tells me that she hears that above 300 houses have been burned down tonight by the fire we saw, and that it is now burning down all Fish Street, by London Bridge. So I made myself ready presently, and walked to the Tower,[9] and there got up upon one of the high places, Sir J. Robinson's little son going up with me; and there I did see the houses at that end of the bridge all on fire, and an infinite great fire on this and the other side the end of the bridge; which, among other people, did trouble me for poor little Michell and our Sarah on the bridge. So down, with my heart full of trouble, to the Lieutenant of the Tower, who tells me that it begun this morning in the King's baker's house in Pudding Lane, and that it hath burned St. Magnus's Church and most part of Fish Street already. So I down to the waterside, and there got a boat and through bridge, and there saw a lamentable fire. Poor Michell's house, as far as the Old Swan, already burned that way, and the fire running farther, that in a very little time it got as far as the steel yard, while I was there. Everybody endeavoring to remove their goods, and flinging into the river or bringing them into lighters that lay off; poor people staying in their houses as long as till the very fire touched them, and then running into boats, or clambering from one

Water bucket used to fight the Great Fire of London

Vocabulary
lamentable (lam′ ən tə bəl) *adj.* causing grief; distressing

Reading Check

How did Pepys hear about the fire in the city?

---

8. tench *n.* type of fish.
9. Tower Tower of London.

Reading Strategy
Verifying and Clarifying
Which facts in this paragraph could you verify in another source?

Vocabulary
combustible (kəm bus´ tə bəl) *adj.* capable of being ignited and burned; flammable

▼ Primary Source: Art
What line from Pepys's account of the fire would be an appropriate caption for this painting? Why? **[Connect]**

pair of stairs by the waterside to another. And among other things, the poor pigeons, I perceive, were loth to leave their houses, but hovered about the windows and balconies till they were, some of them burned, their wings, and fell down. Having stayed, and in an hour's time seen the fire rage every way, and nobody, to my sight, endeavoring to quench it, but to remove their goods, and leave all to the fire, and having seen it get as far as the steel yard, and the wind mighty high and driving it into the city; and everything, after so long a drought, proving combustible, even the very stones of churches, and among other things the poor steeple by which pretty Mrs.— lives, and whereof my old schoolfellow Elborough is parson, taken fire in the very top, and there burned till it fell down. I to Whitehall (with a gentleman with me who desired to go off from the Tower, to see the fire, in my boat), and there up to the King's closet in the chapel, where people come about me, and I did give them an account dismayed them all, and word was carried in to the King. So I was called for, and did tell the King and Duke of York what I saw, and that unless his Majesty did command houses to be pulled down nothing could stop the fire. They seemed much troubled, and the King commanded me to go to my Lord Mayor from him, and command him to spare no houses, but to pull down before the fire every way. The Duke of York bid me tell him that if he would have any more soldiers he shall; and so did my Lord Arlington afterwards, as a great secret. Here meeting with Captain Cocke, I in his coach, which he lent me, and Creed with

The Great Fire of London, 1666

me to Paul's,[10] and there walked along Watling Street, as well as I could, every creature coming away loaden with goods to save, and here and there sick people carried away in beds. Extraordinary good goods carried in carts and on backs. At last met my Lord Mayor in Canning Street, like a man spent, with a handkerchief about his neck. To the King's message he cried, like a fainting woman, "Lord! what can I do? I am spent: people will not obey me. I have been pulling down houses; but the fire overtakes us faster than we can do it." That he needed no more soldiers; and that, for himself, he must go and refresh himself, having been up all night. So he left me, and I him, and walked home, seeing people all almost distracted, and no manner of means used to quench the fire. The houses, too, so very thick thereabouts, and full of matter for burning, as pitch and tar, in Thames Street; and warehouses of oil, and wines, and brandy, and other things. Here I saw Mr. Isaake Houblon, the handsome man, prettily dressed and dirty, at his door at Dowgate, receiving some of his brothers' things, whose houses were on fire; and, as he says, have been removed twice already; and he doubts (as it soon proved) that they must be in a little time removed from his house also, which was a sad consideration. And to see the churches all filling with goods by people who themselves should have been quietly there at this time. By this time it was about twelve o'clock; and so home. Soon as dined, and walked through the city, the streets full of nothing but people and horses and carts loaden with goods, ready to run over one another, and removing goods from one burned house to another. They now removing out of Canning Street (which received goods in the morning) into Lumbard Street, and farther; and among others I now saw my little goldsmith, Stokes, receiving some friend's goods, whose house itself was burned the day after. I to Paul's Wharf, where I had appointed a boat to attend me, and took in Mr. Carcasse and his brother, whom I met in the street, and carried them below and above bridge to and again to see the fire, which was now got farther, both below and above, and no likelihood of stopping it. Met with the King and Duke of York in their barge, and with them to Queenhithe, and there called Sir Richard Browne to them. Their order was only to pull down houses apace, and so below bridge at the waterside; but little was or could be done, the fire coming upon them so fast. Good hopes there was of stopping it at the Three Cranes above, and at Buttolph's Wharf below bridge, if care be used; but the wind carries it into the city, so as we know not by the waterside what it do there. River full of lighters and boats taking in goods, and good goods swimming in the water, and only I observed that hardly one lighter or boat in three that had the goods of a house in, but there was a pair of virginals[11] in it. Having seen as much as I could now, I away to Whitehall by

---

10. **Paul's** St. Paul's Cathedral.
11. **virginals** *n.* small, legless harpsichords.

Reading Strategy
Verifying and Clarifying
From the details in the text, what can you clarify about the role of the River Thames in the Great Fire of London?

World LITERATURE CONNECTION

Famous Diaries in World Literature

Samuel Pepys was not the first to keep a diary. As early as the tenth century, women in the Japanese Imperial Court wrote journals they called "pillow books," because they hid them under their pillows. Sei Shōnagon began hers with a description of dawn, written in graceful Japanese brush strokes. Soon, she was confiding, "I just love it when bad things happen to people I can't stand," believing nobody would ever read her words.

In the eighteenth and nineteenth centuries, diary writing became a popular pastime in Europe and the Americas, as Western culture placed greater emphasis on the individual personality. During World War II, a teenager named Anne Frank kept a diary while hiding from the Nazis in an attic in Amsterdam. She never guessed it would be read around the world someday.

Connect to the Literature

Do you think Pepys would have written a different sort of diary if he had known it would be published? Explain.

Reading Check

What does Pepys learn about the fire from his visit to the Tower?

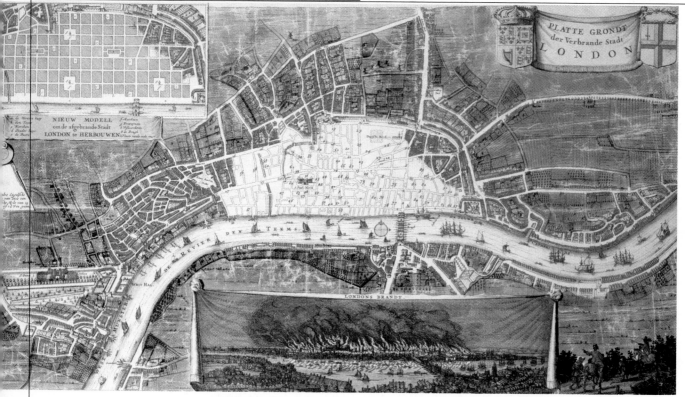

The Great Fire, 1666, Marcus Willemsz Doornik, Guildhall Library, Corporation of London

▲ Primary Source: Art

This map of London includes an inset depicting the area destroyed by the Great Fire. Does this image enhance Pepys's eyewitness description? Explain.
[Make a Judgment]

Vocabulary

malicious (mə lish′ əs) *adj.* deliberately harmful; destructive

Primary Sources

Diary What emotional reaction does Pepys have toward the fire that is sweeping through London? Cite words and phrases that reveal his feelings.

appointment, and there walked to St. James's Park, and there met my wife and Creed and Wood and his wife, and walked to my boat; and there upon the water again, and to the fire up and down, it still increasing, and the wind great. So near the fire as we could for smoke; and all over the Thames, with one's face in the wind, you were almost burned with a shower of firedrops. This is very true; so as houses were burned by these drops and flakes of fire, three or four, nay, five or six houses, one from another. When we could endure no more upon the water, we to a little alehouse on the Bankside, over against the Three Cranes, and there stayed till it was dark almost, and saw the fire grow; and, as it grew darker, appeared more and more, and in corners and upon steeples, and between churches and houses, as far as we could see up the hill of the city, in a most horrid malicious bloody flame, not like the fine flame of an ordinary fire. Barbary and her husband away before us. We stayed till, it being darkish, we saw the fire as only one entire arch of fire from this to the other side the bridge, and in a bow up the hill for an arch of above a mile long: it made me weep to see it. The churches, houses, and all on fire and flaming at once; and a horrid noise the flames made, and the cracking of houses at their ruin. So home with a sad heart, and there find everybody discoursing and lamenting the fire; and poor Tom Hater come with some of his few goods saved out of his house, which is burned upon Fish Street Hill. I invited him to lie at my house, and did receive his goods, but was deceived in his lying there, the news coming every moment of the growth of the fire; so as we were forced to begin to pack up our own goods, and prepare for their removal; and did by moonshine (it being brave dry, and moonshine, and warm weather) carry much of my goods into the garden, and Mr. Hater and I did remove my money and iron chests into my cellar, as thinking that the safest place. And got my bags of gold into my office, ready to carry away, and my chief papers of accounts also there, and my tallies into a box by themselves. So great was our fear, as Sir W. Batten hath carts come out of the country to fetch away his goods this night. We did put Mr. Haters, poor man, to bed a little; but he got but very little rest, so much noise being in my house, taking down of goods.

3rd. About four o'clock in the morning, my Lady Batten sent me a cart to carry away all my money, and plate, and best things, to Sir W. Rider's at Bednall Green. Which I did, riding myself in my nightgown in the cart; and, Lord! to see how the streets and the highways are crowded with people running and riding, and getting of carts at any rate to fetch away things. I find Sir W. Rider tired with being called up all night, and receiving things from several friends. His house full of goods, and much of Sir W. Batten's and Sir W. Pen's. I am eased at my heart to have my treasure so well secured. Then home, with much ado to find a way, nor any sleep all this night to me nor my poor wife.

Vocabulary
accounts (ə kountz´)
n. records of money received and paid out; financial records

Critical Reading

1. **Key Ideas and Details (a)** According to the entry for September 3, 1665, what happened to the saddler's family during the plague? **(b) Infer:** What does Pepys's reaction to this situation show you about his personality?

2. **Key Ideas and Details (a)** What does Pepys recommend to the King and Duke of York during the fire? **(b) Evaluate:** Was the recommendation a good one? Why or why not?

3. **Integration of Knowledge and Ideas (a) Compare and Contrast:** What are some modern disasters that compare with the Great Plague and Great Fire of London? **(b) Evaluate:** Do you think Pepys and others in authority handled disaster as well as their modern counterparts would have? Why or why not?

4. **Craft and Structure (a)** List three details about seventeenth-century London that Pepys includes in his diary. **(b) Evaluate:** How has living in London during the plague and the fire affected what Pepys has to say and the effectiveness with which he says it?

Cite textual evidence to support your responses.

Charles II's
DECLARATION TO LONDON,
1666

BACKGROUND Following the Great Fire of London, Charles II took personal charge of seeing that the city got back on its feet. On the day the fire effectively ended, the king visited a field where a hundred thousand homeless Londoners were camping out and tried to reassure them about the future. Charles would have liked to rebuild his capital on a grand scale but had neither the money nor the time to do so. Instead, he had to move as quickly as possible to address the widespread homelessness and the disruption of London's trade, so vital to the English economy. Charles was nevertheless determined to create a more modern city that would never again face the kind of devastation the fire had caused. Taking advice from architects like Christopher Wren, scientists like Robert Hooke, and officials like Samuel Pepys who had fought the fire, Charles issued the following policy statement giving guidelines to Londoners about rebuilding their streets, shops, and homes.

In the first place the woeful experience in this late heavy visitation hath sufficiently convinced all men of the pernicious consequences which have attended the building with Timber, and even with Stone itself, and the notable benefit of Brick, which in so many places hath resisted and even extinguished the Fire; And we do therefore declare Our express Will and Pleasure, That no man whatsoever shall presume to erect any House or Building, great or small, but of Brick or Stone, and if any man shall do the contrary, the next Magistrate shall forthwith cause it to be pulled down.

. . . all other eminent and notorious Streets, shall be of such a breadth, as may with God's blessing prevent the mischief that one side may suffer if the other be on fire.

. . . nor will we suffer any Lanes or Alleys to be erected, but where upon mature deliberation the same shall be found absolutely necessary.

. . . no house shall be erected within so many foot of the River.

. . . any houses to be inhabited by Brewers, or Dyers, or Sugar-Bakers, which Trades by their continual Smokes contribute very much to the unhealthiness of the adjacent places, but We require the Lord Mayor and Aldermen of London upon a full consideration, and weighing all conveniences and inconveniences that can be foreseen, to propose such a place as may be fit for all those Trades which are carried on by smokes to inhabit together.

Vocabulary

pernicious (pər nish´ is) *adj.* causing great injury, destruction, or ruin; deadly

magistrate (maj´ is trāt) *n.* a local official who administers the law or serves as a judge

eminent (em´ ə nənt) *adj.* noteworthy; of high rank; distinguished

notorious (nō tôr´ ē əs) *adj.* widely but unfavorably known; having a bad reputation

deliberation (di lib´ ər ā´ shən) *n.* careful consideration and discussion before reaching a decision

Primary Sources
Policy Statement
What are the four main guidelines set forth in this policy statement?

Critical Reading

1. Key Ideas and Details (a) What does Charles say the recent fire has shown about building construction? **(b) Infer:** What situation does he want to prevent by getting rid of very narrow streets and keeping lanes and alleys to a minimum? **(c) Speculate:** Why do you think he orders that no house be erected too close to the river?

2. Integration of Knowledge and Ideas (a) Infer: Why does Charles want all London businesses requiring continuous fires to be housed in the same place? **(b) Evaluate:** Do you think this idea is practical? Why or why not?

3. Key Ideas and Details (a) Analyze Cause and Effect: What main concern of Charles II's London has led him to issue this policy statement? **(b) Draw Conclusions:** What does the statement reveal about London buildings before the fire?

Cite textual evidence to support your responses.

Diary • Policy Statement

Comparing Primary Sources

Refer to your note-taking guide to answer these questions.

1. **(a)** Summarize each source, supporting your summary with quotations. **(b)** In the entry for September 3, 1665, what does Pepys imply are the reasons he and others agreed to allow the child "to be received and kept" in Greenwich? Cite textual details in support of your response.

2. **(a)** Outline the sequence of events and interaction of people in Pepys's diary entry for September 2, 1666. **(b)** Identify one point that he leaves unclear, and explain why he probably did not clarify it.

3. Compare and contrast the information Pepys provides about the Great Plague with the information about the Great Fire of London in both sources. **(a)** What do the two disasters have in common, and how do they differ? **(b)** Which seems worse, and why? To help you answer the question, gather details on a Venn diagram like the one shown.

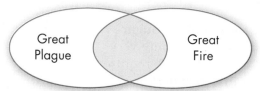

Vocabulary Acquisition and Use

New Vocabulary Answer the questions about the italicized vocabulary words.

1. **(a)** Which word is closest in meaning to *malicious*: *lamentable, pernicious,* or *notorious*? **(b)** What do the two words mean?

2. **(a)** What is similar about the meanings of *eminent* and *notorious*? **(b)** What is different about them?

3. **(a)** Why might a *lamentable* situation prompt *apprehensions*? **(b)** If those *apprehensions* then *abated,* would the person be more or less fearful? Explain your answer.

Content-Area Vocabulary Determine whether each statement is true or false. Explain your answers.

4. Someone who moves with *deliberation* is hasty.

5. Rocks are more *combustible* than paper.

6. A company's bookkeeper is often responsible for keeping *accounts*.

7. A *magistrate* might serve as a judge in a local legal matter.

Etymology Study *Magistrate* comes from the Latin *magnus,* meaning "great." A *magistrate* is a person who exercises great authority in certain legal matters. Use a dictionary to show how these *magnus* terms from political science reflect the idea of greatness: *magisterial, Magna Carta, magnate, magniloquent.*

 **Common Core State Standards**

Writing

7. Conduct short as well as more sustained research projects to answer a question or solve a problem; narrow or broaden the inquiry when appropriate; synthesize multiple sources on the subject, demonstrating understanding of the subject under investigation.

8. Gather relevant information from multiple authoritative print and digital sources, using advanced searches effectively; assess the strengths and limitations of each source in terms of the task, purpose, and audience; integrate information into the text selectively to maintain the flow of ideas, avoiding plagiarism and overreliance on any one source and following a standard format for citation.

Language

6. Acquire and use accurately general academic and domain-specific words and phrases, sufficient for reading, writing, speaking, and listening at the college and career readiness level; demonstrate independence in gathering vocabulary knowledge when considering a word or phrase important to comprehension or expression.

Research Task

Topic: The Great Fire of London

Samuel Pepys's account of the Great Fire takes us right to the scene of the ongoing disaster. You cannot duplicate his eyewitness vantage point. However, you can gain a clear perspective on the causes, sequence of events, or results of the fire.

Assignment: Write a research report on one of the following aspects of the Great Fire:

- causes—geographical, architectural, cultural
- sequence of events from beginning to end
- short-term and long-term effects

Formulate a research plan. Begin with a question open-ended enough to support an in-depth, multi-faceted report, such as, "How did the way of life of seventeenth-century Londoners contribute to the Great Fire?" Then, develop stepping-stone questions the answers to which will help you answer your major question. Finally, devise a research plan by listing the types of sources you will consult. Do not rely entirely on texts written for students. In addition to such texts, consult both primary sources and texts written by experts for informed audiences.

Model: Using Stepping-Stone Questions

How did the way of life of Londoners contribute to the Great Fire?

How did people communicate?
How were neighborhoods arranged?
How were streets designed?
What were buildings made of?

Gather sources. Follow your plan. Assemble and organize your evidence, showing how facts support central ideas. Do not rely entirely on any one source.

Synthesize information. Evaluate your information and determine what to use and what to discard. First, distinguish between reliable and unreliable sources, excluding information you find only in unreliable sources. Then, look for and focus on patterns of ideas, excluding irrelevant details. Be flexible: If your question and research plan result in too little or too much information, revise them.

Organize and present ideas. Write your research paper based on a clear organization or outline. The topic of the Great Fire lends itself to visual aids, so consider including paintings, drawings, blueprints, diagrams, and maps. Avoid plagiarism, citing sources for words, ideas, and visuals not your own, using a standard format.

▲ One effect of the Great Fire was the use of fire marks like this one to identify insured property. Firemen, paid by insurance companies, would try to save marked properties.

RESEARCH TIP

The Great Fire has been treated in books for scholars, for general adult readers, for young adults, and for children. Do not waste time on books that are too specialized or too simplified.

Use a checklist like the one shown to review, and possibly revise, your report.

Research Checklist

☐ Have I answered the major research question?

☐ Have I gathered information from both primary and secondary sources?

☐ Have I organized the information in a logical way?

☐ Have I incorporated visuals appropriately?

London Past

"Don't ever take a city for granted,"

Neil Gaiman wrote in an online essay. "After all, it is bigger than you are; it is older; and it has learned how to wait…." In his novel *Neverwhere,* Gaiman certainly did not take London for granted. Describing a fantastical underground London unknown to the usual inhabitants of "London Above," he pays tribute to the city's long history and to its darker side.

Gaiman's dangerous underground city has a kinship with the London that Pepys describes in his accounts of the Great Plague and the Fire. Both are scary places, filled with turmoil and threat. Pepys may have been unaware that rats were playing a major role in the plague; however, Gaiman gives great power to rodent-like characters called rat-speakers.

A female rat-speaker named Anaesthesia accompanies Gaiman's hero, Richard Mayhew, in this episode from the beginning of the tale. Mayhew has recently arrived in the underground city "from the London Above." Now, he and Anaesthesia, led by a mysterious woman, must cross the fear-inspiring Night's Bridge. It is the first major test of Mayhew's courage.

and Present

Neil Gaiman
Novelist/Graphic Novelist/Poet/Songwriter/Screenwriter

Neverwhere started life in 1996 as a BBC television series in England. Gaiman (b. 1960) later adapted it into a novel in order to develop the characters. The novel became a major success, while the original TV series has faded.

Gaiman is versatile, writing songs and poems as well as screenplays. Even his screenwriting experience is diverse—it includes writing the English-language script for the Japanese anime movie *Princess Mononoke* (1999). Overall, however, Gaiman is best known as the author of the graphic novel series *Sandman*.

Describing his fertile creative process, he wrote, "You get ideas from daydreaming." Clarifying, he continued, "You get ideas from being bored. You get ideas all the time. The only difference between writers and other people is we notice when [it happens]."

from Neverwhere

Neil Gaiman

"If you are crossing the bridge, I will go with you," said a female voice, rich as cream and honey, coming from behind them. Richard was not able to place her accent. He turned, and standing there was a tall woman, with long, tawny hair, and skin the color of burnt caramel. She wore dappled leather clothes, mottled in shades of gray and brown. She had a battered leather duffel bag over her shoulder. She was carrying a staff, and she had a knife at her belt and an electric flashlight strapped to her wrist. She was also, without question, the most beautiful woman that Richard had ever seen.

"Safety in numbers. You're welcome to come with us," he said, after a moment's hesitation. "My name's Richard Mayhew. This is Anaesthesia. She's the one of us who knows what she's doing." The rat-girl preened.

The leather woman looked him up and looked him down. "You're from London Above," she told him.

"Yes." As lost as he was in this strange otherworld, he was at least learning to play the game. His mind was too numb to make any sense of where he was, or why he was here, but it was capable of following the rules.

"Traveling with a rat-speaker. My word."

"I'm his guardian," said Anaesthesia, truculently. "Who are you? Who do you owe fealty to?"

The woman smiled. "I owe no man fealty, rat-girl. Have either of you crossed Night's Bridge before?" Anaesthesia shook her head. "Well. Isn't this going to be fun?"

They walked toward the bridge. Anaesthesia handed Richard her candle-lamp. "Here," she said.

"Thanks." Richard looked at the woman in leather. "Is there anything, really, to be scared of?"

"Only the night on the bridge," she said.

"The kind in armor?"

"The kind that comes when day is over."

Anaesthesia's hand sought Richard's. He held it tightly, her tiny hand in his. She smiled at him, squeezed his hand. And then they set foot on Night's Bridge and Richard began to understand darkness: darkness as something solid and real, so much more than a simple absence of light. He felt it touch his skin, questing, moving, exploring: gliding through his mind. It slipped into his lungs, behind his eyes, into his mouth. . .

With each step they took the light of the candle became dimmer. He realized the same thing was happening to the leather woman's flashlight. It felt not so much as if the lights were being turned down but as if the darkness were being turned up. Richard blinked, and opened his eyes on nothing—nothing but darkness, complete and utter. *Sounds.* A rustling, a squirming. Richard blinked, blinded by the night. The sounds were nastier, hungrier. Richard imagined he could hear voices: a horde of huge, misshapen trolls, beneath the bridge. . . .

Something slithered past them in the dark. "What's that?" squeaked Anaesthesia. Her hand was shaking in his.

"Hush," whispered the woman. "Don't attract its attention."

"What's happening?" whispered Richard.

"Darkness is happening," said the leather woman, very quietly. "Night is happening. All the nightmares that have come out when the sun goes down, since the cave times, when we huddled together in fear for safety and for warmth, are happening. Now," she told them, "now is the time to be afraid of the dark." Richard knew that something was about to creep over his face. He closed his eyes: it made no difference to what he saw or felt. The night was complete. It was then that the hallucinations started.

Richard began to understand darkness: darkness as something solid and real, so much more than a simple absence of light.

He saw a figure falling toward him through the night, burning, its wings and hair on fire.

He threw up his hands: there was nothing there.

Jessica looked at him, with contempt in her eyes. He wanted to shout to her, tell her he was sorry.

Place one foot after another.

He was a small child, walking home from school, at night, down the one road with no streetlights. No matter how many times he did it, it never got any easier, never got any better.

He was deep in the sewers, lost in a labyrinth. The Beast was waiting for him. He could hear a slow drip of water. He knew the Beast was waiting. He gripped his spear. . . . Then a rumbling bellow, deep in its throat, from behind him. He turned. Slowly, agonizingly slowly, it charged at him, through the dark.

And it charged.

He died.

And kept walking.

Slowly, agonizingly slowly, it charged at him, over and over, through the dark.

There was a sputter, and a flare so bright it hurt, making Richard squint and stagger. It was the candle flame, in its lemonade-bottle holder. He had never known how brightly a single candle could burn. He held it up, gasping and gulping and shaking with relief. His heart was pounding and shuddering in his chest.

"We would appear to have crossed successfully," said the leather woman.

Richard's heart was pounding in his chest so hard that, for a few moments, he was unable to talk. He forced himself to breathe slowly, to calm down. They were in a large anteroom, exactly like the one on the other side. In fact, Richard had the strange feeling that it was the same room they had just left. Yet the shadows were deeper, and there were afterimages floating before Richard's eyes, like those one saw after a camera flash. "I suppose," Richard said, haltingly, "we weren't in any real danger. . . . It was like a haunted house. A few noises in the dark . . . and your imagination does the rest. There wasn't really anything to be scared of, was there?"

The woman looked at him, almost pityingly; and Richard realized that there was nobody holding his hand. "Anaesthesia?"

He had never known how brightly a single candle could burn.

From the darkness at the crown of the bridge came a gentle noise, like a rustle or a sigh. A handful of irregular quartz beads pattered down the curve of the bridge toward them. Richard picked one up. It was from the rat-girl's necklace. His mouth opened, but no sound came out. Then he found his voice. "We'd better. We have to go back. She's . . ."

The woman raised her flashlight, shone it across the bridge. Richard could see all the way across the bridge. It was deserted. "Where is she?" he asked.

"Gone," said the woman, flatly. "The darkness took her."

Critical Reading

1. **(a)** What does the leather woman say when she learns that Richard and Anaesthesia have never before crossed Night's Bridge? **(b) Infer:** Do you think that the leather woman has crossed the bridge before? Why or why not?

2. **(a) Summarize:** Briefly summarize what Richard feels and sees in the darkness on Night's Bridge. **(b) Interpret:** What do "night" and "darkness" come to mean to Richard while he is on the bridge?

3. **(a)** Describe the place the leather woman and Richard reach after they cross Night's Bridge. **(b) Speculate:** Are they in the same room they started from? Explain.

Use these questions to focus a class discussion of *Neverwhere:*

4. Do you think that nighttime in Pepys's London would have been a little bit like the night on Gaiman's bridge? Why or why not?

5. Why are writers like Gaiman and Pepys so interested in depicting a city like London?

Connecting to the Essential Question In *A Journal of the Plague Year,* Daniel Defoe vividly describes his hometown, London, during a terrible catastrophe in its past. What landmark event in your own region do you think would make a good story? As you read, note passages that reveal how the plague affected London. They will help you explore the Essential Question: **What is the relationship between literature and place?**

Literary Analysis

Point of view is the perspective from which a narrator tells a story. Stories told from the **first-person point of view** have these qualities:

- The narrator either participates in or observes the events.
- The narrator refers to himself or herself as "I."
- The narrator can tell you his or her thoughts but not those of others.

Nonfiction diaries and journals almost always use the first-person point of view, since they present a person's daily account of his or her thoughts and experiences. Even though *A Journal of the Plague Year* is fiction, Defoe's use of the first-person point of view makes it seem as if he actually witnessed the events he writes about, as in this passage:

It was about the 10th of September that my curiosity led, or rather drove, me to go and see this pit again, . . .

Reporting only his or her own thoughts and experiences, the first-person narrator provides a personal perspective that helps brings readers into a private world of meaning and aesthetic pleasure.

Reading Strategy

© **Preparing to Read Complex Texts** When you realize that you do not understand a passage you are reading, repair your comprehension by **asking questions.** Focus on the basics of the puzzling situation: who is doing what to whom and why? Also, when and where is the action taking place? Use a chart like the one shown to help you ask and answer questions about a passage.

Vocabulary

lamentations (lam′ ən tā′ shənz) *n.* expressions of grief (p. 591)

distemper (dis tem′ pər) *n.* infectious disease, such as the plague (p. 592)

delirious (di lir′ ē əs) *adj.* having hallucinations; ranting (p. 592)

resolution (rez′ ə lo͞o′ shən) *n.* determined state of mind (p. 593)

importuning (im′ pôr to͞on′ iŋ) *v.* pleading with (p. 594)

prodigious (prō′ dij′ əs) *adj.* enormous; huge (p. 595)

Common Core State Standards

Reading Literature
3. Analyze the impact of the author's choices regarding how to develop and relate elements of a story or drama.

Text: Description of Pit

Q. Who was thrown in?
A. Londoners who died of plague

Q. What happened to them?
A. They were buried in a mass grave.

Q. Where was the pit?
A. in Aldgate parish in London

Q. When were they brought there?
A. at night

Q. Why were they put there?
A. to prevent the spread of disease

www.PHLitOnline.com

DANIEL DEFOE

(1660–1731)

Author of *A Journal of the Plague Year*

"A false, shuffling, prevaricating rascal"—that was how fellow author Joseph Addison described Daniel Defoe. In many ways, Addison was not far from wrong. Constantly in debt, Defoe often engaged in shady business deals and declared bankruptcy in 1692, owing a small fortune to his creditors. He was also a sometime government spy and propagandist who even upgraded his own name, originally *Foe*, by adding an aristocratic *De*.

An Innovative Novelist Despite all his flaws, we remember Defoe for an important literary achievement. He practically invented the modern realistic novel. He did so with two books that were written as the memoirs of fictional characters. *Robinson Crusoe* (1719) presents an almost documentary narrative of a man marooned on a desert island. *Moll Flanders* (1722) tells a satirical tale of a poor woman seeking respectability. During his lifetime, Defoe's books were considered so realistic that they were sold as nonfiction. In fact, the first-person narrators were so convincing that Defoe was even accused of "forging a story, and imposing it on the world for truth."

Factual Fiction Defoe brought an even greater factual background to *A Journal of the Plague Year* (1722), his fictional account of the great plague that devastated England from 1664 to 1665. To construct this vivid narrative, Defoe studied official documents, interviewed survivors of the plague, and may have drawn on his own memories as a young child.

The vivid historical re-creation of the plague is a triumph of Defoe's energetic, detailed style in a genre that set English fiction on a new path.

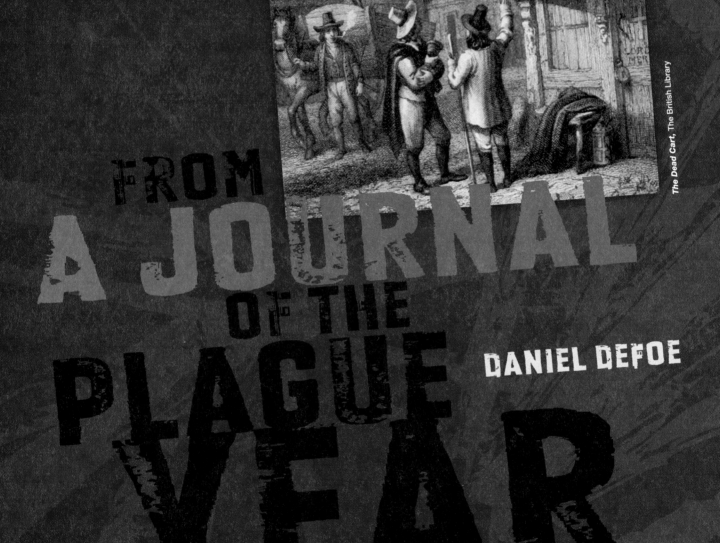

The Dead Cart, The British Library

FROM
A JOURNAL
OF THE
PLAGUE
YEAR

DANIEL DEFOE

The face of London was now indeed strangely altered, I mean the whole mass of buildings, city, liberties, suburbs, Westminster, Southwark, and altogether; for as to the particular part called the city, or within the walls, that was not yet much infected. But in the whole the face of things, I say, was much altered; sorrow and sadness sat upon every face; and though some parts were not yet overwhelmed, yet all looked deeply concerned; and as we saw it apparently coming on, so everyone looked on himself and his family as in the utmost danger. Were it possible to represent those times exactly to those that did not see them, and give the reader due ideas of the horror that everywhere presented itself, it must make just impressions upon their minds and fill them with surprise. London might well be said to be all in tears; the mourners did not go about the streets indeed, for nobody put on black or made a formal dress of mourning for their nearest friends; but the voice of mourning was truly heard in the streets. The shrieks of women and children at the windows and doors of their houses, where their dearest relations were perhaps dying, or just dead, were so frequent to be heard as we passed the streets, that it was enough to pierce the stoutest heart in the world to hear them. Tears and lamentations were seen almost in every house, especially in the first part of the visitation; for toward the latter end men's hearts were hardened, and death was so always before their eyes, that they did not so much concern themselves for the loss of their friends, expecting that themselves should be summoned the next hour. . . .

I went all the first part of the time freely about the streets, though not so freely as to run myself into apparent danger, except when they dug the great pit in the churchyard of our parish of Aldgate. A terrible pit it was, and I could not resist my curiosity to go and see it. As near as I may judge, it was about forty feet in length, and about fifteen or sixteen feet broad, and, at the time I first looked at it, about nine feet deep; but it was said they dug it near twenty feet deep afterwards in one part of it, till they could go no deeper for the water; for they had, it seems, dug several large pits before this. For though the plague was long a-coming to our parish, yet, when it did come, there was no parish in or about London where it raged with such violence as in the two parishes of Aldgate and Whitechapel.

Literary Analysis
Point of View
Where in the first paragraph does the narrator indicate that he is providing a personal account intended to be read by others? Explain.

Vocabulary
lamentations (lam'ən tā′ shənz) *n.* expressions of grief or mourning

Reading Check
In what ways was the "face of London . . . strangely altered"?

Vocabulary
distemper (dis tem′ pər)
n. infectious disease such
as the plague

I saw they had dug several pits in another ground, when the distemper began to spread in our parish, and especially when the dead carts began to go about, which was not, in our parish, till the beginning of August. Into these pits they had put perhaps fifty or sixty bodies each; then they made larger holes, wherein they buried all that the cart brought in a week, which, by the middle to the end of August, came to from 200 to 400 a week; and they could not well dig them larger, because of the order of the magistrates confining them to leave no bodies within six feet of the surface; and the water coming on at about seventeen or eighteen feet, they could not well, I say, put more in one pit. But now, at the beginning of September, the plague raging in a dreadful manner, and the number of burials in our parish increasing to more than was ever buried in any parish about London of no larger extent, they ordered this dreadful gulf to be dug, for such it was rather than a pit.

They had supposed this pit would have supplied them for a month or more when they dug it, and some blamed the churchwardens for suffering[1] such a frightful thing, telling them they were making preparations to bury the whole parish, and the like; but time made it appear the churchwardens knew the condition of the parish better than they did, for the pit being finished the 4th of September, I think, they began to bury in it the 6th, and by the 20th, which was just two weeks, they had thrown into it 1114 bodies, when they were obliged to fill it up, the bodies being then come to lie within six feet of the surface. I doubt not but there may be some ancient persons alive in the parish who can justify the fact of this, and are able to show even in what place of the churchyard the pit lay better than I can. The mark of it also was many years to be seen in the churchyard on the surface, lying in length parallel with the passage which goes by the west wall of the churchyard out of Houndsditch, and turns east again into Whitechapel, coming out near the Three Nuns' Inn.

INTO THESE PITS THEY HAD PUT PERHAPS FIFTY OR SIXTY BODIES EACH

It was about the 10th of September that my curiosity led, or rather drove, me to go and see this pit again, when there had been near 400 people buried in it; and I was not content to see it in the daytime, as I had done before, for then there would have been nothing to have been seen but the loose earth; for all the bodies that were thrown in were immediately covered with earth by those they called the buriers, which at other times were called bearers; but I resolved to go in the night and see some of them thrown in.

Reading Strategy
Questioning From the information in the paragraph beginning, "It was . . .," what reason does the narrator give for wanting to visit the pit at night rather than during the day?

There was a strict order to prevent people coming to those pits, and that was only to prevent infection. But after some time that order was more necessary, for people that were infected and near their end, and delirious also, would run to those pits, wrapped in blankets or rugs, and throw themselves in, and, as they said, bury themselves. I cannot

Vocabulary
delirious (di lir′ ē əs) *adj.* having hallucinations; ranting

---

1. **suffering** allowing.

say that the officers suffered any willingly to lie there; but I have heard that in a great pit in Finsbury, in the parish of Cripplegate, it lying open then to the fields, for it was not then walled about, [some] came and threw themselves in, and expired there, before they threw any earth upon them; and that when they came to bury others, and found them there, they were quite dead, though not cold.

This may serve a little to describe the dreadful condition of that day, though it is impossible to say anything that is able to give a true idea of it to those who did not see it, other than this, that it was indeed very, very, very dreadful, and such as no tongue can express.

I got admittance into the churchyard by being acquainted with the sexton who attended, who, though he did not refuse me at all, yet earnestly persuaded me not to go, telling me very seriously, for he was a good, religious, and sensible man, that it was indeed their business and duty to venture, and to run all hazards, and that in it they might hope to be preserved; but that I had no apparent call to it but my own curiosity, which, he said, he believed I would not pretend was sufficient to justify my running that hazard. I told him I had been pressed in my mind to go, and that perhaps it might be an instructing sight, that might not be without its uses. "Nay," says the good man, "if you will venture upon that score, name of God go in; for, depend upon it, 't will be a sermon to you, it may be, the best that ever you heard in your life. 'T is a speaking sight," says he, "and has a voice with it, and a loud one, to call us all to repentance"; and with that he opened the door and said, "Go, if you will."

His discourse had shocked my resolution a little, and I stood wavering for a good while, but just at that interval I saw two links[2] come over from the end of the Minories, and heard the bellman, and then appeared a dead cart, as they called it, coming over the streets; so I could no longer resist my desire of seeing it, and went in. There was nobody, as I could perceive at first, in the churchyard, or going into it, but the buriers and the fellow that drove the cart, or rather led the horse and cart; but when they came up to the pit they saw a man go to and again,[3] muffled up in a brown cloak, and making motions with his hands under his cloak, as if he was in a great agony, and the buriers immediately gathered about him, supposing he was one of those poor delirious or desperate creatures that used to pretend, as I have said, to bury themselves. He said nothing as he walked about, but two or three times groaned very deeply and loud, and sighed as he would break his heart.

When the buriers came up to him they soon found he was neither a person infected and desperate, as I have observed above, or a person distempered in mind, but one oppressed with a dreadful weight

---

2. **links** torches.
3. **to and again** to and fro.

Literary Analysis
Point of View
In the paragraph beginning, "His discourse . . . ," which details make Defoe's fictional narrator seem like a real person? Why?

Vocabulary
resolution (rez´ə lōō´shən) *n.* fixed or determined state of mind

Reading Check
What provisions does the parish make for disposing of the bodies of plague victims?

Vocabulary
importuning (im′ pôr
t$\overline{oo}$n′ iŋ) *v.* pleading with

of grief indeed, having his wife and several of his children all in the cart that was just come in with him, and he followed in an agony and excess of sorrow. He mourned heartily, as it was easy to see, but with a kind of masculine grief that could not give itself vent by tears; and calmly defying the buriers to let him alone, said he would only see the bodies thrown in and go away, so they left importuning him. But no sooner was the cart turned round and the bodies shot into the pit promiscuously,[4] which was a surprise to him, for he at least expected they would have been decently laid in, though indeed he was afterwards convinced that was impracticable; I say, no sooner did he see the sight but he cried out aloud, unable to contain himself. I could not hear what he said, but he went backward two or three steps and fell down in a swoon. The buriers ran to him and took him up, and in a little while he came to himself, and they led him away to the Pie Tavern over against the end of Houndsditch, where, it seems, the

4. **promiscuously** mixed together without care or thought.

▼ **Critical Viewing** Explain how the *Journal* helps you make sense of details in this picture. **[Connect]**

man was known, and where they took care of him. He looked into the pit again as he went away, but the buriers had covered the bodies so immediately with throwing in earth, that though there was light enough, for there were lanterns, and candles in them, placed all night round the sides of the pit, upon heaps of earth, seven or eight, or perhaps more, yet nothing could be seen.

This was a mournful scene indeed, and affected me almost as much as the rest; but the other was awful and full of terror. The cart had in it sixteen or seventeen bodies: some were wrapped up in linen sheets, some in rags, some little other than naked, or so loose that what covering they had fell from them in the shooting out of the cart, and they fell quite naked among the rest; but the matter was not much to them, or the indecency much to anyone else, seeing they were all dead, and were to be huddled together into the common grave of mankind, as we may call it, for here was no difference made, but poor and rich went together; there was no other way of burials, neither was it possible there should, for coffins were not to be had for the prodigious numbers that fell in such a calamity as this.

Vocabulary
prodigious (prō´ dij´ əs)
adj. enormous; huge

Critical Reading

1. **Key Ideas and Details (a)** What was the purpose of the great pit dug in Aldgate? **(b) Infer:** Why do you think the narrator describes the pit in detail?

2. **Key Ideas and Details (a)** What prompts the narrator to visit the pit? **(b) Interpret:** What does the Sexton mean when he says that visiting the pit will "be a sermon" to the narrator?

3. **Key Ideas and Details (a) Summarize:** Retell the incident concerning the man in the brown cloak. **(b) Draw Conclusions:** In what way does this incident add a new dimension of meaning to the previous general descriptions of the plague? Explain.

4. **Craft and Structure** Does Defoe use informative language, emotional language, or both to describe London during this crisis? In your response, use at least two of these Essential Question words: *city, destruction, struggle. [Connecting to the Essential Question: What is the relationship between literature and place?]*

FOR HERE WAS NO DIFFERENCE MADE, BUT POOR AND RICH WENT TOGETHER

Cite textual evidence to support your responses.

Literary Analysis

**Common Core
State Standards**

Writing

3. Write narratives to develop real or imagined experiences or events using effective technique, well-chosen details, and well-structured event sequences. *(p. 597)*

Language

4.a. Use context as a clue to the meaning of a word or phrase. *(p. 597)*

© **1. Craft and Structure** Referring to specific passages, demonstrate that *A Journal of the Plague Year* is written from the **first-person point of view.**

© **2. Craft and Structure** Why do you think Defoe chose a first-person narrator, an "eyewitness," to present this account of the plague year?

© **3. Key Ideas and Details** What is the first-person narrator like? Use a chart like the one shown to make inferences about his personality traits and attitudes based on what he says, thinks, and does in the selection.

Narrator's Personality Trait or Attitude	Narrator's Statements, Thoughts, or Actions That Support Your Inference

© **4. Key Ideas and Details** Does the narrator seem like an accurate reporter of events, or does he seem unreliable? Cite specific details to support your opinion.

© **5. Integration of Knowledge and Ideas** How does reading an account of the Great Plague from the first-person point of view compare to reading about such events in history textbooks? Explain.

© **6. Integration of Knowledge and Ideas** Which would you prefer to read—Defoe's fictionalized first-person account or an actual journal kept by someone during the Great Plague? Why?

© **7. Integration of Knowledge and Ideas** Defoe's account mixes fiction and nonfiction, combining Defoe's research into the events surrounding the actual plague with a fictional narrator and made-up situations. Do you think literary works should avoid mixing fiction and nonfiction? Why or why not?

Reading Strategy

8. Asking questions is a good way to understand difficult passages. **(a)** If you did not understand the changes described in the first paragraph, what are two questions you might ask to *repair your comprehension?* **(b)** How might you answer those questions?

9. (a) Answer these questions about the man in the next-to-last-paragraph: Who is he? What does he look like? Where is he? Why is he accompanying the cart? How does he behave? **(b)** Then, explain what the narrator's reporting of this incident reveals about himself.

10. You can ask yourself questions to figure out what a puzzling passage means. How could you also use a questioning strategy to monitor your understanding and decide whether a passage has puzzled you?

Integrated Language Skills

Ⓒ Vocabulary Acquisition and Use

Word Analysis: Latin Prefix *dis-*

The word *distemper* includes the Latin prefix *dis-*, which means "the opposite of" or "not." *Distemper* is "the opposite of temper, or balance"—in other words, the state of imbalance when one has a serious disease.

With a small group, write sentences about the selection using at least five of the *dis-* words listed below. Explain the meaning of each *dis-* word you use. Try to figure out the meanings of the following words based on your understanding of the prefix. However, if the meaning of a word is unclear, refer to a dictionary.

disappeared	disinfectant
disbelief	disobey
discomfort	disquiet
disconcert	dispense

Vocabulary: Context Clues

Context clues are words and phrases in a text that help you figure out the meaning of an unfamiliar word. Using context clues in the numbered sentences, choose the word from the vocabulary list on page 588 that best completes the meaning. Then, explain how you arrived at your answers.

1. The death toll from the Great Plague was _____.
2. Many who had the plague became _____ as the disease worsened.
3. Those afflicted with the _____ usually perished in the end.
4. Some mourners made their _____ loudly; others walked in silence.
5. It seemed like the whole city was _____ God to spare their loved ones.
6. It took great _____ for the narrator to walk the streets every night to report on events.

Writing

Ⓒ **Narrative Text** The selection by Defoe begins with an account of great change in London. Try writing your own **essay** about a time of change. It need not be as dramatic as the one in Defoe's account, but it should be a significant change that has affected your life.

Prewriting Jot down notes on the situation before and after the change. Also, briefly explain what caused the change and how it affected you.

Drafting In describing the change and its effect, use types of writing as they are appropriate: *persuasive, narrative, descriptive,* and *expository*. Combine concrete *incidents* with *broader themes* that illustrate your ideas about life.

Revision Exchange drafts with a partner. Accept suggestions for making information, thoughts, and feelings more concrete.

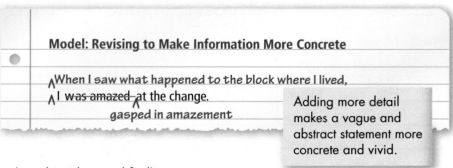

Model: Revising to Make Information More Concrete

ᴧWhen I saw what happened to the block where I lived,
ᴧI was amazed ᴧat the change.
　　　　　gasped in amazement

Adding more detail makes a vague and abstract statement more concrete and vivid.

Analyzing Functional and Expository Texts

Annual Report • Transit Map and Schedule

About the Texts

An **annual report** is a record providing information to the public on the status of an organization's initiatives and finances. Basic features of annual reports include chapter or section headings; bulleted and bold-faced information; and photos, charts, or graphs.

Transit maps and schedules are posters or brochures designed to transmit travel information graphically. They include simplified geographic representations of an area, a key or legend to explain symbols, and charts showing arrivals, departures, and stops.

Reading Strategy

Text features are elements of a text, such as heads, that signal its organization or clarify the information it presents. Follow these steps to **evaluate information from text features** and to evaluate the effectiveness of the structure they create:

- Identify text features, such as heads, legends, or tables, and their function.
- Based on text features, draw conclusions about the topics and subtopics covered in the text, as well as its organization.
- Use the text features to locate information or to guide you as you read.
- Evaluate whether each text feature contributes to the clarity of the text.

As you read, use a chart like the one shown to evaluate text features.

Text Feature Graphic	How It Clarifies/Organizes
Table of Contents/Index	
Head/Subhead	
Bulleted List	
Table/Chart/Graph	
Map	
Legend/Key	

Common Core State Standards

Reading Informational Text
5. Analyze and evaluate the effectiveness of the structure an author uses in his or her exposition or argument, including whether the structure makes points clear, convincing, and engaging.

Language
4.b. Identify and correctly use patterns of word changes that indicate different meanings or parts of speech.

Content-Area Vocabulary

These words may also appear in other subject-area texts:

congestion (kən jes´ chen) *n.* excessive crowding or accumulation

sustainable (sə stān´ ə bəl) *adj.* capable of being maintained or prolonged

consumption (kən sump´ shən) *n.* the using of goods or services

economic (ek´ ə näm´ ik) *adj.* having to do with the production, distribution, and use of goods and services

The Mayor's Annual Report 2004

To reduce congestion in London

Congestion—whether on the roads, on the Underground, on the buses or on the trains—is the scourge of London's current transport system. The result of many years of under-investment combined with significant rates of increase in London's population, it will not be cured overnight. Nevertheless, the Mayor is committed to ensuring that anti-congestion measures are combined with the necessary improvement in the capacity and quality of service of London's transport system to alleviate congestion in a systematic manner.

The heading clearly states the goal that is the topic of this section of the report.

Congestion Charging

The congestion charging scheme commenced in central London in February 2003. The scheme directly tackles four key transport priorities for London:

- reducing congestion
- improving bus services
- improving journey time reliability for car users
- making the distribution of goods and services more reliable, **sustainable** and efficient.

The bulleted list makes the transport priorities easy to read and remember.

TfL are monitoring the impacts and operation of the scheme as set out in the first Annual Monitoring Report in June 2003. They have since produced two reports setting out their findings: Congestion Charging:

Six Months On was published in October 2003; Congestion Charging: February 2004 Update was published after one year's operation. A Second Annual Monitoring Report is currently being prepared for publication in the Spring.

Reduced traffic levels and congestion

TfL estimate that 65,000 fewer cars per day are being driven into or through the charging zone, with the majority of occupants switching to public transport or diverting around the zone. As a result only 4,000 fewer people are coming to the charging zone each day because of the scheme.

Congestion in the zone has dropped by around 30 percent and is at the lowest level seen since the mid-1980s. The number of vehicles with four or more wheels entering the zone during charging hours has dropped by 18 per cent—making journeys to and from the charging zone quicker and more reliable. Journey times to and from the zone have decreased by an average 14 percent and journey time reliability has improved by an average of 30 percent.

Congestion levels in the charging zone during charging hours

Reduced congestion has also assisted the wider improvements in bus service reliability and journey times; the additional waiting time due to unreliability within the charging zone has reduced by around one third since the beginning of the scheme. Routes serving the congestion zone also experience 60 percent less congestion due to traffic disruption than before the charge was introduced.

Economic Impact

Reduced traffic delays, improved journey time reliability, reduced waiting time at bus stops and lower fuel **consumption** resulting from congestion charging all have **economic** benefits which are increasingly being recognised. TfL's cost benefit analysis of the overall impact of congestion charging is that it generates £50 million per annum of net benefits to London, principally through reduced congestion.

The chart shows the progress and effect of the congestion charging program.

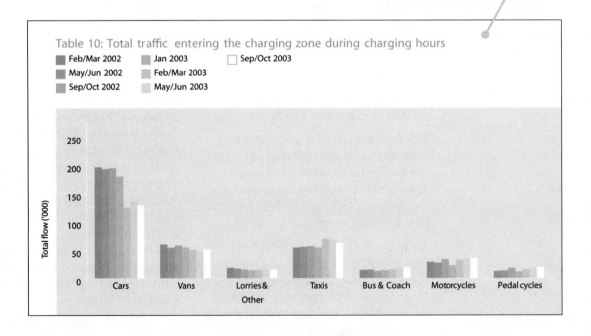

Table 10: Total traffic entering the charging zone during charging hours

■ Feb/Mar 2002	■ Jan 2003	□ Sep/Oct 2003
■ May/Jun 2002	■ Feb/Mar 2003	
■ Sep/Oct 2002	■ May/Jun 2003	

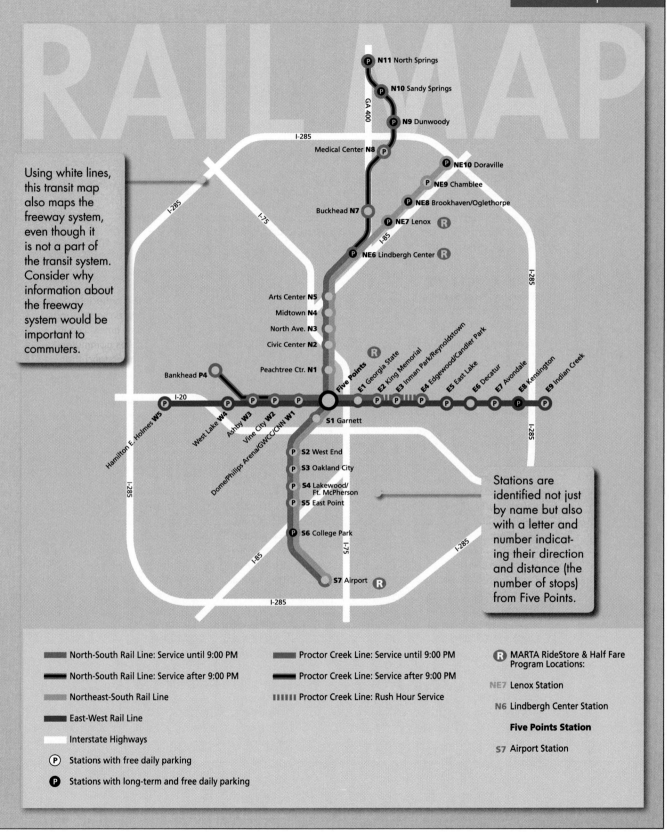

RAIL MAP

N11 North Springs
N10 Sandy Springs
N9 Dunwoody
Medical Center **N8**
NE10 Doraville
NE9 Chamblee
NE8 Brookhaven/Oglethorpe
Buckhead **N7**
NE7 Lenox ⓡ
NE6 Lindbergh Center ⓡ

Arts Center **N5**
Midtown **N4**
North Ave. **N3**
Civic Center **N2**
Peachtree Ctr. **N1**

Five Points
E1 Georgia State
E2 King Memorial
E3 Inman Park/Reynoldstown
E4 Edgewood/Candler Park
E5 East Lake
E6 Decatur
E7 Avondale
E8 Kensington
E9 Indian Creek

Bankhead **P4**
I-20
Hamilton E. Holmes **W5**
West Lake **W4**
Ashby **W3**
Vine City **W2**
Dome/Philips Arena/GWCC/CNN **W1**

S1 Garnett
S2 West End
S3 Oakland City
S4 Lakewood/ Ft. McPherson
S5 East Point
S6 College Park
S7 Airport ⓡ

I-285
I-75
GA 400
I-85
I-285
I-285
I-285

Using white lines, this transit map also maps the freeway system, even though it is not a part of the transit system. Consider why information about the freeway system would be important to commuters.

Stations are identified not just by name but also with a letter and number indicating their direction and distance (the number of stops) from Five Points.

North-South Rail Line: Service until 9:00 PM

North-South Rail Line: Service after 9:00 PM

Northeast-South Rail Line

East-West Rail Line

Interstate Highways

Ⓟ Stations with free daily parking

🅿 Stations with long-term and free daily parking

Proctor Creek Line: Service until 9:00 PM

Proctor Creek Line: Service after 9:00 PM

�𝍇 Proctor Creek Line: Rush Hour Service

ⓡ MARTA RideStore & Half Fare Program Locations:

NE7 Lenox Station

N6 Lindbergh Center Station

Five Points Station

S7 Airport Station

MARTA

North-South Rail Line

Note: If you are traveling Northbound from the Airport to the Buckhead, Medical Center, Dunwoody, Sandy Springs and North Springs rail stations after 9:00 pm, you need to board the northbound train with "Doraville" destination sign, exit at the Lindbergh Center rail station (N6), and transfer to the North Line train with a destination sign of "North Springs."

Train Frequency

Weekday Peak Service:.................................. Every 10 minutes
From 6:00 a.m. until 9:00 a.m.
From 3:00 p.m. until 7:00 p.m.

Weekday Off-Peak Service: .... Every 15 minutes

Weekday Off-Peak Service after 9:00 p.m........... Every 20 minutes
Trains run between Lindbergh Center Station
and North Springs Station after 8:00 p.m.

Weekend (Saturday and Sunday) Service: .... Every 20 minutes

> This schedule does not provide departure times, but it helps commuters understand that trains come along at the specified intervals.

Stations and Average Times to Five Points Station

Airport:	16 minutes	9.0 miles
College Park:	15 minutes	8.2 miles
East Point:	12 minutes	6.4 miles
Lakewood/Ft. McPherson:	08 minutes	4.5 miles
Oakland City:	06 minutes	3.4 miles
West End:	04 minutes	1.9 miles
Garnett:	01 minutes	0.4 miles
Peachtree Center:	01 minutes	0.5 miles
Civic Center:	02 minutes	1.0 miles
North Avenue:	03 minutes	1.4 miles
Midtown:	04 minutes	2.0 miles
Arts Center:	06 minutes	2.5 miles
Lindbergh Center:	10 minutes	5.2 miles
Buckhead:	16 minutes	7.4 miles
Med Center:	20 minutes	12.1 miles
Dunwoody:	22 minutes	13.1 miles
Sandy Springs:	25 minutes	
North Springs:	27 minutes	

Critical Reading

Common Core State Standards

Writing

1. Write arguments to support claims in an analysis of substantive topics or texts, using valid reasoning and relevant and sufficient evidence.

1. **Key Ideas and Details** **(a)** According to the annual report, where was the "congestion charging" plan implemented? **(b)** How often did officials monitor the impact of the plan?

2. **Key Ideas and Details** **(a)** Based on the transit map, how many stops after Georgia State is East Lake? **(b)** Based on the transit schedule, how long does it take to go from Oakland City to Five Points?

3. **Craft and Structure** **(a)** Identify two text features or graphics used in the annual report, and two in the transit map and schedule. **(b)** Explain how effective each is in presenting information or in helping you navigate the text.

4. **Content-Area Vocabulary** *Economic* is an adjective meaning "having to do with the production, distribution, and use of goods or services." Using this definition, along with your knowledge of word forms, give the meaning and part of speech of each of these words: *economize, economist, economical.* Check your answers in a dictionary.

⏱ Timed Writing

Argument [40 minutes]

Format

In a **position paper,** you present your viewpoint on a specific topic. An effective position paper contains a clear thesis logically supported with well-organized evidence and reasons.

Write a **position paper** in which you argue for or against congestion pricing in large cities. Develop a thesis and the support you will use by **synthesizing ideas and making logical connections** between the annual report and the transit map and schedule. Support your claim with textual evidence.

Academic Vocabulary

When you **synthesize ideas and make logical connections,** you combine related ideas from various texts, noting where they reinforce or build on one another, to support a conclusion.

5-Minute Planner

Complete these steps before you begin to write.

1. Read the prompt carefully and underline key words.

2. Scan the text for details that relate to the prompt. **TIP** Consider what the transit map and schedule show about the advantages or disadvantages of public transit.

3. Before writing, create an outline to guide you.

4. Reread the prompt, and begin drafting your essay.

from *Gulliver's Travels* • *A Modest Proposal*

Connecting to the Essential Question Like Jonathan Swift in his time, you might want to criticize social practices of today that you find annoying or disturbing. As you read the excerpts from *Gulliver's Travels* and the essay "A Modest Proposal," identify the subjects that Swift targets in his satire. Doing so will help as you answer the Essential Question: **How does literature shape or reflect society?**

Common Core State Standards

Reading Literature
6. Analyze a case in which grasping point of view requires distinguishing what is directly stated in a text from what is really meant.

Literary Analysis

Satire is writing that uses humor to expose and ridicule vice and folly. Satirical writing can appear in many genres—for example, Swift's *Gulliver's Travels* is a *satirical novel* and "A Modest Proposal" is a *satirical essay*. Although satirists unmask evils, they sometimes conceal their point of view by masking their targets in order to avoid the dangers involved in naming real people, places, or beliefs. Swift uses masks such as the following in *Gulliver's Travels*:

- imaginary lands and people, such as Lilliput and the Lilliputians
- fictional conflicts, like the conflict between Big- and Little-Endians

In his essay, Swift uses these devices:

- *understatement*, in which the literal meaning falls short of the topic; saying you cannot think of one objection to a terrifying proposal is an example.
- *hyperbole*, or exaggeration
- *sarcasm*, or a bitter way of saying the opposite of what you mean

Comparing Literary Works In both his novel and his essay, Swift uses the satirical weapon of **irony,** a surprising contradiction between reality and appearance or between the actual and intended meaning of words.

Reading Strategy

Preparing to Read Complex Texts By **analyzing and evaluating information from text features** such as background and footnotes, you can better understand Swift's irony and his point of view. Use a chart like the one shown to analyze text features and show how they clarify Swift's meaning.

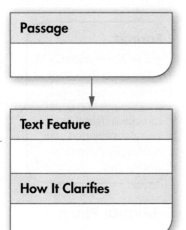

Passage

Text Feature

How It Clarifies

Vocabulary

conjecture (kən jek′ chər) *v.* guess (p. 607)

schism (siz′ əm) *n.* division of a group into factions (p. 608)

expedient (ek spē′ dē ənt) *n.* device used in an emergency (p. 609)

sustenance (sus′ tə nəns) *n.* food or money to support life (p. 618)

commodity (kə mäd′ ə tē) *n.* product that is bought or sold (p. 619)

censure (sen′ shər) *v.* strongly disapprove; condemn (p. 621)

PHLit Online!
www.PHLitOnline.com

Jonathan Swift *(1667–1745)*

Author of *Gulliver's Travels* • "A Modest Proposal"

Swift was born in Dublin, Ireland, to English parents, although his father died before he was born. With the assistance of relatives, he received a good education and then obtained an appointment in the household of Sir William Temple, a wealthy diplomat who lived on an estate in Surrey, England. Swift hoped for a career in politics, but receiving no support from Sir William, he decided on a career in the church. After Temple's death in 1699, he was given a small parish near London.

Satirist The satirical writing Swift had done while in the Temple household was out of character for a clergyman, but its brilliance was widely acknowledged in 1704 when he published his satires as two separate books: *A Tale of a Tub,* which satirizes excesses in religion and learning, and *The Battle of the Books*, which describes a comic encounter between ancient and modern literature.

Ambition and Achievement When the authorship of Swift's religious satires became known, Swift lost favor in the eyes of many church officials and also lost opportunities for advancement. Although he failed to achieve his goal of becoming a bishop in the Church of England, Swift remained a staunch defender of the Anglican faith. His political allegiance, however, shifted completely in 1710 when he left the Whig party to join the Tory party favored by Queen Anne. He benefited immediately from this move. As the leading party writer for the government, he wrote many pamphlets and wielded considerable political influence.

The Story Behind *Gulliver's Travels* Swift's most famous book, the novel *Gulliver's Travels,* began as a humorous assignment from the Scriblerus Club, a group of Swift's sharp-witted literary friends. These writers, who delighted in making fun of literary pretensions, gave Swift the project of writing a series of amusing, imaginary journeys because they knew he enjoyed reading travel books.

Later Years Although embittered by his failure to be named a bishop, Swift served for more than thirty years as dean of St. Patrick's Cathedral in Dublin. His caustic wit did not flag, as shown in the savage satire "A Modest Proposal" (1729), on starvation in Ireland. His death in 1745 deprived the world of a generous and learned man who despised fanaticism, selfishness, and pride.

from Gulliver's Travels

Jonathan Swift

Background *Swift's era was marked by religious and political strife. Reacting against the intolerance displayed in these conflicts, he ridiculed those whose pride overcame their reason. His novel <u>Gulliver's Travels</u> satirizes such intolerance by means of four imaginary voyages of Lemuel Gulliver, the narrator, a well-educated but unimaginative ship's surgeon. In "A Voyage to Lilliput," for example, Swift focuses on disputes between the established Church of England and Roman Catholicism, calling the followers of each Little-Endians and Big-Endians, respectively. He also satirizes the religious wars between Protestant England and Catholic France, disguising them as a conflict between Lilliput and Blefuscu. In "A Voyage to Brobdingnag," he suggests that the politicians leading England are guilty of "ignorance, idleness, and vice."*

from A Voyage to Lilliput

After being shipwrecked, Gulliver swims to shore and drifts off to sleep. When he awakens, he finds that he has been tied down by the Lilliputians (lil′ ə pyo͞o′ shənz), a race of people who are only six inches tall. Though he is held captive and his sword and pistols are taken from him, Gulliver gradually begins to win the Lilliputians' favor because of his mild disposition, and he is eventually granted his freedom. Through Gulliver's exposure to Lilliputian politics and court life, the reader becomes increasingly aware of the remarkable similarities between the English and Lilliputian affairs of state. The following excerpt begins during a discussion between the Lilliputian Principal Secretary of Private Affairs and Gulliver concerning the affairs of the Lilliputian empire.

We are threatened with an invasion from the island of Blefuscu,[1] which is the other great empire of the universe, almost as large and powerful as this of his Majesty. For as to what we have heard you affirm, that there are other kingdoms and states in the world, inhabited by human creatures as large as yourself, our philosophers are in much doubt, and would rather conjecture that you dropped from the moon, or one of the stars; because it is certain, that an hundred mortals of your bulk would, in a short time, destroy all the fruits

---

1. Blefuscu represents France.

◄ **Critical Viewing** What passages in the text reveal that Lilliputians now trust Gulliver more than they did in the episode depicted here? **[Infer]**

Vocabulary
conjecture (kən jek′ chər)
v. guess

Reading Check

From where do the Lilliputians think Gulliver came?

and cattle of his Majesty's dominions. Besides, our histories of six thousand moons make no mention of any other regions, than the two great empires of Lilliput and Blefuscu. Which two mighty powers have, as I was going to tell you, been engaged in a most obstinate war for six and thirty moons past. It began upon the following occasion. It is allowed on all hands, that the primitive way of breaking eggs before we eat them, was upon the larger end; but his present Majesty's grandfather, while he was a boy, going to eat an egg, and breaking it according to the ancient practice, happened to cut one of his fingers. Whereupon the Emperor, his father, published an edict, commanding all his subjects, upon great penalties, to break the smaller end of their eggs. The people so highly resented this law that our histories tell us there have been six rebellions raised on that account; wherein one emperor lost his life, and another his crown.[2] These civil commotions were constantly fomented by the monarchs of Blefuscu; and when they were quelled, the exiles always fled for refuge to that empire. It is computed that eleven thousand persons have, at several times, suffered death rather than submit to break their eggs at the smaller end. Many hundred large volumes have been published upon this controversy; but the books of the Big-Endians have been long forbidden, and the whole party rendered incapable by law of holding employments.[3] During the course of these troubles, the emperors of Blefuscu did frequently expostulate[4] by their ambassadors, accusing us of making a schism in religion, by offending against a fundamental doctrine of our great prophet Lustrog, in the fifty-fourth chapter of the *Brundecral* (which is their Alcoran).[5] This, however, is thought to be a mere strain upon the text, for the words are these: That all true believers shall break their eggs at the convenient end; and which is the convenient end, seems, in my humble opinion, to be left to every man's conscience, or at least in the power of the chief magistrate[6] to determine. Now the Big-Endian exiles have found so much credit in the Emperor of Blefuscu's court, and so much private assistance and encouragement from their party here at home, that a bloody war hath been carried on between the two empires for six and thirty moons with various success; during which time we have lost forty capital ships, and a much greater number of smaller vessels, together with thirty thousand of our best seamen and soldiers; and the damage received by the enemy is reckoned to be somewhat greater than ours. However, they have now equipped a numerous fleet,

Literary Analysis
Satire Why do you think Swift chooses the correct way to break eggs as the cause of conflict between Lilliput and Blefuscu?

Vocabulary
schism (siz´ əm) *n.* division of a group into factions

Spiral Review
Denotation and Word Choice Read the vocabulary word *schism* in context. What conclusions can you draw about the positive or negative nuances of *schism*?

---

2. **It is allowed . . . crown** Here, Swift satirizes the dispute in England between the Catholics (Big-Endians) and Protestants (Little-Endians). King Henry VIII who "broke" with the Catholic church, King Charles I, who "lost his life," and King James, who lost his "crown," are each referred to in the passage.
3. **the whole party . . . employments** The Test Act (1673) prevented Catholics from holding office.
4. **expostulate** (eks päs´ chə lāt´) *v.* reason earnestly with.
5. **Alcoran** Koran, the sacred book of Muslims.
6. **chief magistrate** ruler.

and are just preparing to make a descent upon us; and his Imperial Majesty, placing great confidence in your valor and strength, hath commanded me to lay this account of his affairs before you.

I desired the Secretary to present my humble duty to the Emperor, and to let him know, that I thought it would not become me, who was a foreigner, to interfere with parties; but I was ready, with the hazard of my life, to defend his person and state against all invaders.

The empire of Blefuscu is an island situated to the north-northeast side of Lilliput, from whence it is parted only by a channel of eight hundred yards wide. I had not yet seen it, and upon this notice of an intended invasion, I avoided appearing on that side of the coast, for fear of being discovered by some of the enemy's ships, who had received no intelligence of me, all intercourse between the two empires having been strictly forbidden during the war, upon pain of death, and an embargo laid by our Emperor upon all vessels whatsoever. I communicated to his Majesty a project I had formed of seizing the enemy's whole fleet; which, as our scouts assured us, lay at anchor in the harbor ready to sail with the first fair wind. I consulted the most experienced seamen upon the depth of the channel, which they had often plumbed, who told me, that in the middle at high water it was seventy *glumgluffs* deep (which is about six feet of European measure), and the rest of it fifty *glumgluffs* at most. I walked to the northeast coast over against Blefuscu, where, lying down behind a hillock, I took out my small pocket perspective-glass, and viewed the enemy's fleet at anchor, consisting of about fifty men of war, and a great number of transports. I then came back to my house and gave order (for which I had a warrant) for a great quantity of the strongest cable and bars of iron. The cable was about as thick as packthread, and the bars of the length and size of a knitting-needle. I trebled the cable to make it stronger, and for the same reason I twisted three of the iron bars together, bending the extremities into a hook. Having thus fixed fifty hooks to as many cables, I went back to the northeast coast and, putting off my coat, shoes, and stockings, walked into the sea in my leathern jerkin, about half an hour before high water. I waded with what haste I could, and swam in the middle about thirty yards until I felt ground; I arrived at the fleet in less than half an hour. The enemy was so frightened when they saw me, that they leaped out of their ships, and swam to shore, where there could not be fewer than thirty thousand souls. I then took my tackling, and, fastening a hook to the hole at the prow of each, I tied all the cords together at the end. While I was thus employed, the enemy discharged several thousand arrows, many of which struck in my hands and face and, besides the excessive smart, gave me much disturbance in my work. My greatest apprehension was for my eyes, which I should have infallibly lost, if I had not suddenly thought of an expedient. I kept

Vocabulary
expedient (ek spē′ dē ənt)
n. device used in an emergency

Reading Check

How does Gulliver plan to defend the Lilliputians against invasion?

Literary Analysis
Satire and Irony What is ironic about Gulliver using spectacles as a shield in a military operation?

among other little necessaries a pair of spectacles in a private pocket, which, as I observed before, had escaped the Emperor's searchers. These I took out and fastened as strongly as I could upon my nose and thus armed went on boldly with my work in spite of the enemy's arrows, many of which struck against the glasses of my spectacles, but without any other effect further than a little to discompose them. I had now fastened all the hooks and, taking the knot in my hand, began to pull, but not a ship would stir, for they were all too fast held by their anchors, so that the boldest part of my enterprise remained. I therefore let go the cord, and, leaving the hooks fixed to the ships, I resolutely cut with my knife the cables that fastened the anchors, receiving above two hundred shots in my face and hands; then I took up the knotted end of the cables to which my hooks were tied and, with great ease, drew fifty of the enemy's largest men-of-war after me.

The Blefuscudians, who had not the least imagination of what I intended, were at first confounded with astonishment. They had seen me cut the cables and thought my design was only to let the ships run adrift or fall foul on each other; but when they perceived the whole fleet, moving in order, and saw me pulling at the end, they set up such a scream of grief and despair that it is almost impossible to describe or conceive. When I had got out of danger, I stopped a while to pick out the arrows that stuck in my hands and face, and rubbed on some of the same ointment that was given me at my first arrival, as I have formerly mentioned. I then took off my spectacles, and, waiting about an hour until the tide was a little fallen, I waded through the middle with my cargo and arrived safe at the royal port of Lilliput.

The Emperor and his whole court stood on the shore expecting the issue of this great adventure. They saw the ships move forward in a large half-moon but could not discern me, who was up to my breast in water. When I advanced to the middle of the channel, they were yet more in pain, because I was under water to my neck. The Emperor concluded me to be drowned, and that the enemy's fleet was approaching in a hostile manner; but he was soon eased of his fears; for, the channel growing shallower every step I made, I came in a short time within hearing, and holding up the end of the cable by which the fleet was fastened, I cried in a loud voice, Long live the most puissant[7] Emperor of Lilliput! This great prince received me at my landing with all possible encomiums and created me a *Nardac* upon the spot, which is the highest title of honor among them.

His Majesty desired I would take some other opportunity of bringing all the rest of his enemy's ships into his ports. And so unmeasurable is the ambition of princes, that he seemed to think of nothing less than reducing the whole empire of Blefuscu into a province and governing it by a viceroy; of destroying the Big-Endian exiles and compelling that people to break the smaller end of their eggs,

---

7. puissant (pyo͞o´ i sənt) *adj.* powerful.

A Voyage to Lilliput, Illustration from a nineteenth-century edition of *Gulliver's Travels*

◄ Critical Viewing
What specific details
from the text does this
picture illustrate?
[Connect]

by which he would remain sole monarch of the whole world. But I
endeavored to divert him from this design by many arguments drawn
from the topics of policy as well as justice, and I plainly protested
that I would never be an instrument of bringing a free and brave
people into slavery. And when the matter was debated in council, the
wisest part of the ministry were of my opinion.

This open bold declaration of mine was so opposite to the
schemes and politics of his Imperial Majesty that he could never

Reading
Check

Summarize the action
Gulliver takes against the
fleet of Blefuscu.

forgive me; he mentioned it in a very artful manner at council, where I was told that some of the wisest appeared, at least, by their silence, to be of my opinion; but others, who were my secret enemies, could not forbear some expressions, which by a sidewind reflected on me. And from this time began an intrigue between his Majesty and a junta of ministers maliciously bent against me, which broke out in less than two months and had like to have ended in my utter destruction. Of so little weight are the greatest services to princes when put into the balance with a refusal to gratify their passions.

from 𝔄 𝔙𝔬𝔶𝔞𝔤𝔢 𝔱𝔬 𝔅𝔯𝔬𝔟𝔡𝔦𝔫𝔤𝔫𝔞𝔤

Gulliver's second voyage leads him to Brobdingnag (bräb´ diŋ nag´), an island located near Alaska that is inhabited by giants twelve times as tall as Gulliver. After being sold to the Queen of Brobdingnag, Gulliver describes the English social and political institutions to the King, who reacts to his description with contempt and disgust.

Literary Analysis
Satire Which satirical details in the first paragraph of "A Voyage to Brobdingnag" relate to England and which relate to humanity in general? Explain.

Reading Strategy
Analyzing Text Features Based on what you have learned from text features about this historical period, what is satirical about the King laughingly asking whether Gulliver is "a Whig or a Tory"?

It is the custom that every Wednesday (which, as I have before observed, was their Sabbath) the King and Queen, with the royal issue of both sexes, dine together in the apartment of his Majesty, to whom I was now become a favorite; and at these times my little chair and table were placed at his left hand before one of the saltcellars. This prince took a pleasure in conversing with me, inquiring into the manners, religion, laws, government, and learning of Europe, wherein I gave him the best account I was able. His apprehension was so clear, and his judgment so exact, that he made very wise reflections and observations upon all I said. But I confess, that after I had been a little too copious in talking of my own beloved country, of our trade, and wars by sea and land, of our schisms in religion, and parties in the state, the prejudices of his education prevailed so far, that he could not forbear taking me up in his right hand, and stroking me gently with the other, after an hearty fit of laughing, asked me whether I were a Whig or a Tory.[8] Then turning to his first minister, who waited behind him with a white staff, near as tall as the mainmast of the *Royal Sovereign*,[9] he observed how contemptible a thing was human grandeur, which could be mimicked by such diminutive insects as I. And yet, said he, I dare engage, those creatures have their titles and distinctions of honor, they contrive little nests and burrows, that they call houses and cities; they make a figure in dress and equipage;[10] they love, they fight, they dispute, they cheat, they betray. And thus he continued on, while my color came and went several times, with indignation to hear our noble country, the mistress

---

8. **Whig . . . Tory** British political parties.
9. *Royal Sovereign* one of the largest ships in the British Navy.
10. **equipage** (ek´ wi pij´) horses and carriages.

of arts and arms, the scourge of France, the arbitress of Europe, the seat of virtue, piety, honor and truth, the pride and envy of the world, so contemptuously treated. . . .

He laughed at my odd kind of arithmetic (as he was pleased to call it) in reckoning the numbers of our people by a computation drawn from the several sects among us in religion and politics. He said he knew no reason why those who entertain opinions prejudicial to the public should be obliged to change or should not be obliged to conceal them. And, as it was tyranny in any government to require the first, so it was weakness not to enforce the second; for, a man may be allowed to keep poisons in his closets, but not to vend them about as cordials.

He observed, that among the diversions of our nobility and gentry[11] I had mentioned gaming.[12] He desired to know at what age this entertainment was usually taken up, and when it was laid down. How much of their time it employed; whether it ever went so high as to affect their fortunes. Whether mean vicious people by their dexterity in that art might not arrive at great riches, and sometimes keep our very nobles in dependence, as well as habituate them to vile[13] companions, wholly take them from the improvement of their minds, and force them, by the losses they received, to learn and practice that infamous dexterity upon others.

He was perfectly astonished with the historical account I gave him of our affairs during the last century, protesting it was only an heap of conspiracies, rebellions, murders, massacres, revolutions, banishments, the very worst effects that avarice, faction, hypocrisy, perfidiousness, cruelty, rage, madness, hatred, envy, lust, malice, and ambition could produce.

His Majesty in another audience was at the pains to recapitulate the sum of all I had spoken; compared the questions he made with the answers I had given; then taking me into his hands, and stroking me gently, delivered himself in these words, which I shall never forget, nor the manner he spoke them in. "My little friend Grildrig, you have made a most admirable panegyric upon your country. You have clearly proved that ignorance, idleness, and vice are the proper ingredients for qualifying a legislator. That laws are best explained, interpreted, and applied by those whose interest and abilities lie in perverting, confounding, and eluding them. I observe among you some lines of an institution, which in its original might have been tolerable, but these half erased, and the rest wholly blurred and blotted by corruptions. It doth not appear from all you have said how any one perfection is required toward the procurement of any one station among you, much less that men are ennobled on account of their virtue, that priests are advanced for their piety or learning, soldiers for their con-

> ...after an hearty fit of laughing, (he) asked me whether I were a Whig or a Tory.

Reading Check

What does the King of Brobdingnag say in response to Gulliver's account of European customs and history?

---

11. gentry the class of landowning people ranking just below the nobility.
12. gaming gambling.
13. habituate (hə bich′ oo͞ āt′) **them** to make them used to.

duct or valor, judges for their integrity, senators for the love of their country, or counselors for their wisdom. As for yourself," continued the King, "who have spent the greatest part of your life in traveling, I am well disposed to hope you may hitherto have escaped many vices of your country. But, by what I have gathered from your own relation, and the answers I have with much pains wringed and extorted from you, I cannot but conclude the bulk of your natives to be the most pernicious race of little odious vermin that nature ever suffered to crawl upon the surface of the earth."

Nothing but an extreme love of truth could have hindered me from concealing this part of my story. It was in vain to discover my resentments, which were always turned into ridicule; and I was forced to rest with patience while my noble and most beloved country was so injuriously treated. I am heartily sorry as any of my readers can possibly be that such an occasion was given, but this prince happened to be so curious and inquisitive upon every particular that it could not consist either with gratitude or good manners to refuse giving him what satisfaction I was able. Yet thus much I may be allowed to say in my own vindication that I artfully eluded many of his questions and gave to every point a more favorable turn by many degrees than the strictness of truth would allow. For I have always borne that laudable partiality to my own country, which Dionysius Halicarnassensis[14] with so much justice recommends to an historian. I would hide the frailties and deformities of my political mother and place her virtues and beauties in the most advantageous light. This was my sincere endeavor in those many discourses I had with that mighty monarch, although it unfortunately failed of success.

But great allowances should be given to a king who lives wholly secluded from the rest of the world, and must therefore be altogether unacquainted with the manners and customs that most prevail in other nations: the want of which knowledge will ever produce many prejudices, and a certain narrowness of thinking, from which we and the politer countries of Europe are wholly exempted. And it would be hard indeed, if so remote a prince's notions of virtue and vice were to be offered as a standard for all mankind.

To confirm what I have now said, and further to show the miserable effects of a confined education, I shall here insert a passage which will hardly obtain belief. In hopes to ingratiate myself farther into his Majesty's favor, I told him of an invention discovered between three and four hundred years ago, to make a certain powder, into an heap of which the smallest spark of fire falling, would kindle the whole in a moment, although it were as big as a mountain, and make it all fly up in the air together, with a noise and agitation greater

Literary Analysis
Satire and Irony In Gulliver's remark that he "artfully eluded" the King's questions, what is the difference between the intended meaning and the actual meaning?

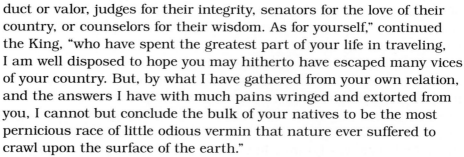

14. Dionysius (dī´ ə nĭsh´ əs) **Halicarnassensis** (hal´ ə kär na sen´ sis) Greek writer who lived in Rome and attempted to persuade the Greeks to submit to their Roman conquerors.

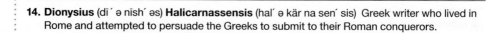

◄ **Critical Viewing**
Compare the relationship between Gulliver and the King of Brobdingnag as portrayed by the artist with that portrayed in the text. **[Compare and Contrast]**

than thunder. That a proper quantity of this powder rammed into an hollow tube of brass or iron, according to its bigness, would drive a ball of iron or lead with such violence and speed as nothing was able to sustain its force. That the largest balls, thus discharged, would not only destroy whole ranks of an army at once, but batter the strongest walls to the ground, sink down ships, with a thousand men in each, to the bottom of the sea; and when linked together by a chain, would cut through masts and rigging, divide hundreds of bodies in the middle, and lay all waste before them. That we often put this powder into large hollow balls of iron, and discharged them by an engine into some city we were besieging, which would rip up the pavement, tear the houses to pieces, burst and throw splinters on

☑ Reading
Check

What is the King's opinion of most of Gulliver's countrymen?

every side, dashing out the brains of all who came near. That I knew the ingredients very well, which were cheap, and common; I understood the manner of compounding them, and could direct his workmen how to make those tubes of a size proportionable to all other things in his Majesty's kingdom, and the largest need not be above two hundred foot long; twenty or thirty of which tubes, charged with the proper quantity of powder and balls, would batter down the walls of the strongest town in his dominions in a few hours, or destroy the whole metropolis, if ever it should pretend to dispute his absolute commands. This I humbly offered to his Majesty as a small tribute of acknowledgment in return of so many marks that I had received of his royal favor and protection.

The King was struck with horror at the description I had given of those terrible engines and the proposal I had made. He was amazed how so impotent and groveling an insect as I (these were his expressions) could entertain such inhuman ideas, and in so familiar a manner as to appear wholly unmoved at all the scenes of blood and desolation which I had painted as the common effects of those destructive machines; whereof he said some evil genius, enemy to mankind, must have been the first contriver. As for himself, he protested that although few things delighted him so much as new discoveries in art or in nature, yet he would rather lose half his kingdom than be privy to such a secret, which he commanded me, as I valued my life, never to mention any more.

> **The** *King was struck with horror at the description I had given . . . and the proposal I had made.*

Critical Reading

© 1. Key Ideas and Details (a) Describe the conflict between Big-Endians and Little-Endians. **(b) Infer:** Do these two groups take their dispute seriously? Why or why not? **(c) Analyze:** What evidence is there that Swift does not want you to take the dispute seriously? Explain.

© 2. Key Ideas and Details (a) Citing the text, give one example of how the King of Brobdingnag shows affection toward Gulliver and one example of how he shows distaste for Gulliver's ideas. **(b) Interpret:** Show how the final disagreement between Gulliver and the King reflects a difference between ingenuity and wisdom.

© 3. Key Ideas and Details (a) What is the most important physical difference between Lilliputians and Brobdingnagians? **(b) Interpret:** How does this physical difference suggest other important ways in which they differ? Explain. **(c) Synthesize:** How do Lilliputians and Brobdingnagians each represent a different way of viewing humanity?

© 4. Integration of Knowledge and Ideas In the final paragraph, how does Swift use the King's reactions to express his own hopes for humankind?

Cite textual evidence to support your responses.

A Modest Proposal

Jonathan Swift

Background

Swift recognized that the best audience for "A Modest Proposal" was the upper class—a group of people who had the ability to make changes for the better in Ireland. On a satirical level, however, Swift's essay mocks this very group of people. He suggests that their relentless pursuit of luxury has developed in them a taste for almost unimaginable delicacies. In this way, they become the perfect target for his modest proposal.

▲ **Critical Viewing**
In what way does this painting embody the "relentless pursuit of luxury" that Swift addresses through his essay? **[Interpret]**

FOR PREVENTING THE CHILDREN OF POOR PEOPLE FROM BEING A BURDEN TO THEIR PARENTS OR COUNTRY, AND FOR MAKING THEM BENEFICIAL TO THE PUBLIC.

It is a melancholy object to those, who walk through this great town,[1] or travel in the country, when they see the streets, the roads, and cabin-doors, crowded with beggars of the female sex, followed by three, four, or six children, all in rags, and importuning every passenger for an alms.[2] These mothers instead of being able to work for their honest livelihood, are forced to employ all their time in strolling, to beg sustenance for their helpless infants, who, as they grow up, either turn thieves for want of work, or leave their dear native country to fight for the Pretender in Spain,[3] or sell themselves to the Barbadoes.[4]

I think it is agreed by all parties, that this prodigious number of children, in the arms, or on the backs, or at the heels of their mothers, and frequently of their fathers, is in the present deplorable state of the kingdom, a very great additional grievance; and therefore whoever could find out a fair, cheap and easy method of making these children sound useful members of the commonwealth would deserve so well of the public, as to have his statue set up for a preserver of the nation.

But my intention is very far from being confined to provide only for the children of professed beggars, it is of a much greater extent, and shall take in the whole number of infants at a certain age, who are born of parents in effect as little able to support them, as those who demand our charity in the streets.

As to my own part, having turned my thoughts, for many years, upon this important subject, and maturely weighed the several schemes of other projectors, I have always found them grossly mistaken in their computation. It is true a child, just dropped from its dam[5] may be supported by her milk for a solar year with little other nourishment, at most not above the value of two shillings, which the mother may certainly get, or the value in scraps, by her lawful occupation of begging, and it is exactly at one year old that I propose to provide for them, in such a manner, as, instead of being a charge upon their parents, or the parish, or wanting food and raiment[6] for the rest of their lives, they shall, on the contrary, contribute to the feeding and partly to the clothing of many thousands.

There is likewise another great advantage in my scheme, that it will prevent those voluntary abortions, and that horrid practice of

1. **this great town** Dublin.
2. **importuning. . . alms** begging passersby for charity.
3. **Pretender in Spain** James Edward Stewart (1688–1766), a Catholic, was a claimant (or "Pretender") to the English throne despite being barred against succession.
4. **sell. . . Barbadoes** commit themselves as indentured servants on Barbadian plantations.
5. **dam** female parent, usually an animal.
6. **raiment** clothing.

women murdering their bastard children, alas, too frequent among us, sacrificing the poor innocent babes, I doubt, more to avoid the expense, than the shame, which would move tears and pity in the most savage and inhuman breast.

The number of souls in this kingdom being usually reckoned one million and a half,[7] of these I calculate there may be about two hundred thousand couple whose wives are breeders, from which number I subtract thirty thousand couples, who are able to maintain their own children, although I apprehend there cannot be so many under the present distresses of the kingdom, but this being granted, there will remain an hundred and seventy thousand breeders. I again subtract fifty thousand for those women who miscarry, or whose children die by accident, or disease within the year. There only remain an hundred and twenty thousand children of poor parents annually born: The question therefore is, how this number shall be reared, and provided for, which, as I have already said, under the present situation of affairs, is utterly impossible by all the methods hitherto proposed, for we can neither employ them in handicraft, or agriculture; we neither build houses, (I mean in the country) nor cultivate land: they can very seldom pick up a livelihood by stealing till they arrive at six years old, except where they are of towardly parts,[8] although, I confess they learn the rudiments much earlier, during which time, they can however be properly looked upon only as probationers, as I have been informed by a principal gentleman in the County of Cavan, who protested to me, that he never knew above one or two instances under the age of six, even in a part of the kingdom so renowned for the quickest proficiency in that art.

I am assured by our merchants, that a boy or a girl, before twelve years old, is no saleable commodity, and even when they come to this age, they will not yield above three pounds, or three pounds and half-a-crown at most on the Exchange, which cannot turn to account[9] either to the parents or the kingdom, the charge of nutriment and rags having been at least four times that value.

I shall now therefore humbly propose my own thoughts, which I hope will not be liable to the least objection.

I have been assured by a very knowing American of my acquaintance in London, that a young healthy child well nursed is at a year old a most delicious, nourishing, and wholesome food, whether stewed, roasted, baked, or boiled, and I make no doubt that it will equally serve in a fricassee, or a ragout.[10]

▲ **Critical Viewing**
Do you think the technique used in this etching best conveys the hardship of poverty? Explain. **[Assess]**

Vocabulary
commodity (kə mäd´ ə tē) *n.* product that is bought or sold

Reading Check
Who first told Swift about the use of children as a source of food?

---

7. **souls . . . half** censuses from the year 1699 put Ireland's population at approximately 1.2 million.
8. **of towardly parts** highly talented or able.
9. **turn to account** bring a profit.
10. **fricassee** (frik ə sē´) **. . . ragout** (ra goo´) meat stews.

Literary Analysis
Satire What effect do words like *breed* and *savages* have on the tone in this paragraph?

I do therefore humbly offer it to public consideration, that of the hundred and twenty thousand children, already computed, twenty thousand may be reserved for breed, whereof only one fourth part to be males, which is more than we allow to sheep, black-cattle, or swine, and my reason is that these children are seldom the fruits of marriage, a circumstance not much regarded by our savages, therefore one male will be sufficient to serve four females. That the remaining hundred thousand may at a year old be offered in sale to the persons of quality, and fortune, through the kingdom, always advising the mother to let them suck plentifully in the last month, so as to render them plump, and fat for a good table. A child will make two dishes at an entertainment for friends, and when the family dines alone, the fore or hind quarter will make a reasonable dish, and seasoned with a little pepper or salt will be very good boiled on the fourth day, especially in winter.

I have reckoned upon a medium,[11] that a child just born will weigh 12 pounds, and in a solar year if tolerably nursed increases to 28 pounds.

Literary Analysis
Satire In what way does Swift's sarcasm sharpen his satirical attack on landlords?

I grant this food will be somewhat dear,[12] and therefore very proper for landlords, who, as they have already devoured[13] most of the parents, seem to have the best title to the children.

Infants' flesh will be in season throughout the year, but more plentiful in March, and a little before and after, for we are told by a grave author an eminent French physician,[14] that fish being a prolific diet, there are more children born in Roman Catholic countries about nine months after Lent, than at any other season; therefore reckoning a year after Lent, the markets will be more glutted than usual, because the number of popish[15] infants, is at least three to one in this kingdom, and therefore it will have one other collateral[16] advantage by lessening the number of Papists[17] among us.

I have already computed the charge of nursing a beggar's child (in which list I reckon all cottagers, laborers, and four-fifths of the farmers) to be about two shillings per annum, rags included, and I believe no gentleman would repine[18] to give ten shillings for the carcass of a good fat child, which, as I have said will make four dishes of excellent nutritive meat, when he has only some particular friend, or his own family to dine with him. Thus the Squire will learn to be a good landlord, and grow popular among his tenants, the mother will have eight shillings net profit, and be fit for work till she produces another child.

---

11. **reckoned upon a medium** estimated as an average.
12. **dear** costly.
13. **devoured** financially destroyed.
14. **grave . . . physician** François Rabelais, a renown humorist and satirist.
15. **popish** Catholic (derogatory).
16. **collateral** parallel; related.
17. **Papists** Roman Catholics (derogatory).
18. **repine** (ri pīn´) *v.* complain.

Those who are more thrifty (as I must confess the times require) may flay the carcass; the skin of which, artificially dressed, will make admirable gloves for ladies, and summer boots for fine gentlemen.

As to our city of Dublin, shambles[19] may be appointed for this purpose, in the most convenient parts of it, and butchers we may be assured will not be wanting, although I rather recommend buying the children alive, and dressing them hot from the knife, as we do roasting pigs.

A very worthy person, a true lover of his country, and whose virtues I highly esteem, was lately pleased, in discoursing on this matter, to offer a refinement upon my scheme. He said, that many gentlemen of this kingdom, having of late destroyed their deer, he conceived that the want of venison might be well supplied by the bodies of young lads and maidens, not exceeding fourteen years of age, nor under twelve, so great a number of both sexes in every country being now ready to starve, for want of work and service: and these to be disposed of by their parents if alive, or otherwise by their nearest relations. But with due deference to so excellent a friend, and so deserving a patriot, I cannot be altogether in his sentiments; for as to the males, my American acquaintance assured me from frequent experience, that their flesh was generally tough and lean, like that of our schoolboys, by continual exercise, and their taste disagreeable, and to fatten them would not answer the charge. Then as to the females, it would, I think with humble submission, be a loss to the public, because they soon would become breeders themselves: And besides, it is not improbable that some scrupulous people might be apt to censure such a practice, (although indeed very unjustly) as a little bordering upon cruelty, which, I confess, has always been with me the strongest objection against any project, however so well intended.

But in order to justify my friend, he confessed that this expedient was put into his head by the famous Psalmanazar,[20] a native of the island Formosa, who came from thence to London, above twenty years ago, and in conversation told my friend, that in his country when any young person happened to be put to death, the executioner sold the carcass to persons of quality, as a prime dainty, and that, in his time, the body of a plump girl of fifteen, who was crucified for an attempt to poison the emperor, was sold to his Imperial Majesty's Prime Minister of State, and other great Mandarins of the Court, in joints from the gibbet, at four hundred crowns. Neither indeed can I deny, that if the same use were made of several plump young girls in this town, who, without one single groat[21] to their fortunes, cannot stir abroad without a chair, and appear at

---

19. **shambles** slaughterhouses.
20. **Psalmanazar** Here, Swift refers to a fictitious account of cannibalism in Formosa as made by impostor George Psalmanazar.
21. **groat** coin, of trivial amount.

LITERATURE IN CONTEXT

The Irish Troubles

In the later seventeenth century, just as Swift was growing up, England encouraged Scottish Protestants to emigrate to Northern Ireland and confiscate land owned by Catholics. Political power in Ireland became concentrated exclusively in the hands of the Protestant upper class, which comprised only about ten percent of the population. Catholics were the targets of relentless discrimination. For example, they were not allowed to reside in towns, but had to content themselves with living in rural settings. England's exploitative economic policies combined with crop failures in the 1720s to trigger a crisis; many farmers found it impossible to pay rent to their English landlords, and the streets teemed with beggars. This desolate situation was the background for "A Modest Proposal."

Connect to the Literature

In his essay, Swift appears to condemn the Irish Catholics in the same way as the social class he mocks. What possible motives might Swift have for using such a strategy?

Vocabulary
censure (sen´ shər) v.
strongly disapprove; condemn

Reading Check

What contribution to society will infants make if Swift's proposal is accepted?

the playhouse, and assemblies in foreign fineries, which they never will pay for, the kingdom would not be the worse.

Some persons of a desponding spirit are in great concern about that vast number of poor people, who are aged, diseased, or maimed, and I have been desired to employ my thoughts what course may be taken to ease the nation of so grievous an encumbrance.[22] But I am not in the least pain upon that matter, because it is very well known, that they are every day dying, and rotting, by cold, and famine, and filth, and vermin, as fast as can be reasonably expected. And as to the younger laborers they are now in almost as hopeful a condition. They cannot get work, and consequently pine away for want of nourishment, to a degree, that if at any time they are accidentally hired to common labor, they have not strength to perform it; and thus the country and themselves are happily delivered from the evils to come.

I have too long digressed, and therefore shall return to my subject. I think the advantages by the proposal which I have made are obvious and many, as well as of the highest importance.

For first, as I have already observed, it would greatly lessen the number of Papists, with whom we are yearly over-run, being the principal breeders of the nation, as well as our most dangerous enemies, and who stay at home on purpose with a design to deliver the kingdom to the Pretender, hoping to take their advantage by the absence of so many good Protestants, who have chosen rather to leave their country, than stay at home, and pay tithes against their conscience, to an Episcopal curate.[23]

Secondly, the poorer tenants will have something valuable of their own, which by law may be made liable to distress,[24] and help to pay their landlord's rent, their corn and cattle being already seized, and money a thing unknown.

Thirdly, whereas the maintenance of an hundred thousand children, from two years old, and upwards, cannot be computed at less than ten shillings a piece per annum, the nation's stock will be thereby increased fifty thousand pounds per annum, besides the profit of a new dish, introduced to the tables of all gentlemen of fortune in the kingdom, who have any refinement in taste, and the money will circulate among ourselves, the goods being entirely of our own growth and manufacture.

Fourthly, the constant breeders, besides the gain of eight shillings sterling per annum, by the sale of their children, will be rid of the charge of maintaining them after the first year.

Fifthly, this food would likewise bring great custom to taverns, where the vintners will certainly be so prudent as to procure the best

Literary Analysis
Satire What realistic solution to Ireland's problems is suggested in Swift's second argument?

---

22. **encumbrance** burden.
23. **tithes . . . curate** taxes, paid to the Catholic Church, which Protestants paid against their conscience.
24. **liable to distress** available for seizure by landlords as payment for debts.

receipts for dressing it to perfection, and consequently have their houses frequented by all the fine gentlemen, who justly value themselves upon their knowledge in good eating; and a skillful cook, who understands how to oblige his guests will contrive to make it as expensive as they please.

Sixthly, this would be a great inducement to marriage, which all wise nations have either encouraged by rewards, or enforced by laws and penalties. It would increase the care and tenderness of mothers toward their children, when they were sure of a settlement for life, to the poor babes, provided in some sort by the public to their annual profit instead of expense. We should see an honest emulation[25] among the married women, which of them could bring the fattest child to the market, men would become as fond of their wives, during the time of their pregnancy, as they are now of their mares in foal, their cows in calf, or sows when they are ready to farrow, nor offer to beat or kick them (as it is too frequent a practice) for fear of a miscarriage.

Many other advantages might be enumerated: For instance, the addition of some thousand carcasses in our exportation of barreled beef; the propagation of swine's flesh, and improvement in the art of making good bacon, so much wanted among us by the great destruction of pigs, too frequent at our tables, which are no way comparable in taste, or magnificence to a well-grown, fat yearling child, which roasted whole will make a considerable figure at a Lord Mayor's feast, or any other public entertainment. But this, and many others I omit being studious of brevity.

Supposing that one thousand families in this city, would be constant customers for infants' flesh, besides others who might have it at merry-meetings, particularly weddings and christenings, I compute that Dublin would take off annually about twenty thousand carcasses, and the rest of the kingdom (where probably they will be sold somewhat cheaper) the remaining eighty thousand.

I can think of no one objection, that will possibly be raised against this proposal, unless it should be urged that the number of people will be thereby much lessened in the kingdom. This I freely own, and was indeed one principal design in offering it to the world. I desire the reader will observe, that I calculate my remedy *for this one individual Kingdom of Ireland, and for no other that ever was, is, or, I think, ever can be upon earth. Therefore let no man talk to me of other expedients:*[26] *Of taxing our absentees at five shillings a pound: Of using neither clothes, nor household furniture, except what is of our own growth and*

25. **emulation** competition.
26. **expedients** Prior to publication, Swift proposed each of the following reasonable means by which Ireland might find relief, but the government ignored his suggestions. Swift used italics in editions printed during his lifetime to indicate that these proposals were, in fact, serious ones.

Literary Analysis
Satire Explain Swift's use of exaggeration in this passage.

Reading Strategy
Analyzing Text Features In what ways do the proposals in italics contrast with Swift's "modest proposal" in the body of the essay?

Reading Check

According to Swift's third argument, what benefit will his plan bring to Ireland?

manufacture: Of utterly rejecting the materials and instruments that promote foreign luxury: Of curing the expensiveness of pride, vanity, idleness, and gaming in our women: Of introducing a vein of parsimony, prudence and temperance: Of learning to love our Country, wherein we differ even from Laplanders, and the inhabitants of Topinamboo:[27] Of quitting our animosities and factions, nor act any longer like the Jews, who were murdering one another at the very moment their city was taken:[28] Of being a little cautious not to sell our country and consciences for nothing: Of teaching landlords to have at least one degree of mercy toward their tenants. Lastly of putting a spirit of honesty, industry and skill into our shopkeepers, who, if a resolution could now be taken to buy only our native goods, would immediately unite to cheat and exact upon us in the price, the measure, and the goodness, nor could ever yet be brought to make one fair proposal of just dealing, though often and earnestly invited to it.

Therefore I repeat, let no man talk to me of these and the like expedients, till he hath at least some glimpse of hope, that there will ever be some hearty and sincere attempt to put them in practice.

But as to myself, having been wearied out for many years with offering vain, idle, visionary thoughts, and at length utterly despairing of success, I fortunately fell upon this proposal, which as it is wholly new, so it hath something solid and real, of no expense and little trouble, full in our own power, and whereby we can incur no danger in disobliging[29] England. For this kind of commodity will not bear exportation, the flesh being of too tender a consistence, to admit a long continuance in salt, although perhaps I could name a country,[30] which would be glad to eat up our whole nation without it.

After all I am not so violently bent upon my own opinion, as to reject any offer, proposed by wise men, which shall be found equally innocent, cheap, easy and effectual. But before something of that kind shall be advanced in contradiction to my scheme, and offering a better, I desire the author, or authors will be pleased maturely to con-

---

27. **Laplanders and . . . Topinamboo** Swift refers to natives of inhospitable lands as examples for the Irish.
28. **city . . . taken** Jerusalem, which was taken by Rome in AD 70 while its Jewish inhabitants were occupied with infighting.
29. **disobliging** offending.
30. **country** England.

sider two points. First, as things now stand, how they will be able to find food and raiment for an hundred thousand useless mouths and backs. And secondly, there being a round million of creatures in human figure, throughout this kingdom, whose whole subsistence put into a common stock, would leave them in debt two millions of pounds sterling adding those, who are beggars by profession, to the bulk of farmers, cottagers and laborers with their wives and children, who are beggars in effect. I desire those politicians, who dislike my overture, and may perhaps be so bold to attempt an answer, that they will first ask the parents of these mortals, whether they would not at this day think it a great happiness to have been sold for food at a year old, in the manner I prescribe, and thereby have avoided such a perpetual scene of misfortunes, as they have since gone through, by the oppression of landlords, the impossibility of paying rent without money or trade, the want of common sustenance, with neither house nor clothes to cover them from the inclemencies of the weather, and the most inevitable prospect of entailing[31] the like, or greater miseries upon their breed for ever.

I profess in the sincerity of my heart that I have not the least personal interest in endeavouring to promote this necessary work, having no other motive than the public good of my country, by advancing our trade, providing for infants, relieving the poor, and giving some pleasure to the rich. I have no children, by which I can propose to get a single penny; the youngest being nine years old, and my wife past child-bearing.

31. entailing passing to a later generation.

Literary Analysis
Satire Why do you think Swift uses the phrases "sincerity of my heart" and "not the least personal interest" in the final paragraph?

Critical Reading

1. **Key Ideas and Details** **(a)** What agreement "by all parties" does Swift seek to establish in the second paragraph of the essay? **(b) Analyze:** Why is this agreement necessary for setting the groundwork for the satire?

2. **Key Ideas and Details** According to Swift's American acquaintance in London, what purpose can be served by well-nursed children who are a year old?

3. **Key Ideas and Details** **(a)** According to Swift, why will children be a very proper food for landlords? **(b) Draw Conclusions:** What satirical point is Swift making in his reference to landlords?

4. **Integration of Knowledge and Ideas** What do these selections suggest that Swift wanted to change about society? In your response, use at least two of these Essential Question words: *values, dissatisfaction, ideal.* [**Connecting to the Essential Question: How does literature shape or reflect society?**]

Cite textual evidence to support your responses.

Literary Analysis

@ 1. **Craft and Structure** Use a chart like the one shown to indicate three targets of Swift's **satire** in *Gulliver's Travels*.

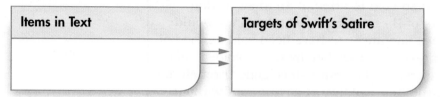

Items in Text		Targets of Swift's Satire
	→	
	→	
	→	

@ 2. **Key Ideas and Details (a)** Compare and contrast Gulliver's impression of the Lilliputians with the King of Brobdingnag's impression of Europeans. **(b)** How does the comparison add to the satire?

@ 3. **Key Ideas and Details** Summarize the universal and timeless points Swift wants to make in his satirical novel.

@ 4. **Key Ideas and Details (a)** What is Swift's chief satirical target in "A Modest Proposal"? **(b)** Why do you think he only gradually reveals the real nature of the "proposal"? **(c)** What is misleading about the word *modest* in the title?

@ 5. **Craft and Structure** Demonstrate how Swift uses each of these elements in his essay: **(a)** *understatement* **(b)** *hyperbole* **(c)** *sarcasm*.

6. **Comparing Literary Works (a)** Focusing on a passage in each work, compare and contrast Swift's use of **irony** in his novel and his essay. **(b)** In which passage is the irony more effective? Why?

@ 7. **Integration of Knowledge and Ideas** Are there any contemporary satires—whether in literature, on television, or in the movies—that resemble Swift's? Explain, citing examples.

8. **Analyze Visual Information** Use your knowledge of *Gulliver's Travels* to explain the humor in the cartoon on this page.

Reading Strategy

9. **(a)** Identify a passage in Swift's work that might require you to **analyze text features** in order to discover what is being satirized. **(b)** Demonstrate step by step how such analysis would work.

10. **(a)** Which text features were most helpful to you in figuring out the targets of Swift's satire in his novel and his essay? Why? **(b)** Which text features helped you better understand Swift's irony? Explain.

**Common Core
State Standards**

Writing
2.a. Introduce a topic; organize complex ideas, concepts, and information so that each new element builds on that which precedes it to create a unified whole; include formatting, graphics, and multimedia when useful to aiding comprehension. *(p. 627)*

Language
5. Demonstrate understanding of word relationships in word meanings. *(p. 627)*

▼ *"Tell me more about these little people that are out to get you."*

© Vocabulary Acquisition and Use

Word Analysis: Latin Root -jec-

The word *conjecture* includes the Latin root *-jec-*, which means "throw." *Conjecture* means "to guess by 'throwing' facts or inferences together." Write sentences using at least four of the following words in a paragraph describing what you might think or feel when traveling to another planet, just as Gulliver traveled to new worlds. If any of the words are unfamiliar, use a dictionary to clarify their meanings.

dejection	eject
object	project
reject	trajectory

Then, choose one of the words you used and write a sentence identifying how the "throw" root helps create its meaning.

Vocabulary: Analogies

Analogies show the relationships between pairs of words. Complete each analogy using a word from the vocabulary list on page 604. In each, your choice should create a word pair that matches the relationship between the first two words given. Then, explain your answers.

1. *Vegetables* : _____ :: *homes* : *shelter.*
2. *A* _____ : *merchandise* :: *help* : *assistance.*
3. *Emergency* : *an* _____ :: *moving* : *truck.*
4. *A transmission* : *a message* :: *a* _____ : *a rupture.*
5. _____ : *criticize* :: *praise* : *approve.*
6. *Night* : *day* :: _____ : *certainty.*

Writing

© **Informative Text** Like a modern-day Swift, make a plan for a satiric **multimedia** using *text, images, and sound.* You might include taped scenes or archival footage; photos, video, or cartoons; and sound effects or music.

Prewriting Start by choosing a target. What foolish behavior, trend, or attitude in today's world merits mockery?

Drafting Outline the sequence of your presentation. Then, decide on the *appropriate medium* to present each idea. Select the words, images, or sounds that will best convey your satire at each stage. Decide whether it is better to create those elements or to identify copyrighted sources that might provide the needed material—for example, television, videos, or films; newspapers, magazines, or books; clip-art collections or original drawings. Use a chart like the one shown to record your ideas.

Point	Media	Possible Sources
Reality shows are not "real."	Video clip from a reality show that reveals a convoluted situation.	Download copyrighted content from Internet
	News headlines showing problems people really face.	Scan from local papers

Revising Read through your plan and make any changes needed to clarify your message and to blend different types of media effectively.

Connecting to the Essential Question In *The Rape of the Lock*, Pope mocks the pretensions of high society. Briefly describe pretentious behavior that you have observed. As you read, noticing the upper-class behavior that Pope mocks will help as you consider the Essential Question: **How does literature shape or reflect society?**

Common Core State Standards

Reading Literature
6. Analyze a case in which grasping point of view requires distinguishing what is directly stated in a text from what is really meant.

Literary Analysis

Used in poetry, prose, drama, and other basic genres, **parody** is writing that makes fun of another, more serious work or of its author's style. *The Rape of the Lock* is a *mock epic,* or poetic parody of a traditional epic about heroes. Pope applies these conventions of classical epics to his trivial subject, the theft of a lady's lock of hair:

- boasting speeches made by heroes and heroines
- elaborate descriptions of warriors and their weapons
- involvement of gods and goddesses in the action
- **epic similes,** or intricate comparisons in the style of Homer that sometimes use the words *like, as,* or *so*

Note Pope's mocking of epic elements in *The Rape of the Lock*. Also note how, in both poems, he uses antithesis, a rhetorical device in which contrasting words, clauses, sentences, or ideas are placed side by side in parallel grammatical structures:

Whether he thinks <u>too little</u>, *or* <u>too much</u>. *(Essay, line 12)*

Reading Strategy

Preparing to Read Complex Texts To **analyze how an author's purpose affects the meaning of a work,** ask yourself why the author is writing. For example, knowing that Pope's purpose is to poke fun at grand literature and high society, you will understand why he chooses certain words to suggest contrasts between heroic deeds and trivial upper-class pursuits to in turn create a humorous **tone.** As you read, notice how his purpose leads him to make such contrasts throughout the poem.

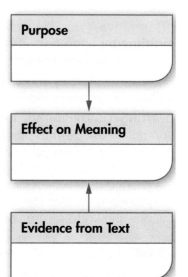

Purpose

↓

Effect on Meaning

↑

Evidence from Text

Vocabulary

stoic (stō´ ik) *n.* person indifferent to joy, grief, or pain (p. 631)

disabused (dis´ ə byo͞ozd´) *adj.* freed from false ideas (p. 631)

obliquely (ə blēk´ lē) *adv.* at a slant; indirectly (p. 634)

plebeian (plē bē´ ən) *adj.* common; not aristocratic (p. 635)

destitute (des´ tə to͞ot´) *adj.* lacking (p. 635)

assignations (as´ ig nā´ shənz) *n.* appointments to meet (p. 639)

Alexander Pope
(1688–1744)

Author of *An Essay on Man* •
The Rape of the Lock

Despite a crippling childhood disease and persistent ill
health, Alexander Pope was determined at a young age
to become a great poet. He triumphantly achieved his
boyhood ambition by the time he was in his twenties,
capturing the attention of the leading literary figures of
England. A brilliant satirist in verse, Pope gave his name to
the literary era in which he wrote, which is now called the
Age of Pope and Swift.

A Struggle Against Prejudice Born into the Roman
Catholic family of a London linen merchant, Pope was
a member of a persecuted religious minority. After the
expulsion of King James II in 1688, English Catholics could
not legally vote, hold office, attend a university, or live
within ten miles of London. Probably to comply with the
rule of residency, his family moved first to the village of
Hammersmith and then to Binfield, near Windsor Forest.
In this rural setting, Pope spent his formative years writing
poetry, studying the classics, and educating himself.

"[T]his long Disease, my Life" In addition to facing
religious prejudice, Pope had severe physical problems.
Deformed by tuberculosis of the bone, or Pott's disease,
Pope stood only about four and a half feet tall—"that little
Alexander the women laugh at," he said about himself. Pope
also suffered from nervousness and excruciating headaches
throughout his life. In a line from his poem *Epistle to Dr.
Arbuthnot* (1735), he refers jokingly but also with sadness to
"this long Disease, my Life."

A Turn to Philosophy In the 1730s, Pope's writing moved
out of the satirical mode to become increasingly philosophical. Leaving humor behind, he embarked on a massive work
concerning morality and government but completed only
An Essay on Man and *Moral Essays*. Nevertheless, the entire
body of his work is so noteworthy that critics and fellow
writers alike frequently accord him exceptionally high
praise. The twentieth-century poet Edith Sitwell, for example, called Pope "perhaps the most flawless artist our race
has yet produced."

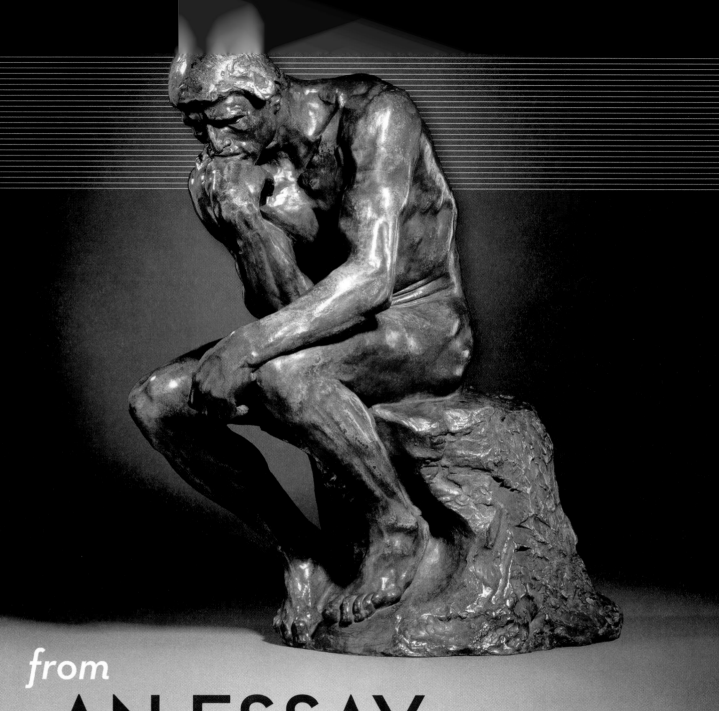

from
AN ESSAY Alexander Pope
ON MAN

▲ **Critical Viewing** Compare and contrast the perspective on humanity indicated by this Rodin sculpture with Pope's perspective in *An Essay on Man*. **[Compare and Contrast]**

Know then thyself, presume not God to scan;
The proper study of mankind is man.
Placed on this isthmus of a middle state,
A being darkly wise, and rudely great:
5 With too much knowledge for the skeptic side,
With too much weakness for the stoic's pride,
He hangs between; in doubt to act, or rest;
In doubt to deem himself a god, or beast;
In doubt his mind or body to prefer;
10 Born but to die, and reasoning but to err;
Alike in ignorance, his reason such,
Whether he thinks too little, or too much:
Chaos of thought and passion, all confused;
Still by himself abused, or disabused;
15 Created half to rise, and half to fall;
Great lord of all things, yet a prey to all;
Sole judge of truth, in endless error hurled:
The glory, jest, and riddle of the world!

Vocabulary
stoic (stō′ ik) *n.* person indifferent to joy, grief, pleasure, or pain
disabused (dis′ ə byo͞ozd′) *adj.* freed from false ideas

Critical Reading

1. **Key Ideas and Details (a)** What does Pope say should be the object of man's study? **(b) Speculate:** Why do you think Pope says, "presume not God to scan"?

2. **Key Ideas and Details (a)** According to Pope, what prevents man from being a skeptic or a stoic? **(b) Analyze Cause and Effect:** What is the result of man's being neither skeptic nor stoic? Explain.

3. **Key Ideas and Details (a)** What does each "half" of man do? **(b) Interpret:** In your own words, express how man can be both a "lord of all things" and "a prey to all."

4. **Integration of Knowledge and Ideas** What twentieth-century events suggest that humans are any or all of the following: "The glory, jest, and riddle of the world!" Explain.

Cite textual evidence to support your responses.

from

The Rape of the Lock

Alexander Pope

BACKGROUND *The Rape of the Lock* is based on an actual incident. Two families, the Petres and the Fermors, became involved in a dispute when Robert Petre flirtatiously cut a lock of hair from the head of lovely Arabella Fermor.

The first of the poem's five cantos opens with a formal statement of theme and an invocation to the Muse for poetic inspiration. Then, Belinda, the poem's heroine, receives a warning from the sylph Ariel that a dreadful event will take place in her immediate future. In Canto II, during a boat ride on the Thames, an adventurous baron admires Belinda's hair and is determined to cut two bright locks from her head and keep them as a prize. Aware of the baron's desires, Ariel urges the spirits to protect Belinda.

The Barge, 1895–96 Aubrey Beardsley

Critical Viewing Does the artist's portrayal of Belinda, who is shown here, correspond to Pope's portrayal of her in Canto III? Explain. **[Connect]**

Canto III

Close by those meads, forever crowned with flowers,
Where Thames with pride surveys his rising towers,
There stands a structure of majestic frame,[1]
Which from the neighboring Hampton takes its name.

5 Here Britain's statesmen oft the fall foredoom
Of foreign tyrants, and of nymphs at home;
Here thou, great Anna![2] whom three realms obey,
Dost sometimes counsel take—and sometimes tea.
    Hither the heroes and the nymphs resort,

10 To taste awhile the pleasures of a court;
In various talk th' instructive hours they passed,
Who gave the ball, or paid the visit last;
One speaks the glory of the British Queen,
And one describes a charming Indian screen;

15 A third interprets motions, looks, and eyes;
At every word a reputation dies.
Snuff, or the fan,[3] supply each pause of chat,
With singing, laughing, ogling, and all that.
    Meanwhile, declining from the noon of day,

20 The sun obliquely shoots his burning ray;
The hungry judges soon the sentence sign,
And wretches hang that jurymen may dine;
The merchant from th' Exchange[4] returns in peace,
And the long labors of the toilet[5] cease.

25 Belinda now, whom thirst of fame invites,
Burns to encounter two adventurous knights,
At omber[6] singly to decide their doom;
And swells her breast with conquests yet to come.
Straight the three bands prepare in arms to join,

30 Each band the number of the sacred nine.[7]
Soon as she spreads her hand, th' aerial guard
Descend, and sit on each important card:
First Ariel perched upon a Matadore,[8]
Then each, according to the rank they bore;

35 For sylphs, yet mindful of their ancient race,
Are, as when women, wondrous fond of place.
    Behold, four kings in majesty revered,
With hoary whiskers and a forky beard;

Meanwhile, declining
from the noon of day,
The sun obliquely
shoots his burning ray.

Vocabulary
obliquely (ə blēk´ lē) *adv.*
at a slant; indirectly

Literary Analysis
Parody To what trivial subject and epic convention does Pope refer in lines 33–36?

---

1. **structure . . . frame** Hampton Court, a royal palace near London.
2. **Anna** Queen Anne, who ruled England, Ireland, and Scotland from 1702 through 1714.
3. **snuff . . . fan** At the time, gentlemen commonly took snuff and ladies usually carried a fan.
4. **Exchange** London financial center where merchants, bankers, and brokers conducted business.
5. **toilet** dressing tables.
6. **omber** popular card game.
7. **sacred nine** reference to the nine Muses of Greek mythology.
8. **Matadore** powerful card that could take a trick.

And four fair queens whose hands sustain a flower,
40 Th' expressive emblem of their softer power;
    Four knaves in garbs succinct,[9] a trusty band,
    Caps on their heads, and halberts[10] in their hand;
    And particolored troops, a shining train,
    Draw forth to combat on the velvet plain.
45   The skillful nymph reviews her force with care:
    Let spades be trumps! she said, and trumps they were.
        Now move to war her sable Matadores,
    In show like leaders of the swarthy Moors.
    Spadillio[11] first, unconquerable Lord!
50 Led off two captive trumps, and swept the board.
    As many more Manillio[12] forced to yield,
    And marched a victor from the verdant field.[13]
    Him Basto[14] followed, but his fate more hard
    Gained but one trump and one plebeian card.
55 With his broad saber next, a chief in years,
    The hoary majesty of spades appears,
    Puts forth one manly leg, to sight revealed,
    The rest, his many-colored robe concealed.
    The rebel knave, who dares his prince engage,
60 Proves the just victim of his royal rage.
    Even mighty Pam,[15] that kings and queens o'erthrew
    And mowed down armies in the fights of loo,
    Sad chance of war! now destitute of aid,
    Falls undistinguished by the victor spade!
65   Thus far both armies to Belinda yield;
    Now to the baron fate inclines the field.
    His warlike Amazon her host invades,
    Th' imperial consort of the crown of spades.
    The club's black tyrant first her victim died,
70 Spite of his haughty mien, and barbarous pride.
    What boots[16] the regal circle on his head,
    His giant limbs, in state unwieldy spread;
    That long behind he trails his pompous robe,
    And, of all monarchs, only grasps the globe?
75   The baron now his diamonds pours apace;
    Th' embroidered king who shows but half his face,
    And his refulgent queen, with powers combined
    Of broken troops an easy conquest find.

Vocabulary
plebeian (plē bē′ ən) *adj.*
common; not aristocratic

Vocabulary
destitute (des′ tə tōōt)
adj. lacking

Reading Check
In what way do Belinda and her friends pass the time?

9. **succinct** (sək siŋkt′) belted.
10. **halberts** long-handled weapons.
11. **Spadillio** ace of spades.
12. **Manillio** two of spades.
13. **verdant field** the card table, covered with a green cloth.
14. **Basto** ace of clubs.
15. **Pam** knave of clubs, the highest card in the game called "loo."
16. **What boots** of what benefit is.

▶ **Critical Viewing**
Which elements of the situation portrayed in this drawing do you think Pope would choose to ridicule? Why? **[Speculate]**

Reading Strategy
Analyzing Author's Purpose How does Pope's purpose affect the meaning of lines 83–86?

Literary Analysis
Mock Epic and Antithesis Why is line 92 an example of antithesis?

Clubs, diamonds, hearts, in wild disorder seen,
80 With throngs promiscuous strew the level green.
Thus when dispersed a routed army runs,
Of Asia's troops, and Afric's sable sons,
    With like confusion different nations fly,
Of various habit, and of various dye,
85 The pierced battalions disunited fall,
In heaps on heaps; one fate o'erwhelms them all.
    The knave of diamonds tries his wily arts,
And wins (oh shameful chance!) the queen of hearts.
At this, the blood the virgin's cheek forsook,
90 A livid paleness spreads o'er all her look;
She sees, and trembles at th' approaching ill,
Just in the jaws of ruin, and codille.¹⁷
And now (as oft in some distempered state)
On one nice trick depends the general fate.

---

17. codille term meaning the defeat of a hand of cards.

The
BRITISH
TRADITION

**Neoclassical Style and
The Heroic Couplet**
Lines 105–106 or any of the rhyming lines in the poem demonstrate Pope's use of the closed heroic couplet, a rhyming pair of iambic pentameter lines that are "closed" because they express a complete thought. This type of couplet is typical of the Neoclassical style of the eighteenth century, which had these characteristics: a reliance on Greek and Roman models, a stress on human limitations, and a concept of the poet as a kind of public speaker addressing society as a whole.

In keeping with the Neoclassical outlook, the closed heroic couplet allows Pope to indicate human follies and frailties with devices from public speaking, such as antithesis.

Connect to the Literature

In what ways do lines 125 and 126 fit the Neoclassical style and outlook?

95   An ace of hearts steps forth; the king unseen
     Lurked in her hand, and mourned his captive queen.
     He springs to vengeance with an eager pace,
     And falls like thunder on the prostrate ace.
     The nymph exulting fills with shouts the sky;
100   The walls, the woods, and long canals reply.
        Oh thoughtless mortals! ever blind to fate,
     Too soon dejected, and too soon elate.
     Sudden, these honors shall be snatched away,
     And cursed forever this victorious day.
105   For lo! the board with cups and spoons is crowned,
     The berries crackle, and the mill turns round;[18]
     On shining altars of Japan[19] they raise
     The silver lamp; the fiery spirits blaze;
     From silver spouts the grateful liquors glide,
110   While China's earth[20] receives the smoking tide.
     At once they gratify their scent and taste,
     And frequent cups prolong the rich repast.
     Straight hover round the fair her airy band;
     some, as she sipped, the fuming liquor fanned,
115   Some o'er her lap their careful plumes displayed,
     Trembling, and conscious of the rich brocade.
     Coffee (which makes the politician wise,
     And see through all things with his half-shut eyes)
     Sent up in vapors to the baron's brain
120   New stratagems, the radiant lock to gain.
     Ah cease, rash youth! desist ere 'tis too late,
     Fear the just gods, and think of Scylla's fate![21]
     Changed to a bird, and sent to flit in air,
     She dearly pays for Nisus' injured hair!
125   But when to mischief mortals bend their will,
     How soon they find fit instruments of ill!
     Just then, Clarissa drew with tempting grace
     A two-edged weapon from her shining case:
     So ladies in romance assist their knight,
130   Present the spear, and arm him for the fight.
     He takes the gift with reverence, and extends
     The little engine[22] on his fingers' ends;
     This just behind Belinda's neck he spread,
     As o'er the fragrant steams she bends her head.
135   Swift to the lock a thousand sprites repair,
     A thousand wings, by turns, blow back the hair;

Reading Check

What is the baron plotting to do?

---

18. The berries . . . round Coffee beans are ground in a hand mill at the table.
19. altars of Japan small imported lacquer tables.
20. China's earth earthenware cups imported from China.
21. Scylla's (sil´ əz) **fate** Scylla, the daughter of King Nisus, was turned into a sea bird because she cut off the lock of her father's hair on which his safety depended and sent it to his enemy.
22. engine instrument.

The Rape of the Lock, 1895–96, Aubrey Beardsley

◢ Critical Viewing

Where in the poem does Pope make a trivial occasion seem important, as the artist does here? Explain. **[Connect]**

And thrice they twitched the diamond in her ear;
Thrice she looked back, and thrice the foe drew near.
Just in that instant, anxious Ariel sought
140 The close recesses of the virgin's thought;
As on the nosegay in her breast reclined,
He watched th' ideas rising in her mind,
Sudden he viewed, in spite of all her art,
An earthly lover lurking at her heart.[23]
145 Amazed, confused, he found his power expired,
Resigned to fate, and with a sigh retired.
    The peer now spreads the glittering forfex[24] wide,
T' enclose the lock; now joins it, to divide.
Even then, before the fatal engine closed,
150 A wretched sylph too fondly interposed;
Fate urged the shears, and cut the sylph in twain,
(But airy substance soon unites again).
The meeting points the sacred hair dissever
From the fair head, forever, and forever!
155   Then flashed the living lightning from her eyes,
And screams of horror rend th' affrighted skies.
Not louder shrieks to pitying heaven are cast,
When husbands, or when lap dogs breathe their last;
Or when rich China vessels fallen from high,
160 In glittering dust, and painted fragments lie!
    "Let wreaths of triumph now my temples twine,"
The victor cried, "the glorious prize is mine!"
While fish in streams, or birds delight in air,
Or in a coach and six the British Fair,
165 As long as *Atalantis*[25] shall be read
Or the small pillow grace a lady's bed,
While visits shall be paid on solemn days,
When numerous wax lights in bright order blaze,
While nymphs take treats, or assignations give,
170 So long my honor, name, and praise shall live!
What time would spare, from steel receives its date,[26]
And monuments, like men, submit to fate!
Steel could the labor of the gods destroy,
And strike to dust th' imperial towers of Troy;
175 Steel could the works of mortal pride confound,
And hew triumphal arches to the ground.
What wonder then, fair nymph! thy hairs should feel,
The conquering force of unresisted steel?

---

23. earthly lover . . . heart If in her heart Belinda wants the baron to succeed, they cannot
    protect her.
24. forfex scissors.
25. *Atalantis* popular book of scandalous gossip.
26. receives its date is destroyed.

Reading Strategy
Analyzing Author's Purpose Why does the author describe the scene in lines 145–160 in such an elevated manner?

Literary Analysis
Parody How is Belinda's reaction to the loss of her hair appropriate for a mock epic?

Vocabulary
assignations
(as´ ig nā´ shənz) *n.* appointments to meet

Reading
Check

What happens to the sylph that flies between the blades of the shears?

from Canto V

LITERATURE IN CONTEXT

Fashions of the Times

Pope's focus on Belinda's hair indicates the importance that women's hairstyles played in the upper-class obsession with fashion at this time. During the eighteenth century, the world's first fashion magazine was launched by the French, suggesting that nation's leadership in setting styles. Leonard, hairdresser to the French queen Marie Antoinette (1755–1793), whose picture appears below, established a fashion in which women's hairdos rose as high as four feet. These "hair statues" were augmented with horsehair pads and decorated with gauze and feathers. English hairdressers quickly took up the challenge, decorating women's heads with horse-drawn carriages, zoos of miniature lions and tigers, and, if accounts can be believed, a lit stove complete with pots and pans!

Connect to the Literature

Explain how Belinda and other women of her class might reflect their status in their hairstyles.

In Canto IV, after Umbriel, "a dusky, melancholy sprite," empties a bag filled with "the force of female lungs, sighs, sobs, and passions, and the war of tongues" onto Belinda's head, the lady erupts over the loss of her lock. Then she "bids her beau," Sir Plume, to "demand the precious hairs," but Plume is unable to persuade the baron to return the hair.

In the beginning of Canto V, Clarissa, a level-headed nymph, tries to bring an end to the commotion, but rather than being greeted with applause, her speech is followed by a battle cry.

"To arms, to arms!" the fierce virago[27] cries,
And swift as lightning to the combat flies.
All side in parties, and begin th' attack;
Fans clap, silks rustle, and tough whalebones crack;
5   Heroes' and heroines' shouts confusedly rise,
And bass and treble voices strike the skies.
No common weapons in their hands are found,
Like gods they fight, nor dread a mortal wound.
    So when bold Homer makes the gods engage,
10   And heavenly breasts with human passions rage;
'Gainst Pallas, Mars, Latona, Hermes[28] arms;
And all Olympus[29] rings with loud alarms:
Jove's[30] thunder roars, heaven trembles all around,
Blue Neptune[31] storms, the bellowing deeps resound;
15   Earth shakes her nodding towers, the ground gives way,
And the pale ghosts start at the flash of day!
    Triumphant Umbriel on a sconce's height[32]
Clapped his glad wings, and sat to view the fight;
Propped on their bodkin spears,[33] the sprites survey
20   The growing combat, or assist the fray.
    While through the press enraged Thalestris[34] flies,
And scatters death around from both her eyes,
A beau and witling[35] perished in the throng,
One died in metaphor, and one in song.
25   "O cruel nymph! a living death I bear,"
Cried Dapperwit, and sunk beside his chair.

---

27. **virago** (vi rā′ gō) scolding woman.
28. **Pallas . . . Hermes** gods who directed the Trojan War. Pallas and Hermes supported the Greeks, while Mars and Latona sided with the Trojans.
29. **Olympus** mountain which was supposed to be the home of the Greek gods.
30. **Jove's** referring to Jupiter, the ruler of the Gods in Roman mythology: identified with Zeus in Greek mythology.
31. **Neptune** Roman god of the sea; identified with Poseidon in Greek mythology.
32. **sconce's height** candleholder attached to the wall.
33. **bodkin spears** large needles.
34. **Thalestris** (thə lēs′ tris) an Amazon (a race of female warriors supposed to have lived in Scythia) who played a role in the medieval tales of Alexander the Great.
35. **witling** person who fancies himself or herself a wit.

◀ **Critical Viewing** In what ways is the elaborate decorative style of the drawing similar to the language of the poem? **[Connect]**

The Battle of the Beaux and Belles Aubrey Beardsley

A mournful glance Sir Fopling[36] upwards cast,
"Those eyes are made so killing"—was his last.
Thus on Maeander's[37] flowery margin lies
30   Th' expiring swan, and as he sings he dies.
     When bold Sir Plume had drawn Clarissa down,
Chloe[38] stepped in, and killed him with a frown;
She smiled to see the doughty hero slain,
But, at her smile, the beau revived again.

Reading
Check

What "weapons" do the combatants use?

---

36. Dapperwit . . . Sir Fopling names of amusing characters in comedies of the time.
37. Maeander's referring to a river in Asia.
38. Chloe (klō´ ē) heroine of the ancient Greek pastoral romance, *Daphnis and Chloe*.

Spiral Review
Couplet
Does Pope's use of
the couplet differ from
Chaucer's use? Explain.

35   Now Jove suspends his golden scales in air,
      Weighs the men's wits against the lady's hair;
      The doubtful beam long nods from side to side;
      At length the wits mount up, the hairs subside.
         See, fierce Belinda on the baron flies,
40   With more than usual lightning in her eyes;
      Nor feared the chief th' unequal fight to try,
      Who sought no more than on his foe to die.
      But this bold lord with manly strength endued,
      She with one finger and a thumb subdued:
45   Just where the breath of life his nostrils drew,
      A charge of snuff the wily virgin threw;
      The gnomes direct, to every atom just,
      The pungent grains of titillating dust.
      Sudden with starting tears each eye o'erflows,
50   And the high dome re-echoes to his nose.
         "Now meet thy fate," incensed Belinda cried,
      And drew a deadly bodkin[39] from her side . . .
         "Boast not my fall," he cried, "insulting foe!
      Thou by some other shalt be laid as low.
55   Nor think, to die dejects my lofty mind;
      All that I dread is leaving you behind!
      Rather than so, ah let me still survive,
      And burn in Cupid's flames—but burn alive."
         "Restore the lock!" she cries; and all around
60   "Restore the lock!" the vaulted roofs rebound.
      Not fierce Othello in so loud a strain
      Roared for the handkerchief that caused his pain.[40]
      But see how oft ambitious aims are crossed,
      And chiefs contend till all the prize is lost!
65   The lock, obtained with guilt, and kept with pain,
      In every place is sought, but sought in vain.
      With such a prize no mortal must be blessed,
      So Heaven decrees! with Heaven who can contest?
         Some thought it mounted to the lunar sphere,
70   Since all things lost on earth are treasured there.
      There heroes' wits are kept in ponderous vases,
      And beaux' in snuffboxes and tweezer cases.
      There broken vows and deathbed alms are found,
      And lovers' hearts with ends of riband bound . . .
75   But trust the Muse—she saw it upward rise,
      Though marked by none but quick, poetic eyes . . .

Literary Analysis
Parody
How are Belinda's words
and actions in lines 51–52
appropriate for a mock epic?

---

39. bodkin ornamental pin shaped like a dagger.
40. Not . . . pain In Shakespeare's *Othello*, the hero is convinced that his wife is being unfaithful to him when she cannot find the handkerchief that he had given her. Actually, the handkerchief had been taken by the villain, Iago, who uses it as part of his evil plot.

A sudden star, it shot through liquid[41] air
And drew behind a radiant trail of hair . . .[42]
    Then cease, bright Nymph! to mourn thy ravished hair,
80 Which adds new glory to the shining sphere!
Not all the tresses that fair head can boast,
Shall draw such envy as the lock you lost.
For, after all the murders of your eye,[43]
When, after millions slain, yourself shall die;
85 When those fair suns shall set, as set they must,
And all those tresses shall be laid in dust,
This lock, the Muse shall consecrate to fame,
And midst the stars inscribe Belinda's name.

---

41. liquid clear.
42. trail of hair The word *comet* comes from a Greek word meaning "long-haired."
43. murders . . . eye lovers struck down by her glances.

> Not all the tresses that
> fair head can boast,
> Shall draw such envy
> as the lock you lost.

Critical Reading

Cite textual evidence to support your responses.

1. **Key Ideas and Details (a)** What happens during the game of cards? **(b) Infer:** What does the way they play reveal about Belinda and the baron?

2. **Key Ideas and Details (a)** What does Clarissa help the baron do to Belinda, and what struggle results from it? **(b) Compare and Contrast:** Compare and contrast the card game with the final conflict in the poem. **(c) Synthesize:** What is really at stake in all of the poem's conflicts?

3. **Key Ideas and Details (a)** What happens to the lock of hair in lines 79–88 of Canto V? **(b) Analyze:** In what way is the claim that Pope makes in these lines ridiculous? In what way is it true? Explain.

4. **Integration of Knowledge and Ideas (a) Interpret:** What do you think is Pope's basic criticism of the rituals he describes in the poem? Explain. **(b) Support:** Which passage or passages indicate that Pope has some positive feelings about the rituals he criticizes? Explain.

5. **Integration of Knowledge and Ideas** Pope based this poem on an actual incident. What contemporary incident might inspire a mock epic? Explain.

6. **Integration of Knowledge and Ideas** Are elaborate social rituals, like the ones Pope mocks, always ridiculous? Why or why not?

7. **Integration of Knowledge and Ideas** Was Pope's main goal to change the behavior he mocked or to entertain readers? In your response, use at least two of the following Essential Question words: *exaggerate, reform, charm, preserve.* *[Connecting to the Essential Question: How does literature shape or reflect society?]*

Literary Analysis

1. Craft and Structure Use a chart like the one shown to identify epic elements and the trivial activities to which they apply in *The Rape of the Lock*, Pope's **mock epic.**

Epic Element	Lines in Poem	Activity
Hero's boasts		
Gods and goddesses		
Description of warriors		

2. Craft and Structure **(a)** Why are lines 8–16 in Canto V an **epic simile? (b)** How does this simile add to the absurdity of the action Pope is describing?

3. Craft and Structure Which of the epic elements Pope uses adds most to his criticism of upper-class courtship rituals? Explain.

4. Key Ideas and Details Referring to a specific passage, show that Pope's criticism of upper-class rituals is affectionate rather than stern.

5. Integration of Knowledge and Ideas Classical epics frequently feature gods and goddesses who intervene in human affairs. What qualities of Pope's sprites distinguish them from the gods and goddesses of a classical epic?

6. Craft and Structure Explain how line 12 of *An Essay on Man* and Canto III, lines 13–14, of *The Rape of the Lock* are examples of **antithesis.**

7. Craft and Structure In what way does antithesis help Pope describe the human condition in *An Essay on Man* and mock upper-class pretensions in *The Rape of the Lock*?

8. Integration of Knowledge and Ideas Is antithesis a device that is equally essential in both poems? Why or why not?

Reading Strategy

9. Analyze Pope's purpose to show how, in Canto III, lines 105–120, Pope's intention is both to make fun of a social ritual and to entertain readers.

10. (a) How does knowing Pope's purpose help you determine the meaning of his comparison of a card game with a serious battle (Canto III, lines 75–86)? **(b)** How might your interpretation of the meaning change if you did not realize Pope's purpose? Explain.

Common Core State Standards

Reading Literature
9. Demonstrate knowledge of eighteenth-, nineteenth- and early-twentieth-century foundational works of American literature, including how two or more texts from the same period treat similar themes or topics. (p. 645)

Reading Informational Text
9. Analyze seventeenth-, eighteenth-, and nineteenth-century foundational U.S. documents of historical and literary significance for their themes, purposes, and rhetorical features. (p. 645)

Writing
4. Produce clear and coherent writing in which the development, organization, and style are appropriate to task, purpose, and audience. (p. 645)

Language
4.a. Use context as a clue to the meaning of a word or phrase. (p. 645)

Integrated Language Skills

ⓒ Vocabulary Acquisition and Use

Words from Political Science

Many English words concerning social or political matters have Latin origins. *Plebeian*, meaning "ordinary or common," comes from the Latin word *plebs* meaning, "the common people." Use your background knowledge and context clues to determine the meanings of the italicized words below, and explain those meanings. Consult a dictionary to confirm the definitions and trace the words' Latin origins.

1. In some cultures, property is inherited along *maternal* lines.
2. The United States is not a direct democracy but a *republic*.
3. People need the *society* of others.
4. *Officials* should act in the public interest.
5. A principle of the American legal system is "equal *justice* under the law."

Vocabulary: Synonyms

A **synonym** is a word that has the same meaning as another word. Replace each italicized word in the following sentences with its synonym from the vocabulary list on page 628.

1. "Your underhanded actions *rid* me of any illusions about you," she said.
2. She delivered the message *slyly* so that anyone overhearing their conversation would not understand it.
3. The shabby clothes showed how *poor* the once-rich prince had become.
4. The secretive pair often had *trysts*.
5. The manager's *unemotional* manner never changed whether the team won or lost.
6. She pretended to be sophisticated, but she spoke in a *common* manner.

Writing

ⓒ **Explanatory Text** The Enlightenment was an eighteenth-century cultural movement favoring reason and balance. To appreciate the wide influence of the Enlightenment, find and read two American works from the period: the Declaration of Independence and Phillis Wheatley's "To His Excellency, General Washington." Compare them to Pope's "Essay on Man."

Prewriting Note details in the Declaration and in Pope's poem that reflect ideas about human nature. Note details about the language, imagery, tone, and rhyme scheme in Pope's and Wheatley's poems.

> **Model: Revising for Parallelism**
> Pope's rhyming couplets emphasize his witty contrasts; Wheately's [are different because they] reinforce her stately voice.

By phrasing contrasting thoughts in grammatically parallel clauses, the writer adds force and clarity.

Drafting In your introduction, briefly summarize Pope's ideas about humanity and describe his poetic style. Then, compare his ideas of human nature to those in the Declaration. Next, compare his style to Wheatley's. Finally, draw a conclusion about Enlightenment values based on your comparisons. (You can learn more about the Enlightenment on page 646.)

Revising Make your comparisons clear by using parallelism, stating similar ideas in similar grammatical form.

Connecting to the Essential Question Samuel Johnson wrote the first true English dictionary. As you read, note passages in which each author sees himself as an innovator to answer the Essential Question: **What is the relationship of the writer to tradition?**

Literary Analysis

A **dictionary** defines words and may provide information about their pronunciation, history, and usage. Samuel Johnson compiled the first standard dictionary of the English language. As you read the excerpt from it, look for features he initiated that are still in use today.

A **biography** is an account of someone's life written by another person. Just as Johnson's *Dictionary* was a landmark, so was Boswell's *Life of Samuel Johnson.* In reading it, note how Boswell uses many details from his own personal knowledge to portray Johnson's character.

Comparing Literary Works Both these selections reveal the *philosophical assumptions and beliefs* of the Enlightenment. This eighteenth-century intellectual movement stressed the following values:

- the importance of regularizing and preserving knowledge
- a perception of reason and judgment as the highest human abilities
- the belief that great authors were authorities on language and life
- elevated **diction,** or word choice, revealing a respect for learning

To comprehend elevated diction, look up unfamiliar words, checking connotations, or emotional associations, as well as literal meanings. As you read, also draw inferences about how Enlightenment beliefs influenced each author.

Reading Strategy

© **Preparing to Read Complex Texts** By **analyzing the author's purpose,** or goal, you will better understand a work's *meaning.* For example, knowing that Boswell's purpose was to record the life of an exemplary man, you will realize why he includes detailed stories about Johnson. Over the course of the text, the complex set of ideas develops into a complete picture of the man. Use a graphic organizer to record the author's purpose and how it affects meaning.

Vocabulary

caprices (kə prēs′ iz) *n.* whims (p. 649)

adulterations (ə dul′ tər ā′ shənz) *n.* impurities; added ingredients that are improper or inferior (p. 649)

risible (riz′ ə bəl) *adj.* prompting laughter (p. 650)

abasement (ə bās′ mənt) *n.* condition of being humbled (p. 656)

credulity (krə dōō′ lə tē) *n.* tendency to believe too readily (p. 659)

malignity (mə lig′ nə tē) *n.* strong desire to harm others (p. 659)

© **Common Core State Standards**

Reading Informational Text

3. Analyze a complex set of ideas or sequence of events and explain how specific individuals, ideas, or events interact and develop over the course of a text.

4. Determine the meaning of words and phrases as they are used in a text, including figurative, connotative, and technical meanings.

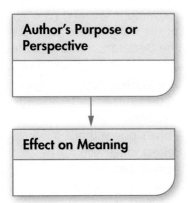

Author's Purpose or Perspective

Effect on Meaning

www.PHLitOnline.com

Samuel Johnson

(1709–1784)

Author of *A Dictionary of the English Language*

With his fine mind and dazzling conversation, Samuel Johnson was at the center of a circle that included most of Britain's leading artists and intellectuals. So great was his influence on English literature that the second half of the eighteenth century is often called the Age of Johnson.

A Life of Hardship Samuel Johnson overcame severe physical and economic hardships. The son of a bookseller in Lichfield, England, he suffered a series of childhood illnesses that left him weak and disfigured. Bright enough to read Shakespeare as a young boy, he was too poor to attend the schools of the aristocracy and pursued his education largely by reading books in his father's shop. Although he was able to enter Oxford in 1728, lack of funds forced him to leave early.

A Great Work In 1737, Johnson moved to London to try to earn his living as a writer; in 1746, he began work on his *Dictionary of the English Language*. This landmark effort took nine years to complete—difficult years during which his wife died and he continued to be dogged by poverty. When at last the *Dictionary* was published, however, it ensured Johnson's place in literary history. Still, it was not until 1762, when he received a pension from the king, that he did not have to rely on writing for a living. In 1775, he received an honorary degree from Oxford, the school he had been forced to leave.

"When a man is tired of London, he is tired of life; for there is in London all that life can afford."

from

A Dictionary of the English Language

Samuel Johnson

BACKGROUND Eighteenth-century thinkers sensed that their era had made great advances in knowledge, and they set down in writing the scientific, philosophical, and historic facts and ideas that were part of this new understanding. Among the intellectual pioneers of this period were Samuel Johnson and James Boswell, whose dictionary and biography, respectively, set the standard for nonfiction works of their type. The eighteenth century also saw the birth of the first *Encyclopaedia Britannica* (1768–1771) as well as Adam Smith's *Wealth of Nations* (1776), which revolutionized the study of economics. As you read the following selections, notice how just as Johnson captures in his dictionary the changing English language, Boswell captures in his biography the changeable personality of Johnson.

from The Preface

It is the fate of those who toil at the lower employments of life, to be rather driven by the fear of evil, than attracted by the prospect of good; to be exposed to censure, without hope of praise; to be disgraced by miscarriage, or punished for neglect, where success would have been without applause, and diligence without reward.

Among these unhappy mortals is the writer of dictionaries; whom mankind have considered, not as the pupil, but the slave of science, the pioneer of literature, doomed only to remove rubbish and clear obstructions from the paths through which learning and genius press forward to conquest and glory, without bestowing a smile on the humble drudge that facilitates their progress. Every other author may aspire to praise; the lexicographer can only hope to escape reproach, and even this negative recompense has been yet granted to very few.

I have, notwithstanding this discourage-ment, attempted a dictionary of the English language, which, while it was employed in the cultivation of every species of literature, has itself been hitherto neglected; suffered to spread under the direction of chance, into wild exuberance; resigned to the tyranny of time and fashion: and exposed to the corruptions of ignorance and caprices of innovation.

When I took the first survey of my undertaking, I found our speech copious without order and energetic without rule: wherever I turned my view, there was perplexity to be disentangled and confu-sion to be regulated; choice was to be made out of boundless variety, without any established principle of selection; adulterations were to be detected, without a settled test of purity; and modes of expression to be rejected or received, without the suffrages of any writers of classical reputation or acknowledged authority.

Having therefore no assistance but from general grammar, I applied myself to the perusal of our writers; and noting whatever might be of use to ascertain or illustrate any word or phrase, accumulated in time the materials of a dictionary, which, by degrees, I reduced to method, establishing to myself, in the progress of the work, such rules as experience and analogy suggested to me; experience, which practice and observation were continually increasing; and analogy, which, though in some other words obscure, was evident in others. . . .

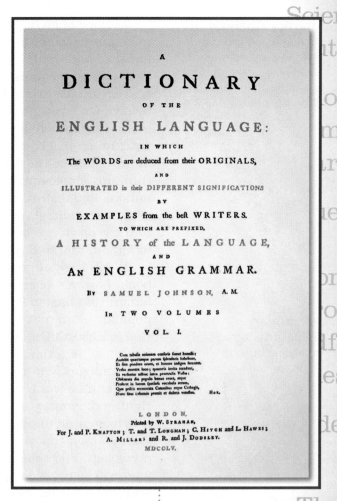

A

DICTIONARY

OF THE

ENGLISH LANGUAGE:

IN WHICH

The WORDS are deduced from their ORIGINALS,

AND

ILLUSTRATED in their DIFFERENT SIGNIFICATIONS

BY

EXAMPLES from the best WRITERS.

TO WHICH ARE PREFIXED,

A HISTORY of the LANGUAGE,

AND

AN ENGLISH GRAMMAR.

BY SAMUEL JOHNSON, A. M.

IN TWO VOLUMES

VOL. I.

LONDON.
Printed by W. STRAHAN,
For J. and P. KNAPTON; T. and T. LONGMAN; C. HITCH and L. HAWES;
A. MILLAR; and R. and J. DODSLEY.
MDCCLV.

▲ **Critical Viewing**
What does this title page of Johnson's *Dictionary* tell you about the contents? **[Infer]**

Vocabulary
caprices (kə prēs´ iz)
n. whims

adulterations (ə dul´ tər ā´ shənz) *n.* impurities; added ingredients that are improper or inferior

Reading Check
In what condition did Johnson find the English language when he began work?

'd,

id;

olish.

when it is cold,

of the churn

of milk.

rubbed

or such like

electricity; but

xperiments of

phical

rned nimbly

uch a quantity

human

to

Literary Analysis

Dictionary What do the first five paragraphs reveal about how Johnson's task differed from that of dictionary makers today?

Vocabulary

risible (riz´ ə bəl) *adj.* prompting laughter

In hope of giving longevity to that which its own nature forbids to be immortal, I have devoted this book, the labor of years, to the honor of my country, that we may no longer yield the palm of philology, without a contest to the nations of the continent. The chief glory of every people arises from its authors. Whether I shall add anything by my own writings to the reputation of English literature, must be left to time. Much of my life has been lost under the pressures of disease; much has been trifled away; and much has always been spent in provision for the day that was passing over me; but I shall not think my employment useless or ignoble, if by my assistance foreign nations and distant ages gain access to the propagators[1] of knowledge, and understand the teachers of truth; if my labors afford light to the repositories of science, and add celebrity to Bacon, to Hooker, to Milton, and to Boyle.[2]

When I am animated by this wish, I look with pleasure on my book, however defective, and deliver it to the world with the spirit of a man that has endeavored well. That it will immediately become popular, I have not promised to myself. A few wild blunders, and **risible** absurdities, from which no work of such multiplicity was ever free, may for a time furnish folly with laughter, and harden ignorance into contempt; but useful diligence will at last prevail, and there never can be wanting some who distinguish desert; who will consider that no dictionary of a living tongue ever can be perfect, since, while it is hastening to publication, some words are budding, and some falling away; that a whole life cannot be spent upon syntax and etymology, and that even a whole life would not be sufficient; that he, whose design includes whatever language can express, must often speak of what he does not understand; that a writer will sometimes be hurried by eagerness to the end, and sometimes faint with weariness under a task which Scaliger[3] compares to the labors of the anvil and the mine; that what is obvious is not always known, and what is known is not always present; that sudden fits of inadvertency will surprise vigilance, slight avocations[4] will seduce attention, and casual eclipses of the mind will darken learning; and that the writer shall often in vain trace his memory at the moment of need, for that which yesterday he knew with intuitive readiness, and which will come uncalled into his thoughts tomorrow.

In this work, when it shall be found that much is omitted, let it not be forgotten that much likewise is performed; and though no book was ever spared out of tenderness to the author, and the world is little solicitous to know whence proceed the faults of that which it condemns; yet it may gratify curiosity to inform it, that the *English Dictionary* was written with little assistance of the learned, and

---

1. **propagators** (präp´ ə gāt´ ərz) *n.* those who cause something to happen or to spread.
2. **Bacon . . . Boyle** writers quoted by Johnson in the *Dictionary*.
3. **Scaliger** Joseph Justus Scaliger (1540–1609), a scholar who suggested that criminals should be condemned to writing dictionaries.
4. **avocations** things that call one away or distract one from something.

without any patronage of the great; not in the soft obscurities of retirement, or under the shelter of academic bowers, but amidst inconvenience and distraction, in sickness and in sorrow. It may repress the triumph of malignant criticism to observe that if our language is not here fully displayed, I have only failed in an attempt which no human powers have hitherto completed. If the lexicons of ancient tongues, now immutably fixed and comprised in a few volumes, be yet, after the toil of successive ages, inadequate and delusive; if the aggregated knowledge and cooperating diligence of the Italian academicians did not secure them from the censure of Beni;[5] if the embodied critics of France, when fifty years had been spent upon their work, were obliged to change its economy[6] and give their second edition another form, I may surely be contented without the praise of perfection, which, if I could obtain, in this gloom of solitude, what would it avail me? I have protracted my work till most of those whom I wished to please have sunk into the grave,[7] and success and miscarriage are empty sounds: I therefore dismiss it with frigid tranquility, having little to fear or hope from censure or from praise.

Selected Entries from A Dictionary

athleʹtick. Strong of body; vigorous; lusty; robust.
   Science distinguishes a man of honor from one of those *athletick* brutes, whom undeservedly we call heroes. Dryden.

bang. A blow; a thump; a stroke: a low word.
   I am a bachelor. That's to say, they are fools that marry; you'll bear me a *bang* for that. Shakespeare, *Julius Caesar*.

to baʹrbecue. A term used in the West Indies for dressing a hog whole; which, being split to the backbone, is laid flat upon a large gridiron, raised about two foot above a charcoal fire, with which it is surrounded.
   Oldfield, with more than harpy throat enduʹd,
   Cries, send me, gods, a whole hog *barbecuʹd*. Pope.

buʹffleheaded. A man with a large head, like a buffalo; dull; stupid; foolish.

cream. The unctuous or oily part of milk, which, when it is cold, floats on the top, and is changed by the agitation of the churn into butter; the flower of milk.

electriʹcity. A property in some bodies, whereby, when rubbed so as to grow warm, they draw little bits of paper, or such like substances, to them. Quincy.

---

5. **Beni** Paolo Beni severely criticized the first Italian dictionary.
6. **economy** organization.
7. **sunk . . . grave** Johnson's wife had died three years earlier.

Reading Strategy
Analyzing the Author's Purpose What information in the last two paragraphs helps you determine Samuel Johnson's purpose for writing his *Dictionary*?

Reading Check

Why, according to Johnson, can "no dictionary of a living tongue ever . . . be perfect"?

A Page from Johnson's Dictionary

Such was the account given a few years ago of electricity; but the industry of the present age, first excited by the experiments of Gray, has discovered in electricity a multitude of philosophical wonders. Bodies electrified by a sphere of glass, turned nimbly round, not only emit flame, but may be fitted with such a quantity of the electrical vapor as, if discharged at once upon a human body, would endanger life. The force of this vapor has hitherto appeared instantaneous, persons at both ends of a long chain seeming to be struck at once. The philosophers are now endeavoring to intercept the strokes of lightning.

to fu´rnace. To throw out as sparks from a furnace. A bad word.
> He *furnaces*
> The thick sighs from him. Shakespeare's
> *Cymbeline.*

gang. A number herding together; a troop; a company;
> a tribe; a herd. It is seldom used but
> in contempt or abhorrence.

ha´tchet-face. An ugly face; such, I suppose, as might be hewn out of a block by a hatchet.
> An ape his own dear image will embrace;
> An ugly beau adores a *hatchet-face.* Dryden.

lifegua´rd. The guard of a king's person.

mo´dern. In Shakespeare, vulgar; mean; common.
> We have our philosophical persons to make *modern*
> and familiar things supernatural and causeless.
> Shakespeare.

pa´tron. One who countenances, supports or protects. Commonly a wretch who supports with insolence, and is paid with flattery.

pi´ckle. Condition; state. A word of contempt and ridicule.
> How cam'st though in this *pickle*? Shakespeare.

plu´mper. Something worn in the mouth to swell out the cheeks.
> She dex'trously her *plumpers* draws, That serve to fill
> her hollow jaws. Swift's *Miscellanies.*

shill-I-shall-I. A corrupt reduplication of *shall I?* The question
> of a man hesitating. To stand *shill-I-shall-I,* is to continue
> hesitating and procrastinating.

Literary Analysis
Dictionary and Style
What effect does Johnson's word choice have on his definition of *patron*?

I am somewhat dainty in making a resolution, because when I make it, I keep it; I don't stand shill-I-shall-I then; if I say't, I'll do't. Congreve's *Way of the World*.

to sneeze. To emit wind audibly by the nose.

wi´llow. A tree worn by forlorn lovers.

to wipe. To cheat; to defraud.
  The next bordering lords commonly encroach one upon another, as one is stronger, or lie still in wait to wipe them out of their lands. Spenser, *On Ireland*.

you´ngster, you´nker. A young person.
  In contempt.

youth. The part of life succeeding to childhood and adolescence; the time from fourteen to twenty-eight.

Critical Reading

Cite textual evidence to support your responses.

1. **Key Ideas and Details (a)** Among what class of workers does Johnson place writers of dictionaries? **(b) Infer:** What does this ranking suggest about his experience in compiling his *Dictionary*?

2. **Key Ideas and Details (a)** What did the English language lack when Johnson undertook his work? **(b) Infer:** What do you think Johnson hoped his *Dictionary* would make available to English speakers and writers?

3. **Key Ideas and Details (a)** What is Johnson's definition of *modern*? **(b) Compare and Contrast:** Compare and contrast Johnson's definition of this word with our definition of it today. Explain what different values each represents. **(c) Draw Conclusions:** What does your comparison indicate about the nature of language?

4. **Integration of Knowledge and Ideas (a) Analyze:** Which definitions are most revealing of Johnson's character and situation? **(b) Draw Conclusions:** What do these definitions reveal about Johnson?

5. **Integration of Knowledge and Ideas (a) Speculate:** Why do you think *electricity* receives such a long definition? **(b) Connect:** In what ways is Johnson similar to the scientists whose work he eagerly discusses in this entry?

6. **Integration of Knowledge and Ideas** What does Johnson's use of quotations suggest about the role of authors in shaping meanings?

7. **Integration of Knowledge and Ideas** Do you find Johnson's definitions more or less useful than those in modern dictionaries? Explain.

James Boswell

(1740–1795)

Author of *The Life of Samuel Johnson*

James Boswell is perhaps the greatest biographer in English letters. In his *Life of Samuel Johnson*, he writes with vigor about his fascinating subject, training his eye on the picturesque and the grotesque.

Celebrity Chaser Born into an aristocratic family in Edinburgh, Scotland, Boswell was educated at several universities. Although he received his degree in law and was admitted to the bar in both Scotland and England, his true passion was literature. His father, a prominent judge, was angered by what he saw as his son's "shallow" values. The extremely sensitive Boswell interpreted this dissatisfaction as rejection. In an effort to overcome his low self-esteem and also find a suitable father figure, he became a celebrity chaser.

In Samuel Johnson, he found not only a friendly celebrity but also the father figure he apparently sought. Deciding to become Johnson's biographer, he devoted many years to compiling detailed records of Johnson's life.

Twentieth-Century Author Boswell's *Life of Samuel Johnson* (1791) was an acclaimed book from its first appearance. Then, in the 1920s, scholars discovered Boswell's private papers, long thought to have been destroyed. In 1950, they began publishing the journals they found among these papers—the first volume was *Boswell's London Journal* (1762–1763)—and the great biographer was reborn as a twentieth-century author!

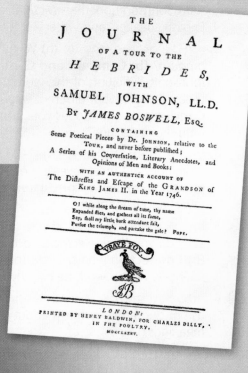

from The Life of Samuel Johnson

James Boswell

Boswell Meets Johnson
1763

This is to me a memorable year; for in it I had the happiness to obtain the acquaintance of that extraordinary man whose memoirs I am now writing; an acquaintance which I shall ever esteem as one of the most fortunate circumstances in my life. Though then but two-and-twenty, I had for several years read his works with delight and instruction, and had the highest reverence for their author, which had grown up in my fancy into a kind of mysterious veneration, by figuring to myself a state of solemn elevated abstraction, in which I supposed him to live in the immense metropolis of London. . . .

Mr. Thomas Davies[1] the actor, who then kept a bookseller's shop in Russel Street, Covent Garden, told me that Johnson was very much his friend, and came frequently to his house, where he more than once invited me to meet him; but by some unlucky accident or other he was prevented from coming to us.

At last, on Monday the 16th day of May, when I was sitting in Mr. Davies's back parlor, after having drunk tea with him and Mrs. Davies, Johnson unexpectedly came into the shop; and Mr. Davies having perceived him through the glass door in the room in which we were sitting, advancing towards us—he announced his aweful[2] approach to me, somewhat in the manner of an actor in the part of Horatio, when he addresses Hamlet on the appearance of his father's ghost, "Look, my Lord, it comes,"[3] I found that I had a very perfect idea of Johnson's figure, from the portrait of him painted by Sir Joshua Reynolds[4] soon after he had published his *Dictionary*, in the attitude of sitting in his easy chair in deep meditation, which was

---

1. **Thomas Davies** English bookseller and unsuccessful actor (1712–1785).
2. **aweful** awe-inspiring.
3. **Horatio ". . . it comes"** from Shakespeare's *Hamlet* (Act I, Scene iv).
4. **Sir Joshua Reynolds** celebrated portrait painter at the time (1723–1792).

> *I had the* **happiness** *to obtain the acquaintance of that extraordinary man . . . which I shall ever esteem as one of the most fortunate circumstances in my life.*

Reading Check

Why is 1763 "a memorable year" for Boswell?

Reading Strategy
Analyzing the Author's Purpose What details in the third paragraph make Boswell's purpose for sharing the story of his first meeting with Johnson clearer?

Vocabulary
abasement (ə bās′ mənt) n. condition of being put down or humbled

the first picture his friend did for him, which Sir Joshua very kindly presented to me, and from which an engraving has been made for this work. Mr. Davies mentioned my name, and respectfully introduced me to him. I was much agitated; and recollecting his prejudice against the Scotch, of which I had heard much, I said to Davies, "Don't tell where I come from." "From Scotland," cried Davies roguishly. "Mr. Johnson," said I, "I do indeed come from Scotland, but I cannot help it." I am willing to flatter myself that I meant this as light pleasantry to soothe and conciliate him, and not as an humiliating abasement at the expense of my country. But however that might be, this speech was somewhat unlucky; for with that quickness of wit for which he was so remarkable, he seized the expression "come from Scotland," which I used in the sense of being of that country; and, as if I had said that I had come away from it, or left, retorted, "That, Sir, I find, is what a very great many of your countrymen cannot help." This stroke stunned me a good deal; and when we had sat down, I felt myself not a little embarrassed, and apprehensive of what might come next. He then addressed himself to Davies: "What do you think of Garrick?[5] He has refused me an order for the play for Miss Williams, because he knows the house will be full, and that an order would be worth three shillings." Eager to take any opening to get into conversation with him, I ventured to say, "O, Sir, I cannot think Mr. Garrick would grudge such a trifle to you." "Sir," said he, with a stern look, "I have known David Garrick longer than you have done: and I know no right you have to talk to me on the subject." Perhaps I deserved this check; for it was rather presumptuous in me, an entire stranger, to express any doubt of the justice of his animadversion upon his old acquaintance and pupil. I now felt myself much mortified, and began to think that the hope which I had long indulged of obtaining his acquaintance was blasted. And, in truth, had not my ardor been uncommonly strong, and my resolution uncommonly persevering, so rough a reception might have deterred me forever from making any further attempts. Fortunately, however, I remained upon the field not wholly discomfited; and was soon rewarded by hearing some of his conversation, of which I preserved the following short minute,[6] without marking the questions and observations by which it was produced.

"People," he remarked, "may be taken in once, who imagine that an author is greater in private life than other men. Uncommon parts require uncommon opportunities for their exertion."

"In barbarous society, superiority of parts is of real consequence. Great strength or great wisdom is of much value to an individual. But in more polished times there are people to do everything for money; and then there are a number of other superiorities, such as those of

---

5. **Garrick** David Garrick (1717–1779), a famous actor who had been educated by Johnson. Garrick was also one of the managing partners of the Drury Lane Theatre in London.
6. **minute** note.

birth and fortune, and rank, that dissipate men's attention, and leave no extraordinary share of respect for personal and intellectual superiority. This is wisely ordered by Providence, to preserve some equality among mankind."

"Sir, this book (*The Elements of Criticism*,[7] which he had taken up) is a pretty essay, and deserves to be held in some estimation, though much of it is chimerical."

Speaking of one[8] who with more than ordinary boldness attacked public measures and the royal family, he said, "I think he is safe from the law, but he is an abusive scoundrel; and instead of applying to my Lord Chief Justice to punish him, I would send half a dozen footmen and have him well ducked."[9]

"The notion of liberty amuses the people of England, and helps to keep off the *taedium vitae*.[10] When a butcher tells you that his heart bleeds for his country, he has, in fact, no uneasy feeling."

"Sheridan[11] will not succeed at Bath with his oratory. Ridicule has gone down before him, and, I doubt,[12] Derrick[13] is his enemy."

"Derrick may do very well, as long as he can outrun his character; but the moment his character gets up with him, it is all over."

It is, however, but just to record, that some years afterwards, when I reminded him of this sarcasm, he said, "Well, but Derrick has now got a character that he need not run away from."

I was highly pleased with the extraordinary vigor of his conversation, and regretted that I was drawn away from it by an engagement at another place. I had, for a part of the evening, been left alone with him, and had ventured to make an observation now and then, which he received very civilly; so that I was satisfied that though there was a roughness in his manner, there was no ill nature in his disposition. Davies followed me to the door, and when I complained to him a little of the hard blows which the great man had given me he kindly took upon him to console me by saying, "Don't be uneasy. I can see he likes you very well."

> *I was highly pleased with the extraordinary vigor of his conversation...*

Reading Check

What quality of Johnson's conversation pleased Boswell?

---

7. **The Elements of Criticism** one of the works of Scottish philosophical writer Henry Home (1696–1782).
8. **one** John Wilkes (1727–1797), an English political agitator.
9. **ducked** tied to a chair at the end of a plank and plunged into water.
10. *taedium vitae* (tē´ dē əm vī´ tē) boredom.
11. **Sheridan** Thomas Sheridan (1719–1788), an Irish actor and author. At the time, Sheridan was reading lectures at the Oratory at Bath.
12. **doubt** fear.
13. **Derrick** the Master of Ceremonies of the Oratory at Bath.

▲ **Critical Viewing**
This engraving shows the ghost of Samuel Johnson haunting Boswell. In what ways does the relationship between the men that it portrays reflect the relationship suggested by Boswell's *Life*? **[Interpret]**

Johnson's Character

The character of Samuel Johnson has, I trust, been so developed in the course of this work, that they who have honored it with a perusal, may be considered as well acquainted with him. As, however, it may be expected that I should collect into one view the capital and distinguishing features of this extraordinary man, I shall endeavor to acquit myself of that part of my biographical undertaking, however difficult it may be to do that which many of my readers will do better for themselves.

His figure was large and well formed, and his countenance of the cast of an ancient statue; yet his appearance was rendered strange and somewhat uncouth by convulsive cramps, by the scars of that distemper[14] which it was once imagined the royal touch could cure,[15] and by a slovenly mode of dress. He had the use only of one eye; yet

---

14. **distemper** scrofula, a type of tuberculosis that causes swelling and scarring of the neck.
15. **royal touch . . . cure** it was at one time believed that the touch of an English monarch had the power to heal. As a child Johnson was taken to Queen Anne to receive her touch in the hope that it would cure him.

so much does mind govern and even supply the deficiency of organs, that his visual perceptions, as far as they extended, were uncommonly quick and accurate. So morbid was his temperament, that he never knew the natural joy of a free and vigorous use of his limbs: when he walked, it was like the struggling gait of one in fetters; when he rode, he had no command or direction of his horse, but was carried as if in a balloon. That with his constitution and habits of life he should have lived seventy-five years, is a proof that an inherent *vivida vis*[16] is a powerful preservative of the human frame.

Man is, in general, made up of contradictory qualities; and these will ever show themselves in strange succession, where a consistency in appearance at least, if not in reality, has not been attained by long habits of philosophical discipline. In proportion to the native vigor of the mind, the contradictory qualities will be the more prominent, and more difficult to be adjusted; and, therefore, we are not to wonder that Johnson exhibited an eminent example of this remark which I have made upon human nature. At different times, he seemed a different man, in some respects; not, however, in any great or essential article, upon which he had fully employed his mind, and settled certain principles of duty, but only in his manners and in the display of argument and fancy in his talk. He was prone to superstition, but not to credulity. Though his imagination might incline him to a belief of the marvelous and the mysterious, his vigorous reason examined the evidence with jealousy.[17] He was a sincere and zealous Christian, of high Church of England and monarchical principles, which he would not tamely suffer to be questioned; and had, perhaps, at an early period, narrowed his mind somewhat too much, both as to religion and politics. His being impressed with the danger of extreme latitude in either, though he was of a very independent spirit, occasioned his appearing somewhat unfavorable to the prevalence of that noble freedom of sentiment which is the best possession of man. Nor can it be denied, that he had many prejudices; which, however, frequently suggested many of his pointed sayings that rather show a playfulness of fancy than any settled malignity. He was steady and inflexible in maintaining the obligations of religion and morality; both from a regard for the order of society, and from a veneration for the Great Source of all order; correct, nay, stern in his taste; hard to please, and easily offended; impetuous and irritable in his temper, but of a most humane and benevolent heart, which showed itself not only in a most liberal charity, as far as his circumstances would allow, but in a thousand instances of active benevolence. He was afflicted with a bodily disease, which made him often restless and fretful; and with a constitutional melancholy, the clouds of which darkened the brightness of his fancy, and gave a gloomy cast to his whole course of thinking: we, therefore, ought not to wonder at his sallies

---

16. *vivida vis* lively force.
17. **jealousy** suspicion.

Vocabulary

credulity (krə dōō′ lə tē) *n.* tendency to believe too readily

malignity (mə līg′ nə tē) *n.* strong desire to harm others

Reading Check

What are some of Johnson's "contradictory qualities"?

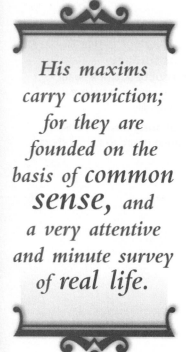

His maxims carry conviction; for they are founded on the basis of common sense, and a very attentive and minute survey of real life.

of impatience and passion at any time; especially when provoked by obtrusive ignorance, or presuming petulance; and allowance must be made for his uttering hasty and satirical sallies even against his best friends. And, surely, when it is considered, that, "amidst sickness and sorrow," he exerted his faculties in so many works for the benefit of mankind, and particularly that he achieved the great and admirable Dictionary of our language, we must be astonished at his resolution. The solemn text, "of him to whom much is given, much will be required," seems to have been ever present to his mind, in a rigorous sense, and to have made him dissatisfied with his labors and acts of goodness, however comparatively great; so that the unavoidable consciousness of his superiority was, in that respect, a cause of disquiet. He suffered so much from this, and from the gloom which perpetually haunted him and made solitude frightful, that it may be said of him, "If in this life only he had hope, he was of all men most miserable."[18] He loved praise, when it was brought to him; but was too proud to seek for it. He was somewhat susceptible of flattery. As he was general and unconfined in his studies, he cannot be considered as master of any one particular science; but he had accumulated a vast and various collection of learning and knowledge, which was so arranged in his mind, as to be ever in readiness to be brought forth. But his superiority over other learned men consisted chiefly in what may be called the art of thinking, the art of using his mind; a certain continual power of seizing the useful substance of all that he knew and exhibiting it in a clear and forcible manner; so that knowledge, which we often see to be no better than lumber[19] in men of dull understanding, was, in him, true, evident, and actual wisdom. His moral precepts are practical; for they are drawn from an intimate acquaintance with human nature. His maxims carry conviction; for they are founded on the basis of common sense, and a very attentive and minute survey of real life. His mind was so full of imagery, that he might have been perpetually a poet; yet it is remarkable, that, however rich his prose is in this respect, his poetical pieces, in general, have not much of that splendor, but are rather distinguished by strong sentiment and acute observation, conveyed in harmonious and energetic verse, particularly in heroic couplets. Though usually grave, and even aweful, in his deportment, he possessed uncommon and peculiar powers of wit and humor; he frequently indulged himself in colloquial pleasantry; and the heartiest merriment was often enjoyed in his company; with this great advantage, that as it was entirely free from any poisonous tincture of vice or impiety, it was salutary to those who shared in it. He had accustomed himself to such accuracy in his common conversation, that he at all times expressed his thoughts with great force, and an elegant choice of language,

---

18. "If . . . miserable" from I Corinthians 15:19.
19. lumber rubbish.

the effect of which was aided by his having a loud voice, and a slow deliberate utterance. In him were united a most logical head with a most fertile imagination, which gave him an extraordinary advantage in arguing: for he could reason close or wide, as he saw best for the moment. Exulting in his intellectual strength and dexterity, he could, when he pleased, be the greatest sophist[20] that ever contended in the lists of declamation; and, from a spirit of contradiction and a delight in showing his powers, he would often maintain the wrong side with equal warmth and ingenuity; so that, when there was an audience, his real opinions could seldom be gathered from his talk; though when he was in company with a single friend, he would discuss a subject with genuine fairness: but he was too conscientious to make error permanent and pernicious[21], by deliberately writing it; and, in all his numerous works, he earnestly inculcated[22] what appeared to him to be the truth; his piety being constant, and the ruling principle of all his conduct.

Such was Samuel Johnson, a man whose talents, acquirements, and virtues, were so extraordinary, that the more his character is considered the more he will be regarded by the present age, and by posterity, with admiration and reverence.

---

20. **sophist** (säf´ ist) *n.* one who makes clever, apparently plausible arguments.
21. **pernicious** (pər nish´ əs) *adj.* wicked; evil.
22. **inculcated** (in kul´ kāt´ əd) *v.* to teach by repetition and urging.

Critical Reading

1. **Key Ideas and Details (a)** How did Boswell meet Johnson? **(b) Infer:** What does their conversation at that meeting tell you about each of them?

2. **Key Ideas and Details (a)** What are some of the topics Johnson discusses that Boswell records "without marking the questions and observations" that produced them? **(b) Infer:** What do Johnson's opinions on these topics suggest about his interests and knowledge?

3. **Key Ideas and Details (a)** Briefly summarize Boswell's remarks on Johnson's character. **(b) Evaluate:** Would Johnson have been less interesting if he had been less "contradictory"? Explain.

4. **Integration of Knowledge and Ideas** Which label, if any, suits each author better, inventor or conservator? Explain. In your response, use at least two of these Essential Question words: *commentary, conventional, authentic. [Connecting to the Essential Question: What is the relationship of the writer to tradition?]*

Cite textual evidence to support your responses.

Literary Analysis

1. Integration of Knowledge and Ideas Use a chart like the one shown to compare the definition of a word in Johnson's *Dictionary* with its definition in a modern **dictionary.**

Johnson's *Dictionary*	Modern Dictionary	Similarities/ Differences

2. Key Ideas and Details (a) Find three examples of facts and three examples of opinions in the **biography** written by Boswell. **(b)** Which is more revealing of Johnson's character, the facts or the opinions? Why?

3. Craft and Structure Find passages from the Preface to the *Dictionary* and from *The Life of Samuel Johnson* that show the formality of the **diction** of the eighteenth-century Enlightenment.

4. Integration of Knowledge and Ideas Citing specific passages, contrast Johnson's mixed *tone* of discouragement and pride in the Preface with Boswell's unmixed tone of admiration in *Life*.

5. Integration of Knowledge and Ideas Referring to specific passages, demonstrate how both works strive to accomplish an Enlightenment goal of bringing order to messy reality.

6. Analyzing Visual Information Using what you know about Johnson and Boswell, explain the humor of the cartoon shown on this page.

Reading Strategy

7. Analyze Johnson's purpose for writing his *Dictionary* by reviewing the Preface. **(a)** Which passage best expresses his purpose? Why? **(b)** Do you think Johnson achieved this purpose? Why or why not? **(c)** Explain how knowing Johnson's purpose helps you understand why he included quotations from famous authors in many definitions.

8. (a) Identify a passage revealing Boswell's purpose for writing. **(b)** How does his purpose explain the space he devotes to his meeting with Johnson?

"More port for Dr. Johnson. And more ink for Mr. Boswell." ▶

Common Core State Standards

Reading Informational Text

9. Analyze seventeenth-, eighteenth-, and nineteenth-century foundational U.S. documents of historical and literary significance for their themes, purposes, and rhetorical features. *(p. 663)*

Writing

9.b. Apply *grades 11–12 Reading standards* to literary nonfiction. *(p. 663)*

Language

4.c. Consult general and specialized reference materials, both print and digital, to find the pronunciation of a word or determine or clarify its precise meaning, its part of speech, its etymology, or its standard usage. *(p. 663)*

Integrated Language Skills

Ⓒ Vocabulary Acquisition and Use

Word Analysis: Latin Root -dict-

The Latin root -dict- conveys the idea of something said. In *dictionary*, it refers to the words "said" in a language. The root also appears in the word *dictator*, which means "a ruler whose pronouncements are the final word." Knowing the meaning of the root -dict-, use context clues to infer the meaning of each italicized word listed here. Then, use a dictionary to verify your inferences.

1. During the Napoleonic Wars, Britain sought to *interdict* the flow of goods to France.

2. In the British legal system, a person must be *indicted* before being tried.

3. A Supreme Court judge releases a *dictum* of his or her position after many cases.

4. Dictators issue *edicts*, but in Britain, Parliament makes the laws.

5. In the past, secretaries used shorthand to record messages *dictated* by their bosses.

6. Skilled playwrights control the *diction* of each character to reflect his or her background.

Vocabulary: Cognates

Cognates are words that share a common origin but may have different meanings. For instance, *patron*, one of Johnson's dictionary entries, shares its origin with *paternal* ("fatherly"). Both come from the Latin *pater*, which means "father." Cognates can also occur across languages, like the English word *night* and the German word *nacht*. Study the pairs of words from Johnson's Preface and Boswell's *Life* that follow. Determine whether each pair is a cognate, explaining your reasoning. Then, check the words in a dictionary to see if you were correct.

1. *caprices* ("whims") and *capacity* ("volume")

2. *adulterations* ("impurities") and *adult* ("individual who has reached maturity")

3. *risible* ("laughable") and *ridiculous* ("deserving ridicule")

4. *abasement* ("being put down") and *debase* ("to corrupt")

5. *malignity* ("desire to harm others") and *aligned* ("in line with")

Writing

Ⓒ **Informative Text** James Boswell's *The Life of Samuel Johnson* and Benjamin Franklin's *The Autobiography* are two eighteenth-century classics. Find a copy of Franklin's autobiography (or download it from a Web site, such as the Gutenberg Project, that provides classic works free of charge), and read his account of his first entry into Philadelphia. Then, write an **essay** comparing two "firsts": Boswell's introduction to Dr. Johnson and Franklin's arrival in Philadelphia. Discuss whether Johnson, an Englishman, and Franklin, a colonial American, possess similar traits or share certain values.

Prewriting As you read both texts, take notes about the ways in which each man presents his younger self. Consider the personality traits each displays and the qualities each seems to value, both in himself and others. Review your findings to arrive at a thesis.

> **Model: Revising for Impact**
>
> At his first meeting with Dr. Johnson, young Boswell felt ~~overwhelmed with a sense of awe and a little fearful.~~
> awestruck and intimidated.

Specific language makes an essay stronger.

Drafting Organize your ideas logically, so that your discussion explores the two texts clearly. Support your ideas with quotations from each work.

Revising Review your draft, highlighting any awkward or wordy phrasing. Revise with more concise and precise word choices.

Connecting to the Essential Question Like each of these authors, you might sometimes seek out a special landscape or place when you want to think things over. Noting the qualities of each author's special place as you read will help as you consider the Essential Question: **What is the relationship between literature and place?**

Literary Analysis

Eighteenth-century **Pre-Romantic poetry** shares characteristics of two different styles. Like earlier, Neoclassical poetry, Pre-Romantic poetry is characterized by these features:

- the polished expression of ideas
- the use of balanced phrases and sophisticated vocabulary

At the same time, Pre-Romantic poetry anticipates Romantic literature by introducing these elements:

- a new focus on nature and the life of common folk
- the expression of heightened, sometimes nameless feelings

Look for all these characteristics as you read the following poems.

Comparing Literary Works Like the Romantics who come after them, Gray and Finch express heightened feelings in their poetry. Gray's stroll through a country churchyard lets him discover life's true value. Finch's nighttime walk allows her to feel a deep connection with nature. As you read, compare the emotions these poets experience and analyze two or more themes or central ideas in the poems. Consider how these themes develop and build on one another to produce a deeper meaning.

Reading Strategy

Preparing to Read Complex Texts **Determine the essential message,** or main idea, of a passage in a poem by *paraphrasing* it—identifying its key ideas and restating them in your own words. Use a chart like the one shown to paraphrase passages from these poems as you read.

Vocabulary

penury (pen´ yōō rē) *n.* poverty (p. 669)

circumscribed (sʉr´ kəm skrībd´) *v.* limited; confined (p. 669)

ingenuous (in jen´ yōō əs) *adj.* candid and frank; naive; simple (p. 669)

nocturnal (näk tʉr´ nəl) *adj.* occurring at night (p. 673)

temperate (tem´ pər it) *adj.* mild (p. 674)

venerable (ven´ ər ə bəl) *adj.* commanding respect because of age, character, or rank (p. 674)

Common Core State Standards

Reading Literature
2. Determine two or more themes or central ideas of a text and analyze their development over the course of the text, including how they interact and build on one another to produce a complex account.

Original
"Now fades the glimmering landscape on the sight,…"

Paraphrase
Nightfall is making it difficult to see the landscape.

www.PHLitOnline.com

Thomas Gray
(1716–1771)

Author of "Elegy Written in a Country Churchyard"

The uncertainty of life was something that Thomas Gray understood all too well. The only one of twelve Gray children to survive infancy, he suffered from convulsions as a child. On at least one occasion, his mother was forced to open a vein to relieve the pressure on his brain.

Lavishing affection on her sickly son, Gray's mother saved money from the shop she kept in London and sent him to Eton and Cambridge.

A Quiet Life After making the Grand Tour of Europe with his friend the author Horace Walpole, Gray lived with his mother and aunts in the sleepy village of Stoke Poges. There, in the summer of 1742, he wrote his first important poems. The church and graveyard at Stoke Poges probably inspired his best-known poem, "Elegy Written in a Country Churchyard."

A Near Mishap This beloved poem nearly went astray. Gray sent a copy to Walpole, and it fell into the hands of a dishonest editor. It was retrieved only after a struggle. In the end, the poem came to belong to its readers: It contains some of the best-remembered lines in English poetry.

A Lonely Romantic After age thirty, Gray returned to Cambridge, where he studied classical literature and Celtic and Norse mythology. He died after an attack of gout. His literary output was small—he wrote slowly, striving for perfection—but his poems are counted among the finest in the English language. In them, he expresses new, Romantic yearnings in the formal style of his times. The poet Matthew Arnold suggested that if Gray had lived in another era, his accomplishments might have been even greater.

Elegy Written in a Country Churchyard

THOMAS GRAY

▲ Critical Viewing The churchyard in this photograph looks untended and forgotten. How does the photograph reflect the meaning of Gray's poem? **[Deduce]**

BACKGROUND In the eighteenth century, many writers championed reason, clarity, and logic. These values led to the articulate, eloquent couplets of Alexander Pope. They also led to the major scientific discoveries of Sir Isaac Newton, of whom Pope wrote: "God said, Let Newton be! And there was light!" These values might be thought of as belonging to daylight. In contrast, the poems in this grouping are set at twilight or at night. They stress emotion—the not-always-reasonable reaction to circumstances—and mystery—those longings and intuitions of human experience that are not clearly communicable or analyzable. By stressing these "nighttime" qualities, these poets anticipate the artistic movement called Romanticism.

The curfew tolls the knell of parting day,
    The lowing herd winds slowly o'er the lea,[1]
The plowman homeward plods his weary way,
    And leaves the world to darkness and to me.

5 Now fades the glimmering landscape on the sight,
    And all the air a solemn stillness holds,
Save where the beetle wheels his droning flight,
    And drowsy tinklings lull the distant folds;

Save that from yonder ivy-mantled tower,
10   The moping owl does to the moon complain
Of such as, wandering near her secret bower,
    Molest her ancient solitary reign.

Beneath those rugged elms, that yew tree's shade,
    Where heaves the turf in many a moldering heap,
15 Each in his narrow cell forever laid,
    The rude[2] forefathers of the hamlet sleep.

---

1. **lea** meadow.
2. **rude** uneducated.

> **✓ Reading Check**
> At what time of day is the poem set?

Reading Strategy
Paraphrasing Restate the main ideas in lines 17–20 in your own words.

Literary Analysis
Pre-Romantic Poetry
What images and phrasings in lines 33–36 show formal polish?

The breezy call of incense-breathing morn,
　　The swallow twittering from the straw-built shed,
The cock's shrill clarion, or the echoing horn,[3]
20　　No more shall rouse them from their lowly bed.

For them no more the blazing hearth shall burn,
　　Or busy housewife ply her evening care;
No children run to lisp their sire's return,
　　Or climb his knees the envied kiss to share.

25　Oft did the harvest to their sickle yield,
　　Their furrow oft the stubborn glebe[4] has broke;
How jocund[5] did they drive their team afield!
　　How bowed the woods beneath their sturdy stroke!

Let not Ambition mock their useful toil,
30　　Their homely joys, and destiny obscure;
Nor Grandeur hear with a disdainful smile
　　The short and simple annals of the poor.

The boast of heraldry,[6] the pomp of power,
　　And all that beauty, all that wealth e'er gave,
35　Awaits alike the inevitable hour.
　　The paths of glory lead but to the grave.

Nor you, ye proud, impute to these the fault,
　　If memory o'er their tomb no trophies[7] raise,
Where through the long-drawn aisle and fretted vault[8]
40　　The pealing anthem swells the note of praise.

Can storied urn,[9] or animated[10] bust,
　　Back to its mansion call the fleeting breath?
Can honor's voice provoke[11] the silent dust,
　　Or Flattery soothe the dull cold ear of Death?

45　Perhaps in this neglected spot is laid
　　Some heart once pregnant with celestial fire;
Hands, that the rod of empire might have swayed,
　　Or waked to ecstasy the living lyre.

---

3. clarion . . . horn A clarion is a trumpet. The horn is a hunter's horn.
4. glebe soil.
5. jocund cheerful.
6. heraldry noble descent.
7. trophies symbolic figures or pictures depicting the achievements of the dead man.
8. fretted vault church ceiling decorated with intersecting lines.
9. storied urn funeral urn with an epitaph inscribed on it.
10. animated lifelike.
11. provoke call forth.

But Knowledge to their eyes her ample page
    Rich with the spoils of time did ne'er unroll;
50 Chill **Penury** repressed their noble rage,
    And froze the genial current of the soul.

Full many a gem of purest ray serene
    The dark unfathomed caves of ocean bear:
55 Full many a flower is born to blush unseen,
    And waste its sweetness on the desert air.

Some village Hampden,[12] that, with dauntless breast,
    The little tyrant of his fields withstood,
Some mute inglorious Milton[13] here may rest,
60   Some Cromwell[14] guiltless of his country's blood.

The applause of listening senates to command,
    The threats of pain and ruin to despise,
To scatter plenty o'er a smiling land,
    And read their history in a nation's eyes,

65 Their lot forbade: nor **circumscribed** alone
    Their growing virtues, but their crimes confined
Forbade to wade through slaughter to a throne,
    And shut the gates of mercy on mankind,

The struggling pangs of conscious truth to hide,
70   To quench the blushes of **ingenuous** shame,
Or heap the shrine of Luxury and Pride
    With incense kindled at the Muse's flame.

Far from the madding[15] crowd's ignoble[16] strife,
    Their sober wishes never learned to stray;
75 Along the cool sequestered vale of life
    They kept the noiseless tenor[17] of their way.

Yet even these bones from insult to protect
    Some frail memorial still erected nigh,
With uncouth rhymes and shapeless sculpture decked,[18]
80   Implores the passing tribute of a sigh.

---

12. Hampden John Hampden (1594–1643), an English statesman who defied King Charles I, resisting the king's efforts to circumvent Parliament.
13. Milton English poet, John Milton (1608–1674).
14. Cromwell Oliver Cromwell (1599–1658), English revolutionary leader who defeated King Charles I and ruled England as Lord Protector of the Commonwealth from 1653 to 1658.
15. madding frenzied.
16. ignoble (ig nō´ bəl) *adj.* not noble; common.
17. tenor general tendency or course.
18. Some . . . decked contrasts with "the storied urn[s] or animated bust[s]" (line 41) inside the church.

Vocabulary
penury (pen´ yōō rē)
n. poverty

Literary Analysis
Pre-Romantic Poetry
How do the images in lines 53–56 give the reader a powerful sense of what is unknown or lost?

Vocabulary
circumscribed (sʉr´ kəm skrībd) *v.* limited; confined

ingenuous (in jen´ yōō əs) *adj.* naive; simple

Reading Check
About whom is the speaker speculating?

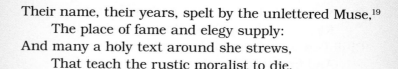

Reading Strategy
Paraphrasing Express the key idea of lines 85–88 in your own words.

Literary Analysis
Pre-Romantic Poetry
What intense, perhaps irrational feelings are expressed in lines 89–92?

Their name, their years, spelt by the unlettered Muse,[19]
    The place of fame and elegy supply:
And many a holy text around she strews,
    That teach the rustic moralist to die.

85 For who, to dumb Forgetfulness a prey,
    This pleasing anxious being e'er resigned,
Left the warm precincts of the cheerful day,
    Nor cast one longing lingering look behind?

On some fond breast the parting soul relies,
90   Some pious drops[20] the closing eye requires;
Even from the tomb the voice of Nature cries,
    Even in our ashes live their wonted fires.

For thee,[21] who, mindful of the unhonored dead,
    Dost in these lines their artless tale relate;
95 If chance, by lonely contemplation led,
    Some kindred spirit shall enquire thy fate,

Haply[22] some hoary-headed swain[23] may say,
    "Oft have we seen him at the peep of dawn
Brushing with hasty steps the dews away,
100   To meet the sun upon the upland lawn.

"There at the foot of yonder nodding beech,
    That wreathes its old fantastic roots so high,
His listless length at noontide would he stretch,
    And pore upon the brook that babbles by.

105 "Hard by yon wood, now smiling as in scorn,
    Muttering his wayward fancies he would rove;
Now drooping, woeful wan, like one forlorn,
    Or crazed with care, or crossed in hopeless love.

"One morn I missed him on the customed hill,
110   Along the heath, and near his favorite tree;
Another came; nor yet beside the rill,[24]
    Nor up the lawn, nor at the wood was he;

---

19. the unlettered Muse In Greek mythology, the Muses were goddesses who inspired artists and writers. *Unlettered* means "uneducated."
20. drops tears.
21. thee Gray himself.
22. Haply perhaps.
23. hoary-headed swain white-haired country laborer.
24. rill brook.

"The next, with dirges due in sad array
        Slow through the churchway path we saw him borne.
115 Approach and read (for thou canst read) the lay
        Graved on the stone beneath yon aged thorn."[25]

The Epitaph

Here rests his head upon the lap of Earth
        A youth, to Fortune and to Fame unknown.
Fair Science[26] frowned not on his humble birth,
120   And melancholy marked him for her own.

Large was his bounty, and his soul sincere,
        Heaven did a recompense as largely send:
He gave to misery (all he had) a tear,
        He gained from Heaven ('twas all he wished) a friend.

125 No farther seek his merits to disclose,
        Or draw his frailties from their dread abode
(There they alike in trembling hope repose),
        The bosom of his Father and his God.

---

25. **thorn** hawthorn tree.
26. **Science** learning.

Critical Reading

1. **Key Ideas and Details** Who are the forefathers to whom the speaker refers in line 16? **(b) Interpret:** In line 35, what is the "inevitable hour" that the rich and ambitious share with their forefathers?

2. **Key Ideas and Details** According to lines 45–48, what types of people might lie among the forefathers? **(b) Infer:** Why did the forefathers not fulfill their potential? **(c) Interpret:** In what way do the images of the gem and the flower in lines 53–56 express the idea of unfulfilled potential?

3. **Key Ideas and Details (a) Summarize:** What mark have the forefathers left on history? **(b) Connect:** According to lines 77–84, how is their memory preserved? **(c) Interpret:** What do lines 85–92 suggest about the need to be remembered after death?

4. **Key Ideas and Details (a) Summarize:** By what standards is the life of the speaker measured in "The Epitaph"? **(b) Draw Conclusions:** What insight into life does the speaker reach?

5. **Integration of Knowledge and Ideas** Do you find the feelings in the poem artificial or moving? Explain.

Cite textual evidence to support your responses.

ANNE FINCH
Countess of Winchilsea (1661–1720)

Author of "A Nocturnal Reverie"

Anne Kingsmill Finch, Countess of Winchilsea, lived in an era that rejected women intellectuals. Even her friend Alexander Pope poked fun at her, satirizing her as the character Phoebe Clinket in the play *Three Hours After Marriage.* Despite this mockery, Finch pursued her interest in poetry, publishing a volume of verse in 1713, during an era when publication by women was rare.

An Uncertain Childhood Anne Kingsmill's father died when she was only five months old, and three years later her mother died as well. For eight years, she and her sister, Bridget, lived with their grandmother, while their brother, William, lived with an uncle. The children were reunited under their uncle's care in 1672. By the standards of the day, the girls' education was quite progressive. Anne studied classical Greek and Roman literature, the Bible, French, Italian, history, poetry, and drama.

A Poet and Countess In 1682, Anne Kingsmill left home to become a maid of honor to the wife of the duke of York, later James II. In the duke's household, she met her husband, Heneage Finch.

When James II was driven from power in 1688, the Finches endured a period of poverty until Heneage Finch inherited the title Earl of Winchilsea and an estate at Eastwell in Kent. Many of Anne Finch's poems celebrate the rural pleasures of Eastwell.

Though she was not the most famous of poets, her work had an impact on later writers. In 1800, Romantic poet William Wordsworth praised her in the Preface to his groundbreaking book, *Lyrical Ballads.*

A Nocturnal Reverie

Anne Finch, Countess of Winchilsea

In such a night, when every louder wind
Is to its distant cavern safe confined;
And only gentle Zephyr[1] fans his wings,
And lonely Philomel,[2] still waking, sings;
5   Or from some tree, famed for the owl's delight,

---

1. Zephyr (zef´ ər) in Greek myth, the west wind; a breeze.
2. Philomel (fil´ ō mel´) in Greek myth, nightingale.

Cottage and Pond, Moonlight, Thomas Gainsborough, Victoria and Albert Museum, London

▲ **Critical Viewing** What visual elements in this picture help create a mood like that of the poem? **[Analyze]**

She, hollowing clear, directs the wanderer right:
In such a night, when passing clouds give place,
Or thinly veil the heavens' mysterious face;
When in some river, overhung with green,

10 The waving moon and trembling leaves are seen;
When freshened grass now bears itself upright,
And makes cool banks to pleasing rest invite,
Whence springs the woodbind, and the bramble-rose,
And where the sleepy cowslip sheltered grows;

15 Whilst now a paler hue the foxglove takes,
Yet checkers still with red the dusky brakes:[3]
When scattered glow-worms, but in twilight fine,
Show trivial beauties watch their hour to shine;
Whilst Salisbury[4] stands the test of every light,

Vocabulary

temperate (tem´ pər it)
adj. mild

venerable (ven´ ər ə bəl)
adj. commanding respect
because of age, character,
or social rank

20 In perfect charms, and perfect virtue bright:
When odors, which declined repelling day,
Through temperate air uninterrupted stray;
When darkened groves their softest shadows wear,
And falling waters we distinctly hear;

25 When through the gloom more venerable shows
Some ancient fabric,[5] awful in repose,
While sunburnt hills their swarthy looks conceal,
And swelling haycocks thicken up the vale:
When the loosed horse now, as his pasture leads,

30 Comes slowly grazing through the adjoining meads,[6]
Whose stealing pace, and lengthened shade we fear,
Till torn-up forage[7] in his teeth we hear:
When nibbling sheep at large pursue their food,
And unmolested kine[8] rechew the cud;

---

3. brakes overgrown areas; thickets.
4. Salisbury This may refer to a Lady Salisbury, daughter of a friend,
not to the town of Salisbury.
5. ancient fabric edifice or large, imposing building.
6. meads archaic term for meadows.
7. forage (fôr ij) *n.* food grazed for by animals.
8. kine archaic plural of cow; cattle.

35 When curlews cry beneath the village walls,
   And to her straggling brood the partridge calls;
   Their shortlived jubilee the creatures keep,
   Which but endures, whilst tyrant man does sleep;
   When a sedate content the spirit feels,
40 And no fierce light disturbs, whilst it reveals;
   But silent musings urge the mind to seek
   Something, too high for syllables to speak;
   Till the free soul to a composedness charmed,
   Finding the elements of rage disarmed,
45 O'er all below a solemn quiet grown,
   Joys in the inferior world, and thinks it like her own:
   In such a night let me abroad remain,
   Till morning breaks, and all's confused again;
   Our cares, our toils, our clamors are renewed,
50 Or pleasures, seldom reached, again pursued.

Critical Reading

1. Key Ideas and Details (a) Describe the setting of the poem, listing specific images from lines 1–24. **(b) Analyze:** What mood do these images create?

Cite textual evidence to support your responses.

2. Key Ideas and Details (a) Analyze: Outline the steps that lead from the speaker's "sedate content" to her joy (lines 39–46). **(b) Interpret:** How does the natural world charm the speaker to "composedness"?

3. Key Ideas and Details (a) Infer: What is the relation between people and their "pleasures" in line 50? **(b) Compare and Contrast:** What is the main difference between the pursuit of pleasures and the "composedness" caused by nature?

4. Integration of Knowledge and Ideas If the speaker were taking a nocturnal walk in modern times, do you think her reactions to nature would be the same? Explain.

5. Integration of Knowledge and Ideas What qualities of a special place help each author to draw conclusions about life? In your response, use at least two of these Essential Question words: *nature, country, isolation.* [Connecting to the Essential Question: What is the relationship between literature and place?]

Literary Analysis

1. Integration of Knowledge and Ideas Explain what is **Pre-Romantic** about Gray's concern for the unknown dead of a country graveyard and Finch's loving attention to humble "creatures." How do these *themes* anticipate Romanticism?

2. Key Ideas and Details (a) What feelings do lines 89–92 of Gray's "Elegy" convey? **(b)** Compare these feelings to the feelings in lines 39–46 of "A Nocturnal Reverie," using a chart like the one shown.

Lines	Stated Ideas	Feelings Expressed	Themes, or Messages, About Life

Common Core State Standards

Writing
2. Write informative/ explanatory texts to examine and convey complex ideas, concepts, and information clearly and accurately through the effective selection, organization, and analysis of content.

Reading Strategy

3. *Paraphrase* to **determine the essential message** in lines 29–32 of Gray's "Elegy" and lines 47–50 of "A Nocturnal Reverie."

PERFORMANCE TASKS
Integrated Language Skills

Vocabulary Acquisition and Use

Use a different vocabulary word from page 664 in place of each familiar underlined word. Explain your choices.

The underlined respected old woman wanted to overcome the underlined poverty in the village. She told young people that underlined nighttime reading could help them escape a underlined limited life. She risked the danger that her underlined mild manner would make her seem underlined naive.

Writing

Explanatory Text The *recitation* of poetry requires attention to *performance details* to convey the *meaning* of a poem in a way that is *forceful and clear.* Choose a brief passage from one of these poems and write **directions** for reciting it:

- Identify which words to emphasize and where to pause.
- Explain when to change volume or pitch.
- Tell how eye contact and appropriate gestures will engage an audience.

Then, follow the directions and have a partner rate your performance.

Focus on Literary Forms:
The Essay

"*A* GOOD ESSAY . . . MUST DRAW ITS CURTAIN ROUND US, BUT IT MUST BE A CURTAIN THAT SHUTS US IN, NOT OUT."

— VIRGINIA WOOLF

Defining the Essay

An **essay** is a short work of nonfiction that explores a specific topic and conveys an author's ideas and opinions. In 1580, the French philosopher Michel de Montaigne published a new form of short prose discussions called *Essais*. Over four hundred years later, Montaigne is still credited with creating the modern essay.

Types of Essays Most essays fall into one of two categories:

- **Formal essays** use a serious tone and dignified language, and often analyze public issues or important events.
- **Informal essays,** also called personal essays, use a more casual tone and explore everyday topics in a relaxed, conversational style.

Modes of Writing Within the two broad categories, essays can be further classified according to the mode of writing used.

- A **narrative essay** tells a true story about real people or events.
- A **persuasive essay,** also called an **argumentative essay,** tries to persuade the reader to accept the writer's opinion or to take a course of action.
- A **descriptive essay,** sometimes called an **observational essay,** uses sensory details to create a portrait of a person, a place, or an object.
- An **expository essay** presents information or discusses an idea.

An essayist often combines different modes of writing. Thus, a persuasive essay might contain narrative examples.

Close Read: Elements of an Essay

These literary elements are called out in the Model text at right.

Author's Purpose: the author's particular reason for writing Example: *Jonathan Swift wrote "A Modest Proposal" to attack British economic and social policies in Ireland.*	**Style:** the author's distinctive way of writing; the overall "sound" of a work Example: *In "The Aims of the Spectator," Joseph Addison uses an elegant style as in the statement "But there will be none to whom this paper will be more useful than to the female world."*
Theme: the main insight into life conveyed by a work Example: *In "Days of Obligation," Richard Rodriguez reflects on what is incomplete or relative in the identity of places and people, using the example of Tijuana.*	**Tone:** the author's attitude toward his or her subject or audience, as expressed in word choice, sentence structure, and so on Example: *In "Shooting an Elephant," George Orwell takes an ironic tone in the sentence "In Moulmein, . . . I was hated by large numbers of people."*

Model

About the Text Besides his novels, short stories (including the Father Brown detective series), literary studies, poems, and works on religion, the British writer G. K. Chesterton (1874–1936) wrote highly regarded essays. This essay is one of his most admired.

from "The Fallacy of Success," in *Selected Essays*
G. K. Chesterton

There has appeared in our time a particular class of books and articles which I sincerely and solemnly think may be called the silliest ever known among men. They are much more wild than the wildest romances of chivalry and much more dull than the dullest religious tract. Moreover, the romances of chivalry were at least about chivalry; the religious tracts are about religion. But these things are about nothing; they are about what is called Success. On every bookstall, in every magazine, you may find works telling people how to succeed. They are books showing men how to succeed in everything; they are written by men who cannot even succeed in writing books. To begin with, of course, there is no such thing as Success. Or, if you like to put it so, there is nothing that is not successful. That a thing is successful merely means that it is; a millionaire is successful in being a millionaire and a donkey in being a donkey. Any live man has succeeded in living; any dead man may have succeeded in committing suicide. But, passing over the bad logic and bad philosophy in the phrase, we may take it, as these writers do, in the ordinary sense of success in obtaining money or worldly position. These writers profess to tell the ordinary man how he may succeed in his trade or speculation—how, if he is a builder, he may succeed as a builder; how, if he is a stockbroker, he may succeed as a stockbroker. They profess to show him how, if he is a grocer, he may become a sporting yachtsman; how, if he is a tenth-rate journalist, he may become a peer; and how, if he is a German Jew, he may become an Anglo-Saxon. This is a definite and business-like proposal, and I really think that the people who buy these books (if any people do buy them) have a moral, if not a legal, right to ask for their money back. Nobody would dare to publish a book about electricity which literally told one nothing about electricity; no one would dare to publish an article on botany which showed that the writer did not know which end of a plant grew in the earth. Yet our modern world is full of books about Success and successful people which literally contain no kind of idea, and scarcely any kind of verbal sense.

It is perfectly obvious that in any decent occupation (such as bricklaying or writing books) there are only two ways (in any special sense) of succeeding. One is by doing very good work, the other is by cheating. Both are much too simple to require any literary explanation. If you are in for the high jump, either jump higher than any one else, or manage somehow to pretend that you have done so.

Theme Chesterton points to his theme at the outset of the essay: The concept of Success is empty—or even evil—and so should not serve as the "value" that some modern people take it to be.

Tone Here, Chesterton delivers a joke, implying that the books are frauds, with breezy efficiency. This passage reflects the overall tone of light satire.

Author's Purpose Chesterton's purpose, or reason for writing, is to mock "how-to" books of his day as well as to entertain his readers. He accomplishes both purposes in passages such as this one.

Style Chesterton's style combines plain, direct diction ("cheating") with a brisk, punchy balance of phrases and clauses. ("One is . . . , the other is. . . .")

Before You Read

The Aims of The Spectator

Connecting to the Essential Question Just as today's bloggers enjoy the Internet, Addison was excited by the new medium of *his* day, the magazine. As you read, notice passages in which Addison expresses what his audience needs from his magazine and how he will meet those needs. These passages will help as you answer the Essential Question: **How does literature shape or reflect society?**

Common Core State Standards

Reading Informational Text

1. Cite strong and thorough textual evidence to support analysis of what the text says explicitly as well as inferences drawn from the text, including determining where the text leaves matters uncertain.

Literary Analysis

An **essay** is a short prose piece that explores a topic as if the author were letting you overhear his or her thoughts. Meaning an "attempt" or a "test," the word *essay* was first applied to writing by the French essayist Michel de Montaigne (1533–1592).

Addison's essay can be seen as a "test," or experiment, to discover connections between experiences and to learn about the self. As you read, notice how the writer links observations and anecdotes to form ideas.

It is no accident that the essay flourished during the eighteenth century. Here are some links between this form and the **historical period:**

- This era saw the development of a rising and well-off middle class.

- Middle-class people wanted to learn more about the world and about themselves. This new class needed a self-definition.

- The essay, often featured in magazines, provided such information, as well as entertainment and moral instruction.

As you read, note how Addison helps readers ask and answer questions such as, *Who am I? What do I need to know and believe?*

Reading Strategy

© **Preparing to Read Complex Texts** To fully appreciate an *author's perspective,* you need to **analyze the author's implicit philosophical assumptions**—unstated beliefs—and **explicit assumptions**—stated beliefs—about a subject. To analyze unstated beliefs, draw inferences and support them with textual evidence. Use a chart like the one shown to find evidence of the *author's perspective.*

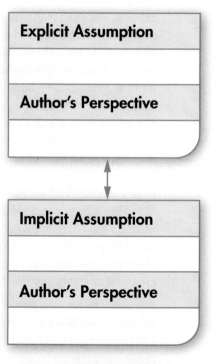

Explicit Assumption
Author's Perspective

Implicit Assumption
Author's Perspective

Vocabulary

transient (tran´ shənt) *adj.* temporary; passing (p. 682)

assiduous (ə sij´ o͞o əs) *adj.* constant in application or attention (p. 682)

affluence (af´ lo͞o əns) *n.* abundant wealth (p. 683)

contentious (kən ten´ shəs) *adj.* quarrelsome (p. 683)

trifles (trī´ fəlz) *n.* things of little value or importance (p. 684)

embellishments (em bel´ ish məntz) *n.* decorative touches; ornamentation (p. 684)

JOSEPH ADDISON
(1672–1719)

Author of "The Aims of *The SPECTATOR*"

Born in a village in Wiltshire, England, Joseph Addison was educated at the Charterhouse School in London, where he became a friend of classmate Richard Steele. Both young men went on to Oxford, but, after their school days, their paths diverged. The impetuous Steele immersed himself in London life, editing an early newspaper and managing the Drury Lane Theatre, while the more cautious Addison pursued prestigious political positions. Their paths, though, were to cross again.

Scholar, Poet, and Bureaucrat A Fellow of Magdalen College, Oxford, Addison was invited by John Dryden to do translations of Virgil. After four years of European study and travel, he produced an epic, *The Campaign*, celebrating a notable English victory. In 1706, Addison was named undersecretary of state and later went on to other important posts.

A Reunion In 1709, the story is told, Addison happened to read an article in *The Tatler*, a new literary magazine that had become all the rage in London coffeehouses. The article was signed "Isaac Bickerstaff," but Addison immediately recognized the style of his old school friend Richard Steele. Addison soon became a contributor to *The Tatler*. When publication of *The Tatler* ended, the two founded another journal, *The Spectator*.

A Lifetime Partnership As a team, Addison and Steele became the most celebrated journalists in England. Their essays in *The Tatler* and *The Spectator* earned them a permanent place in English literature. Almost every magazine you can buy today uses an informal, popular style derived from the one they originated.

> **"** *But there are none to whom this paper will be more useful than to the female world.* **"**

The Spectator, No. 10,
Monday, March 12, 1711

The Aims of
The SPECTATOR

Joseph Addison

Richard Rodriguez
Author's Insight
Addison's point of view is appropriate to a new city of strangers. The writer recommends himself to everyone, addressing none as "you."

Vocabulary
transient (tran´ shənt) *adj.* temporary; passing

assiduous (ə sij´ oo əs) *adj.* constant in application or attention

Literary Analysis
Essay How does Addison make a personal connection with his readers in his opening paragraph?

It is with much satisfaction that I hear this great city inquiring day by day after these my papers, and receiving my morning lectures with a becoming seriousness and attention. My publisher tells me that there are already three thousand of them distributed every day. So that if I allow twenty readers to every paper, which I look upon as a modest computation, I may reckon about three-score thousand[1] disciples in London and Westminster, who I hope will take care to distinguish themselves from the thoughtless herd of their ignorant and unattentive brethren. Since I have raised to myself so great an audience, I shall spare no pains to make their instruction agreeable, and their diversion useful. For which reasons I shall endeavor to enliven morality with wit, and to temper wit with morality, that my readers may, if possible, both ways find their account in the speculation of the day. And to the end that their virtue and discretion may not be short, transient, intermitting[2] starts of thought, I have resolved to refresh their memories from day to day, till I have recovered them out of that desperate state of vice and folly into which the age is fallen. The mind that lies fallow[3] but a single day sprouts up in follies that are only to be killed by a constant and assiduous culture. It was said of Socrates[4] that he brought philosophy down from heaven, to inhabit among men; and I shall be ambitious to have it said of me that I have brought philosophy out of closets and libraries, schools and colleges, to dwell in clubs and assemblies, at tea tables and in coffeehouses.

I would therefore in a very particular manner recommend these my speculations to all well-regulated families that set apart an hour in every morning for tea and bread and butter; and would earnestly advise them for their good to order this paper to be punctually served up, and to be looked upon as part of the tea equipage. . . .

---

1. **three-score thousand** sixty thousand.
2. **intermitting** pausing at times; not constant.
3. **fallow** unused; unproductive.
4. **Socrates** ancient Greek philosopher (470?–399 b.c.), immortalized as a character in Plato's dialogues, who cross-examined ancient Athenians about their lives and values.

> **❝***I have resolved to refresh their memories from day to day, till I have recovered them out of that desperate state of vice and folly into which the age is fallen.***❞**

In the next place, I would recommend this paper to the daily perusal of those gentlemen whom I cannot but consider as my good brothers and allies, I mean the fraternity of spectators, who live in the world without having anything to do in it; and either by the affluence of their fortunes or laziness of their dispositions have no other business with the rest of mankind but to look upon them. Under this class of men are comprehended all contemplative tradesmen, titular physicians, fellows of the Royal Society, Templars[5] that are not given to be contentious, and statesmen that are out of business; in short, everyone that considers the world as a theater, and desires to form a right judgment of those who are the actors on it.

There is another set of men that I must likewise lay a claim to, whom I have lately called the blanks of society, as being altogether unfurnished with ideas, till the business and conversation of the day has supplied them. I have often considered these poor souls with an eye of great commiseration, when I have heard them asking the first man they have met with, whether there was any news stirring? and by that means gathering together materials for thinking. These needy persons do not know what to talk of till about twelve o'clock in the morning; for by that time they are pretty good judges of the weather, know which way the wind sits, and whether the Dutch mail[6] be come in. As they lie at the mercy of the first man they meet, and are grave or impertinent all the day long, according to the notions which they have imbibed in the morning, I would earnestly entreat them not to stir out of their chambers till they have read this paper, and do promise them that I will daily instil into them such sound and wholesome sentiments as shall have a good effect on their conversation for the ensuing twelve hours.

But there are none to whom this paper will be more useful than to the female world. I have often thought there has not been sufficient pains taken in finding out proper employments and diversions for the fair ones. Their amusements seem contrived for them, rather as they are women, than as they are

---

5. **titular physicians, fellows of the Royal Society, Templars** physicians in title only; members of a group dedicated to scientific research; lawyers or law students with offices in the Inner or Middle Temple.
6. **Dutch mail** mail from Europe bearing news of the war.

reasonable creatures; and are more adapted to the sex than to the species. The toilet[7] is their great sense of business, and the right adjusting of their hair the principal employment of their lives. The sorting of a suit of ribbons is reckoned a very good morning's work; and if they make an excursion to a mercer's or a toyshop,[8] so great a fatigue makes them unfit for anything else all the day after. Their more serious occupations are sewing and embroidery, and their greatest drudgery the preparation of jellies and sweetmeats. This, I say, is the state of ordinary women; though I know there are multitudes of those of a more elevated life and conversation, that move in an exalted sphere of knowledge and virtue, that join all the beauties of the mind to the ornaments of dress, and inspire a kind of awe and respect, as well as love, into their male beholders. I hope to increase the number of these by publishing this daily paper, which I shall always endeavor to make an innocent if not an improving entertainment, and by that means at least divert the minds of my female readers from greater trifles. At the same time, as I would fain give some finishing touches to those which are already the most beautiful pieces in human nature, I shall endeavor to point all those imperfections that are the blemishes, as well as those virtues which are the embellishments, of the sex.

---

7. **toilet** act of dressing and grooming oneself.
8. **suit of ribbons . . . mercer's or a toyshop** A suit of ribbons was a set of matching ribbons; a mercer's store sold fabrics, ribbons, and so on; a toyshop sold small items of little value.

Critical Reading

Cite textual evidence to support your responses.

1. **Key Ideas and Details (a)** What reason does Addison give for making his instruction "agreeable"? **(b) Support:** Addison felt *The Spectator* would set high standards for readers. Identify two expressions of this attitude.

2. **Key Ideas and Details (a)** How does Addison define the "spectators" of society? **(b) Infer:** What is Addison's attitude toward the "blanks of society" and toward women? Is he sympathetic, mocking, or both? Explain.

3. **Integration of Knowledge and Ideas Apply:** Do modern media encourage "spectatorship" as Addison defines it? Explain.

4. **Integration of Knowledge and Ideas** What kinds of things would Addison like to change about society? In your response, use at least two of these Essential Question words: *values, dissatisfaction, ideal.* [*Connecting to the Essential Question: How does literature shape or reflect society?*]

After You Read | *The Aims of* The Spectator

Literary Analysis

© **1. Key Ideas and Details** In his **essay** for *The Spectator,* Addison describes audiences for his paper. How does he "test" the usefulness of his paper?

© **2. Integration of Knowledge and Ideas** Using a chart like this one, analyze Addison's portrait of his four readers.

© **Common Core State Standards**

Writing
1.a. Introduce precise, knowledgeable claim(s), establish the significance of the claim(s), distinguish the claim(s) from alternate or opposing claims, and create an organization that logically sequences claim(s), counterclaims, reasons, and evidence.

Passage	Analytic/ Descriptive	General/Of a Specific Era?	Logical/ Humorous?

Reading Strategy

3. Analyze the author's philosophical assumptions in the first paragraph. **(a)** What *explicit assumptions* does he make about the best way to present moral instruction? Cite specific evidence. **(b)** What *implicit assumptions* does he make about using media to promote ideas? Explain.

PERFORMANCE TASKS
Integrated Language Skills

© Vocabulary Acquisition and Use

For each word, choose the letter of its synonym, a word that means the same thing. Explain each choice.

1. affluence: **(a)** speed   **(b)** poverty   **(c)** wealth

2. assiduous: **(a)** diligent   **(b)** aggressive   **(c)** helpful

3. contentious: **(a)** mild   **(b)** argumentative   **(c)** proud

4. embellishments: (a) food   **(b)** remarks   **(c)** decorations

5. transient: **(a)** powerful   **(b)** passing   **(c)** near

6. trifles: **(a)** trivia   **(b)** wonders   **(c)** dangers

Writing

© **Argumentative Text** Like Addison, you observe people in action every day. Write a **letter to the editor** of a local paper describing a kind of behavior you find interesting, amusing, or annoying. Persuade readers to regard the behavior as you do.

- State your position, presenting vivid *examples* of the behavior.
- Support your views with *reasoning* and *emotional appeals.*
- Anticipate and *refute opposing arguments.*

Richard Rodriguez Introduces

from **Days of Obligation:**

from "In Athens Once"

Journalist as Spectator, Then and Now The best journalists achieve a sort of disappearing act, a recitation of facts so transparent it is as though the eye were speaking. Joseph Addison, writing three hundred years ago, styled himself a "spectator" of the great city of London. *Spectator* is a noun I would willingly take for myself, preferring to present myself to the reader as a spectator, at some cool distance from the world I describe.

Joseph Addison, Spectator and Man Joseph Addison was a periodical columnist, writing for magazines. He invented a fictionalized persona who roamed the city of London and reported what he found there. The persona of the Spectator was not Joseph Addison, but resembled him. There is, for instance, a discernible moral sensibility in all Addison's writing that reveals the man. If he writes about that fellow in the corner, with the parrot on his shoulder, it is because he has something in mind to say. It is not simply that he wishes to place a colorful character before us.

Richard Rodriguez, Journalist and Man The journalist in me wants to be informative, to say what is true or factual, and to report exactly what I have seen, without reference to my own sensibility. As a journalist, for example, I visit the teeming, optimistic city of Tijuana, Mexico, situated across the border from San Diego, California.

Tijuana is a city of uncountable millions, and as many aspirations, and as many preoccupations, and as many points of

About the Author

Journalist, essayist, and author Richard Rodriguez won the George Foster Peabody Award in 1997 for his work on PBS's *MacNeil-Lehrer NewsHour*. His writing has appeared in a number of publications, including *The Washington Post*, the *Wall Street Journal*, and *Harper's*.

"The best journalists achieve a sort of disappearing act."

▲ **Critical Viewing**
In what way is the man pictured here a "colorful character" and, like Rodriguez, "at odds" with his surroundings? **[Analyze]**

view. Most Americans have no sense of Tijuana beyond its old-fashioned notoriety as a honky-tonk draw for sailors during the war.

To me, Tijuana appears as raw and exciting, sometimes as appalling, as I imagine eighteenth-century London must have appeared to Joseph Addison. Large, beautiful houses overlook a city of factories, heavy metal rock bands, gypsies, taxis, street cries, stinking canals. It is a city of contradictions.

My journalistic obligation to the reader is to present numbers and dates as correctly as I can. My journalistic impulse always intends to complicate rather than to simplify issues, to suggest two or several points of view rather than to argue a single position. My journalistic obligation, therefore, is to see this border town from both sides—to describe how Mexico, particularly Mexico City, views Tijuana, as well as how people north of the border regard this city.

But I have also come to Tijuana as a Mexican American, as someone born in the United States to Mexican parents. My status here is in question. Indeed, Tijuana, this city that lies on the border between cultures, must finally remind me of myself—the struggle of cultures in my own soul. Tijuana implicates me and fascinates me for being (as I am) confused by its identity.

The Spectator Becomes a Comic Character Thus, you will see how in this piece, Richard Rodriguez becomes a comic character within the city he has been at such pains to describe from a distance. *They* surround the *I*. The diffidence of Richard Rodriguez is exposed as completely at odds with the messy ease of Tijuana—at odds, too, with the airs he gives himself as a traveler-observer.

When the journalist becomes a character within his own report, he enters the realm of bias and prejudice, or he enters the realm of literature—depending.

The pieces I write for newspapers are usually published on an opinion page; they intend to persuade. My television essays are reserved for the last part of a news program; they are clearly identified as "commentary." They circle a point of view, but cannot express a point of view. The only journalistic pride I own is the fact that I have been called by some readers "left" and by other readers "right." The journalist in me does not want to be slotted among one band of partisans in an argument.

But the writing I prefer attempts a marriage: journalism wedded to literature.

The journalist Richard Rodriguez writes as fairly as possible of the world around him. The writer Richard Rodriguez finds himself caught up in the world he is watching. He may be morally outraged. Or he may simply be made petulant by the heat. He shows his hand, at any rate.

Critical Reading

1. **Key Ideas and Details (a)** According to Rodriguez, in what way do good journalists perform a "disappearing act"? **(b) Make a Judgment:** Do you think his ideas apply to today's television and print journalists? Explain.

2. **Key Ideas and Details (a)** What connections does Rodriguez draw between Addison's London and modern-day Tijuana? **(b)** As a journalist, in what way must Rodriguez present the border town of Tijuana? **(c) Speculate:** Because of the parallels Rodriguez notes between himself and Tijuana, do you think he can be objective in his presentation of the city? Why or why not?

3. **Key Ideas and Details (a) Infer:** In what ways might the connection Rodriguez feels to Tijuana make him the perfect person to write about the city? **(b) Interpret:** In your own words, explain what Rodriguez means by "journalism wedded to literature."

4. **Craft and Structure (a)** In this commentary, what is the effect of Richard Rodriguez referring to himself in the third person? **(b)** What, if any, is the difference between the "I" in this essay and "Richard Rodriguez"?

5. **Craft and Structure** Note words and phrases that make this a piece of journalism and words and phrases that make it literature. Explain the differences you note, using what you read in Rodriguez's essay.

6. **Integration of Knowledge and Ideas** Consider whether Rodriguez remains a spectator throughout his essay. Identify any moments when you think he becomes a participant rather than an observer.

Cite textual evidence to support your responses.

from Days of Obligation:
from "In Athens Once"

Richard Rodriguez

Consider Tijuana from Mexico's point of view. Tijuana is farther away from Mexico City than any other city in Mexico. Tijuana is where Mexico comes to an end.

In Mexico City you will waste an afternoon if you go to bookstores looking for books about Tijuana. The clerk will scarcely conceal his amusement. (And what would be in a book about Tijuana?) People in Mexico City will tell you, if they have anything at all to say about Tijuana, that Tijuana is a city without history, a city without architecture, an American city. San Diego may worry about Mexican hordes crawling over the border. Mexico City worries about a cultural spill from the United States.

▲ **Critical Viewing**
What does this image suggest about the contents and tone of the essay to come? **[Predict]**

From prehistory, the North has been the problem. Mexico City (la capital) has been the platform from which all provincialism[1] is gauged. From the North came marauding[2] tribes, iconoclasts,[3] destroyers of high Indian civilization. During the Spanish colonial era, the North was settled, even garrisoned, but scarcely civilized. In the nineteenth century, Mexico's northernmost territories were too far from the center to be defended against America's westward expansion. In after-decades, the North spawned revolutionaries and bandits, or these fled into the North and the North hid them well.

Beyond all the ribbon-cutting palaver[4] about good neighbors, there remains an awesome distance of time. Tijuana and San Diego are not in the same historical time zone. Tijuana is poised at the beginning of an industrial age, a Dickensian[5] city with palm trees. San Diego is a postindustrial city of high-impact plastic and despair diets. And palm trees. San Diego faces west, looks resolutely out to sea. Tijuana stares north, as toward the future. San Diego is the future—secular, soulless. San Diego is the past, guarding its quality of life. Tijuana is the future.

On the Mexican side there is flux, a vast migration, a camp of siege. On the Mexican side is youth, with bad skin or bad teeth, but with a naïve optimism appropriate to youth.

On the American side are petitions to declare English the official language of the United States; the Ku Klux Klan; nativists posing as environmentalists, blaming illegal immigration for freeway congestion.

▼ **Critical Viewing**
In what ways does this photograph depict the contradictory worlds Rodriguez describes?
[Connect]

---

1. **provincialism** narrowness of outlook.
2. **marauding** plundering, raiding.
3. **iconoclasts** those who seek to destroy widely accepted beliefs or ideas.
4. **palaver** conference or discussion.
5. **Dickensian** having the characteristics of a nineteenth century English novel written by Charles Dickens (1812–1870). Dickensian characteristics would include obscure London streets inhabited by scoundrels and villains, wide-eyed innocents, and eccentric characters.

Tijuana
and San Diego are not in the same historical time zone.

And late at night, on the radio call-in shows, hysterical, reasonable American voices say they have had enough. Of this or that. Of trampled flower beds. Of waiting in line or crowded buses, of real or imagined rudeness, of welfare.

In San Diego people speak of "the border" as meaning a clean break, the end of *us*, the beginning of *them.* In Mexican Spanish, the legality takes on distance, even pathos, as *la frontera*, meaning something less fixed, something more akin to the American "frontier." Whereas San Diego remains provincial and retiring, the intrusion of the United States has galvanized Tijuana to cosmopolitanism.[6] There are seven newspapers in Tijuana; there is American television—everything we see they see. Central American refugees and southern California turistas cross paths in Tijuana. There are new ideas. Most worrisome to Mexico City has been the emergence of a right-wing idea, a pro-American politics to challenge the one-party system that has governed Mexico for most of this century.

Because the United States is the richer country, the more powerful broadcaster, Mexicans know more about us than we care to know about them. Mexicans speak of America as "the other side," saying they are going to *el otro lado* when they cross for work, legal or illegal. The border is real enough; it is guarded by men with guns. But Mexicans incline to view the border without reverence, referring to the American side as *el otro cachete,* the other buttock.

Traditionally, Mexican cities are centered by a town square or *zócalo,* on either side of which stand city hall and cathedral, counterweights to balance the secular[7] with the eternal. Tijuana never had a *zócalo.* And, like other California cities, Tijuana is receding from its old downtown.

---

6. cosmopolitanism worldly sophistication.
7. secular related to worldly, rather than religious, things.

Reading Check

Which city is called "la capital"?

The new commercial district of Tijuana, three miles east of downtown, is called the Zona del Río. For several blocks within the Zona del Río, on grass islands in the middle of the Paseo de los Héroes, stand monuments to various of Mexico's heroes. There is one American (Abraham Lincoln) in a line that otherwise connects the good Aztec, Cuauhtémoc,[8] to the victorious Mexican general, Zaragoza.[9] With Kremlin-like dullness, these monuments were set down upon the city, paperweights upon a map. They are gifts from the capital, meant as reminders.

Prominent along the Paseo de los Héroes is Tijuana's Cultural Center, Mexico City's most insistent token of troth.[10] Tijuana might better have done with sewers or streetlights, but in 1982 the Mexican government built Tijuana a cultural center, an orange concrete bomba[11] in the brutal architectural idioms[12] of the 1970s. The main building is a museum, very clean and empty during my visit, except for a janitor who trails me with a vacuum cleaner. Together we tread a ramp past fairly uninteresting displays of Mayan pottery, past folk crafts, past reproductions of political documents and portraits of Mexico's military heroes. The lesson to Tijuana is clear: she belongs to Mexico.

As the exhibits travel in time, south to north, the umbilical approach narrows to gossamer. We reach a display devoted to Tijuana's own history. We find a collection of picture postcards from the

---

8. **Cuauhtémoc** the 11th and last Aztec emperor. When captured in battle, Cuauhtémoc refused to reveal the location of Aztec riches, earning him legendary status among Mexico's leaders.
9. **Zaragoza** General Zaragoza and his militia defeated an invading French army on May 5, 1862. Cinco de Mayo is celebrated each year to commemorate the victory.
10. **troth** loyalty.
11. **bomba** bomb.
12. **idioms** style of expression.

The lesson to
Tijuana is clear:
She belongs
to Mexico.

twenties, emblazoned in English with "Greetings from Old Mexico."

One sympathizes with the curator's dilemma. How does one depict the history of so unmonumental a city, a city occasioned by defeat and submission to the enemy's will?

The treaty ending the Mexican-American War ruled a longitudinal line between the Gulf of Mexico and the Pacific Ocean. For decades thereafter, Tijuana remained vacant land at the edge of the sea, an arid little clause dangling from Mexico's disgraced nineteenth century.

No one in Tijuana is able to fix for me the derivation of the name of the place. Some say it is an Indian name. Some think the town was named for a woman who lived in a shack at the turn of the century, a Mexican Ma Kettle known in the region as Tía Juana.

Mexico City tried to dispose of the name in 1925. By an act of Mexico's congress, Tijuana was proclaimed to be Ciudad Zaragoza. A good name. A patriot's name. The resolution languished in a statute book on a shelf in Mexico City, two thousand miles away.

▲ **Critical Viewing**
Which details in this postcard support the author's message that Tijuana lacks a clear identity as a city? **[Connect]**

Critical Reading

1. Key Ideas and Details (a) According to the residents of Mexico City, what two things does Tijuana lack? **(b) Interpret:** In what way does geography play a part in this reputation? **(c) Speculate:** What effects might a city that lacks a specific urban plan or a sense of identity have on the community and people who live there?

Cite textual evidence to support your responses.

2. Key Ideas and Details (a) According to the essay, which city is actively moving toward its own future? **(b) Hypothesize:** What challenges might arise when a city progresses and grows very quickly? Cite examples from the essay to support your response.

3. Integration of Knowledge and Ideas (a) Instead of a cultural center, which other improvement might have benefited Tijuana? **(b) Compare and Contrast:** In what ways is Tijuana more American than Mexican in its culture? **(c) Analyze Cause and Effect:** What effect might Rodriguez's American background have on his perception of Tijuana's cultural identity?

4. Integration of Knowledge and Ideas (a) Infer: Which characteristics of Tijuana are likely to appear in a positive light in a tourism advertisement? **(b) Evaluate:** Are these characteristics truly assets to the city? Explain.

Write a Reflective Essay

Common Core State Standards

Writing
3.a. Engage and orient the reader by setting out a problem, situation, or observation and its significance.

Reflective Essay In this unit, thought-provoking essays by Joseph Addison and Richard Rodriguez offer revealing glimpses of each writer's personality. These **reflective essays** also encourage readers to consider their own personal experiences more deeply. Follow the steps outlined in this workshop to write a reflective essay.

Assignment Write a reflective essay in which you describe an event from your personal experience and then share insights about its significance.

What to Include The assignment summarizes your *purpose*, and your *audience* will be your classmates. To achieve your purpose and engage the audience, include these elements in your essay:

- an explanation of a personal experience that shaped your beliefs
- an organization that clarifies the significance of the events you describe, and a balance between specific events and beliefs
- clear connections between beliefs and events
- a consistent, personal tone

To preview the criteria on which your reflective essay may be assessed, see the rubric on page 701.

To get a feel for the reflective essay, read this excerpt from *Days of Obligation* by Richard Rodriguez on page 692.

from: Days of Obligation

Prominent along the Paseo de los Héroes is Tijuana's Cultural Center, Mexico City's most insistent token of troth. *Tijuana might better have done with sewers or streetlights, but in 1982 the Mexican government built Tijuana a cultural center, an orange concrete bomba in the brutal architectural idioms of the 1970s.* The main building is a museum, very clean and empty during my visit, except for a janitor who trails me with a vacuum cleaner. Together we tread a ramp past fairly uninteresting displays of Mayan pottery, past folk crafts, past reproductions of political documents and portraits of Mexico's military heroes. The lesson to Tijuana is clear: she belongs to Mexico.

WRITE GUY
Jeff Anderson, M.Ed.

What Do You Notice?

Read the highlighted sentence several times. Then, with a partner, discuss the qualities that make it special. You might consider the following elements:

- word choice
- sentence length
- use of punctuation
- vivid details

Share your group's observations with the class.

Prewriting and Planning

Choosing Your Topic

To choose an event to focus on, use one of these strategies:

- **Freewriting** Write for five minutes about key experiences in your life and beliefs you hold strongly. Jot down as many ideas as you can. Then, look for connections between general beliefs and specific events.

- **Top-Five List** Make a list of five times in your life when you discovered something wonderful. Scan *journals*, if necessary, to help generate this list. For each key event, note what you learned and think about why this discovery has remained important to you.

Narrowing Your Topic

Focus on an insight. Once you have selected an event, focus your essay by stating your key insight in one sentence. Then, develop ideas and examples that explain and support that insight.

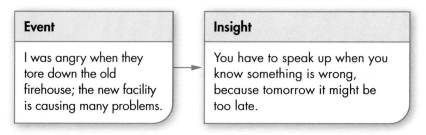

Event	Insight
I was angry when they tore down the old firehouse; the new facility is causing many problems.	You have to speak up when you know something is wrong, because tomorrow it might be too late.

Gathering Details

Make connections. Consider how your experiences relate to themes in the world at large. Organize your thoughts in a diagram like the one shown. Then, conduct research to deepen your knowledge about your subject. Talk with friends and family, or use the library or the Internet to gather details about past events or issues that relate to your personal experience.

Preparing Rhetorical Strategies

While preparing to write about an event, remember that you can use a variety of different rhetorical strategies in addition to narration, or story telling. These strategies include *description* (when you describe people, things, and places), *exposition* (when you set forth general ideas), and *persuasion* (when you try to convince the reader that your beliefs are true).

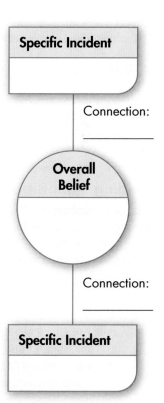

Drafting

Shaping Your Writing

Decide where to start. A well-organized reflective essay alternates between *broader themes* or generalizations and *specific incidents*. Your introduction should include both. Consider these organizations for your opening:

- State your overall belief and then give one or two tantalizing details about the incidents that led you to it.
- Describe an event and then tell the surprising insight you drew from it. Your essay will make the full connection clear.

Establish a tone. Introduce an appropriate tone for your essay from the beginning, and stay with it throughout. A serious, straightforward tone is appropriate, but you might also consider using one of these:

- **Ironic tone:** a good tone to use when your details show that things do not always work out as expected or intended

- **Humorous tone:** a logical choice when your examples are amusing

Model: Experimenting With Specific Tones

Ironic Tone
I welcomed my coach's criticism as warmly as any self-centered ten-year-old might. I was quite comfortable postponing any action until the following year, by which time I expected the matter would be forgotten.

Humorous Tone
Having a little brother is not as big a pain as people say. It's worse. Yet, after years of his tattling and tagging along, one incident brought home to me how important family is—even little brothers. I no longer want to sell him to the circus. Not unless they've raised their prices.

Providing Elaboration

Explode a moment. Expand key descriptions by telling more about what happened, what something looked like, or how the people involved—including you—reacted. Mark moments you can "explode," and use the margin to write the details you want to add.

Model: Revising to Explode a Moment

Julie was cute and dated the most popular boys in our school.
    a cheerleader and
She was a Student Council member. She was also the most
        , and she welcomed an understudy
confident person I knew .

> These additional details provide more description.

Common Core State Standards

Writing

3.c. Use a variety of techniques to sequence events so that they build on one another to create a coherent whole and build toward a particular tone and outcome.

3.d. Use precise words and phrases, telling details, and sensory language to convey a vivid picture of the experiences, events, setting, and/or characters.

Writers on Writing

Richard Rodriguez On Reflective Writing

Richard Rodriguez is the author of *Days of Obligation* (p. 689).

These paragraphs appear in *Days of Obligation*, a philosophical travel book of mine that ranges over several centuries and back and forth across the U.S.-Mexico border. Each chapter, like the fragment below, is autobiographical. But that is only to say, memory is my guide throughout; memory forces me to reflect on the lessons within my life.

"In my reflective essays, the 'I' moves freely."

—Richard Rodriguez

from *Days of Obligation*

Our last house on "Eye" Street was across from an old cemetery. No memory attached to it. The grass was watered and cut once a month by the city. There were no scrolls or wrought-iron fences; no places to put flowers. There were granite plaques level with the ground. Early dates. Solitary names. Men. Men who had come early to California and died young.

No grandsons or granddaughters came forward in the 1950s when Sacramento needed the land to build a school, a new Sutter Junior High School. A plywood fence was hammered up around the cemetery and, within that discretionary veil, bulldozers chugged and grunted, pulling up moist hairy mounds of what had once been the light of day; trucks came to carry it all away.

In early November, white tulle fog rises from the valley floor. My father is easy with this ancient weather reminiscent of the sea. My father is whistling this morning as he scrambles two eggs. My mother turns away from the window, pulling her blue bathrobe closer around her throat. I am sitting at the kitchen table. I am sixteen years old. I am pouring milk onto Sugar Frosted Flakes, watching milk rise in the bowl. My parents will die. I will die. Everyone I know will someday be dead. The blue parakeet my mother has taught to say "pretty boy" swings upon his little trapeze, while my mother pours coffee.

Each paragraph is about remembrance or the refusal to remember: civic amnesia; the forgetfulness of ancestors; the middle-aged writer's teenage discovery of death; the adult's inability to remember winter.

Images of nature are everywhere in this meditation on death—the parakeet, winter fog, clumps of grass upturned by bulldozers. As the contending images suggest: Death is the end of life yet also a part of nature.

Notice here how the most astonishing ideas of life can come not with a drumbeat or violin, but in an instant of a Saturday morning, between spoonfuls of cereal.

Revising

Revising Your Overall Structure

Balance narration with reflection. Review your writing to make sure that you *maintained a balance between specific incidents and general ideas.*

1. Bracket any segments of the essay that describe specific events.
2. Mark in red any passages where you have included a detail that does not set a scene or advance ideas.
3. Use a different color to mark the points where you provide your interpretation of events.

Model: Editing to Omit Unnecessary Details

[I giggled and flirted my way through the next two years.]
✓ [During that time, my Dad got a new job and we moved to a different neighborhood.] Through it all, I felt as if I were putting on an act. [In the middle of my junior year, I received my first ACT results.] I was not happy with my scores.

> The writer deleted this incident because it did not contribute toward her insight or provide necessary background.

4. Looking at your essay as a whole, determine whether you have maintained a balance between specific events and the interpretation of those events.

Revising Your Sentences

Strengthen your connections. Examine the passages where you shift between events and the generalizations to which they have led you. Consider using transitional words or phrases to clarify the connections for your readers.

Examples:

And that is how . . .
Suddenly I understood that . . .
After this happened, . . .
As a result, . . .
For the very first time, . . .
I gradually became aware that . . .

Peer Review: Ask a partner to identify passages in your essay where your connections could be stronger. Discuss ways to strengthen and clarify the connections.

Evaluate your partner's suggestions. Then, make your revisions and share your work with your partner.

Developing Your Style

Moving From Personal to Universal

A reflective essay moves from personal experiences to universal truths. Be careful to maintain your **personal voice** even when generalizing.

- Maintain your personal tone, even when stating general truths. Look for ways to inject your personality into each section of your essay.
- Be sure that you really agree with the statements you make. Your essay may feel insincere if you say something just because you think it sounds good or because you think your audience will agree.

Here is how one writer revised a universal statement that felt stiff and artificial. The revised version feels more personal and sincere.

Stiff Voice	Personal Voice
Families help us learn and grow. We achieve our best when we have their love and support. Your family's encouragement can help you accomplish anything.	For better or worse, your family knows you better than anyone else. As a result, they won't let you get away with doing anything less than your best. That can be a pain, but it also helps you succeed.

Find It in Your Reading

Read or review Richard Rodriguez's introductory essay on page 686.

1. Find two personal experiences that Rodriguez discusses in the essay.
2. Evaluate the lessons that Rodriguez draws from these experiences.
3. Look for the language that lets you "hear" Rodriguez's unique voice.

Apply It to Your Writing

Review your draft. For each paragraph, follow these steps:

1. Underline the specific events and details that you have included.
2. Circle the broader, more general lessons, observations, or beliefs about life to which these events and details have led you. Then, answer these questions:
   - Do you genuinely believe the statement?
   - Do you state your belief in a personal way?
3. Revise your essay, as necessary, to maintain your personal voice.

Student Model: Ashley Philips, Ruston, LA

Coming Home

North Carolina novelist T. R. Pearson told me recently that when he was a teenager, he had set his stories in New York City, though he had never been there. "I thought New York was where it was," he laughed, adding that the fiction he had produced during this period was uniformly bad. Almost accidentally, he had begun to write about the life he really knew—life in little towns like Reidsville, North Carolina. It was only then that he succeeded at what he was attempting. Pearson's remarks set me thinking about my own life. Like Tom Pearson, I had spent a part of my life attempting something foreign and feeling unhappy with the result.

When I was in grade school, I read through every book in our classroom and did special reports. Research thrilled me. Books were the most important part of my life. I knew who I was. And I was happy.

In my freshman year, though, I decided that my own life paled compared with that of my older friend Julie. Julie was popular and dated the most popular boys in our school. She was a cheerleader and a Student Council member. She was also the most confident person I knew, and she welcomed an understudy. I borrowed Julie's clothes and copied her hairstyles, right down to the huge hair bows that were her signature. By the end of the year, I had decided to run for cheerleader.

I giggled and flirted my way through the next two years. Through it all, I felt as if I was putting on an act. In the middle of my junior year, I received my first ACT results. I was not happy with my scores. I began to reevaluate my life. I decided not to run for cheerleader. I paid less attention to who was popular and concentrated on friendships that were comfortable and fun. I threw myself into my science project and was exhilarated when I took top honors at the state science fair. By the end of the year, a teacher had invited me to serve as editor of a literary magazine. I felt that I was home again.

This December, as I sat listening to T. R. Pearson discuss the path that had led him to his true subject, I felt I knew exactly what he was talking about. It was a warm December day. A late fall sun filtered through the pine trees onto my English teacher's deck. Four other students and I sat in deck chairs and listened to Pearson speak about writing. It all felt so natural. This, I thought, is the kind of world I want to live in. I realized then that you can never get anywhere if you leave your true self behind. At that moment, I could not, for all the world, remember why cheerleading or Julie's boys or big hair bows had ever mattered.

Ashley sets up a clear connection between the narrative that follows and her general point: Success depends on being true to oneself.

By carefully selecting details, Ashley includes just enough incidents to support and balance her general insight.

Ashley's short, decisive self-descriptions establish a consistent tone.

Ashley reports incidents that clearly lead to her realization.

In her conclusion, Ashley clearly states her general insight. (See Developing Your Style on p. 699.)

Editing and Proofreading

Focus on commas. Focus on commas between items in a series, commas in compound sentences, and commas that set off appositives.

Focus on spelling. When adding *-ly* to form an adverb from an adjective ending in *-le,* drop the *-le. Reasonable* becomes *reasonably.*

Spiral Review Conventions Earlier in this unit, you learned about comparative and superlative adjectives and adverbs (p. 493); participles, gerunds, and infinitives (p. 503); and fixing misplaced and dangling modifiers (p. 539). Check your persuasive essay to be sure you have used those conventions correctly.

Publishing, Presenting, and Reflecting

Consider one of the following ways to share your writing:

Create a radio broadcast. Use your essay as the basis for a radio opinion piece. Rehearse your presentation, looking for ways to match the tone of your voice to the tone of your essay. Try to "tell" incidents or events rather than read them verbatim. If possible, record your presentation so that you can critique it later.

Publish on the Internet. Post your reflective essay on a Web site for student writing. Invite feedback from other writers.

Reflect on your writing. Jot down your thoughts on the experience of writing a reflective essay. Begin by answering these questions:

- What have I learned about moving from the particular to the general, and back again, in my writing?
- What new aspects of the topic did I discover as I developed plans for my essay?

Common Core State Standards

Writing
5. Develop and strengthen writing as needed by editing, focusing on addressing what is most significant for a specific purpose and audience.
6. Use technology, including the Internet, to produce, publish, and update individual or shared writing products in response to ongoing feedback, including new arguments or information.
Language
2.b. Spell correctly.

Rubric for Self-Assessment

Evaluate your reflective essay using the following criteria and rating scale, or, with your classmates, determine your own reasonable evaluation criteria.

Criteria	Rating Scale
	not very very
Focus: How clearly do you show how a personal experience led you to an insight?	1 2 3 4 5
Organization: How logical is your organization?	1 2 3 4 5
Support/Elaboration: How fully do you describe the events that influenced your beliefs?	1 2 3 4 5
Style: How well do you establish a personal tone?	1 2 3 4 5
Conventions: How correct is your grammar, especially your use of commas?	1 2 3 4 5

Oral Interpretation of a Literary Work

**Common Core
State Standards**

Reading Literature
7. Analyze multiple interpretations of a story, drama, or poem, evaluating how each version interprets the source text.

Speaking and Listening
6. Adapt speech to a variety of contexts and tasks, demonstrating a command of formal English when indicated or appropriate.

An **oral interpretation** is an oral reading of a literary work that conveys the presenter's understanding of the nuances of a text. Long before the invention of the printing press, poets and storytellers performed for their communities, relying on voice and gesture to convey meaning. People still present literary works in this manner today.

Analyze a Literary Work

Review the text. Make a copy of a speech, poem, or soliloquy from this unit. Choose one that you truly enjoy. Then, analyze the work to identify the use of literary elements and stylistic devices, such as the following:

- **Tone:** the author's attitude. Determine if it is formal, earnest, satirical, approving, or critical.

- **Author's Style:** the way a writer uses language to express ideas. Analyze the elements that help reveal a writer's voice. For example, notice sentence lengths, word choice, images, and characters' personalities, as well as uses of symbols, figurative language, and description.

- **Imagery:** descriptions that appeal to the senses. Study the author's images of places, objects, and experiences.

- **Theme:** the overall message of the selection. Consider the writer's purpose and note ideas or images that are repeated.

- **Nuance and Ambiguity:** Literature can be interpreted in many ways. Look for actions or symbols whose meanings are not directly stated, and decide how you understand the author's meaning in these items.

A review of these elements will help you understand the selection's *significant ideas*. Read the work several times to help you understand its layers of meanings or to find areas where you may have questions. Pay attention to denotative, or surface-level meanings. Eventually, connotative meanings—those that are deeper or more subtle—will become apparent. Look to other texts as well to support your ideas. Record your observations by *highlighting, circling words, and making marginal notes*.

Write your analysis. Use your notes to write a brief analytical essay that details your understanding of the text. Focus on your interpretation of any *complexities of the text*. Make specific references to the literary elements noted above and the ways in which they affect your understanding. Also, consider including *rhetorical strategies* in your analysis, such as describing other interpretations or narrating your first impressions of the work. Use this essay to introduce your oral presentation.

Rehearse Speaking Strategies

To perform your oral interpretation effectively, use these techniques:

Technique	Application	Explore It
Eye Contact	Look at everyone in your audience.	Observe how your teachers look at the whole class while teaching.
Gesture/Movement	Use hand gestures and staging to convey action and emotion.	View a recording of a famous actor or poet performing a literary work and note his or her movements.
Vocalization	Reflect characters' accents and dialects, and enunciate and project your voice.	Research the areas in which your characters are said to live and how they might sound.
Voice Register	Use your voice's highs and lows to create emphasis or differentiate characters.	Practice saying the same sentence with different emphasis and pitch.

Enhance your performance. To further develop your interpretation, consider using simple costumes and props, music, pictures, or sound effects. You can ask a friend to assist with such effects during your performance.

Practice. *Rehearse* in front of a mirror and then in front of family or friends. Be sure to practice your *staging* and the use of any props.

Activities: Deliver and Analyze Oral Interpretations

Ⓒ **Comprehension and Collaboration** For both activities, use an evaluation form like the one below.

A. Present your interpretation, starting off with an introduction based on your essay. Afterward, apply listeners' feedback to revise your delivery.

B. With a small group, listen to a variety of interpretations of the same work. You may use audio or video recordings, your own interpretations, or a combination of the two. Analyze how each version interprets the source text.

Evaluation Form for Oral Interpretation

Title and Author of Literary Selection: _____

Which aspects of the work does the interpreter emphasize?_____

Does the interpreter use gestures? How do they help the performance? _____

How does he or she use voice techniques?_____

How well does the interpreter maintain eye contact?_____

Name one thing the interpreter could do better next time. _____

Etymology: Political Science/History Terms

If you were given the original manuscript of *Beowulf,* you would need an Anglo-Saxon scholar to read it for you, so different is Old English from the language we speak today. In contrast, you could read much of *The Canterbury Tales* on your own. By Chaucer's day, Anglo-Saxon had been transformed into Middle English, a language that shares much of the grammar and vocabulary of our modern tongue. The Norman invasion of England in 1066 brought thousands of French and Latin words into the vocabulary. Since French and Latin were the languages of the ruling class, many of the new words referred to administration, government, and law. The chart below introduces you to key affixes and roots stemming from these words. An understanding of these word parts can help you define unfamiliar terms you encounter in political science and history.

**Common Core
State Standards**

Language
4. Determine or clarify the meaning of unknown and multiple-meaning words and phrases based on *grades 11–12 reading and content*, choosing flexibly from a range of strategies.

4.a. Use context as a clue to the meaning of a word or phrase.

4.c. Consult general and specialized reference materials, both print and digital, to find the pronunciation of a word or determine or clarify its precise meaning, its part of speech, its etymology, or its standard usage.

Prefixes

ab- (Latin): away from
ad- (Latin): to; toward
an- (Greek): not; without
ex-, e- (Latin): outside; out of; away
pro- (Latin): forward
syn- (Greek): together; with

Roots

-arch- (Greek): chief; first; highest; ruler
-dict- (Latin): say or tell
-doc- (Latin): teach
-jud-, -jur- (Latin): to judge; law, swear
-urbs- (Latin): city
-ven-, -vent- (Latin): come

Suffixes

-an (Latin): belonging to
-ate (Latin): characterized by
-ation (Latin): action or process; result
-dom (Anglo-Saxon): state; condition; domain; rank
-ity-, ty (Latin): state or quality
-y (Latin): condition or state

Practice

Practice A: Choose the word from the list that fits each numbered definition. Explain your choices with reference to each word's root and affixes.

anarchy	edict	judiciary
adjudicate	urban	syndicate

1. a decree issued by an authority

2. absence of political authority

3. relating to a city

4. government branch that administers justice

5. an association of individuals formed to carry out a project

6. to judge a case

Practice B: Using a dictionary, trace the etymologies of the following political science and history terms: *prerogative, doom, allegiance, property, deed.* Identify the language of origin and the point at which the word entered the English language.

Vocabulary Acquisition and Use: Context Clues

Context clues are words or phrases that help readers clarify the meanings of unfamiliar words in a text. By using context clues, you can determine the word or words that complete a sentence. Sentence Completion questions appear in most standardized tests. In these types of questions, you are given sentences with one or more missing words. Your task is to use the context to choose the correct word or words to complete each sentence logically. Try this strategy: (1) Identify the meaning of each answer option. (2) If you are unsure of the meaning of a word, use roots, prefixes, and suffixes, or similar words to help you understand the meaning. (3) Test those potential meanings in the sentence.

Practice

This exercise is modeled after the Sentence Completion exercises that appear in the Critical Reading section of the SAT.

Directions: Each of the following sentences is missing one or two words. Choose the word or set of words that best completes each sentence.

Test-Taking Tip
Pace yourself: Questions are easier early in the test and more challenging later in the test.

1. The critic praised the actress, calling her performance ___?___.
   A. devout
   B. eminent
   C. lamentable
   D. transcendent
   E. transient

2. Due to the manager's ___?___, the staff was whimsically assigned to different projects.
   A. caprices
   B. credulity
   C. discretion
   D. guile
   E. resolution

3. Her earlier ___?___ forgotten, she enjoyed a life of ___?___.
   A. abasement . . . expedients
   B. dominions . . . covetousness
   C. penury . . . affluence
   D. piety . . . distemper
   E. schism . . . resolution

4. The pleas of the ___?___ peasant did not affect the ___?___ noble.
   A. delirious . . . inconstant
   B. importuning . . . obdurate
   C. ingenuous . . . temperate
   D. prodigious . . . dubious
   E. risible . . . substantial

5. The owl set out each evening on its ___?___ search for food.
   A. amorous
   B. heedless
   C. nocturnal
   D. notorious
   E. venerable

6. The speaker's arguments did nothing to ___?___ the situation.
   A. breach
   B. illumine
   C. presume
   D. reconfigure
   E. transgress

Test-Taking Practice

Reading Test: Humanities Passage

Humanities passages are one of the four types of reading selections found on standardized tests. These passages come from memoirs or essays and cover subjects in the arts and literature, philosophy, and entertainment media. Questions can focus on main ideas and supporting details, on the author's tone and style, and on the meaning of particular words or sentences. They may require you to make generalizations or analyze causes and effects.

**Common Core
State Standards**

RL.11-12.1, RL.11-12.3,
RL.11-12.4; L.11-12.1,
L.11-12.3, L.11-12.4.a
[For the full wording of
the standards, see the
standards chart in the front
of your textbook.]

Practice

The following exercise is modeled after the ACT Reading Test, Humanities section.

Directions: Read the following passage, taken from John Donne's "Meditation 17." Then, choose the *best* answer to each question.

No man is an island, entire of itself: every man is a piece of the continent, a part of the main. If a clod be washed away by the sea, Europe is the less, as well as if a promontory were, as well as if a manor of thy friend's or of thine own were. Any man's death diminishes
5 me because I am involved in mankind, and therefore never send to know for whom the bell tolls; it tolls for thee. Neither can we call this a begging of misery or a borrowing of misery, as though we were not miserable enough of ourselves but must fetch in more from the next house, in taking upon us the misery of our neighbors. Truly it were an
10 excusable covetousness if we did; for affliction is a treasure, and scarce any man hath enough of it. No man hath affliction enough that is not matured and ripened by it, and made fit for God by that affliction. If a man carry treasure in bullion, or in a wedge of gold, and have none coined into current money, his treasure will not defray him as he travels.
15 Tribulation is treasure in the nature of it, but it is not current money in the use of it, except we get nearer and nearer our home, heaven, by it.

Strategy

Scan, then read.

- **First, underline words that indicate the author's attitude.** Look for formal language, diction, and rhetorical devices used to make an argument more persuasive.

- **Second, consider how this language contributes to the writer's message.** Ask yourself what effect the writer's feelings have on the ideas he or she presents.

- Finally, answer the questions using this information to guide you.

1. Which of these best paraphrases lines 1–2?
   A. All men are connected to one another, but that is not true of women.
   B. People who live on islands are not isolated from one another.
   C. All people, by natural right, partly own the land where they live.
   D. No person exists in isolation; we are all connected.

2. Which best explains why Donne refers to the *clod* and the *promontory* in lines 2–3?
   F. Referring to both small and large pieces of land strengthens his argument.
   G. He emphasizes that Europe has both lowland and highland areas.
   H. Citing the landholdings of both the poor and the rich reinforces his point.
   J. Mentioning landforms of all shapes and sizes underlines his point that the world is constantly changing.

3. In the context of lines 1–5, it can reasonably be inferred that *diminishes* means:
   A. reduces the amount of light available.
   B. lessens something in quantity or size.
   C. saddens someone; causes grief.
   D. holds dominion over; controls.

4. Which of these best paraphrases lines 5–6?
   F. When church bells signal that someone has died, we should all attend the services.
   G. When church bells signal that someone has died, a part of each of us dies.
   H. One day, the church bell will toll for each of us, signaling our death.
   J. We should not ask why the church bell tolls but consider how morally we have lived our lives.

5. Why does Donne say in lines 6–7 that feeling the death of another person is not "a begging of misery or a borrowing of misery"?
   A. He believes we will be repaid for it in the end.
   B. He thinks that feeling is false rather than heartfelt.
   C. He argues that we are truly affected by that person's death.
   D. He says that we must pay for these feelings with our treasure.

6. From the context of lines 1–10, it can reasonably be inferred that *affliction* means:
   F. fond feelings for another person.
   G. difficult circumstances that cause suffering.
   H. pretending to have a better social status than one does.
   J. sympathy for people who are suffering.

7. Why is it surprising that Donne uses the phrase "excusable covetousness" in line 10 to refer to afflictions?
   A. It is surprising to say people desire afflictions.
   B. It is surprising to call covetousness excusable, because it is a sin.
   C. It is unusual to say people covet what neighbors own.
   D. Earlier in the piece, Donne condemned covetousness.

8. From the context of lines 12–14, it can reasonably be inferred that *bullion* means:
   F. sores upon the feet.
   G. something of value.
   H. money and jewels.
   J. land and property.

Grammar and Writing: Editing in Context

Editing-in-context segments often appear in the writing sections of standard-ized tests. They are made up of a reading passage with numbered sentences, some of which contain errors in grammar, style, and usage. For each question, you must choose the best way to correct a given sentence.

Practice

This exercise is modeled after the ACT English Test.

Directions: For each underlined sentence or portion of a sentence, choose the best alternative. If an item asks a question about the underlined portion, choose the best answer to the question.

Strategy

Narrow the Answer Options.

Make your task simpler by eliminating any an-swers that you know to be incorrect.

In "A Modest Proposal," Jonathan Swift <u>presents an outrageous and</u>

<u>disgusting idea calmly and rationally</u>. Beginning by establishing his cred-
₁

ibility, <u>the reader's confidence is gained by the anonymous writer</u>. First,
₂

he paints a dismal picture of the difficult lives of the country's poor. Next, the

writer promises great advantages from his solution, declaring it will apply

<u>not only to beggars but also </u>to other families. Then, the author states that
₃

he <u>has spent much time thinking about the problem and weighed</u>
₄

<u>different options carefully</u>. <u>He details his calculations about births. He</u>

<u>uses mathematics to present an image of rationality.</u> <u>Relying on expert</u>
₅   ₆

<u>testimony</u>, the writer dismisses another possible solution. Just before

finally dropping his bombshell, the writer states that he offers this idea

<u>"humbly" or hopes </u>there can be no objection. <u>Only after laying this</u>
₇   ₈

<u>careful groundwork</u> does Swift allow his anonymous writer to present his

insane idea.

1. **A.** NO CHANGE
   B. presents an outrageous and a disgusting idea calmly and rationally.
   C. presents calmly an outrageous, rational, and disgusting idea.
   D. calmly and rationally presents an outrageous and disgusting idea.

2. **F.** NO CHANGE
   G. the reader's confidence is gained by Swift.
   H. the confidence of the reader is gained by the anonymous writer.
   J. the anonymous writer gains the reader's confidence.

3. What is the function of *not only* and *but also*?
   A. They are adjectives.
   B. They are coordinating conjunctions.
   C. They are correlative conjunctions.
   D. They are subordinating conjunctions.

4. **F.** NO CHANGE
   G. has spent careful time thinking about the problem and weighed different options.
   H. has spent much time thinking about the problem and carefully weighing different options.
   J. has carefully spent time thinking about the problem and weighed different options.

5. **A.** NO CHANGE
   B. Because he details his calculations about births, he presents an image of rationality.
   C. He details his calculations about births, but uses mathematics to present an image of rationality.
   D. He details his calculations about births; however, he uses mathematics to present an image of rationality.

6. What word or words are modified by this clause?
   F. the writer
   G. dismisses
   H. another possible
   J. solution

7. **A.** NO CHANGE
   B. "humbly" and hopes
   C. "humbly" but hopes
   D. either "humbly" or hopes

8. What is the function of the underlined words?
   F. prepositional phrase
   G. adverb clause
   H. independent clause
   J. no purpose; the words should be eliminated

Timed Writing: Persuasive Essay [30 minutes]

An old saying goes, "If at first you don't succeed, try, try again." History is full of examples of people who reached their goals by sheer determination. However, persistence alone is not always sufficient to guarantee success.

In an essay, take a position on the above claim. You may argue any point of view. Be sure to back up your statements with sound reasoning and specific examples.

Academic Vocabulary
Carefully read the prompt and the assignment twice. Note key words and phrases, such as "take a position" or "examples," that clarify the assignment.

Performance Tasks

Follow the instructions to complete the tasks below as required by your teacher. As you work on each task, incorporate both general academic vocabulary and literary terms you learned in this unit.

Common Core State Standards

RL.11-12.2, RL.11-12.3, RL.11-12.4;
RI.11-12.2, RI.11-12.4, RI.11-12.5;
W.11-12.2, W.11-12.9.a, W.11-12.9.b;
SL.11-12.6

[For the full wording of the standards, see the standards chart in the front of your textbook.]

Writing

 Task 1: Literature [RL.11-12.2; W.11-12.2, W.11-12.9.a]

Analyze the Development of Themes

*Write an **essay** in which you analyze the development of two or more themes in a literary work from this unit.*

- Identify a literary work from this unit that presents two or more significant themes. State which work you chose and explain your reasons for this choice.

- Explain the themes the work expresses and identify specific ways in which each theme is introduced and developed. Include an analysis of how the themes interact and build on one another.

- Cite specific details from the literary work under discussion to support your analysis.

- Use appropriate and varied transitions to clarify the relationships among your ideas.

 Task 2: Literature [RL.11-12.3; W.11-12.2, W.11-12.9.a]

Analyze the Development of a Narrative

*Write an **essay** in which you analyze and evaluate the development of a narrative work from this unit.*

- Explain which work you chose and briefly summarize the essential elements, such as setting, situation, characters, conflict, and plot.

- Discuss how the author orders events and how he or she introduces and develops characters or new situations.

- Explain how the author's choices about the development of the narrative affect the reading experience and contribute to the narrative's larger meaning or themes.

- Organize your ideas so that each new idea builds on the one it follows to create a unified whole.

- Provide a concluding section that follows from the explanation presented.

 Task 3: Informational Text [RI.11-12.5; W.11-12.9.b]

Analyze and Evaluate Text Structure

*Write an **essay** in which you analyze and evaluate the structure of a work of nonfiction from this unit.*

- Identify a work of nonfiction from this unit and provide a brief summary of its central ideas and key supporting details.

- Explain the structure the author chose. To clarify the work's structure for the reader, provide a list, an outline, or a clear description of its structural elements.

- Evaluate the effectiveness of the author's choice of structure. Identify specific ways in which the structure either contributes to or detracts from the meaning, and consider whether the structure itself helps to add interest to the work.

- Organize your essay logically and use thoughtful transitional words and phrases to clarify the flow of your ideas. Provide a concluding section that follows from and supports the evaluation you presented.

Speaking and Listening

Task 4: Informational Text [RI.11-12.4; SL.11-12.6]

Analyze Word Choice and Meaning

Deliver an ***oral presentation*** *in which you analyze the use of language in a nonfiction work from this unit.*

- Introduce the work you chose. Provide information about the author, explain the work's historical context, and briefly summarize its central ideas.

- Provide a broad overview of the type of diction the author employs. Then, identify specific word choices that are critical to the writer's overall purpose and expression of ideas. State why you chose these words and phrases, and explain their figurative, technical, or connotative meanings.

- Consider any key words or phrases the author uses repeatedly and discuss how the meaning of those terms is modified or refined over the course of the work.

- Include examples from the text that illustrate and support your analysis.

- Speak clearly and precisely so that listeners can follow your line of reasoning.

Task 5: Informational Text [RI.11-12.2; SL.11-12.6]

Analyze Central Ideas

Deliver an ***oral presentation*** *in which you analyze and evaluate the central ideas in a work of nonfiction from this unit.*

- Explain which work you chose and provide information about the historical context, occasion and purpose for the writing, and the author.

- Identify two or more central ideas expressed in the work. Cite specific details to show how the author introduces, develops, and refines each idea.

- Discuss your assessment of the central ideas. Include an evaluation of how well the two central ideas build on and reinforce one another.

- Provide hand-outs or other materials to help your listeners understand your ideas.

- Organize and develop your presentation logically and clearly, avoiding abrupt shifts in focus and using language that provides clear transitions among ideas.

Task 6: Literature [RL.11-12.4; SL.11-12.6]

Analyze Word Choice and Tone

Deliver a ***visual presentation*** *in which you analyze the impact of word choice on tone in a literary work from this unit.*

- State which work you chose and summarize its key elements—setting, characters, events, and themes.

- Describe the tone of the work. Cite at least three specific word choices—especially those with rich connotations or multiple meanings—that contribute to this tone.

- Incorporate visuals, such as drawings, photographs, or word maps, that illustrate the words and phrases you chose and capture the overall tone of the work. Discuss these choices.

- Present your ideas clearly and logically, using formal English and academic vocabulary.

What is the relationship between literature and place?

London as a Character The literature of the period addressed in this unit is filled with vivid personalities, authors, and fictional characters alike. Perhaps the greatest literary star of the period, however, is the city of London.

Assignment Write a **literary analysis** of the work of three authors from this unit. Analyze the role that London played—a "character" in its own drama, a vivid backdrop for action, or an area for a certain social class—in each work.

Featured Titles

In this unit, you have read a variety of British literature from the seventeenth and eighteenth centuries. Continue to read works related to this era on your own. Select books that you enjoy, but challenge yourself to explore new topics, new authors, and works offering varied perspectives or approaches. The titles suggested below will help you get started.

LITERATURE

Moll Flanders
Daniel Defoe

Fiction Moll Flanders starts out life as "a poor desolate girl" in seventeenth-century England. Gradually, she claws her way up to a life of wealth and security, making mistakes along the way. The novel presents an interesting portrait of a woman who is more a victim of society's evils than an evildoer herself.

[An excerpt from Defoe's A Journal of the Plague Year *begins on page 590. Build knowledge by reading another novel by this author.]*

Gulliver's Travels
Jonathan Swift

Satire Shipwrecked and cast adrift, Lemuel Gulliver awakes to find himself in Lilliput, an island inhabited by people whose six-inch height makes their quarrels over fashion and fame seem ridiculous. His subsequent encounters with equally strange individuals give Gulliver new, bitter insights into human behavior. With its wild distortions and undertones of the grotesque, *Gulliver's Travels* defies the reader's expectations of a conventional traveler's tale.

[An excerpt from Gulliver's Travels *begins on page 606 of this book. Build knowledge by reading the full text.]*

Donne: Selected Poetry
John Donne   EXEMPLAR TEXT

Poetry Enjoy the poetry of Donne's romantic youth and the more spiritual poetry of his later life. This collection contains Donne's famous poem "A Valediction: Forbidding Mourning."

[Donne's poems appear on pages 482–490 of this book. Build knowledge by reading other poems by this author.]

INFORMATIONAL TEXTS

Historical Texts

The Diary of Samuel Pepys
Samuel Pepys
Modern Library, 2001

Diary In his diary, Pepys recorded his observations and impressions of some of the great events of his time, including the Great Plague of 1665 and the Great Fire of London in 1666. Equally engaging are his accounts of everyday life in the seventeenth century.

[An excerpt of the diary begins on page 571 in this book. Build knowledge by reading the full text.]

Selected Letters
Lady Mary Wortley Montagu

Letters Writer and essayist Montagu wrote about her experiences with great humor and a unique perspective. Read her selected letters to learn about the life of this extraordinary woman.

Contemporary Scholarship

A Preface to Paradise Lost
C. S. Lewis
Oxford University Press, 1961

Literary Criticism In this critically acclaimed book, C. S. Lewis, a literary scholar and famed children's author, discusses the importance of the epic as a literary form and provides insight into Milton's *Paradise Lost*.

Samuel Johnson
W. Jackson Bate
Counterpoint, 1998

Biography This biography of Samuel Johnson, author of *A Dictionary of the English Language*, describes both the private and the public life of this extraordinary man of letters. Winner of both the National Book Award and the Pulitzer Prize, the book presents an engaging, modern look at this larger-than-life figure.

Preparing to Read Complex Texts

Reading for College and Career In both college and the workplace, readers must analyze texts independently, draw connections among works that offer varied perspectives, and develop their own ideas and informed opinions. The questions shown below, and others that you generate on your own, will help you more effectively read and analyze complex college-level texts.

 **Common Core State Standards**

Reading Literature/Informational Text
10. By the end of grade 12, read and comprehend literature, including stories, dramas, and poems, and literary nonfiction at the high end of the grades 11-CCR text complexity band independently and proficiently.

When reading complex texts, ask yourself...

- What idea, experience, or story seems to have compelled the author to write? Has the author presented that idea, experience, or story in a way that I, too, find compelling?

- How might the author's era, social status, belief system, or personal experiences have affected the point of view he or she expresses in the text?

- How do my circumstances affect what I understand and feel about this text?

- What key idea does the author state explicitly? What key idea does he or she suggest or imply? Which details in the text help me to perceive implied ideas?

- Do I find multiple layers of meaning in the text? If so, what relationships do I see among these layers of meaning?

- How do details in the text connect or relate to one another? Do I find any details unconvincing, unrelated, or out of place?

- Do I find the text believable and convincing?

© Key Ideas and Details

- What patterns of organization or sequences do I find in the text? Do these patterns help me understand the ideas better?

- What do I notice about the author's style, including his or her diction, uses of imagery and figurative language, and syntax?

- Do I like the author's style? Is the author's style memorable?

- What emotional attitude does the author express toward the topic, the story, or the characters? Does this attitude seem appropriate?

- What emotional attitude does the author express toward me, the reader? Does this attitude seem appropriate?

- What do I notice about the author's voice—his or her personality on the page? Do I like this voice? Does it make me want to read on?

© Craft and Structure

- Is the work fresh and original?

- Do I agree with the author's ideas entirely, or are there elements I find unconvincing?

- Do I disagree with the author's ideas entirely, or are there elements I can accept as true?

- Based on my knowledge of British literature, history, and culture, does this work reflect the British tradition? Why or why not?

© Integration of Ideas

Resources

English Glossary

Essential Question vocabulary appears in **blue type**. High-utility Academic vocabulary is <u>underlined</u>.

A

abasement (uh BAYS muhnt) *n.* condition of being put down or humbled

abated (uh BAYT ihd) *v.* lessened

abide (uh BYD) *v.* to stay; remain

absolution (AB suh LOO shuhn) *n.* act of freeing someone of a sin or criminal charge

acceded (ak SEED uhd) *v.* yielded; agreed

accounts (uh KOWNTS) *n.* records of money received and paid out; financial records

adjure (uh JUR) *v.* request solemnly; appeal to earnestly

admonish (ad MON ihsh) *v.* caution

adroitly (uh DROYT lee) *adv.* with physical or mental skill

adulterations (uh duhl tuh RAY shuhnz) *n.* impurities; added ingredients that are improper or inferior

adversary (AD vuhr sehr ee) *n.* opponent; enemy

<u>**advocate**</u> (AD vuh kayt) *v.* speak or write in support of

affably (AF uh blee) *adv.* in a friendly manner

affinities (uh FIHN uh teez) *n.* family connections; sympathies

affluence (AF loo uhns) *n.* abundant wealth

ague (AY gyoo) *n.* a chill or fit of shivering

alderman (AWL duhr muhn) *n.* chief officers in a shire or county

alters (AWL tuhrz) *v.* changes

amiable (AY mee uh buhl) *adj.* friendly; agreeable

amorous (AM uhr uhs) *adj.* full of love or desire

anarchy (AN uhr kee) *n.* absence of government; disorder

anatomize (uh NAT uh myz) *v.* to dissect in order to examine structure

ancestral (an SEHS truhl) *adj.* inherited

anemic (uh NEE mihk) *adj.* lacking power, vigor, vitality, or colorfulness; listless; weak

<u>**annotate**</u> (AN uh tayt) *v.* note or mark with explanation

antic (AN tihk) *adj.* odd and funny; silly

antidote (AN tee doht) *n.* something that works against an unwanted condition; remedy

aperture (AP uhr chur) *n.* opening

apothecary (uh POTH uh kehr ee) *n.* pharmacist; druggist

appalled (uh PAWLD) *v.* filled with consternation or dismay

appendage (uh PEHN dihj) *n.* something added on

apprehension (ap rih HEHN shuhn) *n.* anxious feeling of foreboding; dread

apprehensions (ap rih HEHN shuhnz) *n.* fears; concerns

approbation (AP ruh BAY shuhn) *n.* official approval or sanction

arboreal (ahr BAWR ee uhl) *adj.* of, near, or among trees

<u>**articulate**</u> (ahr TIHK yuh layt) *v.* express clearly

artifice (AHR tuh fihs) *n.* skill; the product of skill, especially a skillful deception

artificiality (AHR tuh fihsh ee AL uh tee) *n.* unnatural; unreal

aspire (uh SPYR) *v.* have high ambitions; yearn or seek after

assault (uh SAWLT) *v.* violently attack

assessing (uh SEHS ihng) *v.* to estimate the value of (property) for taxation

assiduous (uh SIHJ oo uhs) *adj.* constant in application or attention

assignations (AS ihg NAY shuhn) *n.* appointments to meet

asunder (uh SUHN duhr) *adj.* into parts or pieces

atrophy (AT ruh fee) *v.* to waste away

augment (awg MEHNT) *v.* make greater; enlarge

authentic (aw THEHN tihk) *adj.* genuine; real

avarice (AV uhr ihs) *n.* greed

averred (uh VURD) *v.* stated to be true

awe (aw) *n.* mixed feeling of reverence, fear, and wonder

B

balm (bahm) *n.* ointment or other thing that heals or soothes

bar (bahr) *n.* one of the vertical lines dividing written music into equal sections called measures

beliefs (bih LEEFS) *n.* what is held to be true

bequeath (bih KWEETH) *v.* hand down as an inheritance

bilious (BIHL yuhs) *adj.* peevish; irritable; crank

blight (blyt) *n.* condition of withering

blithe (blyTH) *adj.* cheerful

boundary (BOWN duhr ee) *n.* limiting line; border

breach (breech) *n.* breaking or being broken; failure to observe the terms of an agreement

brink (brihngk) *n.* edge; margin

burden (BUR duhn) *n.* something that weighs one down; a heavy load or responsibility

C

cadence (KAY duhns) *n.* measured movement

caprices (kuh PREES ez) *n.* whims

capitalism (KAP uh tuh lihz uhm) *n.* economic system in which private individuals or groups of individuals own land, factories, and other means of production

<u>**categorize**</u> (KAT uh guh ryz) *v.* place in related groups

censure (SEHN shuhr) *v.* strongly disapprove; condemn

certify (SUR tuh fy) *v.* declare a thing true or accurate; verify; attest

<u>**characterize**</u> (KAR ihk tuh ryz) *v.* describe features, qualities, or traits

chronicle (KRON uh kuhl) *n.* historical record of events in chronological order

chrysalis (KRIHS uh lihs) *n.* the third stage in the development of a moth or butterfly

circumscribed (SUR kuhm skrybd) *v.* limited; having a definite boundary

<u>**cite**</u> (syt) *v.* quote from a text

city (SIHT ee) *n.* large and heavily populated town

clamorous (KLAM uhr uhs) *adj.* loud and confused; noisy

<u>**clarify**</u> (KLAR uh fy) *v.* make clear

clasped (klaspt) *v.* firmly grasped or gripped

classics (KLAS ihks) *n.* books or paintings of the highest quality

<u>**classify**</u> (KLAS uh fy) *v.* assign to a category

climacteric (kly MAK tuhr ihk) *n.* any critical period

colonize (KOL uh nyz) *v.* establish a settlement

combatants (KOM buh tuhnts) *n.* fighters

combustible (kuhm BUHS tuh buhl) *adj.* capable of being ignited and burned; flammable

commentary (KOM uhn TEHR ee) *n.* a series of comments

commission (kuh MIHSH uhn) *n.* authorization; act of giving authority to an individual

commodity (kuh MOD uh tee) *n.* product that is bought or sold

compassionate (kuhm PASH uh niht) *adj.* sympathizing

compile (kuhm PYL) *v.* put together

complaisant (kuhm PLAY zuhnt) *adj.* agreeable; willing to please

comprised (kuhm PRYZD) *v.* consisted of; included

concord (KON kawrd) *n.* friendly relations; harmony

condescension (kon dih SEHN shuhn) *n.* a patronizing act

conflagration (KON fluh GRAY shuhn) *n.* great fire

conflict (KON flihkt) *n.* a fight or struggle

conjecture (kuhn JEHK chuhr) *v.* guess

connote (kuh NOHT) *v.* suggest or convey

conquest (KON kwehst) *n.* act of conquering

consciousness (KON shuhs nihs) *n.* state of being aware

constituency (kuhn STIHCH oo uhn see) *n.* the people making up a body of voters

construct (kuhn STRUHKT) *v.* build by fitting parts together systematically

contemporary (kuhn TEHM puh rehr ee) *adj.* belonging to the same period of time

contemptuous (kuhn TEHMP choo uhs) *adj.* scornful

contend (kuhn TEHND) *v.* assert or argue

contention (kuhn TEHN shuhn) *n.* dispute; argument

contentious (kuhn TEHN shuhs) *adj.* quarrelsome

contextualize (kuhn TEHKS choo uh lyz) *v.* place information within a larger background

contrite (kuhn TRYT) *adj.* willing to repent or atone

controversy (KON truh vur see) *n.* act of arguing a question about which differences of opinion exist

contusions (kuhn TOO zhuhnz) *n.* an injury in which the skin is not broken; a bruise

conventional (kuhn VEHN shuh nuhl) *adj.* acting or behaving according to commonly accepted or approved ways

coordinate (koh AWR duh nayt) *v.* relate or link

country (KUHN tree) *n.* land; nation

covetousness (KUHV uh tuhs nuhs) *n.* greediness

conviction (kuhn VIHK shuhn) *n.* belief; faith

countenance (KOWN tuh nuhns) *n.* face

courtly (KAWRT lee) *adj.* elegantly dignified; polite

cower (KOW uhr) *v.* crouched, as from fear or cold

coyness (KOY nuhs) *n.* shyness; aloofness, often as part of a flirtation

credulity (kruh DOO luh tee) *n.* tendency to believe too readily

credulous (KREHJ uh luhs) *adj.* tending to believe too readily

critique (krih TEEK) *v.* examine critically; review

cultivated (KUHL tuh vay tihd) *v.* grown

cynically (SIHN uh kuhl ee) *adv.* like or characteristic of a cynic; distrusting or disparaging the motives of other

D

dappled (DAP uhld) *adj.* a spot or mottled marking, usually occurring in clusters

dauntless (DAWNT lihs) *adj.* fearless; cannot be intimidated

debate (dih BAYT) *v.* discuss opposing reasons

deduce (dih DOOS) *v.* infer from a general principle

deference (DEHF uhr uhns) *n.* courteous regard or respect

deficient (dih FIHSH uhnt) *adj.* lacking an essential quality

define (dih FYN) *v.* tell the qualities that make something what it is

deftly (DEHFT lee) *adv.* with ease and quickness

deism (DEE ihz uhm) *n.* belief in God on the evidence of reason and nature

deliberation (dih lihb uh RAY shuhn) *n.* careful consideration and discussion before reaching a decision

delirious (dih LIHR ee uhs) *adj.* having hallucinations; ranting

demonstrate (DEHM uhn strayt) *v.* show by reasoning or examples

denote (dih NOHT) *v.* refer to clearly

depict (dih PIHKT) *v.* portray an image using words

depredation (dep ruh DAY shuhn) *n.* a predatory attack; a raid

derided (dih RYD ihd) *v.* made fun of; ridiculed

design (dih ZYN) *v.* condescend; lower oneself

desolate (DEHS uh liht) *adj.* deserted; forlorn

despondent (dih SPON duhnt) *adj.* hopeless; dejected

despotic (dehs POT ihk) *adj.* tyrannical

destitute (DEHS tuh toot) *adj.* lacking

destruction (dih STRUHK shuhn) *n.* act of destroying

devise (dih VYZ) *v.* work out or create; plan

diffusive (dih FYOO sihv) *adj.* tending to spread out

disabused (dihs uh BYOOZ) *v.* freed from false ideas

discern (duh ZURN) *v.* recognize as separate or different

discreet (dihs KREET) *adj.* wise; prudent

discretion (dihs KREHSH uhn) *n.* care in what one does and says; good judgment; prudence

dislocation (dihs loh KAY shuhn) *n.* condition of being out of place

dispensation (dihs puhn SAY shuhn) *n.* religious system or beliefs

disposable (dihs POH zuh buhl) *adj.* free for use; available

dissatisfaction (dihs sat ihs FAK shuhn) *n.* state of being discontent

dissect (dih SEHKT) *v.* analyze and interpret minutely

distemper (dihs TEHM puhr) *n.* infectious disease such as the plague

distill (dihs TIHL) *v.* to obtain the essential part

divine (duh VYN) *adj.* heavenly; holy

dominion (duh MIHN yuhn) *n.* rule or power over a territory; authority or control

dominions (duh MIHN yuhnz) *n.* governed territories or lands

dowry (DOW ree) *n.* property brought by a woman's family to her husband upon their marriage

dregs (drehgz) *n.* a small amount; a residue

E

eclipse (ih KLIHPS) *v.* dimming or extinction of power or glory

economic (ee kuh NOM ihk) *adj.* having to do with the management of the income

edit (EHD iht) *v.* alter, adapt, or refine

effigy (EHF uh jee) *n.* portrait or statue of a person

electors (ih LEHK tuhrz) *n.* those who vote

eloquent (EHL uh kwuhnt) *adj.* beautifully expressive

eludes (ih LOODZ) *v.* avoids or escapes

embarked (ehm BAHRKT) *v.* engaged in something, such as a journey

embellishments (ehm BEHL ihsh muhnts) *n.* decorative touches; ornamentation

eminent (EHM uh nuhnt) *adj.* noteworthy; of high rank; distinguished

empire (EHM pyr) *n.* group of nations or states under one ruler or government

encomiums (ehn KOH mee uhmz) *n.* formal expressions of great praise

endeavored (ehn DEHV uhrd) *n.* made a serious attempt; tried

enhance (ehn HANS) *v.* improve or heighten

enigma (ih NIHG muh) *n.* riddle; perplexing statement, person, or situation

entreated (ehn TREET uhd) *v.* begged; pleaded with

enumerate (ih NOO muh rayt) *v.* specify a list

epic (EHP ihk) *n.* long poem that tells of the adventures of one or more great heroes

equate (ih KWAYT) *v.* consider one thing the same as another

equivocate (ih KWIHV uh kayt) *v.* to use terms that have two or more meanings to mislead purposely or deceive

escapade (EHS kuh payd) *n.* adventurous action, especially one that breaks ordinary rules of conduct

esteemed (ehs TEEMD) *adj.* highly respected; held in high regard

etymology (eht uh MOL uh jee) *n.* the study of word origins

evaluate (ih VAL yoo ayt) *v.* determine something's significance, worth, or condition

evanescence (ehv uh NEHS uhns) *n.* vanishing or tendency to vanish

evoke (ih VOHK) *v.* draw out a reaction

exemplary (ehg ZEHM pluhr ee) *adj.* of that which should serve as a model

exile (EHG zyl) *v.* force a person to leave home or country

exotic (ehg ZOT ihk) *adj.* from a foreign country

expedient (ehk SPEE dee uhnt) *n.* device used in an emergency

expiated (EHKS pee ayt uhd) *v.* atoned; made amends for, especially by suffering

extract (ehk STRAKT) *v.* draw out information

extravagant (ehk STRAV uh guhnt) *adj.* going beyond reasonable limits; excessive

F

fantastic (fan TAS tihk) *adj.* very fanciful; unbelievably good

fastidious (fas TIHD ee uhs) *adj.* particular; difficult to please

fate (fayt) *n.* destiny

fathom (FATH uhm) *v.* understand thoroughly

fervent (FUR vuhnt) *adj.* having great warmth of feeling

fidelity (fy DEHL uh tee) *n.* faithfulness

filial (FIHL ee uhl) *adj.* expected of a son or a daughter

form (FAWR myuh layt) *v.* give shape to

format (FAWR mat) *v.* arrange according to a plan

formulate (FAWR myuh layt) *v.* express fully and clearly; devise

fortitude (FAWR tuh tood) *n.* courage; strength to endure

fracture (FRAK chuhr) *n.* the act of breaking; state of being broken

frugally (FROO guhl ee) *adv.* in a way that is careful with money

furrow (FUR oh) *n.* narrow groove made in the ground by a plow

G

gall (gawl) *n.* bitter feeling; deep spite

galled (gawld) *adj.* injured or made sore by rubbing or chafing

galleons (GAL ee uhnz) *n.* large sailing ships used for war or trade

garnished (GAHR nihsht) *v.* decorated; trimmed

garrulous (GAR uh luhs) *adj.* talkative

gaunt (gawnt) *adj.* thin and bony, as from great hunger or age

geography (jee OG ruh fee) *n.* surface features of a place or region

ghastly (GAST lee) *adj.* terrible; very bad

gleaned (gleend) *v.* collected from bit by bit, as when gathering stray grain after a harvest

gout (gowt) *n.* a mass or splash, as of blood; spurt

grandeur (GRAN juhr) *n.* splendor; magnificence

gravity (GRAV uh tee) *n.* weight; seriousness

grievances (GREE vuhns ez) *n.* circumstances that cause people to complain

grieved (greevd) *v.* felt deep grief for; mourned

guile (gyl) *n.* artful trickery

H

haggard (HAG uhrd) *adj.* appearing worn and exhausted; gaunt

harbingers (HAHR bihn juhrz) *n.* forerunners

heedless (HEED lihs) *adj.* not taking notice; inattentive

highlight (HY lyt) *v.* emphasize

hoary (HAWR ee) *adj.* white or gray with age

homespun (hohm spuhn) *adj.* spun or made at home; plain

hypothesize (hy POTH uh syz) *v.* suggest a possible explanation

I

ideal (y DEE uhl) *n.* perfect type

idealism (y DEE uh lihz uhm) *n.* a belief in or pursuit of things as they should be

ignoble (ihg NOH buhl) *adj.* not noble; common

ignominy (IHG nuh mihn ee) *n.* humiliation; dishonor

illumine (ih LOO muhn) *v.* light up

illusion (ih LOO zhuhn) *n.* appearance or feeling that misleads because it is not real

immigrant (IHM uh gruhnt) *n.* person who comes into a foreign country to live

immortal (ih MAWR tuhl) *adj.* living or lasting forever; not dying

impediments (ihm PEHD uh muhnts) *n.* obstacles

imperceptibly (ihm puhr SEHP tuh buhl ee) *adv.* without being noticed

imperial (ihm PIHR ee uhl) *adj.* of an empire; having supreme authority

imperialism (ihm PIHR ee uh lihz uhm) *n.* policy of forming an empire by conquest and colonization

impertinence (ihm PUR tuh nuhns) *n.* rudeness; impudence

imperturbable (ihm puhr TUR buh buhl) *adj.* calm; not easily ruffled

implored (ihm PLAWRD) *v.* begged earnestly

importuning (ihm pawr TOON ihng) *v.* pleading with

impressionistic (ihm prehsh uh NIHS tihk) *adj.* conveying a picture through quickly sketched suggestions of details

impudence (IHM pyuh duhns) *n.* lack of shame; rudeness

impulse (IHM puhls) *n.* force driving forward

inane (ihn AYN) *adj.* lacking sense, significance, or ideas; silly

incessant (ihn SEHS uhnt) *adj.* continuing without interruption; ceaseless

incitement (ihn SYT muhnt) *n.* act of urging; encouragement

inconstancy (ihn KON stuhn see) *n.* fickleness; changeableness

inconstantly (ihn KON stuhnt lee) *adv.* changeably; in a fickle way

incredulously (ihn KR uh luhs lee) *adv.* in a manner expressing doubt or disbelief

independence (ihn dih PEHN duhns) *n.* freedom from the control of others

indignant (ihn DIHG nuhnt) *adj.* outraged; filled with righteous anger

indissoluble (ihn dih SOL yuh buhl) *adj.* not able to be dissolved or undone

inducted (ihn DUHKT ihd) *v.* brought formally into an organization

industry (IHN duh stree) *n.* any branch of business, trade, or manufacture

inevitable (ihn EHV uh tuh buhl) *adj.* unavoidable; certain to happen

infamy (IHN fuh mee) *n.* very bad reputation; disgrace; dishonor

infirmity (n FUR muh tee) *n.* physical or mental defect; illness

ingenuous (ihn JEHN yoo uhs) *adj.* naïve; simple

ingratiating (ihn GRAY shee ay tihng) *adj.* charming; agreeable; pleasing

inheritance (ihn HEHR uh tuhns) *n.* act of inheriting

inklings (IHNGK lihngz) *n.* indirect suggestions; vague ideas

innumerable (ih NOO muhr uh buhl) *adj.* too many to count

insatiableness (ihn SAY shuh buhl nuhs) *n.* the quality of being impossible to fill

instantaneous (IHN stuhn TAY nee uhs) *adj.* done or happening in an instant

integrate (IHN tuh grayt) *v.* bring together distinct parts

intemperance (ihn TEHM puhr uhns) *n.* lack of restraint

interpret (ihn TUR priht) *v.* explain the meaning

interpretation (ihn tur pruh TAY shuhn) *n.* act of explaining

interred (ihn TURD) *v.* buried in the earth

intrigues (ihn TREEGZ) *n.* plots or schemes

intrinsically (ihn TRIHN suh kuhl ee) *adv.* at its core; inherently; innately

invasion (ihn VAY zhuhn) *n.* entering by force

invincible (ihn VIHN suh buhl) *adj.* unconquerable

irrevocable (ih REHV uh kuh buhl) *adj.* unable to be undone or cancelled

isolation (y suh LAY shuhn) *n.* state of being completely separated from others

J

judicious (joo DIHSH uhs) *adj.* showing good judgment

K

keenly (KEEN lee) *adv.* sharply; intensely

ken (kehn) *n.* range of sight or knowledge

kindred (KIHN drihd) *n.* a person's relatives collectively

kingdoms (KIHNG duhm) *n.* countries that are governed by a king or queen

L

label (LAY buhl) *v.* describe or designate

laity (LAY uh tee) *n.* those not initiated into a priesthood

lament (luh MEHNT) *v.* to express grief over; to mourn

lamentable (LAM uhn tuh buhl) *adj.* causing grief; distressing

lamentations (lam uhn TAY shuhnz) *n.* expressions of grief or mourning

languish (LANG gwihsh) *v.* become weak; droop; suffer from longing

languished (LANG gwihsht) *v.* weakened; dulled

languor (LANG guhr) *n.* lack of energy or vitality; sluggishness

largesse (LAHR jihs) *n.* nobility of spirit

larking (LAHRK ihng) *v.* free-spirited, whimsical fun

legacy (LEHG uh see) *n.* money or other property left to a person by the will of someone who has died

lintel (LIHN tuhl) *n.* horizontal bar above a door

loathsome (LOHTH suhm) *adj.* disgusting

loyalties (LOY uhl teez) *n.* loyal feelings or behaviors; faithfulness

loyalty (LOY uhl tee) *n.* loyal feeling or behavior; faithfulness

ludicrous (LOO duh kruhs) *adj.* absurd; ridiculous

lustrous (LUHS truhs) *adj.* having luster; shining; luminous

M

macadam (muh KAD uhm) *n.* the broken stone used in making a road

madrigals (MAD ruh guhlz) *n.* short love poems set to music

magistrate (MAJ uh strayt) *n.* a local official who administers the law or serves as a judge

malevolence (muh LEHV uh luhns) *n.* ill will; spitefulness

malicious (muh LIHSH uhs) *adj.* deliberately harmful; destructive

massive (MAS ihv) *adj.* big and solid; bulky

measure (MEHZH uhr) *n.* a section of written music between two vertical lines called bars; a bill, resolution, or something else proposed or enacted to improve a situation

melodious (muh LOH dee uhs) *adj.* sweet-sounding; tuneful

melody (MEHL uh dee) *n.* a sequence of single tones that together create a tune or song

migrated (MY grayt uhd) *v.* moved from one region or country to another

mobility (moh BIHL uh tee) *n.* ability to move

mockeries (MOK uhr eez) *n.* futile or disappointing efforts; ridicule

modernization (mod uhr nuh ZAY shuhn) *n.* bringing up to the present ways or standards

monarch (MON uhrk) *n.* country ruled by one person

monotonous (muh NOT uh nuhs) *adj.* without variation

morose (muh ROHS) *adj.* gloomy; sullen

mortal (MAWR tuhl) *adj.* of that which must eventually die

multitudinous (muhl tuh TOO duh nuhs) *adj.* existing in great numbers

munificence (myoo NIHF uh suhns) *n.* lavish generosity

N

nature (NAY chuhr) *n.* all things except those made by man

nimble (NIHM buhl) *adj.* able to move quickly and lightly

nocturnal (nok TUR nuhl) *adj.* occurring at night

notorious (noh TAWR ee uhs) *adj.* widely but unfavorably known; having a bad reputation

nuisance (NOO suhns) *n.* act, thing, or condition causing trouble

O

obdurate (OB duhr iht) *adj.* stubborn

obedience (oh BEE dee uhns) *n.* the act of following orders or instructions

obliquely (uh BLEEK lee) *adv.* at a slant; indirectly

obscure (uhb SKYUR) *adj.* not easily seen; not generally known

obscure (uhb SKYUR) *v.* making difficult to see

obstinate (OB stuh niht) *adj.* stubborn; dogged

obstinately (OB stuh niht lee) *adv.* in a determined way; stubbornly

officious (uh FIHSH uhs) *adj.* meddlesome

ordeal (awr DEEL) *n.* difficult or painful experience that tests one

order (AWR duhr) *n.* way one thing follows another

orthodox (AWR thuh doks) *adj.* conforming to established beliefs

outcast (OWT KAST) *n.* person cast out from home and friends

outline (OWT LYN) *v.* develop a general plan

P

pallor (PAL uhr) *n.* unnatural lack of color; paleness

palpable (PAL puh buhl) *adj.* capable of being touched or felt

palpitation (pal puh TAY shuhn) *n.* an unusually or abnormally rapid or violent beating of the heart

paltry (PAWL tree) *adj.* practically worthless; insignificant

paradox (PAR uh doks) *n.* statement that may be true but seems to say two opposite things

paraphrase (PAR uh frayz) *v.* reword something spoken or written

pastoral (PAS tuhr uhl) *n.* simple or naturally beautiful like the country

pathos (PAY thos) *n.* quality that evokes sorrow or compassion

patronize (PAY truh nyz) *v.* to be a customer of a particular merchant or store

penury (PEHN yuhr ee) *n.* poverty

perceive (puhr SEEV) *v.* recognize through the senses

peril (PEHR uhl) *n.* exposure to harm or injury

pernicious (puhr NIHSH uhs) *adj.* causing great injury, destruction, or ruin; fatal; deadly

phantasm (FAN taz uhm) *n.* supernatural form or shape; ghost; figment of the imagination

philosophy (fuh LOS uh fee) *n.* system for guiding life

piety (PY uh tee) *n.* devotion to religion

platitude (PLAT uh tood) *n.* commonplace or overused statement

plebeian (plih BEE uhn) *adj.* common; not aristocratic

power (POW uhr) *n.* strength or force

predominance (prih DOM uh nuhns) *n.* superiority

predominant (prih DOM uh nuhnt) *adj.* foremost; powerful

prefiguring (pree FIHG yuhr ihng) *v.* resembling and so suggesting beforehand

prenatal (pree NAY tuhl) *adj.* existing or taking place before birth

presumed (prih ZOOMD) *v.* taken for granted; assumed

presumption (prih ZUHMP shuhn) *n.* audacity

prevail (prih VAYL) *v.* to succeed; become dominant; win out

prevarication (pree VAR uh KAY shuhn) *n.* evasion of truth

prime (prym) *n.* best stage of a thing or process

pristine (PRIHS teen) *adj.* original; unspoiled

probe (prohb) *v.* search into and explore thoroughly

prodding (PROD ihng) *v.* poking, jabbing, seeking

prodigal (PROD uh guhl) *adj.* recklessly wasteful

prodigious (pruh DIHJ uhs) *adj.* enormous; huge

profanation (PROF uh NAY shuhn) *n.* action showing disrespect for something sacred

proferring (PROF uhr ihng) *n.* offering

profuse (pruh FYOOS) *adj.* abundant; pouring out

progress (PROG rehs) *n.* growth; improvement

promontories (PROM uhn tawr eez) *n.* peaks of high land sticking out into a body of water

prophet (PROF iht) *n.* person who tells what will happen

propitiate (pruh PIHSH ee ayt) *v.* win the goodwill of; appease

propose (pruh POHZ) *v.* set forth a plan or intention

propriety (pruh PRY uh tee) *n.* quality or condition of being proper

prosper (PROS puhr) *v.* to thrive

prowess (PROW ihs) *n.* heroism; distinction

prudence (PROO duhns) *n.* careful management of resources; economy

pulp (puhlp) *n.* the soft, juicy, edible part of a fruit

purge (purj) *v.* purify; cleanse

R

rancor (RANG kuhr) *n.* ill will; continuing and bitter hate

ransacked (RAN sakt) *v.* searched through to find goods to rob; Looted

rapture (RAP chuhr) *n.* joy; great pleasure

rapturous (RAP chuhr uhs) *adj.* filled with joy and love; ecstatic

rational (RASH uh nuhl) *adj.* sensible; reasonable

realms (rehlmz) *n.* regions under the rule of a king or queen

rebellious (rih BEHL yuhs) *adj.* defying authority

rebuild (ree BIHLD) *v.* build or create again

rebuke (rih BYOOK) *v.* criticize strongly

recall (rih KAWL) *v.* remember

reckoning (REHK uhn ihng) *n.* accounting

recoil (rih KOYL) *v.* to draw back in fear, surprise, or disgust

recommend (rehk uh MEHND) *v.* suggest favorably

recompense (REHK uhm pehns) *n.* payment in return for something

recount (rih KOWNT) *v.* tell in detail

reform (rih FAWRM) *v.* make better

reformation (REHF uhr MAY shuhn) *n.* change for the better; improvement

refractory (rih FRAK tuhr ee) *adj.* hard to manage; stubborn

refute (rih FYOOT) *v.* prove wrong

reiterate (ree IHT uh rayt) *v.* state or do over again

relates (rih LAYTS) *v.* tells

remnant (REHM nuhnt) *n.* what is left over; remainder

Renaissance (REHN uh sahns) *n.* great revival of art and learning in Europe during the 1300s, 1400s, and 1500s

reparation (rehp uh RAY shuhn) *n.* compensation for a wrong

reprove (rih PROOV) *v.* to disapprove of strongly; censure

requiem (REHK wee uhm) *n.* musical composition honoring the dead

resolution (rehz uh LOO shuhn) *n.* a resolve or determination

resume (rih ZOOM) *v.* to take up or go on with again after interruption

reticent (REHT uh suhnt) *adj.* silent; reserved

reverence (REHV uhr uhns) *n.* deep respect

reverently (REHV uhr uhnt lee) *adv.* with deep respect or awe

revolution (rehv uh LOO shuhn) *n.* complete overthrow of an established government or political system

righteousness (RY chuhs nihs) *n.* the characteristic of acting in a just, virtuous manner

risible (RIHZ uh buhl) *adj.* prompting laughter

rites (ryts) *n.* ceremonies; rituals

role (rohl) *n.* part or function assumed by any person or thing

roused (rowzd) *v.* stirred up

rue (roo) *n.* sorrow; regret

rummage (RUHM ihj) *v.* to search thoroughly or actively through

S

sanguine (SANG gwihn) *adj.* confident; cheerful

satiety (suh TY uh tee) *n.* state of being filled with enough or more than enough

sauntered (SAWN tuhrd) *v.* walked at an unhurried pace

scales (skaylz) *n.* thin, platelike pieces on an animal or plant

schism (SIHZ uhm) *n.* division of a group into factions

scope (skohp) *n.* range of perception or understanding

scurry (SKUR ee) *v.* to run hastily; to scamper

segmented (SEHG muhnt uhd) *v.* divided into joined parts

semblance (SEHM bluhns) *n.* appearance; image

sentinel (SEHN tuh nuhl) *n.* person or animal that guards

sepulcher (SEHP uhl kuhr) *n.* tomb

sequestered (sih KWEHS tuhrd) *v.* kept apart from others

shrill (shrihl) *adj.* high and sharp in tone; high-pitched

sinews (SIHN yooz) *n.* tendons

sinuous (SIHN yu uhs) *adj.* bending; winding

skeptical (SKEHP tuh kuhl) *adj.* doubting; not easily persuaded

smudge (smuhj) *n.* a smear or stain of dirt

sojourn (SOH jurn) *n.* short stay someplace; visit

solace (SOL ihs) *n.* comfort; relief

solicitous (suh LIHS uh tuhs) *adj.* showing care or concern

sordid (SAWR dihd) *adj.* dirty

sound (sownd) *adj.* healthy; undamaged

sovereign (SOV ruhn) *adj.* supreme in power, rank, or authority

specious (SPEE shuhs) *adj.* deceptively attractive or valid; false

spectral (SPEHK truhl) *adj.* ghostly

spellbound (SPEHL BOWND) *adj.* bound by or as if by a spell

spirit (SPIHR iht) *n.* immaterial part of man

sprawling (SPRAWL ihng) *adj.* spread out

stagnant (STAG nuhnt) *adj.* motionless; foul

stature (STACH uhr) *n.* height; level of achievement

stead (stehd) *n.* position being filled by a replacement

steadfastly (STEHD fast lee) *adv.* fixed in direction; steadily directed

stealthy (STEHL thee) *adj.* secretive; furtive; sly

stoic (STOH ihk) *n.* person indifferent to joy, grief, pleasure, or pain

struggle (STRUHG uhl) *v.* work hard against difficulties

subdued (suhb DOOD) *adj.* quiet; inhibited; repressed; controlled

substantial (suhb STAN shuhl) *adj.* having substance, large in size or strength

succor (SUHK uhr) *v.* help; aid; relief

suffused (suh FYOOZD) *v.* spread throughout; filled

sulk (suhlk) *v.* to show resentment by refusing to interact with others

sullen (SUHL uhn) *adj.* gloomy; dismal

sundry (SUHN dree) *adj.* various; miscellaneous

supine (soo PAHYN) *adj.* lying on the back

supplication (suhp luh KAY shuhn) *n.* act of praying or pleading

surmise (suhr MYZ) *n.* imaginings; speculation; guess

sustenance (SUHS tuh nuhns) *n.* food or money to support life

symbolize (SIHM buh lyz) *v.* represent a thing or concept

symmetry (SIHM uh tree) *n.* balanced form; the beauty resulting from such balance

syntax (SIHN taks) *n.* the study of sentence structure

T

tarry (TAR ee) *v.* to delay or linger

technology (tehk NOL uh jee) *n.* science of the mechanical and industrial arts

teeming (TEE mihng) *v.* filled to overflowing

temperate (TEHM puhr iht) *adj.* mild

tempestuous (tehm PEHS chu uhs) *adj.* turbulent; stormy

tenacity (tih NAS uh tee) *n.* persistence; stubbornness

terrestrial (tuh REHS tree uhl) *adj.* relating to the earth or to this world

topographical (top uh GRAF uh kuhl) *adj.* representing the surface features of a region

tortuous (TAWR chu uhs) *adj.* full of twists, turns, or bends; twisting, winding, or crooked

traditional (truh DIHSH uh nuhl) *adj.* customary

transformation (trans fuhr MAY shuhn) *n.* act or process of changing

transgress (tranz GREHS) *v.* violate a law or command

transgressed (tranz GREHST) *v.* overstepped or broke (a law or commandment)

tranquil (TRANG kwuhl) *adj.* calm; serene; peaceful

transcendent (tran SEHN duhnt) *adj.* exceeding beyond all limits

transient (TRAN shuhnt) *adj.* temporary; passing

treachery (TREHCH uhr ee) *n.* betrayal of trust, faith, or allegiance

treasons (TREE zuhnz) *n.* betrayals of one's country or oath of loyalty

trends (trehndz) *n.* general directions; fashions or styles

trepidation (TREHP uh DAY shuhn) *n.* trembling

tribe (tryb) *n.* group of people united by race and customs

trifles (TRY fuhlz) *n.* things of little value or importance

truculent (TRUHK yuh luhnt) *adj.* cruel; fierce

tumid (TOO mihd) *adj.* swollen

tumult (TOO muhlt) *n.* noisy commotion, often caused by a crowd

turbid (TUR bihd) *adj.* muddy or cloudy; stirred up and confused

turmoil (TUR moyl) *n.* a state of great commotion, confusion, or disturbance

tyrants (TY ruhnts) *n.* cruel, oppressive rulers

U

uncanny (uhn KAN ee) *adj.* mysterious; hard to explain

undeterminable (uhn dih TUR muh nuh buhl) *adj.* not able to be decided or settled

ungenial (uhn JEEN yuhl) *adj.* disagreeable; characterized by bad weather

upbraidings (uhp BRAY dihngz) *n.* stern words of disapproval; scoldings

urban (UR buhn) *adj.* that is or has the essential characteristics of a city

utters (UHT uhrz) *v.* sends forth with the voice

V

vales (vaylz) *n.* valleys; hollows; depressed stretches of ground

valor (VAL uhr) *n.* courageous behavior; bravery

values (VAL yooz) *n.* principles

venerable (VEHN uhr uh buhl) *adj.* commanding respect because of age, character, or social rank

verge (vurj) *n.* edge; rim

vindication (vihn duh KAY shuhn) *n.* act of providing justification or support for

vintage (VIHN tihj) *n.* wine of fine quality

vivacious (vy VAY shuhs) *adj.* lively, spirited

vulnerable (VUHL nuhr uh buhl) *adj.* exposed to attack or harm

W

wallowed (WOL ohd) *v.* rolled around in mud, water, etc.

wan (won) *adj.* sickly pale; faint or weak

waning (WAY nihng) *v.* gradually becoming dimmer or weaker

welfare (WEHL FAIR) *n.* condition of being well; health

winsome (WIHN suhm) *adj.* having a charming appearance or way

wither (WIHTH uhr) *v.* fade or waste away

wreath (reeth) *n.* circle of flowers

writhes (rythz) *v.* twists and turns the body, as in agony

writhing (RYTH ihng) *n.* twisting or turning motion

Spanish Glossary

El vocabulario de Pregunta Essential aparece en **azul**. El vocabulario academico de alta utilidad está <u>subrayado</u>.

A

abasement / humillación *s.* condición de ser degradado o rebajado

abated / disminuido *v.* reducido

abide / permanecer *v.* quedarse; mantenerse

absolution / absolución *s.* acto de librar a alguien de un pecado o acusación criminal

acceded / accedió *v.* cedió; acordó

accounts / cuentas *s.* registros de dinero recibido y pagado; registros financieros

adjure / implorar *v.* solicitar solemnemente; conjurar seriamente

admonish / amonestar *v.* advertir

adroitly / diestramente *adv.* con destreza física o mental

adulterations / adulteraciones *s.* impurezas; ingredientes agregados que son inadecuados o inferiores

adversary / adversario *s.* opositor; enemigo

<u>**advocate / abogar**</u> *v.* hablar o escribir en apoyo de

affably / afablemente *adv.* de manera amistosa

affinities / afinidades *s.* conexiones familiares; simpatías

affluence / opulencia *s.* riqueza abundante

ague / escalofrío *s.* enfriamiento o estremecimiento

alderman / concejal *s.* funcionario principal en un pueblo o condado

alters / altera *v.* cambia

amiable / amigable *adj.* amistoso; afable

amorous / amoroso *adj.* lleno de amor o deseo

anarchy / anarquía *s.* ausencia de gobierno; desorden

anatomize / anatomizar *v.* disecar a fin de examinar su estructura

ancestral / ancestral *adj.* heredado

anemic / anémico *adj.* que le falta fuerza, vigor, vitalidad o colorido; desganado; débil

<u>**annotate / anotar**</u> *v.* hacer anotaciones o señalar con una explicación

antic / bufonesco *adj.* raro y cómico; ridículo

antidote / antídoto *s.* algo que sirve para combatir una condición no deseada; remedio

aperture / abertura *s.* orificio

apothecary / boticario *s.* farmacéutico; titular de droguería

appalled / pasmó *v.* que se llenó de consternación o desaliento

appendage / apéndice *s.* algo que se agrega

apprehension / aprensión *s.* sentimiento ansioso de presentimiento; pavor

apprehensions / aprensiones *s.* temores; preocupaciones

approbation / aprobación *s.* aceptación o ratificación oficial

arboreal / arbóreo *adj.* de, cerca o entre los árboles

<u>**articulate / articular**</u> *v.* expresar claramente

artifice / artificio *s.* habilidad; el producto de una destreza, especialmente un engaño astuto

artificiality / artificialidad *s.* que no es natural; irreal

aspire / aspirar *v.* tener grandes ambiciones; desear o buscar

assault / asaltar *v.* atacar violentamente

assessing / avaluando *v.* estimando el valor (de una propiedad) para fines de impuestos

assiduous / asiduo *adj.* constante en cuanto a aplicación o atención

assignations / asignaciones *s.* citas que deben cumplirse

asunder / en partes *adj.* roto en partes o pedazos

atrophy / atrofiar *v.* deteriorar

augment / aumentar *v.* hacer más grande; expandir

<u>**authentic / auténtico**</u> *adj.* genuino; real

avarice / avaricia *s.* codicia

averred / afirmó *v.* verificó

awe / asombro *s.* sensación mixta de reverencia, temor y asombro

B

balm / bálsamo *s.* ungüento u otra cosa que sana o alivia

bar / barra *s.* una de las líneas verticales que divide la música escrita en secciones iguales llamadas compases

bequeath / heredar *v.* pasar como una herencia

beliefs / creencias *s.* lo que uno sostiene que es cierto

bilious / colérico *adj.* malgeniado; irritable; malhumorado

blight / plaga *s.* condición de estar marchito

blithe / alegre *adj.* Animado

boundary / límite *s.* línea divisoria; frontera

breach / ruptura *s.* rompimiento o estar roto; dejar de cumplir con los términos de un acuerdo

brink / borde *s.* orilla; margen

burden / carga *s.* algo que pone un peso sobre uno; una pesada obligación o responsabilidad

C

cadence / cadencia *s.* movimiento medido

capitalism / capitalismo *s.* sistema económico en el cual personas particulares o grupos de personas son propietarias de tierras, fábricas y otros medios de producción.

caprices / caprichos *s.* extravagancias

<u>**categorize / categorizar**</u> *v.* colocar en grupos relacionados

censure / censurar *v.* desaprobar con firmeza; condenar

certify / certificar *v.* declarar que una cosa es cierta o exacta; verificar; atestar

<u>**characterize / caracterizar**</u> *v.* describir aspectos, cualidades o rasgos

chronicle / crónica *s.* registro histórico de eventos en orden cronológico

chrysalis / crisálida *s.* la tercera fase en el desarrollo de una polilla o mariposa

circumscribed / circunscrito *v.* delimitado; que tiene un lindero definido

<u>**cite / citar**</u> *v.* referirse a un texto

city / ciudad *s.* pueblo grande densamente poblado

clamorous / clamoroso *adj.* bullicioso y confuso; ruidoso

clarify / aclarar *v.* poner en claro

clasped / agarrado *v.* sujetado o estrechado firmemente

classics / clásicos *s.* libros o pinturas de las más alta calidad

<u>**classify / clasificar**</u> *v.* asignar a una categoría

climacteric / crisis s. cualquier período crítico

colonize / colonizar v. establecer un asentamiento

combatants / combatientes s. luchadores

combustible / combustible adj. capaz de ser encendido y quemado; inflamable

commentary / comentario s. serie de observaciones

commission / comisión s. autorización; acto de dar autoridad a un individuo

commodity / mercancía s. producto que es comprado o vendido

compassionate / compasivo adj. simpatizante con

compile / compilar v. reunir

complaisant / complaciente adj. afable; dispuesto a agradar

comprised / comprendió v. consistió de; incluyó

concord / concordia s. relaciones amistosas; armonía

condescension / condescendencia s. el acto o instancia de condescender

conflagration / conflagración s. gran incendio

conflict / conflicto s. lucha o contienda

conjecture / conjeturar v. adivinar

connote / connotar v. sugerir o comunicar

conquest / conquista s. acto de conquistar

consciousness / conciencia s. estar consciente de

constituency / distrito electoral s. la gente que compone un grupo de votantes

construct / construir v. colocar partes sistemáticamente para armar algo

contemporary / contemporáneo adj. que pertenece al mismo período de tiempo

contemptuous / desdeñoso adj. despreciativo

contend / contender v. aseverar o disputar

contention / contienda s. disputa, argumento

contentious / contencioso adj. disputador

contextualize / contextualizar v. colocar información dentro de un plano más amplio

contrite / contrito adj. dispuesto a arrepentirse o a expiar

controversy / controversia s. acto de disputar un tema sobre el cual existen varios puntos de vista

contusions / contusiones s. herida en la que la piel no se rompe; magulladura

conventional / convencional adj. que actúa o se comporta de manera usualmente aceptada o aprobada

conviction / convicción s. creencia; fe

coordinate / coordinar v. relacionar o vincular

countenance / semblante s. cara

country / país s. territorio; nación

courtly / cortésmente adj. elegantemente digno; decoroso

covetousness / codicia s. avaricia

cower / agachar v. encogerse, como de miedo o frío

coyness / modestia s. timidez; afectación, a menudo como parte de un coqueteo

credulity / credulidad s. tendencia a creer con demasiada facilidad

credulous / crédulo adj. que tiende a creer con demasiada facilidad

critique / criticar v. examinar críticamente, revisar

cultivated / cultivó v. sembró

cynically / cínicamente adv. semejante o característico de un cínico; desconfiado o que menosprecia los motivos de otro

D

dappled / manchado adj. pinto o moteado, usualmente en montones

dauntless / intrépido adj. valiente; que nada le intimida

debate / debatir v. discutir razonamientos opuestos

deduce / deducir v. inferir algo de un principio general

deference / deferencia s. consideración o respeto hacia otros

deficient / deficiente adj. que carece de una cualidad esencial

define / definir v. mencionar las cualidades que describen algo

deftly / diestramente adv. con facilidad y rapidez

deism / deísmo s. creencia en Dios basada en la evidencia de la razón y la naturaleza

deliberation / deliberación s. consideración y discusión cuidadosa antes de tomar una decisión

delirious / delirante adj. que tiene alucinaciones; desvariado

demonstrate / demostrar v. mostrar usando el razonamiento o ejemplos

denote / denotar v. referirse claramente a algo

depict / representar v. describir una imagen utilizando palabras

depredation / depredación s. un ataque predatorio; pillaje

derided / mofó v. burló; ridiculizó

deign / dignarse v. condescender; rebajarse a

desolate / desolado adj. desierto; solitario

despondent / desalentado adj. desanimado; abatido

despotic / despótico adj. tiránico

destitute / desprovisto adj. Carente

destruction / destrucción s. el acto de destruir

devise / idear v. inventar o crear; planear

diffusive / difusivo adj. tendiente a esparcirse

disabused / desengañó v. liberó de ideas falsas

discern / discernir v. reconocer como separado o diferente

discreet / discreto adj. sabio; prudente

discretion / discreción s. cuidado en lo que uno hace y dice; buen criterio; prudencia

dislocation / dislocación s. condición de estar fuera de lugar

dispensation / designio divino s. sistema religioso o creencias

disposable / disponible adj. libre para usar; a disposición

dissatisfaction / descontento s. estado de disgusto

dissect / disecar v. analizar e interpretar minuciosamente

distemper / distémper s. enfermedad infecciosa, como la plaga

distill / destilar v. obtener la parte esencial

divine / divino adj. celestial; sagrado

dominion / dominio s. soberanía o poder sobre un territorio; autoridad o control

dominions / dominios s. territorios o tierras gobernadas

dowry / dote s. propiedad que aporta la familia de la mujer a su marido cuando se casan

dregs / vestigios s. una pequeña cantidad; residuo

E

eclipse / eclipsar v. desvanecer o extinguir el poder o la gloria

economic / económico adj. relacionado al manejo de los ingresos

edit / editar v. alterar, adaptar o refinar

effigy / efigie s. retrato o estatua de una persona

electors / electores s. aquellos que votan

eloquent / elocuente adj. bellamente expresivo

eludes / elude v. evita o escapa

embarked / enfrascó v. que participó en algo, como en una conversación

embellishments / adornos s. toques decorativos; ornamentos

eminent / eminente adj. notable; de algo rango; distinguido

empire / imperio s. grupo de naciones o estados bajo un solo soberano o gobierno

encomiums / encomios s. expresiones formales de gran elogio

endeavored / esforzó s. hizo un intento serio; trató

enhance / realzar v. mejorar o elevar

enigma / enigma s. acertijo; declaración, persona o situación perpleja

entreated / suplicó v. imploró; rogó

enumerate / enumerar v. especificar en una lista

epic / epopeya s. poema largo sobre las aventuras de uno o más grandes héroes

equate / igualar v. considerar que una cosa es igual que otra

equivocate / emplear lenguaje ambiguo v. usar términos que tienen dos o más significados para despistar intencionalmente o engañar

escapade / escapada s. aventura, especialmente una que rompe con las reglas normales de conducta

esteemed / estimado adj. altamente respetado; tener en alta estima

etymology / etimología s. el estudio de los orígenes de las palabras

evaluate / evaluar v. establecer el significado, valor o condición de algo

evanescence / desvanecimiento s. desaparición o tendencia a desaparecer

evoke / evocar v. provocar una reacción

exemplary / ejemplar adj. dícese de algo que podría servir de modelo

exile / exiliar v. obligar a una persona a abandonar su hogar o país

exotic / exótico adj. de un país extranjero

expedient / recurso s. dispositivo usado en una emergencia

expiated / expió v. reparó; dio cumplida satisfacción, especialmente mediante el sufrimiento

extract / extraer v. sonsacar información

extravagant / extravagante adj. ir más allá de los límites razonables; excesivo

F

fantastic / fantástico adj. muy extravagante; increíblemente bueno

fastidious / quisquilloso adj. exigente; difícil de satisfacer

fate / sino s. destino

fathom / comprender v. entender cabalmente

fervent / ferviente adj. tener gran calidez de sentimientos

fidelity / fidelidad s. lealtad

filial / filial adj. lo que se espera de un hijo o hija

form / moldear v. dar forma a

format / formatear v. disponer de acuerdo a un plan

formulate / formular v. expresar completa y claramente; idear

fortitude / fortaleza s. valor; fuerza para resistir

fracture / fractura s. el acto de quebrar; condición de estar roto

frugally / frugalmente adv. forma de ser cuidadoso con el dinero

furrow / surco s. carril angosto hecho en la tierra con un arado

G

gall / amargura s. sentimiento amargo; rencor profundo

galled / irritado adj. lastimado o excoriado por rozadura

galleons / galeones s. grandes veleros usados para la guerra o el comercio

garnished / adornó v. decoró; guarneció

garrulous / gárrulo adj. parlanchín

gaunt / demacrado adj. flaco y huesudo, como por desnutrición o edad avanzada

geography / geografía s. aspectos de la superficie de un lugar o región

ghastly / horriblemente adv. terriblemente; muy malo

gleaned / espigó v. juntó poco a poco, como cuando se recolecta granos que quedan después de una cosecha

gout / gota s. una masa o salpicadura de un líquido como la sangre

grandeur / grandeza s. esplendor; magnificencia

gravity / gravedad s. peso; seriedad

grievances / agravios s. circunstancias que hacen que la gente se queje

grieved / afligió v. sintió mucho pesar; lamentó

guile / maña s. embuste habilidoso

H

haggard / demacrado adj. que aparenta estar consumido y agotado; ojeroso

harbingers / precursores s. heraldos

heedless / incauto adj. descuidado; desatento

highlight / realzar v. destacar

hoary / canoso adj. blanco o encanecido con la edad

homespun / doméstico adj. hilado o hecho en casa

hypothesize / formular una hipótesis v. sugerir una explicación posible

I

ideal / ideal s. modelo de perfección

idealism / idealismo s. acto de descuidar asuntos prácticos por seguir los ideales

ignoble / innoble adj. que no es noble; plebeyo

ignominy / ignominia s. humillación; deshonra

illumine / iluminar v. alumbrar

illusion / ilusión s. apariencia o sentimiento que engaña porque no es real

immigrant / inmigrante s. persona que llega a vivir a un país extranjero

immortal / inmortal adj. que vive o perdura para siempre; que no muere

impediments / impedimentos s. obstáculos

imperceptibly / imperceptiblemente adv. sin que se note

imperial / imperial adj. de un imperio; que tiene autoridad suprema

imperialism / imperialismo s. política de crear un imperio por medio de la conquista y la colonización

impertinence / impertinencia s. descortesía; insolencia

imperturbable / imperturbable adj. calmado; que no se enfada fácilmente

implored / imploró v. rogó seriamente

importuning / importunando v. insistiendo con

impressionistic / impresionista adj. que comunica un dibujo mediante sugerencias de detalles con un trazo rápido

impudence / impudencia s. falta de vergüenza; descortesía

impulse / impulso s. fuerza que empuja hacia adelante

inane / vacío adj. que le falta sentido, significado o ideas; necio

incessant / incesante *adj.* que continúa sin interrupción; perenne

incitement / incitación *s.* acto de apremiar; estímulo

inconstancy / inconstancia *s.* inestabilidad; veleidad

inconstantly / inconstantemente *adv.* inestablemente; veleidosamente

incredulously / incrédulamente *adv.* de forma que expresa duda o escepticismo

independence / independencia *s.* estar libre del control de los demás

indignant / indignado *adj.* enfurecido; lleno de cólera justa

indissoluble / indisoluble *adj.* que no puede ser disuelto o deshecho

inducted / admitió *v.* introdujo formalmente a una organización

industry / industria *s.* cualquier rama empresarial, comercial o manufacturera

inevitable / inevitable *adj.* ineludible; que sucederá con seguridad

infamy / infamia *s.* muy mala reputación; desgracia; deshonra

infirmity / enfermedad *s.* defecto físico o mental; dolencia

ingenuous / ingenuo *adj.* inocente; sencillo

ingratiating / congraciador *adj.* encantador; ameno; complaciente

inheritance / herencia *s.* acto de heredar

inklings / indicios *s.* sugerencias indirectas; ideas vagas

innumerable / innumerable *adj.* mucha cantidad para contar

insatiableness / insaciabilidad *s.* la cualidad de ser imposible de satisfacer

instantaneous / instantáneo *adj.* que se hace o sucede en un instante

integrate / integrar *v.* reunir partes distintas

intemperance / intemperancia *s.* falta de moderación

interpret / interpretar *v.* explicar el significado

interpretation / interpretación *s.* el acto de explicar

interred / sepultó *v.* enterró

intrigues / intrigas *s.* tramas o maquinaciones

intrinsically / intrínsecamente *adv.* en su meollo; inherentemente; de manera innata

invasion / invasión *s.* entrar a la fuerza

invincible / invencible *adj.* inconquistable

irrevocable / irrevocable *adj.* incapaz de ser deshecho o cancelado

isolation / aislamiento *s.* acto de estar completamente separado de los demás

J

judicious / juicioso *adj.* que muestra buen criterio

K

keenly / profundamente *adv.* agudamente; intensamente

ken / vista *s.* alcance de la vista o comprensión

kindred / parentela *s.* el grupo de parientes de una persona

kingdoms / reinos *s.* países bajo el mandato de un rey o una reina

L

label / calificar *v.* describir o designar

laity / laicos *s.* aquéllos que no pertenecen al sacerdocio

lament / lamentar *v.* expresar dolor; afligirse

lamentable / lamentable *adj.* que causa dolor; perturbador

lamentations / lamentaciones *s.* expresiones de dolor o aflicción

languish / languidecer *v.* debilitar; marchitar; suspirar por

languished / languideció *v.* se debilitó; se entorpeció

languor / languidez *s.* falta de energía o vitalidad; lentitud

largesse / generosidad *s.* nobleza de espíritu

larking / retozar *v.* divertirse despreocupada y caprichosamente

legacy / legado *s.* dinero u otras pertenencias heredadas a una persona por voluntad de alguien que haya muerto

lintel / dintel *s.* barra horizontal sobre una puerta

loathsome / repulsivo *adj.* repugnante

loyalties / lealtades *s.* sentimientos o comportamientos leales; fidelidad

loyalty / lealtad *s.* sentimiento o comportamiento leal; fidelidad

ludicrous / risible *adj.* absurdo; ridículo

lustrous / lustroso *adj.* que tiene lustre; brillante; luminoso

M

macadam / macadán *s.* piedra quebrada que se usa para hacer una calle con el mismo nombre

madrigals / madrigales *s.* poemas cortos de amor con música

magistrate / magistrado *s.* un funcionario local que hace cumplir la ley o funge como juez

malevolence / malevolencia *s.* mala voluntad; despecho

malicious / malicioso *adj.* deliberadamente dañino; destructivo

massive / masivo *adj.* grande y sólido; voluminoso

measure / medida *s.* una sección de música escrita entre dos líneas verticales llamadas barras; ley, resolución o algo parecido que se propone o ratifica para mejorar una situación

melodious / melodioso *adj.* de sonido placentero; armonioso

melody / melodía *s.* secuencia de tonos solos que juntos crean una tonada o canción

migrated / emigró *v.* que se mudó de una región o país a otro

mobility / movilidad *s.* habilidad de movimiento

mockeries / burlas *s.* esfuerzos fútiles o decepcionantes; ridículo

modernization / modernización *s.* llevar a la actualidad las costumbres o normas

monarch / monarca *s.* persona que gobierna un país

monotonous / monótono *adj.* sin variación

morose / malhumorado *adj.* triste; adusto

mortal / mortal *adj.* dícese de todo lo que eventualmente morirá

multitudinous / numeroso *adj.* que existe en grandes cantidades

munificence / munificencia *s.* esplendidez

N

nature / naturaleza *s.* todas las cosas, excepto aquellas creadas por el hombre

nimble / ágil *adj.* capaz de moverse rápidamente y con ligereza

nocturnal / nocturno *adj.* que ocurre de noche

notorious / notorio *adj.* ampliamente conocido pero desfavorablemente; que tiene una mala reputación

nuisance / fastidio *s.* acto, cosa o condición que causa molestia

O

obdurate / inexorable *adj.* obstinado

obedience / obediencia *s.* el acto de seguir órdenes o instrucciones

obliquely / oblicuamente *adv.* sesgadamente; indirectamente

obscure / oscuro *adj.* que no se ve fácilmente; que por lo general no se conoce

obscure / oscurecer *v.* que hace difícil ver

obstinate / obstinado *adj.* testarudo; terco

obstinately / obstinadamente *adv.* de forma determinante; testarudamente

officious / oficioso *adj.* entremetido

ordeal / prueba severa *s.* experiencia difícil o penosa que lo pone a uno a prueba

order / orden *s.* manera en que una cosa sigue después de otra

orthodox / ortodoxo *adj.* que se conforma a las creencias establecidas

outcast / desterrado *s.* persona exiliada de su hogar y amistades

outline / esbozar *v.* desarrollar un plan general

P

pallor / palor *s.* falta no natural de color; palor

palpable / palpable *adj.* capaz de ser tocado o sentido

palpitation / palpitación *s.* latido del corazón inusual o anormalmente rápido o violento

paltry / miserable *adj.* prácticamente inútil; insignificante

paradox / paradoja *s.* afirmación que puede ser verdadera pero pareciera expresar dos cosas opuestas

paraphrase / parafrasear *v.* poner en otras palabras algo dicho o escrito

pastoral / pastoral *s.* simple o naturalmente bello, como el campo

pathos / patetismo *s.* cualidad que evoca tristeza o compasión

patronize / frecuentar *v.* ser cliente asiduo de un determinado negocio o almacén

penury / penuria *s.* pobreza

perceive / percibir *v.* reconocer a través de los sentidos

peril / peligro *s.* exposición a situación peligrosa o arriesgada

pernicious / pernicioso *adj.* que causa un gran daño, destrucción o ruina; fatal; mortal

pernicious / pernicioso *adj.* que causa un gran daño, destrucción o ruina; mortal

phantasm / fantasma *s.* forma o figura sobrenatural; espectro; producto de la imaginación

philosophy / filosofía *s.* sistema que sirve de guía para la vida

piety / piedad *s.* devoción a una religión

platitude / perogrullada *s.* declaración que carece de autoridad

plebeian / plebeyo *adj.* común; no aristocrático

power / poder *s.* fuerza o vigor

predominance / predominio *s.* superioridad

predominant / predominante *adj.* en primer lugar; poderoso

prefiguring / prefigurando *v.* que se parece, por lo que se sugiere de antemano

prenatal / prenatal *adj.* que existe o tiene lugar antes del nacimiento

presumed / presumió *v.* que dio por sentado; supuso

presumption / presunción *s.* atrevimiento

prevail / prevalecer *v.* tener éxito; obtener el dominio; terminar ganando

prevarication / engaño *s.* evasión de la verdad

prime / plenitud *s.* la mejor etapa de una cosa o proceso

pristine / prístino *adj.* original; intacto

probe / indagar *v.* investigar y explorar minuciosamente

prodding / aguijoneando *v.* picando, punzando, buscando

prodigal / pródigo *adj.* despilfarrador

prodigious / prodigioso *adj.* enorme; inmenso

profanation / profanación *s.* acción que muestra irreverencia hacia algo sagrado

proferring / ofrecimiento *s.* ofrenda

profuse / profuso *adj.* abundante; que se derrama

progress / progreso *s.* crecimiento; mejora

promontories / promontorios *s.* colinas de tierras altas que se introducen en una masa de agua

prophet / profeta *s.* persona que dice lo que ocurrirá

propitiate / propiciar *v.* ganarse la buena voluntad de; aplacar

propose / proponer *v.* presentar un plan o intención

propriety / propiedad *s.* cualidad o condición de ser correcto

prosper / prosperar *v.* medrar

prowess / proeza *s.* heroísmo; distinción

prudence / prudencia *s.* cuidadoso manejo de recursos; economía

pulp / pulpa *s.* la parte suave, jugosa y comestible de una fruta

purge / purgar *v.* purificar; limpiar

R

rancor / rencor *s.* mala voluntad; odio amargo y persistente

ransacked / saqueó *v.* buscó por todo para hallar bienes para robar; pilló

rapture / éxtasis *s.* embeleso; gran placer

rapturous / extasiado *adj.* lleno de embeleso y amor; extático

rational / racional *adj.* sensato; razonable

realms / reinos *s.* regiones bajo el gobierno de un rey o reina

rebellious / rebelde *adj.* que desafía a la autoridad

rebuild / reconstruir *v.* construir o crear de nuevo

rebuke / increpar *v.* criticar fuertemente

recall / recordar *v.* rememorar

reckoning / cálculo *s.* contabilidad

recoil / recular *v.* retroceder por temor, sorpresa o disgusto

recommend / recomendar *v.* sugerir favorablemente

recompense / recompensar *v.* pagar en compensación por algo

recount / narrar *v.* contar con detalles

reform / reformar *v.* mejorar

reformation / reforma *s.* cambio positivo; mejora

refractory / recalcitrante *adj.* difícil de manejar; terco

refute / refutar *v.* demostrar lo contrario

reiterate / reiterar *v.* decir o hacer de nuevo

relates / relata *v.* cuenta

remnant / remanente *s.* lo que queda; residuo

renaissance / renacimiento *s.* gran renacer del arte y de los conocimientos en Europa durante los siglos XIV, XV y XVI

reparation / reparación *s.* compensación por un mal

reprove / criticar v. desaprobar con firmeza; censurar

requiem / réquiem s. composición musical para honrar a los muertos

resolution / resolución s. propósito o determinación

resume / reasumir v. asumir de nuevo o continuar con algo después de una interrupción

reticent / discreto adj. callado; reservado

reverence / reverencia s. respeto profundo

reverently / reverentemente adv. con profundo respeto o admiración

revolution / revolución s. derrocamiento total de un gobierno o sistema político establecido

righteousness / rectitud s. la característica de actuar de forma justa y virtuosa

risible / risible adj. que causa risa

rites / ritos s. ceremonias; rituales

role / papel s. rol o función desempeñada por una persona o cosa

roused / suscitó v. agitó

rue / desilusión s. tristeza; arrepentimiento

rummage / registrar v. buscar detenidamente o activamente

S

sanguine / optimista adj. confiado; esperanzado

satiety / saciedad s. condición de estar lleno con suficiente o más que suficiente

sauntered / deambuló v. caminó a un paso pausado

scales / escamas s. parte delgada, escariosa o membranosa de una planta, como la bráctea de un amento o candelilla

schism / cisma s. separación de un grupo en facciones

scope / alcance s. rango de percepción o entendimiento

scurry / escabullir v. correr rápidamente; escurrirse

segmented / segmentó v. dividió en partes unidas

semblance / apariencia s. aspecto exterior; imagen

sentinel / centinela s. persona o animal que vigila

sepulcher / sepulcro s. tumba

sequestered / secuestró v. mantuvo alejado de los demás

shrill / agudo adj. tono alto y agudo; estridente

sinews / tendones s. fibras

sinuous / sinuoso adj. ondulado; tortuoso

skeptical / escéptico adj. dudoso; que no se persuade fácilmente

smudge / mancha s. un tiznajo o mancha de tierra

sojourn / estada s. corta estadía en algún lugar; visita

solace / solaz s. confortación; desahogo

solicitous / solícito adj. que muestra interés o preocupación

sordid / sórdido adj. sucio

sound / íntegro adj. sano; ileso

sovereign / soberano adj. supremo en poder, rango o autoridad

specious / especioso adj. engañosamente atractivo o válido; falso

spectral / espectral adj. fantasmal

spellbound / encantado adj. atado como por un hechizo

spirit / espíritu s. parte inmaterial del ser humano

sprawling / extendido adj. irregular y grande

stagnant / estancado adj. estático; fétido

stature / estatura s. altura; nivel de realización

stead / lugar s. posición ocupada por un reemplazo

steadfastly / resueltamente adv. con dirección fija; dirigido con firmeza

stealthy / furtivo adj. secreto; clandestino; disimulado

stoic / estoico s. persona indiferente a la alegría, pena, placer o dolor

struggle / luchar v. esforzarse para vencer vicisitudes

subdued / reprimido adj. quieto; inhibido, dominado; controlado

substantial / sustancial adj. que tiene sustancia; grande en tamaño o fuerza

succor / socorrer v. ayudar; asistir; aliviar

suffused / bañó v. se dispersó por todo; llenó

sulk / enfurruñar v. mostrar resentimiento, rehusándose a interactuar con otros

sullen / malhumorado adj. triste; sombrío

sundry / diversos adj. varios; misceláneos

supine / supino adj. que yace sobre su espalda

supplication / súplica s. acto de rezar o rogar

surmise / conjetura s. imaginación; especulación; suposición

sustenance / sustento s. alimento o dinero para subsistir

symbolize / simbolizar v. representar una cosa o un concepto

symmetry / simetría s. forma balanceada; la belleza que resulta de un balance tal

syntax / sintaxis s. el estudio de la estructura de las oraciones

T

tarry / aguardar v. demorarse o quedarse atrás

technology / tecnología s. ciencia de las artes industriales y mecánicas

teeming / rebosar v. llenar hasta que se desborda

temperate / temperado adj. leve

tempestuous / tempestuoso adj. turbulento; tormentoso

tenacity / tenacidad s. persistencia; terquedad

terrestrial / terrestre adj. relativo a la tierra o a este mundo

topographical / topográfico adj. que representa las características superficiales de una región

tortuous / tortuoso adj. lleno de curvas, vueltas o giros; que es sinuoso, curveado o torcido

traditional / tradicional adj. habitual

transformation / transformación s. acto o proceso de cambio

transgress / transgredir v. violar una ley u orden

transgressed / transgredió v. propasó o violó (una ley o mandamiento)

tranquil / tranquilo adj. calmado; sereno; apacible

transcendent / trascendente adj. que excede todos los límites

transient / pasajero adj. temporal; transitorio

treachery / engaño s. el acto de traicionar la confianza, fe o lealtad

treasons / traiciones s. deslealtades hacia su propio país o hacia un juramento de lealtad

trends / tendencias s. direcciones generales; modas o estilos

trepidation / trepidación s. estremecimiento

trifles / bagatelas s. cosas de poco valor o importancia

truculent / truculento adj. cruel; feroz

tumid / túmido adj. hinchado

tumult / tumulto s. conmoción ruidosa, a menudo causada por una muchedumbre

turbid / turbio adj. lodoso o lechoso; revuelto y confuso

turmoil / disturbio s. estado de gran conmoción, confusión o alboroto

tyrants / tiranos s. gobernantes crueles y opresivos

U

uncanny / extraño *adj.* misterioso; difícil de explicar

undeterminable / indeterminable *adj.* no determinable; incierto

ungenial / desfavorable *adj.* desagradable; caracterizado por el mal tiempo

upbraidings / reproches *s.* palabras fuertes de desaprobación; regaños

urban / urbano *adj.* que es o posee las características principales de una ciudad

utters / pronuncia *v.* transmite con la voz

V

vales / valles *s.* hondonadas; hundimientos; depresiones en la superficie terrestre

valor / valor *s.* comportamiento valeroso; coraje

values / valores *s.* valor real; precio correcto

venerable / venerable *adj.* que exige respeto debido a edad, carácter o posición social

verge / borde *s.* filo; margen

vindication / reivindicación *s.* acto de dar justificación o apoyo por

vintage / vendimia *s.* vino de alta calidad

vivacious / vivaz *adj.* vivaracho, fogoso

vulnerable / vulnerable *adj.* expuesto a ataque o perjuicio

W

wallowed / revolcó *v.* rodó por el fango, agua, etc.

wan / pálido *adj.* con palidez enfermiza; desfallecido o débil

waning / menguando *v.* haciendo gradualmente más oscuro o débil

welfare / bienestar *s.* condición de estar bien; salud

winsome / atractivo *adj.* que tiene una apariencia o comportamiento encantador

wither / marchitar *v.* languidecer o deteriorarse

wreath / corona *s.* círculo de flores

writhes / retuerce *v.* que tuerce y contorsiona el cuerpo, como en agonía

writhing / retorciendo *v.* haciendo movimientos de retorcimiento y contorsión

Life of the English Language

The life of every language depends on the people who use it. Whenever you use English by asking a question, talking on the phone, going to a movie, reading a magazine, or writing an e-mail, you keep it healthy and valuable.

Using a Dictionary

Use a **dictionary** to find the meaning, the pronunciation, and the part of speech of a word. Consult a dictionary also to trace the word's *etymology*, or its origin. Etymology explains how words change, how they are borrowed from other languages, and how new words are invented, or "coined."

Here is an entry from a dictionary. Notice what it tells about the word *anthology*.

> **anthology** (an thäl'ə jè) *n., pl.* —gies [Gr. anthologia, a garland, collection of short poems < *anthologos*, gathering flowers < *anthos*, flower + *legein*, to gather] a collection of poems, stories, songs, excerpts, etc., chosen by the compiler.

Dictionaries provide the *denotation* of each word, or its objective meaning. The symbol < means "comes from" or "is derived from." In this case, the Greek words for "flower" and "gather" combined to form a Greek word that meant a garland, and then that word became an English word that means a collection of literary flowers—a collection of literature like the one you are reading now.

Using a Thesaurus

Use a **thesaurus** to increase your vocabulary. In a thesaurus, you will find synonyms, or words that have similar meanings, for most words. Follow these guidelines to use a thesaurus:

- Do not choose a word just because it sounds interesting or educated. Choose the word that expresses exactly the meaning you intend.
- To avoid errors, look up the word in a dictionary to check its precise meaning and to make sure you are using it properly.

Here is an entry from a thesaurus. Notice what it tells about the word *book*.

> **book** *noun* A printed and bound work: tome, volume. See WORDS.
>
> **book** *verb* **1.** To register in or as if in a book: catalog, enroll, inscribe, list, set down, write down. *See* REMEMBER. **2.** To cause to be set aside, as for one's use, in advance: bespeak, engage, reserve. *See* GET.

If the word can be used as different parts of speech, as book can, the thesaurus entry provides synonyms for the word as each part of speech. Many words also have connotations, or emotional associations that the word calls to mind. A thesaurus entry also gives specific synonyms for each connotation of the word.

Activity Look up the words *knight* and *chivalry* in a dictionary. **(a)** What are their etymologies? **(b)** Explain what their etymologies reveal about the development of English. Then, check the word *chivalry* in a thesaurus. **(c)** What are two synonyms for this word? **(d)** In what way do the connotations of the synonyms differ?

The Origin and Development of English

Old Engish English began about the year 500 when Germanic tribes settled in Britain. The language of these peoples—the Angles, Saxons, and Jutes—combined with Danish and Norse when Vikings attacked Britain and added some Latin elements when Christian missionaries arrived. The result was Old English, which looked like this:

> *Hwaet! We Gar-Dena   in gear-dagum,*
> *peod-cyninga,   prym gefrunon,*
> *hu da aepelingas   ellen fremedon!*

These words are the opening lines of the Old English epic poem *Beowulf*, probably composed in the eighth century. In modern English, they mean: "Listen! We know the ancient glory of the Spear-Danes, and the heroic deeds of those noble kings!"

Middle English The biggest change in English took place after the Norman Conquest of Britain in 1066. The Normans spoke a dialect of Old French, and Old English changed dramatically when the Normans became the new aristocracy. From about 1100 to 1500, the people of Britain spoke what we now call Middle English.

> *A Knyght ther was, and that a worthy man,*
> *That fro the tyme that he first bigan*
> *To riden out, he loved chivalrie,*
> *Trouthe and honour, fredom and curtesie.*

These lines from the opening section of Chaucer's *Canterbury Tales* (c. 1400) are much easier for us to understand than the lines from *Beowulf*. They mean: "There was a knight, a worthy man who, from the time he began to ride, loved chivalry, truth, honor, freedom, and courtesy."

Modern English During the Renaissance, with its emphasis on reviving classical culture, Greek and Latin languages exerted a strong influence on the English language. In addition, Shakespeare added about two thousand words to the language. Grammar, spelling, and pronunciation continued to change. Modern English was born.

> *But soft! What light through yonder window breaks?*
> *It is the East, and Juliet is the sun!*

These lines from Shakespeare's *Romeo and Juliet* (c. 1600) need no translation, although it is helpful to know that "soft" means "speak softly." Since Shakespeare's day, conventions of usage and grammar have continued to change. For example, the *th* at the ends of many verbs has become s. In Shakespeare's time, it was correct to say "Romeo *hath* fallen in love." In our time, it is right to say "he *has* fallen in love." However, the changes of the past five hundred years are not nearly as drastic as the changes from Old English to Middle English, or from Middle English to Modern English. We still speak Modern English.

Old Words, New Words

Modern English has a larger vocabulary than any other language in the world. The *Oxford English Dictionary* contains about a half million words, and it is estimated that another half million scientific and technical terms do not appear in the dictionary. Here are the main ways that new words enter the language:

- **War**—Conquerors introduce new terms and ideas—and new vocabulary, such as *anger,* from Old Norse.

- **Immigration**—When large groups of people move from one country to another, they bring their languages with them, such as *boycott,* from Ireland.

- **Travel and Trade**—Those who travel to foreign lands and those who do business in faraway places bring new words back with them, such as *shampoo,* from Hindi.

- **Science and Technology**—In our time, the amazing growth of science and technology adds multitudes of new words to English, such as *Internet.*

English is also filled with **borrowings,** words taken directly from other languages. Sometimes borrowed words keep basically the same meanings they have in their original languages: *pajamas* (Hindi), *sauna* (Finnish), *camouflage* (French), *plaza* (Spanish). Sometimes borrowed words take on new meanings. *Sleuth,* for example, an Old Norse word for trail, has come to mean the person who follows a *trail*—a detective.

Mythology contributed to our language too. Some of the days of the week are named after Norse gods—Wednesday was Woden's Day, Thursday was Thor's Day. Greek and Roman myths have given us many words, such as *jovial* (from Jove), *martial* (from Mars), *mercurial* (from Mercury), and *herculean* (from Hercules).

Americanisms are words, phrases, usages, or idioms that originated in American English or that are unique to the way Americans speak. They are expressions of our national character in all its variety: *easy as pie, prairie dog, bamboozle, panhandle, halftime, fringe benefit, bookmobile, jackhammer, southpaw, lickety split.*

Activity Look up the following words in a dictionary. Describe the ways in which you think these words entered American English.

    sabotage   burrito   moccasin   mecca   megabyte

The Influence of English

English continues to have an effect on world cultures and literature. There are about three hundred million native English speakers, and about the same number who speak English as a second language. Although more people speak Mandarin Chinese, English is the dominant language of trade, tourism, international diplomacy, science, and technology.

Language is a vehicle of both communication and culture, and the cultural influence of English in the twenty-first century is unprecedented in the history of the world's languages. Beyond business and science, English spreads through sports, pop music, Hollywood movies, television, and journalism. A book that is translated into English reaches many more people than it would in its native language alone. Perhaps most significantly, English dominates the Internet. The next time you log on, notice how many Web sites from around the world also have an English version. The global use of English is the closest the world has ever come to speaking an international language.

Activity Choose one area of culture—such as sports, fashion, the arts, or technology—and identify three new words that English has recently added to the *world's* vocabulary. **(a)** How do you think non-English speakers feel about the spread of English? **(b)** Do you think English helps to bring people together? Why or why not?

Tips for Improving Fluency

When you were younger, you learned to read. Then, you read to expand your experiences or for pure enjoyment. Now, you are expected to read to learn. As you progress in school, you are given more and more material to read. The tips on these pages will help you improve your reading fluency, or your ability to read easily, smoothly, and expressively. Use these tips as you read daily.

Keeping Your Concentration

One common problem that readers face is the loss of concentration. When you are reading an assignment, you might find yourself rereading the same sentence several times without really understanding it. The first step in changing this behavior is to notice that you do it. Becoming an active, aware reader will help you get the most from your assignments. Practice using these strategies:

- Cover what you have already read with a note card as you go along. Then, you will not be able to reread without noticing that you are doing it.

- Set a purpose for reading beyond just completing the assignment. Then, read actively by pausing to ask yourself questions about the material as you read. Check the accuracy of your answers as you continue to read.

- Use the Reading Strategy instruction and notes that appear with each selection in this textbook.

- Look at any art or illustrations that accompany the reading and use picture clues to help your comprehension.

- Stop reading after a specified period of time (for example, 5 minutes) and summarize what you have read. To help you with this strategy, use the Reading Check questions that appear with each selection in this textbook. Reread to find any answers you do not know.

Reading Phrases

Fluent readers read phrases rather than individual words. Reading this way will speed up your reading and improve your comprehension. Here are some useful ideas:

- Experts recommend rereading as a strategy to increase fluency. Choose a passage of text that is neither too hard nor too easy. Read the same passage aloud several times until you can read it smoothly. When you can read the passage fluently, pick another passage and keep practicing.

- Read aloud into a tape recorder. Then, listen to the recording, noting your accuracy, pacing, and expression. You can also read aloud and share feedback with a partner.

- Use the *Pearson Prentice Hall Literature Audio Program Hear It!* to hear the selections read aloud. Read along silently in your textbook, noticing how the reader uses his or her voice and emphasizes certain words and phrases.

- Set a target reading rate. Time yourself as you read and work to increase your speed without sacrificing the level of your comprehension.

Understanding Key Vocabulary

If you do not understand some of the words in an assignment, you may miss out on important concepts. Therefore, it is helpful to keep a dictionary nearby when you are reading. Follow these steps:

- Before you begin reading, scan the text for unfamiliar words or terms. Find out what those words mean before you begin reading.
- Use context—the surrounding words, phrases, and sentences—to help you determine the meanings of unfamiliar words.
- If you are unable to understand the meaning through context, refer to the dictionary.

Paying Attention to Punctuation

When you read, pay attention to punctuation. Commas, periods, exclamation points, semicolons, and colons tell you when to pause or stop. They also indicate relationships between groups of words. When you recognize these relationships you will read with greater understanding and expression. Look at the chart below.

Punctuation Mark	Meaning
comma	brief pause
period	pause at the end of a thought
exclamation point	pause that indicates emphasis
semicolon	pause between related but distinct thoughts
colon	pause before giving explanation or examples

Using the Reading Fluency Checklist

Use the checklist below each time you read a selection in this textbook. In your Language Arts journal or notebook, note which skills you need to work on and chart your progress each week.

Reading Fluency Checklist

- ☐ Preview the text to check for difficult or unfamiliar words.
- ☐ Practice reading aloud.
- ☐ Read according to punctuation.
- ☐ Break down long sentences into the subject and its meaning.
- ☐ Read groups of words for meaning rather than reading single words.
- ☐ Read with expression (change your tone of voice to add meaning to the word).

Reading is a skill that can be improved with practice. The key to improving your fluency is to read. The more you read, the better your reading will become.

Approaches to Criticism

By writing **criticism**—writing that analyzes literature—readers share their responses to a written work. Criticism is also a way for a reader to deepen his or her own understanding and appreciation of the work, and to help others to deepen theirs.

The information in this handbook will guide you through the process of writing criticism. In addition, it will help you to refine your critical perceptions to ensure that you are ready to produce work at the college level.

Understanding Criticism

There are a few different types of criticism. Each can enhance understanding and deepen appreciation of literature in a distinctive way. All types share similar functions.

The Types of Criticism

Analysis Students are frequently asked to analyze, or break into parts and examine, a passage or a work. When you write an analysis, you must support your ideas with references to the text.

Archetypal Criticism Archetypal criticism evaluates works of literature by identifying and analyzing the archetypes contained within them. An archetype, sometimes called a "universal symbol," is a plot, character, symbol, image, setting, or idea that recurs in the literature of many different cultures. Archetypes and patterns of archetypes can be seen as representing common patterns of human life and experience.

Biographical Criticism Biographical criticism uses information about a writer's life to shed light on his or her work.

Historical Criticism Historical criticism traces connections between an author's work and the events, circumstances, or ideas that shaped the writer's historical era.

Political Criticism Political criticism involves viewing an author's work with a focus on political assumptions and content—whether explicit or implicit—and, possibly, assessing the political impact of the work. Similar to historical criticism, political criticism draws connections between an author's work and the political issues and assumptions of the times.

Philosophical Criticism In philosophical criticism, the elements of a literary work such as plot, characters, conflict, and motivations are examined through the lens of the author's philosophical arguments and stances. The critic taking a philosophical approach will analyze philosophical arguments presented in a literary work and determine how those arguments have molded the work.

The Functions of Criticism

Critical writing serves a variety of important functions:

Making Connections All criticism makes connections between two or more things. For instance, an analysis of a poem may show similarities among different images.

Making Distinctions Criticism must make distinctions as well as connections. In an analysis of a poem, a critic may distinguish between two possible purposes for poetry: first, to create an enduring image and, second, to present a deeper meaning.

Achieving Insight By making connections and distinctions, criticism achieves insight. An analysis of a poem may reach the insight that the poem stands on its own as a work of beauty apart from any deeper meaning.

Making a Judgment Assessing the value of a work is an important function of criticism. A critic may assess a work by comparing it with other works and by using a standard such as enjoyment, insight, or beauty.

"Placing" the Work Critics guide readers not by telling them *what* to think but by giving them *terms in which to think*. Critical writing may help readers apply varied perspectives to illuminate different aspects of a work.

Writing Criticism

Like all solid writing, a work of criticism presents a thesis (a central idea) and supports it with arguments and evidence. Follow the strategies below to develop a critical thesis and gather support for it.

Formulate a Working Thesis

Once you have chosen a work or works on which to write, formulate a working thesis. First, ask yourself questions like these:

- What strikes you most about the work or the writer that your paper will address? What puzzles you most?

- In what ways is the work unlike others you have read?

- What makes the techniques used by the writer so well-suited to (or so poorly chosen for) conveying the theme of the work?

Jot down notes answering your questions. Then, reread passages that illustrate your answers, jotting down notes about what each passage contributes to the work. Review your notes, and write a sentence that draws a conclusion about the work.

Gather Support

Taking Notes From the Work

Once you have a working thesis, take notes on passages in the work that confirm it. To aid your search for support, consider the type of support suited to your thesis, as in the chart.

Conducting Additional Research If you are writing biographical or historical criticism, you will need to consult sources on the writer's life and era. Even if you are writing a close analysis of a poem, you should consider consulting the works of critics to benefit from their insights and understanding.

If your thesis concerns . . .	look for support in the form of . . .
Character	• dialogue • character's actions • writer's descriptions of the character • other characters' reactions to the character
Theme	• fate of characters • patterns and contrasts of imagery, character, or events • mood • writer's attitude toward the action
Style	• memorable descriptions, observations • passages that "sound like" the writer • examples of rhetorical devices, such as exaggeration and irony
Historical Context	• references to historical events and personalities • evidence of social or political pressures on characters • socially significant contrasts between characters (for example, between the rich and the poor)
Literary Influences	• writer's chosen form or genre • passages that "sound like" another writer • events or situations that resemble those in other works • evidence of an outlook similar to that of another writer

Take Notes

Consider recording notes from the works you are analyzing, as well as from any critical works you consult, on a set of note cards. A good set of note cards enables you to recall details accurately, to organize your ideas effectively, and to see connections between ideas.

One Card, One Idea If you use note cards while researching, record each key passage, theme, critical opinion, or fact on a separate note card. A good note card includes a brief quotation or summary of an idea and a record of the source, including the page number, in which you found the information. When copying a sentence from a work, use quotation marks and check to make sure you have copied it correctly.

Coding Sources Keep a working bibliography, a list of all works you consult, as you conduct research. Assign a code, such as a letter, to each work on the list. For each note you take, include the code for the source.

Coding Cards Organize your note cards by labeling each with the subtopic it concerns.

Present Support Appropriately

As you draft, consider how much support you need for each point and the form that support should take. You can provide support in the following forms:

- **Summaries** are short accounts in your own words of important elements of the work, such as events, a character's traits, or the writer's ideas. They are appropriate for background information.

- **Paraphrases** are restatements of passages from a work in your own words. They are appropriate for background and for information incidental to your main point.

- **Quotations of key passages** are direct transcriptions of the writer's words, enclosed in quotation marks or, if longer than three lines, set as indented text. If a passage is crucial to your thesis, you should quote it directly and at whatever length is necessary.

Quotations of multiple examples are required to support claims about general features of a work, such as a claim about the writer's ironic style or use of cartoonlike characters.

DOs and DON'Ts of Academic Writing

Avoid gender and cultural bias. Certain terms and usages reflect the bias of past generations. To eliminate bias in any academic work you do, edit with the following rules in mind:

- **Pronoun usage** When referring to an unspecified individual in a case in which his or her gender is irrelevant, use forms of the pronoun phrase *he or she*. Example: "A lawyer is trained to use his or her mind."

- **"Culture-centric" terms** Replace terms that reflect a bias toward one culture with more generally accepted synonyms. For instance, replace terms such as primitive (used of hunting-gathering peoples), the Orient (used to refer to Asia), and Indians (used of Native Americans), all of which suggest a view of the world centered in Western European culture.

Avoid plagiarism. Presenting someone else's ideas, research, or exact words as your own is plagiarism, the equivalent of stealing or fraud. Laws protect the rights of writers and researchers in cases of commercial plagiarism. Academic standards protect their rights in cases of academic plagiarism.

To avoid plagiarism, follow these practices:

- Read from several sources.

- Synthesize what you learn.

- Let the ideas of experts help you draw your own conclusions.

- Always credit your sources properly when using someone else's ideas to support your view.

By following these guidelines, you will also push yourself to think independently.

Forming Your Critical Vocabulary

To enhance your critical perceptions—the connections you find and the distinctions you make—improve your critical vocabulary. The High-Utility Academic Words that appear in this textbook and are underlined in the Glossary (pp. R1–R13) are useful in critical writing.

Citing Sources and Preparing Manuscript

In research writing, cite your sources. In the body of your paper, provide a footnote, an endnote, or an internal citation, identifying the sources of facts, opinions, or quotations. At the end of your paper, provide a bibliography or a Works Cited list, a list of all the sources you cite. Follow an established format, such as Modern Language Association (MLA) Style or American Psychological Association (APA) Style.

Works Cited List (MLA Style)

A Works Cited list must contain accurate information sufficient to enable a reader to locate each source you cite. The basic components of an entry are as follows:

- Name of the author, editor, translator, or group responsible for the work
- Title
- Place and date of publication
- Publisher

For print materials, the information required for a citation generally appears on the copyright and title pages of a work. For the format of Works Cited list entries, consult the examples at right and in the chart on page R22.

Parenthetical Citations (MLA Style)

A parenthetical citation briefly identifies the source from which you have taken a specific quotation, factual claim, or opinion. It refers the reader to one of the entries on your Works Cited list. A parenthetical citation has the following features:

- It appears in parentheses.
- It identifies the source by the last name of the author, editor, or translator.
- It gives a page reference, identifying the page of the source on which the information cited can be found.

Punctuation A parenthetical citation generally falls outside a closing quotation mark but within the final punctuation of a clause or sentence. For a long quotation set off from the rest of your text, place the citation at the end of the excerpt without any punctuation following.

Special Cases

- If the author is an organization, use the organization's name, in a shortened version if necessary.
- If you cite more than one work by the same author, add the title or a shortened version of the title.

Sample Works-Cited Lists

Carwardine, Mark, Erich Hoyt, R. Ewan Fordyce, and Peter Gill. *The Nature Company Guides: Whales, Dolphins, and Porpoises.* New York: Time-Life, 1998.

"Discovering Whales." 18 Oct. 1999. <http://whales.magna.com.au/DISCOVER>.

Neruda, Pablo. "Ode to Spring." *Odes to Opposites.* Trans. Ken Krabbenhoft. Ed. and illus. Ferris Cook. Boston: Little, 1995.

The Saga of the Volsungs. Trans. Jesse L. Byock. London: Penguin, 1990.

List an anonymous work by title.

List both the title of the work and the collection in which it is found.

Sample Parenthetical Citations

It makes sense that baleen whales such as the blue whale, the bowhead whale, the humpback whale, and the sei whale (to name just a few) grow to immense sizes (Carwardine, Hoyt, and Fordyce 19–21). The blue whale has grooves running from under its chin to partway along the length of its underbelly. As in some other whales, these grooves expand and allow even more food and water to be taken in (Ellis 18–21).

Author's last name

Page numbers where information can be found

MLA Style for Listing Sources

Book with one author	Pyles, Thomas. *The Origins and Development of the English Language.* 2nd ed. New York: Harcourt, 1971.
Book with two or three authors	McCrum, Robert, William Cran, and Robert MacNeil. *The Story of English.* New York: Penguin, 1987.
Book with an editor	Truth, Sojourner. *Narrative of Sojourner Truth.* Ed. Margaret Washington. New York: Vintage, 1993.
Book with more than three authors or editors	Donald, Robert B., et al. *Writing Clear Essays.* Upper Saddle River: Prentice, 1996.
Single work in an anthology	Hawthorne, Nathaniel. "Young Goodman Brown." *Literature: An Introduction to Reading and Writing.* Ed. Edgar V. Roberts and H. E. Jacobs. Upper Saddle River: Prentice, 1998. 376–385. [Indicate pages for the entire selection.]
Introduction to a work in a published edition	Washington, Margaret. Introduction. *Narrative of Sojourner Truth.* By Sojourner Truth. Ed. Washington. New York: Vintage, 1993. v–xi.
Signed article from an encyclopedia	Askeland, Donald R. "Welding." *World Book Encyclopedia.* 1991 ed.
Signed article in a weekly magazine	Wallace, Charles. (2000, February 14). A Vodacious Deal. *Time* 14 Feb. 2000: 63.
Signed article in a monthly magazine	Gustaitis, Joseph. "The Sticky History of Chewing Gum." *American History* Oct. 1998: 30–38.
Newspaper	Thurow, Roger. "South Africans Who Fought for Sanctions Now Scrap for Investors." *Wall Street Journal* 11 Feb. 2000: A1+. [For a multipage article that does not appear on consecutive pages, write only the first page number on which it appears, followed by the plus sign.]
Unsigned editorial or story	"Selective Silence." Editorial. *Wall Street Journal* 11 Feb. 2000: A14. [If the editorial or story is signed, begin with the author's name.]
Signed pamphlet or brochure	[Treat the pamphlet as though it were a book.]
Work from a library subscription service	Ertman, Earl L. "Nefertiti's Eyes." *Archaeology* Mar.–Apr. 2008: 28–32. *Kids Search.* EBSCO. New York Public Library. 18 June 2008 <http://www.ebscohost.com>.
Filmstrips, slide programs, videocassettes, DVDs, and other audiovisual media	*The Diary of Anne Frank.* Dir. George Stevens. Perf. Millie Perkins, Shelley Winters, Joseph Schildkraut, Lou Jacobi, and Richard Beymer. 1959. DVD. Twentieth Century Fox, 2004.
CD (with multiple publishers)	Simms, James, ed. *Romeo and Juliet.* By William Shakespeare. CD-ROM. Oxford: Attica Cybernetics; London: BBC Education; London: Harper, 1995.
Radio or television program transcript	"Washington's Crossing of the Delaware." Host Liane Hansen. Guest David Hackett Fischer. *Weekend Edition Sunday.* Natl. Public Radio. WNYC, New York. 23 Dec. 2003. Transcript.
Internet Web page	"Fun Facts About Gum." National Association of Chewing Gum Manufacturers. 19 Dec. 1999 <http://www.nacgm.org/consumer/funfacts.html>. [Indicate the date you accessed the information. Content and addresses at Web sites change frequently.]
Personal interview	Smith, Jane. Personal interview. 10 Feb. 2000.

APA Style for Listing Sources

Book with one author	Pyles, T. (1971). *The origins and development of the English language* (2nd ed.). New York: Harcourt Brace Jovanovich.
Book with two or three authors	McCrum, R., Cran, W., & MacNeil, R. (1987). *The story of English.* New York: Penguin Books.
Book with an editor	Truth, S. (1993). *Narrative of Sojourner Truth* (M. Washington, Ed.). New York: Vintage Books.
Book with more than three authors or editors	Donald, R. B., Morrow, B. R., Wargetz, L. G., & Werner, K. (1996). *Writing clear essays.* Upper Saddle River, NJ: Prentice Hall. [With eight or more authors, abbreviate all authors after the sixth as "et al."]
Single work from an anthology	Hawthorne, N. (1998). Young Goodman Brown. In E. V. Roberts, & H. E. Jacobs (Eds.), *Literature: An introduction to reading and writing* (pp. 376–385). Upper Saddle River, NJ: Prentice Hall.
Introduction in a published edition	Washington, M. (1993). Introduction. In M. Washington (Ed.), S. Truth, *Narrative of Sojourner Truth* (pp. v–xi). New York: Vintage Books.
Signed article from an encyclopedia	Askeland, D. R. (1991). Welding. In *World Book Encyclopedia.* (Vol. 21, pp. 190–191). Chicago: World Book.
Signed article in a weekly magazine	Wallace, C. (2000, February 14). A vodacious deal. *Time, 155,* 63. [The volume number appears in italics before the page number.]
Signed article in a monthly magazine	Gustaitis, J. (1998, October). The sticky history of chewing gum. *American History, 33,* 30–38.
Newspaper	Thurow, R. (2000, February 11). South Africans who fought for sanctions now scrap for investors. *Wall Street Journal,* pp. A1, A4. [If an article appears on discontinuous pages, give all page numbers and separate the numbers with a comma.]
Unsigned editorial or story	Selective silence [Editorial]. (2000, February 11). *Wall Street Journal,* p. A14.
Signed pamphlet	Pearson Education. (2000). *LifeCare* (2nd ed.) [Pamphlet]. New York: Smith, John: Author.
Work from a library subscription service	Ertman, Earl L. (2008, March–April). "Nefertiti's Eyes." *Archaeology, 61,* 28–32. Retrieved June 18, 2008, from EBSCO Science Reference Center database.
Filmstrips, slide programs, videocassettes, DVDs, and other audiovisual media	Wallis, H. B. (Producer), & Curtiz, M. (Director). (1942). *Casablanca* [Motion picture]. United States: Warner.
Radio or television program transcript	Hackett Fisher, D. (Guest), Hansen, L. (Host). (2003, December 23). Washington's crossing of the Delaware. [Radio series installment]. *Weekend Edition Sunday.* New York: National Public Radio. Retrieved March 6, 2008 from http://www.npr.org/templates/story/story.php?storyId=1573202
Internet	National Association of Chewing Gum Manufacturers. (1999).Retrieved December 19, 1999, from http://www.nacgm.org/consumer/funfacts.html [References to Websites should begin with the author's last name, if available. Indicate the site name and the available path or URL address.]
CD	Shakespeare, W. (1995). *Romeo and Juliet.* (J. Simms, Ed.) [CD-ROM] Oxford: Attica Cybernetics.
Personal interview	[APA states that, since interviews (and other personal communications) do not provide "recoverable data," they should only be cited in text.]

Literary Terms

ALLEGORY An *allegory* is a literary work with two or more levels of meaning—a literal level and one or more symbolic levels. The events, settings, objects, or characters in an allegory—the literal level—stand for ideas or qualities, such as goodness, tyranny, salvation, and so on. Allegorical writing was common in the Middle Ages. Spenser revived the form in *The Faerie Queene,* and John Bunyan revived it yet again in *The Pilgrim's Progress.* Some modern novels, such as George Orwell's *Animal Farm,* can be read as allegories.

ALLITERATION *Alliteration* is the repetition of initial consonant sounds in accented syllables. Coleridge uses the alliteration of both *b* and *f* sounds in this line from "The Rime of the Ancient Mariner":

> The fair breeze blew, the white foam flew.

Especially in poetry, alliteration is used to emphasize and to link words, as well as to create musical sounds.

See also *Anglo-Saxon Poetry.*

ALLUSION *Allusion* is a reference to a well-known person, place, event, literary work, or work of art.

AMBIGUITY *Ambiguity* is the effect created when words suggest and support two or more divergent interpretations. Ambiguity may be used in literature to express experiences or truths that are complex or even contradictory. For instance, the title of Elizabeth Bowen's short story "The Demon Lover," on page 1298, is ambiguous: It can refer either to the main character, who is a lover of a "demon" (a past love that she has not resolved), to the past that haunts her, or to her demonic lover, a ghost who haunts her. This ambiguous use of words reflects a larger ambiguity in the story.

See also *Irony.*

ANALOGY An *analogy* is an extended comparison of relationships. It is based on the idea or insight that the relationship between one pair of things is like the relationship between another pair. Unlike a metaphor, another form of comparison, an analogy involves an explicit comparison, often using the word *like* or *as.*

See also *Metaphor* and *Simile.*

ANAPEST See *Meter.*

ANGLO-SAXON POETRY The rhythmic poetry composed in the Old English language before A.D. 1100 is known as *Anglo-Saxon poetry.* It generally has four accented syllables and an indefinite number of unaccented syllables in each line. Each line is divided in half by a caesura, or pause, and the halves are linked by the alliteration of two or three of the accented syllables. The following translation from "Wulf and Eadwacer" shows the alliteration and caesuras used in Anglo-Saxon poetry:

> I waited for my Wulf // with far-Wandering yearnings,
> When it was rainy weather // and I sat weeping.

Anglo-Saxon poetry was sung or chanted to the accompaniment of a primitive harp; it was not written but was passed down orally.

See also *Alliteration, Caesura,* and *Kenning.*

ARCHETYPAL LITERARY ELEMENTS *Archetypal literary elements* are patterns in literature found around the world. For instance, the occurrence of events in threes is an archetypal element of fairy tales. Certain character types, such as mysterious guides, are also archetypal elements of such traditional stories. According to some critics, these elements express in symbolic form truths about the human mind.

ARGUMENT See *Persuasion.*

ASSONANCE *Assonance* is the repetition of vowel sounds in stressed syllables containing dissimilar consonant sounds. Robert Browning uses assonance in this line in "Andrea del Sarto":

> Ah, but man's reach should exceed his grasp. . . .

The long *e* sound is repeated in the words *reach* and *exceed.* The syllables containing these sounds are stressed and contain different consonants: *r-ch* and *c-d.*

See also *Consonance.*

BALLAD A *ballad* is a song that tells a story, often about adventure or romance, or a poem imitating such a song. Most ballads are divided into four- or six-line stanzas, are rhymed, use simple language, and depict dramatic action. Many ballads employ a repeated refrain. Some use incremental repetition, in which the refrain is varied slightly each time it appears.

BLANK VERSE *Blank verse* is unrhymed poetry usually written in iambic pentameter (see Meter). Occasional variations in rhythm are introduced in blank verse to create emphasis, variety, and naturalness of sound. Because blank verse sounds much like ordinary spoken English, it is often used in drama, as by Shakespeare, and in poetry.

See also *Meter.*

CAESURA A *caesura* is a natural pause in the middle of a line of poetry. In Anglo-Saxon poetry, a caesura divides each four-stress line in half and thus is essential to the rhythm.

See also *Anglo-Saxon Poetry.*

CARPE DIEM A Latin phrase, *carpe diem* means "seize the day" or "make the most of passing time." Many great literary works have been written with the *carpe diem* theme.

CHARACTER The personality that takes part in the action of a literary work is known as a character. Characters can be classified in different ways. A character who plays an important role is called a *major character.* A character who does not is called a *minor character.* A character who plays the central role in a story is called the **protagonist.** A character who opposes the protagonist is called the **antagonist.** A **round character** has many aspects to his or her personality. A **flat character** is defined by only a few qualities. A character who changes is called **dynamic;** a character who does not change is called **static.**

See also **Characterization.**

CHARACTERIZATION **Characterization** is the act of creating and developing a character. A writer uses **direct characterization** when he or she describes a character's traits explicitly. Writers also use **indirect characterization.** A character's traits can be revealed indirectly in what he or she says, thinks, or does; in a description of his or her appearance; or in the statements, thoughts, or actions of other characters.

See also **Character.**

CLIMAX The **climax** is the high point of interest or suspense in a literary work. Often, the climax is also the crisis in the plot, the point at which the protagonist changes his or her understanding or situation. Sometimes, the climax coincides with the **resolution**, the point at which the central conflict is ended.

See also **Plot.**

COMEDY A **comedy** is a literary work, especially a play, that has a happy ending. A comedy often shows ordinary characters in conflict with their society. Types of comedy include **romantic comedy,** which involves problems among lovers, and the **comedy of manners,** which satirically challenges the social customs of a sophisticated society. Comedy is often contrasted with tragedy, in which the protagonist meets an unfortunate end.

See also **Drama** and **Tragedy.**

CONCEIT A **conceit** is an unusual and surprising comparison between two very different things. This special kind of metaphor or complicated analogy is often the basis for a whole poem. During the Elizabethan Age, sonnets commonly included Petrarchan conceits. **Petrarchan conceits** make extravagant claims about the beloved's beauty or the speaker's suffering, with comparisons to divine beings, powerful natural forces, and objects that contain a given quality in the highest degree. Spenser uses a Petrarchan conceit when he claims in Sonnet 1, on page 254, that the "starry light" of his beloved's eyes will make his book happy when she reads it. Seventeenth-century **metaphysical** poets used elaborate, unusual, and highly intellectual conceits, as in the conceit of the compass in John Donne's "A Valediction: Forbidding Mourning," on page 484.

See also **Metaphor.**

CONFLICT A **conflict** is a struggle between opposing forces. Sometimes, this struggle is internal, or within a character. At other times, the struggle is external, or between the character and some outside force. The outside force may be another character, nature, or some element of society such as a custom or a political institution. Often, the conflict in a work combines several of these possibilities.

See also **Plot.**

CONNOTATION **Connotation** refers to the associations that a word calls to mind in addition to its dictionary meaning. For example, the words *home* and *domicile* have the same dictionary meaning. However, the first has positive connotations of warmth and security, whereas the second does not.

See also **Denotation.**

CONSONANCE **Consonance** is the repetition of final consonant sounds in stressed syllables containing dissimilar vowel sounds. Samuel Taylor Coleridge uses consonance in these lines from "The Rime of the Ancient Mariner," on page 820:

> a frightful fie**nd** / Doth close behi**nd** him tread.

Fiend and the stressed syllable in *behind* have the same final consonat sounds but different vowel sounds.

See also **Assonance.**

COUPLET A **couplet** is a pair of rhyming lines written in the same meter. A **heroic couplet** is a rhymed pair of iambic pentameter lines. In a **closed couplet**, the meaning and syntax are completed within the two lines. These lines from Alexander Pope's "An Essay on Criticism" are a closed heroic couplet:

> True ease in writing comes from art, not chance,
> As those move easiest who have learned to dance.

Shakespearean sonnets usually end with heroic couplets.

See also **Sonnet.**

DACTYL See **Meter.**

DENOTATION **Denotation** is the objective meaning of a word—that to which the word refers, independent of other associations that the word calls to mind. Dictionaries list the denotative meanings of words.

See also **Connotation.**

DIALECT **Dialect** is the form of a language spoken by people in a particular region or group. Dialects differ from one another in grammar, vocabulary, and pronunciation.

DIALOGUE **Dialogue** is a conversation between characters. Writers use dialogue to reveal character, to present events, to add variety to narratives, and to interest readers. Dialogue in a story is usually set off by quotation marks and paragraphing. Dialogue in a play script generally follows the name of the speaker.

DIARY A **diary** is a personal record of daily events, usually written in prose. Most diaries are not written for publication; sometimes, however, interesting diaries or diaries written by influential people are published. One example of a published diary is that of Samuel Pepys, a selection from which appears on page 571.

See also **Journal.**

DICTION **Diction** is a writer's word choice. It can be a major determinant of the writer's style. Diction can be described as formal or informal, abstract or concrete, plain or ornate, ordinary or technical.

See also **Style.**

DIMETER See *Meter.*

DRAMA A *drama* is a story written to be performed by actors. It may consist of one or more large sections, called acts, which are made up of any number of smaller sections, called scenes.

Drama originated in the religious rituals and symbolic reenactments of primitive peoples. The ancient Greeks, who developed drama into a sophisticated art form, created such dramatic forms as tragedy and comedy.

The first dramas in England were the miracle plays and morality plays of the Middle Ages. Miracle plays told biblical stories. Morality plays, such as *Everyman,* were allegories dealing with personified virtues and vices. The English Renaissance saw a flowering of drama in England, culminating in the works of William Shakespeare, who wrote many of the world's greatest comedies, tragedies, histories, and romances. During the Neoclassical Age, English drama turned to satirical comedies of manners that probed the virtues of upper-class society. In the Romantic and Victorian ages, a few good verse plays were written, including Percy Bysshe Shelley's *The Cenci* and *Prometheus Unbound.* The end of the nineteenth and beginning of the twentieth centuries saw a resurgence of the drama in England and throughout the English-speaking world. Great plays of the Modern period include works by Bernard Shaw, Christopher Fry, T. S. Eliot, Harold Pinter, and Samuel Beckett.

DRAMATIC MONOLOGUE A *dramatic monologue* is a poem in which an imaginary character speaks to a silent listener. Robert Browning's "My Last Duchess," on page 978, is a dramatic monologue.

ELEGY An *elegy* is a solemn and formal lyric poem about death. It may mourn a particular person or reflect on a serious or tragic theme, such as the passing of youth or beauty. See Thomas Gray's "Elegy Written in a Country Churchyard," on page 666.

See also *Lyric Poem.*

END-STOPPED LINE An *end-stopped line* is a line of poetry concluding with a break in the meter and in the meaning. This pause at the end of a line is often punctuated by a period, comma, dash, or semicolon. These lines from "Away, Melancholy," by Stevie Smith, are end-stopped:

> Are not the trees green,
> The earth as green?
> Does not the wind blow,
> Fire leap and the rivers flow?

See also *Run-on Line.*

EPIC An *epic* is a long narrative poem about the adventures of gods or of a hero. *Beowulf,* on page 40, is a *folk epic,* one that was composed orally and passed from storyteller to storyteller. The ancient Greek epics attributed to Homer—the *Iliad* and the *Odyssey*—are also folk epics. The *Aeneid,* by the Roman poet Virgil, and *The Divine Comedy,* by the Italian poet Dante Alighieri, are examples of literary epics from the Classical and Medieval periods, respectively. John Milton's *Paradise Lost,* a selection from which appears on page 524, is also a literary epic.

Epic conventions are traditional characteristics of epic poems, including an opening statement of the theme; an appeal for supernatural help in telling the story (an invocation); a beginning *in medias res* (Latin: "in the middle of things"); catalogs of people and things; accounts of past events; and descriptive phrases.

See also *Kenning.*

EPIGRAM An *epigram* is a brief statement in prose or in verse. The concluding couplet in an English sonnet may be epigrammatic. An essay may be written in an epigrammatic style.

EPIPHANY *Epiphany* is a term introduced by James Joyce to describe a moment of insight in which a character recognizes a truth. In Joyce's "Araby," on page 1236, the boy has an epiphany when he sees the falsity of his dream.

EPITAPH An *epitaph* is an inscription written on a tomb or burial place. In literature, epitaphs include serious or humorous lines written as if intended for such use, like the epitaph in Thomas Gray's "Elegy Written in a Country Churchyard," on page 666.

ESSAY An *essay* is a short nonfiction work about a particular subject. Essays are of many types but may be classified by tone or style as formal or informal. Addison's breezy style and tongue-in-cheek descriptions make "The Aims of *The Spectator,*" on page 682, an instance of an informal essay. An essay is often classed by its main purpose as descriptive, narrative, expository, argumentative, or persuasive.

EXTENDED METAPHOR See *Metaphor.*

FICTION *Fiction* is prose writing about imaginary characters and events. Some writers of fiction base their stories on real events, whereas others rely solely on their imaginations.

See also *Narration* and *Prose.*

FIGURATIVE LANGUAGE *Figurative language* is writing or speech not meant to be interpreted literally. Poets and other writers use figurative language to paint vivid word pictures, to make their writing emotionally intense and concentrated, and to state their ideas in new and unusual ways. Among the figures of speech making up figurative language are hyperbole, irony, metaphor, metonymy, oxymoron, paradox, personification, simile, and synecdoche.

See also the entries for individual figures of speech.

FOLKLORE The stories, legends, myths, ballads, riddles, sayings, and other traditional works produced orally by illiterate or semiliterate peoples are known as *folklore*. Folklore influences written literature in many ways. The beheading contest in *Sir Gawain and the Green Knight,* on page 170, is an example of folklore.

FOOT See *Meter.*

FREE VERSE *Free verse* is poetry not written in a regular, rhythmical pattern, or meter. Instead of having metrical feet and lines, free verse has a rhythm that suits its meaning and that uses the sounds of spoken language in lines of different lengths. Free verse has been widely used in twentieth-century poetry. An example is "The Galloping Cat," by Stevie Smith:

> All the same I
> Intend to go on being
> A cat that likes to
> Gallop about doing good
> So
> Now with my bald head I go,
> Chopping the untidy flowers down, to and fro.

GOTHIC *Gothic* is a term used to describe literary works that make extensive use of primitive, medieval, wild, mysterious, or natural elements. Gothic novels, such as Mary Wollstonecraft Shelley's *Frankenstein,* the Introduction to which appears on page 760, often depict horrifying events set in gloomy castles.

HEPTAMETER See *Meter.*

HEXAMETER See *Meter.*

HYPERBOLE *Hyperbole* is a deliberate exaggeration or overstatement. In "Song," on page 482, John Donne uses this figure of speech:

> When thou sigh'st, thou sigh'st not wind,
> but sigh'st my soul away

See also *Figurative Language.*

IAMBIC PENTAMETER See *Meter.*

IMAGE An *image* is a word or phrase that appeals to one or more of the senses—sight, hearing, touch, taste, or smell. In a famous essay on *Hamlet,* T. S. Eliot explained how a group of images can be used as an "objective correlative." By this phrase, Eliot meant that a complex emotional state can be suggested by images that are carefully chosen to evoke this state.

See also *Imagery.*

IMAGERY *Imagery* is the descriptive language used in literature to re-create sensory experiences. Imagery enriches writing by making it more vivid, setting a tone, suggesting emotions, and guiding readers' reactions.

IRONY *Irony* is the general name given to literary techniques that involve surprising, interesting, or amusing contradictions. In *verbal irony,* words are used to suggest the opposite of their usual meaning. In *dramatic irony,* there is a contradiction between what a character thinks and what the reader or audience knows to be true. In *irony of situation,* an event occurs that directly contradicts expectations.

JOURNAL A *journal* is a daily autobiographical account of events and personal reactions. Daniel Defoe adapted this form to fictional use in *A Journal of the Plague Year,* an excerpt from which appears on page 590.

See also *Diary.*

KENNING A *kenning* is a metaphorical phrase used in Anglo-Saxon poetry to replace a concrete noun. In "The Seafarer," on page 20, the cuckoo is called "summer's sentinel" and the sea, "the whale's home."

See also *Anglo-Saxon Poetry* and *Epic.*

LEGEND A *legend* is a widely told story about the past that may or may not be based in fact. A legend often reflects a people's identity or cultural values, generally with more historical truth than that in a myth. English legends include the stories of King Arthur (retold in *Morte d'Arthur,* a selection from which appears on page 185) and Robin Hood.

See also *Myth.*

LETTER A *letter* addresses a specific person or group and is meant to be read within a specific time.

LYRIC POEM A *lyric poem* is a poem expressing the observations and feelings of a single speaker. Unlike a narrative poem, it presents an experience or a single effect, but it does not tell a full story. Types of lyric poems include the elegy, the ode, and the sonnet.

METAPHOR A *metaphor* is a figure of speech in which one thing is spoken of as though it were something else, as in "death, that long sleep." Through this identification of dissimilar things, a comparison is suggested or implied.

An *extended metaphor* is developed at length and involves several points of comparison. A mixed metaphor occurs when two metaphors are jumbled together, as in "The thorns of life rained down on him."

A *dead metaphor* is one that has been so overused that its original metaphorical impact has been lost. Examples of dead metaphors include "the foot of the bed" and "toe the line."

See also *Figurative Language.*

METAPHYSICAL POETRY The term *metaphysical poetry* describes the works of such seventeenth-century English poets as Richard Crashaw, John Donne, George Herbert, and Andrew Marvell. Characteristic features of metaphysical poetry include intellectual playfulness, argument, paradoxes, irony, elaborate and unusual conceits, incongruity, and the rhythms of ordinary speech. Examples of metaphysical poems in this textbook include Donne's "Song," on page 482, and Marvell's "To His Coy Mistress," on page 506.

METER *Meter* is the rhythmical pattern of a poem. This pattern is determined by the number and types of stresses, or beats, in each line. To describe the meter of a poem, you must scan its lines. Scanning involves marking the stressed and unstressed syllables, as follows:

> I ween | that, when | the grave's | dark wall
> Did first | her form | retain,
> They thought | their hearts | could ne'er | recall
> The light | of joy | again.

—Emily Brontë, "Song"

As you can see, each stressed syllable is marked with a slanted line (´) and each unstressed syllable with a horseshoe symbol (˘). The stresses are then divided by vertical lines into groups called feet. The following types of feet are common in English poetry:

1. **Iamb:** a foot with one unstressed syllable followed by one stressed syllable, as in the word **afraid**
2. **Trochee:** a foot with one stressed syllable followed by one unstressed syllable, as in the word **heather**
3. **Anapest:** a foot with two unstressed syllables followed by one stressed syllable, as in the word **disembark**
4. **Dactyl:** a foot with one stressed syllable followed by two unstressed syllables, as in the word **solitude**
5. **Spondee:** a foot with two stressed syllables, as in the word **workday**
6. **Pyrrhic:** a foot with two unstressed syllables, as in the last foot of the word **unspeak | ably**
7. **Amphibrach:** a foot with an unstressed syllable, one stressed syllable, and another unstressed syllable, as in the word **another**
8. **Amphimacer:** a foot with a stressed syllable, one unstressed syllable, and another stressed syllable, as in **up and down**

A line of poetry is described as **iambic**, **trochaic**, **anapestic**, or **dactylic** according to the kind of foot that appears most often in the line. Lines are also described in terms of the number of feet that occur in them, as follows:

1. **Monometer:** verse written in one-foot lines:

> Sound the Flute!
> Now it's mute.
> Birds delight
> Day and Night.
>
> —William Blake, "Spring"

2. **Dimeter:** verse written in two-foot lines:

> Ŏ Róse | thŏu árt sick.
> The invís | ĭble wórm.
> Thăt flíes | ĭn thĕ níght
> Ĭn thĕ hów | lĭng stórm:
> Hăs fóund | ŏut thy̆ béd
> Ŏf crím | sŏn jóy: . . .
>
> —William Blake, "The Sick Rose"

3. **Trimeter:** verse written in three-foot lines:

> Ĭ wént | tŏ thĕ Gárd | ĕn ŏf Lóve
> Ănd sáw | whăt Ĭ név | ĕr hăd séen:
> Ă Cháp | ĕl wăs búilt | ĭn thĕ mídst,
> Whĕre Ĭ úsed | tŏ pláy | ŏn thĕ gréen.
>
> —William Blake, "The Garden of Love"

4. **Tetrameter:** verse written in four-foot lines:

> Ĭ wánd | ĕr thró' | ĕach chárt | ĕr'd stréet
> Neăr whére | thĕ chárt | ĕr'd Thámes |
> dŏes flów
> Ănd márk | ĭn év | ĕry fáce | Ĭ méet
> Márks ŏf | wéaknĕss, | márks ŏf | wóe.
>
> —William Blake, "London"

A six-foot line is called a **hexameter.** A line with seven feet is a **heptameter.**

A complete description of the meter of a line tells both how many feet there are in the line and what kind of foot is most common. Thus, the stanza from Emily Brontë's poem, quoted at the beginning of this entry, would be described as being made up of alternating iambic tetrameter and iambic trimeter lines. Poetry that does not have a regular meter is called **free verse**.

See also **Free Verse.**

METONYMY **Metonymy** is a figure of speech that substitutes something closely related for the thing actually meant. In the opening line of "The Lost Leader," Robert Browning says, "Just for a handful of silver he left us," using "silver" to refer to money paid for a betrayal.

See also **Figurative Language.**

MIRACLE PLAY See **Drama.**

MOCK EPIC A **mock epic** is a poem about a trivial matter written in the style of a serious epic. The incongruity of style and subject matter produces comic effects. Alexander Pope's "The Rape of the Lock," on page 632, is a mock epic.

See also **Epic.**

MODERNISM **Modernism** describes an international movement in the arts during the early twentieth century. Modernists rejected old forms and experimented with the new. Literary Modernists—such as James Joyce, W. B. Yeats, and T. S. Eliot—used images as symbols. They presented human experiences in fragments, rather than as a coherent whole, which led to new experiments in the forms of poetry and fiction.

MONOLOGUE A **monologue** is a speech or performance given entirely by one person or by one character.

See also **Dramatic Monologue** and **Soliloquy.**

MOOD **Mood**, or **atmosphere**, is the feeling created in the reader by a literary work or passage. Mood may be suggested by the writer's choice of words, by events in the work, or by the physical setting. Nadine Gordimer begins "The Train from Rhodesia," on page 1342, with a description of the hot, sandy train station that sets a mood mixing boredom and confinement with the eager expectation of the train.

See also **Setting** and **Tone.**

MORALITY PLAY See *Drama.*

MYTH A *myth* is a fictional tale, originally with religious significance, that explains the actions of gods or heroes, the causes of natural phenomena, or both. Allusions to characters and motifs from Greek, Roman, Norse, and Celtic myths are common in English literature. In addition, mythological stories are often retold or adapted.

See also *Legend.*

NARRATION *Narration* is writing that tells a story. The act of telling a story is also called narration. The *narrative*, or story, is told by a character or speaker called the *narrator.* Biographies, autobiographies, journals, reports, novels, short stories, plays, narrative poems, anecdotes, fables, parables, myths, legends, folk tales, ballads, and epic poems are all narratives, or types of narration.

See also *Point of View.*

NARRATIVE POEM A *narrative poem* is a poem that tells a story in verse. Three traditional types of narrative poems include ballads, epics, and metrical romances.

NATURALISM *Naturalism* was a literary movement among writers at the end of the nineteenth century and during the early decades of the twentieth century. The Naturalists depicted life in its grimmer details and viewed people as hopeless victims of natural laws.

See also *Realism.*

NEOCLASSICISM *Neoclassicism* was a literary movement of the late seventeenth and the eighteenth centuries in which writers turned to classical Greek and Roman literary models and standards. Like the ancients, Neoclassicists, such as Alexander Pope, stressed order, harmony, restraint, and the ideal. Much Neoclassical literature dealt with themes related to proper human conduct. The most popular literary forms of the day—essays, letters, early novels, epigrams, parodies, and satires—reflected this emphasis.

See also *Romanticism.*

NONFICTION *Nonfiction* is prose writing that presents and explains ideas or tells about real places, objects or events. To be classified as nonfiction, a work must be true.

NOVEL A *novel* is an extended work of fiction that often has a complicated plot, many major and minor characters, a unifying theme, and several settings. Novels can be grouped in many ways, based on the historical periods in which they are written (such as Victorian), on the subjects and themes that they treat (such as Gothic or regional), on the techniques used in them (such as stream of consciousness), or on their part in literary movements (such as Naturalism or Realism). Among the early novels were Samuel Richardson's *Pamela* and *Clarissa* and Henry Fielding's *Tom Jones.* Other classic English novels include Jane Austen's *Pride and Prejudice,* Sir Walter Scott's *Waverley,* Charles Dickens's *David Copperfield,* and George Eliot's *The Mill on the Floss*. Major twentieth-century novelists include James Joyce, Virginia Woolf, D. H. Lawrence, Henry James, Graham Greene, and Patrick White. A *novella*—for example, Joseph Conrad's *Heart of Darkness*—is not as long as a novel but is longer than a short story.

OBJECTIVE CORRELATIVE See *Image.*

OCTAVE See *Stanza.*

ODE An *ode* is a long, formal lyric poem with a serious theme. It may have a traditional structure with stanzas grouped in threes, called the *strophe,* the *antistrophe,* and the *epode.* Odes often honor people, commemorate events, or respond to natural scenes.

See also *Lyric Poem.*

ONOMATOPOEIA *Onomatopoeia* is the use of words that imitate sounds. Examples of such words are *buzz, hiss, murmur,* and *rustle.* Onomatopoeia is used to create musical effects and to reinforce meaning.

ORAL TRADITION *Oral tradition* is the body of songs, stories, and poems preserved by being passed from generation to generation by word of mouth. Among the many materials composed or preserved through oral tradition in Great Britain are *Beowulf,* on page 40, and the folk ballads on pages 205–211. In his *Morte d'Arthur,* a selection from which begins on page 185, Sir Thomas Malory drew on Arthurian legends from the oral tradition. Shakespeare drew on materials from the oral tradition to create the sprites and fairies of *A Midsummer Night's Dream* and the witches of *Macbeth,* on page 322. Folk epics, ballads, myths, legends, folk tales, folk songs, proverbs, and nursery rhymes are all products of the oral tradition.

See also *Ballad, Folklore, Legend,* and *Myth.*

OXYMORON An *oxymoron* is a figure of speech that fuses two contradictory ideas, such as "freezing fire" or "happy grief," thus suggesting a paradox in just a few words.

See also *Figurative Language* and *Paradox.*

PARABLE A *parable* is a short, simple story from which a moral or religious lesson can be drawn. The most famous parables are those in the New Testament, an example of which appears on page 302.

PARADOX A *paradox* is a statement that seems to be contradictory but that actually presents a truth. In "Love's Growth," John Donne presents the following paradox:

> Methinks I lied all winter, when I swore
> My love was infinite, if spring make it more.

Because a paradox is surprising or even shocking, it draws the reader's attention to what is being said.

See also *Figurative Language* and *Oxymoron.*

PARODY A *parody* is a humorous imitation of another work or of a type of work.

PASTORAL *Pastoral* refers to literary works that deal with the pleasures of a simple rural life or with escape to a simpler place and time. The tradition of pastoral literature began in ancient Greece with the poetic idylls of Theocritus. The Roman poet Virgil also wrote a famous collection of pastoral poems, the *Eclogues.*

During the European Renaissance, pastoral writing became quite popular. Two famous examples are *The Countess of Pembroke's Arcadia,* by Sir Philip Sidney, and Christopher Marlowe's "The Passionate Shepherd to His Love," on page 266.

Today, the term *pastoral* is commonly applied to any work in which a speaker longs to escape to a simpler rural life. By this definition, both William Wordsworth's "The World Is Too Much With Us," on page 790, and William Butler Yeats's "The Lake Isle of Innisfree," on page 1141, are pastoral poems.

PENTAMETER See *Meter.*

PERSONIFICATION *Personification* is a figure of speech in which a nonhuman subject is given human characteristics. Percy Bysshe Shelley uses personification in these lines:

Swiftly walk o'er the western wave,
Spirit of the Night!

Effective personification of things or ideas makes their qualities seem unified, like the characteristics of a person, and their relationship with the reader seem closer.

See also *Figurative Language* and *Metaphor.*

PERSUASION *Persuasion* is writing or speech that attempts to convince a reader to think or act in a particular way. Persuasion is used in advertising, in editorials, in sermons, and in political speeches. An *argument* is a logical way of presenting a belief, conclusion, or stance. A good argument is supported with reasoning and evidence.

PLOT *Plot* is the sequence of events in a literary work. The two primary elements of any plot are characters and a conflict. Most plots can be analyzed into many or all of the following parts:

1. The *exposition* introduces the setting, the characters, and the basic situation.
2. The *inciting incident* introduces the central conflict and develops the rising action.
3. During the *development,* or rising action, the conflict runs its course and usually intensifies.
4. At the *climax,* the conflict reaches a high point of interest or suspense.
5. The *denouement,* or *falling action,* ties up loose ends that remain after the climax of the conflict.
6. At the *resolution,* the story is resolved and an insight is revealed.

There are many variations on the standard plot structure. Some stories begin *in medias res* ("in the middle of things"), after the inciting incident has already occurred. In some stories, the expository material appears toward the middle, in flashbacks. In many stories, there is no denouement. Occasionally, the conflict is left unresolved.

POETRY *Poetry* is one of the three major types, or genres, of literature, the others being prose and drama. Poetry defies simple definition because there is no single characteristic that is found in all poems and not found in all nonpoems.

Often, poems are divided into lines and stanzas. Poems such as sonnets, odes, villanelles, and sestinas are governed by rules regarding the number of lines, the number and placement of stressed syllables in each line, and the rhyme scheme. In the case of villanelles and sestinas, the repetition of words at the ends of lines or of entire lines is required. (An example of a sestina, Seamus Heaney's "Two Lorries," appears on page 1370. An example of a villanelle, Dylan Thomas's "Do Not Go Gentle into That Good Night," appears on page 1390.) However, some poems are written in free verse. Most poems make use of highly concise, musical, and emotionally charged language. Many also use imagery, figurative language, and devices of sound like rhyme.

Types of poetry include *narrative poetry* (ballads, epics, and metrical romances); *dramatic poetry* (dramatic monologues and dramatic dialogues); *lyrics* (sonnets, odes, elegies, and love poems); and *concrete poetry* (a poem presented on the page in a shape that suggests its subject).

POINT OF VIEW The perspective, or vantage point, from which a story is told is its *point of view.* If a character within the story narrates, then it is told from the *first-person point of view.* If a voice from outside the story tells it, then the story is told from the *third-person point of view.* If the knowledge of the storyteller is limited to the internal states of one character, then the storyteller has a *limited point of view.* If the storyteller's knowledge extends to the internal states of all the characters, then the storyteller has an *omniscient point of view.*

POLITICAL COMMENTARY *Political commentary* offers opinions on political issues, building arguments on evidence and assumptions. Using writing forms such as speeches, poems, and letters, commentators seek to persuade using persuasive devices such as rhetorical questions and balanced clauses.

PROSE *Prose* is the ordinary form of written language and one of the three major types of literature. Most writing that is not poetry, drama, or song is considered prose. Prose occurs in two major forms: fiction and nonfiction.

PSALM A *psalm* is a sacred song or lyric poem in praise of God.

PYRRHIC See *Meter.*

QUATRAIN See *Stanza.*

REALISM *Realism* is the presentation in art of details from actual life. During the last part of the nineteenth century and the first part of the twentieth, Realism enjoyed considerable popularity among writers in the English-speaking world. Novels often dealt with grim social realities and presented realistic portrayals of the psychological states of characters.

REFRAIN A *refrain* is a regularly repeated line or group of lines in a poem or song.

See also *Ballad.*

REGIONALISM *Regionalism* is the tendency to confine one's writing to the presentation of the distinct culture of an area, including its speech, customs, and history. For example, the Brontës wrote about Yorkshire, Thomas Hardy wrote about Dorset and Wessex, and D. H. Lawrence wrote about Nottinghamshire.

RHYME *Rhyme* is the repetition of sounds at the ends of words. *End rhyme* occurs when rhyming words appear at the ends of lines. *Internal rhyme* occurs when rhyming words fall within a line. *Exact rhyme* is the use of identical rhyming sounds, as in *love* and *dove*. *Approximate,* or *slant*, *rhyme* is the use of sounds that are similar but not identical, as in *prove* and *glove*.

RHYME SCHEME *Rhyme scheme* is the regular pattern of rhyming words in a poem or stanza. To indicate a rhyme scheme, assign a different letter to each final sound in the poem or stanza. The following lines from Charlotte Brontë's "On the Death of Anne Brontë" have been marked:

There's little joy in life for me,	**a**
And little terror in the grave;	**b**
I've lived the parting hour to see	**a**
Of one I would have died to save.	**b**

RHYTHM See *Meter.*

ROMANCE A *romance* is a story that presents remote or imaginative incidents rather than ordinary, realistic experience. The term *romance* was originally used to refer to medieval tales of the deeds and loves of noble knights and ladies. These early romances, or tales of chivalry and courtly love, are exemplified by *Sir Gawain and the Green Knight,* on page 170, and by the extract from Malory's *Morte d'Arthur,* on page 185. During the Renaissance in England, many writers, such as Edmund Spenser in *The Faerie Queene,* drew heavily on the romance tradition. From the eighteenth century on, the term *romance* has been used to describe sentimental novels about love.

ROMANTICISM *Romanticism* was a literary and artistic movement of the eighteenth and nineteenth centuries. In reaction to Neoclassicism, the Romantics emphasized imagination, fancy, freedom, emotion, wildness, the beauty of the untamed natural world, the rights of the individual, the nobility of the common man, and the attractiveness of pastoral life. Important figures in the Romantic Movement included William Wordsworth, Samuel Taylor Coleridge, Percy Bysshe Shelley, John Keats, and George Gordon, Lord Byron.

RUN-ON LINE A *run-on line* is a line that does not contain a pause or a stop at the end. It ends in the middle of a statement and a grammatical unit, and the reader must read the next line to find the end of the statement and the completion of the grammatical unit. The beginning of Molly Holden's "The Double Nature of White" illustrates the run-on line:

> White orchards are the earliest, stunning
> the spirit resigned to winter's black, white thorn
> sprays first the bare wet branches of the hedge.

See also *End-Stopped Line.*

SATIRE *Satire* is writing that ridicules or holds up to contempt the faults of individuals or groups. Satires include Jonathan Swift's prose work *Gulliver's Travels,* on page 606, and Alexander Pope's poem *The Rape of the Lock,* on page 632. Although a satire is often humorous, its purpose is not simply to make readers laugh but also to correct the flaws and shortcomings that it points out.

SCANSION *Scansion* is the process of analyzing the metrical pattern of a poem.

See also *Meter.*

SERMON A *sermon* is a speech offering religious or moral instruction. For example, the Sermon on the Mount, on page 301, given by Jesus on a mountain in Galilee, contains the basic teachings of Christianity.

SESTET See *Stanza.*

SETTING The *setting* is the time and place of the action of a literary work. A setting can provide a backdrop for the action. It can be the force that the protagonist struggles against and thus the source of the central conflict. It can also be used to create an atmosphere. In many works, the setting symbolizes a point that the author wishes to emphasize.

See also *Mood* and *Symbol.*

SHORT STORY A *short story* is a brief work of fiction. The short story resembles the longer novel, but it generally has a simpler plot and setting. In addition, a short story tends to reveal character at a crucial moment, rather than to develop it through many incidents.

SIMILE A *simile* is a figure of speech that compares two apparently dissimilar things using *like* or *as.* Christina Rossetti uses simile in "Goblin Market" to describe two sisters:

> Like two blossoms on one stem,
> Like two flakes of new-fallen snow,
> Like two wands of ivory
> Tipped with gold for awful kings.

By comparing apparently dissimilar things, the writer of a simile surprises the reader into an appreciation of the hidden similarities of the things being compared.

See also *Figurative Language.*

SOCIAL COMMENTARY *Social commentary* is writing that offers insight into society, its values, and its customs. For example, Mary Wollstonecraft's *A Vindication of the Rights of Woman* (p. 916) offers social commentary on the debate over women's rights and seeks to attribute this problem to social customs.

SOLILOQUY A *soliloquy* is a long speech in a play or in a prose work made by a character who is alone and thus reveals private thoughts and feelings to the audience or reader. William Shakespeare opens Act III of *Macbeth,* on page 361, with a soliloquy in which Banquo speculates on Macbeth's reaction to the witches' prophecy.

See also *Monologue.*

SONNET A sonnet is a fourteen-line lyric poem with a single theme. Sonnets are usually written in iambic pentameter. The *Petrarchan,* or *Italian sonnet,* is divided into two parts, an eight-line octave and a six-line sestet. The octave rhymes *abba abba,* while the sestet generally rhymes *cde cde* or uses some combination of *cd* rhymes. The octave raises a question, states a problem, or presents a brief narrative, and the sestet answers the question, solves the problem, or comments on the narrative.

The *Shakespearean,* or *English,* *sonnet* has three four-line quatrains plus a concluding two-line couplet. The rhyme scheme of such a sonnet is usually *abab cdcd efef gg.* Each of the three quatrains usually explores a different variation of the main theme. Then, the couplet presents a summarizing or concluding statement.

The *Spenserian* sonnet has three quatrains and a couplet, but the quatrains are joined by linking rhymes like those of an Italian sonnet. The rhyme scheme of this type of sonnet is *abab bcbc cdcd ee.*

See also *Lyric Poem* and *Sonnet Sequence.*

SONNET SEQUENCE A *sonnet sequence* is a series or group of sonnets, most often written to or about a beloved. Although each sonnet can stand alone as a separate poem, the sequence lets the poet trace the development of a relationship or examine different aspects of a single subject. Examples of sonnet sequences are Sir Philip Sidney's *Astrophel and Stella,* Edmund Spenser's *Amoretti,* and Elizabeth Barrett Browning's *Sonnets from the Portuguese.*

See also *Sonnet.*

SPEAKER The *speaker* is the imaginary voice assumed by the writer of a poem; the character who "says" the poem. This character is often not identified by name but may be identified otherwise. For example, the title of William Blake's poem "The Chimney Sweeper," on page 751, identifies the speaker, a child who gives an account of his life.

Recognizing the speaker and thinking about his or her characteristics are often central to interpreting a lyric poem. In Blake's poem, for instance, the speaker's acceptance of his oppressive life is offered for the reader's evaluation.

See also *Point of View.*

SPONDEE See *Meter.*

SPRUNG RHYTHM The term *sprung rhythm* was used by Gerard Manley Hopkins to describe the idiosyncratic meters of his poems. The rhythm is quite varied and contains such violations of traditional metrical rules as several strong stresses in a row or feet containing more than two weak stresses.

STANZA A *stanza* is a group of lines in a poem, which is seen as a unit. Many poems are divided into stanzas that are separated by spaces. Stanzas often function like paragraphs in prose. Each stanza states and develops one main idea.

Stanzas are commonly named according to the number of lines found in them, as follows:

1. *Couplet:* a two-line stanza
2. *Tercet:* a three-line stanza
3. *Quatrain:* a four-line stanza
4. *Cinquain:* a five-line stanza
5. *Sestet:* a six-line stanza
6. *Heptastich:* a seven-line stanza
7. *Octave:* an eight-line stanza

See also *Sonnet.*

STYLE *Style* is a writer's typical way of writing. Determinants of a writer's style include formality, use of figurative language, use of rhythm, typical grammatical patterns, typical sentence lengths, and typical methods of organization. John Milton is noted for a grand, heroic style that contrasts with John Keats's rich, sensory style and with T. S. Eliot's allusive, ironic style.

See also *Diction.*

SUBLIME The *sublime* is an effect created in literature when a writer confronts a power or mystery in nature that exceeds human understanding. The effect is achieved by representing the infinite or endless in sensory terms, as when Byron characterizes the inexhaustible power of the ocean in the "Apostrophe to the Ocean" in *Childe Harold's Pilgrimage,* on page 856.

SYMBOL A *symbol* is a sign, word, phrase, image, or other object that stands for or represents something else. Thus, a flag can symbolize a country, a spoken word can symbolize an object, a fine car can symbolize wealth, and so on. In literary criticism, a distinction is often made between traditional or conventional symbols—those that are part of our general cultural inheritance—and *personal symbols*—those that are created by particular authors for use in particular works. For example, the lamb in William Blake's poem "The Lamb," on page 748, is a conventional symbol for peace, gentleness, and innocence. However, the tiger in Blake's poem "The Tyger," on page 749, is not a conventional or inherited symbol. Blake created this symbol specifically for this poem.

Conventional symbolism is often based on elements of nature. For example, youth is often symbolized by greenery or springtime, middle age by summer, and old age by autumn or winter. Conventional symbols are also borrowed from religion and politics. For example, a cross may be a symbol of Christianity, or the color red may be a symbol of Marxist ideology.

SYNECDOCHE *Synecdoche* is a figure of speech in which a part of something is used to stand for the whole. In the preface to his long poem entitled *Milton,* William Blake includes these lines: "And did those feet in ancient time / Walk upon England's mountains green?" The "feet" stand for the whole body, and "England's mountains green" stand for England.

See also *Figurative Language.*

SYNTAX *Syntax* is the way words are organized—for example, their order is a sentence or phrase.

TETRAMETER See *Meter.*

THEME *Theme* is the central idea, concern, or purpose in a literary work. In an essay, the theme might be directly stated in what is known as a thesis statement. In a serious literary work, the theme is usually expressed indirectly rather than directly. A light work, one written strictly for entertainment, may not have a theme.

TONE *Tone* is the writer's attitude toward the readers and toward the subject. It may be formal or informal, friendly or distant, personal or pompous. For example, John Keats's tone in his poem "On First Looking into Chapman's Homer," on page 882, is earnest and respectful, while James Boswell's tone in *The Life of Samuel Johnson,* which begins on page 655, is familiar and engaging.

See also *Mood.*

TRADITION In literary study and practice, a *tradition* is a past body of work, developed over the course of history. A literary tradition may be unified by form (the tradition of the sonnet), by language (literature in English), or by nationality (English literature). A tradition develops through the acknowledgment of works, forms, and styles as classic. It also develops through critical reappraisals, as when T. S. Eliot, in the early twentieth century, elevated seventeenth-century poet John Donne out of the shadows of critical obscurity and disfavor. Writers participate in a tradition if only by following conventions about the suitable forms and subjects for literature. They make conscious use of the tradition when they use references, stories, or forms from old literature to give authority to their work. For example, John Milton uses the classical form of the epic in *Paradise Lost,* page 524, to retell the biblical story of the Fall. Writers may also break from a tradition, as when Wordsworth rejects elevated poetic language in favor of conversational speech in poems such as "London, 1802," page 791. A tradition may also be used to question itself. For example, Derek Walcott in the extract from *Midsummer,* page 1360, uses references to Shakespeare's works to question the extent to which he, a black poet, can participate in a tradition largely maintained by white society for white society.

TRAGEDY *Tragedy* is a type of drama or literature that shows the downfall or destruction of a noble or outstanding person, traditionally one who possesses a character weakness called a *tragic flaw.* Macbeth, for example, is a brave and noble figure led astray by ambition. The *tragic hero* is caught up in a sequence of events that inevitably results in disaster. Because the protagonist is neither a wicked villain nor an innocent victim, the audience reacts with mixed emotions—both pity and fear, according to the Greek philosopher Aristotle, who defined tragedy in the *Poetics.* The outcome of a tragedy, in which the protagonist is isolated from society, contrasts with the happy resolution of a comedy, in which the protagonist makes peace with society.

See also *Comedy* and *Drama.*

TRIMETER See *Meter.*

TROCHEE See *Meter.*

VOICE The *voice* of a writer is his or her "sound" on the page. It is based on elements such as word choice, sound devices, pace, and attitude.

College Application Essay

If you are applying for admission to a college, you will probably need to submit an essay as part of your application. This essay will help admissions committee members get a sense of you as a person and as a student. Review the chart at right for general strategies, and follow the guidelines below to produce an effective college application essay.

Selecting a Topic

Read the essay question on the application form with care. Mark key criteria and direction words such as *describe* and *explain*. After you have written a first draft, check to make sure you have met all of the requirements of the question. Your essay has a better chance of succeeding if it meets the requirements exactly.

General Questions About You

The essay question on a college application may be as general as "Describe a significant experience or event in your life and explain its consequences for you." To choose the right topic for such a question, think of an event or experience that truly is meaningful to you—a camping trip, a volunteer event, a family reunion. Test the subject by drafting a letter about it to a good friend or relative. If you find that your enthusiasm for the subject grows as you write, and if your discussion reveals something about your growth or your outlook on life, the topic may be the right one for your essay.

Directed Questions

The essay question on an application may be a directed question, rather than a general question. For instance, you may be asked to select three figures from history you would like to meet and to explain your choices.

In such cases, do not give an answer just because you think it will please reviewers. Rely on your own interests and instincts. Your most convincing writing will come from genuine interest in the subject.

> **Strategies for Writing an Effective College Application Essay**
>
> - **Choose the right topic**. If you have a choice of essay topics, choose one that truly interests you.
> - **Organize.** Use a strong organization that carries the reader from introduction to conclusion.
> - **Begin Strongly.** Open with an introduction that has a good chance of sparking the reader's interest.
> - **Elaborate.** Be sure to explain why the experiences you discuss are important to you or what you learned from them.
> - **Show style.** Bring life to your essay through vivid descriptions, precise word choice, and sophisticated sentence structure, such as parallelism. Consider including dialogue where appropriate.
> - **Close with a clincher.** Write a conclusion that effectively sums up your ideas.
> - **Do a clean job**. Proofread your essay carefully. It should be error-free.

Style

Remember that an essay is a formal document addressed to strangers. Use a formal to semiformal style. Avoid incomplete sentences and slang unless you are using them for clear stylistic effect. Use words with precision, selecting one or two accurate words to express your meaning. Do not use a word if you are unsure of its meaning.

Format

Most applications limit the length of essays. Do not exceed the allowed space or word count. Your college application essay should be neatly typed or printed, using adequate margins. Proofread your final draft carefully. If you submit a separate copy of the essay (rather than writing on the application form), number the pages and include your name and contact information on each page.

Reusing Your Essay

Most students apply to a number of different colleges. Once you have written a strong essay for one application, you may adapt it for others. However, do not submit a single essay to several schools blindly. Always read the application essay question carefully to ensure that the essay you submit fulfills all of its requirements.

Workplace Writing

Job Search Document: Cover Letter

A cover letter is a formal letter in which the writer asks to be considered for a job. It usually accompanies, or "covers," a completed job application, a résumé, or both. A good cover letter relates specifically to the job for which the writer is applying.

Write a Cover Letter

Consider a part-time job or a summer job you would like to have. Then, write a cover letter to accompany a job application. Include a header, an inside address, an introductory paragraph, one or two body paragraphs, a closing paragraph, and a signature. Mention your main qualifications, and explain how they make you a good fit for the job.

Cesar Moreno
000 Park Avenue
San Marcos, Texas 00000
512-000-0000
emailaddress@theinternet.com

January 15, 20—

Barbara Jones, Director
River Place Day Camp
500 S. Camp Street
Austin, TX 00000

Dear Ms. Jones:

I am writing to apply for the position of Activities Coordinator for your summer camp. The job description posted on the Texas Summer Camps job board perfectly parallels my own interests and experience.

As noted on the enclosed résumé, I have four years' experience as a camp counselor, including one as Lead Counselor and one as Assistant Activities Director. In these roles, I learned not only to work as a team leader, but also to help tailor a camp's programs to the needs of its campers. As an education student at Texas State University, I have completed basic education courses as well as electives in counseling, recreational learning, and youth leadership. These courses, along with my volunteer work as an after-school mentor, have sparked my interest in non-classroom education. In fact, I plan to base my entire career on the idea that learning can be fun—and can happen anywhere.

I hope to help make River Place Day Camp a fun, educational, and well-organized experience for both its campers and its staff. I look forward to meeting with you and discussing my qualifications in more detail.

Sincerely,

Cesar Moreno

> The heading should include the writer's name, address, phone number, e-mail address, and the date of the letter.

> The inside address includes the name, title, and address of the recipient.

> The body paragraph describes how the writer's experiences relate specifically to the job responsibilities.

Job Search Document: Résumé

A **résumé** is a written summary or outline of a person's job qualifications. It plays a key part in most career or job searches. An effective résumé has the following elements:

- candidate's name, current address, phone number, and e-mail address;
- educational background, work experience, and other relevant life experiences;
- logical organization;
- clearly labled sections.

Compile a Résumé

Write a résumé to use in a job search. Consider a specific job you would like to pursue. Then, brainstorm for relevant information in your schooling, work experience, including important details and maintaining a professional tone. As you develop your document, experiment with different fonts to create a professional, readable document.

CESAR MORENO
000 Park Avenue
San Marcos, Texas 00000
512-000-0000 • emailaddress@theinternet.com

> Place contact information at the top of the résumé.

EDUCATION
- **Texas State University**, San Marcos, TX
  Bachelor of Science in Education
  Expected: May, 20—
- **Austin High School**, Austin, TX
  Graduated with honors, May, 20—

> The headings *Education*, *Work Experience*, and so on indicate that this résumé is organized by topic.

WORK EXPERIENCE
- **Summer 2008–Summer 2010**
  Camp Lazy J, Fredericksburg, TX
  Camp Counselor: Supervised groups of campers aged 8–12. Served as Lead Counselor in 20– and as Assistant Activities Director in 20–.
- **2009–2010**
  YMCA, Austin, Texas
  Life Guard and Swim Instructor: Guarded weekend free-swim sessions and taught beginning and intermediate youth swim classes.

> The items under each topic are bulleted and arranged from most to least recent.

VOLUNTEER EXPERIENCE
- **2009–present**
  San Marcos Community Center, San Marcos, TX
  After-School Mentor: Help elementary and middle school students organize and complete schoolwork, develop skills and interests, and resolve personal issues.
- **2008–2009**
  Stepping Up Preschool, Austin, TX
  Teacher's Aide: Assisted in the 3- and 4-year-old classroom; helped plan and execute special summer programs.

ADDITIONAL SKILLS AND CERTIFICATIONS
- CPR certified, 2007 to the present
- Fluent in Spanish
- Proficient in water sports, including rowing, kayaking, and rafting
- Proficient in Microsoft Word, Excel, and PowerPoint
- Completed childcare training course, YMCA, 2007

> A résumé should be no longer than a single page.

REFERENCES
Furnished on request.

Job Search Document: Job Application

Many employers require job applicants to complete a **job application.** A job application is a standard form that asks for particular kinds of information, including the candidate's contact information, education, and work experience.

Complete a Job Application

Consider a part-time job you would like to have. Then, copy and complete the job application shown here using your own information.

Employment Application

PERSONAL INFORMATION
Full Name: Cesar Moreno
Address: 000 Park Ave., San Marcos, TX, 00000
Phone Number: (512) 000-0000
E-mail Address: emailaddress@theinternet.com

POSITION AND AVAILABILITY
Position Applied For: Activities Coordinator

EDUCATION

School	Degree/Diploma	Graduation Date
Texas State University Austin High School	B.S./Education diploma	expected 5/20— May, 20—
Additional Skills, Qualifications, Licenses, Training, Awards		
CPR and childcare certified, 2007—present Fluent in Spanish		

EMPLOYMENT HISTORY
Present/Last Position and Dates: Camp Counselor, Summer 2006–Summer 2009
Employer: Camp Lazy J
Responsibilities: supervised campers aged 8–12
Supervisor: Mr. Smith
May we contact Supervisor? If so, phone number: yes; (512) 000-0000

Previous Position: Lifeguard and Swim Instructor, 2007–2008
Employer: Austin YMCA
Responsibilities: Guarded free-swim sessions; taught youth swim classes
Supervisor: Mrs. Smith
May we contact Supervisor? If so, phone number: yes; (512) 000-0000

Please list additional employment information on a separate sheet of paper.

I certify that the information contained in this application is true and complete. I authorize the verification of any or all information listed above.

Signature: Cesar Moreno
Date: January 15, 20—

> Include only relevant information, and condense it to fit the space available.

> Get your former supervisor's permission before responding "yes" to this item.

> The applicant's signature gives the employer permission to check the information provided.

Business Communications: Business Letter

Business letters are formal letters in which the content is other than personal. Whatever the subject, an effective business letter has the following elements:

- a heading, inside address, salutation or greeting, body, closing, and signature
- one of several acceptable formats, including *block format,* in which each part of the letter begins at the left margin, and *modified block format,* in which the heading, closing, and signature are indented to the center of the page
- formal and courteous language

Write a Business Letter

Choose one of the following purposes and write a business letter to accomplish it. Include heading, inside address, salutation, body, closing, and signature. Use polite and formal language.

- complain about poor service in a restaurant
- accompany a short story you hope to have published
- praise the work of an artist or musician
- gain support for a beautification plan in your community

Bright Orange Lodge
000 Orange Dr.
Orchard, FL 00000

May 1, 20—

Tom Manager, Business Manager
Universal Bank, Inc.
00000 Adams Park Drive
Miami, FL 00000

> The inside address includes the name, title, company, and address of the recipient.

Dear Mr. Manager:

I am writing to confirm the reservation you have made for your organization's annual corporate retreat.

Per our phone conversation of April 28, you requested that the Bright Orange Lodge facilities be reserved for Universal Bank, Inc. from Friday, June 10, at 6:00 p.m. to Sunday, June 12, at 3:00 p.m. Facilities are to include the large meeting room, the kitchen, and a block of between 20 and 30 double-occupancy rooms. As we discussed, I anticipate a firm room count from you by the end of this month.

> This letter is organized in modified block format.

Per the same conversation, I understand that Universal Bank is planning to use its own caterers for all meals. Should this change, Bright Orange can provide food services in its main dining hall, but we will need advance notice.

A bill for the above-specified services will be sent to your attention under separate cover.

Thank you for choosing Bright Orange for your corporate retreat. If I can be of any further assistance, or if you have any questions, please contact me directly at (352) 000-0000.

Sincerely,
Pat Brown

Pat Brown
Event Coordinator

> Business letters end with formal closings, such as *Sincerely* or *Respectfully yours,* followed by the writer's signature and typed name.

Business Communications: Memo

A **memo**—short for *memorandum*—is a brief printed message between co-workers. It usually focuses on information necessary for the completion of a particular task or project. An effective memo has the following elements:

- block organization, with each new element beginning at the left margin

- sender's name, intended audience, date, and topic

- clear and brief description, including statement of actions required

MEMO

TO: Members of the Corporate Retreat Staff
FROM: Ann Smith, Vice President
DATE: May 11, 20—
RE: PLANNING SESSION

Our annual corporate retreat is fast approaching. To ensure that all aspects of the retreat are coordinated, let's meet this Friday, May 14, at 9:00 a.m. in the second-floor conference room.

We will discuss the following topics, so please be prepared to report the status of your assigned area of responsibility.

- finalized dates, times, and location of the retreat (Tom)
- schedule of sessions and events (Bruno)
- presenters and topics (Yolanda)
- caterers and pricing (Barry)
- employee communications — invitations, RSVPs, etc. (DeShon)

I appreciate the many hours you have already invested in the planning process, and I hope that our meeting on Friday will be brief and productive.

AS

Most memos follow this format: To, From, Date, and Re (Regarding). The word *re:* is Latin for "about." It introduces the subject of the memo.

The body of a memo is brief and informative, and should clearly state a course of action.

Memos are often initialed (either at the conclusion or next to the "FROM" line) in order to indicate that the contents have been approved by the sender.

Business Communications: E-Mail

An **e-mail** is a message sent through an electronic communication system such as a computer network or the Internet. Like a memo, an e-mail may be sent to many recipients at once; however, an e-mail has the added benefit of traveling instantaneously. It can also be used to send an attachment—a file that travels with the e-mail but that must be opened using a separate application. While e-mail messages are often more casual than memos, a workplace e-mail (unlike a personal e-mail) should maintain an appropriately formal tone.

Write a Memo and an E-mail

Choose one of the topics below and write a memo that states the message quickly and efficiently. Then, recast the memo as an e-mail.

- announcement of an upcoming event to members of a club or organization
- reminder to fellow workers in a gift shop about store procedures
- information about a surprise party for a teacher
- details about transportation to a sports competition

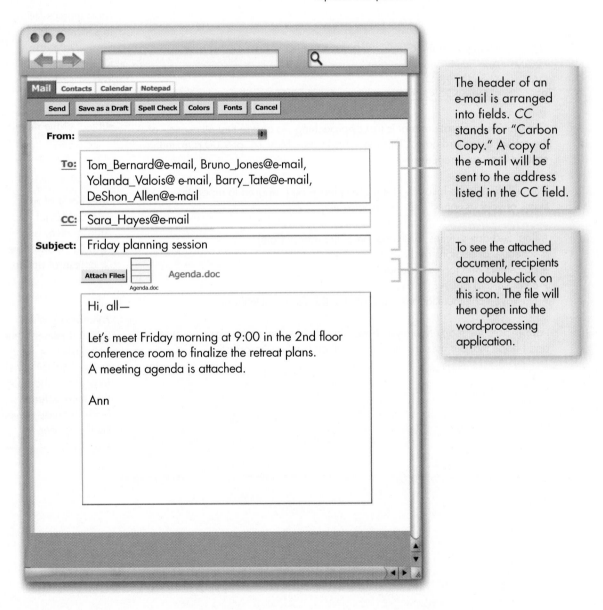

The header of an e-mail is arranged into fields. *CC* stands for "Carbon Copy." A copy of the e-mail will be sent to the address listed in the CC field.

To see the attached document, recipients can double-click on this icon. The file will then open into the word-processing application.

Business Communications: Meeting Minutes

Meeting minutes are notes that tell what transpired at a meeting: what was said, what was decided, and what was left unresolved. Often, the person taking the minutes will jot down abbreviated notes during the meeting, and then rewrite the minutes afterward to distribute to meeting participants.

Write Meeting Minutes

In a small group, conduct a business meeting. Take notes during the meeting. Afterward, write a set of minutes to distribute to your fellow group members.

Meeting to Finalize Corporate Retreat Plans
Friday, May 14, 20–
Main Office, 2nd Floor Conference Room, 9:00 a.m.

> The header should include the name of the meeting and its date, location, and time.

Committee Members Present: Ann Smith, Tom Bernard, Yolanda Valois, DeShon Allen
Committee Members Absent: Bruno Jones
Others Present: Sara Hayes, assistant to Ann Smith

Proceedings:
Meeting called to order at 9:00 a.m. by Ann Smith.
Agenda was distributed by Sara Hayes.

First Agenda Item: Retreat dates, times, and location, presented by Tom Bernard.
  Tom reported that he has received a letter from Bright Orange Lodge that confirms reservation of their retreat facilities for Universal Bank, Inc. from Friday, June 10, at 6:00 p.m. through Sunday, June 12, at 3:00 p.m. A copy of this letter is attached to the minutes.

> These minutes are formatted to show that the meeting followed an agenda.

Second Agenda Item: Schedule of sessions and events, presented by Ann Smith for Bruno Jones.
  Bruno is out of the office today, but e-mailed Ann the finalized retreat schedule. Ann distributed copies of the schedule to all members. MOTION to approve schedule; passed unanimously.

> A *motion* is a proposal to vote on something. All motions and their results should be carefully noted in meeting minutes.

Assessment of the meeting: Members agreed that the retreat promises to be very successful. Jeff congratulated committee members on a job well done.

Meeting adjourned at 10:05 a.m.
Meeting minutes compiled by Sarah Hayes.

Business Communications: Technical Writing

Technical writing refers to any kind of writing that presents specialized information to help someone perform a task. Scientific reports, troubleshooting guides, assembly instructions, and school handbooks are all examples of technical writing. Although the format varies with the purpose, all technical writing must be clear and easy to use—in other words, "user friendly." It must also be absolutely precise.

Write a Section of a Technical Document

Think of something you know how to do well and write a set of procedures for completing the task. Remember to use specific language that accurately describes the details of the task.

Porterdale Community Library rev. 7/09
Policies and Procedures
Section IV: Collection Maintenance

> A page header identifies the publication title, the section, and the revision date.

IV.D. PROCESSING NEW MATERIALS

When new items are delivered to the library, they must be processed, or prepared for use by patrons. The steps for processing a new shipment of items are as follows.

> A brief introduction tells the reader what is included in this section.

1. **Before unpacking the items:**
   a. Remove the packing slip from the box.
   b. Find the matching order form in the main filing cabinet. Order forms are filed alphabetically by vendor.

2. **Unpacking the items:**
   a. Check each item against both the order form and the packing slip.
   b. Place a checkmark on each document next to the title of the item.
   c. If all items in the shipment correspond with those on the order form, send the order form and invoice to the business office for payment. The invoice is usually inside the shipment or affixed to the outside in an envelope.
   d. If an item is missing or damaged, make a note and/or set the item aside. (See section IV.B. for Ordering and Returning procedures.)

(To process books, see item 3, below. To process other media items, proceed to item 4 on the following page.)

> Cross-references and navigational guides are included to help the reader find additional needed information with ease.

3. **Processing books:**
   a. Attach a bar code label to the upper left-hand corner of the front cover.
   b. Stamp books with the library name on the front inside cover and back inside cover.
   c. Prepare a spine label for books. (See section II.A. for call number designation.) Affix the label to the spine with a label protector.
   d. Enter information for the new item into the library catalog database. (See section III.B. for cataloging procedures.)

Guide to Rubrics

What is a rubric?

A rubric is a tool, often in the form of a chart or a grid, that helps you assess your work. Rubrics are particularly helpful for writing and speaking assignments.

To help you or others assess, or evaluate, your work, a rubric offers several specific criteria to be applied to your work. Then the rubric helps you or an evaluator indicate your range of success or failure according to those specific criteria. Rubrics are often used to evaluate writing for standardized tests.

Using a rubric will save you time, focus your learning, and improve the work you do. When you know what the rubric will be before you begin writing a persuasive essay, for example, you will be aware as you write of specific criteria that are important in that kind of an essay. As you evaluate the essay before giving it to your teacher, you will focus on the specific areas that your teacher wants you to master—or on areas that you know present challenges for you. Instead of searching through your work randomly for any way to improve it or correct its errors, you will have a clear and helpful focus on specific criteria.

How are rubrics constructed?

Rubrics can be constructed in several ways.

- Your teacher may assign a rubric for a specific assignment.

- Your teacher may direct you to a rubric in your textbook.

- Your teacher and your class may construct a rubric for a particular assignment together.

- You and your classmates may construct a rubric together.

- You may create your own rubric with criteria you want to evaluate in your work.

How will a rubric help me?

A rubric will help you assess your work on a scale. Scales vary from rubric to rubric but usually range from 6 to 1, 5 to 1, or 4 to 1, with 6, 5, or 4 being the highest score and 1 being the lowest. If someone else is using the rubric to assess your work, the rubric will give your evaluator a clear range within which to place your work. If you are using the rubric yourself, it will help you make improvements to your work.

What are the types of rubrics?

- A holistic rubric has general criteria that can apply to a variety of assignments. See p. R45 for an example of a holistic rubric.

- An analytic rubric is specific to a particular assignment. The criteria for evaluation address the specific issues important in that assignment. See p. R44 for examples of analytic rubrics.

Sample Analytic Rubrics

Rubric With a 4-point Scale

The following analytic rubric is an example of a rubric to assess a persuasive essay.
It will help you evaluate focus, organization, support/elaboration, and style/convention.

	Focus	Organization	Support/Elaboration	Style/Convention
4	Demonstrates highly effective word choice; clearly focused on task.	Uses clear, consistent organizational strategy.	Provides convincing, well-elaborated reasons to support the position.	Incorporates transitions; includes very few mechanical errors.
3	Demonstrates good word choice; stays focused on persuasive task.	Uses clear organizational strategy with occasional inconsistencies.	Provides two or more moderately elaborated reasons to support the position.	Incorporates some transitions; includes few mechanical errors.
2	Shows some good word choices; minimally stays focused on persuasive task.	Uses inconsistent organizational strategy; presentation is not logical.	Provides several reasons, but few are elaborated; only one elaborated reason.	Incorporates few transitions; includes many mechanical errors.
1	Shows lack of attention to persuasive task.	Demonstrates lack of organizational strategy.	Provides no specific reasons or does not elaborate.	Does not connect ideas; includes many mechanical errors.

Rubric With a 6-point Scale

The following analytic rubric is an example of a rubric to assess a persuasive essay.
It will help you evaluate presentation, position, evidence, and arguments.

	Presentation	Position	Evidence	Arguments
6	Essay clearly and effectively addresses an issue with more than one side.	Essay clearly states a supportable position on the issue.	All evidence is logically organized, well presented, and supports the position.	All reader concerns and counterarguments are effectively addressed.
5	Most of essay addresses an issue that has more than one side.	Essay clearly states a position on the issue.	Most evidence is logically organized, well presented, and supports the position.	Most reader concerns and counterarguments are effectively addressed.
4	Essay adequately addresses issue that has more than one side.	Essay adequately states a position on the issue.	Many parts of evidence support the position; some evidence is out of order.	Many reader concerns and counterarguments are adequately addressed.
3	Essay addresses issue with two sides but does not present second side clearly.	Essay states a position on the issue, but the position is difficult to support.	Some evidence supports the position, but some evidence is out of order.	Some reader concerns and counterarguments are addressed.
2	Essay addresses issue with two sides but does not present second side.	Essay states a position on the issue, but the position is not supportable.	Not much evidence supports the position, and what is included is out of order.	A few reader concerns and counterarguments are addressed.
1	Essay does not address issue with more than one side.	Essay does not state a position on the issue.	No evidence supports the position.	No reader concerns or counterarguments are addressed.

Sample Holistic Rubric

Holistic rubrics are sometimes used to assess writing assignments on standardized tests. Notice that the criteria for evaluation are focus, organization, support, and use of conventions.

Points	Criteria
6 Points	• The writing is strongly focused and shows fresh insight into the writing task. • The writing is organized with a logical progression of ideas. • A main idea is fully developed, and support is specific and substantial. • A mature command of the language is evident. • Sentence structure is varied, and writing is free of all but purposefully used fragments. • Virtually no errors in writing conventions appear.
5 Points	• The writing is clearly focused on the task. • The writing is well organized and generally shows a logical progression of ideas. • A main idea is well developed and supported with relevant detail. • Sentence structure is varied, and the writing is free of unintended fragments. • Writing conventions are followed correctly.
4 Points	• The writing is clearly focused on the task, but extraneous material may intrude at times. • Clear organizational pattern is present, though lapses may occur. • A main idea is adequately supported, but development may be uneven. • Sentence structure is generally fragment free but shows little variation. • Writing conventions are generally followed correctly.
3 Points	• Writing is generally focused on the task, but extraneous material may intrude at times. • An organizational pattern is evident, but writing may lack a logical progression of ideas. • Support for the main idea is generally present but is sometimes illogical. • Sentence structure is generally free of fragments, but there is almost no variation. • The work generally demonstrates a knowledge of writing conventions, with occasional misspellings.
2 Points	• The writing is related to the task but generally lacks focus. • There is little evidence of organizational pattern, and there is little sense of cohesion. • Support for the main idea is generally inadequate, illogical, or absent. • Sentence structure is unvaried, and serious errors may occur. • Errors in writing conventions and spellings are frequent.
1 Point	• The writing may have little connection to the task and is generally unfocused. • There has been little attempt at organization or development. • The paper seems fragmented, with no clear main idea. • Sentence structure is unvaried, and serious errors appear. • Poor word choice and poor command of the language obscure meaning. • Errors in writing conventions and spelling are frequent.
Unscorable	The paper is considered unscorable if: • The response is unrelated to the task or is simply a rewording of the prompt. • The response has been copied from a published work. • The student did not write a response. • The response is illegible. • The words in the response are arranged with no meaning. • There is an insufficient amount of writing to score.

Student Model

Persuasive Writing

This persuasive letter, which would receive a top score according to a persuasive rubric, is a response to the following writing prompt, or assignment:

Write a letter to a government official strongly supporting an environmental issue that is important to you and urging the official to take a specific action that supports your cause.

Dear Secretary of the Interior:

It's a normal carefree day in the forest. The birds are singing and all of the animals are relaxing under the refreshing glow of the sun. But suddenly the thunderous sound of a chainsaw echoes throughout the woodlands, and trees fall violently. The creatures of the forest run in terror. Many of these beautiful creatures will starve to death slowly and painfully as their homes are destroyed, and this precious ecosystem will not be able to regrow to its previous greatness for many years to come.

This sad story is a true one in many places around the globe. We must slow deforestation and replant trees immediately to save our breathable air, fertile soil, and fragile ecosystems.

If entire forests continue to be obliterated, less oxygen will be produced and more CO_2 emitted. In fact, deforestation accounts for a quarter of the CO_2 released into the atmosphere each year: about 1–2 billion tons. Forests provide the majority of the oxygen on earth, and if these forests disappear our air will soon be unbreathable.

Second, deforestation results in a loss of topsoil. Many of the companies who are involved in deforestation claim that the land is needed for farms, but deforestation makes the land much less fertile because it accelerates the process of erosion. According to the UN Food and Agriculture Organization, deforestation has damaged almost 6 million square kilometers of soil.

Finally, if cutting doesn't slow, many species will die off and many ecosystems will be destroyed. The 2000 UN Global Environment Outlook says that forests and rain forests have the most diverse plant and animal life in the world. The GEO also notes that there are more than 1,000 threatened species living in the world's forests. Imagine someone destroying all the houses in your neighborhood and leaving all of the residents homeless. This is how it is for the organisms that live in the forests.

In conclusion, deforestation must slow down and trees must be replanted immediately, or we will lose clean air, topsoil, and many precious organisms. Furthermore, a loss in forests will result in a generation that knows very little about nature. So, to prevent the chaotic disturbance of peace in the forests, please do whatever you can to prevent deforestation. Vote YES on any UN bills that would help the condition of our world's forests.

Sincerely Yours,
Jamil Khouri

A descriptive and interesting introduction grabs the reader's attention and shows a persuasive focus.

The writer supports the argument with facts and evidence, and also uses the persuasive appeal to the reader's emotions.

The conclusion restates the argument and presents a call to action.

21st Century Skills

Changing technology creates new ways to communicate. This handbook provides an overview of some ways you can use today's technology to create, share, and find information. You will find brief descriptions of the following topics in this section:

- ✔ Blogs
- ✔ Social Networking
- ✔ Widgets and Feeds
- ✔ Podcasts
- ✔ Wikis
- ✔ Internet Research Guide

BLOGS

A **blog** is a common form of online writing. The word *blog* is a contraction of *Web log*. Most blogs include a series of entries known as posts. The posts appear in a single column and are displayed in reverse chronological order. That means that the most recent post is at the top of the page. As you scroll down, you will find earlier posts.

Blogs have become increasingly popular. Researchers estimate that 75,000 new blogs are launched every day. Blog authors are often called bloggers. They can use their personal sites to share ideas, experiences, and impressions. Because blogs are designed so that they are easy to update, bloggers can post new messages as often as they like, often daily.

Another key component of blogs is interactivity with their audience. Many blogs allow readers to post their responses by using a comments feature found in each new post. Popular blog entries often inspire extended conversations and debates.

Kinds of Blogs

Not all blogs are the same. Many blogs have a single author, but others are group projects.

Blogs also serve a variety of purposes. Here are some common types of blog:

- Personal blogs often have a general focus. Bloggers post about any topic they find interesting in their daily lives.
- Topical blogs focus on a specific theme, such as movie reviews, political news, class assignments, or health care opportunities.
- Open Forum blogs are open to any Internet user.
- Closed Forum blogs are allowed only to members of a site. Bloggers can further limit readership by giving only invited users full access to their site.

Web Safety

Always be aware of the information you post on the Internet. Remember that whatever information you post can be read by everyone with access to that page. Once you post a picture or text, it can be saved on someone else's computer, even if you later remove it.

Using the Internet safely means keeping personal information personal. Do not post sensitive information. Never include your address (e-mail or real), last name, telephone numbers, or mention places you can be frequently found. Do not give out this information for other people. Never give out passwords you use to access other Web sites and do not respond to e-mails from strangers.

Anatomy of a Blog

Here are some of the features you can include in a blog.

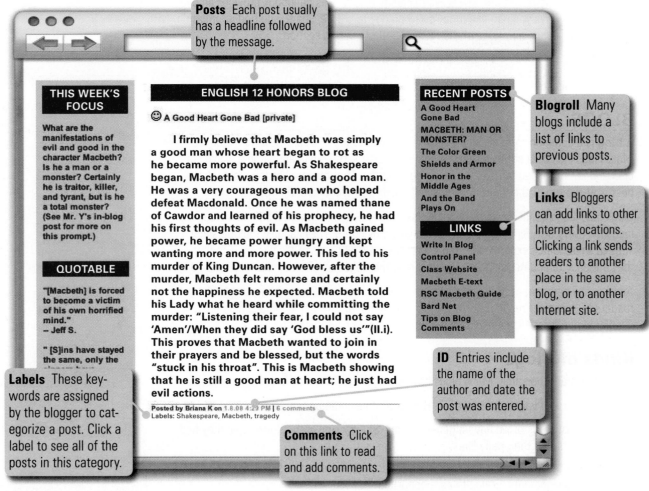

Posts Each post usually has a headline followed by the message.

THIS WEEK'S FOCUS

What are the manifestations of evil and good in the character Macbeth? Is he a man or a monster? Certainly he is traitor, killer, and tyrant, but is he a total monster? (See Mr. Y's in-blog post for more on this prompt.)

QUOTABLE

"[Macbeth] is forced to become a victim of his own horrified mind."
– Jeff S.

"[S]ins have stayed the same, only the ...

ENGLISH 12 HONORS BLOG

☺ A Good Heart Gone Bad [private]

I firmly believe that Macbeth was simply a good man whose heart began to rot as he became more powerful. As Shakespeare began, Macbeth was a hero and a good man. He was a very courageous man who helped defeat Macdonald. Once he was named thane of Cawdor and learned of his prophecy, he had his first thoughts of evil. As Macbeth gained power, he became power hungry and kept wanting more and more power. This led to his murder of King Duncan. However, after the murder, Macbeth felt remorse and certainly not the happiness he expected. Macbeth told his Lady what he heard while committing the murder: "Listening their fear, I could not say 'Amen'/When they did say 'God bless us'"(II.i). This proves that Macbeth wanted to join in their prayers and be blessed, but the words "stuck in his throat". This is Macbeth showing that he is still a good man at heart; he just had evil actions.

Posted by **Briana K** on 1.8.08 4:22 PM | 6 comments
Labels: Shakespeare, Macbeth, tragedy

RECENT POSTS

A Good Heart Gone Bad
MACBETH: MAN OR MONSTER?
The Color Green
Shields and Armor
Honor in the Middle Ages
And the Band Plays On

LINKS

Write In Blog
Control Panel
Class Website
Macbeth E-text
RSC Macbeth Guide
Bard Net
Tips on Blog Comments

Blogroll Many blogs include a list of links to previous posts.

Links Bloggers can add links to other Internet locations. Clicking a link sends readers to another place in the same blog, or to another Internet site.

ID Entries include the name of the author and date the post was entered.

Labels These keywords are assigned by the blogger to categorize a post. Click a label to see all of the posts in this category.

Comments Click on this link to read and add comments.

Creating a Blog

Like any form of writing, blogging is a form of communication. Keep these hints and strategies in mind to help you create an interesting and fair blog:

- Focus each blog entry on a single topic. If you have two ideas you want to write about, create two separate blog entries. This can help readers find topics that interest them.
- Vary the length of your posts. Sometimes, all you need is a line or two to share a quick thought. Other posts will be much longer.
- Make your main ideas pop out by using clear or clever headlines and boldfacing key terms.
- Use labels to categorize entries, allowing readers to find material that interests them.
- Give credit to other people's work and ideas. Mention the names of people whose ideas you are quoting. You can also add a link that will take readers directly to that person's blog or site.
- If you post comments, try to make them brief and polite. Even if you disagree, state the reasons for your disagreement clearly and without exaggeration.

SOCIAL NETWORKING

Social networking refers to any interaction between members of an online community. People can exchange many different kinds of information, from text and voice messages to video images.

Many social network communities, such as MySpace and Facebook, allow users to create permanent pages that describe themselves. Users create home pages to share ideas about their lives and post messages to other members in the network. Each user is responsible for adding and updating the content on his or her profile page. You can create a social network page for an individual or a group, such as a school or special interest club. Many hosting sites do not charge to register, so you can also have fun by creating a page for a pet or a fictional character.

Here are some features you are likely to find on a social network profile:

- A biographical description, including photographs and artwork.

- Lists of favorite things, such as books, movies, music, and fashions.

- Playable media elements, such as videos and sound recordings.

- Message boards, or "walls," in which members of the community can exchange messages.

Privacy in Social Networks

Social networks allow users to decide how open their profiles will be. Be sure to read introductory information carefully before you register at a new site. Once you have a personal profile page, monitor your privacy settings regularly. Remember that any information you post will be available to anyone in your network.

Users often post messages anonymously or using false names, or pseudonyms. People can also post using someone else's name. Judge all information on the net critically. Do not assume that you know who posted information simply because you recognize the name of the post author. The rapid speed of communication on the Internet can make it easy to jump to conclusions. Be careful to avoid this trap.

Think twice before posting anything on a social networking page or blog. Once you have posted a photo or text, it can be saved on someone else's computer. Even if you remove the material later, the Web user still has a copy. Once another user has your photo, he or she might post it to other sites, or alter it using photo editing software. This practice may not be legal, but many users are not familiar with privacy laws, or choose to ignore them.

In fact, the user might not even be a person. A Web crawler is a computer program that browses the Internet and collects and saves data posted on Web sites. Also known as Web spiders or Web robots, these automated programs might gather information for marketing research or targeted sales.

Tips for Sending Effective Messages

Technology makes it easy to share ideas quickly, but writing for the Internet also poses some special challenges. The writing style for blogs and social networks is usually conversational. In blog posts and comments, instant messages, and e-mails, writers express themselves very quickly, using relaxed language, short sentences, and abbreviations. However, in a conversation, we get a lot of information from a speaker's tone of voice and body language. On the Internet, those clues are missing. As a result, Internet writers sometimes use italics or bracketed labels to indicate emotions. An alternative is using emoticons—strings of characters that give visual clues to indicate emotion:

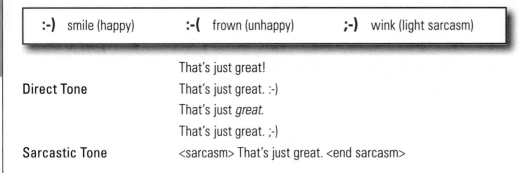

| :-) smile (happy) | :-(frown (unhappy) | ;-) wink (light sarcasm) |

Direct Tone

That's just great!

That's just great. :-)

That's just *great*.

That's just great. ;-)

Sarcastic Tone

\<sarcasm\> That's just great. \<end sarcasm\>

Here are some additional strategies you can use for communicating effectively when using technology:

- Reread your messages. Before you click **Send,** read your message through and make sure that your tone will be clear to the reader

- Don't jump to conclusions—ask for clarification first. Make sure you really understand what someone is saying before you respond.

- Remember that during chat sessions, messages often cross. As a result, messages may not always refer to the message immediately above. Read carefully to make sure you understand which topic a message refers to. If you're not sure, say so.

- Avoid using ALL CAPS. Many people feel this is like shouting for an entire conversation.

WIDGETS and FEEDS

A **widget** is a small application that can be found on many blogs, social network profiles, and other Web sites. Each widget performs a specific task. You might find widgets that give weather predictions, offer dictionary definitions or translations, or provide entertainment such as games. Other widgets present a new item each day, such as a joke, vocabulary word, sports photograph, brain teaser, or inspirational quotation.

A **feed** is a special kind of widget. It displays headlines taken from the latest content on a specific media source. Clicking on the headline will take you to the full article. Feeds can connect you to the latest news or sports. Feeds are convenient because they automatically send new data to your web page. You get news when it occurs.

Many social network communities and other Web sites allow you to personalize your home page by adding widgets and feeds. Browse through the options available to find the applications that are most useful to you. Be aware that loading widgets onto your page can affect the speed with which your page loads and updates. Test a new widget for one or two sessions—if you do not like the way it performs, simply delete it.

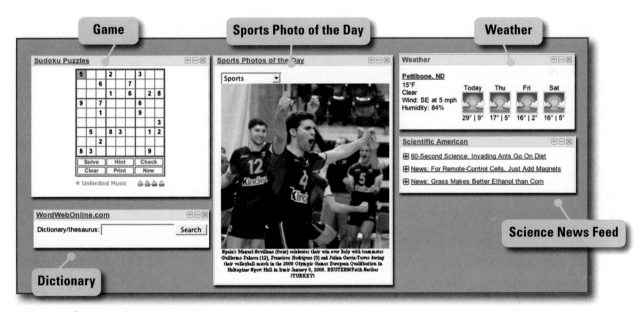

Widget and feeds on a home page.

PODCASTS

A **podcast** is a digital audio or video recording of a program that is made available on the Internet. Users can replay the podcast on a computer, or download and replay it on a personal audio player. You might think of podcasts as radio or television programs that you create yourself. They can be embedded on a Web site or fed to a Web page through a podcast widget.

Creating an Effective Podcast

To make a podcast, you will need a recording device, such as a microphone or digital video camera, as well as editing software. Open source editing software is widely available and free of charge. Most audio podcasts are converted into the MP3 format. Bulleted list of hints and strategies for creating a podcast that is clear and entertaining (such as rehearsing before recording, preparing a time outline, limiting length, and so on).

- Listen to several podcasts by different authors to get a feeling for the medium. Make a list of features and styles you like, as well as those you want to avoid.

- Test your microphone to find the best recording distance. You will stand close to the microphone so that your voice sounds full, but not so close that you create an echo.

- Create an outline that gives your estimated timing for each element.

- Be prepared before you record. Rehearse, but do not create a script. Podcasts are best when they have a natural, easy flow.

- Talk directly to your listeners. Slow down enough so they can understand you.

- Use software to edit your podcast before publishing it.

WIKIS

A **wiki** is collaborative Web site that lets visitors create, add, remove, and edit content. The term comes from the Hawaiian phrase *wiki wiki*, which means "quick." Web users at a wiki are both the readers and the writers of the site. Some wikis are open to contributions from anyone. Others require visitors to register before they can edit the content.

Wikipedia is a well-known wiki encyclopedia. All of the text was created by people who use the site. Articles are constantly changing, as visitors find and correct errors and improve texts.

Wikis have both advantages and disadvantages as sources of information. They are valuable open forums for the exchange of ideas. The unique collaborative writing process allows entries to change over time. However, entries can also be modified incorrectly. Careless or malicious users can delete good content and add inappropriate or inaccurate information.

You can change the information on a wiki, but be sure your information is correct and clear before you add it. Wikis keep track of all changes, so your work will be recorded and can be evaluated by other users.

Wiki users must agree to use the sites responsibly so they can offer accurate information. As with blogs and social networking pages, the informal nature of wikis can lead to trouble. Remember that all information you post to a wiki—including text or images you erase—can not only be seen but also tracked, since all versions of the wiki are saved for security purposes.

Research and Technology Guide

USING THE INTERNET FOR RESEARCH

Key Word Search

Before you begin a search, you should identify your specific topic. To make searching easier, narrow your subject to a key word or a group of key words. These are your search terms, and they should be as specific as possible. For example, if you are looking for the latest concert dates for your favorite musical group, you might use the band's name as a key word. However, if you were to enter the name of the group in the query box of the search engine, you might be presented with thousands of links to information about the group that is unrelated to what you want to know. You might locate such information as band member biographies, the group's history, fan reviews of concerts, and hundreds of sites with related names containing information that is irrelevant to your search. Because you used such a broad key word, you might need to navigate through all that information before you could find a link or subheading for concert dates. In contrast, if you were to type in "Duplex Arena and [band name]," you would have a better chance of locating pages that contain this information.

How to Narrow Your Search

If you have a large group of key words and still do not know which ones to use, write out a list of all the words you are considering. Once you have completed the list, scrutinize it. Then, delete the words that are least important to your search, and highlight those that are most important.

These **key search connectors** can help you fine-tune your search:

AND: Narrows a search by retrieving documents that include both terms. For example: ***baseball*** AND ***playoffs***

OR: Broadens a search by retrieving documents including any of the terms. For example: ***playoffs*** OR ***championships***

NOT: Narrows a search by excluding documents containing certain words. For example: ***baseball*** *NOT* ***history of***

Tips for an Effective Search

1. Remember that search engines can be case-sensitive. If your first attempt at searching fails, check your search terms for misspellings and try again.

2. If you are entering a group of key words, present them in order from the most important to the least important key word.

3. Avoid opening the link to every single page in your results list. Search engines present pages in descending order of relevancy. The most useful pages will be located at the top of the list. However, read the description of each link before you open the page.

4. Some search engines provide helpful tips for specializing your search. Take the opportunity to learn more about effective searching.

Other Ways to Search

Using Online Reference Sites How you search should be tailored to what you are hoping to find. If you are looking for data and facts, use reference sites before you jump onto a simple search engine. For example, you can find reference sites to provide definitions of words, statistics about almost any subject, biographies, maps, and concise information on many topics. Here are some useful online reference sites:

Online libraries
Online periodicals
Almanacs
Encyclopedias

You can find these sources using subject searches.

Conducting Subject Searches As you prepare to go online, consider your subject and the best way to find information to suit your needs. If you are looking for general information on a topic and you want your search results to be extensive, consider the subject search indexes on most search engines. These indexes, in the form of category and subject lists, often appear on the first page of a search engine. When you click on a specific highlighted word, you will be presented with a new screen containing subcategories of the topic you chose.

Evaluating the Reliability of Internet Resources

Just as you would evaluate the quality, bias, and validity of any other research material you locate, check the source of information you find online. Compare these two sites containing information about the poet and writer Langston Hughes:

Site A is a personal Web site constructed by a college student. It contains no bibliographic information or links to sites that he used. Included on the site are several poems by Langston Hughes and a student essay about the poet's use of symbolism. It has not been updated in more than six months.

Site B is a Web site constructed and maintained by the English Department of a major university. Information on Hughes is presented in a scholarly format, with a bibliography and credits for the writer. The site includes links to other sites and indicates new features that are added weekly.

For your own research, consider the information you find on Site B to be more reliable and accurate than that on Site A. Because it is maintained by experts in their field who are held accountable for their work, the university site will be a better research tool than the student-generated one.

Tips for Evaluating Internet Sources

1. Consider who constructed and who now maintains the Web page. Determine whether this author is a reputable source. Often, the URL endings indicate a source.

   - Sites ending in *.edu* are maintained by educational institutions.

   - Sites ending in *.gov* are maintained by government agencies (federal, state, or local).

   - Sites ending in *.org* are normally maintained by nonprofit organizations and agencies.

   - Sites ending in *.com* are commercially or personally maintained.

2. Skim the official and trademarked Web pages first. It is safe to assume that the information you draw from Web pages of reputable institutions, online encyclopedias, online versions of major daily newspapers, or government-owned sites produce information as reliable as the material you would find in print. In contrast, unbranded sites or those generated by individuals tend to borrow information from other sources without providing documentation. As information travels from one source to another, it could have been muddled, misinterpreted, edited, or revised.

3. You can still find valuable information in the less "official" sites. Check for the writer's credentials, and then consider these factors:

   - Do not be misled by official-looking graphics or presentations.

   - Make sure that the information is updated enough to suit your needs. Many Web pages will indicate how recently they have been updated.

   - If the information is borrowed, notice whether you can trace it back to its original source.

Respecting Copyrighted Material

Because the Internet is a relatively new and quickly growing medium, issues of copyright and ownership arise almost daily. As laws begin to govern the use and reuse of material posted online, they may change the way that people can access or reprint material.

Text, photographs, music, and fine art printed online may not be reproduced without acknowledged permission of the copyright owner.

Tips for Discussing Literature

As you read and study literature, discussions with other readers can help you understand, enjoy, and develop interpretations of what you read. Use the following tips to practice good speaking and listening skills in group discussions of literature.

• Understand the purpose of your discussion.

Your purpose when you discuss literature is to broaden your understanding and appreciation of a work by testing your own ideas and hearing the ideas of others. Be sure to stay focused on the literature you are discussing and to keep your comments relevant to that literature. Starting with one focus question will help to keep your discussion on track.

• Communicate effectively.

Effective communication requires thinking before speaking. Plan the points that you want to make and decide how you will express them. Organize these points in logical order and cite details from the work to support your ideas. Jot down informal notes to help keep your ideas focused.

Remember to speak clearly, pronouncing words slowly and carefully so that your listeners will understand your ideas. Also, keep in mind that some literature touches readers deeply—be aware of the possibility of counterproductive emotional responses and work to control them.

• Make relevant contributions.

Especially when responding to a short story or a novel, avoid simply summarizing the plot. Instead, consider *what* you think might happen next, *why* events take place as they do, or *how* a writer provokes a response in you. Let your ideas inspire deeper thought or discussion about the literature.

• Consider other ideas and interpretations.

A work of literature can generate a wide variety of responses in different readers—and that can make your discussions really exciting. Be open to the idea that many interpretations can be valid. To support your own ideas, point to the events, descriptions, characters, or other literary elements in the work that led to your interpretation. To consider someone else's ideas, decide whether details in the work support the interpretation he or she presents. Be sure to convey your criticism of the ideas of others in a respectful and supportive manner.

• Ask questions and extend the contributions of others.

Get in the habit of asking questions to help you clarify your understanding of another reader's ideas. You can also use questions to call attention to possible areas of confusion, to points that are open to debate, or to errors in the speaker's points.

In addition, offer elaboration of the points that others make by providing examples and illustrations from the literature. To move a discussion forward, summarize and evaluate tentative conclusions reached by the group members.

Oral and Visual Communication

You use speaking and listening skills every day. When you talk with your friends, teachers, or parents, or when you interact with store clerks, you are communicating orally. In addition to everyday conversation, oral communication includes class discussions, speeches, interviews, presentations, debates, and performances. The following terms will give you a better understanding of the many elements that are part of communication and help you eliminate barriers to listening by managing any distractions:

Body language refers to the use of facial expressions, eye contact, gestures, posture, and movement to communicate a feeling or an idea.

Connotation is the set of associations a word calls to mind. The connotations of the words you choose influence the message you send. For example, most people respond more favorably to being described as "slim" rather than as "skinny." The connotation of *slim* is more appealing than that of *skinny*.

Eye contact is direct visual contact with another person's eyes.

Feedback is the set of verbal and nonverbal reactions that indicate to a speaker that a message has been received and understood.

Gestures are the movements made with arms, hands, face and fingers to communicate.

Listening is understanding and interpreting sound in a meaningful way. You listen differently for different purposes.

> **Listening for key information:** For example, when a teacher gives an assignment, or when someone gives you directions to a place, you listen for key information.

> **Listening for main points:** In a classroom exchange of ideas or information, or while watching a television documentary, you listen for main points.

> **Listening critically:** When you evaluate a performance, song, or a persuasive or political speech, you listen critically, questioning and judging the speaker's message.

Medium is the material or technique used to present a visual image. Common media include paint, clay, and film.

Nonverbal communication is communication without the use of words. People communicate nonverbally through gestures, facial expressions, posture, and body movements. Sign language is an entire language based on nonverbal communication. Be aware of your nonverbal communication and make sure that your gestures and facial expressions do not conflict with your words.

Projection is speaking in such a way that the voice carries clearly to an audience. It's important to project your voice when speaking in a large space like a classroom or an auditorium.

Viewing is observing, understanding, analyzing, and evaluating information presented through visual means. You might use the following questions to help you interpret what you view:

- What subject is presented?
- What is communicated about the subject?
- Which parts are factual? Which are opinion?
- What mood, attitude, or opinion is conveyed?
- What is your emotional response?

Vocal delivery is the way in which you present a message. Your vocal delivery involves all of the following elements:

> **Volume:** the loudness or quietness of your voice

> **Pitch:** the high or low quality of your voice

> **Rate:** the speed at which you speak; also called pace

> **Stress:** the amount of emphasis placed on different syllables in a word or on different words in a sentence

All of these elements individually, and the way in which they are combined, contribute to the meaning of a spoken message.

Speaking, Listening, and Viewing Situations

Here are some of the many types of situations in which you apply speaking, listening, and viewing skills:

Audience Your audience in any situation refers to the person or people to whom you direct your message. An audience can be a group of people observing a performance or just one person. When preparing for any speaking situation, it's useful to analyze your audience, so that you can tailor your message to them.

Charts and graphs are visual representations of statistical information. For example, a pie chart might indicate how the average dollar is spent by government, and a bar graph might compare populations in cities over time.

Debate A debate is a formal public-speaking situation in which participants prepare and present arguments on opposing sides of a question, states as a **proposition.**

The two sides in a debate are the *affirmative* (pro) and the *negative* (con). The affirmative side argues in favor of the proposition, while the negative side argues against it. Each side has an opportunity for *rebuttal,* in which they may challenge or question the other side's argument.

Documentaries are nonfiction films that analyze news events or other focused subjects. You can watch a documentary for the information on its subject.

Graphic organizers summarize and present information in ways that can help you understand the information. Graphic organizers include charts, outlines, webs, maps, lists, and diagrams. For example, a graphic organizer for a history chapter might be an outline. A Venn diagram is intersecting circles that display information showing how concepts are alike and different.

Group discussion results when three or more people meet to solve a common problem, arrive at a decision, or answer a question of mutual interest. Group discussion is one of the most widely used forms or interpersonal communication in modern society.

Interview An interview is a form of interaction in which one person, the interviewer, asks questions of another person, the interviewee. Interviews may take place for many purposes: to obtain information, to discover a person's suitability for a job or a college, or to inform the public of a notable person's opinions.

Maps are visual representations of Earth's surface. Maps may show political boundaries and physical features and provide information on a variety of other topics. A map's titles and its key identify the content of the map.

Oral interpretation is the reading or speaking of a work of literature aloud for an audience. Oral interpretation involves giving expression to the ideas, meaning, or even the structure of a work of literature. The speaker interprets the work through his or her vocal delivery. **Storytelling,** in which a speaker reads or tells a story expressively, is a form of oral interpretation.

Panel discussion is a group discussion on a topic of interest common to all members of a panel and to a listening audience. A panel is usually composed of four to six experts on a particular topic who are brought together to share information and opinions.

Pantomime is a form of nonverbal communication in which an idea or a story is communicated completely through the use of gesture, body language, and facial expressions, without any words at all.

Political cartoons are drawings that comment on important political or social issues. Often, these cartoons use humor to convey a message about their subject. Viewers use their own knowledge of events to evaluate the cartoonist's opinion.

Readers theatre is a dramatic reading of a work of literature in which participants take parts from a story or play and read them aloud in expressive voices. Unlike a play, however, sets and costumes are not part of the performance, and the participants remain seated as they deliver their lines.

Role play To role-play is to take the role of a person or character and act out a given situation, speaking, acting, and responding in the manner of the character.

Speech A speech is a talk or address given to an audience. A speech may be **impromptu** or **extemporaneous**—delivered on the spur of the moment with no preparation—or formally prepared and delivered for a specific purpose or occasion.

- *Purposes:* the most common purposes of speeches are to persuade, to entertain, to explain, and to inform.

- *Occasions:* Different occasions call for different types of speeches. Speeches given on these occasions could be persuasive, entertaining, or informative, as appropriate.

Visual representation refers to informative texts, such as newspapers and advertisements, and entertaining texts, such as magazines. Visual representations use elements of design—such as texture and color, shapes, drawings, and photographs—to convey the meaning, message, or theme.

Grammar, Usage, and Mechanics Handbook

Parts of Speech

Every English word, depending on its meaning and its use in a sentence, can be identified as one of the eight parts of speech. These are nouns, pronouns, verbs, adjectives, adverbs, prepositions, conjunctions, and interjections.

Understanding the parts of speech will help you learn the rules of English grammar and usage.

Part of Speech	Definition	Examples
Noun	**Names a person, place, or thing**	
Common	• Names any one of a class of persons, places, or things	writer, country, novel
Proper	• Names a specific person, place or thing	Charles Dickens, Great Britain, *Hard Times*
Pronoun	**Stands for a noun or for a word that takes the place of a noun**	
Personal	• Refers to the person speaking (first person); the person spoken to (second person); or the person, place, or thing spoken about (third person)	I, me, my, mine, we, us, our, ours, you, our, yours, he, him, his, she, her, hers, it, its, they, them, their, theirs, myself, ourselves, yourself, yourselves, himself, herself, itself, themselves
Reflexive	• Names the person or thing receiving an action when that person or thing is the same as the one performing the action	"They click upon *themselves*/ As the breeze rises,…" –Robert Frost
Intensive	• Adds emphasis to a noun or pronoun	"The United States *themselves* are essentially the greatest poem…" –Walt Whitman
Demonstrative	• Singles out specific person(s), place(s), or thing(s)	this, that, these, those
Relative	• Begins a subordinate clause and connects it to another idea in the sentence	that, which, who, whom, whose
Interrogative	• Begins a question	what, which, who, whom, whose
Indefinite	• Refers to a person, place, or thing that may or may not be specifically named	another, everyone, nobody, one, both, few, all, most, none

(Parts of Speech continued)

(continued)

Part of Speech	Definition	Examples
Verb	**Expresses time while showing an action, condition, or the fact that something exists**	
Action	• Tells what action someone or something is performing	gather, read, work, jump, imagine, analyze, conclude
Linking	• Connects the subject with another word that identifies or describes the subject	appear, be, become, feel, look,remain, sound, stay, taste
Helping	• Added to another verb to make a verb phrase	be, do, have, should, can, could, may
Adjective	**Used to describe a noun or pronoun or give it a more specific meaning**	*purple* hat, *happy* face, *this* bowl, *three* cars, *enough* food, *a loud* sound
Adverb	**Modifies a verb, an adjective, or another adverb by telling *where, when, how* or *to what extent***	will answer *soon, extremely* sad, calls *more* often
Preposition	**Relates a noun or pronoun that appears with it to another word in the sentence**	Dad made a meal *for* us. We talked *till* dusk. Bo missed school *because of* his illness.
Conjunction	**Connects words or groups of words**	
Coordinating	• Connects equal words or word groups	bread *and* cheese, brief *but* powerful
Correlative	• Used in pairs to connect equal words or word groups	*both* Luis *and* Rosa, neither you *nor* I
Subordinating	• Indicates the connection between two ideas by placing one below the other in rank or importance	We will miss her *if* she leaves. Hank shrieked *when* he slipped on the ice.
Interjection	**Expresses feeling or emotion**	ah, hey, ouch, well, yippee

Phrases and Clauses

Phrases A **phrase** is a group of words that does not have a subject and verb and that functions as one part of speech.

Prepositional Phrases A **prepositional phrase** is a group of words that includes a preposition and a noun or pronoun.
  before dawn   **as a result of** the rain

An **adjective phrase** is a prepositional phrase that modifies a noun or pronoun.
  Eliza appreciates the beauty of a well-crafted poem.

An **adverb phrase** is a prepositional phrase that modifies a verb, an adjective, or an adverb.
  She reads Spenser's sonnets **with great pleasure.**

Appositive Phrases An **appositive phrase** is a noun or pronoun with modifiers, placed next to a noun or pronoun to add information.
  Mr. Roth, **my music teacher,** is sick.

Verbal Phrases A **participial phrase** is a participle that is modified by an adverb or an adverb phrase or that has a complement. The entire phase acts as an adjective.
  Jenna's backpack, **loaded with equipment,** was heavy.

A **gerund** is a noun formed from the present participle of a verb (ending in –*ing*). A **gerund phrase** is a gerund with modifiers or a complement, all acting together as a noun.

Taking photographs of wildlife **is her main hobby.**

An **infinitive phrase** is an infinitive with modifiers, complements, or a subject, all acting together as a single part of speech.

She tries **to get out into the wilderness often.**

Clauses A **clause** is a group of words with its own subject and verb.

Independent Clauses An independent clause can stand by itself as a complete sentence.

George Orwell wrote with extraordinary insight.

Subordinate Clauses A subordinate clause cannot stand by itself as a complete sentence.

George Orwell, **who wrote with extraordinary insight,** produced many politically relevant works.

An **adjective clause** is a subordinate clause that modifies a noun or pronoun by telling *what kind* or *which one.*

"The Lamb" is the poem **that I memorized for class.**

An **adverb clause** is a subordinate clause that modifies a verb, an adjective, an adverb, or a verbal by telling *where, when, in what way, to what extent, under what condition,* or *why.*

When I recited the poem, Mr. Lopez was impressed.

A **noun clause** is a subordinate clause that acts as a noun.

William Blake survived on **whatever he made as an engraver.**

Sentence Structure

Subject and Predicate A **sentence** is a group of words with two main parts: a *subject* and a *predicate.* Together, these parts express a complete thought.

The **complete subject** tells *whom* or *what* the sentence is about. The **complete predicate** tells what the complete subject of the sentence does or is.

Complete Subject	Complete Predicate
Both of those girls	have already read *Macbeth.*

The **simple subject** is the essential noun, pronoun, or group of words acting as a noun that cannot be left out of the complete subject. The **simple predicate** is the essential verb or verb phrase that cannot be left out of the complete predicate.

Simple Subject	Simple Predicate
Both of those girls	**have** already **read** *Macbeth.*

Complements A **complement** is a word or word group that completes the meaning of the predicate. There are five kinds of complements: *direct objects, indirect objects, objective complements, predicate nominatives,* and *predicate adjectives.*

A **direct object** is a noun, a pronoun, or a group of words acting as a noun that receives the action of a transitive verb.

Joseph Addison held important political **posts.**

An **indirect object** is a noun or pronoun that appears with a direct object and names the person or thing that something is given to or done for.

Oxford awarded **Samuel Johnson** an honorary degree. [The direct object is *degree.*]

An **objective complement** is an adjective or noun that appears with a direct object and describes or renames it.

Many consider Shakespeare the greatest **playwright.** [The direct object is *Shakespeare.*]

A **predicate nominative** is a noun or pronoun that appears with a linking verb and tells something about the subject.

"A Modest Proposal" is a **pamphlet.**

A **predicate adjective** is an adjective that appears with a linking verb and describes the subject of the sentence.

"A Modest Proposal" is **satirical.**

Classifying Sentences by Structure

Sentences are often classified according to the kind and number of clauses they contain. The four basic sentence structures are *simple, compound, complex,* and *compound-complex.*

A **simple sentence** consists of one independent clause.

Terrence enjoys modern British literature.

A **compound sentence** consists or two or more independent clauses.

Terrence enjoys modern British literature, but his brother prefers the classics.

A **complex sentence** consists of one independent clause and one or more subordinate clauses.

Terrence, who reads voraciously, enjoys modern British literature.

A **compound-complex sentence** consists of two or more independent clauses and one or more subordinate clauses.

Terrence, who reads voraciously, enjoys modern British literature, but his brother prefers the classics.

Paragraph Structure

An effective paragraph is organized around one **main idea,** which is often stated in a **topic sentence.** The other sentences support the main idea. To give the paragraph **unity**, make sure the connection between each sentence and the main idea is clear.

Usage

Lessons throughout your literature book will help you with many usage problems. See Unit 1 for help with **using coordinating conjunctions** (p. 67) and **using correlative conjunctions** (p. 154). See Unit 2 for help with **using subordinating conjunctions** (p.263) and **using adjective and adverb clauses** (p. 419). In Unit 3 you will find lessons on **comparative and superlative adjectives** and **adverbs** (p. 493), **using participles, gerunds,** and **infinitives** (p. 503), and **misplaced and dangling modifiers** (p. 539). Unit 4 has lessons on the following topics: **introductory phrases** and **clauses** (p. 755), **subject-verb agreement problems** (p. 767), and **pronoun-antecedent agreement problems** (p. 795). See Unit 5 for help with **avoiding shifts in verb tense** (p. 1009) and **using active, not passive, voice** (p. 1085). Go to Unit 6 for lessons on **sentence fragments** and **run-ons** (p. 1151), **transitional expressions** (p. 1169), **using parallel structure** (p. 1207), and **creating sentence variety** (p. 1339).

Unintended Shift in Person

Do not change needlessly from one person to another. Keep the person consistent in your sentences.

> **Max** went to the bakery, but *you* can't buy mints there. [shift from third person to second person]

> **Max** went to the bakery, but **he** can't buy mints there. [consistent]

Modifier Placement

To avoid confusion, a modifying word, phrase, or clause should be placed as close as possible to the word or words it is supposed to modify.

> My cousin has a ferret **who works in a pet store.** [misplaced modifier]

> My cousin, **who works in a pet store,** has a ferret. [correct placement]

Agreement

Subject and Verb Agreement

A singular subject must have a singular verb. A plural subject must have a plural verb.

> **Dr. Boone uses** a telescope to view the night sky.

> The **students use** a telescope to view the night sky.

A phrase or clause that comes between a subject and verb does not affect subject-verb agreement.

> His **theory,** as well as his claims, **lacks** support.

Two subjects joined by *and* usually take a plural verb.

> The **dog** and the **cats are** healthy.

Two singular subject joined by *or* or *nor* must have a singular verb.

> The **dog** or the **cat is** hiding.

Two plural subjects joined by *or* or *nor* must have a plural verb.

> The **dogs** and the **cats are** coming home with us.

Pronoun and Antecedent Agreement

Pronouns must agree with their antecedents in number and gender. Use singular pronouns with singular antecedents and plural pronouns with plural antecedents.

> **Doris Lessing** uses **her** writing to challenge ideas about women's roles.

> **Writers** often use **their** skills to effect social change.

Use a singular pronoun when the antecedent is a singular indefinite pronoun such as *anybody, each, either, everybody, neither, no one, one,* or *someone*.

> Judge **each** of the articles on **its** merits.

Use a plural pronoun when the antecedent is a plural indefinite pronoun (*both, few, many,* or *several*).

> **Both** of the articles have **their** flaws.

The indefinite pronouns *all, any, more, most, none,* and *some* can be singular or plural depending on the number of the word to which they refer.

> **Most** of the books are in **their** proper places.

> **Most** of the *book* has been torn from **its** binding.

Using Verbs

Principal Parts of Regular and Irregular Verbs

A verb has four principal parts:

Present	Present Participle	Past	Past Participle
learn	learning	learned	learned
discuss	discussing	discussed	discussed
stand	standing	stood	stood
begin	beginning	began	begun

Regular verbs such as *learn* and *discuss* form the past and past participle by adding *−ed* to the present form. **Irregular verbs** such as *stand* and *begin* form the past and past participle in other ways. If you are in doubt about the principal parts of an irregular verb, check a dictionary.

The Tenses of Verbs

The different tenses of verbs indicate the time an action or condition occurred.

The **present tense** is most often used to show one of the following:

Present action or condition:	Jamal **hikes** to the lake. The sky **is** clear.
Regularly occurring action or condition:	Tourists **flock** to the site yearly. **I am** usually tired by 9:00.
Constant action or condition:	The earth **orbits** the sun. Pets **are** good for our health.

The **past tense** is used to express a completed action or condition.

The squirrel **dropped** the nut and **ran** up the tree.

The **present perfect tense** is used to express (1) an action or condition that happened at an indefinite time in the past or (2) an action or condition from the past that is continuing into the present.

We **have seen** improvements in the neighborhood.

The puppy **has been** under the bed all day.

The **past perfect tense** shows an action or condition completed before another past action or condition.

Gerard **had revised** his essay before he turned it in.

The **future tense** is used to show a future action or condition.

The Glazers **will visit** us tomorrow.

The future perfect tense is used to show a future action or condition that is completed before another future action or condition.

Mimi **will have painted** the kitchen by the time we finish the shutters.

Using Modifiers

Degrees of Comparison

Adjectives and adverbs take different forms to show the three degrees of comparison: the *positive,* the *comparative,* and the *superlative.*

Positive	Comparative	Superlative
fast	faster	fastest
crafty	craftier	craftiest
abruptly	more abruptly	most abruptly
badly	worse	worst
much	more	most

Using Comparative and Superlative Adjectives and Adverbs

Use comparative adjectives and adverbs to compare two things. Use superlative adjectives and adverbs to compare three or more things.

Jake practices **more often** than Jamal.

Of everyone in the band, Jake practices **most often.**

Using Pronouns

Pronoun Case

The **case** of a pronoun is the form it takes to show its use in a sentence. There are three pronoun cases: *nominative, objective,* and *possessive.*

Nominative	Objective	Possessive
I, you, he, she, it, we, you, they	me, you, him, her, it, us, you, them	my, your, his, her, its, our, their, mine, yours, his, hers, its, ours, theirs

Use the **nominative case** for the *subject* or for a *predicate nominative.*

They are going to the movies. [subject]

The biggest movie fan is **she.** [predicate nominative]

Use the **objective case** for a *direct object,* an *indirect object,* or the *object of a preposition.*

The ending of the play surprised **me.** [direct object]

Mary gave **us** two tickets to the play. [indirect object]

The audience cheered for **him.** [object of preposition]

The **possessive case** is used to show ownership.

The red suitcase is **hers.**

Commonly Confused Words

Diction refers to word choice. The words you choose contribute to the overall effectiveness of your writing. One aspect of diction has to do with choosing between commonly confused words, such as the pairs listed below.

amount, number

Amount refers to quantity or a unit. *Number* refers to individual items that can be counted.

The **amount** of attention that great writers have paid to Faust is remarkable.

A **number** of important English writers have been fascinated by the legend of King Arthur.

bad, badly

Use bad after a linking verb such as *feel, look,* or *seem.* Use *badly* when an adverb is required.

> In "My Last Duchess," the duke does not seem to feel **bad** about the death of his wife.
>
> The announcement of Lady Macbeth's death **badly** unnerves Macbeth.

fewer, less

Use *fewer* for things that can be counted. Use *less* for amounts of quantities that cannot be counted.

> Wordsworth uses **fewer** end-stopped lines than Pope does.
>
> The prodigal son shows **less** respect for the father than the older son does.

lay, lie

Lay is a transitive verb meaning "to set or put something down." Its principal parts are *lay, laying, laid, laid. Lie* is an intransitive verb meaning "to recline." Its principal parts are *lie, lying, lay, lain.*

> Coleridge implies that the mariner's reckless act of killing the albatross **lays** a curse on the crew.
>
> By the end of D.H. Lawrence's story, Paul **lies** dead.

who, whom

Remember to use *who* only as a subject in clauses and sentences and *whom* only as an object.

> V.S. Naipaul, **who** wrote "B. Wordsworth," has also written some well-received novels.
>
> V.S. Naipaul, **whom** many critics have praised as one of the best contemporary writers in English, was born and raised in Trinidad.

Editing For English Language Conventions

Capitalization

First Words

Capitalize the first word of a sentence.

> **S**tories about knights and their deeds interest me.

Capitalize the first word of a direct quotation.

> **S**haron asked, "**D**o you like stories about knights?"

Proper Nouns and Proper Adjectives

Capitalize all proper nouns.

> **T**hames **R**iver   **J**ohn **K**eats   the **R**enaissance

Capitalize all proper adjectives.

> **S**hakespearean play   **D**anish invaders
>
> **E**lizabethan period   **B**ritish literature

Academic Course Names

Capitalize course names only if they are language courses, are followed by a number, or are preceded by a proper noun or adjective.

> **S**panish   **H**onors Chemistry   **H**istory 101
>
> **g**eology   **a**lgebra   **s**ocial **s**tudies

Titles

Capitalize titles showing family relationships when they refer to a specific person unless they are preceded by a possessive noun or pronoun.

> **U**ncle Oscar   Mangan's **s**ister   his **a**unt Tessa

Capitalize the first word and all other key words in the titles of books, stories, songs, and other works of art.

> *F*rankenstein   "**S**hooting an **E**lephant"

Punctuation

End Marks

Use a **period** to end a declarative sentence or an imperative sentence.

> We are studying the structure of sonnets.
>
> Read the biography of Mary Shelley.

Use periods with abbreviations.

> D.H. Lawrence   Mrs. Browning

Use a **question mark** to end an interrogative sentence.

> What is Macbeth's fatal flaw**?**

Use an **exclamation mark** after an exclamatory sentence or a forceful imperative sentence.

> That's a beautiful painting**!**   Let me go now**!**

Commas

Use a **comma** before the conjunction to separate two independent clauses in a compound sentence.

> The game was very close**,** but we were victorious.

Use commas to separate three or more words, phrases, or clauses in a series.

> William Blake was a writer**,** artist**,** and printer.

Use a comma after an introductory word, phrase, or clause.

> When Grendel was killed**,** his mother sought revenge.

Use commas to set off nonessential expressions.

> Old English**,** of course**,** requires translation.

Use commas with places and dates.

> Coventry**,** England   September 1**,** 1939

Semicolons

Use a **semicolon** to join closely related independent clauses that are not already joined by a conjunction.

> Tanya likes to write poetry; Heather prefers prose.

Use semicolons to avoid confusion when items in a series contain commas.

> They traveled to London, England; Madrid, Spain; and Rome, Italy.

Colons

Use a **colon** before a list of items following an independent clause.

> Notable Victorian poets include the following: Tennyson, Arnold, Housman, and Hopkins.

Use a colon to introduce an independent clause that summarizes or explains the sentence before it.

> Malcolm loves volunteering: He reads to sick children every Saturday afternoon.

Quotation Marks

Use **quotation marks** to enclose a direct quotation.

> "Short stories," Ms. Hildebrand said, "should have rich, well-developed characters."

An **indirect quotation** does not require quotation marks.

> Ms. Hildebrand said that short stories should have well-developed characters.

Use quotation marks around the titles of short written works, episodes in a series, songs, and titles of works mentioned as parts of collections.

> "The Lagoon"   "Boswell Meets Johnson"

Italics

Italicize the titles of long written works, movies, television and radio shows, lengthy works of music, paintings, and sculptures.

> *Howards End*   *60 Minutes*   *Guernica*

For handwritten material, you can use underlining instead of italics.

> The Princess Bride   Mona Lisa

Dashes

Use **dashes** to indicate an abrupt change of thought, a dramatic interrupting idea, or a summary statement.

> I read the entire first act of *Macbeth*—you won't believe this—in less than an hour.

Parentheses

Use **parentheses** to set off asides and explanations when the material is not essential or when it consists of one or more sentences.

> He listened intently (it was too dark to see who was speaking) to try to identify the voices.

In the example above, the sentence in parentheses interrupts the larger sentence, so it does not have a capital letter and a period. When a sentence in parentheses falls between two other complete sentences, it should start with a capital letter and end with a period.

> The quarterback threw three touchdown passes. (We knew he could do it.) Our team won the game by two points.

Apostrophes

Add an **apostrophe** and an *s* to show the possessive case of most singular nouns and of plural nouns that do not end in *−s* or *−es*.

> Blake's poems   the mice's whiskers

Names ending in *s* form their possessives in the same way, except for classical and biblical names, which add only an apostrophe to form the possessive.

> Dickens's   Hercules'

Add an apostrophe to show the possessive case of plural nouns ending in *−s* and *−es*.

> the girls' songs   the Ortizes' car

Use an apostrophe in a contraction to indicate the position of the missing letter or letters.

> She's never read a Coleridge poem she didn't like.

Brackets

Use **brackets** to enclose a word or words you insert in a quotation when you are quoting someone else.

> Use brackets to enclose a word or words you insert in a quotation when you are quoting someone else.
> Arthur C. Clarke writes about changes in travel: "Over the seas where Odysseus wandered for a decade, the Rome-Beirut Comet [an airplane] whispers its way within the hour."

Ellipses

Use three **ellipses** to indicate where you have omitted words from quoted material.

> Wollestonecraft wrote, "The education of women has of late been more attended to than formerly; yet they are still . . . ridiculed or pitied . . . ."

In the example above, the four dots at the end of the sentence are the three ellipses plus the period from the original sentence.

Spelling

Spelling Rules

Learning the rules of English spelling will help you make **generalizations** about how to spell words.

Rules for Spelling with Word Parts

The three word parts that can combine to form a word are roots, prefixes, and suffixes. Many of these word parts come from the Greek, Latin, and Anglo-Saxon languages.

The **root word** carries a word's basic meaning.

Root and Origin	Meaning	Examples
-leg- (-log-) [Gr.]	to say, speak	*leg*al, *log*ic
-pon- (-pos-) [L.]	to put, place	post*pone*, deposit

A **prefix** is one or more syllables at the beginning of a word. A prefix adds to the meaning of the root.

Prefix and Origin	Meaning	Examples
anti- [Gr.]	against	*anti*pathy
inter- [L.]	between	*inter*national
mis- [A.S.]	wrong	*mis*place

A **suffix** is added to the end of a root word and can change the word's meaning or part of speech.

Suffix and Origin	Meaning	Part of Speech
-ful [A.S.]	full of: scorn*ful*	adjective
-ity [L.]	state of being: advers*ity*	noun
-ize (-ise) [Gr.]	to make: idol*ize*	verb
-ly [A.S.]	in a manner: calm*ly*	adverb

Rules for Adding Suffixes to Root Words

When adding a suffix to a root word ending in *y* preceded by a consonant, change *y* to *i* unless the suffix begins with *i*.

    ply + -able = pliable   happy + -ness = happiness
    defy + -ing = defying   cry + -ing = crying

For a root word ending in *e,* drop the *e* when adding a suffix beginning with a vowel.

    drive + -ing = driving   move + -able = movable
    SOME EXCEPTIONS: traceable, seeing, dyeing

For root words ending with a consonant + vowel + consonant in a stressed syllable, double the final consonant when adding a suffix that begins with a vowel.

    mud + -y = muddy   submit + -ed = submitted
    SOME EXCEPTIONS: mixing, reference

Rules for Adding Prefixes to Root Words

When a prefix is added to a root word, the spelling of the root remains the same.

    un- + certain = uncertain   mis- + spell = misspell

With some prefixes, the spelling of the prefix changes when joined to the root to make the pronunciation easier.

    in- + mortal = immortal   ad- + vert = avert

Orthographic Patterns

Certain letter combinations in English make certain sounds. For instance, *ph* sounds like *f, eigh* usually makes a long *a* sound, and the *k* before an *n* is often silent.

    pharmacy   n**eigh**bor   ac**k**nowledge

Understanding **orthographic patterns** such as these can help you improve your spelling.

Forming Plurals

The plural form of most nouns is formed by adding —*s* or —*es* to the singular.

    computer**s**   gadget**s**   Washington**s**

For words ending in *s, ss, x, z, sh, ch,* add —*es.*

    circus**es**   tax**es**   wish**es**   bench**es**

For words ending in *y* or *o* preceded by a vowel, add —*s.*

    key**s**   patio**s**

For words ending in *y* preceded by a consonant, change the *y* to an *i* and add —*es.*

    cit**ies**   enem**ies**   troph**ies**

For most words ending in *o* preceded by consonant, add —*es.*

    echo**es**   tomato**es**

Some words form the plural in irregular ways.

    oxen   children   teeth   deer

Foreign Words Used in English

Some words used in English are actually foreign words we have adopted. Learning to spell these words requires memorization. When in doubt, check a dictionary.

    sushi   enchilada   au pair   fiancé
    laissez faire   croissant

Index of Authors and Titles

Note: Page numbers in *italics* refer to biographical information for authors, or commentary on titles or literary and historical issues. Nonfiction and informational text appears in red.

Index of Skills

Boldface numbers indicate pages where terms are defined.

Writing Applications

Writing Strategies

Prewriting

Drafting

Revising

Test-Taking Practice

Grammar

ACT: English Test, 228, 708, 1114
SAT: Writing, Identifying Sentence Errors, 456
SAT: Writing, Improving Paragraphs, 1482
SAT: Writing, Improving Sentences, 934

Reading

ACT: Natural Science Reading, 226
ACT: Reading Test, Humanities, 706
ACT: Reading Test, Prose Fiction, 1112
SAT: Critical Reading, Long Reading
  Passages, 932
SAT: Critical Reading, Paired Passages, 454
SAT: Critical Reading, Short Reading
  Passages, 1480

Timed writing:

ACT: Position Statement, 229, 1115
ACT: Persuasive Essay, 709
SAT: Position Statement, 457, 935

Vocabulary in context

SAT: Critical Reading, Sentence Completion,
  225, 453, 705, 931, 1111
SAT: Reading Comprehension, Sentence
  Completion, 1479

Index of Features

Acknowledgments

Grateful acknowledgment is made to the following for copyrighted material:

Aitken Alexander Associates Ltd "B. Wordsworth" from *Miguel Street* by V. S. Naipaul. Copyright © 1959 by V. S. Naipaul. Used with permission of Aitken Alexander Associates Limited.

Anvil Press Poetry Ltd. "Prayer" from *Mean Time* by Carol Ann Duffy. Published by Anvil Press Poetry in 1993. Copyright © Carol Ann Duffy, 1985, 1987, 1990, 1993, 1994. Used by permission of Anvil Press Poetry.

Georges Borchardt, Inc. From "Disappearing Act" by John Lahr from *The New Yorker*, February 12, 2007. Used by permission of Georges Borchardt, Inc.

Professor Geoffrey Bownas "When I went to visit" by Ki Tsurayuki, "Was it that I went to sleep" by Ono Kamachi, "Once cannot ask loneliness" by Priest Jakuren. Copyright © 1964 by Penguin Books, revised edition 1998. Translation copyright © Geoffrey Bownas and Anthony Thwaite, 1964, 1998. Used by permission of Geoffrey Bownas.

Broadway Video "Where's Frankenstein" from a *Saturday Night Live* episode that originally aired on October 28, 2006, hosted by Hugh Laurie. Copyright © 2006 NBC Studios, Inc. Distributed by Broadway Video Enterprises. Courtesy of Broadway Video Enterprises and NBC Studios, Inc.

Curtis Brown London "Be Ye Men of Valor" (retitled "Wartime Speech"), BBC London, May 19, 1940, from *Blood, Toil, Tears and Sweat: The Speeches of Winston Churchill* edited and with an introduction by David Cannadine. Speeches Copyright © 1989 by Winston Churchill. Used courtesy of Curtis Brown Ltd. on behalf of The Estate of Winston Churchill.

California State Parks Jack London State Historic Park brochure, copyright © 2001 California State Parks. Used by permission of California State Parks.

Cambridge University Press, NY Excerpt from "Letter to Thomas Flower Ellis from Thomas Babington Macaulay on the Passing of the Reform Bill" written in 1831, from *The Selected Letters of Thomas Babington Macaulay*, ed. Thomas Pinney, 5 vols. Used with the permission of Cambridge University Press.

Citysearch.com "A Thoughtful, Poignant, and Chilling Macbeth" October 7, 1999 from *www.shakespearefest.org/macbeth_99.htm#Reviews*. Copyright © Citysearch.com. Citysearch is a registered trademark of Bluefoot Ventures, Inc. and is used under license. Used by permission of Citysearch.com.

Arthur C. Clarke "Extra-Terrestrial Relays" by Arthur C. Clarke from *Wireless World*, October 1945, pp 305-308 © 1945. Used by permission of the author and the author's agents, Scovil Chichak Galen Literary Agency, Inc.

Jonathan Clowes Ltd. "No Witchcraft for Sale," from *African Short Stories* by Doris Lessing. Copyright © 1981 Doris Lessing. Used by kind permission of Jonathan Clowes, Ltd., London, on behalf of Doris Lessing.

Copyright Clearance Center, Inc. for Hearst Communications, Inc. 'Kingdom of Desire' a sensual 'Macbeth' remake Peking opera style" by Robert Hurwitt from San Francisco Chronicle, May 23, 2005, *www.sfgate.com/cgi-bin/article.cgi?f=/c/a/2005/05/23/DDG9LCSIOH1.DTL&hw=kingdom+of+desire&sn=002&sc=981*. Copyright © 2005 by San Francisco Chronicle. Reproduced with permission of San Francisco Chronicle via Copyright Clearance Center.

Cumbria County Council Table of Traffic Flow at Waterhead, Ambleside. A591 from *Transport and Policies 1999/2000, and Local Transport Plan 2001/2–2005/6*. Copyright © Cumbria County Council. Used by permission of Cumbria County Council.

The Charles Dickens Museum Charles Dickens Museum in London Homepage & Online Tour retrieved from *http://www.dickensmuseum.com*. Copyright © 2005 Charles Dickens Museum. Reproduced courtesy of The Charles Dickens Museum, London.

Dorling Kindersley Ltd. "Lancashire and the Lakes" from *DK Eyewitness Travel Guides: Great Britain* by Michael Leapman. Copyright © 1995, 2001 Dorling Kindersley Limited, London. Reproduced by permission of Dorling Kindersley Ltd.

Dutton Signet From *Beowulf* by Burton Raffel, translator. Translation copyright © 1963, renewed © 1991 by Burton Raffel. Used by permission of Dutton Signet, a division of Penguin Group (USA) Inc.

Encyclopædia Britannica Search results: Anglo-Saxon Poetry from *http://search.eb.com/search?query=anglo+saxon+poetry&x=0&y=0*. "English Literature: The Old English Period: Poetry: The major manuscripts" from *http://search.eb.com/eb/article-12747*. Copyright © 2007 by Encyclopædia Britannica. Used with permission from Encyclopædia Britannica, Inc.

Faber and Faber Limited "Journey of the Magi" from *Collected Poems 1909–1962* by T. S. Eliot, copyright 1936, copyright © 1964, 1963 by T. S. Eliot. "The Horses" from *New Selected Poems* by Ted Hughes. Copyright © 1957, 1960 by Ted Hughes. Published in the UK in The Hawk in the Rain by Ted Hughes. "Follower" from *Poems 1965–1975* by Seamus Heaney. Copyright © 1980 by Seamus Heaney. "The Hollow Men" from *Collected Poems 1909–1962* by T. S. Eliot, copyright 1936 and renewed 1964, 1963 by T. S. Eliot. "Two Lorries" from *The Spirit Level* by Seamus Heaney. Copyright © 1996 by Seamus Heaney. "The Explosion" from *Collected Poems* by Philip Larkin. Copyright © 1988, 1989 by the Estate of Philip Larkin. "An Arundel Tomb" from *Collected Poems* by Philip Larkin. Copyright © 1988, 1989 by the Estate of Philip Larkin. "That's All" from *Complete Works: Three* by Harold Pinter. Copyright © 1966 by H. Pinter Ltd. "Not Palaces" by Stephen Spender. From *Collected Poems 1928–1985*. Copyright © 1986 by Stephen Spender. Copyright © 1934 by The Modern Library, Inc. and renewed 1962, 1964, 1986 by Stephen Spender. Used by permission of Faber and Faber.

Farrar, Straus & Giroux, LLC "Follower" from *Poems 1965–1975* by Seamus Heaney. Copyright © 1980 by Seamus Heaney. "The Horses" from *Collected Poems* by Ted Hughes. Copyright © 2003 by The Estate of Ted Hughes. "Two Lorries" from *The Spirit Level* by Seamus Heaney. Copyright © 1996 by Seamus Heaney. "The Explosion" from *Collected Poems* by Philip Larkin. Copyright © 1988, 1989 by the Estate of Philip Larkin. "An Arundel Tomb" from *Collected Poems* by Philip Larkin. Copyright © 1988, 1989 by the Estate of Philip Larkin. "Chapter XXVIII, Part I" from *Omeros* by Derek Walcott. Copyright © 1990 by Derek Walcott. "Midsummer XXIII" from *Collected Poems 1948–1984* by Derek Walcott. Copyright © 1986 by Derek Walcott. Used by permission of Farrar, Straus and Giroux, LLC.

Florida Department of Environmental Protection Marjorie Kinnan Rawlings Historic State Park Brochure from *http://www.floridastateparks.org/marjoriekinnanrawlings/docs/brochure.pdf*. Printed 02/07. Used by permission of Florida Department of Environmental Protection.

Fondo de Cultura Economica From *The Nine Guardians* by Rosario Castellanos, translated by Irene Nicholson. Balún Canán de Rosario Castellanos. D.R. © 1957 Fondo de Cultura Economica. Carretera Picacho-Ajusco 227, C.P. 14200, Mexico, D.F. Used by permission of Fondo de Cultura Económica.

Professor Norman Gash "The case for parliamentary reform: 1831: Lord John Russell: 1 March 1831" by Lord John Russell from *The Age of Peel* by Norman Gash (London, Edward Arnold, 1973) *www.dialspace.dial.pipex.com/town/terrace/adw03/peel/refact/refbill.htm*. Copyright © Norman Gash. "A conservative criticism of parliamentary reform: 1831" by Sir Robert Peel, 2nd Baronet from *The Age of Peel* by Norman Gash (London, Edward Arnold, 1973) *www.dialspace.dial.pipex.com/town/terrace/adw03/peel/refact/refpeel.htm*. Copyright © Norman Gash. Used by permission of Norman Gash.

Greater London Authority From *The Mayor's Annual Report 2004* from *http://www.london.gov.uk/mayor/annual_report/docs/ann_rpt_2004.pdf*. Copyright April 2004, Greater London Authority. Used by permission.

Grove/Atlantic, Inc. "That's All" from *Complete Works: Three* by Harold Pinter. Copyright © 1966 by H. Pinter Ltd. "Come and Go" from Collected Shorter Plays by Samuel Beckett. Copyright © 1968, 1984 by Samuel Beckett. "Next Term We'll Mash You" from *Pack of Cards* by Penelope Lively. Copyright © 1978, 1980 1981, 1982, 1984, 1985, 1986 by Penelope Lively. Used by permission of Grove/Atlantic, Inc.

Grove/Atlantic, Inc. From *Pedro Paramo* by Juan Rulfo, translated by Margaret Sayers Peden. Originally published in Mexico in 1955. English translation by Margaret Sayers Peden. Copyright © 1994 by Northwestern University Press.

J.C. Hall "Vergissmeinnicht" by Keith Douglas from *The Complete Poems of Keith Douglas,* Faber and Faber Ltd. Used by permission of Faber and Faber Ltd. and J.C. Hall.

Harcourt, Inc. Excerpt from *Mrs. Dalloway* by Virginia Woolf, copyright 1925 by Harcourt, Inc. and renewed 1953 by Leonard Woolf. Used by permission of the publisher. "The Hollow Men" from Collected Poems 1909–1962 by T. S. Eliot, copyright 1936 by Harcourt, Inc. and renewed 1964 by T. S. Eliot. "The Lady in the Looking Glass: A Reflection" from *A Haunted House and Other Short Stories* by Virginia Woolf, copyright 1944 and renewed 1972 by Harcourt, Inc. "Shooting an Elephant" from *Shooting an Elephant and Other Essays* by George Orwell, copyright 1950 by Sonia Brownell Orwell and renewed 1978 by Sonia Pitt-Rivers. "Journey of the Magi" from *Collected Poems 1909–1962* by T. S. Eliot, copyright 1936 by Harcourt Brace & Company, copyright © 1964, 1963 by T. S. Eliot. "Charles Baudelaire: L'Invitation au Voyage" from *Things of This World,* copyright © 1956 and renewed 1984 by Richard Wilbur. From A Room of One's Own by Virginia Woolf, copyright 1929 by Harcourt, Inc. and renewed 1957 by Leonard Woolf. Used by permission of the publisher. This material may not be reproduced in any form or by any means without the prior written permission of the publisher.

HarperCollins Publishers, Inc. "A Devoted Son" from *Games at Twilight and Other Stories* by Anita Desai. Copyright © 1978 by Anita Desai. Used by permission of HarperCollins Publishers, Inc.

HarperCollins Publishers, Ltd. UK "Post-Script: For Gweno" from *Raiders' Dawn and Other Poems* by Alun Lewis. First published in March, 1942. Second Impression June, 1942. Third Impression August, 1942. Fourth Impression October, 1943. Fifth Impression 1945. Reprinted 1946. Copyright © Alun Lewis. Used by permission of HarperCollins Publishers Ltd.

A.M. Heath & Company Limited "Shooting an Elephant" from *Shooting an Elephant and Other Essays* by George Orwell. Copyright © George Orwell, 1936. Used by permission of Bill Hamilton as the Literary Executor of the Estate of the Late Sonia Brownell Orwell and Secker & Warburg Ltd.

David Higham Associates Limited "On the Patio" from *Poems 1954–1987* by Peter Redgrove. Copyright © Peter Redgrove, 1959, 1961, 1963, 1966, 1972, 1973, 1975, 1977, 1979, 1981, 1985, 1986, 1987. "A Shocking Accident" from *Collected Stories of Graham Greene* by Graham Greene. Copyright © 1957 by Graham Greene. "In the Kitchen" from *Redgrove's Wife* by Penelope Shuttle. First published 2006 by Bloodaxe Books Ltd. Copyright © Penelope Shuttle 2006. "from Faust" from *Goethe's Faust: Parts I and II* by Louis Macneice. Originally published by Faber and Faber Limited. "Next Term We'll Mash You" from Pack of Cards by Penelope Lively. Copyright © 1978, 1980 1981, 1982, 1984, 1985, 1986 by Penelope Lively. Used by permission of David Higham Associates.

Hughes Network Systems, LLC "Satellite Network Keeps Florida Communicating During Emergencies" from *http://www.hughes.com/HUGHES/Doc/0/P6KO209FS0KK3E3H417TPTVSD6/florida_emergency.pdf.* Used by permission of Hughes Network Systems, LLC, www.hughes.com.

Johnson & Alcock Ltd. (formerly John Johnson Ltd.) "I have visited again" by Alexander Pushkin. Copyright © *The Bronze Horseman: Selected Poems of Alexander Pushkin,* translated by D.M. Thomas, Secker & Warburg UK 1981/Viking US 1982. Used by permission of Johnson & Alcock Ltd.

Alfred A. Knopf, Inc. "The Demon Lover" from *The Collected Stories of Elizabeth Bowen* by Elizabeth Bowen, copyright © 1981 by Curtis Brown Ltd., Literary Executors of the Estate of Elizabeth Bowen. Used by permission of Alfred A. Knopf, a division of Random House, Inc.

Lake District National Park Authority Education Service Tracking Management from *Education Service Traffic Management.* Copyright © Lake District National Park Authority. Used by permission of Lake District National Park Authority.

Barbara Levy Literary Agency "Wirers" from *Collected Poems Of Siegfried Sasson* by Siegfried Sassoon, copyright 1918, 1920 by E. P. Dutton. Used by kind permission of George Sassoon.

MARTA Metropolitan Atlanta Rapid Transit Authority Map and Schedule" from *www.itsmarta.com/getthere/schedules/index-rail.htm.* Copyright © 2004 MARTA. All rights reserved. Used by permission of MARTA.

Metropolitan Transportation Authority Go Metro Map and Metro Red Line East Schedule from *www.mta.net/riding_metro/riders_guide/planning_trip. htm.* Copyright © 2007 LACMTA. Used by permission of Metropolitan Transportation Authority.

Michelin Travel Publications "Tintern Abbey" by Staff from *The Green Guide.* Copyright © Michelin et Cie, proprietaires-editeurs. Used by permission of Michelin Travel Publications.

William Morrow & Company, Inc. From *Neverwhere* by Neil Gaiman. Copyright © 1996, 1997 by Neil Gaiman. Used by permission of HarperCollins Publishers.

NASA Johnson Space Center "Anticipating Earthquakes" by Patrick L. Barry from *www.nasa.gov/vision/earth/environment/earthquakes_prt.htm.* Copyright © National Aeronautics and Space Administration.

The National Archives of the UK "Government Evacuation Scheme (Source 1)" from *Learning Curve: The National Archives of the UK.* www.learningcurve.gov.uk/homefront/evacuation/britain/source1.htm. "The Interrogation of Don Lewes from Cordoba in Andalucia, Simplified Transcript (Source 4)" by from Learning Curve: The National Archives of the UK *www.learningcurve.gov.uk/snapshots/snapshot39/39_images_am/39_trans/SP63_1137Am4_pg1_simp.htm.*

New Beacon Books Ltd. "Time Removed" from *Fractured Circles* by James Berry, published by New Beacon Books Ltd. Copyright © 1979, James Berry. "Freedom" from *Fractured Circles* by James Berry, published by New Beacon Books Ltd. Copyright © 1979, James Berry. From "Lucy: Englan' Lady" from *Lucy's Letter and Loving* by James Berry. Copyright © 1982 by James Berry. First published by New Beacon Books Ltd. in 1982. Used by permission of New Beacon Books, Ltd

New Directions Publishing Corporation "Do Not Go Gentle Into That Good Night" by Dylan Thomas, from *The Poems of Dylan Thomas.* Copyright © 1952 by Dylan Thomas. "Anthem for Doomed Youth" by Wilfred Owen, from *The Collected Poems Of Wilfred Owen,* copyright © 1963 by Chatto & Windus, Ltd. "Jade Flower Palace" by Tu Fu, translated by Kenneth Rexroth from *One Hundred Poems from The Chinese.* Copyright © 1971 by Kenneth Rexroth. "Not Waving But Drowning" by Stevie Smith, from *Collected Poems of Stevie Smith,* copyright © 1972 by Stevie Smith. "Fern Hill" by Dylan Thomas, from *The Poems of Dylan Thomas,* copyright © 1945 by The Trustees for the Copyrights of Dylan Thomas. Used by permission of New Directions Publishing Corp.

The New York Times Agency c/o PARS International "The Scottish Play, Told With Sound and Fury and Puppets" by Lawrence Van Gelder from The New York Times Arts & Culture Section, 4/26/2007 Issue, Page E5, *http://theater2.nytimes.com/2007/04/26/theater/reviews/26macb. html?pagewanted=print.* Copyright © 2007 The New York Times. All rights reserved. Used by permission and protected by the Copyright Laws of the United States. The printing, copying, redistribution, or retransmission of the Material without express written permission is prohibited. www.nytimes.com.

W. W. Norton & Company, Inc. "Outside History" from *Outside History: Selected Poems, 1980–1990* by Eavan Boland. Copyright © 1990 by Eavan Boland. "The Inferno: Canto XXXIV", from *The Divine Comedy* by Dante Alighieri, translated by John Ciardi. Copyright 1954, 1957, 1959, 1960, 1961, 1965, 1967, 1970 by the Ciardi Family Publishing Trust. From *Sir Gawain And The Green Knight: A New Verse Translation* by Marie Borroff, translator. Copyright © 1967 by W.W. Norton & Company, Inc. Used by permission of W.W. Norton & Company, Inc.

The Flannery O'Connor-Andalusia Foundation Andalusia: Home of Flannery O'Connor brochure. Used courtesy of Flannery O'Connor-Andalusia Foundation.

Jen O'Leary "Weather in the Palm of Your Hand" by Jennifer O'Leary, University of Wisconsin-Madison Space Science and Engineering Center from *www.ssec.wisc.edu/media/features/jan10_06.htm*. Used by permission of the author.

Oxford University Press, Inc. "The Wanderer," from *An Anthology of Old English Poetry,* edited and translated by Charles W. Kennedy. Copyright © 1960 by Oxford University Press, Inc. Used by permission of Oxford University Press, Inc.

Oxford University Press, UK "The Naming of Parts," from *A Map of Verona* by Henry Reed, 1946, copyright © by Henry Reed. Used by permission of Oxford University Press, UK.

Oxford University Press, UK "To Lucasta, Going To the Wars" from *The Poems Of Richard Lovelace,* edited by C.H. Wilkinson, copyright © 1953. "To the Virgins, to Make Much of Time" from The Poems of Robert Herrick, edited by L.C. Martin.

Penguin Books Ltd., London "The Wife of Bath's Tale" from *The Canterbury Tales* by Geoffrey Chaucer, translated by Nevill Coghill (Penguin Classics 1951, Fourth revised edition 1977). Copyright 1951 by Nevill Coghill. Copyright © the Estate of Nevill Coghill, 1958, 1960, 1975, 1977. From *A History of The English Church and People* by Bede (pp 37-40), translated by Leo Sherley-Price, revised by R.E. Latham (Penguin Classics 1955, Revised edition 1968). Copyright © Leo Sherley-Price, 1955, 1968. "Prologue" from *The Canterbury Tales* by Geoffrey Chaucer, translated by Nevill Coghill (Penguin Classics 1951, Fourth revised edition 1977). Copyright 1951 by Nevill Coghill. Copyright © the Estate of Nevill Coghill, 1958, 1960, 1975, 1977. "Pardoner's Tale" from *The Canterbury Tales* by Geoffrey Chaucer, translated by Nevill Coghill (Penguin Classics 1951, Fourth revised edition 1977). Copyright 1951 by Nevill Coghill. Copyright © the Estate of Nevill Coghill, 1958, 1960, 1975, 1977. From *The Decameron* by Giovanni Boccaccio, translated with an introduction and notes by G. H. McWilliam (Penguin Classics 1972, Second Edition 1995). Copyright © G. H. McWilliam, 1972, 1995. "Next Term We'll Mash You" from Pack of Cards by Penelope Lively. Copyright © 1978, 1980 1981, 1982, 1984, 1985, 1986 by Penelope Lively. Used by permission of Penguin Group Ltd., UK.

Random House, Inc. "In Memory of W. B. Yeats", copyright 1940 & renewed 1968 by W.H. Auden from *Collected Poems* by W.H. Auden. "Musee des Beaux Arts", copyright 1940 & renewed 1968 by W.H. Auden from *Collected Poems* by W.H. Auden. Used by permission of Random House, Inc. "Home" by Anton Chekhov from *Modern Library,* copyright © 1999 by Random House, Inc.

Riverbend From "Baghdad Burning" by Riverbend (baghdad.burning@gmail.com)from *The Great Wall of Segregation...*, *http://riverbendblog.blogspot.com*, April 26, 2007.

Riverhead Books, an imprint of Penguin Group (USA) Inc. "I'm Like a Bird" from *Songbook* by Nick Hornby, copyright © 2002 by Nick Hornby. Used by permission of Riverhead Books, an imprint of Penguin Group (USA) Inc.

Rogers, Coleridge & White Ltd. "A Devoted Son" from *Games at Twilight and Other Stories* by Anita Desai. Copyright © 1978 Anita Desai. Reproduced by permission of the author c/o Rogers, Coleridge & White Ltd., 20 Powis Mews, London W11 1JN.

Russell & Volkening, Inc. "The Train from Rhodesia" from *Selected Stories* by Nadine Gordimer. Copyright © 1950 by Nadine Gordimer, renewed in 1978 by Nadine Gordimer. Used by the permission of Russell & Volkening as agents for the author.

Scovil Chichak Galen Literary Agency, Inc. "We'll Never Conquer Space" by Arthur C. Clarke, from *Science Digest,* June 1960. Copyright © 1960 by Popular Mechanics Company. Used by permission of the author and the author's agents, Scovil Chichak Galen Literary Agency, Inc.

Scribner, an imprint of Simon & Schuster "The Second Coming" from *The Collected Works of W.B. Yeats, Volume 1: The Poems* edited by Richard J. Finneran. Copyright © 1924 by The Macmillan Company; copyright renewed © 1952 by Bertha Georgie Yeats. Used with the permission of Scribner, an imprint of Simon & Schuster Adult Publishing Group, All rights reserved.

Smithsonian Institution "Recasting Shakespeare's Stage" by Eric Jaffe from *www.smithsonianmag.com/arts-culture/globe.html.* Copyright 2008 Smithsonian Institution. Used with permission from Smithsonian Business Ventures. All rights reserved. Reproduction in any medium is strictly prohibited without permission from Smithsonian Institution. Such permission may be requested from Smithsonian Business Ventures.

Stage Three Music (US) Inc. "Eli, the Barrow Boy" written by Colin Meloy from *Picaresque.* Copyright © 2005 music of Stage Three/Osterozhna! Music (BMI). Used by permission of Stage Three Music (US), Inc.

The Estate of Ann Stanford "The Wife's Lament" by Ann Stanford from *The Women Poets In English: An Anthology.* Copyright © 1972 by Ann Stanford. Used with permission of the Estate of Ann Stanford.

Taylor & Francis From "The Rape Of The Lock", reprinted from *The Poems of Alexander Pope,* edited by John Butt. Reproduced by permission of Taylor & Francis Books UK.

University of California Press & Carmen Balcells Agencia Literaria *Selected Odes of Pablo Neruda,* by Pablo Neruda, translated by Margaret Sayers Peden, copyright © 1990 by the Fundacion Pablo Neruda, published by the University of California Press. All rights reserved.

The University of Chicago Press Excerpt from "Oedipus The King" by Sophocles, D. Grene, trans., from *The Complete Greek Tragedies,* R. Lattimore and D. Grene, eds. Used with permission of The University of Chicago Press.

Ed Victor, Ltd. "Not Palaces" from *Collected Poems 1928–1985* by Stephen Spender, copyright © 2004 by Stephen Spender. Used by permission of Ed Victor Ltd.

Viking Penguin, Inc. "Araby", from *Dubliners* by James Joyce, copyright 1916 by B. W. Heubsch. Definitive text Copyright © 1967 by The Estate of James Joyce. "Wirers" from *Collected Poems Of Siegfried Sasson* by Siegfried Sassoon, copyright 1918, 1920 by E. P. Dutton. Copyright 1936, 1946, 1947, 1948 by Siegfried Sassoon. "The Rocking-Horse Winner" from *Complete Short Stories Of D.H. Lawrence* by D.H. Lawrence. Copyright © 1933 by the Estate of D. H. Lawrence, renewed © 1961 by Angelo Ravagli and C. M. Weekley, Executors of the Estate of Frieda Lawrence. "The Book of Sand", from *Collected Fictions,* by Jorge Luis Borges, translated by Andrew Hurley, copyright © 1998 by Maria Kodama; translation copyright © 1998 by Penguin Putnam, Inc. From "In Athens Once", from *Days Of Obligation* by Richard Rodriguez, copyright © 1992 by Richard Rodriguez. Used by permission of Viking Penguin, a division of Penguin Group (USA) Inc. All rights reserved.

Wake Forest University Press "Carrick Revisited" from *Selected Poems of Louis MacNeice,* edited by Michael Longley. Copyright © Wake Forest University Press, 1990. Used by permission of Wake Forest University Press.

The Arthur Waley Estate Excerpts from *The Analects of Confucius,* translated and annotated by Arthur Waley. Copyright © 1938 by George Allen and Unwin Ltd, London. From "The Book of Songs, Song 34 (Thick Grow the Rush Leaves)" translated by Arthur Waley from *The Book Of Songs.* Copyright © 1919, 1941 by Alfred A. Knopf, Inc. Used by permission of The Arthur Waley Estate.

Wikipedia.org "Zorro" retrieved from http://en.wikipedia.org accessed on 6/6/07. "Space Mirror Memorial" retrieved from http://en.wikipedia.org accessed on 6/15/07. "Davy Crockett" retrieved from http://en.wikipedia.org accessed on 6/18/07.

Yale University Press "The Seafarer" from *Poems from the Old English,* translated by Burton Raffel. Copyright © 1960, 1964; renewed 1988, 1922 by The University of Nebraska Press. Copyright © 1994 by Burton Raffel. Used by permission of Yale University Press.

Note: Every effort has been made to locate the copyright owner of material reproduced on this component. Omissions brought to our attention will be corrected in subsequent editions.

Credits

Photo Credits

xlvi: Amra Pasic/Shutterstock; **1:** Bridgeman Art Library, London/SuperStock; **2:** r. **2:** m. © The Board of Trinity College, Dublin, Ireland/The Bridgeman Art Library; **2:** l. Stapleton Collection/CORBIS; **3:** rt. Erich Lessing/Art Resource, NY; **3:** rm. British Museum/Art Resource, NY; **3:** rb. Andy Crawford/© Dorling Kindersley; **3:** bl. Historical Picture Archive/CORBIS; **3:** tl. Werner Forman/CORBIS; **4:** br. Archivo Iconografico, S.A./CORBIS; **4:** bl. The Art Archive / British Museum / Eileen Tweedy; **5:** br. **5:** bl. Abbie Enock; Travel Ink/CORBIS; **6:** bm. The Granger Collection, New York; **6:** br. The Art Archive / British Library; **7:** bl. Christophe Boisvieux/CORBIS; **7:** br. Frans Lanting/CORBIS; **8:** br. The Granger Collection, New York; **9:** br. The Granger Collection, New York; **9:** bl. Werner Forman/CORBIS; **10:** bl. The Gallery Collection/CORBIS; **10:** br. The Granger Collection, New York; **11:** bl. The Granger Collection, New York; **11:** br. Bettmann/CORBIS; **12:** bl. Archivo Iconografico, SA/CORBIS; **12:** br. Danny Lehman/CORBIS; **13:** br. Stephano Bianchetti/CORBIS; **13:** bl. HIP/Art Resource, NY; **15:** br. Prentice Hall; **17:** Bridgeman Art Library, London/SuperStock; **20–21:** Barry Lewis/CORBIS; **24:** t. St. Cuthbert's Holy Island, 1797 (w/c over pencil on textured paper) by Thomas Girtin (1775–1802); Yale Center for British Art, Paul Mellon Collection, USA/ / The Bridgeman Art Library; **26:** Matthias Kulka/CORBIS; **31:** r. Clive Druett;Papilio/CORBIS; **33:** The Grandsons of Gostosmysl: Rurick, Truvori and Sineus, 1986 (oil on canvas), Glazunov, Ilya (b. 1930) / Private Collection, / The Bridgeman Art Library; **34:** The Granger Collection, New York; **37:** Boris Vallejo, Inc.; **42:** b. Kerstin Hamburg/CORBIS; **46:** l. istockphoto.com; **47:** b. ©The Trustees of the British Museum; **47:** TR ©The Trustees of the British Museum; **49:** r. HIP/Art Resource, NY; **55:** tr. British Museum/Art Resource, NY; **59:** BEOWULF: A TALE OF BLOOD, HEAT, AND ASHES. Text copyright ©27 by Nicky Raven. Illustrations copyright ©27 by John Howe. Reproduced by permission of the publisher Candlewick Press, Inc., Cambridge, MA; **61:** t. **62:** bl. The Granger Collection, New York; **63:** t. BEOWULF: A TALE OF BLOOD, HEAT, AND ASHES. Text copyright ©27 by Nicky Raven. Illustrations copyright ©27 by John Howe. Reproduced by permission of the publisher Candlewick Press, Inc., Cambridge, MA; **68:** t. ©Smith Richard Frank/CORBIS Sygma; **68:** m. Concept and design by Cynthia Krupt; b. The Art Archive/British Library; **69:** tr. Richard Cummings/CORBIS; **76:** b. **77: 78: 80:** t. **83:** tr. David Reed/CORBIS; **84: 87:** tr. M-Sat Ltd / Photo Researchers, Inc.; **90:** l. The Granger Collection, New York; **92–93:** The Granger Collection, New York; **93:** t. Stapleton Collection/CORBIS; **96–97:** Reproduced with the cooperation of Alexandra Szyk Bracie and Historicana www.szyk.com; **100:** l. The Yeoman, Arthur Szyk for The CANTERBURY TALES, Reproduced with permission of Alexadra Szyk Bracie and Irvin Ungar; **102:** l. The Monk, Arthur Szyk for The CANTERBURY TALES, Reproduced with permission of Alexadra Szyk Bracie and Irvin Ungar; **104:** l. The Student, Arthur Szyk for The CANTERBURY TALES, Reproduced with permission of Alexadra Szyk Bracie and Irvin Ungar; **109:** The Wife of Bath, Arthur Szyk for The CANTERBURY TALES, Reproduced with permission of Alexadra Szyk Bracie and Irvin Ungar; **111:** r. Matt Stroshane/Getty Images, Inc.; **111:** no credit necessry; **111:** The Miller, Arthur Szyk for The CANTERBURY TALES, Reproduced with permission of Alexadra Szyk Bracie and Irvin Ungar; **112:** Richard Ross/CORBIS; **113:** The Summoner Arthur Szyk for The CANTERBURY TALES, Reproduced with permission of Alexadra Szyk Bracie and Irvin Ungar; **114:** l. The Pardoner, Arthur Szyk for The Canterbury Tales, Reproduced with permission of Alexadra Szyk Bracie and Irvin Ungar; **118:** b. Three Monks, Arthur Szyk for The CANTERBURY TALES, Reproduced with permission of Alexadra Szyk Bracie and Irvin Ungar; **124: 131:** t. Lambeth Palace Library, London, UK/Bridgeman Art Library, London/New York; **144:** Bridgeman Art Library; **151:** br. www.cartoonStock.com; **157:** r. Summerfield Press/CORBIS; **158:** The Decameron, 1916 (oil on canvas), Waterhouse, John William (1849–1917) / © Lady Lever Art Gallery, National Museums Liverpool, / The Bridgeman Art Library; **160:** b. Scala/Art Resource; **162:** l. The Granger Collection, New York; **167:** St. George and the Dragon, c.1606 (oil on canvas), Rubens, Peter Paul (1577–1640) / Prado, Madrid, Spain, Giraudon / The Bridgeman Art Library; **185:** Michel Setboun/CORBIS; **188–189:** Photo by Mansell/Time & Life Pictures/Getty Images; **190–191:** Fine Art Photographic Library, London/Art Resource, NY; **193** Giraudon/Art Resource, NY; **193:** Giraudon/Art Resource, NY; **196:** b. www.cartoonStock.com; **201:** Photographersdirect.com; **207:** tr. The Granger Collection, New York; **211:** t. The Gallery Collection/CORBIS; **211:** bl. Geoff Dann/© Dorling Kindersley, Courtesy of the Anthony Barton Collection; **211:** bmr. Geoff Dann/© Dorling Kindersley, Courtesy of the Anthony Barton Collection; **211:** bml. Geoff Dann/© Dorling Kindersley, Courtesy of the Anthony Barton Collection; **211:** br. Geoff Dann/© Dorling Kindersley, Courtesy of the Anthony Barton Collection; **214:** b. CORBIS; **234–235:** Scala/Art Resource, NY; **236:** br. Private Collection/ The Stapleton Collection/ The Bridgeman Art Library; **236:** t. **237:** br. Scala/Art Resource, NY; **237:** bl. The Granger Collection, New York; **237:** bmr. The Granger Collection, New York; **237:** bml. Science Museum/Science & Society Picture Library; **238:** br. Gianni Dagli Orti/CORBIS; **238:** bl. Bettmann/CORBIS; **239:** King Richard I and his Barons, Anonymous / British Library, London, UK, © British Library Board. All Rights Reserved / The Bridgeman Art Library; **239:** bl. Jim Zuckerman/CORBIS; **239:** br. **240:** bl. Paule Seux/Hemis/CORBIS; **241:** bl. The Granger Collection, New York; **242:** b. The Granger Collection, New York; **243:** tr. National Trust/Art Resource, NY; **243:** br. Gregg Newton/Gregg Newton/CORBIS; **243:** bl. Andy Willimams/Loop Images/CORBIS; **243:** rm. Victoria & Albert Museum, London / Art Resource, NY; **244:** bl. Blue Lantern Studio/CORBIS; **244:** Bettmann/CORBIS; **245:** br. Bettmann/CORBIS; **247:** br. Bettmann/CORBIS; **249:** b. Prentice Hall; **249:** t. ©Edinburgh University Library, Scotland/ The Bridgeman Art Library; **250:** t. ©Hatfield House, Hertfordshire, UK/ The Bridgeman Art Library; **251:** Burstein Collection/CORBIS; **251:** **253:** r. **255:** Burstein Collection/CORBIS; **257:** r. **258:** Victoria & Albert Museum, London/Art Resource, NY; **265** rt. www.cartoonStock.com; **267–268:** Museum of Fine Arts, Houston, Texas, USA/ Agnes Cullen Arnold Endowment Fund/ The Bridgeman Art Library; **273:** r. **274:** Private Collection/ The Stapleton Collection/ The Bridgeman Art Library; **277:** tr. The Granger Collection, New York; **277:** ml. Private Collection/ © Philip Mould Ltd, London/ The Bridgeman Art Library; **277:** rm. **277:** rb. No. 3856 Henry Wriothesley, 3rd Earl of Southampton (1573–1624), c.1594 (gouache on vellum) by Nicholas Hilliard (1547–1619) Fitzwilliam Museum, University of Cambridge, UK/ The Bridgeman Art Library; **277:** bml. **277:** bl. North Wind Picture Archives; **277:** tl. The Art Archive/Victoria and Albert Museum London/Sally Chappell; **277:** tm. The Art Archive/Victoria and Albert Museum London/Sally Chappell; **277:** tr. Judith Miller/© Dorling Kindersley/Joseph H. Bonner; **277:** ml. istockphoto.com; **281:** Hans the Younger Holbein (1497/8–1543), Dutch, "Portrait of Henry VIII", 16th century. Oil on canvas. Belvoir Castle, Leicestershire. The Bridgeman Art Library Ltd.; **285:** tr. "Dangers Averted" medal, celebrating the defeat of the Spanish Armada, c. 1589, gold cast and chased by Nicholas Hilliard (1537–1619) Fitzwilliam Museum, University of Cambridge/Bridgeman Art Library , London/New York; **286:** Elizabeth I, Armada Portrait, c. 1588 (oil on panel) by George Gower (1540–1596) (attr. to). Woburn Abbey, Bedfordshire, UK/Bridgeman Art Library, London/New York; **288:** bl. Picture Desk, Inc./Kobal Collection; **290:** t. istockphoto.com; **292:** m. Getty Images; **292:** b. Getty Images; **293:** t. **294:** l. Polygram/The Kobal Collection, Bailey, Alex; **295:** t. Studio Canal/Working Title/The Koball Collection/Sparham, Laurie; **297:** Private Collection/The Bridgeman Art Library; **298:** RÈunion des MusÈes Nationaux / Art Resource, NY; **303:** The Return of the Prodigal Son, Lionello Spada/Erich Lessing/Art Resource, NY; **307:** Ellen Terry (as Lady Macbeth), 1889, oil on canvas 87″ x 45″, Tate Gallery on loan to National Portrait Gallery London, Art Resource, NY; **313:** b. Photofest; **313:** tr. MIRISCH-7 ARTS/UNITED ARTISTS / THE KOBAL COLLECTION; **313:** tl. MGM / THE KOBAL COLLECTION; **316:** b. National Portrait Gallery, London/Superstock; **318:** ml. Mary Evans Picture Library; **318–319:** b. **324:** t. Erich Lessing / Art Resource, NY; **328:** t. New Walk Museum, Leicester City Museum Service, UK/ The Bridgeman Art Library; **330:** b. Darren Robb/Getty Images; **332:** b. t. City of Westminster Archive Centre, London, UK/ The Bridgeman Art Library; **343:** t. Steve Gorton/ Dorling Kindersley; **347:** Photofest; **350:** b. The Pierpont Morgan Library, Art Resource, NY; **352:** t. The Granger Collection, New York; **366:** t. The Art Archive / Garrick Club; **371:** t. Scene from Macbeth, Cattermole, By Permission of the Folger Shakespeare Library, Washington, D.C.; **379:** t. Earl & Nazima Kowall/CORBIS; **380:** Victoria & Albert Museum, London / Art Resource, NY; **387:** b. The Granger Collection, New York; **393:** b. Corel Professional Photos CD-ROMô; **394: 399:** r. Yale Center for British Art, Paul Mellon Collection, USA/ The Bridgeman Art Library; **401:** r. Geoff Dann© Dorling Kindersley, Courtesy of David Edge; **402:** RÈunion des MusÈes Nationaux / Art Resource, NY; **410:** t. The Art

Images; **1144:** Underwood & Underwood/CORBIS; **1144:** age fotostock / SuperStock; **1145:** The Image Bank/Getty Images; **1147:** Gilles Mermet / Art Resource, NY; **1147:** Gilles Mermet / Art Resource, NY; **1148:** Gilles Mermet / Art Resource, NY; **1155:** Hulton-Deutsch Collection/CORBIS; **1156:** E.O. HoppÈ/CORBIS; **1158:** Jean Kugler/Getty Images; **1163:** PhotothÈque R. Magritte-ADAGP / Art Resource, NY, ©1998 C. Herscovici, Brussels/ Artists Rights Society (ARS), New York.; **1171:** Bettmann/CORBIS; **1172:** The Granger Collection, New York; **1172:** Bkgrnd Freyda Miller/CORBIS; **1174:** Michael Goldman/Getty Images; **1176:** Art Projects International; **1177:** **1179:** Getty Images; **1180:** Michael St. Maur Sheil/CORBIS; **1182:** Sophie Bassouls/Sygma/CORBIS; **1182:** **1183:** Paul Hardy/CORBIS; **1184:** Paul Hardy/CORBIS; **1187:** © Gilles Mermet / Art Resource; **1188:** Getty Images; **1189:** t. Private Collection, © The Bloomsbury Workshop, London / The Bridgeman Art Library International; **1189:** b. Private Collection, The Stapleton Collection/ The Bridgeman Art Library International; **1190:** t. Marilyn Monroe, Andy Warhol, © Andy Warhol Foundation/CORBIS. TM 2006 Marilyn Monroe, LLC by CMG Worldwide, Inc / www.MarilynMonroe.com © Andy Warhol Foundation for the Visual Arts / ARS, New York; **1190:** br. Getty Images; **1190:** bl. **1192:** RÈunion des MusÈes Nationaux / Art Resource, NY; **1193:** **1195:** The Garden of Love, Walter Richard Sickert, Fitzwilliam Museum, Cambridge; **1196:** RÈunion des MusÈes Nationaux / Art Resource, NY; **1197:** age fotostock / SuperStock; **1198:** Private Collection, / The Bridgeman Art Library International; **1200:** Julian Barrow/Getty Images; **1200:** **1201:** Andreas Altwein/dpa/CORBIS; **1210:** b. Library of Congress, Prints & Photographs Division, NYWT&S Collection; **1217:** Getty Images **1219:** Hulton-Deutsch Collection/CORBIS; **1220–1221:** Ron Dahlquist / Super; **1223:** Image1 / SuperStock; **1224–1225:** border Gala / SuperStock; **1226:** Michael Halminski / SuperStock; **1228–1229:** Steve Vidler / SuperStock; **1230–1231:** age fotostock / SuperStock; **1231:** Ben Mangor / SuperStock; **1232:** Digital Vision Ltd. / SuperStock; **1233:** The Granger Collection, New York; **1234:** St. Patrick's Close, Walter Osborne, National Gallery of Ireland; **1235:** Robbie Pleck / SuperStock; **1238:** © The Metropolitan Museum of Art / Art Resource, NY; **1239:** British Museum / Art Resource, NY; **1243:** Bettmann/CORBIS; **1244:** Stockbyte /Getty Images; **1245:** Stockbyte /Getty Images; **1247:** Izzy Schwartz/Getty Images; **1249:** Marvin E. Newman/Getty Images; **1250:** Jonathan Kitchen/ Getty Images; **1251:** C Squared Studios/Getty Images; **1255:** Stockbyte / Getty Images; **1256:** Marvin E. Newman/Getty Images; **1258:** Bettmann/ CORBIS; **1259:** Kevin Summers/Getty Images; **1260:** Kevin Summers/ Getty Images; **1262:** Kevin Summers/Getty Images; **1264:** Beth Dixson/ Getty Images; **1267:** Bildarchiv Preussischer Kulturbesitz / Art Resource, NY; **1269:** t. Michael Nicholson/CORBIS; **1269:** m. Hulton-Deutsch Collection/CORBIS; **1269:** b. The Granger Collection, New York; **1270:** Bettmann/CORBIS; **1271:** t. Nathan Benn/CORBIS; **1272:** Bettmann/ CORBIS; **1276:** Getty Images; **1278–1279:** AFP/Getty Images; **1282:** Bettmann/CORBIS; **1283:** Snark/Art Resource, NY; **1293:** Hulton-Deutsch Collection/CORBIS; **1296:** Portrait of N. Pietrunkevic, Nikolai Ge, Scala/Art Resource, NY; **1297:** Sleepless Night, Nikolai Romadin, Scala/Art Resource, NY; **1302–1303:** Hulton-Deutsch Collection/CORBIS; **1305:** b. courtesy of Royal Literary Fund and Special Collections, U of Birmingham; **1306:** Hulton-Deutsch Collection/CORBIS; **1308:** The Art Archive / Imperial War Museum; **1308:** The Art Archive / Imperial War Museum; **1313:** The Granger Collection, New York; **1314:** Paul Souders/ CORBIS; **1319:** Steve McDonough/CORBIS; **1320:** ©Orwell Archive/ **1323:** Colin McPherson/CORBIS; **1324:** HIP / Art Resource, NY; **1327:** HIP / Art Resource, NY; **1330:** Private Collection/ The Stapleton Collection/ The Bridgeman Art Library; **1337:** Micheline Pelletier/CORBIS; **1338:** Ron Stroud/Masterfile; **1340:** Jean Miele/CORBIS; **1343:** Peter Turnley/ CORBIS; **1344:** David Bergman/CORBIS; **1355:** BASSOULS SOPHIE/ CORBIS SYGMA; **1356:** ©Bettmann/CORBIS; **1358:** "Boy on a Wall: Rat Island, 1989" from TIEPOLO'S HOUND by Derek Walcott. Copyright © 20 by Derek Walcott. Reprinted ty Permission of Farrar, Straus and Giroux, LLC. From the collection of Michael and Judy Chastanet.; **1358:** Ryan McVay/Getty Images; **1363:** ©Smith Richard Frank/CORBIS Sygma; **1366:** Hulton-Deutsch Collection/CORBIS; **1369:** The Irish Times; **1370:** Starry Night, Vincent van Gogh, Digital Image © The Museum of Modern Art/Licensed by SCALA / Art Resource, NY; **1373:** JLImages / Alamy; **1375:** Thierry Orban/CORBIS SYGMA; **1376:** Ulrik Tofte/Getty Images; **1376:** Ulrik Tofte/Getty Images; **1379:** Getty Images; **1380:** Getty Images; **1385:** Getty Images; **1386:** Arthur S. AubryGetty Images; **1388:** Daniel Nevins / SuperStock; **1391:** AP/Wide World Photos; **1392:** Scott Stulberg/CORBIS; **1394:** Scott Stulberg/CORBIS; **1397:** Getty Images; **1398:** image reproduced with the kind permission of the Dean and Chapter of Chichester Cathedral; **1402:** t. Nicolas Elder/Globe Photos; **1402:** b. Hulton-Deutsch Collection/CORBIS; **1403:** GK Hart/Vicky Hart/Getty Images; **1404:** PIER/Getty Images; **1406:** Getty Images; **1407:** t. Colin McPherson/CORBIS; **1407:** b. Getty Images; **1408:** Artkey/ CORBIS; **1408:** Artkey/CORBIS; **1410:** Getty Images; **1410:** Getty Images; **1412:** l. Fridmar Damm/zefa/Corbis; **1412:** r. Colin McPherson/CORBIS; **1413:** istockphoto.com; **1415:** Colin McPherson/CORBIS; **1416:** Franck Guiziou/Hemis/CORBIS; **1417:** Martin Harvey/CORBIS; **1422:** Grace Davies/Omni-Photo Communications, Inc.; **1423:** Blaine Harrington III/ CORBIS; **1431:** Getty Images; **1432:** © David Noton Photography / Alamy; **1434:** © Orit Allush / Alamy; **1434:** © Orit Allush / Alamy; **1436:** Christopher Pillitz/Getty Images; **1438:** Tim Graham/Getty Images; **1441:** William Coupon/CORBIS; **1442:** Steve Nagy/Design Pics/CORBIS; **1443:** NASA/ JPL; **1444:** US Geological Service; **1444:** Hiroyuki Matsumoto /Getty Images; **1448:** AITCH/Getty Images; **1449:** t. CORBIS; **1449:** b. istockphoto. com; **1449:** mb. ESA/K. Horgan/Getty Images; **1449:** mt. DRA/Getty Images; **1459:** mc. PHERSON COLIN/CORBIS SYGMA; **1460:** Luke MacGregor/Reuters/CORBIS; **1462:** Tim Mosenfelder/CORBIS; **1462:** Tim Mosenfelder/CORBIS; **1486:** bcl. ©Bettmann/Corbis

Staff Credits

The people who made up the Pearson Prentice Hall Literature team— representing design, editorial, editorial services, education technology, manufacturing and inventory planning, market research, marketing services, planning and budgeting, product planning, production serv- ices, project office, publishing processes, and rights and permissions— are listed below. Boldface type denotes the core team members.

Tobey Antao, Margaret Antonini, Rosalyn Arcilla, Penny Baker, James Ryan Bannon, Stephan Barth, **Tricia Battipede,** Krista Baudo, Rachel Beckman, Julie Berger, Lawrence Berkowitz, Melissa Biezin, **Suzanne Biron,** Rick Blount, **Marcela Boos, Betsy Bostwick,** Kay Bosworth, Jeff Bradley, Andrea Brescia, Susan Brorein, Lois Brown, **Pam Carey,** Lisa Carrillo, **Geoffrey Cassar,** Patty Cavuoto, Doria Ceraso, Jennifer Ciccone, Jaime Cohen, Rebecca Cottingham, Joe Cucchiara, Jason Cuoco, **Alan Dalgleish, Karen Edmonds, Irene Ehrmann,** Stephen Eldridge, Amy Fleming, Dorothea Fox, Steve Frankel, Cindy Frederick, Philip Fried, Diane Fristachi, Phillip Gagler, **Pamela Gallo,** Husain Gatlin, **Elaine Goldman,** Elizabeth Good, John Guild, Phil Hadad, Patricia Hade, Monduane Harris, Brian Hawkes, Jennifer B. Heart, Martha Heller, John Hill, Beth Hyslip, Mary Jean Jones, Grace Kang, Nathan Kinney, Roxanne Knoll, **Kate Krimsky,** Monisha Kumar, Jill Kushner, Sue Langan, Melisa Leong, Susan Levine, Dave Liston, **Mary Luthi, George Lychock, Gregory Lynch, Joan Mazzeo, Sandra McGloster,** Salita Mehta, Eve Melnechuk, Kathleen Mercandetti, Artur Mkrtchyan, Karyn Mueller, Alison Muff, Christine Mulcahy, Kenneth Myett, Elizabeth Nemeth, Stefano Nese, Carrie O'Connor, April Okano, Kim Ortell, Sonia Pap, Raymond Parenteau, Dominique Pickens, Linda Punskovsky, **Sheila Ramsay,** Maureen Raymond, Mairead Reddin, **Erin Rehill-Seker, Renee Roberts, Laura Ross,** Bryan Salacki, Sharon Schultz, Jennifer Serra, **Melissa Shustyk,** Rose Sievers, Christy Singer, Yvonne Stecky, **Cynthia Summers,** Steve Thomas, Merle Uuesoo, Roberta Warshaw, Patricia Williams, Daniela Velez

Additional Credits

Lydie Bemba, Victoria Blades, Denise Data, Rachel Drice, Eleanor Kostyk, Jill Little, Loraine Machlin, Evan Marx, Marilyn McCarthy, Patrick O'Keefe, Shelia M. Smith, Lucia Tirondola, Laura Vivenzio, Linda Waldman, Angel Weyant